Rick Steves'
BEST OF EUROPE
2000

John Muir Publications
Santa Fe, New Mexico

Other JMP travel guidebooks by Rick Steves
Rick Steves' Europe Through the Back Door
Europe 101: History and Art for the Traveler (with Gene Openshaw)
Rick Steves' Postcards from Europe
Rick Steves' Mona Winks: Self-Guided Tours of Europe's Top Museums
   (with Gene Openshaw)
Rick Steves' France, Belgium & the Netherlands (with Steve Smith)
Rick Steves' Germany, Austria & Switzerland
Rick Steves' Great Britain & Ireland
Rick Steves' Italy
Rick Steves' London (with Gene Openshaw)
Rick Steves' Paris (with Steve Smith and Gene Openshaw)
Rick Steves' Rome (with Gene Openshaw)
Rick Steves' Scandinavia
Rick Steves' Spain & Portugal
Rick Steves' Phrase Books: German, French, Italian,
   Spanish/Portuguese, and French/Italian/German
Asia Through the Back Door (with Bob Effertz)

John Muir Publications, P.O. Box 613, Santa Fe, NM 87504
Copyright © 2000, 1999, 1998, 1997, 1996 by Rick Steves
Cover copyright © 2000, 1999, 1998 by John Muir Publications
All rights reserved.

Printed in the United States of America
Second printing January 2000

For the latest on Rick Steves' lectures, guidebooks, tours, and public television series, contact Europe Through the Back Door, Box 2009, Edmonds, WA 98020, tel. 425/771-8303, fax 425/771-0833, www.ricksteves.com, or e-mail: rick@ricksteves.com.

ISBN: 1-56261-496-7
ISSN: 1096-7702

Europe Through the Back Door Editor Risa Laib
John Muir Publications Editors Laurel Gladden Gillespie,
   Krista Lyons-Gould, Elizabeth Wolf
Research Assistance Steve Smith, Dave Fox, Brian Carr Smith,
   and Risa Laib
Production & Typesetting Kathleen Sparkes, White Hart Design
Design Linda Braun
Cover Design Janine Lehmann
Maps David C. Hoerlein
Printer Banta Company
Cover Photo Il Duomo (cathedral and temple), Siena, Italy;
   Leo de Wys Inc./Jacobs

Distributed to the book trade by
Publishers Group West
Berkeley, California

Although the author and publisher have made every effort to provide accurate, up-to-date information, they accept no responsibility for loss, injury, loose stools, or inconvenience sustained by any person using this book.

Europe's Best Destinations

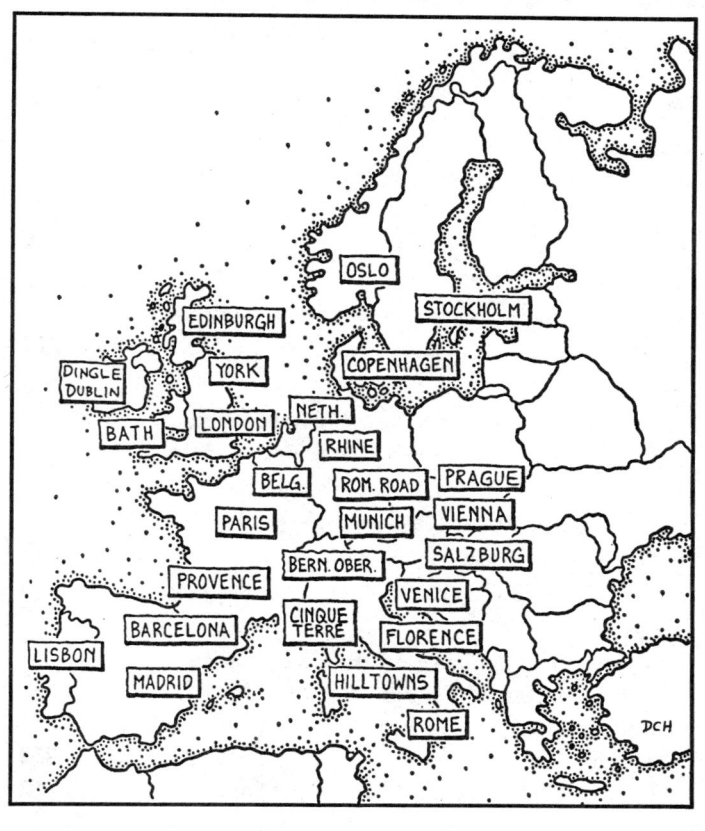

CONTENTS

INTRODUCTION 1

BACK DOOR TRAVEL PHILOSOPHY 23

AUSTRIA
From *Rick Steves' Germany, Austria & Switzerland*
- Vienna 24
- Salzburg, Salzkammergut, and Hallstatt 56

BELGIUM
From *Rick Steves' France, Belgium & the Netherlands*
- Bruges 75

CZECH REPUBLIC
From *Rick Steves' Germany, Austria & Switzerland*
- Prague 90

FRANCE
From *Rick Steves' France, Belgium & the Netherlands*
- Paris 113
- Provence 171

GERMANY
From *Rick Steves' Germany, Austria & Switzerland*
- Rhine and Mosel Valleys 187
- Rothenburg 214
- Munich 232
- Bavaria (Germany) and Tirol (Austria) 252

GREAT BRITAIN
From *Rick Steves' Great Britain & Ireland*
- London 270
- Bath 327
- York 340
- Edinburgh 352

IRELAND
From *Rick Steves' Great Britain & Ireland*
- Dublin 371
- Dingle Peninsula 389

ITALY
From *Rick Steves' Italy*
- Rome 405
- Florence 449
- Venice 471
- Hill Towns 499
- The Cinque Terre 533

THE NETHERLANDS
From *Rick Steves' France, Belgium & the Netherlands*
- Amsterdam 551
- Haarlem 571

PORTUGAL
From *Rick Steves' Spain & Portugal*
- Lisbon 581

SCANDINAVIA
From *Rick Steves' Scandinavia*
- Copenhagen, Denmark 602
- Stockholm, Sweden 625
- Oslo, Norway 643

SPAIN
From *Rick Steves' Spain & Portugal*
- Barcelona 660
- Madrid 679

SWITZERLAND
From *Rick Steves' Germany, Austria & Switzerland*
- Gimmelwald and the Berner Oberland 700

APPENDIX 718

INDEX 725

INTRODUCTION

This book breaks Europe into its top big-city, small-town, and rural destinations. It then gives you all the information and opinions necessary to wring the maximum value out of your limited time and money in each of them. If you plan two months or less in Europe, this lean and mean book is all you need.

Experiencing Europe's culture, people, and natural wonders economically and hassle free has been my goal for more than 25 years of traveling, tour guiding, and travel writing. With this book, I pass on to you the lessons I've learned, updated for 2000.

Rick Steves' Best of Europe is the crème de la crème of places featured in my Country Guides. This book is balanced to include a comfortable mix of exciting big cities and cozy small towns: from Paris, London, and Rome to traffic-free Riviera ports, avalanche-zone Alpine villages, and mom-and-pop châteaus. It covers the predictable biggies and mixes in a healthy dose of Back Door intimacy. Along with Leonardo in the Louvre, you'll enjoy Caterina in her Cantina. I've been selective. For example, rather than listing the countless castles, hill towns, and Riviera resorts, I recommend the best three or four of each.

The best is, of course, only my opinion. But after more than two decades of travel writing, lecturing, and tour guiding, I've developed a sixth sense for what tickles the traveler's fancy.

This Information Is Accurate and Up-to-Date

This book is updated every year. Most publishers of guidebooks that cover Europe from top to bottom can afford an update only every two or three years (and even then, it's often by letter). Since this book covers only my favorite places, I am able to update it personally each year. Even with an annual update, things change. But if you're traveling with the current edition of this book, I guarantee you're using the most up-to-date information available. If you're packing an old book, you'll learn the seriousness of your mistake... in Europe. Your trip costs at least $10 per waking hour. Your time is valuable. This guidebook saves lots of time.

Planning Your Trip

This book is organized by destinations. Each destination is covered as a minivacation on its own, filled with exciting sights and homey, affordable places to stay. In each chapter, you'll find the following:

Planning Your Time, a suggested schedule, with thoughts on how to best use your limited time.

Orientation, including tourist information, city transportation, and an easy-to-read map designed to make the text clear and your arrival smooth.

Sights with ratings: ▲▲▲—Don't miss; ▲▲—Try hard to see; ▲—Worthwhile if you can make it; No rating—Worth knowing about.

Sleeping and Eating, with addresses and phone numbers of my favorite budget hotels and restaurants.

Transportation Connections to nearby destinations by train, bus, or car.

The **Appendix** is a traveler's tool kit, with telephone tips, a climate chart, and a list of national tourist offices.

Browse through this book, choose your favorite destinations, and link them up. Then have a great trip! You'll travel like a temporary local, getting the absolute most out of every mile, minute, and dollar.

You won't waste time on mediocre sights because this guidebook, unlike others, covers only the best. Since your major financial pitfalls are lousy, expensive hotels, I've worked hard to assemble the best accommodations values for each stop. And as you travel the route I know and love, I'm happy you'll be meeting some of my favorite Europeans.

Trip Costs

Five components make up your trip cost: airfare, surface transportation, room and board, sightseeing/entertainment, and shopping/miscellany.

Airfare: Don't try to sort through the mess yourself. Get and use a good travel agent. A basic round-trip U.S.A.-to-Europe flight should cost $600 to $1,000, depending on where you fly from and when. Always consider saving time and money in Europe by flying "open-jaws" (flying into one city and out of another, such as flying into London and out of Rome).

Surface Transportation: Your best mode depends upon the time you have and the scope of your trip. For many it's a Eurailpass (3 weeks-$718; 1 month-$890; 2 months-$1,260; 15 days in 2 months-$862). Train passes are normally available only outside of Europe. You may save money by simply buying tickets as you go (see "Transportation," below).

Drivers can figure $200 per person per week (based on two people splitting the cost of the car, tolls, gas, and insurance). Car rental is cheapest to arrange from the U.S.A. Leasing, for trips over three weeks, is even cheaper.

Room and Board: You can thrive in Europe in 2000 on an overall average of $70 a day per person for room and board (less for the smaller cities). A $70 a day budget allows $10 for lunch, $15 for dinner, and $45 for lodging (based on two people splitting the cost of a $90 double room that includes breakfast). That's doable. Students and tightwads will do it on $35 or $40 ($15–20 per bed, $20 for meals and snacks). But budget sleeping and eating require the skills and information covered below (or much more extensively in *Rick Steves' Europe Through the Back Door 2000*).

Sightseeing and Entertainment: In big cities, figure $5 to $10 per major sight, $2 for minor ones, and $25 for splurge experiences (e.g., tours, concerts, gelato binges). An overall average of $15 a day works for most. Don't skimp here. After all, this category directly powers most of the experiences all the other expenses are designed to make possible.

Shopping and Miscellany: Figure $1 per postcard and $2 per coffee, beer, and ice-cream cone. Shopping can vary in cost from nearly nothing to a small fortune. Good budget travelers find that this category has little to do with assembling a trip full of lifelong and wonderful memories.

Exchange Rates
I've priced things in local currencies throughout this book.

Country	$1 equals roughly . . .
Austria	12 Austrian schillings (AS)
Belgium	40 Belgian francs (BF)
Czech Republic	32 koruna (kč)
Denmark	7 kroner (kr)
France	6 francs (F)
Germany	1.70 Deutsche marks (DM)
Great Britain	.60 pound (£)
Ireland	.70 punt (£)
Italy	1,900 lire (L)
Netherlands	2 guilders (f)
Norway	7 kroner (kr)
Portugal	190 escudos ($)
Spain	160 pesetas (ptas)
Sweden	7 kroner (kr)
Switzerland	1.40 Swiss francs (SF)

Prices, Times, and Discounts
The prices in this book, as well as the hours and telephone numbers, are accurate as of late 1999. But Europe is always changing. I know you'll understand that this, like any other guidebook, starts to yellow even before it's printed.

In Europe—and in this book—you'll be using the 24-hour clock. After 12:00 noon, keep going—13:00, 14:00, and so on. For anything over 12, subtract 12 and add p.m. (14:00 is 2 p.m.).

This book lists peak-season hours for sightseeing attractions (May–September). Off-season, roughly October through April,

Europe's Best 70 Days

expect generally shorter hours, more lunchtime breaks, fewer activities, and fewer guided tours in English. If you're traveling off-season, be careful to confirm opening times.

While discounts for sights and transportation are not listed in this book, seniors (60 and over), students (with International Student Identity Cards), and youths (under 18) can sometimes get discounts—but only by asking.

When to Go

May, June, September, and October are the best travel months. Generally, peak season (July and August) offers the sunniest weather and the most exciting slate of activities—but the worst crowds. During this crowded time, it's best to arrive early in the day or to call your next hotel in advance. (Your fluent receptionist can help you.) As a general rule of thumb any time of year, the climate north of the Alps is mild (like Seattle), and south of the Alps it's like southern California. For information on weather, check the Climate Chart in the Appendix. If you wilt in the heat, avoid the Mediterranean in the summer. If you want blue skies in the Alps, Britain, and Scandinavia, travel in the height of summer.

Introduction 5

Plan your itinerary to beat the heat (spring trip, start in the south and work north) but also to moderate culture shock (start in mild Britain and work south and east) and minimize crowds. Touristy places in the core of Europe (Germany, the Alps, France, Italy, and Greece) suffer most from crowds.

Sightseeing Priorities

Depending on the length of your trip, here are my recommended priorities. Assuming you're traveling by train, I've taken geographical proximity into account.

5 days:	London, Paris
7 days, add:	Amsterdam, Haarlem
10 days, add:	Rhine, Rothenburg, Munich
14 days, add:	Salzburg, Swiss Alps
17 days, add:	Venice, Florence
21 days, add:	Rome, Cinque Terre
24 days, add:	Siena, Bavarian sights
30 days, add:	Arles, Barcelona, Madrid, Toledo
36 days, add:	Vienna, Berlin, Bath/Cotswolds
40 days, add:	Copenhagen, Edinburgh
70 days:	See Europe's Best 70 Days map on page 4.

Red Tape, News, and Banking

Red Tape: You currently need a passport but no visa and no shots to travel in Europe. Crossing borders is easy. Sometimes you won't even realize it's happened. When you do change countries, however, you change money, postage stamps, phone cards, gas prices, ways to flush a toilet, words for "hello," figurehead monarchs, and breakfast breads. Plan ahead for these changes. Coins and stamps are worthless outside their home countries. Just before crossing a border, I use up my coins on gas, candy, souvenirs, or a telephone call home.

News: Americans keep in touch with the *International Herald Tribune* (published almost daily via satellite throughout Europe). Every Tuesday, the European editions of *Time* and *Newsweek* hit the stands with articles of particular interest to European travelers. Sports addicts can get their fix from *USA Today*. News in English will only be sold where there's enough demand: in big cities and tourist centers. If you're concerned about how some event might affect your safety as an American traveling abroad, call the U.S. consulate or embassy in the nearest big city for advice.

Banking: Bring plastic (ATM, credit, or debit cards) along with traveler's checks in dollars.

To get a cash advance from a bank machine, you'll need a four-digit PIN (numbers only, no letters) with your bank card. Before you go, verify with your bank that your card will work, then use it whenever possible (bring two cards in case one gets demagnetized

The Best of Europe in Three Weeks

Day 1	Arrive in Amsterdam, stay in Haarlem
Day 2	Amsterdam
Day 3	To Rhine, Bacharach
Day 4	Cruise Rhine, tour Rheinfels Castle
Day 5	Rothenburg
Day 6	Munich
Day 7	Castle Day in Bavaria and Tirol, Reutte
Day 8	To Venice
Day 9	Venice
Day 10	Florence
Day 11	Siena, Florence
Day 12	Rome
Day 13	Rome
Day 14	Civita di Bagnoregio
Day 15	Italian Riviera, Cinque Terre, Vernazza
Day 16	Beach time or hiking Riviera trails
Day 17	To the Alps, Gimmelwald
Day 18	Alps Appreciation Day
Day 19	To Beaune in Burgundy
Day 20	Versailles, drop car
Day 21	Paris
Day 22	Paris

While this itinerary is designed to be done by car, with a few small modifications, it works great by train. Stay in Füssen in Bavaria rather than Reutte in Triol. The hill town of Orvieto is easier to reach than Civita. Consider skipping Beaune if you'd perfer to take an overnight train from Switzerland to Paris. Do Versailles as an easy day trip from Paris.

---

or eaten by a machine). But beware that the distances between these machines can be great, and bring enough traveler's checks as backup.

Visa and MasterCard are more commonly accepted than American Express. Just like at home, credit or debit cards work easily at larger hotels, restaurants, and shops, but smaller businesses prefer payment in local currency.

Regular banks have the best rates for cashing traveler's checks. For a large exchange, it pays to compare rates and fees. Post offices and train stations usually change money if you can't get to a bank.

Europe's Best Three Weeks

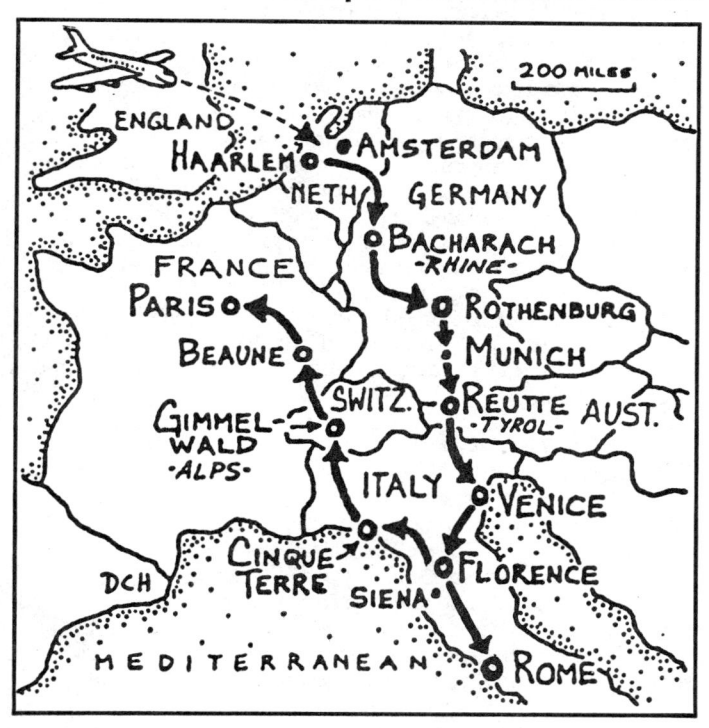

[Map showing travel route through Europe: Amsterdam → Haarlem → Bacharach (Rhine) → Rothenburg → Munich → Reutte (Tyrol) → Venice → Florence → Siena → Rome → Cinque Terre → Gimmelwald (Alps) → Beaune → Paris. Countries labeled: England, Netherlands, Germany, France, Switzerland, Austria, Italy. Mediterranean Sea shown. Scale: 200 miles.]

You should use a money belt. Thieves target tourists. A money belt (call 425/771-8303 for our free newsletter/catalog) provides peace of mind. You can carry lots of cash safely in a money belt.

Don't be petty about changing money. You don't need to waste time every few days returning to a bank or tracking down a cash machine. Change a week's worth of money, get big bills, stuff it in your money belt, and travel!

Travel Smart

Upon arrival in a new town, lay the groundwork for a smooth departure. Reread this book as you travel and visit local tourist information offices. Buy a phone card and use it for reservations, reconfirmations, and double-checking hours. Enjoy the friendliness of the local people. Ask questions. Most locals are eager to point you in their idea of the right direction. Wear your money belt, learn the local currency, and develop a simple formula to estimate rough prices in dollars quickly. Keep a notepad in your pocket for organizing your thoughts. Those who expect to travel smart, do.

As you read this book, note the days of markets and festivals and when sights are closed. Anticipate problem days: Mondays are bad in Munich, Dachau, and Florence; Tuesdays are bad in Paris. Museums and sights, especially large ones, usually stop admitting people 30 to 60 minutes before closing time.

Sundays have the same pros and cons as they do for travelers in the United States. Sightseeing attractions are generally open, shops and banks are closed, and city traffic is light. Rowdy evenings are rare on Sundays. Saturdays in Europe are virtually weekdays with earlier closing hours. Hotels in tourist areas are most crowded on Fridays and Saturdays.

Plan ahead for banking, laundry, post office chores, and picnics. Mix intense and relaxed periods. Every trip (and every traveler) needs at least a few slack days. Pace yourself. Assume you will return.

Tourist Information

The tourist information office is your best first stop in any new city. Try to arrive, or at least telephone, before it closes. In this book, I'll refer to a tourist information office as a TI. Throughout Europe, you'll find TIs are usually well organized and English speaking.

As national budgets tighten, many TIs have been privatized. This means they become sales agents for big tours and hotels, and their "information" becomes unavoidably colored. While the TI has listings of all the rooms and is eager to book you one, use their room-finding service only as a last resort. Across Europe, room-finding services are charging commissions from hotels, taking fees from travelers, blacklisting establishments that buck their materialistic rules, and are unable to give hard opinions on the relative value of one place over another. The accommodations stakes are too high to go potluck through the TI. By using the listings in this book, you can avoid that kind of "help."

Tourist Offices, U.S.A. Addresses: Each country has a national tourist office in the U.S.A. (see the Appendix for addresses). Before your trip, you can ask for the free general information packet and any specific information you may want (such as city maps and schedules of upcoming festivals).

Recommended Guidebooks

You may want some supplemental information, especially if you'll be traveling beyond my recommended destinations. When you consider the improvements they'll make in your $3,000 vacation, $25 or $35 for extra maps and books is money well spent. Especially for several people traveling by car, the weight and expense are negligible.

The Lonely Planet guides to various European countries are thorough, well researched (though not updated annually), and packed with good maps and hotel recommendations for low- to moderate-budget travelers. The hip, insightful Rough Guide series (by British researchers, not updated annually) and the highly opinionated Let's Go series (annually updated by Harvard students) are great for students and vagabonds. If you're a backpacker with a train pass and interested in the youth and night scene, get Let's Go. The popular, skinny green Michelin guides to most southern countries and French regions are excellent, especially if you're driving. They're known for their city and sightseeing maps, dry but concise and helpful information on all major sights, and good cultural and historical background. English editions are sold locally at tourist shops and gas stations.

Rick Steves' Books and Videos

Rick Steves' Europe Through the Back Door 2000 (John Muir Publications) gives you budget travel tips on minimizing jet lag, packing light, planning your itinerary, traveling by car or train, finding budget beds without reservations, changing money, avoiding rip-offs, outsmarting thieves, hurdling the language barrier, staying healthy, taking great photographs, using your bidet, and much more. The book also includes chapters on my 34 favorite "Back Doors."

Rick Steves Country Guides are a series of seven guidebooks—including this one—covering Britain & Ireland; France, Belgium & the Netherlands; Italy; Spain & Portugal; Germany, Austria & Switzerland; and Scandinavia. These are updated annually and come out each January. If you wish this book covered more of any particular country, my Country Guides are for you.

My **City Guides** cover Paris, London, and—new for 2000—Rome. For more thorough coverage of Europe's three greatest cities, complete with self-guided, illustrated tours through the greatest museums, consider these handy, easy-to-pack guidebooks.

Europe 101: History and Art for the Traveler (co-written with Gene Openshaw, John Muir Publications, 1996) gives you the story of Europe's people, history, and art. Written for smart people who were sleeping in their history and art classes before they knew they were going to Europe, *101* helps Europe's sights come alive.

Rick Steves' Mona Winks (also co-written with Gene Openshaw, John Muir Publications, 1998) gives you fun, easy-to-follow self-guided tours of the major museums and historic highlights featured in this book, including Amsterdam's Rijksmuseum and Van Gogh Museum; London's British Museum, British Library, National Gallery, Tate Gallery, Westminster Abbey, and a Westminster Walk; Venice's St. Mark's, Doge's Palace, and Accademia Gallery; Florence's Uffizi Gallery, Bargello, Michelangelo's *David*, and a Renaissance Walk; Rome's Colosseum, Forum, Pantheon,

Vatican Museum, and St. Peter's Basilica; Spain's Prado; and Paris' Louvre, the exciting Orsay Museum, and a tour of Europe's greatest palace, Versailles. If you're planning on touring these sights, *Mona* will be a valued friend.

Rick Steves' Phrase Books: After more than 25 years as an English-only traveler struggling with other phrase books, I've designed a series of practical, fun, and budget-oriented phrase books to help you ask the gelato man for a free little taste and the hotel receptionist for a room with no street noise. If you want to chat with your cabbie and make hotel reservations over the phone, my pocket-sized Rick Steves' Phrase Books (for French; German; Italian; combined French/Italian/German; and Spanish/Portuguese) will come in very handy (John Muir Publications, 1999).

My television series, *Travels in Europe with Rick Steves*, includes 52 half-hour shows on Europe. A new series of 13 shows—featuring London, Paris, and Rome, among others—will air in 2000. All of the earlier shows are run throughout the United States on public television stations and on the Travel Channel. The shows are also available as information-packed videotapes, along with my two-hour slideshow lectures (call us at 425/771-8303 for our free newsletter/catalog).

Rick Steves' Postcards from Europe (John Muir Publications, 1999), my autobiographical book, packs more than 25 years of travel anecdotes and insights into the ultimate 3,000-mile European adventure. Through my guidebooks, I share my favorite European discoveries with you. *Postcards* introduces you to my favorite European friends.

Maps

The maps in this book, drawn by Dave Hoerlein, are concise and simple. Dave, who is well-traveled in Europe, has designed the maps to help you locate recommended places and get to the tourist offices, where you can pick up a more in-depth map (usually free) of the city or region.

European bookstores, especially in tourist areas, have good selections of maps. For drivers, I'd recommend a 1:200,000 or 1:300,000 scale map for each country. Train travelers can usually manage fine with the freebies they get with their train pass and at the local tourist offices.

Transportation in Europe

By Car or Train?

Each has pros and cons. Cars are an expensive headache in big cities but give you more control for delving deep into the countryside. Groups of three or more go cheaper by car. If you're packing

Railpasses

2000 EURAILPASSES

These passes cover all 17 Eurail countries: Austria, Belgium, Denmark, Finland, France, Germany, Greece, Hungary, Ireland, Italy, Luxembourg, Netherlands, Norway, Portugal, Spain, Sweden, and Switzerland.

	1st cl	1st cl Saver*	2nd cl Youth**
10 days in 2 months flexi	$654	$556	$458
15 days in 2 months flexi	862	732	599
15 consecutive days	554	470	388
21 consecutive days	718	610	499
1 month consec. days	890	756	623
2 months consec. days	1260	1072	882
3 months consec. days	1558	1324	1089

2000 EUROPASSES

All Europasses include France, Germany, Italy, Spain and Switzerland. Up to two of the following extra-cost "zones" may be added: ▼ Austria/Hungary; ▼ Belgium/Netherlands/Luxembourg; ▼ Portugal; ▼ Greece (includes the Brindisi, Italy to Patras, Greece boat).

	1st cl	1st cl Saver*	2nd cl Youth**
5 days in 2 months	$348	$296	$233
6 days in 2 months	$368	$314	$253
8 days in 2 months	$448	$382	$313
10 days in 2 month	$528	$450	$363
15 days in 2 months	$728	$620	$513
With one add-on zone	+$60	+$52	+$45
With two add-on zones	+$100	+$86	+$78

*__Saverpasses:__ When 2 or more adults _travel together at all times_, they each save 15% by sharing a Saverpass, compared to buying individual Eurail or Europasses.
**__Youthpasses:__ Under age 26 only. Kids 4-11 pay half adult fare; under 4: free.

For a Eurail/Europass order form, or for Rick's complete Railpass Guide, visit www.ricksteves.com or call us at 425/771-8303. To order Rail & Drive passes, call DER at 800/549-3737 or Rail Europe at 800/438-7245.

heavy (with kids), go by car. Trains are best for city-to-city travel and give you the convenience of doing long stretches overnight. By train, I arrive relaxed and well rested—not so by car. A rail 'n' drive pass allows you to mix train and car travel. When thoughtfully used, this pass economically gives you the best of both transportation worlds.

Traveling by Train

A major mistake Americans make is relating public transportation in Europe to the pathetic public transportation they're used to at home. By rail you'll have the Continent by the tail. And every year the trains of Europe are getting speedier and more comfortable. While many simply buy tickets as they go ("point to point"), the

Rail 'n' Drive Passes

2000 FIRST CLASS EURAILDRIVE PASSES
4 first class rail days and 2 car days in a 2 month period.

Car categories	2 adults	1 adult	Extra car day	Extra rail day
Economy	$339	$399	$61	$59
Compact	359	439	80	59
Intermediate	369	459	90	59

Prices are per person. Third and fourth persons sharing car get a 4-day out of 2-month railpass for approx. $280 (kids 4-11: $140). You can add rail days (max. 5) and car days (no limit).

2000 FIRST CLASS EUROPASS DRIVE
3 first class rail days and 2 car days in a 2 month period.

Car categories	2 adults	1 adult	Extra car day	Extra rail day
Economy	$284	$345	$59	$45
Compact	304	379	79	45
Intermediate	314	399	89	45
Small Automatic	334	445	109	45

Prices are per person. You can add rail days (max. 7) and car days (no limit). *Prices may vary in 2000. To order Rail 'n Drive passes, call Rail Europe at 800/438-7245 or DER at 800/549-3737.*

various train passes give you the simplicity of ticket-free, unlimited travel and, depending on how much traveling you do, often offer a tremendous savings over regular point-to-point tickets. The Eurailpass gives you several options (explained in the box on page 11). For a free 40-page Railpass Guide analyzing the railpass and point-to-point ticket deals available in both the U.S.A. and in Europe, call my office at 425/771-8303 (or download it at www.ricksteves.com). This booklet is updated each January. Regardless of where you get your train pass, this information will help you know you're getting the right one for your trip. To study train schedules in advance on the Web, check http://bahn.hafas.de/english.html.

Eurailpass and the Europass

The granddaddy of European railpasses, Eurail gives you unlimited rail travel on the national trains of 17 European countries. That's 100,000 miles of track through all of western Europe, including Ireland, Greece, and Hungary (but excluding Great Britain and most of eastern Europe). The pass includes many bonuses, such as free boat rides on the Rhine, Mosel, Danube, and lakes of Switzerland; several international ferries (Sweden–Finland and Italy–Greece, plus a 50 percent discount on the Ireland–France route); and a 75 percent discount on the Romantic Road bus tour through Germany.

The cheaper Europass is more focused than the Eurailpass, covering five countries (France, Germany, Switzerland, Italy, and Spain), with an extra-cost option to add several more. Both

Introduction 13

Europe by Rail: Time and Cost

This map can help you determine quickly and painlessly whether a railpass is right for your trip. Add up the ticket prices for your route. If your total is about the same or more than the cost of a pass, buy the pass.

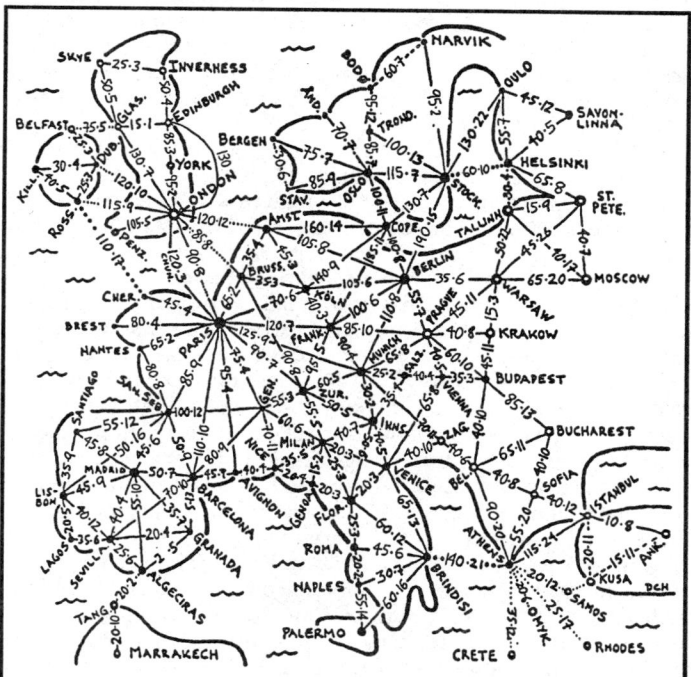

The **first number** between cities = **cost** in $US for a one-way, second-class ticket. The **second number** = number of **hours** the trip takes.
- ● = Cities served by Eurailpass
- ○ = Cities not served by Eurailpass (for example, if you want to go from Munich to Prague, you'll need to pay extra for the portion through the Czech Republic)
- ••• = Boat Crossings

Important: These fares and times are based on the Eurail Tariff Guide. Actual prices may vary due to currency fluctuations and local promotions. Local competition can cut the actual price of some boat crossings (from Italy to Greece, for example) by 50% or more. For approximate first-class rail prices, multiply the prices shown by 1.5. In some cases, faster trains (like the TGV in France) are available, cutting the hours indicated on the map. Travelers under age 26 can receive up to 1/3 off the second-class fares shown. Eurailpasses are not honored in the United Kingdom, Turkey, or Eastern Europe (except for Hungary).

Eurailpasses and Europasses come in a discounted Saverpass version available to groups of two or more.

Eurail Analysis

Break-even point? For an at-a-glance break-even point, remember that a one-month Eurailpass pays for itself if your route is Amsterdam–Rome–Madrid–Paris on first class or Copenhagen–Rome–Madrid–Copenhagen on second class. A one-month Eurail Youthpass saves you money if you're traveling from Amsterdam to Rome to Madrid and back to Amsterdam. Passes pay for themselves quicker in the north, where the cost per kilometer is higher. Check the "Europe by Rail: Time and Cost" map, on page 13 to see if your planned travels merit the purchase of a train pass. If it's about even, go with the pass for the convenience of not having to wait in line to buy tickets and for the fun and freedom to travel "free."

Using one Eurailpass versus a series of country passes: While nearly every country has its own miniversion of the Eurailpass, trips covering several countries are usually cheapest with the budget whirlwind traveler's old standby, the Eurailpass, or its budget cousin, the Europass. This is because the more rail days included in a pass, the cheaper your per-day cost is. A group of country passes with a few rail days apiece will have a high per-day cost, while a Eurailpass with a longer life span offers a better deal overall. However, if you're traveling in a single country, an individual country railpass (such as Francerail or Germanrail) is a better value than a Eurail or Europass.

EurailDrive Pass: The EurailDrive Pass is for those who want to combine train travel with the freedom of having a car a day here and a day there. Great areas for a day of joyriding include the Dutch countryside; Germany's Rhine, Mosel, or Bavaria; France's Loire, Burgundy, Alsace, Provence, or Pyrenees; Italy's Tuscany, Umbria, or Dolomites; Spain's Andalusian hill towns; Norway's fjord country; or "car hiking" in the Alps. When comparing prices, remember that each day of car rental comes with about $30 of extra expenses (CDW insurance, gas, parking), which you'll divide among the people in your party.

Car Rental

It's cheaper to arrange European car rentals in the United States, so check rates with your travel agent. Rent by the week with unlimited mileage. If you'll be renting for three weeks or more, ask your agent about leasing, which is a scheme to save on insurance and taxes. I normally rent the smallest, least expensive model. Explore your drop-off options (and costs).

For peace of mind, I spring for the Collision Damage Waiver insurance (CDW, about $10–15 per day), which has a zero-deductible rather than the standard value-of-the-car "deductible."

Introduction

Standard European Road Signs

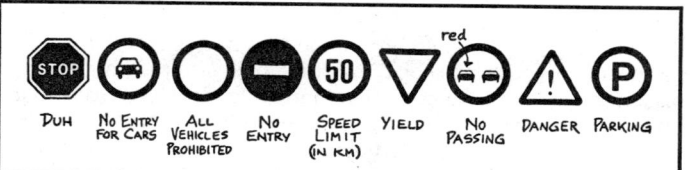

STOP	🚗	⊘	⊖	50	▽	🚗🚗 (red)	⚠	Ⓟ
DUH	NO ENTRY FOR CARS	ALL VEHICLES PROHIBITED	NO ENTRY	SPEED LIMIT (IN KM)	YIELD	NO PASSING	DANGER	PARKING

Ask your travel agent about money-saving alternatives to CDW. A few gold credit cards cover CDW insurance; quiz your credit-card company on the worst-case senario. Or consider Travel Guard, which offers CDW insurance for $6 a day (U.S. tel. 800/826-1300); it'll cover you on the Continent but not in Ireland and Britain.

Driving

For most of Europe, all you need is your valid U.S. driver's license and a car. Ask your rental company whether an international license is required. While gas is expensive, if you keep an eye on the big picture, paying $4 per gallon is more a psychological trauma than a financial one. I use the freeways whenever possible. They are free in the Netherlands and Germany. You'll pay a one-time road fee of about $30 as you enter Switzerland and about $10 for Austria. The Italian autostradas and French autoroutes are punctuated by toll booths (charging about $1 for every 10 minutes). The alternative to these superfreeways often is being marooned in rural traffic. The autobahn/autostrada route usually saves enough time, gas, and nausea to justify its expense. Mix scenic country-road rambling with high-speed autobahning, but don't forget that in Europe, the shortest distance between two points is the autobahn.

Metric: Outside of Britain, get used to metric. A liter is about a quart, four to a gallon. A kilometer is six-tenths of a mile. I figure kilometers to miles by cutting them in half and adding back 10 percent of the original (120 km: 60 + 12 = 72 miles, 300 km: 150 + 30 = 180 miles).

Parking: Parking is a costly headache in big cities. You'll pay about $20 a day to park safely. Ask at your hotel for advice. I keep a pile of coins in my ashtray for parking meters, public phones, Laundromats, and wishing wells.

Telephones and Mail

Smart travelers learn the phone system and use it daily to reserve or reconfirm rooms, find out tourist information, or phone home. Many European phone booths take phone cards rather than coins.

Each country sells phone cards good for use in that country's phones. (For example, you can use a Swiss phone card to make local and international calls from Switzerland, but it won't do a thing for you in France.) Buy a phone card from post offices, newsstands, or tobacco shops. Insert the card into the phone and make your call, and the value is automatically deducted from your card. If you use coins instead, have a bunch handy. Newly popular PIN cards allow you to dial from any phone, even your hotel room; after you buy the card (at exchange bureaus, newsstands, or minimarts), just follow the instructions. You'll end up dialing lots more numbers (whether it's a local or international call), but you'll save money per minute, especially on international calls. There's no one brand name; just ask for an international calling card. Available in Britain, Ireland, France, and Italy, these will likely catch on soon throughout Europe.

Dialing Direct: You'll usually save money by dialing direct. You just need to learn to break the codes.

Here are the general guidelines: When calling long-distance within a country, first dial the area code (which starts with zero), then dial the local number. For example, Munich's area code is 089, and the number of one of my recommended Munich hotels is 264-349. To call it from Frankfurt, dial 089/264-349. When dialing internationally, dial the international access code (of the country you're calling from), the country code (of the country you're calling to), the area code (without the initial zero), and the local number. To call the Munich hotel from the U.S.A., dial 011 (U.S.A.'s international access code), 49 (Germany's country code), 89 (Munich's area code without the zero), then 264-349. To call my office from Munich, I dial 00 (Europe's international access code), 1 (U.S.A.'s country code), 425 (Edmonds' area code), and 771-8303.

There are always exceptions. Some countries, such as France, Spain, Portugal, Italy, Norway, and Denmark, do not use area codes. To make an international call to these countries, dial the international access code of the country you're calling from, the country code of the country you're calling, and the local number in its entirety. (Okay, so there's one exception to the exception; for France, you drop the initial zero of the local number.) To make long-distance calls within any of these countries, simply dial the local number in its entirety (whether you're calling across the street or across the country).

European time is six/nine hours ahead of the east/west coast of the U.S.A. For a listing of international access codes and country codes, see the Appendix.

USA Direct Services: Calling home from Europe is easy with AT&T, MCI, or Sprint calling cards, but since direct-dial rates have dropped, calling cards aren't as good a deal as they were a few years ago. It's cheaper to call direct. But if you prefer to use a calling card, here's the scoop: Each card company has a toll-free number in each European country that puts you in touch with an English-speaking operator who takes your card number and the number you want to call, puts you through, and bills your home phone number for the call (about $2.50 for the first minute, plus a $4 service charge and $1.50 per additional minute). Calling an answering machine is a $6.50 mistake. Avoid this by making a five-second call using a small-value coin or a phone card. For about 25 cents you can get through long enough to make sure an answering machine is off so you can call back using your USA Direct number. For a list of AT&T, MCI, and Sprint calling-card operators, see the Appendix. It's a rip-off to use your calling card to make calls between European countries; it's much cheaper to call direct using a phone card or coins.

Mail: To arrange for mail delivery, reserve a few hotels along your route in advance and give their addresses to friends or use American Express Company's mail services (available to anyone who has at least one Amex traveler's check). Allow 10 days for a letter to arrive. Federal Express makes two-day deliveries—for a price. Phoning is so easy that I've dispensed with mail stops all together.

Sleeping

In the interest of smart use of your time, I favor hotels and restaurants handy to your sightseeing activities. Rather than list hotels scattered throughout a city, I describe my favorite two or three neighborhoods and recommend the best accommodations values in each, from $10 bunks to $150 doubles.

Now that hotels are so expensive and tourist information offices' room-finding services are so greedy, it's more important than ever for budget travelers to have a good listing of rooms and call directly to make reservations. This book gives you a wide range of budget accommodations to choose from: hostels, bed-and-breakfasts, guest houses, pensions, small hotels, and splurges. I like places that are quiet, clean, small, central, traditional, friendly, and not listed in other guidebooks. Most places I list are a good value, having at least five of these seven virtues.

Rooms with private bathrooms are often bigger and renovated, while the cheaper rooms without bathrooms often will be on the top floor or not yet refurbished. Any room without a bathroom has access to a bathroom in the corridor (free unless otherwise noted). Rooms with tubs often cost more than rooms with showers. All rooms have a sink. Unless I note a difference, the cost of a room includes a continental breakfast. When breakfast is not included, the price is usually posted in your hotel room.

Before accepting a room, confirm your understanding of the complete price. The only tip my recommended hotels would like is a friendly, easygoing guest. I appreciate feedback on your hotel experiences.

Sleep Code

To give maximum information in a minimum of space, I use this code to describe accommodations listed in this book. Prices listed are per room, not per person. When there is a range of prices in one category, the price will fluctuate with the season, size of room, or length of stay.

S = Single room (or price for one person in a double).

D = Double or Twin. Double beds are usually big enough for non-romantic couples.

T = Triple (often a double bed with a single bed moved in).

Q = Quad (an extra child's bed is usually less).

b = Private bathroom with toilet and shower or tub.

t = Private toilet only (the shower is down the hall).

s = Private shower or tub only (the toilet is down the hall).

CC = Accepts credit cards (Visa, MasterCard, American Express). If CC isn't mentioned, assume you'll need to pay cash.

SE = Speaks English. This code is used only when it seems predictable that you'll encounter English-speaking staff.

NSE = Does not speak English. Used only when it's unlikely you'll encounter English-speaking staff.

According to this code, a couple staying at a "Db-6,000 ptas, CC:V, SE" hotel in Spain would pay a total of 6,000 pesetas (about $38) for a double room with a private bathroom. The hotel will accept Visa or Spanish cash in payment, and the staff speaks English.

Hotels

While most hotels listed in this book cluster around $60 to $80 per double, they range from $25 (very simple, toilet and shower down the hall) to $150 (maximum plumbing and more) per double. The cost is higher in big cities and heavily touristed cities and lower off the beaten track. Three or four people can save money by requesting one big room. Traveling alone can get expensive: A single room is often only 20 percent cheaper than a double. If you'll accept a room with twin beds and you ask for a double, you may be turned away. Ask for "a room for two people" if you'll take a twin or a double.

Rooms are generally very safe, but don't leave valuables lying around. More (or different) pillows and blankets are usually in the closet or available on request. Remember, in Europe towels and linen aren't always replaced every day. Drip-dry and conserve.

A very simple continental breakfast is almost always included. (Breakfasts in Europe, like towels and people, get smaller as you go south.) If you like juice and protein for breakfast, supply it yourself. I enjoy a box of juice in my hotel room and often supplement the skimpy breakfast with a piece of fruit and cheese.

Making Reservations

It's possible to travel at any time of year without reservations, but given the high stakes, erratic accommodations values, and the quality of the gems I've found for this book, I'd highly recommend calling for rooms a day or two in advance as you travel. Even if a hotel clerk says the hotel is full, you can try calling between 9:00 and 10:00 on the day you plan to arrive. That's when the hotel clerk knows who'll be checking out and just which rooms will be available. I've taken great pains to list telephone numbers with long distance instructions (see "Telephones," above and the Appendix). Use the telephone and the convenient phone cards. Most hotels listed are accustomed to English-only speakers. A hotel receptionist will trust you and hold a room until 16:00 (4:00 p.m.) without a deposit, though some will ask for a credit-card number. Honor (or cancel by phone) your reservations. Long distance is cheap and easy from public phone booths. Don't let these people down—I promised you'd call and cancel if for some reason you won't show up. Don't needlessly confirm rooms through the tourist office; they'll take a commission.

If you know exactly which dates you need and really want a particular place, reserve a room well in advance before you leave home. To reserve from home, call, fax, e-mail, or write the hotel. Phone and fax costs are reasonable, e-mail is a steal, and simple English is usually fine. To fax, use the form in the Appendix (or find it online at www.ricksteves.com/reservation). If you're writing, add the zip code and confirm the need and method for a deposit. A two-night stay in August would be "2 nights, 16/8/00 to 18/8/00" (Europeans write the date in this order—day/month/year—and hotel jargon counts your stay from your day of arrival through your day of departure). You'll often receive a letter or fax back requesting one night's deposit. A credit-card number and expiration date will usually be accepted as a deposit, though you may need to send a signed traveler's check or a bank draft in the local currency. If you use your credit card for the deposit, you can pay with your card or cash when you arrive; if you don't show up, you'll be billed for one night. Reconfirm your reservations a day in advance for safety.

Bed-and-Breakfasts

You can stay in private homes throughout Europe and enjoy double the cultural intimacy for about half the cost of hotels. You'll find them mainly in smaller towns and in the countryside (so they are most handy for those with a car). In Germany, look for *Zimmer* signs. For Italian *affitta camere* and French *chambre d'hôte* (CH), ask at local tourist offices. Doubles cost about $50, and you'll often share a bathroom with the family. While your European hosts will rarely speak English (except in Switzerland, the Netherlands, Belgium, and Scandinavia), they will almost always be enthusiastic and a delight to share a home with.

Hostels
For $10 to $20 a night, you can stay at one of Europe's 2,000 youth hostels. While most hostels admit nonmembers for an extra fee, it's best to join the club and buy a youth hostel card before you go (call Hostelling International at 202/783-6161 or order online at www.hiayh.org). Except in Bavaria (where you must be under 27 to stay in a hostel), travelers of any age are welcome as long as they don't mind dorm-style accommodations and making lots of traveling friends. Cheap meals are sometimes available, and kitchen facilities are usually provided for do-it-yourselfers. Expect crowds in the summer, snoring, and lots of youth groups giggling and making rude noises while you try to sleep. Family rooms and doubles are often available on request, but it's basically boys' dorms and girls' dorms. Many hostels are locked up from about 10:00 until 17:00, and a 23:00 curfew is often enforced. Hosteling is ideal for those traveling single: prices are per bed, not per room, and you'll have an instant circle of friends. More and more hostels are getting their business acts together, taking credit-card reservations over the phone and leaving sign-in forms on the door for each available room. If you're serious about traveling cheaply, get a card, carry your own sheets, and cook in the members' kitchens.

Camping
For $4 to $10 per person per night, you can camp your way through Europe. "Camping" is an international word, and you'll see signs everywhere. All you need is a tent and a sleeping bag. Good campground guides are published, and camping information is also readily available at local tourist information offices. Europeans love to holiday camp. It's a social rather than a nature experience and a great way for traveling Americans to make local friends. Camping is ideal for families traveling by car on a tight budget.

Eating European
Europeans are masters at the art of fine living. That means eating long and eating well. Two-hour lunches, three-hour dinners, and endless hours sitting in outdoor cafés are the norm. Americans eat on their way to an evening event and complain if the check is slow in coming. For Europeans, the meal is an end in itself, and only rude waiters rush you.

Even those of us who liked dorm food will find that the local cafés, cuisine, and wines become a highlight of our European adventure. This is sightseeing for your palate, and even if the rest of you is sleeping in cheap hotels, your taste buds will want an occasional first-class splurge. You can eat well without going broke. But be careful: You're just as likely to blow a small fortune on a mediocre meal as you are to dine wonderfully for $15.

Restaurants

When restaurant hunting, choose a place filled with locals, not the place with the big neon signs boasting "We Speak English and Accept Credit Cards." Look for menus posted outside; if you don't see one, move along. Especially in France and Italy, look for set-price menus (called the tourist menu, *menu del giorno*, *prix-fixe*, or simply *le menu*) that give you several choices of courses. Combination plates (*le plat* in France, *plato combinado* in Spain) provide house specialties at reasonable prices. Galloping gourmets bring a menu translator. (The *Marling Menu Master*, available in French, Italian, and German editions, is excellent.) These days, tipping is included in the bill in most cafés and restaurants. If it's not, the menu will tell you. Still, it's polite to leave the change (under 5 percent) if the service was good.

When you're in the mood for something halfway between a restaurant and a picnic meal, look for take-out food stands, delis with stools or a table, a department store cafeteria, or simple little eateries for fast and easy sit-down restaurant food. Many restaurants offer a good value three- to five-course "menu" at lunch only. The same menu often costs much more at dinner.

Picnics

So that I can afford the occasional splurge in a nice restaurant, I like to picnic. In addition to the savings, picnicking is a great way to sample local specialties. And, in the process of assembling your meal, you get to plunge into local markets like a European.

Gather supplies early. Many shops close for a lunch break. While it's fun to visit the small specialty shops, a *supermarché* gives you more efficiency with less color for less cost.

When driving, I organize a backseat pantry in a cardboard box: plastic cups, paper towels, a water bottle (the standard disposable European half liter plastic mineral water bottle works fine), a damp cloth in a Zip-loc baggie, a Swiss army knife, and a petite tablecloth. To take care of juice once and for all, stow a rack of liter boxes of orange juice in the trunk. (Look for "100%" on the label or you'll get a sickly sweet orange drink.)

Picnics (especially French ones) can be an adventure in high cuisine. Be daring: Try the smelly cheeses, midget pickles, ugly pâtés, and minuscule yogurts. Local shopkeepers sell small quantities of produce and even slice and stuff a sandwich for you.

A typical picnic for two might be fresh bread (half loaves on request), two tomatoes, three carrots, 100 grams of cheese (about a quarter-pound, called an *etto* in Italy), 100 grams of meat, two apples, a liter box of orange juice, and yogurt. Total cost for two: about $8.

Stranger in a Strange Land

We travel all the way to Europe to enjoy differences—to become temporary locals. You'll experience frustrations. Certain truths that we find "God-given" or "self-evident," like cold beer, ice in drinks, bottomless cups of coffee, hot showers, body odor smelling bad, and bigger being better, are suddenly not so true. One of the benefits of travel is the eye-opening realization that there are logical, civil, and even better alternatives. A willingness to go local ensures that you'll enjoy a full dose of local hospitality.

Tours of Europe

Travel agents will tell you about typical tours of Europe, but they won't tell you about ours. At Europe Through the Back Door, we run 20-day tours of Europe featuring most of the highlights in this book (departures April–October, 26 people on a big bus with lots of empty seats). We also offer regional tours of Britain, Ireland, Spain/Portugal, Italy, Germany/Austria/Switzerland, Scandinavia, and Turkey as well as weeklong winter getaways to London, Paris, and Rome. For details, call us at 425/771-8303 or visit www.ricksteves.com.

Send Me a Postcard, Drop Me a Line

If you enjoy a successful trip with the help of this book and would like to share your discoveries, please fill out the survey at the end of this book and send it to me at Europe Through the Back Door, Box 2009, Edmonds, WA 98020. I personally read and value all feedback.

For our latest travel information, tap into our Web site: www.ricksteves.com. To check on updates for this book, visit www.ricksteves.com/update. My e-mail address is rick@ricksteves.com. Anyone is welcome to request a free issue of our *Back Door* quarterly newsletter.

Judging from all the positive feedback I receive from travelers who have used this book, it's safe to assume you're on your way to a great vacation—with the finesse of an experienced, independent traveler. Thanks, and happy travels!

BACK DOOR TRAVEL PHILOSOPHY
As Taught in Rick Steves' Europe Through the Back Door

Travel is intensified living—maximum thrills per minute and one of the last great sources of legal adventure. Travel is freedom. It's recess, and we need it.

Experiencing the real Europe requires catching it by surprise, going casual... "Through the Back Door."

Affording travel is a matter of priorities. (Make do with the old car.) You can travel—simply, safely, and comfortably—anywhere in Europe for $70 a day plus transportation costs. In many ways, spending more money only builds a thicker wall between you and what you came to see. Europe is a cultural carnival and, time after time, you'll find that its best acts are free and the best seats are the cheap ones.

A tight budget forces you to travel close to the ground, meeting and communicating with the people, not relying on service with a purchased smile. Never sacrifice sleep, nutrition, safety, or cleanliness in the name of budget. Simply enjoy the local-style alternatives to expensive hotels and restaurants.

Extroverts have more fun. If your trip is low on magic moments, kick yourself and make things happen. If you don't enjoy a place, maybe you don't know enough about it. Seek the truth. Recognize tourist traps. Give a culture the benefit of your open mind. See things as different but not better or worse. Any culture has much to share.

Of course, travel, like the world, is a series of hills and valleys. Be fanatically positive and militantly optimistic. If something's not to your liking, change your liking. Travel is addicting. It can make you a happier American as well as a citizen of the world. Our Earth is home to 6 billion equally important people. It's humbling to travel and find that people don't envy Americans. They like us, but with all due respect, they wouldn't trade passports.

Globetrotting destroys ethnocentricity. It helps you understand and appreciate different cultures. Travel changes people. It broadens perspectives and teaches new ways to measure quality of life. Many travelers toss aside their hometown blinders. Their prized souvenirs are the strands of different cultures they decide to knit into their own character. The world is a cultural yarn shop. And Back Door Travelers are weaving the ultimate tapestry. Come on, join in!

VIENNA (WIEN)

Vienna is a head without a body. For 600 years the capital of the once-grand Habsburg Empire, she started and lost World War I and, with it, her far-flung holdings. Today you'll find an elegant capital of 1.6 million people (20 percent of Austria's population) ruling a small, relatively insignificant country. Culturally, historically, and from a sightseeing point of view, this city is the sum of its illustrious past. The city of Freud, Brahms, a gaggle of Strausses, Maria Theresa's many children, and a dynasty of Holy Roman Emperors is right up there with Paris, London, and Rome.

Vienna has always been the easternmost city of the West. In Roman times it was Vindobona, on the Danube facing the Germanic barbarians. In medieval times Vienna was Europe's bastion against the Ottoman Turks (a "horde" of 300,000 was repelled in 1683). While the ancient walls held out the Turks, World War II bombs destroyed 22 percent of the city's buildings. In modern times Vienna took a big bite out of the USSR's Warsaw Pact buffer zone.

The truly Viennese person is not Austrian but a second-generation Habsburg cocktail, with grandparents from the distant corners of the old empire—Polish, Serbian, Hungarian, Romanian, Czech, or Italian. Vienna is the melting-pot capital of an empire of 60 million—of which only 8 million are Austrian.

In 1900, Vienna's 2.2 million inhabitants made it the world's fifth-largest city (after New York, London, Paris, and Berlin). But the average Viennese mother has 1.3 children, and the population is down to 1.6 million. (Dogs are the preferred "child.")

Some ad agency has convinced Vienna to make Elisabeth, wife of Emperor Franz Josef, with her narcissism and difficulties with royal life, the darling of the local tourist scene. You'll see Sissy all over town. But stay focused on the Habsburgs who mattered.

Vienna Overview

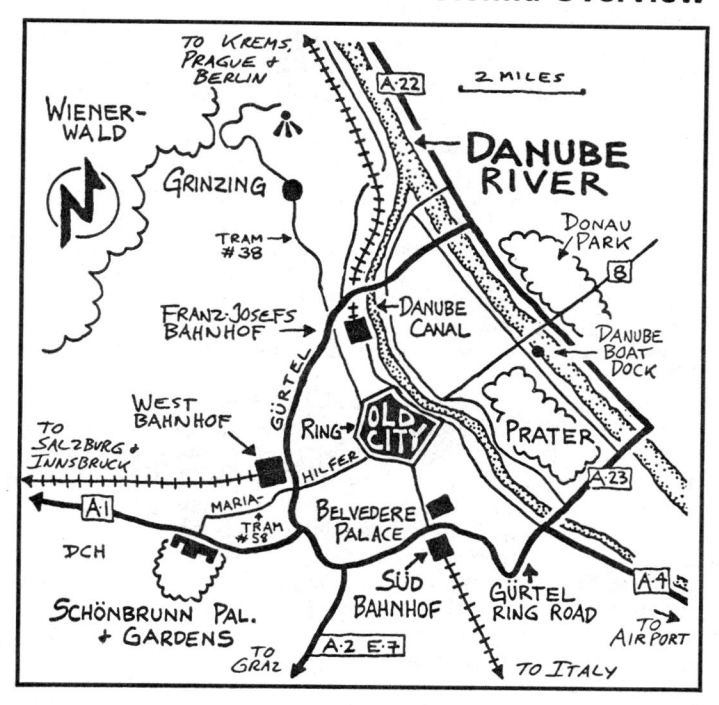

Of the Habsburgs who ruled Austria from 1273 to 1918, Maria Theresa (ruled 1740–1765) and Franz Josef (ruled 1848–1916) are the most famous. People are quick to remember Maria Theresa as the mother of 16 children (12 survived). This was actually no big deal back then (one of her daughters had 18 kids, and a son fathered 16). Maria Theresa's reign followed the Austrian defeat of the Turks, when Europe recognized Austria as a great power. She was a strong and effective queen. (Her rival, the Prussian emperor, said, "When at last the Habsburgs get a great man, it's a woman.")

Maria Theresa was a great social reformer. During her reign she avoided wars and expanded her empire by skillfully marrying her children into the right families. With daughter Marie Antoinette's marriage into the French Bourbon family (to Louis XVI), for instance, a country that had been an enemy became an ally. (Unfortunately for Marie, she arrived in time for the Revolution, and she lost her head.)

In tune with her age and a great reformer, Maria Theresa's "Robin Hood" policies helped Austria slip through the "age of revolution" without turmoil. She taxed the church and the nobility and provided six years of obligatory education to all children and free health care to all in her realm. She also welcomed the boy genius Mozart into her court.

As far back as the 12th century, Vienna was a mecca for musicians—both sacred and secular (troubadours). The Habsburg emperors of the 17th and 18th centuries were not only generous supporters of music but fine musicians and composers themselves. (Maria Theresa played a mean double bass.) Composers like Haydn, Mozart, Beethoven, Schubert, Brahms, and Mahler gravitated to this music-friendly environment. They taught each other, jammed together, and spent a lot of time in Habsburg palaces. Beethoven was a famous figure, walking—lost in musical thought—through Vienna's woods.

After the defeat of Napoleon and the Congress of Vienna in 1815 (which shaped 19th-century Europe), Vienna enjoyed its violin-filled belle époque, which shaped our romantic image of the city—fine wine, chocolates, cafés, and waltzes. "Waltz King" Johann Strauss and his brothers kept Vienna's 300 ballrooms spinning.

This musical tradition that continues in our century leaves some prestigious Viennese institutions for today's tourists to enjoy: the Opera, the Boys' Choir, and the great Baroque halls and churches, all busy with classical and waltz concerts.

Planning Your Time

For a big city, Vienna is pleasant and laid-back. Vienna is worth two days and two nights. Not only is it packed with great sights, but it's also a joy to spend time in. It seems like Vienna was designed to help people simply meander through a day. To be grand-tour efficient, you could sleep in and sleep out on the train (Berlin, Venice, Rome, the Swiss Alps, Paris, and the Rhine are each handy night trains away). I'd come in from Salzburg via Hallstatt and spend two days this way:

Day 1: 9:00–Circle the Ring by tram, following the self-guided tour (below), 10:00–Tour Opera (take care of any TI and ticket needs), 11:00–Horse lovers tour the Lipizzaner Museum and see the horses practicing; art fans can visit the Academy of Fine Arts or the Art Nouveau sights at Karlsplatz; people watchers wander Naschmarkt, 12:00–Lunch at Buffet Trzesniewski or Rosenberger Markt Restaurant, 13:00–Tour Hofburg, visiting Augustinian church, royal apartments, treasury, Neue Burg, and Kaisergruft, 16:30–Stroll Kärntner Strasse, tour cathedral, and stroll Graben and Kohlmarkt, 19:00–Choose classical music, Heurige wine garden, Prater amusement park, or an opera performance; spend some time wandering the old center.

Vienna 27

Day 2: 9:00–Schönbrunn Palace, 13:00–Kunsthistorisches Museum after lunch, 15:00–Your choice of the many sights left to see in Vienna, Evening–See Day 1 evening options.

Orientation (tel. code: 01)

Vienna, or Wien (veen) in German, is bordered on three sides by the Vienna Woods (Wienerwald) and the Danube (Donau). To the southeast is industrial sprawl. The Alps, which arc across Europe from Marseilles, end at Vienna's wooded hills. These provide a popular playground for walking and new-wine drinking. This greenery's momentum carries on into the city. You'll notice more than half of Vienna is parkland, filled with ponds, gardens, trees, and statue memories of Austria's glory days.

Think of the city map as a target. The bull's-eye is the cathedral, the first circle is the Ring, and the second is the Gürtel. The old town snuggles around towering St. Stephan's Cathedral south of the Donau, and is bound tightly by the Ringstrasse. The Ring, marking what was the city wall, circles the first district (or *Bezirk*). The Gürtel, a broader ring road, contains the rest of downtown (*Bezirkes* 2–9).

Addresses start with the *Bezirk*, followed by street and building number. Any address higher than the ninth *Bezirk* is beyond the Gürtel, far from the center. The middle two digits of Vienna's postal codes show the district, or *Bezirk*. The address "7, Lindengasse 4" is in the seventh district, #4 on Linden Street. Its postal code would be 1070. Nearly all your sightseeing will be done in the core first district or along the Ringstrasse. As a tourist, concern yourself only with this small old center. When you do, sprawling Vienna suddenly becomes manageable.

Tourist Information

Beware of "tourist offices" at the train stations, airport, and around town, which are hotel agencies in disguise. Vienna's real main tourist office, currently near the Opera House at Kärntner Strasse 38, is planning to move sometime in 2000 to Albertinaplatz, next to the Albertina Museum, a block behind the Opera (daily 9:00–19:00, tel. 01/211-140 or 01/513-8892, www.info.wien.at/). Stop here first with a list of needs and questions. Confirm your sightseeing plans and pick up the free and essential city map (also available at most hotels), the museum brochure (listing hours), the monthly program of concerts, (called "Programm"), Vienna's bike route brochure (*Tips for Radfahrer*), and the fact-filled *Young Vienna Scene* magazine.

Consider the TI's handy 50-AS *Vienna from A to Z* booklet. Every important building has a numbered flag banner that keys into this guidebook. A to Z numbers are keyed into the TI's city map. When lost, find one of the "famous-building flags" and match its number to your map. If you're at a "famous building," check the map to see what other key numbers are nearby, then check the A to Z book description to see if you want to go in.

I skip the much promoted 210-AS "Vienna Card," which gives you a three-day transit pass (worth 180 AS) and tiny discounts at museums on the push list (which you probably won't visit). But check the list of discounts; some travelers find it worthwhile.

Arrival in Vienna

By Train at the West Station (Westbahnhof): Most train travelers arrive at the Westbahnhof. The Reisebüro am Bahnhof, under the clock, can help with hotels (for a fee) and answer questions. Skip their 30-AS city map, free at hotels. To get to the city center (and most likely, your hotel) catch the U-3 subway (buy the 60-AS 24-hour pass from a *Tabak*/tobacco shop in the station or from a machine—good on all city transit). U-3 signs lead down long escalators to the subway tracks. Catch a subway in the direction of U-3 Erdberg. If your hotel is along Mariahilfer Strasse, your stop is on this line (see "Sleeping," below). If you're sleeping in the center or just sightseeing, ride five stops to Stephansplatz, escalate in the exit direction "Stephansplatz," and you'll hit the cathedral. The TI is a five-minute stroll down the busy Kärntner Strasse pedestrian street.

The Westbahnhof has a grocery store (daily 5:30–23:00), change offices (station ticket windows offer better rates than change offices and are open long hours), storage facilities, and rental bikes (see "Getting around Vienna," below). Airport buses and taxis await in front of the station.

By Train at the South Station (Sudbahnhof): This station has all the services, including bike rental, left luggage, and a TI (Mon–Fri 8:00–19:00, Sat 8:00–13:00, closed Sun). To reach Vienna's center, follow the "S" (Schnellbahn) signs to the right and down the stairs, and take any train in the direction "Floridsdorf"; transfer in two stops (at Landsstrasse/Wien Mitte) to the U-3 (yellow) line, direction "Ottakring." Stephensplatz is one stop away.

By Plane: The airport (16 km from town, tel. 01/7007-2233) is connected by 70-AS shuttle buses (2/hrly) to either the Westbahnhof (35 min) or the City Air Terminal (20 min) near the river in the old center. Taxis into town cost about 400 AS.

Getting around Vienna

By Bus, Tram, and Subway: To take simple and economical advantage of Vienna's fine transit system of buses, trams, and sleek, easy subways, buy the 24-hour (60-AS) or 72-hour (150-AS) subway/bus/tram pass at a station machine or at *Tabak* shops near any station. There are no manned ticket windows; it's all by machine, even on the trams. Take a moment to study the eye-friendly city center map on metro station walls to internalize how the metro and tram system can help you (subway routes are signed by the end-of-the-line stop). I use it mostly to zip along the Ring (tram #1 or #2) and subway to more outlying sights or hotels. The 30-AS transit map is overkill. All necessary routes are listed on the free tourist city map. Without a pass, either buy individual tickets (19 AS, good for one journey with necessary changes) from metro ticket machines or buy blocks of five tickets for 95 AS (19 AS apiece). Tickets are 22 AS on the trams (exact change only). Eight-strip, eight-day, 300-AS transit passes, called "8 Tage Umwelt Streifennetzkarte," can be shared (for instance, four people for two days each—a 33 percent savings over the already cheap 24-hour pass).

Stamp a time on your pass as you enter the system or tram (stiff 500-AS fine if caught without a valid ticket). Rookies miss stops because they fail to open the door. Push buttons, pull latches, do whatever it takes. Study your street map before you exit the subway; by choosing the right exit—signposted from the moment you step off the train—you'll save yourself lots of walking.

By Taxi: Vienna's comfortable, honest, and easy-to-flag-down taxis start at 27 AS. You'll pay 90 AS to go from the Opera to the South or West Train Station.

By Bike: Good as the city's transit system is, you may want to rent a bike and follow one of the routes recommended in the TI's biking brochure. Bikes are available at any train station (daily 04:00–24:00, 100 AS/day with railpass or train ticket, 150 AS without; rent early in morning before supply runs out). Pedal Power offers rental bikes (300 AS/half day, 395 AS/day, includes delivery and pickup from your hotel) and 3.5-hour two-language city tours (daily at 10:00, 280 AS includes bike and guide, Austellungsstrasse 3, U-1 to Praterstern and long walk, tel. 01/729-7234, www.pedalpower.co.at).

By Buggy: Rich romantics get around by traditional horse and buggy. You'll see the Fiakers clip-clopping tourists on tours lasting 20 minutes (500 AS), 40 minutes (800 AS), or one hour (1,300 AS).

Helpful Hints

Bank Alert: Banking is expensive in Vienna. Save 3 percent by comparing rates. (Warning: "Rieger Bank" is not a bank; it's an expensive exchange bureau in disguise.) Banks are open weekdays roughly from 8:00 to 15:00 and until 17:30 on Thursday. After-hours you can change money at train stations, the airport, or post offices. Commissions of 100 AS are sadly normal. A happy exception is the American Express Company office, which charges no commissions to change Amex checks (Mon–Fri 9:00–17:30, Sat 9:00–12:00, Kärntner Strasse 21–23, tel. 01/51540). ATMs are abundant.

Post Offices: The main post office is on Postgasse in the city center (open 24 hours daily, also has handy metered phones). The West and South train stations each have full-service post offices (open 4:00–24:00).

English Bookstores: Consider the British Bookshop (at the corner of Weihburggasse and Seilerstätte) or Shakespeare & Co. (Sterngasse 2, north of Höher Markt Square, tel. 01/535-5053).

Internet Access: The TI has an updated list. News Café Buchandlung is central (Mon–Fri 9:30–19:00, Sat–Sun 9:30–17:00, Kärntner Strasse 19, tel. 01/513-1450) and Internet Aktiv is near the Mariahilfer Strasse hotels (small sign, Zieglergasse 29, tel. 01/526-7389).

Laundry: These are few and far between; ask at your hotel. Gottshalks will do your laundry in a day (50 AS for one kilo, Mon–Fri 8:00–18:00, Sat 9:00–12:00, near St. Stephan's at Singerstrasse 22). Laundrette, near Mariahilfer Strasse, is handy (Mon–Fri 8:00–18:00, closed Sat–Sun, Siebensternstrasse 52, walk 4 blocks up Zollergasse from Mariahilfer Strasse).

City Tours

Walks: The *Walks in Vienna* brochure at the TI describes Vienna's many guided walks. Unfortunately, only a few are in English (130 AS, not including admissions, 90 min, tel. 01/894-5363). Eva Prochaska can book you a private guide who charges 1,230 AS for a half-day tour (Weihburggasse 13–15, tel. 01/513-5294).

Bus Tours: Vienna Line offers hop-on hop-off tours covering the 14 predictable sightseeing stops. Given Vienna's excellent public transportation and this outfit's meager one-bus-per-hour frequency, I'd take this not to hop on and off, but only to get a 2.5-hour narrated (in German and English) orientation drive through town (250 AS, good for two days, for this and more tours tel. 01/714-1141).

Do-It-Yourself Bus Orientation Tour

▲▲**Ringstrasse Tour**—In the 1860s Emperor Franz Josef had the city's ingrown medieval wall torn down and replaced with a grand boulevard 190 feet wide. The road, arcing nearly three miles around the city's core, predates all the buildings that line it. So what you'll see is neo-Gothic, neoclassical, and neo-Renaissance. One of Europe's great streets, it's lined with many of the city's top sights. Trams #1 and #2 and an ideal bike path circle the whole route and so should you.

This self-service tram tour gives you a fun orientation and a ridiculously quick glimpse of the major sights as you glide by (20-AS, 30-minute circular tour). For an actual look at these sights, consider biking or hiking most of the route. Tram #1 goes clockwise; tram #2, counterclockwise. Most sights are on the outside, so tram #2 is best (sit on right). The tour assumes you're

Vienna

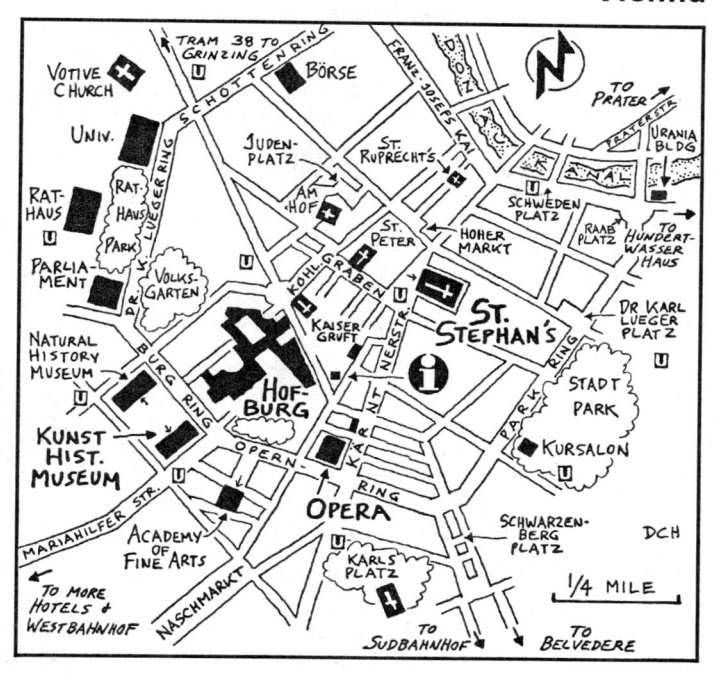

sitting in front of the front car. Start at the Opera House. With a 24-hour ticket, you can jump on and off as you go—trams come every five minutes. (Otherwise, buy your 22-AS one-ride ticket as you board, exact change only.) Read ahead and pay attention, these sights can fly by. Let's go:

☛ Immediately on the left: The city's main pedestrian drag, Kärntner Strasse, leads to the zigzag roof of St. Stephan's Cathedral. This tour makes a 360-degree circle, staying about this far from that spire.

☛ At first bend: Look right toward the tall fountain (if it's not going, look for the equestrian statue). Schwartzenberg Platz—with its equestrian statue of Prince Charles Schwartzenberg, who fought Napoleon—leads to the Russian monument (behind the fountain). This monument was built in 1945 as a forced thanks to the Soviets for liberating Austria from the Nazis. Formerly a sore point, now it's just ignored.

☛ Going down Schubertring, you reach the huge *Stadtpark* (city park) on the right, which honors 20 great Viennese musicians and composers with statues. At the beginning of the park, the white and yellow concert hall behind the trees is the Kursalon, opened in 1867 by the Strauss brothers, who directed many waltzes here (see "Music," below).

☛ Immediately after next stop: In the same park, the gilded statue of Waltz King Johann Strauss holds his violin as he did when he conducted his orchestra.

☛ While at next stop at end of park: On the left, a green statue of Dr. Karl Lueger honors the popular man who was mayor of Vienna until 1910.

☛ At next bend: On the right, the white quaint building with military helmets decorating the windows was the Austrian ministry of war, back when that was a serious operation. Field Marshal Radetzky, a military big shot in the 19th century under Franz Josef, still sits on his high horse.

☛ At next corner: The white-domed building over your right shoulder as you turn is the Urania, Franz Josef's 1910 observatory. Lean forward and look behind it for a peek at the huge red cars of the giant 100-year-old Ferris wheel in Vienna's Prater Park.

☛ Now you're rolling along the Danube Canal. This "Baby Danube" is one of the many small arms of the river that once made up the Danube at this point. The rest have been gathered together in a mightier modern-day Danube, farther away. This was the site of the original Roman town, Vindobona. In three long blocks, on the left (opposite BP station, be ready—it passes fast), you'll see the ivy-covered walls and round Romanesque arches of St. Ruprechts, the oldest church in Vienna (built in the 11th century on a bit of Roman ruins). By about 1200, Vienna had grown to fill the area within this ring road.

☛ Leaving the canal, turning up Schottenring, at first stop: On the left, the pink-and-white, neo-Renaissance temple of money, the Börse, is Vienna's stock exchange.

☛ Next stop, at corner: The huge, frilly, neo-Gothic church on the right is a "votive church," built in 1853 as a thanks to God when an assassination attempt on Emperor Franz Josef failed. Ahead on the right is the Vienna University building, which faces (on the left, behind the gilded angel) a chunk of the old city wall.

☛ At next stop on right: The neo-Gothic city hall, flying the flag of Europe, towers over Rathaus Platz, a festive site of outdoor movies and concerts. Immediately across the street (on left) is the Hofburg Theater, Austria's national theater.

☛ At next stop on right: The neo-Greek temple of democracy houses the Austrian Parliament. The lady with the golden helmet is Athena, goddess of wisdom. Across the street (on left) is the royal park called the "Volksgarten." (Get ready, the next stop is packed with sights.)

Vienna

☛ At next stop on the right is the Natural History Museum, the first of Vienna's huge twin museums. Next door is the Kunsthistorisches Museum, containing the city's greatest collection of paintings. A statue of Empress Maria Theresa sits between the museums, facing the grand gate to the Hofburg, the emperor's palace (on left). Of the five arches, only the center one was used by the emperor. The gate, a modern addition, is located where Vienna's medieval city wall once stood.

☛ Fifty yards after next stop, through a gate in the black iron fence: On the left is the statue of Mozart in the Burggarten, which until 1880 was the private garden of the emperor. A hundred yards farther (on left, just out of the park), Goethe sits in a big, thought-provoking chair playing Trivia with Schiller (across the street on your right). Behind the statue of Schiller is the Academy of Fine Arts. Vienna had its share of intellectual and creative geniuses.

☛ Hey, there's the Opera again. Jump off the bus and see the rest of the city.

Sights—Vienna's Old Center

(Sights are listed in a logical walking order.)

▲▲▲**Opera (Staatsoper)**—The Opera, facing the Ring and near the TI, is a central point for any visitor. While the critical reception of the building 130 years ago led the architect to commit suicide, and though it's been rebuilt since the World War II bombings, it's a dazzling place (65 AS, by guided 35-minute tour only, daily in English, Jul–Aug at 11:00, 13:00, 14:00, 15:00, and often at 10:00 and 16:00; other months, afternoons only). Tours are often canceled for rehearsals and shows, so check the posted schedule or call 01/51444 or 01/514-442-959.

The Vienna State Opera, with not the Vienna Philharmonic Orchestra but its farm team in the pit (you can't get into the best orchestra in town without doing time here), is one of the world's top opera houses. There are 300 performances a year—nearly nightly, except in July and August (when the singers rest their voices). Expensive seats are normally sold out. Unless Pavarotti is in town, it's easy to get one of 567 *Stehplatz* (standing-room spots, 30–50 AS for the very top, better 30-AS spots downstairs). If fewer than 567 people are in line, there's no need to line up early. The *Stehplatz* ticket window in the front lobby opens 80 minutes before each performance (*Stehplatz* information tel. 01/5144-42419, e-mail: tickets@volksoper.at). Dress is casual (but do your best) at the standing-room bar.

Rick's crude tip: For me, three hours is a lot of opera. But just to see and hear the Opera House in action for half an hour is a treat. You can buy a ticket intending to just drop in for part of the show. Ushers don't mind letting tourists with standing-room tickets in for a short look. Ending time is posted in the lobby—you could drop in for just the finale. If you go for the start or finish you'll see Vienna dressed up. With all the time you save, consider stopping by...

Sacher Café, home of every chocoholic's fantasy, the *Sachertorte*, faces the rear of the Opera (on Philharmoniker Strasse). A coffee and slice of cake here is 100 AS well invested.

Monument against War and Fascism—Behind the Opera House, on Albertinaplatz, a modern, white split statue is Vienna's monument remembering the victims of the 1938–1945 Nazi rule of Austria. In 1938, Germany annexed Austria, saying Austrians were wannabe-Germans anyway. Austrians are not Germans—never were, never will be. They're quick to tell you that, while Austria was founded in 976, Germany wasn't born until 1870. For seven years (1938–1945), there was no Austria. In 1955, after 10 years of joint occupation by the victorious Allies, Austria regained her independence.

▲**Kärntner Strasse**—This grand mall (traffic-free since 1974) is the people-watching delight of this in-love-with-life city. It points south in the direction of the southern Austrian state of Kärnten (for which it's named). Starting from the Opera, you'll find the TI, city casino (at #41, the former Esterhazy Palace), many fine stores, pastry shops, an American Express office (#21–23), and then, finally, the cathedral.

▲▲**St. Stephan's Cathedral**—Stephansdom is the Gothic needle around which Vienna spins. It's survived Vienna's many wars and symbolizes the city's freedom. Locals call it "Steve" (*Steffl*, church open daily 6:00–22:00, most tours are in German—1/day in English at best, information board inside entry has tour schedules and time of impressive 50-minute daily Mass).

Outside, the last bit of the 11th-century Romanesque church can be seen in the west end (above the entry): the portal and the round windows of the towers. The church survived the bombs of World War II, but in the last days of the war, fires from the street fighting between Russian and Nazi troops leapt to the rooftop; the original timbered Gothic rooftop burnt, and the cathedral's huge bell crashed to the ground. With a financial outpouring of civic pride, the roof of this symbol of Austria was rebuilt in its original splendor by 1952. The ceramic tiles are purely decorative (and each has the name of a local who contributed money to the rebuilding). Photos of the war damage can be seen inside.

The interior is grand in general, but it's hard to get thrilled about any particular bit. An exception is the Gothic sandstone pulpit in the middle of the nave (on left or north). A spiral stairway winds up to the lectern, surrounded and supported by the four Latin Church fathers: St. Ambrose, St. Gerome, St. Gregory, and St. Augustine. The work of Anton Pilgram, this has all the elements of Flamboyant Gothic in miniature. But this was 1515. The Italian Renaissance was going strong in Italy and, while Gothic persisted in the north, the Renaissance spirit had already arrived. Pilgram included a rare self-portrait bust in his work (the guy with sculptor's tools, looking out a window under the stairs). Gothic art was to the glory of God. Artists were anonymous. In the more humanist Renaissance, man was allowed to shine—and artists became famous.

Hundreds of years of history are carved in its walls and buried in its crypt (left transept, 40 AS, open at odd times, tel. 01/515-523-526). You can ascend both towers, the north (via crowded elevator inside on the left) and the south (by spiral staircase). The north shows you a big bell (the 21-ton Pummerin, cast from the cannon captured from the Turks in 1683) but a mediocre view (40 AS, daily 9:00–18:00, enter inside). The 450-foot-high south tower, called St. Stephan's Tower, offers a great view—343 tightly wound steps away, up the spiral staircase at the watchman's lookout (30 AS, daily 9:00–17:30, enter outside right transept and burn about one *Sachertorte* of calories). From the top, use your *Vienna from A to Z* to locate the famous sights.

The peaceful Cathedral Museum (Dom Museum, outside left transept past horses) gives a close-up look at piles of religious paintings, statues, and a treasury (50 AS, Tue–Sat 10:00–17:00, closed Mon, behind church and past buggy stand, Stephansplatz 6). Near the church entrance, descend into the Stephansplatz subway stop for a peek into the 13th-century Virgilkapelle.

▲▲**Stephansplatz, Graben, and Kohlmarkt**—The atmosphere of the church square, Stephanplatz, is colorful and lively. At nearby Graben Street (which was once a *Graben*, or "ditch"), top-notch street entertainment dances around an exotic plague monument (at Brauner Strass). In medieval times people did not understand the causes of plagues and figured they were a punishment from God. It was common for survivors to thank God with a monument like this one from the 1600s.

Just beyond the monument is a fine set of Jugendstil public toilets more than worth the effort to explore (men must go through the door in the first area, women pay 5.50 AS). St. Peter's Church faces the toilets. Step into this festival of Baroque (from 1708) and check out the jeweled skeletons—anonymous martyrs donated by the pope.

Kohlmarkt (end of Graben), Vienna's most elegant shopping street (except for "American Catalog Shopping," at #5, second floor), leads left to the palace. Wander down here, checking out the edible window displays at Demel (Kohlmarkt 14). Then drool through the interior (coffee and cake for 100 AS). Shops like this boast "K. u. K." This means a shop considered good enough for the *König und Kaiser* (king and emperor—same guy).

Kohlmarkt leads to Michaelerplatz. The stables of the Spanish Riding School face this square a block to the left. Notice the Roman excavation in the center. Enter the Hofburg Palace by walking through the gate and into the first square (In der Burg).

Sights—Vienna's Hofburg Palace

▲▲**Hofburg**—The complex, confusing, imposing Imperial Palace, with 640 years of architecture, demands your attention. This first Habsburg residence grew with the family empire from the 13th century until 1913, when the new wing was opened. The winter residence of the Habsburg rulers until 1918, it's still the home of the Spanish Riding School, the Vienna Boys' Choir, the Austrian president's office, and several important museums.

While you could lose yourself in its myriad halls and courtyards, I'd focus on three things: the Imperial Apartments, Treasury, and Neue Burg (New Palace).

Orient from **In der Burg Square**. The statue is of Emperor Franz II (grandson of Maria Theresa and grandfather of Franz Josef). Behind him is a tower with three kinds of clocks—the yellow disc shows the stage of the moon tonight. On the right, a door leads to the Imperial Apartments and Hofburg model. Franz II is facing the oldest part of the palace. The gate, which used to have a drawbridge, leads to the 13th-century Swiss Court (named for the Swiss mercenary guards who used to be stationed here) with the Schatzkammer (treasury) and Hofburgkappelle (palace chapel)— where the Boys' Choir sings the mass. Continuing out opposite the way you entered In der Burg, you'll pass through the left-most tunnel (with a handy sandwich bar—Hofburg Stüberl) to the Hero's Square and the Neue Burg. Tour the Imperial Apartments first.

▲▲**Imperial Apartments (Kaiserappartements)**—These lavish, Versailles-type "wish-I-were-God" royal rooms are a small, downtown version of the grander Schönbrunn Palace. If rushed, and you have time for only one, these suffice. The Imperial Apartments share a ticket booth with the Silver and Porcelain Collection (Silberkammer). You can tour either for 80 AS or get a Kombi-Ticket for 95 AS and see them both (daily 9:00–17:00, from courtyard through St. Michael's Gate, just off Michaelerplatz, tel. 01/533-7570). While combo tickets are cheap, for most, the rooms of plates and fancy silverware are not worth the extra 15 AS or time. (Study the great Hofburg model outside near the ticket line; from there, see enough of the collection through the window.) Palace visits are a one-way romp through 20 rooms. You'll find some helpful English information within, and together with the following description, you won't need the 95-AS Hofburg guidebook.

Get your ticket and climb two flights. The first two rooms give an overview (in English) of Empress Elisabeth's assortment of luxury homes, including the Hofburg. Her mantra was to not stay put in one spot too long.

Amble through the first several furnished rooms to:

The audience chamber: Three huge paintings would entertain guests waiting here before an audience with the emperor. Every

Vienna's Hofburg Palace

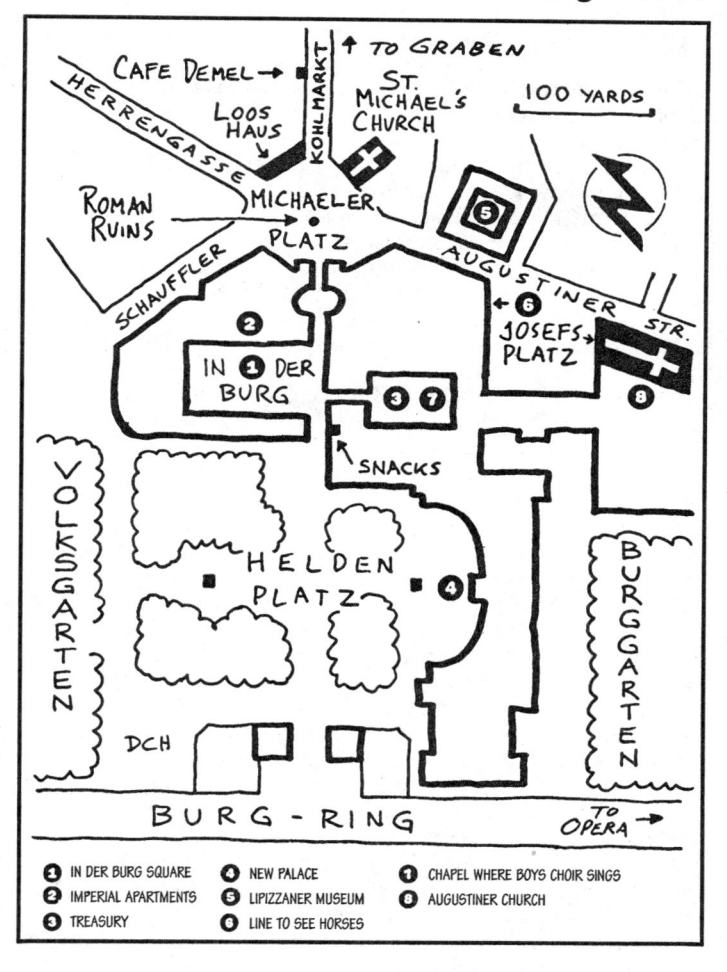

- **1** IN DER BURG SQUARE
- **2** IMPERIAL APARTMENTS
- **3** TREASURY
- **4** NEW PALACE
- **5** LIPIZZANER MUSEUM
- **6** LINE TO SEE HORSES
- **7** CHAPEL WHERE BOYS CHOIR SINGS
- **8** AUGUSTINER CHURCH

citizen had the right to meet privately with the emperor. Paintings in this room show crowds of commoners enthusiastic about their Habsburg royalty. On the right: the emperor returning to Vienna celebrating news that Napoleon had begun his retreat in 1809. Left: the return of the emperor from the 1814 Peace of Paris, the treaty that ended the Napoleonic wars. (The 1815 Congress of Vienna that followed was the greatest assembly of diplomats in European history.

Its goal: to establish peace through a "balance of power" among nations. While rulers ignored nationalism in favor of continued dynastic rule, this worked for about 100 years, when a colossal war wiped out Europe's royal families.) Center: Less importantly, the emperor makes his first public appearance to adoring crowds after recovering from a life-threatening illness (1826). The chandelier is Baroque of Bohemian crystal.

Audience room: Suddenly you were face to face with the emp. The portrait shows Franz Josef (my vote for the greatest Habsburg emperor) in 1915 when he was over 80 years old. Famously energetic, he lived a spartan life dedicated to duty. He'd stand at the high table here to meet with commoners who came to show gratitude or make a request. (Standing kept things moving.) On the table you see a partial list of 56 appointments he had on June 3, 1910.

Conference room: The emperor presided here over the equivalent of cabinet meetings.

Emperor Franz Josef's study: The desk was originally between the windows. Franz Josef could look up from his work and see his lovely empress Elisabeth's reflection in the mirror. "Sissy's" main purpose in life seemed to be to preserve her reputation as a beautiful empress and maintain her fairy-tale hair. In spite of severe dieting and fanatic exercise, age took its toll. After turning 30, she had no portraits painted and was seen in public generally with a delicate fan covering her face. Notice the trompe l'oeil paintings above each door giving the believable illusion of marble relief.

The walls between the rooms are wide enough to hide **servants' corridors**. The emperor lived with a personal staff of 14: "3 valets, 4 lackeys, 2 doormen, 2 manservants, and 3 chambermaids." Look for window shades with English info in the next several rooms.

Emperor's bedroom: This features his famous spartan iron bed and portable washstand (necessary until 1880 when the palace got running water). A small painted porcelain portrait of the newlywed royal couple sits on the dresser. Franz Josef lived here after his estrangement from Sissy. An etching shows the empress—an avid hunter—riding sidesaddle while jumping a hedge. The big ornate stove in the corner was fed from behind. Through the 19th century, this was a standard form of heating.

Great salon: See the paintings of the emperor and empress in grand gala ballroom outfits from 1865.

The emperor's smoking room: This is dedicated to the memory of the assassinated Emperor Maximillian of Mexico (bearded portrait, killed in 1867). A smoking room was necessary in the early 19th century, when smoking was newly fashionable but only for men and then not in the presence of women.

The empress' bedroom and drawing room: This was Sissy's, refurbished neorococo in 1854. She lived here until her death in 1898.

Sissy's dressing/gymnastic room: This was the marital bedroom of the newlywed couple. The open bathroom door shows her huge copper tub. Servants worked two hours a day on Sissy's famous ankle-length hair here. She'd exercise on the wooden structure. While she had a tough time with people, she did fine with animals. Her favorite circus horses, Flick and Flock, prance on the wall.

The empress' great salon: The room is painted with Mediterranean escapes, the 19th-century equivalent of travel posters. The statue is of Elisa, Napoleon's oldest sister (by the neoclassical master Canova). At the end of the hall admire the empress' hard-earned thin waist. Turn the corner and pass through the anterooms of Alexander's apartments.

Reception room: This has Gobelin wall hangings, a 1776 gift from Marie Antoinette and Louis XVI in Paris to their Viennese counterparts.

The dining room: It's dinner time, and Franz Josef has called his large family together. The settings are of modest silver. Gold was saved for formal state dinners. Next to each name card was a menu with the chef responsible for each dish. (Talk about pressure.) While the Hofburg had tableware for 4,000, feeding 3,000 was a typical day. The cellar was stocked with 60,000 bottles of wine—fit for an emperor. The kitchen was huge—50 birds could be roasted on the hand-driven spits at once.

Small salon: The last room is dedicated to Franz Josef's first two heirs: Rudolf (his troubled son, who committed suicide in 1889) and Franz Ferdinand (his liberal nephew, assassinated in Sarajevo in 1914). Two quick lefts out of the exit will take you back to the palace square (In der Burg) and the treasury.

▲▲▲**Treasury**—The Weltliche und Geistliche Schatzkammer (Secular and Religious Treasure Room) contains by far the best jewels on the Continent. Slip through the vault doors and reflect on the glitter of 21 rooms filled with scepters, swords, crowns, orbs, weighty robes, a 96-inch-tall and 500-year-old unicorn horn (or maybe the tusk of a narwhal), double-headed eagles, gowns, dangles, and gem-studded bangles. Remember that these were owned by the Holy Roman Emperor—a divine monarch (100 AS, Wed–Mon 10:00–18:00, closed Tue, follow "Schatzkammer" signs through the black, red, and gold arch leading from the main courtyard into Schweizerhof, tel. 01/533-7931). Take advantage of the ingenious and helpful Art-Guide minivideo (deposit: passport or 500 AS). Point this infrared computer at display cases to get information.

Study the Throne Cradle (room 5). Napoleon's son was born in 1811 and made king of Rome. The little eagle at the foot is symbolically not yet able to fly, but glory bound. "Glory" is the star with his dad's big "N" raised high.

The collection's highlight is the 10th-century crown of the Holy Roman Emperor (room 11). The imperial crown swirls with symbolism "proving" that the emperor is both holy and Roman. The jeweled arch over the top is reminiscent of the parade helmet of ancient Roman emperors whose successors the HRE claimed to be. The cross on top says that the HRE rules as Christ's representative on earth. King Solomon's portrait is Old Testament proof that kings can be wise and good. The crown's eight sides represent the celestial city of Jerusalem's eight gates. The jewels on the front panel symbolize the Twelve Apostles. The honorary 13th stone is the HRE.

Two cases in this room have jewels from the reign of Karl der Grosse (Charlemagne), the greatest ruler of medieval Europe. Notice Charlemagne modeling the crown in the tall painting adjacent. Room 12 features a painting of the coronation of Josef II in 1764, wearing the crown and royal garb you've just seen.

▲Neue Burg (New Palace)—The New Palace is labeled "Kuntistorisches Museum" because it contains one wing from the main museum across the way. This last grand addition to the palace, from just before World War I, was built for Franz Ferdinand but never used. Its grand facade arches around Heldenplatz, or Hero's Square. Notice statues of the two great Austrian heroes on horseback: Prince Eugene of Savoy (who saved the city from the Turks) and Archduke Charles Schwartzenberg (first to beat Napoleon in a battle, breaking Nappy's image of invincibility and heralding the end of the Napoleonic age). The Neue Burg houses three small but fine museums (same ticket): an armory, historical musical instruments, and classical statuary from ancient Ephesus. The musical instruments are particularly entertaining, and free radio headsets (when they work) play appropriate music in each room. Wait for the brief German description to finish, and you might hear the instruments you're seeing. Stay tuned in, as graceful period music accompanies your wander through the neighboring halls of medieval weaponry—a killer collection of crossbows, swords, and armor. An added bonus is the chance to wander all alone among those royal Habsburg halls, stairways, and painted ceilings. Gavotte to the music down the royal stairs and out (60 AS for all three collections, Wed–Mon 10:00–18:00, closed Tue, almost no tourists).

Sights—Schönbrunn Palace

▲▲▲Schönbrunn Palace—Among Europe's palaces, only Schloss Schönbrunn rivals Versailles. Located seven kilometers from the center, it was the Habsburgs' summer residence. It is big—1,441 rooms—but don't worry, only 40 rooms are shown to the public. (The families of 260 civil servants actually rent simple apartments in the rest of the palace.)

While the exterior is Baroque, the interior was finished under Maria Theresa in the let-them-eat-cake rococo style. The chandeliers are either of hand-carved wood with gold-leaf gilding or of Bohemian crystal. Thick walls hid the servants as they ran around stoking the ceramic stoves from the back, and so on. Most of the public rooms are decorated in neo-Baroque as they were under Franz Josef (ruled 1848–1916). While World War II bombs rained on the city and the palace grounds, the palace itself took only one direct hit. Thankfully, that bomb, which crashed through three floors, including the sumptuous central ballroom, was a dud.

Choose between the Imperial Tour and the bigger Grand Tour. Both come with free headphones that describe the sights in English as you walk through the rooms on your own. The Imperial Tour covers 22 rooms (90 AS, 30 min, Grand Palace rooms plus apartments of Franz Josef and Elisabeth). I'd recommend the Grand Tour, which covers those 22 rooms plus 18 more (120 AS, 45 min, adds apartments of Maria Theresa). Optional guided tours do all 40 rooms in English (departing roughly every two hours, 25 AS extra). The headphones are so good I'd skip the tour.

Schönbrunn suffers from serious crowd problems. To avoid the long delays, make a reservation by telephone (01/8111-3239). You'll get an appointment time and ticket number. Upon arrival, go to the first desk for group leaders, give your number, pick up your ticket, and jump in ahead of the masses. If you show up without calling first, wait in line, buy your ticket, and wait until the listed time to enter (which could be tomorrow). Kill time in the gardens or coach museum (palace open daily 8:30–17:45, last entry 17:00; off-season until 17:15, last entry 16:30; take tram #58 from Westbahnhof or U-4 to Schönbrunn; U-4 leaves you 300 yards from entry; tel. 01/8111-3239). Crowds are worst around 10:00 and on weekends; it's least crowded from 12:00 to 14:00 and after 16:00. The main entrance is on the left side of the palace.

Coach Museum Wagenburg: The Schönbrunn coach museum is a 19th-century traffic jam of 50 impressive royal carriages and sleighs. Highlights include silly sedan chairs, the death-black hearse carriage (used for Franz Josef in 1916 and most recently for Empress Zita in 1989), and an extravagantly gilded imperial carriage pulled by eight Cinderella horses (60 AS, daily 9:00–18:00, off-season 10:00–16:00 and closes on winter Mon, 200 meters from palace, exit through right arch as you face palace).

Palace Gardens: A stroll through the emperor's garden with countless commoners (after strolling through all the Habsburgs tucked neatly into their crypts) is a celebration of the natural (and necessary) evolution of civilization from autocracy into real democracy. We're doing well. The sculpted gardens (with a palm house, 45 AS, 9:30–18:00) lead past Europe's oldest zoo (Tiergarten, 100 AS, built by Maria Theresa's husband for the entertainment and education of the court in 1752) up to the Gloriette, a purely decorative monument celebrating an obscure Austrian military victory and offering a fine city view (and an expensive cup of coffee). The park is free and open until dusk; entrance is on either side of the palace.

More Sights—Vienna

▲**Lipizzaner Museum**—This is a must for horse lovers. This tidy new museum in the Renaissance Stallburg Palace shows the 400-year history of the famous riding school. Videos show the horses in action (on TVs throughout and in the basement theater—45-minute movie in German, but great horse footage). A highlight for many is the opportunity to view the stable from a museum window and actually see the famous white horses just sitting there looking common (50 AS, daily 9:00–18:00, Reitschulgasse 2 between Josefsplatz and Michaelerplatz, tel. 01/533-7811). At the end of World War II, knowing that the Soviets were about to take control of Vienna, U.S. General Patton ordered a raid on the stable to save the horses and insure the survival of their fine old bloodlines.

Seeing the Lipizzaner Stallions: Seats for performances by Vienna's prestigious Spanish Riding School are always booked in advance, but standing room is usually available the same day (tickets 250–900 AS, standing room-200 AS, one or two shows per week Apr–Jun and Sept–Oct). Lucky for the masses, training sessions in a chandeliered Baroque hall are open to the public (100 AS at the door, Tue–Fri 10:00–12:00 roughly Feb–Jun and Sept–Dec; occasional rehearsals with music on Sat are especially entertaining). The gang lines up early at Josefsplatz, gate 2. Save money and avoid the wait by buying admission to the training session together with a ticket to the museum. Or, better yet, simply show up late. Tourists line up for hours to get in at 10:00. Anyone can just waltz in with no wait at all after 11:00. Almost no one stays for the full two hours—except for the horses.

▲**Augustinian Church**—Step into the nearby Augustinerkirche (on Josefsplatz), the church where the Habsburg weddings took place. Don't miss the exquisite Canova tomb (neoclassical, 1805) of Maria Theresa's favorite daughter, Maria Christina, with its incredibly sad white-marble procession. The church has the burial vault for the hearts of the Habsburgs (by appointment only).

▲▲**Kaisergruft, the Remains of the Habsburgs**—Visiting the imperial remains is not as easy as you might imagine. These original organ donors left their bodies—147 in all—in the Kaisergruft (Capuchin Crypt), their hearts in St. George Chapel in the Augustinian Church (church open daily, but to see the goods you'll have to talk to a priest; near the Hofburg, Augustinerstrasse 3), and their entrails in the crypt below St. Stephan's Cathedral. Don't tripe.

Upon entering the Kaisergruft (40 AS, daily 9:30–16:00, behind Opera on Neuer Markt), buy the 5-AS map with a Habsburg family tree and a chart locating each coffin from the Capuchin brother at the door. The double coffin of Maria Theresa and her husband is worth a close look for its artwork. Don't miss the tomb of Franz Josef and—the latest addition—Empress Zita, buried in 1989.

Vienna

Rather than chasing down all these body parts, remember that the magnificence of this city is the real remains of the Habsburgs. Pan up. Watch the clouds glide by the ornate gables of Vienna.

▲▲▲**Kunsthistorisches Museum**—This exciting museum across the Ring from the Hofburg Palace showcases the great Habsburg art collection—masterpieces by Dürer, Rubens, Titian, Raphael, and especially Brueghel. There's also a fine display of Egyptian, classical, and applied arts, including a divine golden salt bowl by Cellini. The museum sells a 20-AS pamphlet on the top 21 paintings and offers 90-minute English tours (30 AS, Apr–Oct Tue–Sun usually at 11:00 and 15:00). The paintings are hung on one floor (100 AS, higher depending on special exhibitions, Tue–Sun 10:00–18:00, Thu until 21:00, closed Mon, tel. 01/525-240).

Natural History Museum—In the twin building facing the art museum, you'll find moon rocks, dinosaur stuff, and the fist-sized *Venus of Willendorf*—at 30,000 years old, the world's oldest sex symbol, found in the Danube Valley (30 AS, Wed–Mon 9:00–18:30, Wed until 21:00, closed Tue, off-season 9:00–15:00).

▲**Academy of Fine Arts**—This small but exciting collection includes works by Bosch, Botticelli, and Rubens; a Venice series by Guardi; and a self-portrait by 15-year-old Van Dyck (50 AS, Tue–Sun 10:00–16:00, closed Mon, 3 blocks from Opera at Schillerplatz 3, tel. 01/5881-6225).

KunstHausWien—This "make yourself at home" modern-art museum is a hit with lovers of modern art. It features the work of local painter/environmentalist Hundertwasser (95 AS, 48 AS on Mon, daily 10:00–19:00; 3, Weissgerberstrasse 13, nearest metro: U-3 Landstrasse, tel. 01/712-0491). Nearby, the one-with-nature Hundertwasserhaus (at Löwengasse and Kegelgasse) is a complex of 50 lived-in apartments. This was built in the 1980s as a breath of architectural fresh air in a city of boring blocky apartment complexes. It's not open to visitors but is worth visiting for its fun-loving and colorful patchwork exterior, the Hundertwasser festival of shops across the street, and for the pleasure of annoying its residents.

▲**Belvedere Palace**—The elegant palace of Prince Eugene of Savoy (the still-much-appreciated conqueror of the Turks), and later home of Franz Ferdinand, houses the Austrian Gallery of 19th- and 20th-century art. Skip the lower palace and focus on the garden and the top floor of the upper palace (Oberes Belvedere) for a winning view of the city and a fine collection of Jugendstil art, Klimt, and Kokoschka (60 AS, Tue–Sun 10:00–17:00, closed Mon, entrance at Prinz Eugen Strasse 27, tel. 01/7955-7134). Your ticket includes the Austrian Baroque and Gothic art in the lower palace.

Top People-Watching and Strolling Sights

▲**City Park**—Vienna's Stadtpark is a waltzing world of gardens, memorials to local musicians, ponds, peacocks, music in bandstands, and local people escaping the city. Notice the Jugendstil entry at the Stadtpark subway station. The Kursalon orchestra plays Strauss waltzes nightly in summer (see "Music," below).

▲**Prater**—Vienna's sprawling amusement park tempts any visitor with its huge 220-foot-high, famous, and lazy Ferris wheel (*Riesenrad*), roller coaster, bumper cars, Lilliputian railroad, and endless eateries. This is a fun, goofy place to share the evening with thousands of Viennese (daily 9:00–24:00 in summer, U-Bahn: Praterstern). For a local-style family dinner, eat at Schweizerhaus (good food, great beer) or Wieselburger Bierinsel.

Sunbathing—Like most Europeans, the Austrians worship the sun. Their lavish swimming centers are as much for tanning as for swimming. For the best man-made island beach scene, head for the "Danube Sea," Vienna's 20 miles of beach along Danube Island (subway: Donauinsel).

▲**Naschmarkt**—Vienna's ye olde produce market bustles daily, near the Opera along Wienzeile Street. It's likably seedy and surrounded by sausage stands, Turkish *döner kebab* stalls, cafés, and theaters. Each Saturday it's infested by a huge flea market where, in olden days, locals would come to hire a monkey to pick little critters out of their hair (Mon–Fri 6:00–18:30, Sat 6:00–17:00). For a picnic park, walk a block down Schleifmuhlgasse.

Summer Music Scene

Vienna is Europe's music capital. It's music *con brio* from October through June, with things reaching a symphonic climax during the Vienna Festival each May and June. Sadly, in July and August, the Boys' Choir, the Opera, and many more music companies are—like you—on vacation. But Vienna hums year-round with live classical music. In the summer, you have these basic choices:

Touristy Mozart and Strauss Concerts—If the music comes to you, it's touristy—designed for flash-in-the-pan Mozart fans. Powdered-wig orchestra performances are given almost nightly in grand traditional settings (400–600 AS). Pesky wigged and powdered Mozarts peddle tickets in the streets with slick sales pitches about the magic of the venue and the quality of the musicians. Second-rate orchestras, clad in historic costumes, perform the greatest hits of Mozart and Strauss. While there's not a local person in the audience, the tourists generally enjoy the evening.

Strauss in the Kursalon—Two rival companies offer Strauss concerts inside the Kursalon, where the Waltz King himself directed wildly popular concerts 100 years ago. To accommodate antsy groups, concert tickets are sold in two sections: 20:00–21:00 and 21:30–22:30 (260 AS for one with a glass of wine, 490 AS for both, tel. 01/718-9666; for the other company, tel. 01/710-5580). Or pick up the brochures from racks all over town. Shows are a touristy mix of ballet, waltzing, 15-piece orchestra in wigs and old outfits, and a

Vienna 45

chance to get on the floor and waltz yourself. On balmy summer evenings, the concert moves into the romantic garden.
Serious Concerts—These events, including the Opera, are listed in the monthly *Programm* (available at the TI). Tickets run from 300 to 700 AS (plus a stiff 25 percent booking fee when booked in advance or through a box office like the one next to the TI behind the Opera). If you call a concert hall directly, they can advise you on the availability of (cheaper) tickets at the door. Vienna takes care of its starving artists (and tourists) by offering cheap standing-room tickets to top-notch music and opera. Locals are amazed at the stiff prices tourists pay to see otherwise affordable concerts.

Vienna's Summer of Music Festival assures that even from June through September you'll find lots of great concerts, choirs, and symphonies (special *Klang Bogen* brochure at TI; get tickets at Wien Ticket pavilion off Kärntner Strasse next to Opera House, or go directly to location of particular event, tel. 01/4000-8410 for information).

▲▲**Vienna Boys' Choir**—The boys sing (heard but not seen, from a high balcony) at Mass in the Imperial Chapel (Hofburgkapelle) of the Hofburg (entrance at Schweizerhof) at 9:15 on Sundays, except from July through mid-September. Seats must be reserved at least two months in advance (60–340 AS), but standing room inside is free and open to the first 60 who line up. Rather than line up early, you can simply swing by and stand in the narthex just outside, from where you can hear the boys and see the Mass on a TV monitor. Boys' Choir concerts (on stage in the Konzerthaus) are also given Fridays at 15:30 in May, June, September, and October (390–430 AS, tel. 01/5880-4141, fax 011-431-533-992-775 from the U.S., or write Hofmusikkapelle, Hofburg, A-1010 Wien). They're nice kids, but for my taste, not worth all the commotion.

Vienna's Cafés and Wine Gardens
▲**Viennese Coffeehouse**—In Vienna the living room is down the street at the neighborhood coffeehouse. This tradition is just another example of the Viennese expertise in good living. Each of Vienna's many long-established (and sometimes even legendary) coffeehouses has its individual character (and characters). They offer newspapers, pastries, sofas, elegance, a smoky ambience, and a "take all the time you want" charm for the price of a cup of coffee. You may want to order *malange* (with a little milk) rather than *schwarzer* (black).

My favorites are: **Café Hawelka**, with a dark, "brooding Trotsky" atmosphere, paintings on the walls by struggling artists who couldn't pay, a saloon-wood flavor, chalkboard menu, smoked velvet couches, an international selection of newspapers, and a phone that rings for regulars (8:00–02:00, Sun from 16:00, closed Tue, Dorotheergasse 6, just off Graben); crowded **Café Central**, with Jugendstil decor and great *Apfelstrudel* (rude staff, Mon–Sat

8:00–20:00, closed Sun, Herrengasse 14); the **Jugendstil Café Sperl**, dating from 1880 (Mon–Sat 7:00–23:00, closed Sun in summer, Gumpendorfer 11, just off Naschmarkt near Mariahilfer Strasse); and the basic, untouristy **Café Ritter** (daily 8:00–20:00, Mariahilfer Strasse 73, at Neubaugasse subway stop near several of my recommended hotels).

▲**Wine Gardens**—The *Heurige* is a uniquely Viennese institution celebrating the *Heurige*, or new wine. It all started when the Habsburgs let Vienna's vintners sell their own wine tax free for 300 days a year. Several hundred families opened *Heurigen* (wine-garden restaurants) clustered around the edge of Vienna, and a tradition was born. Today they do their best to maintain their old-village atmosphere, serving the homemade new wine (the last vintage, until November 11) with light meals and strolling musicians. For a *Heurige* evening, rather than go to a particular place, tram to the wine-garden district of your choice and wander around, choosing the place with the best ambience.

Of the many *Heurige* suburbs, **Grinzing** (tram #38 or #38A) is the most famous and lively—but it comes with too many tour buses. **Nussdorf** is less touristy but still characteristic and popular with locals (two fine places are right at the end of tram D). Pfarrplatz has many decent spots. **Beethoven's home** in Heiligenstadt comes with crowds and live music (Pfarrplatz, tram #38A or #37 and a 10-minute walk, tel. 01/371-287). While Beethoven lived here in 1817 (to be near a spa that he hoped would cure his worsening deafness), he composed his Sixth Symphony (*Pastoral*). These suburbs are all within a 15-minute stroll of each other.

Gumpoldskirchen is a small medieval village farther outside of Vienna with more *Heurige* ambience than tourists. Ride the commuter train from the Opera to Gumpoldskirchen and you'll find plenty of places to choose from.

At any *Heurige*, fill your plate at a self-serve cold-cut buffet (75–125 AS for dinner). Waitresses will then take your wine order (30 AS per quarter liter). Many locals claim it takes several years of practice to distinguish between *Heurige* and vinegar. For a near-*Heurige* experience right downtown, drop by Gigerl Stadtheuriger (see "Eating," below).

Nightlife

If old music or new wine isn't your thing, Vienna has plenty of alternatives. For an up-to-date rundown on fun after dark, get the TI's free *Young Vienna Scene* booklet. An area known as the "Bermuda Dreieck" (Triangle), north of the cathedral between Rotenturmstrasse and Judengasse, is the hot local nightspot, with lots of classy pubs, or *Beisl* (such as Krah Krah, Salzamt, Kitch, and Bitter), and popular music spots. On balmy summer evenings the liveliest scene is at Danube Island.

Vienna

Sleeping in Vienna
(12 AS = about $1, tel. code: 01)
Sleep Code: **S** = Single, **D** = Double/Twin, **T** = Triple, **Q** = Quad, **b** = bathroom, **t** = toilet only, **s** = shower only, **CC** = Credit Card (Visa, MasterCard, Amex). English is spoken at each place.

Call accommodations a few days in advance. Most places will hold a room without a deposit if you promise to arrive before 17:00. My recommendations stretch mainly along the likeable Mariahilfer Strasse from the Westbahnhof (West Station) to the town center. These hotels are listed starting from the not-so-appealing Westbahnof and working toward the city center. The smaller places don't have signs; look for the family name at the door and push the buzzer. If you can't make it, please call to cancel; these B&B owners turn customers away to hold your reserved room for you. Unless otherwise noted, prices include a continental breakfast. Postal code is 1XX0, with XX being the district. Most have elevators (thankfully) one floor up, which usually means two, counting the mezzanine level.

Sleeping near the Westbahnhof Train Station
Pension Funfhaus is big, clean, stark, and quiet. Although the neighborhood is run-down, this place is a good value (S-395 AS, Sb-480 AS, D-570 AS, Db-650 AS, T-850 AS, Tb-930 AS, two-bedroom apartments for four-1,140 AS, closed mid-Nov–Feb; 15, Sperrgasse 12, 1150 Wien, tel. 01/892-3545 or 01/892-0286, fax 01/892-0460, Frau Susi Tersch SE). Half the rooms are in the fine main building and half are in the annex, which has good rooms but is near the train tracks and a bit scary on the street at night. From the station, ride tram #52 or #58 two stops or walk seven blocks away from downtown on Mariahilfer Strasse, to Sperrgasse.

Hotel Ibis Wien, a modern high-rise hotel with American charm, is ideal for anyone tired of quaint old Europe. Its 340 cookie-cutter rooms are bright, comfortable, modern, and with all the conveniences. It has a friendly, spirited staff, lots of smoke-free rooms, some easy-access rooms, and air-conditioning—rare in this price range (Sb-890 AS, Db-1,090 AS, Tb-1,290 AS, breakfast-120 AS, CC:VMA, elevator, 3 blocks to the right leaving Westbahnhof, Mariahilfer Gürtel 22–24, A-1060 Wien, tel. 01/59998, fax 01/597-9090, e-mail: resamariahilf@hotel-ibis.co.at).

Hotel Furstenhof, right across from the station, charges top schilling for its Old World, red-floral, and spacious rooms; cable TV; and Internet access (S-550 AS, Sb-880–1,150 AS, D-800, Db-1,320 AS, Tb-1410 AS, Qb-1440 AS, CC:VMA, Europlatz 4, tel. 01/523-3267, fax 01/523-326-726, www.hotelfuerstenhof.com).

Hotels along Mariahilfer Strasse
Lively Mariahilfer Strasse connects the West Station with the center. The U-3 subway line, starting at the Westbahnhof, goes down

Vienna: Hotels Outside the Ring

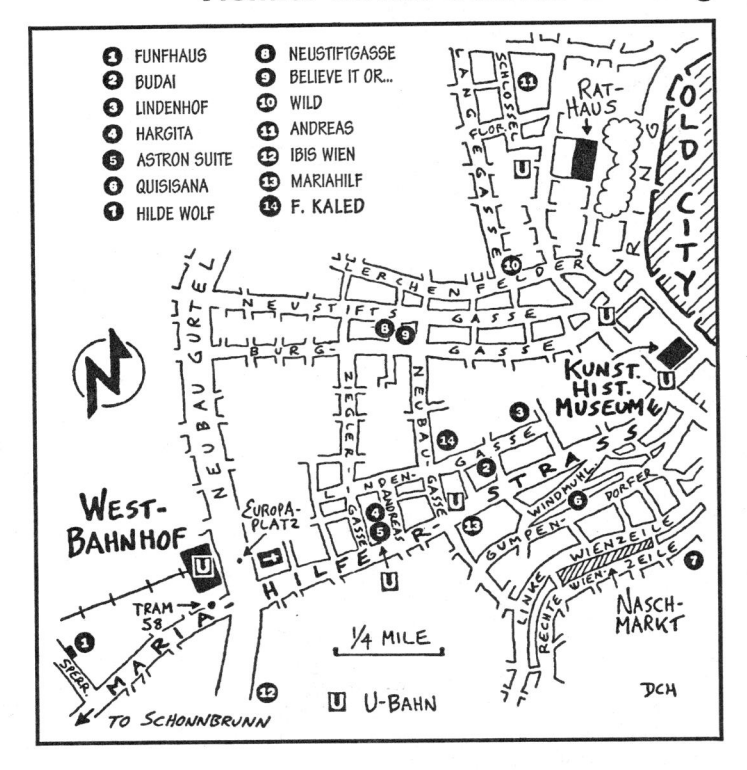

- **1** FUNFHAUS
- **2** BUDAI
- **3** LINDENHOF
- **4** HARGITA
- **5** ASTRON SUITE
- **6** QUISISANA
- **7** HILDE WOLF
- **8** NEUSTIFTGASSE
- **9** BELIEVE IT OR...
- **10** WILD
- **11** ANDREAS
- **12** IBIS WIEN
- **13** MARIAHILF
- **14** F. KALED

Mariahilfer Strasse to the cathedral. This very Viennese street is a comfortable and vibrant area filled with local shops and cafés. Most are within a few steps of the subway station, just one or two stops from the West train station.

Pension Hargita, with 19 generally small, bright, and tidy rooms (mostly twins), is handy—right at the U-3 Zieglergasse stop—and next to a sex shop (S-400 AS, Ss-450 AS, D-600 AS, Ds-700 AS, Db-800 AS, Ts-850 AS, Tb-1,050 AS, Qb-1,100 AS, breakfast-40 AS, cheaper off-season for longer stays, U-Bahn: Zieglergasse, on corner of Mariahilfer Strasse and Andreasgasse at 7, Andreasgasse 1, 1070 Wien, tel. 01/526-1928, fax 01/526-0492, e-mail: pension-hargita@magnet.at).

Astron Suite Hotel Wien/Atterseehaus is a business hotel with 54 family-ideal suites. Each has a living room, two TVs, bathroom, desk, and kitchenette (Db-1,980–2,880 AS, kids under 12 free,

400 AS per kid over 12, breakfast-140 AS, CC:VMA, nonsmoking rooms, elevator, at U-3 Zieglergasse subway stop, Mariahilfer Strasse 78, A-1070 Wien, tel. 01/5245-6000, fax 01/524-560-015, www.astron-hotels.de). Nearby they have a bigger suite hotel (same prices, Mariahilfer Strasse 32, tel. 01/521-720, fax 01/521-7215).

At Mariahilfer Strasse 57, you'll find two handy hotels. **Pension Corvinus**, on the fifth floor, is small, bright, modern, and warmly run. Its comfortable rooms have small bathrooms and cable TV (Sb-750 AS, Db-1,150 AS, Tb-1,350, extra bed-350 AS, CC:VM, elevator, portable air-conditioning available, garage-150 AS, tel. 01/587-7239, fax 01/587-723-920, e-mail: corvinus@teleweb.at). On the first floor, **Haydn Hotel** is a big, hotelesque place with spacious, airy rooms. This is where the Old World meets the motel world—get a room off the street (Sb-850 AS, Db-1,200 AS, extra bed-400 AS, garage-120 AS, cable TV, CC:VM, tel. 01/587-4414, fax 01/586-1950, e-mail: info@haydn-hotel.at).

Pension Mariahilf is a four-star place offering a clean aristocratic air in an affordable and cozy pension package. Its 12 rooms are spacious and feel new, but with a Jugendstil flair. With four stars, everything's done right. You'll find the latest American magazines and even free Mozart balls at the reception desk (Sb-800 AS, Db-1,300 AS, Tb-1,700 AS, including an all-you-can eat breakfast, at U-3 Neubaugasse station, Mariahilfer Strasse 49, tel. 01/586-1781, fax 01/586-178-122, warmly run by Frau and Herr Ender).

The next three places are run by Hungarian friends who can help even if their places are booked up.

Privatzimmer F. Kaled is bright, airy, and homey (S-400 AS, Sb-450 AS, D-550 AS, Db-650 AS, T-800 AS, skip breakfast, reserve with CC but pay cash, cable TV, Lindengasse 42, 1070 Wien, near Neubaugasse, tel. & fax 01/523-9013). The same friendly owners have just renovated a fine old building, **K&T Boardinghouse**, with four comfortable spacious rooms right on Mariahilfer Strasse at #72, three flights up at door 18 (no elevator, above harmless blue sex shop, Internet access, no breakfast, laundry, nonsmoking, TV with CNN, tel. 01/523-2989, fax 01/522-0345).

Budai Ildiko has high-ceilinged rooms, Old World furnishings, and a warm, homey feeling. It's run by charming and English-speaking Frau Budai (S-370 AS, D-580 AS, T-840 AS, Q-1,070 AS, no breakfast but free coffee, three rooms share one bath, laundry-40 AS, great elevator but no need as she's only half a floor up, Lindengasse 39, 1070 Wien, no sign, look for her buzzer, tel. 01/523-1058, tel. & fax 01/526-2595, e-mail: budai@hotmail.com). In the same building one floor up, delightful **Maria Pribojszki**, who speaks a smidgen of English, has two cavernous rooms plus one narrow but good twin, all right out of grandma's house (D-550 AS, one shared bath, no sign, first floor, tel. 01/523-9006).

Pension Lindenhof is worn but clean, filled with plants, and run with Bulgarian and Armenian warmth (S-370 AS, Sb-470 AS, D-620 AS, Db-840 AS, cheaper in winter, hall showers-20 AS, Lindengasse 4, 1070 Wien, take U-3 to Neubaugasse, tel. 01/523-0498, fax 01/523-7362).

Don't judge the **Hotel Admiral** by its lobby. This huge, quiet hotel has spacious and comfortable, just-renovated rooms, and is well located a block from charming art galleries and cafés—see "Eating," below (Sb-750–860 AS, Db-990–1,490 AS, extra bed-310 AS, cable TV, U-2 or U-3 Volkstheater, 3 blocks from Mariahilfer Strasse near the old city, Karl Schweighofer Gasse 7, tel. 01/521-410, fax 01/521-4116, www.admiral.co.at).

Pension Quisisana is tired and ramshackle, but cheap and sleep-worthy for vagabonds (S-330 AS, Ss-380 AS, D-520 AS, Ds-600–640 AS, Db-700–740 AS, third person-260 AS, Windmuhlgasse 6, 1060 Wien, tel. 01/587-7155, fax 01/587-715-633).

Seven blocks off Mariahilfer Strasse and three blocks below the Naschmarkt is **Hilde Wolf**'s homey place (no sign, find her buzzer and wait). Her four huge rooms are like old libraries. Hilde loves her work and will do your laundry if you stay two nights. From the Westbahnhof, take tram #6 or #18 five stops to Eichenstrasse, then take tram #62 six stops to Paulanergasse. For a real home in Vienna, unpack here (S-450 AS, D-650 AS, T-955 AS, Q-1,225 AS, includes big, friendly, family-style breakfast, prices good through 2000, reserve by phone and CC but pay in cash, elevator, three blocks off Naschmarkt near U-2 Karlsplatz, Schleifmühlgasse 7, 1040 Vienna, tel. 01/586-5103).

Sleeping North of Mariahilfer Strasse, Closer to the Rathaus

Values in this slightly less central but nontouristy area tend to be very good. The hotels are listed in the order you'll find them walking from Mariahilfer Strasse toward the Rathaus.

Jugendherbergen Neustiftgasse is a well-run youth hostel. They'll hold rooms until 16:00, have a 01:00 curfew, and 65-AS meals (185 AS per person, nonmembers pay 40 AS extra, includes sheets and breakfast, 3- to 6-bed rooms, Myrthengasse 7, 1070 Wien, tel. 01/523-6316, fax 01/523-5849, e-mail: oejhv-wien-jgh-neustiftg@oejhv.or.at). They try to accommodate couples and families with private rooms but can make no promises.

Believe It or Not, across the street (no sign, first floor), is a friendly and basic place with two big coed rooms for up to 10 travelers under age 30. It's locked up from 10:30 to 12:30, has kitchen facilities, and no curfew (160 AS per bed, 110 AS Nov–Easter, Myrthengasse 10, ring Apt. #14, tel. 01/526-4658, run by Gosha).

Pension Wild, with 14 delightful, just-renovated rooms, two family apartments, and a good, keep-it-simple-and-affordable attitude is one of the best values I've found. Reserve ahead (S-490 AS,

Sb-690 AS, D-690 AS, Db-990 AS, reserve with CC:VMA but pay cash, elevator, kitchen privileges, TV cable, airport shuttle-300 AS, train shuttle-100 AS, near U-2 Rathaus, Langegasse 10, 1080 Vienna, tel. 01/406-5174, fax 01/402-2168, www.pension-wild.com).

Pension Andreas is past-its-prime classy and quiet with high ceilings and compact bathrooms (40 rooms, St-690–740 AS, Ds-850 AS, Db-930 AS, big Db-990 AS, big-family room deals, CC:VMA, elevator, 2 blocks behind Rathaus U-2 stop, walk up Floriangasse to Schlösselgasse 11, 1080 Wien, tel. 01/405-3488, fax 01/4053-48850, e-mail: andreas.hotelpension@vienna.at).

Sleeping within the Ring, in the Old City Center

These places offer less room per schilling but are comfortable (with elevators), right in the town center, and near the subway. The first three are nearly in the shadow of St. Stephan's Cathedral, on or near the Graben, where the elegance of Old Vienna strums happily over the cobbles. The next two listings are near the Opera (subway: Karlsplatz) just off the famous Kärntner Strasse, near the TI and five minutes from the cathedral. If you can afford it, staying here gives you the best classy Vienna experience. The last two are past the cathedral, closer to the Danube Canal.

At **Pension Nossek** an elevator takes you above any street noise into Frau Bernad's and Frau Gundolf's world, where the children seem to be placed among the lace and flowers by an interior designer. Right on the wonderful Graben, this is the best value of these first three (Ss-700 AS, Sb-850–1,100 AS, Db-1,300 AS, apartment-1,700–2,000 AS, Graben 17, tel. 01/5337-0410, fax 01/535-3646).

Pension Pertschy, in a beautiful building, is bigger and more hotelesque than the others. Its rooms are huge (ask to see a couple), and those on the courtyard are quietest (Sb-880 AS, Db-1,280–1,560 AS depending on size, apartments with kitchenette for same price—just ask, cheaper off-season, extra person-350 AS, CC:VM, Habsburgergasse 5, tel. 01/53449, fax 01/534-4949, e-mail: pertsch@pertsch.com).

Pension Neuer Markt has narrow halls caused by a Mickey Mouse cramming on of bathrooms to each room, but the rooms are comfy and pleasant and the location is great (Ds-1,150 AS, Db-1,450 AS, prices soft when slow, CC:VMA, Seilergasse 9, 1010 Wien, tel. 01/512-2316, fax 01/513-9105).

Pension Suzanne, as Baroque and doily as you'll find in this price range, is wonderfully located a few yards from the Opera. It's quiet, with pink elegance bouncing on every bed (Sb-890 AS, Db-1,090–1,300 AS, third person-500 AS, huge discounts in winter, reserve with CC but cash preferred, a block from Opera, U-Bahn to Karlsplatz—Opera exit, Walfischgasse 4, 1010 Wien, tel. 01/513-2507, fax 01/513-2500).

Hotels in Central Vienna

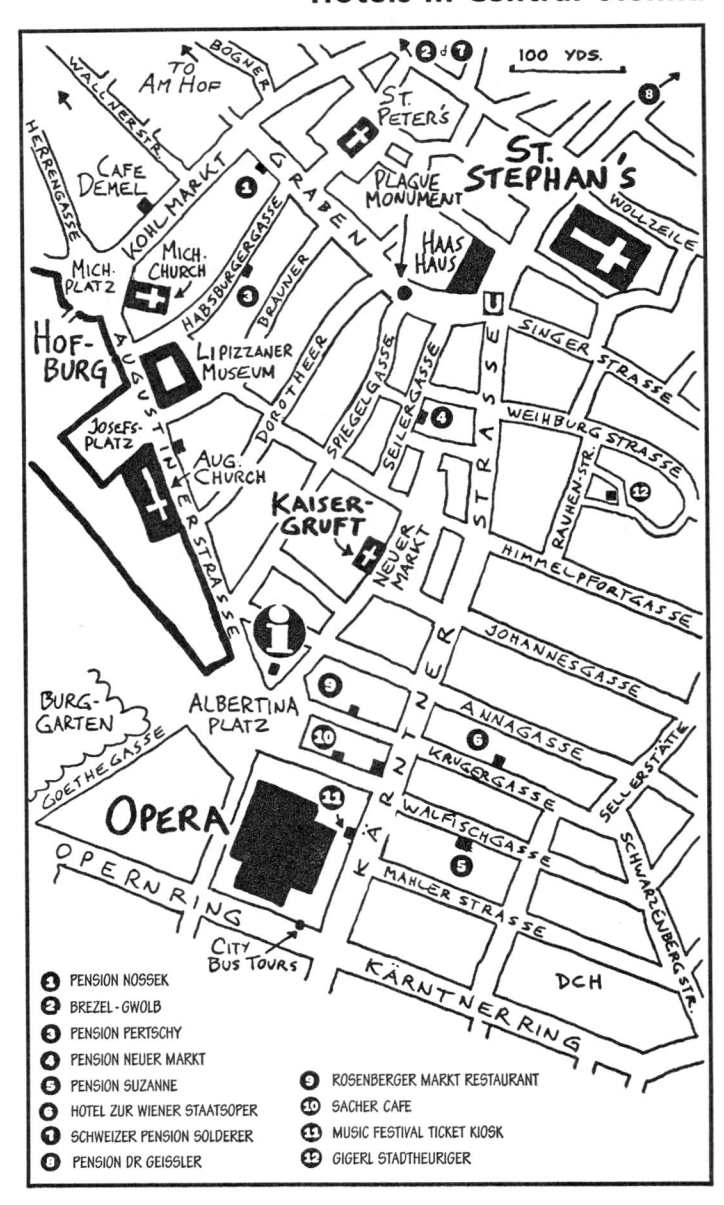

1. PENSION NOSSEK
2. BREZEL-GWOLB
3. PENSION PERTSCHY
4. PENSION NEUER MARKT
5. PENSION SUZANNE
6. HOTEL ZUR WIENER STAATSOPER
7. SCHWEIZER PENSION SOLDERER
8. PENSION DR GEISSLER
9. ROSENBERGER MARKT RESTAURANT
10. SACHER CAFE
11. MUSIC FESTIVAL TICKET KIOSK
12. GIGERL STADTHEURIGER

Hotel zur Wiener Staatsoper is quiet, rich, and hotelesque. Its smallish rooms come with high ceilings, chandeliers, and fancy carpets on parquet floors—a good value for this locale and ideal for people whose hotel tastes are a cut above mine (Sb-1,200 AS, Db-1,750 AS, Tb-2,050 AS, family deals, CC:VMA; a block from Opera at Krugerstrasse 11, 1010 Wien, tel. 01/513-1274, fax 01/5131-27415).

Schweizer Pension Solderer, family owned for three generations, is warmly run by two friendly sisters, Monica and Anita. Enjoy the homey feel, 11 big, comfortable rooms, parquet floors, and lots of tourist info (S-485 AS, Ss-700 AS, Sb-850 AS, D-750 AS, Ds-950 AS, Db-1,050 AS, elevator, laundry-150 AS, nonsmoking; from West station take U-3 to Volkstheater, then U-2 to Schottenring; Heinrichsgasse 2, 1010 Wien, tel. 01/533-8156, fax 01/535-6469).

Pension Dr. Geissler has comfortable rooms on the eighth floor of a modern building about 10 blocks northeast of St. Stephen's, just below the canal (S-450–580 AS, Sb-650–850 AS, D-600–780 AS, Ds-620–980 AS, Db-800–1,200 AS, prices vary with season, CC:VMA, U-Bahn: Schwedenplatz, Postgasse 14, 1010 Wien, tel. 01/533-2803, fax 01/533-2635).

Eating in Vienna

The Viennese appreciate the fine points of life, and right up there with the waltz is eating. The city has many atmospheric restaurants. As you ponder the Slavic and eastern European specialties on menus, remember that Vienna's diverse empire may be gone, but its flavor lingers.

On nearly every corner, you can find a colorful *Beisl* (Viennese tavern) filled with poetry teachers and their students, couples loving without touching, housewives on their way home from cello lessons, and waiters who thoroughly enjoy serving hearty food and good drink at an affordable price. Ask at your hotel for a good *Beisl*. Wherever you're eating, some vocabulary will help. Try the *grüner Veltliner* (dry white wine, any time), *Traubenmost* (a heavenly grape juice on the verge of wine, autumn only, sometimes just called *Most*), and *Sturm* (barely fermented *Most*, autumn only). The local red wine (called *Portuguese*) is pretty good. Since the Austrian wine is often very sweet, remember the word *Trocken* (dry). You can order your wine by the *Viertel* (quarter liter) or *Achtel* (eighth liter). Beer comes in a *Krugel* (half liter) or *Seidel* (.3 liter).

Eating in the City Center

These eateries are within a five-minute walk of the cathedral.

Gigerl Stadtheuriger offers a near-*Heurige* experience (à la Grinzing, see "Vienna's Cafés and Wine Gardens," above) without leaving the center. Just point to what looks good. Food is sold by the weight (cheese and cold meats cost about 35 AS/100 grams, salads are about 15 AS/100 grams; price sheet is posted, 10 dag equals 100 grams). They also have menu entrées, along with spinach strudel, quiche, *Apfelstrudel*, and, of course, casks of new and local wines. Meals run from 100 AS to 150 AS (daily 11:00–24:00, indoor/outdoor seating, behind cathedral, a block off Kärntner Strasse, a few cobbles off Rauhensteingasse on Blumenstock, tel. 01/513-4431).

The next four places are within a block of Am Hof square (U-3 Herrengasse). **Brezel-Gwölb**, a wonderfully atmospheric wine cellar with outdoor dining on a quiet square, serves delicious light meals, fine *Krautsuppe*, and old-fashioned local dishes. It's ideal for a romantic late-night glass of wine (daily 11:30–01:00, Ledererhof 9, take Drahtgasse 50 feet off Am Hof, then look left, tel. 01/533-8811). Around the corner, **Zum Scherer Sitz u. Stehbeisl** is just as untouristy, with indoor or outdoor seating, a soothing woody atmosphere, intriguing decor, and local specialties (Mon–Sat 11:00–01:00, Sun 17:00–24:00, Judenplatz 7, near Am Hof). Just below Am Hof, **Stadtbeisl** offers a good mix of value, local cuisine, and atmosphere (open nightly, Naglergasse 21, tel. 01/533-3507). Around the corner the ancient and popular **Esterhazykeller** has traditional fare deep underground or outside on a delightful square (open daily, Haarhof 1, tel. 01/533-9340).

These wine cellars are fun and touristic but typical, in the old center of town, with reasonable prices and plenty of smoke: **Melker Stiftskeller**, less touristy, is a *Stadtheurige* in a deep and rustic cellar with hearty, inexpensive meals and new wine (Mon–Sat 17:00–24:00, closed Sun, halfway between Am Hof and the Schottentor subway stop at Schottengasse 3, tel. 01/533-5530). **Zu den Drei Hacken** is famous for its local specialties (Mon–Fri 9:00–24:00, Sat 10:00–24:00, closed Sun, indoor/outdoor seating, CC:VA, Singerstrasse 28). **Augustinerkeller** is fun, reasonably priced, and very touristy with live music nightly (daily 10:00–24:00, next to Opera under Albertina Museum on Augustinerstrasse).

For a fast, light, and central lunch, **Rosenberger Markt Restaurant**, a popular highway chain, has an elegant super-branch a block toward the cathedral from the Opera. This place, while not cheap, is brilliant: friendly and efficient, with special theme rooms for dining, it offers a fresh, smoke-free, and healthy cornucopia of food and drink (daily 11:00–23:00, lots of fruits, veggies, fresh-squeezed juices, just off Kärntner Strasse at Maysedergasse 2, ride the glass elevator downstairs). You can stack a small salad or veggie plate into the tower of gobble for 30 AS.

Buffet Trzesniewski is justly famous for its elegant and cheap finger sandwiches and small beers (9 AS each). Three sandwiches and a *kleines Bier* (*Pfiff*) make a fun, light lunch (Mon–Fri 8:30–19:30, Sat 9:00–17:00, just off Graben, nearly across from the brooding Café Hawelka, on Dorotheergasse).

Eating near Mariahilfer Strasse

Mariahilfer Strasse is filled with reasonable cafés serving all types of cuisine. **Café Ritter** is good (daily 8:00–20:00, Mariahilfer Strasse 73). I walk the few extra blocks to the romantic streets just north of Siebensterngasse (take Stiftgasse from Mariahilfer Strasse), where several cobbled alleys open their sidewalks and courtyards to appreciative locals (ideal for dinner or a relaxing drink). Stroll adorable Spitellberggasse, Schrankgasse, and Gutenberggassse and pick your favorite place. Check out the courtyard inside Spittelberggasse 3, and don't miss the vine-strewn wine garden inside Schrankgasse 1. For traditional Viennese cuisine, try **Witwe Bolte** (Gutenberggasse 13, closed Sun).

Naschmarkt, five minutes beyond the Opera a few blocks off Mariahilfer Strasse, is Vienna's best Old World market, with plenty of fresh produce, cheap local-style eateries, cafés, and *döner kebab* and sausage stands (Mon–Fri 6:00–18:30, Sat until 17:00, closed Sun).

Transportation Connections—Vienna

Vienna has two main train stations: the Westbahnhof, serving Munich, Salzburg, Melk, and Budapest; and the Südbahnhof, serving Italy, Budapest, and Prague. A third station, Franz Josefs, serves Krems and the Danube Valley (but Melk is served by the Westbahnhof). Subway line U-3 connects the Westbahnhof with the center, tram D takes you from the Südbahnhof and the Franz Josefs to downtown, and tram #18 connects West and South stations. Train info: tel. 01/1717.

By train to: Melk (hrly, 75 min), **Krems** (10/day, 1 hr), **Salzburg** (hrly, 3 hrs), **Innsbruck** (3/day, 5.5 hrs), **Budapest** (3/day, 3 hrs), **Prague** (4/day, 5.5 hrs), **Munich** (10/day, 4.5 hrs), **Berlin** (2/day 14 hrs), **Zurich** (4/day, 9 hrs), **Rome** (3/day, 14 hrs), **Venice** (6/day, 9 hrs), **Frankfurt** (7/day, 7.5 hrs), **Amsterdam** (2/day, 14 hrs).

To Eastern Europe: Vienna is the springboard for a quick trip to Prague and Budapest—three hours by train from Budapest (344 AS, 688 AS round-trip, free with Eurail) and 5.5 hours from Prague (486 AS one way, 972 AS round-trip, 664 AS round-trip with Eurail). Visas are not required. Purchase tickets at most travel agencies (such as the Austrian National Travel Office at Operngasse 3–5, tel. 01/588-6238; or Intropa, next to TI and Opera on Kärntner Strasse).

SALZBURG AND HALLSTATT

Enjoy the sights, sounds, and splendor of Mozart's hometown, Salzburg, then commune with nature in the Salzkammergut, Austria's *Sound of Music* country. Amid hills alive with the S.O.M., you'll find the tiny town of Hallstatt, as pretty as a postcard (and not much bigger).

SALZBURG

Salzburg is forever smiling to the tunes of Mozart and *The Sound of Music*. Thanks to its charmingly preserved old town, splendid gardens, Baroque churches, and Europe's largest intact medieval castle, Salzburg feels made for tourism.

Eight million tourists crawl its cobbles each year. That's a lot of Mozart balls—all that popularity has led to a glut of businesses hoping to catch the tourist dollar, and an almost desperate greediness. The town's creative energy is invested in ways to soak the tourist rather than share its rich cultural heritage. Salzburg makes for a pleasant visit, but for most, a day is plenty.

Planning Your Time

While Vienna measures much higher on the Richter scale of sightseeing thrills, Salzburg is simply a stroller's joy—a touristy and expensive joy. If you're going into the nearby Salzkammergut lake country, skip the *Sound of Music* tour—if not, allow half a day for it. The S.O.M. tour kills a nest of sightseeing birds with one ticket (city overview, S.O.M. sights, a luge ride, and a fine drive through the lakes). You'll probably need two nights for Salzburg; nights are important for swilling beer in atmospheric local gardens and attending concerts in Baroque halls and chapels. Seriously consider one of Salzburg's many evening musical events (about

Salzburg and Hallstatt 57

Salzburg

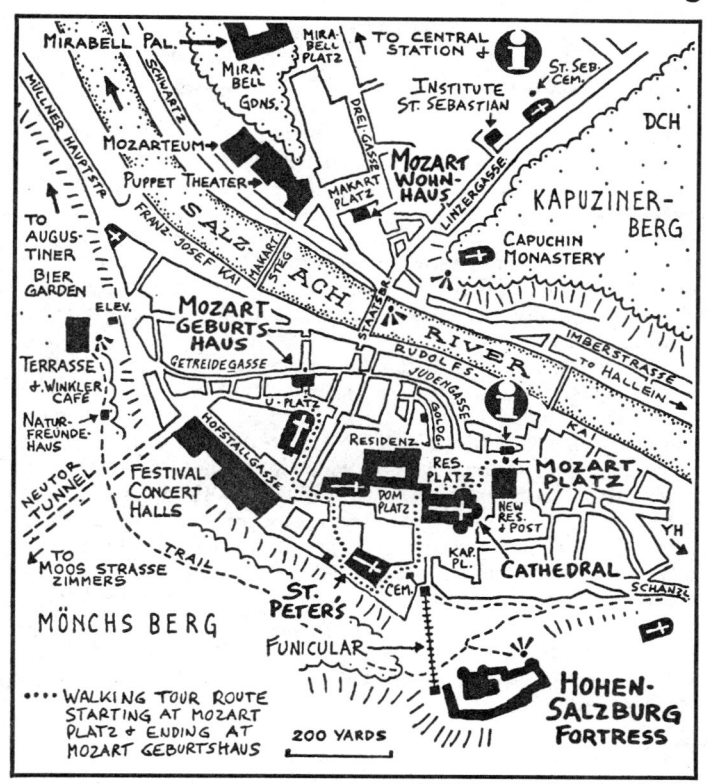

350–400 AS). While the sights are mediocre, the town is an enjoyable Baroque museum of cobbled streets and elegant buildings. But if you like to get away from it all, bike down the river or hike across the Mönchsberg.

Orientation (tel. code: 0662)

Salzburg, a city of 150,000 (Austria's fourth largest), is divided into old and new. The old town, sitting between the Salzach River and the 1,600-foot-high hill called Mönchsberg, holds all the charm and most of the tourists.

Tourist Information: Salzburg's many TIs are helpful (at the train station—daily 8:15–21:00; on Mozartplatz in the old center—daily 9:00–20:00 in summer, closes at 19:00 off-season; on freeway exits; and at the airport, tel. 0662/88987, www.salzburginfo.or.at).

You can pick up a city map (10 AS, free at most hotels), a list of sights with current hours, and a schedule of events. The TI sells a "Salzburg Card" (200 AS for a 24-hour bus pass and 24 hours free entrance to all the city sights), which pays for itself after two admissions and one bus ride. The new "Salzburg Plus Light" adds 145 AS to the Salzburg Card for a dinner and two drinks at your choice of the city's big hotels. Book a concert upon arrival. The TIs also book rooms (30-AS fee, or 60 AS for 3 people or more).

Arrival in Salzburg

By Train: The little Salzburg station makes it easy. The TI is at track 2A. Downstairs, at street level, you'll find a place to store your luggage, rent bikes, buy tickets, and get train information. The bus station (where buses #1, #5, #6, and #51 go to the old center; get off at the first stop after you cross the river for most sights and city center hotels, or before the bridge for Linzergasse hotels; see "Sleeping on Linzergasse and Rupertgasse," below) is across the street. Figure 90 AS for a taxi to the center. To walk downtown (15 min), leave the station ticket hall to the left near the Bankomat and walk straight down Rainerstrasse, which leads under the tracks past Mirabellplatz, turning into Dreitaltigkeitsgasse. From here you can turn left onto Paris-Lodron Strasse or Linzergasse for many hotels listed in this book, or cross the *Staatsbrücke* (bridge) for the old town (and more hotels). For a more dramatic approach, leave the station the same way but follow the tracks to the river, turn left, and walk the riverside path toward the castle.

By Car: Follow "Zentrum" signs to the center and park short term on the street or longer under Mirabellplatz. Ask at your hotel for suggestions.

Getting around Salzburg

By Bus: Single-ride tickets are sold on the bus for 20 AS. Daily passes called Tageskarte cost 40 AS (good for one calendar day only). Bus information: tel. 0662/872-145.

By Bike: Salzburg is bike friendly. From 7:00 until midnight, the train station rents good road bikes for 100 AS and mountain bikes for 175 AS; if you don't have a railpass or train ticket, you'll pay 25 to 50 AS more (no deposit required, pay at counter #3, pick it up at "left luggage"). Georg runs Velo-Active, renting bikes on Residenzplatz under the Glockenspiel in the old town (190 AS/day, 150 AS with this book, daily 9:00–19:00 but hours unreliable, less off-season and in bad weather, passport number for security, extra charge for mountain bikes, tel. 0663/868-827).

By Funicular and Elevator: The old town is connected to Mönchsberg (and great views) via funicular and elevator. The funicular whisks you up to the imposing Hohensalzburg fortress (69 AS includes fortress admission). The elevator on the east side of the old town propels you to Café Winkler, the recommended Naturfreundehaus (see "Sleeping," below), and lots of wooded paths (27 AS round-trip).

Helpful Hints

Laundromat: You'll find it two blocks from recommended Linzergasse hotels at the corner of Paris-Lodron Strasse and Wolf-Dietrich Strasse (Mon–Fri 7:30–8:00, Sat 8:00–12:00, self-serve or drop-off service).

Internet Access: Cyber Cafe is at Gstattengasse 27; turn right where Griesgasse meets the hill (80 AS/hr, daily 14:00–20:00, tel. 0662/8426-1622).

American Express: Amex charges no commission to cash Amex checks (Mon–Fri 9:00–17:30, Sat 9:00–12:00, Mozartplatz 5, A-5010 Salzburg, tel. 0662/8080).

Sights—Salzburg's Old Town

▲▲**Old Town Walking Tour**—The two-language, one-hour guided walks of the old town are informative and worthwhile if you don't mind listening to a half hour of German (80 AS, start at TI on Mozartplatz daily at 12:15, not on winter Sun, tel. 0662/847-568), but you can easily do it on your own. Here's a basic old-town orientation walk (start on Mozartplatz in the old town):

Mozartplatz features a statue of Mozart erected in 1842. Mozart spent most of his first 20 years (1756–1777) in Salzburg, the greatest Baroque city north of the Alps. Walk to the next big square with the huge fountain.

Residenz Platz: Salzburg's energetic Prince-Archbishop Wolf Dietrich (who ruled from 1587–1612) was raised in Rome, counted the Medicis as his buddies, and had grand Renaissance ambitions for Salzburg. After a convenient fire destroyed much of the old town, he set about building "the Rome of the North." This square, with his new cathedral and palace, was the centerpiece of his new, Italian-designed Baroque city. A series of interconnecting squares lead from here through the old town.

For centuries, Salzburg's leaders were both important church leaders and princes of the Holy Roman Empire, hence their title—mixing sacred and secular authority. Wolf Dietrich abused his power and spent his last five years imprisoned in the Salzburg castle.

The fountain is as Italian as can be, with a Triton matching Bernini's famous *Triton Fountain* in Rome. As the north became aware of the exciting things going on in Italy, things Italian were respected. Local architects even Italianized their names in order to raise their rates. A picnic-friendly grocery with an orange awning is near the fountain (Mon–Fri 8:30–18:00, Sat 8:00–17:00).

Dietrich's palace, the **Residenz**, is connected to the cathedral by a skyway. A series of ornately decorated rooms and an art gallery are open to visitors with time to kill (80 AS with audio-guide, open 10:00–17:00, tel. 0662/8042-2690).

Opposite the Residenz is the new Residenz, which has long been a government administration building with the central post office. Atop the new Residenz is the famous **Glockenspiel**, or bell tower. Its carillon of 35 17th-century bells (cast in Antwerp) chimes throughout the day and plays a tune (that changes each month) at 7:00, 11:00, and 18:00. There was a time when Salzburg could afford to take tourists to the top of the tower to actually see the big adjustable barrel turn...pulling the right bells in the right rhythm—a fascinating show.

Look back past Mozart's statue to the 4,220-foot-tall Gaisberg (the forested hill with the television tower). A road leads to the top for a commanding view. It's a favorite destination for local bikers. Walking under the Prince-Archbishop's skyway, step into Domplatz, the cathedral square.

Salzburg Cathedral, built in the 17th century, claims to be the first Baroque building north of the Alps (free, daily 10:00–18:30). The dates on the iron gates refer to milestones in the church's history: In 774 the previous church (long since destroyed) was founded by St. Virgil, to be replaced in 1628 by the church you see today. In 1959 the reconstruction was completed after a bomb blew through the dome in World War II.

Check out the organ draped over the entrance; it was played only when the archbishop walked in and out of the cathedral. Gape up. The interior is marvelous. Concert and Mass schedules are posted at the entrance; the Sunday Mass at 10:00 is famous for its music.

Under the skyway, a stairway leads down to the excavation site under the church with a few second-century Christian Roman mosaics and the foundation stones of the previous Romanesque and Gothic churches (20 AS, Wed–Sun 9:00–17:00). The Cathedral (or *Dom*) Museum has a rich collection of church art (entry at portico).

The cathedral square is surrounded by "ecclesiastical palaces." The statue of Mary (1771) is looking away from the church, but if you stand in the rear of the square immediately under the middle arch, you'll see how she's positioned to be crowned by the two angels on the church facade.

From the arch, walk back across the square to the front of the cathedral and turn right (going past the underground public toilets) to the next square, where you'll see locals playing chess on the giant board. Past the chessboard, a small road leads up to the castle (and castle lift). On the right, a gate reading "St. Peter" leads past a traditional old bakery (near the waterfall, hard to beat their rocklike *Roggenbrot*) and into a cemetery.

St. Peter's Cemetery is a collection of lovingly tended minigardens (butted up against the Mönchberg's rock wall). The

Salzburg and Hallstatt

graves are cared for by relatives; anyone residing in the cemetery for more than 30 years without living kin gets dug up. Early Christian catacombs are carved into the rock wall above the graveyard (12 AS, Tue–Sun 10:30–17:00, closed Mon). This was where the von Trapp family hid out in the S.O.M. movie. Walk through the cemetery (silence is requested) and out the opposite end. Drop into St. Peter's Church, a Romanesque basilica done up beautifully Baroque. Continue (through arch opposite hillside, left at church, second right, pass public WC, another square, and church) to Universitätsplatz, with its busy open-air produce market. This is Salzburg at its liveliest and most real (mornings, daily except Sun). Check out the urban waterfall, then exit through the covered arcade at #10 to Getreidegasse.

Getreidegasse was old Salzburg's busy, colorful main drag. Famous for its old wrought-iron signs, it still looks much as it did in Mozart's day. *Schmuck* means jewelry. Wolfgang was born on this street. Find his very gold house.

▲**Mozart's Birthplace (Geburtshaus)**—Mozart was born here in 1756. It was in this building that he composed most of his boy-genius works. This most popular Mozart sight in town, filled with scores of scores, portraits, and old keyboard instruments and violins, is almost a pilgrimage. If you're a fan, you'll have to check it out (70 AS, or 110 AS for combined ticket to Mozart's Wohnhaus—see below, daily 9:00–18:00, shorter hours off-season, Getreidegasse 9). Note the cobbled entryway. All Salzburg used to be paved this way.

▲**Hohensalzburg Fortress**—Built on a rock 400 feet above the Salzach River, this castle, one of Europe's mightiest, dominates Salzburg's skyline and offers incredible views. You can walk up and up and up to the fortress, or take the busy *festungsbahn* (funicular, 69 AS round-trip includes fortress courtyard, 59 AS one way, pleasant to walk down). The courtyard (35 AS, unless you took the funicular) is poorly signed and disorienting. The fortress interior (entrance near the public WCs) is worth the 40 AS extra admission (everyone pays) because you came this far and the view is incredible from the high tower (Room 204). The new, included audioguide takes about 40 minutes and gives good information but makes a short story long (feel free to skip rooms). It ends at the museum showing the fortress through its battle-torn years including World War II (pass on the detailed 10-AS English leaflet, fortress open daily 8:00–19:00, off-season 9:00–18:00, tel. 0662/842-430). Kids may enjoy the Marionette exhibit in the fortress courtyard (35 AS, 20 AS for kids).

▲**The Hills Are Alive Walk**—For a most enjoyable approach to the castle, consider riding the elevator to Café Winkler and walking 20 minutes through the woods high above the city to Festung Hohensalzburg (stay on the high paved paths, or you'll have a needless climb back up to the castle).

Sights—Across the River

▲▲**Mozart's Wohnhaus (a.k.a. Mozarts Ton- und Filmmuseum)**—Better than the birthplace is this newly renovated museum, a reconstruction of Mozart's second home (his family moved here when he was 17). You need patience to work the English-language audiophone (free with admission); keep it pointed at the transmitters and follow the numbers religiously or you're lost. Along with the usual scores and old pianos, the highlight is an intriguing film that leaves you wanting to know more about Mozart and his remarkable family (65 AS, or 110 AS for combined ticket to birthplace, guidebook-59 AS, daily 10:00–18:00, allow one hour for visit, just over the river at Marktplatz 8, tel. 0662/889-4040).

▲**Mirabell Gardens and Palace (Schloss)**—The bubbly gardens are always open and free. You may recognize the statues featured in the S.O.M. To properly enjoy the lavish Mirabell Palace, get a ticket to a *Schlosskonzert*. Baroque music flying around a Baroque hall is a happy bird in the right cage. Tickets are around 400 AS (250 AS student) and are rarely sold out (tel. 0662/848-586).

More Sights—Salzburg

▲▲*Sound of Music* **Tour**—I took this tour skeptically (as part of my research chores) and liked it. It includes a quick but good general city tour, stops for a luge ride (in season, fair weather, 35 AS extra), hits all the S.O.M. spots (including the stately home, gazebo, and wedding church), and shows you a lovely stretch of the Salzkammergut. The Salzburg Panorama Tours Company charges 350 AS for the four-hour, English-only tour (from Mirabellplatz daily at 9:30 and 14:00, tel. 0662/874-029, www.panoramatours.at; ask for a reservation and a free hotel pickup; travelers with this book who buy their tickets with cash at the Mirabellplatz ticket booth get a 10 percent discount on this and any other tour they do). This is worthwhile for S.O.M. fans without a car, or those who won't otherwise be going into the Salzkammergut. Warning: Many think rolling through the Austrian countryside with 30 Americans singing "Doe, a deer" is pretty schmaltzy. And local Austrians don't understand all the commotion.

Several similar and very competitive tour companies offer every conceivable tour of and from Salzburg (Mozart sights, Berchtesgaden, salt mines, Salzkammergut lakes and mountains). Some hotels have their brochures and get a healthy commission. Bob's Special Tours uses a minibus (several different tours, Kaigasse 19, tel. 0662/849-511, e-mail: bobs-specialtours @net4you.co.at).

▲**Hellbrunn Castle**—The attractions here are a garden full of clever trick fountains and the sadistic joy the tour guide gets from soaking tourists. The archbishop's mediocre 17th-century palace is open by tour only (30 AS, 2/hrly, 20 minutes). His Baroque garden, one of the oldest in Europe, is pretty enough and now features the "I am 16, going on 17" gazebo (70 AS for 35-minute tour and admission, daily 9:00–17:30, until 22:00 Jul–Aug, until 16:30 in Apr and Oct, closed Nov–Mar, tel. 0662/820-372). The castle is three miles south of Salzburg (bus #55 from the station or downtown, 2/hrly, 20 min). It's most fun on a sunny day or with kids, but, for many, it's a lot of trouble for a few water tricks.

Music Scene

▲▲Salzburg Festival—Each summer from late July to the end of August, Salzburg hosts its famous Salzburger Festspiele, founded in 1920 partly to employ Vienna's musicians in the summer. This fun and festive time is crowded, but there are plenty of beds (except for a few August weekends). Except for the big shows, tickets are normally available the day of the concert (ticket office on Mozartplatz, in TI). You can contact the Austrian National Tourist Office in the United States for specifics on this year's festival schedule and tickets (Box 1142, New York, NY 10108, tel. 212/944-6880, fax 212/730-4568, www.anto.com), but I've never planned in advance and have enjoyed great concerts with every visit.

▲▲Musical Events outside of Festival Time—Salzburg is busy throughout the year with 2,000 classical performances in its palaces and churches annually. Pick up the events calendar at the TI (free, comes out monthly). Whenever you visit, you'll have a number of concerts to choose from. There are nearly nightly concerts at the Mirabell Palace and up in the fortress (both with open seating and 400-AS tickets, concerts at 19:30 or 20:30, doors open 30 minutes early). The *Schlosskonzerte* at the Mirabell Palace offer a fine Baroque setting for your Mozart (tel. 0662/848-586). The fortress concerts, called *Festungskonzerte*, are held in the "prince's chamber" (usually chamber music—a string quartet, tel. 0662/825-858 to reserve, you can pick up tickets at the door). This medieval-feeling room atop the castle has windows overlooking the city, and the concert gives you a chance to enjoy a stroll through the castle courtyard and enjoy the grand city view (69-AS funicular, round-trip).

The almost daily "5:00 Concert" next to St. Peter's is cheaper, since it features young artists (120 AS, daily except Wed, 45 minutes, tel. 0662/8445-7619). While the series is named after the brother of Joseph Haydn, it features music from various masters.

Salzburg's impressive Marionette Theater performs operas with remarkable marionettes and recorded music (350–480 AS, nearly nightly May–Sept, tel. 0662/872-406, www.tcs.at/mario/).

The *S.O.M.* musical at the Stieglkeller restaurant (see "Eating," below) gets good reviews from couples and families.

Sleeping in Salzburg
(12 AS = about $1, tel. code: 0662, zip code: 5020)
Sleep Code: **S** = Single, **D** = Double/Twin, **T** = Triple, **Q** = Quad, **b** = bathroom, **t** = toilet only, **s** = shower only, **CC** = Credit Card (Visa, MasterCard, Amex).

Finding a room in Salzburg, even during the music festival, is usually easy. Unless otherwise noted, all my listings come with breakfast and at least some English is spoken. Rates rise significantly during the music festival (late July and August). Don't expect a warm welcome from your hotelier here; most are serious and hardworking with little time for small talk.

Sleeping in (or above) the Old Town

Gasthaus zur Goldenen Ente, run by the family Steinwender, is a good splurge if you'd like to sleep in a 600-year-old building above a fine restaurant as central as you can be on a pedestrian street in old Salzburg. Somehow the 15 modern and comfortable doubles fit into this building's medieval-style stone arches and narrow stairs (Sb-750 AS, Db-1,100 AS with this book off-season, higher prices in high season, extra person-450 AS, CC:VMA, elevator, parking deals, Goldgasse 10, tel. 0662/845-622, fax 0662/845-6229, e-mail: ente@eunet.at). The breakfast is buffet-big and their restaurant is a treat (see "Eating," below).

Hotel Restaurant Weisses Kreuz is a classy, comfy, family-run place on a cobbled back street under the castle away from the crowds with a fine restaurant (Sb-800 AS, Db-1,200 AS, Tb-1,600 AS, CC:VMA, reserve ahead, Bierjodlgasse 6, tel. 0662/845-641, fax 0662/845-6419).

Gasthof Hinterbrühl is a smoky, ramshackle old place with a handy location, minimal plumbing, and not a tourist in sight (S-420 AS, D-520 AS, T-600 AS, plus optional 50-AS breakfast, above a bar that can be noisy, workable parking, on a village-like square under the castle's river end at Schanzlgasse 12, tel. 0662/846-798, fax 0662/841-859, e-mail: hinterbruhl@kronline.at).

Naturfreundehaus, also called "Gasthaus Bürgerwehr," is a local version of a mountaineer's hut. It's a great budget alternative in a forest guarded by singing birds and snuggled in the remains of a 15th-century castle wall. It has magnificent town and mountain views (D-280 AS, 120 AS per person in 4- to 6-bed dorms, breakfast-30 AS, dinner-68–108 AS, curfew-01:00, open May–Sept, Mönchsberg 19, 2 minutes from the top of the 27-AS round-trip Mönchsberg elevator, tel. 0662/841-729). High above the old town, it's the stone house to the left of the glass Café Winkler.

Sleeping on Linzergasse and Rupertgasse

These listings are between the train station and the old city in a pleasant neighborhood (with easy parking), a 15-minute walk from

Salzburg and Hallstatt 65

Salzburg Hotels

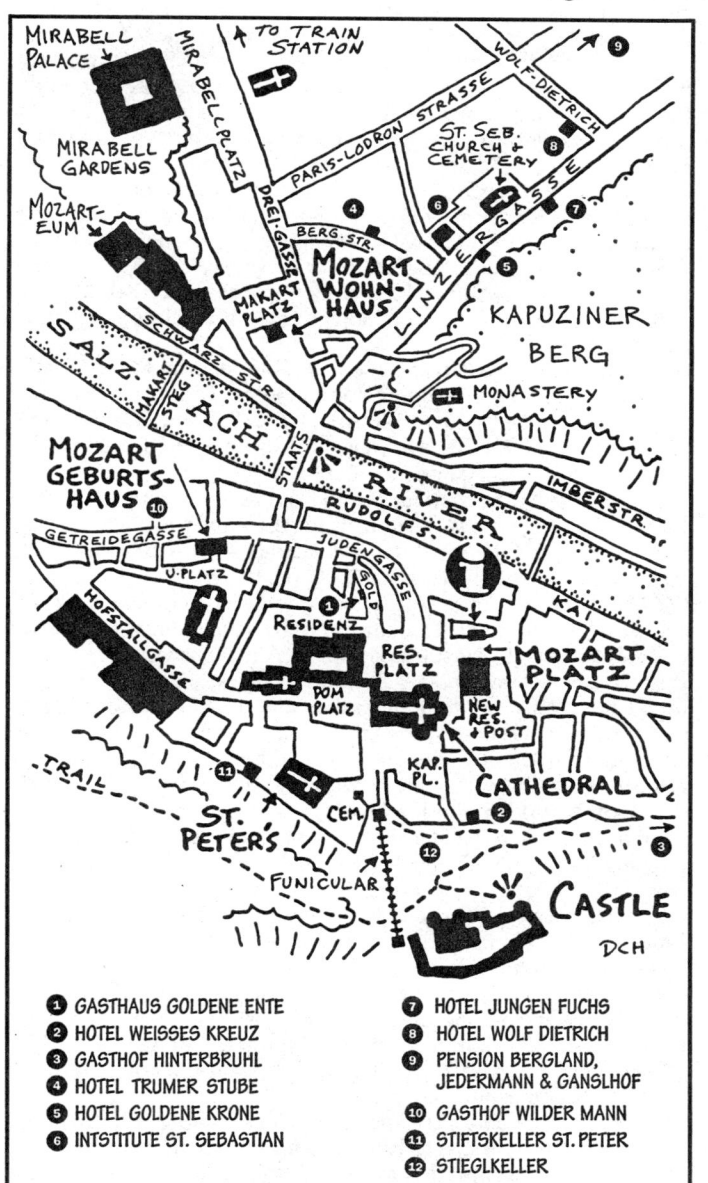

① GASTHAUS GOLDENE ENTE
② HOTEL WEISSES KREUZ
③ GASTHOF HINTERBRUHL
④ HOTEL TRUMER STUBE
⑤ HOTEL GOLDENE KRONE
⑥ INTSTITUTE ST. SEBASTIAN
⑦ HOTEL JUNGEN FUCHS
⑧ HOTEL WOLF DIETRICH
⑨ PENSION BERGLAND, JEDERMANN & GANSLHOF
⑩ GASTHOF WILDER MANN
⑪ STIFTSKELLER ST. PETER
⑫ STIEGLKELLER

the train station and 10 to 15 minutes to the old city. From the old city simply cross the main bridge (Staatsbrücke) to Linzergasse (see above for directions from the station). Linzergasse's bustling crowds of shoppers overwhelm the few shy cars that venture onto it. The first five listings are on or very near Linzergasse, across the bridge from Mozartville. The last three listings are farther out Linzergasse with easiest parking and a 15-minute walk to the old city.

Hotel Trumer Stube, a comfy little hotel-pension a few blocks from the river just off Linzergasse, has clean new rooms and a friendly can-do owner (Sb-750 AS, Db-1,280 AS, Tb-1,420 AS, Qb-1,790 AS, higher in August, lower in winter, CC to reserve but pay cash, elevator, parking-100 AS, Bergstrasse 6, tel. 0662/874-776, fax 0662/874-326, e-mail: hotel.trumer-stube.sbg@eunet.at, Sylvia SE).

Hotel Goldene Krone, about five blocks from the river, is big, quiet, and creaky-traditional but modern, with comforts rare in this price range (Sb-500–570 AS, D-700–800 AS, Db-850–970 AS, Tb-1,000–1,300 AS, elevator, Linzergasse 48, tel. 0662/872-300, 0662/872-30066).

Institute St. Sebastian, across from Hotel Krone, offers the town's best doubles and dorm beds for the money (Sb-390 AS, Db-680 AS, Tb-900 AS, elevator, Linzergasse 41, enter through arch at #37, reception closes at 21:00, tel. 0662/871-386, fax 0662/8713-8685). They usually have rooms when others don't, and 210-AS spots in 10-bed dorms (30 AS less if you have sheets, no lockout time, lockers, free showers). Anyone is welcome to use the self-service kitchen on each floor. Fridge space is free; just ask for a key. Ask also about their washer and dryer. This somewhat sterile but very clean, historic building has spacious public areas and a roof garden. The doubles come with modern baths and head-to-toe twin beds. Some Mozarts are buried in the courtyard.

Hotel zum Jungen Fuchs turns on troglodytes. It's very plain but clean and wonderfully located in a funky, dumpy old building (S-280 AS, D-400 AS, T-500 AS, no breakfast, just up from Hotel Krone at Linzergasse 54, tel. 0662/875-496).

Altstadthotel Wolf Dietrich, one block above Hotel zum Jungen Fuchs, around the corner on Wolf-Dietrich, is the most formal and comfortable I list in Salzburg. Broad sidewalks, outdoor tables, and an elegant coffeehouse greet its guests. Upstairs the decor is flawless and the rooms are plush (Sb-1,000 AS, Db-1,580–1,780 AS, mini apartments-1,980–2,440 AS, CC:VMA, Wolf-Dietrich Strasse 7, tel. 0662/871-275, fax 0662/882-320, e-mail: office@salzburg-hotel.at).

These three hotels are about five blocks farther from the river up Paris-Lodron Strasse to Rupertgasse, a breeze for drivers.

Pension Bergland is a totally charming, classy oasis of calm, with rustic rooms and musical evenings (Sb-560 AS, Db-920 AS, Tb-1,060 AS, music room open 17:00–21:30, Internet access, bike rental, English library, Rupertgasse 15, tel. 0662/872-318, fax 0662/872-3188, www.sol.at/bergland, e-mail: pkuhn@sol.at).

The similar boutiquelike **Hotel Jedermann**, a few doors down, is tastefully done and comfortable with friendly owners (Walter SE), a cheery breakfast room, and a bird-chirping backyard garden (Sb-650 AS, Db-1,250 AS, Qb-1, 700 AS, CC:VMA, cable TV, Internet access, Rupertgasse 25, tel. 0662/873-241, fax 0662/873-2419, e-mail: jedermann@salzburginfo.at).

Gasthaus Ganslhof, around the corner to the right, facing a hill of trees, is concrete basic with Motel 6 ambience, a parking lot, and surprisingly comfortable rooms (Db-850–1,100 AS, elevator, TV, and phone, CC:VMA, Vogelweiderstrasse 6, tel. 0662/873-853, fax 0662/8738-5323).

Zimmer

These are generally roomy and comfortable and come with a good breakfast, easy parking, and tourist information. Off-season, competition softens prices. They are a bus ride from town, but with a day pass and the frequent service, this shouldn't keep you away. Unsavory *Zimmer* skimmers lurk at the station. If you have a reservation, ignore them. If you need a place, they need a customer.

Brigitte Lenglachner fills her big, traditional home with a warm welcome (S-290 AS, D-480 AS, bunk bed D-390 AS, Db-550 AS, T-690 AS, Tb-830 AS, apartment available, Scheibenweg 8, tel. & fax 0662/438-044). It's a 10-minute walk northeast of the station (cross the pedestrian Pioneer bridge, turn right, and walk along the river 200 yards, then left to Scheibenweg).

Trude Poppenberger's three pleasant rooms enjoy a mountain-view balcony (S-280 AS, D-480 AS, T-720 AS; stay 2 nights and she'll do your laundry for 80 AS; Wachtelgasse 9, tel. & fax 0662/430-094). It's a 20-minute walk from the station: cross the pedestrian Pioneer bridge, turn right, walk along the river 200 yards, then take a left to Scheibenweg (or she'll pick you up for free).

***Zimmers* on Moosstrasse:** The street called Moosstrasse, southwest of Mönchsberg, is lined with *Zimmer*. Those farther out are farmhouses. From the station, catch bus #1 and change to bus #60 immediately after crossing the river. From the old town, ride bus #60 (get off after the American High School at Sendleweg). If you're driving from the center, go through the tunnel, straight on Neutorstrasse, and take the fourth left onto Moosstrasse.

Maria Gassner rents 10 sparkling clean, comfortable rooms in her modern house (St-250 AS, Sb-400 AS, D-440 AS, Db-500 AS, big Db-600 AS, 10 percent more for one-night stays, family deals, CC:VM, 60-AS coin-op laundry, Moosstrasse 126-B, tel. 0662/824-990, fax 0662/822-075).

Frau Ballwein offers cozy, charming rooms in an old farmhouse (S-200 AS, Ss-240 AS, D-400 AS, Db-480 AS, farm-fresh breakfasts, Moosstrasse 69A, tel. & fax 0662/824-029).

Haus Reichl also has good rooms (Db-550 AS, Tb-800 AS, Qb-1,000 AS, family deals, Q rooms have balcony and view, between Ballwein and Bankhammer B&Bs at Reiterweg 52, tel. & fax 0662/826-248).

Helga Bankhammer rents recently renovated, pleasant rooms in a farmhouse with farm animals nearby (D-450 AS, Db-500 AS, Moosstrasse 77, tel. & fax 0662/830-067).

Gästehaus Blobergerhof is rural and comfortable (Sb-350 AS, Db-550 AS, 10 percent more for 1-night stays, CC:VM; breakfast buffet, bike rental, laundry service, will pick up at station, Hammerauerstrasse 4, Querstrasse zur Moosstrasse, tel. 0662/830-227, fax 0662/827-061).

Eating in Salzburg

Salzburg boasts many inexpensive, fun, and atmospheric places to eat. I'm a sucker for big cellars with their smoky Old World atmosphere, heavy medieval arches, time-darkened paintings, antlers, hearty meals, and plump patrons. These places are famous with visitors but are also enjoyed by the locals. The first seven are central in the old city.

Gasthaus zum Wilder Mann is the place if the weather's bad and you're in the mood for Hofbräu atmosphere and a hearty, cheap meal at a shared table in one small, well-antlered room (Mon–Sat 11:00–21:00, closed Sun, smoky, 2 minutes from Mozart's birthplace, enter from Getreidegasse 20 or Griesgasse 17, tel. 0662/841-787). For a quick lunch, get the *Bauernschmaus*, a mountain of dumplings, kraut, and peasant's meats.

Stiftskeller St. Peter has been in business for more than 1,000 years. It's classy (with strolling musicians), more central, and a good splurge for traditional Austrian cuisine in medieval sauce (meals 100–200 AS, daily 11:00–24:00, indoor/outdoor seating, CC:VMA, next to St. Peter's church at foot of Mönchsberg, tel. 0662/841-268).

Gasthaus zur Goldenen Ente (see "Sleeping in (or above) the Old Town," above) serves great food in a classy, subdued hotel dining room. The chef, Robert, specializes in roast duck (*Ente*) and seafood, along with "Salzberger *Nockerl*," the mountainous sweet soufflé served all over town. It's big enough for four (Mon–Fri 11:00–21:00, closed Sat–Sun, Goldgasse 10, tel. 0662/845-622).

Stieglkeller is a huge, atmospheric institution that has several rustic rooms and outdoor garden seating with a great rooftop view of the old town (daily 10:00–22:00, 50 yards uphill from the lift to the castle, Festungsgasse 10, tel. 0662/842-681). They offer a well-done *Sound of Music* spin-off—a dinner show, featuring songs from the movie and local dances (520 AS

Salzburg and Hallstatt

includes dinner at 19:30, 360 AS for 20:30 show only when booked in advance, ideal for families, daily May–Sept, tel. 0662/832-029). Since the Stieglkeller has lots of rooms, you can skip the show and still enjoy the restaurant.

Café Glockenspiel, on Mozartplatz 2, is the place to see and be seen (pricey lunch, 90–190 AS). Nearby, **Hotel Restaurant Weisses Kreuz** serves a fine meal in a pleasant dining room (see "Sleeping in (or above) the Old Town," above).

Picnickers will appreciate the bustling morning produce market (daily except Sun) on University Square, just behind Mozart's house. On the same square I enjoyed a great chicken salad at the reasonable **Restaurant Zipfer Bierhaus**.

The next two places are on the old-town side of the river, about a 10-minute walk along the river (river on your right) from the Staatsbrücke bridge.

Krimplestätter employs 450 years of experience serving authentic old-Salzburger food in its authentic old-Austrian interior or its cheery garden (Tue–Sun 10:00–24:00, closed Mon all year and winter Sun, Müllner Hauptstrasse 31). For fine food with a wild finale, eat here and drink at the nearby Augustiner Bräustübl.

Augustiner Bräustübl, a monk-run brewery, is rustic and crude. On busy nights it's like a Munich beer hall with no music but the volume turned up. When it's cool you'll enjoy a historic setting with beer-sloshed and smoke-stained halls. On balmy evenings you'll eat under trees in a pleasant outdoor beer garden. Local students mix with tourists eating hearty slabs of schnitzel with their fingers or cold meals from the self-serve picnic counter (daily 15:00–23:00, Augustinergasse 4, head up Müllner Hauptstrasse northwest along the river, and ask for "Müllnerbräu," its local nickname). Don't be fooled by second-rate gardens serving the same beer nearby—this huge, 1,000-seat place is in the Augustiner brewery. Order carefully, prices can sting. Pick up a half-liter (28–32 AS) or full-liter mug (56–64 AS) of the great beer, pay the lady, and give Mr. Keg your empty mug. For dessert, after a visit to the strudel kiosk, enjoy the incomparable floodlit view of old Salzburg from the nearby pedestrian bridge, and then stroll home along the river.

Eating on or near Linzergasse

These cheaper places are near the recommended hotels on Linzergasse. **Frauenberger** is friendly, picnic-ready, and inexpensive, with indoor or outdoor seating (Mon–Fri 8:00–14:00, across from Linzergasse 16). **Spicy Spices** is a vegetarian-Indian lunch take-out restaurant (with a few tables) serving tasty curry and rice boxes, *samosas*, organic salads, and fresh juices (Wolf-Dietrich Strasse 1). **Mensa Aicherpassage** serves some of Salzburg's cheapest meals in the basement (Mon–Fri 11:30–14:30, near Mirabellplatz walk into

Aicherpassage, go under arch, enter metal door to "Mozarteum," and go down 1 floor). Closer to the hotels on Rupertgasse and away from the tourists is the very local **Biergarten Weisse** (daily 11:00–24:00, on Rupertgasse east of Bayerhamerstrasse).

For a painless view over the city spires, find **Hotel Stein** near where Linzergasse meets the main bridge and take the elevator to the seventh floor.

Transportation Connections—Salzburg
By train to: **Innsbruck** (every 2 hrs, 2 hrs), **Vienna** (2/hrly, 3.5 hrs), **Hallstatt** (hrly, 50 min to Attnang Puchheim, 20-minute wait, 90 min to Hallstatt), **Reutte** (every 2 hrs, 4 hrs, transfer in Innsbruck), **Munich** (hrly, 90 min).

SALZKAMMERGUT LAKE DISTRICT AND HALLSTATT
Commune with nature in Austria's Lake District. "The hills are alive," and you're surrounded by the loveliness that has turned on everyone from Emperor Franz Josef to Julie Andrews. This is *Sound of Music* country. Idyllic and majestic, but not rugged, it's a gentle land of lakes, forested mountains, and storybook villages, rich in hiking opportunities and inexpensive lodging. Settle down in the postcard-pretty, fjord-cuddling town of Hallstatt.

Planning Your Time
While there are plenty of lakes, Hallstatt is really the only one that matters. One night and a few hours to browse are all you'll need to fall in love. To relax or take a hike in the surroundings, give it two nights and a day. It's a good stop between Salzburg and Vienna. A visit here, a bike ride along the Danube, and the two big cities—Salzburg and Vienna—make an ideal Austrian itinerary.

Orientation (tel. code: 06134)
Lovable Hallstatt is a tiny town bullied onto a ledge between a selfish mountain and a swan-ruled lake, with a waterfall ripping furiously through its middle. It can be toured on foot in about 15 minutes. The town is one of Europe's oldest, going back centuries before Christ. The charm of Hallstatt is the village and its lakeside setting. Go there to relax, nibble, wander, and paddle. (In August, tourist crowds can trample much of Hallstatt's charm.) The lake is famous for its good fishing and pure water.

Tourist Information: The TI is on the main drag (a block from Marktplatz toward the lakefront parking, above the post office, Seestrasse 169). They can find you a room and get you a holiday "guest card" allowing free parking (Mon–Fri 9:00–17:00, Sat–Sun 10:00–14:00, less off-season, tel. 06134/8208, e-mail: hallstatt-info@eunet.at).

Hallstatt

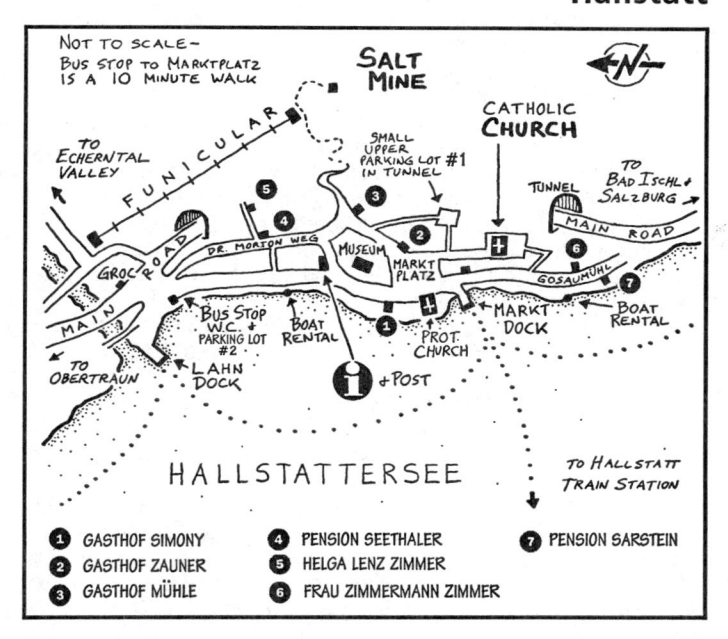

(Map of Hallstatt with legend:)
1. GASTHOF SIMONY
2. GASTHOF ZAUNER
3. GASTHOF MÜHLE
4. PENSION SEETHALER
5. HELGA LENZ ZIMMER
6. FRAU ZIMMERMANN ZIMMER
7. PENSION SARSTEIN

Arrival in Hallstatt

By Train: Hallstatt's train station is a wide spot on the tracks across the lake. *Stefanie* (a boat) meets you at the station and glides across the lake into town (23 AS, with each train until 18:40—don't arrive after that). The boat ride is gorgeous. Last departing boat-train connection leaves Hallstatt at 18:15. Walk left from the boat dock for the TI and most hotels.

By Car: Hallstatt has several numbered parking areas outside the town center. Skip the tunnel parking (lot 1) and park on the lake in lot 2 (just after the tunnel, coming from Salzburg or Vienna). You can drive into the village to drop bags, but parking is best at lot 2. It's a lovely, level, 10-minute walk to the center of town from here.

Helpful Hints

A Laundromat is at the campground near the bathing island (wash, dry, and soap, 100 AS). The post office is below the TI (see above). You can rent a bike at Hotel Gruner Baum, next to recommended Hotel Simony (80 AS/half day, 120 AS/day).

Views: For a relatively easy, great view over Hallstatt, hike above Helga Lenz's *Zimmer* as far as you like (see "Sleeping," below), or climb any path leading up the hill. The 40-minute steep hike down from the salt mine tour gives the best views.

Sights—Hallstatt

Prehistory Museum—The humble Prehistory Museum adjacent to the TI is interesting because little Hallstatt was the important salt-mining hub of a culture that spread from France to the Balkans during what archaeologists call the "Hallstatt Period" (800–400 B.C.). Back then, Celtic tribes dug for precious salt, and Hallstatt was, as its name means, the "home of salt." Your 50-AS Prehistory Museum ticket also gets you into the cute Heimatmuseum of folk culture (daily 10:00–18:00 in summer). Historians like the English booklet that covers both museums (25 AS). The Janu sport shop across from the TI dug into a prehistoric site, and now its basement is another small museum (free).

▲▲**Hallstatt Church and Cemetery**—Hallstatt has two churches. The Protestant church is at lake level. The more interesting Catholic church, with a giant St. Christopher (protector of us travelers) on its outside wall, overlooks the town from above. From near the boat dock, hike up the covered wooden stairway to the church. The lovely church has 500-year-old altars and frescoes dedicated to the saints of mining and salt. Space is so limited in Hallstatt that bones have only 12 peaceful buried years in the church cemetery before making way for the freshly dead. The result is a fascinating chapel of bones in the cemetery (Beinhaus, 10 AS, daily 10:00–18:00). Each skull is lovingly named, dated, and decorated, with the men getting ivy, and the women, roses. They stopped this practice in the 1960s, about the same time the Catholic Church began permitting cremation.

▲▲**Salt Mine Tour**—If you have yet to do a salt mine, Hallstatt's is as good as any. You'll ride a steep funicular high above the town (97 AS round-trip), take a 10-minute hike, put on old miners' clothes, take an underground train, slide down the banisters, and listen to an English tape-recorded tour while your guide speaks German (135 AS, May–mid-Oct daily 9:30–16:30, no children under age 4, tel. 06134/8251). The well-publicized ancient Celtic graveyard excavation sites nearby are really dead. The scenic 40-minute hike back into town is (with strong knees) a joy.

▲**Boating, Hiking, and Spelunking**—Those into relaxation can rent a sleepy electric motorboat to enjoy town views from the water (75 AS/30 min, 120 AS/60 min, 1 or 2 people, 2 speeds: slow and stop, rental place next to ferry dock). Mountain lovers, hikers, and spelunkers keep busy for days using Hallstatt as their home base. Get information from the TI on the various caves with their ice formations, the thunderous rivers, mountain lifts, nearby walks, and harder hikes. The Dachstein Giant Ice Cave gets rave reviews (90 AS, 9:00–16:00).

Salzburg and Hallstatt 73

Salzkammergut Lakes

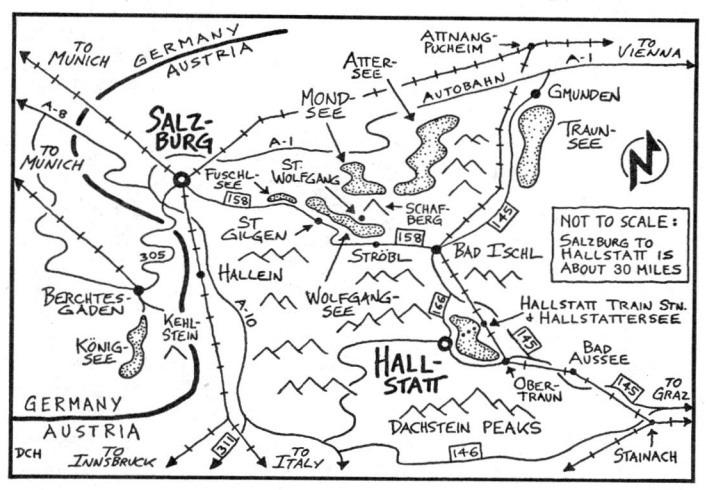

Sleeping in Hallstatt
(12 AS = about $1, tel. code: 06134, zip code: 4830)
Hallstatt's TI can almost always find you a room. Mid-July and August can be tight, and early August is worst. A bed in a private home costs about 200 AS with breakfast. It's hard to get a one-night advance reservation. But if you drop in and they have a spot, they're happy to have you. Prices include breakfast, lots of stairs, and a silent night. "*Zimmer mit Aussicht?*" means "Room with view?"—worth asking for. Only one of my listings accepts plastic, which goes for most businesses here.

Gasthof Simony is my stocking-feet-tidy, 500-year-old favorite. It's right on the square with a lake view, balconies, creaky wood floors, slippery rag rugs, antique furniture, a lakefront garden, and a huge breakfast. Call friendly Susan Scheutz for a reservation. For safety, reconfirm a day or two before you arrive (S-380 AS, Sb-650 AS, D-550 AS, Db-900 AS, price varies according to the plumbing, view, season, and length of stay, 250 AS for 3rd person, cheaper for families, Markt 105, tel. 06134/8231, SE). Downstairs and in the lakefront garden, Frau Zopf runs a traditional Austrian restaurant—try her delicious homemade desserts.

Gasthof Zauner, at the opposite end of the square from the Simony, is my only listing that accepts credit cards. It's a business machine offering modern rooms with all the comforts and a restaurant specializing in grilled meat and fish (Db-1,210 AS, CC:VM, Marktplatz 51, tel. 06134/8246, fax 06134/82468).

Gasthaus Mühle Naturfreunde-Herberge, below the waterfall with the best cheap beds in town, is clearly the place to eat well on a budget—great pizzas (120 AS per bed in 2- to 20-bed coed dorms, add 40 AS if you need sheets, breakfast-40 AS, closed Nov, restaurant closed Wed, Kirchenweg 36, below tunnel car park, tel. & fax 06134/8318, run by Ferdinand Törö).

Pension Seethaler is a homey old lodge with 45 beds and a breakfast room mossy with antlers, perched above the lake (215 AS per person in S, D, T, or Q, 280 AS/person in rooms with private bath, 20 AS cheaper if you stay more than 1 night, no extra for views; from the Boote paddleboats between the lake parking lot and Marktplatz, find and climb the steps then turn right, Dr. Morton Weg 22, tel. 06134/8421, fax 06134/84214, Frau Seethaler).

Helga Lenz is a five-minute climb above the Seethaler (look for the green "*Zimmer*" sign). This big, sprawling, woodsy house has a nifty garden perch, wins the best-view award, and is ideal for those who sleep well in tree houses (D-360 AS, T-540 AS, Q-720 AS, 20 AS more for 1-night stays, Hallberg 17, tel. 06134/8508, SE).

These two listings are 100 yards to the right of the ferry boat dock, with your back to the lake: **Frau Zimmermann** runs a small *Zimmer* (as her name implies) in a 500-year-old ramshackle house with low beams, time-polished wood, and fine lake views (S-210 AS, D-400 AS, T-600 AS, can be musty, Gosaumühlstrasse 69, tel. 06134/86853). **Pension Sarstein** has 25 beds in basic, sometimes dirty rooms with flower-bedecked lake-view balconies, in a charming building run by friendly Frau Fisher. You can swim from her lakeside garden (D-420 AS, Ds-520 AS, Db-620 AS with this book; 1-night stays cost 20 AS per person extra; Gosaumühlstrasse 83, tel. 06134/8217).

Transportation Connections—Hallstatt
By train to: Salzburg (hrly, 90 min to Attnang Puchheim, short wait, 50 min to Salzburg), **Vienna** (hrly, 90 min to Attnang Puchheim, short wait, 2.5 hrs to Vienna). Day-trippers to Hallstatt can check bags at the Attnang Puchheim station. But connections there and back can be very fast—about five minutes. Have three 10-AS coins ready for the lockers.

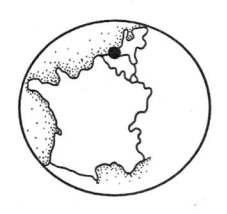

BRUGES (BRUGGE)

With Renoir canals, pointy gilded architecture, time-tunnel art, and stay-awhile cafés, Bruges is a heavyweight sightseeing destination as well as a joy. Where else can you ride a bike along a canal, munch mussels, wash them down with the world's best beer, savor heavenly chocolate, and see Flemish Primitives and a Michelangelo, all within 300 yards of a bell tower that rings out "Don't worry, be happy" jingles every 15 minutes? And there's no language barrier.

The town is Brugge (broo-gha) in Flemish...Bruges (broozh) in French and English. Before it was Flemish or French, the name was a Viking word for "wharf" or "embarkment." Right from the start, Bruges was a trading center. In the 11th century it grew wealthy on the cloth trade. By the 14th century Bruges' population was 40,000, in a league with London and one of the largest in the world. Bruges was the most important cloth market in northern Europe. In the 15th century Bruges was the favored residence of the Dukes of Burgundy. Commerce and the arts boomed. Jan van Eyck and Hans Memling had studios here. But by the 16th century the harbor had silted up, and the economy collapsed. The Burgundian court left, Spain conquered Belgium in 1548, and Bruges' Golden Age was over. For generations it was known as a mysterious and dead city. In the 19th century a new port, Zeebrugge, brought renewed vitality to the area. And 20th-century tourists discovered the town. Today Bruges prospers because of tourism: It's a uniquely well preserved Gothic city and a handy gateway to Europe. Bruges is no secret to vacationers and travelers, but even with the crowds it's the kind of city where you don't mind being a tourist.

Planning Your Time

Bruges needs at least two nights and a full, well-organized day. Even nonshoppers enjoy browsing here, and the Belgian love of life makes a hectic itinerary seem a little senseless. With one day, the speedy visitor could do this: 9:30–Climb the belfry, 10:00–Tour the Burg sights (visit the TI if necessary), 11:30–Take a boat tour, 12:15–Walk to the brewery, have lunch, and catch the 13:00 tour, 14:30–Walk through the Beguinage, 15:00–Tour the Memling Museum (six paintings), 15:45–See the Michelangelo in the church, 16:00–Tour the Groeninge Museum (closes at 17:00). Rent a bike for an evening ride through the quiet backstreets (or take a 900BF half-hour horse-and-buggy tour). Lose the tourists and find a dinner. (If this schedule seems insane, skip the belfry and the brewery—or stay another day.)

Orientation (tel. code: 050)

The tourists' Bruges (you'll be sharing it) is contained within a one-kilometer-square canal, or moat. Nearly everything of interest and importance is within a cobbled and convenient swath between the train station and Market Square (a 15-minute walk).

Tourist Information: The main office is on Burg Square (Mon–Fri 9:30–18:30, Sat–Sun 10:00–12:00, 14:00–18:30, off-season closes at 17:00, lockers and money exchange desk, tel. 050/448-686, public WC in courtyard). The other TI is at the train station (Mon–Sat 10:30–13:15, 14:00–18:30, closed Sun and off-season at 17:00, www.bruges.be). Both TIs sell a great 25BF all-inclusive Bruges visitors guide with a map and listings of all of the sights and services. The free *Exit* includes a monthly calendar of the many events the town puts on to keep its hordes of tourists entertained. It's in Dutch but almost readable (i.e., van Gershwin tot Clapton). Skip the TI's "combo" museum ticket. They also have train schedule information and specifics on the various kinds of tours available. Bikers will want the *5X on the Bike around Bruges* map/guide, which sells for 20BF and shows five routes through the countryside.

Internet Access: A cyber café is at Katelijnestraat 67, halfway between the station and Market Square near Walplein (60BF/15 min, also word processing and printing, Mon–Wed 9:30–21:30, Thu–Sat 9:30–17:30, tel. 050/349-352, e-mail: Kdenys@unicall.be).

Laundromat: You can wash clothes at Gentportstraat 28 (daily 7:00–22:00, English instructions, machines use 20BF coins; you'll need about 10 total) or at Mr. Wash (near Hotel Hansa on St. Jakobsstraat).

Arrival in Bruges

By Train: From the train (and from the TI near the station), you'll see the square belfry tower marking the main square. Upon arrival, stop by the station TI to pick up the Bruges visitors' guide (map in centerfold). There are no ATMs at the station, but you can change money at ticket windows. Buses marked "CENTRUM" go fast-as-a-taxi to the Market Square (40BF ticket, buy from driver, good for an hour). Buses #4 and #8 go farther, near the recommended Carmerstraat-area hotels. The taxi fare to most hotels is 250BF. It's a 20-minute walk from the station to the center: Cross the busy street and canal in front of the station, head up Oostmeers, and turn right on Steenstraat to reach Market Square. You could rent a bike at the station for the duration of your stay (325BF/day with a 500BF deposit, tel. 050/302-329), but other bike-rental shops are closer to the center (see "Bruges Experiences," below).

By Car: Park at the train station for just 100BF a day and pretend you arrived by train; show your parking receipt on the bus to get a free ride into town. The pricier underground parking garage at t'Zand costs 350BF/day.

Helpful Hints

You can change traveler's checks at Best Change (daily 9:00–21:00, until 19:00 in winter, just off Market Square on Steenstraat). The post office is on Market Square near the belfry (Mon–Fri 9:00–19:00, Sat 9:00–12:00). Shops are open 9:00–18:00, a little later on Friday. Grocery stores are usually closed on Sunday. Market day is Wednesday morning (Market Square) and Saturday morning (t'Zand). On Saturday and Sunday afternoons, there's a flea market along Dijver in front of the Groeninge Museum. October through March is off-season (when some museums close on Tuesday). A botanical garden blooms in the center of Astrid Park.

Sights—Bruges

Bruges' sights are listed here in walking order, from Market Square to the Burg to the cluster of museums around the Church of Our Lady to the Beguinage (a 10-minute walk from beginning to end). Like Venice, the ultimate sight is the town itself, and the best way to enjoy that is to get lost on the back streets away from the lace shops and ice-cream stands.

Market Square (Markt)—Ringed by banks, the post office, lots of restaurant terraces, great old gabled buildings, and the belfry, this is the modern heart of the city. Most city buses go from here to the station. Under the belfry are two great Belgian French-fry stands and a quadrilingual Braille description and model of the tower. In its day, a canal went right up to the central square of this formerly great trading center. Geldmuntstraat, just off the square, is a delightful street with many fun and practical shops and eateries.

▲▲**Belfry (Belfort)**—Most of this bell tower has stood over Market Square since 1300. In 1486 the octagonal lantern was added, making it 88 meters high—that's 366 steps (daily 9:30–17:00, Oct–Mar closed 12:30–13:30, ticket window closes 45 minutes

Belgium

Bruges

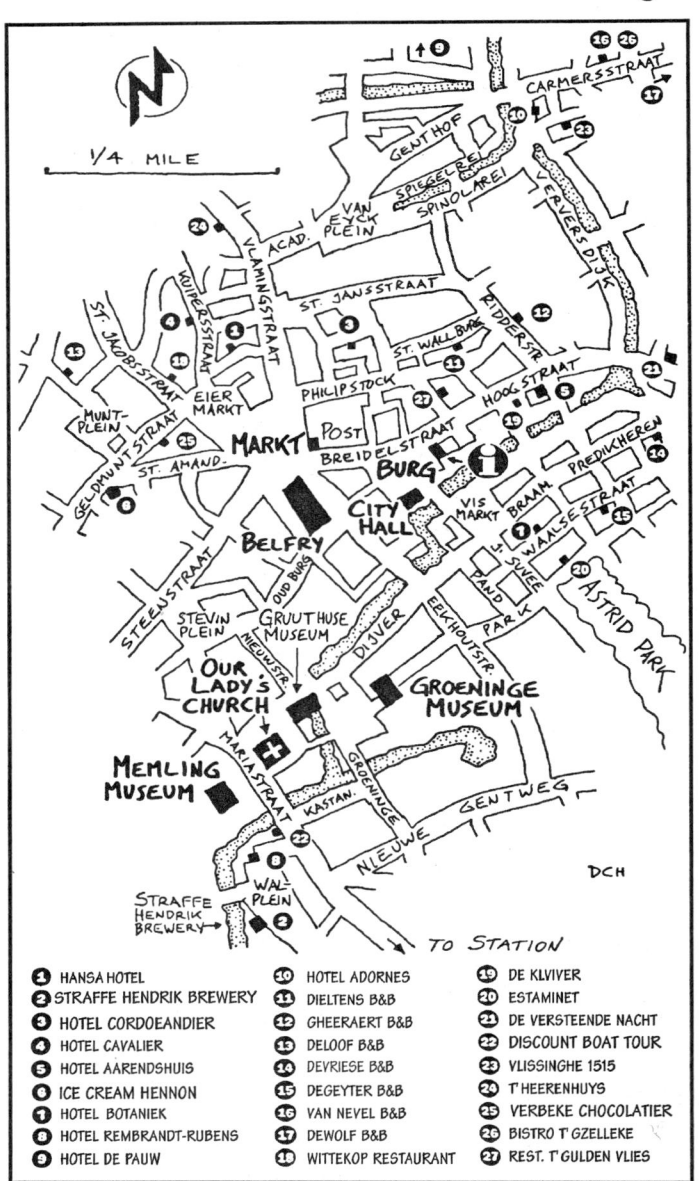

- ❶ HANSA HOTEL
- ❷ STRAFFE HENDRIK BREWERY
- ❸ HOTEL CORDOEANDIER
- ❹ HOTEL CAVALIER
- ❺ HOTEL AARENDSHUIS
- ❻ ICE CREAM HENNON
- ❼ HOTEL BOTANIEK
- ❽ HOTEL REMBRANDT-RUBENS
- ❾ HOTEL DE PAUW
- ❿ HOTEL ADORNES
- ⓫ DIELTENS B&B
- ⓬ GHEERAERT B&B
- ⓭ DELOOF B&B
- ⓮ DEVRIESE B&B
- ⓯ DEGEYTER B&B
- ⓰ VAN NEVEL B&B
- ⓱ DEWOLF B&B
- ⓲ WITTEKOP RESTAURANT
- ⓳ DE KLVIVER
- ⓴ ESTAMINET
- ㉑ DE VERSTEENDE NACHT
- ㉒ DISCOUNT BOAT TOUR
- ㉓ VLISSINGHE 1515
- ㉔ T'HEERENHUYS
- ㉕ VERBEKE CHOCOLATIER
- ㉖ BISTRO T'GZELLEKE
- ㉗ REST. T'GULDEN VLIES

early, WC in courtyard). The view is worth the climb and the 100BF. Survey the town. On the horizon you can see the towns along the coast. Just before you reach the top, peek into the carillon room. The 47 bells can be played mechanically with the giant barrel and movable tabs (as they do on each quarter hour), or with a manual keyboard (as it does for regular concerts) with fists and feet rather than fingers. Be there on the quarter hour, when things ring. It's *bellissimo* at the top of the hour. Carillon concert times are listed at the base of the belfry (usually Mon, Wed, and Sat at 21:00 and Sun at 14:15). Back on the square, with your back to the belfry, turn right onto pedestrian-only Breidelstraat and thread yourself through the lace and *wafels* to Burg Square.

▲▲**Burg Square**—The opulent square called Burg is Bruges' civic center, historically the birthplace of Bruges and the site of the ninth-century castle of the first Count of Flanders. Today it's the scene of outdoor concerts and home of the TI (with a 10BF WC). It's surrounded by six centuries of architecture. Sweeping counterclockwise 360 degrees, you'll go from Romanesque (the round arches and thick walls of the brick basilica in the corner, best seen inside the lower chapel) to the pointed Gothic arches of the Town Hall (with its "Gothic Room") to the well-proportioned Renaissance windows of the Old Recorder's House (next door, under the gilded statues) and past the TI and the park to the elaborate 17th-century Baroque of the Provost's House. Complete your spin and walk to that corner.

▲**Basilica of the Holy Blood**—Originally the Chapel of Saint Basil, it is famous for its relic of the blood of Christ, which, according to tradition, was brought to Bruges in 1150 after the Second Crusade (and is displayed only during Friday worship services). The lower chapel (through the door labeled "*Basiliek*") is dark and solid—a fine example of Romanesque style (with some beautiful statues). The upper chapel (separate entrance, climb the stairs) is decorated Gothic and usually filled with appropriately contemplative music. A 10BF English flier tells about the relic, art, and history. The small but sumptuous Basilica Museum (well described in English) contains the gem-studded hexagonal reliquary (c. 1600) that carries the relic on its yearly Ascension Day trip through the streets of Bruges (museum is next to upper chapel, 40BF, daily 9:30–11:50, 14:00–17:50; shorter hours and closed Wed afternoon off-season).

▲**City Hall's Gothic Room**—Your ticket gives you a room full of old town maps and paintings and a grand, beautifully restored "Gothic Hall" from 1400. Its painted and carved wooden ceiling features hanging arches (explained by an English flier). Notice the New Testament themes carved into the circular "vault keys." The wall murals are late-19th-century Romantic paintings of episodes from the city's history (described in the flier). The free ground-level lobby (closed on weekends) is a picture gallery of

Belgium's colonial history, from the Spanish Bourbon king to Napoleon (100BF, includes admission to Renaissance Hall, daily 9:30–17:00, closed 12:30–14:00 off-season, Burg 12).

Renaissance Hall (Brugse Vrije)—This is just one ornate room with an impressive Renaissance chimney. If you're into heraldry, the symbolism, explained in the free English flier, makes this worth a five-minute stop. If you're not, you'll wonder where the rest of the museum is (100BF, includes admission to City Hall, daily 9:30–12:30, 13:15–17:00, longer lunch—until 14:00—in winter, entry in the corner of the square).

From Burg to Fish Market to View—From Burg, walk under the Goldfinger family down Blinde Ezelstraat. Just after you cross the bridge, the persistent little fish market (Vismarkt, fresh North Sea catch sold Tue–Fri 6:00–13:00) is on your left. Take an immediate right to Huidevettersplein, a tiny, picturesque, and restaurant-filled square. Continue a few steps to Rozenhoedkaai Street, where you can get a great photo of the belfry reflected in the canal. Can you see its tilt? It leans about four feet. Down the canal (past a flea market on weekends) looms the huge spire of the Church of Our Lady (tallest brick spire in the Low Countries). Between you and the church are the next three museums.

▲▲▲**Groeninge Museum**—This diverse and classy collection shows off mostly Flemish art from Memling to Magritte. Rooms 1 through 18 take you from 1400 to 1945. While it has plenty of worthwhile modern art, the highlights are its vivid and pristine Flemish Primitives. (*Primitive* here really means before the Renaissance.) Flemish art is shaped by its love of detail, its merchant patrons' egos, and the power of the Church. Lose yourself in the halls of Groeninge: Gaze across 15th-century canals, into the eyes of reassuring Marys, and through town squares littered with leotards, lace, and lopped-off heads (200BF, daily 9:30–17:00, Oct–Mar closed 12:30–14:00 and Tue, Dijver 12). The **Brangwyn Museum** (Arentshuis), next door, is only interesting if you are into lace or the early-20th-century art of Brangwyn (80BF, daily 9:30–17:00, off-season closed 12:30–14:00 and Tue, Dijver 16).

▲**Gruuthuse Museum**—A wealthy brewer's home, this is a sprawling smattering of everything from medieval bedpans to a guillotine. There's no information inside, so to understand the crossbows, dark old paintings, and what a beer merchant's doing with box seats peeking down on the altar of the Church of Our Lady next door, you'll have to buy or browse through the 600BF guidebook (130BF, daily 9:30–17:00, shorter hours off-season, Dijver 17). Leaving the museum, contemplate the mountain of bricks towering 120 meters above as they have for 600 years.

▲▲**Church of Our Lady**—The church stands as a memorial to the power and wealth of Bruges in its heyday. A delicate *Madonna and Child*, by Michelangelo, is near the apse (to the right if you're facing the altar). It's said to be the only Michelangelo statue to leave Italy in his lifetime (thanks to the wealth generated by Bruges' cloth trade). If you like tombs and church art, pay to wander through the apse (70BF, Michelangelo free, art-filled apse Mon–Fri 10:00–11:30, 14:30–17:00, closes at 16:00 on Sat, Sun 14:30–17:00, on Mariastraat).

▲▲St. Jans Hospital/Memling Museum—Across the street from the Church of Our Lady is a medieval hospital with six much-loved paintings by the greatest of the Flemish Primitives, Hans Memling. His *Mystical Wedding of St. Catherine* triptych deserves a close look. Catherine and her "mystical groom," the baby Jesus, are flanked by a headless John the Baptist and a pensive John the Evangelist. The chairs are there so you can study it. If you understand the Book of Revelations, you'll understand St. John's wild and intricate vision. The Reliquary of St. Ursula, an ornate little mini-church in the same room, is filled with impressive detail (100BF, daily 9:30–17:00, off-season closed 12:30–14:00 and Wed, Mariastraat 38).

▲▲Straffe Hendrik Brewery Tour—Belgians are Europe's beer connoisseurs. This fun and handy tour is a great way to pay your respects. The happy gang at this working family brewery gives entertaining and informative 45-minute, four-language tours (usually by friendly Inge, 140BF including a beer, piles of very steep steps, a great rooftop panorama, daily on the hour 11:00–17:00, Oct–Mar 11:00 and 15:00 only, 1 block past church and canal, take a right down skinny Stoofstraat to #26 on Walplein square, tel. 050/332-697). At Straffe Hendrik ("Strong Henry") they remind their drinkers: "The components of the beer are vitally necessary and contribute to a well-balanced life-pattern. Nerves, muscles, visual sentience, and a healthy skin are stimulated by these in a positive manner. For longevity and lifelong equilibrium, drink Straffe Hendrik in moderation!"

Their bistro, where you'll be given your included-with-the-tour beer, serves a quick and hearty lunch plate (the 150BF "bread with pâté and vegetables" is the best value, although the 250BF "meat selection and vegetables" is a beer-drinker's picnic for two). On sunny summer days they offer a barbecue and salad bar for 350BF. You can eat indoors with the smell of hops or outdoors with the smell of hops. This is a great place to wait for your tour or to linger afterward. From here the lacy cuteness of Bruges crescendos as you approach the Beguinage.

▲▲Beguinage—For military (and various other) reasons, there were more women than men in the medieval Low Countries. Towns provided Beguinages, dignified places in which these "Beguines" could live a life of piety and service (without having to take the same vows a nun would). You'll find Beguinages all over Belgium and Holland. Bruges' Beguinage—now inhabited not by

Beguines but by Benedictine nuns—almost makes you want to don a habit and fold your hands as you walk under its wispy trees and whisper past its frugal little homes. For a good slice of Beguinage life, walk through the simple museum (Beguine's House, left of entry gate, 60BF with English flier, daily 10:00–12:00, 13:45–17:00, shorter hours off-season).

Minnewater—Beyond the Beguinage is Minnewater, an idyllic, clip-clop world of flower boxes, canals, swans, and tour boats packed like happy egg cartons. Beyond that is the train station.

Almshouses—Walking from the Beguinage back to the center, you might detour along Nieuwe Gentweg to visit one of about 20 almshouses in the city. At #8, go through the door dated 1613 (free) into the peaceful courtyard. This was a medieval form of housing for the poor. The rich would pay for someone's tiny room here in return for lots of prayers. The Diamond Museum (at the start of Nieuwe Gentweg) is less interesting than an encyclopedia (200BF).

Bruges Experiences

Chocolate—Bruggians are connoisseurs of fine chocolate. You'll be tempted by chocolate-filled display windows all over town. Godiva is the best big-factory/high-price/high-quality local brand, but for the finest small-family operation, drop by **Maitre Chocolatier Verbeke**. While Mr. Verbeke is busy downstairs making chocolates, Mrs. Verbeke makes sure customers in the shop get the chocolate of their dreams. Ask her to assemble a bag of your favorites. (The smallest amount sold is 100 grams—about seven pieces—for 90BF). Most are pralines, which means they're filled. While the "hedgehogs" are popular, be sure to get a "pharaoh's head." Pray for cool weather, since it's closed when it's very hot. (Open at least in the mornings on Tue, Wed, Fri, and Sat; open cooler afternoons as well; a block off Market Square at Geldmuntstraat 25; can ship overseas except during hot summer months, tel. 050/334-198.)

Lace and Windmills by the Moat—A 10-minute walk from the center to the northeast end of town brings you to four windmills strung out along a pleasant grassy setting on the "big moat" canal (between Kruispoort and Dampoort, on the Bruges side of the moat). One of the windmills (St. Janshuismolen) is open to visitors (40BF, daily 9:30–12:30, 13:15–17:00, closed Oct–Mar, at the end of Carmersstraat).

To actually see lace being made, drop by the nearby Lace Centre, where ladies toss bobbins madly while their eyes go bad (60BF includes afternoon demonstrations and a small lace museum called Kantcentrum, as well as the adjacent Jerusalem church; Mon–Fri 10:00–12:00, 14:00–18:00, until 17:00 on Sat, closed Sun, Peperstraat 3). The Folklore Museum, in the same neighborhood, is cute but forgettable (80BF, daily 9:30–17:00, less off-season, Rolweg 40). To find either place, ask for the Jerusalem church.

▲▲**Biking**—While the sights are close enough for easy walking, the town is a treat to bike through, and you'll be able to get away from the tourist center. Consider a peaceful evening ride through the back streets and around the outer canal. Rental shops have maps and ideas. The TI sells a handy *5X on the Bike around Bruges* map/guide for 20BF; it narrates five different bike routes (18–30 kms) through the idyllic nearby countryside. The best trip is 30 minutes along the canal out to Damme and back. The Netherlands/Belgium border is a 40-minute pedal beyond Damme. Two shops rent bikes in the center of town (70BF for 1 hour, 150BF for 4 hours, or 250BF/day). Both offer free city maps and child seats. **Popelier Eric's** requires no deposit and sells a good map of the countryside for 80BF (daily 9:00–21:00 in summer, 10:00–19:00 in winter, 50 meters from Church of Our Lady at Mariastraat 26, tel. 050/343-262). **'T Koffieboontje** asks for a deposit of 1,000BF, your passport, or a credit-card imprint. They sell an annoying double-sided photocopy of the TI's biking brochure for 20BF; the map is on one side, and the directions—inconveniently—are on the other (Hallestraat 4, closer to the belfry, tel. 050/338-027). The less central **De Ketting** rents bikes for less (150BF/day, Gentpoortstraat 23, tel. 050/344-196). **Dolfinarium**—At Boudewijnpark, just outside of town, dolphins make a splash at 11:15, 14:00, and 16:00 (280BF for the 40-min show, Debaeckestraat 12, call to confirm show times, tel. 050/383-838). The theme park's roller-skating rink is open in the afternoon (and turns into an ice-skating rink off-season). From Bruges, catch the "Sint Michiels" bus #7 or #17 from Kuipersstraat.

Tours of Bruges

Bruges by Boat—The most relaxing and scenic (if not informative) way to see this city of canals is by boat, with the captain narrating. Boats leave from all over town (190BF, 4/hrly, 10:00–18:00, copycat 30-min rides). Boten Stael (just over the canal from the Memling Museum) offers a 30BF discount with this book.
City Minibus Tours—"City Tour Bruges" gives 50-minute/380BF rolling overviews of the town in an 18-seat, two-skylight minibus with dial-a-language headsets and video support. The tour leaves hourly (on the hour, 9:00–19:00 in summer, until 18:00 in spring and fall, less in winter) from Market Square. The narration, while clean, is slow-moving and boring. But the tour is a lazy way to cruise by every sight I've described here.
Walking Tours—Local guides walk small groups through the core of town daily in July and August (150BF, depart from TI at 15:00). The tours, while earnest, are heavy on history and in two languages, so they may be less than peppy. Still, to propel you beyond the pretty gables and canal swans of Bruges, they are good medicine. A private guided tour costs 1,500BF (reserve at least 3 days in advance through a TI).

Bus Tours of Countryside—Quasimodo Tours offers those with extra time two excellent all-day tours through the rarely visited Flemish countryside. The "Flanders Fields" tour concentrates on World War I battlefields, trenches, memorials, and poppy-splattered fields (Sun, Tue, and Thu 9:00–16:30). The other is "Triple Treat": the port of Damme, a castle, a monastery, a brewery, and a chocolate factory as well as a sampling of the the treats—a waffle, chocolate, and beer (Mon, Wed, and Fri 9:00–16:00). Hardworking Lote leads all the tours himself, in English only (1,500BF, 1,200BF for people under 26, CC:VM, 29-seat non-smoking bus, lunch included, lots of walking, pickup at your hotel or the train station, tel. 050/370-470 to book, fax 050/374-960).
Bruges by Bike—The **Backroad Bike Company** leads daily bike tours through the nearby countryside (550–650BF, 30 km, 3 hrs, tel. 050/370-470). Shorter, longer, and evening tours are available.
Bus and Boat Tour—**Sightseeing Line** offers a bus trip to Damme and a boat ride back (660BF, Apr–Jun daily at 14:00 and 16:00, 2 hrs, leaves from Market Square).

Sleeping in Bruges
(40BF = about $1, tel. code 050, zip code: 8000)
Sleep Code: **S** = Single, **D** = Double/Twin, **T** = Triple, **Q** = Quad, **b** = bathroom, **t** = toilet only, **s** = shower only, **CC** = Credit Card (**V**isa, **M**asterCard, **A**mex). Everyone speaks English.

Most places are located between the train station and the old center, with the most distant (and best) being a few blocks beyond Market Square to the north and east. B&Bs offer the best value. All include breakfast, are on quiet streets, and (with a few exceptions) keep the same prices throughout the year. Bruges is most crowded Friday and Saturday evenings Easter through October—with July and August weekends being worst. Otherwise, finding a room is easy.

Hotels
Hansa Hotel offers 20 rooms in a completely modernized old building. Tastefully decorated in elegant pastels, it has all the amenities. This is a great splurge (Db-4,360–5,770BF depending on size of room, extra bed-1,250BF, CC:VMA, air-con, nonsmoking, elevator, Niklaas Desparsstraat 11, a block north of Market Square, tel. 050/338-444, fax 050/334-205, www.hansa.be, e-mail: information@hansa.be, run by cheery, hardworking Johan and Isabelle).

Hotel Aarendshuis, an old merchant's mansion, is well worn but comfortable. It's family run and has 25 spacious rooms, dingy carpets, chandeliered public places, and a small garden (prices vary with size and luxury: Sb-2,400BF, Db-3,000–4,000BF, Tb-4,000BF, Qb-4,500BF, kids under 10 free, car park-350BF, CC:VMA, elevator, 2 blocks off Burg Square at Hoogstraat 18, tel. 050/337-889, fax 050/330-816, e-mail: hotelaarendshuis@village.uunet.be).

Hotel Cordoeandier, another family-run place, rents 22 bright, simple, modern rooms on a quiet street two blocks off Market Square (Sb-1,950BF, Db-2,300BF, Tb-2,900–3,200BF, Qb-3,400BF, 5b-3,900BF, CC:VM, nearly free Internet access, Cordoeanierstraat 16, tel. 050/339-051, fax 050/346-111, www.cordoeanier.be, Kris and Veerie). Equally central and even cheaper but smoky and not the same value is **Hotel Nicolas** (Sb-1,600BF, Db-2,000BF, CC:VMA, elevator, next to Hotel Hansa at N. Desparsstraat 9, tel. 050/335-502, Chinese-run and decorated).

Hotel Cavalier, with less character and more stairs, serves a hearty buffet breakfast in a royal setting (Sb-1,900BF, Db-2,400BF, Tb-3,000BF, Qb-3,300BF, 2 lofty "backpackers' doubles" on the 4th floor-1,600BF or 1,800BF with WC, CC:VMA, Kuipersstraat 25, tel. 050/330-207, fax 050/347-199, e-mail: cavalier@skynet.be, run by friendly Viviane De Clerck).

Hotel Botaniek has three stars, nine small rooms, and a quiet location a block from Astrid Park. This friendly hotel is basic, small, and comfy (Sb-2,500BF, Db-2,900BF, Tb-3,500BF, CC:VMA, Waalsestraat 23, tel. 050/341-424, fax 050/345-939).

Hotel Rembrandt-Rubens has 15 rooms in a creaky 500-year-old building with tipsy floors, a mysterious floor plan, tacky rooms, ancient dippy beds, elephant tusks, a gallery of creepy old paintings, and probably the Holy Grail in a drawer somewhere (S-1,100BF, Ss-1,500BF, one D-1,600BF, Ds-2,100BF, Db-2,400BF, Tb-3,000BF, Qb-3,900BF, locked up at 24:00, on a quiet square between the Memlings and the brewery at Walplein 38, tel. 050/336-439). The breakfast room (which must have been the knights' hall) overlooks a canal (while Rembrandt and Rubens overlook you from an ornately carved and tiled 1648 chimney). There's a little warmth behind Mrs. DeBuyser's crankiness. The hotel has been in her family for 50 years.

Hotel Adornes is a great value and has 20 comfy new rooms in a 17th-century canalside house. They offer free parking and free loaner bikes; a cellar game and video lounge; and clean, simple rooms with full, modern bathrooms (Db-2,900–3,700BF depending upon size, CC:VMA, elevator, near Van Nevel B&B, below, and Carmersstraat at St. Annarei 26, tel. 050/341-336, fax 050/342-085, e-mail: hotel.adornes@proximedia.be, Nathalie runs the family business).

Hotel De Pauw is tall, skinny, and family run, with straightforward rooms on a quiet street across from a church (2 top-floor D-1,850BF, Db-2,100–2,450BF, CC:VMA, free and easy parking, cable TV and phones, Sint Gilliskerkhof 8, tel. 050/337-118, fax 050/345-140, info@hoteldepauw.be, Josine).

Hotel t'Keizershof is a dollhouse of a hotel that lives by its motto, "Spend a night, not a fortune." It's simple and tidy, with eight small, cheery old-time rooms split between two floors, a shower and toilet on each (S-950BF, D-1,400BF, T-2,100BF, Q-2,500BF, free and easy parking, laundry service-300BF, Oostmeers 126, a block in front of train station, tel. 050/338-728, e-mail: stefaan.persyn@skynet.be, run by Stefaan and Hilde).

Crowne Plaza Hotel Brugge is the most modern, comfortable, and central hotel option. Each of its 90 air-conditioned rooms comes with a magnifying mirror and trouser press (rack rate: Db-8,000BF, prices drop as low as 5,100BF on weekdays and off-season, CC:VMA, elevator, pool, Burg 10, tel. 050/345-834, fax 050/345-615, www.crowneplaza.com).

Bed-and-Breakfasts

These places offer the best value. Each is central and run by people who enjoy their work and offers lots of stairs and three or four doubles you'd pay 4,000BF for in a hotel. Parking is generally easy on the street.

Koen and Annemie Dieltiens are a friendly couple who enjoy getting to know their guests, who eat a hearty breakfast around a big table in their bright, homey, comfortable house. They are a wealth of information on Bruges (S-1,300BF, Sb-1,700BF, D-1,600BF, Db-1,900BF, T-2,100BF, Tb-2,400BF, Qb-2,900BF, 1-night stops pay 200BF extra per room, nonsmoking, Sint-Walburgastraat 14, 3 blocks east of Market Square, tel. 050/334-294, fax 050/335-230, e-mail: koen.dieltiens@skynet.be). The Dieltiens also rent a cozy studio and apartment for two to six people in a nearby 17th-century house (2 pay 13,300BF per week for studio, 14,700BF for apartment, prices higher for shorter stays and more people; cheaper off-season).

Paul and Roos Gheeraert live on the first floor, while their guests take the second. This neoclassical mansion with big, bright, comfy rooms is another fine value (Sb-1,600BF, larger Sb-1,700BF, Db-1,800BF, larger Db-1,900BF, Tb-2,400BF; rooms have coffeemakers and fridges; Ridderstraat 9, 4 blocks east of Market, tel. 050/335-627, fax 050/345-201, e-mail: paul.gheeraert@skynet.be). They also rent three modern, fully-equipped apartments and a large loft nearby (minimum 3 nights, view at http://users.skynet.be/brugge-gheeraert).

Chris Deloof's big, homey rooms are a good bet in the old center. The ones with showers are more elegant, but the upstairs A-frame lofty room is fun (Ss-1,400BF, D-1,500BF, Ds-1,900BF, pleasant breakfast room, free loaner bikes, nonsmoking, communal kitchen, Geerwijnstraat 14, tel. & fax 050/340-544, www.sin.be/chrisdeloof, e-mail: chris.deloof@ping.be). Chris also rents a nearby apartment, great for a family or group (Qb-3,500BF).

The **Van Nevel family** rents two attractive top-floor rooms with built-in beds in a 16th-century house (S-1,200–1,500BF, D-1,500–1,800BF, Carmersstraat 13, 10-min walk from Market

Square, tel. 050/346-860, fax 050/347-616, e-mail: robert.vannevel@advalvas.be). Robert enthusiastically shares the culture and history of Bruges with his guests.

Yvonne De Vriese rents three tidy but neglected B&B rooms on a corner overlooking two canals (1 S-1,000BF, D-1,500BF, Db-1,800BF, 500BF extra for 3rd or 4th person; breakfast served in your room; canal views come with mosquitoes; CC:VMA, Predikherenstraat 40, 4 blocks east of Burg Square, take bus #6 or #16 from station and get off at the first stop on Predikheren Rei, tel. 050/334-224). **Jan Degeyter**, a block away, rents two airy, spacious, wood-floored rooms on a quiet street (Db-1,800BF, Tb-2,300BF, Qb-2,800BF, CC:VMA, Waalsestraat 40, tel. 050/331-199, fax 050/347-857).

Arnold Dewolf's B&B is in a stately, quiet neighborhood on a dead-end street (D-1,400BF, 1 big family room-1,400–2,200BF, depending on number of people, Oostproostse 9, 20-min walk from center, near the windmills, tel. 050/338-366). Going down Carmersstraat, turn left on Peterseliestraat then right on Leestenburg to Oostprootse.

Hostels

Bruges has several good hostels offering beds for around 400BF in two- to eight-bed rooms (singles go for around 600BF). Pick up the hostel info sheet at the station TI. Smallest, loosest, and closest to the center are the dull **Snuffel Travelers Inn** (Ezelstraat 47, tel. 050/333-133), the **Bauhaus International Party Hotel** (Langestraat 135, tel. 050/341-093), and the funky **Passage** (Dweerstraat 26, tel. 050/340-232; its hotel next door rents 1,200BF doubles). The new, American-style **Charlie Rockets** bar and hostel is the liveliest and most central hostel (56 beds, 2 to 6 per room, 500BF per bed, Hoogstraat 19, tel. 050/330-660).

Eating in Bruges

Specialties include mussels cooked a variety of ways (one order can feed two people), fish dishes, grilled meats, and French fries. Touristy places on the square come with great views and are affordable; candle-cool bistros flicker on back streets. Don't eat before 19:30 unless you like eating alone. Tax and service are always included.

Wittekop is very Flemish—a cluttered, laid-back, old-time place specializing in the beer-soaked equivalent of beef bourguignonne (600BF plates, Tue–Sat 18:00–24:00, closed Sun–Mon, terrace in the back, Sint Jakobsstraat 14, tel. 050/332-059).

The classy **'T Heerenhuys**, famous for its top-notch Flemish/French cooking, serves a much-raved-about 375BF lunch special (12:00–14:30, closed Thu and Sun, Vlamingstraat 53, tel. 050/346-178).

De Kluiver is a pub serving hot snacks, light 400BF meals, and great "seasnails in spiced bouillon" simmered in a whispering jazz ambience (Wed–Mon 18:00–01:00, closed Tue, Hoogstraat 12, tel. 050/338-927).

Pannekoekenhuisje, the little pancake house, is a cute restaurant serving delicious, inexpensive pancake meals (just off Geldmuntstraat at Helmstraat 3, tel. 050/340-086).

Lotus Vegetarisch Restaurant serves good veggie lunches only (300BF plates, Mon–Sat 11:45–13:45, closed Sun, just off the Burg at Wapenmakersstraat 5, tel. 050/331-078).

Two youthful, trendy, jazz-filled eateries: For hearty budget spaghetti (210BF), head for **Estaminet**, on the northern border of peaceful Astrid Park (open from 11:30 on, closed Mon afternoon and all day Thu, Park 5). Or try **De Versteende Nacht Jazzcafe** on Langestraat 11 (500BF meals, Tue–Sat 19:00–2:00, closed Sun–Mon).

Vlissinghe 1515, the oldest pub in town, serves hot snacks in great atmosphere (open from 11:30 on, closed Tue, Blekersstraat 2).

Bistro 't Gezelleke (next door to the Van Nevel B&B and near Bauhaus hostel) offers fine fresh food at bring-'em-in prices (300–400BF meals, Mon–Fri 12:00–24:00, Saturday from 18:00, closed Sun, Carmersstraat 15, tel. 050/338-102). **Restaurant 't Gulden Vlies**, just off Burg, is good for a late dinner (600BF plates, closed Mon–Tue, Mallebergplaats 17).

Picnics: Geldmuntstraat is a handy street when you're hungry. A block off Market Square, **Pickles Frituur** serves the best sit-down fries in town (Mon–Sat 11:00–24:00, closed Sun). A block farther, past the Verbeke chocolate shop, **Nopri Supermarket** is great for picnics (push-button produce pricer lets you buy as little as one mushroom, Mon–Sat 9:00–18:30, closed Sun). The small **Delhaize grocery** is on Market Square opposite the belfry (Mon–Sat 8:00–12:00, 13:30–18:00, closed Sun). **Selfi** has cheap sandwiches to go (Breidelstraat 16, between Burg and Market Square). For midnight munchies, you'll find Indian-run corner grocery stores.

Frietjes: These local French fries are a treat. Proud and traditional *frituurs* serve tubs of fries and various local-style shish kebabs. Belgians dip their *frietjes* in mayonnaise, but ketchup is there for the Yankees (along with spicier sauces). For a quick, cheap, and scenic meal, hit a *frituur* and sit on the steps or benches overlooking Market Square, about 50 yards past the post office.

Beer: Belgium boasts more than 350 types of beer. Straffe Hendrik ("Strong Henry"), a potent and refreshing local brew, is, even to a Bud Lite kind of guy, obviously great beer. Among the more unusual of the others to try: Dentergems (with coriander and orange peel) and Trappist (a dark, malty, monk-made beer). Non-beer drinkers enjoy Kriek (a cherry-flavored beer) and

Frambozen Bier (raspberry-flavored beer). Each beer is served in its own unique glass. Any pub carries the basic beers, but for a selection of more than 300 types, drink at **t'Brugs Beertje** (16:00–01:00, closed Wed, Kemelstraat 5). When you've finished those, step next door, where **Dreupel Huisje "1919"** serves more than 100 Belgian gins and liqueurs (closed Tue). Another good place to gain an appreciation of the Belgian beer culture is **de Garre**. Rather than a noisy pub scene, it has a sit-down-and-focus-on-your-friend-and-the-fine-beer ambience (huge selection, off Breidelstraat, between Burg and Markt, on the tiny Garre alley, daily 12:00–24:00).

Belgian Waffles: While Americans think of "Belgian" waffles for breakfast, the Belgians (who don't eat waffles or pancakes for breakfast) think of *wafels* as Leige-style (dense, sweet, eaten plain and heated up, served take-away) and Brussels-style (lighter, often with powdered sugar or whipped cream and fruit, served in teahouses). For the best Leige-style *wafels* in town, drop by **Ice Cream Hennon** for a Luikse Wafel (50BF, across from Nopri Supermarket, corner of Guldmuntstraat and Sind Amandstraat, daily 10:00–24:00). Hennon's *wafels* and ice cream (18 flavors) are extremely fresh... and tasty. Any number of teahouses serve Brussels-style *wafels*.

Transportation Connections—Bruges
From nearby Brussels, all of Europe is at your fingertips. Train info: tel. 050/382-382.

By train to: Brussels (2/hrly, 1 hr), **Ghent** (3/hrly, 20 min), **Oostende** (3/hrly, 15 min), **Köln** (6/day, 4 hrs), **Paris** (3 direct, high-speed Thalys trains/day, 2.5 hrs, 400BF supplement for Eurail), **Amsterdam** (hrly, 3.5 hrs).

Trains from England: Bruges is an ideal "welcome to Europe" stop after London. Take the Eurostar train from London to Brussels under the English Channel (6/day, 3 hrs), then transfer to Bruges (hrly, 1 hour). Or, if you'd prefer to cross the Channel by boat, catch the London–Dover train (2 hrs, from London's Victoria station), then the catamaran to Oostende (2 hrs; train station at Oostende catamaran terminal), then the Oostende–Bruges train (15 min). Five boats run daily (1,500BF one way, same price for the cheap five-day return ticket; call to reserve a seat and pay at the dock, CC:VMA, tel. 059/559-955).

PRAGUE

It's amazing what 10 years of freedom can do. Prague has always been historic. Now it's fun, too. No place in Europe has become so popular so quickly. And for good reason: The capital of the Czech Republic—the only major city of central Europe to escape the bombs of this century's wars—is Europe's best-preserved Baroque city. It's slinky with sumptuous Art Nouveau facades, offers tons of cheap Mozart and Vivaldi, and brews the best beer in Europe. But more than the architecture and traditional culture, it's an explosion of pent-up entrepreneurial energy jumping for joy after 50 years of Communist rule. And its low prices will make your visit enjoyable and nearly stressless.

Planning Your Time

Two days (with three nights, or two nights and a night train) makes the long train ride in and out worthwhile and gives you time to get beyond the sightseeing and enjoy Prague's fun-loving ambience. Many wish they'd scheduled three days for Prague. From Munich, Berlin, and Vienna, it's a six-hour train ride (during the day) or an overnight ride.

With two days I'd spend a morning seeing the castle and a morning in the Jewish Quarter—the only two chunks of sightseeing that demand any brainpower. Spend your afternoons around the Old Town, Charles Bridge, and the Little Quarter and split your nights between beer halls and live music. Remember: state museums close on Monday, and Jewish sites close on Saturday.

History

Medieval Prague: Prague's castle put it on the map in the ninth century. In the 10th century, the region was incorporated into the

Prague

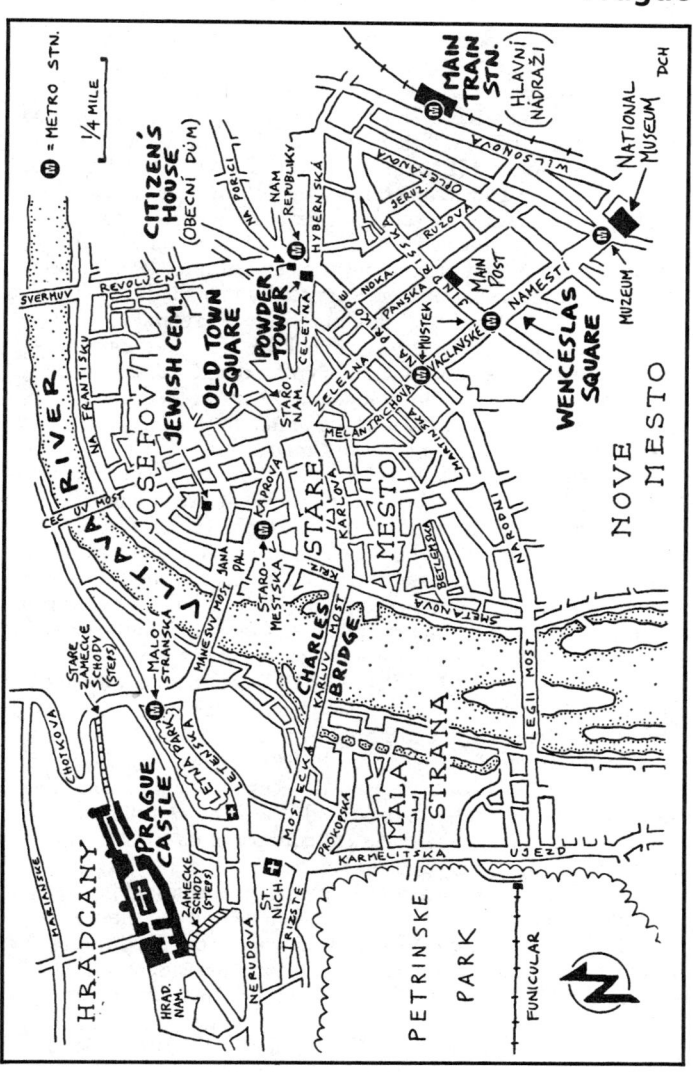

German "Holy Roman" Empire. The 14th century was Prague's Golden Age, when it was one of Europe's largest and most highly cultured cities. During this period Prague built St. Vitus Cathedral and Charles Bridge and established the first university in central Europe.

Bucking the Pope and Germany: Jan Hus was a local preacher who got in trouble with the Vatican a hundred years before Martin Luther. Like Luther, he preached in the people's language rather than Latin. To add insult to injury, he complained about church corruption. Tried for heresy and burned in 1415, Hus roused nationalist (Bohemian) as well as religious feelings and became a symbol of Czech martyrdom. His followers are Hussites.

Religious Wars: The reformist times of Jan Hus (around 1400, when Czechs rebelled against both German and Roman control) led to a period of religious wars and ultimately subjugation under Austrian rule. Prague stagnated under the Habsburgs of Austria with the brief exception of Rudolf II's reign.

Under the late-16th-century rule of the Habsburg king Rudolf II, Prague emerged again as a cultural and intellectual center. Johannes Kepler, Tycho Brahe, and others worked here. Much of Prague's great art can be attributed to this Habsburg king who lived not in Vienna but in Prague.

The Thirty Years' War (1618–1648) began in Prague when locals tossed two Catholic/Habsburg officials (Czechs sympathetic to the Germans) out the window of the Prague Castle. Often called "the first world war" because it engulfed so many nations, the 30 years were particularly tough on Prague. During this period its population dropped from 60,000 to 25,000. The result of this war was 300 years of Habsburg rule: German and Catholic culture, not Czech. Prague became a backwater of Vienna.

Czech Nationalist Revival: The 19th century was a time of nationalism for people throughout Europe, including the Czechs, as the age of divine kings and ruling families was coming to a fitful end. The arts (such as the paintings by Mucha and the building of the massive National Museum atop Wenceslas Square) stirred the national spirit. With the end of World War I the Habsburgs were history, and in 1918 the independent country of Czechoslovakia was proclaimed with Prague as its capital.

Troubled 20th Century: Independence had lasted barely 20 years when the Nazis swept in (1939). Prague escaped the bombs of World War II but went almost directly from the Nazi frying pan into the Communist fire. Almost. A local uprising freed the city from the Nazis on May 8, 1945. The Russians "liberated" them again on May 9.

The Communist chapter of Czech subjugation (1948–1989) was grim. The student- and artist-led "Prague Spring" revolt in 1968 was crushed. The charismatic leader Alexander Dubcek was exiled into a job in the backwoods, and the years after 1968 were particularly tough. But eventually the Soviet empire crumbled. Czechoslovakia regained its freedom in the 1989 "Velvet Revolution" (so called because there were no casualties). Until 1989, May 9 was the Czech day of liberation. Now Czechs celebrate their liberation on May 8. In 1993 the Czech and Slovak Republics agreed on the "Velvet Divorce" and became two separate countries.

Today, while not without its problems, the Czech Republic is enjoying a growing economy and a strong democracy. While some have profited from the new capitalism, many are anxiously awaiting their share. Prague has emerged as one of the most popular tourist destinations in Europe. You're about to find out why.

Orientation (tel. code: 02)

Locals call their town "Praha." It's big, with 1.2 million people, but for the quick visit you should think of it as small and focus on the core of the city. I will refer to the tourist landmarks in English (with the Czech name in parentheses). Study the map and learn these key places:

    Main Train Station: *Hlavní Nádraží* (hlav-nee nah-dra-shzee)
    Old Town: *Staré Město* (sta-rey mnyess-toh)
    Old Town Square: *Staroměstské Náměstí* (starro-min-yes-ststi-keh nah-mnyess-tee)
    New Town: *Nové Město* (no-vay mnyess-toh)
    Little Quarter: *Malá Strana* (mah-lah strah-nah)
    Jewish Quarter: *Josefov* (yoo-zef-fohf)
    Castle Area: *Hradčany* (hrad-chah-nee)
    Charles Bridge: *Karluv most* (kar-loov most)
    Wenceslas Square: *Václavske Náměstí* (vah-slawf-skeh nah-mnyess-tee)
    The River: *Vltava* (vul-tah-vah)

The Vltava River divides the west side (castle and Little Quarter) from the east side (train station, Old Town, New Town, and nearly all of the recommended hotels). Prague addresses come with a general zone. Praha 1 is in the old center on either side of the river. Praha 2 is in the new city south of Wenceslas Square. Praha 3 and higher indicates a location farther from the center.

Tourist Information

TIs are at four key locations: at the main train station, on the Old Town Square, below Wenceslas Square at Na Prikope 20, and in the West Tower of Charles Bridge (Mon–Fri 9:00–19:00, until 18:00 Sat–Sun and in winter, tel. 02/2448-2202). They offer maps, information on guided walks and bus tours, and bookings for concerts, hotel rooms, and rooms in private homes. Get the brochure listing of all Prague's museums and hours.

Helpful Hints

Formalities: Travel in Prague is like travel in Western Europe, only it's not covered by the Eurailpass and it seems 15 years behind the times. Americans and Canadians need no visa. Just flash your passport at the border. The U.S. embassy in Prague is near the Little Quarter Square, or Malostranske Náměstí (Trziste 15, tel. 02/5732-0663).

Rip-offs: Prague's new freedom comes with new scams. There's no particular risk of violent crime, just green, rich tourists getting taken by con artists. Simply be on guard: on trains (thieves on overnight trains and corrupt conductors intimidating Western tourists for a bribe); changing money (tellers anywhere with bad arithmetic and inexplicable pauses while counting back your change); and dealing with taxis (see "Getting around Prague," below). In restaurants, understand the price clearly before ordering.

Telephoning: Czech phones work like any in Europe. For international calls, buy a phone card at a kiosk or your hotel (180 kč). It costs about $1 a minute to call the United States directly (dial 001, the area code, and the number) from a public phone booth that accepts the local phone card. To call Prague from abroad, dial the international code (00 in Europe or 011 in the U.S.), the Czech Republic code (420), then Prague's city code (2), followed by the local number. To call within the Czech Republic, simply dial the number as listed, beginning with a 0 and the city code. To dial a local number within a city, drop the city code (to call Prague's TI from your Prague hotel, dial 2448-2202). Hotels often list phone numbers with the country code (420), a number you don't need to dial when inside the Czech Republic.

Money: 32 Koruna (kč) = about U.S. $1. There is no black market. Assume anyone trying to sell money on the streets is peddling obsolete currency. Buy and sell easily at the station (4 percent fees), banks, or hotels. ATMs are everywhere. Czech money is tough to change in the West. Before leaving the Czech Republic, change your remaining Koruna into your next country's currency (at Prague's train station change bureaus).

American Express: Vaclavske Náměstí 56, Praha 1 (daily 9:00–19:00) or Mosteka 12, Praha 1 (open 9:30–19:30, tel. 02/5731-3636).

Internet Access: The Internet Café is central at Nadroni Trida 25 (Mon–Fri 9:00–23:00, Sat–Sun 10:00–23:00, tel. 02/2108 5284). Near Wenceslas Square is Cybeteria (Mon–Fri 10:00–20:00, Sat–Sun 9:00–18:00, Stepanska 18, tel. 02/2223-0703). Cafe.Com is also central (daily 11:00–24:00, Na Porici 36, tel. 02/241-9435).

Local Help: Magic Praha is a tiny travel service run by hardworking English-speaking Lida Steflova. She is a charming jack-of-all-trades, and particularly helpful with accommodations, private tours, and airport or train station transfers anywhere in the Czech Republic (tel. 02/302-5170, cellular 060-686-6190, e-mail: mp.ludmila@post.cz).

Best Views: Enjoy "the golden city of a hundred spires" during the early evening when the light is warm and the colors are rich. Good viewpoints include the castle square, the top of the east tower of Charles Bridge, the Old Town Square clock tower, and the steps of the National Museum overlooking Wenceslas Square.

Language: Czech, a Slavic language, has little resemblance to Western European languages. These days, English is "modern" and you'll find the language barrier minimal. If you speak German, it's helpful. An acute accent means you linger on that vowel. The little smile above the c, s, or z makes it ch, sh, or zh.

Learn these key Czech words:

Hello/Goodbye (familiar)	*Ahoj* (ah-hoi)
Good day, Hello (formal)	*Dobrý den* (DOH-bree den)
Yes/No	*Ano* (AH-no)/*Ne* (neh)
Please	*Prosím* (proh-zeem)
Thank you	*Děkuji* (dyack-quee)
You're welcome	*Prosím* (proh-zeem)
Where is...?	*Kde je...?* (gday yeh)
Do you speak English?	*Mluvíte anglicky?* (MLOO-vit-eh ANG-litz-key)
krown (the money)	*koruna* (koh-roo-nah)

Arrival in Prague

Prague unnerves many travelers—it's relatively run-down, it's behind the former Iron Curtain, and you've heard stories of rip-offs and sky-high hotel prices. But in reality, Prague is charming, safe, and welcomes you with open cash registers and smiles.

By Train: Prague has several train stations. Most travelers coming from and going to the West use the main station (Hlavní Nádraží) or the secondary station (Holešovice Nádraží). Trains to other points within the country use Masarykovo or Smíchov stations.

Upon arrival, change money. Rates vary—compare by asking at two exchange windows what you'll get for $100. Count carefully. At the same window, buy a city map (about 35 kč, with trams and metro lines marked and tiny sketches of the sights for ease in navigating). You'll be constantly referring to this map. Confirm your departure plans at the train information window. Consider arranging a room or tour at the TI or AVE travel agency (free maps occasionally available at AVE). The left-luggage counter is reportedly safer than the lockers.

At Prague's main train station (Hlavní Nádraží), you'll be met at the tracks by room hustlers (snaring tourists for cheap rooms—illegally). A huge highway (Wilson Boulevard) obliterates the front of the formerly elegant station (go upstairs to see its original Art Nouveau interior). The orange low-ceilinged main hall is downstairs and is filled with travelers, kiosks, loitering teenagers, and older riffraff.

From the main station it's an easy 10-minute walk to Wenceslas Square (turn left out of the station and follow Washingtonova to the huge Narodini Museum and you're there). You can also catch trams #5, #9, or #26 (to find the stop, walk into the park and head two minutes to the right), or take the metro (just before leaving the station, look for the red "M" with two directions: "Muzeum" or "Florenc;" take "Muzeum," then transfer to the green line—direction "Dejvicka"—and get off at either Můstek or Staroměstske; these stops straddle the Old Town). The courageous and savvy get a cabbie to treat them fairly and get to their hotel fast and sweat-free for no more than 130 kč (see "Getting around Prague" below).

Holešovice Nádrazí station is suburban mellow. The main hall has all the services of the main station in a compact area. Outside the first glass doors, the ATM is on the left, the metro is straight ahead (follow "Vstup," which means "entrance," take it three stops to the main station, four stops to the city center Muzeum stop), and taxis and trams are outside to the right (allow 150 kč for a cab to the center).

By Plane: A couple of minibus services get you between the airport and downtown. The Cedaz minibus costs 100 kč and runs hourly (5:00–22:00) between the airport and Náměstí Republiky.

Getting around Prague

You can walk nearly everywhere. But the metro is slick, the trams fun, and the taxis quick and easy once you're initiated.

Public Transport: The trams and metro work on the same tickets. Buy from machines (press "enter" after the ticket type before inserting coins in the machines) at kiosks, or from hotels. For convenience, buy all the tickets you think you'll need for your stay: 15-minute ticket—8 kč, 60-minute ticket—12 kč, 24-hour ticket—70 kč, three-day pass—180 kč. The metro closes at midnight, but some trams keep running all night (identified with white numbers on blue backgrounds at tram stops).

City maps show the tram/bus/metro lines. The metro system is handy and simple (just three lines) but doesn't get to many hotels and sights. Trams are also easy to use; track your route with your city map. They run every 5 to 10 minutes, less on weekends. Get used to hopping on and off. Validate your ticket on the bus by sticking it in the machine (which stamps a time on it).

Taxis: The most infamous taxis in Europe are being tamed. While bandito cabbies still have meters that spin like pinwheels, the city has made great strides in civilizing these thugs. While most guidebooks advise avoiding taxis, this is defeatist. I find Prague is a great taxi town and use them routinely. Get the local rate and they're cheap. Use only registered taxis: These are marked by a roof lamp with the word "TAXI" in black on

Prague Metro

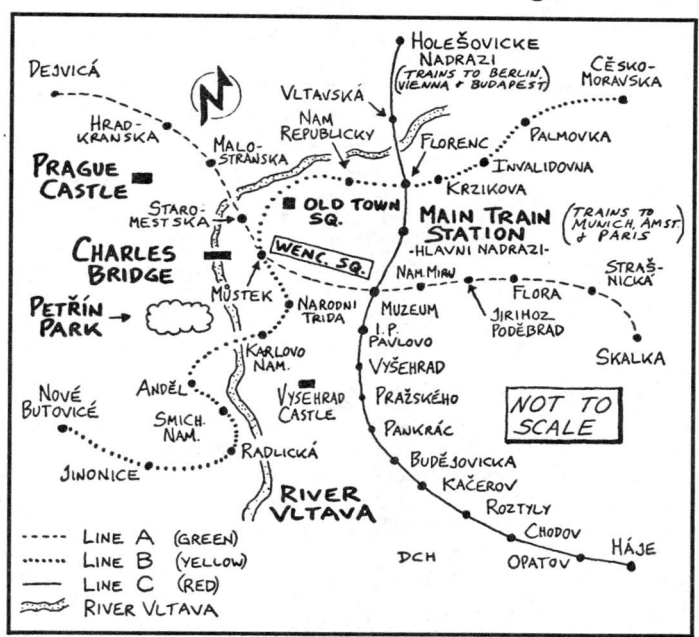

[Map of Prague Metro showing:]

- Line A (Green)
- Line B (Yellow)
- Line C (Red)
- River Vltava

Stations shown include: Dejvicá, Hradkranska, Malostranska, Staroměstska, Můstek, Vltavská, Nam Republicky, Florenc, Holešovicke Nadrazi (Trains to Berlin, Vienna & Budapest), Česko-Moravska, Palmovka, Invalidovna, Krzikova, Main Train Station - Hlavni Nadrazi- (Trains to Munich, Amst & Paris), Nam Miru, Muzeum, I.P. Pavlovo, Flora, Jirihoz Poděbrad, Strašnicka, Skalka, Narodni Trida, Karlovo Nam., Vyšehrad, Pražského, Pankrác, Budějovicka, Kačerov, Roztyly, Chodov, Opatov, Háje, Anděl, Smich. Nam., Radlicka, Jinonice, Nové Butovice, Vysehrad Castle, DCH

Also shown: Prague Castle, Charles Bridge, Petřín Park, Old Town Sq., Wenc. Sq., River Vltava

NOT TO SCALE

---

both sides, and the front doors sport a black-and-white checkered ribbon, the company name, license number, and rates (three rows: drop charge—25 kč, per-kilometer charge—17 kč, and wait time per minute—4 kč). The key is the tiny "*sazba*" box on the magic meter showing the rate. This should read "1," unless you called for a pickup (which adds 30–50 kč). If a cabbie tries to rip you off, simply pay 100 kč. Let him follow you into the hotel if he insists you owe him more. (He won't.) The receptionist will defend you. Rip-offs are most likely around tourist sites and the train station. To remind him to turn on the meter, say "*Zapnete taximetr*" (zappa-nyet-ay tax-ah-met-er). Leny Taxi is reliable and honest (tel. 02/6126-2121 or cellular 060-120-1305).

Tours of Prague

Walking Tours—Prague Walks offers walking tours of the Old Town, the castle, and Jewish Quarter. Most last two hours and cost 230 kč. Get the current schedule from any TI (e-mail: pwalks@comp.cz).

Bus Tours—Cheap big-bus orientation tours provide an efficient once-over-lightly look at Prague and a convenient way to see the castle. Premiant City Tours offers 15 different tours including: quick city (350 kč, 2 hrs, 5/day); grand city (570 kč, 3.5 hrs, 2/day); Jewish Quarter (590 kč, 2 hrs); Prague by night, Bohemian glass, Terezin Concentration Camp memorial, Karlštejn Castle, Český Krumlov (1600 kč, 8 hrs), and a river cruise. The tours feature live guides (in German and English) and depart from near the bottom of Wenceslas Square at Na Príkope 23. Get tickets at an AVE travel agency, hotel, on the bus, or at Na Príkope 20 (tel. 02/2423-0072 or cellular 060-121-2625, www.sos.cz/premiant).
Tram Joyride—Trams #22 and #23 make a fine joyride through town. Consider this as a scenic lead-up to touring the castle. Catch it at metro: Náměstí Míru, roll through a bit of the New Town, the Old Town, across the river, and hop out just above the castle.

Self-Guided Walking Tour
The King's Walk (Královská cesta), the ancient way of coronation processions, is touristy but great. Pedestrian friendly and full of playful diversions, it connects the essential Prague sites. The king would be crowned in St. Vitus Cathedral in the Prague Castle, walk through the Little Quarter to the Church of St. Nicholas, cross Charles Bridge, and finish at the Old Town Square. If he hurried, he'd be done in 20 minutes. Like the main drag in Venice between St. Mark's and the Rialto bridge, this walk mesmerizes tourists. Use it as a spine, but venture off it—especially to eat.

This walk laces together all the following recommended sights except the Jewish Quarter. From the castle, stairs lead down into the Little Quarter. They dump you into the Little Quarter Square a few blocks from the Church of St. Nicholas. Farther downhill, a medieval gate announces Charles Bridge. Over the river another gate welcomes you to the Old Town. A well-trod, shop-lined street under glorious Baroque and Art Nouveau facades leads to the Old Town Square. For the sake of completeness, extend the King's Walk from there past the Havelska Market and up Wenceslas Square. See the view from the National Museum steps.

Sights—Prague's Castle Area
▲▲**Prague Castle**—For a thousand years, Czech rulers have ruled from the Prague Castle. It's huge (by some measures, the biggest castle on earth), with a wall more than a kilometer long. It's confusing with plenty of sights not worth seeing. Rather than worry about rumors that you should spend all day here with long lists of museums within to see, keep things simple. Four stops matter and are explained here: St. Vitus Cathedral, the old Royal Palace, Basilica of St. George, and the Golden Lane. (120 kč for entrance to all

sights within, daily 9:00–17:00, last entry at 16:00; the 145 kč audio guide is good but requires 2 hours and makes it impossible to exit the castle area from the bottom.) To reach the castle by metro, get off at the Malostranská metro stop, climb through the Little Quarter and up the castle steps (Zamecke Schody). Or, better, ride tram #22 or #23, which stop above the castle, or take a cab.

Castle Square (Hradčanske Náměstí)—The big square facing the castle offers fine string-quartet street music (their CD is terrific; say hello to friendly, mustachioed Josef), an awesome city view, and stairs down to the Little Quarter. The National Gallery's collection of European paintings is in the neighboring Sternberg Palace (contains works by Dürer, Rubens, Rembrandt, El Greco). A tranquil café hides a few steps down immediately to the right as you face the castle.

Survey the castle from this square, the tip of a 500-meter-long series of courtyards, churches, and palaces. The offices facing this first courtyard belong to the Czech president, Vaclav Havel (left side). The guard changes on the hour. Walk under the fighting giants, under an arch, and find your way to St. Vitus. You can enter the cathedral without a ticket, but will need one to climb the spire and to visit the other sights (120 kč, ticket office opposite cathedral entry). Your ticket is good for three days and covers the cathedral spire, Old Royal Palace, Basilica of St. George, and the Powder Tower. English tours depart from the ticket office regularly (60 kč).

▲**St. Vitus Cathedral**—This cathedral symbolizes the Czech spirit. It was finished in 1929 on about the 1,000th anniversary of the assassination of St. Wenceslas, patron saint of the Czechs. This most important church in Prague houses the crown jewels (thoroughly locked up and out of sight) and the tomb of "Good King" Wenceslas as well as other Czech royalty. Wenceslas' tomb sits in the fancy chapel (right transept). Murals here show scenes of his life. More kings are buried in the royal mausoleum in front of the high altar and in the crypt underneath. The cathedral, a mix of Gothic and neo-Gothic, is 124 meters long and offers a great view from the top of its spire (daily 9:00–17:00, 287 steps). The windows are brilliant. The rose window above the entry shows the creation. The Art Nouveau window from 1931 is by Czech artist Alfons Mucha (look for Saints Cyril and Methodius, third chapel on left). If you like Mucha's work, visit the Mucha Museum near Wenceslas Square (see below). Seek out the newly restored mosaic of the Last Judgment outside the right transept.

Old Royal Palace—This was the seat of the Bohemian princes in the 12th century. While extensively rebuilt, the large hall is late Gothic. It's big enough for jousts—even the spiral staircases were designed to let a mounted soldier gallop up. Look up at the impressive vaulted ceiling, look down on the chapel from the end, and go out on the balcony for a fine Prague view. Is that Paris in the distance? No, it's an observation tower built for an exhibition in 1891 (60 meters tall, a quarter of the height of its big brother in Paris built in 1889). The spiral stairs on the left lead up to several rooms with painted coats of arms and no English explanations. There's nothing to see downstairs in the palace. Across from the palace exit is the basilica.

Basilica of St. George and Convent—The first Bohemian convent was established here near the palace in 973. Today the convent houses the Czech Gallery (best Czech paintings from Gothic, Renaissance, and Baroque periods). The beautifully lit basilica is the best-preserved Romanesque church in Prague. St. Ludmila was buried here in 973. Admire the wood ceiling and find the helpful English explanations in the rear. Continue walking downhill through the castle grounds. Turn left on the first street, which leads into a cute lane.

Golden Lane—This street of old buildings, which originally housed goldsmiths, is now jammed with tourists and lined with expensive gift shops, boutiques, galleries, and cafés. The Czech writer Franz Kafka lived at #22. There's a pricey deli/bistro at the top and a convenient public WC at the bottom. Beyond that, at the end of the castle, are fortifications beefed up in anticipation of the Turkish attack—the cause for most medieval arms buildups in Europe—and steps leading down. Turn right at the bottom and parallel the river to reach the Little Quarter (Malá Strana).

Sights—From the Little Quarter to Charles Bridge

▲▲**Little Quarter (Malá Strana)**—This is the most characteristic fun-to-wander old section of town. It's one of four medieval towns (along with Hradčany, Staré Město, and Nové Město) which eventually grew to become Prague. It centers on the Little Quarter Square (Malostranské Náměstí) with its plague monument facing the entry to the commanding church, at the upper end of the square.

Church of St. Nicholas—Dominating the Little Quarter, this is the best example of High Baroque in town (daily 9:00–16:00, built 1703–1760, 230-foot-high dome, you can climb the tower outside the right transept for more views, 30 kč, daily 10:00–18:00). Normally, every night there are concerts at two venues in this square: in the Church of St. Nicholas (about 400 kč) and in Lichtenstein Palace across from the church (450–1,000 kč). Charles Bridge is a short walk down Mostecka from the square. But there's no hurry—wander off the main drag onto smaller lanes and into tiny squares.

▲▲▲**Charles Bridge (Karluv Most)**—This much-loved bridge, commissioned by the Holy Roman Emperor Charles IV in 1357, offers one of the most pleasant 500-meter strolls in Europe. Be on the bridge when the sun is low for the warmest people watching and photography. At one time, the black crucifix (1657) standing near the east end stood alone. The other saints, near and dear to old Praguers, were added later. Today most are replicas; the originals are in museums and out of the pollution.

A TI is at the west end tower (climbable, 30 kč). The tower at the east end is considered one of the finest Gothic gates in existence. Climb it for a fine view but nothing else (30 kč, daily 10:00–18:30). After crossing the bridge, follow the flow straight ahead to the Old Town Square (hint: turn left when you reach Jilska).

Sights—Prague's Old Town Square

▲▲▲Old Town Square (Staroměstske Náměstí)—The focal point for most visits, this has been a market square since the 11th century. It became the nucleus of a town (Staré Město) in the 13th century when its city hall was built. Today the old-time market stalls have been replaced by cafés, touristic horse buggies, and souvenir hawkers. Walk to the center.

The Hus Memorial—erected in 1915, 500 years after his burning—marks the center of the square and symbolizes the long struggle for Czech freedom. The Czech reformer Jan Hus stands tall between two groups of people: victorious Hussite patriots and Protestants defeated by the Habsburgs. A mother with her children behind Hus represents the ultimate rebirth of the Czech nation. The steps are a popular local hangout—young Czechs gawking at gawking tourists.

A spin tour from the center gives you a look at architectural styles: Romanesque, Gothic, Renaissance, Baroque, and Art Nouveau.

Spin clockwise from the green domes of the Baroque Church of St. Nicholas. There has been a church on this site since the 12th century. This one, dating from the early 18th century, is now a Hussite church (evening concerts). The Jewish Quarter (Josefov) is a few blocks behind it. Spin to the right past the Hus Memorial and the fine golden and mosaic Art Nouveau facade of the Prague City Insurance Company. Notice the fanciful Gothic Tyn Church with its Disneyesque spires flanking a solid gold effigy of the Virgin Mary. For 200 years after Hus' death, this was the leading Hussite church in Prague (enter through arcade facing the square; a diagram at the door locates spots of touristic interest such as the tomb of astronomer Tycho Brahe). Lining the south side of the square an interesting row of pastel houses. Their Gothic, Renaissance, and Baroque facades are ornamented with interesting statues that symbolize the original use of each building. The pointed 230-foot-tall spire marks the 14th-century Old Town Hall, famous for its astronomical clock (see below). In front of the city hall, 27 white inlaid crosses mark the spot where 27 Protestant nobles were beheaded in 1621 after rebelling against Catholic Habsburgs.

▲▲Old Town Hall Astronomical Clock—Join the gang, ignoring the ridiculous human sales racks, for the striking of the hour

Central Prague

- ❶ PICK UP BUS TOUR (AT #20)
- ❷ MUCHA MUSEUM
- ❸ NEAT PARK
- ❹ HOTEL JULIAN
- ❺ HOTEL CENTRAL
- ❻ BETHLEM CLUB
- ❼ HOTEL U STARÉ PANI
- ❽ HOTEL U KLENOTNIKA
- ❾ HOTEL LUNIK
- ❿ HOTEL UNION
- ⓫ HOTEL EUROPA
- ⓬ PENSION UNITAS
- ⓭ EXPRESS PENSION
- ⓮ PENSION U MEDVIDKU

(daily 8:00–20:00) on the 15th-century town hall clock. As you wait for the show, see if you can figure out how the clock works.

With revolving disks and sweeping hands, this clock keeps several versions of time. Two outer rings show the hour: Bohemian time (Gothic numbers, with hours counted from sunset) and our time (24 Roman numerals, XII at the top being noon, XII at the bottom being midnight). Everything revolves around the earth (the fixed middle background, with Prague at the center). Arcing lines and moving spheres combine with the big hand (a sweeping golden sun) and the little hand (the moon showing various stages) to indicate the times of sunset and sunrise. Look for the orbits of the sun and moon as they rise through day (the blue zone) and night (the black zone). If this seems complex today, it must have been a marvel in 1490.

Four statues flank the clock representing 15th-century Prague's four biggest worries: invasion (the Turk), death (skeleton), greed (a moneylender, which used to have "Jewish" features until after World War II, when anti-Semitism became politically incorrect), and vanity (enjoying the mirror).

At the top of the hour, (1) death tips his hourglass and pulls the cord ringing the bell, (2) the windows open and the Twelve Apostles parade by acknowledging the gang of onlookers, (3) the rooster crows, and (4) the hour is rung. The hour is often off because of daylight saving time (which made no sense at all in the 15th century).

Next to the clock you'll find the main TI, the local guides desk, and the opportunity to pay three admissions: for the city hall (by tour only), Gothic chapel (nothing to see except a close-up of the Twelve Apostles and the clock mechanism well described in English), and the tower (climb for one more fine city view). Leave the Old Town Square via Zelezna to reach Havelská Market.

Sights—Around Wenceslas Square

▲Havelská Market—Central Prague's best open-air flower and produce market scene is a block toward the Old Town Square from the bottom of Wenceslas Square. Laid out in the 13th century by King Wenceslas for the German trading community, it keeps hungry locals and vagabonds fed cheaply today.

▲▲Wenceslas Square (Václavske Náměstí)—More a broad boulevard than a square, it's named for the statue of King Wenceslas that stands on a horse at the top. The square is a stage for modern Czech history: The Czechoslovak state was proclaimed here in 1918. In 1968 the Soviets put down huge popular demonstrations here. And in 1969 Jan Palach set himself on fire here to protest against the puppet Soviet government. The next day 200,000 local protesters gathered here. Starting at the top (metro: Muzeum), stroll down the square:

The National Museum stands grandly at the top. The only thing exciting about it is the view (60 kč, daily 10:00–18:00, halls of Czech fossils and animals).

St. Wenceslas, commemorated by the statue, is the "good king" of Christmas carol fame. He was never really a king, but the wise and benevolent 10th-century Duke of Bohemia. After being assassinated in 935, he became a symbol of Czech nationalism.

The metro stop (Muzeum) is the cross point of two metro lines. From here you could roll a ball straight down the boulevard and through the heart of Prague to Charles Bridge. It is famous locally as the downtown meeting place. They say, "I'll see you under the horse's ass."

Thirty meters below the big horse is a small round garden with a low-key memorial "to the victims of Communism." Pictured here is Jan Palach. The massive demonstrations here in the days following his death led to the overthrow of the Czech Communist government. From the balcony of the Grand Hotel Europa (farther down), Vaclav Havel stood with Alexander Dubcek, hero of the 1968 revolt, and declared the free Republic of Czechoslovakia in December 1989.

Continue people watching your way downhill. American Express is on the corner (on left, daily 9:00–19:00). The Grand Hotel Europa (halfway down Wenceslas Square) is hard to miss. Notice its Art Nouveau exterior and step inside for the smoky, elegant Old World ambience of the hotel's Art Nouveau restaurant (see "Three-Star Hotels," below).

The bottom of Wenceslas Square meets another spacious pedestrian mall. Na Príkope (meaning "the moat") leads from Wenceslas Square right to the Municipal House and the Powder Tower (the Powder Tower sounds interesting but is a dud). City tour buses leave from along this street.

Sights—Prague's Jewish Quarter

▲▲▲Jewish Quarter (Josefov)—The Jewish people were dispersed by the Romans 2,000 years ago. "Time was their sanctuary which no army could destroy" as their culture survived in enclaves throughout the Western world. Jews first came to Prague in the 10th century. The main intersection of Josefov (Maiselova and Siroka Streets) was the meeting point of two medieval trade routes. Jewish traders settled here in the 13th century and built a synagogue.

When the pope declared Jews and Christians should not live together, Jews had to wear yellow badges, and their quarter was walled in so that it became a ghetto. In the 16th and 17th centuries Prague had the biggest ghetto in Europe with 11,000 inhabitants—nearly half the population of Prague.

The "outcasts" of Christianity relied on profits from moneylending (forbidden to Christians) and community solidarity to survive. While their money protected them, it was also a curse. Throughout Europe, when times got tough and Christian debts to the Jewish community mounted, entire Jewish communities were burned, evicted, or killed.

Within its six gates, Prague's Jewish Quarter was a gaggle of 100 wooden buildings. Someone wrote: "Jews nested rather than dwelled." In the 1780s Emperor Joseph II eased much of the discrimination against Jews. In 1848 the walls were torn down and the neighborhood, named Josefov in honor of the emperor who was less anti-Semitic than the norm, was incorporated as a district of Prague.

In 1897 ramshackle Josefov was razed and replaced with a new modern town—the original 31 streets and 220 buildings became 10 streets and 83 buildings. This is what you'll see today: an attractive neighborhood of fine, mostly Art Nouveau buildings, with a few surviving historic Jewish buildings. In the 1930s some 50,000 Jews lived in Josefov. Today only a couple of thousand remain.

Prague's Jewish Quarter

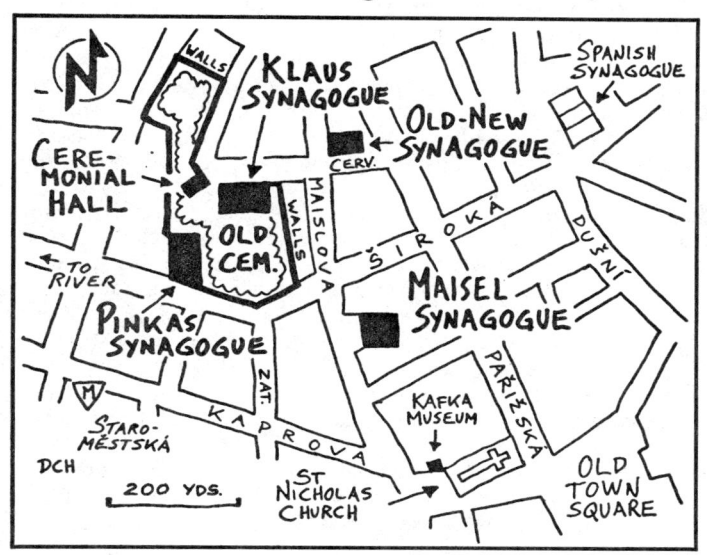

Strangely, the museums of the Jewish Quarter are, in part, the work of Hitler. He preserved Josefov to be his museum of the "exterminated race." Six sites scattered over a three-block area make the tourists' Jewish Quarter. Five, called "the Museum," are treated as one admission. Go early or late, as crowds can be fierce. Your ticket comes with a map locating the sights and five admission appointments: times you'll be let in if it's very crowded. (Without crowds, ignore the times.)

Westerners pay more than locals: 450 kč (250 kč for the "Museum" and 200 kč for the Old-New Synagogue). The sites are open from Sunday to Friday 9:00 to 17:30, and closed on Saturday (the Jewish Sabbath). The audio guide provides a good historic background and an easy-to-follow orientation for each site (125 kč, available at Pinkas Synagogue). There are also occasional live guided walks (often at 14:00, 40 kč). Most stops are wonderfully described in English. These museums are well presented and profoundly moving: For me, this is the most interesting Jewish site in Europe.

Start at the Maisel Synagogue unless you want to rent the audio guide at the Pinkas Synagogue.

Maisel Synagogue—This shows a thousand years of Jewish history in Bohemia and Moravia. Ironically, the collection was assembled from synagogues throughout the region by Nazis planning to archive the "extinct Jewish culture" here in Josefov with a huge

museum. Exhibits include topics such as the origin of the Star of David, Jewish mysticism, and the creation of the Prague Ghetto.
Pinkas Synagogue—A site of Jewish worship for 400 years, today this is a moving memorial to the victims of the Nazis. Of the 120,000 Jews living around here in 1939, only 15,000 lived to see liberation in 1945. The walls are covered with the handwritten names of 77,297 local Jews who were sent from here to the gas chambers of Auschwitz. Family names are in gold, followed by the individuals' first names in black, with birthdays and the last date known to be alive (usually the date of transport). Notice how families generally perished together. Climb six steps into the women's gallery. The names near the ceiling in poor condition are from 1953. When the Communists moved in, they closed the synagogue and erased everything. With freedom, in 1989, the Pinkas Synagogue was reopened, and all the names rewritten.

Upstairs is the Terezin Children's Art Exhibit. Terezin, near Prague, was a fortified town of 7,000 Czechs. The Nazis moved these people out and moved in 60,000 Jews, creating their model "Jewish town," a concentration camp dolled up for propaganda purposes. The town's medieval walls, which used to prevent people from getting in, were used by Nazis to prevent people from getting out. Jewish culture seemed to thrive in Terezin as "citizens" put on plays and concerts, published a magazine, and raised their families in ways impressive to Red Cross inspectors. Virtually all of the Jews ended up at Auschwitz. The art of the children of Terezin survives as a poignant testimony to the horror of the Holocaust. While the Communists kept the art away from the public, today it's well displayed and described in English.

Terezin is a powerful day trip from Prague for those interested in touring the concentration camp memorial/museum; you can either take a tour bus (see "Tours of Prague," above) or public bus (6/day, 60 min, leaves from Prague's Florenc bus station).
Old Jewish Cemetery—From 1439 until 1787, this was the only burial ground allowed for the Jews of Prague. With limited space and over 100,000 graves, tombs were piled atop each other. With as many as 12 layers, the cemetery became a small plateau. The Jewish word for cemetery means "House of Life"; like Christians, Jews believe that death is the gateway into the next world. Today visitors wander among more than 12,000 evocative stones.
Ceremonial Hall—Leaving the cemetery you'll find a neo-Romanesque mortuary house built in 1911 for the purification of the dead. It's filled with an interesting exhibition on Jewish burial traditions with historic paintings of the cemetery.
Klaus Synagogue—This 17th-century synagogue (also at the exit of the cemetery) is the final wing of this museum, devoted to Jewish religious practices.
Old-New Synagogue—For over 700 years this has been the

most important synagogue and central building in Josefov. Standing like a bomb-hardened bunker, it feels like it's survived plenty of hard times. Stairs take you down to the street level of the 13th century and into the Gothic interior. Built in 1270, it's the oldest synagogue in Europe. Originally called the "New Synagogue," it was renamed "Old-New" as other synagogues were built. The Shrine of the Arc in front is the focus of worship. It holds the sacred scrolls of the Torah, the holiest place in the synagogue. The old rabbi's chair to the right is left empty out of respect. Twelve is a popular number (e.g., windows) because it symbolizes the 12 tribes of Israel. The windows on the left are an 18th-century addition allowing women to view the men-only services.

Art Nouveau

▲▲**Mucha Museum**—I find the art of Alfons Mucha (moo-kah, 1860–1939) insistently likeable. Read about this popular Czech artist's posters, which were patriotic banners in disguise, see the crucifixion scene he painted as an eight-year-old, and check out the photographs of his models. Prague isn't much on museums, but if you're into Art Nouveau, this one is great. Run by Mucha's grandson, it's two blocks off Wenceslas Square and wonderfully described and displayed on one comfortable floor (130 kč, daily 10:00–18:00, Panska 7, tel. 02/628-4162, www.mucha.cz). While the exhibit is well described in English, the 30 kč English brochure on the art is a good supplement. The video is also worthwhile (30 min, hrly in English, ask upon entry).

More Art Nouveau—Prague is the best Art Nouveau town in Europe. Check out St. Vitus Cathedral (the Mucha stained glass window), the main train station (dome on top floor), and Hotel Europa overlooking Wenceslas Square (inside and out). The Municipal House (Obecní Dům, built 1906–1912, near Powder Tower) features Prague's largest concert hall and a great Art Nouveau café with handy cyber access. Look for the *Homage to Prague* mosaic on the building's striking facade; it stoked cultural pride and nationalist sentiment.

Nightlife in Prague

Prague booms with live (and inexpensive) theater, opera, classical, jazz, and pop entertainment. Everything's listed in *Test the Best*, Prague's monthly cultural events program (free at TI). The Prague Spring International Music Festival runs the last three weeks in May.

Six or eight classical "tourist" concerts a day resound throughout the famous Old Town halls and churches. The music is of the crowd-pleasing sort: Vivaldi, Best of Mozart, Most Famous Arias, and works by local boy Anton Dvorak. Leafleteers are everywhere announcing the evening's events. Concerts typically cost 400 kč, start anywhere from 17:00 to 21:00, last one hour, and are usually quartets (e.g., flute, French horn, cello, violin). Common venues are in the Little Quarter Square (Malostranské Náměstí, at the Church of St. Nicholas and the Prague Academy of Music in the Lichtenstein Palace), at the east end of Charles Bridge (St. Francis Church), and on the Old Town Square (another St. Nicholas Church).

Sleeping in Prague
(32 kč = about $1, tel. code: 02)
Sleep Code: **S** = Single, **D** = Double/Twin, **T** = Triple, **Q** = Quad, **b** = bathroom, **t** = toilet only, **s** = shower only, **CC** = Credit Card (**V**isa, **M**asterCard, **A**mex).

Finding a bed in Prague worries Western tourists. It shouldn't. You have several options. Capitalism is working as Adam Smith promised: With a huge demand, the supply is increasing and the price is going up. Peak time is May, June, September, October, Christmas, and Easter. July and August are not too bad. Virtually every place listed speaks English. Reserve by telephone, then confirm with a fax. Generally you simply promise to come and need no deposit.

Room-Booking Services: The city is awash with fancy rooms on the push list and private small-time operators with rooms to rent in their apartments. Numerous booking services connect these places with travelers for a small fee.

At the main train station, the AVE is a helpful and well-organized booking service (daily 6:00–23:00, tel. 02/2422-3226, fax 02/2423-0783). With the railroad tracks at your back, walk down to the orange ceiling—it's the small window just before the exit on your right. Their main office is by the exit to the taxis on the left; another AVE office is at Holešovice station). Their display board shows three-star hotels with $100 rooms available for half price (though many look unappealing). They have a slew of private rooms and small pensions available ($50 pension doubles in the old center, $35 doubles a metro ride away). You can reserve by e-mail (using your credit card as a deposit) or just show up at the office and request a room. For a more personal touch, contact Lida at Magic Praha for help with accommodations (see "Helpful Hints," above).

Three-Star Hotels
Prague's three-star hotels come with cookie-cutter standards. They're cheap, perfectly professional, and hotelesque, with English-speaking receptionists, comfortable modern furnishings, modern full bathrooms, included buffet breakfasts, and rarely an elevator. These hotels are often beholden to agencies that have a lock on rooms (generally until six weeks in advance). Agencies get a 30 percent

discount and can sell the rooms at whatever price they like between that and the "rack rate." Because of these agencies, Prague has a reputation of being perpetually booked up. But as they rarely use up their allotment, it almost never is. You need to make reservations either very long in advance, when the few rooms not reserved for agencies are still available, or not long in advance, after the agencies have released their rooms.

These recommended three-star hotels all cost about the same and have rooms any normal person would find pleasant. While I've listed them in order of value for the dollar, characteristics such as location and price need to be considered. Hotels Julian, Lunik, and Union are away from the center; the rest cluster in the Old Town, mainly near metro: Můstek, unless otherwise noted.

Hotel Julian is an oasis of professional, predictable decency in a quiet neighborhood a five-minute taxi or tram ride from the action. Its 29 spacious, well-furnished rooms and big, homey public spaces hide behind a noble neoclassical facade. The staff is friendly and helpful (Sb-2,680 kč, Db-3,080 kč, suite Db-3,680 kč, extra bed-800 kč, CC:VMA, 5 percent discount off best quoted rate with this book, parking lot, elevator, Internet services, nonsmoking rooms, Elisky Peskove 11, Prague 5, tel. 02/5731-1150, reception tel. 02/5731-1144, fax 02/5731-1149, e-mail: casjul@vol.cz).

Hotel Central is likeable like an old horse. I stayed there in the Communist days, and it hasn't changed a lot since. Even Charlie is still at the reception desk. The 62 rooms are proletarian plain, but the place is well run and the location, three blocks east of the old square, is excellent (Sb-3,000 kč, Db-3,500 kč, Tb-4,000 kč, CC:VMA, elevator, Rybna 8, Praha 1, metro: Náměstí Republiky, tel. 02/2481-2041, fax 02/232-8404, e-mail: what?).

Bethlem Club is an impersonal, shiny jewel of comfort on a pleasant medieval square in the heart of the Old Town across from the Bethlem Chapel where Jan Hus preached his trouble-making sermons. Its 22 modern and comfy rooms face a quiet inner courtyard, and breakfast is served in a Gothic cellar (Sb-2,600 kč, Db-3,400 kč, extra bed-600 kč, elevator, Betlémské Náměstí 9, Praha 1, tel. 02/2222-1575, fax 02/2222-0580).

Hotel U Staré Pani is well located in the Old Town above a jazz club that quits around midnight. The bright rooms are pastel-cheery and wicker-cozy (Db-3,950 kč, apartment Tb-5,760 kč, apartment Qb-6,660 kč, CC:VMA, no elevator, Michalska 9, Praha 1, 2 blocks from metro: Můstek, tel. 02/267-267, fax 02/267-9841).

Hotel U Klenotnika, with 10 modern and comfortable rooms in a plain building, is the most central of my recommendations. It's only three blocks off the old square (Sb-2,500 kč, Db-3,700 kč, Tb-4,300 kč, CC:VMA, no elevator, Rytirska 3, Praha 1, tel. 02/2421-1699, fax 02/261-782).

Hotel Lunik is a stately no-nonsense place out of the

medieval faux-rustic world and in a normal, pleasant business district two metro stops from the main station (direction: Muzeum, stop: I.P. Pavlova) or a 10-minute walk from Wenceslas Square. It's friendly, spacious, and rents 35 pleasant rooms (Db-2,500 kč, Tb-2,900 kč, CC:VMA, elevator, Londynska 50, Praha 2, tel. 02/2425-3974, fax 02/2425-3986).

Hotel Union is a grand 1906 Art Nouveau building filling its street corner. Like Hotel Lunik, it's away from the touristic center but in a more laid-back neighborhood a direct 10-minute ride to the station on tram #24 or to Charles Bridge on tram #18 (Sb-2,815 kč, Db-3,380 kč, Db deluxe-3,580 kč, extra bed-865 kč, Nusle Ostrcilovo Náměstí 1, Praha 2, tel. 02/6121-4812, fax 02/6121-4820, e-mail: hotel.union@telecom.cz).

Hotel Europa is in a class by itself. This landmark place, in all the guidebooks for its wonderful 1903 Art Nouveau facade, is the centerpiece of Wenceslas Square. But someone pulled the plug on the hotel about 50 years ago, and it's a mess, not even meriting its two stars. It offers haunting beauty in all the public spaces with 90 dreary, ramshackle rooms and a weary staff (S-1,300 kč, Sb-2,700 kč, D-2,160 kč, Db-3,740 kč, T-2,800 kč, Tb-4,4780 kč, CC:VMA, elevator, Václavské Náměstí 25, Praha 1, tel. 02/2422-8117, fax 02/2422-4544).

Three-Star Hotels near the Castle in Malá Strana

Hotel Sax is wonderfully located on a quiet corner a block below the action, and will delight the artsy yuppie with its airy atrium and modern, stylish decor (Sb-3,600 kč, Db-4,300 kč, Db suite-4,950 kč, CC:VMA, elevator, near St. Nicholas church, 1 block below Nerudova (Jansky Vrsek 3, tel. 02/5753-1268, fax 02/5753-4101).

Domus Henrici, a rare find just above the castle square, is a quiet retreat that charges (and gets) top kroner for its smartly appointed rooms, some of which include good views (Sb-4,250 kč, Db-4,600 kč, deluxe Db-5,600, extra bed-1,050 kč, pleasant breakfast terrace, Loretanska 11, tel. 02/2051-1369, fax 02/2051-1502, www.domus-henrici.cz).

Pensions

With the rush of tourists into Prague, small 6- to 15-room pensions are popping up everywhere. Most have small, basic, clean rooms with no plumbing at all; sinks, showers, and toilets are down the hall. Breakfast is included in the price. Some of these places take bookings no more than a month in advance. All are within 100 meters of each other in the Old Town, close to the Můstek metro station.

Pension Unitas is the best pension in the city. It's located right in the center of town and includes lots of modern rooms rented from a convent. It's next to the city police station—site of the old Communist secret police headquarters, which still gives locals the creeps. Pension Unitas' 34 rooms are small and tidy with spartan furnishings and no sinks (S-1,020 kč, D-1,200 kč, T-1,650 kč, Q-2,000 kč, T and Q are cramped with bunks in D-sized rooms, book long in advance). Unitas shares the building with the three-star **Cloister Inn** (Db-3,400 kč, a great value but nearly always booked by agencies, address and phone for both: Bartolomejska 9, 11000 Praha 1, tel. 02/232-7700, fax 02/232-7709, www.cloister-inn.cz). The place was actually a prison recently—Vaclav Havel spent a night here...free.

Express Pension is a quiet and creative little place renting 16 simple rooms and serving a lousy continental breakfast (Sb-2,400 kč, D-1,500 kč, 2 on ground floor and 2 on 4th floor, Db-2,600 kč, Tb-3,000 kč, no elevator, small patio with tables, Skorepka 5, Praha 1, tel. 02/2421-1801, fax 02/261-672).

Penzion U Medvidku, with indifferent management, rents a few big and plain rooms with no sinks and 11 sharp, just-renovated rooms (Sb-2,265 kč, D-1,600 kč, Db-3,000 kč, T-2,400 kč, Tb-3,800 kč, CC:VMA, Na Perstyne 7, Praha 1, tel. 02/2421-1916, fax 02/2422-0930, www.umedvidu.cz). They run a popular restaurant that has live music until 23:00 nightly.

Eating in Prague

The beauty of Prague is wandering aimlessly through the winding old quarters marveling at the architecture, people watching, and sniffing out restaurants. You can eat well and for very little money. What you'd pay for a basic meal in Vienna or Munich will get you an elegant meal in Prague. Your basic decision is: traditional dark Czech beerhall-type ambience, elegant Jugendstil turn-of-the-century atmosphere, or a modern place. For traditional, wander the Old Town (Staré Město). For fun, look around the Little Quarter Square (Malostranské Náměstí).

Here are a few places (between the bottom of Wenceslas Square and Charles Bridge) that I enjoyed:

Plzenska Restaurace U Dvou Kocek is a typical Czech pub with cheap, local, no-nonsense, hearty Czech food; great beer; and a local crowd (150 kč for three courses and beer, serving original Pilsner Urquell with traditional music daily until 23:00, under an arcade, facing the tiny square between Perlova and Skorepka Streets, tel. 02/267-729). **Restaurant U Staré Pani** is a good place for Czech or international food (2 blocks from metro: Můstek at Michalska 9 in recommended hotel by same name). **Restaurant U Plebana** is a quiet little place with good service, Czech cuisine, and a more modern yet elegant setting (daily until 24:00, Betlemske Náměstí 10, tel. 02/2222-1568). **Restaurant Mucha** is smoky with decent but pricey Czech food in a formal Art Nouveau dining room (300 kč meals, daily until 24:00, Melantrichova 5, tel. 02/263-586).

For a basic, very local cafeteria, slide your tray down the Czech-out line in the Můstek metro station at **37 Patro Fast Food** (extremely cheap, downstairs under Jungmannovo Náměstí). At least once, eat in a restaurant with no English menu.

Czech Beer

For many, *pivo* (beer) is the top Czech tourist attraction. After all, the Czechs invented lager in nearby Pilsen. This is the famous Pilsner Urquell, a great lager available on tap everywhere. Budvar is the local Budweiser, but it's not related to the American brew. Czechs are among the world's biggest beer drinkers—adults drink about 80 gallons a year. Order beer from the tap (*sudove pivo*) in either small (.3 liter, *male pivo*) or large (.5 liter, *pivo*). In many restaurants a beer hits your table like a glass of water in the United States.

Transportation Connections—Prague

Getting to Prague: Those with railpasses need to purchase tickets to cover the portion of their journey from the border of the Czech Republic to Prague (buy at station before you board train for Prague). Or supplement your pass with a "Prague Excursion" pass, giving you passage from any Czech border station into Prague and back to any border station within seven days. Ask about this pass—and get reservations—at the EurAide offices in Munich (089/593-889, www.euraide.de) or Berlin (90 DM first class, 60 DM second class, 45 DM for youths under 26). EurAide's U.S. office sells these passes for a bit less (tel. 941/480-1555, fax 941/480-1522). You can also try DER (tel. 800/549-3737), us (tel. 425/771-8303), or your travel agent. Direct trains leave Munich for Prague daily around 7:00, 14:00, and 23:00, arriving five or six hours later. Tickets cost about 100 DM from Munich or 30 DM from the border (if you have a railpass covering Germany).

By train to: Berlin (5/day, 5 hrs), **Munich** (3/day, 5 hrs), **Frankfurt** (3/day, 6 hrs), **Vienna** (3/day, 5 hrs), **Budapest** (6/day, 9 hrs). Train information: tel. 02/2422-4200. Czech Rail Agency, tel. 02/800-805.

PARIS

Paris offers sweeping boulevards, sleepy parks, world-class art galleries, chatty crêpe stands, Napoleon's body, sleek shopping malls, the Eiffel Tower, and people watching from outdoor cafés. Climb Notre-Dame and the Eiffel Tower, cruise the Seine and the Champs-Élysées, and master the Louvre and Orsay museums. Save some after-dark energy for one of the world's most romantic cities. Many people fall in love with Paris. Some see the essentials and flee, overwhelmed by the huge city. With the proper approach and a good orientation, you'll fall head over heels for Europe's capital city.

Planning Your Time: Paris in One, Two, or Three Days

Day 1
Morning: Follow "Historic Core of Paris Walk" (see "Sights," below) featuring Île de la Cité, Notre-Dame, Latin Quarter, and Sainte-Chapelle.
Afternoon: Tour Louvre Museum.
Evening: Cruise Seine River or take illuminated Paris by Night bus tour.

Day 2
Morning: Métro to l'Arc de Triomphe and saunter down the Champs-Élysées.
Midday: Tour Orsay Museum.
Afternoon: Catch RER from Orsay to Versailles. To avoid crowds, see the park first and the palace late.
Evening: Enjoy Trocadero scene and ride up Eiffel Tower.

> **Daily Reminder**
>
> **Monday:** These museums—Orsay, Rodin, Marmottan, Montmartre, Pompidou, and Versailles—are closed; the Louvre is more crowded because of this, but the Richelieu wing stays open until 21:45. Many small stores don't open until 14:00. Some restaurants close on Mondays. It's discount night at most cinemas.
> **Tuesday:** The Louvre, Picasso, Cluny, and most other national museums are closed today. Versailles and the Orsay can be jammed.
> **Wednesday:** All museums are open. The weekly *Pariscope* magazine comes out today.
> **Thursday:** All museums are open.
> **Friday:** All museums are open. Afternoon trains and roads leaving Paris are crowded; TGV reservation fees are much higher.
> **Saturday:** Avoid weekend crowds at area châteaus. Paris department stores are busy.
> **Sunday:** Organ concerts at St. Sulpice and possibly at other churches. Free evening concert at the American Church (18:00). The fountains run at Versailles. Some museums are two-thirds price all day (Louvre, Orsay, Cluny, Picasso). The Marais is the place to window shop and café hop; many of Paris' stores are closed on Sunday, but as this is the Jewish Quarter, it bustles.

Day 3
Morning: Tour Rodin Museum and nearby Napoleon's Tomb and Military Museum (Les Invalides).
Afternoon: Your choice—museums, shopping, walking tour, stroll rue Cler or Marais neighborhoods.
Evening: Explore Montmartre and Sacre Coeur.

Orientation

Paris is split in half by the Seine River, divided into 20 arrondissements (proud and independent governmental jurisdictions) and circled by a ring-road freeway (the *périphérique*). You'll find Paris easier to negotiate if you know which side of the river you're on, which arrondissement you're in, and which subway (Métro) stop you're closest to. If you're north of the river (above on any city map), you're on the Right Bank (*rive droite*). If you're south of it, you're on the Left Bank (*rive gauche*).

Arrondissements are numbered, starting at Notre-Dame (ground zero) and moving in a clockwise spiral out to the ring road. The last two digits in a Parisian zip code are the arrondissement

Paris

Paris Overview

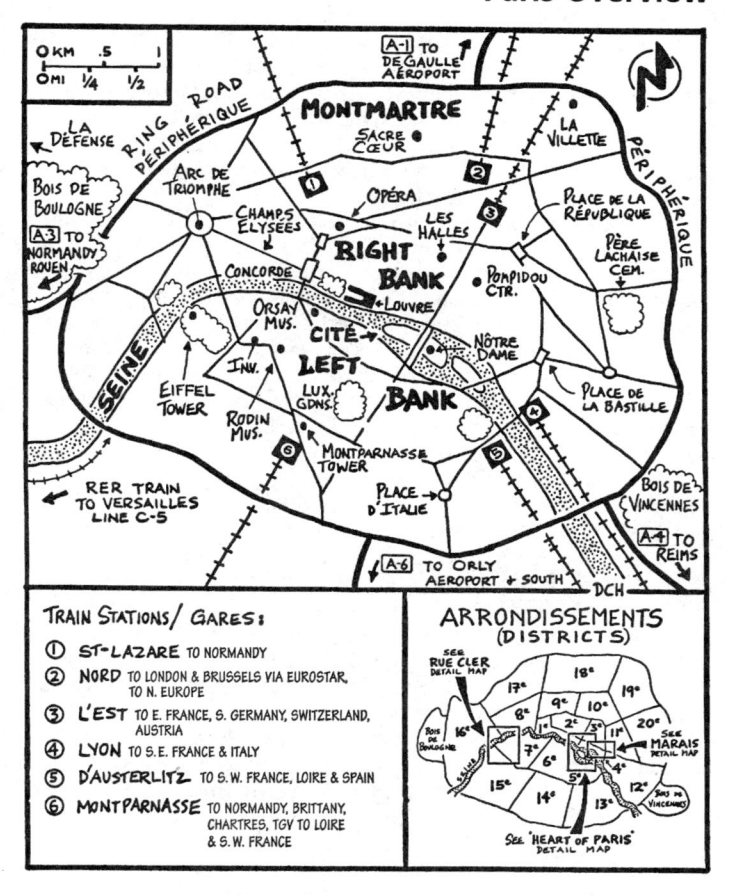

Train Stations / Gares:
1. **ST-LAZARE** TO NORMANDY
2. **NORD** TO LONDON & BRUSSELS VIA EUROSTAR, TO N. EUROPE
3. **L'EST** TO E. FRANCE, S. GERMANY, SWITZERLAND, AUSTRIA
4. **LYON** TO S.E. FRANCE & ITALY
5. **D'AUSTERLITZ** TO S.W. FRANCE, LOIRE & SPAIN
6. **MONTPARNASSE** TO NORMANDY, BRITTANY, CHARTRES, TGV TO LOIRE & S.W. FRANCE

number, and the notation for the Métro stop is "Mo." In Parisian jargon, Napoleon's tomb is on *la rive gauche* (the Left Bank) in the *7ème* (seventh arrondissement), zip code 75007, Mo: Invalides. Paris Métro stops are used as a standard aid in giving directions, even for those not using the Métro.

Tourist Information

Avoid the Paris TIs—long lines, short information, and a 5F charge for maps. This book, the *Pariscope* magazine (described below), and one of the freebie maps available at any hotel are all you need. The main TI is at 127 avenue des Champs-Élysées (daily 9:00–20:00), but the TIs at the Louvre, Eiffel Tower, and Gare de Lyon train station are handier (daily 8:00–20:00).

The *Pariscope* weekly magazine (or one of its clones, 3F at any newsstand, explained below) lists museum hours, special art exhibits, concerts, music festivals, plays, movies, and nightclubs. For a complete list of museum hours and scheduled English museum tours, pick up the free *Musées, Monuments Historiques, et Expositions* booklet from any museum.

While Paris is littered with free maps, they don't show all the streets. You may want the huge Michelin #10 map of Paris. For an extended stay we prefer the pocket-size and street-indexed *Paris Pratique* (40F). For supplemental background on the city, sights, and neighborhoods, you may want to buy an additional guidebook. The *Michelin Green Guide*, which is somewhat scholarly, and the more readable *Paris Access Guide* are both well researched. Consider *Rick Steves' Paris* or *Rick Steves' Mona Winks*, for their extensive self-guided walking tours of the Louvre, Orsay, Versailles, and the Historic Core of Paris.

There are many English-language bookstores in Paris where you can pick up guidebooks (for nearly double their American price). A few are Shakespeare and Company (12:00–24:00, lots of used travel books, 37 rue de la Boucherie, across the river from Notre-Dame), W. H. Smith (248 rue de Rivoli), and Brentanos (37 avenue de L'Opéra).

The American Church is a nerve center for the American émigré community and distributes the *Free Voice*, a handy and insightful monthly English-language newspaper with useful reviews of concerts, plays, and current events in Paris; and *France—U.S.A. Contacts*, an advertisement paper full of useful information for those looking for work or long-term housing (facing the river between Eiffel Tower and Orsay at 65 quai d'Orsay, Mo: Invalides tel. 01 40 62 05 00).

Arrival in Paris

By Train: Paris has six train stations, all connected by Métro and bus, most with banks, and all with lockers (*consigne automatique*). Hop the Métro to your hotel (see "Getting around Paris," below).

Paris' six train stations are well organized and efficient. The Gare de l'Est handles the east, the Gare du Nord and Gare St. Lazare serve northern and central Europe, the Gare d'Austerlitz and Gare du Lyon cover southern Europe, and the Gare Montparnasse handles western France and TGV service to France's southwest. (Any train station can give you the schedule information you need, make reservations, and sell tickets for any destination.) Buying tickets is handier from an SNCF neighborhood office (e.g., Louvre, Orsay, Versailles, airports) or at your neighborhood travel agency, and it's worth their small fee ("SNCF" signs in their window indicate they sell train tickets).

By Plane: For detailed information on getting from Paris' airports to downtown Paris (and vice versa), see "Transportation Connections" at the end of this chapter.

Helpful Hints

Theft Alert: Use your money belt and never carry a wallet in your back pocket or a purse over your shoulder. Thieves thrive in tourist areas, subway stations, and on the Métro.

Museums: Most museums offer reduced prices and shorter hours on Sunday. Many begin closing rooms 45 minutes before the actual closing time. For the fewest crowds, visit very early, at lunch, or very late. The best Impressionist art museums are the Orsay and Marmottan (another, L'Orangerie, is closed for renovation). Most museums have slightly shorter hours October through March. French holidays can really mess up your sightseeing plans (Jan 1, May 1, May 8, Jul 14, Nov 1, Nov 11, and Dec 25). See "Daily Reminder," above, for other "closed" days.

Paris Museum Pass: In Paris there are two classes of sightseers: those with a museum pass and those without. Serious sightseers save time (less time in lines) and money by getting this pass. Sold at museums, main Métro stations, and tourist offices, it pays for itself in two admissions and gets you into sights with no lining up (1 day-80F, 3 consecutive days-160F, 5 consecutive days-240F; no discounts for kids). Included sights (and admission prices without the pass) you're likely to visit: Louvre (45F), Orsay (40F), Sainte-Chapelle (32F), l'Arc de Triomphe (40F), Napoleon's Tomb and the Army Museum (38F), Carnavalet Museum (35F), Conciergerie (32F), Sewer Tour (25F), Cluny Museum (38F), Notre-Dame towers (35F) and crypt (32F), Picasso Museum (30F), Rodin Museum (28F), and the elevator to the top of the Grand Arche de la Defense (43F). Outside Paris, the pass covers the Palace of Versailles (45F), its Grand Trianon (30F), and Château Chantilly (39F). Notable sights not covered: Marmottan Museum, the new Museum of Art and History of Judaism, Eiffel Tower, Montparnasse Tower, the ladies of Pigalle, and Disneyland Paris. Tally it up—but remember, an advantage of the pass is that you skip to the front of the line—saving hours of waiting in the summer (though everyone must pass through the slow-moving metal-detector lines at a few sights). And with the pass, you'll pop painlessly into sights that you're walking by (even for a few minutes) that might otherwise not be worth the expense (e.g., Notre-Dame crypt, Cluny Museum, Conciergerie, Victor Hugo's House). The free museum and monuments directory that comes with your pass lists the latest hours, phone numbers, and specifics on what kids pay (the cutoff age for free entry varies from 5 to 18. Most major, serious art museums let young people up to age 18 in for free). If you're buying a pass at a museum with a long line, skip to the front and find the sales window.

Local Guides: Arnaud Servignat (tel. 01 42 57 03 35, fax 01 42 62 68 62, e-mail: arnoud.saigon@wanadoo.fr) and Marianne Siegler (tel. 01 42 52 32 51) are licensed local guides who freelance for individuals and families ($150/4 hrs, $250/day).

Telephone Cards: Pick up the essential France *télécarte* or KOSMOS card at any *tabac* (tobacco shop), post office, or tourist office (*une petite télécarte* is 42F; *une grande* is 98F). Smart travelers check things by telephone. Most public phones use *télécartes* (KOSMOS cards work at any phone).

Useful Telephone Numbers: American Hospital, 01 46 41 25 25; American pharmacy, 01 47 42 49 40 (Mo: Opéra); Police, 17; United States Embassy, 01 43 12 22 22; Paris and France directory assistance, 12; AT&T operator, 0800 99 00 11; MCI, 0800 99 00 19; Sprint, 0800 99 00 87. (See Appendix for additional numbers.)

Toilets: Carry small change for pay toilets or walk into any outdoor café like you own the place and find the toilet in the back. Remember, the toilets in museums are free and generally the best you'll find. Modern super-sanitary street booths provide both relief and a memory.

Getting around Paris

By Métro: Europe's best subway is divided into two systems—the Métro (puddle-jumping everywhere in Paris) and the RER (which makes giant speedy leaps around town and connects suburban destinations). You'll be using the Métro for most of your trips.

In Paris you're never more than a 10-minute walk from a Métro station. One ticket takes you anywhere in the system with unlimited transfers. Save 40 percent by buying a *carnet* (car-nay) of 10 tickets for 54F at any Métro station (a single ticket is 8F). Métro tickets work on city buses, though one ticket cannot be used as a transfer between subway and bus.

The Mobilis ticket (30F) allows unlimited travel for a single day on all bus and Métro lines. If you're staying longer, the Carte Orange pass gives you free run of the bus and Métro system for one week (80F plus a photo of yourself, ask for the Carte Orange Coupon Vert) or a month (280F, ask for the Carte Orange Coupon Orange). These pass prices cover only central Paris; you can pay more for passes covering regional destinations (e.g., Versailles). The weekly pass begins Monday and ends Sunday, and the monthly pass begins the first day of the month and ends the last day of that month, so midweek or midmonth purchases are generally not worthwhile. All passes can be purchased at any Métro station (most have photo booths).

Paris

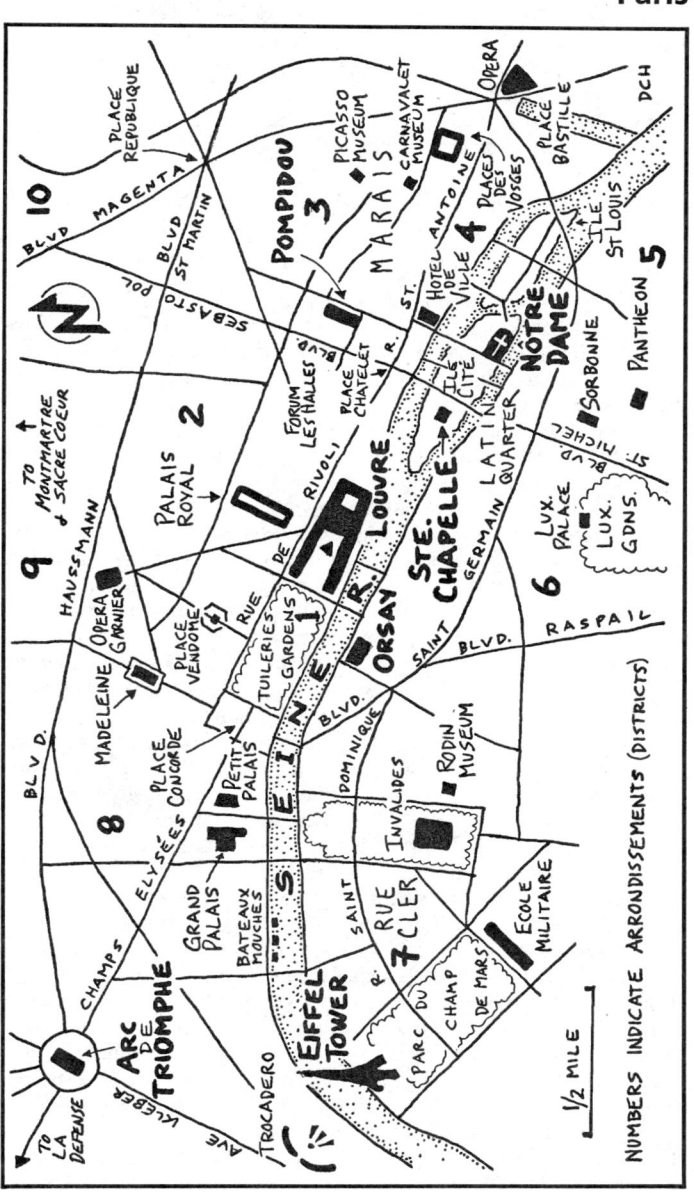

Key Words for the Métro and RER

direction (dee-rek-see-ohn): direction
correspondance (kor-res-pohn-dahns): transfer
sortie (sor-tee): exit
carnet (kar-nay): cheap set of 10 tickets
Pardon, madame/monsieur (par-dohn, mah-dahm/mes-yur):
Excuse me, lady/bud.
Je descend (juh day-sahn): I'm getting off.
Donnez-moi mon porte-monnaie!: Give me back my wallet!

To get to your destination, determine which "Mo." stop is closest to it and which line or lines will get you there. The lines have numbers, but they're best known by their direction or end-of-the-line stop. (For example, the La Defense/Château de Vincennes line runs between La Defense in the west and Vincennes in the east.)

Once in the Métro station, you'll see blue-and-white signs directing you to the train going in your direction (e.g., *direction*: La Defense). Insert your ticket in the automatic turnstile, pass through, and then reclaim and keep your ticket until you exit the system (fare inspectors accept no excuses from anyone). Transfers are free and can be made wherever lines cross. When you transfer, look for the orange *correspondence* (connections) signs when you exit your first train and then follow the proper *direction* sign.

Before you *sortie* (exit), check the helpful *plan du quartier* (map of the neighborhood) to get your bearings, locate your destination, and decide which *sortie* you want. At stops with several *sorties*, you can save lots of walking by choosing the best exit.

Thieves thrive in the Métro. Be on guard. A pocket picked as you pass through a turnstile leaves you on the wrong side and the thief strolling away. Any jostle or commotion (especially when boarding or leaving trains) is likely the sign of a thief or team of thieves in action. Paris is most dangerous late at night.

Paris has a huge homeless population and over 12 percent unemployment; expect a warm Métro welcome by panhandlers, musicians, and those selling magazines produced by the homeless community.

By RER: The RER (Réseau Express Régionale, air-uh-air) suburban train system (thick lines on your subway map identified by letters A, B, C, and so on) works like the Métro but is much speedier because it makes only a few stops within the city. One Métro ticket is all you need for RER rides within Paris. You can transfer between the Métro and RER systems with the same ticket. Unlike the Métro, you need to insert your ticket in a turnstile to exit the RER system. To travel outside the city (for example, to Versailles or the airport—both covered by railpass but uses up a day or the airport) you'll need to buy a separate, more expensive ticket at the station window before boarding and make sure your stop is served by checking the signs over the train platform (not all trains serve all stops).

By City Bus: The trickier bus system is worth figuring out. Métro tickets are good on both bus and Métro, though you can't use the same ticket to transfer between the two systems. One ticket gets you anywhere in central Paris, but if you leave the city center (shown as section 1 on the diagram onboard the bus), you must validate a second ticket. While the Métro shuts down at about 00:30, some buses continue much later. Schedules are posted at bus stops. Handy bus-system maps are available in any Métro station (*plan des autobus*) and are provided in your *Paris Pratique* map book if you invest (40F).

Big system maps, posted at each bus and Métro stop, display the routes. Individual route diagrams show the exact route of the lines serving that stop. Major stops are painted on the side of each bus. Enter through the front doors. Punch your Métro ticket in the machine behind the driver or pay the higher cash fare. Get off the bus using the rear door. Even if you're not certain you've figured it out, do some joyriding (outside of rush hour). Lines #24, #63, and #69 are Paris' most scenic routes and make a great introduction to the city. Bus #69 is particularly handy, running between the Eiffel Tower, the recommended hotels around rue Cler, the Orsay Museum, the Louvre, the Marais/Bastille area (more recommended hotels), and Père Lachaise Cemetery. The most handy bus routes are listed for each hotel area recommended (below).

By Taxi: Parisian taxis are almost reasonable. A 10-minute ride costs about 50F (versus about 5.5F to get anywhere in town on the Métro). You can try waving one down, but it's easier to ask for the nearest taxi stand ("oo ay la tet de stah-see-oh taxi?") or ask your hotel to call for you. Higher rates are charged from 22:00 to 6:30, all day Sunday, and to the airport. If you call from your hotel, the meter starts as soon as the call is received. Taxis are tough to find on Friday and Saturday nights, especially after the Métro closes (around 00:30).

By Foot: Be careful out there! Parisian drivers are notorious for ignoring pedestrians. Never assume you have the right of way, even in a crosswalk. When crossing a street, keep your pace constant and don't stop suddenly. Parisian drivers carefully calculate your speed and will miss you, provided you don't alter your route or pace.

Organized Tours of Paris

Bus Tours: Paris Vision offers handy bus tours of Paris, day and night (advertised in hotel lobbies, 150F, 100 min, audio guide, tel. 01 42 60 30 01, www.parisvision.com). Paris also has a hop-on hop-off bus service called Open Deck Tours that connects all the major sights and includes a running commentary; you can get off at a site, explore, and catch a later bus (135F for 1 day, 150F for 2 days, buy from driver, 2 buses per hour). You'll see these bright yellow topless double-decker buses all over town.

Boat Tours: Several companies offer one-hour boat cruises on the Seine. The Bateaux-Mouches boats depart every 30 minutes (10:00–23:00, best at night) from the pont de l'Alma, the pont Neuf, and Eiffel Tower (40F, 20F for children under age 14, tel. 01 42 25 96 10). The much smaller and more intimate **Vedettes de pont Neuf** depart only once an hour from the center of the pont Neuf but come with a live guide giving explanations in French and English only and are convenient to Marais and Contrescarpe hotels (50F, 25F under age 14, tel. 01 46 33 98 38). From April to October, **Bateau-Bus** operates boats on the Seine connecting six key stops about every 25 minutes: Eiffel Tower, Orsay/place de la Concorde, Louvre, Notre-Dame, Hôtel de Ville, and St. Germain-des-Prés. Pick up their schedule at any stop (or TI) and use this as a scenic alternative to the Métro. Tickets are available for single trips (20F), one day (60F), and two days (90F). Boats run from 10:00 to 19:00, until 22:00 in summer.

Walking Tours: Consider Paris Walking Tours, which offers a daily walk for 60F. Choose from architecture, Montmartre, Hemingway's Paris, Medieval Paris, French Revolution, Marais, and museum tours (admission extra), and more (tel. 01 48 09 21 40, fax 01 42 43 75 51, http://ParisWalkingtours.com). Paris Literary Promenades takes you through areas once popular with literary giants, from Joyce to Beckett to Hemingway (60F, 2 hrs., depart from place de l'Odeon, daily except Wed at 14:30 and 19:00, late May–mid-Oct, tel. 01 48 07 80 72, cellular 06 03 27 73 52).

Bike Tours: Bullfrog Bike Tours will show you Paris on two wheels at a relaxed pace (120F, 3–4-hr tours in English at 11:00 and 15:30, May–mid-Sept, no bikes or reservations needed, meet at fountain on Avenue Joseph 100 yards from the Eiffel Tower in Champs de Mars park, http://BullfrogBikes.com, e-mail: bullfrogbikes@hotmail.com, cellular 06 09 98 08 60).

Sights—The "Historic Core of Paris" Walk

(This information is distilled from the Historic Paris Walk chapter in *Rick Steves' Mona Winks*, by Gene Openshaw and Rick Steves.) Allow four hours for this self-guided tour, including sightseeing. Start where the city did—on the Île de la Cité—face Notre-Dame, and follow the dotted line on the "Core of Paris" map. To get to Notre-Dame, ride the Métro to Cité, Hôtel de Ville, or St. Michel and walk to the big square facing the...

▲▲**Notre-Dame Cathedral**—The 700-year-old cathedral is packed with history and tourists. Study its sculpture (Notre-Dame's forte) and windows, take in a Mass, eavesdrop on guides, and walk all around the outside. (Free, daily 8:00–18:45; treasury-

Core of Paris

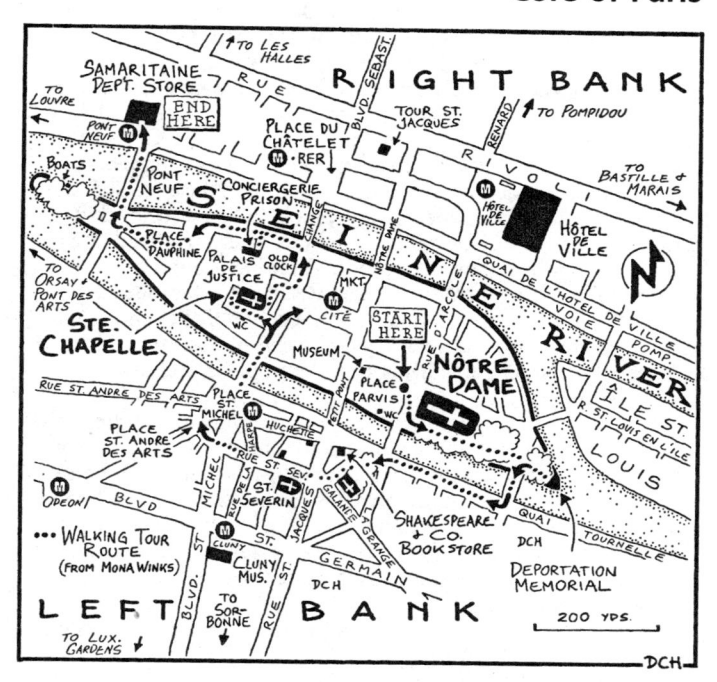

15F, daily 9:30–17:30. Ask about the free English tours, normally Wed and Thu at 12:00 and Sat at 14:30.) Sunday Masses are at 8:00, 8:45, 10:00, 11:30, 12:30, and 18:30. Climb to the top for a great gargoyle's-eye view of the city; you get 400 steps for only 35F (entrance on the outside, north tower open 9:30–17:30, closed at lunch and earlier off-season). There are clean 2.70F toilets in front of the church near Charlemagne's statue.

The cathedral facade is worth a close look. The church is dedicated to "Our Lady" (Notre-Dame). Mary is center stage—cradling Jesus, surrounded by the halo of the rose window. Adam is on the left, and Eve is on the right.

Below Mary and above the arches is a row of 28 statues known as the Kings of Judah. During the French Revolution, these Biblical kings were mistaken for the hated French kings. The citizens stormed the church, crying, "Off with their heads!" All were decapitated but have since been recapitated.

Speaking of decapitation, look at the carving above the doorway on the left. The man with his head in his hands is St. Denis. Back when there was a Roman temple on this spot, Christianity began making converts. The fourth-century bishop of Roman Paris, Denis, was beheaded. But these early Christians were hard to keep down. The man who would become St. Denis got up, tucked his head under his arm, and headed north until he found just the right place to meet his maker: Montmartre, which means "mountain of the martyr." The Parisians were convinced of this miracle, Christianity gained ground, and a church soon replaced the pagan temple.

Medieval art was OK if it embellished the house of God and told Bible stories. For a fine example, move to the base of the central column (at the foot of Mary, about where the head of St. Denis could spit if he was real good). Working around from the left, find God telling a barely created Eve, "Have fun but no apples." Next, the sexiest serpent I've ever seen makes apples à la mode. Finally, Adam and Eve, now ashamed of their nakedness, are expelled by an angel. This is a tiny example in a church covered with meaning.

Now move to the right and study the carving above the central portal. It's the end of the world, and Christ sits on the throne of Judgment (just under the arches, holding his hands up). Below him an angel and a demon weigh souls in the balance. The "good" stand to the left, looking up to heaven. The "bad" ones to the right are chained up and led off to...Versailles on a Tuesday. The "ugly" ones must be the crazy sculpted demons to the right, at the base of the arch.

Wander through the interior. You'll be routed around the ambulatory, much as medieval pilgrims would have been. Don't miss the rose windows filling each of the transepts. Back outside, walk around the church through the park on the riverside for a close look at the flying buttresses.

The neo-Gothic 90-meter spire is a product of the 1860 reconstruction. Around its base are apostles and evangelists (the green men) as well as Viollet-le-Duc, this work's architect. The apostles look outward, blessing the city, while the architect (at top, seen from behind the church) looks up, admiring his spire.

The archaeological crypt is a worthwhile 15-minute stop with your museum pass (enter 100 yards in front of church, 32F, 50F with Notre-Dame's tower, daily 10:00–18:00, closes at 17:00 Oct–Apr). You'll see Roman ruins, trace the street plan of the medieval village, and see diagrams of how the earliest Paris grew and grew, all thoughtfully explained in English.

If you're hungry near Notre-Dame, the only grocery store on the Île de la Cité is tucked away at 16 rue Chanoinesse, one block north of the church (Mon–Sat 9:00–13:30, 16:00–20:30, closed Sun). Nearby Île St. Louis has inexpensive *crêperies* and grocery stores open daily on its main drag. Plan a picnic for the quiet bench-filled park immediately behind the church (public WC).

Paris

Behind Notre-Dame, squeeze through the tourist buses, cross the street, and enter the iron gate into the park at the tip of the island. Look for the stairs and head down.

▲▲**Deportation Memorial (Mémorial de la Déportation)**—This memorial to the 200,000 French victims of the Nazi concentration camps draws you into their experience. As you descend the steps, the city around you disappears. Surrounded by walls, you have become a prisoner. Your only freedom is your view of the sky and the tantalizing glimpse of the river below.

Enter the single-file chamber ahead. Inside, the circular plaque in the floor reads, "They descended into the mouth of the earth and they did not return." A hallway stretches in front of you, lined with 200,000 lighted crystals, one for each French citizen that died. Flickering at the far end is the eternal flame of hope. The tomb of the unknown deportee lies at your feet. Above, the inscription reads, "Dedicated to the living memory of the 200,000 French deportees sleeping in the night and the fog, exterminated in the Nazi concentration camps."

Above the exit as you leave is the message you'll find at all Nazi sights: "Forgive but never forget." (Free, Mon–Fri 8:30–21:45, Sat–Sun and holidays from 9:00, sometimes closes 12:00–14:00, shorter hours off-season, east tip of the island near Île St. Louis, behind Notre-Dame, Mo: Cité.)

Île St. Louis—Back on street level, look across the river to the Île St. Louis. If the Île de la Cité is a tug laden with the history of Paris, it's towing this classy little residential dinghy laden only with boutiques, famous sorbet shops, and characteristic restaurants (see "Eating in Paris," below). This island wasn't developed until much later (18th century). What was a swampy mess is now harmonious Parisian architecture. The pedestrian bridge, Pont Saint Louis, connects the two islands, leading right to rue Saint Louis en l'Île. This spine of the island is lined with interesting shops. A short stroll takes you to the famous Bertillon ice-cream parlour (#31). Loop back to the pedestrian bridge along the parklike quays (walk north to the river and turn left). This riverside walk is about as peaceful and romantic as Paris gets.

Before walking to the opposite end of the Île de la Cité, loop through the Latin Quarter (as indicated on the map). From the Deportation Memorial cross the bridge onto the Left Bank and enjoy the riverside view of Notre-Dame and window shop among the green book stalls, browsing through used books, vintage posters, and souvenirs. At the little park and church (over the bridge from the front of Notre-Dame), venture inland a few blocks, basically arcing through the Latin Quarter and returning to the island two bridges down at place St. Michel.

▲**Latin Quarter**—This area, which gets its name from the language used here when it was an exclusive medieval university district, lies between the Luxembourg Gardens and the Seine, centering around the Sorbonne University and boulevards St. Germain and St. Michel. This is the core of the Left Bank—it's crowded with international eateries, far-out bookshops, street singers, and jazz clubs. For colorful wandering and café sitting, afternoons and evenings are best (Mo: St. Michel).

Along rue Saint-Séverin you can still see the shadow of the medieval sewer system (the street slopes into a central channel of bricks). In the days before plumbing and toilets, when people still went to the river or neighborhood wells for their water, "flushing" meant throwing it out the window. Certain times of day were flushing times. Maids on the fourth floor would holler "*Garde de l'eau!*" ("Look out for the water!") and heave it into the streets, where it would eventually be washed down into the Seine.

Consider a visit to the Cluny Museum for its medieval art and unicorn tapestries (listed under "Sights—Southeast Paris," below).

Place St. Michel (facing the St. Michel bridge) is the traditional core of the Left Bank's artsy, liberal, hippie, Bohemian district of poets, philosophers, winos, and tourists. In less commercial times, place St. Michel was a gathering point for the city's malcontents and misfits. Here, in 1871, the citizens took the streets from the government troops, set up barricades *Les Mis*–style, and established the Paris Commune. In World War II the locals rose up against their Nazi oppressors (read the plaques by the St. Michael fountain). And in the spring of 1968, a time of social upheaval all over the world, young students—battling riot batons and tear gas—took over the square and demanded change.

From place St. Michel, look across the river and find the spire of Sainte-Chapelle church and its weathervane angel (below). Cross the river on the Pont St. Michel and continue along boulevard du Palais. On your left you'll see the high-security doorway to Sainte-Chapelle. But first, carry on another 30 meters and turn right at a wide pedestrian street, the rue de Lutece.

Cité "Métropolitain" Stop—Of the 141 original turn-of-the-century subway entrances, this is one of 17 survivors now preserved as a national art treasure. The curvy, plantlike ironwork is a textbook example of Art Nouveau, the style that rebelled against the erector-set squareness of the Industrial Age (e.g., Mr. Eiffel's tower).

The flower market right here on place Louis Lepine is a pleasant detour. On Sundays this square chirps with a busy bird market. And across the way is the Prefecture de Police, where Inspector Clouseau of *Pink Panther* fame used to work and where the local resistance fighters took the first building from the Nazis in August 1944, leading to the Allied liberation of Paris a week later.

Pause here to admire the view. Sainte-Chapelle is a pearl in an ugly architectural oyster, part of a complex of buildings that includes the Palace of Justice (to the right of Sainte-Chapelle, behind the fancy gates). Return to the entrance of Sainte-Chapelle. You'll need to pass through a metal detector to get in. Free toilets are ahead on the left. The line into the church may be long. (Museum card holders can go directly in; pick up the excellent English info sheet.) Enter the humble ground floor of...

▲▲▲**Sainte-Chapelle**—The triumph of Gothic church architecture is a cathedral of glass like no other. It was speedily built from 1242 to 1248 for St. Louis IX (France's only canonized king) to house the supposed Crown of Thorns. Its architectural harmony is due to the fact that it was completed under the direction of one architect in only six years—unheard of in Gothic times. (Notre-Dame took more than 200 years to build.)

The design clearly shows an Old Regime approach to worship. The basement was for staff and other common folk. Royal Christians worshiped upstairs. The ground-floor paint job, a 19th-century restoration, is a reasonably accurate copy of the original.

Climb the spiral staircase to the Chapelle Haute. Fill the place with choral music, crank up the sunshine, face the top of the altar, and really believe that the Crown of Thorns was there, and this becomes one awesome space.

"Let there be light." In the Bible, it's clear: Light is divine. Light shining through stained glass was a symbol of God's grace shining down to earth. Gothic architects used their new technology to turn dark stone buildings into lanterns of light. The glory of Gothic shines brighter here than in any other church.

There are 15 separate panels of stained glass (6,500 square feet—two-thirds of it 13th-century original), with more than 1,100 different scenes, mostly from the Bible. In medieval times, scenes like these helped teach Bible stories to the illiterate.

The altar was raised up high to better display the relic—the Crown of Thorns—around which this chapel was built. The supposed Crown cost King Louis three times as much as this church. Today it is kept in Notre-Dame Treasury and shown only on Good Friday.

Louis' little private viewing window is in the wall to the right of the altar. Louis, both saintly and shy, liked to go to church without dealing with the rigors of public royal life. Here he could worship still dressed in his jammies.

Lay your camera on the ground and shoot the ceiling. Those pure and simple ribs growing out of the slender columns are the essence of Gothic.

Books in the gift shop explain the stained glass in English. There are concerts (120F) almost every summer evening. (32F, daily 9:30–18:00, off-season 10:00–17:00, call 01 48 01 91 35 for concert information, Mo: Cité.)

Palais du Justice—Back outside, as you walk around the church exterior, look down and notice how much Paris has risen in the

800 years since Sainte-Chapelle was built. You're in a huge complex of buildings that has housed the local government since ancient Roman times. It was the site of the original Gothic palace of the early kings of France. The only surviving medieval parts are the Sainte-Chapelle church and the Conciergerie prison.

Most of the site is now covered by the giant Palais de Justice, home of France's supreme court (built in 1776). "Liberté, Egalité, Fraternité" over the doors is a reminder that this was also the headquarters of the revolutionary government.

Now pass through the big iron gate to the noisy boulevard du Palais and turn left (toward the Right Bank). On the corner is the site of the oldest public clock (built in 1334) in the city. While the present clock is said to be Baroque, it somehow still manages to keep accurate time.

Turn left onto quai de l'Horologe and walk along the river. The round medieval tower just ahead marks the entrance to the Conciergerie. Pop in to visit the courtyard and lobby (free). Step past the serious-looking guard into the courtyard.

Conciergerie—The Conciergerie, a former prison, is a gloomy place. Kings used it to torture and execute failed assassins. The leaders of the Revolution put it to similar good use. The tower next to the entrance, called "the babbler," was named for the painful sounds that leaked from it.

Look at the stark lettering above the doorways. This was a no-nonsense revolutionary time. Everything, even lettering, was subjected to the test of reason. No frills or we chop 'em off.

Step inside; the lobby, with an English-language history display, is free. Marie Antoinette was imprisoned here. During a busy eight-month period in the Revolution, she was one of 2,600 prisoners kept here on the way to the guillotine. The interior, with its huge vaulted and pillared rooms, echoes with history but is pretty barren (32F, daily 9:30–18:30, 10:00–17:00 in winter, good English descriptions). You can see Marie Antoinette's cell, housing a collection of her mementoes. In another room, a list of those made "a foot shorter at the top" by the "national razor" includes ex-King Louis XVI, Charlotte Corday (who murdered Marat in his bathtub), and the chief revolutionary who got a taste of his own medicine, Maximilien Robespierre.

Back outside, wink at the flak-proof vested guard, fake right, and turn left. Listen for babbles and continue your walk along the river. Across the river you can see the rooftop observatory—flags flapping—of the Samaritaine department store, where this walk will end. At the first corner, veer left past France's supreme-court building and into a sleepy triangular square called place Dauphine. Marvel at how such quaintness could be lodged in the midst of such greatness as you walk through the park to the end of the island. At the equestrian statue of Henry IV, turn right onto the bridge and take refuge in one of the nooks on the Eiffel Tower side.

Pont Neuf—This "new bridge" is now Paris' oldest. Built during Henry IV's reign (around 1600), its 12 arches span the widest part of the river. The fine view includes the park on the tip of the island (note Seine tour boats), the Orsay Museum, and the Louvre. These turrets were originally for vendors and street entertainers. In the days of Henry IV, who originated the promise of "a chicken in every pot," this would have been a lively scene.

Directly over the river, the first building you'll hit on the Right Bank is the venerable old department store, Samaritaine.

▲**Samaritaine Department Store Viewpoint**—Enter the store and go to the rooftop. Ride the glass elevator from near the Pont Neuf entrance to the ninth floor (you'll be greeted by a WC—check out the sink). Pass the 10th-floor *terrasse* for the 11th-floor panorama (tight spiral staircase; watch your head). Quiz yourself. Working counterclockwise, find the Eiffel Tower, Invalides/Napoleon's Tomb, Montparnasse Tower, Henry IV statue on the tip of the island, Sorbonne University, the dome of the Panthéon, Sainte-Chapelle, Notre-Dame, Hôtel de Ville (city hall), Pompidou Center, Sacré-Coeur, Opéra, and Louvre. The Champs-Élysées leads to the Arc de Triomphe. Shadowing that—even bigger, while two times as distant—is the Grand Arche de la Defense. You'll find light, reasonably priced, and incredibly scenic meals on the breezy terrace and a supermarket in the basement. (Rooftop view is free, daily 9:30–19:00, tel. 01 40 41 20 20, Mo: Pont Neuf.)

Sights—Paris' Museums near the Tuileries Gardens

The newly renovated Tuileries Gardens was once private property of kings and queens. Paris' grandest public park links these museums.

▲▲▲**Louvre**—This is Europe's oldest, biggest, greatest, and maybe most-crowded museum. There is no grander entry than through the pyramid, but metal detectors create a long line at times. To avoid the line, you have two choices. Museum pass holders can use the nearby entrance over the Richelieu wing (facing the pyramid with your back to the Tuileries Gardens, go to your left, which is north; under the arches you'll find the Richelieu entrance and escalator down). Or anyone can get into the Louvre from the slick underground shopping mall that connects with the museum; enter the mall either at 99 rue de Rivoli at the door with the red awning or get off the Métro at the "Palais Royal Musée du Louvre" stop and follow signs to "Musée du Louvre"; don't get off at the "Louvre Rivoli" Métro stop, which is farther away.

Pick up the free *Louvre Handbook* in English at the information desk under the pyramid as you enter. Don't try to cover the museum thoroughly. The 90-minute English-language tours,

Paris' Museums near Tuileries Gardens

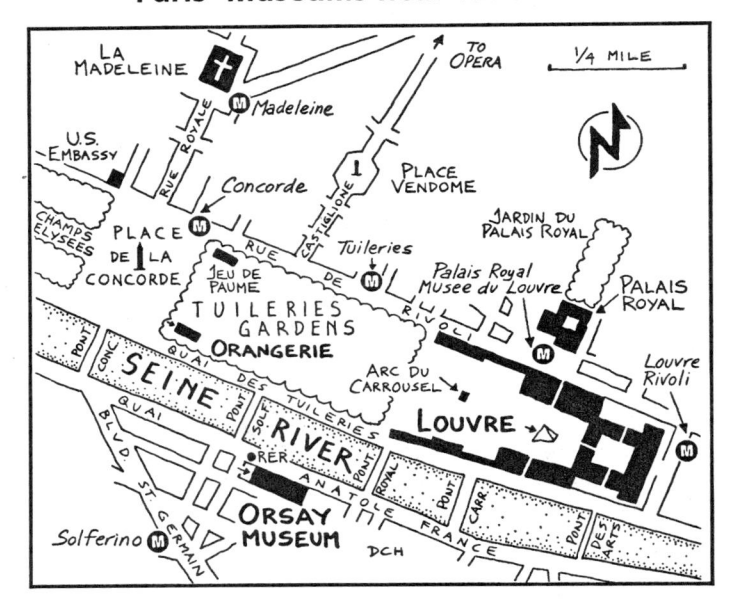

which leave six times daily except Sunday, boil this overwhelming museum down to size (33F, tour tel. 01 40 20 52 09). Clever new 30F digital audio tours (after ticket booths, at top of stairs) give you a receiver and a directory of about 130 masterpieces, allowing you to dial a (rather dull) commentary on included works as you stumble upon them. Rick Steves' and Gene Openshaw's museum guidebook *Rick Steves' Mona Winks* (buy in the United States) includes a self-guided tour of the Louvre.

If you can't get a guide, start in the Denon wing and visit these highlights, in this order: Michelangelo's *Slaves*, Ancient Greek and Roman works (Parthenon frieze, *Venus de Milo*, Pompeii mosaics, Etruscan sarcophagi, Roman portrait busts, *Nike of Samothrace*); Apollo Gallery (jewels); French and Italian paintings in the Grande Galerie (a quarter-mile long and worth the hike); the *Mona Lisa* and her Italian Renaissance roommates; the nearby neoclassical collection (*Coronation of Napoleon*); and the Romantic collection, with works by Delacroix (*Liberty at the Barricades*) and Géricault (*Raft of the Medusa*).

Cost: 45F, 26F after 15:00 and on Sun, those under 18 enter free; free on first Sun of the month. Tickets good all day. Reentry allowed.

Hours: Wed–Mon 9:00–18:00, closed Tue, all wings open Wed until 21:45, Richelieu Wing (only) open until 21:45 on Mon. Galleries start closing 30 minutes early. Closed Jan 1, Easter, May 1, Nov 1, and Christmas Day. Crowds are worst on Sun, Mon, Wed, and mornings. Save money by visiting after 15:00. (You can enter the pyramid for free until 21:30. Go in at night and see it glow.) Tel. 01 40 20 51 51 or 01 40 20 53 17 for recorded information (www.louvre.fr).

The newly renovated Richelieu wing and the underground shopping-mall extension add the finishing touches to Le Grand Louvre Project (which started in 1989 with the pyramid entrance). To explore this most recent extension of the Louvre, enter through the pyramid, walk toward the inverted pyramid, and uncover a post office, a handy TI and SNCF office, glittering boutiques and a dizzying assortment of good-value eateries (up the escalator), and the Palais-Royal Métro entrance. Stairs at the far end take you right into the Tuileries Gardens, a perfect antidote to the stuffy, crowded rooms of the Louvre.

Jeu de Paume—This one-time home to the Impressionist art collection (now located in the Orsay Museum) hosts rotating exhibits of top contemporary artists (38F, Tue 12:00–21:30, Wed–Fri 12:00–19:00, Sat–Sun 10:00–19:00, closed Mon; on place de la Concorde, just inside Tuileries Gardens on the rue de Rivoli side; Mo: Concorde).

L'Orangerie—Closed for renovation.

▲▲▲**Orsay Museum**—Paris' 19th-century art museum (actually, art from 1848 to 1914) includes Europe's greatest collection of Impressionist works. The museum is housed in a former train station (Gare d'Orsay) across the river and 10 minutes downstream from the Louvre. (The RER-C train line zips you right to "Musée d'Orsay"; the Métro stop Solferino is three blocks south of the Orsay.)

Start on the ground floor. The "pretty" conservative establishment art is on the right. Then cross left into the brutally truthful and, at that time, very shocking art of the realist rebels and Manet. Then ride the escalators at the far end (detouring at the top for a grand museum view) to the series of Impressionist rooms (Monet, Renoir, Dégas, et al). Don't miss the Grand Ballroom (room 52, Arts et Decors de la IIIème République) and Art Nouveau on the mezzanine level.

Cost: 40F, 27F for people ages 18 to 25 or over 60, under 18 free, tickets good all day. The booth near the entrance gives free floor plans in English. English-language tours usually run daily except Sun at 11:30, cost 38F, take 90 minutes, and are also available on audiotape. Paris museum passes are sold in the basement; if there's a long line you can skip it by buying one there, but you can't skip the metal detector line into the museum. Tel. 01 40 49 48 48.

Hours: Tue–Wed, Fri–Sat 10:00–18:00, Thu 10:00–21:45,

Sun 9:00–18:00, closed Mon. Museum opens at 9:00 Jun 20 through Sept 20. Last entrance is 45 minutes before closing. Galleries start closing 30 minutes early. The Orsay is very crowded on Tuesday, when the Louvre is closed.

Sights—Southwest Paris: The Eiffel Tower Neighborhood

▲▲▲Eiffel Tower—It's crowded and expensive but worth the trouble. Go early (arrive by 9:15) or late in the day (after 18:00) to avoid most crowds; weekends are worst. Pilier Nord (the north pillar) has the biggest elevator and, therefore, the fastest-moving line.

It's 1,000 feet tall (six inches taller in hot weather), covers 2.5 acres, and requires 50 tons of paint. The tower's 7,000 tons of metal are spread out so well at the base that it's no heavier per square inch than a linebacker on tiptoes. Visitors to Paris may find *Mona Lisa* to be less than expected, but the Eiffel Tower rarely disappoints, even in an era of skyscrapers.

Built a hundred years after the French Revolution (and in the midst of an industrial one), the tower served no function but to impress. Gustave Eiffel won an architectural contest at the 1889 Centennial world's fair by beating out such rival proposals as a giant guillotine. To a generation hooked on technology, the tower was the marvel of the age, a symbol of progress and of man's ingenuity. To others it was a cloned-sheep monstrosity. The writer de Maupassant routinely ate lunch in the tower just so he wouldn't have to look at it.

Delicate and graceful when seen from afar, it's massive—even a bit scary—from close up. You don't appreciate the size until you walk toward it—like a mountain, it seems so close but takes forever to reach. There are three observation platforms, at 200, 400, and 900 feet. The higher you go the more you pay. Each requires a separate elevator (and a line), so plan on at least 90 minutes if you want to go to the top and back. The view from the 400-foot-high second level is plenty. Begin at the first floor, read the informative signs (in English) describing the major monuments, see the entertaining free movie on the history of the tower, and consider a drink overlooking all of Paris at the café or at the reasonable restaurant Altitude 95 (decent 110F meals until 20:00, and Paris' best view bar). Take the elevator to the second floor for even greater views. As you ascend through the metal beams, imagine being a worker, perched high above nothing, riveting this giant erector set together.

On top you can see all of Paris, aided by a panorama guide. On a good day you can see 40 miles. It costs 21F to go to the first level, 43F to the second, and 60F to go all the way for the 1,000-foot view (not included with museum pass). On a budget? You can climb the stairs to the second level for only 15F (summers

Eiffel Tower to Invalides

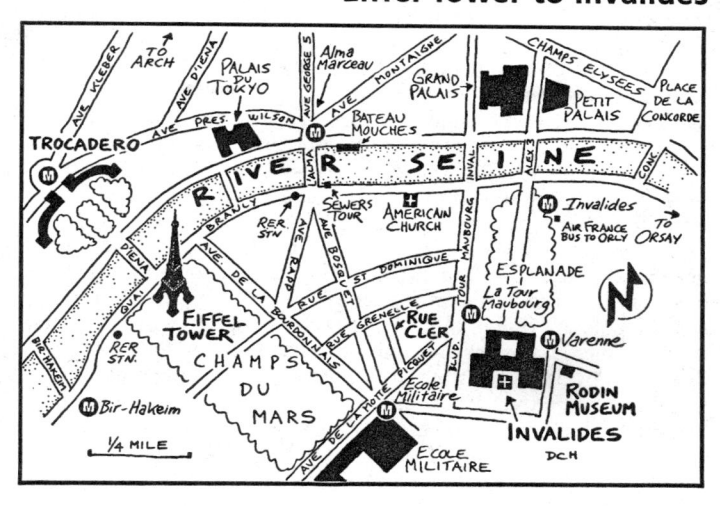

daily 9:00–24:00, off-season 9:30–23:00, tel. 01 44 11 23 23, Mo: Trocadero, RER: Champs de Mars).

For a great view, especially at night, enjoy the tower—and the wild in-line skating scene on Trocadero square—by approaching via the Trocadero Métro stop (from here the tower is a 10-minute walk north, across the river. Another super view is from the long, grassy fields of the Champs du Mars (to the south). After about 21:00 the gendarmes look the other way as Parisians stretch out or picnic on the grass. However impressive it may be by day, it's an awesome thing to see at twilight, when the tower becomes engorged with light and virile Paris lies back and lets night be on top.

▲**Paris Sewer Tour (Egouts)**—This quick and easy visit takes you along a few hundred yards of underground water tunnel lined with interesting displays, well described in English, explaining the evolution of the world's longest sewer system. (If you lined up Paris' sewers they would reach beyond Istanbul.) Don't miss the slideshow, the fine WCs just beyond the gift shop, and the occasional tours in English (25F, Sat–Wed 11:00–17:00, closed Thu–Fri, where the pont de l'Alma hits the Left Bank, tel. 01 47 05 10 29).

▲▲ **Napoleon's Tomb and Army Museum (Les Invalides)**—The emperor lies majestically dead inside several coffins under a grand dome—a goose-bumping pilgrimage for historians. Napoleon is surrounded by the tombs of other French war heroes and Europe's greatest military museum in the Hôtel des Invalides.

Follow signs to the "crypt," where you'll find Roman Empire–style reliefs listing the accomplishments of Napoleon's administration. The restored dome glitters with 26 pounds of gold (38F, daily 10:00–17:45, off-season 16:45, tel. 01 44 42 37 67, Métros: La Tour Maubourg or Varennes).

▲▲Rodin Museum—This user-friendly museum is filled with passionate works by the greatest sculptor since Michelangelo. See *The Kiss, The Thinker, The Gates of Hell,* and many more. Don't miss the room full of work by Rodin's student and mistress, Camille Claudel (28F, 18F on Sun; 5F for gardens only, which may be Paris' best deal, as many works are well displayed in the beautiful gardens; Tue–Sun 9:30–17:45, closed Mon and at 17:00 off-season, 77 rue de Varennes, tel. 01 44 18 61 10, Mo: Varennes, near Napoleon's Tomb). There's a good self-serve cafeteria as well as idyllic picnic spots in the family-friendly back garden.

▲▲Marmottan—In this private, intimate, less-visited museum you'll find more than 100 paintings by Claude Monet (thanks to his son Michel), including the *Impressions of a Sunrise* painting that gave the movement its start—and name (40F, Tue–Sun 10:00–17:30, closed Mon, no museum pass, 2 rue Louis Boilly, Mo: La Muette, follow the museum signs 6 blocks through a park to the museum, tel. 01 42 24 07 02). Combine this fine museum with a stroll down one of Paris' most pleasant shopping streets, the rue de Passy (from la Muette Mo. stop).

Sights—Southeast Paris: The Latin Quarter

▲Latin Quarter—This Left Bank neighborhood just opposite Notre-Dame is the Latin Quarter. (For more information and a walking tour, see "'Historic Core of Paris' Walk," above.) This was a center of Roman Paris. But its touristic fame relates to the Latin Quarter's intriguing artsy, bohemian character. This was perhaps Europe's leading university district in the Middle Ages—home, since the 13th century, to the prestigious Sorbonne University. Back then, Latin was the language of higher education. And, since students here came from all over Europe, Latin served as their linguistic common denominator. Locals referred to the quarter by its language: Latin. In modern times this was the center of Paris' café culture. The neighborhood's main boulevards (St. Michel and St. Germain) are lined with cafés—once the haunts of great poets and philosophers but now the hangout of tired tourists. While still youthful and artsy, the area has become a tourist ghetto filled with cheap North African eateries.

▲Cluny Museum (Musée National du Moyen Age)—This treasure trove of medieval art fills the old Roman baths, offering close-up looks at stained glass, Notre-Dame carvings, fine goldsmithing and jewelry, and rooms of tapestries—the best of which is the exquisite *Lady with the Unicorn*. In five panels, a delicate-as-medieval-can-be noble lady introduces a delighted unicorn to the senses of taste, hearing, sight, smell, and touch (38F, Wed–Mon 9:15–17:45, closed Tue, 6 place Paul-Painlevé near the corner of boulevards St. Michel and St. Germain, tel. 01 53 73 78 00, Mo: Cluny).

St. Germain des Prés—A church was first built on this site in A.D. 452. The church you see today was constructed in 1163. The area around the church hops at night with fire eaters, mimes, and scads of artists (Mo: St. Germain-des-Prés).

▲**St. Sulpice Organ Concert**—For pipe-organ enthusiasts, this is a delight. The Grand-Orgue at St. Sulpice has a rich history, with a line of 12 world-class organists (including Widor and Dupre) going back 300 years. Widor started the tradition of opening the loft to visitors after the 10:30 service on Sundays. Daniel Roth continues to welcome guests in three languages while playing five keyboards at once. The 10:30 Sunday Mass is followed by a 20-minute recital at 11:40. If you're lucky, at 12:00 the small unmarked door will open (left of entry as you face the rear) and allow visitors to scamper like sixteenth notes up spiral stairs to a world of 7,000 pipes, where they can watch the master perform the next Mass, friends warming his bench, and a committee scrambling to pull and push the 102 stops (Mo: St. Sulpice or Mabillon).

▲**Luxembourg Gardens**—Paris' most beautiful, interesting, and enjoyable garden/park/recreational area is a great place to watch Parisians at rest and play. Bring your kids to the playground (southwest corner) or afternoon puppet shows (*guignols*). Challenge the card and chess players to a game (near the tennis courts) or find a chair near the main pond and take a breather. Paris Walking Tours offers a good tour of the park (see "Organized Tours," above). The grand neoclassical-domed Panthéon (now a mausoleum housing the tombs of several great Frenchmen) is a block away but only worth entering if you have a museum pass. The park is open until dusk (Mo: Odéon). If you enjoy these gardens and want to see more, visit the more elegant Parc Monceau (Mo: Monceau) and the colorful Jardin des Plantes (Mo: Jussieu).

▲**Montparnasse Tower**—This 59-floor superscraper—it's cheaper and easier to get to the top than to that of the Eiffel Tower—offers one of Paris' best views, since the Eiffel Tower is in it and the Montparnasse tower isn't. Buy the photo guide to the city, then go to the rooftop and orient yourself (46F, daily in summer 9:30–23:00, off-season 10:00–22:00, disappointing after dark, entrance on rue l'Arrivé, Mo: Montparnasse). This is efficient when combined with a day trip to Chartres, which begins at the Montparnasse train station.

Sights—Northwest Paris
▲▲**Place de la Concorde and the Champs-Élysées**—This famous boulevard is Paris' backbone and greatest concentration

of traffic. All of France seems to converge on the place de la Concorde, the city's largest square. It was here that the guillotine took the lives of thousands—including King Louis XVI and Marie Antoinette. Back then it was called the place de la Revolution.

Catherine de Médici wanted a place to drive her carriage, so she started draining the swamp that would become the Champs-Élysées. Napoleon put on the final touches, and it's been the place to be seen ever since. The Tour de France bicycle race ends here, as do all parades (French or foe) of any significance. While the boulevard has become a bit hamburgerized, a walk here is a must. Take the Métro to the Arc de Triomphe (Mo: Étoile) and saunter down the Champs-Élysées (Métro stops every few blocks: FDR, George V, and Étoile).

▲▲▲**Arc de Triomphe**—Napoleon had the magnificent Arc de Triomphe commissioned to commemorate his victory at the Battle of Austerlitz. There's no triumphal arch bigger (50 meters high, 40 meters wide). And, with 12 converging boulevards, there's no traffic circle more thrilling to experience—either behind the wheel or on foot (take the underpass). An elevator or a spiral staircase leads to a cute museum about the arch and a grand view from the top, even after dark (40F, daily 9:30–23:00, Oct–May daily 9:30–22:00, tel. 01 43 80 31 31, Mo: Étoile).

▲**Grande Arche de la Defense**—The centerpiece of Paris' ambitious skyscraper complex (La Defense) is the Grande Arche. Built to celebrate the 200th anniversary of the 1789 French Revolution, the place is big—38 floors on more than 200 acres. It holds offices for 30,000 people. Notre-Dame Cathedral could fit under its arch. The La Defense complex is an interesting study in 1960s land-use planning. More than 100,000 workers commute here daily, directing lots of business and development away from downtown and allowing central Paris to retain its more elegant feel. This aspect makes sense to most Parisians, regardless of whatever else they feel about the controversial complex. You'll enjoy city views from the Arche elevator (43F includes a film on its construction and art exhibits, daily 10:00–19:00, tel. 01 49 07 27 57, Métro or RER: La Defense, follow signs to Grande Arche).

Sights—Northeast Paris: Marais Neighborhood and More

▲▲**Museum of Art and History of Judaism (Hotel d'Aignan)**—This remarkable new museum located in a beautifully restored Marais mansion tells the story of *Judaisme* throughout Europe, from the Roman destruction of Jerusalem to the theft of famous art works during World War II. Helpful audiophones and many English explanations make this an enjoyable history lesson (red numbers on small signs indicate the number you should press on your audiophone followed by the play button). Move along at your own speed. The emphasis of the museum is to illustrate the cultural unity maintained by this continually dispersed population. You'll learn about the history of Jewish traditions, from bar mitzvahs to menorahs, and see exquisite traditional costumes and objects around which daily life revolved. Don't miss the explanation of the Dreyfus affair, a major event in early 1900 French politics. You'll also see photographs of and paintings by famous Jewish artists, including Chagall, Modigliani, and Soutine. The small section devoted to the deportation of Jews from Paris is very moving (40F, not covered with museum pass, Sun 10:00–18:00, Mon–Fri 11:00–18:00, closed Sat, 71 rue du Temple, tel. 01 53 01 86 53).

▲Picasso Museum (Hôtel Salé)—This is the world's largest collection of Pablo Picasso's paintings, sculpture, sketches, and ceramics and includes his personal collection of Impressionist art. It's well explained in English and worth ▲▲▲ if you're a fan (30F, Wed–Mon 9:30–18:00, closed Tue, 5 rue Thorigny, Mo: St. Paul or Chemin Vert, tel. 01 42 71 25 21).

▲Carnavalet Museum—The tumultuous history of Paris is well displayed in this converted Marais mansion. Unfortunately, explanations are in French only, but many displays are fairly self-explanatory. You'll see paintings of Parisian scenes, French Revolution paraphernalia, old Parisian store signs, a small guillotine, a model of 16th-century Île de la Cité (notice the bridge houses), and rooms full of 15th-century Parisian furniture. The medieval rooms and Revolution rooms are the most interesting (35F, Tue–Sun 10:00–17:00, closed Mon, 23 rue de Sévigné, Mo: St Paul, tel. 01 42 72 21 13).

Victor Hugo's House—France's literary giant lived in this fine house on the place des Vosges from 1832 to 1848. Inside you'll find many posters advertising theater productions of his works, paintings of some of his most famous character creations, and a few furnished rooms (22F, Tue–Sun 10:00–17:40, closed Mon, 6 place des Vosges).

Promenade Plantée Park—This three-kilometer narrow garden walk, once a train track and now a joy, runs from place de la Bastille (Mo: Bastille) along avenue Daumesnil to Saint-Mandé (Mo: Michel Bizot). Part of the park is elevated. At times you'll walk along the street till you pick up the next segment. From place de la Bastille, take avenue Daumesnil (past Opéra building) to the intersection with avenue Ledru Rollin; walk up the stairs and through the gate (free, hours vary with season, open roughly 8:00–20:00).

▲Père Lachaise Cemetery—Littered with the tombstones of many of the city's most illustrious dead, this is your best one-stop look at the fascinating, romantic world of permanent Parisians. The place is confusing, but maps will direct you to the graves of Chopin, Molière, Edith Piaf, Oscar Wilde, Gertrude Stein, Héloïse

and Abelard, and even the American rock star Jim Morrison (who died in Paris). In section 92, a series of statues memorializing the war makes the French war experience a bit more real (helpful 10F maps at the flower store near the entry, across the street from Métro stop, closes at dusk, Mo: Père Lachaise or bus #69).
▲▲**Pompidou Center**—Europe's greatest collection of far-out modern art, the Musée National d'Art Moderne, is housed on the top floor of this newly renovated and colorful exoskeletal building. Once ahead of its time, this 20th-century art (remember that century?) has been waiting for the world to catch up with it. After so many Madonnas and Children, a piano smashed to bits and glued to the wall is refreshing. The center and its square are lively, with lots of people, street theater, and activity inside and out—a perpetual street fair. Ride the escalator for a great city view from the café terrace on top and don't miss the free exhibits on the ground floor (50F, Tue–Fri 10:00–17:30, Sat–Sun and most holidays 10:00–19:00, closed Mon, Mo: Rambuteau, tel. 01 44 78 12 33). Kids of any age enjoy the fun, colorful fountain (called *Homage to Stravinsky*) next to the Pompidou Center.

Sights—North Paris: Montmartre

▲**Sacré-Coeur and Montmartre**—This Byzantine-looking church, while only 130 years old, is impressive. It was built as a "praise the Lord anyway" gesture after the French were humiliated by the Germans in a brief war in 1871. The church is open daily until 23:00. One block from the church, the place du Tertre was the haunt of Toulouse-Lautrec and the original Bohemians. Today it's mobbed by tourists and unoriginal bohemians but still fun. Wander down the rue Lepic to the two remaining windmills (once there were 30). Rue des Saules leads to Paris' only vineyard. Métros: Anvers (an extra Métro ticket buys your way up the funicular and avoids the stairs) or the closer but less scenic Abbesses. A taxi to the top of the hill saves time and sweat.
Pigalle—Paris' red-light district, the infamous "Pig Alley," is at the foot of Butte Montmartre. Ooh la la. More shocking than dangerous. Walk from place Pigalle to place Blanche, teasing desperate barkers and fast-talking temptresses. In bars a 1,000F bottle of cheap champagne comes with a friend. Stick to the bigger streets, hang on to your wallet, and exercise good judgment. Cancan can cost a fortune, as can con artists in topless bars. After dark, countless tour buses line the streets, reminding us that tour guides make big bucks by bringing their groups to touristic nightclubs like the famous Moulin Rouge (Mo: Pigalle and Abbesses).

Best Shopping

Forum des Halles is a huge subterranean shopping center. It's fun, mod, and colorful but lacks a soul (Mo: Les Halles). The

Galeries Lafayette behind the opera house is your best elegant, Old World, one-stop Parisian department store/shopping center. Also visit the adjacent **Printemps** store and the historic (as well as handy) **Samaritaine** department store in several buildings near Pont Neuf (Mo: Pont Neuf). Ritzy shops surround the Ritz Hotel at **place Vendôme** (Mo: Tuileries).

Disappointments *de* Paris

While Paris can drive you in-Seine with superlatives, here are a few negatives to help you manage your limited time:

La Madeleine is a big, stark, neoclassical church with a postcard facade and a postbox interior. The famous aristocratic deli behind the church, Fauchon, is elegant, but so are many others handier to your hotel.

The old Opéra Garnier has a great Chagall-painted ceiling but is in a pedestrian-mean area. Don't go to American Express (behind the Opéra) just to change money. You'll get a better rate at many other banks.

Paris' Panthéon (nothing like Rome's) is another stark, neoclassical edifice filled with mortal remains of great Frenchmen who mean little to the average American tourist.

The Bastille is Paris' most famous nonsight. The square is there, but confused tourists look everywhere and can't find the famous prison of Revolution fame. The building's gone.

The Latin Quarter is a frail shadow of its characteristic self. It's more Tunisian, Greek, and Woolworth's than old-time Paris. The café life that turned on Hemingway and endeared Boul Miche and boulevard St. Germain to so many poets is also trampled by modern commercialism.

Palace of Versailles

Every king's dream, Versailles was the residence of the French king and the cultural heartbeat of Europe for about 100 years—until the Revolution of 1789 ended the notion that God deputized some people to rule for Him on Earth. Louis XIV spent half a year's income of Europe's richest country turning his dad's hunting lodge into a palace fit for a divine monarch. Louis XV and Louis XVI spent much of the 18th century gilding Louis XIV's lily. In 1837, about 50 years after the royal family was evicted, King Louis Philippe opened the palace as a museum. Europe's next-best palaces are Versailles wanna-bes.

Information: There's a helpful TI across the street from Versailles' R.G. station (tel. 01 39 50 36 22), two information desks on the approach to the palace, and a very helpful TI at entrance C. The useful brochure, "Versailles Orientation Guide," explains your sightseeing options. Versailles info: tel. 01 30 84 76 18 or 01 30 84 74 00. WC and phones are near the main entrance.

Versailles

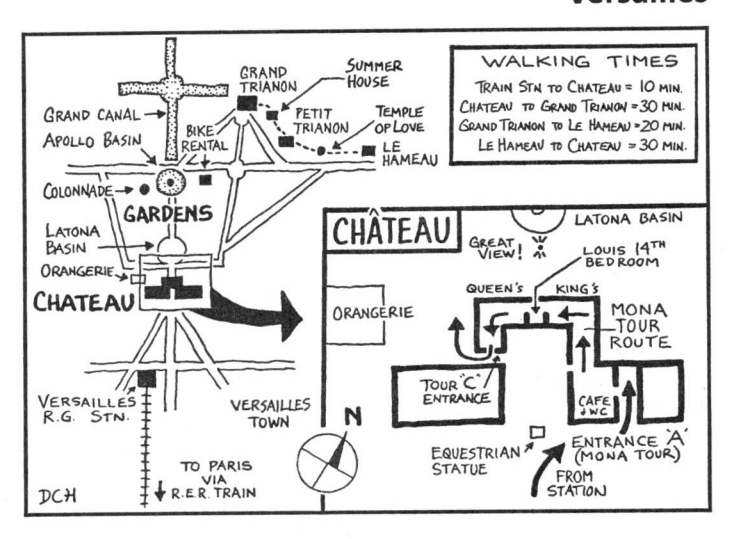

Ticket Options: The self-guided one-way palace romp, including the Hall of Mirrors, costs 45F (covered by museum pass, 35F after 15:30, on Sun, or for those over 60 or ages 18–25; under 18 free). To supplement this with a guided tour through the other sections, you'll need to pay the 45F base price then add 25F for a one-hour guided tour, 37F for a 90-minute guided tour, or 30F for a self-guided Walkman-cassette tour—tours aren't covered by the museum pass. (Tip: If you're waiting for your tour time, have finished a tour, or have a museum pass, you can go directly into the main palace with no line at the B gate and explore the palace on your own.) In the gardens, you can see the Grand and Petit Trianon palaces for 30F total (payable at the site).

Hours: Tue–Sun 9:00–18:30, closed Mon; Oct–Apr Tue–Sun 9:00–17:30; last entry 30 minutes before closing. Versailles is especially crowded around 10:00 and 13:00, Tue and Sun. To minimize crowds and get a reduced entry ticket, arrive after 15:30. Tour the gardens after the palace closes. The palace is great late. On my last visit, at 18:00, I was the only tourist in the Hall of Mirrors...even on a Tuesday.

Time to Allow: Six hours round-trip from Paris (an hour each way in transit, two hours for the palace, two for the grounds).

Self-Guided Tour: For the basic self-guided tour, join the line at entrance A1. Those with a Paris Museum Card are allowed in through entrance B without a wait. Enter the palace and take a one-way walk through the state apartments from the "King's Wing," through the magnificent Hall of Mirrors, and out via the "Queen's Wing."

The Hall of Mirrors was the ultimate hall of the day—250 feet long, 17 arched mirrors matching 17 windows with royal garden views, 24 gilded candelabra, eight busts of Roman emperors, and eight classical-style statues (seven of them actually ancient originals). The ceiling is decorated with stories of Louis' triumphs. Imagine this place filled with silk gowns and powdered wigs, lit by thousands of candles. The mirrors—a luxurious rarity at the time—were a reflection of a time when aristocrats felt good about their looks and their fortunes. In another age altogether, this was the room in which the Treaty of Versailles was signed, ending World War I.

Before going downstairs at the end, take a stroll clockwise around the long room filled with the great battles of France murals. If you don't have *Rick Steves' Paris* or *Rick Steves' Mona Winks*, the guidebook called *The Châteaux, The Gardens, and Trianon* gives a room-by-room rundown.

Guided Tours: For a guided tour, pay the 45F base-price admission at the same time you pay for your tour (at entrance D). The 60- or 90-minute tours, led by an English-speaking art historian, take you through sections of Versailles not included in the base-price visit. Groups are limited to 30. Of the several tours offered, the 90-minute version covering Louis XV and Louis XVI's apartments and the opera is best. Pay and get your tour appointment at entrance D. Tour times are normally all allotted for the day by 13:00. Tours leave from entrance F.

Walkman Tour: If you're in a hurry, the self-guided Walkman-cassette tour of the king's chamber (30F, entrance C, last entry at 15:00) covers Louis XIV's rooms and is a good option.

Palace Gardens: The gardens offer a world of royal amusements. Outside the palace is L'Orangerie. Louis, the only one who could grow oranges in Paris, had an orange grove on wheels that could be wheeled in and out of his greenhouses according to the weather. A promenade leads from the palace to the Grand Canal, an artificial lake that, in Louis' day, was a mini-sea with nine ships, including a 32-cannon warship. France's royalty used to float up and down the canal in Venetian gondolas.

While Louis cleverly used palace life at Versailles to "domesticate" his nobility, turning otherwise meddlesome nobles into groveling socialites, all this pomp and ceremony hampered the royal family as well. For an escape from the public life at Versailles, they built more intimate palaces as retreats in their garden. Before the Revolution there was plenty of space to retreat—the grounds were enclosed by a 25-mile-long fence.

The beautifully restored **Grand Trianon Palace** is as sumptuous as the main palace but much smaller. With its pastel pink colonnade and more human scale, this is a place you'd like to call home. (See hours and prices below.)

The nearby **Petit Trianon**, which has a fine neoclassical exterior with a skippable interior, was Marie Antoinette's favorite residence.

You can almost see princesses bobbing gaily in the branches as you walk through the enchanting forest, past the white marble temple of love (1778) to the queen's fake-peasant hamlet (*hameau*; interior not tourable). Palace life really got to Marie Antoinette. Sort of a back-to-basics queen, she retreated further and further from her blue-blooded reality. Her happiest days were at the hamlet, under a bonnet, tending her perfumed sheep and her manicured gardens in a thatch-happy wonderland.

Getting around the Gardens: It's a 30-minute hike from the palace, down the canal, past the two mini-palaces to the hamlet. You can rent bikes (30F/hr). The pokey tourist train, which costs only 10F, runs between the canal and château (30F, 5/hrly, 4 stops, you can hop on and off as you like; nearly worthless commentary).

Garden Hours and Admissions: Except for fountain-filled Sundays (below), the gardens are free and open from 7:00 to sunset (as late as 21:30). Grand and Petit Trianon are open May–Sept Tue–Sun 10:00–18:00, closed Mon; off-season 10:00–17:00 (Grand Trianon-25F, Petit Trianon-15F, 30F for both). The park is picnic-perfect. Food is not allowed into the palace, but those with a picnic can check bags (and picnics) at doors A or C. There's a kiosk selling good sandwiches, and there's a decent restaurant on the canal in the gardens.

Fountain Spectacles: Every Sunday from May through October, music fills the king's backyard and the garden's fountains are in full squirt (from 11:15–11:35 and 15:30–17:00, 25F garden admission on these days only). Louis had his engineers literally reroute a river to fuel these fountains. Even by today's standards they are impressive.

Getting to Versailles: From Paris, take the RER-C train (28F round-trip, 30 min) to "Versailles R.G.," not "Versailles C.H.," which is farther from the palace. Trains, usually named "Vick," leave about five times an hour for the palace. Get off at Versailles Rive Gauche (the end of the line). RER-C trains leave from these RER/Metro stops: "Invalides" (Napoleon's Tomb, Military Museum, Rodin Museum), "Champ de Mars" (Eiffel Tower), "Musée d'Orsay," "St. Michel" (Notre-Dame, Latin Quarter), and "Gare d'Austerlitz." Leaving the station, turn right, then left on the major boulevard (10-minute walk). (The RER trip is free with a railpass but uses up a flexi-day; consider seeing Versailles on your way in or out of Paris. To get free passage, show your railpass at an SCNF ticket window—for example at the Les Invalides or Musée d'Orsay RER stops—to get a *contremarque de* *passage*; keep this ticket to exit the system.) When returning look through the windows past the turnstiles for the departure board. Any train leaving Versailles goes as far as downtown Paris (they're marked "all stations until Austerlitz"). If you're uncertain, confirm with a local by asking, "*À Paris?*" ("To Paris?").

The 100F Paris–Versailles taxi fare is economical for groups of three or four or for people with more money than time. To cut your park walking by 50 percent, consider having the taxi drop you at the Hamlet (Hameau).

Town of Versailles (zip code: 78000): After the palace closes and the tourists go, the prosperous, wholesome town of Versailles feels a long way from Paris. The central market thrives on Tuesday, Friday, and Saturday until 13:00 (place du Marché; leaving the RER station, turn right and walk 10 minutes). Consider the wisdom of picking up or dropping your rental car in Versailles rather than in Paris. In Versailles, the Hertz and Avis offices are at the Gare des Chantiers (Versailles C.H., served by Paris' Montparnasse station). Versailles makes a fine home base; see Versailles accommodations under "Sleeping," below.

More Day Trips from Paris

▲▲▲**Chartres**—In 1194 a terrible fire destroyed the church at Chartres that housed the much-venerated veil of Mary. With almost unbelievably good fortune, the monks found the veil miraculously preserved in the ashes. Money poured in for the building of a bigger and better cathedral—decorated with 2,000 carved figures and some of France's best stained glass. The cathedral feels too large for the city because it was designed to accommodate huge crowds of pilgrims. One of those pilgrims, an impressed Napoleon, declared after a visit in 1811: "Chartres is no place for an atheist." Rodin called it "the Acropolis of France." British Francophile Malcolm Miller or his impressive assistant give great "Appreciation of Gothic" tours Monday through Saturday, usually at 12:00 and 14:45 (verify times in advance, no tours off-season, call TI at 02 37 18 26 26). Each 40F tour is different; many people stay for both tours. Just show up at the church (daily 7:00–19:00).

Explore Chartres' pleasant city center and discover the picnic-friendly park behind the cathedral. The helpful TI, next to the cathedral, has a map with a self-guided tour of Chartres (daily 9:30–18:45). Chartres is a one-hour train trip from the Gare Montparnasse (75F one way, 10/day, last train on Sat departs at about 19:00). Upon arrival, confirm your return schedule to avoid an unplanned night in Chartres.

▲**Giverny**—Monet spent 43 of his most creative years (1883–1926) here at the Camp David of Impressionism. Monet's gardens and home are split by a busy road. Buy your ticket, walk through

Chartres

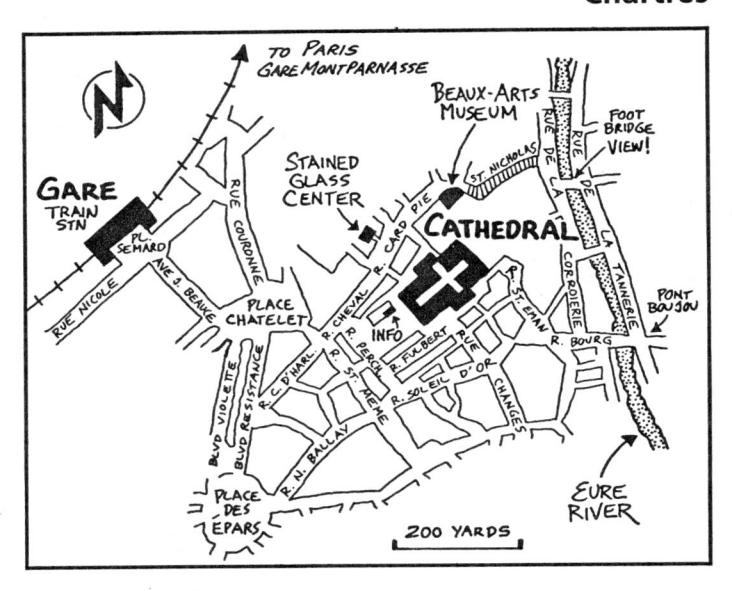

the gardens, and take the underpass into the artist's famous lilypad land. The path leads you over the Japanese Bridge, under weeping willows, and past countless scenes that leave artists aching for an easel. For Monet fans, it's strangely nostalgic. Back on the other side, continue your visit with a wander through his more robust and structured garden and his mildly interesting home. The jammed gift shop at the exit is the actual skylit studio where Monet painted his waterlily masterpieces.

While lines may be long and tour groups may trample the flowers, true fans still find magic in those lilypads. Avoid crowds by arriving after 16:00 (35F, 25F for gardens only, Apr–Oct Tue–Sun 10:00–18:00, closed Mon and off-season, tel. 02 32 51 94 65). Take the Rouen-bound train from Paris' Gare St. Lazare station to Vernon (about 140F round-trip, long gaps in service, know the schedule before you go). To get from the Vernon train station to Monet's garden (4 kilometers away), take the Vernon–Giverny bus (5/day, scheduled to meet most trains), hitch, taxi (60F), or rent a bike at the station (60F, busy road). Get return bus times from the ticket office in Giverny or ask them to call a taxi. Big tour companies do a Giverny day trip from Paris for around $60.

The new **American Impressionist Art Museum** (100 yards

Paris Day Trips

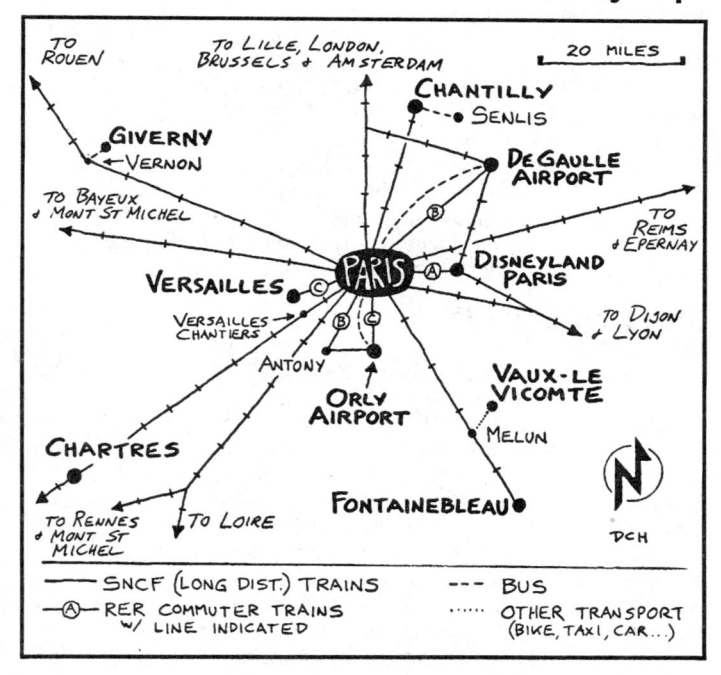

Map showing Paris and surrounding day trip destinations including Rouen, Lille/London/Brussels/Amsterdam, Chantilly, Senlis, Giverny, Vernon, De Gaulle Airport, Bayeux & Mont St Michel, Reims & Epernay, Versailles, Versailles Chantiers, Disneyland Paris, Dijon & Lyon, Antony, Vaux-le Vicomte, Orly Airport, Melun, Chartres, Fontainebleau, Rennes & Mont St Michel, Loire. Legend: SNCF (long dist.) trains, RER commuter trains w/ line indicated, Bus, Other transport (bike, taxi, car...). 20 miles scale. DCH.

from Monet's place) is devoted to American artists who followed Claude to Giverny. Giverny had a great influence on American artists of Monet's day. This bright, modern gallery is well explained in English, has a good little Mary Cassatt section, and gives Americans a rare chance to see French people appreciating our artists (same price and hours as Monet's home, pleasant café).

▲▲**Disneyland Paris**—Europe's Disneyland is basically a modern remake of California's, with most of the same rides and smiles. The main difference is that Mickey Mouse speaks French (and you can buy wine with your lunch). My kids went ducky. Locals love it. It's worth a day if Paris is handier than Florida or California. If possible, avoid Saturday, Sunday, Wednesday, school holidays, and July and August. The park can get very crowded. When 60,000 have entered, they close the gates (tel. 01 64 74 30 00 for the latest). After dinner, crowds are gone, and you'll walk right onto rides that had a 45-minute wait three hours earlier. Food is fun but expensive. Smuggle in a picnic.

Disney brochures are in every Paris hotel. The RER (43F

each way, direct from downtown Paris to Marne-la-Vallee in 30 minutes) drops you right into the park. The last train back into Paris leaves shortly after midnight (220F for adults, 170F for kids ages 3–11, 25F less in spring and fall, daily 9:00–23:00 late Jun–early Sept and Sat and Sun off-season, shoulder-season weekdays 9:00–19:00, off-season 10:00–18:00, tel. 01 60 30 60 30, fax 01 60 30 60 65 for park and hotel reservations).

To sleep reasonably at the huge Disney complex, try Hotel Sante Fe (780F family rooms for two to four people includes breakfast, less off-season; ask for their hotel-and-park package deal). If all this ain't enough, a new Planet Hollywood restaurant opened just outside the park a five-minute walk from the RER stop.

Sleeping in Paris
(6F = about $1)
Sleep Code: **S** = Single, **D** = Double/Twin, **T** = Triple, **Q** = Quad, **b** = bathroom, **t** = toilet only, **s** = shower only, **CC** = Credit Card (Visa, MasterCard, Amex), * = French hotel rating system (0–4 stars).

I've focused on three safe, handy, and colorful neighborhoods: rue Cler, Marais, and Contrescarpe. For each, I list good hotels, helpful hints, and restaurants (see "Eating," below). At the end of this section you'll find accommodations listed for Versailles.

Reserve ahead for Paris—the sooner the better. Conventions clog Paris in September (worst), October, May, and June. In August, when Paris is quiet, some hotels offer lower rates to fill their rooms (if you're planning to visit Paris in the summer, the extra expense of an air-conditioned room is money well spent for some). Most hotels accept telephone reservations, require prepayment with a credit-card number, and prefer a faxed follow-up to be sure everything is in order. For more information, see "Making Reservations" in this book's introduction.

French hotels are rated by stars (indicated in this chapter by an *). One star is simple, two has most of the comforts, and three is, for this book, plush. If you need maximum comfort, go for the three-star places.

Old, characteristic, budget Parisian hotels have always been cramped. Retrofitted with elevators, toilets, and private showers (as most are today), they are even more cramped. Even three-star hotel rooms are small and generally not worth the extra expense in Paris. Some hotels include the hotel tax (*taxe de sejour*, about 5F per person per day), though most will add this to your bill. Two-star hotels are required to have an English-speaking staff. Nearly all hotels listed will have someone who speaks English.

Quad rooms usually have two double beds. Recommended hotels have an elevator unless otherwise noted. Because rooms with double beds and showers are cheaper than rooms with twin beds and baths, room prices vary within each hotel.

You can save as much as 100F by finding the increasingly rare room without a private shower, though some hotels charge for down-the-hall showers. Breakfasts cost 20F to 50F extra. Café or picnic breakfasts are cheaper, but hotels usually give unlimited coffee. Singles (except for the rare closet-type rooms that fit only one twin bed) are simply doubles used by one person. They rent for only a little less than a double.

Get advice for safe parking from your hotel. Meters are free in August. Garages are plentiful (90–140F per day, with special rates through some hotels). Self-serve Laundromats are common; ask your hotelier for the nearest one (*"Où est un laverie automatique?"*; ooh ay uh lah-vree auto-mah-teek).

Sleeping in the Rue Cler Neighborhood
(7th arrondissement, Mo: École Militaire, zip code: 75007)
Rue Cler, a villagelike pedestrian street, is safe and tidy and makes me feel like I must have been a poodle in a previous life. How such coziness lodged itself between the high-powered government/business district and the expensive Eiffel Tower and Invalides areas I'll never know. Living here ranks with the top museums as one of the city's great experiences (but if you're into nightlife, consider one of the other two neighborhoods I list).

The street called rue Cler is the glue that holds this pleasant neighborhood together. From rue Cler you can walk to the Eiffel Tower, Napoleon's Tomb, the Seine, and the Orsay and Rodin Museums. The first six hotels listed below are within Camembert-smelling distance of the rue Cler; the others are within a 5- or 10-minute stroll. Warning: The first two hotels are popular with my readers.

Hôtel Leveque** is ideally located and has an air-conditioned lobby (with ice machine), helpful staff, and a singing maid. Its well-designed, comfortable rooms have ceiling fans, cable TV, hair dryers, direct phone lines, French modem outlets, and safes (S-300F, Db-400–470F, Tb-580F, breakfast-30F, 1st breakfast free for readers of this book, CC:VMA, 29 rue Cler, tel. 01 47 05 49 15, fax 01 45 50 49 36, www.hotel-leveque.com, e-mail: leveque @gofornet.com).

Hôtel du Champs de Mars**, with charming, pastel rooms and helpful English-speaking owners Françoise and Stephane, is an even cosier rue Cler option. The hotel has a Provence-style small-town feel from top to bottom. Rooms are comfortable and a very good value. Single rooms can work as tiny doubles (Sb-390F, Db-430–460F, Tb-550F, CC:VMA, cable TV, hair dryers, etc., 30 yards off rue Cler at 7 rue du Champs de Mars, tel. 01 45 51 52 30, fax 01 45 51 64 36, www.adx.fr/hotel-du-champ-de-mars, e-mail: stg@club-internet.fr).

Hôtel la Serre*, across the street from the Hotel Leveque, is

Rue Cler Hotels

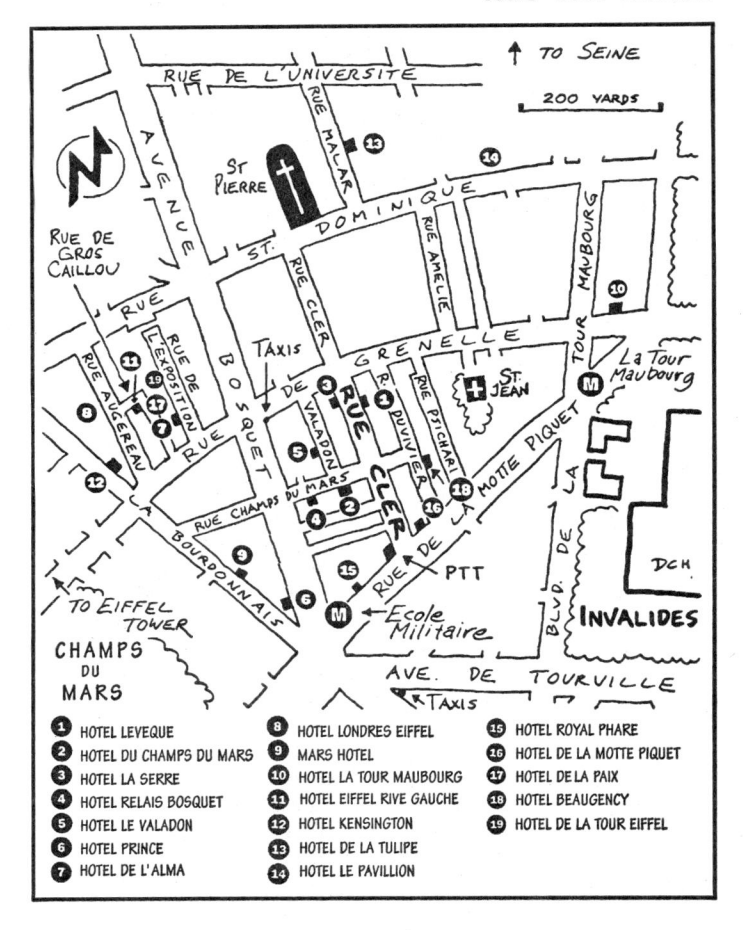

1. HOTEL LEVEQUE
2. HOTEL DU CHAMPS DU MARS
3. HOTEL LA SERRE
4. HOTEL RELAIS BOSQUET
5. HOTEL LE VALADON
6. HOTEL PRINCE
7. HOTEL DE L'ALMA
8. HOTEL LONDRES EIFFEL
9. MARS HOTEL
10. HOTEL LA TOUR MAUBOURG
11. HOTEL EIFFEL RIVE GAUCHE
12. HOTEL KENSINGTON
13. HOTEL DE LA TULIPE
14. HOTEL LE PAVILLON
15. HOTEL ROYAL PHARE
16. HOTEL DE LA MOTTE PIQUET
17. HOTEL DE LA PAIX
18. HOTEL BEAUGENCY
19. HOTEL DE LA TOUR EIFFEL

a simple hotel with basic rooms, thin walls, tattered hallways, and a charming location. Beware: You'll likely be asked to pay before seeing the room, and refunds are rarely given (D-280F, Db-280–450F, Tb-550F, cable TV in some rooms, CC:VM, 24 rue Cler, tel. 01 47 05 52 33, fax 01 40 62 95 66, e-mail: laserre@easynet.fr).

Hôtel Relais Bosquet*** is bright, spacious, and a bit upscale with sharp, comfortable rooms (Sb-600–800F, Db-650–1,000F, most at 850F, more expensive rooms with air-con, CC:VMA, 19 rue de Champs de Mars, tel. 01 47 05 25 45, fax 01 45 55 08 24, www.relaisbosquet.com).

Hotel Beaugency*** offers basic three-star comfort for less (Sb-680F, Db-730F, Tb-830F includes a buffet breakfast, 21 rue Duvivier, tel. 01 47 05 01 63, fax 01 45 51 04 96).

Hôtel Le Valadon**, on a quiet street with spacious, tired rooms, has a shy Parisian cuteness (Db-410–530F, Tb-560F, CC:VMA, 16 rue Valadon, tel. 01 47 53 89 85, fax 01 44 18 90 56).

These listings are a 5- to 10-minute walk west of the rue Cler and are listed in order of proximity.

Hotel Prince**, just across avenue Bosquet from École Militaire Métro, has fair-value rooms, many overlooking a busy street (Db-450–510F, CC:VMA, 66 avenue Bosquet, tel. 01 47 05 40 90, fax 01 47 53 06 62).

Hotel le Tourville**** is the most classy and expensive of my Paris listings. This four-star gem is surprisingly intimate and friendly from its welcoming lobby to air-conditioned pink-pastel rooms (small standard Db-690–900F, superior Db-800–1,150F, Db with private terrace-1,450F, 16 avenue de Tourville, Mo: École Militaire, tel. 01 47 05 62 62, fax 01 47 05 43 90, e-mail: hotel@tourville.com).

Hotel de Turenne**, with small, air-conditioned rooms, is a good value when it's hot (Sb-360F, Db-430–500F, Tb-590F, extra bed-60F, CC:VM, 20 avenue de Tourville, tel. 01 47 05 99 92, fax 01 45 56 06 04, e-mail: hotel.turenne.paris7@wanadoo.fr).

Hôtel de l'Alma*** is a very good value, with 32 small but pleasant look-alike rooms all with cable TV and a minibar (Sb-450F, Db-500F, includes breakfast, no triples but a kid's bed can be moved in for free, CC:VMA, 32 rue de l'Exposition, tel. 01 47 05 45 70, fax 01 45 51 84 47).

Hotel Londres Eiffel*** is just renovated and has cheerful attention to detail and a melt-in-your-chair breakfast room. Its cozy rooms are thoughtfully appointed, and the owners seem eager to please (Sb-545F, Db-645F, Tb-825F, extra bed-70F, CC:VMA, 40 percent deposit required to reserve, 1 rue Augerau, tel. 01 45 51 63 02, fax 01 47 05 28 96, www.Londres-Eiffel.com).

Mars Hôtel** is a very good, truly Old World value with formal owners, a richly decorated lobby, and a beam-me-up-Maurice coffin-sized elevator. Rooms and bathrooms are spacious; front rooms are noisier but have views of the Eiffel Tower (large Sb-320F, Db-380F, Twin/b-480F, CC:VM, 117 avenue de la Bourdonnais, tel. 01 47 05 42 30, fax 01 47 05 45 91).

Hôtel Kensington** has just been renovated into a reasonable value but has a rude staff (Sb-315F, Db-400–500F, extra bed-80F, CC:VMA, 79 avenue de La Bourdonnais, tel. 01 47 05 74 00, fax 01 47 05 25 81).

Hotel de la Bourdonnais***, more famous for its highly respected restaurant, is a superb three-star value. This perfectly Parisian place mixes Old World elegance with top-notch service, very comfortable and spacious rooms, and pleasant public spaces

(Sb-630F, Db-720F, Tb-780F, Qb-830F, cable TV, CC:VMA, 111 aveune de la Bourdonnais, tel. 01 47 05 45 42, fax 01 45 55 75 54, e-mail: labourdonnais@adi.fr).

Hôtel de la Tulipe**, two blocks from the rue Cler toward the river, charges top franc for its tastefully done rooms, which surround a wood-beamed lounge and a leafy courtyard (Db-650F–680F, no elevator, 33 rue Malar, tel. 01 45 51 67 21, fax 01 47 53 96 37, www.hoteldelatulipe.com).

Hôtel La Tour Maubourg*** lies alone five minutes east of the rue Cler, just off the Esplanade des Invalides, and feels like a slightly faded elegant manor house with spaciously comfortable Old World rooms. It overlooks a cheery green lawn within sight of Napoleon's tomb (Sb-700F, Db-800–900F, suites for up to 4-1,100–1,800F, prices include breakfast with fresh-squeezed juice, prices reduced mid-Jul–mid-Aug, CC:VM, immediately at the La Tour Maubourg Métro stop, 150 rue de Grenelle, tel. 01 47 05 16 16, fax 01 47 05 16 14, e-mail: victor@worldnet.fr).

These places are lesser values but, in this fine area, acceptable last choices: **Hôtel de la Tour Eiffel**** (Sb-350F, Db-400F, Tb-520F, CC:VMA, 17 rue de l'Exposition, tel. 01 47 05 14 75, fax 01 47 53 99 46, Muriel speaks English); the quiet but tired **Hotel le Pavillon**, which has a small courtyard (Db-460F, family suites-575F, 54 rue St. Dominique, tel. 01 45 51 42 87, fax 01 45 51 32 79); **Hôtel Royal Phare**** (Db-310–410F, CC:VMA, facing École Militaire Métro stop, 40 avenue de la Motte Piquet, tel. 01 47 05 57 30, fax 01 45 51 64 41); **Hôtel de la Motte Piquet**** (Db-370–470F, duplex suites-650–760F, CC:VM, 30 avenue de la Motte Piquet, tel. 01 47 05 09 57, fax 01 47 05 74 36); and simple, quiet **Hôtel de la Paix**, run agreeably by English-speaking Noël (S-180F, Ds-330F, Db-350F, Tb-480F, no elevator, 19 rue du Gros-Caillou, tel. 01 45 51 86 17, fax 01 45 55 93 28).

Rue Cler Orientation

Become a local at a rue Cler café for breakfast or join the afternoon crowd for *une bière pression* (a draft beer). On rue Cler you can eat and browse your way through a street full of tart shops, delis, cheeseries, and colorful outdoor produce stalls. (For cafés and restaurants, see "Eating," below.) For an after-dinner cruise on the Seine, it's just a short walk to the river and the Bâteaux Mouches (see "Organized Tours of Paris," above).

Your neighborhood TI is at the Eiffel Tower (May–Sept daily 11:00–18:00, tel. 01 45 51 22 15). The Métro station (École Militaire) and a post office are at the end of rue Cler on avenue de la Motte Piquet, and there's a very handy SNCF office under the Aerogare at the Invalides Métro stop where you can get information, buy tickets, and make seat reservations. Michelle runs the Laundromat Pressing Laverie with panache (daily 7:00–22:00,

Paris

16 rue Cler); or try Lav Club at 27 rue Augereau (same hours). The nearest Internet access is Cyber Cube (5 rue Mignon, tel. 01 53 10 30 50). Taxi stands are on avenue de Tourville at avenue de la Motte Piquet (near Métro stop), and on avenue Bosquet at rue St. Dominique. The Banque Populaire (across from Hôtel Leveque) changes money and has an ATM. Rue St. Dominique is the area's boutique-browsing street. The Epicerie de la Tour grocery shop is open until midnight at 197 rue de Grenelle.

The American Church and College is the community center for Americans living in Paris (65 quai d'Orsay, tel. 01 40 62 05 00). The interdenominational service at 11:00 on Sunday, the coffee hour after church, and the free Sunday concerts (18:00) are a great way to make some friends and get a taste of émigré life in Paris. Stop by and pick up copies of the *Free Voice* for a monthly review of Paris entertainment and *France U.S.A. Contacts* for information on housing and employment through the community of 30,000 Americans living in Paris.

Afternoon *boules* (lawn bowling) on the esplanade des Invalides is a relaxing spectator sport. Look for the dirt area to the upper right as you face the Invalides.

Helpful bus routes: Line #69 runs along rue St. Dominique and serves Les Invalides, Orsay, Louvre, Marais, and Père-Lachaise Cemetery. Line #92 runs along avenue Bosquet and serves the Arc de Triomphe and Champs-Élysées in one direction and the Montparnasse tower in the other. Line #49 runs on boulevard La Tour Maubourg and serves St. Lazare and Gare du Nord stations.

Sleeping in the Marais Neighborhood
(4th arrondissement, Mo: St. Paul or Bastille, zip code: 75004)

Those interested in a more Soho/Greenwich, gentrified, urban-jungle locale should make the Marais their Parisian home. The Marais is a more happening locale than rue Cler. It's narrow medieval Paris at its finest, where elegant stone mansions sit side by side with trendy bars and antique shops. Only 15 years ago it was a forgotten Parisian backwater, but now the Marais is one of Paris' most popular residential and shopping areas. For us, the Marais runs from the Hôtel de Ville to the Bastille (a 15-minute walk), with most hotels located a few blocks north of the main east-west drag, rue de Rivoli/St. Antonie. It's about 15 minutes on foot from any hotel in this area to Notre-Dame, Île St. Louis, and the Latin Quarter. The St. Paul Métro stop puts you right in the heart of the Marais, while the Hôtel de Ville stop serves its western end and the Bastille stop serves its eastern limit.

Hôtel Castex**, a clean and cheery place, is a great value, with comfortable rooms, many stairs, and a good location on a relatively quiet street (Ss-240F, Sb-260–290F, Ds-320–340F, Db-340–360F,

Marais Hotels

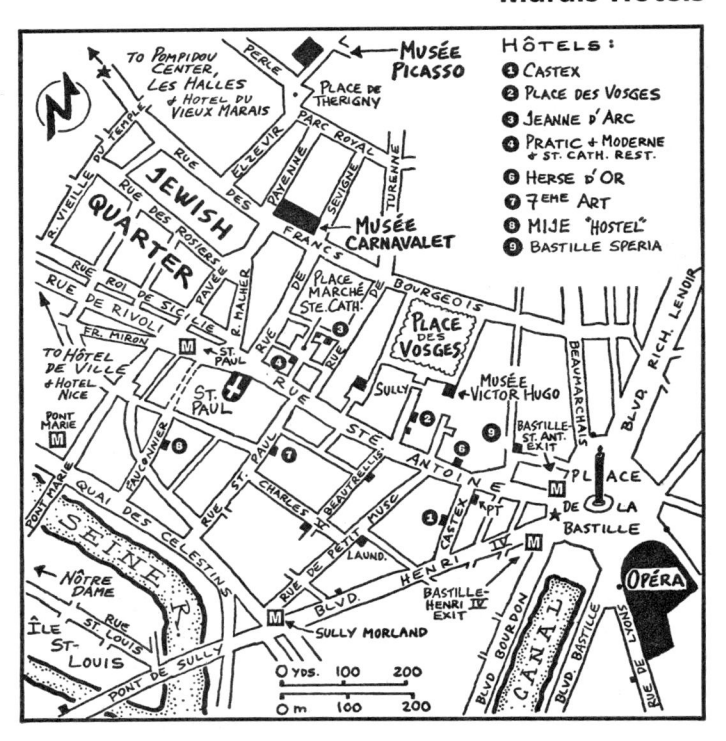

HÔTELS:
1. Castex
2. Place des Vosges
3. Jeanne d'Arc
4. Pratic + Moderne & St. Cath. Rest.
5. Herse d'Or
6. 7ème Art
7. MIJE "Hostel"
8. Bastille Speria

Tb-460F, CC:VM, no elevator, 5 rue Castex, just off place de la Bastille and rue St. Antoine, Mo: Bastille, tel. 01 42 72 31 52, fax 01 42 72 57 91, www.castexhotel.com). Reserve by phone and leave your credit-card number. The security code marked on your key opens the front door after hours. The owners have another good-value hotel two Métro stops away in a less appealing location that often has rooms when others don't: **Hotel de la Republique****, Db-380F, elevator, cable TV, 31 rue Albert Thomas, 75010, Mo: Republique, tel. 01 42 39 19 03, fax 01 42 39 22 66.

Grand Hôtel Jeanne d'Arc**, is a cozy, welcoming place with thoughtfully appointed rooms and is ideally located for connoisseurs of the Marais. Rooms on the street are noisy until the bars close (small Db-310F, Db-425–500F, Tb-540F, Qb-600F, extra bed-75F, CC:VM, 3 rue Jarente, Mo: St. Paul, tel. 01 48 87 62 11, fax 01 48 87 37 31). Sixth-floor rooms have a view. Corner rooms are wonderfully bright in the City of Light.

Hotel Bastille Speria*** feels family run while offering a serious business-type service. Its spacious lobby and 45 newly redecorated rooms are modern, cheery, and pastel, and it's English-language friendly, from the *Herald-Tribune*s in the lobby to the history of the Bastille in the elevator (Sb-540–580F, Db-600–680F, Tb-790F, extra bed-110F, CC:VMA, 1 rue de la Bastille, Mo: Bastille, tel. 01 42 72 04 01, fax 01 42 72 56 38, e-mail: speria@micronet.fr).

Hotel Lyon-Mulhouse**, on a busy street just off place de la Bastille, is a good value, with pleasantly renovated rooms and helpful owners (Sb-355–425F, Db-360–530F, Tb-545–575F, Qb-600–640F, CC:VM, elevator, 8 blvd. Beaumarchais, tel. 01 47 00 91 50, fax 01 47 00 06 31).

Hôtel de la Place des Vosges**, quasi-classy with a linoleum/antique feel, is ideally located on a quiet street (Sb-385F, Db-560–610F, CC:VMA, 12 rue de Biraque, just off the elegant place des Vosges and just as snooty, Mo: St. Paul, tel. 01 42 72 60 46, fax 01 42 72 02 64).

Hotel des Chevaliers***, one block northwest of the place des Vosges, offers small but pleasant and comfortable rooms with all the comforts, from hair dryers to cable TV. Rooms off the street are quiet (Db-640–830F, CC:VMA, skip the overpriced breakfast, 30 rue de Turenne, Mo: St. Paul, tel. 01 42 72 73 47, fax 01 42 72 54 10).

Hotel de la Herse d'Or is industrial-strength, three-coats-of-paint simple, with a good location, tortured floor plan, and hard-to-beat prices for its relatively comfortable rooms (S-170F, D-210F, Db-290F, shower-10F, no elevator, 20 rue St. Antoine, Mo: Bastille, tel. 01 48 87 84 09, fax 01 48 87 94 01).

Hotel Sévigné** provides basic and cramped two-star comfort at fair prices and the cheapest breakfast in Paris—20F (Sb-355F, Db-375–470F, CC:VM, 2 rue Malher, Mo: St. Paul, tel. 01 42 72 76 17, fax 01 42 78 68 26).

Hôtel Pratic* has a slightly Arabic feel in its cramped lobby. The tidy, just-renovated rooms are simple but not confined, stairs are many, and it's right on a great people-friendly square. Single rooms are tiny (S-230F, D-280F, Ds-310F, Db-400F, no elevator, 9 rue d'Ormesson, Mo: St. Paul, tel. 01 48 87 80 47, fax 01 48 87 40 04).

The bare-bones and dumpy **Hôtel Moderne**, next to the Hôtel Pratic, might be better than a youth hostel if you need privacy. The only thing *moderne* about it is the name, which is illegible on the broken sign (S-150F, D-190F, Db-320F, 3 rue Caron, Mo: St. Paul, tel. 01 48 87 97 05).

Hôtel de 7ème Art**, two blocks south of rue St. Antoine, is a Hollywood-nostalgia place run by young, friendly Marais types, with a full-service café/bar and Charlie Chaplin murals. Most rooms are average, but the few large double rooms, at 670F, are very nice (Sb-300F, Db-420–490F, extra bed-100F, CC:VMA, 20 rue St. Paul, Mo: St. Paul, tel. 01 44 54 85 00, fax 01 42 77 69 10).

Grand Hotel du Loiret**, just north of rue de Rivoli, is a fair enough value, has laid-back management, and seems filled with American students (S-190F, D-220F, Db-310–410F, Tb-400F, Qb-500F, CC:VMA, 8 rue des Garçons Mauvais, Mo: Hôtel de Ville, tel. 01 48 87 77 00, fax 01 48 04 96 56).

Hôtel de Nice** is a cozy Marie-Antoinette-does-tie-dye place with lots of thoughtful touches on the Marais' busy main drag (Sb-380F, Db-500F, Tb-630F, CC:VM, 42 bis rue de Rivoli, Mo: Hôtel de Ville, tel. 01 42 78 55 29, fax 01 42 78 36 07). Twin rooms, which cost the same as doubles, are roomier but on the street side (effective double-paned windows).

Hotel de la Bretonnerie***, three blocks north and east of the Hôtel de Ville, is my favorite Marais splurge. It has elegant decor; tastefully decorated and spacious rooms with an antique, open-beam coziness; and an efficient, helpful staff (standard Db-650F, Db with character-795F, the standard Db has enough character for me, fine family-friendly suites-990F, CC:VMA, between rue du Vielle du Temple and rue des Archives at 22 rue St. Croix de la Bretonnerie, Mo: Hôtel de Ville, tel. 01 48 87 77 63, fax 01 42 77 26 78, www.HoteldelaBretonnerie.com).

Hotel Caron de Beaumarchais*** is an 18th-century Marais manor house that charges top prices for its charming and very comfortable rooms (Db-730–810F, CC:VMA, air-con, 12 rue Vielle du Temple, Mo: Hôtel de Ville, tel. 01 42 72 34 12, fax 01 42 72 34 63).

Hotel de Vieux Marais**, tucked away on a quiet street two blocks east of the Pompidou Center, offers spotless and fairly spacious rooms with air-conditioning, pleasing decor, and we-try-harder owners (Db-660–690F, extra bed-100F, CC:VM, just off rue des Archives at 8 rue du Platre, Mo: Hôtel de Ville, tel. 01 42 78 47 22, fax 01 42 78 34 32).

MIJE Youth Hostels: The Maison Internationale de la Jeunesse des Étudiants (MIJE) runs three classy old residences clustered a few blocks south of rue St. Antoine. Each offers simple, clean, single-sex, one- to four-bed rooms for travelers under the age of 30 and families. Prices are per person; you can pay more to have your own room or be roomed with as many as three others (Sb-220, Db-170F, Tb-150F, Qb-140F, includes breakfast but not towels—which you can get from a machine; rooms are locked 12:00–15:00 and at 01:00). MIJE Fourcy (cheap dinners, 6 rue de Fourcy, just south of the rue Rivoli), MIJE Fauconnier (11 rue Fauconnier), and the best, MIJE Maubisson (12 rue des Barres), share the same number (01 42 74 23 45, fax 01 40 27 81 64, e-mail: MIJE@wanadoo.fr) and Métro stop (St. Paul). Reservations are accepted.

Marais Orientation

The nearest TIs are in the Louvre and Gare du Lyon (arrival level, open 8:00–20:00, tel. 01 43 43 33 24). The Banque de France changes money, offering good rates and sometimes long lines (where rue St. Antoine hits place de la Bastille, Mon–Fri 9:00–11:45, 13:30–15:30). Most banks and other services are on the main drag, rue de Rivoli/St. Antoine. You'll find one taxi stand on the north side of St. Antoine, where it meets rue Castex, and another on the south side of St. Antoine in front of the St. Paul church.

The new Bastille opera house, Promenade Plantée Park, place des Vosges (Paris' oldest square), the Jewish Quarter (rue des Rosiers), and the Pompidou Center are all nearby. Be sure to stroll into place des Vosges after dark. A fine budget department store is BHV, next to the Hôtel de Ville. Marais post offices are on rue Castex and on the corner of rues Pavée and Francs Bourgeois.

Helpful bus routes: Line #69 on rue St. Antoine takes you to the Louvre, Orsay, Rodin, and Napoleon's Tomb and ends at the Eiffel Tower. Line #86 runs down boulevard Henri IV, crossing the Île St. Louis and serving the Latin Quarter along boulevard St. Germain. Line #96 runs on rues Turenne and Francois Miron and serves the Louvre and boulevard St. Germain (near Luxembourg Gardens). Line #65 serves the train stations Austerlitz, Est, and Nord from place de la Bastille.

Sleeping in the Contrescarpe Neighborhood
(5th arrondissement, Mo: place Monge, zip code: 75005)

This lively, colorful neighborhood reminds me of Montmartre without all the tourists. It's just over the hill from the Latin Quarter, behind the Panthéon, and is walking distance from Notre-Dame, Île de la Cité, Île St. Louis, Luxembourg Gardens, and the grand boulevards St. Germain and St. Michel. Most of our hotels are on or very near rue Mouffetard, the spine of this area, running from the perfectly Parisian place Contrescarpe south to the rue Bazelles. Rue Mouffetard is a market street by day and touristy restaurant row by night. Fewer tourists sleep here, and I find the hotel values generally better than most other neighborhoods. These hotels are listed in order by proximity to the Seine River (and Notre-Dame).

The low-energy, bare-bones **Hôtel du Commerce** is run by Monsieur Mattuzzi, who must be a pirate gone good (S-130F, D-150F, Ds-170F, Ts-220F, Qs-280F, shower-15F, no elevator, takes no reservations, call at 10:00 and he'll say *"oui"* or *"non,"* 14 rue de La Montagne Ste. Geneviève, Mo: Maubert-Mutualité, tel. 01 43 54 89 69). This 300-year-old place (with vinyl that looks it) is a great rock-bottom deal and as safe as any dive next to a police station can be. In the morning, the landlady will knock and chirp, *"Restez-vous?"* ("Are you staying tonight?")

Contrescarpe Hotels

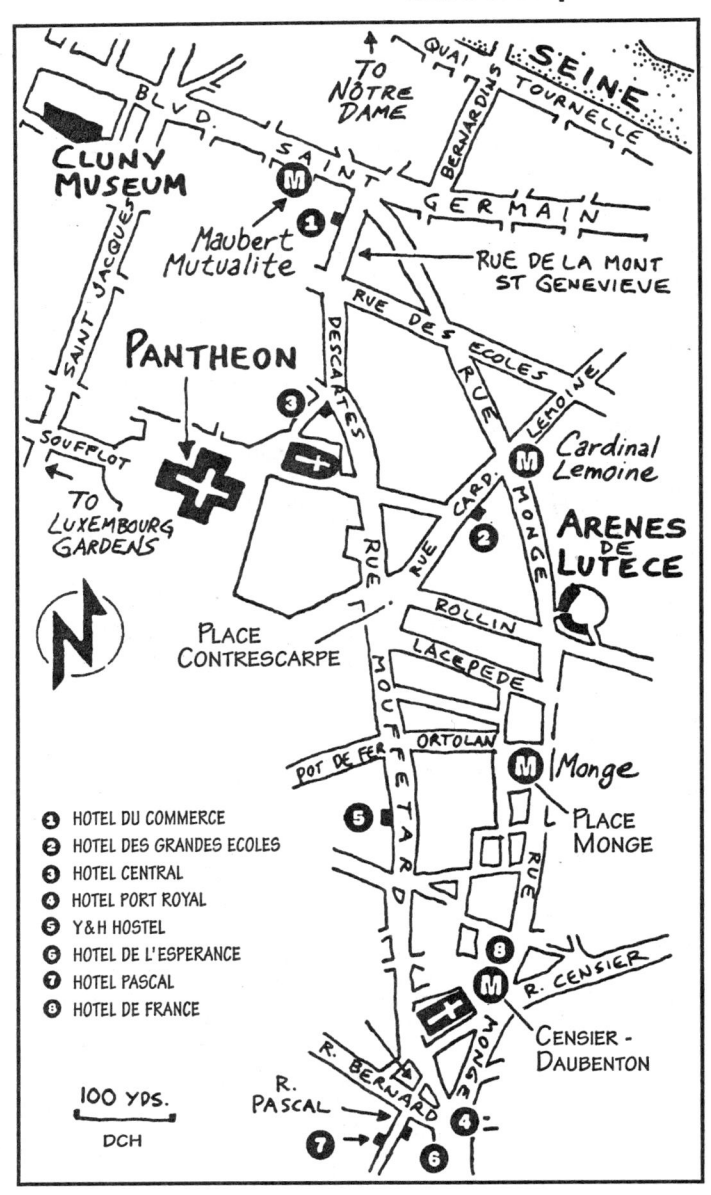

1. HOTEL DU COMMERCE
2. HOTEL DES GRANDES ECOLES
3. HOTEL CENTRAL
4. HOTEL PORT ROYAL
5. Y&H HOSTEL
6. HOTEL DE L'ESPERANCE
7. HOTEL PASCAL
8. HOTEL DE FRANCE

Paris

Hôtel Central* is unpretentious, with a charming location, a steep and slippery castlelike stairway, simple rooms (all with showers, though toilets are down the hall), so-so beds, and plenty of smiles. It's a fine budget value (Ss-165–190F, Ds-240–270F, no elevator, 6 rue Descartes, Mo: Cardinal Lemoine, tel. 01 46 33 57 93).

Hôtel des Grandes Écoles*** is simply idyllic. A short alley leads to three buildings protecting a flowering garden courtyard and preserving a tranquility rare in a city this size. This romantic place is deservedly popular, so call well in advance (Db-530–690F, Tb-630–780F, Qb-680–890F, extra bed-100F, 75 rue de Cardinal Lemoine, Mo: Cardinal Lemoine, tel. 01 43 26 79 23, fax 01 43 25 28 15, www.hotel-grandes-ecoles.com).

The hotels listed below lie on or at the bottom of the rue Mouffetard and may have rooms when others don't.

Y&H Hostel offers a great location, easygoing English-speaking management, and basic but acceptable hostel-like conditions (110F-beds in 4-bed rooms, 130F-beds in double rooms, 15F for sheets, rooms closed 11:00–17:00, though reception stays open, curfew at 02:00, reservations must be paid in advance, 80 rue Mouffetard, Mo: Cardinal Lemoine, tel. 01 45 35 09 53, fax 01 47 07 22 24).

Hotel de l'Esperance**, located at the bottom of rue Mouffetard, gives you nearly three stars for the price of two. It's quiet, fluffy, and comfortable, with thoughtfully appointed rooms complete with canopy beds, hair dryers, cable TV, and a flamboyant owner (Sb-440F, Db-450–520F, Tb-600F, CC:VM, 15 rue Pascal, Mo: Censier-Daubenton, tel. 01 47 07 10 99, fax 01 43 37 56 19).

Hotel Pascal*, across from Hotel de l'Esperance, is a good value, with a Byzantine floor plan; simple, less-than-clean rooms; small double beds; and minuscule bathrooms (S-205F, Db-305F, Tb-455F, Qb-605–705F, funky studio lofts with kitchenettes-460F, CC:VMA, 20 rue Pascal, Mo: Censier-Daubenton, tel. 01 47 07 41 92, fax 01 47 07 43 80, e-mail: hotpascal@mail.opsion.fr).

Hotel de France**, on a busy street, has fine, modern rooms and hardworking, helpful owners (Sb-380F, Db-410–440F, CC:VM, 108 rue Monge, Mo: Censier-Daubenton, tel. 01 47 07 19 04, fax 01 43 36 62 34, e-mail: hotel.de.fce@wanadoo.fr). The best and quietest rooms are *sur le cour* (on the courtyard).

Hotel Port Royal*, a well-run hotel, has a small, pleasant courtyard and incredibly clean, comfortable rooms at very fair prices; ask for a room off the street (S-195–240F, D-245F, Db-365–450F, climb the stairs from the rue Pascal to the busy boulevard Port Royal, 8 boulevard de Port Royal, Mo: Gobelins, tel. 01 43 31 70 06, fax 01 43 31 33 67).

Contrescarpe Orientation

The nearest TI is at the Louvre Museum. The post office (PTT) is between rue Mouffetard and rue Monge at 10 rue de l'Épée du

Bois. Place Monge hosts a colorful outdoor market on Wednesdays, Fridays, and Sundays until 13:00. The street market at the bottom of rue Mouffetard bustles Tuesday through Saturday 8:00 to 12:00 and 15:30 to 19:00 and on Sundays 8:00 to 12:00 (5 blocks south of the place Contrescarpe), and the lively place Contrescarpe hops in the afternoon and evening until the wee hours.

The flowery Jardin des Plantes park is close by and great for afternoon walks, as are Luxembourg Gardens, which easily justify the 15-minute walk. The doorway at 49 rue Monge leads to a hidden Roman arena (Arènes de Lutèce). Today, *boules* players occupy the stage, while couples cuddle on the seats. Walk to the Panthéon, admire it from the outside (it's not worth paying to go in), and go into the wildly beautiful St. Étienne-du-Mont church.

Sleeping near Paris, in Versailles
(zip code: 78000)
For a laid-back alternative to Paris within easy reach of the big city by RER train (5/hrly, 30 min) and with easy, safe parking, Versailles can be a good overnight stop.

Hôtel Le Cheval Rouge**, built in 1676 as Louis XIV's stables, now houses tourists comfortably. It's a block behind place du Marché on a large, quiet courtyard in a quaint corner of town (Ds-290F, Db-350–400F, extra bed-90F, CC:VMA, 18 rue Andre Chenier, tel. 01 39 50 03 03, fax 01 39 50 61 27).

Ibis Versailles**, a slick business-class place, offers all the comfort with none of the character (Db-420F, CC:VMA, across from RER station, 4 avenue du Gen. de Gaulle, tel. 01 39 53 03 30, fax 01 39 50 06 31).

Hotel du Palais, facing the RER station, has cheap and handy beds; get a room off the street. It's a pink and funky place, dumpy enough to lack even one star but proud enough to put candy on the beds (D-180F, Ds-220F, Db-250F, extra person-30F, miles of stairs, 6 place Lyautey, tel. 01 39 50 39 29, fax 01 39 50 80 41).

Hotel d'Angleterre** is a peaceful, well-worn old place near the palace (Db-300, 350, and 450F, extra bed-100F, CC:VMA, 1st-floor rooms are best, 2 rue de Fontenay, tel. 01 39 51 43 50, fax 01 39 51 45 63).

Eating in Paris
Paris is France's wine and cuisine melting pot. While it lacks a style of its own, it draws from the best of France. Paris could hold a gourmets' Olympics and import nothing.

Picnic or go to bakeries for quick take-out lunches or stop at a café for a lunch salad or *plat du jour* but linger longer over dinner. You can eat well, restaurant-style, for 100F to 140F. Your hotel can usually recommend nearby restaurants in the 70F-to-100F range. Remember, cafés and simple small restaurants are happy to serve a *plat du jour* (garnished plate of the day, about 60F) or a chef-like salad (45–60F) day or night. Famous places are often overpriced, overcrowded, and overrated. Find a quiet neighborhood and wander or follow a local recommendation. Restaurants open for dinner around 19:00, and small local favorites get crowded after 21:00. To save piles of francs, review the budget eating tips in this book's introduction. Our recommendations are centered around the same three great neighborhoods for which we listed hotels so that you can come home exhausted after a busy day of sightseeing and have a good selection of restaurants right around the corner. And evening is a fine time to explore any of these delightful neighborhoods even if you're sleeping elsewhere.

Restaurants

The Parisian eating scene is kept at a rolling boil. Entire books (and lives) are dedicated to the subject. If you are traveling outside of Paris, save your splurges for the countryside, where you'll enjoy better cooking for less money. I've listed places that conveniently fit a busy sightseeing schedule and places near recommended hotels. If you'd like to visit a district specifically to eat, consider the many romantic restaurants that line the cozy Île St. Louis' main street and the colorful, touristic but fun string of eateries along rue Mouffetard behind the Panthéon (in the Contrescarpe neighborhood). Beware, many restaurants close Sunday and Monday.

Cafeterias and Picnics

Many Parisian department stores have huge supermarkets hiding in the basement and top-floor cafeterias offering not really cheap but low-risk, low-stress, what-you-see-is-what-you-get meals.

For lunch and dinner picnics, you'll find handy little groceries (*épiceries*) and delis (*charcuteries*) all over town but rarely near famous sights. Good picnic fixings include roasted chicken, drinkable yogurt, fresh bakery goods, melons, exotic pâtés, and cheeses. Great take-out deli-type foods, such as gourmet salads and quiches, abound. *Boulangeries* make good cheap miniquiches and sandwiches. While wine is taboo in public places in the United States, it's *pas de problème* (no problem) in France.

Romantic Picnic Spots: My favorite dinner-picnic places are the pedestrian bridge (Pont des Arts) across from the Louvre, with unmatched views and plentiful benches; the Champs de Mars park under the Eiffel Tower (after dusk); and the western tip of Île St. Louis overlooking the Île de la Cité. Bring your own dinner feast and watch the riverboats or the Eiffel Tower light up the city for you. The Palais Royal (across the street from the Louvre) is a good spot for a peaceful, royal picnic, as is the little triangular Henry IV Park on the west tip of the Île de la Cité. For lunch picnics with great people watching, try the Pompidou Center (by the *Homage to Stravinsky* fountain), the elegant place des Vosges (closes at dusk), the gardens at the Rodin Museum, and Luxembourg Gardens.

Eating in the Rue Cler Neighborhood

Restaurants: The rue Cler neighborhood isn't famous for its restaurants. That's why I enjoy eating here. Several small, family-run places serve great dinner *menus* for 100F and *plats du jour* for 60F to 80F. My first three recommendations are easygoing cafés, ideal if what you want is a light dinner (good dinner salads) or more substantial, but simple, meals.

Café du Marché, with the best seats, coffee, and prices on rue Cler, serves hearty salads and good 60F *plats du jour* for lunch or dinner to a trendy, mainly French crowd. Arrive before 19:30 or wait at the bar. A chalkboard listing the plates of the day—each a meal—will momentarily be hung in front of you (at the corner of rue Cler and rue Champs de Mars). You'll find the same *menu* and prices with better indoor seating at their other restaurant, **Le Comptoir du Septième**, at the École Militaire Métro stop (39 avenue de la Motte Piquet, tel. 01 45 55 90 20).

Café La Roussillon also offers relaxed, good bistro fare at reasonable prices with fewer crowds (their *la Planche* is a board of cheese, meats, pâtés, and some salad; corner of Grenelle and Cler).

Café le Bosquet is owned by the nicest guy in Paris. Jean Francois will make you feel very welcome at his classic Parisian café (many good choices including French onion soup, 98F *menu*, 46 avenue Bosquet, tel. 01 45 51 38 13).

Leo le Lion has been run by Mimi for 20 years and is a very easygoing place. A warm, charming souvenir of old Paris, it's popular with locals. The 115F *menu* comes with a first course that could feed two for an entire meal (but no splitting) and a fully garnished main course (closed Sun, 23 rue Duvivier, tel. 01 45 51 41 77).

Vegetarians will appreciate the Mediterranean cuisine at **7ème Sud** (closed Sun, at the corner of rue de Grenelle and rue Duvivier).

Thoumieux, the neighborhood's classy, traditional Parisian brasserie, is deservedly popular (basic 82F and fine 160F *menu*, complete *à la carte*, 79 rue St. Dominique, tel. 01 47 05 49 75).

For a special dinner, survey the handful of fine places that line the rue de l'Exposition one block west of avenue Bosquet between rue St. Dominique and rue de Grenelle: **Restaurant La Serre**, at #29, has fun ambience, usually great food, but unpredictable staff (*plats* 50–70F, daily from 19:00, often a wait after 21:00, good onion soup and duck specialties, tel. 01 45 55 20 96, Marie-Alice and intense Philippe speak English). Across the street at #28, **Le P'tit Troquet** is delightfully Parisian, popular with locals, and ideal for a last-night splurge—allow 160F per person for dinner (closed Sun–Mon, tel. 01 47 05 80 39). The quieter **La Maison de Cosima** at #20 offers refined, creative French cuisine and excellent 100F and 150F *menus* that include a vegetarian option (closed Sun, tel. 01 45 51 37 71, run by friendly Helene).

The softly lit tables and red velvet chairs of **Auberge du Champs de Mars** at #18 draw a romantic crowd (closed Mon). For top *à la carte*–only cuisine, locals reserve early for the charmingly situated **La Fontaine de Mars** (allow 250F per person with wine, open daily, 129 rue St. Dominique, tel. 01 47 05 46 44). Around the corner, just off rue de Grenelle, the friendly and unpretentious **La Varanque** is a good budget bet, with 60F *plats* and an 80F *menu* (27 rue Augereau, tel. 01 47 05 51 22).

Ambassade du Sud-Ouest, a wine and food boutique/restaurant, specializes in French Southwest cuisine, such as *daubes de canard*—duck meatballs (46 avenue de la Bourdonnais, tel. 01 45 55 59 59). **L'Ami de Jean** is a lively place to sample Basque cuisine (closed Sun, 27 rue Malar, tel. 01 47 05 86 89).

Picnicking: The rue Cler is a moveable feast that gives "fast food" a good name. The entire street is clogged with connoisseurs of good eating. Only the health-food store goes unnoticed. A festival of food, the street is lined with people whose lives seem to be devoted to their specialty: stacking polished produce, rotisserie chicken, crêpes, or cheese squares.

For a magical picnic dinner at the Eiffel Tower, assemble it in no fewer than six shops on rue Cler and lounge on the best grass in Paris (the police don't mind after dusk) with the dogs, Frisbees, a floodlit Tower, and a cool breeze in the Parc du Champs de Mars.

The **crêpe stand** next to Café du Marché does a wonderful top-end dinner crêpe for 25F. An Asian deli, **Traiteur Asie** (across from Hôtel Leveque, another across from Hotel du Champs de Mars), has tasty, low-stress, low-price take-out treats. Its two tables offer the cheapest place to sit, eat, and enjoy the rue Cler ambience. For quiche, cheese pie, or a pear/chocolate tart, try Tarte Julie's (takeout or stools, 28 rue Cler). The elegant **Flo Prestige** *charcuterie* (at École Militaire Métro stop) is open until 23:00 and offers mouthwatering meals to go. **Real McCoy** is a little shop selling American food and sandwiches (194 rue de Grenelle). There's a good, small, late-night grocery at 197 rue de Grenelle.

The bakery (*boulangerie*) on the corner of rue Cler and rue de Champs de Mars is the place for a fresh baguette, sandwich, tiny quiche, or *pain au chocolat*, but the almond croissants at the *boulangerie* on rue de Grenelle at rue Cler make my day. The bakery at 112 rue St. Dominique is in a league by itself and worth the detour, with classic decor and tables to enjoy your café au lait and croissant.

Cafés and Bars: If you want to linger over coffee or a drink at a sidewalk café, try **Café du Marché** (see above), **Brasserie PTT** (opposite #53 rue Cler), or the **Café le Bosquet** (46 avenue

Bosquet, tel. 01 45 51 38 13). **Café La Roussillon**, peopled and decorated á la belle epoche, also offers a quintessential café experience (corner of Grenelle and Cler). **Le Sancerre** wine bar/café is wood-beam warm and ideal for a light lunch or dinner (great omelettes), or just a glass of wine after a long day of sightseeing—served by the owner whose cheeks are the same color as his wine (open until 21:30, 22 avenue Rapp, tel. 01 45 51 75 91). The almost no-name **Maison Altmayer** is a hole-in-the-wall place for a drink quietly festooned with reality (9:00–19:30, 6 rue du Gros Caillou, next to Hôtel Eiffel Rive Gauche). Cafés like this originated (and this one still functions) as a place where locals enjoyed a drink while their heating wood, coal, or gas was prepared for delivery.

Nightlife: This sleepy neighborhood is not the place for night owls, but there are three notable exceptions: **Café du Marché** and its brother, **Le Comptoir du Septième** (see above), hop with a Franco-American crowd until about midnight. **O'Brien's Pub** is a relaxed Parisian rendition of an Irish pub (77 St. Dominique). **Café Thoumieux** is a sophisticated place with big-screen sports and a trendy young crowd (4 rue de la Comete, Mo: Latour Maubourg).

Eating in the Marais Neighborhood

The windows of the Marais are filled with munching sophisticates and crowd-pleasing eateries. And with Île St. Louis a short walk away (see below), those sleeping in the Marais have a great selection of good-value restaurants.

The place du Marche Ste. Catherine, a tiny square just off rue St. Antoine between the St. Paul Métro stop and place des Vosges, is home to several good places. **Le Marais Ste. Catherine** is a good value (110F menu, daily from 19:00, non-smoking, extra seating in their candlelit cellar, 5 rue Caron, tel. 01 42 72 39 94), but if it's warm, I prefer the outdoor tables at **Le Marche** (2 place Marche Ste. Catherine, tel. 01 42 77 34 88). Just off the square, **l'Auberge de Jarente** offers a well-respected and traditional cuisine (120F menu, closed Sun–Mon, 7 rue Jarente, tel. 01 42 77 49 35).

Dinners under the candlelit arches of the place des Vosges are *très* romantic: **Nectarine** at #16 serves fine salads, quiches, and reasonable *plats du jour* daily and nightly, while **Ma Bourgogne** is where locals go for a splurge (open daily, at northwest corner, no CC, reserve dinner ahead, tel. 01 42 78 44 64).

For a fast, cheap change of pace, eat at (or take out from) the Chinese/Japanese **Delice House**. Two can split 200 grams of chicken curry (or whatever, 28F) and a heaping helping of rice (20F). There's lots of seating, with pitchers of tap water at the ground-floor tables and a roomier upstairs (81 rue St. Antoine, open until 21:00).

The *crêperie* near Hôtel Castex serves a 60F *menu*, and the cozy restaurant **de la Poste** (13 rue Castex) offers inexpensive, light meals (both closed Sun). I like **La Bastoche**'s warm ambience and good 100F *menu* (7 rue St. Antoine, tel. 01 48 04 74 34). Across the street, **Le Paradis de Fruit** serves salads and organic foods to a young local crowd (on the small square at rues Tournelle and St. Antoine).

Near Hotel du 7ème Art, try the romantic and traditional **L'Excuse** for a worthwhile splurge (190F *menu*, closed Sun, 14 rue Charles V, call ahead, tel. 01 42 77 98 97). Across the street, **L'Énoteca** (wine bar) has lively and reasonable Italian cuisine in a relaxed, open setting (closed Sun, 20 rue St. Paul, tel. 01 42 78 91 44).

Wine lovers shouldn't miss the superb Burgundy wines and exquisite, though limited, *menu* selection at **Au Bourguignon du Marais** (52 rue Francois Miron, closed Sat–Sun, call by 19:00 to reserve, tel. 01 48 87 15 40).

Vegetarians will appreciate the excellent cuisine at the popular **Picolo Teatro** (closed Mon, 6 rue des Ecouffes, tel. 01 42 72 17 79) and **l'As du Falafel**, serving the best falafel on the rue Rosier, at #34.

Le Petit Gavroche, closer to Hôtel de Ville at 15 Ste. Croix de la Bretonniere, attracts a local crowd in search of a simple, good value (tel. 01 48 87 74 26).

Picnicking: Picnic at the peaceful place des Vosges (closes at dusk). Hobos stretch their francs at the supermarket in the basement of the **Monoprix** department store (close to place des Vosges on rue St. Antoine), and connoisseurs prefer the gourmet take-out places all along rue St. Antoine, such as **Flo Prestige** (open until 23:00, on the tiny square where rue Tournelle and rue St. Antoine meet). A few small grocery shops are open until 23:00 on the rue St. Antoine (near intersection with rue Castex). An open-air market, held Sunday morning, is just off place de la Bastille on boulevard Richard Lenoir.

For a cheap breakfast, try the tiny *boulangerie/pâtisserie* where the hotels buy their croissants (coffee machine, 3F; 10F baby quiches, 5F *pain au chocolat*, 1 block off place de la Bastille, corner of rue St. Antoine and rue de Lesdiguieres).

Cafés and Bars: The trendiest cafés and bars are clustered on the rues Vielle du Temple, Archives, and Ste. Croix de la Bretonniere (open generally till 02:00) and are popular with gay men. **Hamman** is an ethnically hip cyber café (4 rue des Rosiers, on place du Marche Ste. Catherine). The *très* local wine bar at **Au Temps des Cerises** is amiably run and a welcoming, if smoky, place (rue du Petit Musc and rue de Cerisaie, around the corner from Hôtel Castex).

Nightlife: Le Vieux Comptoir is tiny, lively, and not too hip (just off place des Vosges at 8 rue Biraque). **La Perla** is trendy and filled with Parisian yuppies in search of the perfect margarita (26 rue Francois Miron). **The Quiet Man** is a traditional Irish pub with a happy hour from 16:00 to 20:00 (5 rue des Haudriettes).

Eating in the Contrescarpe Neighborhood

The rue Mouffetard and rue du Pot-de-Fer are lined with inexpensive, lively, and forgettable restaurants. Study the many menus, compare crowds, and dive in. **Le Jardin d'Artemis** is one of the better values on rue Mouffetard at #34 (89F *menu*). **Restaurant l'Epoque**, a fine neighborhood restaurant, has excellent-value *menus* at 78F and 118F (1 block off place Contrescarpe at 81 rue Cardinal Lemoine, tel. 01 46 34 15 84). **Savannah Café**'s creative Mediterranean cuisine attracts a loyal, artsy crowd (27 rue Descartes, tel. 01 43 29 45 77). **Le Jardin des Pates** is popular with vegetarians, serving pastas and salads at fair prices (4 rue Lacepede, near Jardins des Plantes, tel. 01 43 31 50 71). **Le Villaret** serves excellent cuisine from France's southwest (*menus* from 110F, closed Sun, near recommended Hotel Central at 44 rue Montagne Ste. Genevieve, tel. 01 46 34 26 46).

Cafés: **Brasserie La Chope**, a classic Parisian brasserie right on the place Contrescarpe, is popular until the wee hours. Sit indoors or out for good people watching. **Café Le Mouffetard** is in the thick of the street-market hustle and bustle (at the corner of rue Mouffetard and rue de l'Arbalete). The outdoor tables at **Cave de la Bourgogne**, at the bottom of rue Mouffetard on rue Bazelles, are picture perfect. At **Café de la Mosque** you'll feel like you've been beamed to Morocco. In this purely Arab café, order a mint tea, pour in the sugar, and enjoy the authentic interior and peaceful outdoor terrace (2 rue Daubenton, behind the mosque).

Eating in the Latin Quarter

La Petite Bouclerie is a cozy place with classy family cooking (70F *menu*, closed Mon, 33 rue de la Harpe, center of touristy Latin Quarter, tel. 01 43 54 18 03). The popular **Restaurant Polidor** is an old turn-of-the-century-style place with great *cuisine bourgeois*, a vigorous local crowd, and a historic toilet. Arrive at 19:00 to get a seat in the restaurant (65F *plat du jour*, 100F *menus*, 41 rue Monsieur le Prince, midway between Odéon and Luxembourg Métro stops, tel. 01 43 26 95 34).

Eating on the Île St. Louis

Cruise the island's main street for a variety of good options, from cozy *crêperies* to romantic restaurants. Sample Paris' best sorbet and ice cream at any place advertising *les glaces Berthillon*; the original **Berthillon** shop is at 31 rue St. Louis-en-l'Île.

All listings below are on the rue St. Louis-en-l'Île and listed from the Île de la Cité end. **Café Med** at #73 serves inexpensive salads, crêpes, and lighter menus in a cheery setting. **La Castafiore** at #51–53 serves fine Italian dishes in a cozy setting (160F *menu*). Farther down lie two fine romantic splurges: **Le Tastevin** (150F and 220F *menus*, #46, tel. 01 43 54 17 31) and **Au Gourmet de l'Isle** (150F and 185F *menus*, closed Mon–Tue), next door.

For crazy, touristy cellar atmosphere and hearty fun food, feast at **La Taverne du Sergeant Recruiter**. The Sergeant Recruiter used to get young Parisians drunk and stuffed here and then sign them into the army. It's all-you-can-eat, including wine and service, for 190F (daily from 19:00, #41, tel. 01 43 54 75 42). There's a near-food-fight clone next door at **Nos Ancêtres Les Gaulois** ("Our Ancestors the Gauls," 190F, daily at 19:00, tel. 01 46 33 66 07).

Elegant Dining on the Seine
La Plage Parisienne is a nearly dress-up riverfront place popular with locals that serves elegant, healthy meals at good prices (Port de Javel-Haut, Mo: Javel, tel. 01 40 59 41 00).

Nightlife in Paris
Paris is brilliant after dark. Save energy from your day's sightseeing and get out at night. Whether it's a concert at Sainte-Chapelle, an elevator up the Arc de Triomphe, or a late-night café, experience the city of light lit. If a night bus tour or a Seine River cruise appeals, see "Organized Tours of Paris," above.

The *Pariscope* magazine (3F at any newsstand) offers a complete weekly listing of music, cinema, theater, opera, and other special events; we decipher this useful periodical for you below. The *Free Voice* newspaper, in English, has a monthly review of Paris entertainment (available at any English-language bookstore, French-American establishments, or the American Church).

A Tour of Pariscope
The weekly *Pariscope* (3F) or *L'Officiel des Spectacles* (2F) are both cheap and essential if you want to know what's happening. Pick one up and page through it. For a headstart, *Pariscope* has a Web site: www.pariscope.fr.

Each begins with culture news. Skip the bulky "Theatres" and "Diners/Spectacles" sections and anything listed as "*des environs*" (outside of Paris). "Musique" or "Concerts Classiques" follow, listing each day's events (program, location, time, and price). Venues with phone numbers and addresses are listed in an "Adresses des Salles de Concerts" sidebar. Touristic venues (such as Sainte-Chapelle and Église de la Madeleine) are often featured in display ads. "Opéras," "Musique Traditionelle," "Ballet/Danse," and "Jazz/Rock" listings follow.

Half of these magazines are devoted to Cinema—a Paris

forte. After the "Films Nouveaux" section trumpets new releases, the "Films en Exclusivite" pages list all the films playing in town. While a code marks films as Historique, Karate, Erotisme, and so on, the key mark for tourists is "v.o.," which means *version original* (American films have their English soundtracks and French subtitles). Films are listed alphabetically, with theaters and their arrondissements at the end of each entry. Later films are listed by neighborhood ("Salles Paris") and by genre. First runs are shown at cinemas on the Champs-Élysées and on place de l'Odeon; art films and older films are best found in the Latin Quarter. To find a showing near your hotel, simply match the arrondissement (but don't hesitate to hop on the Métro for the film you want). "Salles Périphérie" is out in the suburbs. Film festivals are also listed.

Pariscope has a small English "Time Out" section listing the week's events. The "Musées" sections (Monuments, Jardins, Autres Curiosites, Promenades, Activites Sportives, Piscines) give the latest hours of the sights, gardens, curiosities, boat tours, sports, swimming pools, and so on. "Clubs de Loisirs" are various athletic and social clubs. "Pour les Jeunes" is for young people (kids' films, animations/cartoons, marionettes, circuses, and amusement parks, such as Asterix and Disney). "Conferences" are mostly lectures. For cancan mischief, look under "Paris la Nuit, Cabarets," or the busty "Spectacles Erotiques."

Finally, you'll find a TV listing. Paris has four country-wide stations: TF1, France 2, France 3, and the new Arte station (a German/French cultural channel). M6 is filled with American series. Canal Plus (channel 4) is a cable channel that airs an American news show at 7:00 and an American sports event on Sunday evening.

Music

Jazz Clubs

With a lively mix of American, French, and international musicians, Paris has been an internationally acclaimed jazz capital since World War II. You'll pay from 30F to 130F to enter a jazz club (1 drink may be included; if not, expect to pay 30–60F per drink; beer is cheapest). See *Pariscope* under "Musique" for listings or, better, the American Church's *Free Voice* paper for a good monthly review (in English)—or drop by to check out their calendars posted on the front door. Music starts after 22:00 in most clubs. Some offer dinner concerts from about 20:30 on. Here are a few good bets:

Caveau de la Huchette, a characteristic old jazz club for visitors, fills an ancient Latin Quarter cellar with live jazz and frenzied dancing every night (60F weekday, 75F weekend admission, 30F drinks, 21:30–02:30 or later, closed Mon, 5 rue de la Huchette, recorded info tel. 01 43 26 65 05).

For a hotbed of late-night activity and jazz, go to the

two-block-long rue des Lombards, at boulevard Sebastopol, midway between the river and Pompidou Center (Mo: Chatelet).

Au Duc des Lombards is one of the most popular and well-respected jazz clubs in Paris (42 rue des Lombards, tel. 01 42 33 23 88, www:jazzvalley.com/duc). **Le Sunset** is a block to the west and offers more traditional jazz—Dixieland, Big Band—and fewer crowds (60 rue des Lombards, Mo: Chatelet, tel. 01 40 26 46 60).

All Jazz Club, more expensive than the rest, is a happening club in the heart of the St. Germain area attracting a more mature crowd in search of recognizable names (7 rue St. Benoit, Mo: St. Germain-des-Près, tel. 01 42 61 53 53).

At the more down-to-earth and mellow **Le Cave du Franc Pinot**, you can enjoy a glass of chardonnay at the main-floor wine bar then drop downstairs for a cool jazz scene (1 quai de Bourbon, good dinner values as well, located on Île St. Louis where the Pont Marie meets the island, Mo: Pont Marie, tel. 01 46 33 60 64).

The **American Church** regularly plays host to fine jazz musicians for the best price in Paris (free, 65 quai d'Orsay, Mo: Invalides, RER-C: Pont de l'Alma, tel. 01 40 62 05 00).

Classical Concerts

For classical music on any night, consult *Pariscope* magazine; the "Musique" section under "Concerts Classique" lists concerts (free and fee). Look for posters at the churches. Churches that regularly host concerts include St. Sulpice, St. Germain-des-Près, Basilique de Madeleine, St. Eustache, and Sainte-Chapelle. It's worth the 100F to 150F entry for the pleasure of hearing Mozart while you're surrounded by the stained glass of the tiny Sainte-Chapelle. Even the Galleries Lafayette department store offers concerts. Many are free (*entrée libre*), such as the Sunday Atelier concert sponsored by the American Church (18:00, 65 quai d'Orsay, Mo: Invalides, RER: Pont de l'Alma, tel. 01 47 05 07 99).

Opera

Paris is home to two well-respected operas. The **Opéra Garnier**, Paris' first opera house, hosts opera and ballet performances. Come here for less-expensive tickets and grand belle epoque decor (Mo: Opéra, tel. 01 44 73 13 99). The **Opéra de la Bastille** is the massive modern opera house that dominates place de la Bastille. Come here for state-of-the-art special effects and modern interpretations of classic ballets and operas (Mo: Bastille, tel. 01 43 43 96 96). For tickets, either call 01 44 73 13 00, go to the opera ticket offices (open 11:00–18:00), or, best, reserve on the Web at www.ticketavenue.com (for both operas).

Transportation Connections—Paris

Paris is Europe's transportation hub. You'll find trains and buses (day and night) to most any French or European destination. Paris has six central rail stations, each serving different regions. For train schedule information, call 08 36 35 35 35 (3F/min).

Gare St. Lazare: Serves Upper Normandy. To **Giverny** (train to Vernon, 5/day, 45 min; then bus or taxi 10 min to Giverny), **Rouen** (15/day, 75 min), **Honfleur** (6/day, 3 hrs, via Lisieux then bus), **Bayeux** (9/day, 2.5 hrs), **Caen** (12/day, 2 hrs).

Gare Montparnasse: Serves Lower Normandy and Brittany and offers TGV service to Loire Valley and southwestern France. To **Chartres** (10/day, 1 hr), **Mont St. Michel** (2/day, 4.5 hrs, via Rennes), **Dinan** (7/day, 3 hrs, via Rennes and Dol), **Bordeaux** (14/day, 3.5 hrs), **Sarlat** (5/day, 6 hrs, transfer in Bordeaux), **Toulouse** (7/day, 5 hrs, possible transfer in Bordeaux), **Albi** (6.5 hrs, via Toulouse), **Carcassonne** (6.5 hrs, via Toulouse), **Tours** (14/day, 1 hr).

Gare d'Austerlitz: Provides non-TGV service to the Loire Valley, southwestern France, and Iberia. To **Amboise** (8/day, 2.5 hrs), **Sarlat** (5/day, 6 hrs), **Cahors** (5/day, 7 hrs), **Barcelona** (3/day, 13 hrs), **Madrid** (5/day, 16 hrs), **Lisbon** (1/day, 24 hrs).

Gare du Nord: Serves northern France and several international destinations. To **Brussels** (10/day, 3.5 hrs), **Bruges** (3/day, 2.5 hrs), **Amsterdam** (10/day, 5.5 hrs), **Copenhagen** (3/day, 16 hrs), **Koblenz on the Rhine** (3/day, 7 hrs), **London** via the Eurostar Chunnel (12/day, 3 hrs, Full fare: $239 1st class/$159 2nd class; nonexchangeable Leisure Ticket—restrictions on refunds; $199 1st class/$119 2nd class; U.S. tel. 800/EUROSTAR, www.eurostar.com).

Gare de l'Est: Serves eastern France and points east. To **Colmar** (6/day, 5.5 hrs, transfer in Strasbourg or Mulhouse), **Strasbourg** (10/day, 4.5 hrs), **Reims** (8/day, 2 hrs), **Verdun** (5/day, 3 hrs), **Munich** (4/day, 8.5 hrs), **Vienna** (3/day, 13 hrs), **Zurich** (4/day, 6 hrs), **Prague** (2/day, 16 hrs).

Gare du Lyon: Offers TGV and regular service to southeastern France, Italy, and other international destinations. To **Beaune** (8/day, 2–3 hrs), **Dijon** (13/day, 90 min), **Chamonix** (3/day, 9 hrs, transfer in Lyon and St. Gervais, 1 direct and very handy night train), **Annecy** (8/day, 4–7 hrs), **Lyon** (12/day, 2.5 hrs), **Avignon** (10/day, 4 hrs), **Arles** (10/day, 5 hrs), **Nice** (8/day, 7 hrs), **Venice** (5/day, 11 hrs), **Rome** (3/day, 15 hrs), **Bern** (5/day, 5 hrs).

Buses: Long-distance buses provide cheaper, although less comfortable and less flexible, transportation to major European cities. The main bus station in Paris is the Gare Routière du Paris-Gallieni (avenue du General de Gaulle, in a suburb of Bagnolet, Mo: Gallieni, tel. 01 49 72 51 51). Eurolines buses depart from this station.

Charles de Gaulle Airport

Charles de Gaulle Airport is Paris' primary airport. It has three main terminals: T-1, T-2, and T-9. (Air France uses T-2; charters dominate T-9.) Terminals are connected every few minutes by a free *navette* (bus), and the RER (Paris subway) stops at T-1 and T-2 terminals. There is no bag storage at the airport.

Those flying to or from the United States will probably use T-1. Here you'll find an American Express cash machine, an automatic bill changer (at baggage claim 30), and an exchange window (at baggage claim 18). A bank (with barely acceptable rates) and an ATM machine are near gate 16. At the Meeting Point, you'll find the TI, with free Paris maps and information (daily 7:00–22:00), and Relais H (sells phone cards). Car rental offices are on the arrival level from gates 10 to 22; the SNCF (train) office is at gate 22. For flight info, call 01 48 62 22 80.

Transportation between Charles de Gaulle Airport and Paris: There are plenty of choices. Three efficient public-transportation routes, taxis, and airport shuttle vans link the airport's T-1 and T-2 terminals with central Paris. At T-1 (where most will land), the free *navette* (bus) runs between gate 36 (confirm) and the RER Roissy Rail station, where a train zips you into Paris' subway system in 30 minutes (49F, stops at Gare du Nord, Chatelet, St. Michel, and Luxembourg Gardens). The Roissy Bus runs every 15 minutes between gate 30 and the old Paris Opéra (stop is on rue Scribe, in front of American Express), costs 45F (use the automatic ticket machine), and takes 40 minutes but can be jammed. The Air France Bus leaves every 15 minutes from gate 34 and serves the Arc de Triomphe in about 40 minutes for 60F and the Montparnasse tower in 60 minutes for 75F (from any of these stops you can reach your hotel by taxi). For most people the RER Roissy Rail works best. A taxi ride with luggage costs about 230F (a taxi stand at gate 16). The Disneyland Express bus departs from gate 32. (The RER Roissy Rail, Roissy Bus, and Air France bus described above also serve the T-2 terminal efficiently.)

For a stress-free trip between either of Paris' airports and downtown, consider an airport shuttle minivan. Reserve from home, and they'll meet you at the airport. Consider Airport Shuttle (allow 150F for 1 person, 89F per person for 2, cheaper for larger groups and kids, plan on a 30-minute wait if you ask them to pick you up at the airport, tel. 01 45 38 55 72, fax 01 43 21 35 67, www.paris-anglo.com/clients/ashuttle.html) or Paris Airport Services (tel. 01 49 62 78 78, fax 01 49 62 78 79, www.magic.fr/pas).

Sleeping at or near Charles de Gaulle Airport: Those with early flights can sleep in T-1 at Cocoon (60 cabins, Sb-250F, Db-300F, CC:VM, take elevator down to boutique level or walk down from departure level, tel. 01 48 62 06 16, fax 01 48 62 56

97). You get 16 hours of silence buried under the check-in level with TV and toilet. Hôtel IBIS, at the Roissy Rail station, is comfortable (Db-420F, CC:VMA, free shuttle bus to airport takes 2 minutes, tel. 01 49 19 19 19, fax 01 49 19 19 21).

Orly Airport

This airport feels with two terminals: Sud and Ouest. International flights arrive at Sud. After exiting baggage claim (near gate H), you'll be greeted by signs directing you to city transportation, car rental, and so on. Turn left to enter the main terminal area and you'll find exchange offices with barely acceptable rates, an ATM machine, the ADP (a quasi–tourist office that offers free city maps and basic sightseeing information), and an SNCF French rail desk (sells train tickets and Eurailpasses). Downstairs is a sandwich bar, a bank (lousy rates), a newsstand (sells *télécartes*), and a post office (great rates for cash or Amex traveler's checks). For flight info call 01 49 75 15 15.

Transportation between Paris and Orly Airport: There are three efficient public-transportation routes, taxis, and a couple of airport shuttle services linking Orly and central Paris. The Air France bus (outside gate F) runs to Paris' Invalides Métro stop (40F, 4/hrly, 30 min) and is best for those staying in or near the rue Cler neighborhood (from Invalides terminal, take the Métro 2 stops to École Militaire). The Jetbus #285 (outside gate F, 24F, 4/hrly) is the quickest way to the Paris subway and the best way to the recommended hotels in the Marais and Contrescarpe neighborhoods (take Jetbus to Villejuif Métro stop, buy a *carnet* of 10 Métro tickets, then take the Métro to the Sully Morland stop for Marais or the Cardinal Lemoine stop for Contrescarpe). The Orlybus (outside gate H, 30F, 4/hrly) takes you to the Denfert-Rochereau RER-B line and the Métro, offering subway access to central Paris. The Orlyval trains are overpriced (57F). Allow 150F for a taxi into central Paris.

Consider airport shuttle minivans (see "Charles de Gaulle Airport," above). From Orly, figure about 120F for one person, 80F per person for two, or less for larger groups and kids.

Sleeping near Orly Airport: IBIS is cheaper (Db-420F, CC:VMA, tel. 01 46 87 33 50, fax 01 46 87 29 92) than the more comfortable Hilton (Db-680F, tel. 01 45 12 45 12, fax 01 45 12 45 00). Both offer free airport shuttle service.

PROVENCE

This magnificent region is shaped like a wedge of quiche. From its sunburnt crust fanning out along the Mediterranean coast from Nîmes to Nice, it stretches north along the Rhône Valley to Orange. The Romans were here in force and left many ruins—some of the best anywhere. Seven popes; great artists, such as van Gogh, Cézanne, and Picasso; and author Peter Mayle all enjoyed their years in Provence. Provence offers a splendid recipe of arid climate (but brutal winds known as the mistral), captivating cities, exciting hill towns, and remarkably varied landscapes.

Wander through the ghost town of ancient Les Baux and under France's greatest Roman ruin, Pont du Gard. Spend your starry, starry nights where van Gogh did, in Arles. Explore its Roman past then find the linger-longer squares and café corners that inspired Vincent. Some may prefer Avignon's more elegant feel and softer edge as a home base. Youthful but classy Avignon bustles in the shadow of its brooding popes' palace.

Planning Your Time

Make Arles or Avignon your base. Italophiles prefer Arles, while poodles pick Avignon. If you're driving, consider basing in a town nearby and leave absolutely nothing in your car at any stop. Avignon (well connected to Arles by train) is the regional transportation hub for Pont du Gard, Uzès, and Orange. You'll want a full day for Arles (ideally on Wed or Sat, when the morning market rages), a half day for Avignon, and a day or two for countryside villages and sights.

Getting around Provence

The yellow Michelin map to this region is essential for drivers. Public transit is fairly good: Frequent trains link Avignon, Arles, and

Provence

Nîmes (about 30 mins between each). Les Baux is accessible by bus from Arles. Pont du Gard, St. Rémy, Vaison la Romaine, and some Luberon villages are all accessible by bus from Avignon. While a tour of the villages of Luberon is worthwhile only by car, Isle sur la Sorgue is an easy hop by train from Avignon. The TIs in Arles and Avignon have information on bus excursions to regional sights that are hard to reach *sans* car (95F/half day, 150F/day).

Cuisine Scene—Provence

The almost extravagant use of garlic, olive oil, herbs, and tomatoes makes Provence's cuisine France's liveliest. To sample it, order anything *à la Provençale*. Among the area's spicy specialties are ratatouille (a thick mixture of vegetables in an herb-flavored tomato sauce), *brandade* (a salt cod, garlic, and cream mousse), aioli (a garlicky mayonnaise often served atop fresh vegetables), *tapenade* (a paste of puréed olives, capers, anchovies, herbs, and sometimes tuna), *soupe au pistou* (vegetable soup with basil, garlic, and cheese), and *soupe à l'ail* (garlic soup). Look also for *riz Camarguaise* (rice from the Camargue) and *taureau* (bull meat). Banon (wrapped in chestnut leaves) and Picodon (nutty taste) are the native cheeses. Provence also produces some of France's great wines at relatively reasonable prices. Look for Gigondas, Sablet, Côtes du Rhône, and Côte de Provence. If you like rosé, try the Tavel. This is the place to splurge for a bottle of Châteauneuf-du-Pape.

Provence Market Days

Provençal market days offer France's most colorful and tantalizing outdoor shopping. Here's a list to help plan your excursions. The best markets are Wednesday in St. Rémy, Thursday in Nyons, Saturday in Arles, and, best of all, Sunday in Isle sur la Sorgue. Crowds and parking problems abound at these popular events—arrive by 9:00 or, better, sleep in the town the night before.
Monday: Cadenet (near Vaison la Romaine), Cavaillon
Tuesday: Avignon, Tarascon, Gordes, Vaison la Romaine, Beaumes de Venise
Wednesday: Arles, Avignon, St. Rémy, Violes (near Vaison la Romaine)
Thursday: Carianne (near Vaison la Romaine), Nyons, Orange, Avignon, Beaucaire, Vacqueyras, Isle sur la Sorgue
Friday: Remoulins (Pont du Gard), Carpentras, Bonnieux, Visan, Châteauneuf-du-Pape
Saturday: Arles, Avignon, Oppède, Valreas
Sunday: Avignon, Isle sur la Sorgue, Uzès, Coustelet, Beaucaire

ARLES

By helping Julius Caesar defeat Marseille, Arles earned the imperial nod and was made an important port city. With the first bridge over the Rhône, Arles was a key stop on the Roman road from Italy to Spain, the Via Domitia. After reigning as a political center of the early Christian church (the seat of an archbishopric for centuries) and thriving as a trading city on and off until the 18th century, Arles all but disappeared from the map. Van Gogh settled here a hundred years ago but left only memories. American bombers destroyed much of Arles in World War II, but today Arles thrives again. This compact city is alive with great Roman ruins, some fine early Christian art, an eclectic assortment of museums, made-for-ice-cream pedestrian zones, and squares that play hide-and-seek with visitors.

Tourist Information: The small TI at the train station will likely be closed in 2000, but check anyway. The main TI, on the ring road esplanade Charles de Gaulle, is a high-powered mega-information site (daily 9:00–19:00, in winter Mon–Sat 9:00–19:00, Sun 9:00–13:00, tel. 04 90 18 41 20). Pick up the "Arles et

Vincent Van Gogh" walking tour brochure (5F) and the free *Guide Touristique 2000* and ask about bullfights and bus excursions to regional sights.

Arrival in Arles
By Train and Bus: Both stations sit side by side on the river a 10-minute walk from the city center. Lockers are available at the train station. Pick up (or note) the bus schedule to Les Baux on your way into Arles. To reach the old town, walk to the river and turn left.

By Car: Follow signs to *centre-ville* then follow signs toward the *gare SNCF* (train station). You'll come to a huge roundabout (place Lamartine) with a Monoprix department store to the right. There is parking on the left, along the city wall (pay attention to no-parking signs on Wed and Sat until 13:00—they mean it). Theft is a problem; park at your hotel if possible. Take everything out of your car for safety. From place Lamartine, walk into the city through the two stumpy towers.

Helpful Hints
Supermarket: Place Lamartine has a big, handy Monoprix supermarket/department store (Mon–Sat 8:30–19:25, closed Sun).

Banks: Several banks on place de la République across from St. Trophime change money.

Laundry: A Laundromat is at 12 rue Portagnel (Mon–Sat 8:00–12:00, 14:00–19:00). Another, nearby at 6 rue Cavalarie, near place Voltaire (daily 7:00–21:00, later once you're in), has a confusing central-command panel: 20F for wash (push machine number on top row), 10F for 25 minutes of dryer (push dryer number on third row five times slowly), 2F for flakes (button #11). Dine at the recommended L'Arlatan restaurant, across the street, while you clean.

Getting around Arles
Arles faces the Mediterranean more than Paris. Its spaghetti street plan disorients the first-time visitor. Landmarks hide in the medieval tangle of narrow, winding streets. Everything is deceptively close. While Arles sits on the Rhône, it completely ignores the river. The elevated riverside walk does provide a direct route to the excellent Ancient History Museum and an easy return to the station. Hotels have free city maps, but Arles works best if you simply follow the numerous street-corner signs pointing you toward the sights and hotels of the town center. Racing cars seem to enjoy Arles' medieval lanes, turning sidewalks into tightropes and pedestrians into leaping targets.

By Minibus: The free "Starlette" shuttle minibus, which circles the town's major sights twice an hour, is worthwhile only to get to or from the distant Ancient History Museum (just wave

Provence

at the driver and hop in; Mon–Sat 7:30–19:30, never on Sun), though I prefer the 20-minute walk along the river.

By Bike: While Isle sur la Sorgue makes a better biking base (see below), rides to Les Baux or into the Camargue work well from Arles. The Peugeot store rents bikes (15 rue du Pont, tel. 04 90 96 03 77), as does the newsstand next to the main TI (tel. 04 90 96 44 20).

By Taxi: Arles' taxis charge a minimum flat 50F fee. Nothing in town is worth a taxi ride (figure 100F to Les Baux, tel. 04 90 96 90 03).

Car Rental: You can rent cars at ADA (cheapest, 22 avenue Stalingrad, tel. 04 90 52 93 69), Avis (at train station, tel. 04 90 96 82 42), and Europcar (downtown at 15 boulevard Victor Hugo, tel. 04 90 93 23 24).

Sights—Arles' Museums

Arles' Global Billet covers all of the following sights (60F, sold at each sight). Otherwise, it's 15F per sight and museum (35F for the ancient history museum). While any sight is worth a few minutes of your time, many aren't worth the individual admission. For the small price of a Global Billet, the city is yours. (All sights except the Ancient History Museum and Arlatan folk museum are open Jun–mid-Sept 9:00–19:00; Apr–May and latter half of Sept 9:00–12:30, 14:00–19:00; otherwise 10:00–12:30, 14:00–17:30; closes 1 hour earlier in winter.) See Ancient History Museum and Musée Arlatan listings, below, for their hours.

▲▲▲**Ancient History Museum (Musée de L'Arles Antique)**— The sights of Roman Arles make maximum sense if you start your visit in this superb, air-conditioned museum. Models and original sculpture (with the help of the free English handout) re-create the Roman city of Arles, making workaday life and culture easier to imagine. Notice what a radical improvement the Roman buildings were over the simple mud-brick homes of pre-Roman peoples. Models of Arles' arena even illustrate the moveable stadium cover, good for shade and rain. While virtually nothing is left of Arles' chariot racecourse, the model shows how it must have rivaled Rome's Circus Maximus. Jewelry, fine metal and glass artifacts, and fine mosaic floors make it clear that Roman Arles was a city of art and culture. The finale is an impressive row of pagan and early Christian sarcophagi (second to fifth centuries). In the early days of the Church, Jesus was often portrayed beardless and as the good shepherd—with a lamb over his shoulder.

Built at the site of the chariot racecourse, this museum is a 20-minute walk from Arles along the river. Turn left at the river and follow it to the big modern building just past the new bridge—or ride the free Starlette shuttle bus. (35F, daily 9:00–19:00 Apr–Sept, otherwise Wed–Mon 10:00–18:00, closed Tue, tel. 04 90 18 88 88.)

Arles

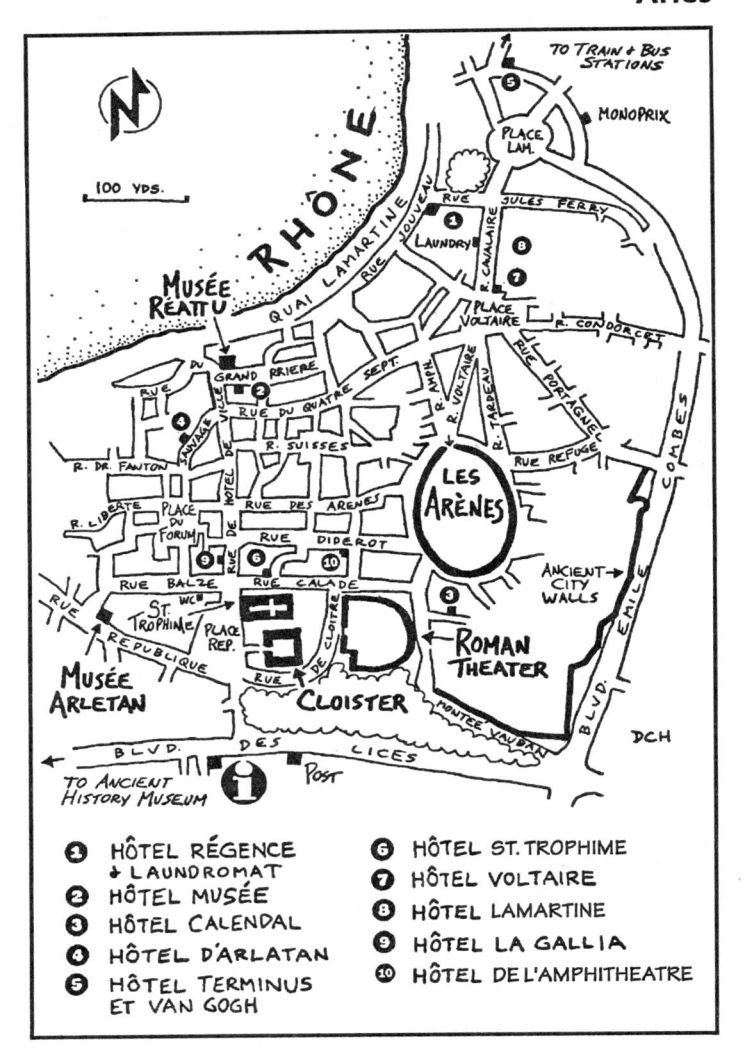

[Map of Arles showing the Rhône river, Musée Réattu, Les Arènes, Roman Theater, Cloister, Musée Arletan, and streets including Quai Lamartine, Rue du Quatre Septembre, Rue des Arènes, Rue Diderot, Rue Calade, Blvd. des Lices, Blvd. Emile Combes, etc. Scale: 100 yds.]

Hotel Key:
1. HÔTEL RÉGENCE & LAUNDROMAT
2. HÔTEL MUSÉE
3. HÔTEL CALENDAL
4. HÔTEL D'ARLATAN
5. HÔTEL TERMINUS ET VAN GOGH
6. HÔTEL ST. TROPHIME
7. HÔTEL VOLTAIRE
8. HÔTEL LAMARTINE
9. HÔTEL LA GALLIA
10. HÔTEL DE L'AMPHITHEATRE

▲▲**Roman Arena (Amphithéâtre)**—Nearly 2,000 years ago, gladiators fought wild animals here to the delight of 20,000 screaming fans—cruel. Today matadors fight wild bulls to the delight of local fans—still cruel. While the ancient third row of arches is long gone, three towers survive from medieval times, when the arena was used as a fortress. In the 1800s it corralled 200 humble homes and functioned as a town within the town. Climb the tower. Walk through the inner corridors of this 440-by-350-foot oval and notice the similarity to 20th-century stadium floor plans. And if you don't mind the gore, a bullfight is an exciting show.

Classical Theater (Théâtre Antique)—Precious little survives from this Roman theater, which served as a handy town quarry throughout the Middle Ages. Two lonely Corinthian columns look from the stage out over the audience. The 10,000 mostly modern seats are still used for concerts and festivals. Take a stroll backstage through broken bits of Rome.

Musée Réattu—Highlights of this mildly interesting museum are a fun collection of 70 Picasso drawings (some two-sided and all done in a flurry of creativity) and a room of Henri Rousseau's Camargue watercolors.

▲**Musée Arlatan**—This cluttered folklore museum, given to Arles by Monsieur Mistral, is filled with interesting odds and ends of Provence life. The employees wear the native costumes. It's like a failed turn-of-the-century garage sale: You'll find shoes, hats, wigs, old photos, bread cupboards, and the beetle-dragon monster. If you're into folklore, this museum is for you (Apr–Sept daily 9:00–12:00, 14:00–19:00, otherwise closes at 17:00).

▲▲**St. Trophime Cloisters and Church**—This church, named after a third-century bishop of Arles, sports the finest Romanesque west portal (main doorway) I've seen anywhere.

But first enjoy the place de la République. Sit on the steps opposite the church. The Egyptian obelisk used to be the centerpiece of Arles' Roman Circus. Watch the peasants—pilgrims, locals, buskers. There's nothing new about this scene. Like a Roman triumphal arch, the church trumpets the promise of Judgment Day. The tympanum is filled with Christian symbolism. Christ sits in majesty, surrounded by symbols of the four evangelists (Matthew—the winged man, Mark—the winged lion, Luke—the ox, and John—the eagle). The Twelve Apostles are lined up below Jesus. Move up closer. This is it. Some are saved and others aren't. Notice the condemned—a chain gang on the right bunny-hopping over the fires of hell. For them the tune trumpeted by the three angels on the very top isn't a happy one. Ride the exquisite detail back to a simpler age. In an illiterate medieval world long before the vivid images of our Technicolor age, this message was a neon billboard over this town's square. A chart just inside the church (on the right) helps explain the carvings. On the right side of the nave, a fourth-century early-Christian sarcophagus is used as an altar.

The adjacent cloisters are the best in Provence (15F, enter from the square, 20 meters to right of church). Enjoy the sculpted capitals of the rounded Romanesque columns (12th century) and the pointed Gothic columns (14th century). The second floor offers only a view of the cloisters from above.

More Sights—Arles
▲▲**Place du Forum**—This café-crammed square, while always lively, is best at night. Named for the Roman Forum that stood here, only two columns from a second-century temple survive. They are incorporated into the wall of Hotel Nord Pinus. (After a few drinks at Café van Gogh, the corner of that hotel actually starts to look phallic.) Van Gogh hung out here under these same plane trees. In fact, his *Le Café de Nuit* was painted from this square. The bistros on the square, while no place for a fine dinner, put together a good salad, and when you sprinkle in the ambience, that's 45F well spent. The guy on the pedestal is Frederic Mistral; in 1904 he received the Nobel Prize for literature. He used his prize money to preserve and display the folk identity of Provence at a time when France was rapidly centralizing. (He founded the Arlatan folk museum—see above.)

▲▲**Wednesday and Saturday Markets**—On these days until around noon, Arles' ring road (boulevard Emile Combes on Wednesday, boulevard Lices on Saturday) erupts into an outdoor market of fish, flowers, produce, and you-name-it. Join in, buy flowers, try the olives, sample some wine, and slap a pickpocket. On the first Wednesday of the month it's a grand flea market.

Fondation Van Gogh—A two-star sight for his fans, this small gallery features works by several well-known contemporary artists who pay homage to Vincent through their thought-provoking interpretations of his art (30F, not covered by Global Billet, Apr–Sept daily 10:00–19:00, otherwise 10:00–12:30, 14:00–17:00, facing the Roman arena at #24).

The 5F "Arles et Vincent Van Gogh" brochure (available at TI) takes you on several interesting walks through Arles using pavement markers as guides; by far the most interesting walk follows the footsteps of Vincent van Gogh.

▲▲**Bullfights (Courses Camarguaise)**—You can occupy the same seats fans have been sitting in for 1,900 years and take in one of Arles' most memorable treats—a bullfight *à la Provençale*. Three classes of bullfights take place here. The *course protection* is the class for aspiring matadors; it's a daring dodge-bull game of scraping hair off the angry bull's nose for prize money offered by local businesses (no blood). The *trophée de l'avenir* is the next class, and it's for amateur matadors. The *trophée des as excellence* is the real thing à la Spain: outfits, swords, spikes, and the whole gory shebang (tickets 30–50F; Apr–Oct Sat, Sun, and holidays; skip the "rodeo" spectacle, tel. 04 90 96 03 70 or ask at TI). There are bullfights in small wooden bullrings in nearby villages nearly every weekend (TI has schedule).

Sleeping in Arles
(6F = about $1, zip code: 13200)
Sleep Code: **S** = Single, **D** = Double/Twin, **T** = Triple, **Q** = Quad, **b** = bathroom, **t** = toilet only, **s** = shower only, **CC** = Credit Card (Visa, MasterCard, Amex), **SE** = Speaks English, **NSE** = No English, * = French hotel rating system (0–4 stars).

Hôtel Régence** sits right on the river and has immaculate and comfortable rooms, good beds, and easy access to the train station and safe parking. Helpful and gentle Sylvie speaks English (Db-200–290F, Tb-260–350F, Qb-360F; choose riverview or quiet, air-con courtyard rooms; CC:VM, 5 rue Marius Jouveau, from place Lamartine turn right immediately after passing through the towers, tel. 04 90 96 39 85, fax 04 90 96 67 64).

Hotel de l'Amphithéâtre**, a boutique hotel, is small, friendly, and *très* cozy, with thoughtfully decorated and air-conditioned rooms and a pleasant atrium breakfast room. It's located one block from the arena toward place du Forum (Db-290–350F, Tb-450–490F, parking-25F, CC:VMA, 5 rue Diderot, tel. 04 90 96 10 30, fax 04 90 93 98 69, SE).

Hôtel du Musée** is a quiet, delightful manor house hideaway with air-conditioned rooms and a terrific courtyard terrace. M. and Mme. Dubreuil speak some English (Sb-230F, Db-290–360F, Tb-370–410F, Qb-480F, parking-40F, CC:VMA, 11 rue de la Grande Prieure, follow signs to Musée Réattu, tel. 04 90 93 88 88, fax 04 90 49 98 15).

Hotel St. Trophime** is another fine, very central place with a grand entry, large rooms, and helpful owners (Sb-210F, Db-290F, spacious Db-340F, Tb-385F, huge Qb-430F, CC:VM, 16 rue de la Calade, near place de la République, tel. 04 90 96 88 38, fax 04 90 96 92 19).

Hôtel Calendal** is Provençal chic, with a tranquil outdoor garden, smartly decorated rooms, and a seductive ambience (Db-380–430F, Tb-470F, Qb-510F, extra bed-115F, parking-60F, air-con, strong beds, modern bathrooms, CC:VMA, located above arena at 22 place Dr. Pomme, tel. 04 90 96 11 89, fax 04 90 96 05 84, www.lecalendal.com, SE).

Hôtel d'Arlatan***, one of France's more affordable classy hotels, has a beautiful lobby; a courtyard terrace; and air-conditioned, antique-filled rooms. In the lobby of this 15th-century building, a glass floor looks down into Roman ruins (Db-500–800F, Db/suites-1,000–1,400F, parking-80F, CC:VMA, elevator, very central, a block off place du Forum at 26 rue du Sauvage, tel. 04 90 93 56 66, fax 04 90 49 68 45, e-mail: hotel-arlatan@provnet.fr, SE).

Hotel Terminus et Van Gogh* has bright, cheery rooms facing a busy square at the gate of the old town, a block from the train station. This building is in the painting of van Gogh's house, which was bombed in World War II (D-150F with no shower available, Ds-185F, Db-225F, CC:VM, 5 place Lamartine, tel. & fax 04 90 96 12 32).

Starving artists can afford these two clean but spartan places: **Hôtel Voltaire*** rents 12 small rooms with great balconies overlooking a caffeine-stained square a block below the arena (D-160F, Ds-180F, Db-200F, add 50F per person for 3 or 4, CC:VM, 1 place Voltaire, tel. 04 90 96 49 18). **Hôtel La Gallia** has small but clean rooms and is a steal (Ds-125–150F, above friendly café, 22 rue de l'Hôtel de Ville, tel. 04 90 96 00 63, fax 04 90 96 45 49).

Sleeping near Arles, in Fontvielle

Many drivers, particularly those with families, prefer setting up in the peaceful countryside with good access to the area's sights. Just 10 minutes from Arles and Les Baux (20 minutes to Avignon) you'll find the Provençal farmhouse/resort **Le Domaine de la Forêt**, which has modern apartments for five to six people (kitchen, 2 bedrooms, private terrace). Surrounded by vineyards and rice fields, this retreat offers a pool, swings, and a volleyball court. While most spend a full week here, shorter stays are possible (nightly-600F, weekly in summer only-3,450F, 2,750F in shoulder season, 2,250F in low season, from Arles take the D-17 toward Fontvieille, veer right in 6 km onto D-82, follow the Gites Ruraux signs, route de L'Aqueduc Romain, 13990 Fontvielle, tel. 04 90 54 70 25, fax 04 90 54 60 50).

Eating in Arles

You can eat basic food with great atmosphere on place du Forum or, better, have a drink there and then try one of these places for dinner. Near Hotel Regence, **L'Arlatan** is unpretentious and friendly and serves a fine meal and great desserts (95F *menu*, opposite Laundromat on rue Cavalarie, closed Wed). Just up the street on the place Voltaire, **La Giraudiere** offers excellent regional cooking (110F *menu*, closed Tue, tel. 04 90 93 27 52). Near Hotel du Musée, **L'Olivier** is my Arles splurge, offering exquisite *Provençale* cuisine (160F *menu*, 1 bis rue Reattu, reserve ahead, tel. 04 90 49 64 88). Vegetarians love **La Vitamine**'s salads and pastas (closed Sat–Sun, just below place du Forum on 16 rue Dr. Fanton, tel. 04 90 93 77 36). Almost next door, **La Paillotte** specializes in tradional *Provençale* cuisine (95F *menu*, 28 rue Dr. Fanton). **Le Criquet** is cheap, fun, and good (1 block from Hôtel Calendal at 12 Porte de Laure).

Transportation Connections—Arles

By bus to: Les Baux (4/day, 30 min; none on Sun, ideal departure about 8:30 with a return from Les Baux about 11:20 or 12:40, departs Arles bus station and 16 boulevard Clemenceau downtown; service reduced Nov–Mar; tel. 04 90 93 74 90).

By train to: Paris (2 direct TGVs, 4.5 hrs; otherwise transfer in Avignon, 8/day, 5.5 hrs), **Avignon** (8/day, 20 min, check for afternoon gaps), **Carcassonne** (8/day, 3 hrs, a few direct, most require a painless transfer in Narbonne), **Beaune** (3/day, 5 hrs, transfer in Lyon), **Nice** (8/day, 3.5 hrs, likely transfer in Marseille), **Barcelona** (3/day, 7 hrs, at least 1 transfer), **Italy** (3/day, via Marseille and Nice; from Arles it's 5 hrs to Ventimiglia on the border, 9 hrs to the Cinque Terre, 9 hrs to Milan, 11 hrs to Florence, 13 hrs to Venice or Rome). Train info: tel. 04 90 96 43 94.

AVIGNON

Famous for its nursery rhyme, medieval bridge, and brooding Palace of the Popes, contemporary Avignon bustles and prospers behind its walls. During the 68 years (1309–1377) that Avignon played Franco Vaticano, it grew from a quiet village to the thriving city it still is. Today this city combines a youthful student population with a white-collar, sophisticated city feel. Street mimes play to crowds enjoying Avignon's slick cafés and chic boutiques. If you're here any time in July, save evening time for Avignon's rollicking theater festival and reserve your hotel early. The streets throng with jugglers, skits, and singing, as visitors from around the world converge on Avignon.

Orientation

The cours Jean Jaurés (which turns into the rue de la République) leads from the train station to place de l'Horloge and the Palace of the Popes, forming Avignon's spine. Climb to the parc de Rochers des Doms for a fine view, enjoy the people scene on place de l'Horloge, and meander the back streets (see below). Avignon's shopping district fills the pedestrian streets where rue de la République meets place de l'Horloge (great gelato just off place de l'Horloge, where St. Agricol meets Joseph-Vernet). Walk across Pont Daladier (bridge) for a great view of Avignon and the Rhône River.

Tourist Information: The main TI is between the train station and the old town at 41 cours Jean Juarés (Mon–Fri 9:00–13:00, 14:00–18:00, Sat–Sun until 17:00, closed Sun in winter, tel. 04 90 82 65 11, e-mail: information@avignon.fr), while a smaller branch is just inside the city wall at the entrance to Pont St. Bénezet (same hours as main TI). Pick up their Avignon discovery guide, which has a good, but long, walking tour, "Strolling along the Old Streets" (consider shortcutting the route after place St. Pierre and continuing from there to the Palace of the Popes). The TI offers English-language walking tours of Avignon (50F, Tue and Thu at 10:00). They also have regional bus and train schedules to all destinations described in this chapter and information on bus excursions to popular regional sights.

Arrival in Avignon

By Train: Cross the big street and walk through the city walls onto the cours Jean Juarés (TI 3 blocks down at #41). The bus station (*halte routière*) and car rentals are 100 yards to the right as you exit the train station, near the IBIS hotel.

By Car: Drivers enter Avignon following *centre-ville* signs. Park along the wall close to Pont St. Bénezet (ruined old bridge) and use that TI. Hotels have advice for smart overnight parking.

Sights—Avignon

▲**Palace of the Popes (Palais des Papes)**—In 1309 a French pope was elected (Pope Clement V). At the urging of the French king, His Holiness decided he'd had enough of unholy Italy. So he loaded up his carts and moved out of the chaos north to Avignon for a steady rule under a friendly, supportive king. The Catholic Church literally bought Avignon, then a two-bit town, and popes resided here until 1403. From 1378 on, there were twin popes, one in Rome and one in Avignon, causing a split in the Catholic Church that wasn't fully resolved until 1417.

The pope's palace is two distinct buildings, one old and one older. Along with lots of big, barren rooms, you'll see frescoes, tapestries, and remarkable floor tiles. The new audiophone self-guided tours do a good job overcoming the lack of furnishings and give a great history lesson while allowing you to tour this vast place at your own pace (don't miss the view and windswept café from the tower, 45–55F, occasional supplements for special exhibits, Apr–Oct daily 9:00–19:00, until 20:00 in summer, off-season 9:00–17:45, ticket office closes 1 hour earlier, tours in English twice daily Mar–Oct, call 04 90 27 50 74 to confirm.)

▲**Musée du Petit Palais**—This palace superbly displays collections of 14th- and 15th-century Italian painting and sculpture. Since the Catholic Church was the patron of the arts in those days, all 350 paintings deal with Christian themes. Visiting this museum before going to the Palace of the Popes gives you a sense of art and life during the Avignon papacy. Notice the improvement in perspective in the later paintings (30F, Wed–Mon 9:30–18:00 in summer, otherwise 9:30–12:00, 14:00–18:00, closed Tue).

▲**Parc de Rochers des Doms and Pont St. Bénezet**—Hike above the Palace of the Popes for a panoramic view over Avignon and the Rhône valley. At the far end, drop down a few steps for a good view of Pont St. Bénezet. This is the famous "sur le Pont d'Avignon," whose construction and location were inspired by a shepherd's religious vision. Imagine a 22-arch, 3,000-foot-long bridge extending across two rivers to that lonely Tower of Philippe the Fair (the bridge's former tollgate on the distant side). The island the bridge spanned is now filled with campgrounds. You can pay 15F to walk along a section of the ramparts and do

Provence

your own jig on the bridge (good view), but it's best appreciated from where you are. The castle on the right, the St. André Fortress, was once another island in the Rhône. Cross Daladier Bridge for the best view of the old bridge and Avignon's skyline.
Fondation Anglandon Dubrujeaud—This newly opened museum displays an engaging collection of art from Postimpressionists to contemporary artists (30F, Wed–Sun 13:00–18:00, closed Tue, 5 rue Laboureur).
Avignon 2000—Avignon has been selected as one of several European Capitals of Culture for the millennium. Many projects and events are under consideration to celebrate this event (including rebuilding Pont St. Benezet). Check at the TI for year 2000 events that might coincide with your visit.

Sleeping in Avignon
(6F = about $1, zip code: 84000)

These hotels are listed in the order you would pass them from the train station.

Hôtel Splendid* rents firm beds in good rooms for a fair price near the station, on the small park near the TI (S-165F, Ds-170-220F, Db-180F–270F, 17 rue Agricol Perdiguier, tel. 04 90 86 14 46, fax 04 90 85 38 55). Across the street at #18, **Hotel du Parc***'s sharply renovated rooms are a better value but have small beds (D-165F, Ds-215F, Db-230-260F, tel. 04 90 82 71 55, fax 04 90 85 64 86).

Hotel Colbert**, one block down, is a one-star hotel masquerading as a two-star hotel, but it does have air-conditioning and cheap rates (Sb-180–250F, Db-210–290F, Tb-260-350F, 7 rue Agricol Perdiguier, tel. 04 90 86 20 20 , fax 04 90 85 97 00).

Hôtel Blauvac** offers cozy rooms with stone walls in an old manor home near the pedestrian zone (Sb-350F, Db-370–450F, Tb/Qb-400–525F, CC:VMA, 1 block off rue de la République, 11 rue de La Bancasse, tel. 04 90 86 34 11, fax 04 90 86 27 41, M. Surcouf SE). Right on the loud rue de la République at #17, the bright and cheery **Hotel Danieli**** offers modern and comfortable rooms in shiny surroundings at Parisian prices (Db-330–475F, Tb-570F, CC:VM, tel. 04 90 86 46 82, fax 04 90 27 09 24).

Hotel Medieval** is a fine value in an old mansion with friendly owners and kitchenettes in all of its unimaginative, but comfortable and fairly spacious, rooms (Db-240–350F, Tb-380F, extra bed-50F, 15 rue Petite Saunerie, 5 blocks east of place de l'Horloge, behind Eglise St. Pierre, tel. 04 90 86 11 06, fax 04 90 82 08 64).

For reliable, ultramodern comfort and a great location, try one of two **Hotel Mercures***** (Db-550–650F). One is just inside the walls near Pont St. Bénezet (Quartier de la Balance, tel. 04 90 85 91 23, fax 04 90 85 32 40); the other is near the Palace of the

Popes (Cité des Papes, 1 rue Jean Vilar, tel. 04 90 86 22 45, fax 04 90 27 39 21).

You'll find good cheap beds across Pont Daladier on the Island (Ile de la) Barthelasse at the **Auberge Bagatelle's hostel/campground,** which has a pool, laundry, a cheap café, and campers for neighbors (dorm bed-61F, Ile de la Barthelasse, tel. 04 90 86 30 39).

Eating in Avignon

L'Epicerie is charmingly located on a tiny square a few blocks east of place de l'Horloge, and offers a good selection of à la carte items (10 place St. Pierre, tel. 04 90 82 74 22).

Transportation Connections—Avignon

By train to: Arles (8/day, 20 min), **Orange** (hrly, 15 min), **Nîmes** (hrly, 20 min), **Nice** (10/day, 4 hrs; a few direct, most require transfer in Marseille), **Carcassonne** (8/day, 3 hrs, possible transfer in Narbonne), **Lyon** (14/day, 2.5 hrs), **Paris'** Gare du Lyon (10 TGVs/day, 4 hrs), **Barcelona** (2/day, 5 hrs, possible transfer in Narbonne; direct night train is convenient).

By bus to Pont du Gard: Bus service can leave you stranded for hours (3/day, 45 min, to Auberge Blanche stop, a 15-min walk to Pont du Gard). Consider visiting Pont du Gard, continuing on to Nîmes or Uzès (both merit exploration), and returning to Avignon from there (try these plans: Take the noon bus from Avignon, arriving at Pont du Gard at 12:45; then take either the 14:45 bus from there to Nîmes, where trains run hourly back to Avignon, or a 16:00 bus, Mon–Fri, on to Uzès, arriving at 16:30, with a return bus to Avignon at 18:30). Make sure you're waiting for the bus on the right side of the road at the Pont du Gard Auberge Blanche stop (ask at the small inn: *"Nîmes? Uzès? Avignon? Par ici?"*). The Avignon TI has all schedules. Service is reduced or nonexistent on Sunday and holidays. In Avignon, the bus station (tel. 04 90 82 07 35) is adjacent to the train station (tel. 08 36 35 35 35).

By bus to: St. Rémy (6/day, 45 min, handy way to visit its Wed market).

Sights—Provence

▲▲▲**Les Baux**—This rock-top ghost town is worth visiting for the lunar landscape alone. Arrive by 9:00 or after 17:00 to avoid the crowds. A 12th-century regional powerhouse with 6,000 fierce residents, Les Baux was razed in 1632 by a paranoid Louis XIII, afraid of these troublemaking upstarts. What remains are a reconstructed "live city" of tourist shops and snack stands and the "dead city" ruins carved into, out of, and on top of a 600-foot-high rock. Spend most of your time in the dead city—it's most dramatic and enjoyable in the morning or early-evening light. Don't miss the slideshow on van

Gogh, Gaugin, and Cézanne in the small chapel near the entry. Spend some time in the small museum as you enter (good exhibits) and pick up the English explanations before exploring the dead city. In the tourist-trampled live city, you'll find artsy shops, several interesting Renaissance homes, and a fine exhibit of paintings by Yves Brayer (20F), who spent his final years here (entrance to dead city costs 36F, includes entry to all the town's sights; Easter–Oct 9:00–19:00, until 20:00 in summer, otherwise 9:30–17:00; pick up the excellent brochure, "A Sense of Place," at TI, tel. 04 90 54 34 39). To best experience the bauxite rock quarries and enjoy a great view of Les Baux, drive or hike one kilometer up D-27 and sample wines with atmosphere at **Caves de Sarragnan** (tel. 04 90 54 33 58). Nearby, the **Cathedrale d'Images** uses 48 projectors showing 3,000 images inside a rock quarry to immerse its visitors in themes from the region (43F, daily 10:00–18:00, on D-27 as you leave Les Baux toward St. Rémy). If you're tempted to spend the night, try the enchanting **Hotel Reine Jeanne****, 50 yards on your right after the main entry (Db-270–360F, great family suite-520F, ask for a *chambre avec terasse*, *menus* from 110F, CC:VM, 13520 Les Baux, tel. 04 90 54 32 06, fax 04 90 54 32 33).

Four daily buses serve Les Baux from the Arles train station, and two daily buses (summers only) leave from Avignon. Les Baux is 15 kilometers northeast of Arles, just past Fontvieille.

St. Rémy—This chic Provençal town is a scenic ride just over the hill from Les Baux. Here you'll find a thriving Wednesday market (until noon); the crumbled ruins of **Glanum**, a once-thriving Roman city located at the crossroads of two ancient trade routes between Italy and Spain; and the mental ward where Vincent van Gogh was sent after cutting off his ear. Glanum is just outside St. Rémy on the road to Les Baux (D-5). Walk to the gate and peek in to get a feel for its scale. The ruins are worth the effort if you have the time and haven't been to Pompeii or Ephesus (33F, Apr–Sept daily 9:00–12:00, 14:00–19:00, otherwise 9:30–12:00, 14:00–17:00). Across the street, opposite the entrance, is a Roman arch and tower. The arch marked the entry into Glanum. The tower is a memorial to the grandsons of Emperor Augustus.

Across the street from Glanum is the still-functioning mental hospital that housed van Gogh (Clinique St. Paul). Wander into the small chapel and intimate cloisters. Vincent's favorite walks outside the hospital are clearly signposted. If St. Rémy charms you into a longer visit, sleep dead center at the comfortable **Hotel du Cheval Blanc**** (Db-280–300F, CC:VM, 6 avenue Fauconnet, tel. 04 90 92 09 28, fax 04 90 92 69 05) or just outside town at the tranquil **Canto Cigalo** (Db-280–340F, chemin Canto Cigalo, tel. 04 90 92 14 28, fax 04 90 92 24 48).

▲▲▲**Pont du Gard**—One of Europe's great treats, this remarkably well preserved Roman aqueduct was built before the time of

Christ. It was the missing link of a 35-mile canal that, by dropping one foot for every 300, supplied 44 million gallons of water to Nîmes daily. While the top is now closed to daredevils, just walking under it is a marvel. Study it up close. There's no mortar—just expertly cut stones. Signs direct you to "panaromas" above the bridge on either side. The best view of the aqueduct is from the cool of the river below, floating flat on your back—bring a swimsuit and sandals for the rocks (always open and free). Consider renting a canoe from Collas to Remoulins, ending at the Pont du Gard (2-hour trip, 175F per 2-person canoe; shuttle to bus stop, car park, or Remoulins included; Collas Canoes, tel. 04 66 22 85 54).

Buses run to Pont du Gard from Nîmes, Uzès, and Avignon. Combine Uzès (see below) and Pont du Gard for an ideal day excursion from Avignon (see "Transportation Connections—Avignon," above). By car, Pont du Gard is an easy 30-minute drive due west of Avignon (follow signs to Nîmes) and 45 minutes northwest of Arles (via Tarascon). Park on the *rive gauche* side (you'll see signs) and leave nothing in your car.

Uzès—An intriguing, less-trampled town near Pont du Gard, Uzès is best seen slowly on foot, with a long coffee break in its mellow main square, the place aux Herbes (not so mellow during the colorful Sunday morning market). Check out the round Tour Fenestrelle (all that remains of a 12th-century cathedral) and the Duché de Uzès. Uzès is a short hop west (by bus) of Pont du Gard and is well served from Nîmes (9/day) and Avignon (3/day).

The Camargue—This is one of the few truly "wild areas" of France, where pink flamingos, wild bulls, and the famous white horses wander freely amid rice fields and lagoons. Skip it. The Camargue's biggest town is Aigue Mortes. That means "dead town," and it should stay that way.

▲▲**Orange**—This most northern town in Provence is notable for its Roman arch and theater. Its 60-foot-tall Roman arch (from 25 B.C.) shows off Julius Caesar's defeat of the Gauls in 49 B.C. Its best-preserved Roman theater in existence still seats 10,000; the 120-foot-high stage wall is awesome (30F, Apr–early Oct daily 9:00–18:30, off-season 9:00–12:00, 13:30–17:00; ticket includes entrance to city museum across street, which has more Roman art; Orange TI tel. 04 90 34 70 88). Trains run hourly between Avignon and Orange (15-min ride; bus #2 takes you the mile from Orange station to the old town center).

RHINE AND MOSEL VALLEYS

These valleys are storybook Germany, a fairy-tale world of Rhine legends and robber-baron castles. Cruise the most castle-studded stretch of the romantic Rhine as you listen for the song of the treacherous Loreley. For hands-on castle thrills, climb through the Rhineland's greatest castle, Rheinfels, above the town of St. Goar. Then, for a sleepy and laid-back alternative, mosey through the neighboring Mosel Valley. On the Rhine, stay in St. Goar or Bacharach. On the Mosel, choose Zell.

Planning Your Time

The Rhineland does not take much time to see. The blitziest tour is an hour looking at the castles from your train window. For a better look, however, cruise in, tour a castle or two, sleep in a genuine medieval town, and take the train out. If you have limited time, cruise less and be sure to get into a castle.

Ideally, spend two nights here, sleep in Bacharach, cruise the best hour of the river (from Bacharach to St. Goar), and tour the Rheinfels Castle. Those with more time can ride the riverside bike path. With two days and a car, visit the Rhine and the Mosel. With two days by train, see the Rhine. With three days by train, do the Rhine and Mosel, and with four days include a sleepy night in the Mosel River Valley.

THE RHINE

Ever since Roman times, when this was the Empire's northern boundary, the Rhine has been one of the world's busiest shipping rivers. You'll see a steady flow of barges with 1,000- to 2,000-ton loads. Tourist-packed buses, hot train tracks, and highways line both banks.

Rhine and Mosel Valleys

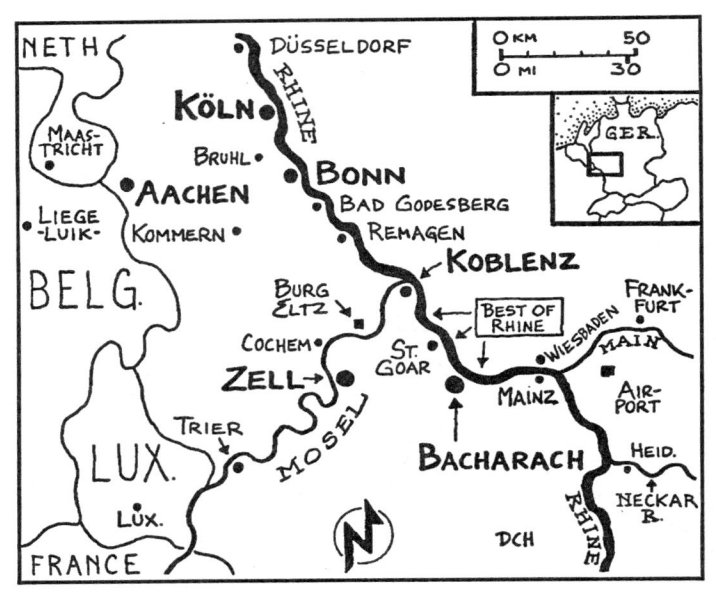

Many of the castles were "robber-baron" castles, put there by petty rulers (there were 300 independent little countries in medieval Germany) to levy tolls on passing river traffic. A robber baron would put his castle on, or even in, the river. Then, often with the help of chains and a tower on the opposite bank, he'd stop each ship and get his toll. There were 10 customs stops between Mainz and Koblenz alone (no wonder merchants were early proponents of the creation of larger nation-states).

Some castles were built to control and protect settlements, and others were the residences of kings. As times changed, so did the lifestyles of the rich and feudal. Many castles were abandoned for more comfortable mansions in the towns.

Most Rhine castles date from the 11th, 12th, and 13th centuries. When the pope successfully asserted his power over the German emperor in 1076, local princes ran wild over the rule of their emperor. The castles saw military action in the 1300s and 1400s, as emperors began reasserting their control over Germany's many silly kingdoms.

The castles were also involved in the Reformation wars, in which Europe's Catholic and "protesting" dynasties fought it out using a fragmented Germany as their battleground. The Thirty Years' War (1618–1648) devastated Germany. The outcome: Each ruler got the freedom to decide if his people would be Catholic or Protestant, and one-third of Germany was dead. Production of Gummi Bears ceased entirely.

The French—who feared a strong Germany and felt the Rhine was the logical border between them and Germany—destroyed most of the castles prophylactically (Louis XIV in the 1680s, the revolutionary army in the 1790s, and Napoleon in 1806). They were often rebuilt in neo-Gothic style in the Romantic Age—the late 1800s—and today are enjoyed as restaurants, hotels, hostels, and museums. Check out the Rhine Web site at www.loreleytal.com.

Getting around the Rhine

While the Rhine flows from Switzerland to Holland, the stretch from Mainz to Koblenz hoards all the touristic charm. Studded with the crenelated cream of Germany's castles, it bustles with boats, trains, and highway traffic. Have fun exploring with a mix of big steamers, tiny ferries, bikes, and trains.

By Boat: While many travelers do the whole trip by boat, the most scenic hour is from St. Goar to Bacharach. Sit on the top deck with your handy Rhine map-guide (or the kilometer-keyed tour in this chapter) and enjoy the parade of castles, towns, boats, and vineyards.

There are several boat companies, but most travelers sail on the bigger, more expensive and romantic Köln-Düsseldorf (K-D) line (free with Eurailpass or a dated Europass, otherwise about 15.40 DM for the first hour, then progressively cheaper per hour; the recommended Bacharach–St. Goar trip costs 15.40 DM one way, 18.80 DM round-trip; tel. 06741/1634 in St. Goar). Boats run daily in both directions from April through October, with fewer boats off-season. Complete, up-to-date schedules are posted in any station, Rhineland hotel, TI, or current Thomas Cook Timetable. Purchase tickets at the dock five minutes before departure. The boat is never full. (Confirm times at your hotel the night before.)

The smaller Bingen-Rüdesheimer line is 25 percent cheaper than K-D (Eurail not valid, buy tickets on boat, tel. 06721/14140), with three two-hour round-trip St. Goar–Bacharach trips daily in summer (about 12 DM one way, 16 DM round-trip; departing St. Goar at 11:00, 14:10, and 16:10; departing Bacharach at 10:10, 12:30, and 15:00).

Drivers have these options: (1) skip the boat; (2) take a round-trip cruise from St. Goar or Bacharach; (3) draw pretzels and let the loser drive, prepare the picnic, and meet the boat; (4) rent a bike, bring it on the boat for free, and bike back; or (5) take the boat one way and return by train.

By Train: Hourly milk-run trains down the Rhine hit every town: St. Goar–Bacharach, 12 min; Bacharach–Mainz, 60 min;

Mainz–Frankfurt, 45 min. Some train schedules list St. Goar but not Bacharach as a stop, but any schedule listing St. Goar also stops at Bacharach. Tiny stations are unmanned—buy tickets at the platform machines or on the train.

By Bike: In Bacharach try Hotel Hillen (10 DM/half day, 15 DM/day, cheaper for guests, 20 bikes) or Hotel Gelberhof (20 DM/day for 10-speeds, 25 DM for "trekking" bikes, 5 DM for child's seat, tel. 06743/910-100, ring bell when closed). There are no bike rentals in St. Goar. The best riverside bike path is from Bacharach to Bingen (leaving from Bacharach, head down after campground to path bordering river). The path is also good from St. Goar to Bacharach, but it's closer to the highway. Consider renting a bike in Bacharach and taking it on the boat to Bingen and biking back, visiting Rheinstein Castle (you're on your own to wander the well-furnished castle) and Reichenstein Castle (admittance with groups), and maybe even taking a ferry across the river to Kaub (where a tiny boat shuttles sightseers to the better-from-a-distance castle on the island). While there are no bridges between Koblenz and Mainz, several small ferries do their job constantly and cheaply.

Sights—The Romantic Rhine

(These sights are listed from north to south, Koblenz to Bingen.)
▲▲▲**Der Romantische Rhein Blitz Zug Fahrt**—One of Europe's great train thrills is zipping along the Rhine in this fast train tour. Here's a quick and easy, from-the-train-window tour (also works for car, bike, or best by boat, you can cut in anywhere) that skips the syrupy myths and the life story of Dieter von Katzenelnbogen that fill normal Rhine guides. For more information than necessary, buy the handy *Rhine Guide from Mainz to Cologne* (7-DM book with foldout map, at most shops).

Sit on the left (river) side of the train or boat going south from Koblenz. While nearly all the castles listed are viewed from this side, clear a path to the right window for the times I yell, "Crossover!"

You'll notice large black-and-white kilometer markers along the riverbank. I erected these years ago to make this tour easier to follow. They tell the distance from the Rhinefalls where the Rhine leaves Switzerland and becomes navigable. Now the river-barge pilots have accepted these as navigational aids as well. We're tackling just 36 miles of the 820-mile-long Rhine. Your Blitz Rhine Tour starts at Koblenz and heads upstream to Bingen. If you're going the other direction, it still works. Just hold the book upside down.

Km 590: Koblenz—This Rhine blitz starts with Romantic Rhine thrills—at Koblenz. Koblenz is not a nice city (it was really hit hard in World War II), but its place as the historic *Deutsche-Ecke* (German corner)—the tip of land where the Mosel joins the Rhine—gives it a certain historic charm. Koblenz, Latin for "confluence," has Roman origins. Walk through the park, noticing the

Rhine and Mosel Valleys 191

reconstructed memorial to the Kaiser. Across the river, the yellow Ehrenbreitstein Castle now houses a hostel. It's a 30-minute hike from the station to the Koblenz boat dock.

Km 585: Burg Lahneck—Above the modern Autobahn bridge over the Lahn River, this castle (*Burg*) was built in 1240 to defend local silver mines, ruined by the French in 1688 and rebuilt in the 1850s in neo-Gothic style. Burg Lahneck faces the yellow Schloss Stolzenfels (out of view above the train, a 10-minute climb from tiny car park, open for touring, closed Mon).

Km 580: Marksburg—This castle (black and white with the three modern chimneys behind it, just after town of Spay) is the best-looking of all the Rhine castles and the only surviving medieval castle on the Rhine. Because of its commanding position, it was never attacked. It's now open as a museum with a medieval interior second only to the Mosel's Burg Eltz (9 DM, daily 10:00–17:00, call ahead to see if a rare English tour is scheduled, tel. 02627/206).

Km 570: Boppard—Once a Roman town, Boppard has some impressive remains of fourth-century walls. Notice the Roman towers and the substantial chunk of Roman wall near the Boppard's train station. Boppard is worth a stop. Just above the main square are the remains of the Roman wall. Below the square is a fascinating church. Notice the carved Romanesque crazies at the doorway. Inside, to the right of the entrance, you'll see Christian symbols from Roman times. Also notice the painted arches and vaults. Originally most Romanesque churches were painted this way. Down by the river, look for the high water (*Hochwasser*) marks on the arches from various flood years. (You'll find these flood marks throughout the Rhine and Mosel Valleys.)

Km 567: Burg Sterrenberg and Burg Liebenstein—These are the "Hostile Brothers" castles, across from Bad Salzig. Take the wall between the castles (actually designed to improve the defenses of both castles), add two greedy and jealous brothers and a fair maiden, and create your own legend. The castles are restaurants today.

Km 559: Burg Maus—The Maus ("Mouse") got its name because the next castle was owned by the Katzenelnbogen family. ("Katz" means "cat.") In the 1300s it was considered a state-of-the-art fortification...until Napoleon had it blown up in 1806 with state-of-the-art explosives. It was rebuilt true to its original plans around 1900.

Km 557: St. Goar and Rheinfels Castle—Cross to the other side of the train. The pleasant town of St. Goar was named for a sixth-century hometown monk. It originated in Celtic times (really old) as a place where sailors would stop, catch their breath, send home a postcard, and give thanks after surviving the seductive and treacherous Loreley crossing. St. Goar is worth a stop to explore its mighty Rheinfels Castle. (For information on a guided castle tour and accommodations, see below.)

Best of the Rhine

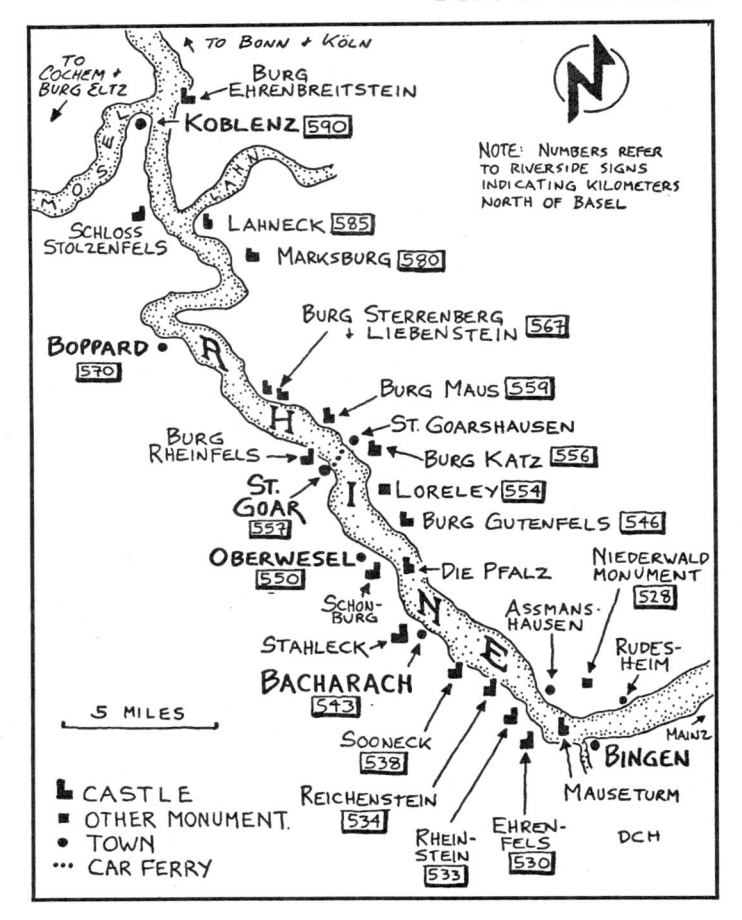

Map legend:
- TO COCHEM + BURG ELTZ
- TO BONN + KÖLN
- BURG EHRENBREITSTEIN
- KOBLENZ 590
- NOTE: NUMBERS REFER TO RIVERSIDE SIGNS INDICATING KILOMETERS NORTH OF BASEL
- SCHLOSS STOLZENFELS
- LAHNECK 585
- MARKSBURG 580
- BURG STERRENBERG + LIEBENSTEIN 567
- BOPPARD 570
- BURG MAUS 559
- ST. GOARSHAUSEN
- BURG RHEINFELS
- BURG KATZ 556
- ST. GOAR 557
- LORELEY 554
- BURG GUTENFELS 546
- OBERWESEL 550
- DIE PFALZ
- NIEDERWALD MONUMENT 528
- SCHÖNBURG
- ASSMANSHAUSEN
- STAHLECK
- RÜDESHEIM
- BACHARACH 543
- 5 MILES
- SOONECK 538
- MAINZ
- BINGEN
- REICHENSTEIN 534
- MAUSETURM
- RHEINSTEIN 533
- EHRENFELS 530
- DCH
- ■ CASTLE
- ■ OTHER MONUMENT
- ● TOWN
- ⋯ CAR FERRY

Km 556: Burg Katz—From the town of St. Goar, you'll see Burg Katz (Katzenelnbogen) across the river. Together, Burg Katz (built in 1371) and Rheinfels Castle had a clear view up and down the river and effectively controlled traffic. There was absolutely no duty-free shopping on the medieval Rhine. Katz got Napoleoned in 1806 and rebuilt around 1900. Today it's a convalescent home.

About km 555: You'll see the statue of the Loreley, the beautiful but deadly nymph (see next listing for legend), at the end of a long spit—built to give barges protection from vicious

2000 Rhine Cruise Schedule

Koblenz	Boppard	St. Goar	Bacharach
—	9:00	10:15	11:35
9:00	10:50	12:05	13:15
11:00	12:50	14:05	15:15
14:00	15:50	17:05	18:15
11:05*	11:30*	11:50*	12:10*
13:00	11:40	10:45	10:00
14:20	13:10	12:15	11:30
—	14:00	13:15	12:30
18:00	16:40	15:45	15:00
20:00	18:50	18:00	17:20

* Hydrofoil, Koblenz–Bacharach, 30 DM with Eurail, 70 DM without.
Note: Schedule applies May through September and mostly April and October; no boats run November through March.

icebergs that occasionally rage down the river in the winter. The actual Loreley, a cliff, is just ahead.

Km 554: The Loreley—Steep a big slate rock in centuries of legend and it becomes a tourist attraction, the ultimate Rhinestone. The Loreley (two flags on top, name painted near shoreline), rising 450 feet over the narrowest and deepest point of the Rhine, has long been important. It was a holy site in pre-Roman days. The fine echoes here—thought to be ghostly voices—fertilized the legendary soil.

Because of the reefs just upstream (at km 552), many ships never made it to St. Goar. Sailors (after days on the river) blamed their misfortune on a *wunderbares Fräulein* whose long blonde hair almost covered her body. Heinrich Heine's *Song of Loreley* (the Cliffs Notes version is on local postcards) tells the story of a count who sent his men to kill or capture this siren after she distracted his horny son, causing him to drown. When the soldiers cornered the nymph in her cave, she called her father (Father Rhine) for help. Huge waves, the likes of which you'll never see today, rose from the river and carried Loreley to safety. And she has never been seen since.

But alas, when the moon shines brightly and the tour buses

River Trade and Barge Watching

The river is great for barge watching. Since ancient times this has been a highway for trade. Today the world's biggest port (Rotterdam) waits at the mouth of the river. Barge workers are almost a subculture. Many own their own ships. The captain (and family) live in the stern. Workers live in the bow. The family car often decorates the bow like a shiny hood ornament. In the Rhine town of Kaub there's even a boarding school for the children of the Rhine merchant marine. The flag of the boat's home country flies in the stern (German, Swiss, Dutch—horizontal red, white, and blue; or French—vertical red, white, and blue). Logically, imports go upstream (Japanese cars, coal, and oil) and exports go downstream (German cars, chemicals, and pharmaceuticals). A clever captain manages to ship goods in each direction.

At this point tugs can push a floating train of up to five barges at once. Upstream it gets steeper and they can push only one at a time. Before modern shipping, horses dragged boats upstream (the faint remains of the towpaths survive at points along the river). From 1873 to 1900 they actually laid a chain from Bonn to Bingen, and boats with cogwheels and steam engines hoisted themselves slowly upstream. Today 265 million tons are shipped each year along the 528 navigable miles from Basel on the Swiss border to Rotterdam on the Atlantic.

While riverside navigational aids are ignored by camera-toting tourists, they are of vital interest to captains who don't wish to meet the Loreley. Boats pass on the right unless they clearly signal otherwise with a large blue sign. Since downstream ships can't stop or maneuver as freely, upstream boats are expected to do the tricky do-si-do work. Cameras monitor traffic all along and relay warnings of oncoming ships via large triangular signals posted before narrow and troublesome bends in the river. There may be two or three triangles per signpost, depending upon how many "sectors," or segments, of the river are covered. The lowest triangle indicates the nearest stretch of river. Each triangle tells if there's a ship in that sector. When the bottom side of a triangle is lit, that sector is empty. When the left side is lit, an oncoming ship is in that sector.

are parked, a soft, playful Rhine whine can still be heard from the Loreley. As you pass, listen carefully ("Sailors... sailors... over my bounding mane").

Km 552: Killer reefs, marked by red-and-green buoys, are called the "Seven Maidens."

Km 550: Oberwesel—Cross to the other side of the train. Oberwesel was a Celtic town in 400 B.C., then a Roman military station. It now boasts some of the best Roman wall and tower remains on the Rhine and the commanding Schönburg Castle. Notice how many of the train tunnels have entrances designed like medieval turrets—they were actually built in the Romantic 19th century. OK, back to the riverside.

Km 546: Burg Gutenfels and Pfalz Castle: The Classic Rhine View—Burg Gutenfels (see the white painted "Hotel" sign) and the shipshape Pfalz Castle (built in the river in the 1300s) worked very effectively to tax medieval river traffic. The town of Kaub grew rich as Pfalz raised its chains when boats came and lowered them only when the merchants had paid their duty. Those who didn't pay spent time touring its prison, on a raft at the bottom of its well. In 1504 a pope called for the destruction of Pfalz, but a six-week siege failed. Notice the overhanging "outhouse" (tiny white room with the faded medieval stains between the two wooden ones). Pfalz is tourable but bare and dull (3-DM ferry from Kaub, 4 DM, Tue–Sun 9:00–13:00, 14:00–18:00, closed Mon, tel. 06774/570).

In Kaub a green statue honors the German General Blücher. He was Napoleon's nemesis. In 1813, as Napoleon fought his way back to Paris after his disastrous Russian campaign, he stopped at Mainz—hoping to fend off the Germans and Russians pursuing him—by controlling that strategic bridge. Blücher tricked Napoleon. By building the first major pontoon bridge of its kind, here at the Pfalz Castle, he crossed the Rhine and outflanked the French. Two years later Blücher and Wellington teamed up to defeat Napoleon once and for all at Waterloo.

Km 544: The "Raft Busters"—Immediately before Bacharach, at the top of the island, buoys mark a gang of rocks notorious for busting up rafts. The Black Forest is upstream. It was poor, and wood was its best export. Black Foresters would ride log booms down the Rhine to the Ruhr (where their timber fortified coal-mine shafts) or to Holland (where logs were sold to shipbuilders). If they could navigate the sweeping bend just before Bacharach and then survive these "raft busters," they'd come home reckless and romantic, the German folkloric equivalent of American cowboys after payday.

Km 543: Bacharach and Burg Stahleck—Cross to the other side of the train. Bacharach is a great stop (see details and accommodations below). Some of the Rhine's best wine is from this town, whose name means "altar to Bacchus." Local vintners brag that the medieval Pope Pius II ordered it by the cartload. Perched above the town, the 13th-century Burg Stahleck is now a hostel.

Km 540: Lorch—This pathetic stub of a castle is barely visible from the road. Notice the small car ferry (3/hrly, 10 min), one of several between Mainz and Koblenz, where there are no bridges.

Km 538: Castle Sooneck—Cross back to the other side of the train. Built in the 11th century, this castle was twice destroyed by people sick and tired of robber barons.

Km 534: Burg Reichenstein, and **Km 533: Burg Rheinstein**—Stay on the other side of the train to see two of the first castles to be rebuilt in the Romantic era. Both are privately owned, tourable, and connected by a pleasant trail.

Km 530: Ehrenfels Castle—Opposite Bingerbrück and the Bingen station, you'll see the ghostly Ehrenfels Castle (clobbered by the Swedes in 1636 and by the French in 1689). Since it had no view of the river traffic to the north, the owner built the cute little *Mäuseturm* (Mouse Tower) on an island (the yellow tower you'll see near the train station today). Rebuilt in the 1800s in neo-Gothic style, today it's used as a Rhine navigation signal station.

Km 528: Niederwald Monument—Across from the Bingen station on a hilltop is the 120-foot-high Niederwald monument, a memorial built with 32 tons of bronze in 1877 to commemorate "the reestablishment of the German Empire." A lift takes tourists to this statue from the famous and extremely touristy wine town of Rüdesheim.

Our tour is over. From Bingen you can continue your journey (or return to Koblenz) by train or boat.

BACHARACH

Once prosperous from the wine and wood trade, Bacharach is now just a pleasant half-timbered village working hard to keep its tourists happy.

The slick new TI is on the main street in the Posthof courtyard next to the church (Mon–Fri 9:00–12:30, 13:30–17:00, Sat 10:00–12:00, closed Sun, Oberstrasse 45, from station walk down main street with castle high on your left and walk about five blocks, tel. 06743/919-303).

The Jost beer stein "factory outlet" carries most everything a shopper could want. It has one shop across from the church in the main square and a slightly cheaper shop a block away on Rosenstrasse 16 (Mon–Fri 8:30–18:00, Sat 8:30–17:00, Sun 10:00–17:00, ships overseas, 10 percent discount with this book, CC:VMA, tel. 06743/1224).

Get acquainted with Bacharach by taking a walking tour. Charming Herr Rolf Jung, retired headmaster of the Bacharach school, is a superb English-speaking guide (50 DM, 90 min, call TI to reserve a tour with him, or call him directly, tel. 06743/1519). Or take the self-guided walk, described below. For accommodations, see "Sleeping on the Rhine," below.

Sights—Bacharach

▲▲**Introductory Bacharach Walk**—Start at the Köln-Düsseldorf ferry dock (next to a fine picnic park). View the town from the parking lot—a modern landfill. The Rhine used to lap against Bacharach's town wall, just over the present-day highway. Every few years, the river floods, covering the highway under several feet of water. The castle on the hill is a youth hostel. Two of its original 16 towers are visible from here (up to five if you look real hard). The huge roadside wine keg declares this town was built on the wine trade.

Reefs up the river forced boats to unload upriver and reload here. Consequently, Bacharach became the biggest wine trader on the Rhine. A riverfront crane hoisted huge kegs of prestigious "Bacharach" wine (which in practice was from anywhere in the region). The tour buses next to the dock and the flags of the biggest spenders along the highway remind you today's economy is basically tourism.

At the big town map and public WC, take the underpass, ascend on the right, make a U-turn, then walk under the tracks through the medieval gate (one of six 14th-century gates) and to the two-tone Protestant church, which marks the town center.

From this intersection, Bacharach's main street (Oberstrasse) goes right to the half-timbered red-and-white Altes Haus (from 1368, the oldest house in town) and left way down to the train station. To the left (or south) of the church, the golden horn hangs over the old Posthof (and new TI). The post horn symbolizes the postal service throughout Europe. In olden days, when the postman blew this, traffic stopped and the mail sped through. Step into the courtyard. Notice the fascist eagle (from 1936, on the left as you enter) and the fine view of a chapel and church. This post station dates from 1724, when stagecoaches ran from Köln to Frankfurt.

Two hundred years ago this was the only road along the Rhine. Napoleon widened it to fit his cannon wagons. The steps alongside the church lead to the castle. Return to the church.

Inside the church you'll find grotesque and brightly painted capitals and a mix of round Romanesque and pointed Gothic arches. In the upper left corner some medieval frescoes survive where an older Romanesque arch was cut by a pointed Gothic one.

Continue down Oberstrasse past the Altes Haus to the old mint (*Münze*), marked by a crude coin in its sign. Across from the mint, the wine garden of Fritz Bastian is the liveliest place in town after dark. Above you in the vineyards stands a ghostly black-and-gray tower—your destination.

Bacharach

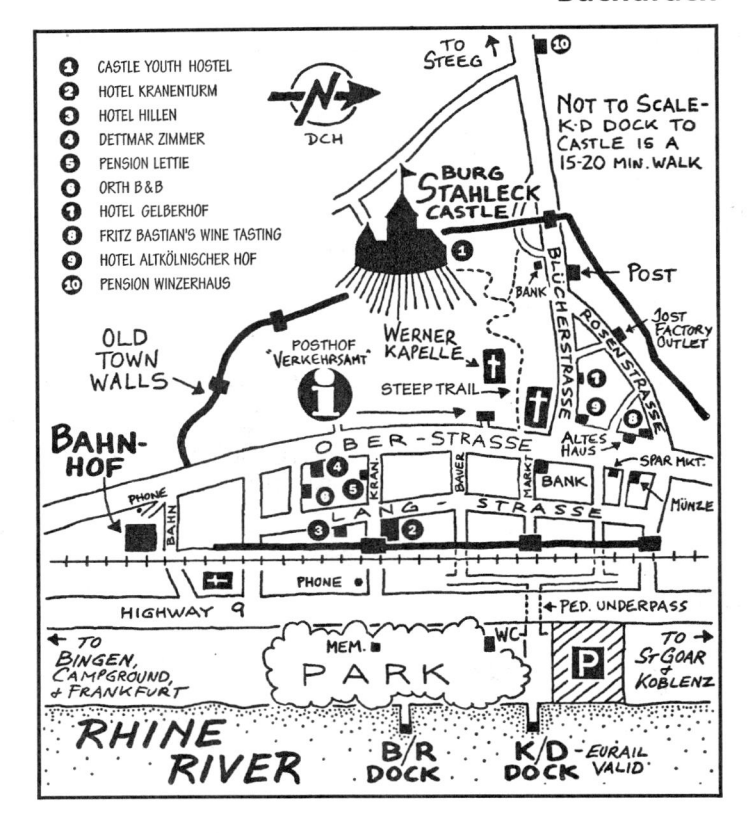

    Take the next left (Rosenstrasse) and wander 30 meters up to the well. Notice the sundial and the wall painting of 1632 Bacharach with its walls intact. Climb the tiny-stepped lane behind the well up into the vineyard and to the tower. The slate steps lead to a small path that deposits you at a viewpoint atop the stubby remains of the old town wall, just above the tower's base (if signs indicate that the path is closed get as close to the tower base as possible).

    A grand medieval town spreads before you. When Frankfurt had 15,000 residents, medieval Bacharach had 6,000. For 300 years (1300–1600) Bacharach was big, rich, and politically powerful.

    From this perch you can see the chapel ruins and six of the nine surviving city towers. Visually trace the wall to the castle, home of one of seven electors who voted for the Holy Roman Emperor in

1275. To protect their own power, these elector princes did their best to choose the weakest guy on the ballot. The elector from Bacharach helped select a two-bit prince named Rudolf von Habsburg (from a two-bit castle in Switzerland). The underestimated Rudolf brutally silenced the robber barons along the Rhine and established the mightiest dynasty in European history. His family line, the Habsburgs, ruled the Austro-Hungarian Empire until 1918.

Plagues, fires, and the Thirty Years' War (1618–1648) finally did Bacharach in. The town has slumbered for several centuries, with a population of about a thousand.

In the mid-19th century, artists and writers such as Victor Hugo were charmed by the Rhineland's romantic mix of past glory, present poverty, and rich legend. They put this part of the Rhine on the old "grand tour" map as the "Romantic Rhine." Victor Hugo pondered the ruined 15th-century chapel, which you can see under the castle. In his 1842 travel book, *Rhein Reise (Rhine Travels)*, he wrote, "No doors, no roof or windows, a magnificent skeleton puts its silhouette against the sky. Above it, the ivy-covered castle ruins provide a fitting crown. This is Bacharach, land of fairy tales, covered with legends and sagas." If you're enjoying the Romantic Rhine, thank Victor Hugo and company. To get back into town, take the path that leads along the wall up the valley to the next tower, then down onto the street. Follow the road under the gate and back into the center.

ST. GOAR

St. Goar is a classic Rhine town—its hulk of a castle overlooking a half-timbered shopping street and leafy riverside park busy with sightseeing ships and contented strollers. From the boat dock, the main drag—a pedestrian mall—cuts through town before winding up to the castle. Rheinfels Castle, once the mightiest on the Rhine, is the single best Rhineland ruin to explore.

The St. Goar TI is on the pedestrian street, three blocks from the K-D boat dock, and offers free left-luggage service (May–Oct Mon–Fri 8:00–12:30, 14:00–17:00, Sat 10:00–12:00, closed Sun and earlier in winter, tel. 06741/383). St. Goar's waterfront park is hungry for a picnic. The small EDEKA supermarket on the main street is fine for picnic fixings (Mon–Fri 8:00–19:00, Sat 8:00–16:00, limited hours on Sun in summer). There is no bike rental in St. Goar.

The friendly and helpful Montag family in the shop under Hotel Montag has Rhine guidebooks (Koblenz-Mainz), fine steins, and copies of this year's *Rick Steves' Germany, Austria & Switzerland* guidebook. They offer 10 percent off any of their souvenirs for travelers with this book.

For a good two-hour hike from St. Goar to the Loreley viewpoint, catch the ferry across to St. Goarshausen (2.5-DM round-trip, 4/hrly), hike up past the Katz castle (now a convalescent home), and traverse along the hillside, always bearing right toward the river. You'll pass through a residential area, hike down a 50-meter path through trees, then traverse a wheat field until you reach an amphitheater adjacent to the Loreley overview (restaurant available). From here it's a steep 15-minute hike down to the river where a riverfront trail takes you back to the St. Goarshausen-to-St. Goar ferry.

Sights—St. Goar's Rheinfels Castle
▲▲▲Self-Guided Tour—Sitting like a dead pit bull above St. Goar, this mightiest of Rhine castles rumbles with ghosts from its hard-fought past. Burg Rheinfels (built in 1245) withstood a siege of 28,000 French troops in 1692. But in 1797 the French Revolutionary army destroyed it.

Rheinfels was huge. In fact, it was the biggest on the Rhine and was used as a quarry. Today this hollow but interesting shell offers your single best hands-on ruined castle experience on the river (5 DM, daily 9:00–18:00, last entry at 17:00, only Sat–Sun in winter, gather 10 English-speaking tourists and get a nearly free English tour, tel. 06741/7753). The cruel castle map is not worth the .30 DM, nor is the English booklet worth its price (3.50 DM). If planning to explore the underground passages, bring a flashlight, buy a tiny one (5 DM at entry), or do it by candlelight (museum sells candles with matches, 1 DM). To get to the castle from St. Goar's boat dock or train station, take a steep 15-minute hike, a 7-DM taxi ride (11 DM for a minibus, tel. 06741/93100), or the goofy tourist train (3 DM, 3/hrly, from square between station and dock, complete with lusty music). A handy WC is in the castle courtyard by the restaurant entry. If it's damp, be careful of slippery stones.

Rather than wander aimlessly, visit the castle by following this tour: From the ticket gate walk straight and uphill. Pass Grosser Keller on left (where we'll end this tour), walk through an internal gate past the "zu den gedeckten Wehrgängen" sign on the right (where we'll pass later) to the museum (daily 9:00–12:00, 13:00–17:00) in the only finished room of the castle.

1. Museum and castle model: The seven-foot-tall carved stone ("Keltische Säule von Pfalzfeld") immediately inside the door—a tombstone from a nearby Celtic grave—is from 600 years before Christ. There were people here long before the Romans... and this castle. The chair next to the door is an old library chair. Fold it up and it becomes stairs for getting to the highest shelves.

The castle history exhibit in the center of the room is well described in English. At the far end is a model reconstruction of the castle showing how much bigger it was before Louis XIV destroyed it. Study this. Find where you are (hint: Look for the

St. Goar

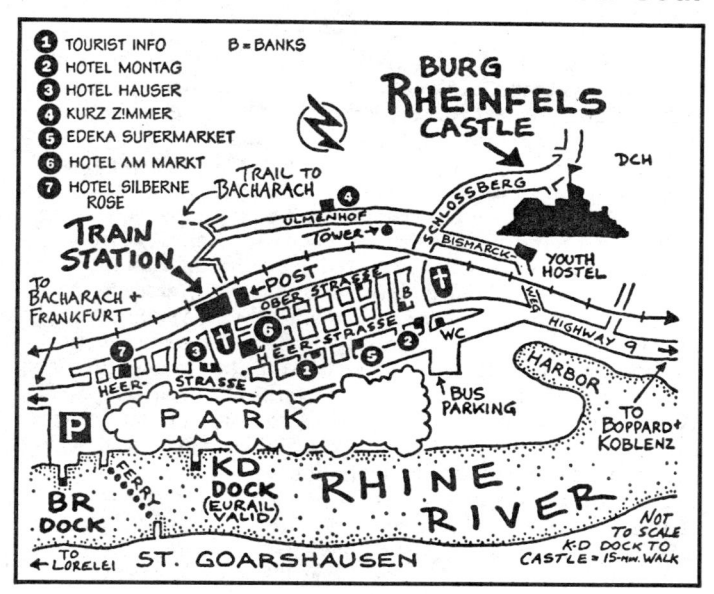

Map Legend:
- ① TOURIST INFO
- ② HOTEL MONTAG
- ③ HOTEL HAUSER
- ④ KURZ ZIMMER
- ⑤ EDEKA SUPERMARKET
- ⑥ HOTEL AM MARKT
- ⑦ HOTEL SILBERNE ROSE
- B = BANKS

Map features: BURG RHEINFELS CASTLE, TRAIL TO BACHARACH, TRAIN STATION, TO BACHARACH + FRANKFURT, ULMENHOF TOWER, SCHLOSSBERG, BISMARCK-, YOUTH HOSTEL, POST, OBER-STRASSE, HEER-STRASSE, WC, HIGHWAY 9, BUS PARKING, HARBOR, TO BOPPARD + KOBLENZ, PARK, P, KD DOCK (EURAIL VALID), BR DOCK, FERRY, RHINE RIVER, TO LORELEI, ST. GOARSHAUSEN, DCH, NOT TO SCALE, KD DOCK TO CASTLE = 15-min. WALK

tall tower). This was the living quarters of the original castle, which was only the smallest ring of buildings around the tiny central courtyard (13th century, marked by red well). The ramparts were added in the 14th century. In 1605 the entire fortress was completed. The vast majority of the place was destroyed in 1796. It has had no military value since. While no WWII bombs were wasted on this ruin, it served St. Goar as a quarry for generations. The basement of the museum shows the castle pharmacy and an exhibit on Rhine region odds and ends, including tools and an 1830 loom.Exit the museum and walk 30 meters directly out, slightly uphill into the castle courtyard.

2. Medieval castle courtyard: Five hundred years ago the entire castle circled this courtyard. The place was self-sufficient and ready for a siege with a bakery, pharmacy, herb garden, animals, brewery, well (top of yard), and livestock. During peacetime, 300 to 600 people lived here; during a siege there would be as many as 4,500. The walls were plastered and painted white. Bits of the original 13th-century plaster survive.

Continue through the courtyard, out "Erste Schildmauer," turn left into the next courtyard, and walk to the two old, black, upright posts. Find the pyramid of stone catapult balls.

3. Castle garden: Catapult balls like these were too expensive not to recycle. If ever used, they'd be retrieved after the battle. Across from the balls is a well—essential for any castle during the age of sieging. The old posts are for the ceremonial baptizing of new members of the local trading league. While this guild goes back centuries, today it's a social club that fills this court with a huge wine party the first weekend of each August.

If weary, skip to 5; otherwise, climb the cobbled path up to the castle's best viewpoint up where the German flag waves.

4. Highest castle tower lookout: Enjoy a great view of the river, castle, and the forest that was once all part of this castle. Remember, the fortress once covered five times the land it does today, and this castle was no bigger than the two you see over the river. Notice how the other castles don't poke above the top of the canyon. That would make them easy for invading armies to see.

Return to the catapult balls, walk down the road, go through the tunnel, veer left through the arch marked "zu den Gedeckten Wehrgängen," go down two flights of stairs, and turn left into the dark covered passageway. We now begin a rectangular walk taking us completely around the perimeter of the castle.

5. Covered defense galleries: Soldiers—the castle's "minutemen"—had a short commute: defensive positions on the outside, home in the holes below on the left. Even though these living quarters were padded with straw, life was unpleasant. A peasant was lucky to live beyond age 28.

Continue straight through the gallery and to the corner of the castle, where you'll see a white painted arrow at eye level.

6. Corner of castle: Look up. A three-story, half-timbered building originally rose beyond the highest stone fortification. The two stone tongues near the top just around the corner supported the toilet. (Insert your own joke here.) Turn around. The crossbow slits below the white arrow were once steeper. The bigger hole on the riverside was for hot pitch, etc.

Follow that white arrow along the outside to the next corner. Midway you'll pass stairs leading down "zu den Minengängen" (sign on upper left). Adventurers with flashlights can detour here. You may come out around the next corner. Otherwise, stay with me, walking level to the corner. At the corner, turn left.

7. Thoop...you're dead. Look ahead at the smartly placed crossbow arrow slit. While you're lying there, notice the stone work. The little round holes were for scaffolds used as they built up. They indicate this stonework is original. Notice also the fine stonework on the shoots. More boiling oil...now you're toast too. Continue along. At the railing, look up the valley and uphill where the fort existed. Below, just outside the wall, is land where attackers would gather. Tunnels filled with explosives ran under the land just outside the walls. With clever thin slate roofs, the force of their detonation went up, killing masses of attackers without damaging the actual castle. In 1626 a handful of underground Protestant Germans blew 300 Catholic Spaniards to—they figured—hell. You can explore these underground passages from the next courtyard.

Continue along the perimeter, jog left, go down five steps and into an open field, and walk toward the wooden bridge. You may detour here into the passageway marked "13 Hals Graben." The old wooden bridge is actually modern. Angle left through two arches and through the rough entry to "Verliess" on the left.

8. Prison: This is one of six dungeons. You walked through a door prisoners only dreamed of 400 years ago. They came and went through the little square hole in the ceiling. The holes in the walls supported timbers that gave residents something to sit on to keep them out of the filth that gathered on the floor. Twice a day they were given bread and water. Some prisoners actually survived five years in here. The town could torture and execute. The castle had permission only to imprison in these dungeons.

Continue through the next arch, under the white arrow, and turn left and walk 40 yards to the *Schlachthaus*.

9. Slaughterhouse: A castle was prepared to survive a six-month siege. With 4,000 people, that's a lot of provisions. The cattle that lived within the walls were slaughtered here. Notice the drainage gutters for water and blood. "Running water" came through from above...one bucket at a time.

Back outside, climb the modern stairs to the left. A skinny passage leads you into...

10. The big cellar: This "Grosser Keller" was a big pantry. When the castle was smaller, this was the original moat—you can see the rough lower parts of the wall. The original floor was five feet deeper. When the castle expanded, the moat became the cellar. Above the entry, holes mark spots where timbers made a storage loft, perhaps filled with grain. Kegs of wine lined the walls. Part of a soldier's pay was three liters of wine a day. In the back, an arch leads to the wine cellar where finer wine was kept. The castle consumed 200,000 liters of wine a year. The count owned the surrounding farmland. Farmers got to keep 20 percent of their production. Later, in more liberal feudal times, the nobility let them keep 40 percent. Today the German government leaves the workers with 60 percent...and provides a few more services.

Climb out, turn right, and leave. For coffee on a great view terrace, visit the Rheinfels Castle Hotel, opposite the entrance (good WC at the base of steps).

Sleeping on the Rhine
(1.70 DM = about $1)
Sleep Code: **S** = Single, **D** = Double/Twin, **T** = Triple, **Q** = Quad, **b** = bathroom, **t** = toilet only, **s** = shower only, **CC** = Credit Card

(Visa, MasterCard, Amex), **SE** = Speaks English, **NSE** = No English. All hotels speak some English. Breakfast is included unless otherwise noted.

The Rhine is an easy place for cheap sleeps. *Zimmer* and *Gasthäuser* with 35-DM beds abound (and *Zimmer* normally discount their prices for longer stays). A few exceptional Rhine-area hostels offer 20-DM beds (for travelers of any age). Each town's TI is eager to set you up, and finding a room should be easy any time of year (except for wine-festy weekends in September and October). Bacharach and St. Goar, the best towns for an overnight stop, are about 10 miles apart, connected by milk-run trains, riverboats, and a riverside bike path. Bacharach is more interesting and less touristy, but St. Goar has the famous castle (see "St. Goar," above). Parking in Bacharach is simple along the highway next to the tracks (three-hour daytime limit is generally not enforced) or in the boat parking lot. Parking in St. Goar is tighter; ask at your hotel.

Sleeping in Bacharach
(tel. code: 06743, zip code: 55422)

Hotels

Hotel Kranenturm gives you castle ambience without the climb. It offers a good combination of comfort and hotel privacy with *Zimmer* coziness, a central location, and a medieval atmosphere. Run by hardworking Kurt Engel, his intense but friendly wife, Fatima, and faithful Schumi, this hotel is actually part of the medieval fortification. Its former *Kran* (crane) towers are now round rooms—great for medievalists. When the riverbank was higher, cranes on this tower loaded barrels of wine onto Rhine boats. Hotel Kranenturm is five yards from the train tracks, but a combination of medieval sturdiness, triple-paned windows, and included earplugs makes the riverside rooms sleepable (Sb-60–70 DM, Db-90–105 DM, Tb-130–140 DM, Qb-165–175 DM with this book, prices include breakfast; the lower price is for off-season or stays of at least three nights in high season; CC:VMA but prefer cash, Rhine views come with ripping train noise, back rooms—some with castle views—are quieter, all rooms with cable TV, kid-friendly, Langstrasse 30, tel. 06743/1308, fax 06743/1021, e-mail: hotel-kranenturm@t-online.de). Kurt, a good cook, serves 15- to 25-DM dinners. Trade travel stories on the terrace with new friends over dinner, letting screaming trains punctuate your conversation. Kurt's big-enough-for-three Kranenturm ice-cream special is a delight (10.50 DM). Drivers park along the highway at the Kranenturm tower. Eurailers walk down Oberstrasse, then turn right on Kranenstrasse.

Hotel Hillen, a block south of the Hotel Kranenturm, has less charm and more train noise, with friendly owners and lots of rental bikes. To minimize train noise, ask for *"ruhige Seite,"* the quiet side (S-50 DM, Sb-65 DM, D-85 DM, Db-10C Tb-140 DM, 10 percent less for two nights, 10 percent more with CC, Langstrasse 18, tel. 06743/1287, fax 06743/1037).

Hotel Altkölnischer Hof, a grand old building near the church, rents 20 rooms with modern furnishings and bathrooms, some with balconies over an Old World restaurant. Public rooms are old-time elegant (Sb-90–95 DM, Db-110–130 DM, Db with terrace-140 DM, with balcony-150–160 DM, CC:VA, TV in rooms, elevator, tel. 06743/1339 or 06743/2186, fax 06743/2793).

Hotel Gelberhof, a few doors up from the Jost store, has spiffy public spaces but unimaginative rooms (S-55 DM, Sb-75–85 DM, small Db-110 DM, Db-120–140 DM, possible cash or two-night discounts, CC:M, popular with groups, elevator, bike rental, Blücherstrasse 26, tel. 06743/910-100, fax 06743/910-1050, e-mail: gelberhof@fh-bingen.de).

Pensions and Private Rooms

At **Pension Lettie**, effervescent and eager-to-please Lettie offers four modern, bright rooms (Sb-55 DM, Db-75 DM, Tb-110 DM with this book and cash, discount for three-night stays, strictly nonsmoking, no train noise, a few doors inland from Hotel Kranenturm, Kranenstrasse 6, tel. & fax 06743/2115, e-mail: pension.lettie@t-online.de). Lettie speaks English (worked for the U.S. Army before we withdrew) and does laundry (16 DM per load).

Delightful **Ursula Orth** rents five, airy rooms—a great value, around the corner from Pension Lettie (Sb-35 DM, Db-55–65 DM, Tb-75 DM for one night and less for two, nonsmoking, Rooms 4 and 5 on ground floor—easy access; from Hotel Hillen walk up Spurgasse, her *Zimmer* is on the right at #3; tel. 06743/1557, minimal English spoken).

Around the corner, **Annelie und Hans Dettmar**, entrepreneurial but curiously lacking in warmth, rent several smoke-free rooms and two great family rooms with kitchenette (20 DM to use it) in a modern house on the main drag (big Sb-50 DM, Db-60–70 DM, Tb-75 DM, Qb-100 DM, includes breakfast, free use of two old bikes, laundry-17 DM, Oberstrasse 8, tel. & fax 06743/2661, SE). Readers give this couple mixed reviews, but their rooms are good. Their unsmiling son, **Jürgen Dettmar**, runs the adjacent bakery and rents five fine, very central rooms with a common kitchen and small bathrooms, near the church behind Restaurant Braustube. Ask for a room with balcony for a bird's-eye view over the town center (Db-60 DM, Tb-90 DM, Oberstrasse 64, tel. & fax 06743/1715, e-mail: PensionDettmar@gmx.de, SE).

Very nearby, the cozy home of **Herr und Frau Theilacker** is a German-feeling *Zimmer* with comfortable rooms and no outside sign. It's likely to have a room when others don't (S-30 DM,

Germany

D-60 DM, in the town center, walk 30 steps straight out of Restaurant Braustube to Oberstrasse 57, tel. 06743/1248, NSE).

Pension Winzerhaus, a 10-room place run by Herr Petrescu, is 200 yards up the valley from the town gate, so the location is less charming, but it has no train noise and easy parking. Rooms are simple, clean, and modern (Sb-50 DM, Db-85 DM, Tb-90 DM, Qb-95 DM, 10 percent off with this book, free bikes for guests, Blücherstrasse 60, tel. 06743/1294, fax 069/283-927).

Bacharach's hostel, **Jugendherberge Stahleck**, is a 12th-century castle on the hilltop—500 steps above Bacharach—with a royal Rhine view. Open to travelers of any age, this is a newly redone gem with eight beds and a private modern shower and WC in each room. A steep 15-minute climb on the trail from the town church, the hostel is warmly run by Evelyn and Bernhard Falke (FALL-kay), who serve hearty, 9.5-DM all-you-can-eat buffet dinners. The hostel pub serves cheap local wine until midnight (25.50-DM dorm beds with breakfast and sheets, 6 DM extra without a card or in a double, couples can share rooms, groups pay 34.50 DM per bed with breakfast and dinner, no smoking in rooms, easy parking, beds normally available but call and leave your name, they'll hold a bed until 18:00, tel. 06743/1266, SE).

Eating in Bacharach

Several places offer good, inexpensive, and atmospheric indoor or outdoor dining, all for about 20 to 30 DM. The oldest building in town, **Altes Haus** (by the church, closed Wed), and **Kurpfälzische Münze** (open daily, in the old mint, a half block down from Altes Haus; claims to be even older), are both good values with great ambience. **Weingut zum Gruner Baum** offers delicious appetizers (also next to Altes Haus, good ambience indoors and out). **Hotel Kranenturm** is another good value with hearty meals and good main course salads (see hotel listing above).

Wine Tasting: Drop in on entertaining Fritz Bastian's **Weingut zum Grüner Baum** wine bar (just past Altes Haus, evenings only, closed Thu, tel. 06743/1208). As the president of the local vintner's club, Fritz's mission is to give travelers an understanding of the subtle differences among the Rhine wines. Groups of 2 to 10 people pay 26 DM for a "carousel" of 15 glasses of 14 different white wines, one lonely red, and a basket of bread. Your mission: Team up with others with this book to rendezvous here after dinner. Spin the lazy Susan, share a common cup, and discuss the taste. Fritz insists, "After each wine, you must talk to each other."

Sleeping in St. Goar
(tel. code: 06741, zip code: 56329)
Hotel am Markt, well run by Herr and Frau Velich, is rustic with all the modern comforts. It features a hint of antler with a pastel

flair and bright rooms and a good restaurant. It's a good value and a stone's throw from the boat dock and train station (Ss-65 DM, Sb-80 DM, Db-100 DM, Tb-140 DM, Qb-160 DM, cheaper off-season, closed Dec–Feb, CC:VMA, Am Markt 1, tel. 06741/1689, fax 06741/1721, e-mail: hotel_am_markt_st.goar@t-online.de).

Hotel Hauser, facing the boat dock, is another good deal, warmly run by another Frau Velich and Sigrid (S-42 DM, D-88 DM, Db-98 DM, great Db with Rhine-view balconies-110 DM, small bathrooms, show this book to get these prices, cheaper in off-season, CC:VMA, Heerstrasse 77, telephone reservations easy, tel. 06741/333, fax 06741/1464, SE).

A few doors upriver, the strangely vacant **Rhein Hotel** has modern, unimaginative rooms, a few of which have Rhine-view balconies. No prices are posted but it seems to be a fair deal (Sb-60–80 DM, Db-90–130 DM, Heerstrasse 71, tel. 06741/355, fax 06741/2835). Next door **Hotel Silberne Rose** is musty with older decor and some rooms with Rhine views (Sb-60–70 DM, Db-100–120 DM, Tb-125–140 DM, cheaper price for longer stays, CC:VM, across from K-D dock, Heerstrasse 63, tel. 06741/7040, fax 06741/2865).

Hotel Montag is on the castle end of town just across the street from the world's largest free-hanging cuckoo clock. Manfred and Maria Montag and their son Mike speak New Yorkish. Even though the hotel gets a lot of bus tours, it's friendly, laid-back, and comfortable; ask about its luxurious apartments (Sb-70 DM, Db-130 DM, price can drop if things are slow, CC:VMA, Heerstrasse 128, tel. 06741/1629, fax 06741/2086, e-mail: hotelmontag @01019freenet.de). Check out their adjacent crafts shop (heavy on beer steins).

St. Goar's best *Zimmer* deal is the home of **Frau Kurz**. It includes a breakfast terrace, a garden, a fine view, easy parking, and most of the comforts of a hotel (S-34 DM, D-60 DM, Db-70 DM, showers-5 DM, one-night stays cost extra, confirm prices, honor your reservation or call to cancel, Ulmenhof 11, tel. & fax 06741/459, some English spoken). It's a steep five-minute hike from the train station (exit left from station, take immediate left at the yellow phone booth, go under tracks to paved path, take a right partway up stairs, climb a few more stairs to Ulmenhof).

The Germanly run **St. Goar Hostel**, the big beige building under the castle (veer right off the road up to the castle), has 2 to 12 beds per room, a 22:00 curfew, and hearty 9.50-DM dinners (20-DM beds with breakfast, 5-DM sleep sacks, open all day, check-in from 17:00–18:00 and 19:00–20:00, Bismarckweg 17, tel. 06741/388, SE).

Rheinfels Castle Hotel is the town splurge. Actually part of the castle, but an entirely new building, this luxury place is good for those with money and a car (Db-240–265 DM depending on river views and balconies, CC:VMA, elevator, dress-up restaurant, Schlossberg 47, tel. 06741/8020, fax 06741/802-802, e-mail: rheinfels.st.goar@t-online.de).

Eating in St. Goar
Hotel Am Markt and **Hotel Hauser** offer excellent meals at fair prices. For your Rhine splurge, walk, taxi, or drive up to **Rheinfels Castle Hotel** for its incredible view and elegant setting, and consider a sunset drink on the view terrace (see hotel listing above; reserve a table by the window).

Transportation Connections—Rhine
Milk-run trains stop at all Rhine towns each hour starting as early as around 6:00. Koblenz, Boppard, St. Goar, Bacharach, Bingen, and Mainz are each about 15 minutes apart. From Koblenz to Mainz takes 75 minutes. To get a faster big train, go to Mainz or Koblenz.

From Mainz by train to: **Bacharach/St. Goar** (hrly, 1 hr), **Cochem** (hrly, 2.5 hrs, changing in Koblenz), **Köln** (3/hrly, 90 min), **Baden-Baden** (hrly, 2.5 hrs), **Munich** (hrly, 4 hrs), **Frankfurt** (3/hrly, 45 min), **Frankfurt Airport** (3/hrly, 25 min).

From Frankfurt by train to: **Koblenz** (hrly, 90 min), **Rothenburg** (hrly, 3 hrs, transfers in Würzburg and Steinach), **Würzburg** (hrly, 90 min), **Munich** (hrly, 3.5 hrs), **Amsterdam** (8/day, 5 hrs), **Paris** (4/day, 6.5 hrs).

MOSEL VALLEY
The misty Mosel is what some visitors hoped the Rhine would be—peaceful, sleepy, romantic villages slipped between the steep vineyards and the river; fine wine; a sprinkling of castles; and lots of friendly *Zimmer*. Boat, train, and car traffic here is a trickle compared to the roaring Rhine. While the swan-speckled Mosel moseys 300 miles from France's Vosges Mountains to Koblenz, where it dumps into the Rhine, the most scenic piece of the valley lies between the towns of Bernkastel-Kues and Cochem. I'd savor only this section.

Throughout the region on summer weekends and during the fall harvest time, wine festivals with oompah bands, dancing, and colorful costumes are powered by good food and wine.

Getting around the Mosel Valley
By Train and Bus: The train zips you to Cochem, Bullay, or Trier in a snap. Frequent buses connect Zell with the Bullay station in 10 minutes, and six buses a day connect tiny Beilstein with Cochem in 20 minutes (last bus about 15:10). Four buses a day link Zell and Beilstein.

By Boat: A few daily departures allow you to cruise the most scenic stretch between Cochem, Beilstein, and Zell: between

Mosel Valley

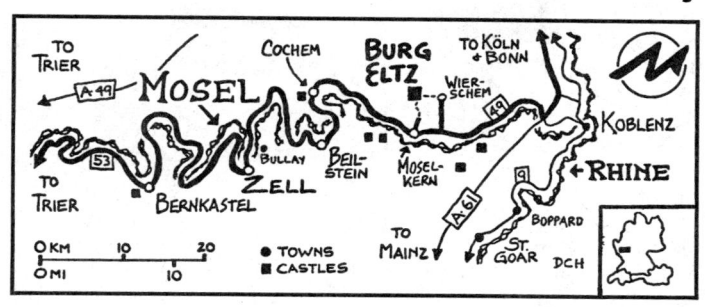

Cochem and Zell (2/day May–Aug but none on Fri and Mon May–Jun, 3 hrs, 23 DM one way, 35 DM round-trip, on Kolb-Line); between Cochem and Beilstein (5/day, 60 min, 13 DM one way, 18 DM round-trip, tel. 02673/151); and between Zell and Beilstein (1–2/day May–Oct, 2 hrs, 18 DM one way, 26 DM round-trip). The K-D (Köln-Düsseldorf) line sails once a day in each direction but only as far as Cochem (May–Sept, Koblenz to Cochem 10:00–14:30, or Cochem to Koblenz 15:50–20:10, free with Eurailpass or a dated Flexi- or Europass).

By Bike: You can rent bikes in most Mosel towns (see listings per village below).

Sights—Mosel Valley

Cochem—With a majestic castle and picturesque medieval streets, Cochem is the very touristic hub of this part of the river. The TI's free map includes the town's history and a walking tour. The pointy Cochem Castle is the work of overly imaginative 19th-century restorers (7 DM, daily mid-Mar–Oct 9:00–17:00, 15-minute walk from Cochem, follow one of the frequent German-language tours while reading English explanation sheets or call ahead to see if any English tours are planned, tel. 02671/255). Cochem has frequent train service (to Koblenz, hrly, 60 min; to Bullay, hrly, 10 min; to Trier, hrly, 45 min).

Arrival in Cochem: Make a hard right out of the station (lockers available) and walk about 10 minutes to the town center and TI (just past the bus lanes). Drivers can park near the bridge (TI right there). To get to the main square (*Markt*), continue under the bridge, then angle right and follow Bernstrasse.

The information-packed TI is by the bridge at the main bus stop. They book rooms (same day only) and keep a thorough 24-hour room listing in the window. Ask about public transportation to Burg Eltz (see below) and pick up the well-done *Moselle Wine*

Road brochure and info on area hikes (May–Oct Mon–Sat 10:00–17:00, Sun 10:00–12:00, off-season closed weekends and at lunch, tel. 02671/3974). For accommodations, see "Sleeping," below.

Burg Eltz Area

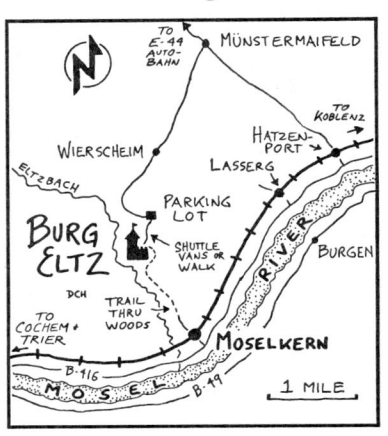

Stroll along the pleasant paths that line the river and hike up to the Aussichtspunkt (the cross on the hill) for a great view. You can rent bikes from the K-D boat kiosk at the dock (summers only) or year-round from Kreutz near the station on Ravenstrasse 42 (7 DM/4 hrs, 14 DM/day, no deposit required, just your passport number, tel. 02671/91131). Consider taking a bike on the boat and riding back. If stranded, many hitchhike.

▲▲▲**Burg Eltz**—My favorite castle in all of Europe lurks in a mysterious forest. It's been left intact for 700 years and is furnished throughout as it was 500 years ago. Thanks to smart diplomacy and clever marriages, Burg Eltz was never destroyed. (It survived one five-year siege.) It's been in the Eltz family for 820 years. The countess arranges for new flowers in each room weekly. The only way to see the castle is with a one-hour tour (included in admission ticket). German tours (with pathetic English fact sheets) go constantly. Organize an English tour by corralling 20 English-speakers in the inner courtyard—they'll thank you for it. (Then push the red button on the white porch and politely beg for an English guide. This is well worth a short wait. You can also telephone ahead to see if there's an English-language group scheduled that you could tag along with.)

Reaching Burg Eltz by train, walk one steep hour from Moselkern station (midway between Cochem and Koblenz, no lockers at station; trail is slippery when wet, follow white "park and walk" signs) through a pine forest where sparrows carry crossbows, and maidens, disguised as falling leaves, whisper "watch out." In 1999 the first-ever public bus to Burg Eltz ran from Cochem (15 DM round-trip, gives you two hours in castle, six-person minimum, find fellow travelers or call to see if bus will run, tel. 02671/980-098 or ask at TI); if enough travelers use the bus, it will run in 2000.

Drivers often get lost on the way to Burg Eltz. Use your map and do this: Leave the river at Moselkern (shortest drive) following the white "Burg Eltz Park & Ride" signs through the towns of Münstermaifeld and Wierschem. The castle parking lot is two kilometers past Wierschem. From the lot, hike 10 minutes downhill or wait for the red castle shuttle bus
(2 DM). There are three "Burg Eltz" parking lots; only the Hatzenport lot is close enough for an easy walk (9 DM, Apr–Oct daily 9:30–17:30, tel. 02672/950-500).

▲Beilstein—Farther upstream is the quaintest of all Mosel towns. Beilstein is Cinderella land. Explore the narrow lanes, ancient wine cellar, resident (and very territorial) swans, and ruined castle. The small 2-DM ferry goes constantly back and forth. Two shops rent bikes for the pleasant riverside stroll (toward Zell is best). The TI is in a café (summer Tue–Sun 9:00–19:00, closed Mon, tel. 02673/1417). Four buses a day connect Zell and Beilstein.

▲Zell—This is the best Mosel town for an overnight stop (see "Sleeping," below). It's peaceful, with a fine riverside promenade, a pedestrian bridge over the water, plenty of *Zimmer*, and a long pedestrian zone filled with colorful shops, restaurants, *Weinstuben* (wine bars), and a fun oompah folk band on weekend evenings on the main square. The TI is on the pedestrian street, four blocks downriver from the pedestrian bridge (Mon–Fri 8:00–12:30, 13:30–17:00, Sat 10:00–13:00, off-season closed Sat, tel. 06542/4031). The fine little Wein und Heimatmuseum features Mosel history (same building as TI, Wed and Sat 15:00–17:00). Walk up to the medieval wall's gatehouse and through the cemetery to the old munitions tower for a village view. You can rent bikes from Frau Klaus (Hauptstrasse 5, tel. 06542/2589).

Locals know Zell for its Schwarze Katz (Black Cat) wine. Franz Josef Weis (who learned his English as a POW in England) and his son Peter give an entertaining tour of their 40,000-bottle-per-year wine cellar. The clever tour lasts an hour, and you'll want to leave with a bottle or two. A green flag marks their *Weinkeller* north of town, past the bridge, at Notenau 26. They also rent two luxurious apartments for 100 DM (CC:M, tel. & fax 06542/5789 or tel. 06542/41398).

Sleeping on the Mosel
(1.70 DM = about $1)

Sleeping in Cochem
(tel. code: 02671, zip code: 56812)
All rooms come with breakfast.

Gästezimmer Hüsgen is a good and handy value that welcomes one-night stays (Ss-40–45 DM, D-64 DM, Ds-68 DM, Db-82 DM, family deals, ground-floor rooms, small view terrace,

Ravenestrasse 34, 150 meters from station, tel. 02671/5817, charming Andrea SE). Ask about their beautiful new rooms wedged between vineyards and train tracks, with a pleasant garden and a big common kitchen (Db-82 DM, same phone number). Across the street above a local *Weinstube*, the light-hearted and ever-so-funky **Gasthaus Ravene** offers six rooms varying in size and comfort (several are spacious and airy). The stairway needs new carpeting, but the rooms are fine (Sb-60 DM, Db-80–100 DM, Tb-133 DM, Ravenestrasse 43, tel. 02671/980-177, fax 02671/91119, www.gasthaus-ravene.de, some English spoken).

The rustic **Hotel Lohspeicher**, just off the main square on a tiny-stepped street, is for those who want a real hotel in the thick of things (and much higher prices, Sb-85–95 DM, Db-170 DM, CC:VMA, elevator, Obergasse 1, tel. 02671/3976, fax 02671/1772, Ingo SE).

Haus Andreas has many small but modern rooms at fair prices (S-25 DM, Sb-40 DM, Db-60 DM, Schlosstrasse 9 or 16, tel. 02671/1370 or 02671/5155, fax 02671/1370). From the main square, take Herrenstrasse; after a block, angle right uphill on Schlosstrasse.

For a top-dollar view of Cochem, cross the bridge and find the balconied rooms at **Hotel Am Hafen** (180 DM, skip cheaper no-view rooms, Uferstrasse 3, tel. 02671/97720, fax 02671/977-227).

Sleeping in Zell
(tel. code: 06542, zip code: 56856)
If the Mosel charms you into spending the night, do it in Zell. By car, this is a natural. It's also easy by boat (2/day from Cochem) or train (go to Bullay—hrly from Cochem or Trier; from Bullay the bus takes you to little Zell—2.80 DM, 2/hrly, 10 min; bus stop is across street from Bullay train station, check yellow MB schedule for times, last bus at about 19:00). The central Zell stop is called Lindenplatz.

Zell's hotels are a disappointment, but its private homes are great. The owners speak almost no English and discount their rates if you stay more than one night. They can't take reservations long in advance for one-night stays; just call a day ahead. My favorites are on the south end of town, a five-minute walk from the town hall square (TI) and the bus stop. Breakfast is included. These places are listed in the order you would find them from the pedestrian bridge.

Friendly **Natalie Huhn** (no sign), your German grandmother, has the cheapest beds in town in her simple but comfortable house (S-30 DM, D-60 DM, cheaper for 2-night stays, 2 blocks to left of church at Jakobstrasse 32, tel. 06542/41048).

Weinhaus zum Fröhlichen Weinberg offers cheap, basic rooms (D-70 DM, 60 DM for 2 or more nights, family *Zimmer*,

Mittelstrasse 6, tel. 06542/4308) above a *Weinstube* disco (noisy on Friday and Saturday nights).

Homey **Gästehaus am Römerbad** is a few blocks from the church and a decent value (Db-80 DM, Am Römerbad 5, tel. 06542/41602, Elizabeth Münster).

Zell's best *Zimmer* values lie at the end of the pedestrian street about five blocks from the pedestrian bridge:

Gasthaus Gertrud Thiesen is classy, with a TV-living-breakfast room and a river view. The Thiesen house has big, bright rooms and is on the town's first corner overlooking the Mosel from a great terrace (S or D-70 DM, Balduinstrasse 1, tel. 06542/4453, SE). Notice the high-water flood marks on the wall across the street.

Gästezimmer Rosa Mesenich is another friendly little place facing the river 100 yards from Thiesen (S-30 DM, Sb-35 DM, D-60 DM, Db-70 DM, Brandenburg 48, tel. 06542/4297).

Almost next door, the vine-strewn doorway of **Gastehaus Eberhard** leads to gregarious owners, cushy rooms, and potential wine tastings (Sb-58 DM, Db-70 DM, Brandenburg 42, tel. 06542/41216, NSE).

If you're looking for room service, a sauna, a pool, and an elevator, sleep at **Hotel Grüner Kranz** (Db-160 DM, CC:VMA, tel. 06542/98610, fax 06542/986-180). **Weinhaus Mayer**, a classy—if stressed-out—old pension next door, is perfectly central with Mosel-view rooms (Db-120–160 DM, Balduinstrasse 15, tel. 06542/4530, fax 06542/61160). They have newly renovated rooms with top comforts, many with river-view balconies (ask for Neues Gastehaus, view Db-160 DM, big Tb-180 DM, same tel. and fax). The freshly remodeled **Hotel Ratskeller** (above a classy pizzeria) has rooms on the pedestrian street that are less cozy but sharp with tile flooring and fair rates (Sb-65–75 DM, Db-90–110 DM, CC:VM, Balduinstrasse 36, tel. 06542/98620, fax 06542/986-244).

ROTHENBURG AND THE ROMANTIC ROAD

From Munich or Füssen to Frankfurt, the Romantic Road takes you through Bavaria's medieval heartland, a route strewn with picturesque villages, farmhouses, onion-domed churches, Baroque palaces, and walled cities.

Dive into the Middle Ages via Rothenburg (ROE-ten-burg), Germany's best-preserved walled town. Countless travelers have searched for the elusive "untouristy Rothenburg." There are many contenders (such as Michelstadt, Miltenberg, Bamberg, Bad Windsheim, and Dinkelsbühl), but none holds a candle to the king of medieval German cuteness. Even with crowds, overpriced souvenirs, Japanese-speaking night watchmen, and yes, even with *Schneebälle*, Rothenburg is best. Save time and mileage and be satisfied with the winner.

Planning Your Time

The best one-day look at the heartland of Germany is the Romantic Road bus tour. Eurail travelers, who get a 75 percent discount, pay only 39 DM for the ride (daily, Frankfurt to Munich or Füssen, and vice versa). Drivers can follow the route laid out in the tourist brochures (available at any TI). The only stop worth more than a few minutes is Rothenburg. Twenty-four hours is ideal for this town. Two nights and a day are a bit much, unless you're actually relaxing on this trip.

Rothenburg in a day is easy, with four essential experiences: the Medieval Crime and Punishment Museum, the Riemenschneider wood carving in St. Jakob's Church, the city walking tour, and a walk along the wall. With more time there are several mediocre but entertaining museums, walking and biking in the nearby countryside, and lots of cafés and shops. Make a point to spend at least

Rothenburg

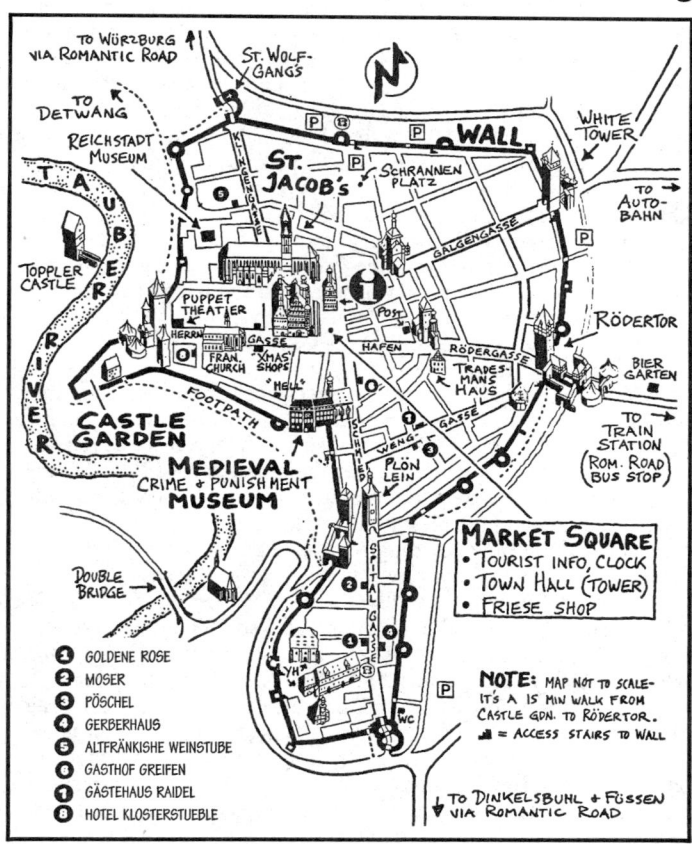

one night. The town is yours after dark when the groups vacate and the town's floodlit cobbles wring some romance out of any travel partner.

ROTHENBURG

In the Middle Ages, when Frankfurt and Munich were just wide spots on the road, Rothenburg was Germany's second-largest free imperial city, with a whopping population of 6,000. Today it's her best-preserved medieval walled town, enjoying tremendous tourist popularity without losing its charm. Get medievaled in Rothenburg.

During Rothenburg's heyday, from 1150 to 1400, it was the

crossing point of two major trade routes: Tashkent-Paris and Hamburg-Venice. Today the great trade is tourism; two-thirds of the townspeople are employed to serve you. Too often Rothenburg brings out the shopper in visitors before they've had a chance to appreciate the historic city. True, this is a great place to do your German shopping, but first see the town. While 2.5 million people visit each year, a mere 500,000 spend the night. Rothenburg is most enjoyable early and late, when the tour groups are gone.

Orientation (tel. code: 09861)

To orient yourself in Rothenburg, think of the town map as a human head. Its nose—the castle garden—sticks out to the left, and the neck is the skinny lower part, with the hostel and my favorite hotels in the Adam's apple. The town is a joy on foot. No sight or hotel is more than a 15-minute walk from the train station or each other.

Most of the buildings you'll see were built by 1400. The city was born around its long-gone castle—built in 1142, destroyed in 1356, and now the site of the castle garden. You can see the shadow of the first town wall, which defines the oldest part of Rothenburg, in its contemporary street plan. A few gates from this wall still survive. The richest and biggest houses were in this central part. The commoners built higgledy-piggledy (read: picturesquely) farther from the center near the present walls.

Tourist Information: The TI is on Market Square (Mon–Fri 9:00–12:30, 13:00–18:00, unreliably Sat–Sun 10:00–15:00, shorter hours off-season, tel. 09861/40492, after-hours board lists rooms still available). Pick up a map and the *Sights Worth Seeing and Knowing* brochure (a virtual walking guide to the town). The free "Hotels and Pensions of Rothenburg" map has the greatest detail and names all of the streets. Confirm sightseeing plans and ask about the daily 14:00 walking tour (Apr–Dec) and evening entertainment. The best town map is available free at the Friese shop, two doors toward Rothenburg's "nose."

Festivals: Rothenburgers dress up in medieval costumes and beer gardens spill out into the street to celebrate Mayor Nusch's Meistertrunk victory (Whitsun, 6 weeks after Easter) and 700 years of history in the Imperial City Festival (2nd weekend in September, with fireworks).

Internet Access: Try Planet Internet (9 DM/hr, Paradeisgasse 5, tel. 09861/934 415).

Arrival in Rothenburg: Exit left from the train station and turn right on the first busy street (Ansbacher Strasse). It'll take you to Rothenburg's Market Square within 10 minutes. Leave luggage in lockers at the station (2 DM). The travel agency in the station is the place to arrange train and *couchette*/sleeper reservations. Taxis wait at the station and can take you to any hotel for 8 DM.

Rothenburg and the Romantic Road 217

Tours of Rothenburg

The TI on Market Square offers one-hour guided walking tours in English (6 DM, Apr–Oct daily at 14:00 from Market Square). A bit less informative but wonderfully entertaining, the **Night Watchman's Tour** takes tourists on his one-hour rounds each evening at 20:00 (6 DM, Apr–Dec, in English). This is the best evening activity in town. Or you can hire a private guide. For 85 DM, a local historian who's an intriguing character as well will bring the ramparts alive. Eight hundred years of history are packed between Rothenburg's cobbles. (Manfred Baumann, tel. 09861/4146, and Anita Weinzierl, tel. 09868/7993, are good guides.) If you prefer riding to walking, **horse-and-buggy rides** last 30 minutes and cost 10 DM per person for a minimum of three people.

Sights—Rothenburg's Town Hall Square

▲▲**Town Hall Tower**—The best view of Rothenburg and the surrounding countryside and a close-up look at an old tiled roof from the inside are yours for 1 DM and a rigorous (214 steps, 180 feet) but interesting climb (daily 9:30–12:30, 13:00–17:00, off-season weekends 12:00–15:00 only). The entrance is on Market Square. Women, beware: Some men find the view best from the bottom of the ladder just before the top.

Meistertrunk Show—Be on Market Square at 11:00, 12:00, 13:00, 14:00, 15:00, 20:00, 21:00, or 22:00 for the ritual gathering of the tourists to see the less-than-breathtaking reenactment of the Meistertrunk story. In 1631 the Catholic army took the Protestant town and was about to do its rape, pillage, and plunder thing when, as the story goes, the mayor said, "Hey, if I can drink this entire three-liter tankard of wine in one gulp, will you leave us alone?" The invading commander, sensing he was dealing with an unbalanced people, said, "Sure." Mayor Nusch drank the whole thing, the town was saved, and the mayor slept for three days. Hint: For the best show, don't watch the clock; watch the open-mouthed tourists gasp as the old windows flip open. At the late shows, the square flickers with flash attachments. While you wait for the show, give yourself the spin tour below.

Market Square Spin Tour—Stand at the bottom of Market Square (10 feet below the wooden post) and spin 360 degrees clockwise starting with the city hall tower. Now, do it slower following these notes: 1) The city's tallest tower, at 200 feet, stands atop the old city hall, a white, Gothic, 13th-century building. Notice the tourists enjoying the view from the black top of the tower. 2) When the town had more money and Gothic went out of style, a new town hall was built in front of the old one. This is in Renaissance style from 1570. (Access to the old town hall tower is through the middle of the new town hall arcade.) 3) At the top of the square stands the proud Councilors' Tavern (clock tower, from 1466). In its day, the city council drank here. Today it's the TI and the focus of all the attention when the little doors on either side of the clock flip open and the wooden figures (from 1910) reenact the Meistertrunk. 4) Across the street, the green building is the oldest pharmacy in town—Löwen Apotheke, from 1374. Peek inside. 5) On the bottom end of the square, the grey building is a fine print shop (see "Shopping," below; free brandy). 6) Adjoining that is the Baumeister's House with its famous Renaissance facade featuring statues of the seven virtues and the seven vices—the former supporting the latter. 7) The green house below that is the former house of Mayor Toppler, today the fine old Greifen Hotel; next to it is a famous Scottish restaurant. 8) Continue circling to the big 17th-century St. George's fountain. The long metal gutters slid, routing the water into the villagers' buckets. Rothenburg's many fountains had practical functions beyond providing drinking water. The water was used for fighting fires and the fountains were stocked with fish during times of siege. Two fine buildings behind the fountain show the old-time lofts with warehouse doors and pulleys on top for hoisting. All over town, lofts were filled with grain and corn. A year's supply was required by the city so they could survive any siege. One building is a free art gallery showing off the work of Rothenburg's top artists. The other is another old-time pharmacy. 9) The broad street running under the town hall tower is Herrngasse. The town originated with its castle (1142). Herrngasse leads from the castle (now gone) to Market Square where you stand now.

▲**Historical Town Hall Vaults**—Under the town hall tower is a city history museum that gives a waxy but good look at medieval Rothenburg. With the best English descriptions in town, it offers a look at "the fateful year 1631," a replica of the famous Meistertrunk tankard, and a dungeon complete with three dank cells and some torture lore (3 DM, 9:30–18:00, closed in winter, well described in English).

Sights—Rothenburg

▲▲**Walk the Wall**—Just over a mile around, providing great views and a good orientation, this walk can be done by those under six feet tall and without a camera in less than an hour, and requires no special sense of balance. Photographers go through lots of film, especially before breakfast or at sunset, when the lighting is best and the crowds are fewest. The best fortifications are in the Spitaltor (south end). Walk from there counterclockwise to the "forehead." Climb the Rödertor en route. The names you see along the way are people who donated money to rebuild the wall after World War II.

▲**Rödertor**—The wall tower nearest the train station is the only one you can climb. It's worth the hike up for the view and a fascinating rundown on the bombing of Rothenburg in the last weeks of World War II when the northeast corner of the city was destroyed (2 DM, daily 9:00–17:00, closed off-season, photos, English translation).

▲▲**St. Jakob's Church**—Built in the 14th century, it's been Lutheran since 1544. Take a close look at the Twelve Apostles altar in front (from 1546, left permanently in its open festival-day position). Six saints are below Christ. St. James (Jacob in German) is the one with the staff. He's the saint of pilgrims, and this was on the medieval pilgrimage route to Santiago de Compostela in Spain. Study the painted panels. Around the back (upper left) is a great painting of Rothenburg's Market Square in the 15th century looking like it does today. Before leaving the front of the church, notice the old medallions above the carved choir stalls featuring the coats of arms of Rothenburg's leading families and portraits of early Reformation preachers.

Next, climb the stairs in the back. Behind the pipe organ stands the artistic highlight of Rothenburg and perhaps the most wonderful woodcarving in all Germany: the glorious 500-year-old, 30-foot-high *Altar of the Holy Blood*. Tilman Riemenschneider, the Michelangelo of German woodcarvers, carved this from 1499 to 1504 to hold a precious rock crystal capsule set in a cross containing a drop of the holy blood (1270). Below, in the scene of the Last Supper, Jesus gives Judas a piece of bread marking him as the traitor while John lays his head on Christ's lap. On the left: Jesus entering Jerusalem. On the right: Jesus praying in the Garden of Gethsemane (2.50 DM, Mon–Sat 9:00–17:30, Sun 10:45–17:30, off-season 10:00–12:00, 14:00–16:00, free helpful English info sheet).

▲▲**Medieval Crime and Punishment Museum**—It's the best of its kind, full of fascinating old legal bits and *Kriminal* pieces, instruments of punishment and torture, even a special cage complete with a metal gag—for nags. Exhibits are well described in English (6 DM, 10 DM combo includes Imperial City Museum, daily 9:30–17:15, shorter hours in winter, fun cards and posters).

Museum of the Imperial City (Reichsstadt Museum)—This less sensational museum, housed in the former Dominican Convent, gives a more scholarly look at old Rothenburg. Highlights include *The Rothenburg Passion*, a 12-panel series of paintings from 1492 showing scenes leading up to Christ's crucifixion, an exhibit of Jewish culture through the ages in Rothenburg, and a 14th-century convent kitchen (5 DM, daily 9:30–17:30, in winter 13:00–16:00). The convent garden is a peaceful place to work on your tan.

▲**Toy Museum**—Two floors of historic *Kinder*-cuteness is a hit with many (6 DM, 12 DM per family, daily 9:30–18:00, just off Market Square, downhill from the fountain, Hofbronneng 13).

▲▲**Herrngasse and the Castle Garden**—Any town's *Herrngasse*, where the richest patricians and merchants (the *Herren*) lived, is your chance to see its finest old mansions. Wander from Market Square down Herrngasse (past Rothenburg's old official measurement rods on the city hall wall) and drop into the lavish front rooms of a ritzy hotel or two. Pop into the Franciscan Church (free, Mon–Sat 10:00–12:00, 14:00–16:00, Sun 14:00–16:00, built in 1285—the oldest in town, with a Riemenschneider altarpiece), continue on down past the old-fashioned puppet theater, through the old gate (notice the tiny after-curfew door in the big door and the frightening mask mouth from which hot Nutella was poured onto attackers), through the garden and to the end of what used to be the castle (great picnic spots and Tauber Riviera views at sunset). This is the popular kissing spot for romantic Rothenburg teenagers.

▲**Walk in the Countryside**—Just below the *Burggarten* (castle garden) in the Tauber Valley is the cute, skinny, 600-year-old castle/summer home of Mayor Toppler (2 DM, Fri–Sun 13:00–16:00, closed Mon–Thu). On the top floor, notice the photo of bombed-out Rothenburg in 1945. Then walk on past the covered bridge and huge trout to the peaceful village of Detwang. Detwang (from 968, the second-oldest village in Franconia) is actually older than Rothenburg and also has a Riemenschneider altar piece in its church. For a scenic return, loop back to Rothenburg through the valley along the river, past a café with outdoor tables, great desserts, and a town view to match.

Swimming—Rothenburg has a fine modern recreation center with an indoor/outdoor pool and sauna. It's just a few minutes' walk down the Dinkelsbühl Road (Fri–Wed 9:00–20:00, Thu 10:00–20:00, tel. 09861/4565).

Sightseeing Lowlights—St. Wolfgang's Church is a fortified Gothic church built into the medieval wall at Klingentor. Its dungeon-like passages and shepherd's dance exhibit are pretty lame (2 DM, daily 10:00–13:00, 14:00–17:00). The cute-looking Bäuerliches Museum (farming museum) next door is even worse. The Rothenburger Handwerkerhaus (tradesman's house, 700 years old) shows the typical living situation of a Rothenburger in the town's heyday (3 DM, daily 10:00–18:00, closed in winter, Alter Stadtgraben 26, near the Markus Tower).

Sights—Near Rothenburg

Franconian Bike Ride—For a fun, breezy look at the countryside around Rothenburg, rent a bike from Rad & Tat (25 DM/day, Mon–Fri 9:00–18:00, Sat–Sun 9:00–14:00, Bensenstrasse 17, outside of town behind the "neck," near corner of Bensenstrasse and Erlbacherstrasse, no deposit except passport number, tel. 09861/87984). Return the bike the next morning before 10:00. For a pleasant half-day pedal, bike south down to Detwang via Topplerschlosschen. Go north along the level bike path to

Tauberscheckenbach, then huff and puff uphill about 20 minutes to Adelshofen and south back to Rothenburg.

Franconian Open-Air Museum—A 20-minute drive from Rothenburg in the undiscovered "Rothenburgy" town of Bad Windsheim is a small, open-air folk museum that, compared with others in Europe, isn't much. But it's trying very hard and gives you the best look around at traditional rural Franconia (6 DM, Tue–Sun 9:00–18:00, closed Mon and Nov–Feb).

Shopping

Be careful... Rothenburg is one of Germany's best shopping towns. Do it here, mail it home, and be done with it. Lovely prints, carvings, wineglasses, Christmas-tree ornaments, and beer steins are popular.

The Käthe Wohlfahrt Christmas trinkets phenomenon is spreading across the half-timbered reaches of Europe. In Rothenburg tourists flock to two Käthe Wohlfahrt Christmas Villages (on either side of Herrngasse, just off Market Square). This Christmas wonderland is filled with enough twinkling lights to require a special electric hookup, instant Christmas mood music (best appreciated on a hot day in July), and American and Japanese tourists hungrily filling little woven shopping baskets with 5- to 10-DM goodies to hang on their trees. (OK, I admit it, my Christmas tree sports a few KW ornaments.) Note: Prices have hefty tour-guide kickbacks built into them. The Käthe Wohlfahrt discount store sells damaged and discontinued items. It's unnamed at Kirchgasse 5 across from the entrance of St. Jakob's Church (Mon–Fri 9:00–18:00, less on weekends, closed Jan–Feb, tel. 09861/4090).

The Friese shop offers a charming contrast (just off Market Square, west of TI, on corner across from public WC). Cuckoo with friendliness, it gives shoppers with this book tremendous service: a 10 percent discount, 16 percent tax deducted if you have it mailed, and a free map. Anneliese, who runs the place with her sons, Frankie and Berni, charges only her cost for shipping, changes money at the best rates in town with no extra charge, and lets tired travelers leave their bags in her back room for free. Her pricing is good, but to comparison shop, go here last.

The Ernst Geissendörfer print shop sells fine prints, etchings, and paintings. If you show this book they'll offer 10 percent off marked prices for all purchases in cash (or credit card purchases of at least 100 DM) and a free shot of German brandy whether you buy anything or not (enter through bear shop on corner where Market Square hits Schmiedgasse; go to first floor).

For characteristic wineglasses and oinkology gear, drop by the Weinladen am Plonlein (Plonlein 27).

Shoppers who mail their goodies home can get handy boxes

at the post office (Mon–Fri 9:00–12:30, 14:00–17:00, Sat 9:00–12:00, Milchmarkt 5, 2 blocks east of Market Square).

Those who prefer to eat their souvenirs shop the *Bäckereien* (bakeries). Their succulent pastries, pies, and cakes are pleasantly distracting. Skip the bad-tasting Rothenburger *Schneebälle*.

Sleeping in Rothenburg
(1.70 DM = about $1, tel. code: 09861, zip code: 91541)
Sleep Code: **S** = Single, **D** = Double/Twin, **T** = Triple, **Q** = Quad, **b** = bathroom, **t** = toilet only, **s** = shower only, **CC** = Credit Card (**V**isa, **M**asterCard, **A**mex), **SE** = Speaks English, **NSE** = No English. Unless otherwise indicated, room prices include breakfast.

Rothenburg is crowded with visitors. But when the sun sets, most retreat to the predictable plumbing of their big-city high-rise hotels. Except for the rare Saturday night and festivals (see "Orientation," above), room-finding is easy throughout the year. Unless otherwise noted, enough English is spoken.

Many hotels and guest houses will pick up desperate heavy packers at the station. You may be greeted at the station by *Zimmer* skimmers who have rooms to rent. If you have reservations, resist. But if you don't have a reservation, try talking yourself into one of these more desperate bed-and-breakfast rooms for a youth-hostel price. Be warned: These people are notorious for taking you to distant hotels and then charging you for the ride back if you decline a room. There's a handy Laundromat near the station (Johannitergasse 8, tel. 09861/5177).

Hotels
I like **Hotel Goldene Rose**, where scurrying Karin serves breakfast and stately Henni keeps everything in good order. Other than its annex and apartment, the hotel has only one shower for two floors of rooms, but the rooms are clean and you're surrounded by cobbles, flowers, and red-tiled roofs (1 small S-25 DM, S-35 DM, D-65 DM, Ds-85 DM, Db-90 DM in classy annex behind the garden; some triples; spacious family apartment: for 4-190 DM, for 5-225 DM; CC:VMA; streetside rooms can be noisy; closed Jan–Feb; kid-friendly; ground-floor rooms in annex; Spitalgasse 28, tel. 09861/4638, fax 09861/86417, Henni SE). The Favetta family also serves good, reasonably priced meals. Remember to keep your key to get in after they close (at the side gate in the alley). The hotel is a 15-minute walk from the station or a seven-minute walk downhill from Market Square.

Gasthof Greifen, once the home of Mayor Toppler, is a big, traditional, 600-year-old place with large rooms and all the comforts. It's family run and creaks just the way you want it to (small Sb-64, Sb-80 DM, one big D-74 DM with no shower available, Db-115–135 DM, Tb-180 DM, 10 percent off for 3-night stay,

CC:VMA, laundry self- or full-service, free and easy parking, half a block downhill from Market Square at Obere Schmiedgasse 5, tel. 09861/2281, fax 09861/86374, Brigitte and Klingler family).

Gasthof Marktplatz, right on Market Square, has eight tidy rooms and a cozy atmosphere (S-40 DM, D-72 DM, Ds-82 DM, Db-90 DM, T-92 DM, Ts-107 DM, Tb-117 DM, Grüner Markt 10, tel. & fax 09861/6722, Herr Rosner SE).

Gästehaus Raidel, a creaky 500-year-old house packed with antiques, offers large rooms with cramped facilities down the hall. Run by grim people who make me want to sing the *Addams Family* theme song, it works in a pinch (S-35 DM, Sb-69 DM, D-69 DM, Db-89 DM, Wenggasse 3, tel. 09861/3115, fax 09861/935-255, e-mail: gaesthaus-raidel@t-online.de).

Hotel Gerberhaus, a classy new hotel in a 500-year-old building, is warmly run by Inge and Kurt, who mix modern comforts into bright and airy rooms while maintaining a sense of half-timbered elegance. Enjoy the great buffet breakfasts and pleasant garden in back (Sb-80 DM, Db-100–140 DM depending on size, Tb-165 DM, Qb-185 DM, all with TV and telephones, CC:VM but use cash for 5 percent off and a free *Schneebälle*, Spitalgasse 25, tel. 09861/94900, fax 09861/86555, e-mail: gerberhaus@t-online.de). The downstairs café serves good salads and sandwiches.

Hotel Klosterstueble, deep in the old town near the castle garden, is even classier. Jutta greets her guests while husband Rudolf does the cooking (Sb-100 DM, Db-130–170 DM, Tb-200 DM, some luxurious family rooms, 10 DM extra on weekends, discounts for families, CC:V, Heringsbronnengasse 5, tel. 09861/6774, fax 09861/6474, www.klosterstueble.rothenburg.de).

Bohemians enjoy the **Hotel Altfränkische Weinstube am Klosterhof**. Mario and Hanne run this dark and smoky pub in a 600-year-old building. Upstairs they rent six cozy rooms with upscale Monty Python atmosphere, TVs, modern showers, open-beam ceilings, and *"Himmel"* beds—canopied four-poster "heaven" beds (Sb-79 DM, Db-89 DM, Tb-109–119 DM, CC:VM, most rooms have tubs with hand-held showers, kid-friendly, walk under St. Jakob's Church, take second left off Klingengasse at Klosterhof 7, tel. 09861/6404, fax 09861/6410). Their pub is a candlelit classic, serving hot food until 22:30 and closing at 01:00. Drop by on Wednesday evening (19:30–24:00) for the English Conversation Club.

Top Private Rooms

For the best real, with-a-local-family, comfortable, and homey experience, stay with **Herr und Frau Moser** (D-65 DM, T-95 DM, no single rooms, Spitalgasse 12, tel. 09861/5971). This charming retired couple speak little English but try very hard. Speak slowly, in clear, simple English. Reserve by phone and reconfirm by phone one day ahead of arrival.

Pension Pöschel is friendly with seven cozy rooms on the second floor of a concrete but pleasant building (S-35 DM, D-60 DM, T-90 DM, small kids free, Wenggasse 22, tel. 09861/3430, e-mail: pension.poeschel@t-online.de).

Frau Guldemeister, who rents two simple ground-floor rooms, takes reservations by phone only, no more than a day or two in advance (Ss-40 DM, Ds with twin beds-60 DM, bigger Db-70 DM, breakfast in room, minimum 2-night stay, off Market Square behind the Christmas shop, Pfaffleinsgasschen 10, tel. 09861/8988, some English).

Last-Resort Accommodations

These are all decent places, just lesser values compared to the places mentioned above. **Pension Kreuzerhof** has seven big, modern, ground-floor, motel-style rooms with views of parked cars on a quiet street (Sb-45-50 DM, Db-78-87 DM, Millergasse 6, tel. & fax 09861/3424). **Erich Endress** offers five airy, comfy rooms above his grocery store (S-45 DM, D-80 DM, Db-110 DM, nonsmoking, Rodergasse 6, tel. 09861/2331, fax 09861/935 355). The **Zum Schmolzer** restaurant at Rosengasse 21 rents 14 nice but drab-colored rooms (Sb-55 DM, Db-90 DM, Stollengasse 29, tel. 09861/3371, fax 09861/7204, SE). **Cafe Uhl** offers 10 fine, slightly frayed rooms over a bakery (Sb-58-75 DM, Db-95-110 DM, CC:VA, Plonlein 8, tel. 09861/4895, fax 09861/92820). **Gästehaus Flemming** has seven plain yet comfortable rooms behind St. Jakob's Church (Db-86, Klingengasse 21, tel. 09861/92380). **Gästehaus Viktoria** is a peaceful and cheery little place with a tiny garden and two rooms (Ds-75 DM, Klingenschütt 4, tel. 09861/87682, Hanne).

In the modern world, a block from the train station, **Pension Willi und Helen Then** is run by a cool guy who played the sax in a jazz band for seven years after the war and is a regular at the English Conversation Club (D-100 DM, Db-120 DM, tel. 09861/5177, fax 09861/86014).

Hostel

Here in Bavaria, hosteling is limited to those under 27, except for families traveling with children under 18. The fine **Rossmühle Youth Hostel** has 184 beds in two buildings. The droopy-eyed building (the old town horse-mill, used when the town was under siege and the river-powered mill was inaccessible) houses groups and the hostel office. The adjacent and newly renovated hostel is mostly for families and individuals (dorm beds-23 DM, Db-56 DM, sheets-5.50 DM, includes breakfast, dinner-9 DM, self-serve laundry, Muhlacker 1, tel. 09861/94160, fax 09861/941-620, e-mail: JHRothen@aol.com, SE). This popular place takes reservations (even more than a year in advance) and will hold rooms until 18:00.

Sleeping in Nearby Detwang and Bettwar

The town of Detwang, a 15-minute walk below Rothenburg, is loaded with quiet *Zimmer*. The clean, quiet, and comfortable old **Gasthof zum Schwarzen Lamm** in Detwang (D-85 DM, Db-110-130 DM, tel. 09861/6727, fax 09861/86899) serves good food, as does the popular and very local-style **Eulenstube** next door. **Gästehaus Alte Schreinerei** offers good food and 18 quiet, comfy, reasonable rooms a little farther down the road in Bettwar (Db-76 DM, 8801 Bettwar, tel. 09861/1541, fax 09861/86710).

Eating in Rothenburg

Most places serve meals only from 11:30 to 13:30 and 18:00 to 20:00. At **Goldene Rose** (see "Sleeping," above), Reno cooks up traditional German fare at good prices (Thu–Mon 11:30–14:00, 17:30–21:00, closed Tue–Wed, in sunny weather the leafy garden terrace is open in the back, Spitalgasse 28).

Galgengasse (Gallows Lane) has two cheap and popular standbys: **Pizzeria Roma** (11:30–24:00, 10-DM pizzas and normal schnitzel fare, Galgengasse 19) and **Gasthof zum Ochsen** (Fri–Wed 11:30–13:30, 18:00–20:00, closed Thu, uneven service but decent 10-DM meals, Galgengasse 26). **Landsknechtstuben,** at Galgengasse 21, is pricey but friendly, with some cheaper schnitzel choices.

Gasthaus Siebersturm serves up tasty, reasonable meals in a bright, airy dining room (Spitalgasse). For a break from schnitzel, **Lotus China** serves good Chinese food daily (2 blocks behind TI near the church, Eckele 2, tel. 09861/86886). **Gasthaus Greifen** serves typical Rothenburg cuisine at moderate prices (just below Market Square).

Two **supermarkets** are near the wall at Rödertor (the one outside the wall to the left is cheaper; the one inside is nicer).

Evening Fun and Beer Drinking

For beer-garden fun on a balmy summer evening (dinner or beer), you have three fine choices: Nearby is **Gasthof Rödertor**, just outside the wall at the Rödertor (red gate, near discos, below). In the valley along the river and worth the 20-minute hike is **Unter den Linden** beer garden. A more central and touristy beer garden is behind Hotel Eisenhut (nightly until 22:00, access from Burggasse or through the hotel off Herrngasse).

Trinkstube zur Hölle (Hell) is dark and foreboding. But they serve good ribs from 18:00 and offer thick wine-drinking atmosphere until late (a block past Criminal Museum on Burggasse, with devil hanging out front, tel. 09861/4229). For mellow ambience, try the beautifully restored **Alte Keller's Weinstube** under walls festooned with old pots and jugs (closed Tue, Alter Keller 8). Wine lovers enjoy the **Glocke Hotel's Stube**

Romantic Road

(Plonlein 1). And perhaps the most elegant place in town is the courtyard of **Baumeister Haus** (behind statue-festooned facade a few doors below Market Square).

Two popular **discos** are near the Gasthof Rödertor's beer garden, a few doors farther out near the Sparkasse bank (T.G.I. Friday's at Ansbacher 15, in alley next to bank, open Wed, Fri–Sat; Check Point, around corner from, open Wed, Fri–Sun).

For a rare chance to mix it up with locals who aren't selling anything, bring your favorite slang and tongue twisters to the **English Conversation Club** at Mario's Altfränkische Weinstube (Wed 19:30–24:00, Anneliese from the Friese shop is a regular). This dark and smoky pub is an atmospheric hangout any night but Tuesday, when it's closed (Klosterhof 7, off Klingengasse, behind St. Jakob's Church, tel. 09861/6404).

2000 Romantic Road Bus Schedule (Daily, April–October)

Frankfurt	8:00	—
Würzburg	9:45	—
Arrive Rothenburg	12:45	—
Depart Rothenburg	14:30	—
Arrive Dinkelsbühl	15:25	—
Depart Dinkelsbühl	16:15	15:30
Munich	19:50	—
Füssen	—	20:10
Check www.euraide.de for updates.		
Füssen	8:00	—
Arrive Wieskirche	8:35	—
Depart Wieskirche	8:55	—
Munich	—	9:00
Arrive Dinkelsbühl	12:50	12:45
Depart Dinkelsbühl	—	14:00
Arrive Rothenburg	—	14:40
Depart Rothenburg	—	16:15
Würzburg	—	18:30
Frankfurt	—	20:30

Transportation Connections—Rothenburg

The Romantic Road bus tour takes you in and out of Rothenburg each afternoon (Apr–Oct) heading to Munich, Frankfurt, or Füssen. See the Romantic Road bus schedule this page.

A tiny train line runs between Rothenburg and Steinach (almost hrly, 15 min, but only until early evening). **Steinach by train to: Würzburg** (hrly, 30 min), **Munich** (hrly, 2 hrs), **Frankfurt** (hrly, 2 hrs, change in Würzburg).

ROMANTIC ROAD

The Romantic Road (Romantische Strasse) winds you past the most beautiful towns and scenery of Germany's medieval heartland. Once Germany's medieval trade route, now it's the best way to connect the dots between Füssen, Munich, and Frankfurt.

Wander through quaint hills and rolling villages, and stop wherever the cows look friendly or a town fountain beckons. My favorite sections are from Füssen to Landsberg and Rothenburg to Weikersheim. (If you're driving with limited time, you can connect Rothenburg and Munich by Autobahn, but don't miss these two best sections.) Caution: The similarly promoted "Castle Road" sounds intriguing but is nowhere near as interesting.

Throughout Bavaria you'll see colorfully ornamented Maypoles decorating town squares. Many are painted in Bavaria's colors, blue and white. The decorations that line each side of the pole symbolize the crafts or businesses of that community. Each May Day they are festively replaced. Traditionally, rival communities try to steal each other's Maypole. Locals will guard their new pole night and day as May Day approaches. Stolen poles are ransomed only with lots of beer for the clever thieves.

Getting around the Romantic Road

By Bus: The Europa Bus Company runs buses daily between Frankfurt and Munich in each direction (Apr–Oct). A second route goes daily between Dinkelsbühl and Füssen. Buses leave from train stations in towns served by a train. The 120-DM, 11-hour ride costs only 39 DM with a Eurailpass (including the 10-DM registration fee which allows 1 free piece of baggage, 3 DM per additional bag). Each bus stops in Rothenburg (about 2 hours) and Dinkelsbühl (about an hour) and briefly at a few other attractions, and has a usually mediocre guide who hands out brochures and narrates the journey in English. There is no quicker or easier way to travel across Germany and get such a hearty dose of its countryside. Bus reservations are free, easy, and smart—without one you can lose your seat to someone who has one (especially on summer weekends; call Munich's EurAide office at 089/593-889 at least 1 day in advance to reserve). You can start, stop, and switch over where you like, but you'll be guaranteed a seat only if you reserve each segment.

By Car: Follow the brown "Romantische Strasse" signs.

FRANKFURT

Frankfurt, the northern terminus of the Romantic Road, is actually pleasant for a big city and offers a good look at today's no-nonsense urban Germany.

Orientation (tel. code: 069)

Tourist Information: For a quick look at the city, pick up a 1-DM map at the TI in the train station (Mon–Fri 8:00–21:00, Sat–Sun 9:00–18:00, tel. 069/2123-8849). It's a 20-minute walk from the station down Kaiserstrasse past Goethe's house (great

Rothenburg and the Romantic Road

man, mediocre sight, Grosser Hirschgraben 23) to Römerberg, Frankfurt's lively Market Square (or you can take subway U-4 or U-5 from the station to Römerberg). A string of museums is just across the river along Schaumainkai (Tue–Sun 10:00–17:00, Wed until 20:00, closed Mon). The TI also has info on bus tours of the city (44 DM, 10:00 and 14:00 in summer, 14:00 only off-season, 2.5 hrs).

A browse through Frankfurt's red-light district offers a fascinating way to kill time between trains. Wander down Taunusstrasse two blocks in front of the station and you'll find 20 "eros towers," each a five-story-tall brothel filled with prostitutes. Climbing through a few of these may be one of the more memorable experiences of your European trip. It feels safe, the atmosphere is friendly, and browsing is encouraged (40 DM, daily, tel. 069/32422).

Romantic Road Bus: If you're taking the bus out of Frankfurt, you can buy your ticket either at the train station or the Deutsches Touring office, which is part of the train station complex but has an entrance outside (Mon–Fri 7:30–18:00, Sat 7:30–14:00, Sun 7:30–14:00, CC:VMA, entrance at Mannheimer Strasse 4, tel. 069/230-735); or pay cash when you board the bus. Eurail and Europass holders, who get a 75 percent discount, pay only 39 DM (including the 10-DM registration fee). The bus waits at stall #9 (right of the train station as you leave).

Sleeping in Frankfurt
(1.70 DM = about $1, tel. code: 069, zip code: 60329)
Avoid driving or sleeping in Frankfurt, especially during the city's numerous trade fairs (about five days a month), which send hotel prices skyrocketing. Pleasant Rhine or Romantic Road towns are just a quick train ride or drive away. But if you must spend the night in Frankfurt, here are some places within a block of the train station (and its handy train to the airport). This isn't the safest neighborhood; be careful after dark. For a rough idea of directions to hotels, stand with your back to the main entrance of the station: Using a 12-hour clock, Hotel Manhattan is across the street at 10:00, Pension Schneider at 12:00, Hotel Europa and Wiesbaden at 4:00, and Hotel Paris at 5:00. Breakfast is included in all listings and English is spoken.

Hotel Manhattan, with newly remodeled, sleek, arty rooms, is expensive—best for a splurge on a first or last night in Europe (Sb-140 DM, Db-160 DM, show this book to get a break during nonconvention times, CC:VMA, elevator, riffraff in front of hotel, Düsseldorfer Strasse 10, tel. 069/234-748, fax 069/234-532, e-mail: manhattan-hotel@t-online.de).

Pension Schneider is a strange little oasis of decency and quiet three floors above the epicenter of Frankfurt's red-light district, two blocks in front of the train station. The street is safe in spite of the pimps and pushers. Its 10 rooms are big, bright, and comfortable (D-80 DM, Db-100 DM, Tb-120 DM, CC:VMA, elevator, corner of Moselstrasse at Taunusstrasse 43, tel. 069/251-071, fax 069/259-228).

Hotel Europa, with well-maintained rooms, is a fine value (Sb-80 DM, Db-120 DM, Tb-150 DM, prices soft on weekends, some nonsmoking rooms, garage, CC:VMA, Baseler Strasse 17, tel. 069/236-013, fax 069/236-203).

Hotel Wiesbaden has worn rooms and a kind manager (S-80 DM, Sb-115 DM, Db-140–165 DM depending on size, Tb-180–200 DM, CC:VMA, a little smoky, elevator, Baseler Strasse 52, tel. 069/232-347, fax 069/252-845).

Hotel Paris, just renovated with modern, Impressionist rooms, is the most cushy of my listings (Sb-110 DM, Db-150 DM, CC:VMA, Karlsruherstrasse 8, tel. 069/273-9963, fax 069/2739-9651).

Farther from the station is **Pension Backer** (S-50 DM, D-60 DM, showers-3 DM, near the botanical gardens; take S-Bahn 2 stops to Hauptwache, then transfer to U-6 or U-7 for 2 stops to Westend; Mendelssohnstrasse 92, tel. 069/747-992).

The **hostel** is open to members of any age (8-bed rooms, 32 DM per bed with sheets and breakfast, bus #46 from station to Frankenstein Place, Deutschherrnufer 12, tel. 069/619-058).

Transportation Connections—Frankfurt

By train to: Rothenburg (hrly, 3 hrs, changes in Würzburg and Steinach; the tiny Steinach-Rothenburg train often leaves from the "B" section of track, away from the middle of the station, shortly after the Würzburg train arrives), **Würzburg** (hrly, 90 min), **Munich** (hrly, 3.5 hrs), **Baden-Baden** (hrly, 90 min), **Freiburg** (hrly, 2 hrs, change in Mannheim), **Bonn** (hrly, 2 hrs), **Koblenz** (hrly, 90 min), **Köln** (hrly, 2 hrs), **Berlin** (hrly, 5 hrs), **Amsterdam** (8/day, 5 hrs), **Bern** (14/day, 4.5 hrs, changes in Mannheim and Basel), **Brussels** (6/day, 5 hrs), **Copenhagen** (3/day, 10 hrs), **London** (5/day, 9.5 hrs), **Milan** (6/day, 9 hrs), **Paris** (4/day, 6.5 hrs), **Vienna** (7/day, 7.5 hrs).

Frankfurt's Airport

The airport (*Flughafen*) is a 12-minute train ride from downtown (4/hrly, 5.90 DM, ride included in Frankfurt's 8.5-DM all-day city transit pass or the 13-DM 2-day city pass). The airport is user-friendly. It offers showers, a baggage check, fair banks with long hours, a grocery store, a train station, a lounge where you can sleep overnight, a business lounge (Europe City Club—30 DM to anyone with a plane ticket), easy rental-car pickup, plenty of parking, an information booth, and even McBeer. McWelcome to Germany.

Airport English-speaking info: tel. 069/6901 (will transfer you to any of the airlines for booking or confirmation). Lufthansa—069/255-255, American Airlines—069/271-130, Delta—069/664-1212, Northwest—0180/525-4650.

To Rothenburg: Train travelers can validate railpasses or buy tickets at the airport station and catch a train to Würzburg, connecting to Rothenburg via Steinach (hrly, 3 hrs). If driving to Rothenburg, follow Autobahn signs to Würzburg.

Flying Home from Frankfurt: The airport has its own train station, and many of the trains from the Rhine stop there on their way into Frankfurt (e.g., hrly 90-min rides direct from Bonn; hrly 2-hr rides from Bacharach with a change in Mainz; earliest train from Bacharach to Frankfurt leaves just before 6:00). By car, head toward Frankfurt on the Autobahn and follow the little airplane signs to the airport.

MUNICH (MÜNCHEN)

Munich, Germany's most livable and "yuppie" city, is also one of its most historic, artistic, and entertaining. It's big and growing, with a population of more than 1.4 million. Just a little more than a century ago, it was the capital of an independent Bavaria. Its imperial palaces, jewels, and grand boulevards constantly remind visitors that this was once a political and cultural powerhouse. And its recently-bombed-out feeling reminds us that 75 years ago it provided a springboard for Nazism, and 55 years ago it lost a war.

Orient yourself in Munich's old center with its colorful pedestrian mall. Immerse yourself in Munich's art and history—crown jewels, Baroque theater, Wittelsbach palaces, great paintings, and beautiful parks. Munich evenings are best spent in frothy beer halls, with their oompah, bunny-hopping, and belching Bavarian atmosphere. Pry big pretzels from no-nonsense, buxom beer maids.

Planning Your Time

Munich is worth two days, including a half-day side trip to Dachau. If necessary, its essence can be captured in a day (walk the center, tour a palace and a museum, and enjoy a beer-filled evening). Those without a car and in a hurry can do the Bavarian castles of Ludwig as a day trip from Munich by tour. Even Salzburg can be a handy day trip from Munich.

Orientation (tel. code: 089)

The tourist's Munich is circled by a ring road (which was the town wall) marked by four old gates: Karlstor (near the train station, known as the Hauptbahnhof), Sendlinger Tor, Isartor (near the river), and Odeonsplatz (near the palace). Marienplatz is the city center. A great pedestrian-only street cuts this circle in half, running nearly from Karlstor and the train station through Marienplatz to Isartor. Orient yourself along this east-west axis. Most sights are within a few blocks of this people-filled walk. Ninety percent of the sights and hotels I recommend are within a 20-minute walk of Marienplatz and each other.

Tourist Information

Munich has two helpful TIs: in front of the station (with your back to the arrival/departure board, walk through the central hall and turn right outside; Mon–Sat 9:00–20:00, Sun 10:00–18:00, tel. 089/2333-0257 or 089/2333-0272) and on Marienplatz (Mon–Fri 10:00–20:00, Sat 10:00–16:00, closed Sun, www.muenchen-tourist.de). Have a list of questions ready, confirm sightseeing plans, and pick up brochures. The excellent Munich city map is one of the handiest in Europe. Consider the *Monats-programm* (3 DM, a German-language list of sights and an events calendar), *Hits for Kids* (1 DM), and the free twice-monthly magazine *In München* (lists in German all the movies and entertainment in town, available at TI or any big cinema till supply runs out). The TI can refer you to hotels for a 10 to 15 percent fee, but you'll get a better value with my recommended hotels—contact them directly. If the line at the TI is bad, go to EurAide (below). The only essential item is the TI's great city map (also available at EurAide and many hotels).

EurAide: The industrious, eager-to-help EurAide office in the train station is a godsend for Eurailers and budget travelers (daily in summer 7:45–12:00, 13:00–18:00; in winter it closes at 16:00 on weekdays, 12:00 on Sat, and all day Sun; Room 3 at track 11; tel. 089/593-889, fax 089/550-3965, www.euraide.de, e-mail: euraide @compuserve.com). Alan Wissenberg and his staff know your train travel and accommodations questions and have answers in clear American English. The German rail company pays them to help you design your best train travels. They make train and Romantic Road bus reservations and sell train tickets, *couchettes*, and sleepers. They can find you a room for a 7-DM fee (but not at my hotels), and they offer a 1-DM city map and a free, useful newsletter. They sell a "Prague Excursion" train pass, convenient for Prague-bound Eurailers—good for train travel from any Czech border station to Prague and back to any border station within seven days (first class-90 DM, second class-60 DM, youth second-45 DM; a bit cheaper through their U.S. office: 941/480-1555, fax 941/480-1522). Every Wednesday in June and July, EurAide provides an excellent "Two Castle" tour of Neuschwanstein and Linderhof that includes Wieskirche (frustrating without a car, see "Sights–Near Munich" below).

Arrival in Munich

By Train: Munich's train station is a sight in itself—one of those places that can turn an accountant into a vagabond. For a quick orientation in the station, use the big wall maps showing the train station, Munich, and Bavaria (through the center doorway as you leave the tracks on the left). For a quick rest stop, the Burger King upstairs has toilets as pleasant and accessible as its hamburgers. A classier and more peaceful hangout is the vast, generally empty, old restaurant opposite track 14. The Internationale Presse (across from track 24) is great for English-language books, papers, and magazines, including *Munich Found* (informative English-speaking residents' monthly, 4.5 DM). You'll also find two TIs (the city TI and EurAide, see above) and lockers (track 31). Europcar and Hertz are up the steps opposite track 21. The U-Bahn, S-Bahn, and buses connect the station to the rest of the city (though many hotels listed in this book are within walking distance of the station).

By Plane: There are two good ways to connect the airport and downtown Munich: Take an easy 40-minute ride on subway S-8 (from Marienplatz, 14.4 DM or free with train pass) or take the Lufthansa airport bus to (or from) the train station (15 DM, 3/hrly, 45 min, buy tickets on bus or from EurAide). Airport info tel. 089/9759-1313.

Getting around Munich

Much of Munich can be walked. To reach sights away from the city center, use the fine tram, bus, and subway systems. Taxis are expensive and generally unnecessary (except perhaps to avoid the time-consuming trip to Nymphenburg).

By Public Transit: Subways are called U- or S-Bahns. Subway lines are numbered (e.g., S-3 or U-5). Eurailpasses are good on the S-Bahn (actually an underground-while-in-the-city commuter railway). Regular tickets cost 3.60 DM and are good for two hours of changes in one direction. For the shortest rides (one or two stops) buy the 1.80-DM ticket (*Kurzstrecke*). The 9-DM all-day pass is a great deal (valid until 6:00 the next morning). The Partner Daily Ticket (for 13 DM) is good all day for up to five adults and a dog (two kids count as one adult, so two adults, six kids and a dog can travel with this ticket). Tickets are available from easy-to-use ticket machines (which take bills and coins), subway booths, and TIs. The entire system (bus/tram/subway) works on the same tickets. You must punch your own ticket before boarding (stamping a date and time on it). Plainclothes ticket-checkers enforce this "honor system," rewarding freeloaders with stiff 60-DM fines.

Important: All S-Bahn lines connect the Hauptbahnhof (main station) with Marienplatz (main square). If you want to use the S-Bahn and you're either at the station or Marienplatz, follow signs to the S-Bahn (U is not for you) and concern yourself only with the direction—in German, *richtung* (Hauptbahnhof/Pasing or Marienplatz).

Munich   235

By Bike: Munich—level and compact, with plenty of bike paths—feels good on two wheels. Bikes can be rented quickly and easily at the train station at **Radius Bikes** (May–mid-Oct daily 10:00–18:00, near track 30, tel. 089/596-113, three-speed bikes-5 DM/hr, 25 DM/day, 30 DM/24 hrs, 45 DM/48 hrs, mountain bikes-20 percent more; credit-card imprint, 100 DM, or passport for a deposit). They also offer excellent Munich and Dachau tours (see below) and dispense all the necessary tourist information (city map, bike routes), including a do-it-yourself bike tour booklet (5 DM).

Helpful Hints

Monday Tips: Most Munich sights (including Dachau) are closed on Monday. If you're in Munich on Monday, here are some suggestions: visit the Deutsches Museum, BMW Museum, or churches; take a walking tour or bus tour; climb high for city views; stroll the pedestrian streets; have lunch at the Viktualien Markt (see "Eating," below); rent a bike for a spin through Englischer Garten; day-trip to Salzburg or Ludwig's castles; or, if Oktoberfest is on, join the celebration.

Useful Phone Numbers: Pharmacy (at train station, tel. 089/594-119), EurAide train info (tel. 089/593-889, SE), German train info (tel. 089/19419, NSE), U.S. consulate (Königinstrasse 5, tel. 089/28880), American Express Company (on main pedestrian drag at Kaufingerstrasse 24, tel. 089/2280-1387), taxi (tel. 089/21610).

Laundromat: A handy *Waschcenter* is near the station at Paul Heyse Strasse 21 (6 DM/load, daily 7:00–23:00).

Car Rental: Munich's cheapest is Allround Car Rental (Boschetsrieder Strasse 12, U-3 to Obersendling, tel. 089/723-8383).

Internet Access: There's plenty of on-line access in Munich. The best deal is across from the main entrance of the station on Bahnhofplatz at the Hertie department store (6 DM/hr, open weekdays until 20:00). Times Square OnLine Bistro can connect you for 10 DM/hr (outside south exit of the station).

Sights—Central Munich

▲▲**Marienplatz and the Pedestrian Zone**—Riding the escalator out of the subway into sunlit Marienplatz (Mary's Square) gives you a fine first look at the glory of Munich: great buildings bombed flat and rebuilt, outdoor cafés, and people bustling and lingering like the birds and breeze they share this square with. Notice the ornate facades of the gray, pointy old city hall (Altes Rathaus) and the neo-Gothic new city hall (Neues Rathaus, built 1867–1910) with its *Glockenspiel*. The not-very-old *Glockenspiel* "jousts" on Marienplatz daily through the tourist season at 11:00, 12:00, and 17:00.

From here the pedestrian mall (Kaufingerstrasse and Neuhauserstrasse) leads you through a great shopping area, past carnivals of street entertainers and good old-fashioned slicers and

Munich Center

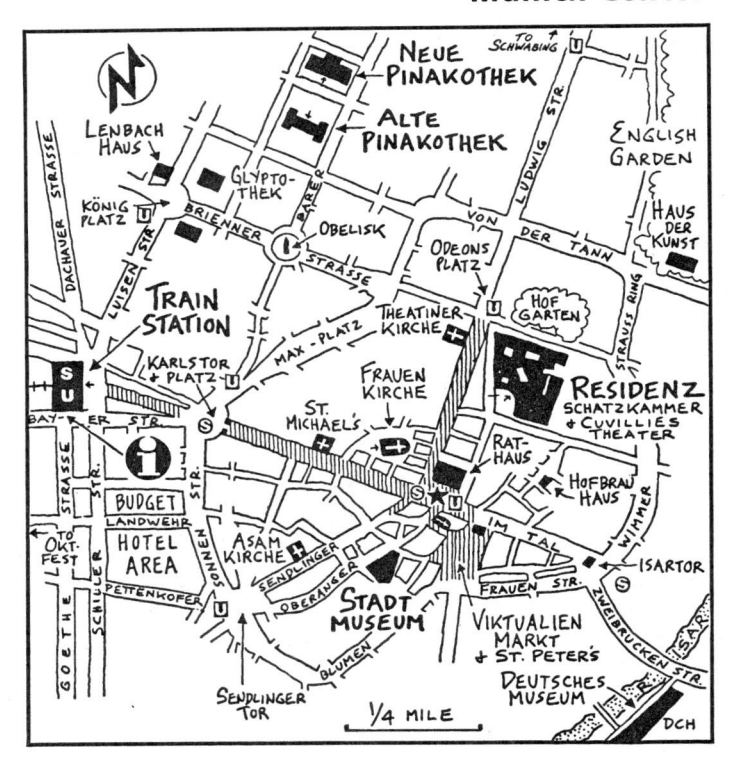

dicers, the twin-towering Frauenkirche (built in 1470, rebuilt after World War II), and several fountains, to Karlstor and the train station. As one of Europe's first pedestrian zones, the mall enraged shopkeepers when it was built in 1972. Today it is "Munich's living room." Nine thousand shoppers pass through it each hour...and the shopkeepers are very happy. Imagine this street in hometown U.S.A.

In the pedestrian zone around Marienplatz, there are three noteworthy churches. **St. Michael's Church**, while one of the first great Renaissance buildings north of the Alps, has a brilliantly Baroque interior. You can borrow the tiny English booklet to read in a pew; see the interesting photos of the bombed-out city center near the entry; and go into the crypt to see the tomb of King Ludwig II, the "mad" king still loved by romantics (2 DM, 40 stark royal tombs).

The twin onion domes of the 500-year-old **Frauenkirche**

(Church of Our Lady) are the symbol of the city. While much of the church was destroyed in World War II, the towers survived. Gloriously rebuilt since, the church is worth a visit. It was built in Gothic style, but money problems meant the domes weren't added until Renaissance times. These domes were inspired by the typical arches of the Venetian Renaissance. And the church domes we think of as "typically Bavarian" were inspired by these.

St. Peter's Church, the oldest in town, overlooks Marienplatz. Built upon the hill where the first monks founded the city in the 12th century, it has a fine interior with photos of the WWII bomb damage near the entrance. It's a long climb to the top of the spire (no elevator), much of it with two-way traffic on a one-way staircase, but the view is dynamite (2.50 DM, Mon–Sat 9:00–19:00, Sun 10:00–19:00). Try to be two flights from the top when the bells ring at the top of the hour, and when your friends back home ask you about your trip, you'll say, "What?"

▲▲**City Views**—Downtown Munich's three best city viewpoints are from the tops of: 1) St. Peter's Church (described above); 2) Frauenkirche (also described above), the highest viewpoint at 350 feet (4 DM, elevator, Mon–Sat 10:00–17:00, closed Sun); and 3) the Neues Rathaus, or new city hall (3 DM, elevator from under the Marienplatz *Glockenspiel*, Mon–Fri 9:00–19:00, Sat–Sun 10:00–19:00).

▲**Münchner Stadtmuseum**—The Munich city museum has four floors of exhibits: first floor—life in Munich through the centuries (including World War II) illustrated in paintings, photos, and models; second floor—special exhibits (often more interesting than the permanent ones); third floor—historic puppets and carnival gadgets; and fourth floor—a huge collection of musical instruments from around the world (5 DM, 7.50 DM for families, Tue–Sun 10:00–17:00, Wed until 20:30, closed Mon, no English descriptions, no crowds, bored and playful guards, 3 blocks off Marienplatz at St. Jakob's Platz 1, a fine children's playground faces the entry).

▲▲**Alte Pinakothek**—Bavaria's best painting gallery is newly renovated to show off a great collection of European masterpieces from the 14th to 19th centuries featuring work by Fra Angelico, Botticelli, da Vinci, Raphael, Dürer, Rubens, Rembrandt, El Greco, and Goya (7 DM, Tue–Sun 10:00–17:00, closed Mon, U-2 to Königsplatz or tram #27, tel. 089/238-05216).

▲**Neue Pinakothek**—The Alte Pinakothek's hip sister is a twin building across the square, showing off paintings from 1800 to 1920: Romantic, Realistic, Impressionism, Jugendstil, Monet, Renoir, van Gogh, Klimt (7 DM, Tue–Sun 10:00–17:00, closed Mon).

▲**Haus der Kunst**—Built by Hitler as a temple of Nazi art, this bold and fascist building now houses modern art, the kind the Führer censored. It's a playful collection—Kandinsky, Picasso,

Dalí, and much more from the 20th century (6 DM, Tue–Sun 10:00–17:00, closed Mon, Prinzregentenstrasse 1, at south end of Englischer Garden).
Bayerisches Nationalmuseum—An interesting collection of Riemenschneider carvings, manger scenes, traditional living rooms, and old Bavarian houses (3 DM, Tue–Sun 9:30–17:00, closed Mon, tram #20 or bus #53 or #55 to Prinzregentenstrasse 3).
▲▲▲**Deutsches Museum**—Germany's answer to our Smithsonian Institution, the Deutsches Museum traces the evolution of science and technology. With 10 miles of exhibits from astronomy to zymurgy, even those on roller skates will need to be selective. Blue dots on the floor mark someone's idea of the top 12 stops, but I had a better time just wandering through well-described rooms of historic bikes, cars (Benz's first car...a three-wheeler from the 1880s), trains, airplanes (Hitler's flying bomb from 1944), spaceships (step inside a rocket engine), mining, the harnessing of wind and water power, hydraulics, musical instruments, printing, photography, computers, astronomy, clocks...it's the Louvre of science and technology.

Most sections are lovingly described in English. The much-vaunted "high voltage" demonstrations (3/day, 15 minutes, all in German) show the noisy creation of a five-foot bolt of lightning—not that exciting. There's also a state-of-the-art planetarium (German only) and an adjacent IMAX theater (museum entry-10 DM, daily 9:00–17:00, self-serve cafeteria; S-Bahn to Isartor, then walk 300 meters over the river, following signs; tel. 089/217-9369). Save this for a Monday, when virtually all of Munich's museums are closed.
▲**Müllersches Volksbad**—This elegant Jugendstil (1901) public swimming pool is just across the river from the Deutsches Museum (5 DM, Rosenheimerstrasse 1, tel. 089/2361-3434).
Schwabing—Munich's artsy, bohemian university district, or "Greenwich Village," has been called "not a place but a state of mind." All I experienced was a mental lapse. The bohemians run the boutiques. I think the most colorful thing about Schwabing is the road leading back downtown. U-3 or U-6 will take you to the Münchener-Freiheit Center if you want to wander. Most of the jazz and disco joints are near Occamstrasse. The Haidhausen neighborhood (U-Bahn: Max Weber Platz) is becoming the "new Schwabing."
▲**Englischer Garden**—Munich's "Central Park," the largest on the Continent, was laid out in 1789 by an American. A huge beer garden sprawls near the Chinese pagoda. A rewarding respite from the city, it's especially fun on a bike under the summer sun (bike rental at train station). Caution: While a new local law requires sun worshipers to wear clothes on the tram, this park is sprinkled with nude sunbathers—quite a spectacle to most Americans (they're the ones riding their bikes into the river and trees).

Asam Church—Near the Stadtmuseum, this private church of the Asam brothers is a gooey, drippy, Baroque-concentrate masterpiece by Bavaria's top two rococonuts. A few blocks away, the small Damenstift Church has a sculptural rendition of the Last Supper so real you feel you're not alone (at intersection of Altheimer Ecke and Damenstiftstrasse, a block south of the pedestrian street).

Sights—Residenz

▲**Residenz**—For a long hike through rebuilt corridors of gilded imperial Bavarian grandeur, tour the family palace of the Wittelsbachs, who ruled Bavaria for more than 700 years. With a worthless English guidebook and not a word of English within, it's one of Europe's worst-presented palaces. Think of it as doing laps at the mall, with better art. Follow the "Führungslinie" signs: The first room shows a WWII exhibit. After long, boring halls of porcelain and dishes behind glass, you enter the king's apartments with a little throne-room action. The best Romantic-era dish art is on the top floor (7 DM, Tue–Sun 10:00–16:30, closed Mon, enter on Max-Joseph Platz, 3 blocks north of Marienplatz).

▲▲**Schatzkammer**—This treasury, next door to the Residenz, shows off a thousand years of Wittelsbach crowns and knickknacks (another 7 DM from the same window, same hours as Residenz, the only English you'll encounter is the "do not touch" signs). Vienna's palace and jewels are better, but this is Bavaria's best, with fine 13th and 14th century crowns and delicately carved ivory and glass. For a more efficient ramble, consider the eight rooms as one big room and make a long clockwise circle.

▲**Cuvillies Theater**—Attached to the Residenz, this national theater designed by Cuvillies is dazzling enough to send you back to the days of divine monarchs. Visitors see simply the sumptuous interior. There is no real exhibit (3 DM, Mon–Sat 14:00–17:00, Sun 10:00–17:00; facing the Residenz entry, go left around the Residenz about a half block to reach the theater entrance).

Sights—Greater Munich

▲▲**Nymphenburg Palace**—This royal summer palace is impressive only by Bavarian standards. If you do tour it, meditate upon the theme: nymphs. Something about the place feels highly sexed in a Prince Charles kind of way. Two rooms deserve special attention: the riotous rococo Great Hall (at entry, 1756 by Zimmermann) and King Ludwig's Gallery of Beauties. This room (#15, 1825–1848) is stacked with portraits of 36 of Bavaria's loveliest women...according to Ludwig. If only these creaking floors could tell a story. Don't miss the photos (in the glass cases) of Ludwig II and his Romantic composer friend Richard Wagner.

The Amalienburg—another rococo jewel designed by Cuvillies and decorated by Zimmermann—is 300 meters from the

Greater Munich

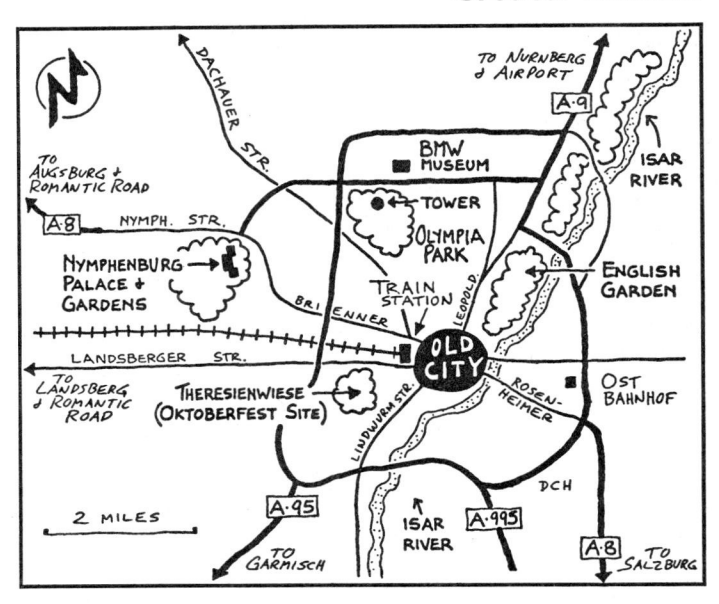

palace. Every rich boy needs a hunting lodge like this. Above the pink and white grand entry, notice Diana, goddess of the chase, flanked by busts of satyrs. Tourists enter around back. Highlights in this tiny getaway include: first room—dog houses under gun cupboards; the fine yellow and silver bedroom—see Vulcan forging arrows for amorous cupids at the foot of the bed; the mini-Hall of Mirrors—a blue-and-silver commotion of rococo nymphs and a kitchen with blue Dutch Bible scene tiles.

The sleigh and coach collection (Marstallmuseum, closes from 12:00–13:00) is a huge garage lined with gilded Cinderella coaches. It's especially interesting for Ludwig fans.

The palace park, which is good for a royal stroll or bike ride, contains more playful extras. You'll find things like a bathhouse, a pagoda, and artificial ruins (8 DM for everything, less for individual parts; Tue–Sun 9:00–12:30, 13:30–17:00, shorter hours Oct–Mar; the 5-DM English guidebook does little to make the palace meaningful; U-1 direction: Westfriedhof to Rotkreuzplatz, then tram or bus #12 to Romanplatz and a 10-minute walk or tram #17 from downtown or the station direct; tel. 089/179-080).

BMW Museum—The BMW headquarters, located in a striking building across the street from the Olympic Grounds, offers a good museum popular with car buffs (5.50 DM, daily 9:00–17:00, last ticket sold at 16:00, closed much of Aug, U-3 to the end: Olympia-zentrum, tel. 089/3822-3307). BMW fans should ask about factory tours (unreliable hours).

▲**Olympic Grounds**—Munich's great 1972 Olympic stadium and sports complex is now a lush park offering a tower (5 DM, commanding but so-high-it's-boring view from 820 feet, daily 9:00–24:00, last trip 23:30), an excellent swimming pool (5 DM, Fri–Wed 7:00–22:30, Thu 7:00–18:00), a virtual sports center where you can return Stefi Graf's serve, a good look at the center's striking "cobweb" style of architecture, and plenty of sun, grass, and picnic potential. Take U-3 to Olympia-zentrum direct from Marienplatz.

Tours of Munich: By Foot, Bike, and Bus

Walking Tours—Munich Walks offers two excellent walking tours: an introduction to the old town and "Infamous Third Reich Sites" (15 DM per tour, 12 DM if under 26, 3 hrs, tel. 0177-227-5901, e-mail: berlinwalks@berlin.de). The old-town tour starts daily at 10:30 early April through October (also at 14:30 May–Aug, but not Sun). The Third Reich tour is offered at 10:30 on Monday, Thursday, and Saturday from June through early October (less in off-season). Both tours depart from the EurAide office (track 11) in the train station. There's no need to register—just show up. Bring any city transport ticket (like a Kurzstrecke) or buy one from your guide. Renate Suerbaum is a good local guide (170 DM for private 2-hour walking tour, tel. 089/283-374).

Bike Tours—Radius Bikes (track 31 in the station) organizes fun and informative three-hour guided bike tours covering the best of historic and scenic downtown Munich (daily May 1–Oct 6 at 10:30, 2nd tour at 14:30 May 15–Sept 5; 25 DM, 22 DM with this book in 2000, 2 per book, 10 percent discount if you also take their Dachau tour; tel. 089/596-113). Those missing their fraternity may prefer Mike's four-hour bike tours (29 DM, flyers all over town).

City Bus Tour—Panorama Tours offers one-hour orientation bus tours (17 DM, Apr–Oct daily 10:00, 11:30, 13:00, 14:30, and 16:00; Nov–Mar 10:00 and 14:30; guide speaks German and English; Arnulfstrasse 8, near train station; tel. 089/5490-7560).

Oktoberfest

When King Ludwig I had a marriage party in 1810, it was such a success that they made it an annual bash. These days the Oktoberfest lasts 16 days, ending on the first full weekend in October. It starts (Sept 16–Oct 1 in 2000) with an opening parade of more than 6,000 participants and fills eight huge beer tents with about 6,000 people each. A million gallons of beer later, they roast the last ox.

Sights near Munich

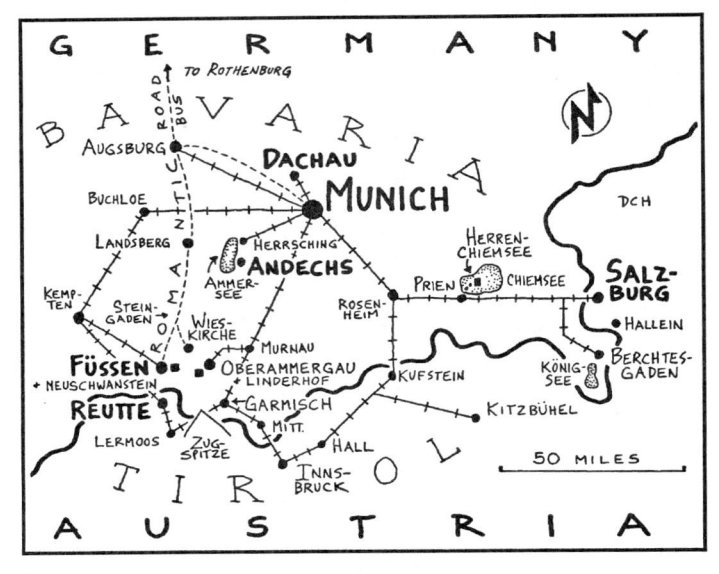

It's best to reserve a room before you go, but if you arrive in the morning (except Friday or Saturday) and haven't called ahead, the TI can normally find you a place. The fairground, known as the "Wies'n" (a few blocks south of the train station), erupts in a frenzy of rides, dancing, and strangers strolling arm-in-arm down rows of picnic tables while the beer god stirs tons of beer, pretzels, and wurst in a bubbling caldron of fun. The three-loops roller coaster must be the wildest on earth (best before the beer drinking).

During the fair the city functions even better than normal. It's a good time to sightsee, even if beer-hall rowdiness isn't your cup of tea.

Sights—Near Munich
Castle Tours—Two of King Ludwig's castles, Neuschwanstein and Linderhof, are an easy day trip by tour. Without a tour, only Neuschwanstein is easy (2 hours by train to Füssen, 10-minute bus ride to Neuschwanstein). Panorama Tours offers all-day bus tours of the two castles with 30 minutes in Oberammergau (78 DM, plus 19 DM for 2 castle admissions, live guide, 2 languages, departing 8:30 from north side of the station at Arnulfstrasse 8, tickets sold at EurAide office at track 11 with a discount for

Dachau

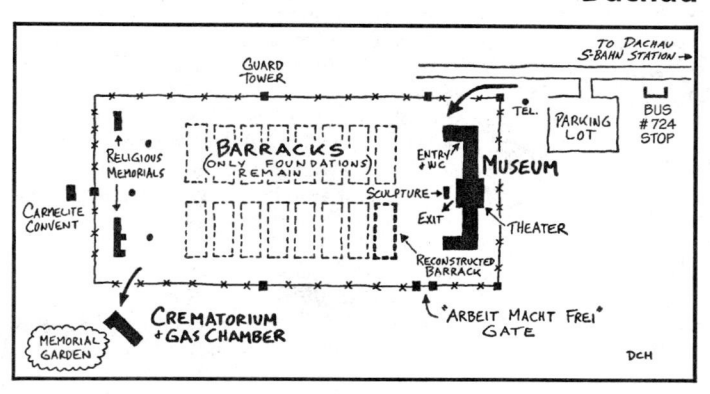

railpass or ISIC holders, tel.089/593-889). On Wednesdays in June and July, EurAide operates an all-day train/bus Neuschwanstein-Linderhof-Wieskirche day tour (70 DM, 55 DM with a train pass, admissions not included, departs at 7:30 and beats most groups to avoid the long line, tel. 089/593-889). For info on Ludwig's castles, see the Bavaria and Tirol chapter.

▲▲**Dachau**—Dachau was the first Nazi concentration camp (1933). Today it's the most accessible camp to travelers and a very effective voice from our recent but grisly past, warning and pleading "Never Again," the memorial's theme. This is a valuable experience and, when approached thoughtfully, well worth the trouble. In fact, it may change your life. See it. Feel it. Read and think about it. After this most powerful sightseeing experience, many people gain more respect for history and the dangers of not keeping tabs on their government.

Upon arrival, pick up the miniguide and note when the next documentary film in English will be shown (25 min, normally shown at 11:30 and 15:30 and often at 14:00). Both the museum and the movie are exceptional. Notice the Expressionist fascist-inspired art near the theater, where you'll also find English books, slides, and a WC. Outside, see the reconstructed barracks and the memorial shrines at the far end (Tue–Sun 9:00–17:00, closed Mon). For maximum understanding, consider the English guided walk (daily in summer at 12:30, 2 hrs, donation, call 08131/1741 to confirm) or the Radius tour from Munich (see below). It's a 45-minute trip from downtown Munich: Take S-2 (direction: Petershausen) to Dachau, then from the station, catch bus #724 or #726, Dachau-Ost, to Gedenkstätte (the camp). The two-zone 7-DM ticket covers the entire trip (one way); with a train pass, just pay for the bus (1.80 DM one way). Drivers follow Dachauerstrasse from downtown Munich to Dachau-Ost. Then follow the KZ-Gedenkstätte signs. The town of Dachau is more pleasant than its unfortunate image (TI tel. 08131/84566).

Radius Touristik at track 31 in the Munich train station offers hassle-free and thoughtful tours of the Dachau camp from Munich (20 DM plus cost of public transportation, May–Sept, Tue–Sun at 13:50, allow 4 hours for round-trip, reserve ahead, tel. 089/596-113).

Sleeping in Munich
(1.70 DM = about $1, tel. code: 089)
Sleep Code: **S** = Single, **D** = Double/Twin, **T** = Triple, **Q** = Quad, **b** = bathroom, **t** = toilet only, **s** = shower only, **CC** = Credit Card (Visa, MasterCard, Amex). English is nearly always spoken, unless otherwise noted. Prices include breakfast and increase with conventions and festivals.

There are no cheap beds in Munich. Youth hostels strictly enforce their 26-year-old age limit, and side-tripping in is a bad value. But there are plenty of decent, moderately priced rooms. I've listed places in three areas: within a few blocks of the central train station (Hauptbahnhof), in the old center, and near the Deutsches Museum. Prices can triple during Oktoberfest (Sept 16–Oct 1 in 2000), when Munich is packed. While rooms can generally be found through the TI, Oktoberfest revelers should reserve in advance.

Sleeping near the Train Station
Budget hotels (90-DM doubles, no elevator, shower down the hall) cluster in the area immediately south of the station. It's seedy after dark (erotic cinemas, barnacles with lingerie tongues, men with moustaches in the shadows) but dangerous only to those in search of trouble. Still, I've listed places in more polite neighborhoods, generally a 5- or 10-minute walk from the station and handy to the center. Places are listed roughly in order of proximity to the station. The nearest Laundromat is at Paul-Heyse Strasse 21, near the intersection with Landswehrstrasse (daily 7:00–23:00, 8-DM wash and dry).

Hotel Haberstock, a classic old-European hotel less than a block from the station, is homey, a little worn but in the process of renovating, old-fashioned, and relatively quiet (S-65–78 DM, Ss-85 DM, Sb-115 DM, D-120 DM, Ds-140 DM, Db-180 DM, good breakfast, CC:VMA, cable TV, Schillerstrasse 4, 80336 Munich, tel. 089/557-855, fax 089/550-3634, friendly Alfred at the desk). Ask about weekend and winter discounts.

Hotel Europäischer Hof München is a huge business

Munich

Munich, Hotels near the Train Station

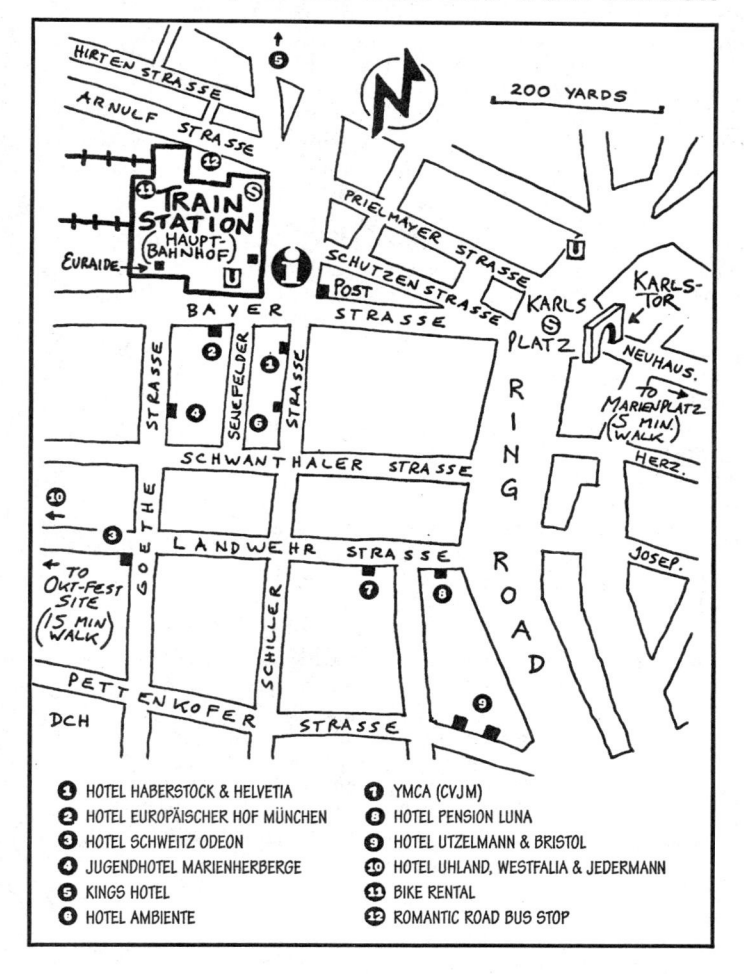

- ❶ HOTEL HABERSTOCK & HELVETIA
- ❷ HOTEL EUROPÄISCHER HOF MÜNCHEN
- ❸ HOTEL SCHWEITZ ODEON
- ❹ JUGENDHOTEL MARIENHERBERGE
- ❺ KINGS HOTEL
- ❻ HOTEL AMBIENTE
- ❼ YMCA (CVJM)
- ❽ HOTEL PENSION LUNA
- ❾ HOTEL UTZELMANN & BRISTOL
- ❿ HOTEL UHLAND, WESTFALIA & JEDERMANN
- ⓫ BIKE RENTAL
- ⓬ ROMANTIC ROAD BUS STOP

hotel with fine rooms and elegant public spaces (S-73–93 DM, Sb-123–163 DM, D-106–146 DM, Db-146–196 DM, these prices only with this book during slow times, Bayerstrasse 31, 80335 Munich, tel. 089/551-510, fax 089/5515-1222, www.heh.de).

Hotel Schweitz Odeon is ugly outside and run-down inside, but is a good place to sleep for the price. They also serve a good buffet breakfast and have nonsmoking rooms (Sb-95 DM, Db-140 DM,

Tb-170 DM, 15-DM garage, CC:VMA, elevator, Goethestrasse 26, from the station walk 2 blocks down Goethestrasse, tel. 089/539-585, fax 089/550-4383).

Jugendhotel Marienherberge is clean and pleasant and has the best cheap beds in town for young women only (25-year age limit can flex upward a couple of years for 10 DM extra, S-40 DM, 35 DM per bed in D and T, 30 DM per bed in 6-bed rooms, nonsmoking, office open 8:00–24:00, a block from station at Goethestrasse 9, tel. 089/555-805, fax 089/5502-8260).

Hotel Helvetia is an on-the-ball, backpacker's favorite (S-55–65 DM, D-78–99 DM, Ds-99–120 DM, T-105–126 DM, laundry service, elevator, Schillerstrasse 6, 80336 Munich, tel. 089/590-6850, fax 089/5906-8570, e-mail: hotel-helvetia@t-online.de).

Kings Hotel, a fancy, old business-class hotel, is a good, elegant splurge on weekends. You'll get carved wooden ceilings, canopy beds, chandeliers, and a sauna (Db-275 DM; weekend special: Db-175 DM except during fairs; CC:VMA; some nonsmoking rooms; 150 meters north of station at Dachauer Strasse 13, 80335 Munich, tel. 089/551-870, fax 089/5518-7300, www.king-group.com).

Hotel Ambiente has dark halls but clean, bright, newly refurbished rooms with all the comforts and a friendly professional staff (Sb-138–182 DM, Db-150–230 DM depending on season, CC:VMA, a block from station at Schillerstrasse 12, 80336 Munich, tel. 089/545-170, fax 089/5451-7200).

CVJM (YMCA), open to all ages and sexes, has modern rooms (S-56 DM, D-86 DM, T-120 DM, 40 DM/bed in a shared triple, those over 26 pay 16 percent more, free showers, elevator, Landwehrstrasse 13, 80336 Munich, tel. 089/552-1410, fax 089/550-4282, www.cvjm.org/muenchen/hotel).

Hotel Pension Luna is a dumpy building with cheery rooms (S-55 DM, Ss-65 DM, Sb-69 DM, D/twin-90 DM, D-95 DM, Ds-110 DM, T-130 DM, Ts-140 DM, CC:VMA, lots of stairs, free showers, Landwehrstrasse 5, tel. 089/597-833, fax 089/550-3761).

Hotel Pension Utzelmann feels less welcoming thanks to its huge rooms—especially the curiously cheap room #6. Each lacy room is richly furnished. It's in a pleasant neighborhood just a 10-minute walk from the station and a block off Sendlinger (S-50–85 DM, Ss-95 DM, Sb-125 DM, D-90 DM, Ds-110 DM, Db-145 DM, T-130 DM, Ts-150 DM, Tb-175 DM, hall showers-5 DM, Pettenkoferstrasse 6, enter through the iron gate, tel. 089/594-889, fax 089/596-228, Frau Schlee NSE).

Hotel Bristol, nearly next door to Hotel Utzelmann, has comfortable rooms and is a fine value (Sb-99 DM, Db-139 DM, Tb-170 DM; to get these cash-only prices—which are 20 to 30 DM below the hotel's normal rates—ask for friendly Johannes and mention this book; nonsmoking; hearty buffet breakfast on terrace, parking

Munich

available, bike rental-20 DM/day, CC:VMA, Pettenkoferstrasse 2, 80336 Munich, 1 metro stop on U-1 or U-2 from station, tel. 089/595-151, fax 089/591-451, www.bristol-muc.com). Johannes also has an apartment (45 DM per person; up to 4 people).

Hotel Uhland, an elegant mansion, is a worthwhile splurge with spacious rooms (Sb-110 DM, Db-150 DM, Tb-180 DM, huge breakfast, elevator, free bikes, cable TV, Internet access, free parking, Uhlandstrasse 1, 80336 Munich, near Theresienwiese Oktoberfest grounds, 15 min from station, walk up Goethestrasse and turn right on Pettenkoferstrasse, tel. 089/543-350, fax 089/5433-5250, e-mail: Hotel_Uhland@compuserve.com).

Pension Westfalia overlooks the Oktoberfest grounds from the top floor of a quiet and classy old building. Well run by Peter and Mary Deiritz, this is a great value if you prefer sanity and personal touches to centrality (S-65 DM, Sb-85–95 DM, D-90 DM, Db-110–130 DM, cheaper off-season, extra bed-25 DM, hallway showers-3 DM, buffet breakfast, CC:VA, elevator, easy parking, U-3 or U-6 to Goetheplatz, Mozartstrasse 23, 80336 Munich, tel. 089/530-377, fax 089/543-9120, e-mail: pension-westfalia @t-online.de). Around the corner, tidy **Pension Schubert** rents four simple but elegant rooms (S-50 DM, D-85 DM, Db-95 DM, Schubertstrasse 1, tel. 089/535-087).

Hotel Jedermann is an old business hotel offering comfortable rooms with baths and basic, well-worn rooms without baths (S-65–85 DM, Sb-95–160 DM, D-95–140 DM, Ds-110–160 DM, Db-130–240 DM depending on season, extra bed-25–40 DM, kids' cot-15 DM, CC:VMA, nonsmoking rooms available, Internet access, elevator, rental bikes, turn right out of station and walk 15 minutes to Bayerstrasse 95, or take tram #18 or #19, 80335 Munich, tel. 089/533-617, fax 089/536-506, www .hotel-jedermann.de).

Sleeping in the Old Center

Pension Lindner is clean, quiet, and modern, with pastel-bouquet rooms (S-65 DM, D-110 DM, Ds-135 DM, Db-150 DM, elevator, just off Sendlinger Strasse, Dultstrasse 1, 80331 Munich, tel. 089/263-413, fax 089/268-760, run by cheery Marion Sinzinger). One floor below, the quirky **Pension Stadt Munich** isn't as homey, but is OK if the Lindner is full (4 Ds-120 DM, a tad smoky, Dultstrasse 1, tel. 089/263-417, fax 089/267-548, some English spoken).

Pension Seibel is ideally located with cozy rooms and a friendly, family atmosphere, one block off the Viktualienmarkt in a fun neighborhood (S-70–90 DM, Sb-89–119 DM, D-99–129 DM, Db-129–159 DM, Tb-150–189 DM, these prices are promised through 2000 during nonfair periods if you show them this book and pay cash, family apartment for up to 5 people-45 DM each,

Munich Center Hotels and Restaurants

- ① PENSION LINDNER & STADT MUNICH
- ② PENSION SEIBEL
- ③ HOTEL MÜNCHNER KINDL
- ④ HOTEL ISARTOR
- ⑤ PENSION BECK
- ⑥ HOFBRÄUHAUS
- ⑦ WEISSES BRÄUHAUS
- ⑧ JODLERWIRT REST.
- ⑨ NÜRNBERGER BRATWURST GLÖCKL
- ⑩ ALTES HACKERHAUS
- ⑪ VIKTUALIEN MARKT
- ⑫ ALOIS DALLMAYR

big breakfast, CC to reserve but pay cash, tries to be smoke-free, no elevator, Reichenbachstrasse 8, 80469 Munich, tel. 089/264-043, fax 089/267-803, e-mail: pension.seibel@t-online.de, Mercedes, Moe, and Kirstin). If you're stuck, ask about their not-as-central but still comfortable Hotel Seibel on the fairgrounds (same rates).

Hotel Münchner Kindl is a jolly place with decent rooms but high prices above a friendly local bar (S-90 DM, Sb-120 DM, D-130 DM, Ds-150 DM, Db-170 DM, Tb-205 DM, Qb-220 DM, prices with this book, CC:VM, night noises travel up central courtyard, no elevator, easy telephone reservations, 2 blocks off main pedestrian drag from "Thomas" sign at Damenstiftstrasse 16, 80331 Munich, tel. 089/264-349, fax 089/264-526, run by Gunter and English-speaking Renate Dittertt).

Munich

Sleeping away from the Center

Hotel Isartor is a modern, comfortable, concrete-feeling place just a two-minute walk from the Isartor S-Bahn stop (26 rooms, Sb-145 DM, Db-170 DM, 10 percent discount with cash in July, August, and during slow times, parking garage-12 DM/day, CC:VMA, elevator, refrigerators in rooms, Baaderstrasse 2, 80469 Munich, tel. 089/216-3340, fax 089/298-494, e-mail: hotel-isartor@t-online.de, family Pangratz).

Pension Beck is well worn and farther away but a good budget bet (S-from 60 DM, D-86–95 DM, Db-120 DM, larger rooms available; family, youth, and 2-night deals; CC:VM, lots of stairs, Thierschstrasse 36, take streetcar #17 direct from station or any S-Bahn to Isartor and 400-meter walk, tel. 089/220-708, fax 089/220-925, e-mail: pension.beck@bst-online.de).

American **Audrey Bauchinger** rents quiet, tidy rooms and spacious apartments east of the Deutsches Museum in a quiet residential area a 20-minute walk from Marienplatz (Ss-45 DM, D-75 DM, 1 D with private bath across hall-125 DM, Ds-80–105 DM, spacious Db/Tb with kitchenette-160 DM/200 DM, no breakfast, CC:VMA, corner of Schweigerstrasse, at Zeppelinstrasse 37, 81669 Munich, tel. 089/488-444, fax 089/489-1787, e-mail:106437.3277@compuserve.com). From the station, take any S-Bahn to Marienplatz, then take bus #52 (the only bus there) to Schweigerstrasse.

Cheap Beds

Munich's International **Youth Camp Kapuzinerhölzl** (a.k.a. "The Tent") offers 400 places on the wooden floor of a huge circus tent. If you're under 25 you'll get a mattress (14 DM) or bed (18 DM), blankets, good showers, washing machines, and breakfast. It can be a fun experience—kind of a cross between a slumber party and Woodstock. There's a cool Ping-Pong-and-Frisbee atmosphere throughout the day, and no curfew at night (Jul–Aug only, confirm first at TI that it's open, then catch tram #17 from train station to Botanischer Garten, direction: Amalienburgstrasse, and follow crowd down Franz-Schrankstrasse, tel. 089/141-4300, e-mail: see-you@the-tent).

Eating in Munich

Munich cuisine is best seasoned with beer. For beer halls, you have two basic choices: the Hofbräuhaus, where you'll find music and tourists, or the mellower beer gardens, where you'll find the Germans.

The world's most famous and touristy beer hall is the **Hofbräuhaus** (daily 9:30–24:00, music during lunch and dinner, Platzl 6, 5-minute walk from Marienplatz, tel. 089/221-676). Even if you don't eat here, check it out; it's fun to see 200 Japanese people drinking beer in a German beer hall...across from a Planet

Hollywood. Germans go for the entertainment—to sing "Country Roads," see how Texas girls party, and watch salaried professionals from Tokyo chug beer. The music-every-night atmosphere is thick, and the fat, shiny-leather bands even get church mice to stand up and conduct three-quarter time with breadsticks. Meals are inexpensive (for a light 10-DM meal, I like the local favorite, 2 *paar Schweinswurst mit Kraut*); white radishes are salted and cut in delicate spirals; and surly beer maids pull mustard packets from their cleavages. Huge liter beers (called *eine Mass* in German or "*ein* pitcher" in English) cost 10.50 DM. You can order your beer *helles* (light but not "lite," which is what you'll get if you say "*ein* beer"), *dunkles* (dark), or *Radler* (half lemonade, half light beer). Notice the vomitoriums in the WC. (They host a gimmicky folk evening upstairs in the *Festsaal* nightly at 19:00 for 9 DM, food and drinks are sold from the same menu, tel. 089/2901-3610.)

Weisses Bräuhaus is more local and features good food and the region's fizzy wheat beer (daily 8:00–24:00, Tal 10, between Marienplatz and Isartor, 2 blocks from Hofbräuhaus). Hitler met with fellow fascists here in 1920 when his Nazi party had yet to ferment.

Augustiner Beer Garden is a sprawling haven for trendy local beer lovers on a balmy evening (10:00–23:00, across from train tracks, 3 loooong blocks from station, away from the center, on Arnulfstrasse 52). For a true under-the-leaves beer garden packed with locals, this is best.

The tiny **Jodlerwirt** is a woodsy, smart-alecky, yodeling kind of pub. The food is great and the ambience is as Bavarian as you'll find. Avoid the basic ground-floor bar and climb the stairs into the action (accordion act from 19:00, closed Sun, Altenhofstrasse 4, between the Hofbräuhaus and Marienplatz, tel. 089/221-249). Good food, lots of belly laughs... completely incomprehensible to the average tourist.

For a classier evening stewed in antlers and fiercely Bavarian, eat under a tree or inside at the **Nürnberger Bratwurst Glöckl am Dom** (daily 9:30–24:00, 25-DM dinners, Frauenplatz 9, at the rear of the twin-domed cathedral, tel. 089/295-264). Almost next door, the more trendy **Andechser am Dom** serves Andechs beer to appreciative locals.

Locals enjoy the **Altes Hackerhaus** for traditional Bayerischer fare with a dressier feel (daily until 24:00, 25–30 DM meals, Sendlingerstrasse 14, tel. 089/260-5026).

For outdoor atmosphere and a cheap meal, spend an evening at the Englischer Garden's **Chinesischer Turm** (Chinese pagoda) **Biergarten.** You're welcome to BYO food and grab a table or buy from the picnic stall (*Brotzeit*) right there. Don't bother to phone ahead—they have 6,000 seats. For a more intimate place with

Munich

more local families and fewer tourists, venture deeper into the garden (past the Isarring road) to the **Hirschau Biergarten**.

For similar BYOF atmosphere right behind Marienplatz, eat at **Viktualien Markt's** beer garden (closed Sun). Lunch or dinner here taps you into about the best budget eating in town. Countless stalls surround the beer garden and sell wurst, sandwiches, produce, and so on. This BYOF tradition goes back to the days when monks were allowed to sell beer but not food. To picnic, choose a table without a tablecloth. This is a good place to grab the most typical meal in town: *Weisswurst* (white sausage) with *süss* (sweet) mustard, a salty pretzel, and *Weissbier*. **Suppenküche** is fine for a small, cozy, sit-down lunch (soup kitchen, 6–9-DM soup meals, in Viktualien Markt near intersection of Frauenstrasse and Reichenbachstrasse, everyone knows where it is). For your strudel and coffee, consider **Marktcafe** (closed Sun, 7-DM fresh strudel, on a tiny street a block below the market, Heiliggeiststrasse 2, tel. 089/227-816).

For a fun and easy (though not cheap) cafeteria meal near Karlstor on the pedestrian mall, consider the **Mövenpick Marche**. Climb downstairs into the marketplace fantasy and pick up a card. Your card will be stamped as you load your tray. Choose your table from several typical Munich themes, and pay after you eat (daily 12:00–22:00, smoke-free zones, reasonable small-plate veggie and salad buffets, distracting men's room, on Neuhauser pedestrian street across from St. Michael's church).

The crown in its emblem indicates that the royal family assembled its picnics in the historic and expensive **Alois Dallmayr** delicatessen (Mon–Fri 9:30–19:30, Sat 9:00–16:00, closed Sun, Dienerstrasse 14, behind the Neues Rathaus). An elegant café serves light meals behind the bakery on the ground floor. Explore this dieter's purgatory and put together a royal picnic to munch in the nearby Hofgarten. To save money, browse at Dallmayr's but buy in the basement **supermarkets** of the Kaufhof stores across Marienplatz or at Karlsplatz.

Transportation Connections—Munich

Munich is a super transportation hub (one reason it was the target of so many WWII bombs).

By train to: Füssen (10/day, 2 hrs, the 8:51 departure is good for a Neuschwanstein castle day trip), **Berlin** (6/day, 8 hrs), **Würzburg** (hrly, 3 hrs), **Frankfurt** (14/day, 3.5 hrs), **Salzburg** (12/day, 2 hrs), **Vienna** (4/day, 5 hrs), **Venice** (3/day, 9 hrs), **Paris** (4/day, 9 hrs), **Prague** (3/day, 7–10 hrs), and just about every other point in western Europe. Munich is three hours from **Reutte**, Austria (every 2 hours, 3 hrs, transfer in Garmisch).

BAVARIA AND TIROL

Two hours south of Munich, between Germany's Bavaria and Austria's Tirol, is a timeless land of fairy-tale castles, painted buildings shared by cows and farmers, and locals who still yodel when they're happy.

In Germany's Bavaria, tour "Mad" King Ludwig's ornate Neuschwanstein Castle, Europe's most spectacular. Stop by the Wieskirche, a textbook example of Bavarian rococo bursting with curly curlicues, and browse through Oberammergau, Germany's wood-carving capital and home of the famous Passion Play.

In Austria's Tirol, hike to the Ehrenberg ruined castle, scream down a nearby ski slope on an oversized skateboard, then catch your breath for an evening of yodeling and slap dancing.

In this chapter I'll cover Bavaria first, then Tirol. Austria's Tirol is easier and cheaper than touristy Bavaria. My favorite home base for exploring Bavaria's castles is actually in Austria, in the town of Reutte. Füssen, in Germany, is a handier home base for train travelers.

Planning Your Time

While locals come here for a week or two, the typical speedy American traveler will find two days' worth of sightseeing. With a car and more time you could enjoy the more remote corners, but the basic visit ranges anywhere from a long day trip from Munich to a three-night, two-day visit. If the weather's good and you're not going to Switzerland, be sure to ride a lift to an Alpine peak.

A good schedule for a one-day circular drive from Reutte is: 7:30–Breakfast, 8:15–Depart hotel, 8:45–Arrive at Neuschwanstein, park and hike to the castle for a tour, 12:00–Drive to the Wieskirche (20-minute stop) and on to Oberammergau for a stroll

Highlights of Bavaria and Tirol

and lunch, 14:00–Drive to Linderhof, 14:30–Tour Linderhof, 16:30–Drive along Plansee back into Austria, 17:30–Back at hotel, 19:00–Dinner at hotel and perhaps a folk evening. In peak season you might arrive later at Linderhof to avoid the crowds. The next morning you could stroll Reutte, hike to the Ehrenberg ruins, and ride the luge on your way to Innsbruck, Munich, Venice, Switzerland, or wherever.

Train travelers can base in Füssen and bus or bike the short distance to Neuschwanstein. If you base in Reutte, you can bike to Neuschwanstein, Ehrenberg ruins, and the luge. You can hike to Neuschwanstein from the recommended Gutshof zum Schluxen.

Getting around Bavaria and Tirol
By Car: This region is ideal by car. All the sights are within an easy 60-mile loop from Reutte or Füssen.

By Train and Bus: It can be frustrating by train. Local bus service in the region is spotty for sightseeing. If you're rushed and without wheels, Reutte, the Wieskirche, and the luge rides are probably not worth the trouble (but there is a small luge near Neuschwanstein that's within walking distance).

Füssen (with a two-hour train ride to/from Munich every hour, transfer in Buchloe) is three miles from Neuschwanstein Castle with easy bus and bike connections. Reutte has five buses per day from Füssen (30 minutes, not Sunday) and is a good place to catch a train to Innsbruck and Munich. Oberammergau (2-hour trains from Munich every hour with 1 change) has decent bus connections to nearby Linderhof Castle. Oberammergau to Füssen is sparse (1 bus/day, 2 hrs).

By Rental Car: You can rent a car in either Füssen or Reutte (see below).

By Tour: If you're interested only in Bavarian castles, consider an all-day organized bus tour of the Bavarian biggies as a side trip from Munich (see Munich chapter).

By Bike: This is great biking country. Many train stations (including Reutte and Füssen) and hotels rent bikes for 15 to 20 DM per day. The rides from Reutte to Neuschwanstein, Ehrenberg ruins, and the luge are great for those with the time and energy.

By Thumb: Hitchhiking, always risky, is a slow-but-possible way to connect the public transportation gaps.

FÜSSEN

Füssen has been a strategic stop since ancient times. Its main street sits on the Via Claudia Augusta, which crossed the Alps (over Brenner Pass) in Roman times. The town was the southern terminus of the medieval trade route known among 20th-century tourists as the "Romantic Road." Dramatically situated under a renovated castle on the lively Lech River, Füssen just celebrated its 700th birthday.

Unfortunately, in the summer Füssen is entirely overrun by tourists. Traffic can be exasperating, but by bike or on foot it's not bad. Off-season, the town is a jester's delight.

Everyone is very excited about a daring new theater built right into the lake (Forgensee) with a view of Neuschwanstein Castle. It will be home to the new musical *Ludwig II*. The show, which opens in March 2000, will be costly (95–220 DM per seat; for more information or tickets call 01805/583-944, www.ludwigmusical.com). Apart from this and Füssen's cobbled and arcaded town center, there's little real sightseeing. The striking-from-a-distance castle houses a boring picture gallery. The mediocre city museum in the monastery below the castle exhibits lifestyles of 200 years ago and the story of the monastery, and offers displays on the development of the violin, for which Füssen was famous (5 DM, Tue–Sun 11:00–16:00, closed Mon, explanations in German only). Halfway between Füssen and the border (as you drive, or a woodsy walk from the town) is the Lechfall, a thunderous waterfall with a handy potty stop.

Orientation (tel. code: 08362)

Füssen's train station is a few blocks from the TI, the town center (a cobbled shopping mall), and all my hotel listings (see "Sleeping," below). The TI has a room-finding service (look for Kurverwaltung, three blocks down Bahnhofstrasse from the station, Mon–Fri 9:00–19:00, Sat 9:00–14:00, shorter hours off-season, tel. 08362/93850, fax 08362/938-520, www.fuessen.de). After-hours try the little self-service info pavilion near the front of the TI. It dispenses Füssen maps for 1 DM.

Arrival in Füssen: Exit left as you leave the train station (lockers available) and walk a few straight blocks to the center of town and the TI. Bus stops to Neuschwanstein and Reutte are at the station.

Bike Rental: Rent at the station (15 DM/day, 9:00–19:00) or, for a bigger selection, at Rad Zacherl (14 DM/day, mountain bikes-20 DM, passport number for deposit, Mon–Fri 9:00–12:00, 14:00–18:00, Sat 9:00–13:00, 2 blocks from front of station—turn left onto Rupprechtstrasse and walk to 8.5, tel. 08362/3292).

Car Rental: Antes & Huber is more central (Kemptenenerstrasse 59, tel. 08362/91920) than Hertz (Füssenerstrasse 112, tel. 08362/986 580).

Sights—Neuschwanstein Castle Area, Bavaria

▲▲▲**Neuschwanstein Castle**—The fairy-tale castle of Neuschwanstein looks medieval, but it's only about as old as the Eiffel Tower and feels like something you'd see at a home show for 19th-century royalty. It was built (1869–1886) to suit the whims of Bavaria's King Ludwig II and is a textbook example of the Romanticism that was popular in 19th-century Europe.

Getting to the castle: It's a steep 20- to 30-minute hike to Neuschwanstein from the parking lot (TI at parking lot/bus stop, open 9:00–18:00). If you arrive by bus, the quickest (and steepest) way to the castle starts in parking lot D. A more gradual ascent starts at the parking lot near the lake (Parkplatz am Alpsee, best for drivers, all lots cost 6 DM). To minimize hiking, you can take advantage of the frequent shuttle buses (3.50 DM up, 5 DM round-trip; drops you off at Mary's Bridge, a steep 10 minutes above the castle) or horse carriages (8 DM up, 4 DM down; slower than walking, stops 5 minutes short of the castle).

Touring the castle: To beat the crowds, see Neuschwanstein, Germany's most popular castle, by 9:00 (best)

Neuschwanstein

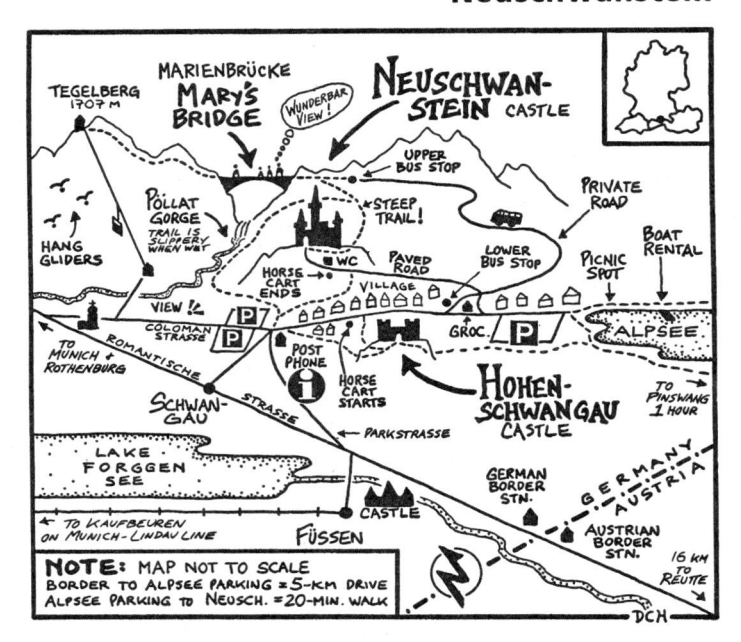

or late in the afternoon (OK). The castle is open every morning at 8:30; by 11:00 it's packed. Rushed 35-minute English-language tours are less rushed early. Tours, which leave regularly, tell the sad story of Bavaria's "Mad" King Ludwig and how he drowned under suspicious circumstances at age 41 after nearly bankrupting Bavaria to build his castles. You'll go up and down more than 300 steps through lavish Wagnerian dream rooms, a royal state-of-the-19th-century-art kitchen, the king's gilded-lily bedroom, and his extravagant throne room. You'll see 15 rooms with their original furnishings and fanciful wall paintings. The rest of the castle is unfinished; the king lived here fewer than 200 days before he died (12 DM, Apr–Sept daily 8:30–17:30, Mar and Oct 9:30–16:30, Nov–Feb 10:00–16:00, no photography inside). Guided tours are mandatory. To cut down on lines, the castle's ticket office gives out appointment times for tours. When you get to the castle go right to the ticket office (it's just below the castle) and pick up a time; if you have a long wait, hike up to Mary's Bridge.

Before or after the tour, climb up to Mary's Bridge to marvel at Ludwig's castle, just as Ludwig did. This bridge was quite an engineering accomplishment 100 years ago. From the bridge, the frisky can hike even higher to the "Beware—Danger of Death" signs and an even more glorious castle view. For the most interesting descent (15 minutes longer and extremely slippery when wet), follow signs to the Pöllat Gorge. Castle-lovers save time for Hohenschwangau.

▲▲Hohenschwangau Castle—Standing quietly below Neuschwanstein, the big yellow Hohenschwangau Castle was Ludwig's boyhood home. It's more lived-in and historic, and actually gives a better glimpse of Ludwig's life. There are only three ways to get an English tour: gather 21 people together; wait in line until 20 English speakers join you; or politely ask your German guide to say a few words in English after her German spiels. (Same hours and price as Neuschwanstein, but closed in winter.)

The "village" at the foot of Europe's "Disney" castle feeds off the droves of hungry, shop-happy tourists. The Alpsee lake is ideal for a picnic; the souvenir shop nearest the Bräustüberl restaurant (open daily) has a microwave fast-food machine and the makings for a skimpy lunch. Picnic at the lakeside park or in one of the old-fashioned rowboats (rented by the hour in summer). The bus stop, post/telephone office, and helpful TI cluster around the main intersection (TI open daily 9:00–18:00, until 17:00 off-season, tel. 08362/819-840).

Getting to the Castles from Füssen or Reutte: From Füssen, three miles away from the castles, catch a bus from the train station (2/hrly, 10 min, 2.5 DM one way, 5 DM round-trip) or ride a rental bike. From Reutte it's a bus ride to Füssen (5/day, 30 min, then city bus to castle); or, for a romantic twist, hike or mountain bike from the trailhead at the recommended hotel Gutshof zum Schluxen in Pinswang (see "Sleeping near Reutte"). When the dirt road forks at the top of the hill go right (downhill), cross the border (marked by a sign and deserted hut), and follow the narrow paved road to the castles. It's a 60- to 90-minute hike or a great circular bike trip (allow 90 minutes from Reutte or 30 minutes from Gutshof zum Schluxen; return by bus via Füssen).

▲Tegelberg Gondola—Just north of Neuschwanstein, hang gliders circle like vultures. Their pilots jumped from the top of the Tegelberg Gondola. For 28 DM you can ride high to the 5,500-foot summit and back down (daily from 9:00, last lift at 17:00, closes earlier in winter, tel. 08362/98360). On a clear day you get great views of the Alps and Bavaria and the vicarious thrill of watching hang gliders and parasailors leap into airborne ecstasy. Weather permitting, scores of German thrill-seekers line up and leap from the launch ramp at the top of the lift. With one leaving every two or three minutes, it's great spectating. Thrill seekers with exceptional social skills may talk themselves into a tandem ride with a parasailor. From there it's a steep 2.5-hour hike down to Ludwig's castle.

Tegelberg Luge—Next to the lift is a luge (like a bobsled on wheels; for details see "Sights—Tirol, Near Reutte," below). The track, made of stainless steel, is often open when rainy weather shuts down the concrete luges. It's not as fast or scenic as Bichlbach and Biberwier (below), but it's close and cheap (4 DM per run, 10 percent less when using 6-trip cards, can be crowded on sunny summer weekends, tel. 08362/98360). A funky cable system pulls lugers to the top without a ski lift.

More Sights—Bavaria

(These are listed in driving order from Füssen.)

▲▲Wies Church (Wieskirche)—Germany's greatest rococo-style church, Wieskirche ("the church in the meadow") is newly restored and looking as brilliant as the day it floated down from heaven. Overripe with decoration but bright and bursting with beauty, this church is a divine droplet, a curly curlicue, the final flowering of the Baroque movement. The ceiling depicts the Last Judgment.

This is a pilgrimage church. In the early 1700s a carving of Christ too graphic to be accepted by that generation's church was the focus of worship in a peasant's private chapel. Miraculously, it wept. And pilgrims came from all around.

Bavaria's top rococo architects, the Zimmermann brothers, were then commissioned to build the Wieskirche, which features the amazing carving above its altar and still attracts countless pilgrims (donation requested, daily 8:00–20:00, less off-season). Take a commune-with-nature-and-smell-the-farm detour back through the meadow to the car park.

Wieskirche is 30 minutes north of Neuschwanstein. The northbound Romantic Road bus tour stops here for 15 minutes. Füssen–Wieskirche buses run several times a day. By car, head north from Füssen, turn right at Steingaden, and follow the signs.

If you can't visit Wieskirche, visit one of the other churches that came out of the same heavenly spray can: Oberammergau's church, Munich's Asam Church, the Würzburg Residenz Chapel, or the splendid Ettal Monastery (free and near Oberammergau).

If you're driving from Wieskirche to Oberammergau, you'll cross the Echelsbacher Bridge, which arches 250 feet over the Pöllat Gorge. Thoughtful drivers let their passengers walk across (for the views) and meet them at the other side. Any kayakers? Notice the painting of the traditional village woodcarver (who used to walk from town to town with his art on his back) on the first big house on the Oberammergau side, a shop called Almdorf Ammertal. It has a huge selection of overpriced carvings and commission-hungry tour guides.

▲Oberammergau—The Shirley Temple of Bavarian villages and exploited to the hilt by the tourist trade, Oberammergau wears way

Bavaria and Tirol

too much makeup. It's worth a wander only if you're passing through anyway. But with the crowds expected for the 2000 Passion Play, I'd stay far away. If you have tickets or just can't resist overly cute villages, you can browse through the woodcarvers' shops—small art galleries filled with very expensive whittled works—or see folk art at the town's Heimatmuseum (TI tel. 08822/92310, closed weekends off-season, www.oberammergau.de).

Visit the church, a poor cousin of the one at Wies. This church looks richer than it is. Put your hand on the "marble" columns. If they warm up, they're painted fakes. Wander through the graveyard. Ponder the deaths that two wars dealt Germany. Behind the church are the photos of three Schneller brothers, all killed within two years in World War II.

Passion Play: Still making good on a deal the townspeople made with God when they were spared devastation by the Black Plague 350 years ago, once each decade Oberammergau performs the Passion Play. It happens in 2000, when 5,000 people a day for 100 summer days will attend Oberammergau's all-day dramatic story of Christ's crucifixion. It's sold out. Unless you miraculously get a ticket, you'll have to settle for browsing through the theater's exhibition hall (4 DM, daily 9:30–12:00, 13:30–16:00, closed Mon off-season, tel. 08822/32278), seeing Nicodemus tool around town in his VW, or reading the Book. Oberammergau is connected to Füssen by one direct two-hour bus per day.

Gasthaus zum Stern is friendly, serves good food (closed Tue low season), and is a good value for this touristy town (Sb-45 DM, Db-90 DM, closed Nov–Dec, Dorfstrasse 33, 82487 Oberammergau, tel. 08822/867, fax 08822/7027). **Hotel Bayerische Lowe** is central with a good restaurant and comfortable rooms (Db-99 DM, Dedlerstrasse 2, tel. 08822/1365). Oberammergau's modern **youth hostel** is on the river a short walk from the center (20-DM beds, open all year, tel. 08822/4114).

Driving into town from the north, cross the bridge, take the second left, follow "Polizei" signs, and park by the huge gray Passionsspielhaus. Leaving town, head out past the church and turn toward Ettal on Road 23. You're 20 miles from Reutte via the scenic Plansee.

▲▲**Linderhof Castle**—This was "Mad" King Ludwig's home, his most intimate castle. It's small and comfortably exquisite, good enough for a minor god. Set in the woods 15 minutes from Oberammergau by car or bus (3/day) and surrounded by fountains and sculpted, Italian-style gardens, it's the only palace I've toured that actually had me feeling envious. Don't miss the grotto (10 DM, daily 9:00–17:30, Oct–Mar 10:00–16:00 with lunch break, fountains often erupt on the hour, English tours when 20 gather—easy in summer but sparse off-season, tel. 08822/3512). Plan for lots of crowds, lots of walking, and a two-hour stop.

▲▲Zugspitze—The tallest point in Germany is a border crossing. Lifts from Austria and Germany go to the 10,000-foot summit of the Zugspitze. Straddle two great nations while enjoying an incredible view. Restaurants, shops, and telescopes await you at the summit. The 75-minute trip from Garmisch on the German side costs 75 DM round-trip; family discounts are available (buy a combo cogwheel train and cable car ride, tel. 08821/7970). On the Austrian side, from the less crowded Talstation Obermoos above the village of Erwald, the tram zips you to the top in 10 minutes (420 AS or 61 DM round-trip, late May–Oct daily 8:40–16:40, tel. in Austria 05673/2309). The German ascent is easier for those without a car, but buses do connect the Erwald train station and the Austrian lift almost every hour. Hikers enjoy the easy 10-kilometer walk around the lovely Elbsee lake (German side, 5 minutes downhill from cable "Seilbahn").

Sleeping in Füssen
(1.70 DM = about $1, tel. code: 08362, zip code: 87629)
Sleep Code: **S** = Single, **D** = Double/Twin, **T** = Triple, **Q** = Quad, **b** = bathroom, **t** = toilet only, **s** = shower only, **CC** = Credit Card (Visa, MasterCard, Amex).

Unless otherwise noted, breakfast is included, hall showers are free, and English is spoken. Prices listed are for one-night stays. Some places give a discount for longer stays. Always ask. Competition is fierce and off-season prices are soft.

While I prefer sleeping in Reutte (see below), convenient Füssen is just three miles from Ludwig's castles and offers a cobbled, riverside retreat. But it also happens to be very touristy (notice *das* sushi bar). It has just about as many rooms as tourists, though, and the TI has a free room-finding service. All places I've listed (except the hostel) are within a few blocks of the train station and the town center. They are used to travelers getting in after the Romantic Road bus arrives (20:40) and will hold rooms for a telephone promise. Parking is easy at the station. Hotels will be busier than usual in 2000, thanks to the Passion Play in nearby Oberammergau.

Hotel Kurcafé is deluxe, with spacious rooms and all of the amenities. Its bakery can ruin your budget any time of year (Sb-130 DM, Db-180 DM, Tb-220 DM, less off-season, CC:VM, on the tiny traffic circle a block in front of train station at Bahnhofstrasse 4, tel. 08362/6369, fax 08362/39424, e-mail: hotel.kurcafe@t-online.de). The attached restaurant has good and reasonable daily specials.

Hotel Gasthaus zum Hechten offers all the modern comforts in a friendly, traditional shell right under the Füssen Castle in the old-town pedestrian zone (S-65 DM, Sb-80 DM, D-100 DM, Db-120 DM, Tb-160 DM, Qb-190 DM, these prices and free parking

Bavaria and Tirol

Füssen

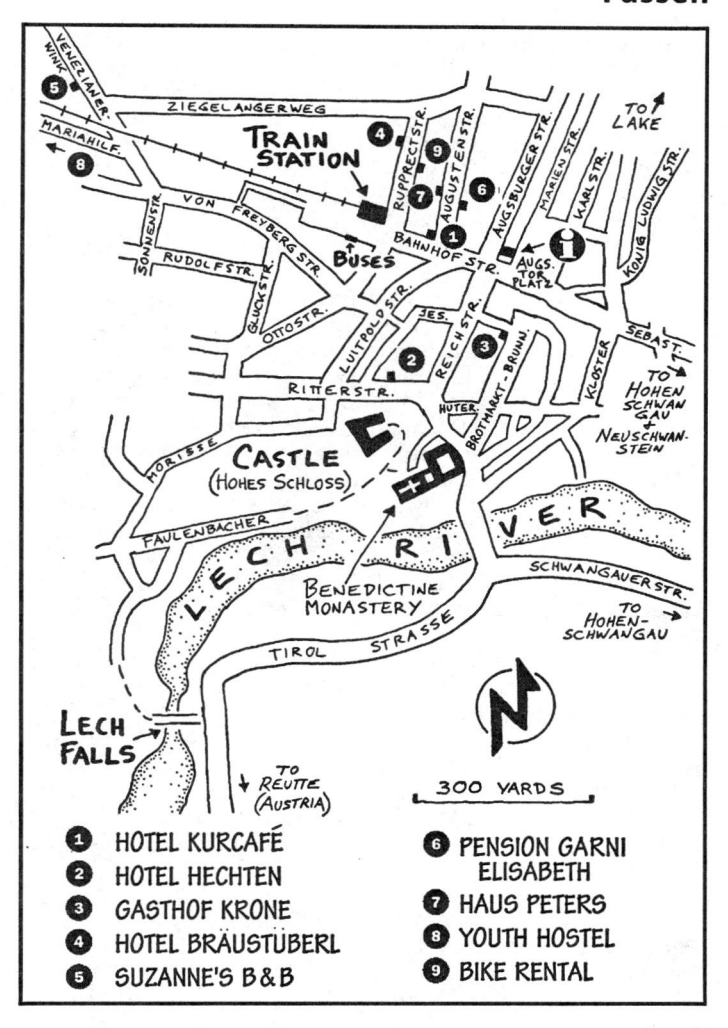

Map Legend:
1. HOTEL KURCAFÉ
2. HOTEL HECHTEN
3. GASTHOF KRONE
4. HOTEL BRÄUSTÜBERL
5. SUZANNE'S B&B
6. PENSION GARNI ELISABETH
7. HAUS PETERS
8. YOUTH HOSTEL
9. BIKE RENTAL

promised with this book in 2000, cheaper off-season and for multi-night stays, fun mini–bowling alley in basement; from TI, walk down pedestrian street, take 2nd right to Ritterstrasse 6; tel. 08362/91600, fax 08362/916-099; Frau Margaret has taken fine care of travelers for 40 years). The attached restaurant Zum Hechten serves hearty Bavarian specialties and specializes in pike (*Hecht*), pulled from the Lech River.

Gasthof Krone, a rare bit of pre-glitz Füssen in the pedestrian zone, has dumpy halls and stairs but bright, cheery, comfy rooms at good prices (S-53 DM, D-90 DM, extra bed-48 DM, prices drop 6 DM for 2-night stays, CC:VMA, reception in restaurant; from TI, head down pedestrian street, take 1st left to Schrannengasse 17, tel. 08362/7824, fax 08362/37505).

Hotel Bräustüberl has clean, bright, newly renovated rooms in a musty old beer hall–type place at fair rates (Sb-50 DM, Db-100 DM, Rupprechtstrasse 5, a block from the station, tel. 08362/7843, fax 08362/38781).

American-run **Suzanne's B&B** does everything right, from backyard-fresh eggs to local cheese, a children's yard, affordable laundry, common kitchen, bright and spacious rooms, and feel-good balconies. Big families should ask about her attic special (D-90 DM, Db-130 DM, Tb-170 DM, Qb-200 DM, room for up to 6 costs 220–240 DM, nonsmoking, bike rental, backtrack 2 blocks from station, Venetianerwinkel 3, tel. 08362/38485, fax 08362/921-396, www.pension-suzanne.at).

The funky, old, ornately furnished **Pension Garni Elisabeth** exudes an Addams-family friendliness. Floors creak, dust balls wander, and the piano is never played (S-50 DM, D-80–90 DM, Db-120–180 DM, T-120 DM, Tb-150–190 DM, showers-6 DM, Augustenstrasse 10, 2 blocks from the station toward town, take 2nd left, tel. 08362/6275).

Haus Peters, across the street, is comfy, smoke free, and friendly, but often closed (Db-86 DM, Tb-120 DM, Augustenstrasse 5, tel. 08362/7171).

Füssen Youth Hostel, a fine, German-run youth hostel, welcomes travelers under 27 (2- to 6-bed rooms, 23 DM for bed and breakfast, 7 DM for dinner, 5.50 DM for sheets, laundry-7 DM/load, nonsmoking, Mariahilferstrasse 5, tel. 08362/7754, fax 08362/2770). From the station, backtrack 10 minutes along the tracks.

Sleeping in Hohenschwangau, near Neuschwanstein Castle
(tel. code: 08362, zip code: 87645)

Inexpensive farmhouse *Zimmer* (B&Bs) abound in the Bavarian countryside around Neuschwanstein and are a good value. Look for signs that say "Zimmer Frei" ("room free," or vacancy). The going rate is about 80 DM per double including breakfast. **Pension Weiher** has lots of balconies and floodlit Neuschwanstein views (S-35–38 DM, D-77 DM, Db-95 DM, Hofwiesenweg 11, tel. & fax 08362/81161). **Pension Schwansee** has clean, basic rooms (Db-100–110 DM, CC:VM, bike rental, 2.5 kilometers

Bavaria and Tirol

from the castle, right on the road to Füssen at Parkstrasse 9, 87645 Alterschrofen, tel. 08362/8353, fax 08362/987-320, family Strössner).

For more of a hotel, try **Alpenhotel Meier**. It's located in a rural setting within walking distance of the castle, just beyond the lower parking lot. Its rooms have new furnishings and porches (Sb-80–90 DM, Db-130–150 DM, 2-night discounts, larger rooms available, easy parking, Schwangauerstrasse 37, tel. 08362/ 81152, fax 08362/987-028).

Eating in Füssen

Infooday is a clever and modern self-service eatery that sells its hot meals and salad bar by weight and offers English newspapers (8 DM/filling salad, 12 DM meals, Mon–Fri 10:30–18:30, Sat 10:30–14:30, closed Sun, under Füssen Castle in Hotel zum Hechten, Ritterstrasse 6). A couple of blocks away, **Pizza Blitz** offers good take-out or eat-at-the-counter pizzas and hearty salads for about 8 DM apiece (Mon–Sat 11:00–23:00, Sun 12:00–23:00, Luitpoldstrasse 14). For more traditional fare, **Hotel Bräustüberl** (see above) has famous home-brewed beer and a popular kitchen (Tue–Sun 10:00–24:00, closed Mon, Rupprechtstrasse 5, near station). For picnicking, try the **Plus supermarket** on the tiny traffic circle a block from the train station (Mon–Fri 8:30–19:00, Sat 8:00–14:00, closed Sun, basement level of shopping complex).

Transportation Connections—Füssen

To: Neuschwanstein (2 buses/hrly, 10 min, 2.5 DM one way, 5 DM round-trip; taxis cost 20 DM), **Reutte** (5 buses/day, 30 min, no service on Sun; taxis cost 40 DM), **Munich** (hrly, 2 hrs, transfer in Buchloe).

Romantic Road Buses: The northbound Romantic Road bus departs Füssen at 8:00; the southbound bus arrives at Füssen at 20:10 (bus stops at train station). Railpasses get you a 75 percent discount on the Romantic Road bus (and best of all, the ride doesn't use up a day of a flexipass)—this is a great value. For more information, see the Rothenburg chapter.

REUTTE, AUSTRIA
(12 AS = about $1)

Reutte (ROY-teh, rolled "r"), a relaxed town of 5,500, is located 20 minutes across the border from Füssen. It's far from the international tourist crowd, but popular with Germans and Austrians for its climate. Doctors recommend its "grade 1" air. Reutte isn't in any other American guidebook. Its charms are subtle, though its generous sidewalks are filled with smart boutiques and lazy coffee houses. It never was rich or important. Its castle is ruined, its buildings have painted-on "carvings," its churches are full, its men yodel for each other on birthdays, and lately its energy is spent soaking its Austrian and German guests in *Gemütlichkeit*. Most guests stay for a week, so the town's attractions are more time-consuming than thrilling. If the weather's good, hike to the mysterious Ehrenberg ruins, ride the luge, or rent a bike. For a slap-dancing bang, enjoy a Tirolean folk evening. For accommodations, see "Sleeping," below.

Orientation (tel. code: 05672)

Tourist Information: Reutte's TI is a block in front of the train station (Mon–Fri 8:00–12:00, 13:00–17:00, Sat 8:30–12:00, tel. 05672/62336 or, from Germany, 0043-5672/62336). Go over your sightseeing plans, ask about a folk evening, pick up city and biking maps, and ask about discounts with the hotel guest cards.

Arrival in Reutte: Head straight out of the station one long block to the TI. At the TI, turn left to reach the center of town.

Bike Rental: The train station rents bikes (city bike-150 AS, mountain bike-200 AS, kid's bike-100 AS, 50 percent discount with a railpass). In the center, the Heinz Glatzle also rents good mountain bikes (Obermarkt 61, tel. 05672/2752). Most of the sights described in this chapter make good biking destinations. Ask about the bike path (*Radwanderweg*) along the Lech River.

Kids' Play Areas: Reutte's pool (see below) has a playground. The TI can recommend several others.

Laundry: Don't ask the TI about a Laundromat. Unless you can infiltrate the local campground, Hotel Maximilian, or Gutshof zum Schluxen (see "Sleeping," below), the town has none.

Sights—Reutte

▲▲**Ehrenberg Ruins**—The brooding ruins of Ehrenberg Castle are a mile outside of Reutte on the road to Lermoos and Innsbruck. This 13th-century rock pile, a great contrast to King Ludwig's "modern" castles, is a super opportunity to let your imagination off its leash. Hike up from the parking lot at the base of the hill; it's a 25-minute walk to the castle for a great view from your own private ruins. (Facing the hill from the parking lot, the steeper trail is to the right, the easy gravelly road is to the left.) Imagine how proud Count Meinrad II of Tirol (who built the castle in 1290) would be to know that his castle repelled 16,000 Swedish soldiers in the defense of Catholicism in 1632.

The easiest way down is via the small road leading from the gully. The car park, with a café/guest house (Gasthor Klaus, closed Wed, offers a German-language flyer about the castle and has a wall painting of the intact castle), is just off the Lermoos/Reutte road. Reutte is a pleasant one-hour walk away. If you're biking, use the trail (*Radwanderweg*) along the Lech River (the TI has a good map).

Bavaria and Tirol

Reutte

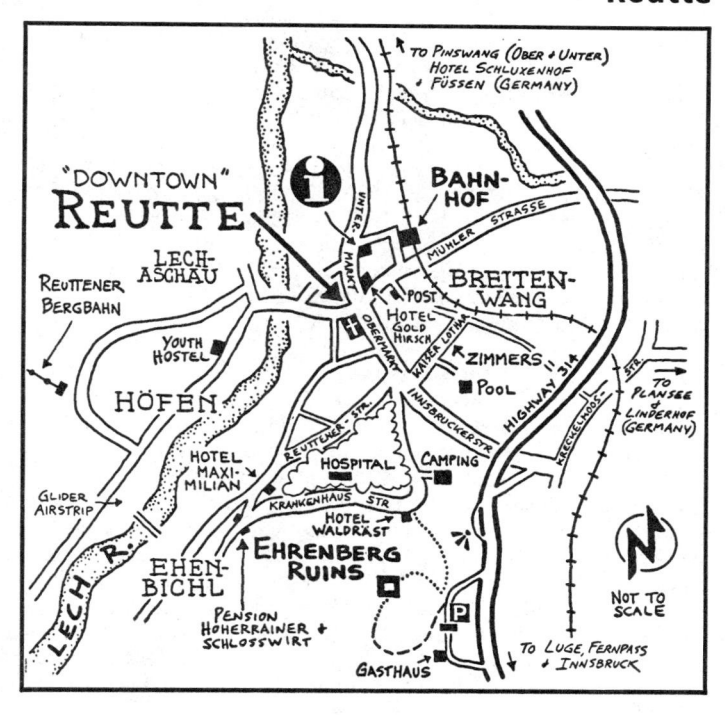

Folk Museum—Reutte's Heimatmuseum, offering a quick look at the local folk culture and the story of the castle, is more cute than impressive and comes without English explanations (20 AS, Tue–Sun 10:00–12:00, 14:00–17:00, closed Mon and off-season, in the bright green building on Untermarkt, around the corner from Hotel Goldener Hirsch, 1 block away).

▲▲**Tirolean Folk Evening**—Ask the TI or your hotel if there's a Tirolean folk evening scheduled. About once a week in the summer, Reutte or a nearby town puts on an evening of yodeling, slap dancing, and Tirolean frolic usually worth the 80 AS and short drive. Off-season, you'll have to do your own yodeling. There are also weekly folk concerts in the park (ask at TI).

Swimming—Plunge into Reutte's Olympic-size swimming pool to cool off after your castle hikes (60 AS, daily 10:00–21:00, off-season 14:00–21:00 and closed Mon, new pool planned for 2000 at same site, 15 minutes on foot from Reutte center, head out Obermarkt and turn left on Kaiser-Lothar).

Reuttener Bergbahn—This mountain lift swoops you high above the tree line to a starting point for several hikes and an Alpine flower park with special paths leading you past countless local varieties (good bike ride with an uphill at the end).

Flying and Gliding—For a major thrill on a sunny day, drop by the tiny airport in Hofen across the river, and fly. A small single-prop plane can buzz the Zugspitze and Ludwig's castles and give you a bird's-eye peek at Reutte's Ehrenberg ruins (2 people for 30 minutes-1,350 AS, 1 hour-2,400 AS, tel. 05672/63207). Or, for something more angelic, how about *Segelfliegen*? For 500 AS you get 30 minutes in a glider for two (you and the pilot). Just watching the towrope launch the graceful glider like a giant, slow-motion rubber-band gun is thrilling (late May–Oct 11:00–19:00, in good weather only, tel. 05672/71550).

Sights—Tirol, Near Reutte

▲▲**The Luge (*Sommerrodelbahn*)**—Near Lermoos, on the Innsbruck-Lermoos-Reutte road, you'll find two rare and exciting luge courses, or *Sommerrodelbahn*. To try one of Europe's great $5 thrills, take the lift up, grab a sledlike go-cart, and luge down. The concrete course banks on the corners, and even a novice can go very, very fast. Most are cautious on their first run and speed demons on their second. (A woman once showed me her journal illustrated with her husband's dried five-inch-long luge scab. He disobeyed the only essential rule of luging: Keep both hands on your stick.) No one emerges from the course without a windblown hairdo and a smile-creased face. Both places charge the same price (75 AS per run, 5- and 10-trip discount cards) and shut down when it rains (call ahead to make sure they're open).

The short and steep luge: Bichlbach, the first course (100-meter drop over 800-meter course), is six kilometers beyond Reutte's castle ruins. Look for a chairlift on the right and exit on the tiny road at the yellow "Riesenrutschbahn" sign (open only Sat–Sun 9:00–17:00 in late May, then daily mid-Jun–Sept or Oct, call first, tel. 05674/5350, or contact the local TI at 05674/5354). If you're without wheels, catch the train from Reutte to Bichlbach (6/day, 20 min) and walk one kilometer to the luge.

The longest luge: The Biberwier Sommerrodelbahn is a better luge and, at 1,300 meters, the longest in Austria (15 minutes farther from Reutte than Bichlbach, just past Lermoos in Biberwier—the first exit after a long tunnel). The only drawbacks are its shorter season and that it's open only on weekends until July (then daily 9:00–16:30 through Sept, call first, tel. 05673/2111, TI tel. 05673/2922). One or two blocks downhill from this luge, behind the Sport und Trachtenstüberl shop, is a wooden church dome with a striking Zugspitze backdrop. If you have sunshine and a camera, don't miss it. Without a car, the bus from Reutte to Biberwier is your best bet

Bavaria and Tirol

(8/day, fewer on Sun, 30 min, bus stop and posted schedule near Reutte's Hotel Goldener Hirsch on Untermarket). The nearest train station is Lermoos, four kilometers from the luge.
▲**Fallerschein**—Easy for drivers and a special treat for those who may have been Kit Carson in a previous life, this extremely remote log-cabin village is a 4,000-foot-high, flower-speckled world of serene slopes and cowbells. Thunderstorms roll down the valley like it's God's bowling alley, but the pint-size church on the high ground, blissfully simple in a land of Baroque, seems to promise that this huddle of houses will survive and the river and breeze will just keep flowing. The couples sitting on benches are mostly Austrian vacationers who've rented cabins here. Many of them, appreciating the remoteness of Fallerschein, are having affairs.

For a rugged chunk of local Alpine peace, spend a night in the local Matratzenlager Almwirtschaft Fallerschein, run by Kerle Erwin (about 120 AS per person with breakfast; open, if weather permits, mid-May–Oct; 27 cheap beds in a very simple loft dorm, good, inexpensive meals; 6671 Weissenbach Pfarrweg 18, Reutte, tel. 0567 8/5142, rarely answered, and then not in English). It's crowded only on weekends. Fallerschein, at the end of the two-kilometer Berwang Road, is near Namlos and about 45 minutes southwest of Reutte.

Sleeping in and near Reutte
(12 AS = about $1, tel. code: 05672, zip code: 6600)
Reutte is a mellow Füssen with fewer crowds and easygoing locals with a contagious love of life. Come here for a good dose of Austrian ambience and lower prices. Those with a car should homebase here; those without should consider it. (To call Reutte from Germany, dial 00-43-5672, then the local number.) You'll drive across the border but probably won't even have to stop. Reutte is popular with Austrians and Germans who come here year after year for one- or two-week vacations. The hotels are big, elegant, and full of comfy, carved furnishings and creative ways to spend so much time in one spot. They take great pride in their restaurants, and the owners send their children away to hotel management schools. All include a generally great breakfast but few accept credit cards. Those that do are identified; those that don't will generally accept traveler's checks. Hotels will be busier than usual in 2000, thanks to the Passion Play in Oberammergau, so reserve ahead.

Hotels and Guest Houses
Hotel Goldener Hirsch, located in the center of Reutte just two blocks from the station, is a grand old hotel renovated with a mod Tirolean Jugendstil flair. It includes minibars, cable TV, and one lonely set of antlers. For those without a car, this is convenient (Sb-550 AS, Db-880 AS, 2-night discounts, CC:VMA, a few family rooms, elevator, pleasant restaurant, try the fitness salad, 6600

Reutte-Tirol, tel. 05672/62508, fax 05672/625-087, e-mail: gold.hirsch@netway.at).

Moserhof Hotel is a plush Tyrolian splurge with polished service and facilities. The dining room is elegant (older but fine Db-860 AS, newer and larger Db-920 AS, extra person-430 AS, all rooms with balconies, elevator, from Reutte train station walk to post office roundabout then to Planseestrasse 44, in village of Breitenwang, tel. 05672/62020, fax 05672/620-2040).

The next four listings are a few miles upriver from Reutte in the village of Ehenbichl; all are along an enjoyable hike to Ehrenburg ruins.

Hotel Maximilian is a fine splurge. It includes free bicycles, Ping-Pong, a sauna, a children's playroom, and the friendly service of the Koch family. Daughter Gabi speaks flawless English and is clearly in charge. There always seems to be a special event here, and the Kochs host many Tirolean folk evenings (Sb-450 AS, Db-940–1,000 AS, cheaper for families, no CC, laundry service available even to nonguests, good restaurant, far from the train station in the next village but can often pick up, A-6600 Ehenbichl-Reutte, tel. 05672/62585, fax 05672/625-8554, e-mail: maxhotel@netway.at). From central Reutte, go south on Obermarkt and turn right on Reuttenerstrasse (25 minutes on foot). They rent cars to guests only (one VW Golf, one VW van, must book in advance).

Pension Hohenrainer is a quiet, good value with some castle-view balconies (Sb-280–320 AS, Db-580–640 AS). The same family runs the simpler **Gasthof Schlosswirt** across the green field (S-180–200 AS, D-360 AS, D with view-400 AS, no CC, traditional Tirolean-style restaurant). Both are up the road behind Hotel Maximilian (turn right and continue 100 meters to Unterreid 3, A-6600 Ehenbichl, tel. 05672/62544, fax 05672/62052, e-mail: hohenrainer@aon.at).

Gasthof-Pension Waldrast, separating a forest and a meadow, is run by the farming Huter family. The place feels hauntingly quiet and has no restaurant, but it does include very nice rooms with sitting areas and castle-view balconies (Db-about 700 AS, on Ehrenbergstrasse, a mile from Reutte just off the main drag toward Innsbruck, past the campground and under the castle ruins, 6600 Reutte-Ehenbichl, tel. & fax 05672/62443, www.waldrast.com).

Closer to Füssen but still in Austria, **Gutshof zum Schluxen**, run by helpful Hermann, gets the "remote-old-hotel-in-an-idyllic-setting" award. This family-friendly working farm offers modern rustic elegance draped in goose down and pastels, and a chance to pet a rabbit. Its picturesque meadow setting will turn you into a dandelion picker, and its proximity to Neuschwanstein will turn you into a hiker (free pickup at Reutte or Füssen station, Sb-560 AS, Db-1,120 AS; cheaper with cash, traveler's checks, or 2 nights; extra person-300 AS, CC:VM, good restaurant, fun bar, self-service laundry, mountain bike rental for guests, A-6600 Pinswang-Reutte, between Reutte and Füssen in the village of Pinswang, tel. 05677/8903, fax 05677/890-323, www.schluxen.com).

Private Homes in Breitenwang, near Reutte
The Reutte TI has a list of more than 50 private homes (*Zimmer*) that rent out generally good rooms with facilities down the hall, pleasant communal living rooms, and breakfast. Most charge 200 AS per person per night and speak little if any English. Reservations are nearly impossible for one- or two-night stays. But short stops are welcome if you just drop in and fill in available gaps. Most *Zimmer* charge 15 AS to 20 AS extra for heat in winter (worth it). The TI can always find you a room when you arrive.

Right next door to Reutte is the older and quieter village of Breitenwang. It has all the best *Zimmer*, the recommended Moserhof Hotel (above), and a bakery (a 20-minute walk from the Reutte train station—at the post office roundabout, follow Planseestrasse past the onion dome to the pointy straight dome; unmarked Kaiser Lothar Strasse is the first right past this church). The following three *Zimmer* are comfortable, quiet, have few stairs, and are within two blocks of the Breitenwang church steeple: **Helene Haissl** (S-190 AS, D-380 AS, less for a 2-night stay, fine rooms, beautiful garden, separate entrance for rooms, across from the big Alpenhotel at Planseestrasse 63, tel. 05672/67913); **Inge Hosp** (S-200 AS, D-400 AS, an old-fashioned place, includes antlers over the breakfast table, Kaiser Lothar Strasse 36, tel. 05672/62401); and **Walter and Emilie Hosp**, Inge's more formal cousins who have a modern house across the street (D-400 AS for 1 night, otherwise D-380 AS, extra person-160 AS, Kaiser Lothar Strasse 29, tel. 05672/65377).

Eating in Reutte
Hotels in this region take great pleasure in earning the loyalty of their guests by serving local cuisine at reasonable prices. Rather than go to a cheap restaurant, I'd order low on a hotel menu. For cheap food, the **Metzgerei Storf** (Mon–Fri 8:30–15:00), above the deli across from the Heimatmuseum on Untermarkt Street, is good. The modern **Alina** restaurant in Breitenwang is a fine Italian establishment with decent prices (near recommended *Zimmer*, 2 blocks behind church at Bachweg 17).

Transportation Connections—Reutte
To: Füssen (6 buses/day, 30 min, no service on Sun; taxis cost 35 DM), **Garmisch** (2 trains/hr, 60 min), **Munich** (hrly trains, 3 hrs, transfer in Garmisch), **Innsbruck** (6/day, 3 hrs), **Salzburg** (6/day, 6 hrs, transfer in Innsbruck).

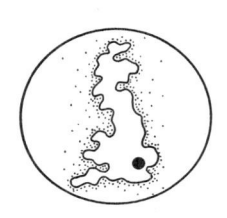

LONDON

London is more than 600 square miles of urban jungle. With 9 million struggling people—many of whom speak English—it's a world in itself and a barrage on all the senses. On my first visit I felt very, very small. London is much more than its museums and famous landmarks. It's a living, breathing, thriving organism.

London has changed dramatically in recent years, and many visitors are surprised to find how "un-English" it is. Whites are now a minority in major parts of the city that once symbolized white imperialism. Arabs have nearly bought out the area north of Hyde Park. Chinese take-outs outnumber fish-and-chips shops. Many hotels are run by people with foreign accents (who hire English chambermaids), while outlying suburbs are home to huge communities of Indians and Pakistanis. London is learning—sometimes fitfully—to live as a microcosm of its formerly vast empire. With the English Channel Tunnel complete, many see more foreign threats to the Britishness of Britain.

With just a few days here, you'll get no more than a quick splash in this teeming human tidal pool. But, with a quick orientation, you'll get a good taste of its top sights, history, and cultural entertainment, as well as its ever-changing human face.

Have fun in London. Blow through the city on the open deck of a double-decker orientation tour bus, and take a pinch-me-I'm-in-Britain walk through downtown. Ogle the crown jewels at the Tower of London, hear the chimes of Big Ben, and see the Houses of Parliament in action. Hobnob with the tombstones in Westminster Abbey, duck WWII bombs in Churchill's underground Cabinet War Rooms, and brave the earthshaking Imperial War Museum. Overfeed the pigeons at Trafalgar Square. Visit with Leonardo, Botticelli, and Rembrandt in the National Gallery. Whisper across the dome of St. Paul's Cathedral and rummage through our civilization's attic at the British Museum. Cruise down the Thames River. You'll enjoy some of Europe's best people watching at Covent Garden and snap to at Buckingham Palace's Changing of the Guard. Just sit in Victoria Station, at a major tube station, at Piccadilly Circus, or in Trafalgar Square, and observe. Spend one evening at a theater and the others catching your breath.

Planning Your Time

The sights of London alone could easily fill a trip to Britain. It's a great one-week getaway. On a three-week tour of Britain I'd give it three busy days. If you're flying in, consider starting your trip in Bath and make London your British finale. Especially if you hope to enjoy a play or concert, a night or two of jet lag is bad news.

Here's a suggested schedule:

Day 1: 9:00–Tower of London (Beefeater tour, crown jewels), 12:00–Munch a sandwich on the Thames while cruising from the Tower to Westminster Bridge, 13:00–Follow the self-guided "Hello London" walk (see below) with a quick visit to the Cabinet War Rooms, 15:30–Trafalgar Square and National Gallery, 17:30–Visit the National Tourist Information Centre near Piccadilly, planning ahead for your trip, 18:30–Dinner in Soho. Take in a play or 19:30 concert at St. Martin-in-the-Fields.

Day 2: 9:00–If traveling around Britain, spend 30 minutes at a phone nailing down all the essentials of your trip. If you know where you'll be and when, call those B&Bs now. 9:30–Take the Round London bus tour (hop off for the 11:30 Changing of the Guard at Buckingham Palace), 12:30–Covent Gardens for lunch and people watching, 14:00–Tour the British Museum. Have a pub dinner before a play, concert, or evening walking tour.

Days 3 and 4: Choose among these remaining London highlights: Tour Westminster Abbey, the British Library, the Imperial War Museum, the two Tate Galleries (British art on the north bank and modern art on the south bank), St. Paul's Cathedral, or the Museum of London; cruise to Kew or Greenwich (Millennium Dome); do some serious shopping at one of London's elegant department stores or open-air markets; or consider another historic walking tour.

After considering nearly all of London's tourist sights, I have pruned them down to just the most important (or fun) for a first visit of up to seven days. You won't be able to see all of these, so don't try. You'll keep coming back to London. After 25 visits myself, I still enjoy a healthy list of excuses to return.

Orientation
(tel. code: 020)

To grasp London comfortably, see it as the old town without the modern, congested sprawl. Most of the visitor's London lies

Millennium London

London seems hell-bent on hosting the world's grandest millennium celebrations. The year 2000 brings London revamped museums, a huge Ferris wheel, and a giant dome at Greenwich.

Greenwich, site of the world's prime meridian and "the place from where time is measured," kicked off the millennium with gusto, playing host to Her Majesty and Prince Charles' big New Year's Eve 2000 bash in the Millennium Dome. This exhibition hall, 50 meters high and a kilometer around, is the biggest millennium project anywhere. Fourteen theme zones (such as Mind, Body, Spirit, Work, National Identity, Play, and a display of Princess Diana's dresses) surround a vast central stage. Expect lots of live entertainment, huge video screens, virtual reality gimmicks, and enthusiastic interactivity. After 2000, the dome will be redeveloped as a theme park or exhibition center. In the town of Greenwich, the Queen's House hosts the new *The Story of Time* exhibit (until Sept 24) and the Old Royal Naval College opens its Painted Hall and Chapel to the public. (For details, see "Greenwich," below.)

On London's South Bank, a grand Ferris wheel spins opposite Big Ben—at 450 feet high, it's the highest public viewpoint in London. The new Tate Gallery of Modern Art, opening this May, will be linked to St. Paul's Cathedral by the new pedestrian Millennium Bridge, London's first bridge in a hundred years. And the Globe Theater has expanded its exhibit on the history of the Globe to cover Shakespeare, his contemporaries, and the beginnings of theater. (For details, see "Sights—South London," below.)

The British Museum opens its Great Court and elegant, round Reading Room (which Karl Marx liked so much) to the public this fall. The museum hosts a thought-provoking exhibit exploring the legacy of the book of Revelations—*The Apocalypse and the Shape of Things to Come*—tracing ideas about the devil and the apocalypse from the 11th century to World War II (through April 24, 2000).

The "Arts 2000" movement plans to free art from its normal places all over Britain and hang it in unusual, everyday places, from train stations to shopping malls.

Like nowhere else in Europe, London and Greenwich know how to throw a party. They make it easy to turn 2000.

between the Tower of London and Hyde Park—about a three-mile walk. Mentally—maybe even physically—scissor down your map to include only the area between the Tower, King's Cross Station, Paddington Station, the Victoria and Albert Museum, and Victoria Station. With this focus and a good orientation, you'll find London manageable and even fun.

Tourist Information

The **British Visitors Centre** is the best information service in town (Mon–Fri 9:00–18:30, Sat–Sun 10:00–16:00, just off Piccadilly Circus at 1 Lower Regent Street, tel. 020/8846-9000, www.visitbritain.com). It's great for London information. If you're traveling beyond London, take advantage of its well-equipped London/England desk, Wales desk (tel. 020/7803-3838), Ireland desk (tel. 020/7493-3201), and Scotland desk. At the center's extensive bookshop, gather whatever guidebooks, youth hostel directories, maps, and information you'll need. If venturing beyond London, consider the *Michelin Green Guide* to London or Britain (£9), the Britain road atlas (£10), and Ordnance Survey maps for areas you'll be exploring by car. There's also a travel agency upstairs.

The **Scottish Tourist Centre** (19 Cockspur Street, tel. 020/7930-8661) and the slick new **French National Tourist Office** (Mon–Sat 9:00–17:30, closed Sun, 179 Piccadilly Street, tel. 0990-848-848) are nearby.

Unfortunately **London's Tourist Information Centres** (TIs) are now owned by the big hotels and are simply businesses selling advertising space to companies with flyers to distribute. They are not very helpful. Avoid their 50p-per-minute telephone information service (instead try the **British Visitors Centre** at 020/8846-9000). Locations include Heathrow Airport's Terminal 3 (daily 6:00–23:00, most convenient and least crowded); Heathrow Airport's Terminal 1 and 2 tube station (daily 8:00–18:00); Victoria Station (daily 8:00–18:00, shorter hours in winter, crowded and commercial); and Waterloo International Terminal Arrivals Hall (serving trains from Paris, daily 8:30–22:30).

At any of the TIs, bring your itinerary and a checklist of questions. Pick up these publications: *London Planner* (a great free monthly that lists all the sights, events, and hours), walking-tour schedule flyers, and a theater guide. Consider buying their fine £1.40 London map, which rivals the £4 maps sold in newsstands (free from the British Tourist Authority in the U.S.A.: tel. 800/462-2748 or 212/986-2200, 551 Fifth Avenue, 7th floor, New York, NY 10176, www.visitbritain.com). The TIs sell BT phone cards, long-distance bus tickets and passes, British Heritage Passes, and tickets to plays (steep booking fee). They also book rooms (avoid their £5 booking fee by calling hotels direct).

Helpful Hints

Theft Alert: The Artful Dodger is alive and well in London. Be on guard, particularly on public transportation and in places crowded with tourists. Tourists, considered naive and rich, are targeted. Over 7,500 handbags are stolen annually at Covent Garden alone. Thieves paw you so you don't feel the pickpocketing.

Changing Money: ATMs are really the way to go. Standard transaction fees at banks are £2–4. American Express Offices offer a fair rate and change any brand of traveler's checks for no fee. There are several offices (Heathrow Terminal 4 tube station and at 6 Haymarket near Piccadilly, daily 9:00–18:00, tel. 020/7930-4411). Avoid changing money at exchange bureaus. Their latest scam: They advertise very good rates with a same-as-the-banks fee of 2 percent. But the fine print explains that the fee of 2 percent is for buying pounds. The fee for *selling* pounds is 9.5 percent. Ouch!

What's Up: For the best listing of what's happening (plays, movies, restaurants, concerts, exhibitions, protests, walking tours, shopping, and children's activities) and a look at the trendy London scene, pick up a current copy of *Time Out* (£1.80, www.timeout.co.uk) or *What's On* at any newsstand. The TI's free monthly *London Planner* lists sights, plays, and events at least as well. For a fun Web site on London's entertainment, theater, restaurants, and news, go to www.thisislondon.com.

Free Sights: The British Museum, British Library, National Gallery, National Portrait Gallery, and both Tate Galleries are always free. These museums are free from 16:30 to closing (17:30 or 18:00), saving you £5 or so: The Imperial War Museum, Museum of London, Natural History Museum, and Victoria and Albert Museum. More museums will be free in the next few years.

Travel Bookstores: Stanfords Travel Bookstore—near Victoria Station (52 Grosvenor Gardens), at Covent Garden (12 Long Acre, tel. 020/7836-1321), and at 156 Regent Street—is good and stocks current editions of my books. Waterstones Bookstore, on the corner of Trafalgar Square, is also handy, with a fine travel selection next to the Coffee Republic café (WC upstairs, tel. 020/7839-4411). The best London map I've seen is the Bensons Mapguide of London (£2, May 1999 edition has the Greenwich Dome).

Travel Agency: The student travel agency USIT, across from Victoria Station, has great deals on flights for people of all ages (Mon–Fri 9:00–18:00, Sat–Sun 10:00–17:00, Buckingham Palace Road, tel. 0870-240-1010, www.usitcampus.co.uk). Also, look in the Sunday *Times* travel section for great deals on flights.

Arrival in London

By Train: London has eight train stations, all connected by the tube (subway), all with exchange offices and luggage storage. From any station, ride the tube or taxi to your hotel.

By Bus: The bus station is one block southwest of Victoria Station, which has a TI and tube entrance.

By Plane: For detailed information on getting from London's airports to downtown London, see "Transportation Connections" at the end of this chapter.

Getting around London

London's taxis, buses, and subway system make a private car unnecessary. To travel smart in a city this size, you must get comfortable with public transportation.

By Taxi: London is the best taxi town in Europe. Big, black, carefully regulated cabs are everywhere. I never met a crabby cabbie in London. They love to talk and know every nook and cranny in town. I ride in one a day just to get my London questions answered. Rides start at £1.40 and cost about £1.50 per tube stop. Connecting downtown sights is quick and easy and will cost you about £4 (e.g., St. Paul's to the Tower of London). For a short ride, three people in a cab travel at tube prices. Groups of four or five should taxi everywhere. If a cab's top light is on, just wave it down. (Drivers flash lights when they see you.) They have a tiny turning radius, so you can wave at cabs going both directions. If waving doesn't work, ask someone where you can find a taxi stand. Stick with metered cabs. While telephoning a cab gets one in minutes, it's generally not necessary and adds to the cost. London is such a great wave-'em-down taxi town that most cabs don't even have a radio phone.

By Bus: London's extensive bus system is easy to follow. Just pick up a free map from a TI or tube station. Signs at stops list routes clearly. Conductors are terse but helpful. Ask to be reminded when it's your stop. Just hop on, tell the driver where you're going, pay what he says, grab a ticket, take a seat, and relax. (The best views are upstairs.) Rides start at 90p. If the driver is not taking money, hop in and grab a seat. The conductor will eventually sell you a ticket. If you have a transit pass, get in the habit of hopping buses for quick little straight shots (even just to get to a metro stop). During bump-and-grind rush hours (8:00–10:00 and 16:00–19:00), you'll go faster by tube.

By Tube: London's subway is one of this planet's great people movers and the fastest (and cheapest) long-distance transport in town. Any ride in the Central Zone (on or within the Circle Line, including virtually all my recommended sights and hotels) costs £1.40. You can avoid ticket window lines in tube stations by buying tickets from coin-op machines; practice on the punchboard to see how the system works (hit "adult single" and your destination). Again, nearly every ride will be £1.40. (These tickets are valid only on the day of purchase.) Beware: Overshooting your zone will get you a £10 fine.

Most city maps include a tube map with color-coded lines and names (free at any station window). Each line has a name (such as Circle, Northern, or Bakerloo) and two directions (indicated by end stop). In stations you'll have a choice of two platforms per line. Navigate by signs leading to the platforms (usually labeled north, south, east, or west) and clearly listing the stops served by each line, or ask a local or an orange-vested staff person for help. All city maps have north on top. Know which general direction you're heading, and tube navigation suddenly becomes easier. Some tracks are shared by several lines, and electronic signboards announce which train is next and the minutes remaining until various arrivals. Each train has its final destination or line name above its windshield. Read the system notices clearly posted at the platform; they explain the tube's latest flood, construction, or bomb scare. Bring something to do to pass the waits productively. And always... mind the gap.

You can't leave the system without feeding your ticket to the turnstile. Save time by choosing the best street exit (look at the maps on the walls). "Subway" means pedestrian underpass in "English." For tube and bus information, call 020/7222-1234.

London Tube and Bus Passes: Consider using these passes, valid on both the tube and buses. The "Travel Card," covering Zones 1 and 2, gives you unlimited travel for a day, starting after 9:30 and anytime on weekends, for £3.80. The all-zone version of this card costs £4.50 (and includes Heathrow airport). The "LT Card," a one-day, two-zone pass with no time restriction, costs £4.80. Families save with the one-day "Family Travel Card." The "Weekend Travel Card," covering Zones 1 and 2 for £5.70, costs 25 percent less than two one-day cards. The "7-Day Travel Card" costs £18, covers Zone 1, and requires a passport-type photo (cut one out of any snapshot and bring it from home). All passes are available for more zones and are purchased as easily as a normal ticket at any station. If you figure you'll take three rides in a day, get a day pass.

If you want to travel a little each day or if you're part of a group, a £10 "carnet" is a great deal: You get 10 separate tickets for tube travel in Zone 1 (£1 each rather than £1.40). Wait for the machine to lay all 10 tickets.

Tours of London

▲▲▲**Hop-on Hop-off Double-Decker Bus Tours**—Two very competitive companies ("Original" and "Big Bus") offer essentially the same tours, with live (English-only) guides on board. This two-hour, once-over-lightly bus tour drives by all the most famous sights, providing a stressless way to get your bearings and at least see the biggies. You can sit back and enjoy the entire two-hour orientation tour (a good idea if you like the guide and the weather) or "hop on and hop off" at any of the 20 plus stops and catch a

London Tube Map

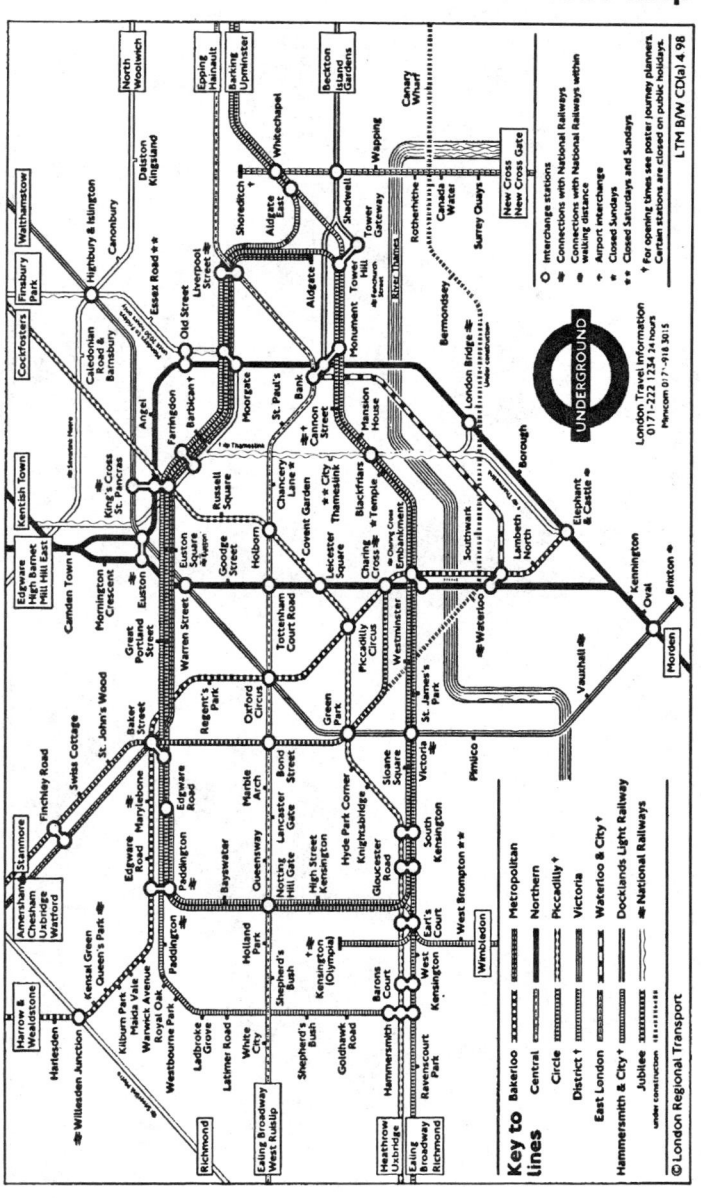

London

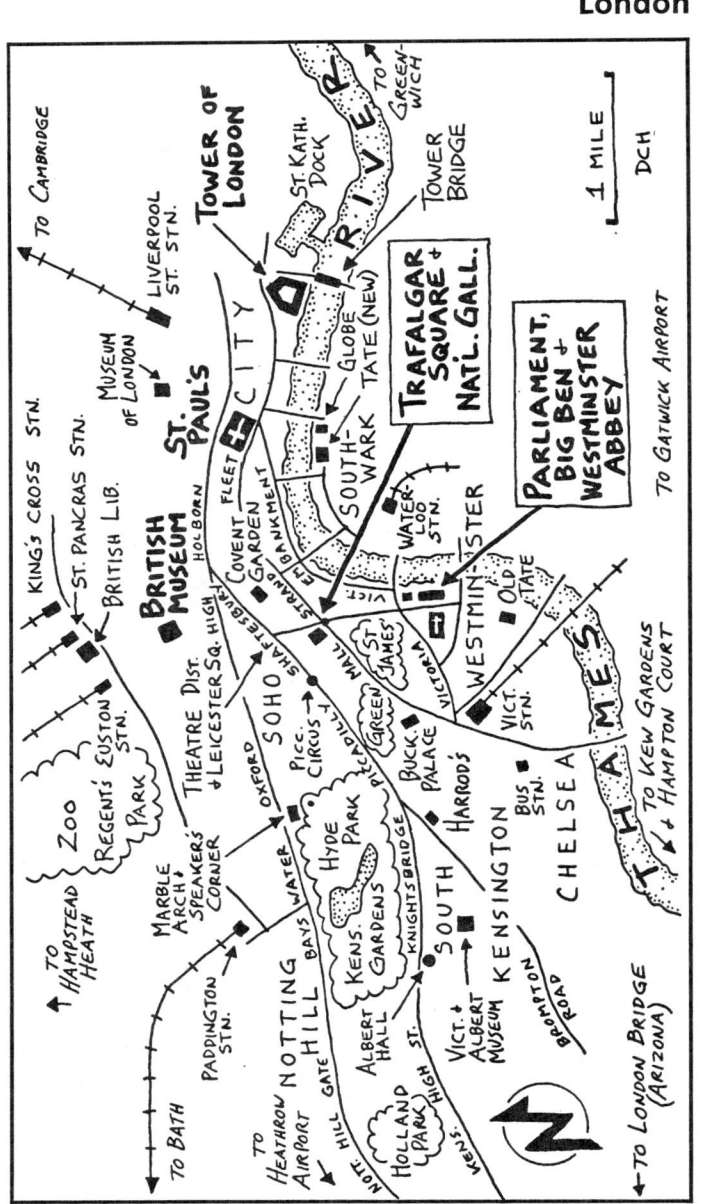

later bus. Buses run about every 10 minutes in summer, every 20 minutes in winter. It's an inexpensive form of transport as well as an informative tour. Grab one of the maps and study it. Buses run daily, except on Christmas (from about 9:00 in summer—9:30 in winter—until early evening), from Victoria Street (1 block north of Victoria Station), Marble Arch, Piccadilly Circus, Trafalgar Square, and so on. Each company offers a core two-hour overview tour and two other routes (buy ticket from driver, ticket good for 24 hours; bring a sweater and extra film). Note: If you start at Victoria at 9:30, you can hop off near the end of the two-hour loop at the Buckingham Palace stop (Bressenden Place), a five-minute walk from the palace and the Changing of the Guard at 11:30. Sunday morning, with light traffic and many museums closed, is a fine time for the tour.

Original London Sightseeing Bus Tour: Live guided buses have a Union Jack flag and a yellow triangle on the front of the bus. If the front has many flags or a green triangle, it's a tape-recorded multilingual tour—avoid it, unless you have kids who'd enjoy the more entertaining recorded kids' tour (£12.50, £3.50 off with this book—limit 2 discounts per book, they'll rip off the corner of this page, ticket good for 24 hours, tel. 020/8877-1722).

Big Bus Hop-on Hop-off London Tours: These are also good. For £15 you get the same basic tour plus coupons for four different one-hour London walks and the scenic and entertainingly guided Thames boat ride (normally £4.60) between Westminster Pier and the Tower of London. The pass and extras are valid for 24 hours. While the price is steeper, Big Bus guides seem more dynamic than the Original guides, and the Big Bus system is probably better organized (tel. 020/8944-7810, www.bigbus.co.uk).

▲▲**Walking Tours**—Many times a day top-notch local guides lead small groups through specific slices of London's past. Schedule flyers litter the desks of TIs, hotels, and pubs. (The beefy, plain black-and-white *Original London Walks* newsletter lists their extensive daily schedule.) *Time Out* lists many but not all scheduled walks. Simply show up at the announced location, pay £5, and enjoy two chatty hours of Dickens, the Plague, Shakespeare, Legal London, the Beatles, Jack the Ripper, or whatever is on the agenda. Original London Walks is the dominant company (for schedule, tel. 020/7624-3978, www.walks.com). They do private tours for £80.

Robina Brown, who winters in Seattle (a bizarre concept), leads tours on foot or with small groups in her Toyota Previa. Standard rates for London's registered guides: £83/4 hrs, £125/9 hrs. For car and guiding she charges £145 for 3 hours and about £300 per day per group (tel. & fax 020/7228-2238, e-mail: robina.brown@which.net). Brit Lonsdale, an energetic mother of twins, is another registered London guide (tel. 020/7386-9907, fax 020/7386-9807). Chris Salaman, while semiretired, tailors specialty walks (his favorite: industrial tours). He does daylong private walks, including lunch, a tube travel card, and museum admissions, for £120 for up to six people (tel. 020/8871-9048). For other guides call 020/7403-2062, www.touristguides.org.uk.

▲▲Cruise the Thames—Boat tours with an entertaining commentary sail regularly from Westminster Pier (at the base of Westminster Bridge under Big Ben). You can cruise to the Tower of London (£4.60, round-trip £5.80, included with Big Bus London tour, 3/hrly, 10:20–21:00 in peak season, until 18:00 in winter, 30 min, tel. 020/7930-9033), Greenwich (£6, round-trip £7.30, 2/hrly, 10:00–17:00, 50 min, tel. 020/7930-4097), and Kew Gardens (£6, round-trip £10, 5/day, 90 min, 30 min narrated, tel. 020/7930-2062). For pleasure and efficiency, consider combining a one-way cruise with a tube ride back.

Sights—From Westminster Abbey to Trafalgar Square

▲▲"Hello London" Walk—Just about every visitor to London strolls the historic Whitehall boulevard from Big Ben to Trafalgar Square. Beneath London's modern traffic and big-city bustle lies 2,000 fascinating years of history. This three-quarter-mile, self-guided orientation walk gives you a whirlwind tour and connects the sights listed in this section.

Start halfway across **Westminster Bridge** for the great view. For that "Wow, I'm really in London!" feeling, get a close-up view of the **Houses of Parliament** and **Big Ben** (floodlit at night). Downstream you'll see the new **Millennium Ferris wheel**. Downstairs are boats to the Tower of London and Greenwich.

To thrill your loved ones (or bug the envious), call home from a pay phone near Big Ben at about three minutes before the hour. You'll find a phone on Great George Street, across from Parliament Square. As Big Ben chimes, stick the receiver outside the booth and prove you're in London: Ding dong ding dong... dong ding ding dong.

Wave hello to Churchill in the park. To his right is **Westminster Abbey** with its two stubby, elegant towers.

Walk north up Parliament Street (which turns into Whitehall) toward Trafalgar Square. As you stroll along this center-of-government boulevard, you'll see the thought-provoking **Cenotaph** in the middle of the street, reminding passersby of Britain's many war dead. To visit the Cabinet War Rooms (see "Sights," below) take a left before the Cenotaph, on King Charles Street.

Continuing on Whitehall, stop at the barricaded and guarded little **Downing Street** to see the British "White House" at **#10**, home of the prime minister. Break the bobby's boredom and ask him a question.

Central London

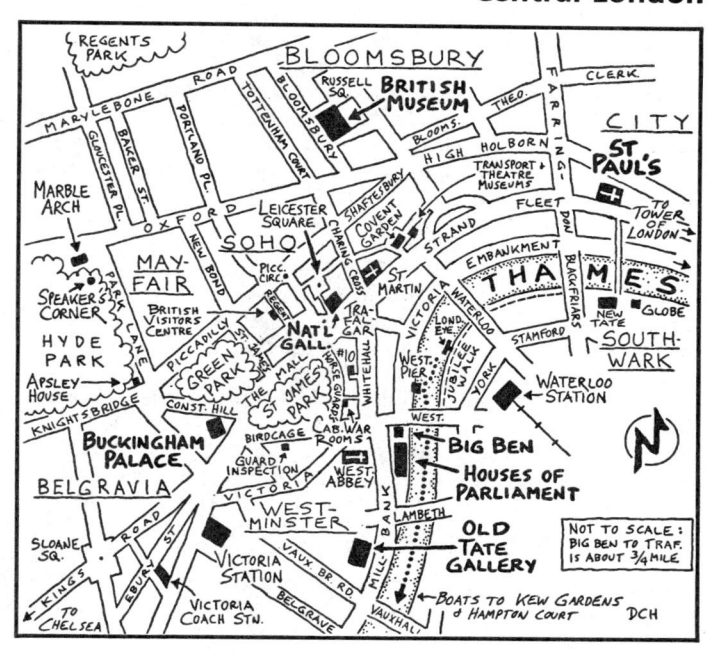

Nearing Trafalgar Square, look for the **Horse Guards** behind the gated fence (11:00 inspection Mon–Sat, 10:00 on Sun; dismounting ceremony daily at 16:00) and the 17th-century **Banqueting House** across the street (see "Sights," below).

The column topped by Lord Nelson marks **Trafalgar Square**. The stately domed building on the far side of the square is the **National Gallery** (free) which has a classy café (upstairs in the Sainsbury wing). To the right of the National Gallery is **St. Martin-in-the-Fields Church** and its Café in the Crypt (see "Eating," below).

To get to Piccadilly from Trafalgar Square, walk up Cockspur Street to Haymarket and then take a short left on Coventry Street to colorful **Piccadilly Circus**.

Near Piccadilly you'll find the **British Tourist Information Centre** and piles of theaters. **Leicester Square** (with its half-price ticket booth for plays) thrives just a few blocks away. Walk through seedy **Soho** (north of Shaftesbury Avenue) for its fun pubs (see "Eating," below, for "Food is Fun" Dinner Crawl). From Piccadilly or Oxford Circus, you can taxi, bus, or tube home.

▲▲▲**Westminster Abbey**—England's historic coronation church is a crowded collection of famous tombs. Like a stony refugee camp huddled outside St. Peter's gates, this is an English hall of fame. Choose among tours (Walkman-£2 or live-£3). Consider attending an evensong (weekdays except Wed at 17:00, Sat and Sun at 15:00) or the Sunday 17:45 organ recital (£5 for abbey entry, tours extra; Mon–Fri 9:15–16:45, Sat 9:00–14:45, technically no visitors on Sun, also open for half price on Wed 18:00–19:45—the only time photography is allowed; last admission one hour before closing, lattés in the cloister, tube: Westminster, tel. 020/7222-7110). For a free peek at the nave with no line, enter via Deans Yard (arch near west end of church) and go through the group entrance as if you're going to the museum. At the cloister, turn left and enter the nave. Since the church is often closed to the public for special services, it's wise to call first. Praying is free; use separate marked entrance.

▲▲**Houses of Parliament (Palace of Westminster)**—This neo-Gothic icon of London, the royal residence from 1042 to 1547, is now the meeting place of the legislative branch of government. While Parliament is too tempting to terrorists to be opened wide to tourists, you can view debates in either the bickering House of Commons or the genteel House of Lords if they're in session—indicated by a flag flying atop the Victoria Tower (Mon, Tue, and Thu 14:30–22:00, Wed 9:30–22:00, Fri 9:30–15:00, generally less action and no lines after 18:00, use St. Stephen's entrance, tube: Westminster, tel. 020/7219-4272 for schedule).

While it's not worth a long wait and the actual action is generally extremely dull, it is a thrill to be inside and see the British government inaction. The House of Lords has more pageantry, shorter lines, and less-interesting debates (tel. 020/7219-3107 for schedule). If confronted with a too-long House of Commons line, see the House of Lords first. Once you've seen the Lords (hide your HOL flyer), you can often slip directly to the Commons—joining the gang waiting in the lobby. If there's only one line outside, it's for the House of Commons. Go to the gate and tell the guard you want the Lords. You may pop right in. While other guidebooks tout the U.S. Embassy "entry cards," which get you directly in, they give out only four per day, and landing one is most likely hopeless.

After passing security, slip to the left and study the big dark **Westminster Hall,** which survived the 1834 fire. The hall is 11th century, and its famous self-supporting hammer-beam roof was added in 1397. The Houses of Parliament are located in what was once the Palace of Westminster, long the palace of England's medieval kings, until it was largely destroyed by fire in 1834. The palace was rebuilt in Victorian Gothic style (a move away from neoclassicism back to England's Christian and medieval heritage, true to the Romantic age). It was completed in 1860; only a few of its 1,000 rooms are open to the public.

The **Jewel Tower** is (along with Westminster Hall) about the only surviving part of the old Palace of Westminster. It contains a fine little exhibit on Parliament: first floor—history, second floor—Parliament today, with a 30-minute video and lonely picnic-friendly benches (£1.50, daily 10:00–18:00, closing at 16:00 or 17:00 off-season, across the street from St. Stephen's Gate, tel. 020/7222-2219).

The clock tower (315 feet high) is named for its 13-ton bell, Ben. The light above the clock is lit when the House of Commons is sitting. For a hip HOP view, walk halfway over Westminster Bridge.

▲▲**Cabinet War Rooms**—This is a fascinating walk through the underground headquarters of the British government's fight against the Nazis in the darkest days of the Battle for Britain. The 21-room nerve center of the British war effort was used from 1939 to 1945. Churchill's room, the map room, and so on, are just as they were in 1945. For all the blood, sweat, toil, and tears details, pick up the headsets at the entry and follow the included and excellent 45-minute audio guide (£4.80, daily 9:30–18:00, last admission 17:15, on King Charles Street 200 yards off Whitehall, follow the signs, tube: Westminster, tel. 020/7930-6961).

Horse Guards—The Horse Guards change daily at 11:00 (10:00 on Sunday), and there's a colorful dismounting ceremony daily at 16:00. The rest of the day they just stand there—terrible for camcorders (on Whitehall, between Trafalgar Square and #10 Downing Street, tube: Westminster). While Buckingham Palace pageantry is canceled when it rains, the horse guards change regardless of the weather.

▲**Banqueting House**—England's first Renaissance building was designed by Inigo Jones around 1620. It's one of the few London landmarks spared by the 1666 fire and the only surviving part of the original Palace of Whitehall. Don't miss its Rubens ceiling, which, at Charles I's request, drove home the doctrine of the legitimacy of the divine right of kings. In 1649, divine right ignored, Charles I was beheaded on the balcony of this building by a Cromwellian parliament. Admission includes a restful 15-minute audiovisual history, which shows the place in banqueting action, a 30-minute tape-recorded tour that is interesting only to history buffs, and a look at a fancy banqueting hall (£3.80, Mon–Sat 10:00–17:00, last entry at 16:15, subject to closure for government functions, aristocratic WC, immediately across Whitehall from the Horse Guards, tube: Westminster, tel. 020/7930-4179). Just up the street is...

Sights—Trafalgar Square

▲▲**Trafalgar Square**—London's central square is a thrilling place to just hang out. Lord Nelson stands atop his 185-foot-tall fluted granite column, gazing out to Trafalgar, where he lost his

National Gallery Highlights

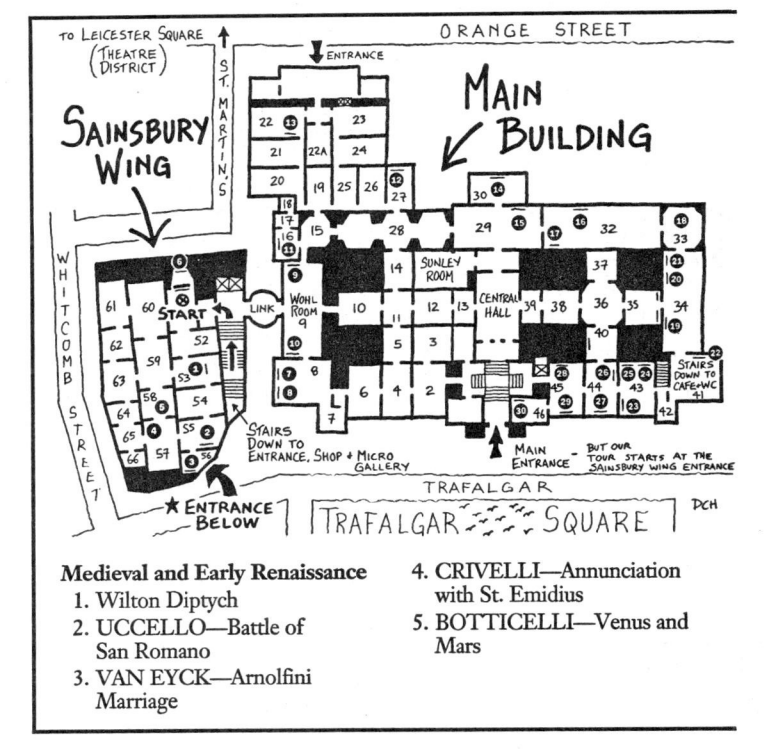

Medieval and Early Renaissance
1. Wilton Diptych
2. UCCELLO—Battle of San Romano
3. VAN EYCK—Arnolfini Marriage
4. CRIVELLI—Annunciation with St. Emidius
5. BOTTICELLI—Venus and Mars

life but defeated the French fleet. Part of this 1842 memorial is made from the melted-down cannons of his victims at Trafalgar. He's surrounded by giant lions, hordes of people, and even more pigeons. Buy a 25p cup of bird-pleasing seed. To make the birds explode into flight, simply toss a sweater into the air. This high-profile square is the climax of most marches and demonstrations (tube: Charing Cross).

▲▲▲**National Gallery**—Wonderfully renovated, displaying Britain's top collection of European paintings from 1250 to 1900 (works by Leonardo, Botticelli, Velázquez, Rembrandt, Turner, van Gogh, and the Impressionists), this is one of Europe's great galleries. While the collection is huge, following the 30-stop route suggested on these pages will give you my best quick tour. Don't miss the "Micro Gallery," a computer room even your dad could have fun in (closes 30 minutes earlier than museum). You can study

High Renaissance
6. LEONARDO DA VINCI—Virgin and Child (painting and cartoon)
7. MICHELANGELO—Entombment
8. RAPHAEL—Pope Julius II

Venetian Renaissance
9. TINTORETTO—Origin of the Milky Way
10. TITIAN—Bacchus and Ariadne

Northern Protestant Art
11. VERMEER—Young Woman Standing at a Virginal
12. REMBRANDT—Self-Portrait
13. REMBRANDT—Belshazzar's Feast

Baroque and Rococo
14. RUBENS—The Judgment of Paris
15. VAN DYCK—Charles I on Horseback
16. VELÁZQUEZ—The Rokeby Venus
17. CARAVAGGIO—Supper at Emmaus
18. BOUCHER—Pan and Syrinx

British
19. CONSTABLE—The Hay Wain
20. TURNER—The Fighting Téméraire
21. TURNER—Rain, Steam, Speed

Impressionism and Beyond
22. DELAROCHE—The Execution of Lady Jane Grey
23. MONET—Gare St. Lazare
24. MANET—The Waitress (La Servante de Bocks)
25. DEGAS— Miss La La at the Cirque Fernando
26. RENOIR—The Umbrellas
27. SEURAT—Bathers at Asnieres
28. VAN GOGH—Sunflowers
29. CÉZANNE—Bathers
30. MONET—Water Lilies

any artist, style, or topic in the museum and even print out a tailor-made tour map (free, daily 10:00–18:00, Wed until 21:00, free 1-hour tours weekdays at 11:30 and 14:30, on Trafalgar Square, tube: Charing Cross or Leicester Square, tel. 020/7747-2885). The CD Walkman tours are the best I've used in Europe (£3 donation requested).

▲**National Portrait Gallery**—Put off by halls of 19th-century characters who meant nothing to me, I used to call this "as interesting as someone else's yearbook." But a select walk through this five-centuries-long Who's Who of British history is quick and free and puts faces on the story of England. A bonus is the chance to admire some great art by painters such as Holbein, Van Dyck, Hogarth, Reynolds, and Gainsborough. The collection is well described, not huge, and in historical sequence, from the 16th century on the top floor to today's royal family on the bottom.

Some highlights: Henry VIII and wives; several fascinating portraits of the "Virgin Queen" Elizabeth I, Sir Francis Drake, and Sir Walter Raleigh; the only real-life portrait of Shakespeare; Oliver Cromwell and Charles I with his head on; self-portraits and other portraits by Gainsborough and Reynolds; the Romantics (Blake, Byron, Wordsworth, and company); Queen Victoria and her era; and the present royal family, including the late Princess Diana. For more information, follow the fine CD Walkman tours (£3 donation requested, tells more about history than art, hear actual interviews with 20th-century subjects) or get the 60p quick overview guidebooklet (free, Mon–Sat 10:00–18:00, Sun 12:00–18:00, entry 100 yards off Trafalgar Square, around the corner from the National Gallery, opposite Church of St. Martin-in-the-Fields, tel. 020/7306-0055).

▲St. Martin-in-the-Fields—This church, built in the 1720s, with a Gothic spire placed upon a Greek-type temple, is an oasis of peace on wild and noisy Trafalgar Square. St. Martin cared for the poor. "In the fields" was where the first church stood on this spot (in the 13th century), between Westminster and the City. Stepping inside, you still feel a compassion for the needs of the people in this community. The church is famous for its concerts. Consider a free lunchtime concert (most weekdays at 13:05) or an evening concert (Thu, Fri, and Sat at 19:30, £6–15, tel. 020/7930-0089). Downstairs you'll find a ticket office for concerts, a good shop, a brass-rubbing centre, and a fine budget support-the-church cafeteria (see "Eating").

More Top Squares: Piccadilly, Soho, and Covent Garden

▲▲Piccadilly Circus—London's touristy "Town Square" is surrounded by fascinating streets and swimming with youth on the rampage. The Rock Circus offers a commercial but serious history of rock music with Madame Tussaud wax stars. While overpriced, it's an entertaining hour under radio earphones for rock 'n' roll romantics—many enter with a beer buzz and sing happily off-key under their headphones—nearly as entertaining as the exhibit itself (£8, daily 10:00–20:00, plenty of photo ops, tube: Piccadilly Circus). For overstimulation, drop by the extremely trashy Pepsi Trocadero Center's "theme park of the future" for its Segaworld virtual reality games, nine-screen cinema, and thundering IMAX theater (admission to Trocadero is free; individual attractions cost £2–8; find a discount ticket at brochure racks at TI or hotels before paying full price for IMAX; between Coventry and Shaftesbury, just off Piccadilly). Chinatown, to the east, has swollen since Hong Kong lost its independence. Nearby Shaftesbury Avenue and Leicester Square teem with fun seekers, theaters, Chinese restaurants, and street singers.

Soho—North of Piccadilly, seedy Soho is becoming trendy and is well worth a gawk. Soho is London's red-light district, where "friendly models" wait in tiny rooms up dreary stairways and scantily clad con artists sell strip shows. While venturing up a stairway to check out a model is interesting, anyone who goes into any one of the shows will be ripped off. Every time. Even a £3 show comes with a £100 cover or minimum (as it's printed on the drink menu) and a "security man." You may accidently buy a £200 bottle of bubbly. And suddenly, the door has no handle. By the way, telephone sex is hard to avoid these days in London. Phone booths are littered with racy flyers of busty ladies "new in town." Some travelers gather six or eight phone booths' worth of flyers and take them home for kinky wallpaper.

▲▲**Covent Garden**—This boutique-ish shopping district is a people watcher's delight with cigarette eaters, Punch-and-Judy acts, food that's good for you (but not your wallet), trendy crafts, sweet whiffs of pot, two-tone hair (neither natural), and faces that could set off a metal detector (tube: Covent Garden). For better Covent Garden lunch deals, walk a block or two away from the eye of this touristic hurricane (check out the places a block or two north of the tube station along Endell Street and Neal Street—try Food for Thought at #31 Neal), and for a "Food is Fun" Dinner Crawl from Covent Garden to Soho, see "Eating," below.

Sights—North London

▲▲▲**British Museum**—This is the greatest chronicle of our civilization anywhere. Visiting this immense museum is like hiking through Encyclopedia Britannica National Park. After an overview ramble, cover just two or three sections of your choice more thoroughly. The Egyptian, Mesopotamian (Assyrian), and Greek (Parthenon) sections are highlights.

The huge winged lions (which guarded Assyrian palaces 800 years before Christ) guard the museum's three great ancient galleries. For a brief tour, connect these ancient dots:

Start with the **Egyptian**. Wander from the Rosetta Stone past the many statues. At the end of the hall, climb the stairs to mummy land.

Back at the winged lions, wander through the dark, violent, and mysterious **Assyrian** rooms. The Nimrud Gallery is lined with royal propaganda reliefs and wounded lions.

The most modern of the ancient art fills the **Greek** section. Find room 1 behind the winged lions and start your walk through Greek art history with the simple and primitive Cycladic fertility figures. Later, painted vases show a culture really into partying. The finale is the Elgin Marbles. The much-wrangled-over bits of the Athenian Parthenon (from 450 B.C.) are even more impressive than they look. To best appreciate these ancient carvings, read through the orientation material in the tiny area between rooms 7 and 8 (free, £2 donation requested, Mon–Sat 10:00–17:00, Sun

12:00–18:00, least crowded weekday late afternoons, guided 90-minute £7 tours offered daily—4/day—call museum for times, free "eye-opener" 50-minute talks on particular subjects nearly hourly—schedule at entry, Great Russell Street, tube: Tottenham Court Road, tel. 020/7636-1555, www.british-museum.ac.uk).

The British Museum is undergoing a major transformation for the millennium and for its 250th birthday in 2003. With more than 6 million visitors a year, Britain's most popular museum was due for an upgrade. In the fall, the Great Court, previously unused, will become the two-acre, glass-domed hub of a new cultural complex. From here you enter a reorganized (better-flowing) British museum, a restored and once-again-public Round Reading Room (Marx's hangout), new Ethnographic Galleries (collections on life in Africa, Asia, and the Americas), and a bustling people zone of shops and restaurants. For the latest, see www.british-museum.ac.uk.

▲▲▲British Library—In the new and impressive British Library, wander through the manuscripts that have enlightened and brightened our lives for centuries. While the library contains 180 miles of bookshelves in London's deepest basement, one beautiful room filled with state-of-the-art glass display cases shows you the treasures: ancient maps, early Gospels on papyrus, illuminated manuscripts from the early Middle Ages, the Gutenberg Bible, the Magna Carta, pages from Leonardo's notebooks, and original writing by the titans of English literature, from Chaucer and Shakespeare to Dickens and Wordsworth. There's also a wall dedicated to music, with manuscripts from Beethoven to the Beatles. To virtually flip through the pages of a few precious books, drop by the "Turning the Pages" room (free, Mon–Fri 9:30–18:00, Tue 9:30–20:00, Sat 9:30–17:00, Sun 11:00–17:00, tube: King's Cross/St. Pancras, leaving station, turn right and walk a block to 96 Euston Road, tel. 020/7412-7332, www.bl.uk).

▲Madame Tussaud's Waxworks—This is expensive but dang good. The original Madame Tussaud did wax casts of heads lopped off during the French Revolution (e.g., Marie Antoinette). She took her show on the road and ended up in London. And now it's much easier to be featured. The gallery is one big Who's Who photo op—a huge hit with the kind of travelers who skip the British Museum. Don't miss the "make a model" exhibit (showing Jerry Hall getting waxed) or the gallery of has-been heads that no longer merit a body (such as Sammy Davis Jr. and Nikita Khrushchev). After looking a hundred famous people in the glassy eyes and surviving a silly hall of horror, you'll board a Disney-type ride and cruise through a kid-pleasing "Spirit of London" time trip (£11, children £7, under five free, daily 9:00–18:00, last admission 17:30, closes at 17:00 in winter, Marylebone Road, tube: Baker Street, tel. 020/7935-6861; combined ticket for Tussaud's

and Planetarium is £13 adults, £8.50 kids). Avoid a wait by arriving late in the day—90 minutes is plenty of time for the exhibit.
Sir John Soane's Museum—Architects and fans of eclectic knick-knacks love this quirky place (free, Tue–Sat 10:00–17:00, closed Sun and Mon, 13 Lincoln's Inn Fields, 5 blocks east of British Museum, tube: Holborn, tel. 020/7405-2107).

Sights—Buckingham Palace
▲**Buckingham Palace**—This has been the royal residence since 1837. When the queen's at home, the royal standard flies; otherwise the Union Jack flaps in the wind. To pay for the restoration of fire-damaged Windsor Castle, the royal family is opening its lavish home to the public through 2000 (£10 to see the state apartments and throne room, open Aug and Sept only, daily 9:30–16:30, only 8,000 visitors a day—come early to get an appointed visit time or call 020/7321-2233 and reserve a ticket with your credit card, tube: Victoria).
▲▲**Changing of the Guard at Buckingham Palace**—The guards change with much fanfare at 11:30 daily through May and June and generally every even-numbered day July through April (no band when wet; worth a phone call any day to confirm that they'll change; tel. 020/7930-4832). Join the mob at the back side of the palace (the front faces a huge and extremely private park). You'll need to be early or tall to see much of the actual changing of the guard, but for the pageantry in the street you can pop by at 11:30. Stake out the high ground on the circular Victoria Monument for the best general views. The marching troops and bands are colorful and even stirring, but the actual changing of the guard is a nonevent. It is interesting, however, to see nearly every tourist in London gathered in one place at the same time. Hop into a big black taxi and say, "Buck House, please." The show lasts about 30 minutes: Three troops parade by, the guard changes with much shouting, the band plays a happy little concert, and then they march out. On a balmy day, it's a fun happening.

For all the color with none of the crowds, see the **Inspection of the Guard Ceremony** at 11:00 in front of the **Wellington Barracks**, 500 yards east of the palace on Birdcage Walk. Afterwards, stroll through nearby St. James' Park (tube: Victoria, St. James' Park, or Green Park).

Sights—West London
▲**Hyde Park and Speakers' Corner**—London's "Central Park"—originally Henry VIII's hunting ground—has more than 600 acres of lush greenery, a huge man-made lake, the royal Kensington Palace (not worth touring), and the ornate neo-Gothic Albert Memorial across from the Royal Albert Hall. Early afternoons on Sunday, Speaker's Corner offers soapbox oratory at its

best (tube: Marble Arch). "The grass roots of democracy" is actually a holdover from when the gallows stood here and the criminal was allowed to say just about anything he wanted to before he swung. I dare you to raise your voice and gather a crowd—it's easy to do.

▲**Apsley House (Wellington Museum)**—Having beat Napoleon at Waterloo, the Duke of Wellington was the most famous man in Europe. He was given London's ultimate address, #1 London. His newly refurbished mansion offers one of London's best palace experiences. An 11-foot-tall marble statue (by Canova) of Napoleon clad only in a fig leaf greets you. Downstairs is a small gallery of Wellington memorabilia (including a 30-minute video and a pair of Wellington boots). The lavish upstairs shows off the duke's fine collection of paintings, including works by Velázquez and Steen (well described by included CD tour wand, £4.50, Tue–Sun 11:00–17:00, closed Mon, 20 yards from Hyde Park Corner tube station, tel. 020/7499-5676). Hyde Park's pleasant and picnic-wonderful rose garden is nearby.

▲▲**Victoria and Albert Museum**—The world's top collection of decorative arts is a gangly (150 rooms over 12 miles of corridors) but surprisingly interesting assortment of artistic stuff from the West as well as Asian and Islamic cultures. The V&A, which grew out of the Great Exhibition of 1851—that ultimate festival celebrating the Industrial Revolution and the greatness of Britain—was originally for manufactured art. But after much support from Queen Victoria and Prince Albert, it was renamed after the royal couple, and its present building was opened in 1909. The idealistic Victorian notion that anyone can be continually improved by education and example remains the driving force behind this museum.

While just wandering works well here, consider catching one of the regular 60-minute orientation tours, buying the fine £5 Hundred Highlights guidebook, or walking through these ground-floor highlights: Medieval Treasury (room 43, well-described treasury of Middle Age European art), the finest collection of Indian decorative art outside India (room 41), the Dress Gallery (room 40, 400 years of English fashion corseted into 40 display cases), the Raphael Gallery (room 48a, seven huge watercolor "cartoons" painted as designs for tapestries to hang in the Sistine Chapel, among the greatest art treasures in Britain and the best works of the High Renaissance), reliefs by the Renaissance sculptor Donatello (room 16), a close-up look at medieval stained glass (room 28, much more upstairs), the fascinating Cast Courts (rooms 46a and 46b, filled with plaster copies of the greatest art of our civilization—such as Trajan's Column and Michelangelo's *David*—made for the benefit of 19th-century art students who couldn't afford a railpass), and the hall of "great" fakes and forgeries (room 46). Upstairs you can walk through the British Galleries for centuries of aristocratic living

London 291

rooms (£5, daily 10:00–18:00, and usually Wed evenings until 21:30 in summer, free after 16:30; the museum café is in the delightfully ornate Gamble Room from 1868, just off room 14, tube: South Kensington, a long tunnel leads directly from the tube station to the museum, tel. 020/7938-8500).

▲**Natural History Museum**—Across the street from the Victoria and Albert Museum, this mammoth museum is housed in a giant and wonderful Victorian neo-Romanesque building. Built in the 1870s specifically to house the huge collection (50 million specimens), it presents itself in two halves: the Life Galleries (creepy-crawlies, human biology, the origin of the species, "our place in evolution," and awesome dinosaurs) and the Earth Galleries (meteors, volcanoes, earthquakes, and so on). Exhibits are wonderfully explained with lots of creative interactive displays (£6.50, children under 16 free, free to anyone after 16:30 on weekdays and after 17:00 on weekends—pop in if only for the wild collection of dinosaurs, Mon–Sat 10:00–18:00, Sun 11:00–18:00, a long tunnel leads directly from the South Kensington tube station to the museum, tel. 020/7938-9123, www.nhm.ac.uk).

Sights—East London: "The City"

▲▲**The City of London**—When Londoners say "The City," they mean the one-square-mile business, banking, and journalism center that 2,000 years ago was Roman Londinium. The outline of the Roman city walls can still be seen in the arc of roads from Blackfriars Bridge to Tower Bridge. Within the City are 24 churches designed by Christopher Wren. Today, while home to only 5,000 residents, the City thrives with over 500,000 office workers coming and going daily. It's a fascinating district to wander, but since almost nobody actually lives there, it's dull on Saturday and Sunday.

▲**Old Bailey**—An hour sitting in the public galleries of the City's Central Criminal Courts, known as "Old Bailey," is always interesting (free, Mon–Fri 10:30–13:00, 14:00–16:30, quiet in August, ask at door which trials are where, no cameras, no bags, no cloakroom, no kids under 14, at Old Bailey and Newgate Streets, tube: St. Paul's, tel. 020/7248-3277).

▲▲▲**St. Paul's Cathedral**—Wren's most famous church is the great St. Paul's, its elaborate interior capped by a 365-foot dome. During World War II, when Nazi bombs failed to blow it up, St. Paul's became Britain's symbol of resistance. The crypt (free with admission) is a world of historic bones and memorials, including Admiral Nelson's tomb and interesting cathedral models. This was the wedding church of Prince Charles and the late Princess Diana (1981). Sit under the second-largest dome in the world and eavesdrop on guided tours. Climb the dome for some fun in the whispering gallery (where the precisely designed barrel of the dome lets sweet nothings circle audibly around to the

The City

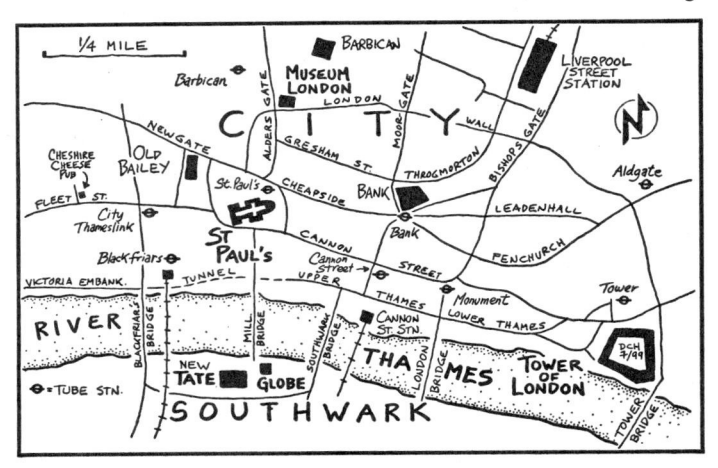

opposite side) and a great city view (£4 entry, free on Sun but restricted viewing due to services, £3.50 extra to climb dome—allow an hour to climb up and down; open daily 9:00–16:30, last entry 16:00, £3.50 for guided 90-minute cathedral and crypt tours offered at 11:00, 11:30, 13:30, and 14:00 or £3 for a Walkman tour anytime, Sunday services at 8:00, 10:15, 11:30, and 15:15, evensong weekdays at 17:00, good restaurant and cheap and cheery café in the crypt, tube: St. Paul's, tel. 020/ 7236-8348).

▲**Museum of London**—Stroll through London history from pre-Roman times through the Blitz up to today. This regular stop for the local schoolkids gives the best overview of London history in town (£5, free after 16:30, Mon–Sat 10:00–18:00, Sun 12:00–18:00, tube: Barbican or St. Paul's, tel. 020/7600-3699).

Geffrye Decorative Arts Museum—Walk through British front rooms from 1600 to 1990 (free, Tue–Sat 10:00–17:00, Sun 12:00–17:00, closed Mon, tube: Liverpool Street, then bus 149 or 242 north, tel. 020/7739-9893).

▲▲▲**Tower of London**—The Tower has served as a castle in wartime, a king's residence in peace, and, most notorious, as the prison and execution site of rebels. This historic fortress is host to more than 3 million visitors a year. Enjoy the free, and riotously entertaining, 50-minute Beefeater tour (leaves regularly from inside the gate, last one is usually at 15:25). The crown jewels, dating from the Restoration, are the best on earth—and come with hour-long lines for most of the day. To avoid the crowds, arrive at

9:00 and go straight for the jewels, doing the tour and tower later—or do the jewels after 16:30 (£10.50, Mon–Sat 9:00–18:00, Sun 10:00–18:00, the long but fast-moving ticket line is worst on Sundays, last entry at 17:00, tube: Tower Hill, tel. 020/7709-0765, recorded info: 020/7680-9004).

Ceremony of the Keys: Every night at 21:30, with pageantry-filled ceremony, the Tower of London is locked up (as it has been for the last 700 years). To attend this free 30-minute event, you need to request an invitation at least five weeks before your visit. Write to: Ceremony of the Keys, H.M. Tower of London, London EC3N 4AB. Include your name; the addresses, names, and ages of all people attending (up to 7, nontransferable); requested date; alternative dates; and an international reply coupon (buy at a U.S. post office).

Sights next to the Tower—The best remaining bit of London's **Roman Wall** is just north of the tower (at the Tower Hill tube station). Freshly painted and restored, **Tower Bridge**—the neo-Gothic maritime gateway to London—has an 1894 to 1994 history exhibit (£6.20, daily 10:00–18:30, last entry at 17:15, good view, poor value, tel. 020/7403-3761). **St. Katherine Yacht Harbor**, chic and newly renovated, just east of the Tower Bridge, has mod shops and the classic old Dickens Inn, fun for a drink or pub lunch. Across the bridge is the South Bank, with the upscale Butlers Wharf area, museums, and promenade.

Sights—South London, on the South Bank

The South Bank is rapidly becoming a thriving arts and cultural center tied together by a riverside path. This trendy, pub-crawling walk—called the Jubilee Promenade—stretches from the Tower of London bridge past Westminster Bridge, with grand views of the Houses of Parliament. (The promenade hugs the river except just east of London Bridge, where it cuts inland for a couple of blocks.)

▲▲**Globe Theater**—The original Globe Theater has been rebuilt—half-timbered and thatched—exactly as it was in Shakespeare's time. It's open as a museum and hosts authentic old-time performances of Shakespeare's plays. The theater is open to tour when there are no plays (£6, daily 9:00–12:00, Oct–Apr 10:00–17:00, includes guided 30-minute tour offered on the half hour). In 2000 the Globe expands its exhibition on the history of the Globe Theater to include the beginnings of theater plus more on Shakespeare, his workplace, and his contemporaries. Expect interactive displays and possibly film presentations, a sound lab, a script factory, and a costume exhibit (included in £6 theater admission, daily 10:00–17:00, Oct–Apr 9:00–16:00, on the South Bank directly across the Thames over Southwark Bridge from St. Paul's, tube: Mansion House, tel. 020/7902-1500, for details on seeing a play, see "Entertainment," below).

▲▲**Tate Gallery of Modern Art**—Open in May of 2000, this new museum across the river from St. Paul's opens the new century with art from the old one (remember the 20th century?). This powerhouse collection of Monet, Matisse, Dalí, Picasso, Warhol, and much more is displayed in a converted power house (free, special exhibitions cost extra, probably daily 10:00–18:00, Walkman tours, free guided tours, call for schedule, walk the new Millennium Bridge from St. Paul's or tube: Southwark plus a 7-minute walk, tel. 020/7887-8000).

▲▲**Millennium Bridge**—Linking St. Paul's Cathedral and the new Tate Gallery of Modern Art, this new bridge opens in April 2000. Its sleek minimalist design—370 meters long, 4 meters wide, stainless steel with teak planks—has clever aerodynamic handrails to deflect wind over the heads of pedestrians. London's only pedestrian bridge is the first new bridge in a century (free, always open).

▲▲▲**Millennium Ferris Wheel (a.k.a. The British Airways London Eye)**—Sponsored by British Airways, the Ferris wheel towers above London opposite Big Ben on the South Bank of the Thames. At 450 feet tall, the world's highest observational wheel offers you the highest public viewpoint in London—and a chance to fly British Air without leaving the city. Built like a giant bicycle wheel, it's a pan-European undertaking: British steel and Dutch engineering, with Czech, German, French, and Italian mechanical parts. It's also very "green," running extremely efficiently and virtually silently. Twenty-five people will ride in each of its 32 capsules for the 30-minute rotation. In 2005 it will be dismantled and moved to a lower-profile location (probably £5, tel. 020/7738-8080).

▲▲**Imperial War Museum**—This impressive museum covers the wars of this century, from heavy weaponry to love notes and Varga Girls, from Monty's Africa campaign tank to Schwartzkopf's Desert Storm uniform. You can trace the development of the machine gun, watch footage of the first tank battles, hold your breath through the gruesome WWI trench experience, and buy WWII-era toys in the fun museum shop. Rather than glorify war, the museum does its best to shine a light on the powerful human side of one of mankind's most persistent traits (£5.20, free for kids under 16, daily 10:00–18:00, free for anyone after 16:30, 90 minutes is enough time for most visitors, tube: Lambeth North, tel. 020/7416-5000).

Bramah Tea and Coffee Museum—Aficionados of tea or coffee will find this small museum fascinating. It tells the story of each drink almost passionately. The owner, Mr. Bramah, comes from a big tea family and wants the world to know how the advent of commercial television, with breaks not long enough to brew a proper pot of tea, required a faster hot drink. In came the horrible English instant coffee. Tea countered with finely chopped leaves in tea bags, and it's gone downhill ever since

(£4, daily 10:00–18:00, in the Butlers Wharf complex just across the bridge from the Tower, behind the Design Museum, tel. 020/7378-0222). Its café, which serves more kinds of coffees and teas than cakes, is open to the public, not just museum goers (same hours as museum).

Sights—South London, on the North Bank

▲▲Tate Gallery of British Art—One of Europe's great art houses, the Tate specializes in British painting: 16th century through the 20th, including Pre-Raphaelites. Commune with the mystical Blake and romantic Turner (free, daily 10:00–18:00, fine £3 CD Walkman tours, free tours weekdays, call for schedule, tube: Pimlico, tel. 020/7887-8000). In May 2000 the Tate's modern collection opens at the new Tate Gallery of Modern Art (on the South Bank; see above).

Sights—Greater London

▲Kew Gardens—For a fine riverside park and a palatial greenhouse jungle to swing through, take the tube or the boat to every botanist's favorite escape, Kew Gardens. While to most visitors the Royal Botanic Gardens of Kew is simply a delightful opportunity to wander among 33,000 different types of plants, it's run by a hardworking organization committed to understanding and preserving the botanical diversity of our planet. The Kew tube station drops you in an herbal little business community a two-block walk from Victoria Gate (the main garden entry). Watch the five-minute orientation video and pick up a map brochure with a monthly listing of best blooms.

Garden lovers could spend days exploring Kew's 300 acres. For a quick visit, spend a fragrant hour wandering through three buildings: the Palm House—a humid Victorian world of iron, glass, and tropical plants—built in 1844; a Waterlily House—hottest in the gardens—that Monet would swim for; and the Princess of Wales Conservatory—a modern greenhouse with many different climate zones growing countless cacti, bug-munching carnivorous plants, and more (£5, Mon–Sat 9:30–18:00, Sun 9:30–19:30, until 16:30 off-season, galleries and conservatories close a half hour earlier, entry discounted to £3.50 90 minutes before closing, consider the £2 narrated floral joyride on the little train departing from Victoria Gate, tube: Kew Gardens, tel. 020/8332-5000). For a sun-dappled lunch, hike 10 minutes from the Palm House to the Orangery (£6 hot meals, daily 10:00–17:30). For tea, consider the Maids of Honor (280 Kew Road, near garden entrance, tel. 020/8940-2752).

▲Hampton Court Palace—Fifteen miles up the Thames from downtown (£16 taxi ride from Kew Gardens) is the 500-year-old palace of Henry VIII. Actually, it was the palace of his minister,

Greater London

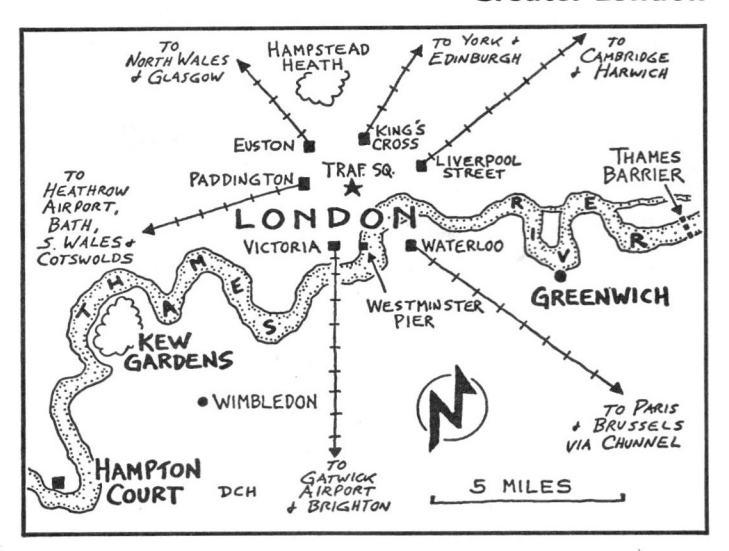

Cardinal Wolsey. When Wolsey, a clever man, realized Henry VIII was experiencing a little palace envy, he gave it to his king. The Tudor palace was also home to Elizabeth I and Charles I. And parts were updated by Christopher Wren for William and Mary. The palace stands stately overlooking the Thames and includes some impressive Tudor rooms, including a Great Hall, with its magnificent hammer-beam ceiling. The industrial-strength Tudor kitchen was capable of keeping 600 schmoozing courtesans thoroughly—if not well—fed. The sculpted garden features a rare Tudor tennis court and a popular maze. The palace, fully restored since its 1986 fire, tries hard to please, but it doesn't quite sparkle. From the information center in the main courtyard, visitors book times for tours with tired costumed guides or grab CD-ROM wands for self-guided tours of various wings of the palace (all free). The Tudor Kitchens, Henry VIII's Apartments, and the King's Apartments are most interesting. The Georgian Rooms are pretty dull. The maze in the nearby garden is a curiosity some find fun. The train (2/hrly, 30 min) from London's Waterloo station drops you just across the river from the palace (£10, Tue–Sun 9:30–18:00, 10:15–18:00 on Mondays, Nov–Mar until 16:30, tel. 020/8781-9500).

▲▲▲**Greenwich and New Millennium Dome**—See "Near London" at the end of this chapter.

Disappointments of London

The venerable BBC broadcasts from Broadcasting House. Of all its productions, its "BBC Experience" tour for visitors is among the worst. On the South Bank, the London Dungeon, a much-visited but amateurish attraction, is just a highly advertised, overpriced haunted house—certainly not worth the £10 admission, much less your valuable London time. It comes with long and rude lines. Wait for Halloween and see one in your hometown to support a better cause. The Design Museum (next to Bramah Tea and Coffee Museum) and "Winston Churchill's Britain at War Experience" (next to London Dungeon) waste your time. The Kensington Palace State Apartments are lifeless and not worth a visit.

Shopping in London

Harrods—Filled with wonderful displays, Harrods is London's most famous and touristy department store. Big yet classy, Harrods has everything from elephants to toothbrushes. The food halls are sights to savor, with cafeterias (Mon, Tue, and Sat 10:00–18:00, Wed–Fri 10:00–19:00, closed Sun, on Brompton Road, tube: Knightsbridge, tel. 020/7730-1234). Many readers report that Harrods is now overpriced (its £1 toilets are the most expensive in Europe), snooty, and teeming with American and Japanese tourists. Still, it's the palace of department stores—an experience for even nonshoppers. The nearby Beauchamp Place is lined with classy and fascinating shops.

Harvey Nichols—Princess Diana's favorite, this is the department store du jour. Its fifth floor is a food fest with a fancy restaurant and a Yo! Sushi bar. Consider a take-away tray of sushi to eat on a bench in the Hyde Park rose garden two blocks away (Mon–Tue and Sat 10:00–19:00, Wed–Fri 10:00–20:00, Sun 12:00–18:00, near Harrods, 109 Knightsbridge, tube: Knightsbridge).

Street Markets—Antique buffs, people watchers, and folks who brake for garage sales love London's street markets. There's good early morning market activity somewhere any day of the week. The best are Portobello Road (Fri–Wed 9:00–18:00, Thu 9:00–13:00, go Saturday for antiques until 16:00—plus the regular junk, clothes, and produce; tube: Notting Hill Gate) and Camden Market (Sat–Sun 10:00–18:00, trendy arts and crafts, tube: Camden Town). The tourist office has a complete, up-to-date list. If you like to haggle, there are no holds barred in London's street markets. Warning: Markets attract two kinds of people—tourists and pickpockets.

Famous Auctions—London's famous auctioneers welcome the curious public for viewing and bidding. For schedules, call Sotheby's (Mon–Fri 9:00–16:30, 34 New Bond Street, tube: Oxford Circus, tel. 020/7293-5000) or Christie's (during sales season:

Mon and Wed–Fri 9:00–16:30, Tue 9:00–20:00, 8 King Street, tube: Green Park, tel. 020/7839-9060).

Entertainment and Theater in London

London bubbles with top-notch entertainment seven days a week. Everything's listed in the weekly entertainment magazines, available at newsstands. Choose from classical, jazz, rock, and far-out music, Gilbert and Sullivan, dance, comedy, Baha'i meetings, poetry readings, spectator sports, film, and theater.

London's theater rivals Broadway's in quality and beats it in price. Choose from the Royal Shakespeare Company, top musicals, comedy, thrillers, sex farces, and more. Performances are nightly except Sunday, usually with one matinee a week. Matinees (Wed, Thu, or Sat) are cheaper and rarely sold out. Tickets range from about £8 to £35.

Most theaters, marked on tourist maps, are in the Piccadilly–Trafalgar area. Box offices, hotels, and TIs have a handy "Theater Guide" brochure listing what's playing.

To book a seat, simply call the theater box office directly, ask about seats and dates available, and buy one with your credit card. You can call from the U.S.A. as easily as from England (photocopy your hometown library's London newspaper theater section or check out www.officiallondontheatre.co.uk). Pick up your ticket 15 minutes before the show.

Ticket agencies are scalpers with an address. Booking through an agency (at most TIs or scattered throughout London) is quick and easy, but prices are inflated by a standard 25 percent fee. If buying from an agency, look at the ticket carefully (your price should be no more than 30 percent over the printed face value; the 17 percent VAT tax is already included in the face value) and understand where you're sitting according to the floor plan (if your view is restricted it will state this on ticket). Agencies are worthwhile only if a show you've got to see is sold out at the box office. They scarf up hot tickets, planning to make a killing after the show is sold out. U.S.A. booking agencies get their tickets from another agency, adding even more to your expense by involving yet another middleman. Many tickets sold on the streets are forgeries. With cheap international phone calls and credit cards, there's no reason not to book direct.

Theater lingo: stalls (ground floor), dress circle (first balcony), upper circle (second balcony), balcony (sky-high third balcony).

Cheap theater tricks: Most theaters offer cheap returned tickets, standing room, matinee, and senior or student standby deals. These "concessions" are indicated with a *conc* or *s* in the listings. Picking up a late return can get you a great seat at a cheap-seat price. Standing room can be very cheap. If a show is "sold out," there's usually a way to get a seat. Call the theater box office and ask how. I buy the second-cheapest tickets directly from the theater box office. The famous "half-price booth" in Leicester (pronounced "Lester") Square sells discounted tickets for good seats to shows on the push list the day of the show only (Mon–Sat 12:00–18:30). Note: The real half-price booth is a free-standing kiosk at the edge of the garden actually in Leicester Square. Several dishonest outfits advertise "official half-price tickets" at agencies closer to the tube station. Avoid these. Many theaters are so small that there's hardly a bad seat. After the lights go down, "scooting up" is less than a capital offense. Shakespeare did it.

Royal Shakespeare Company—If you'll ever enjoy Shakespeare, it'll be in Britain. The RSC splits its season between the Royal Shakespeare Theatre in Stratford (Jun–Sept, tel. 01789/403-403) and the Barbican Centre in London (Oct–May, daily 9:00–20:00, credit-card booking, tel. 020/7638-8891, or for recorded information, tel. 020/7628-9760). To get a schedule, either request it by phone (tel. 020/7638-8891), write to the Royal Shakespeare Theatre, Stratford-upon-Avon, CV37 6BB Warwickshire, or visit www.rsc.org.uk. Tickets range in price from £10 to £30. The best way to book is direct, by telephone and credit card. You can pick up your ticket at the door (Barbican Centre, Silk Street, tube: Barbican). Students, seniors, and those under 16 can get tickets for half price.

Shakespeare at the Globe Theater—To see Shakespeare in an exact replica of the theater for which he wrote his plays, attend a play at the Globe. This thatch-roofed, open-air round theater does the plays as Shakespeare intended (with no amplification). There are performances from May through September (usually Tue–Sat 14:00 and 19:30, Sun at either 13:00 and 18:30 or at 16:00 only, and no plays on Monday). You'll pay £5 to stand and £10 to £25 to sit (usually on a backless bench; only a few rows and the pricier Gentlemen's Rooms have seats with backs). The £5 "yard" (or "groundling") tickets—while the only ones open to rain—are most fun. You're a crude peasant. You can walk around, munch a picnic dinner, lean your elbows on the stage, and even interact with the actors. I've never enjoyed Shakespeare as much as here, performed as it was meant to be in the "wooden O." The theater is on the South Bank directly across the Thames over Southwark Bridge from St. Paul's (tube: Mansion House, tel. 020/7902-1500, box office 020/7401-9919 to book a ticket with your credit card). Plays are long. Many groundlings leave before the end. If you like, hang out an hour before the finish and beg or buy a ticket off someone leaving early (groundlings are allowed to come and go). The Globe is far from public transport, but the courtesy phone in the lobby gets a minicab in minutes. Confirm the cost, but they seem to be much cheaper than the official black cabs (£5 or £6 to Victoria Station).

London Day Trips

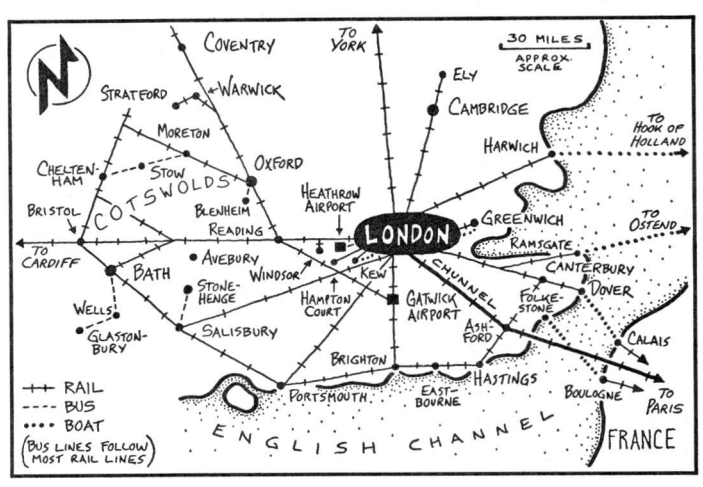

Music—For easy, cheap, or free concerts in historic churches, check the TI's listings for lunch concerts (especially Wren's St. Bride's Church, tel. 020/7353-1301, St. James at Piccadilly, and St. Martin-in-the-Fields, Mon–Tue and Fri at 13:00, tel. 020/7930-1862). St. Martin-in-the-Fields also hosts fine evening concerts by candlelight (Thu–Sat at 19:30, £6–16, tel. 020/7839-8362). For a fun classical event (Jun–Sept only), attend a "Prom Concert." This is an annual music festival with almost nightly concerts in the Royal Albert Hall at give-a-peasant-some-culture prices (£3 standing-room spots sold at the door, tel. 020/7589-8212).

Day Trips from London

You could fill a book with the many easy and exciting day trips from London (Earl Steinbicker did: *Daytrips London: Fifty One-Day Adventures by Rail or Car, in and around London and Southern England*). Several tour companies take London-based travelers out and back every day. Original London Walks offers a variety of day trips using the train for about £10 plus transportation costs (see their walking-tour brochure). Some big bus tours can be used by those without a car as a "free" way to get to Bath or Stow-on-the-Wold (saving you, for instance, the £32.50 London–Bath train ticket). Evan Evans' tours leave from behind Victoria Station daily at 9:00 (with your bag stowed under the bus), include a day of sightseeing, and leave you in Bath before returning to London (£25 for Stonehenge and Bath covers transportation only, or £46 to include tours and admissions; tel. 020/8332-2222). Travelline does a tour of Bath and Stonehenge for £25 (tel. 020/8668-7261, office in Fountain Square directly south of Victoria Station).

The British rail system uses London as a hub and normally offers round-trip fares (after 9:30) that cost virtually the same as one-way fares. "Day return" tickets are best (and cheapest) for day trips. You can save a little money if you purchase Super Advance tickets before 14:00 on the day before your trip. But given the high cost of big-city living and the charm of small-town England, rather than side-tripping I'd see London and get out.

Sleeping in London
(£1 = about $1.70, tel. code: 020)

Sleep Code: **S** = Single, **D** = Double/Twin, **T** = Triple, **Q** = Quad, **b** = bathroom, **t** = toilet only, **s** = shower only, **CC** = Credit Card (Visa, MasterCard, Amex). Unless otherwise noted, prices include a generous breakfast and all taxes.

London is expensive. For £50 ($80), you'll get a sleepable double with breakfast in a safe, cramped, and dreary place with minimal service. For £60 ($95) you'll get a basic, clean, reasonably cheery double in a usually cramped, cracked-plaster building or a soulless but comfortable room without breakfast in a huge Motel 6–type place. My London splurges, at £100 to £140 ($170–240), are spacious, thoughtfully appointed places you'd be happy to entertain or make love in. Hearty English or generous buffet breakfasts are included unless otherwise noted, and TVs are nearly standard in rooms.

Reserve your London room with a phone call or e-mail as soon as you can commit to a date. A few places will hold a room with no deposit if you promise to arrive by midday. Most take your credit-card number as security. Most have expensive cancellation policies. Some fancy £120 rooms rent for half price if you arrive late on a slow day and ask for a deal.

Sleeping in Victoria Station Neighborhood, Belgravia

The streets behind Victoria Station teem with budget B&Bs. It's a safe, surprisingly tidy, and decent area without a hint of the trashy touristy glitz of the streets in front of the station. Here in Belgravia, your neighbors include Andrew Lloyd Webber and Margaret Thatcher (her policeman stands outside 73 Chester Square). Decent eateries abound (see "Eating"). The cheaper listings are dumpy. Don't expect £90 cheeriness in a £50 room. Off-season save money by arriving late without a reservation and checking around. Fierce competition softens prices, especially for multinight stays. Particularly for Warwick Way hotels (and on hot summer nights), request a quiet back room. All are within a five-minute walk of the Victoria tube, bus, and train stations. There's

London, Victoria Station Neighborhood

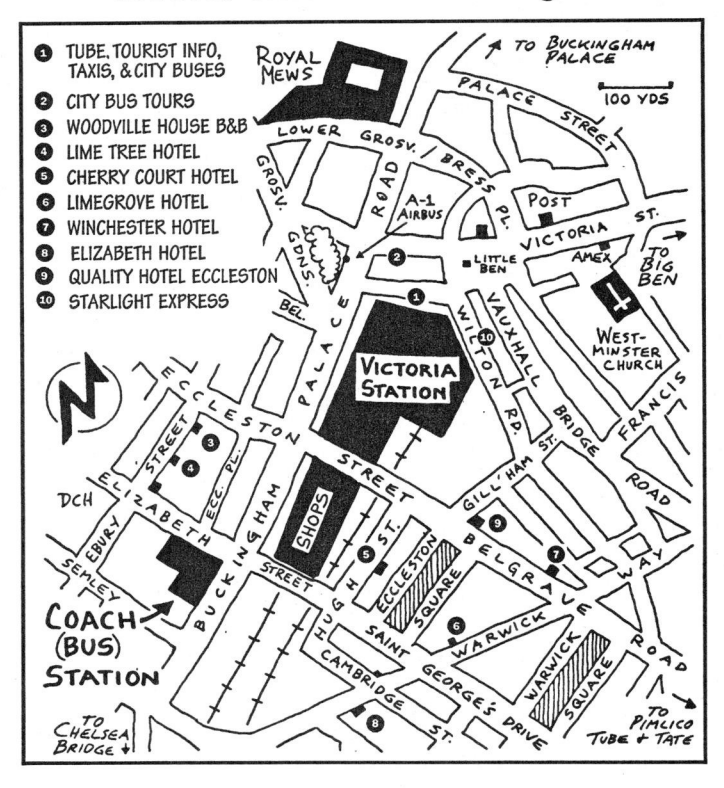

1. TUBE, TOURIST INFO, TAXIS, & CITY BUSES
2. CITY BUS TOURS
3. WOODVILLE HOUSE B&B
4. LIME TREE HOTEL
5. CHERRY COURT HOTEL
6. LIMEGROVE HOTEL
7. WINCHESTER HOTEL
8. ELIZABETH HOTEL
9. QUALITY HOTEL ECCLESTON
10. STARLIGHT EXPRESS

an £8-per-day garage and a nearby launderette (daily 8:00–20:30, self-serve or full-serve, past Warwick Square at 3 Westmoreland Terrace, tel. 020/7821-8692).

Winchester Hotel is family run and perhaps the best value, with 18 fine rooms, no claustrophobia, and a wise and caring management (Db-£75, Tb-£100, Qb-£115, no CC, no groups, no small children, 17 Belgrave Road, London SW1V 1RB, tel. 020/7828-2972, fax 020/7828-5191, Jimmy #1 cooks, Jimmy #2 greets).

In **Woodville House,** the quarters are dollhouse tight, showers are down the hall, and several rooms are on the noisy street (doubles on quiet backside, twins and singles on street), but this well-run, well-worn place is a good value, with lots of travel tips and friendly chat—especially about the local rich and famous—from Rachel

Joplin (S-£42, D-£62, bunky family deals-£80–110 for up to 5, CC:VM, 107 Ebury Street, SW1W 9QU, tel. 020/7730-1048, fax 020/7730-2574, e-mail: woodville.house@cwcom.net).

Lime Tree Hotel, enthusiastically run by David and Marilyn Davies, comes with spacious and thoughtfully decorated rooms and a fun-loving breakfast room. While priced a bit steep, the place has character plus (Sb-£75, Db-£95–105, Tb-£130, family room-£145, David deals in slow times and is creative at helping travelers in a bind, CC:VMA, 135 Ebury Street, SW1W 9RA, tel. 020/7730-8191, fax 020/7730-7865).

Elizabeth House feels institutional and a bit bland—as you might expect from a former YMCA—but the rooms are clean and bright, and the price is right (S-£30, D-£50, Db-£60, T-£75, Q-£85, CC:VM, 118 Warwick Way, SW1 4JB, tel. 020/7630-0741, fax 020/7630-0740).

Quality Hotel Eccleston is big, modern, well located, and a fine value for no-nonsense comfort (Db-£96, on slow days drop-ins can ask for "saver prices"—33 percent off on first night, breakfast extra, CC:VMA, nonsmoking floor, elevator, 82 Eccleston Square, SW1V 1PS, tel. 020/7834-8042, fax 020/7630-8942, e-mail: admin@gb614.u-net.com).

These three places come with cramped rooms and claustrophobic halls. While they generate a lot of reader complaints, I list them because they offer cheap beds at youth hostel prices and are beautifully located a few minutes' walk from Victoria Station: **Cherry Court Hotel** is run by the friendly and industrious Patel family (S-£30, Sb-£40, Db-£45, T-£50, Tb-£65, price promised with this book, CC:VMA, fruit basket breakfast in room, no twins—only double beds, 23 Hugh Street, SW1V 1QJ, tel. 020/7828-2840, fax 020/7828-0393, e-mail: info@cherrycourthotel.co.uk). **Cedar Guest House**, run by a Polish organization to help Poles afford London, welcomes all (D-£38, Db-£45, T-£54, 30 Hugh Street, SW1V 1RP, tel. 020/7828-2625). **Limegrove Hotel,** run by harried Joyce, more musty and run-down, serves a humble breakfast in the room (S-£28, D-£38, Db-£50, T-£48, Tb-£60, cheaper off-season, lots of stairs, 101 Warwick Way, SW1V 1QL, tel. 020/7828-0458). Back rooms are quieter.

Big, Cheap, Modern Hotels

These places—popular with budget tour groups—are well run and offer elevators and all the modern comforts in a no-frills practical package. Their £60 doubles are a great value for London.

London County Hall Travel Inn, literally down the hall from a $400-a-night Marriott Hotel, fills one end of London's massive former City Hall. This place is wonderfully located across the Thames from Big Ben. Its 300 slick and no-frills rooms come with all the necessary comforts (Db-£60 for 2 adults and up to

2 kids under age 17, couples can request a bigger family room—same price, breakfast extra, book in advance, no-show rooms are released at 16:00, elevator, some smoke-free and easy-access rooms, CC:VMA, 500 yards from Westminster tube stop and Waterloo Station where the Chunnel train leaves for Paris, Belvedere Road, SE1 7PB, tel. 020/7902-1600, fax 020/7902-1619, www.travelinn.co.uk).

Other London Travel Inns charging £60 per room include **London Euston** (141 Euston Road, NW1 2AU, tube: Euston), **Tower Bridge** (tube: London Bridge), and **London Putney Bridge** (farther out, tube: Putney Bridge). For any of these, call 01582/414-341.

Hotel Ibis London Euston, which feels classier than a Travel Inn, is located on a quiet street a block behind Euston Station (Sb-£60, Db-£63, breakfast extra, CC:VMA, nonsmoking floor, 3 Cardington St, NW1 2LW, tel. 020/7388-7777, fax 020/7388-0001, e-mail: ho921@accor-hotels.com).

Jurys Inn rents 200 mod, compact, and comfy rooms near King's Cross station (Db/Tb-£75, 2 adults and 2 kids in 1 room is OK, breakfast extra, CC:VMA, nonsmoking floors, 60 Pentonville Road, Islington, N1 9LA, tube: Angel, tel. 020/7282-5500, fax 020/7282-5511).

"South Kensington," She Said, Loosening His Cummerbund

To live on a quiet street so classy it doesn't allow hotel signs, surrounded by trendy shops and colorful restaurants, call "South Ken" your London home. Shoppers like being a short walk from Harrods and the designer shops of King's Road and Chelsea. When I splurge, I splurge here. Sumner Place is just off Old Brompton Road, 200 yards from the handy South Kensington tube station (on Circle Line, two stops from Victoria Station, direct Heathrow connection). There's a taxi rank in the meridian at the end of Harrington Road. The handy "Wash & Dry" Laundromat is on the corner of Queensberry Place and Harrington Road (daily 8:00–21:00, bring 20p and £1 coins).

Aster House Hotel—run by friendly and accommodating Simon and Leona Tan—has a sumptuous lobby, lounge, and breakfast room. Its well-worn rooms are comfy and quiet, with TV, phone, and fridge but ramshackle bathrooms. Enjoy breakfast or just lounging in the whisper-elegant Orangery, a Victorian greenhouse (Sb-£65-85, Db-£125, deluxe four-poster Db-£145, CC:VM, entirely nonsmoking, 3 Sumner Place, SW7 3EE, tel. 020/7581-5888, fax 020/7584-4925, www.welcome2london.com).

Five Sumner Place Hotel was recently voted "the best small hotel in London." In this 150-year-old building, rooms are tastefully decorated and the breakfast room is a Victorian-style conservatory/

greenhouse (13 rooms, Sb-£88, Db-£141, 3rd bed-£24; Oct–Mar 10 percent discount with this book—this makes it the best Sumner Place value off-season; CC:VMA, TV, phones, and fridge in rooms, nonsmoking rooms, elevator, 5 Sumner Place, South Kensington, SW7 3EE, tel. 020/7584–7586, fax 020/7823-9962, www.sumnerplace.com, reservations@sumnerplace.com, run by Tom).

Sixteen Sumner Place—a lesser value for classier travelers—has over-the-top formality and class packed into its 37 unnumbered but pretentiously named rooms, plush lounges, and quiet garden (Db-£160 with showers, £185 with baths, CC:VMA, breakfast in your room, elevator, 16 Sumner Place, SW7 3EG, tel. 020/7589-5232, fax 020/7584-8615, U.S. tel. 800/592-5387, e-mail: reservations@numbersixteenhotel.co.uk).

Kensington Jurys Hotel is big and stately (Sb/Db/Tb-£100–170 depending upon "availability," ask for a deal, breakfast extra, CC:VMA, piano lounge, nonsmoking floor, elevator, Queen's Gate, South Kensington, SW7 5LR, tel. 020/7589-6300, fax 020/7581-1492).

The Claverley, two blocks from Harrods, is on a quiet street similar to Sumner Place. The warmly furnished rooms come with all the comforts (S-£70, Sb-£75–115, Db-£110–145, sofabed Tb-£160–215, flexible during slow times, CC:VMA, plush lounge, nonsmoking rooms, elevator, 13–14 Beaufort Gardens, SW3 1PS, tube: Knightsbridge, tel. 020/7589-8541, fax 020/7584-3410, U.S. tel. 800/747-0398).

Sleeping in Notting Hill Gate Neighborhood

Residential Notting Hill Gate has quick bus and tube access to downtown, is on the A2 Airbus line from Heathrow, and, for London, is very "homely." It has a self-serve launderette, an artsy theater, a late-hours supermarket, and lots of fun budget eateries (see "Eating").

Westland Hotel is comfortable, convenient, and hotelesque, with a fine lounge, an impersonal staff, and spacious 1970s-style rooms (Sb-£80, Db-£95, cavernous deluxe Db-£110, sprawling Tb-£120, gargantuan Qb-£135, 10 percent discount with this book through 2000, CC:VMA, elevator, free garage, between Notting Hill Gate and Queensway tube stations, 154 Bayswater Road, W2 4HP, tel. 020/7229-9191, fax 020/7727-1054, e-mail: 106411.3060@compuserve.com).

Vicarage Private Hotel, understandably popular, is family run and elegantly British in a quiet, classy neighborhood. It has 19 rooms furnished with taste and quality, a TV lounge, and facilities on each floor. Mandy, Richard, and Tere maintain a homey and caring atmosphere. Reserve long in advance. There's no better room for the price (S-£43, D-£68, T-£87, Q-£92, a 6-minute walk from the Notting Hill Gate and High Street Kensington tube

London, Notting Hill Gate Neighborhood

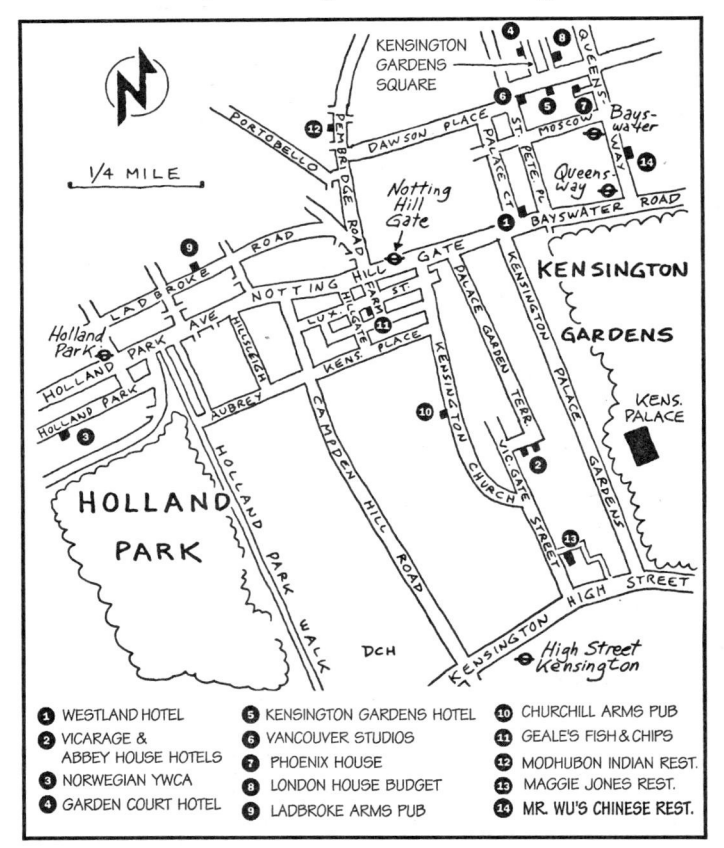

- ❶ WESTLAND HOTEL
- ❷ VICARAGE & ABBEY HOUSE HOTELS
- ❸ NORWEGIAN YWCA
- ❹ GARDEN COURT HOTEL
- ❺ KENSINGTON GARDENS HOTEL
- ❻ VANCOUVER STUDIOS
- ❼ PHOENIX HOUSE
- ❽ LONDON HOUSE BUDGET
- ❾ LADBROKE ARMS PUB
- ❿ CHURCHILL ARMS PUB
- ⓫ GEALE'S FISH & CHIPS
- ⓬ MODHUBON INDIAN REST.
- ⓭ MAGGIE JONES REST.
- ⓮ MR. WU'S CHINESE REST.

stations, near Kensington Palace at 10 Vicarage Gate, Kensington, W8 4AG, tel. 020/7229-4030, fax 020/7792-5989, www.london-vicaragehotel.com).

Abbey House Hotel, next door, is similar, but—while also a fine value—it has no lounge and is less cozy (16 rooms, S-£43, D-£68, T-£85, Q-£95, Quint-£105, 11 Vicarage Gate, Kensington, W8 4AG, tel. 020/7727-2594, Rodrigo).

Norwegian YWCA (Norsk K.F.U.K.) is for women under 30 only (and men with Norwegian passports). Located on a quiet, stately street, it offers nonsmoking rooms, a study, TV room, piano lounge, and an open-face Norwegian ambience. They have mostly quads, so those willing to share with strangers are most likely to get a place (Jul–Aug: Ss-£27, bed in shared double-£25, shared triple-£21 apiece, shared quad-£18 apiece, with breakfast; Sept–Jun: same prices include dinner; CC:VM, 52 Holland Park, W11 3R5, tel. & fax 020/7727-9897). With each visit I wonder which is easier to get—a sex change or a Norwegian passport?

Sleeping on Kensington Gardens

Several big old hotels line the quiet Victorian Kensington Gardens, a block off the bustling Queensway shopping street near the Bayswater tube station. Popular with young travelers from around the world, Queensway is a multicultural festival of commerce and lively eateries (such as Mr Wu's Chinese buffet, stuffing locals for £4.50, on Queensway, see "Eating," below). These hotels come with the least traffic noise of all my downtown recommendations. Brookford Wash & Dry is at Queensway and Bishop's Bridge Road (daily 7:00–19:30, service from 9:00–17:30, computerized pay point takes all coins).

Garden Court rents 34 large, comfortable rooms, offering one of London's best accommodations values. The breakfast room is sticky, and the public bathrooms are a bit unkempt, but it's friendly, with a great lounge and super prices (S-£34, Sb-£48, D-£52, Db-£76, T-£72, Tb-£86, Q-£78, Qb-£92, CC:VM, 30 Kensington Gardens Square, W2 4BG, tel. 020/7229-2553, fax 020/7727-2749, e-mail: gardencourthotel@londonw24bg.freeserve.co.uk).

Kensington Gardens Hotel laces 17 fine, fresh rooms together in a tall, skinny place with lots of stairs (S-£50, Sb-£55, Db-£75, 9 Kensington Gardens Square, W2 4BH, tel. 020/7221-7790, fax 020/7792-8612, www.kensingtongardenshotel.co.uk).

Vancouver Studios is a different concept, giving you a fully equipped kitchenette (plates, stove, microwave, and fridge) rather than breakfast (Sb-£55–72, Db-£85–100, Tb-£123, CC:VMA, homey lounge and private garden, rooms with all the modern comforts, 30 Prince's Square, W2 4NJ, tel. 020/7243-1270, fax 020/7221-8678, e-mail: hotels@vienna-group.co.uk).

Phoenix Hotel, a Best Western modernization of a 130-room hotel, offers American business-class comforts; spacious, plush public spaces; and big, fresh, modern-feeling rooms (Sb-£72, Db-£92, Tb-£120, CC:VMA, nonsmoking rooms, elevator, 8 Kensington Gardens Square, W2 4BH, tel. 020/7229-2494, fax 020/7727-1419, U.S. tel. 800/528-1234, www.phoenixhotel.co.uk).

London House Budget Hotel is a threadbare, nose-ringed slumber mill renting 220 beds in 76 stark but sleepable rooms (S-£40, twin-£54, dorm bed-£20, includes continental breakfast, CC:VMA, lots of school groups, 81 Kensington Gardens Square, W2 4DJ, tel. 020/7727-0696, fax 020/7243-8626, e-mail: hotels@vienna-group.co.uk).

Sleeping in Other Neighborhoods

Euston Station: The **Methodist International Centre** (new in 1998) is a youthful Christian residence, its lower floors filled with international students and its top floor open to travelers. Rooms are modern and simple yet comfortable, with fine bathrooms, phones, and desks. The atmosphere is friendly, safe, clean, and controlled, with a spacious lounge and game room (Sb-£38, Db-£58, Tb-£70, includes breakfast, 3-course buffet dinner-£11, CC:VM, nonsmoking rooms, elevator, on a quiet street a block southwest of Euston Square, 81–103 Euston Street, not Euston Road, W1 2EZ, tube: Euston Station, tel. 020/7380-0001, fax 020/7387-5300, e-mail: sales@micentre.com).

Cottage Hotel is tucked away a block off the west exit of Euston Station. Established in 1950—a bit tired, cramped, and smoky—it feels like 1950. But it's cheap, quiet, and has a fine breakfast room (40 rooms, S-£35, Sb-£45, D-£45, Db-£55, 67 Euston Street, tel. 020/7387-6785, fax 020/7383-0859).

Bloomsbury, near the British Museum: The **Cambria House**, a fine value, is run by the Salvation Army (a plus when it comes to cheap big-city hotels). This smoke-free old building with a narrow maze of halls is all newly painted and superclean, if institutional. The rooms are large and perfectly good. You'll find ample showers and toilets on each floor, a TV lounge, and a warm welcome (S-£29, D-£46, Db-£57, T-£70, CC:VM, north of Russell Square, 37 Hunter Street, WC1N 1BJ, tel. 020/7837-1654, fax 020/7837-1229).

Downtown near Baker Street: For a less hotelesque alternative in the center, consider renting one of 18 stark, hardwood, comfortable rooms in **22 York Street B&B** (Db-£94, Tb-£141, CC:VMA, strictly smoke-free, inviting lounge, social breakfast, from Baker Street tube station walk 2 blocks down Baker Street and take a right, 22 York Street, tel. 020/7224-3990, fax 020/7224-1990, e-mail: mc@22yorkstreet.prestel.co.uk, energetically run by Liz and Michael).

Near St. Paul's: The **City of London Youth Hostel** is clean, modern, friendly, and well run. You'll pay about £24 for a bed in three- to five-bed rooms, £26 in a single (youth hostel membership required, 200 beds, CC:VM, cheap meals, 36 Carter Lane, EC4V 5AD, tube: St. Paul's, tel. 020/7236-4965, fax 020/7236-7681).

South of London: Caroline Cunningham's humble guest house is on a quiet street in a well-worn neighborhood south of Victoria near Clapham Common (3 rooms, S-£15, D-£30 with English breakfast, 98 Hambalt Road, Clapham Common, London SW4 9EJ, tel. 020/8673-1077). It's 15 minutes by tube to Clapham Common, then a bus ride or a 12-minute walk—exit left down Clapham South Road, left on Elms, right on Abbeville

Road, left on Hambalt. Rooms in Caroline's brother's house are an equally good value. A good, cheap Thai restaurant (the Pepper Tree) is near the tube station.

Near Gatwick Airport: These two B&Bs are both in the peaceful countryside and have tennis courts, small swimming pools, and a good pub within walking distance. **Barn Cottage,** a converted 17th-century barn, has two wood-beamed rooms, antique furniture, and a large garden that makes you forget Gatwick is 10 minutes away (S-£35, D-£50, can drive you to airport or train station for £5–6—a taxi costs £10—Leigh, Reigate, Surrey, RH2 8RF, tel. 01306/611-347, warmly run by Pat and Mike Comer). The idyllic **Crutchfield Farm B&B** offers three comfortable rooms, a great sitting room, and an elegant dining room in a 600-year-old renovated farmhouse surrounded by lots of greenery and a pond. Gillian Blok includes a ride to the airport and its train station, whether you're leaving Britain or day-tripping to London (Sb-£45, Db-£75, Tb-£85, Qb-£95, 2 miles from Gatwick Airport—£5 by taxi, 30 minutes by train from London, at Hookwood, Surrey, RH6 OHT, tel. 01293/863-110, fax 01293/863-233, e-mail: TonyBlok@compuserve.com).

Near Heathrow Airport: It's so easy to get to Heathrow from central London, I see no reason to sleep there. But for budget beds near the airport, consider the **Heathrow Ibis** (Db-£60, breakfast extra, CC:VMA, shuttle bus to terminals, 112 Bath Road, tel. 020/8759-4888, fax 020/8564-7894).

Sleeping and Eating in Hampstead, the Small-Town Alternative

If you must "do" London but wish it was a small town, make Hampstead your home-base-on-the-hill. Just 15 to 25 minutes north of the center by tube (to Hampstead on the sometimes tardy Northern Line) and you're in the former resort of wealthy Londoners—drawn by spas in the 1700s and the brilliant views of London from the popular Hampstead Heath, an 800-acre park.

Hampstead today glows with Georgian village elegance—narrow cobblestone lanes, gas lamps (now electrified), blue plaques noting where Keats, Freud, and other famous locals lived. Even McDonald's has a mock-Tudor facade.

The tube station marks the center of the town (note that in tube terms, Hampstead is in Zone 2, covered by day passes but not carnet tickets). From the station, busy High Street cuts downhill though the center. Following it downhill takes you into a cheery business district with side streets flickering with gaslit charm. The hotel is a three-minute walk uphill. The B&B is a brisk 10-minute walk downhill. The **Freemason's Arms** pub (best for dinner) is a couple of blocks beyond the B&B. And all other pubs and restaurants are within five minutes of the tube station. Everything's near the park.

Make a point to explore the back lanes, where you can pop into churches and peek into windows—drapes are left open so their elegant interiors can be envied.

Hampstead Village Guesthouse is run in a laissez-faire style by Anne Marie van der Meer, who rents eight rooms and raised her family in this Victorian house. The homey rooms, most named after her children, don't have locks, but the house is secure. All rooms come with a phone, miniature fridge, TV, and even a hot-water bottle (small S-£40, S-£45, Sb-£55, D-£60, Db-£70, price varies for studio/kitchenette for 1–5 people; £100 for 2, breakfast-£6, CC:VMA for reservation deposit only, payment in cash, nonsmoking, extremely quiet, book well in advance, walk 10 minutes from tube downhill on High Street, left at Lloyds Bank on Pilgrims Lane to 2 Kemplay Road, Hampstead, NW3 1SY, tel. 020/7435-8679, fax 020/7794-0254, e-mail: hvguesthouse @dial.pipex.com).

La Gaffe Hotel is a sweet Italian-run hotel and restaurant right on Heath Street. Its 14 rooms are small and worn but floral, comfy, and quiet (Sb-£60–75, Db-£85–120, 4-poster room priciest, includes breakfast, CC:VM, TV, phones, nonsmoking, walk uphill from tube station 3 minutes to 107 Heath Street, Hampstead, London, NW3 6SS, tel. 020/7435-8965, fax 020/7794-7592, e-mail: la-gaffe@msn.com).

Eating in Hampstead: Freemason's Arms is the place for classy pub grub. If the lighting doesn't make your partner look delicious, the Czech lager will. Set on the edge of the heath, with a spacious interior and sprawling beer garden for summer outdoor seating, the Freemason's Arms serves great English food (£9 meals, Mon–Sat 11:00–23:00, Sun 12:00–23:00, CC:VM, skittles downstairs on Thursday and Saturday night—private but peeking permitted; down High Street, left on Downshire Hill Road to #32, tel. 020/7433-6811).

Down High Street from the tube stop you'll find Hampstead swinging at **The House on Rosslyn Hill**. Serving international cuisine, this trendy, modern brasserie attracts a young crowd wearing black, grey, and white (meals start at £10, daily 11:00–24:00, CC:VM, 34 Rosslyn Hill, tel. 020/7435-8037).

French Hampstead cooks a block below the tube station. For a quick bite, **Maison Blanc** on Hampstead High Street not only has the best croissants in town but also makes great savories, like Roquefort and walnut *fougasse* (focaccia pockets) or tarte Provençal (tomato, zucchini, and Gruyère miniquiche)—all this for £3 to £4, including lovely strong French coffee. **Cafe des Arts** serves French food in a rustic, candlelit English setting (daily 12:00–23:30, CC:VMA, 82 Hampstead High Street), but just around the corner, a little crêpe cart in search of Paris is more popular (on Perrins Lane, a few steps off High Street).

For village atmosphere, shop at the **Hampstead Foodhall** on Fitzjohn Avenue (within a block of the tube, cross High Street to the only level street). There's no place better for a dinner picnic with a view than Hampstead Heath (a 10-minute hike away, up Heath Street).

For a laid-back crowd, visit the **Holly Bush** pub (daily 12:00–23:30, serves sandwiches 12:00–15:00 except Sunday, hidden on a quiet lane uphill from the tube, from Heath Street turn left on Holly Bush Steps). For a livelier, spit-and-sawdust pub, toss your darts with the locals at **The Flask** (on Flask Walk, 2 blocks below the tube station).

Eating in London

If you want to dine (as opposed to eat), check out the extensive listings in the weekly entertainment guides sold at London newsstands (or catch a train for Paris). The thought of a £30 meal in Britain generally ruins my appetite, so my London dining is limited mostly to easygoing, fun, but inexpensive alternatives. I've listed places by neighborhood—handy to your sightseeing or hotel.

Your £6 budget choices are pub grub, a café, fish and chips, pizza, ethnic, or picnic. Pub grub is the most atmospheric budget option. Many of London's 7,000 pubs serve fresh, tasty buffets under ancient timbers, with hearty lunches and dinners priced from £6 to £8. Ethnic restaurants from all over the world add spice to England's lackluster cuisine scene. Eating Indian or Chinese is "going local" in London. It's also going cheap (cheaper if you take out). Most large museums (and many churches) have inexpensive, cheery cafeterias. Sandwich shops are a hit with local workers eating on the run. Of course, picnicking is the fastest and cheapest way to go. Good grocery stores and sandwich shops, fine park benches, and polite pigeons abound in Britain's most expensive city.

Eating near Trafalgar Square

For a tasty meal on a monk's budget sitting on somebody's tomb in an ancient crypt, descend into the **St. Martin-in-the-Fields Café in the Crypt** (Mon–Sat 10:00–20:00, Sun 12:00–20:30, £5–7 cafeteria plates, cheaper sandwich bar, profits go to the church; underneath St. Martin-in-the-Fields on Trafalgar Square, tel. 020/7839-4342).

Chandos Bar's Opera Room floats amazingly apart from the tacky crush of tourism around Trafalgar Square. Look for the pub opposite the National Portrait Gallery (corner of William Street and St. Martin's Lane) and climb the stairs to the Opera Room. They serve £6 pub lunches and dinners (last orders at 19:00, 18:00 on weekends, tel. 020/7836-1401). This is a fine Tragalfar rendezvous point—smoky, but wonderfully local.

Gordon's Wine Bar is ripe with atmosphere. A simple steep staircase leads into a 14th-century cellar filled with candlelight, dusty old wine bottles, faded British memorabilia, and local nine-to-fivers (hot meals only for lunch, fine cheese-and-salad buffet all day until 21:00—one plate of each feeds two for £7). While it's crowded, you can normally corral two chairs and grab the corner of a table (Mon–Sat 11:00–23:00, closed Sun, 2 blocks from Trafalgar Square, bottom of Villiars Street at #47, near Embankment tube station, tel. 020/7930-1408).

Down Whitehall (toward Big Ben), a block from Trafalgar Square, you'll find the touristy but atmospheric **Clarence Pub** (decent grub) and several cheaper cafeterias and pizza joints.

For a classy lunch in the National Gallery, treat your palate to the pricier **Brasserie** (hot meals £8–10, open daily, 1st floor of Sainsbury Wing).

Simpson's in the Strand serves a stuffy, aristocratic, old-time carvery dinner—where the chef slices your favorite red meat from a fancy trolley at your table—in their elegant smoky old dining room (£20, Mon–Sat 12:15–14:30, 17:30–23:00, tel. 020/7836-9112).

Eating near Piccadilly

Hungry and broke in the theater district? Head for Panton Street (off Haymarket, 2 blocks southeast of Piccadilly Circus) for a line of decent eateries. **Stockpot** is a mushy-peas kind of place, famous and rightly popular for its edible, cheap meals (Mon–Sat 8:00–23:00, Sun 8:00–22:00, 40 Panton Street). The **West End Kitchen** (across the street at #5, same hours and menu) is a direct competitor that's just as good. The original **Stockpot,** a few blocks away, has better atmosphere (daily 12:00–23:00, a block north of Shaftesbury near Cambridge Circus at 18 Old Compton Street).

The palatial **Criterion Brasserie** serves a £15 two-course "Anglo-French" menu under gilded tiles and chandeliers in a dreamy Byzantine church setting from 1880. It's right on Piccadilly Circus but a world away from the punk junk (12:00–14:30, 18:00–18:30 only, pricier later, tel. 020/7930-0488).

Just off Leicester Square, **Luigi Malone's**, a chain restaurant, serves inexpensive salads and pasta (12 Irving Street, tel. 020/7925-0457).

Near Covent Garden, the area around Neal's Yard is busy with fun eateries. One of the best is **Food for Thought** (serving until 20:15, closed Sun, very good £4 vegetarian meals, nonsmoking, 2 blocks north of tube: Covent Garden, 31 Neal Street, tel. 020/7836-0239). Neal's Yard itself is a food circus of trendy, healthy eateries.

Eating near St. Paul's

Ye Olde Cheshire Cheese Pub, rebuilt a year after the great fire of 1666, is a creaky half-timbered tangle of eateries (explained on a chart outside the door). Characteristic restaurants are upstairs, while fast, cheap pub meals are served in the rustic cellar bar (Mon–Fri 11:30–23:00, 145 Fleet Street, tel. 020/7353-6170). There's also a good restaurant and cafe in St. Paul's crypt.

The "Food Is Fun" Dinner Crawl: From Covent Garden to Soho

London has a trendy, Generation X scene that most Beefeater seekers miss entirely. For a multicultural movable feast and a chance to sample some of London's most popular eateries, consider sampling these. Start around 18:00 to avoid lines, get in on early specials, and find waiters willing to let you split a meal. Prices, while reasonable by London standards, add up. Servings are large enough to share. All are open nightly.

Suggested nibbler's dinner crawl for two: Arrive before 18:00 at **Belgo** and split the early-bird dinner special: a kilo of mussels, fries, and dark Belgian beer; at **Yo! Sushi,** have beer or sake and a few dishes; slurp your last course at **Wagamama;** for dessert, people watch at Leicester Square, where the serf's always up.

Belgo Centraal is a space-station world overrun with Trappist monks serving hearty Belgian specialties. The classy restaurant section requires reservations, but just grabbing a bench in the boisterous beer hall is more fun. Belgians claim they eat as well as the French and as hearty as the Germans. Specialties include mussels, great fries, and a stunning array of dark, blond, and fruity Belgian beers. Belgo actually makes things Belgian trendy—a formidable feat (£12 meals; open daily till very late; Mon–Fri 17:00–18:30 "beat the clock" meal specials cost only the time... £5 to £6.30, and you get mussels, fries, and beer; no meal-splitting after 18:30; £5 lunch special daily, 12:00–17:00; 1 block north of Covent Garden tube station at the intersection of Neal and Shelton Streets, 50 Earlham Street, tel. 020/7813-2233).

Soho Spice Indian is where modern Britain meets Indian tradition—fine Indian cuisine in a trendy jewel-tone ambience. The £15 "Tandoori selections" meal is the best "variety" dish and big enough for two (daily 12:00–24:00, nonsmoking section, 5 blocks due north of Piccadilly Circus at 124 Wardour Street, tel. 020/7434-0808).

Yo! Sushi is a futuristic Japanese food extravaganza experience. With thumping rock, Japanese cable TV, a 60-meter-long conveyor-belt sushi bar (the world's longest), automated sushi machines, and a robotic drink trolley, just sipping a sake on a bar stool here is a trip. For £1 you get unlimited tea (on request), water (from spigot at bar, with or without gas), or miso soup.

From Covent Garden to Soho, "Food is Fun"

Map legend:
1. CHANDO'S BAR
2. GORDON'S WINE BAR
3. CRITERION BRASSERIE
4. NEAL'S YARD
5. BELGO CENTRAAL
6. SOHO SPICE INDIAN
7. YO! SUSHI
8. WAGAMAMA NOODLE BAR
9. SOHO SOHO BISTRO
10. ANDREW EDMUNDS REST.

Grab dishes as they rattle by (priced by color of dish; see their chart) and a drink off the trash-talking robot (daily 12:00–24:00, 2 blocks south of Oxford Street, where Lexington Street becomes Poland Street, 52 Poland Street, tel. 020/7287-0443). For more serious drinking on tatami mats, go downstairs into "Yo Below."

Wagamama Noodle Bar is a noisy, pan-Asian slurp-athon. As you enter, check out the kitchen and listen to the roar of the basement, where benches rock with happy eaters. Everything's organic—stand against the wall to feel the energy of all this "positive eating" (daily 12:00–23:00, crowded after 20:00, just past the porno and prostitution core of Soho but entirely smoke free, 10A Lexington Street, tel. 020/7292-0990).

Soho Soho French Bistro-Rotisserie is a chance to go French in a Matisse-esque setting. The ground floor is a trendy wine bar. Upstairs is an oasis of peace serving £17 three-course

French "pretheater specials"—order from 18:00 to 19:30 (near Cambridge Circus, 2 blocks east of Charing Cross Road at 11 Frith Street, tel. 020/7494-3491).

Andrew Edmunds Restaurant is a tiny candlelit place where you'll want to hide your camera and guidebook and act as local as possible. The modern-European cooking is worth the splurge (3 courses for £20, 12:30–15:00, 18:00–23:00, 46 Lexington Street in Soho, reservations are smart, tel. 020/7437-5708).

Eating near Recommended Victoria Station Accommodations

Here are places a couple of blocks southwest of Victoria Station where I've enjoyed eating:

Jenny Lo's Tea House is a simple, for-the-joy-of-good-food kind of place serving up £5 Chinese-style meals to locals in the know (Mon–Sat 12:00–15:00, 18:00–22:00, 14 Eccleston Street, tel. 020/7259-0399).

For pub grub with good local atmosphere, consider the **Plumbers Arms** (filling £5 hot meals and cheaper sandwiches Mon–Fri only, indoor/outdoor seating, 14 Lower Belgrave Street, tel. 020/7730-4067—ask about the murdered nanny).

Next door, the small but classy **La Campagnola** is Belgravia's favorite budget Italian restaurant (£12–15, closed Sun, 10 Lower Belgrave Street, tel. 020/7730-2057).

Across the street, the **Maestro Bar** is the closest thing to an English tapas bar I've seen, with salads, sandwiches, and 10 bar stools (very cheap, closed Sat).

The **Ebury Wine Bar** offers a French candlelit ambience and pricey but delicious meals (£15, daily 12:00–15:00, 18:00–22:30, 139 Ebury Street, at the intersection with Elizabeth Street, near the bus station, tel. 020/7730-5447). Several cheap places are around the corner on Elizabeth Street (#23 for take-out or eat-in fish and chips).

The **Duke of Wellington** pub is good, if smoky, for dinner (£5 meals, Mon–Sat 12:00–15:00, 18:00–21:30, Sun 12:00–15:00, 63 Eaton Terrace). **Peter's Restaurant** is the cabbie's hangout for cheap food, smoke, and chatter (closed Sun, end of Ebury, at the intersection with Pimlico).

The **Country Pub in London** lives up to its name and serves good £6 to £12 meals (12:00–15:00, 19:00–21:30, corner of Warwick and Cambridge Streets, tel. 020/7834-5281).

The late-hours **Whistle Stop** grocery at the station has decent sandwiches and a fine salad bar. The **Marche** is an easy cafeteria a couple of blocks north of Victoria Station at Bressenden Place. If you miss America, there's a mall-type food circus at Victoria Place, upstairs in Victoria Station. **Cafe Rouge** is probably the best food there.

Eating near Recommended Notting Hill Gate B&Bs and Bayswater Hotels

The exuberantly rustic and very English **Maggie Jones** serves my favorite £20 London dinner. You'll get solid English cuisine, with huge plates of crunchy vegetables, by candlelight (daily 18:30–23:00, CC:VMA, 6 Old Court Place, just east of Kensington Church Street, near High Street Kensington tube stop, reservations recommended, tel. 020/7937-6462). If you eat well once in London, eat here (and do it quick, before it burns down).

The **Churchill Arms** pub is a local hangout, with good beer and old English ambience in front and hearty £5 Thai plates in an enclosed patio in the back (you can bring the Thai food into the more atmospheric pub section, Mon–Sat 12:00–15:00, 18:00–21:30, closed Sun, 119 Kensington Church Street, tel. 020/7792-1246).

The friendly **Ladbroke Arms Pub** serves country-style meals that are one step above pub grub in quality and price (£8 meals, daily 12:00–14:30, 19:00–22:00, great indoor/outdoor ambience, 54 Ladbroke Road, behind Holland Park tube station, tel. 020/7727-6648).

For fish and chips, the almost-too-popular **Geale's** has long been considered one of London's best (£8, Mon–Sat 12:00–15:00, 18:00–23:00, closed Sun, 2 Farmer Street, just off Notting Hill Gate behind Gate Cinema, tel. 020/7727-7528). Get there early for a place to sit (they take no reservations) and the best selection of fish.

The **Modhubon** Indian restaurant is not too spicy, "vedy, vedy nice," and has cheap lunch specials (Sun–Fri 12:00–15:00, 18:00–24:00, Sat 12:00–24:00, 29 Pembridge Road, tel. 020/7727-3399). Next door is a cheap Chinese take-out (daily 17:30–24:00, 19 Pembridge Road) and the tiny **Organic Restaurant** at #35, which busily keeps yuppie vegetarians as well as carnivores happy (£10, 100 percent organic, Mon–Fri 17:30–23:00, Sat–Sun 10:30–23:00, 35 Pembridge Road, tel. 020/7727-9620).

Cafe Diana is a healthy little sandwich shop decorated with photos of Princess Diana (daily 8:00–22:30, 5 Wellington Terrace, on Bayswater Road, opposite Kensington Palace Garden Gates, tel. 020/7792-9606).

Mr Wu's Chinese Restaurant serves a tasty 10-course buffet in a bright and cheery little place. Just grab a plate and help yourself (£4.50, daily 12:00–23:00, across from Bayswater tube station, 54 Queensway, tel. 020/7243-1017). Queensway is lined with lively and inexpensive eateries.

Eating near Recommended Accommodations in South Kensington

Popular eateries line Old Brompton Road and Thurloe Street (tube: South Kensington).

Luigi Malone's is an Italian-food chain restaurant serving good £6 salads and pasta (73 Old Brompton Road, tel. 020/7584-4323). Its twin brother is just off Leicester Square at 12 Irving Street.

Daquise, an authentic-feeling Polish place, is ideal if you're in the mood for kielbasa and kraut. It's fast, cheap, faded, family run, and a part of the neighborhood (£8 meals, daily until 23:00, nonsmoking, 20 Thurloe Street, tel. 020/7589-6117).

For Indian food, the **Khyber Pass Tandoori Restaurant** is a nondescript but handy place serving good £8 dinners nightly (12:00–15:00, 18:00–24:00, 21 Bute Street, tel. 020/7589-7311).

La Bouchee Bistro Café is a classy hole-in-the-wall touch of France serving early bird three-course £11 meals before 19:30 and *plats du jour* for £8 all *jour* (daily 12:00–23:00, CC:VM, 56 Old Brompton Road, tel. 020/7589-1929).

La Brasserie fills a big plain room with a Parisian ambience and good French-style food at reasonable prices (2-course £14 "regional menu," £12 bottle of house wine, CC:VMA, nightly until midnight, 272 Brompton Road, tel. 020/7581-3089).

PJ's Bar and Grill is popular with the yuppie Chelsea crowd for a good reason. Traditional "New York Brasserie"–style yet trendy, it serves modern Mediterranean cuisine (£15 meals, nightly until 23:30, 52 Fulham Road, tel. 020/7581-0025).

Transportation Connections—London

Flying into London's Heathrow Airport

Heathrow Airport is the world's busiest. Think about it: 60 million passengers a year on 425,000 flights from 200 destinations riding 90 airlines... some kind of global Maypole dance. While many complain about it, I like it. It's user-friendly. Read signs, ask questions. For Heathrow's airport, flight, and transfers information, call 020/8759-4321. It has four terminals: T-1 (mostly domestic flights), T-2 (mostly European flights), T-3 (mostly flights from the U.S.), T-4 (British Air trans-Atlantic flights).

Each terminal has an airport information desk, car-rental agencies, exchange bureaus and ATMs, a pharmacy, a VAT refund desk (VAT info tel. 020/8745-4216; you must present the VAT claim form from the retailer here to get your 17.5 percent tax rebate on items purchased in Britain), and a £3.50/day baggage check desk (open 5:30–23:00). There's a post office in T-2 and T-4. The best value eating at T-3 and T-4 is the cheap and cheery **Granary** self-service cafeteria. The American Express desk (with rates no better than the exchange bureaus) is in the tube station at Terminal 4.

Heathrow's TI gives you all the help that London's Victoria Station does, with none of the crowds (daily 8:30–18:00, a 5-minute walk from Terminal 3 in the tube station, follow signs to "underground"). If you're riding the Airbus into London, have your partner stay with the bags at the terminal. At the TI, get a free simple map and brochures, and if you're taking the tube (subway) into London, buy a Travel Card day pass to cover the ride (see below).

Transportation to London from Heathrow Airport
By Tube (Subway): For £3.40, the tube takes you 14 miles to Victoria Station in 45 minutes (6/hrly, 1 change). Even better, buy a £4.50 Travel Card that covers your trip into London and all your tube travel for the day (starting at 9:30).

By Airbus: The A2 Airbus serves the Notting Hill Gate and Kensington Gardens/Queensway neighborhoods—see recommended hotels, above (departs from each terminal, £6, 4/hrly, 5:15–22:00, buy ticket on bus, tel. 020/8400-6655 or 020/7222-1234). The tube works fine, but with baggage I prefer the Airbus—there are no connections underground and a lovely view from the top of the double-decker bus. Ask the driver to remind you when to get off. If you're going to the airport, exact pick-up times are clearly posted at each bus stop.

By Taxi: Taxis from the airport cost about £35. For four traveling together this can be a deal. Hotels can often line up a cab back to the airport for £30. For the cheapest taxi to the airport don't order one from your hotel. Simply flag down a few and ask them for their best "off-meter" rate (I managed a ride for £25).

By Heathrow Express Train: This new train service zips air travelers between Heathrow and London's Paddington Station; at Paddington, you're in the thick of the tube system, with easy access to any of my recommended neighborhoods—Notting Hill Gate is just two stops away (£10 but ask about discount promos at Heathrow ticket desk, children under 16 ride free if you buy tickets before boarding, 4/hrly, 5:10–23:00, 15 min to downtown from Terminals 1, 2, 3; 20 min from T-4; works as a free transfer between terminals, tel. 0845/600-1515). For one person, the tube or a taxi to Paddington and the Express to Heathrow is as fast and half the cost of a cab to the airport.

Buses from Heathrow to Destinations beyond London
The **National Express Central Bus Station** offers direct bus connections to **Cambridge** (hrly, 3.5 hrs, £17), **Cheltenham** (6/day, 2 hrs, £19), **Gatwick Airport** (2/hrly, 1 hr, £12), and **Bath** (10/day, at 8:40, 10:10, 11:40, 13:10, 14:40, 16:40, 18:10, 19:10, 20:10, 21:40, 2.5 hrs, £19.50, direct, tel. 0990-808-080). Or try the slick 2.5-hour Heathrow–Bath bus/train connection via Reading. Either use your BritRail pass or buy the £26 ticket at the desk in the terminal (credit cards accepted), then catch the twice-hourly

RailAir Link shuttle bus to Reading (RED-ding) to hop on the hourly express train to Bath. Most Heathrow buses depart from the common area serving Terminals 1, 2, and 3, although some depart from T-4 (bus info tel. 0990-747-777).

Flying into London's Gatwick Airport

More and more flights, especially charters, land at Gatwick Airport, halfway between London and the southern coast. Trains—clearly the best way into London from here—shuttle conveniently between Gatwick and London's Victoria Station (4/hrly, 30 min, £9).

Trains and Buses

London, Britain's major transportation hub, has a different train station for each region. Waterloo handles the Eurostar to Paris. King's Cross covers northeast England and Scotland (tel. 08457/225-225). Paddington covers west and southwest England (Bath) and South Wales (tel. 08457/000-125). For the others, call 0345-484-950. Also see the BritRail map in the introduction.

National Express' excellent bus service is considerably cheaper than trains. (For a busy signal, call 0990-808-080, or visit www.nationalexpress.co.uk or the bus station a block southwest of Victoria Station.)

To Bath: Trains leave London's Paddington Station every hour (at a quarter after) for the £32.50, 75-minute ride to Bath. As an alternative, consider taking a guided bus tour from London to Stonehenge and Bath and abandoning the tour in Bath. Both Evan Evans (tel. 020/7950-1777) and Travelline (tel. 020/8668-7261) offer Stonehenge/Bath day trips from London. Evan Evans' tours come fully guided, with admissions for £46 or just the bus transportation (free time at Stonehenge and then in Bath) for £25.

To points north: Trains run hourly from London's King's Cross Station, stopping in York (2 hrs), Durham (3 hrs), and Edinburgh (5 hrs).

To Dublin, Ireland: The boat/rail journey takes 10 hours, all day or all night (£40–60). Consider a cheap 70-minute Ryanair or British Midland flight instead (see below).

Discounted Flights from London

British Midland, the local discount airline, can often get you somewhere cheaper than the train. You can fly cheaply domestically (as little as £60 for a round-trip London–Edinburgh ticket if you stay over Saturday), to Ireland (as little as £70 return to Dublin if you stay over a Saturday), and to Paris, Amsterdam, or Frankfurt (round-trip over a Saturday for around £110). For the latest, call 0870-607-0555 or in the U.S., 800/788-0555.

Virgin Air is a Belgian company with incredible rates (no advance purchase deals, one way is half the round-trip, book by phone with credit card and pick up at the airport an hour before your flight, tel. 020/7744-0004, www.virgin-express.com). Virgin Air flies from Stansted and Gatwick in London to Shannon, Ireland (£47) and Brussels (£30 from Stansted, £40 from Gatwick). From its hub in Brussels you can connect cheaply to Barcelona, Madrid, Nice, Copenhagen, Rome, or Milan (e.g., London–Milan, £50).

Ryanair is a creative Irish airline with more complicated but potentially even cheaper fares. They fly mostly from London's Stansted airport to Dublin, Glasgow, Frankfurt, Lyons, Stockholm, Oslo, Venice, and Turin. Sample fares: London–Dublin—£80 round-trip or £30 one way if purchased a week in advance; London–Frankfurt—£70 round-trip or £30 with three-day advance purchase. They tend to book up a couple of weeks in advance (tel. 0541/569-569, www.ryanair.ie).

Crossing the English Channel

By Eurostar Train: The fastest and most convenient way to get from Big Ben to the Eiffel Tower is by rail. In London, advertisements claim "more businessmen travel from London to Paris on the Eurostar than on all airlines combined." Eurostar is the speedy passenger train that zips you (and up to 800 others in 18 sleek cars) from downtown London to downtown Paris (12/day, 3 hrs) or Brussels (6/day, 3 hrs) faster and easier than flying. The train goes 80 mph in England and 190 mph on the Continent. (When the English segment gets up to speed the journey time will shrink to two hours.) The actual Tunnel crossing is a 20-minute black, silent, 100 mph nonevent. Your ears won't even pop. You can change at Lille to catch a TGV directly to Paris' Charles de Gaulle Airport or Disneyland Paris. Yes!

Channel fares (essentially the same to Paris or Brussels) are reasonable but complicated. For the latest, call 800/EUROSTAR in the U.S. (or go to www.eurostar.com). These are prices for 2000: The "Leisure Ticket" is cheap ($119 second class, $199 first class, 50 percent refundable up to 3 days before departure). "Full Fare" first class costs $239 and includes a meal (a dinner departure nets you more grub than breakfast); second class (or "standard") costs $159 (fully refundable even after departure date).

Discounts for first- or second-class travel are available to railpass holders ($84 off "Full Fare"), youths under 26 ($80 off "Full Fare"), and children under 12 (about half the fare of your ticket). Cheaper seats can sell out. Book from home if you're ready to commit to a date and time. Call your travel agent or call direct (800/EUROSTAR). Prices do not include Fed Ex delivery. Note: Britain's time zone is one hour earlier than the Continent's. Times listed on tickets are local times.

Buying your Eurostar ticket in London is also easy. Here are some sample London–Paris standard—that's second-class—fares (London–Brussels fares are up to £20 less). Avoid the basic standard fare: one way—£145, round-trip—£249. Those with a railpass pay £50 one way, any day. Without a railpass, a same-day round-trip on a Saturday or Sunday costs £99. Those staying at least three nights pay £130 round-trip. Excursion fares (round-trip over a Saturday) are cheaper: £100. "Saturday Night Away" tickets (round-trip, purchased a week in advance, and staying over a Saturday) are the best deal: £90 standard, £160 first class. One-way tickets for departures after 14:00 Friday or anytime Saturday or Sunday cost £90. Youth tickets (for those under 26) are £80 to Paris, £65 to Brussels (round-trip any time and changeable). First-class and business-class fares are substantially higher. The only seven-day advance deal is the Saturday Night Away. Remember, round-trip tickets over a Saturday are much cheaper than the basic one-way fare... you know the trick.

In Europe, get your Eurostar ticket at any major train station (in any country) or at any travel agency that handles train tickets (expect a booking fee). In Britain, you can book and pay for tickets over the phone with a credit card by calling 0990-186-186; pick up your tickets at London's Waterloo station an hour before the Eurostar departure.

By Bus and Boat or Train and Boat: The old-fashioned way of crossing the Channel is competitive and cheaper than Eurostar; it's also twice as romantic, complicated, and time-consuming. You'll get better prices arranging your trip in London than you would in the U.S. Taking the bus is cheapest, and round-trips are a bargain. By bus to Paris or Amsterdam from Victoria Coach Station: £40 one way, £50 round-trip, 10 hours, day or overnight, on Eurolines (tel. 0990-143-219) or Hoverspeed (tel. 0990-240-241). By train and ship: £42 one way overnight, £59 by day, seven hours.

By Plane: Typical fares are £110 regular, less for student standby. Call in London for the latest fares. Consider British Midland (see "Discounted Flights," above) for its cheap round-trip fares.

NEAR LONDON: GREENWICH

The palace at Greenwich was favored by the Tudor kings. Henry VIII was born here. Later kings commissioned Inigo Jones and Christopher Wren to beautify the town and palace. In spite of Greenwich's architectural and royal treats, this is England's maritime capital, and visitors go for things salty. Greenwich hosts historic ships, nautical shops, and hordes of tourists. Now, in 2000, the home of the Zero Meridian will host more visitors than ever, drawn by the huge Millennium Dome.

If you plan to tour the Millennium Dome and Greenwich, do the Dome first (to get your money's worth out of the hefty ticket price—£25), and go straight to the Dome, rather than Greenwich, from London via tube (on the Jubilee Line, tube: North Greenwich) or boat (from Westminster Pier). If you decide to roam the Dome all day, it's easy to return to Greenwich another day to see the sights.

When you tour Greenwich, visit the two great ships upon arrival. Then walk the shoreline promenade with a possible lunch or drink in the venerable Trafalgar Tavern before heading up to the National Maritime Museum and Old Royal Observatory. Or, if you're rushed or tired, consider taking the handy shuttle bus that runs from Greenwich Pier (near the *Cutty Sark*) to the Old Royal Observatory, saving a 15-minute gradual uphill walk; then walk down, sightseeing as you go (£1.50, 4/hrly 10:45–17:00, Apr–Sept, Meridian Line Shuttle).

Getting to the town of Greenwich is a joy by boat or a snap by tube. You have good choices: Cruise down the Thames from central London's piers at Westminster, Charing Cross, or Tower of London; tube to Cutty Sark in Zone 2 (free with tube pass); or catch the train from Charing Cross station (2/hrly, £2). I'd take the tube to Greenwich, see the sights, and cruise back.

The TI is on 46 Greenwich Church Street (daily 10:00–17:00, tel. 020/8858-6376). Most of Greenwich's sights are covered by combo tickets, a pricier one for nearly everything and sometimes a cheaper one for a couple of sights; each year the combination of sights is shuffled slightly and the prices go up. Greenwich throbs with day-trippers on weekends, particularly on Sunday because of its arts and craft market; to avoid crowds, visit on a weekday.

Sights—Greenwich

▲▲*Cutty Sark*—The Scottish-built *Cutty Sark* was the last of the great China tea clippers. Handsomely restored, she was the queen of the seas when first launched in 1869. With 32,000 square feet of sail, she could blow with the wind 300 miles in a day. Below deck you'll see the best collection of merchant-ship figureheads in Britain and exhibits giving a vivid peek into the lives of Victorian sailors back when Britain ruled the waves. Stand at the big wheel and look up at the still-rigged main mast towering 150 feet above. During summer afternoons costumed storytellers tell tales of the high seas (£3.50, £12 combo ticket covers most Greenwich town sights, Mon–Sat 10:00–18:00, Sun 12:00–18:00; Oct–Apr Mon–Sat 10:00–17:00, Sun 12:00–17:00, tel. 020/8858-3445, www.cuttysark.org.uk).

▲*Gipsy Moth IV*—Tiny next to the *Cutty Sark*, the 53-foot *Gipsy Moth IV* is the boat Sir Francis Chichester used for the first solo circumnavigation of the world in 1966 and 1967. Upon

Greenwich

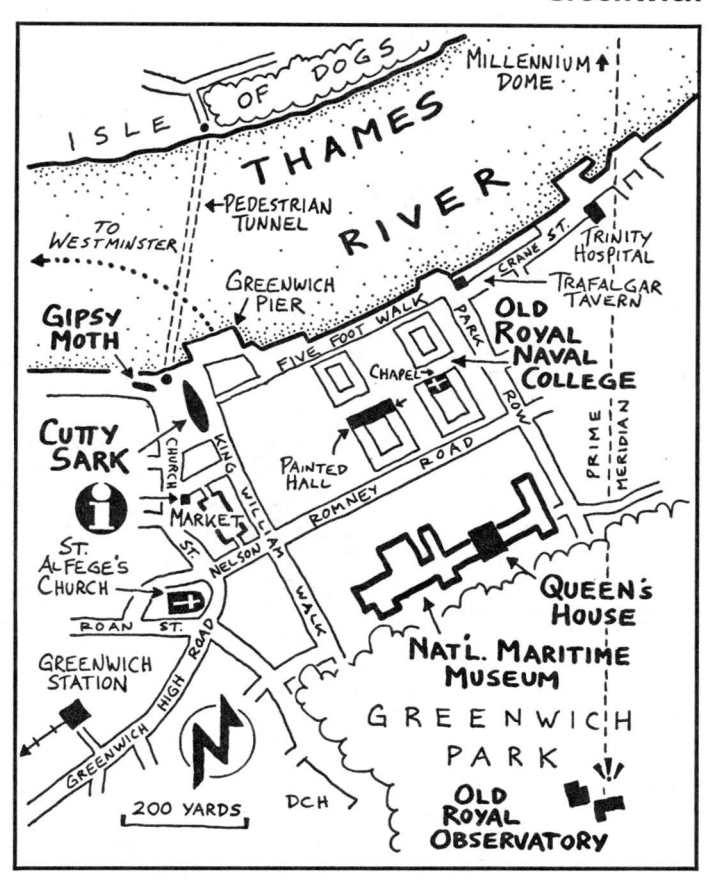

Chichester's return, Queen Elizabeth II knighted him in Greenwich, using the same sword Elizabeth I had used to knight Francis Drake in 1582 (free, viewable anytime, but interior not open to public).

Stroll the Thames to Trafalgar Tavern—From the *Cutty Sark* and *Gipsy Moth*, pass the pier and wander east along the Thames on Five Foot Walk (the width of the path) for grand views in front of the Old Royal Naval College (listed below). Founded by William III as a naval hospital and designed by Wren, the college was split in two because Queen Mary didn't want the view from

Queen's House blocked. The riverside view's good, too, with the twin-domed towers of the college (one giving the time; the other the direction of the wind) framing Queen's House and the Old Royal Observatory crowning the hill beyond.

Continuing downstream, just past the college, you'll see the Trafalgar Tavern. Dickens knew the pub well and even used it as the setting for the wedding breakfast in *Our Mutual Friend*. Built in 1837 in the Regency style to attract Londoners downriver, the tavern is still popular with Londoners for its fine lunches. And the upstairs Nelson Room is still used for weddings. Its formal moldings and elegant windows with balconies over the Thames are a step back in time (Mon–Sat 11:30–23:00, Sun 12:00–23:00, lunch 12:00–15:00, dinner 17:00–21:00, CC:VM, Park Row, tel. 020/8858-2437).

From the Trafalgar Tavern, you can walk the two long blocks up Park Row and turn right onto the park leading up to the Royal Observatory.

Old Royal Naval College—Now that the Royal Navy has moved out, the public is invited in to see the elaborate Painted Hall and Chapel, grandly designed by Wren and completed by other architects in the 1700s (fee not yet set, Mon–Sat 10:00–17:00, Sun 12:00–17:00, in the two college buildings farthest from river, choral service Sunday at 11:00 in chapel—all are welcome).

▲**Queen's House**—In 2000, this royal house—the architectural centerpiece of Greenwich—will host an exhibit, *The Story of Time* (until Sept 24). The building, the first Palladian-style villa in Britain, was designed in 1616 by Inigo Jones for James I's wife, Anne of Denmark. Exploring its Great Hall and Royal Apartments offers a sumptuous look at royal life in the 17th century—or lots of stairs if you're suffering from manor-house fatigue (£12 combo ticket covers most Greenwich town sights, daily 10:00–17:00).

▲▲▲**National Maritime Museum**—At the largest and most important maritime museum in the world visitors can taste both the romance and harshness of life at sea. Experience 20th-century naval warfare on a WWII frigate or get to know Britain's greatest naval hero, Nelson, whose display covers both his public career and his scandalous private life (don't miss the uniform coat in which he was fatally shot). The museum's newly opened Neptune Court greatly increases the number of galleries and better profiles the sweep of the Empire and the role of the sea in British history (£12 combo ticket covers most Greenwich town sights, daily 10:00–17:00, look for the events board at entrance: singing, treasure hunts, storytelling, particularly on weekends, tel. 020/8312-6565, www.nmm.ac.uk).

▲▲**Old Royal Observatory**—Whether you think the millennium starts in 2000 or 2001, it happened/happens here first.

All time is measured from longitude zero degrees, the prime meridian line—the point from which the millennium began/begins. However, the observatory's early work had nothing to do with coordinating the world's clocks to GMT, Greenwich mean time. The observatory was founded in 1675 by Charles II to find a way to determine longitude at sea. Today the Greenwich time signal is linked with the BBC (which broadcasts the "pips" worldwide at the top of the hour). In the courtyard, set your wristwatch to the digital clock showing GMT to a 10th of a second and straddle the prime meridian (called the Times meridian at the observatory, in deference to the *London Times*, which paid for the courtyard sculpture and the inset meridian line that runs banner headlines of today's *Times*—I wish I were kidding). It's less commercial—and cheaper—to straddle the meridian marked on the path outside the museum's courtyard. Nearby (also outside the courtyard), see how your foot measures up to the foot where the public standards of length are cast in bronze. Look up to see the orange Time Ball, also visible from the Thames, which drops daily at 13:00. Inside, check out the historic astronomical instruments and camera obscura. Finally, enjoy the view: the symmetrical royal buildings; the Thames; the square-mile "City" of London, with its skyscrapers and the dome of St. Paul's; the Docklands, with its busy cranes; and the Millennium Dome itself (£12 combo ticket covers most Greenwich town sights, daily 10:00–17:00). Planetarium shows twinkle on weekdays at 14:30, sometimes on weekends—ask (£2, buy tickets at the observatory, a 2-minute walk from the planetarium).

Greenwich Town—Save time to browse the town. Sunday is best for markets: The arts-and-crafts market is an entertaining mini–Covent Garden between College Approach and Nelson Road (Fri–Sun, best on Sun), and the antique market sells old ends and odds at high prices on Greenwich High Road near the post office. Wander beyond the touristy Church Street and Greenwich High Road to where flower stands spill into the side streets and antique shops sell brass nautical knickknacks. King William Walk, College Approach, Nelson Road, and Turnpin Lane are all worth a look. Covered markets and outdoor stalls make weekends colorful and lively.

Sights—Near Greenwich

▲▲▲**Millennium Dome**—Housed under a vast dome a mile from Greenwich, the show's theme is "who we are, how we live, what we do." The dome—at 20 acres the largest ever built—is separated into 14 zones, each with a focus: body, mind, spirit, work, rest, and so on. In the body zone, listen to the magnified sounds of human organs as you walk through the giant 90-foot-tall sculptures of a reclined man and woman (exit through leg). The town zone daily features a different British town telling its story. At center stage, an acrobatic drama troupe performs five times daily.

Your admission includes a filmed 30-minute joke history of Britain by Mr. Bean (Rowan Atkinson) shown at the Skyscape "baby dome," a 5,000-seat theater boasting the two biggest screens in Britain (in the Millennium Plaza in front of the dome).

The organizers plan (or pray) for 12 million visitors this year; a limit of 35,000 tickets will be sold daily. Even from the outside the dome will be a spectacle, especially on the nights it becomes an outdoor light show, with bright lights flickering over its white surface.

Skeptical media, an upset church, and problems getting transportation connections together in time have tempered this Y2K blowout. Still, it's an awesome construction and promises to be a happening worth the steep admission—£25 (daily from Jan 1– Dec 31, 10:00–18:00, until 23:00 in peak times). Tickets are sold at the door, in advance at National Lottery Ticket outlets in Britain, or over the phone at tel. 0870-606-2000, www.dome2000 .co.uk and www.greenwich2000.com. At the end of 2000, the contents of the Dome will be dismantled, and the Dome will be sold.

From London, it's easiest to reach the Dome by tube. The new Jubilee Line Extension, with the largest tube station in Europe, will zip up to 22,000 people an hour from central London directly to the Millennium Dome in 12 minutes (tube: North Greenwich). Boats shuttle people more scenically in about 45 minutes (6/hrly from Westminster Pier). To get to the Dome from the town of Greenwich, take a boat, bus, or the mile-long path.

Thames Barrier—East of Greenwich, the world's largest movable flood barrier welcomes visitors. You'll get a good video and exhibition on the river they claim is the cleanest urban waterway in the world, its floods, and how it was tamed (£3.40, Mon–Fri 10:00– 17:00, Sat–Sun 10:30–17:30; catch the 70-minute boat from Westminster Pier or take the 30-minute boat from Greenwich Pier— first boats from either location leave about 11:00; or a 20-minute train ride from London's Charing Cross station to Charlton, then a 15-minute walk, tel. 020/8305-4188).

BATH

Any tour of Britain that skips Bath stinks. Two hundred years ago this city of 80,000 was the trendsetting Hollywood of Britain. If ever a city enjoyed looking in the mirror, Bath's the one. It has more "government-listed" or protected historic buildings per capita than any other town in England. The entire city, built of the creamy warm-tone limestone called "Bath stone," beams in its cover-girl complexion. An architectural chorus line, it's a triumph of the Georgian style. Proud locals remind visitors that the town is routinely banned from the "Britain in Bloom" contest to give other towns a chance to win. Bath's narcissism is justified. Even with its mobs of tourists, it's a joy to visit.

Long before the Romans arrived in the first century, Bath was known for its hot springs. What became the Roman spa town of Aquae Sulis has always been fueled by the healing allure of its 116-degree mineral hot springs. The town's importance carried through Saxon times, when it had a huge church on the site of the present-day Abbey and was considered the religious capital of Britain. Its influence peaked in 973, when England's first king, Edgar, was crowned in the Abbey. Bath prospered as a wool town.

Bath then declined until the mid-1600s, when it was just a huddle of huts around the Abbey and some hot springs, with 3,000 residents oblivious to the Roman ruins 18 feet below their dirt floors. Then, in 1687, Queen Mary, fighting infertility, bathed here. Within 10 months she gave birth to a son... and a new age of popularity for Bath.

The town boomed as a spa resort. Ninety percent of the buildings you'll see today are from the 18th century. Local architect John Wood was inspired by the Italian architect Palladio to build a "new Rome." The town bloomed in the neoclassical style, and streets were lined not with scrawny sidewalks but with wide "parades," upon which the women in their stylishly wide dresses could spread their fashionable tails.

Beau Nash (1673–1762) was Bath's "master of ceremonies." He organized both the daily regimen of the aristocratic visitors and the city, lighting and improving street security, banning swords, and opening the Pump Room. Under his fashionable baton, Bath became a city of balls, gaming, and concerts and the place to see and be seen in England. This most civilized place became even more so with the great neoclassical building spree that followed.

Planning Your Time

Bath needs two nights even on a quick trip. There's plenty to do, and it's a joy to do it.

Here's how I'd spend a day in Bath: 9:00–Tour the Roman Baths, 10:30–Catch the free city walking tour, 12:30–Picnic on the open deck of a Guide Friday bus tour, 14:30–Free time in the shopping center of old Bath, 16:00–Tour the Costume Museum. Evening: Consider a Bizarre Bath Walk.

Orientation (tel. code: 01225)

Bath's town square, three blocks in front of the bus and train station, is a bouquet of tourist landmarks, including the Abbey, Roman and medieval baths, and the royal Pump Room.

Tourist Information: The TI is in the Abbey churchyard (Mon–Sat 9:30–18:00, Sun 10:00–16:00; Oct–Apr closes at 17:00 Mon–Sat, tel. 01225/477-101). Pick up the 25p Bath map/guide; the free "Museums in Bath" brochure; and the free, info-packed *This Month in Bath*. Browse through scads of flyers, books, and maps (including the Cotswolds) in their bookshop. Skip their room-finding service (£3 fee for walk-ins, £5 for callers) and go direct. An American Express office is tucked into the TI (decent rates, no commission on any checks, open same hours as TI).

Arrival in Bath: The Bath train station is a pleasure (small-town charm, an international tickets desk, and a Guide Friday office masquerading as a tourist information service). The bus station is immediately in front of the train station. To get to the TI, walk two blocks up Manvers Street from either station and turn left, following TI signs. My recommended B&Bs are all within a 10- or 15-minute walk or a £3.50 taxi ride from the station.

Driving within Bath is a nightmare of one-way streets. Nearly everyone gets lost. Ask for advice from your hotelier and minimize driving in town.

Helpful Hints

Festivals: The International Music Festival bursts into song from mid-May to early June (classical, folk, jazz, contemporary, tel. 01225/462-231) overlapped by the eclectic Fringe Festival from late May to mid-June (theater, walks, talks, bus trips, tel. 01225/480-079, www.bathfringe.co.uk). The Mozart festival strikes a universal chord every November. Bath's box office sells tickets for most every event (2 Church Street, tel. 01225/463-362).

Internet Access: Try the Itchy Feet Café & Travel Store (Bartlett Street), the click-cafe.com (Broad Street, near the YMCA), or the Bath Backpackers Hostel (13 Pierrepont Street, near train station, you pass hostel on your way to TI).

Farmers' Market: First and third Saturday of the month at Green Park Station (9:00–15:00).

Car Rental: Avis (behind the station and over the river at Unit 4B Riverside Business Park, Lower Bristol Road, tel. 01225/446-680), Enterprise (Lower Bristol Road, tel. 01225/443-311), and Hertz (just outside the train station, tel. 01225/442-911) are all trying harder. Most offices are a 10-minute walk from most recommended accommodations. Consider hotel delivery (usually £5, free with Enterprise). Most offices close Saturday afternoon and all day Sunday, complicating weekend pickups. Ideally, pick up your car only on the way out and into the countryside. Take the train or bus from London to Bath and rent a car as you leave Bath rather than in London.

Tours of Bath

▲▲**City Bus Tours**—The Guide Friday green-and-cream open-top tour bus makes a 70-minute figure-eight circuit of Bath's main sights with an exhaustingly informative running commentary. For one £8.50 ticket (buy from the driver), tourists can stop and go at will for a whole day. The buses cover the city center and the surrounding hills (17 signposted pick-up points, 5/hrly in summer, hrly in winter, about 9:30–18:00, until 16:00 in winter, tel. 01225/464-446). This is great in sunny weather and a feast for photographers. You can munch a sandwich, work on a tan, and sightsee at the same time. Several competing hop-on hop-off tour bus companies offer basically the same tour, but in 45 minutes and without the swing through the countryside, for a couple pounds less. (Ask a local what he or she thinks about all of these city-tour buses.) Generally, the Guide Friday guides are better. Save your ticket to get a £1 discount on a Guide Friday tour in another town.

▲▲▲**Walking Tours**—These two-hour tours, offered free by trained local volunteers who want to share their love of Bath with its many visitors, are a chatty, historical, gossip-filled joy, essential for your understanding of this town's amazing Georgian social scene. How else will you learn that the old "chair ho" call for your sedan chair evolved into today's "cheerio" greeting? Tours leave from in front of the Pump Room (year-round daily at 10:30, plus May–Oct 14:00 weekdays, 14:30 Sunday, and several evenings a week at 19:00; confirm at TI). For Ghost Walks and Bizarre Bath Comedy Walks, see "Nightlife," below. For a private walking tour from a local gentleman who's an excellent guide, contact Patrick Driscoll (2 hours for £41, tel. 01225/462-010).

Sights—Bath

▲▲▲**Roman and Medieval Baths**—In ancient Roman times, high society enjoyed the mineral springs at Bath. From Londinium, Romans traveled so often to Aquae Sulis, as the city was called, to "take a bath" that finally it became known simply as Bath. Today a fine museum surrounds the ancient bath and is, with its well-documented displays, a one-way system leading you past Roman artifacts, mosaics, a temple pediment, and the actual mouth of the spring, piled high with Roman pennies. Enjoy some quality time looking into the eyes of Minerva, goddess of the hot springs. The included self-guided tour audio-wand makes the visit easy and plenty informative. For those with a big appetite for Roman history, in-depth 40-minute tours leave from the end of the museum at the edge of the actual bath (included, on the hour, a pool-side clock is set for the next departure time). You can revisit the museum after the tour (£6.70, £8.70 combo ticket includes Costume Museum at a good savings, a family combo costs £22.60, combo tickets good for 1 week; daily 9:00–18:00, in August also 20:00–22:00, Oct–Apr closes at 17:00, tel. 01225/477-000).

▲**Pump Room**—After a centuries-long cold spell, Bath was reheated when the previously barren Queen Mary bathed here and in due course bore a male heir to the throne (1687). Once Bath was back on the aristocratic map, high society soon turned the place into one big pleasure palace. The Pump Room, an elegant Georgian hall just above the Roman baths, offers the visitor's best chance to raise a pinky in this Chippendale elegance. Drop by to sip coffee or tea to the rhythm of a string trio or pianist (live music all year 10:00–12:00, summers until 17:00, tea/coffee and pastry available for £4 anytime except during lunch, traditional high tea served after 14:30). Above the newspaper table and sedan chairs a statue of Beau Nash himself sniffles down at you. Now's your chance to have a famous (but forgettable) "Bath bun" and split (and spit) a 45p drink of the awfully curative water. Public WCs are in the entry hallway that connects the Pump Room with the Baths. You can't bathe in the baths, but a new spa facility will open here in 2001.

▲**Abbey**—Bath town wasn't much in the Middle Ages. But an important church has stood on this spot since Anglo-Saxon times. In 973, Edgar, the first king of England, was crowned here. Dominating the town center, the present church—the last great medieval church of England—is 500 years old and a fine example of Late Perpendicular Gothic, with breezy fan vaulting and enough stained glass to earn it the nickname "Lantern of the West"

Bath

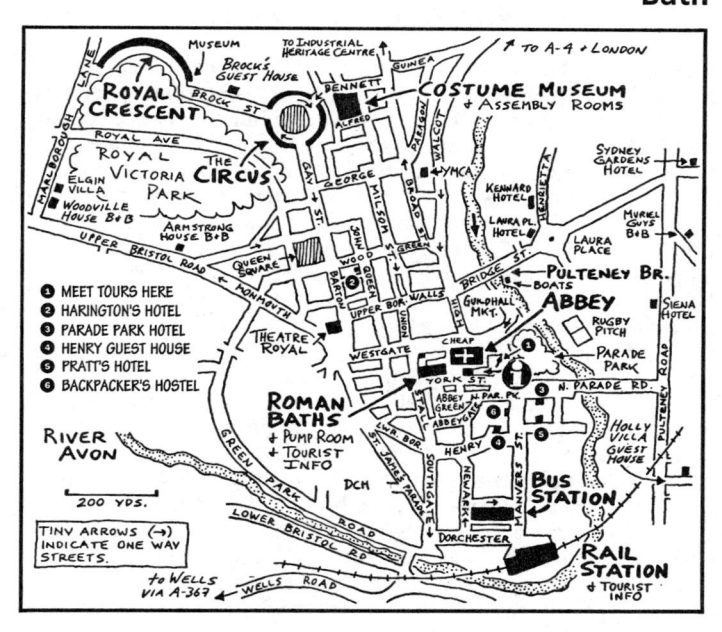

(Mon–Sat 9:00–18:00, Sun 13:00–17:30 with 15:15 evensong service; closes at 16:30 in winter; concert and evensong schedule posted on door, worth the £2 donation, handy flyer narrates an 18-stop tour). The *Abbey's Heritage Vaults*, a small but interesting exhibit, tells the story of Christianity in Bath since Roman times (£2, Mon–Sat 10:00–16:00, closed Sun). Take a moment to really appreciate the Abbey's architecture from the Abbey Green square.

▲**Pulteney Bridge and Cruises**—Bath is inclined to compare its shop-lined Pulteney Bridge to Florence's Ponte Vecchio. That's pushing it. To best enjoy a sunny day, pay £1 to enter the Parade Gardens below the bridge (daily 10:00–20:00, free after 20:00).

Across the bridge at Pulteney Weir, tour boats run cruises from under the bridge (£4, up to 7/day if the weather's good, 50 minutes to Bathampton and back, WCs on board). Just take whatever boat is running. Avon Cruisers stop in Bathampton if you'd like to walk back; Pulteney Cruisers come with a sundeck ideal for picnics.

▲▲**Royal Crescent and the Circus**—If Bath is an architectural cancan, these are the kickers. These first elegant Georgian "condos" by John Wood (the Elder and the Younger) are well explained in the city walking tours. "Georgian" is British for "neoclassical," or dating from the 1770s. Pretend you're rich. Pretend you're poor. Notice the "ha ha fence," a drop in the front yard offering a barrier, invisible from the windows, to sheep and peasants.

▲▲**Georgian House at #1 Royal Crescent**—This museum (on the corner of Brock Street and the Royal Crescent) offers your best look into a period house. It's worth the £4 admission to get behind one of those classy exteriors. The volunteers in each room are determined to fill you in on all the fascinating details of Georgian life... like how high-class women shaved their eyebrows and pasted on carefully trimmed strips of furry mouse skin in their place (Tue–Sun 10:30–17:00, closed Mon, closes at 16:00 in Nov, closed Dec–Jan, "no stiletto heels, please," tel. 01225/428-126).

▲▲▲**Costume Museum**—One of Europe's great museums, displaying 400 years of fashion—one frilly decade at a time—is housed within Bath's elegant Assembly Rooms. Follow the included and excellent CD-wand self-guided tour. Learn why Yankee Doodle "stuck a feather in his cap and called it macaroni" and much more (£4, an £8.70 combo ticket includes Roman Baths, family combo costs £22.60, daily 10:00–17:00, tel. 01225/477-789).

▲▲**Industrial Heritage Centre**—This is the grand title for Mr. Bowler's Business, a turn-of-the-century engineer's shop, brass foundry, and fizzy-drink factory with a Dickensian office. It's just a pile of meaningless old gadgets until a volunteer guide lovingly resurrects Mr. Bowler's creative genius. Fascinating hour-long tours go regularly; just join the one in session upon arrival. (£3.50, plus a few pence for a glass of genuine Victorian lemonade, daily 10:00–17:00, weekends only in winter, 2 blocks up Russell Street from the Assembly Rooms, call to be sure a volunteer is available to give a tour, café upstairs, tel. 01225/318-348.)

The Building of Bath Museum—This offers a fascinating look behind the scenes at how the Georgian city was actually built. It's just one large room of exhibits, but those interested in construction find it worth the £3.50 (Tue–Sun 10:30–17:00, closed Mon, near the Circus on a street called "the Paragon," tel. 01225/333-895).

Royal Photographic Society—A hit with shutterbugs, this focuses on the earliest cameras and photos, and their development (£3, daily 9:30–17:30, on Milsom Street, tel. 01225/462-841).

More Museums—Consider the new **Jane Austen Centre** (£4, daily 9:30–17:00, 40 Gay Street, just south of the Circus), the **Museum of East Asian Art** (daily, 12 Bennett Street, near the Circus), or the **Bath Postal Museum** (daily, 8 Broad Street). For the rundown, get the TI's brochure "Museums in Bath."

▲**American Museum**—This museum offers a fascinating look at colonial and early-American lifestyles. Guides fill you in on the details that make domestic Yankee history surprisingly interesting (£5, Tue–Sun 14:00–17:00, closed Mon and early Nov–late Mar, at Claverton Manor, tel. 01225/460-503).

Activities in Bath
Walking, Biking, and Swimming—Get brochures at the TI. Consider the idyllic walk up the canal path to Bathampton: From downtown, walk over Pulteney Bridge, through Sydney Gardens, turn left on canal, and in 30 minutes you'll hit Bathampton, with its much-loved Old George Pub. The Bath Skyline Walk is a six-mile wander around the hills surrounding Bath (95p leaflet at TI). Consider *Country Walks around Bath*, by Tim Mowls (£5 at TI). Sailors enjoy the river cruise up to Bathampton; hikers like walking back (see "Pulteney Bridge and Cruises," above). From Bathampton it's two hours along the canal to the fine old town of Bradford-on-Avon, from which you can train back to Bath. You can bike this route (rent bikes at Avon Valley Cyclery behind train station, £9/half day, £14/all day, tel. 01225/442-442). The scenic 12-mile path along the old Bath–Bristol train tracks is also popular. Cyclists like *Short Cycles around Bath*, by John Plaxton (£4.50, available at TI).

The Bath Sports and Leisure Centre has a swimming pool and more (£2.50, daily 8:00–22:00, just across North Parade Bridge, call for free swim times, tel. 01225/462-563).

Shopping—There's great browsing between the Abbey and the Assembly Rooms (Costume Museum). Shops close at 17:30, later on Thursday. Explore the antique center on Bartlett Street just below the Assembly Rooms. You'll find the most stalls open on Wednesday. Pick up the local paper (usually out on Friday) and shop with the dealers at estate sales and auctions listed in *What's On*.

Nightlife in Bath
This Month in Bath (available at TI) lists events.

Plays—The Theatre Royal, newly restored and one of England's loveliest, offers a busy schedule of London West End–type plays, including many "pre-London" dress rehearsal runs (£10–25, cheap standby tickets and late returns, tel. 01225/448-844).

Bizarre Bath Walks—For a walking comedy act "with absolutely no history or culture," follow J. J. or Noel Britten on their creative and entertaining Bizarre Bath walk. This 90-minute "tour," which plays off local passersby as well as tour members, is a kick (£3.50, 20:00 nightly Apr–Sept; heavy on magic, careful to insult all minorities and sensitivities, just racy enough but still good family fun; leave from Huntsman pub near the Abbey, confirm at TI or call 01225/335-124). **Ghost Walks** are another way to pass the after-dark hours (£4, 20:00, 2 hrs, unreliably Mon–Sat Apr–Oct; in winter Fridays only; leave from Garrick's Head pub near Theatre Royal, tel. 01225/463-618). Scholarly types can try the free historical walking tours offered several times a week (19:00, 2 hrs, May–Oct, ask at TI).

Drinks—Drink real ale at the Star Pub (top of Paragon Street).

Sleeping in Bath
(£1 = about $1.70, tel. code: 01225)
Sleep Code: **S** = Single, **D** = Double/Twin, **T** = Triple, **Q** = Quad, **b** = bathroom, **t** = toilet only, **s** = shower only, **CC** = Credit Card (Visa, MasterCard, Amex).

Bath is a busy tourist town. To get a good B&B, make a telephone reservation in advance. Competition is stiff, and it's worth asking any of these places for a nonweekend, three-nights-in-a-row, or off-season deal. Friday and Saturday nights are tightest, especially if you're staying only one night, since B&Bs favor those staying longer. If staying only Saturday night, you're very bad news. Expect lots of stairs and no lifts. A launderette is around the corner from Brock's Guest House on the pedestrian lane Margaret's Buildings (Sun–Fri 8:00–21:00, Sat 8:00–20:00), and another scruffier launderette, closer to the Marlborough Lane listings, is on Upper Bristol Road (daily 9:00–20:00, tel. 01225/429-378).

Sleeping in B&Bs near the Royal Crescent

From the train station, these listings are all a 10- to 15-minute uphill walk or an easy £3.50 taxi ride.

Brock's Guest House will put bubbles in your Bath experience. Marion and Geoffrey Dodd have redone their Georgian townhouse (built by John Wood in 1765) in a way that would make the famous architect proud. It's located between the prestigious Royal Crescent and the elegant Circus (Db-£60–67, 1 deluxe Db-£72, Tb-£83–85, Qb-£95–99, reserve with a credit-card number far in advance, CC:VM, strictly nonsmoking, little library on top floor, 32 Brock Street, BA1 2LN, tel. 01225/338-374, fax 01225/334-245, e-mail: marion@brocks.force9.net). Marion can occasionally arrange a reasonable private car hire.

Woodville House is run by Anne and Tom Toalster. This grandmotherly little house has three charming rooms, one shared shower/WC, an extra WC, and a TV lounge. Breakfast is served at a big, family-style table (D-£40, minimum 2 nights, strictly nonsmoking, below the Royal Crescent at 4 Marlborough Lane, BA1 2NQ, tel. & fax 01225/319-335, e-mail: toalster@compuserve.com).

Other recommended B&Bs on Marlborough Lane: **Elgin Villa** is also a fine value, with five comfy, well-maintained rooms (Ds-£45, Db-£50, discounts for 3-night stays, kids £15 extra, continental breakfast served in room, parking, nonsmoking, 6 Marlborough Lane, BA1 2NQ Bath, tel. & fax 01225/424-557, www.elginvilla.co.uk, Alwyn and Carol Landman).

Athelney Guest House, which also serves a continental breakfast in your room, has three spacious rooms with two shared bathrooms (D-£38, T-£57, nonsmoking, parking, 5 Marlborough Lane, BA1 2NQ, tel. & fax 01225/312-031, Sue and Colin Davies).

Parkside Guest House is more upscale, renting four classy

Edwardian rooms (Db-£60, nonsmoking, access to pleasant backyard, 11 Marlborough Lane, BA1 2NQ, tel. & fax 01225/429-444, e-mail: parkside@lynall.freeserve.co.uk, Erica and Inge Lynall).

Marlborough House is both Victorian and vegetarian, with five comfortable rooms and optional £12 veggie dinners (Sb-£45–55, Db-£70–85, CC:VM, room service, 1 Marlborough Lane, BA1 2NQ, tel. 01225/318-175, fax 01225/466-127, www.s-h-systems.co.uk/hotels/marlbor1.html, Americans Laura and Charles).

Prior House B&B, with four rooms, is run by helpful, friendly Lynn and Keith Shearns (D-£35, Db-£40, nonsmoking, 3 Marlborough Lane, tel. 01225/313-587, fax 01225/443-543, e-mail: keith@shearns.freeserve.co.uk).

Armstrong House B&B is basic, well run, and closer to town on a busier road, with five rooms behind double-paned windows (Db-£50–55, continental breakfast in room, nonsmoking, 41 Crescent Gardens, Upper Bristol Road, BA1 2NB, tel. 01225/442-211, fax 01225/460-665, Tony Conradi).

Sleeping in B&Bs East of the River

These listings are about a 10-minute walk from the city center.

Near North Parade Road: Holly Villa Guest House, with a cheery garden and a cozy TV lounge, is enthusiastically and thoughtfully run by Jill and Keith McGarrigle (Ds-£42, Db-£48, deluxe Db-£50, Tb-£65, 6 rooms, strictly nonsmoking, easy parking, 8-minute walk from station and city center, 14 Pulteney Gardens, BA2 4HG, tel. 01225/310-331, fax 01225/339-334, e-mail: hollyvilla.bb@ukgateway.net). From the city center, walk over North Parade Bridge, take the first right, then the second left.

Near Pulteney Road: Muriel Guy's B&B is another good value, mixing Georgian elegance with homey warmth and fine city views (Db-£48, 4 rooms, nonsmoking, 10-minute walk from city center, go over bridge on North Parade Road, left on Pulteney Road, cross to church, Raby Place is first row of houses on hill, 14 Raby Place, BA2 4EH, tel. 01225/465-120, fax01225/465-283).

Siena Hotel next door to a lawn bowling green, has comfy, attractive rooms that hint of a more genteel time. Though this well-maintained hotel fronts a busy street, it feels tranquil inside, with double-paned windows. Rooms in the back have pleasant views of sports greens and Bath beyond (Db-£70–90, 4-poster Db-£100, CC:VMA, access to garden in back, easy parking, 10-minute walk from center, 24/25 Pulteney Road, BA2 4EZ, tel. 01225/425-495, fax 01225/469-029).

In Sydney Gardens: Sydney Gardens Hotel is a classy Casablanca-type place with six tastefully decorated rooms, garden views, and an entrance to Sydney Gardens park. The elegant breakfast room overlooking the park is a magnet (Db-£69/weekdays, £75/weekends, Tb-£95, CC:VM, 2 nights preferred, request garden view, located between park and canal, easy parking, 10-minute walk from center, Sydney Road, BA2 6NT, tel. 01225/464-818, fax 01225/484-347, Geraldine and Peter Beaven).

Sleeping in Hotels near Pulteney Bridge

These listings are just a few minutes' walk from the center.

Kennard Hotel is comfortable, with 14 charming Georgian rooms. Richard Ambler runs this place warmly, with careful attention to detail (S-£48, Db-£88–98 depending upon size, CC:VMA, nonsmoking, just over Pulteney Bridge, turn left at Henrietta, 11 Henrietta Street, BA2 6LL, tel. 01225/310-472, fax 01225/460-054, www.kennard.co.uk).

Laura Place Hotel is another elegant Georgian place (8 rooms, 2 on the ground floor, Db-£80–90 from small and high up to huge and palatial, 2-night minimum stay, 10 percent discount with cash and this book, CC:VMA, family suite, nonsmoking, easy parking, 3 Laura Place, Great Pulteney Street, BA2 4BH, just over Pulteney Bridge, tel. 01225/463-815, fax 01225/310-222, Patricia Bull).

Henrietta Hotel is a very plain place with nearly no character in the same elegant neighborhood (10 rooms, Db-£45–65, cash discount when quiet, CC:VM, 32 Henrietta Street, tel. 01225/447-779, fax 01225/444-150).

Sleeping in Hotels in the Town Center

Harington's of Bath Hotel, with 13 newly renovated rooms on a quiet street in the town center, is run by Susan Pow (Db-£78–95, Tb-£95–120, prices decrease midweek and increase on weekends, CC:VMA, nonsmoking, lots of stairs, attached restaurant/bar serves simple meals throughout day, extremely central at 10 Queen Street, BA1 1HE, tel. 01225/461-728, fax 01225/444-804, www.haringtonshotel.co.uk).

Parade Park Hotel, in a Georgian building, has comfortable rooms, helpful owners, and a central location (35 rooms, Db-£60–65, special 4-poster Db-£75, Tb-£90, Qb-£105, CC:VM, nonsmoking, beaucoup stairs, attached restaurant/bar, 10 North Parade, BA2 4AL, tel. 01225/463-384, fax 01225/442-322, www.paradepark.co.uk, Nita and David Derrick).

Henry Guest House is a plain, vertical little eight-room, family-run place two blocks in front of the train station on a quiet side street (S-£20, D-£40, T-£57, TVs in rooms, lots of narrow stairs, 1 shower and 1 bath for all, 6 Henry Street, BA1 1JT, tel. 01225/424-052). This kind of decency at this budget price, centrally located, is found nowhere else in Bath.

Pratt's Hotel is as proper and old English as you'll find in Bath. Its creaks and frays are aristocratic. Its public places make you want to sip a brandy, and its 46 rooms are bright, spacious, and come with all the comforts (Sb-£75, Db-£105, prices promised with this book in 2000, dogs £2.95 but children free, CC:VMA, attached restaurant/bar, elevator, 2 blocks immediately in front of the station on South Parade, BA2 4AB, tel. 01225/460-441, fax 01225/448-807, e-mail: admin@prattshotel.demon.co.uk).

The Abbey Hotel, a Best Western hotel, overprices its 60 slightly worn rooms, but has a great location and offers a rare elevator as well as some ground-floor rooms (standard Db-£115, deluxe Db-£125, CC:VMA, attached restaurant, nonsmoking rooms available, North Parade, BA1 1LF, tel. 01225/461-603, fax 01225/447-758, e-mail: ahres@compasshotels.co.uk).

Sleeping in Dorms

The **YMCA,** institutional but friendly, and wonderfully central on a leafy square down a tiny alley off Broad Street, has industrial-strength rooms and scuff-proof halls (S-£15, D-£28, T-£42, Q-£55, beds in big dorms-£11, cheaper for 2-night stays, includes breakfast, families offered a day nursery for kids under 5, cheap dinners, CC:VM, Broad Street Place, BA1 5LH, tel. 01225/460-471, fax 01225/462-065, e-mail: info@ymcabath.u-net.com).

Bath Backpackers Hostel bills itself as a totally fun-packed, mad place to stay. This Aussie-run dive/hostel rents bunk beds in 6- to 10-bed coed rooms (£12 per bed, no lockers, Internet access for nonguests as well, a couple of blocks toward the city center from the station, 13 Pierrepont Street, tel. 01225/446-787, fax 01225/446-305, www.backpackers-uk.demon.co.uk, e-mail: backpackers_uk@hotmail.com).

The **Youth Hostel** is in a grand old building on Bathwick Hill outside of town (£11 per bed without breakfast in 2- to 12-bed rooms, bus #18 from station, tel. 01225/465-674).

Eating in Bath

While not a great pub grub town, Bath is bursting with quaint eateries. There's something for every appetite and budget—just stroll around the center of town. A picnic dinner of take-out fish and chips in the Royal Crescent Park is ideal for aristocratic hoboes.

Eating between the Abbey and the Station

Three fine and popular places share North Parade Passage, a block south of the Abbey: **Tilley's Bistro** serves healthy French, English, and vegetarian meals with ambience (£15 3-course lunches, £20 dinners, daily 12:00–14:30, 18:30–23:00, CC:VM, nonsmoking, North Parade Passage, tel. 01225/484-200). **Sally Lunn's House** is a cutesy, quasi-historic place for expensive doily meals, tea, pink pillows, and lots of lace (£12 meals, nightly, CC:VM, 4 North Parade Passage, tel. 01225/461-634). It's fine for tea and buns, and customers get a free peek at the basement museum (otherwise 30p). Next door, **Demuth's Vegetarian Restaurant** serves good three-course £15 meals (daily 10:00–22:00, CC:VM, vegan options available, tel. 01225/446-059).

Crystal Palace Pub, with hearty meals under rustic timbers or in the sunny courtyard, is a handy standby (£6 meals, Mon–Fri 11:00–20:30, Sat 11:00–15:30, Sun 12:00–14:30, children welcome on patio, not indoors; 11 Abbey Green, tel. 01225/423-944).

Seafoods offers the best eat-in or take-out fish-and-chips deal in town (daily from noon until near midnight, 27 Kingsmeads Street, just off Kingsmead Square). For more cheap meals, try **Spike's Fish and Chips** (open very late) and the neighboring café just behind the bus station.

Eating between the Abbey and the Circus

George Street is lined with cheery eateries: Thai, Italian, wine bars, and so on. **Caffé Martini** is purely Italian with class (£9 entrées, £7 pizzas, daily 12:00–14:30, 18:00–22:00, CC:VM, 9 George Street, tel. 01225/460-818), while the **Mediterraneo,** also Italian, is homier (12 George Street, tel. 01225/429-008).

Eastern Eye serves Indian food under the domes of a Georgian auction hall (£15 meals, £9 minimum, daily 12:00–14:30, 18:00–23:00, CC:VMA, 8a Quiet Street, tel. 01225/422-323).

The **Old Green Tree Pub** on Green Street is a rare pub with good grub, microbrews, and a nonsmoking room (lunch only, served 12:00–14:15, no children).

Browns, a popular chain, offers affordable English food throughout the day without the customary afternoon closure (£5 lunch special, Mon–Sat 11:00–23:30, Sun 12:00–23:30, CC:VMA, live music sometimes Sun–Thu eves, half block east of the Abbey, Orange Grove, tel. 01225/461-199).

Locals prize **The Moon and Sixpence** for its quality (£7 lunch, 3-course dinner menu for £18–22, daily 12:00–14:30, 17:30–22:30, CC:VM, indoor/outdoor seating, 6a Broad Street, tel. 01225/460-962).

Pasta Galore serves decent Italian food and homemade pasta outside on a patio or inside; the ground floor is brighter than the basement (daily 12:00–14:30, 18:00–22:30, CC:VM, 1 Barton Street, tel. 01225/463-861).

Devon Savouries serves greasy, delicious take-out pasties, sausage rolls, and vegetable pies (Mon–Sat 9:00–17:30, hours vary on Sun; on Burton Street, the main walkway between New Bond Street and Upper Borough Walls).

The **Waitrose supermarket,** at the Podium shopping center, is great for groceries (Mon–Fri 8:30–20:00, Sat 8:30–19:00, Sun 11:00–17:00, just west of Pulteney Bridge and across from post office on High Street).

Guildhall Market, across from Pulteney Bridge, is fun for browsing and picnic shopping, with an inexpensive Market Café if you'd like to sip tea surrounded by stacks of used books, overripe bananas, and honest-to-goodness old-time locals (Mon–Sat 7:30–17:00, closed Sun).

Eating East of Pulteney Bridge

For a classy, intimate setting and "new English" cuisine worth the splurge, dine at **No. 5 Bistro** (main courses with vegetables £12–15, Mon and Tue are "bring your own bottle of wine" nights—no corkage charge, Mon–Sat 18:30–22:00, closed Sun, just over Pulteney Bridge at 5 Argyle Street, smart to reserve, tel. 01225/444-499).

Eating near the Circus and Brock's Guest House

Circus Restaurant is intimate and a good value, with Mozartian ambience and candlelight prices: £16.50 for a three-course dinner special including great vegetables and a selection of fine desserts (daily 12:00–14:00, 18:30–23:00, 34 Brock Street, tel. 01225/318-918, Felix Rosenow).

Woods Restaurant serves modern English cuisine to well-dressed locals in a sprawling candlelit brasserie (£7 lunches, £13–25 3-course dinners, daily 12:00–15:00, 18:00–23:00 except closed Sun eve, CC:VM, 9–13 Alfred Street, near Assembly Rooms, tel. 01225/314-812).

Transportation Connections—Bath

To London's Paddington Station: By train (hrly, 75 min, £32.50 one way), or cheaper by National Express bus (nearly hrly, 3 hrs, £11.25 one way, £19.50 round-trip, ask about £11.50 day returns). To get from London to Bath, consider an all-day Stonehenge-and-Bath organized bus tour from London. For about the same cost as the train ticket, you can see Stonehenge, tour Bath, and leave the tour before it returns to London (they'll let you stow your bag underneath). Evan Evans (£25 for transportation only, £46 includes admissions and tour, tel. 020/8332-2222) and Travelline (tel. 020/8668-7261) offer Stonehenge/Bath day trips from London. Train info tel. 0345/484-950.

To London's airports: By National Express bus to **Heathrow** Airport—and continuing on to London (10/day, leaving Bath at 5:00, 6:30, 7:30, 8:45, 10:00, 12:00, 13:30, 15:00, 16:30, and 18:30, 2.5 hrs, £11.50, tel. 0990-808-080), and to **Gatwick** (2/hrly, 4.5 hrs, £19.50, change at Heathrow). Trains are faster but more expensive (hrly, 2.5 hrs, £28.20). Coming from Heathrow you can also take the tube from the airport to London's Paddington station and then catch the Exeter train to Bath.

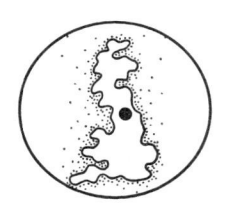

YORK

Historical York is loaded with world-class sights. Marvel at the York Minster, England's finest Gothic church. Ramble through the Shambles, York's wonderfully preserved medieval quarter. Enjoy a walking tour led by an old Yorker. Hop a train at Europe's greatest Railway Museum, travel to the 1800s in York Castle Museum, and head back a thousand years to Viking York at the Jorvik exhibit.

York has a rich history. In A.D. 71 it was Eboracum, a Roman provincial capital. Constantine was proclaimed emperor here in A.D. 306. In the fifth century, as Rome was toppling, a Roman emperor sent a letter telling England it was on its own, and York became Eoforwic, the capital of the Anglo-Saxon kingdom of Northumbria. A church was built here in 627, and the town was an early Christian center of learning. The Vikings later took the town, and from about 860 to 950 it was a Danish trading center called Jorvik. The invading and conquering Normans destroyed then rebuilt the city, giving it a castle and the walls you see today. Medieval York, with 9,000 inhabitants, grew rich on the wool trade and became England's second city. Henry VIII spared the city's fine minster and used York as his Anglican church's northern capital. The Archbishop of York is second only to the Archbishop of Canterbury in the Anglican Church. In the Industrial Age, York was the railway hub of North England. When it was built, York's train station was the world's largest. Today, except for its huge chocolate factory (Kit-Kats are made here), York's leading industry is tourism.

Planning Your Time

York rivals Edinburgh as the best sightseeing city in Britain after London. On even a 10-day trip through Britain, it deserves two nights and a day. For the best 36 hours, follow this plan: Catch the 19:00 city walking tour on the evening of your arrival. The next morning be at Jorvik at 9:00 when it opens (to avoid the midday crowds, or prebook at least a day ahead; see "Sights" below). The nearby Castle Museum is worth the rest of the morning (10:00–noon, I could spend even more time here). Three options for your early afternoon: Shoppers browse the Shambles, train buffs tour the National Railway Museum, and scholars do the Yorkshire Museum. Tour the Minster at 16:00 before catching the 17:00 evensong service. Finish your day with an early evening stroll along the wall and perhaps through the abbey gardens. This schedule assumes you're there in the summer (evening orientation walk) and that there's an evensong on. Confirm your plans with the TI.

Orientation (tel. code: 01904)

The sightseer's York is small. Virtually everything is within a few minutes' walk: the sights, train station, TI, and B&Bs. The longest walk a visitor might take (from a B&B across the old town to the Castle Museum) is 15 minutes.

Bootham Bar, a gate in the medieval town wall, is the hub of your York visit. At Bootham Bar (and on Exhibition Square facing it) you'll find the TI, the starting points for most walking tours and bus tours, handy access to the medieval town wall, Gillygate (pronounced "jilly-gate," lined with good eateries), and Bootham Street, which leads to the recommended B&Bs. (In York, a "bar" is a gate and a "gate" is a street. Go ahead, blame the Vikings.)

Tourist Information: The TI at Bootham Bar sells a 75p "York Map and Guide." Ask for the free monthly *What's On* guide and the monthly *Gig Guide* for live music (Apr–Oct Mon–Sat 9:00–18:00, Sun 9:00–18:00; Jul–Aug until 19:00; Nov–Mar Mon–Sat 9:00–17:00, Sun 9:30–15:00, tel. 01904/621-756, pay WCs next door, built into gate of Bootham Bar). The TI books rooms for a £3 fee, sells theater tickets, and can help with bus and train schedules. The train station TI is smaller but provides all the same information and services (Apr–Sept Mon–Sat 9:00–20:00, Sun 9:30–17:00, shorter hours off-season).

Arrival in York: The station is a five-minute walk from town; turn left down Station Road and follow the crowd toward the Gothic towers of the Minster. After the bridge, a block before the Minster, signs to the TI send you left on St. Leonard's Place. Recommended B&Bs are a five-minute walk from there. (For a shortcut to B&B area from station, walk along river to railway bridge, cross bridge on walkway, cross car park for B&Bs on St. Mary's Street, or duck through pedestrian walkway under tracks to B&Bs on Sycamore and Queen Anne's Road). With lots of luggage, consider a quick taxi ride (£3).

York

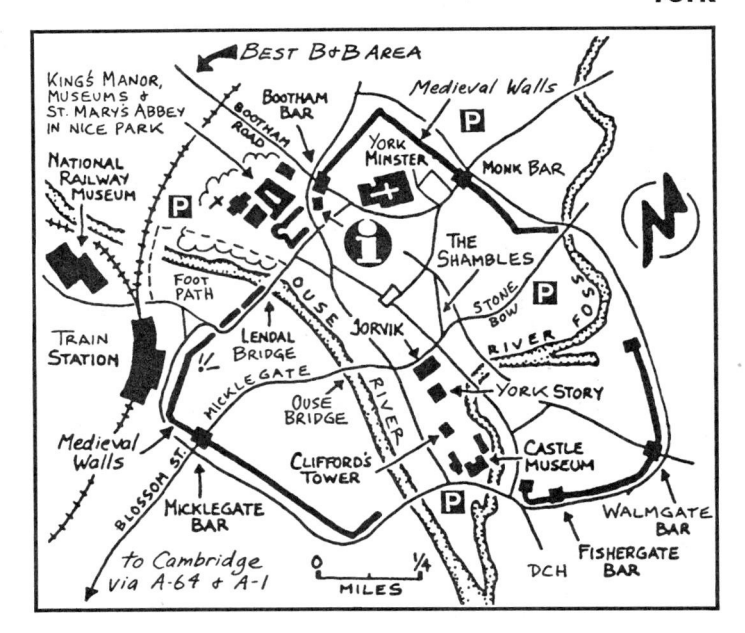

Helpful Hints

Festivals: *York Millennium Mystery Plays,* a series of dramas based on the Bible and involving 200 actors, covering nothing less than the story of humankind, will run from June 22 to July 22 in 2000. York's annual Early Music festival strums and hums from July 7 to 16. Book a room well in advance during festival times.

Internet Access: The Gateway, an Internet café, has eight computers (£5/hr, Mon–Wed 10:00–20:00, Thu–Sat 10:00–23:00, Sun 12:00–16:00, 26 Swinegate, tel. 01904/646-446). The Impressions Gallery has two in a hallway (£5/hr, Mon–Fri 9:30–17:30, on Castlegate, next to Fairfax House, near Jorvik).

Bike Rental: Try Trotters, just outside Monk Bar (£10/day, helmets-£2, Mon–Sat 9:30–17:00, Sun 10:30–15:30, tel. 01904/622-868).

Car Rental: If you're nearing the end of your trip, consider dropping your car upon arrival in York. The money saved by turning it in early nearly pays for the train ticket that whisks you effortlessly to Edinburgh or London. Avis (1 Layerthorpe, tel. 01904/610-460), Hertz (at train station, tel. 01904/612-586), Kenning Car & Van Rental (Micklegate, tel. 01904/659-328), and Budget (Foss Islands Road, tel. 01904/644-919) all have offices in York. Beware, car rental agencies close Saturday afternoon and all day Sunday—when dropping off is OK but picking up is impossible.

Tours of York

▲▲▲**Walking Tours**—Charming local volunteer guides give energetic, entertaining, and free two-hour walks through York (daily 10:15 all year, plus 14:15 Apr–Oct, plus 19:00 Jun–Aug, from Exhibition Square across from TI). There are many other commercial York walking tours. YorkWalk Tours, for example, has reliable guides and many themes to choose from (£4.50, tel. 01904/622-303, TI has schedule). The various ghost tours, all offered after nightfall, are more fun than informative.

▲**Guide Friday Hop-on Hop-off Bus Tours**—York's Guide Friday offers tour guides on speed who can talk enthusiastically to three sleeping tourists in a gale on a topless double-decker bus for an hour without stopping. Buses make the hour-long circuit, covering secondary York sights that the city walking tours skip—the workaday perimeter of town. Tickets cost £8 on the bus or from the TI (hop on and off all day, departures every 10–15 minutes from 9:20 until around 17:00; includes vouchers for discounts on York's sights, read brochure; tel. 01904/640-896). While you can hop on and off where you like, the York route is of no value from a transportation-to-the-sights point of view. I'd catch it at the Bootham Bar TI and ride it for an orientation all the way around (one hour) or get off at the Railway Museum, skipping the last five minutes. Guide Friday's competitors give you a little less for a little less.

Sights—York

▲**City Walls**—The historic walls of York provide a fine two-mile walk. Walk from Bootham Bar (gate) to Monk Bar for outstanding cathedral views. Open from dawn till dusk (barring attacks) and free.

▲▲▲**York Minster**—The pride of York, this largest Gothic church north of the Alps (540 feet long, 200 feet tall) brilliantly shows that the High Middle Ages were far from dark. The word *minster* means a place from which people go out to minister or spread the word of God.

Your first impression might be the spaciousness and brightness of the nave (built 1280–1350). The nave—from the middle period of Gothic, called "Decorated Gothic"—is one of the widest Gothic naves in Europe. Notice the Great West Window (1338) above the entry. The heart in the tracery is called "the heart of Yorkshire." The mysterious dragon's head (sticking out over the nave) was probably used as a crane to lift a font cover.

The north and south transepts are the oldest part of today's church (1220–1270). The oldest complete window in the minster, with the modern-looking grisaille pattern, is the Five Sisters' Window in the north transept (1260).

The fanciful choir and the east end (high altar) is from the last stage of Gothic, Perpendicular (1360–1470). The Great East Window (1405), the largest medieval glass window in existence, shows the beginning and the end of the world, with scenes from Genesis and the Book of Revelation. A chart (on the right, with a tiny, more helpful chart within) highlights the core Old Testament scenes in this hard-to-read masterpiece. Enjoy the art close up on the chart and then step back and find the real thing.

The "foundations" (£2) give you a chance to climb down—archaeologically and physically—through the centuries to see the roots of the much smaller, but still huge, Norman church (Romanesque, 1100) that stood on this spot and, below that, the Roman excavations. Constantine was proclaimed Roman emperor here in the fourth century A.D. Peek also at the modern concrete save-the-church foundations and the church treasury.

There are three more extra visits to consider. The chapter house, an elaborately decorated 13th-century Gothic dome, features playful details carved in the stonework (pointed out in the flyer that comes with the 80p admission). You can step into the crypt—an actual bit of the Romanesque church excavated in modern times—which features 12th-century Romanesque art (80p) or scale the tower (£2.50, 275 steps, great view).

The cathedral opens daily at 7:00 and closes at 20:30 in summer, 18:00 in winter (tel. 01904/624-426). The chapter house, tower, and "foundations" have shorter hours, usually 9:30–18:30 (off-season 10:00–16:30 or 17:30). The crypt's hours are roughly Mon–Sat 9:30–16:30, Sun 13:30–16:30. Follow the "Welcome to the York Minster" flyer and ask about a free guided tour at the reception desk at the entry (tours go frequently, even with just 1 or 2 people; you can join 1 in progress). The helpful blue-armbanded Minster guides are happy to answer your questions. While a donation of £2.50 to visit the church is reasonably requested, by visiting all the small extra spots inside I give that (and more) in the form of those admissions. Just pay for and enjoy all the little extras.

Evensong is a chance to experience the cathedral in musical and spiritual action. The 45-minute evensong services are held at 17:00 on weekdays and 16:00 on weekends but are usually spoken on Monday and when the choir is off.

▲**The Shambles**—This is the most colorful old York street in the half-timbered, traffic-free core of town. Ye olde downtown York, while very touristy, is a window-shopping, busker-filled, people watcher's delight. Don't miss the more frumpy Newgate Market or the old-time candy store just opposite the bottom end of the Shambles.

▲▲▲**York Castle Museum**—Truly one of Europe's top museums, this is a Victorian home show, the closest thing to a time-tunnel experience England has to offer. It includes the 19th-century Kirkgate: a fine collection of old shops well stocked exactly as they were 150 years ago, along with costumes, armor, an eye-opening Anglo-Saxon helmet (from A.D. 750), and the entertaining "every home should have one" exhibit showing the evolution of vacuum cleaners, toilets, TVs, bicycles, stoves, and so on, from their crude beginnings to now. The one-way plan allows you to see everything: a working watermill (Apr–Oct), prison cells, man traps, World War II fashions, and old toys (£5, combined ticket with York Story-£6.30, daily 9:30–17:00, Nov–Mar daily 9:30-16:30, cafeteria midway through museum, shop, car park; the £2.50 guidebook, while not necessary, makes a nice souvenir; CC:VM, tel. 01904/653-611). Clifford's Tower (across from Castle Museum, not worth the £1.80, daily 10:00–18:00) is all that's left of York's castle (13th century, site of an 1190 massacre of local Jews—read about this at base of hill).

▲**Jorvik**—Sail the "Pirates of the Caribbean" north and back 800 years and you get Jorvik—more a ride than a museum. Innovative 10 years ago, the commercial success of Jorvik (yor-vik) inspired copycat ride/museums all over England. You'll ride a little Disney-type train car for 13 minutes through the re-created Viking street of Coppergate. It's the year 948, and you're in the village of Jorvik. Next your little train takes you through the actual excavation sight that inspired this. Finally you'll browse through a small gallery of Viking shoes, combs, locks, and other intimate glimpses of that redheaded culture (£5.35, daily 9:00–17:30, Nov–Mar closing varies from 15:30–16:30, last entry 30 minutes before closing, tel. 01904/643-211). Midday lines can be an hour long, and even past the turnstile there's a 25-minute wait. Avoid the line by going very early or very late in the day or by prebooking (call 01904/543-403 at least a day ahead, Mon–Fri 9:00–17:00, office closed on weekends, CC:VM, you're given a time slot, add £1 per ticket for entry 10:00–16:00). Some love this "ride"; others call it a gimmicky rip-off. If you're looking for a serious museum, see the Viking exhibit at the Yorkshire Museum. It's better. If you're thinking Disneyland with a splash of history, Jorvik's great. I like Jorvik, but it's not worth a long line.

▲▲**National Railway Museum**—This thunderous museum shows 150 fascinating years of British railroad history. Fanning out from a grand roundhouse is an array of historic cars and engines, including Queen Victoria's lavish royal car and the very first "stagecoaches on rails." There's much more, including exhibits on dining cars, post cars, sleeping cars, train posters, and videos. This biggest and best railroad museum anywhere is interesting even to people who think *Pullman* is Japanese for "tug-o-war" (£6, kids under 17 free, daily 10:00–18:00, tel. 01904/621-261). Cute little "road trains" shuttle you between the Minster and the Railway Museum (£1, leaves Railway Museum every 30 minutes from 10:00–17:30, leaves Minster—from Duncombe Place—every 30 minutes from 10:15–17:45).

▲Yorkshire Museum—Located in a lush and lazy park next to the stately ruins of St. Mary's Abbey, Yorkshire Museum is the city's forgotten serious "archaeology of York" museum. While the hordes line up at Jorvik, the best Viking artifacts are here—with no crowds and in a better historical context. You have to walk through this museum, but the stroll takes you through Roman, Saxon, Viking, Norman, and Gothic York. Its prize piece is the delicately etched 15th-century pendant called the Middleham Jewel. The video about the creation of the abbey is worth a look (£4, various exhibitions can increase price, daily 10:00–17:00, tel. 01904/629-745).

Theatre Royal—Fine plays, usually British comedies, entertain the locals (20:00 almost nightly, 19:30 off-season, tickets easy to get, £6.50–14, on St. Leonard's Place next to TI and a 5-minute walk from recommended B&Bs, recorded info tel. 01904/610-041, tickets tel. 01904/623-568).

Honorable Mention—York has a number of other sights and activities (described in TI material) that, while interesting, pale in comparison to the biggies. **Fairfax House** is perfectly Georgian inside, with docents happy to talk with you (£4.25, Sat–Thu 11:00–17:30 except Sun 13:30–17:30, closed Fri except in Aug; possible guided tours offered at 11:00 and 14:00 on Fri during summer—ask in advance at TI; a tour helps bring this well-furnished building to life; on Castlegate, near Jorvik and York Story). **The York Story** offers an exhibit on the building of York and a 45-minute video on the city's past; it's good, straight history (£2, £6.30 combo ticket with Castle Museum, daily 9:30–16:45, Nov–Mar 9:30–16:00, associated with, across the car park from, and promoted by the Castle Museum). The **Hall of the Merchant Adventurers** claims to be the finest medieval guild hall in Europe (from 1361). It's basically a vast half-timbered building with marvelous exposed beams and 15 minutes worth of interesting displays about life and commerce back in the days when York was England's second city (£2, daily 8:30–17:00, Nov–Mar until 15:00, below the Shambles off Piccadilly).

Sleeping in York
(£1 = about $1.70, tel. code: 01904)
Sleep Code: **S** = Single, **D** = Double/Twin, **T** = Triple, **Q** = Quad, **b** = bathroom, **t** = toilet only, **s** = shower only, **CC** = Credit Card (Visa, MasterCard, Amex).

I've listed peak-season, book-direct prices. Don't use the TI. Outside of July and August some prices go soft.

Sleeping in B&Bs near Bootham Gate

These recommendations are in the handiest B&B neighborhood, a quiet residential neighborhood just outside the old-town wall's Bootham gate, along the road called Bootham. All are within a five-minute walk of the Minster and TI and a 10-minute walk or £3 taxi ride from the station. If driving, head for the cathedral and follow the medieval wall to the gate called Bootham Bar. Bootham "street" leads away from Bootham Bar. These B&Bs are all small, smoke free, and family run and come with plenty of steep stairs but no traffic noise. For a good selection, call well in advance. One-nighters will have a tougher time snagging a room, particularly on Saturday. B&Bs will generally hold a room with a phone call and work hard to help their guests sightsee and eat smartly. Most have permits for street parking. And most don't take credit cards. Regency Dry Cleaning does small loads for £8 (drop off by 9:30 for same-day service, Mon–Fri 8:30–18:00, Sat 9:00–17:00, closed Sun, 75 Bootham, tel. 01904/613-311). The cheaper Washeteria launderette is a 10- to 15-minute walk from the B&B neighborhood (Mon and Fri 8:00–20:00, Tue–Thu 8:00–18:00, Sat–Sun 8:00–17:30, last wash 1.5 hrs before closing, 124 Haxby Road, at north end of Gillygate, continue on Clarence, then Haxby, tel. 01904/623-379).

Airden House, the most central of my Bootham-area listings, has eight spacious rooms, a grandfather clock–cozy TV lounge, and brightness and warmth throughout. Susan and Keith Burrows, a great source of local travel tips, keep their place simple, clean, comfortable, and friendly (D-£40, Db-£50, 1 St. Mary's, York YO30 7DD, tel. 01904/638-915). They also rent a fully equipped apartment and a house for weeklong stays starting Saturdays (Db-£210-250, Qb-£320-350, a 5-minute walk from the Minster).

The Sycamore, run by Margaret and David Tyce, is a fine value, with seven homey rooms strewn with silk flowers and personal touches. It's at the end of a dead end opposite a fun-to-watch bowling green (D-£33, Db-£42, family deals, 19 Sycamore Place off Bootham Terrace, YO30 7DW, tel. & fax 01904/624-712).

The Hazelwood is my most hotelesque listing in this neighborhood. Ian and Carolyn McNabb, who run this spacious old house, decorate its 14 rooms with modern furnishings, pay fussy attention to details, and serve a classy breakfast (Db-£53–75 depending on room size, 2 ground-floor rooms, CC:VM, £5 laundry service; a fridge, ice, and great travel library in the plush basement lounge; CC:VM, 24 Portland Street, Gillygate, YO31 7EH, tel. 01904/626-548, fax 01904/628-032, e-mail: hazwdyork @aol.com).

York, Our Neighborhood

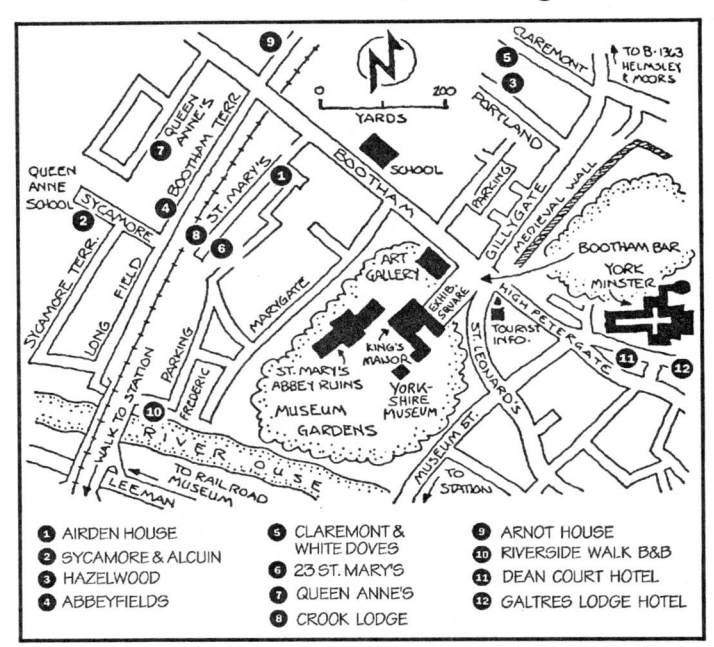

- **1** AIRDEN HOUSE
- **2** SYCAMORE & ALCUIN
- **3** HAZELWOOD
- **4** ABBEYFIELDS
- **5** CLAREMONT & WHITE DOVES
- **6** 23 ST. MARY'S
- **7** QUEEN ANNE'S
- **8** CROOK LODGE
- **9** ARNOT HOUSE
- **10** RIVERSIDE WALK B&B
- **11** DEAN COURT HOTEL
- **12** GALTRES LODGE HOTEL

Abbeyfields Guest House has nine cozy, bright rooms and a quiet lounge. This doily-free place comes without the usual clutter (S-£22, Sb-£30, Db-£50, 19 Bootham Terrace, YO30 7DH, tel. & fax 01904/636-471, www.abbeyfields.co.uk, Richard and Gwen Martin).

Claremont Guest House is a friendly house offering two delightful rooms and many thoughtful touches, including £3 laundry service (D-£32–40, Db-£36–50, 18 Claremont Terrace off Gillygate, YO31 7EJ, tel. 01904/625-158, e-mail: claremont.york@dial.pipex .com, run by Gill—pronounced Jill—and Martyn Cornell).

White Doves is a cheery little Victorian place with a comfy lounge and four tastefully decorated rooms in soothing pastels (Db-£45–48, family deals, 20 Claremont Terrace off Gillygate, YO31 7EJ, tel. 01904/625-957, Pauline and David Pearce).

23 St. Mary's is extravagantly decorated. Mrs. Hudson has done everything super-correctly and offers nine comfortable rooms, a classy lounge, and all the doily touches (Sb-£30–34, Db-£58–64 depending on season and size, 23 St. Mary's, YO30 7DD, tel. 01904/622-738, fax 01904/628-802).

Queen Anne's Guest House has six compact, clean, and cheery rooms (D-£32, Db-£36 through 2000 with this book, CC:V, family deals, 24 Queen Anne's Road, Y030 7AA, tel. 01904/629-389, fax 01904/619-529, Judy and David West).

Crook Lodge B&B is a bit more elegant than the rest, with seven tight and charming rooms (Db-£46–54, car park, 26 St. Mary's, Y030 7DD, tel. & fax 01904/655-614, Susan and John Arnott).

Alcuin Lodge is a good value, with seven pleasant rooms (Db-£42–50, 1 small top-floor D-£35, no kids, CC:VM, 15 Sycamore Place, Y030 7DW, tel. 01904/632-222, fax 01904/626-630, e-mail: Alcuinlodg@aol.com, Susan Taylor).

Arnot House, run by a friendly daughter and mother team, is lushly decorated with early 1900s memorabilia. Cluttered but homey, the quirky museum-quality interior merits a photo. The four well-furnished rooms have little libraries (Db-£50–55, CC:VM with £1 fee, minimum 2-night stay, nonsmoking, 17 Grosvenor Terrace, Y030 7AG, tel. 01904/641-966, Kim and Ann Robbins).

Riverside Walk B&B, on a pedestrian street along the river, has 14 small shipshape rooms, steep stairs, and a breakfast room decorated in nautical green that feels like a fisherman's cottage. Request a river view or you'll overlook a car park (2 D-£37–47, Db-£52–57, nonsmoking, sun terrace on river, quiet, CC:VM for 3.5 percent extra, 8 Earlsborough Terrace, Y030 7BQ, tel. 01904/620-769, fax 01904/646-249, Julie Mett).

York's Youth Hotel is well run, with lots of extras, like a kitchen, a launderette, a game room, a bar, and a bike rental (S-£14, D-£26, £12 in 4- to 6-bed dorms, sheets and breakfast extra, £1 less for multinight stays, CC:VM, 10-minute walk from station at 11 Bishophill Senior Road, YO1 1EF, tel. 01904/625-904 or 01904/612-494, e-mail: youth-hotel@ymn.co.uk).

Sleeping in Hotels in the Center of York

Dean Court Hotel, facing the Minster, is a big stately place marketed by Best Western that has classy lounges and 40 comfortable rooms (small Db-£105, standard Db-£125, superior Db-£140 includes fruit, spacious deluxe Db-£155, CC:VMA, some nonsmoking rooms but even smoking rooms OK, elevator, Duncombe Place, YO1 7EF, tel. 01904/625-082, fax 01904/620-305, www.deancourt-york.co.uk). Ask for a room in front with a Minster view; the rooms in back stare at a brick wall.

Galtres Lodge Hotel, a block from the Minster, offers narrow hallways but comfy rooms above a restaurant in the old town center (S-£25, Sb-£35, Dt-£50, Db-£65, 1 refurbished Db-£75 and worth it, CC:VM, no kids under 14, nonsmoking, 54 Low Petergate, Y01 7HZ, tel. 01904/622-478, fax 01904/627-804).

Eating in York

Lunch in the Shambles
For cuteness, consider the tiny **St. Crux Parish Hall,** a medieval church now used by a medley of charities selling tea and simple snacks (Mon–Sat 10:00–16:00, at bottom end of the Shambles, at intersection with Pavement). For a smoky place with the floor still sticky from last night's spilled beer, the **Golden Fleece** pub is busy at lunch, serving famous Yorkshire pudding and hearty meals (daily 12:00–21:00, CC:VM, on Pavement and Shambles, near St. Crux). Twee, quaint eateries line the street called Pavement. **Ye Olde Starre Inn,** the oldest pub in town, has yet to learn the art of cooking.

Traditional Tea
York is famous for its elegant teahouses. Drop into one around 16:00 for tea and cakes. Ladies love **Betty's Teahouse** (£5 cream tea, daily 9:00–21:00, mostly nonsmoking, St. Helen's Square, fine people watching from a window seat on the main floor; downstairs near WC is a mirror signed by World War II bomber pilots). If there's a line for Betty's, come back at dinnertime, when the line usually disappears—because for the English, "tea time" is over, but tea time is any time at Betty's. If Betty's is just too crowded, many other tearooms can satisfy your king- or queen-for-a-day desires.

Eating near the Minster
Café Concerto has a loyal following for good reason. Their £17 three-course meal is the best I've had in York (daily 10:00–22:00, serves meals all day, traditional English or Continental cuisine, CC:VM, Petergate 21, under Bootham Bar, smart to reserve at 01904/610-478).

The Viceroy of India—just outside Monk Bar and therefore outside the tourist zone—serves great Indian food at good prices to mostly locals; if you've yet to eat Indian on your trip, do it here (nightly 18:00–24:00, £8 plates, friendly staff, CC:VM, continue straight through Monk Bar to 26 Monkgate, notice the big old "Bile Beans keep you healthy, bright-eyed, and slim" sign on your left, tel. 01904/622-370). For Italian food, consider the popular **Little Italy** for dinner (£6–12, Tue–Sun 17:00–23:00, plus Sat 12:00–14:00, closed Mon, Goodramgate 12, just inside Monk Bar, tel. 01904/623-539). The **Royal Oak** offers pub grub throughout the day, a small nonsmoking room, and hand-pulled ale (daily 11:30–20:00, CC:VM, Goodramgate, a block from Monk Bar, a block east of the Minster, tel. 01904/653-856). **St. Williams Restaurant,** just behind the great east window of the Minster in a wonderful half-timbered 15th-century building, serves quick and tasty lunches and elegant candlelit dinners (open daily, 2 courses-£14, 3 courses-£16, traditional and Mediterranean, CC:VM, College Street, tel. 01904/634-830).

Eating near Bootham Bar and Your B&B

Walk along Gillygate and choose from an enjoyable array of eateries: For authentic Italian, consider **Mama Mia's** (£6–9, daily 11:30–14:00, 17:30–23:00, fun, *domani* service, indoor/outdoor patio, CC:VM, 20 Gillygate, tel. 01904/622-020). **Gillygate Fisheries** is a wonderfully traditional little fish-and-chips joint where tattooed people eat in and housebound mothers take out (Mel serves £3–4 meals, eat your mushy peas, 11:30–13:30, 18:00–23:30, closed Mon lunch and all day Sun, smoke-free seating, 59 Gillygate). The **Waggon and Horses** pub has local color and £5 meals (daily 11:30–14:00, 17:30–21:00 but no Sunday dinner, across from Fisheries joint, Gillygate 48). There's a pub serving grub on every block. Eat where you see lots of food. Consider the **Coach House** (nightly 18:30–21:30, 20 Marygate, tel. 01904/652-780). For the closest you'll get to Mexico in Britain, try **Fiesta Mehicana** (nightly 18:00–22:00, sit-down or take-out, CC:VM, 14 Clifford Street, tel. 01904/610-243). The **Grange Hotel's Brasserie** is easy, a couple of blocks from the B&Bs, and classier than a pub. Go downstairs—avoid the pricey ground-floor restaurant (£9 meals, Mon–Sat 12:00–14:00, 18:00–22:00, Sun dinner only, CC:VM, 1 Clifton, tel. 01904/644-744). The people who run your B&B know the latest on what's good.

Grocery stores: In the B&B neighborhood you'll find **Spar** (daily 9:00–21:00, on Queen Anne's Road and Bootham), and near Bootham Bar is **Jackson,** a little run-down but open late (daily 7:00–23:00, on Bootham). In the old town is **Marks & Spencers** (Mon–Sat 9:30–18:00, Sun 11:00–17:00, on Parliament Street); go to the top floor for a striking view of the south wall of the Minster from the menswear department.

Most atmospheric picnic spot: In the Museum Gardens (near Bootham Bar), at the evocative 12th-century ruins of **St. Mary's Abbey.**

Transportation Connections—York

By train to: Durham (hrly, 60 min), **Edinburgh** (2/hrly, 2 hrs), **London** (2/hrly, 2 hrs), **Bath** (via Bristol, hrly, 5 hrs), **Cambridge** (nearly hrly, 2 hrs with a change in Petersborough), **Birmingham** (8/day, 3 hrs). Luggage storage at York's train station: £2, Mon–Sat 8:30–20:30, Sun from 9:00. Train info: tel. 0345-484-950.

By bus to: Keswick (1/day, 4 hrs; X9 bus runs early May–early Sept Mon–Sat, leaves York in afternoon, Keswick in morning; off-season, when bus runs only on Sat, train is doable though tiring: Allow 4 hrs, with transfers at Newcastle, Carlisle, and Penrith, then bus to Keswick).

EDINBURGH

Edinburgh, the colorful city of Robert Louis Stevenson, Sir Walter Scott, and Robert Burns, is Scotland's showpiece and one of Europe's most entertaining cities. Historical, monumental, fun, and well organized, it's a tourist's delight.

Promenade down the Royal Mile through the Old Town. Historic buildings pack the Royal Mile between the castle (on the top) and Holyrood Palace (on the bottom). Medieval skyscrapers stand shoulder to shoulder, hiding peaceful courtyards connected to High Street by narrow lanes or even tunnels. This colorful jumble—in its day the most crowded city in the world—is the tourist's Edinburgh.

Edinburgh (ED'n-burah) was once two towns divided by a lake. To alleviate crowding, the lake was drained, and a magnificent Georgian city, today's New Town, was laid out to the north. Georgian Edinburgh, like the city of Bath, shines with broad boulevards, straight streets, square squares, circular circuses, and elegant mansions decked out in colonnades, pediments, and sphinxes in the proud, neoclassical style of 200 years ago.

While the Georgian city celebrated the union of Scotland and England (with streets and squares named after English kings and emblems), "devolution" is the latest craze. In a 1998 election the Scots voted for more autonomy and to bring their parliament home. Though Edinburgh has been the historic capital of Scotland for centuries, parliament has not met in Scotland since 1707. In 2000—while London will still call the strategic shots—Edinburgh will resume its position as home to the Scottish Parliament. And a strikingly modern new parliament building, opening in 2002, will be one more jewel in Edinburgh's crown.

Planning Your Time

While the major sights can be seen in a day, on a three-week tour of Britain I'd give Edinburgh two days. Ideally on your arrival day, take an introductory Guide Friday bus tour in the late afternoon (when it's discounted to half price).

Day 1: Spend the morning touring the castle. The rest of the day is easily spent exploring (downhill) the Royal Mile—museum-going, lunching, shopping. Catch a walking tour of the Royal Mile at 14:00. If you tour the Holyrood Palace, do it at the end of the day and the bottom of the mile. Evening–Scottish show, folk music at pub, literary pub crawl, or haunted walk.

Day 2: Tour the National Gallery and stroll the adjacent Princes Street Gardens. After lunch, browse the New Town and visit the Georgian House; hike up King Arthur's Seat; or go swimming at the Commonwealth Pool. Evening–Show, pubs, walks, whatever you didn't do last night.

Orientation (tel. code: 0131)

The center of Edinburgh holds the Princes Street Gardens park and Waverley Bridge, where you'll find the TI; Waverley Shopping and Eating Center; the train station; the bus info office, the starting point for most city bus tours; the festival office; the National Gallery; and a covered dance-and-music pavilion. Weather blows in and out—bring your sweater.

Tourist Information: The crowded TI is as central as can be atop the Waverley Market on Princes Street (May–Jun & Sept: Mon–Sat 9:00–19:00, Sun 10:00–19:00; Jul–Aug: daily until 20:00; Nov–Mar: daily until 17:00, tel. 0131/473-3800). Buy a map (£1) but skip the misnamed *Essential Guide to Edinburgh* (£1), which shuffles a little information between lots of ads. Ask for the monthly entertainment *Gig Guide* (free) and browse the racks for brochures on the various Scottish folk shows and walking tours. *The List*, the best monthly entertainment listing, is sold for £1.95 at newsstands. Book your room direct without the TI's help. Haggis Backpackers Ltd is a good source of budget travel information (Mon–Sat 8:00–18:00, Sun 12:00–18:00, just off High Street at 11 Blackfriars Street).

Arrival in Edinburgh: Arriving by train at Waverley Station puts you in the city center and a few steps from the TI (go up the stairs) and the city bus to my recommended B&Bs. Both National Express and Scottish Citylink buses use the bus station a block from the train station in the Georgian town on St. Andrew Square.

Edinburgh's slingshot-of-an-airport is 10 miles northwest of the center and well connected by shuttle buses with Waverley Bridge (LRT "Airline" bus, £3.30 or £4.40 with all-day city bus pass, 4/hrly, 30 min, roughly 6:00–22:00; I'd skip Guide Friday's Airbus Express, which costs more, runs less often, and has shorter

Edinburgh

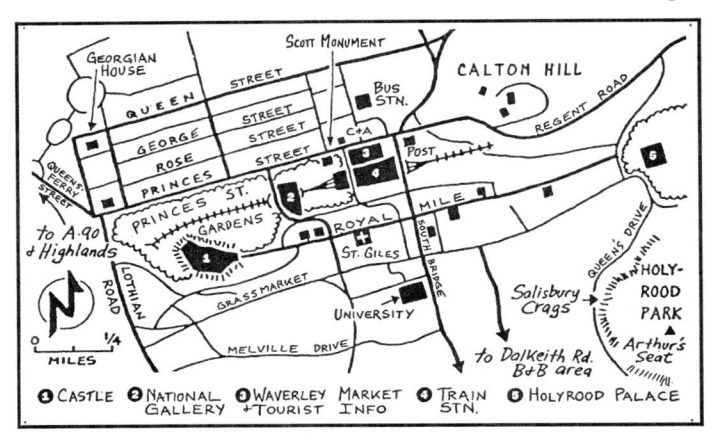

Map legend:
① CASTLE ② NATIONAL GALLERY ③ WAVERLEY MARKET + TOURIST INFO ④ TRAIN STN. ⑤ HOLYROOD PALACE

hours; flight info tel. 0131/333-1000, British Midlands tel. 0870-607-0555, British Air tel. 0345-222-111). Taxi to airport: £15.

Helpful Hints

Sunday Activities: Many sights close on Sunday, but there's still a lot to do: Royal Mile walking tour, Edinburgh Castle, St. Giles Cathedral, Holyrood Palace, Royal Botanic Gardens, Arthur's Seat hike, and city bus tour. An open-air market including antiques is held every Sunday from 10:00 to 16:00 at New Street Car Park near Waverley Center. The Georgian House and National Gallery open Sunday afternoon.

Internet Access: It's a cinch to get plugged in. Try International Telecom Centre on the Royal Mile (£1/15 min, daily 9:00–22:00, 52 High Street, half-block east of Tron Kirk and South Bridge), Café Cyberia in the New Town (Mon–Sat 10:00–22:00, Sun 12:00–19:00, 83 Hanover Street, near recommended restaurants, a few blocks northeast of TI), and Web 13 (13 Bread Street, near Grassmarket, below the castle).

Car Rental: Avis is at 100 Dairy Road, Haymarket, tel. 0131/337-6363.

Getting around Edinburgh

Nearly all Edinburgh sights are within walking distance. City buses are handy and inexpensive (average fare 70p, LRT info office, Old Town end of Waverley Bridge, tel. 0131/555-6363). Tell the driver where you're going, drop exact change into the box or lose the excess, grab your ticket as you board, push the stop button as you near your stop (so your stop isn't skipped), and exit from the middle door. All-day "Freedom Ticket" passes are sold on buses (£2.40—four rides make it worthwhile). Buses run from about 6:00 to 23:00. Taxis are reasonable (easy to flag down, £1.20 drop charge, 80p extra after 18:00, average ride between downtown and B&B district £4.50).

Bus Tours of Edinburgh

▲**Hop-on Hop-off City Bus Tours**—Two companies, Guide Friday and LRT's "Edinburgh Classic Tour," offer buses that circle the town center—Waverley Bridge, around the castle, Royal Mile, Calton Hill, Georgian New Town, and Princes Street—in about an hour, with pickups about every 15 minutes and an informative narration. You can hop on and off with one ticket all day, not 24 hours. The pricier Guide Friday has a live guide, often uninspired—you'll learn the location and opening hours of sights but not much more (£8, CC:VM if bought at office at 133 Canongate, tel. 0131/556-2244). Classic Tour uses headphones and a recorded narration (£6.50; tel. 0131/555-6363). On sunny days they go topless (the buses) but can suffer from traffic noise and congestion. First and last buses leave Waverley Bridge at 9:10 and 19:10 late May through late September (otherwise 17:10). These tours can be half-hearted—pay only half price. Prices drop 50 percent late in the afternoon (Classic Tour after 17:10 late May–late Sept, otherwise after 15:10; Guide Friday sometime between 16:00–17:00, discounts start at Waverley Bridge, later elsewhere).

Sights—Edinburgh

▲▲▲**Edinburgh Castle**—The fortified birthplace of the city 1,300 years ago, this imposing symbol of Edinburgh sits proudly on a rock high above the city. While the castle has been both a fort and a royal residence since the 11th century, most of the buildings today are from its more recent use as a military garrison (£6.50, daily 9:30–18:00, Oct–Mar until 17:00, cafeteria, tel. 0131/225-9846; consider avoiding the long uphill walk from the nearest bus stop by taking a cab to the castle gate).

Entry Gate: Start with the wonderfully droll 30-minute guided introduction tour (free with admission, departs every 15 minutes from entry, see clock for the next departure; few tours run off-season). The CD-ROM audio guide is excellent, with four hours of quick digital dial descriptions (free with admission, pick up at entry gate before meeting the live guide). The clean WC at the entry annually wins "British Loo of the Year" awards (see plaques near men's room), but they use one-way mirrors above the sinks in the women's room. It's to check for cleanliness, but still—complain.

In the castle there are four essential stops: Crown Jewels,

Great Hall, National War Memorial, and St. Margaret's Chapel with city view. All are at the highest and most secure point—on or near the castle square—and where your guided tour ends.

The **Royal Palace** (facing castle square under the flag pole) has two unimpressive rooms (through door reading 1566). Remember, Scottish royalty only lived here when safety or protocol required. They preferred the **Holyrood Palace** at the bottom of the Royal Mile. The line of tourists leads from the square directly to the jewels. Skip this line and enter the building around to the left where you'll get to the jewels via a wonderful *Honors of Scotland* exhibition about the crown jewels.

Scotland's **Crown Jewels** are older than England's. While Cromwell destroyed England's, the Scots hid theirs successfully. Longtime symbols of Scottish nationalism, they were made in Edinburgh—of Scottish gold, diamonds, and gems—in 1540 for a 1543 coronation. They were last used to crown Charles II in 1651. Apparently there was some anxiety about the Act of Union, which dissolved Scotland's parliament into England's to create the United Kingdom in 1707—the Scots locked up and hid their jewels. In 1818 Walter Scott and a royal commission rediscovered the jewels intact.

The **Stone of Scone** sits plain and strong next to the jewels. This big gray rock is the coronation stone of Scotland's ancient kings (ninth century). Swiped by the English, it sat under the coronation chair at Westminster Abbey from 1296 until 1996. With major fanfare, Scotland's treasured Stone of Scone returned to Edinburgh on November 15, 1996. Talk to the guard for more details.

Enter the **Mary Queen of Scots room**, where in 1666 the queen gave birth to James VI of Scotland, later King James I of England. The **Presence Chamber** leads into **Laich Hall** (Lower Hall), the dining room of the royal family.

The **Great Hall** was the castle's ceremonial meeting place in the 16th and 17th centuries. In modern times it was a barracks and a hospital. While most of what you see is Victorian, two medieval elements survive: the fine hammer-beam roof and the iron-barred peephole (above fireplace on right). This allowed the king to spy on his partying subjects.

The imposing **Scottish National War Memorial** commemorates the 148,000 Scottish soldiers lost in World War I, the 57,000 lost in World War II, and the 750 lost in British battles since. Each bay is dedicated to a particular Scottish regiment. The main shrine, featuring a green Italian-marble memorial containing the original WWI rolls of honor, actually sits upon an exposed chunk of the castle rock. Above you, the archangel Michael is busy slaying the dragon. The bronze frieze accurately shows the attire of various wings of Scotland's military. The stained glass starts with Cain and Abel on the left and finishes with a celebration of peace on the right.

St. Margaret's Chapel, the oldest building in Edinburgh, is dedicated to Queen Margaret, who died here in 1093 and was sainted in 1250. Built in 1130 in the Romanesque style of the Norman invaders, it is wonderfully simple, with classic Norman zigzags decorating the round arch that separates the tiny nave from the sacristy. Used as a powder magazine for 400 years, very little survives. You'll see an 11th-century Gospel book of St. Margaret's and small windows featuring St. Margaret, St. Columba (who brought Christianity to Scotland via Iona), and William Wallace (the brave defender of Scotland). The place is popular for weddings and, since it seats only 20, particularly popular with brides' fathers.

Belly up to the bannister (across the terrace outside the chapel) to enjoy the great view. Below you are the guns—which fire the one o'clock salute—and a sweet little line of doggie tombstones, the **soldier's pet cemetery.** Beyond stretches the **Georgian New Town** (read the informative plaque).

The castle could keep you entertained all day (for instance, below, in the vaults, you can see a fine military museum and Mons Meg—a huge 15th-century siege cannon that fired 500-pound stones nearly two miles). But you've seen the essentials.

When leaving the castle, turn around and look back at the gate. There stand King Robert the Bruce (on the left, 1274–1329) and Sir William Wallace (Braveheart—on the right, 1270–1305). Wallace (newly famous, thanks to Mel Gibson) fought long and hard against English domination before being executed in London—his body cut to pieces and paraded through the far corners of jolly olde England. Bruce beat the English at Bannockburn in 1314. Bruce and Wallace still defend the spirit of Scotland.

Sights—Along the Royal Mile
(In walking order from top to bottom.)

▲▲▲**Royal Mile**—This is one of Europe's most interesting historic walks. Start at the top and amble down to the palace. I've listed the top sights of the Royal Mile working downhill.

The Royal Mile, which consists of a series of four different streets—Castlehill, Lawnmarket, High Street, and Canongate—is actually 100 yards longer than a mile. And every inch is packed with shops, cafés, and lanes leading to tiny squares. By poking down the many side alleys, you'll find a few rough edges of a town well on its way to becoming a touristic mall. See it now. In a few years tourists will be slaloming through the postcard racks on bagpipe skateboards.

Royal Mile Terminology: A "close" is a tiny alley between two buildings (originally with a door that closed it at night). A close usually leads to a "court" or courtyard. A "land" is a tenement block

Royal Mile

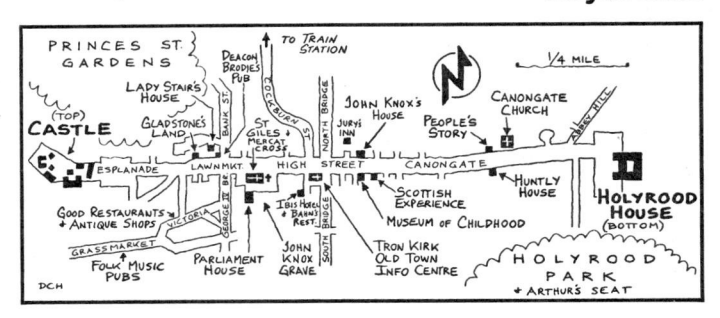

of apartments. A "pend" is an arched gateway. A "wynd" is a narrow winding lane. And "gate" is from an old Scandinavian word for street.

Royal Mile Walking Tours: Mercat Tours offers two-hour guided walks of the mile—more entertaining than historic (£5, daily at 11:00 and 14:00 year-round, from Mercat Cross on the Royal Mile, tel. 0131/225-6591). The guides, who enjoy making a short story long, ignore the big sights, taking you behind the scenes with piles of barely historic gossip, bully-pulpit Scottish pride, and fun but forgettable trivia. For a private guide, consider Robin Sinton (tel. 0131/661-6051) or the Voluntary Guides Association (tel. 0131/664-7180).

Castle Esplanade—At the top of the Royal Mile, the big parking lot leading up to the castle was once a military parade ground. It's often cluttered with bleachers under construction for the military tattoo—a spectacular massing of the bands that fills the square nightly for most of August (see "Edinburgh Festival," below). At the bottom, on the left, the tiny witch's fountain memorializes 300 women who were accused of witchcraft and burned here. Scotland burned more witches per capita than any other country—17,000 between 1479 and 1722. But in a humanitarian gesture, rather than burning them alive as was the custom in the rest of Europe, Scottish "witches" were strangled to death before they were burned. The plaque shows two witches: one good and one bad. (For 90 minutes of this kind of Royal Mile trivia, take the guided tour described above.)

Scotch Whiskey Heritage Centre—This touristy ambush is designed only to distill £5 out of your pocket. You get a video history, a little whiskey-keg train-car ride, and a free sample before finding yourself in the shop 45 minutes later. Small-time thrill seekers prefer the 15-minute tour—just a whiskey-keg ride and a sample—for £3.25. People do seem to enjoy it, but that might have something to do with the sample (tel. 0131/220-0441). The Camera Obscura, across the street, is just as rewarding.

▲▲**Gladstone's Land**—Take a good look at this typical 16th- to 17th-century merchant's house, complete with a lived-in furnished interior and guides in each room who love to talk (£3.40, Mon–Sat 10:00–17:00, Sun 14:00–17:00, last entry at 16:30). For a good Royal Mile photo, lean out the upper-floor window or climb the entry stairway with the golden eagle.

▲**Writers' Museum at Lady Stair's House**—This interesting house, built in 1622, is filled with manuscripts and knickknacks of Scotland's three greatest literary figures: Robert Burns, Sir Walter Scott, and Robert Louis Stevenson. It's worth a few minutes for anyone and is fascinating for fans (free, Mon–Sat 10:00–17:00, closed Sun). Wander around the courtyard here. Edinburgh was a wonder in the 17th and 18th centuries. Tourists came here to see its skyscrapers, which towered 10 stories and higher. No city in Europe was so densely populated as "Auld Reekie."

Deacon Brodie's Tavern—This is a decent place for a light meal (see "Eating," below). Read the story of its notorious namesake on the wall facing Bank Street.

▲**St. Giles Cathedral**—Wander through Scotland's most important church. Stepping inside, find John Knox's statue. Look into his eyes from 10 inches away. Knox, the great reformer and founder of austere Scottish Presbyterianism, first preached here in 1559. His insistence that every person should be able to read the word of God gave Scotland an educational system 300 years ahead of the rest of Europe. For this reason it was Scottish minds that led the way in math, science, medicine, engineering, and so on. Voltaire called Scotland "the intellectual capital of Europe."

The neo-Gothic **Chapel of the Knights of the Thistle** (from 1911, in far corner) was built in two years entirely with Scottish material and labor. Find the angel tooting the bagpipes (above the door on right). The Scottish crown steeple from 1495 is a proud part of Edinburgh's skyline (daily 9:00–19:00, until 17:00 off-season; ask about concerts—some are free, usually Thu at 13:00; fine café downstairs; see "Eating," below).

John Knox is buried out back—austerely, under the parking lot, at spot 44. The statue among the cars shows King Charles II riding to a toga party back in 1685.

Parliament House—Stop in to see the grand hall with its fine 1639 hammer-beam ceiling and stained glass. This hall housed the Scottish Parliament until the Act of Union in 1707 (explained in history exhibition adjacent). Today it's busy with wigged and robed lawyers hard at work in the old library (peek through the door) or pacing the hall deep in discussion. Greater eminence… longer wig. The friendly doorman is helpful (free, public welcome Mon–Fri 9:00–16:30, best action midmornings Tue–Fri, open-

to-the-public trials 10:00–16:00—doorman has day's docket, entry behind St. Giles Cathedral near parking spot 21).
Mercat Cross—This stands on the downhill side of the church. Royal proclamations were read from here in the 14th century. Today it's the meeting point of various walking tours. Pop into the police information center, a few doors downhill, for a little local law-and-order history (free, daily 10:00–22:00).
▲**Tron Kirk**—This fine old building houses an interesting (free) Old Town history display and sometimes a TI.
▲**Museum of Childhood**—This five-story playground of historical toys and games—called the noisiest museum in the world because of its delighted tiny visitors—is rich in nostalgia and history (free, Mon–Fri 10:00–16:30, closed Sun). Just downhill is a fragrant fudge shop offering free samples.
▲**John Knox House**—Fascinating for Reformation buffs, this fine 16th-century house offers a well-explained look at the life of the great reformer (£2, Mon–Sat 10:00–16:30, closed Sun, 43 High Street). While Knox never actually lived here, it was called "his house" to save it from the wrecking ball in 1850.
▲**People's Story**—This interesting exhibition traces the lot of the working class through the 18th, 19th, and 20th centuries (free, Mon–Sat 10:00–17:00, closed Sun). Curiously, while this museum is dedicated to the proletariat, immediately around the back is the tomb of Adam Smith—the author of *Wealth of Nations* and the father of modern capitalism (1723–1790).
▲**Huntly House**—Another old house full of old stuff, Huntly is worth a look for its early Edinburgh history and handy ground-floor WC. Don't miss the original copy of the National Covenant (written in 1638 on an animal skin) or the sketches of pre-Georgian Edinburgh with its lake still wet (free, Mon–Sat 10:00–17:00, closed Sun). Just a toot farther downhill is Bagpipes Galore.
Somerville Playing Cards—This quirky little shop sells over 2,000 kinds of playing cards, from different countries and eras, in various shapes and sizes (Mon–Sat 10:30–17:30, 82 Canongate, tel. 0131/556-5225).
White Horse Close—Step into this 17th-century courtyard (bottom of Canongate, on the left, a block before Holyrood Palace). It was from here that the Edinburgh stagecoach left for London. Eight days later, the horse-drawn carriage pulled into its destination: Scotland Yard.
▲**Holyrood Palace**—The palace marks the end of the Royal Mile. The queen spends a week in Scotland each summer, during which this is her official residence and office. The abbey—part of a 12th-century Augustinian monastery—stood here first. It was named for a piece of the cross brought here as a relic by queen-then-saint Margaret. Scotland's royalty preferred living here to the blustery castle on the rock, and, gradually, the palace grew. The

building is rich in history and decor. But without information or a guided tour ("there's none of either," snickered the guy who sells the boring £3.70 museum guidebooks), you're just another peasant in the dark. Docents in each room are happy to give you the answer if you know the question. After wandering through the elegantly furnished rooms and a few dark older rooms filled with glass cases of historic bits and Scottish pieces that must be fascinating, you're free to wander through the ruined abbey and the queen's gardens (£5.50, daily 9:30–18:00, Nov–Apr until 16:30—guided tour mandatory off-season, last admission 45 minutes before closing; closed last 2 weeks in May, 10 days in early July, when the queen's home, and whenever a prince drops in; tel. 0131/556-7371).

The building lot near the palace entrance is the site of the new Scottish Parliament, slated for completion in 2002.

More Bonnie Wee Sights

▲**Georgian New Town**—Cross Waverley Bridge and walk through Georgian Edinburgh. The grand George Street, connecting St. Andrew and Charlotte Squares, was the centerpiece of the elegantly planned New Town. The entire city plan—laid out in the late 18th century when George was king—celebrates the notion of the United Kingdom. Look at the map. You'll see George Street, Queen Street, Hanover (the royal family surname) Street, and even Thistle and Rose Streets are emblems of the two happily paired nations.

▲▲**Georgian House**—This refurbished Georgian house, set on Edinburgh's finest Georgian square, is a trip back to 1796. A volunteer guide in each room is trained in the force-feeding of stories and trivia. Start your visit with two interesting videos (architecture/Georgian lifestyles) totaling 30 minutes (£4.40, Mon–Sat 10:00–17:00, Sun 14:00–17:00, 7 Charlotte Square, tel. 0131/225-2160).

Princes Street Gardens—This grassy park, a former lake bed, separates Edinburgh's New and Old Towns and offers a wonderful escape from the city. There are plenty of free concerts and country dances in the summer and the oldest floral clock in the world. Join the local office workers for a picnic lunch break.

▲**National Gallery**—This elegant neoclassical building has a small but impressive collection of European masterpieces, from Raphael to van Gogh, and offers the best look you'll get at Scottish paintings (free, Mon–Sat 10:00–17:00, Sun 14:00–17:00, tel. 0131/624-6200).

▲**Walter Scott Monument**—Built in 1840, this elaborate, neo-Gothic monument honors the great author, one of Edinburgh's many illustrious sons. The 200-foot monument shelters a marble statue of Scott. He is surrounded by busts of 16 great Scottish poets and 64 characters from his books. Climb 287 steps for a fine

view of the city (£1, Mon–Sat 9:00–18:00, until 17:00 off-season, closed Sun).
Royal Botanic Garden—Britain's second-oldest botanical garden, established in 1670 for medicinal herbs, is now one of Europe's best (free, daily 9:30–19:00 in season, £2 90-minute "rainforest to desert" tours daily at 11:00 and 14:00, 1 mile north of the center at Inverleith Row, tel. 0131/552-7171).
Museum of Scotland—Learn the story of Scotland, from 2,400 million years ago through today. Take advantage of the free 60-minute orientation tour (usually daily at 14:15 and 15:15, plus Tuesday at 18:00) or take the included audio tour (£3, free Tue 16:30–20:00; Mon–Sat 10:00–17:00, Tue until 20:00, Sun 12:00–17:00, Chambers Street, off George IV bridge, 2 long blocks south of the Royal Mile). Admission includes entry to the Royal Museum, next door.
Dynamic Earth—Using special effects, this new museum showcases the power of the planet, from the big bang to the whole shebang: volcanoes, earthquakes, glaciers, oceans, rainforests. A time machine rewinds history from the world wars back to kings and queens and other dinosaurs. It's family fun with an epic theme (£6, family £16.50, Apr–Oct daily 10:00–18:00, Nov–Mar Wed–Sat 10:00–17:00, on Holyrood Road, near palace and park, tel. 0131/550-7800).

Sights—Outer Edinburgh

Edinburgh Crystal—Blowing, molding, cutting, polishing, and engraving, the Edinburgh Crystal Company glassworks tour smashes anything you'll see in Venice (£3, 35-minute tours offered year-round Mon–Fri 9:15–15:30, Apr–Sept weekends 11:00–14:30, children under 8 and large dogs not allowed in for safety reasons). There is a shop full of "bargain" second-quality pieces, a video show, and a cafeteria. A free red minibus shuttle service from Waverley Bridge departs hourly (Apr–Sept, weekdays 10:00–15:00, weekends 11:00–13:00), or you can drive 10 miles south of town on A701 to Penicuik. You can schedule a more expensive supertour where you actually blow and cut glass (tel. 01968/675-128).

Activities in Edinburgh

▲▲**Arthur's Seat Hike**—A 45-minute hike up the 822-foot volcanic mountain (surrounded by a fine park overlooking Edinburgh), starting from the Holyrood Palace, gives you a rewarding view. You can drive up most of the way from behind (follow the one-way street from the palace, park by the little lake) or run up like they did in *Chariots of Fire*. From the parking lot (south of Holyrood Palace), you'll see 2 trails going up. The steep one with steps skirts the base of the cliffs; the other is longer, with an easier grade.
Brush Skiing—If you'd rather be skiing, the Midlothian Ski

Centre in Hillend has a hill on the edge of town with a chairlift, T-bar, two slopes plus jump slope, and rentable skis, boots, and poles (£6/hr with gear, Mon–Sat 9:30–21:00, Sun 9:30–19:00, closed last 2 weeks of June, probably closed if it snows, bus LRT #4 from Princes Street—garden side, tel. 0131/445-4433).
▲**Royal Commonwealth Games Swimming Pool**—The biggest pool I've ever seen is open to the public, with a Time Out cafeteria (overlooking the pool), weight room, sauna (£6.50 extra), and plenty of water rides, including Europe's biggest waterslide flume (£2.60, Mon–Fri 9:00–21:00, Wed from 10:00, Sat–Sun 10:00–16:00, no suit rentals, tel. 0131/667-7211).
Shopping—The best shopping is along Princes Street (look for elegant old Jenner's Department Store), Victoria Street (antiques galore), and the Royal Mile (touristy but competitively priced, shops usually open 9:00–17:30, later on Thu, some closed Sun).

Edinburgh Festival

One of Europe's great cultural events, Edinburgh's annual festival turns the city into a carnival of culture. There are enough music, dance, art, drama, and multicultural events to make even the most jaded traveler drool with excitement. Every day is jammed with formal and spontaneous fun. The official and fringe festivals rage simultaneously for about three weeks each summer, with the Military Tattoo starting a week earlier. Many city sights run on extended hours, and those that normally close on Sunday (Writers' Museum, Huntly House, and Museum of Childhood) open in the afternoon. It's a glorious time to be in Edinburgh.

The official festival (Aug 13–Sept 2 in 2000) is more formal and serious, with entertainment by festival invitation only. Major events sell out well in advance (show office at 21 Market Street, £4–45, CC:VMA, booking from Apr on, office open Mon–Fri 10:00–16:30, tel. 0131/473-2000, www.edinburghfestivals.co.uk).

The less-formal **Fringe Festival** features "on the edge" comedy and theater (Aug 6–28 in 2000, ticket/info office just below St. Giles Cathedral on the Royal Mile, tel. 0131/226-5257, bookings tel. 0131/226-5138, www.edfringe.co.uk). Its many events have, it seems, more performers than viewers. Tickets are usually available at the door (or strewn on the streets).

The **Military Tattoo** is a massing of bands, drums, and bagpipes with groups from all over what was the British Empire. Displaying military finesse with a stirring lone-piper finale, this grand spectacle fills the castle esplanade nightly except Sunday, normally from a week before the festival starts until a week before it finishes: August 4 to 26 in 2000 (£8.50–20, CC:VMA, booking starts in Jan; Fri and Sat shows sell out, Mon–Thu shows rarely do; 33 Market Street, behind Waverley train station, tel. 0131/225-1188). If nothing else, it is a really big show. The BBC airs the Tattoo in a grand

TV spectacle throughout Britain on the last day of its run—August 26 in 2000. It's worth watching from anywhere in Britain.

If you do manage to hit Edinburgh during the festival, book a room far in advance and extend your stay by a day or two. While Fringe tickets and most Tattoo tickets are available the day of the show, you may want to book a couple of official events in advance. Do it directly by telephone, leaving your credit-card number. Pick up your ticket at the office the day of the show or at the door just before curtain time. Several publications—including the festival's official schedule, the *Festival Times*, *The List*, the *Fringe Program*, and the *Daily Diary*—list and evaluate festival events.

Nightlife in Edinburgh

▲▲**Evening Walking Tours**—These walks, more than a pile of ghost stories, are an entertaining and cheap night out (offered nightly, usually 19:00 and 21:00, easy socializing for solo travelers). The theatrical and creatively staged **Witchery Tours** are the most established of the ghost tours (£7, 90 min, leave from the Royal Mile, reservations required, book your spot by calling 0131/225-6745). The fascinating-for-those-who-care **Literary Pub Tour** leaves from the Beehive Pub on Grassmarket, lasts two hours, and includes two actors and four pub stops (£7, Apr–Jun and Sept–Oct at 19:30 from Thu–Sun; Jul–Aug daily at 18:00 and 20:30; Nov–Mar Fri only at 19:30; tel. 0131/226-6665).

▲**Scottish Folk Evenings**—These £35 to £40 dinner shows, generally for tour groups, are held in huge halls of expensive hotels. (Prices are bloated to include 20 percent commissions.) Your "traditional" meal is followed by a full slate of swirling kilts, blaring bagpipes, and Scottish folk dancing with an "old-time music hall"–type emcee. You can often see the show without dinner for about half price. The TI has flyers on all the latest venues. **Carlton Highland Hotel** offers its Scottish folk evening with or without dinner, nearly nightly—ask when the next show is scheduled (£12 for show at 20:45–22:30, £36.50 includes dinner at 19:30, CC:VM, at High Street and North Bridge, tel. 0131/556-7277).

▲▲**Folk Music in Pubs**—Edinburgh is a good place for folk music. There's always a pub or two with a folk evening on. The monthly *Gig Guide* (free at TI) lists most of the live music action. **Whistle Binkies** offers nightly ad-lib traditional music from about 20:30 until late (just off the Royal Mile on South Bridge, another entrance on Niddry Street, tel. 0131/557-5114).

Grassmarket Street (below the castle) is sloppy with live music—mostly folk. This noisy nightlife center is fun to just wander through late at night. **Finnigan's Wake** has live music—often Irish folk songs—nightly (starts at 22:00, a block off Grassmarket at 9 Victoria Street, tel. 0131/226-3816). The **Fiddlers Arms, Biddy Mulligan,** and **White Hart Inn** (Tue only), among others, all feature live folk music. By the noise and crowds you'll know where to go and where not to. Have a beer and follow your ear.

Theater—Even outside of festival time, Edinburgh is a fine place for lively and affordable theater. Pick up *The List* for a complete rundown of what's on.

Sleeping in Edinburgh
(£1 = about $1.70, tel. code: 0131)

Sleep Code: **S** = Single, **D** = Double/Twin, **T** = Triple, **Q** = Quad, **b** = bathroom, **t** = toilet only, **s** = shower only, **CC** = Credit Card (Visa, MasterCard, Amex).

Book ahead! The annual festival fills Edinburgh each August. Conventions, school holidays, and other surprises can make finding a room tough at almost any time. Call in advance or pay 30 percent extra for a relative dump. For the best prices, book directly rather than through the TI, which charges a £4 booking fee. "Standard" rooms, with toilets and showers a tissue-toss away, save you £10 a night.

My recommendations are south of town near the Royal Commonwealth Pool, just off Dalkeith Road. This comfortably safe neighborhood is a 20-minute walk or 10-minute bus ride from the Royal Mile. All listings are on quiet streets, a two-minute walk from a bus stop, and well served by city buses. Near the B&Bs you'll find plenty of eateries (see "Eating," below), easy free parking, and the handy Capital Laundrette (Mon–Fri 9:00–17:00, Sat 9:00–16:00, £4 for self-serve, £5.50 if they do it, drop off by 11:00 for same-day service, Jun–Sept they'll deliver your clean clothes to B&B for £1 extra, 208 Dalkeith Road, tel. 0131/667-0825).

To reach the hotel neighborhood from the train station, TI, or Scott Monument, cross Princes Street and wait at the bus stop under the small C&A sign on the department store (70p, buses #14, #21, #33, #82, or #86; red bus: exact change or pay more; green bus: makes change; ride 10 minutes to first stop 100 yards after the pool, push the button, exit middle door). These buses also stop at the corner of North Bridge and High Street on the Royal Mile. Buses generally run from about 6:00–23:00, except on Sunday morning—buses don't start running from Dalkeith into town until 9:00. Taxi fare between the station or Royal Mile and the B&Bs is about £4.50.

Room prices in this section are usually listed as a range, from low season (winter) to high season (Jul–Sept), though prices can go even higher during the August festival. Off-season prices go soft, particularly for longer stays. All recommended B&Bs have no traffic noise and are strictly nonsmoking in the bedrooms and breakfast room.

Millfield Guest House, run by Liz and Ed Broomfield, is thoughtfully furnished with antique class, a rare sit-and-chat ambience, and a comfy TV lounge. Since the showers are down the hall, you'll get spacious rooms and great prices (S-£23, D-£36–40, T-£48–52, CC:VM, CC reservation allows for late arrival, 12 Marchhall Road, EH16 5HR, tel. & fax 0131/667-4428). Decipher the breakfast prayer by Robert Burns. Then try the "Taste of Scotland" breakfast option. See how many stone (14 pounds) you weigh in the elegant throne room. This place is worth calling well in advance.

Turret Guest House is teddy-on-the-beddy cozy, with a great bay-windowed family room and a vast breakfast menu that includes haggis and vegetarian options (7 rooms, S-£20–26, D-£40–44, Db-£44–56, £2-per-person discount with this book, cheaper off-season, 8 Kilmaurs Terrace, EH16 5DR, tel. 0131/667-6704, www.turret.clara.net, Mrs. Jackie Cameron).

Kenvie Guest House, well and warmly run by Dorothy Vidler, comes with six rooms and lots of personal touches (1 small twin-£38, D-£41, Db-£49, family deals, 3 percent more with CC, 16 Kilmaurs Road, EH16 5DA, tel. 0131/668-1964, fax 0131/668-1926).

Highland Park House is simple, bright, and friendly (S-£20–25, D-£44–50 with this book, family deals, 16 Kilmaurs Terrace, EH16 5DR, tel. & fax 0131/667-9204, Margaret and Brian Love).

Ard-Na-Said B&B is an elegant 1875 Victorian house with a comfy lounge and classy rooms (1 S-£22–26, Db-£44–52, family deals, 5 Priestfield Road, EH16 5HH, tel. 0131/667-8754, fax 0131/271-0960, www.ardnasaid.freeserve.co.uk, enthusiastically run by Jim and Olive Lyons).

Amaragua Guest House, next door to Turret, is an inviting Victorian home-away-from-home decorated with a Malaysian twist—art and some furniture accumulated when the English owners lived in Kuala Lumpur (S-£18–25, Db-£36–50, £2-per-person discount with this book, 10 Kilmaurs Terrace, EH16 5DR, tel. & fax 0131/667-6775, cell 0789-987-8722, run by gracious Helen and Dave Butterworth).

Dunedin Guest House (dun-EE-din) is bright, plush, Scottish, and a good value (7 rooms, S-£20–30, Db-£40–60, family rooms and deals, strong showers, good lighting, TVs with satellite channels, 8 Priestfield Road, EH16 5HH, tel. 0131/668-1949, fax 0131/668-3636, e-mail: dunedin-guesthouse@edinburgh-EH16 .freeserve.co.uk, Marcella Bowen).

Dorstan Private Hotel is personable but professional and hotelesque, with all the comforts. Several of its 14 thoughtfully decorated rooms are on the ground floor (2 Ds-£58, Db-£66, family rooms, CC:VMA, 7 Priestfield Road, EH16 5HJ, tel. 0131/667-6721, fax 0131/668-4644, e-mail: reservations@dorstan-hotel .demon.co.uk, Mairae Campbell).

Hotel Ceilidh-Donia (cal-uh-DOH-nee-uh) has 13 rooms:

Edinburgh, Our Neighborhood

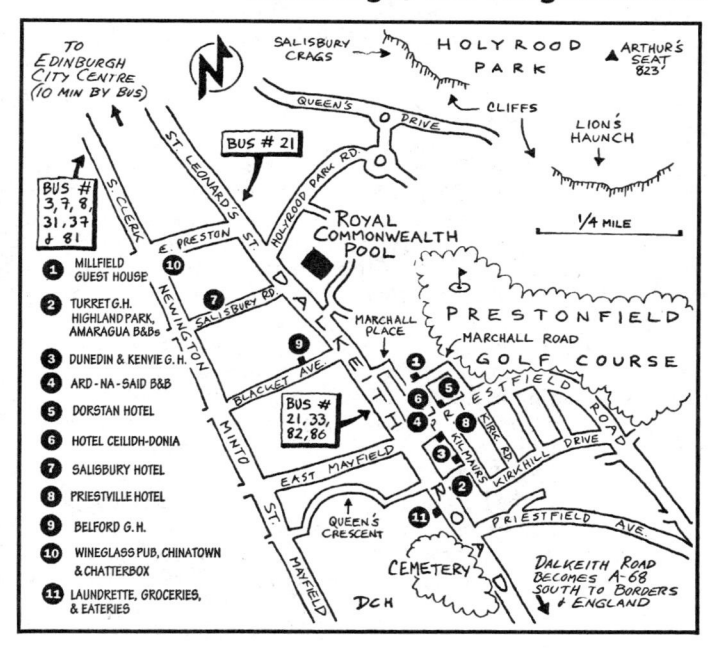

1. MILLFIELD GUEST HOUSE
2. TURRET G.H. HIGHLAND PARK, AMARAGUA B&Bs
3. DUNEDIN & KENVIE G.H.
4. ARD-NA-SAID B&B
5. DORSTAN HOTEL
6. HOTEL CEILIDH-DONIA
7. SALISBURY HOTEL
8. PRIESTVILLE HOTEL
9. BELFORD G.H.
10. WINEGLASS PUB, CHINATOWN & CHATTERBOX
11. LAUNDRETTE, GROCERIES, & EATERIES

half are state-of-the-art new and comfortable, and the other half are being refurbished. Owners Max and Annette Preston offer dinner (£5–6 entrees), run a bar, and have a high-tech security system (two D-£50–54, unrenovated Db-£50–62, deluxe Db-£55–70, CC:VM, nonsmoking except in part of bar, 14 Marchhall Crescent, EH16 5HL, tel. 0131/667-2743, fax 0131/668-2181, www.hotelceilidh-donia.freeserve.co.uk).

Salisbury Hotel fills a classy old Georgian building with 12 rooms, a large lounge, and even a dumbwaiter in the breakfast room. It's more like a hotel than its neighbors but run with B&B warmth by Brenda Wright (D-£40–56, Db-£50–60, 5 percent off with cash and this book, CC:VM, 45 Salisbury Road, EH16 5AA, tel. & fax 0131/667-1264, http://members.edinburgh.org/salisbury/).

Priestville B&B is a spacious place, with six faded rooms and charming rough edges (D-£44–50, Db-£50–56, CC:VM, family deals, small fridge per floor, 10 Priestfield Road, EH16 5HJ, tel. 0131/667-2435, e-mail: priestville@hotmail.com, Angela and Alan Aberdein).

Belford House is a tidy, homey place offering seven good rooms and a warm welcome (D-£40–44, Db-£50–54, family deals, CC:VM, 13 Blacket Avenue, tel. 0131/667-2422, Isa and Tom Borthwick).

Big, Modern, Cheap Hotels in the Center

Ibis Hotel, mid–Royal Mile behind Tron Church, is perfectly located and has 98 soulless but clean and comfy rooms and American charm (Sb-£59.50, Db-£62.50 all year, skip the £4.50 continental buffet breakfast, CC:VMA, nonsmoking rooms available, elevator, 6 Hunter Square, EH1 1QW, tel. 0131/240-7000, fax 0131/240-7007, e-mail: H2039@accor-hotels.com). Considering its location and the costs of other hotels in town, this is a great deal for couples.

Jurys Inn is another cookie-cutter place, with 186 dependably comfortable rooms; unlike Ibis, prices fluctuate, dropping in winter and soaring in August (Db-£39–82, CC:VM, breakfast extra, nonsmoking rooms available, some views, on quiet street just off Royal Mile, 43 Jeffrey Street, EH1 1DG, tel. 0131/200-3300, fax 0131/200-0400, www.jurys.com).

Travel Inn, the biggest hotel in Edinburgh, has even less character but a great price and a mediocre location about a mile west of the Mile. Each of its 280 rooms is modern and comfortable, with a sofa that folds out for two kids if necessary (Db-£50 for 2 adults and up to 2 kids under 15, breakfast is extra, CC:VMA, elevators, nonsmoking rooms, weekends booked long in advance, near Haymarket station west of the castle at 1 Morrison Link, EH3 8DN, tel. 0131/228-9819, fax 0131/228-9836, www.travelinn.co.uk).

Hostels

Although Edinburgh's hostels are well run and open to all and provide £12 bunk beds (an £8–12 savings over B&Bs), they don't include breakfast and are scruffy.

Castle Rock Hostel is hip and easygoing, offering cheap beds, plenty of friends, and a great central location just below the castle and above the pubs with all the folk music (15 Johnston Terrace, tel. 0131/225-9666). Their sister hostels are nearly across the street from each other: **High Street Hostel** (8 Blackfriars Street, just off High Street/Royal Mile, tel. 0131/557-3984) and **Royal Mile Backpackers** (105 High Street, tel. 0131/557-6120).

For more regulations and less color, try the IYH hostels: **Bruntsfield Hostel** (near golf course, 6 to 12 beds per room, 7 Bruntsfield Crescent, buses #11, #15, and #16 from Princes Street, tel. 0131/447-2994) and **Edinburgh Hostel** (4 to 12 beds per room, 18 Eglinton Crescent, 5-minute walk from Haymarket station, tel. 0131/337-1120).

Eating in Edinburgh

Eating along the Royal Mile

Historic pubs and doily cafés with reasonable, unremarkable meals abound. But, since chefs seem to come and go with the seasons, I have no splurge meals to recommend. These are simply handy, affordable places for a good bite to eat (listed in downhill order). **Deacon Brodie's Pub** serves soup, sandwiches, and snacks on the ground floor and good £7 meals upstairs (daily 12:00–22:00, CC:VM, tel. 0131/225-6531). Or munch prayerfully in the **Lower Aisle** restaurant under St. Giles Cathedral (Mon–Fri 8:30–16:30; Jul–Sept also Sun 11:00–14:00). **Bann's Vegetarian Café** serves carnivore-pleasing veggie cuisine that goes way beyond tofu and granola (daily 10:00–23:00, CC:VM, just off South Bridge behind the Tron Church at 5 Hunter Square, tel. 0131/226-1112). For a break from the touristic grind, consider the **Elephant House**, where locals browse newspapers, listen to classic rock, and sip coffee or munch a light meal (daily, 3 blocks south of Royal Mile at 21 George IV Bridge, tel. 0131/220-5355). **Food Plantation** has good, inexpensive fresh sandwiches to eat in or take out (Mon–Fri 7:30–17:00, 274 Canongate). **Brambles Tea Room** serves light lunches and Starbucks coffee (Mon–Sat 10:30–16:45, Sun 11:00–16:45, next to Huntly House at 158 Canongate). **Clarinda's Tea Room**, near the bottom of the Royal Mile, is a charming and tasty place for a break after touring the Mile or palace (daily 9:30–16:45).

Grassmarket Street, below the castle, is lined with sloppy eateries and noisy pubs. This is the place for live folk music. If you want dinner to melt into your beer, eat here.

Lunch in the New Town

Waverley Center Food Court, below the TI and above the station, is a food circus of sticky fast-food joints—including **The Scot's Pantry** for quick traditional edibles—littered with paper plates and shoppers (Mon–Sat 8:30–18:00, Thu until 19:00, Sun 11:00–17:00). Local office workers pile into the friendly and family-run **La Lanterna** for good Italian food (Mon–Sat 12:00–14:00, 17:15–22:00, closed Sun, CC:VMA, 83 Hanover Street, 2 blocks off Princes Street, dinner reservations wise, tel. 0131/226-3090). For a generation, New Town vegetarians have munched salads at **Henderson's Salad Table and Wine Bar** (Mon–Sat 8:00–22:45, closed Sun, nonsmoking section, strictly vegetarian, between Queen and George Streets at 94 Hanover Street, tel. 0131/225-2131). Rose Street has tubs of pubs.

Tesco is the only supermarket in town (Mon–Sat 8:00–21:00, Sun 9:00–19:00, on Nicolson, just south of intersection with W. Richmond Street, 5 long blocks south of the Royal Mile, and on the way home to B&B neighborhood).

Eating in Dalkeith Road Area, near Your B&B

All of these places except Howie's are within a five-minute walk of the recommended B&Bs. The following eateries are on or near the intersection of Newington and East Preston Streets. For a fun local atmosphere, the smoky **Wine Glass Pub** serves filling meals (£4, daily 12:00–14:30, 17:30–21:00 but no dinner on Fri, closes 19:30 on Sat). **Chinatown**, next to the Wine Glass, is a delightful—though not cheap—Chinese restaurant (£7–10 entrées, Tue–Fri 12:00–14:00, 17:30–23:00, Sat–Sun 17:30–23:00, closed Mon, CC:VM, reservations wise, tel. 0131/662-0555). **Chatterbox**, on the other side of the Wine Glass, is fine for a light meal with tea (£3.50 meals, Mon–Fri 8:30–18:00, Sat 9:00–18:00, Sun 11:00–18:00). **Brattisanis** is your basic fish-and-chips joint serving lousy milkshakes and great haggis (daily 11:30–24:00, 87 Newington Road).

Two affordable splurges feature Scottish cooking with a French flair, are open daily, and charge about £5 to £7 for lunch and £16 to £17 for a three-course dinner. **Fenwicks** is cozy and reliable, with tasty food (daily 12:00–14:00, dinner 18:00–late, all day Sunday, CC:VM, 15 Salisbury Place, tel. 0131/667-4265). **Howies**, with a more adventurous menu, is a bit pricier and a longer walk, about 10 minutes north of the B&B neighborhood; you could get off the bus at Clerk Street on the way home (daily 12:00–14:00, 16:00–22:00, can bring own wine for £2 corkage fee, 75 St. Leonard's Street, tel. 0131/668-2917).

Hotel Ceilidh-Donia (see above) serves dinner nightly (£5 to £6 meal), runs a bar with a nonsmoking section, and is open to the public (14 Marchhall Crescent, tel. 0131/667-2743).

On Dalkeith Road, the huge Commonwealth Pool's **Time Out** is a noisy cafeteria (pass the entry without paying, Mon–Fri 10:00–20:00, Sat–Sun 10:00–17:00). **Jade Palace**, several blocks south of the pool, has tasty Chinese food—takeout only (Wed–Mon 16:30–23:00, closed Tue, 212 Dalkeith Road).

Minto Hotel's bar/restaurant serves a filling high tea—hot meaty dinner with tea and scones—for £7 to £8.50 (Mon–Sat 17:00–21:00, Sun 16:00–21:00, CC:VM, on Minto Street just north of intersection with Mayfield Terrace, tel. 0131/668-1234).

Transportation Connections—Edinburgh

By train to: Inverness (7/day, 4 hrs), **Oban** (3/day, change in Glasgow, 4.5 hrs), **York** (hrly, 2.5 hrs), **London** (hrly, 5 hrs), **Durham** (hrly, 2 hrs, less frequent in winter), **Newcastle** (hrly, 1.5 hrs), **Lake District** (south past Carlisle to Penrith, catch bus to Keswick; hrly except Sun 3/day, 40 min), **Birmingham** (6/day, 4.5 hrs), **Crewe** (6/day, 3.5 hrs). Train info: tel. 0345-484-950.

By bus to: Oban (3/day, 4 hrs), **Fort William** (3/day, 4 hrs), **Inverness** (4/day, 4 hrs). For bus info, call National Express (tel. 0990-808-080) or Scottish Citylink (tel. 0990-505-050).

DUBLIN

With reminders of its stirring history and rich culture on every corner, Ireland's capital and largest city is a sightseer's delight. Dublin's fair city will have you humming "Alive, alive-O."

Founded as a Viking trading settlement in the ninth century, Dublin grew to be a center of wealth and commerce second only to London in the British Empire. Dublin, the seat of English rule in Ireland for 700 years, was the heart of a "civilized" Anglo-Irish area (eastern Ireland) known as "the Pale." Anything "beyond the Pale" was considered uncultured and almost barbaric...purely Irish.

The Golden Age of English Dublin was the 18th century. Britain was on a roll, and Dublin was Britain's second city. Largely rebuilt during this Georgian era, Dublin—even with its "tale of two cities" miserable underbelly—became an elegant and cultured capital.

Then nationalism and human rights got in the way. The ideas of the French Revolution inspired Irish intellectuals to buck British rule, and after the revolt of 1798, life in Dublin was never quite the same. But the 18th century left a lasting imprint on the city. Georgian (that's British for neoclassical) squares and boulevards gave the city a grandness. The National Museum, National Gallery, and many government buildings are in the Georgian section of town. Few buildings (notably St. Patrick's Cathedral and Christchurch Cathedral) predate this Georgian period.

In the 19th century, with the closing of the Irish Parliament, the famine, and the beginnings of the struggle for independence, Dublin was treated—and felt—more like a colony than a partner. The tension culminated in the Rising of 1916, independence, and the tragic civil war. With many of Dublin's grand streets left in ruins, the city emerged as the capital of the only former colony in Europe.

While bullet-pocked buildings and dramatic statues keep memories of Ireland's recent struggle for independence alive, it's boom time now, and the city is looking to a bright future. Locals are enjoying the "Celtic Tiger" economy—the best in Europe—while visitors enjoy a big-town cultural scene wrapped in a small-town smile.

Planning Your Time

On a two-week trip through Ireland, Dublin deserves three nights and two days. Consider this sightseeing plan:
Day 1: 10:00–Trinity College walk, 11:00–*Book of Kells* and Old Library, 12:00–Browse Grafton Street, lunch there or picnic on St. Stephen's Green, 13:30–National Museum, 15:00–Historical town walk, 17:00–Return to hotel, rest, dinner—eat well for less during "early bird specials," 19:30–Evening walk (musical or literary), 22:00–Irish music in Temple Bar area.
Day 2: 10:00–Kilmainham Jail, 12:00–Guinness Brewery tour, 13:30–Lunch (with a faint buzz), 15:00–Tour Dublin Castle, Evening–Catch a play or concert.

Orientation (tel. code: 01)

Greater Dublin sprawls with over a million people—nearly a third of the country's population. But the center of touristic interest is a tight triangle between O'Connell Bridge, St. Stephen's Green, and Christchurch Cathedral. Within this triangle you'll find Trinity College (*Book of Kells*), Grafton Street (top pedestrian shopping zone), Temple Bar (trendy nightlife center), Dublin Castle, and the hub of most city tours and buses.

The River Liffey cuts the town in two. Focus on the southern half (where nearly all your sightseeing will take place). Dublin's main drag, O'Connell Street (near Abbey Theater and the outdoor produce market) runs north of the river to the central O'Connell Bridge then continues as the main city axis—mostly as Grafton Street—to St. Stephen's Green. The only major sights outside your easy-to-walk triangle are the Kilmainham Jail and the Guinness Brewery (both west of the center).

Tourist Information

The TI fills an old church on Suffolk Street (a block off Grafton Street, Mon–Sat 9:00–17:30, Sun 9:00–14:30, closed off-season Sun, no telephone help). While packed with tourists, promotional brochures, an American Express office, a café, and traditional knick-knacks, it's short on hard info. Less crowded but equally helpful TI branches are on Baggot Street and at the airport (daily 8:00–22:00). The TI gives a free newspaper with a lousy map, lots of advertisements, and the same flyers that fill racks all over town. The handy

Dublin's Top Visitor Attractions booklet has a map and the latest on all the town's sights—many more than I list here (£2.50, sold at TI bookshop without any wait). For a schedule of happenings in town, buy the excellent *In Dublin* at any newsstand (fortnightly, £2).

Arrival in Dublin

By Train: Trains arrive at Heuston Station (serving the west and southwest) on the west end of town. Dublin's second train station, Connolly Station (serving the north, northwest, and Rosslare), is closer to the center—a 10-minute walk from O'Connell Bridge. Each station has a luggage-check facility.

Bus 90 connects both train stations, the bus station, and the city center (60p flat fee, 6/hrly, runs along river).

By Bus: Bus Eireann, Ireland's national bus company, uses the Busaras Central Bus Station next to Connolly Station (catch bus 90 to the city center).

By Ferry: Irish Ferries dock at the mouth of the River Liffey (near the town center), while the Stena Line docks at Dun Laoghaire (easy DART train connections into Dublin, at least 3/hrly, 15 min).

By Plane: From the airport, milk-run buses 41 and 41C go to Talbot Street, a five-minute walk to O'Connell Bridge (£1.10, 3/hrly). The faster Airlink direct bus connects the airport with the Heuston Station and Busaras Central Bus Station near Connolly Station (£3, 4/hrly, 30 min). Taxis from the airport into Dublin cost about £13.

Helpful Hints

Internet Access: On the north side of O'Connell Bridge, try Global Internet Café (£5/hr, 8 Lower O'Connell St., tel. 01/878-0295). On the south side, try Planet Cybercafé (£5/hr, off Dame Street below the castle at 23 South Great George's Street, tel. 01/679-0583).

Laundry: Capricorn Dry Cleaners is behind Jury's Christchurch on Patrick Street (Mon–Fri 7:30–20:00, Sat 9:00–18:00, Sun 10:00–16:00, tel. 01/473-1779).

Getting around Dublin

You'll do most of Dublin on foot. Big green buses are cheap and cover the city thoroughly. Most lines start at the four quays nearest O'Connell Bridge. If you're away from the center, nearly any bus takes you back downtown. Tell the driver where you're going, and he'll ask for 60p (1 to 3 stops) or 80p (4 to 7 stops). The bus office at 59 Upper O'Connell Street has free "route network" maps and sells bus passes (1-day pass £3.30 adults, £5.50 family, 4-day adult Explorer pass £10.00, bus info tel. 01/873-4222). DART trains connect Dublin with Dun Laoghaire (ferry terminal, at least 3/hrly,

Dublin

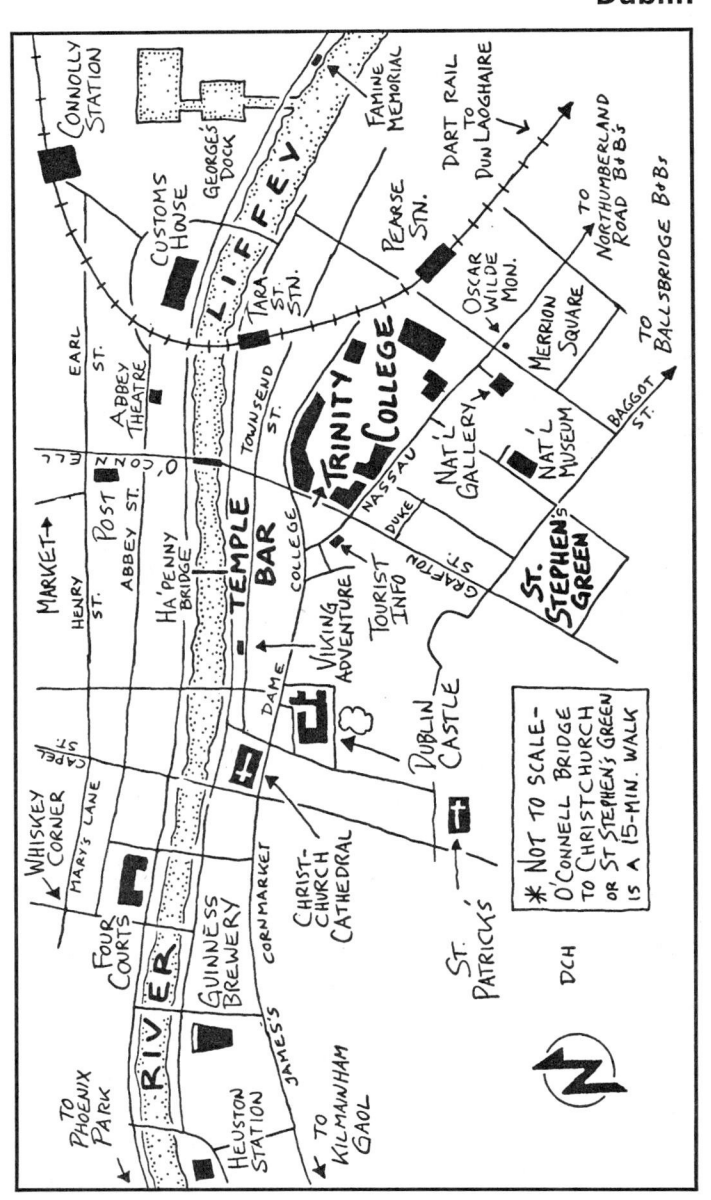

15 min, £1.10). Taxis are honest, plentiful, friendly, and good sources of information (under £4 for most downtown rides, £20 per hour for a guided joyride, City Cabs tel. 01/872-2688).

Tours of Dublin

While the physical treasures of Dublin are mediocre by European standards, the city has a fine story to tell and people with a natural knack for telling it. It's a good town for walking tours—and the competition is fierce. Pamphlets touting creative walks are posted all over town. There are medieval walks, literary walks, Georgian Dublin walks, and more. The two evening walks are great ways to meet other travelers.

▲▲**Historical Walking Tour**—This is your best introductory walk. A group of hardworking history graduates—many of whom claim to have done more than just kiss the Blarney Stone—fill Dublin's basic historic strip (Trinity College, Old Parliament House, Dublin Castle, and Christchurch Cathedral) with the story of their city, from its Viking origin to the present. As you listen to your guide's story, you stand in front of buildings that aren't much to see but are lots to talk about. Guides speak at length about the roots of Ireland's struggle with Britain (£6, 2 hours, depart from front gate of Trinity College, May–Sept daily 11:00 and 15:00 plus Sat–Sun at 12:00; Oct–Apr only Fri, Sat, and Sun at 12:00; tel. 01/878-0227). For a private walk, contact Historical Insights (tel. 01/878-0227, www.historicalinsights.ie).

▲**Jameson Literary Pub Crawl**—Two actors take 30 or so tourists on a walk, stopping at four pubs. Half the time is spent enjoying their entertaining banter, which introduces the novice to the high craic (conversation) of Joyce, O'Casey, and Yeats. The 2.5-hour tour is punctuated with 20-minute pub breaks (free time). While the beer lubricates the social fun, it dilutes the content of the evening. Meet any night at 19:30 (plus Sun at noon) in the Duke Pub off Grafton on Duke Street (£6.50, runs Thu–Sun in winter, tel. 01/670-5602).

▲▲**Traditional Irish-Music Pub Crawl**—This is like the Literary Pub Crawl but features music. You meet upstairs at 19:30 at Gogarty's Pub (in the Temple Bar area) and spend 40 minutes in the upstairs rooms of four pubs listening to two musicians talk about, play, and sing traditional Irish music. While having only two musicians makes the music a bit thin and Irish music aficionados will tell you you're better off just finding a good session, the evening—while touristy—is not gimmicky. The musicians demonstrate four instruments and really enjoy introducing rookies to their art (£6, boss Vinnie offers a £1 discount with this book, beer extra, nightly May–Oct, weekends only in winter, allow 2.5 hours, expect up to 50 tourists, tel. 01/478-0193).

▲**Bus Tours**—Several companies offer the basic center-of-Dublin orientation (3 hrs, £10, departing 10:15 and 14:15, from 59 Upper O'Connell Street, tel. 01/783-4222). For a hop-on hop-off bus tour, consider either **Dublin City Tour** (£7, tel. 01/873-4222) or **Guide Friday** (£7, tel. 01/676-5377). Both do identical 90-minute circuits of the town, allowing you to hop on and hop off at your choice of 12 stops (mostly topless—with running commentaries; they go to Guinness Brewery but not to Kilmainham Jail). Pay the driver when you hop on. Your ticket's good for the entire day. Buses, which leave about every 10 minutes from about 9:30 to 18:00, are especially enjoyable for photographers on sunny days. One ticket gets you on either company's buses.

Sights—Dublin's Trinity College

▲**Trinity College**—Started in 1592 by Queen Elizabeth I to establish a Protestant way of thinking about God, Trinity has long been Ireland's most prestigious college. Originally the student body was limited to rich, Protestant males. Women were admitted in 1903, and Catholics, while allowed entrance by the school much earlier, were given formal permission to study at Trinity in the 1970s. Today half of Trinity's 11,000 students are women, and 70 percent are culturally Catholic (although only about 20 percent of Irish youth are churchgoing).

▲**Trinity College Tour**—Inside the gate of Trinity, students organize and lead 30-minute tours of their campus. You'll get a rundown on the mostly Georgian architecture; a peek at student life, both in the early days and today; and enjoy a chance to hang out with a witty Irish college kid as he talks about his school (daily 10:00–15:30, the £5.50 tour fee includes the £4.50 fee to see the *Book of Kells*, where the tour leaves you).

▲▲▲***Book of Kells*/Trinity Old Library**—The only Trinity campus interior welcoming tourists—just follow the signs—is the Old Library with its precious *Book of Kells*. The first-class *Turning Darkness into Light* exhibit puts the 680-page illuminated manuscript in its historical and cultural context and prepares you for the original book and other precious manuscripts in the treasury. The exhibit is a one-way affair leading to the actual treasury, which shows only three books under glass. Take your time in the exhibit.

Written on vellum (baby calfskin) in the eighth (or early ninth) century—probably by Irish monks in Iona (Scotland)—this enthusiastically decorated copy of the four Gospels was taken to the Irish monastery at Kells in 806 after a series of Viking raids. Arguably the finest piece of art from what is generally called the Dark Ages, the *Book of Kells* shows that monastic life in this far fringe of Europe was far from dark. It has been bound into four separate volumes. At any given time, two of the gospels are on display. You'll see four richly decorated 1,200-year-old pages—two text and two decorated cover pages—under glass. The library

Dublin Center

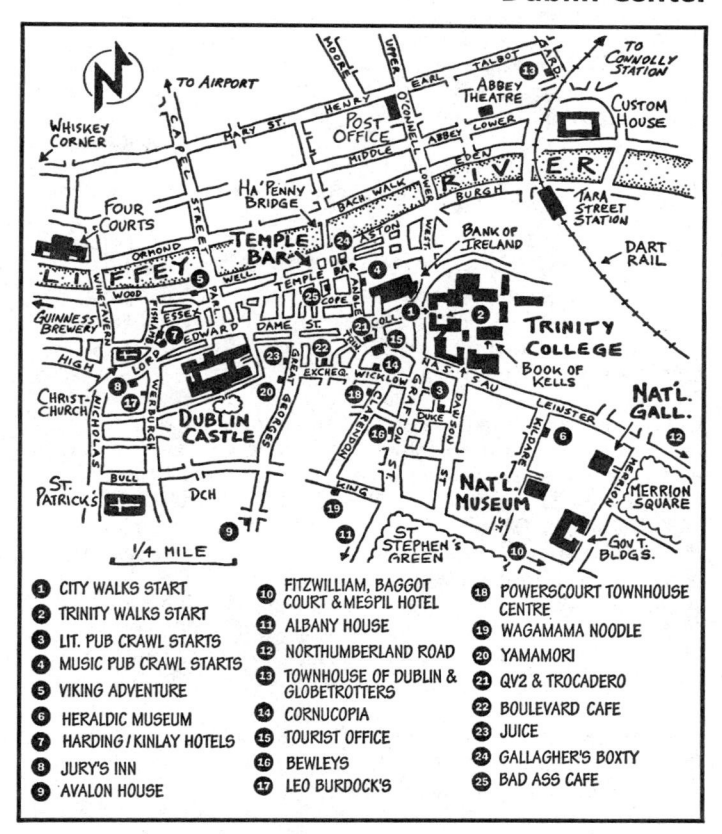

Map legend:
1. CITY WALKS START
2. TRINITY WALKS START
3. LIT. PUB CRAWL STARTS
4. MUSIC PUB CRAWL STARTS
5. VIKING ADVENTURE
6. HERALDIC MUSEUM
7. HARDING / KINLAY HOTELS
8. JURY'S INN
9. AVALON HOUSE
10. FITZWILLIAM, BAGGOT COURT & MESPIL HOTEL
11. ALBANY HOUSE
12. NORTHUMBERLAND ROAD
13. TOWNHOUSE OF DUBLIN & GLOBETROTTERS
14. CORNUCOPIA
15. TOURIST OFFICE
16. BEWLEYS
17. LEO BURDOCK'S
18. POWERSCOURT TOWNHOUSE CENTRE
19. WAGAMAMA NOODLE
20. YAMAMORI
21. QV2 & TROCADERO
22. BOULEVARD CAFE
23. JUICE
24. GALLAGHER'S BOXTY
25. BAD ASS CAFE

treasury also displays the *Book of Armagh* (A.D. 807) and the *Book of Durrow* (A.D. 680), neither of which can be checked out.

Next, a stairway leads to the 65-meter-long main chamber of the Old Library (from 1732), stacked to its towering ceiling with 200,000 of the library's oldest books. Here you'll find one of a dozen surviving original copies of the 1916 Proclamation of the Irish Republic. Patrick Pearse read these words outside the General Post Office on April 24 to start the Easter Rising which led to Irish Independence. Read the entire thing... imagining it was yours. Notice the inclusive opening phrase. (The seven signatories were each executed.) Another national icon is nearby—the oldest surviving Irish harp. From the 15th century, it's the one

featured on Irish coins. Crowds are gone by the end of the day (£4.50, at Trinity College Library, Mon–Sat 9:30–17:00 all year, Sun 9:30–16:30, off-season Sun 12:00–16:30, tel. 01/608-2308).
▲▲The Dublin Experience—This 40-minute video giving a historic introduction to Dublin is one more tourist movie with the sound turned up. It's good—offering a fine sweeping introduction to the story of Ireland—but pricey and riding on the coattails of the *Book of Kells* (£3, discounted with combo Kells/video ticket, daily Jun–Sept 10:00–17:00 on the hour, in modern arts building next to Trinity Old Library).

Sights—Dublin, South of the River Liffey
▲▲Dublin Castle—Built on the spot of the first Viking fortress, this castle was the seat of British rule in Ireland for 700 years (until 1922). Located where the Poddle and Liffey Rivers came together making a black pool ("dubh linn" in Irish), Dublin Castle was the official residence of the viceroy, who implemented the will of the British royalty. Today it's used for fancy state and charity functions. The 45-minute tours offer a room-by-room walk through the lavish state apartments of this most English of Irish palaces (£3, about 4/hrly, Mon–Fri 10:00–17:00, Sat–Sun 14:00–17:00, tel. 01/677-7129). The tour finishes with a look at the foundations of the Norman tower and the best remaining chunk of the 13th-century town wall.
▲Dublin's Viking Adventure—This really is an adventure. You start in a box of seats that transforms into a Viking ship. Your chieftain—who hasn't washed since Norway—joins you, and suddenly you're in a storm, waves splash, smoke rolls, and you land in a kind of Viking summer camp, where you spend 30 minutes being shuttled from one friendly original Dubliner to the next (a trader, a sassy maiden, a monk building a church, and so on). A short film about the Vikings follows, with a look at artifacts recently uncovered in the adjacent excavation sight. It feels hokey, but the cast is certainly hardworking, and you leave feeling as though you'd visited, if not a Viking town, at least the set for a B-grade Viking movie. It's on Essex Street a block off the riverside Essex Quay in Temple Bar—where the Vikings established their first Dublin settlement in 841 (£4.75, Tue–Sat 10:00–16:30, closed Sun and Mon, tel. 01/679-6040).
Christchurch Cathedral—The oldest building in Dublin, the cathedral marks the spot where the Vikings established their town on the river. The first church here was built of wood in 1038 by King Sitric. The present structure dates from a mix of periods: Norman and Gothic but mostly Victorian neo-Gothic (1870s restoration work). Because of its British past, neither of Dublin's top two churches is Catholic. Christchurch Cathedral and the nearby St. Patrick's Cathedral are both from the Church of

Ireland. In Catholic Ireland they feel hollow and are more famous than visit-worthy. A choral evensong is sung at 18:00 on Wednesday and Thursday and 17:00 on Saturday.

▲▲▲**National Museum**—Showing off the treasures of Ireland from the Stone Age to the 20th century, this museum is wonderfully digestible under one dome. Ireland's Bronze Age gold fills the center. The prehistoric Ireland exhibit rings the gold, and in a corner you'll find the treasury with the most famous pieces (brooches, chalices, and other examples of Celtic metalwork) and an 18-minute video giving an overview of Irish art through the 13th century. The collection's superstar: the gold, enamel, and amber eighth-century Tara Brooch. Jumping way ahead, a special corridor features "The Road to Independence," with guns, letters, and death masks recalling the fitful birth of the "Terrible Beauty" (1900–1921, with a focus on the Easter Rising of 1916). The best Viking artifacts in town are upstairs (museum is free, Tue–Sat 10:00–17:00, Sun 14:00–17:00, closed Mon, between Trinity College and St. Stephen's Green on Kildare Street, tel. 01/677-7444). Greatest-hits tours are given several times a day (£1, 45 minutes, call for schedule).

National Gallery—Along with a hall featuring the work of top Irish painters, this has Ireland's best collection of paintings by the European masters. It's impressive—unless you've been to London or Paris (free, Mon–Sat 10:00–17:30, Thu until 20:30, Sun 14:00–17:00, tel. 01/661-5133).

▲▲**Grafton Street**—Once filled with noisy traffic, today Grafton Street is Dublin's liveliest pedestrian shopping mall. A five-minute people- and busker-filled stroll takes you from Trinity College up to St. Stephen's Green (and makes you wonder why American merchants are so terrified of a car-free street). Walking by a buxom statue of "sweet" Molly Malone, you'll soon pass two venerable department stores: the Irish Brown Thomas and the English Marks & Spencer. An alley leads to the Powerscourt Townhouse Shopping Centre tastefully filling a converted Georgian mansion. The huge, glass-covered St. Stephen's Green Shopping Center and the peaceful and green green itself mark the top of Grafton Street.

▲**St. Stephen's Green**—This city park, originally a medieval commons, was enclosed in 1664 and gradually surrounded with fine Georgian buildings. Today it provides 22 acres of grassy refuge for Dubliners. On a sunny afternoon, it's a wonderful world apart from the big city.

Number 29—Tour the carefully restored house at Number 29 Lower Fitzwilliam Street for a walk through a Dublin home in 1790 (£2.50, Tue–Sat 10:00–17:00, Sun 14:00–17:00, closed Mon, includes introductory video and eager-to-teach guides scattered throughout). Nearby Merrion Square is decorated with fine doors—a Dublin trademark—and elegant Georgian knobs and knockers.

▲**Temple Bar**—This was a Georgian center of craftsmen and merchants. When it grew poor in the 19th century, lower rents attracted students and artists, giving the neighborhood a bohemian flair. With recent government tax incentives and lots of development money, the Temple Bar district has become a thriving cultural (and beer-drinking) hot spot. Today, this much-promoted center of trendy shops, cafés, theaters, galleries, pubs with live music, and restaurants feels like the heart of Dublin. Dublin's "Left Bank" (actually on the right bank) fills the cobbled streets between Dame Street and the river. The central **Meeting House Square** (just off Essex Street) hosts free street theater, a lively organic produce market (Sat 9:30–15:00), and a book market (Sat 11:00–18:00). The square is surrounded by interesting cultural centers. For a listing of events and galleries, visit the **Temple Bar Information Centre** (Eustace Street, tel. 01/671-5717, www.temple-bar.ie). Rather than follow particular pub or restaurant recommendations (mine are below under "Eating"), venture down a few side lanes off the main drag to see what looks good. The pedestrian-only **Ha' Penny Bridge**, named for the half-pence toll people used to pay to cross it, leads over the Liffey to Temple Bar. ("Bar" means a walkway along the river.)

Sights—Dublin, North of the River Liffey

▲▲**O'Connell Bridge**—The bridge crosses the River Liffey, which has historically divided the town into the wealthy and cultivated south side and the poorer, cruder north side. While there's plenty of culture on the north, even today "the north" is considered rougher and less safe.

From the bridge look upriver. The high point, near Christchurch (marked by the eyesore of the city planning commission building), is where the Vikings established Dublin in the ninth century. Across the river, the green dome marks the Four Courts, today's Supreme Court building—tragically bombed and burned in 1922 during the civil war that followed Irish independence. Between you and the dome is the elegant iron Ha' Penny Bridge, leading into the Temple Bar district. Looking downstream you'll see the tall ugly union headquarters—for now the tallest building in the Republic—and lots of cranes. Booming Dublin is developing downstream. The Irish—forever clever tax fiddlers—have subsidized and revitalized this formerly dreary quarter with great success. A short walk downstream along the north bank leads to a powerful series of modern statues memorializing the great famine of 1845.

▲**O'Connell Street**—Dublin's grandest street leads from O'Connell Bridge through the heart of north Dublin. Since the 1740s it's been a 45-meter-wide promenade. Ever since the first O'Connell Bridge connected it to the Trinity side of town in 1794, it's been Dublin's main drag. The street, while lined with fast-food and souvenir shops, echoes with history. Much of the fighting during the 1916 Easter Rising and the civil war a few years later took place here. The imposing **General Post Office** is where Patrick Pearse read the Proclamation of Irish Independence. The GPO building itself—a kind of Irish Alamo—was the rebel headquarters and scene of a five-day bloody siege during the Rising. While there's little to see, its facade remains pockmarked with bullet holes (open for business and sightseers Mon–Sat 8:00–20:00, Sun 10:00–18:30).

Statues lining O'Connell Street celebrate great figures in Ireland's fight for independence. Daniel O'Connell (1775–1847), known as "the Liberator," founded the Irish Labor Party and was a strong voice for Irish Catholic rights in the British parliament. James Larkin founded the Irish Workers' Union. One monument that didn't wave an Irish flag—a tall column crowned by a statue of the British hero of Trafalgar, Admiral Nelson—was blown up in 1966 as locals celebrated the 50th anniversary of the Rising.

Make a point to get away from tourists' Dublin. Stroll the smaller streets north of the Liffey. Just a block west of O'Connell Street, the **Moore Street Market** is a colorful commotion of produce and hawkers. For workaday Dublin, the long pedestrian mall of Mary Street, Henry Street, and Talbot Street is a people-watchers' delight.

The prestigious **Abbey Theatre,** now a modern, ugly building, is still the much-loved home of the Irish National Theater (a block off the river on Abbey Street**). St. Mary's Pro-Cathedral** is the leading Catholic church in town but curiously is not a cathedral since Christchurch was made one in the 12th century (the Vatican has chosen to ignore the fact that it hasn't been Catholic for centuries). The **Georgian Parnell Square** has a Garden of Remembrance honoring the victims of the 1916 Rising.

The **Dublin Writers' Museum** fills a splendidly restored Georgian mansion. No country so small produced such a wealth of literature. As interesting to those interested in Irish literature as it is boring to those who aren't, this museum features the lives and works of Dublin's great writers (£3, includes slow-moving audio tour, daily 10:00–18:00, Sun and off-season till 17:00, 18 Parnell Square North, tel. 01/872-2077). With hometown wits such as Swift, Yeats, Joyce, and Shaw, literary fans will have a checklist of residences and memorials to see.

Sights—Outer Dublin

The Jail and the Guinness Brewery are the main sights outside of the old center. Combine these in one visit.

▲▲▲**Kilmainham Gaol (Jail)**—Opened in 1796 as the Dublin County Jail and a debtors' prison and considered a model in its day, it was used frequently as a political prison by the British. Many of those who fought for Irish independence were held or executed here, including leaders of the rebellions of 1798, 1803, 1848, 1867, and 1916. National heroes Robert Emmett and Charles Stewart Parnell each did time here. The last prisoner to be held here was Eamon de Valera (later president of Ireland). He was released on July 16, 1924, the day Kilmainham was finally shut down. The buildings, virtually in ruins, were restored in the 1960s. Today it's a shrine to the Nathan Hales of Ireland.

Start your visit with a guided tour (60 min, including 30 min in the prison chapel for a rebellion-packed video). It's touching to tour the cells and places of execution while hearing tales of terrible colonialism and heroic patriotism—alongside Irish schoolkids who know these names well. Then browse through the excellent exhibit on Victorian prison life and Ireland's fight for independence. Don't miss the dimly lit hall off the second floor displaying the stirring last letters patriots sent to loved ones hours before facing the firing squad (£3, daily 9:30–18:00, 2 tours/hrly, last tour at 16:45; off-season Sun–Fri 10:00–17:00, closed Sat; £4 taxi, bus #51, #78a, or #79 from Aston Quay, tel. 01/453-5984).

▲**Guinness Brewery**—A visit to the Guinness Hop Store is, for many, a pilgrimage. The home of Ireland's national beer welcomes visitors (for £5) with a museum, video, and drink. Arthur Guinness began brewing the famous stout here in 1759. By 1868 it was the biggest brewery in the world. Today the sprawling brewery fills several city blocks. Around the world Guinness brews more than 10 million glasses a day. You can learn as much or as little about the brewing process as you like. Highlights are the cooperage (with old film clips showing the master wood-keg makers plying their now-extinct trade) and a display of the brewery's clever ads. The video is a well-done ad for the brew that makes you feel almost patriotic as you run down to the sample bar to turn in your coupons for a pint of the real thing (£5, Mon–Sat 9:30–17:00, Sun 10:30–16:30, enter on Crane Street off Thomas Street, bus #78A from Aston Quay near O'Connell Bridge, or bus 123 from Dame Street and O'Connell Street, tel. 01/408-4800). Hop-on hop-off bus tours stop here. (Why is there no museum of Irish alcoholism, which is a serious but rarely discussed problem in this land where the social world seems to float in a sea of beer?)

Entertainment and Theater in Dublin

Ireland produced some of the finest writers in both English and Gaelic, and Dublin houses some of Europe's finest theaters. While Handel's *Messiah* was first performed in Dublin (1742), these days Dublin is famous for its rock bands (U2, Thin Lizzie, and Sinead O'Connor all got started here).

You have much to choose from: **Abbey Theatre** is Ireland's national theater. **Gate Theatre** does foreign plays as well as Irish classics. **Point Theatre,** once a railway terminus, is now the country's top live music venue. At the **National Concert Hall**, the National Symphony Orchestra performs most Friday evenings. Street theater takes the stage in Temple Bar on summer evenings. Folk music rings in the pubs, and street entertainers are everywhere. For the latest on live theater, music, cultural happenings, restaurant reviews, pubs, and current museum hours, pick up the free *Dublin Event Guide* or a copy of the twice-monthly *In Dublin* (£2, any newsstand).

Irish Music in nearby Dun Laoghaire

For an evening of pure Irish music, song, and dance, check out the **Comhaltas Ceoltoiri Eireann**, an association working to preserve this traditional slice of Irish culture. It got started when Elvis and company threatened to steal the musical heart of the new generation. Judging by the pop status of traditional Irish music these days, Comhaltas accomplished its mission. Their "Fonntrai" evening is a costumed stage show mixing traditional music, song, and dance (£5, mid-Jun–Aug Mon–Thu at 21:00, followed by informal music session at 22:30). Fridays all year long they have a ceilidh where everyone dances (£5, 21:30–00:30). Saturday nights feature an informal session by the fireside. Performances are held in the Cuturlann na Eireann, near the Seapoint DART stop or a 20-minute walk from Dun Laoghaire, at 32 Belgrave Square, Monkstown (tel. 01/280-0295). Their bar is free and often filled with music.

Sleeping in Dublin
(£1 = about $1.50, tel. code: 01)
Sleep Code: **S** = Single, **D** = Double/Twin, **T** = Triple, **Q** = Quad, **b** = bathroom, **t** = toilet only, **s** = shower only, **CC** = Credit Card (**V**isa, **M**asterCard, **A**mex). Breakfast is included unless otherwise noted.

Dublin is popular and rooms can be tight. Get a reservation for weekends—especially in summer. Big and practical places (both cheap and moderate) are most central at Christchurch on the edge of Temple Bar. For classy, older Dublin accommodations you'll pay more and stay a bit farther out (east of St. Stephen's Green).

Sleeping in Christchurch

These places face Christchurch Cathedral, a great locale a five-minute walk from the best evening scene at Temple Bar and 10 minutes from the sightseeing center (Trinity College).

Harding Hotel is a hardwood, 20th-century, Viking-style place with 53 hotelesque rooms. The rooms are simpler than Jurys' but it's more intimate, without the tour-group mob scenes (Sb-£45, Db/Tb-£65, breakfast extra, CC:VM, elevator with an obnoxious gift of gab, Copper Alley across the street from Christchurch, tel. 01/679-6500, fax 01/679-6504, www.iol.ie/usitaccm/, e-mail: harding@usit.ie).

Jurys Christchurch Inn (like its sisters across town, in Galway and in Belfast) is well located and offers business-class comfort in all of its identical rooms. This no-nonsense, modern, American-style hotel chain has a winning keep-it-simple-and-affordable formula. If old is getting old (and you don't mind big bus-tour groups), you won't find a better value in town. All 180 rooms cost the same: £65 for one, two, or three adults or two adults and two kids, breakfast not included. Each room has a modern bathroom, direct-dial telephone, and TV. Two floors are strictly nonsmoking. Request a room far from the noisy elevator (CC:VMA, Christchurch Place, Dublin 8, tel. 01/454-0000, fax 01/454-0012, U.S. tel. 800/843-3311, e-mail: inquiry@jurys.com).

A 234-room **Jurys Custom House Inn,** on Custom House Quay, offers the same value. Bigger and not quite as well located (in a boring neighborhood, a 10-minute riverside hike from O'Connell Bridge), this Jurys is more likely to have rooms available (£62, tel. 01/607-5000, fax 01/829-0400).

Kinlay House, across the square from Jurys Christchurch Inn, is its backpackers' equivalent—definitely the place to go for cheap beds with a good location, privacy, and an all-ages-welcome atmosphere. This huge, red-brick, 19th-century Victorian building has 120 metal, prison-style beds in spartan, smoke-free rooms: singles, doubles, four- to six-bed dorms (generally coed), and a few giant dorms. It fills up most days. Call well in advance, especially for summer weekends (S-£20, D-£30, Db-£34, dorm beds-£11–13, includes continental breakfast, self-catering kitchen, launderette, Internet access, left luggage, and so on, Christchurch, 2–12 Lord Edward Street, Dublin 2, tel. 01/679-6644, fax 01/679-7437, e-mail: kindub@usit.ie).

Avalon House is 300 beds of backpacker heaven. Well located, cheap, and institutional, it's much like Kinlay House (D-£30, Db-£32, dorm beds-£8.50–13.50, CC:VMA, including continental breakfast, a few minutes off Grafton Street at 55 Aungier Street, tel. 01/475-0001, fax 01/475-0303, www.avalon-house.ie).

Sleeping East of St. Stephen's Green

Two small luxurious hotels are a five-minute walk east of St. Stephen's Green on fashionable Baggot Street. Both are newly renovated, include a fine cooked breakfast, are run with class, and offer the best value for Georgian elegance with modern comforts near the center. **The Fitzwilliam** rents 13 delightful rooms (Sb-£45, Db-£80, CC:VMA, 10 percent discount with cash, children stay for less or free, 41 Upper Fitzwilliam Street, Dublin 2, tel. 01/662-5155, fax 01/676-7488). **Baggot Court**

Accommodations rents 11 similarly elegant rooms a block farther away (Sb-£35–40, Db-£80, Tb-£120, CC:VMA, nonsmoking, free car park, 92 Lower Baggot Street, Dublin 2, tel. 01/661-2819, fax 01/661-0253).

Mespil Hotel is a huge, modern, business-class hotel renting 153 identical three-star rooms at a good price with all the comforts. Half the rooms overlook a canal greenbelt (Sb, Db, or Tb-£85, continental breakfast £6, Irish breakfast £9, elevator, 1 nonsmoking floor, CC:VMA, Mespil Road, Dublin 4, tel. 01/667-1222, fax 01/667-1244, e-mail: mespil@leehotels.ie).

Albany House's 33 rooms come with Georgian elegance, modern comfort, and street noise. Request the huge "superior" rooms, which are the same price (Sb-£70, Db-£100, £80 in slow times, back rooms are quieter, smoke free, CC:VMA, 1 block south of St. Stephen's Green at 84 Harcourt Street, Dublin 2, tel. 01/475-1092, fax 01/475-1093, e-mail: albany@indigo.ie).

The next two listings are on Northumberland Road. While Trinity College is only a 15-minute walk away, buses #5, #6, #7, #8, and #45 (to O'Connell Street) lumber down Northumberland Road to the city center every 10 minutes.

Northumberland Lodge is a quiet, elegant mansion (Sb-£45–55, Db-£70–90, highest on weekends and in summer, CC:VM, 68 Northumberland Road, Ballsbridge, Dublin 4, tel. 01/660-5270, fax 01/668-8679). **Glenveagh Town House** has 13 classy rooms—Victorian upstairs, modern downstairs (a new management expects to charge about Sb-£42, Db-£75, less in slow times, CC:VMA, 31 Northumberland Road, tel. 01/668-4612, fax 01/668-4559, e-mail: glenveagh@tinet.ie).

Sleeping near the Station

The **Townhouse of Dublin** is a smartly run hotel with 80 comfortable rooms filling the richly decorated, carpeted, and furnished home of a famous 19th-century playwright. It's located in a handy but grotty area midway between the train station and O'Connell Bridge (Sb-£38–47, D-£50–60, Db-£60–80, T-£65–70, depending on season and day of the week, weekends are most expensive, CC:VMA, nonsmoking rooms, 47 Lower Gardiner Street, Dublin 1, tel. 01/878-8808, fax 01/878-8787, e-mail: grotter@indigo.ie).

Globetrotters, adjacent to and run by the Townhouse (described above), is a fine slumber mill with 94 beds in 6- to 12-bed dorms (£12–15 per bed, all with private bathrooms and lockers, often special deals for 3-night stays in either place).

Eating in Dublin

As Dublin does its boom-time jig, fine and creative eateries are popping up all over town. While you can get decent pub grub for £6 on just about any corner, consider holding off on pub grub for the more spit-and-potatoes countryside. And there's no pressing reason to eat Irish in cosmopolitan Dublin. Dublin's good restaurants are packed from 20:00 on, especially on weekends. Eating early (18:00–19:00) saves time and usually money (as many better places offer an early-bird special).

Eating Quick and Easy around Grafton Street

Cornucopia is a small, earth-momma, vegetarian self-serve place a block off Grafton. It's friendly, smoke free, and youthful, with great breakfasts, hearty £5 lunches, and dinner specials (Mon–Sat 9:00–20:00, closed Sun, 19 Wicklow St, tel. 01/677-7583).

Graham O'Sullivan Restaurant and Coffee Shop is a cheap and cheery cafeteria serving soup, sandwiches, and a salad bar in unpretentious ambience (Mon–Fri 8:00–19:00, Sat 9:00–17:00, closed Sun, 12 Duke St.). Two pubs on the same street (**The Duke** and **Davy Burns**) serve pub lunches. The **Cathach Rare Books** shop (10 Duke Street) displays a rare first edition of *Ulysses* signed by James Joyce, among other treasures in its window.

Bewleys Restaurant is an old-time local favorite serving traditional Irish and contemporary food in a fresh and bright space decorated by local art students. Light meals start at £3.50, full meals from £6.50 (daily 7:30–23:00, table service on ground floor, cafeteria upstairs, 78 Grafton Street, tel. 01/635-5470).

Blazing Salads, a crowd-pleasing vegetarian place, is just off Grafton Street, upstairs in the trendy Powerscourt Townhouse Centre (£5 meals, Mon–Sat 9:00–18:00, closed Sun, tel. 01/671-9552).

Wagamama Noodle Bar, like its popular sisters in London, is a pan-Asian slurp-athon with great noodle and rice dishes served by walkie-talkie-toting waiters at communal tables (daily 12:00–23:00, nonsmoking, South King Street, tel. 01/478-2152).

Yamamori is a plain, bright, and mod Japanese place serving seas of sushi and noodles (£5 lunch deal served daily 12:30–17:30, £5–10 dinner 17:30–23:00, 71 South Great George's Street, tel. 01/475-5001).

Marks & Spencer department store (on Grafton Street) has a fancy grocery store in the basement with fine take-away sandwiches and salads.

Eating Fast and Cheap near Christchurch

Many of Dublin's **late-night grocery stores** (along Dame Street at top of Temple Bar near Christchurch hotels and elsewhere) sell fine cheap salads, microwaved meat pies, and made-to-order sandwiches. A £3 picnic dinner back at the hotel might be a good option after a grueling day of sightseeing.

Leo Burdocks Fish & Chips is popular with locals (takeout only, Mon–Fri 11:00–23:00, Sat 14:00–23:00, 2 Werburgh Street, off Christchurch).

Dining at Classy Restaurants and Cafés

QV2 Restaurant serves "international with an Irish twist"—great cooking at reasonable prices with an elegant yet comfy atmosphere (£20 meals, Mon–Sat 12:00–15:00, 18:00–24:00, closed Sun, nonsmoking section, 14 St. Andrew Street, tel. 01/677-3363, run by John Count McCormack). They offer a quick £7.50 lunch special and an 18:00–19:30 early-bird special for people on the way to a theater.

Trocadero serves beefy European cuisine to locals interested in a slow romantic meal. The dressy red-velvet interior is draped with photos of local actors. Come early or make a reservation (£20 meals, nightly 18:00–24:00, nonsmoking section, 3 St. Andrew's Street, tel. 01/677-5545). The three-course early-bird special at £11.50 is a fine value (18:00–19:30, leave by 20:45).

Boulevard Cafe is a mod, local, and likeably trendy place serving Mediterranean cuisine heavy on the Italian. They serve salads, pasta, and sandwiches for around £4, two-course business lunch specials (12:00–15:00, Mon–Sat), and dinner plates for £7 to £10 (nightly 18:00–24:00, 27 Exchequer Street, tel. 01/679-2131).

Eating at Temple Bar

Gallagher's Boxty House is touristy and traditional, with good, basic value in a fun old Dublin ambience (£7 meals, stews, corned beef, and boxties—the traditional Irish potato pancake filled and rolled with various meats, veggies, and sauces; daily 12:00–23:30, nonsmoking section, 20 Temple Bar, tel. 01/677-2762). Gallagher's is extremely popular. After 17:00 you'll likely get an appointment and time to wander Temple Bar.

Bad Ass Cafe is a grunge diner serving cowboy/Mex/veggie/pizzas to old and new hippies. No need to dress up (£5 lunch and £11 dinner deals, open nearly all the time, kids specials, Crown Alley, tel. 01/671-2596).

The Brazen Head, famous as Dublin's oldest pub, is a hit for dinner early and live music late. A sprawling complex of smoky atmospheric rooms with a courtyard made to order for balmy evenings, it overlooks the River Liffey (on Bridge Street, a 10-minute walk upstream from Temple Bar).

Transportation Connections—Dublin

By bus to: Belfast (7/day, 3 hrs), **Ennis** (7/day, 4.5 hrs), **Galway** (10/day, 3.5 hrs), **Limerick** (10/day, 3 hrs), **Tralee** (5/day, 6 hrs), **Dingle** (4/day, 8 hrs, £16). Bus info: tel. 01/836-6111.

The **Dublin Airport** is well connected to the city center, seven miles away (see "Arrival in Dublin," above). British Air flies to London's Gatwick Airport (4/day, from £69 return, tel. 01/814-5201 or toll-free tel. 800/626-747 in Ireland, U.S. tel. 800/247-9297), as do Aer Lingus (tel. 01/886-8888) and British Midland (tel. 01/283-8833 in Ireland, U.S. tel. 800/788-0555). Dublin

Airport info: tel. 01/814-4222. Ryanair is a new Irish cut-rate airline with unbelievable fares to European destinations (£70 flights to Frankfurt, tel. 01/609-7800, www.ryanair.ie).

Transportation Connections— Ireland and Britain

Dublin and London: The boat/rail journey takes eight hours (4/day, £40–75). Dublin train info: tel. 01/836-6222. If going directly to London, flying is your best bet.

Dublin and Holyhead: Irish Ferries sails between Dublin and Holyhead in North Wales (dock a mile from O'Connell Bridge, 2/day, 3 hrs, £25 one-way walk-on fare, Dublin tel. 01/661-0511, Holyhead tel. 0990-329-129).

Dun Laoghaire and Holyhead: Stena Line sails between Dun Laoghaire (near Dublin) and Holyhead in North Wales (4/day, 2 hrs on new HSS *Catamaran*, £36 one-way walk-on fare, reserve by phone—they book up long in advance on summer weekends, Dublin tel. 01/204-7777, recorded info tel. 01/204-7799).

Ferry Connections—Ireland and France

Irish Ferries connect Ireland (Rosslare) with France (Cherbourg and Roscoff) every other day (less Jan–Mar). While Cherbourg has the quickest connection to Paris, your overall time between Ireland and Paris is about the same regardless of which port is used on the day you sail. One-way fares vary from £40 to £80 (round-trips are much cheaper). Except for a £5 port tax, Eurailers go half price. In both directions departures are generally between 16:00 and 18:00 and arrive late the next morning. While passengers can nearly always get on, reservations are wise in summer and easy by phone. If you anticipate a crowded departure you can reserve a seat for £5. Beds in a quad start at £15. Doubles (or singles) start at £34. The easiest way to get a bed (except during summer) is from the information desk upon boarding. The cafeteria serves bad food at reasonable prices. Upon arrival in France, buses and taxis connect you to your Paris-bound train (Irish Ferries: Dublin tel. 01/661-0511, recorded info tel. 01/661-0715, Paris tel. 01 44 94 20 40, www.irishferries.ie, e-mail: info@irishferries.ie, European Ferry Guide www.youra.com/ferry/intlferries.html).

DINGLE PENINSULA

Dingle Peninsula, the westernmost tip of Ireland, offers just the right mix of far-and-away beauty, ancient archaeological wonders, and desolate walks or bike rides all within convenient reach of its main town. Dingle Town is just big enough to have all the necessary tourist services and a steady nocturnal beat of Irish folk music.

While the big tour buses clog the neighboring Ring of Kerry before heading east to slobber all over the Blarney Stone, Dingle—while crowded in the summer—still feels like the fish and the farm really matter. Forty fishing boats sail from Dingle, and a faint whiff of peat fills its nighttime streets.

For 20 years my Irish dreams have been set here on this sparse but lush peninsula where locals are fond of saying "The next parish is Boston." There's a closeness to the land on Dingle. When I asked a local if he was born here, he thought for a second and said, "No, it was about six miles down the road." When I told him where I was from, a faraway smile filled his eyes, he looked out to sea and sighed, "Ah, the shores of Americay."

Dingle feels so traditionally Irish because it's a Gaeltacht, a region where the government subsidizes the survival of the Irish language and culture. While English is always there, the signs, menus, and songs come in Gaelic. Children carry hurling sticks to class, and even the local preschool brags "ALL Gaelic."

Of the peninsula's 10,000 residents, 1,300 live in Dingle Town. Its few streets, lined with ramshackle but gaily painted shops and pubs, run up from a rain-stung harbor always busy with fishing boats and yachts. Traditionally, the buildings were drab grey or whitewashed. Thirty years ago Ireland's "tidy town" competition started everyone painting their buildings in playful pastels.

It's a peaceful town. The court house (1832) is open one hour a month. The judge does his best to wrap up business within a half hour. During the day you'll see teenagers—already working on ruddy beer-glow cheeks—roll kegs up the streets and into the pubs in preparation for another night of music and craic (fun conversation).

Dingle History

The wet sod of Dingle is soaked with medieval history. In the darkest depths of the Dark Ages, peace-loving, bookwormish monks fled the chaos of the Continent and its barbarian raids. They sailed to the drizzly fringe of the known world—places like Dingle. These monks kept literacy alive in Europe. Charlemagne, who ruled much of Europe in the year 800, imported Irish monks to be his scribes.

It was from this peninsula that the semimythical explorer monk St. Brandon is said to have set sail in the sixth century in search of a legendary western paradise. Some think he beat Columbus to North America by nearly a thousand years.

Dingle (An Daingean in Gaelic) was a busy seaport in the late Middle Ages. Along with Tralee, it was the only walled town in Kerry—castles stood at the low and high ends of Main Street, protecting the Normans from the angry and dispossessed Irish outside. Dingle was a gateway to northern Spain—a three-day sail due south. Many 14th- and 15th-century pilgrimages left from Dingle for Santiago di Compostela.

In Dingle's medieval heydays, locals traded cowhides for wine. When Dingle's position as a trading center ended, the town faded in importance. In the last century it was a linen-weaving center. Until 1970 fishing dominated. The only visitors were scholars and students of old Irish ways. In 1970 the movie *Ryan's Daughter* introduced the world to Dingle. The trickle of Dingle fans has grown to a flood as word of its musical, historical, gastronomical, and scenic charms—not to mention its friendly dolphin—has spread.

Planning Your Time

For the shortest visit, give Dingle two nights and a day. It takes six to eight hours to get there from Dublin, Galway, or the boat dock in Rosslare. I like two nights because you feel more like a local on your second evening in the pubs. You'll need the better part of a day to explore the 30-mile loop around the peninsula by bike, car, or tour bus (see "Circular Tour," below). To do any serious walking or relaxing you'll need two or three days. It's not uncommon to find Americans slowing way, way down in Dingle.

Orientation (tel. code: 066)

Dingle—extremely comfortable on foot—hangs on a medieval grid of streets between the harbor front (where the Tralee bus stops) and Main Street (three blocks inland). Nothing in town is more than a

Southwest Ireland

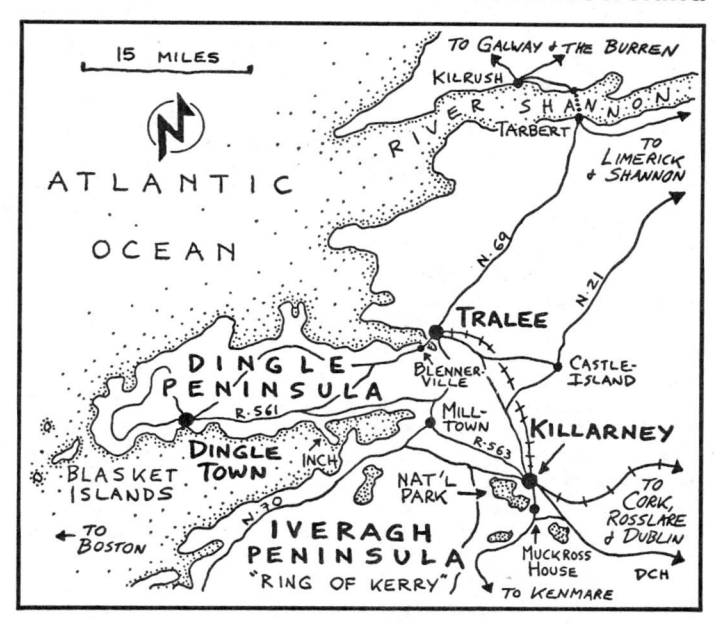

five-minute walk away. Street numbers are used only when more than one place is run by a family of the same name. Most locals know most locals, and people on the street are fine sources of information. Remember, locals love their soda bread, and tourism provides the butter. You'll find a warm and sincere welcome.

Tourist Information: The Bord Failte (TI) is on Strand Street by the water (Mar–Oct Mon–Sat 9:00–19:00, Sun 10:00–13:00, 14:15–18:00, off-season shorter hours and closed Sun, tel. 066/915-1188). In the summer the TI organizes town walks. For more creative help, drop by the Mountain Man shop (on Strand Street, see "Helpful Hints," below).

Helpful Hints

Before You Go: Look up old issues of *National Geographic* (Apr '76, Sept '94, and for the Aran Islands, Apr '81). The local Web site (www.dingle-peninsula.ie) lists festivals and events.

Crowds: Crowds trample Dingle's charm for the first three weeks in August. The absolute craziest are the Dingle Races (second weekend in August) and Dingle Regatta (third weekend in August). July is also packed. Dingle's metabolism (prices, schedules, activities) rises and falls with the tourist crowds—October through April is pretty sleepy.

Banking: Two banks in town, both uphill from the TI on Main Street, offer the same rates (Mon 10:00–17:00, Tue–Fri 10:00–16:00). Both have cash machines.

Supermarket: The Super Valu supermarket/department store, at the base of town, has everything and is ideal for assembling a peninsula picnic (Mon–Sat 8:00–21:00, Sun 8:00–19:00, until 22:00 in summer).

Launderette: Full-service only—drop off a load and pick it up dry and folded three hours later (tiny-£3.50, regular load-£5.50, Mon–Sat 9:00–17:00, on Green Street down alley across from the church, tel. 066/915-1837).

Internet Access: Dingleweb is on Main Street (£5/hour, £1.50 per quarter hour, Mon–Sat 10:00–22:00, less on Sun and off-season, tel. 066/915-2477, e-mail: postmaster@dingleweb.com).

Bike Rental: Bike rental shops abound. Consider Paddy's Bike Hire (£6/day, £7/24 hrs, daily 9:00–19:00, helmets included, on Dykegate next to Grapevine Hostel, tel. 066/915-2311), Sciuird Tours, the Mountain Man, or the Ballintaggert Hostel. If you're biking the peninsula, get a bike with skinny street tires, not slow and fat mountain-bike tires. Plan on leaving a credit card, driver's license, or passport as security.

Dingle Activities: The Mountain Man, a hiking shop run by a local guide, Mike Shea, is a clearinghouse for information, local tours, and excursions (daily 9:00–21:00 in summer, less off-season, just off harbor at Strand Street, tel. 066/915-2400, fax 066/915-2396). Stop by for bike rentals and ideas on biking, hiking, horse riding, climbing, peninsula tours (which they offer), and trips to the Blaskets. They are the Dingle Town contact for the Dunquin–Blasket Islands boats and shuttle bus rides to the harbor.

Travel Agency: Maurice O'Connor at Galvin's Travel Agency can book you bus, train, and plane tickets and boat rides to France (John Street, tel. 066/915-1409).

Sights—Dingle Town

▲**Oceanworld**—The only place charging admission in Dingle is worth considering. This new aquarium offers a little peninsula history, 160 different species of local fish and other sea creatures in thoughtfully described tanks (including a chance to walk under the fish in the "ocean tank"), and the easiest way to see Fungi the dolphin—on video. Their mission is to teach; guided tours are available. The petting pool is fun. Splashing attracts the rays—they're unplugged (£4.50, £12 for families, daily 10:00–20:30 in summer, until 18:00 or earlier in off-season, cafeteria; just past the harbor on the west edge of town; tel. 066/915-2111).

Dingle Peninsula 393

Dingle Town

1 HEATON'S GUEST HOUSE	21 DICK MACK
2 OCEANWORLD	22 CRAFT GALLERIES
3 DINGLE SAILING CLUB	23 LAUNDRY
4 CRUISEBOAT OFFICES	24 EL TORO
5 MAIRE DE BARRA RESTAURANT	25 BENNERS HOTEL & POST
6 MOUNTAIN MAN	26 BANK
7 BUS STATION	27 BIKE RENTAL
8 GREANY'S RESTAURANT	28 AN CAFE LITEARTA
9 SUPER VALUE	29 MACCARTHY'S PUB
10 GRAPEVINE HOSTEL	30 CAPTAIN'S HOUSE B&B
11 O'FLAHERTY'S	31 CINEMA
13 BAMBURY'S B&B	32 ADAM'S BAR & RESTAURANT
14 TRAIL TO LIGHTHOUSE	33 SMALL BRIDGE BAR
15 BALLINTAGGERT HOSTEL	34 DOYLE'S & HALF DOOR RESTAURANTS
16 ALPINE HOUSE	35 SRAID EOIN B&B
17 SCIUIRD TOURS & KIRRARY B&B	36 KELLIHER'S BALLYEGAN HOUSE
18 CORNER HOUSE B&B	37 GREENMOUNT HOUSE
19 CONNORS B&B	38 HILLGROVE HOTEL
20 CITY PARK	39 ARD NA GREINE HOUSE B&B

▲**Fungi**—In 1983 a dolphin moved into Dingle Harbor and became a local celebrity. Fungi is now the darling of the town's tourist trade and one reason you'll find so many tour buses parked along the harbor. With a close look at Fungi as bait, tour boats are thriving (£6, kids £3; while virtually every boat sees him, you don't pay until you've seen him; 1- to 2-hour trips depart between 10:00

and 19:00 depending upon demand; book behind TI at Dolphin Trips office, tel. 066/915-2626). A hardy little fishing boat motors 4 to 30 passengers out to the mouth of the harbor, where you troll around looking for Fungi. To actually swim with Fungi, rent wetsuits and catch the morning trip.

▲**Short Harbor Walk from Dingle**—For an easy stroll along the harbor out of town (and a chance to see Fungi, 90 min roundtrip), head east from the roundabout past the Esso station. Just after Bambury's B&B, take a right following signs to Skelligs Hotel. At the beach, climb the steps over the wall and follow the seashore path to the mouth of Dingle harbor (marked by a tower—some 19th-century fat cat's folly). Ten minutes beyond that is a lighthouse. This is Fungi's neighborhood. If you see tourist boats out, you're likely to see him. The trail continues to a dramatic cliff.

The Harbor—The harbor was built on land reclaimed (with imported Dutch expertise) in 1992. The new roundabout allows traffic to skirt the town center. The string of old stone shops facing the harbor was the loading station for the narrow-gauge railway that hauled the fish from Dingle to Tralee (1891–1953). The Esk Tower on the distant hill is a marker built in 1847 during the famine as a make-work project. In pre-radar days, it helped ships locate Dingle's hidden harbor. The fancy mansion across the harbor is Lord Ventry's 17th-century manor house.

Cruises—The Dingle Marina Center offers diving, sailing, and traditional currach rowing. One-man sailboats can be lent to those wanting to blow around the bay with a day membership in the Sailing Club (£15, tel. 066/915-2422). Currachs—stacked behind the building—are Ireland's traditional lightweight fishing boats, easy to haul and easy to make; cover a wooden frame with canvas and paint with tar. The currachs are owned by the Dingle Rowing Club and go out many summer evenings.

Dingle Pitch & Putt—For 18 scenic holes and a driving range, hike 10 minutes past Ocean World (£3 with gear, driving range £3 for 100 balls, daily 10:00–20:00, over bridge take first left and follow signs, Milltown, tel. 066/915-1819).

Nightlife in Dingle Town

▲▲▲**Folk Music in Dingle Pubs**—Even if you're not into pubs, take a nap and then give these a whirl. Dingle is renowned among traditional musicians as a place to get work ("£30 a day, tax-free, plus drink"). The town has 50 pubs. There's music every night and never a cover charge. The scene is a decent mix of locals, Americans, and Germans. Music normally starts around 21:30, and the last call for drinks is "half eleven" (23:30). For a seat near the music, arrive early. If the place is chockablock, power in and find breathing room in the back. By midnight the door is closed and the chairs are stacked. While two pubs, the Small Bridge Bar (An Droicheed) and O'Flahertys are the most famous for their good beer and folk music, make a point to wander the town and follow your ear. Smaller pubs may feel a bit foreboding to a tourist, but people—locals as well as travelers—are out for the craic. Irish culture is so accessible in the pubs—highly interactive museums waiting to be explored. Have a glass in an empty no-name pub and chat up the publican. Pubs are smoky and hot (leave your coat home). The more offbeat pubs are more likely to erupt into leprechaun karaoke.

The best pub crawl is along the Strand to O'Flaherty's. Rough-and-tumble Murphy's is liveliest, offering rock as well as traditional music. O'Flaherty's, with a high ceiling and less smoke, dripping in old-time photos and town memorabilia, is touristy but lots of fun, with nightly music. Then head up Green Street. Dick Mack (across from the church and therefore nicknamed "the last pew") is a tiny leather shop by day and a pub by night, with a fine snug (private booth, originally designed to allow women to drink discreetly), reliably good beer, and a smoky and strangely fascinating ambience. Notice the Hollywood-type stars on the sidewalk recalling famous visitors. Established in 1899, the original Dick Mack's grandson now runs the place. A painting in the window shows Dick Mack II with the local gang. Wander Main Street from top to bottom. MacCarthy's Pub, a smoke-stained relic at the top, is less touristy and has some fine traditional music sessions (tel. 066/915-1205). The Small Bridge Bar at the bottom—with live music nightly—is popular for good reason. Finally, head up Spa Road a few doors to An Conair—a.k.a. John Benny's, a pub attracting a more alternative Celtic folk talent (often less crowded but with good music). Further up Spa Road, the big hotel has late night dancing (see below).

Dancing—Somewhere almost every night, a pub hosts "Set Dancing," with live music (An Conair Bar Mondays after 21:30, Small Bridge Bar on Wednesdays). Hillgrove Hotel (up Spa Road a few hundred meters) is a modern hotel with traditional dances every Thursday at 23:00 and pop dancing other nights in summer. Locals say the Hillgrove "is a good time if you're pissed."

During the day, music lovers will enjoy dropping by Danlann Gallery, a music shop on Dykegate Street (Mon–Sat 10:00–22:00, Sun 11:00–18:00, less off-season). The music office, also on Dykegate—next to the Grapevine Hostel—has the latest on musical happenings.

Theater—Dingle's great little theater is The Phoenix on Dykegate. Its film club (50 or 60 locals) meets here Tuesdays (Oct–Jun at 20:30). The leader runs it almost like a religion, with a homily on the film before he rolls it. Afterward, locals and tourists chat over coffee and cookies.

Sleeping in Dingle Town
(£1 = about $1.50, tel. code: 066, mail: Dingle, County Kerry)

Sleep Code: **S** = Single, **D** = Double/Twin, **T** = Triple, **Q** = Quad, **b** = bathroom, **t** = toilet only, **s** = shower only, **CC** = Credit Card (Visa, MasterCard, Amex). Prices vary with the season, with August tops.

Sraid Eoin B&B, on the quiet end of town, has four spacious and modern pastel rooms and giant bathrooms and is warmly run by Kathleen and Maurice O'Connor (Db-£34–40, family deals, 10 percent discount with this book and cash, CC:VM, smoke free, John Street, tel. 066/915-1409, fax 066/915-2156). Maurice runs Galvin's Travel Agency on the ground floor (same phone number).

Kellihers Ballyegan House is a big, plain building with six fresh, comfortable rooms on the edge of town and great harbor views. It's run by friendly Mrs. Hannah Kelliher, who provides rare strictly smoke-free rooms (Sb-£18–20, Db-£36–40, 10 percent off with this book, no CC or smokers, Upper John Street, tel. 066/915-1702).

Greenmount House sits among palm trees at the top of town, in the countryside, with a commanding view of the bay and mountains, a five-minute hike up from the town center. John and Mary Curran run one of Ireland's classiest B&Bs, with six fine rooms (Db-£40–50) and six sprawling suites (Db-£50–70) in a modern building with lavish public areas and breakfast in a solarium (CC:VM, no singles during high season or children under eight, most rooms at ground level, top of John Street, reserve in advance, tel. 066/915-1414, fax 066/915-1974, e-mail: greenmount@tinet.ie).

O'Neill's B&B is a plain but homey and friendly place with six decent rooms (Sb-£19, Db-£36–38, family deals, strictly non-smoking, John Street, tel. 066/915-1639, Mary O'Neill).

Corner House B&B is my longtime Dingle home. It's a simple, traditional place with five rooms run with a twinkle and a grandmotherly smile by Kathleen Farrell (S-£19, D-£34, T-£48, plenty of plumbing, but it's down the hall, no CC, reserve with a phone call and reconfirm a day or two ahead or risk losing your bed, central as can be on Dykegate Street, tel. 066/915-1516).

Captain's House B&B is a shipshape place fit for an admiral in the town center, with eight classy rooms and a stay-awhile garden (Sb-£35, Db-£50, great suite-£60, CC:VMA, the Mall, tel. 066/915-1531, fax 066/915-1079, e-mail: captigh@tinet.ie, Jim and Mary Milhench).

Kirrary B&B and **O Coileain B&B** stand side by side on a quiet corner in the town center, offering small, simple rooms and a homey friendliness (Db-£34–40, 10 percent discount with this book outside of August, £6 bike rental, tel. & fax 066/915-1606 or

066/915-1937, e-mail: arch@iol.ie). These are run by the same Collins—Coileain in Gaelic—family that runs the Sciuird tours recommended below. **Connor's B&B,** with 15 basic rooms, is a lesser value (Db-£40–50, CC:VMA, quiet but central on Dykegate Street, tel. 066/915-1598, fax 066/915-2376, Mrs. Connor).

Ard Na Greine House B&B is a charming, windblown, modern house on the edge of town. Mrs. Mary Houlihan rents four well-equipped, comfortable rooms to nonsmokers (Sb-£25, Db-£36, Tb-£50, CC:VM, on the edge of town an 8-minute walk up Spa Road, 3 doors beyond the Hillgrove Hotel, tel. 066/915-1113, fax 066/915-1898).

Alpine House Guest House looks like a monopoly hotel, but that means comfortable and efficient. Its 13 spacious, bright, and fresh rooms come with wonderful sheep and harbor views, a cozy lounge, great breakfast, and friendly management (Db-£40 except £50 in Aug, Tb-£60, less off-season, 10 percent discount with this book, CC:VM, Mail Road, tel. 066/915-1250, fax 066/915-1966). Driving into town from Tralee, you'll see this a block uphill from the Dingle roundabout and Esso station.

Bambury's Guesthouse, another big, modern place with views of sheep and the harbor, rents 12 big, airy, comfy rooms with a family-friendly feeling (Db-£40–55, depending on size and season, family deals, 10 percent discount with this book, CC:VM, on your left coming in from Tralee on Mail Road 2 blocks before Esso station, tel. 066/915-1244, fax 066/915-1786, e-mail: berniebb @tinet.ie).

Ocean View B&B rents three tidy rooms in a little waterfront row house overlooking the bay (S-£16, D-£28, 5-minute walk from the center, 100 meters past Ocean World at 133 The Wood, tel. 066/915-1659, Mrs. Brosnan).

Heatons Guesthouse is a big, peaceful place on the water just west of town at the end of Dingle Bay. Their 12 rooms are thoughtfully appointed with all the comforts (Db-£50–66, CC:VM, 5-minute walk past Ocean World on The Wood, tel. 066/915-2288, fax 066/915-2324, e-mail: heatons@iol.ie, run by Cameron and Nuala Heaton).

Benners Hotel was the only place in town a hundred years ago. It stands bewildered by the modern world on Main Street, with plush and abundant public spaces and sprawling hallways leading to 52 musty but comfortable rooms (Db-£120 Jul–Aug, £90 Jun & Sept, £70 Oct–May, kids-£15 extra, CC:VMA, tel. 066/915-1638, fax 066/915-1412, e-mail: benners@tinet.ie).

Hostels in Dingle Town

Ballintaggart Hostel, a backpacker's complex, is housed in a stylish old manor house used by Protestants during the famine as a soup kitchen (for those hungry enough to renounce their

Catholicism). It comes complete with bike rental, laundry service, kitchen, café, classy study, family room with a fireplace, and a resident ghost (148 beds, £8 in 10-bed dorms, £10 in quads, £14 in singles and doubles, breakfast extra, a mile east of town on Tralee Road, tel. 066/915-1454, fax 066/915-2207, e-mail: btaggart@iol.ie, run by Johnny V). Their shuttle bus meets each arriving inter-city bus and does a nightly pub run—into town at 21:30, back at 23:30.

Grapevine Hostel is a clean and friendly establishment with a cozy fireplace lounge and a fine members' kitchen. Each four- to eight-bed dorm has its own bathroom. Dorms are coed, but there's usually a girls' room established (32 beds, £8–9.50 each, Dykegate Lane, tel. 066/915-1434, e-mail: grapevine@dingleweb.com, run by Siobhan).

The new and modern **Marina Hostel** plans to open by mid-2000 (next to Ocean World, tel. 066/915-1065).

Eating in Dingle Town

For a rustic little village, Dingle is swimming in good food. Budget tips: The **supermarket** stays open late nightly, fancy restaurants serve early-bird specials from 18:00–19:00, many "cheap & cheery" places close at 18:00, and pubs do amazing £5 dinners all over town. Most pubs stop serving food around 21:00 (to make room for maximum beer).

Adam's Bar and Restaurant is a tight, smoky place popular with locals for traditional food at great prices. Try their corned beef and cabbage (£5 meals, last meal at 20:30 in summer, 17:30 off-season, closed Sun, Upper Main Street).

An Cafe Litearta, a popular and friendly eatery hiding behind an inviting bookstore, has good snacks and sandwiches (10:00–17:30, Dykegate Street).

Greany's Restaurant, just off the roundabout, is a local hit serving fine food at decent prices in a cheery, modern atmosphere (£10–15 dinners, fine salmon, Mon–Fri 12:30–22:00, Sat–Sun 11:00–17:30, Holyground, tel. 066/915-2244).

Vittle's Restaurant offers good food and prices with an early-bird special and good vegetarian selections (near the roundabout at Holyground).

The **Global Village Restaurant** is where Martin Bealin serves his favorite dishes, gleaned from travels around the world. It's a smoky and eclectic healthy meat-eaters place popular with locals for its interesting cuisine (£5 lunches, £10 dinners, daily 9:30–21:30, the Thai Curry is great, top of Main Street, tel. 066/915-2325).

El Toro offers a candlelit splash of the Mediterranean, with good seafood, salads, and pizzas (£10–15 meals, 18:00–22:30, Green Street, tel. 066/915-1820).

Maire De Barra's pub serves perhaps the best £5 dinners in town—traditional and seafood (daily 12:30–21:30, music after 21:30, the Pier). **Paudie Brosnan's** pub, a few doors down, is also good.

Dingle's long-established top-notch restaurants are **Doyle's Seafood Bar** (more famous, John Street, tel. 066/915-1174) and the **Half Door** (heartier portions, John Street, tel. 066/915-1600). Both offer £17 three-course early-dinner specials between 18:00 and 19:00 and £25 meals after that. Reservations are necessary in both places.

Transportation Connections—Dingle Town
The nearest train station is in Tralee.

Dingle bus connections: Galway (3/day, 6.5 hrs), **Dublin** (3/day, 8 hrs), **Rosslare** (2/day, 9 hrs), **Tralee** (4/day, 75 min, £6), fewer departures on Sundays. Dingle has no bus station and only one stop, on the waterfront behind the Super Valu supermarket (bus info tel. 01/830-2222 or 066/972-3566).

Drivers choose two roads into town, the easy southern route or the much more dramatic and treacherous Conor Pass. It's 30 miles from Tralee either way.

Dingle Peninsula: Circular Tour by Bike or Car
A ▲▲▲ sight, the Dingle Peninsula loop trip is about 30 miles long (7 hrs by bike, 3 hrs by car, including stops; do only in clockwise direction). While you can take a guided tour of the peninsula (see "Dingle Peninsula Tours," below), it's not necessary with the route described in this section. A fancy map is also unnecessary with my instructions. I've keyed in mileage to help you locate points of interest. If you're driving, as you leave Dingle, reset your odometer at Oceanworld. Even if you get off track or are biking, derive distances between points from these numbers. To get the most out of your circle, read through this entire section before departing. Then go step by step (staying on R559 and following the "The Slea Head Drive" signs). Note: Roads are very congested in August.

The Dingle Peninsula is 10 miles wide and runs 40 miles from Tralee to Slea Head. The top of its mountainous spine is Mount Brandon—at 3,130 feet, the second-tallest mountain in Ireland. While only tiny villages lie west of Dingle Town, the peninsula is home to 500,000 sheep.

Leave Dingle Town west along the waterfront (0.0 miles at Oceanworld). There's an eight-foot tide here. The seaweed was used to nourish reclaimed land. Across the water the fancy Milltown House B&B (with flags) was Robert Mitchum's home for a year during the filming of *Ryan's Daughter*. Look back out

Dingle Peninsula Tour

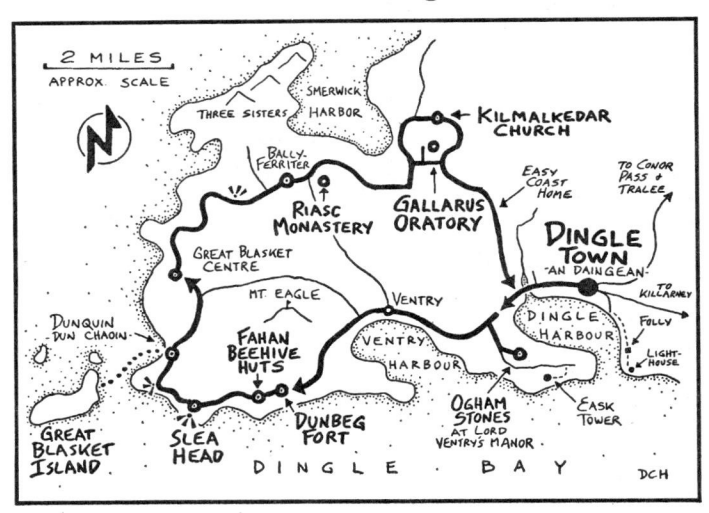

the harbor to see the narrow mouth of this blind harbor. (That's where Fungi frolics.) Dingle Bay is so hidden, ships needed the tower (1847) on the hill to find its mouth.

0.4 miles: Turn left over the bridge. The building on the right was a corn-grinding mill in the 18th century.

0.8 miles: The Milestone B&B is named for the pillar stone (Gallaun in Gaelic) in its front yard. This may have been a prehistoric grave marker or a boundary marker between two tribes. The stone goes down as far as it sticks up. Another pillar stone stands in the field across the street in the direction of the yellow manor house of Lord Ventry. The peninsula, literally an open-air museum, is dotted with more than 2,000 monuments dating from the Bronze Age through early Christian times.

2.1 miles: Pass through a rare grove of trees and turn left ("Leather Workshop" sign). After 100 yards enter the Lord Ventry's Manor, take the first left (unmarked, through white gate—it's private but they don't seem to mind sightseers). The long one-lane drive leads past small 18th-century estate houses through a lush garden (turn right at the fork) to the Ventry Manorhouse. Lord Ventry, whose family came to Dingle as post–Cromwell War landlords in 1666, built this mansion in about 1750. Today it houses an all-Gaelic boarding school for 140 high school–age girls.

Fifty yards before the mansion, stop at the six stones. The Ogham Stones (dating from the third to seventh century, named for the Celtic goddess of writing) decorating the drive are rare examples of early Celtic writing. With variations on five straight lines, they could make 20 letters—the original bar code. Of the 380 known Ogham Stones, 80 are in Dingle. Return to the main road and turn left (3.1 miles).

In the Ventry estate and beyond you'll pass palms, magnolias, fuschias, and exotic flora introduced to Dingle by Ventry. Because of the mild climate (cradled by the gulf stream), fuschias—imported from Chile and spreading like weeds—line the roads all over the peninsula and fill the countryside with red from June to September. The mild climate—it never snows—is OK for subtropical plants.

4.1 miles: Stay off the "soft margin" as you enjoy views of Ventry Bay and its four-mile-long beach. Mount Eagle (1,660 feet), rising across the bay, marks the end of Ireland. In the village of Ventry, Gaelic is the first language.

6.0 miles: The rushes on either side of the road are the kind used to make the local thatched roofs. Thatching, which nearly died out because of the fire danger, is more popular now that anti-flame treatments are available. Magpies fly.

6.6 miles: The Irish football star Paidi O Se (Paddy O'Shea) is a household name in Ireland. He now trains the Kerry team and runs the pub on the left.

6.9 miles: The blue house hiding in the trees 100 meters off the road on the left (view through the white gate) was kept cozy by Tom Cruise and Nicole Kidman during the filming of *Far and Away*.

7.9 miles: "Taisteaal go Mall" means "go slowly"; there's a peach-colored schoolhouse on the right. On the left is the Celtic and Prehistoric Museum, a strange private collection of dinosaur eggs, Celtic and Viking tools, coins, weapons, and an odd mechanical sheep (£3.50, closed Mon).

8.2 miles: The circular mound on the right is a late–Stone Age ring fort. In 500 B.C. it was a petty Celtic chieftain's headquarters, a stone-and-earth stockade filled with little stone houses. These survived untouched through the centuries because of superstitious beliefs that they were "fairy forts." While this is unexcavated, recent digging has shown that people have lived on this peninsula since 4000 B.C.

8.6 miles: Look ahead up Mount Eagle at the patchwork fields created by the stone fences.

9.0 miles: Dunbeg Fort, a series of defensive ramparts and ditches around a central clochan, while ready to fall into the sea, is open to tourists. While there are no carvings to be seen, the small (beg) fort (dun) is dramatic (£1, daily 9:00–20:00, descriptive handout). Forts like this are the most important relics left from Ireland's Iron Age (500 B.C. to A.D. 500). Since erosion will someday take this fort, it has been excavated.

9.6 miles: A group of beehive huts, or *clochans*, is a short walk uphill. These mysterious stone igloos cluster together within a circular wall (£1, daily 9:00–19:00, WC). These are a better sight than the similar group of beehive huts a mile down the road. Farther on, you'll ford a stream. There has never been a bridge here; the road was designed as a ford.

10.6 miles: Pull off to the left at this second group of beehive huts. Look downhill at the scant remains of the scant home that was burned as Lord Ventry tried to evict the tenants in *Far and Away*. Even without Hollywood, this is a bleak and godforsaken land. Look above at the patches of land slowly reclaimed by the inhabitants of this westernmost piece of Europe. Rocks were cleared and piled into fences. Sand and seaweed were laid on the clay, and in time it was good for grass. The created land was generally not tillable. Much has fallen out of use now. Look behind at the Ring of Kerry in the distance and ahead at the Blasket Islands.

11.4 miles: At Slea Head, marked by a crucifix, a pullout, and great views of the Blasket Islands, you turn the corner on this tour.

11.9 miles: Pull out here to view the Blaskets and Dunmore Head (the westernmost point in Europe) and to review the roadside map (which traces your route) posted in the parking lot. The scattered village of Dunquin has many ruined rock homes—abandoned during the famine. They were built with small windows to minimize taxation. Some are fixed up, as this is a popular place these days for summer homes. You can see more good examples of land reclamation, patch by patch, climbing up the hillside. Mount Eagle was the first bit of land Charles Lindberg saw after crossing the Atlantic on his way to Paris. Villagers here were as excited as he. Ahead, down a road on the left, a plaque celebrates the 30th anniversary of the filming of *Ryan's Daughter*.

13.4 miles: The Blasket Islanders had no church or cemetery on the island. This was their cemetery. The famous Blasket storyteller Peig Sayers (1873–1958) is buried in the center. Just past a washed-out bit of road, a lane leads left (100 yards) to a marker remembering the 1588 shipwreck of the *Santa Maria de la Rosa* of the Spanish Armada. Below that is the often tempestuous Dunquin Harbor, from where the Blasket ferry departs. Island farmers—who on a calm day could row across in 20 minutes—would dock here and hike 12 miles into Dingle to sell their produce.

13.5 miles: Back on the main road, follow signs to the Great Blasket Centre.

15 miles: Leave the Slea Head Road left for the Great Blasket Centre to learn more about the islands considered the symbol of ancient Gaelic culture (£2.50, Easter–Oct daily 10:00–18:00, tel. 066/915-6444).

15.7 miles: Back at the turnoff, head left (sign to Louis Mulcahy Pottery).

16.4 miles: Passing land that was never reclaimed, think of the work it took to pick out the stones, pile them into fences, and bring up sand and seaweed to nourish the clay and make soil for growing potatoes. On the left is a shadow of the main street of the fake poor village built to film *Far and Away*. Beyond that is the aptly named "Sleeping Giant" island—hand resting happily on his beer belly.

16.8 miles: The view is spectacular, especially when the waves are "racing in like white horses." Ahead on the right, study the top fields, untouched since the planting of 1845, when the potatoes rotted in the ground. The vertical ridges of the potato beds can still be seen—a reminder of the famine. Before the famine, 60,000 people lived on this peninsula. Today it's home to only 10,000.

20.2 miles: Ballyferriter (Baile an Fheirtearaigh), established by a Norman family in the 12th century, is the largest town on this side of Dingle. The pubs serve grub, and the old schoolhouse is a museum (£1.50, daily Easter–Sept 10:00–16:30, closed off-season). The early Christian cross looks real. Tap it... it's fiberglass—a prop from *Ryan's Daughter*.

21.0 miles: At the T-junction, signs direct you to Dingle (An Daingean, 11 km) either way. Go left, via Gallarus. Take a right over the bridge, still following signs to Gallarus.

21.4 miles: Just beyond the bridge and a few yards before the sign to Mainistir Riaise (Reask Monastic enclosure), detour right up the lane. After 0.2 mile (the unsigned turnout on your right) you find the scant remains of the walled Riasc Monastery (dating from the 5th to 12th centuries). The inner wall divided the community into work and religious sections. The layer of black felt marks where the original rocks stop and the excavators' reconstruction begins. The pillar stone is Celtic (from 1000 B.C.). When the Christians arrived in the fifth century, they didn't throw out the Celtic society. Instead, they carved a Maltese-type cross over the Celtic scrollwork. The square building was an oratory (church—you'll see an intact oratory at the next stop). The round buildings would have been stone igloo-type dwellings. The monasteries had cottage industries. Just outside the wall (opposite the oratory), find a stone hole with a passage facing the southwest wind. This was a kiln. Locals would bring their grain to be dried and ground, and the monks would keep a "tithe." With the arrival of the Normans in the 12th century, these small religious communities were replaced by relatively big-time state and church governments.

21.9 miles: Back on the main road, continue to the right.

23.0 miles: At the big restaurant, turn left (signs to Gallarus Oratory).

23.7 miles: At another restaurant, go right up an unmarked one-lane road.

24.0 miles: The Gallarus Oratory, built about 1,300 years ago, is one of Ireland's best-preserved early-Christian churches. Shaped like an upturned boat, its finely fitted dry-stone walls are still waterproof. Notice the holes for some covering at the door and the fine alternating stonework on the corners. A small tourist center (shop, WC, video theater, parking) charges £1.50 (you get a 17-minute video overview of Dingle Peninsula's historic sights). To park free, drive past the "Visitor Centre" sign and grab one of four spots farther up the one-lane road at the access path marked "public right-of-way" to the oratory. Continue up the rugged one-lane road.

Optional detour: The ruined Kilmalkedar church is two miles from Gallarus. This was the Norman center of worship for this end of the peninsula when England replaced the old monastic settlements in an attempt to centralize their rule.

24.6 miles: Turn left on the two-lane road, then right (to An Daingean, 7 km), where you'll crest and enjoy a three-mile coast back into Dingle Town in the direction of the Esk Tower.

27.6 miles: At the intersection, find the happy dolphin on the left. He leads the way over the bridge and back into Dingle Town (28.4 miles). Well done.

Dingle Peninsula Tours

▲▲**Sciuird Archaeology Tours**—These tours are offered by a father-son team with Dingle history—and a knack for sharing it—in its blood. Tim Coileain (a retired Dingle policeman) and his son Michael give serious 2.5-hour minibus tours (£8, departing at 10:30 and 14:00, depending upon demand). Drop by the Kirrary B&B (Dykegate and Grey's Lane) or call 066/915-1937 or 066/915-1606 to put your name on the list. Call early. Tours fill quickly in summer. Off-season you may have to call back to see if the necessary four people signed up. While skipping the folk legends and the famous sights, your guide will drive down tiny farm roads (the Gaelic word for road is "cow path"), over hedges, and up ridges to hidden Celtic forts, mysterious stone tombs, and forgotten castles with sweeping seaside views. The running commentary gives an intimate peek into Dingle's history. Sit as close to the driver as possible to get all the information. They do two different tours: west (Gallarus Oratory) and east (Minard Castle and a wedge tomb). I enjoyed both. Dress for the weather. In a literal gale with horizontal winds Tim kept saying, "You'll survive it."

Moran's Tour does three-hour guided minibus trips around the peninsula with a more touristic slant (£8, normally at 10:00 and 14:00 from the Dingle TI, tel. 087/241-2488 or 066/915-1155). There are always enough seats. If no one shows up, consider a private Moran taxi trip around the peninsula (3 people, £24, cabby narrates the ride). The **Mountain Man** also offers three-hour minibus tours of the peninsula (tel. 066/915-2400).

ROME
(ROMA)

Rome is magnificent and brutal at the same time. Your ears will ring, if you're careless you'll be run down or pickpocketed, you'll be frustrated by the kind of chaos that only an Italian can understand. You may even come to believe Mussolini was a necessary evil. But Rome is required—and in the Jubilee Year 2000, it's more exciting than ever.

If your hotel provides a comfortable refuge (book in advance for 2000), if you pace yourself and accept and even partake in the siesta plan, if you're well organized for sightseeing, and if you protect yourself and your valuables with extra caution and discretion, you'll do fine. You'll see the sights and leave satisfied.

Rome at its peak meant civilization itself. Everything was either civilized (part of the Roman Empire, Latin- or Greek-speaking) or barbarian. Today Rome is Italy's political capital, the capital of Catholicism, and a splendid... *junk pile* is not quite the right term... of Western civilization. As you peel through its fascinating and jumbled layers, you'll find its buildings, cats, laundry, traffic, and 2.6 million people endlessly entertaining. And then, of course, there are its magnificent sights.

Tour St. Peter's, the greatest church on earth, and scale Michelangelo's 100-yard-tall dome, the world's largest. Learn something about eternity by touring the huge Vatican Museum. You'll find the story of creation—bright as the day it was painted—in the newly restored Sistine Chapel. Do the "Caesar Shuffle" through ancient Rome's Forum and Colosseum. Savor Europe's most sumptuous building—the Borghese Gallery—and take an early evening "*Dolce Vita* Stroll" down the Via del Corso with Rome's beautiful people. Enjoy an after-dark walk from Trastevere to the Spanish Steps, lacing together Rome's Baroque and bubbly night spots.

Rome Area

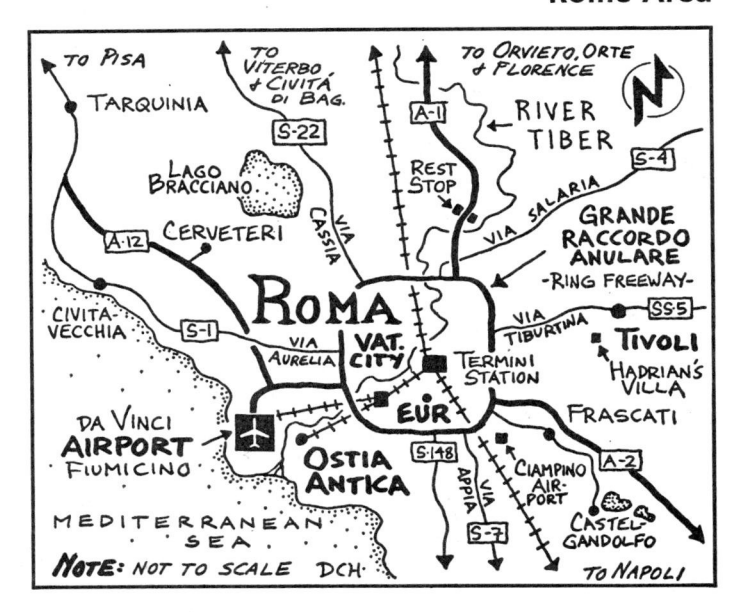

Map: Rome Area (not to scale). Shows major roads and landmarks including To Pisa, Tarquinia, To Viterbo & Civita di Bag., To Orvieto, Orte & Florence, River Tiber, A-11, S-22, S-4, Lago Bracciano, Rest Stop, Via Cassia, Via Salaria, Cerveteri, A-12, Grande Raccordo Anulare - Ring Freeway -, Civitavecchia, S-1, Via Aurelia, ROMA, Vat. City, Via Tiburtina, SS-5, Tivoli, Hadrian's Villa, Termini Station, Da Vinci Airport Fiumicino, EUR, Frascati, Ostia Antica, S-148, Via Appia, Ciampino Airport, A-2, Castel Gandolfo, S-7, Mediterranean Sea, To Napoli. NOTE: NOT TO SCALE DCH.

Planning Your Time

For most travelers, Rome is best done quickly. It's a great city, but exhausting. Time is normally short, and Italy is more charming elsewhere. To "do" Rome in a day, consider it as a side trip from Orvieto or Florence and maybe before the night train to Venice. Crazy as that sounds, if all you have is a day, it's a great one.

Rome in a day: Vatican (2 hours in the museum and Sistine Chapel and 1 hour in St. Peter's), taxi over the river to the Pantheon (munch a bar-snack picnic on its steps), then hike over Capitol Hill, through the Forum, and to the Colosseum. Have dinner on Campo de' Fiori and dessert on Piazza Navona.

Rome in two days: Do the "Caesar Shuffle" from the Colosseum and Forum over Capitol Hill to the Pantheon. After a siesta, join the locals strolling from Piazza del Popolo to the Spanish Steps. Have dinner near your hotel. On the second day, see Vatican City (St. Peter's, climb the dome, tour the Vatican Museum). Spend the evening walking from Trastevere to Campo de' Fiori (atmospheric place for dinner) to the Trevi Fountain. With a third day, add the Borghese Gallery (reservations required) and the National Museum of Rome.

Jubilee Crowds: Given the crowds anticipated for 2000,

you'll need to book your hotel well in advance, get entry appointments for bookable sights in advance (explained below), and do what you can to avoid peak hours (explained below).

Orientation

The modern sprawl of Rome is of no interest to us. Our Rome actually feels small when you know it. It's the old core—within the triangle formed by the train station, Colosseum, and Vatican. Get a handle on Rome by considering it in these layers:

The ancient city had a million people. Tear it down to size by walking through just the core. The best of the classical sights stand in a line from the Colosseum to the Pantheon.

Medieval Rome was little more than a hobo camp of 50,000—thieves, mean dogs, and the pope, whose legitimacy required a Roman address. The medieval city, a colorful tangle of lanes, lies between the Pantheon and the river.

Window-shoppers' Rome twinkles with nightlife and ritzy shopping near medieval Rome, on or near Rome's main drag—Via del Corso—and around the ritzy Spanish Steps.

Vatican City is a compact world of its own with two great, huge sights: St. Peter's Basilica and the Vatican Museum.

Trastevere, the seedy, colorful, wrong-side-of-the-river neighborhood/village, is Rome at its crustiest—and perhaps most "Roman."

Baroque Rome is an overleaf that embellishes great squares throughout the town with fountains and church facades.

Since no one is allowed to build taller than St. Peter's dome, the city has no modern skyline. And the Tiber River is ignored. It's not navigable, and after the last floods (1870), the banks were built up very high and Rome turned its back on its naughty river.

Tourist Information

While Rome has three main tourist information offices, the dozen or so handy TI kiosks scattered around the town at major tourist centers are handier and just as helpful. The main offices are: airport (tel. 06-6595-6074), train station (daily 8:15–19:15, near track 1, very crowded, the only one open on Sun, marked with a large "i," in the middle of the station, tel. 06-487-1270 or 06-482-4078), and the central office (for the city and the region, Mon–Fri 8:15–19:15, Sat 8:15–13:45, next to SAAB dealership, Via Parigi 5, tel. 06-4889-9253, www.comune.roma.it, e-mail: mail@informaroma.it).

The central TI office, near Piazza della Repubblica's huge fountain, is a five-minute walk out the front of the train station. It's air-conditioned, less crowded, and more helpful than the station TI and has a table to plan on—or sit under to overcome your frustration. Ask for the better "long stay" city map and *L'Evento*, the bimonthly periodical entertainment guide for evening events

Rome

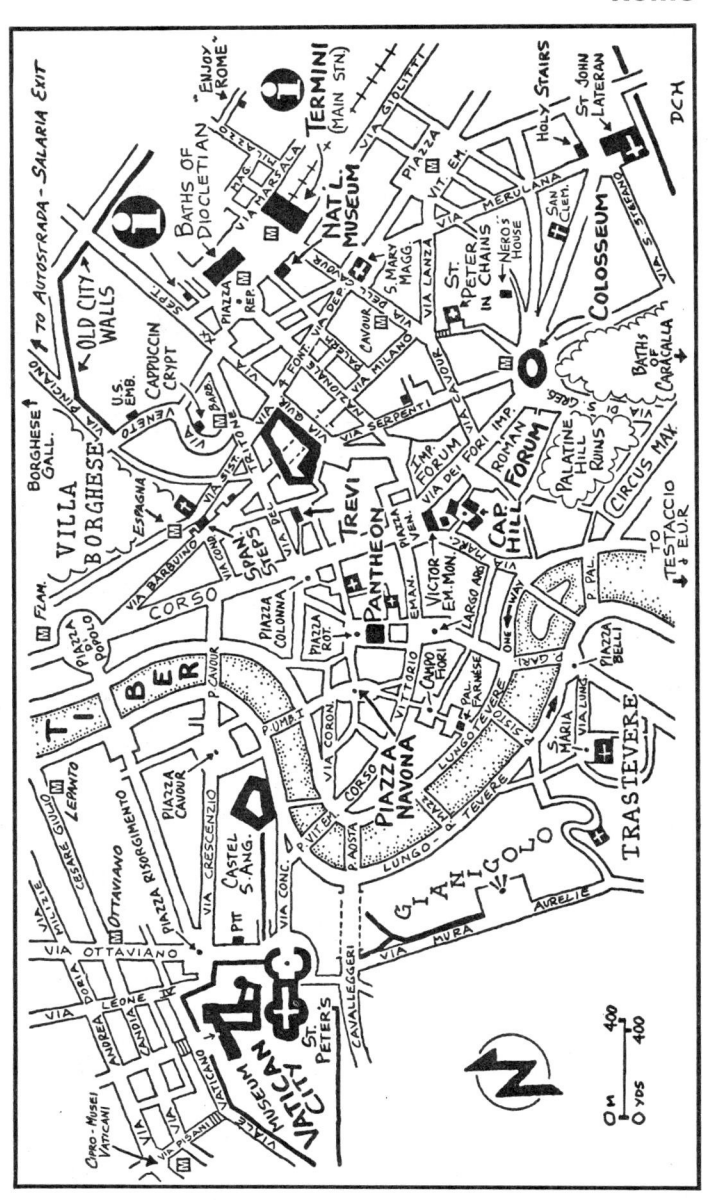

and fun (www.comune.roma.it/comunicazione/evento/). If all you need is a map, forget the TI and pick one up at your hotel. All hotels list an inflated rate to cover the hefty commission any TI room-finding service charges. Save money by booking direct.

The smaller TIs (daily 9:00–16:00) include kiosks near the entrance to the Forum (on Piazza del Tempio della Pace), at Via del Corso (on Largo Goldoni), in Trastevere (on Piazza Sonnino), on Via Nazionale (at Palazzo delle Esposizione), at Castel Sant' Angelo, and at St. John in Lateran.

Romanc'e is a cheap little weekly entertainment guide with a helpful English section on musical events and the pope's schedule for the week. It's sold on newsstands. Fancy hotels carry a free English monthly, *Un Ospite a Roma* (A Guest in Rome).

Enjoy Rome is a free, friendly—if entrepreneurial—information service providing maps, a free useful city guide, lots of tours (see "Tours of Rome," below) and a room-finding service (Mon–Fri 8:30–14:00, 15:30–18:30, Sat 8:30–14:00, closed Sun, 3 blocks northeast of train station at Via Varese 39, tel. 06-445-1843, fax 06-445-0734, www.enjoyrome.com).

Helpful Hints

Plan Ahead: The marvelous Borghese Gallery and newly opened Nero's Golden House both require reservations. Don't go to Rome hoping to see these without having made a reservation (see "Sights," below, for specifics).

Rome on the Web: www.roma2000.it (sight listings and itineraries), www.wantedinrome.com (job openings but also listings of exhibitions and festivals), www.museionline.it (museums in Italy), www.informaroma.it (general Rome info), www.vatican.va (the pope's Web site), www.fs-on-line.com (train info and schedules).

Museum Hours: Most museums close on Monday (except the Vatican) and at 13:00 on Sunday. Outdoor sights like the Colosseum, Forum, and Ostia Antica are open roughly 9:00 to 18:00. For 2000, museum hours will probably be extended into the evening. Hours listed anywhere can vary. Confirm sightseeing plans each morning with a quick L200 telephone call asking, "Are you open today?" (*"Aperto oggi?"*) and "What time do you close?" (*"A che ora chiuso?"*). I've included telephone numbers for this purpose. The last pages of the daily *Messaggero* newspaper list current events, exhibits, and hours.

Churches: Churches generally open early (around 7:00), close for lunch (roughly 12:00–15:00), and close late (around 19:00). Kamikaze tourists maximize their sightseeing hours by visiting churches before 9:00 and seeing the major sights that stay open during the siesta (St. Peter's, Pantheon, Capitol Hill Museums, and Forum) while all good Romans are taking it cool and easy. Many churches have "modest dress" requirements for men and women,

The Jubilee Year—2000

While Rome sees thousands of pilgrims every year, Jubilee Years are festival years, offering Catholics around the world the Roman pilgrimage of a lifetime. The Jubilee Year is based on an Old Testament idea that every 50 years God has mandated we should free slaves, forgive debts, and return land to the original owners. In 1470 the Church shortened the time between Jubilee Years from 50 to 25 years. The year 2000 happens to be the granddaddy of all Jubilee Years. Rome and the Vatican expect millions of extra tourists to visit. As this is the first Holy Year since the fall of the USSR, this Jubilee will be huge among Eastern European Catholics, finally free to travel.

Secular travelers will be coming to Rome on a cultural pilgrimage—to see the grand city of Western Civilization all dolled up with newly restored monuments. While some predict pandemonium, most are now expecting no unmanageable crowds, and some hoteliers even fear a Jubilee Year bust with the expected crowds avoiding the expected crowds. I predict huge crowds of pilgrims staying in institutions outside the city (the Church has massive places available) but otherwise a city that has more than ever to show off and is better equipped than ever to do it. You'll find fleets of new buses, tourist info kiosks scattered all over town, well-organized sights with extended hours, a pedestrian-friendly old town, and lots of healthy competition keeping service up and prices reasonable. For the latest, check out www.jubil2000.org.

If you're thinking this Jubilee commotion is outdated, consider its origin. The purpose of this redistribution of wealth is based on the notion that, when left unbridled, aggressive people take about 50 years to create such an imbalance that society as a whole becomes threatened. Ignoring that imbalance can lead to a regrettably violent redistribution of wealth. (Central America's history substantiates this point. Roughly twice a century, rather than celebrate a Jubilee Year, landowners violently put down uprisings by their "unruly poor.") The pope's wish for this Jubilee Year is for the rich world to forgive the Third World debt (see the page at the end of this book). While Jubilee 2000 has become a tourist event, it's still a global celebration . . . and a necessity.

---

which mean shoulders covered and no shorts (although you'll find many tourists in shorts touring many churches).

Shop Hours: Shops are usually open 9:00 to 13:00 and 16:00 to 19:00. Grocery stores are often closed on Sunday. While the summer break is not what it used to be, during the holiday month of August many shops and restaurants still close up for vacation, and "*Chiuso per ferie*" signs decorate locked doors all over town.

Laundromats: Your hotel can point you to the nearest one (usually open daily 8:00–22:00, about L12,000 to wash and dry a 15-pound load). The Bolle Blu chain now has Internet access (L8,000/hr, near train station at Via Palestro 59, Via Milazzo 20, and Via Principe Amedeo 116, tel. 06-4470-3098).

Travel Agencies: Your hotel can direct you to the nearest travel agency. Buy train tickets and get railpass-related reservations and supplements at travel agencies rather than dealing with the congested train station. The cost is the same.

Books: The American Bookstore sells all the major guidebooks (Via Torino 136, Metro: Repubblica, tel. 06-4746877).

Facing (and Avoiding) Problems

Theft Alert: With sweet-talking con artists meeting you at the station, well-dressed pickpockets on buses, and thieving gangs of children at the ancient sights, Rome is a gauntlet of rip-offs. Other than getting run-down, there's no great physical risk. But green tourists will be ripped off. Thieves strike when you're distracted. Don't trust kind strangers. Keep nothing important in your pockets. Assume you're being stalked. (Then relax and have fun.) Be most on guard while boarding and leaving buses and subways. Thieves crowd the door and then stop and turn while others crowd and push from behind. Gypsies are less dangerous, since you can identify them. The sneakiest thieves are well-dressed businessmen (generally with something in their hands). Lately many are posing as tourists with Tevas, fanny packs, and cameras. The terrace above the bus stop near the Colosseum Metro stop is a fine place to watch the action and maybe even pick up a few moves of your own.

Reporting Losses: To report lost or stolen passports and documents or to file an insurance claim, you must file a police report (*carabinieri* or *polizia* office at the train station near platform 1 or at Piazza Venezia). To replace a passport, file the police report and then go to your embassy (see below). To report lost traveler's checks, call your bank (Visa tel. 800/874-155, Amex tel. 800/872-000, Thomas Cook/Mastercard tel. 800/872-050) and then file a police report. To report stolen or lost credit cards, call the company (Amex tel. 06-7228-0371, Visa tel. 800-877-232, Mastercard tel. 800-870-866) and then file a police report.

Embassies: U.S. (Mon–Fri 8:30–13:00, 14:00–17:30, Via Veneto 119, tel. 06-46741), Canada (Via Zara 30, tel. 06-445-981), Australia (Corso Trieste 25, tel. 06-852-721), Great Britain (Via XX Septembre 80, tel. 06-482-5441).

Emergency Numbers: Police tel. 113. Ambulance tel. 112.

Hit and Run: Walk with extreme caution. Scooters don't

need to stop at red lights, and even cars exercise what drivers call the "logical option" of not stopping if they see no oncoming traffic. As Vespa scooters become electric, they'll get quieter (hooray) but more dangerous for pedestrians. Cross streets following locals like a shadow (or spend a good part of your visit stranded on curbs).

Staying/Getting Healthy: The siesta is a key to survival in summertime Rome. Lie down and contemplate the extraordinary power of gravity in the eternal city. I drink lots of cold, refreshing water from Rome's many drinking fountains (the Forum has three). There are pharmacies (marked by a green cross) in every neighborhood, including a handy one in the train station (open 7:30–22:00). A 24-hour pharmacy is on Piazza dei Cinquecento 51 (next to train station on Via Cavour, tel. 06-488-0019). Embassies can recommend English-speaking doctors. Anyone is entitled to free emergency treatment at public hospitals. The hospital closest to the train station is Policlinico Umberto 1 (entrance for emergency treatment on Via Lancisi, translators available, Metro: Policlinico).

Buyer Beware: I carefully understand the final price before I order anything, and I deliberately count my change. Expect the "slow count"; wait for the last bits of your change to straggle over to you. Never part with a 100,000 lire (say "chen-to mee-la") note without making clear you know it's not a 10,000. There are legitimate extras (café prices as much as double when you sit down instead of stand at the bar, taxis get L5,000 extra after 22:00, and so on) at which paranoid tourists wrongly take offense. But the waiter who charges you L70,000 for a pizza and beer assumes you're too polite to involve the police. If you have any problem with a restaurant, hotel, or taxi, get a cop to arbitrate. Rome is trying to civilize itself.

Arrival in Rome

By Train: Rome's main train station, Termini, is a minefield of tourist services: a late-hours bank, public showers, luggage lockers, 24-hour thievery, the city bus station, a subway stop, and Chef Express (a handy and cheery self-service restaurant, daily 11:00–22:30). Multilingual charts make locations fairly clear. The station is crawling with sleazy sharks with official-looking cards. Generally, avoid anybody selling anything at the station if you can. Most of my hotel listings are easily accessible by foot (near the train station) or by Metro (Colosseum and Vatican neighborhoods). The train station has its own Metro stop (Termini).

By Plane: If you arrive at the airport, catch a train (hrly, 30 min, L16,000) to Rome's train station or take (or share) a taxi to your hotel. For details, see "Transportation Connections," below.

Getting around Rome

Sightsee on foot, by city bus, or by taxi. I've grouped your sightseeing into walkable neighborhoods. Public transportation is efficient, cheap, and part of your Roman experience. It starts running around 5:30 and stops around 23:30. After midnight there are a few very crowded night buses and taxis become more expensive and hard to get. Don't try to hail one—go to a taxi stand.

By Subway: The Roman subway system (Metropolitana) is simple, with two clean, cheap, fast lines. While much of Rome is not served by its skimpy subway, these stops are helpful: Termini (train station, National Museum of Rome at Palazzo Massimo, recommended hotels), Repubblica (Octagonal Hall/Baths of Diocletian, main tourist office, recommended hotels), Barberini (Cappuccin Crypt, Trevi Fountain), Spagna (Spanish Steps, Villa Borghese, classy shopping area), Flaminio (Piazza del Popolo, start of recommended Via del Corso *"Dolce Vita"* stroll, below), Ottaviano (St. Peter's and Vatican City), Cipro-Musei Vaticani (Vatican Museum, recommended hotels), Colosseo (Colosseum, Roman Forum, recommended hotels), and E.U.R. (Mussolini's futuristic suburb).

By Bus: Bus routes are clearly listed at the stops. Buses and subways use the same ticket. You can buy tickets at newsstands, tobacco shops, or major stations or bus stops but not on board (L1,500, good for 75 minutes—one Metro ride and unlimited buses). Punch your ticket in the orange stamping machine as you board—or you are cheating. Riding without a stamped ticket on the bus (or subway), while relatively safe, is stressful. Inspectors fine even innocent-looking tourists L100,000. If you hop a bus without a ticket, locals who use tickets rather than a monthly pass can sell you a ticket from their wallet bundle. Ideally buy a bunch of tickets so you can hop a bus without searching for an open tobacco shop. All-day bus/Metro passes cost L6,000.

Buses, especially the touristic #64 (running between the train station and the Vatican), and the subway, are havens for thieves and pickpockets. Assume any commotion is a thief-created distraction. Bus #64 gets horribly crowded.

Learn which buses serve your neighborhood. Here are a few worth knowing about:

#64: Termini (train station), Piazza della Repubblica, Via Nazionale (recommended hotels), Piazza Venezia (near Forum), Largo Argentina (near Pantheon), St. Peter's Basilica. Ride it for a city overview and to watch pickpockets in action.

#8: This tram connects Largo Argentina with Trastevere (get off at Piazza Mastai).

#492: Stazione Tiburtina, Termini, Piazza Barberini, Piazza Venezia, Corso Rinascimento, Piazza Cavour (Castel Sant' Angelo), Piazza Risorgimento (near Vatican Museum).

#714: Termini, Santa Maria Maggiore, San Giovanni in Laterano, Terme di Caracalla.

By Taxi: Taxis start at about L5,000 (surcharges of L2,000 on Sun, L5,000 for night hours of 22:00–7:00, L2,000 surcharge

Metropolitana: Rome's Subway

```
═══ LINE A
━━━ LINE B
--- BUS
+++ RAIL
```

OTTAVIANO-VATICAN & ST. PETER'S
LEPANTO
FLAMINIO
SPAGNA - SPANISH STEPS
BARBERINI
REPUBBLICA
TERMINI - MAIN TRAIN STATION
VITT. EMAN.
ANAGNINA
TO FRASCATI & CIAMPINO AIRPORT

TO CERVETERI & TARQUINIA
TO DA VINCI AIRPORT

PIAZZA CAVOUR
COLOSSEO - COLOSSEUM & FORUM
CIRCO MASSIMO
PIRAMIDE/OSTIENSE
GARBATELLA
SAN PAOLO
MAGLIANA
EUR MARCONI
EUR FERMI
LAURENTINA

TO OSTIA ANTICA

DCH

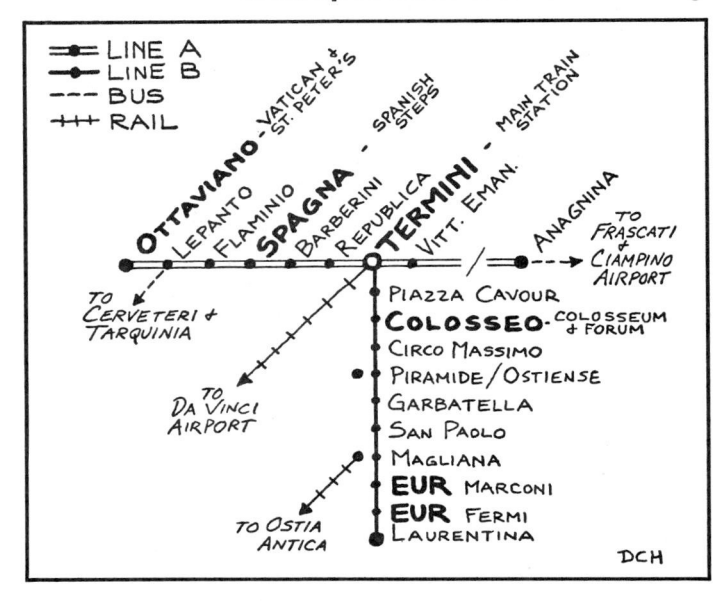

for luggage, L14,000 for airport). Sample fares: Train station to Vatican-L16,000; train station to Colosseum-L10,000; Colosseum to Trastevere-L12,000. Three or four companions with more money than time should taxi almost everywhere. It's tough to wave down a taxi in Rome. Find the nearest taxi stand. (Ask a local or in a shop "*Dov'è* [DOH-vay] *una fermata dei tassi?*" They're listed on my maps.) Taxis listing their telephone number on the door have fair meters—use them. To save time and energy, have your hotel call a taxi (the meter starts when the call is received), enjoy a few extra minutes in the room, and enjoy curb service. (Some Rome cab telephone numbers: 06-6645, 06-8822, 06-3570.)

Tours of Rome

You can choose from an assortment of walking tours or a bus tour. **Enjoy Rome**—This company offers several English-only city walking tours daily (such as greatest ancient and Baroque hits, Vatican, Rome at night, Trastevere, and Jewish Ghetto, 3 hrs, L30,000 per tour, L25,000 if under 26, kids under 15 free). Ask about bike tours of Rome (L35,000 includes bike rental, helmet, and guide, 3 hrs) or their air-conditioned bus to Pompeii (L70,000, 3-hr drive each way, offered every other day, tour and admission not included).

For specifics on Enjoy Rome, see listing in "Tourist Information," above (tel. 06-445-1843, www.enjoyrome.com).

Walks of Rome—Lately students working for "Walks of Rome" have been giving free 45-minute tours of the Colosseum in order to promote their other guided walks. The tours bring the Colosseum to life, and they hope you'll join—and pay for—their other walks: Forum (2 hrs), Vatican City (full-day church, museum, Sistine chapel), night tour (great Renaissance and Baroque squares, nightly at 19:00), and catacombs (3 hrs by bus with some of city included). Their pub crawl tour meets at 20:00 on the Spanish Steps and finishes at a disco six pubs later around midnight. I've never seen 50 young and drunk people having so much fun. (Tel. 06-484-853 or 0347-795-5175, e-mail: walkingtours@yahoo.com.)

Scale Reale—Tom Rankin (an American architect in love with Rome and his Roman wife) runs Scala Reale, a small company committed to sorting out the rich layers of Rome for small groups with a longer-than-average attention span. Their excellent walking tours vary in length from two to four hours and start at L30,000 per person. Try to book in advance, since their small groups are limited to six and fill up fast. Their fascinating Rome Orientation walks lace together lesser-known sights from antiquity to the present, helping you get a sense of how Rome works (toll-free number in U.S.: 888/467-1986, Italy tel. 06-445-1477, fax 06-4470-0898, www.scalareale.org, e-mail: scalareale@mail.nexus.it).

Bus Tour—The ATAC city bus tour offers your best budget orientation tour of Rome. In 2.5 hours you'll have 80 sights pointed out to you (by a live guide in English and maybe one other language) and get out for 15-minute stops at St. Peter's Square, the Colosseum, and Piazza Venezia (L15,000, bus #110 departs daily at 10:30, 14:00, 15:00, 17:00, and 18:00 from in front of train station at platform C, buy tickets at information kiosk there, tel. 06-4695-2252).

Sights—From the Colosseum Area to Capitol Hill

▲**St. Peter-in-Chains Church (San Pietro in Vincoli)**—Built in the fifth century to house the chains of St. Peter, this church is most famous for its Michelangelo statue. Check out the much-venerated chains under the high altar and then focus on *Moses* (free, but pop in L500 to light the statue, Mon–Sat 7:00–12:30, 15:30–19:00, Sun 7:30–12:30, a short walk uphill from the Colosseum; modest dress required).

Pope Julius II commissioned Michelangelo to build a massive tomb with 48 huge statues crowned by a grand statue of this egomaniac pope. When Julius died, the work had barely started, and no one had the money or concern for Julius to finish the project. Michelangelo finished one statue, *Moses*, and left a few unfinished statues: *Leah* and *Rachel* flanking *Moses* in this church, the *Prisoners* now in Florence's Accademia, and the *Slaves* now in Paris' Louvre. Study the powerful statue; it's mature Michelangelo. He worked on it in fits and starts for 30 years. Moses has received the Ten Commandments. As he holds the stone tablets, his eyes show a man determined to stop his tribe from worshiping the golden calf and idols...determined to win salvation for the people of Israel. Why the horns? Centuries ago, the Hebrew word for "rays" was mistranslated as "horns."

▲▲**Nero's Golden House (Domus Aurea)**—The remains of Emperor Nero's "Golden House" are newly opened to the public. Nero's huge house used to sprawl across the valley where the Colosseum now stands. Nero was your quintessential bad emperor: killed his mom and crucified St. Peter. The story goes that he fiddled while Rome burned in A.D. 64; Romans suspected he started the fires to clear land for an even bigger house. While only hints of the splendid colored frescoes survive, the towering vaults and basic immensity of the place is impressive. As you wander, look up at the holes in the ceiling and imagine how much of Rome hides underground...and why the subway is limited to two lines. Visits are allowed only with an escort (25 people every 15 minutes) and a reservation (L12,000, daily 9:00–20:00, last entry at 19:00, tour lasts 40 min, escort speaks Italian, audio guides-L3,000, 200 yards northeast of Colosseum, through a park gate, up a hill, and on the left). To reserve a place, call 06-3974-9907 or 199-199-100 (Mon–Sat 8:00–20:00, information tel. 06-481-5576).

▲▲**Colosseum**—This 2,000-year-old building is the great example of Roman engineering. Using concrete, brick, and their trademark round arches, Romans constructed much larger buildings than the Greeks. But in deference to the higher Greek culture, notice how they finished their no-nonsense megastructure by pasting all three orders of Greek columns (Doric, Ionic, and Corinthian) as exterior decorations. The Flavian Amphitheater's popular name, "Colosseum," comes from the colossal statue of Nero that once stood in front of it.

Romans were into "big." By putting two theaters together, they created a circular amphitheater. They could fill and empty its 50,000 numbered seats as quickly and efficiently as we do our superstadiums. Teams of sailors hoisted canvas awnings over the stadium to give fans shade. This was where ancient Romans, whose taste for violence was the equal of modern America's, enjoyed their Dirty Harry and *Terminator*. Gladiators, criminals, and wild animals fought to the death in every conceivable scenario. The floor of the Colosseum is missing, exposing underground passages. Animals in cages were kept here and then lifted up in elevators; they'd pop out from behind blinds into the arena, and the gladiator didn't know where, when, or by what he'd be attacked (L10,000, daily 9:00–19:00, off-season 9:00–15:00, tel. 06-481-5576 or

06-700-4261). As you stand in the ticket line, students may offer you a free tour. The tours are good (and free because they'll try to get you to pay for their other tours—see "Tours of Rome," above). The stairs to the upper level are near the exit (west end).

▲**Arch of Constantine**—The well-preserved arch that stands between the Colosseum and the Forum commemorates a military coup and, more important, the acceptance of Christianity in the Roman Empire. In A.D. 312 an upstart general named Constantine (who had a vision he could win under the sign of the cross) defeated the Emperor Maxentius. Constantine became Emperor and promptly legalized Christianity.

▲▲▲**Roman Forum (Foro Romano)**—Ancient Rome's birthplace and civic center, the Forum was the common ground between Rome's famous seven hills (free admission to Forum, L12,000 for Palatine Hill, both keep the same hours: daily 9:00–19:30 or an hour before dark, off-season 9:00–15:00, tel. 06-699-0110).

To help resurrect this confusing pile of rubble, study the before-and-after pictures in the cheap city guidebooks sold on the streets. (Check out the small red *Rome, Past and Present* books with plastic overlays to un-ruin the ruins. They're priced at L20,000—pay no more than L15,000.) With the help of the map in this section, follow this basic walk (assuming you enter from the Colosseum side, near the Arch of Constantine):

1. Start by the small **Arch of Titus** (drinking fountain opposite) overlooking the remains of what was the political, social, and commercial center of the Roman Empire. The Via Sacra—the main street of ancient Rome—cuts through the Forum from here to the Capitol Hill and the Arch of Septimus Severus on the opposite side. On the left a ticket booth welcomes you to the Palatine Hill (described below)—once filled with the palaces of Roman emperors. Study the Arch of Titus—carved with propaganda celebrating the A.D. 70 defeat of the Jews, which began the Diaspora that ended with the creation of Israel in 1947. Notice the gaggle of soldiers carrying the menorah.

2. Ahead of you on the right are the massive ruins of the **Basilica Maxentius.** Follow the path leading there from the Via Sacra. Only the giant barrel vaults remain, looming crumbly and weed-eaten. As you stand in the shadow of the Bas Max, reconstruct it in your mind. The huge barrel vaults were just side niches. Extend the broken nub of an arch out over the vacant lot and finish your imaginary Roman basilica with rich marble and fountains. People it with plenty of toga-clad Romans. Yeow.

3. Next hike past the semicircular Temple of Vesta to the **House of the Vestal Virgins.** Here, the VVs kept the eternal flame lit. A set of ponds and a marble chorus line of Vestal Virgins mark the courtyard of the house.

4. The grand **Basilica Julia,** a first-century law court, fills the

The Forum Area

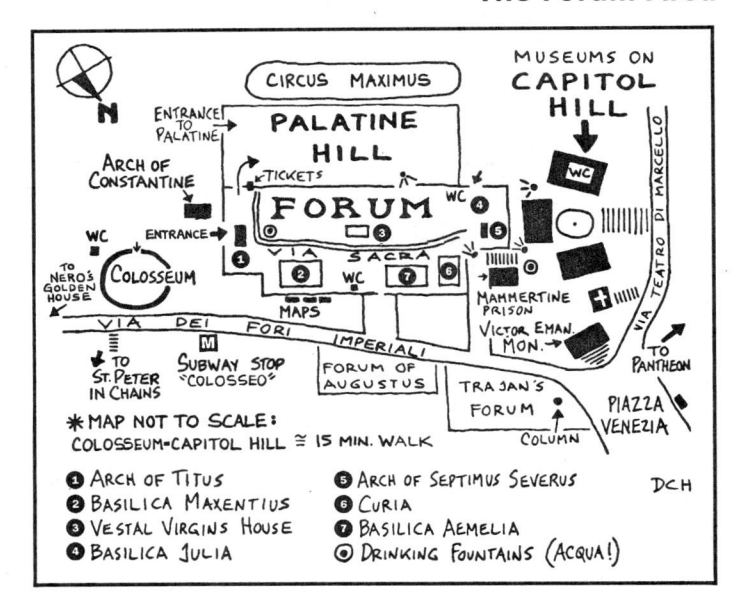

```
                                    MUSEUMS ON
                 CIRCUS MAXIMUS      CAPITOL
         ENTRANCE                    HILL
         TO
         PALATINE   PALATINE
                    HILL
    ARCH OF         TICKETS                    WC
    CONSTANTINE                          WC
                    FORUM
            ENTRANCE
                      VIA  SACRA
    WC                                  
    TO       COLOSSEUM   WC                    MAMMERTINE
    NERO'S                                     PRISON
    GOLDEN                MAPS                 VICTOR EMAN.
    HOUSE                                      MON.
         VIA   DEI   FORI                                  TO
                    IMPERIALI                              PANTHEON
         TO     SUBWAY STOP  FORUM OF
         ST. PETER "COLOSSEO" AUGUSTUS   TRAJAN'S
         IN CHAINS                       FORUM       PIAZZA
    *MAP NOT TO SCALE:                               VENEZIA
    COLOSSEUM-CAPITOL HILL ≅ 15 MIN. WALK   COLUMN

    ❶ ARCH OF TITUS           ❺ ARCH OF SEPTIMUS SEVERUS    DCH
    ❷ BASILICA MAXENTIUS      ❻ CURIA
    ❸ VESTAL VIRGINS HOUSE    ❼ BASILICA AEMELIA
    ❹ BASILICA JULIA          ⊙ DRINKING FOUNTAINS (ACQUA!)
```

corner opposite the Curia. Notice how the Romans passed their time; ancient backgammon-type game boards are cut into the pavement.

5. The **Arch of Septimus Severus,** from about A.D. 200, celebrates that emperor's military victories. In front of it a stone called Lapis Niger covers the legendary tomb of Romulus. To the left of the arch, the stone bulkhead is the Rostra, or speaker's platform. It's named for the ship's prows that used to decorate it as big shots hollered, "Friends, Romans, countrymen...."

6. The plain, intact brick building near the Arch of Septimus Severus was the **Curia,** where the Roman senate sat. (Peek inside.) Roman buildings were basically brick and concrete, usually with a marble veneer, which in this case is long lost.

7. The **Basilica Aemilia** (second century B.C.) shows the floor plan of an ancient palace. This pre-Christian "basilica" design was later adopted by medieval churches. From here a ramp leads up and out (past a WC and a fun headless statue to pose with). Eventually, the entire area between here and Trajan's Column will be an archeological park.

Palatine Hill—The hill above the Forum contains scanty remains of the Imperial palaces and the Roman Quadrata (Iron Age huts and the legendary house of Romulus—under corrugated tin roof in far corner). We get our word *palace* from this hill, where the emperors chose to live. The Palatine was once so filled with palaces that later emperors had to build out. (Looking up at it from the Forum you see the substructure that supported these long-gone palaces.) The newly opened Palatine museum has sculptures and fresco fragments but is nothing special. From the pleasant garden, you'll get an overview of the Forum. On the far side, look down into an emperor's private stadium and then beyond at the dusty Circus Maximus, once a chariot course. Imagine the cheers, jeers, and furious betting. But considering how ruined the ruins are, the heat, the hill to climb, the L12,000 entry fee, and the relative difficulty in understanding what you're looking at, the Palatine Hill is a disappointment.

▲**Thief Gangs**—If you know what to look out for, the gangs of children picking the pockets and handbags of naive tourists are no threat but an interesting, albeit sad, spectacle. Gangs of city-stained children, too young to prosecute but old enough to rip you off, troll through the tourist crowds around the Forum, Colosseum, Piazza Repubblica, and train and Metro stations. Watch them target tourists distracted with a video camera or overloaded with bags. The kids look like beggars and use newspapers or cardboard signs to confuse their victims. They scram like stray cats if you're onto them. A fast-fingered mother with a baby is often nearby.

▲**Mammertine Prison**—The 2,500-year-old cisternlike prison that once imprisoned saints Peter and Paul is worth a look. Stepping into the room you hit a modern floor. Erase that in your mind and look up at the hole in the ceiling through which prisoners were lowered. Then take the stairs down to the actual prison floor level. Imagine humans, amid rotting corpses, awaiting slow deaths. Then consider the legend of the saints baptizing the prisoners from a miraculous spring. On the walls near the entry are lists of notable prisoners (Christian and non-Christian) and how they were executed: *strangolati, decapitato, morto di fame* ... (donation requested, daily 9:00–12:00, 14:30–18:00).

Leaving the prison, turn right and climb the stairs leading to Capitol Hill. Halfway up, you'll find a refreshing water fountain. Block the spout with your fingers; it spurts up for drinking. Romans call this *il nasone* (the nose). A cheap Roman boy takes his date out for a drink to *il nasone*.

▲▲**Capitol Hill (Campidoglio)**—This hill was the religious and political center of ancient Rome. It's still the home of the city's government. Michelangelo's Renaissance square is bounded by two fine museums and the mayoral palace. Its centerpiece is a copy of the famous equestrian statue of Marcus Aurelius (the original is behind glass in the adjacent museum). To approach the great square the way Michelangelo wanted you to, walk halfway down the grand stairway toward Piazza Venezia, spin around, and walk back up. This was the new Renaissance face of Rome, with its back to the Forum and facing the new city. Notice how Michelangelo gave the buildings the "giant order," with huge pilasters making the existing two-story buildings feel one story and a more harmonious part of the new square. Notice also how the statues atop these buildings first welcome you and then draw you in. There's a fine view of the Forum from the terrace just past the mayor's palace (downhill on the right).

The two **Capitol Hill Museums** (Palazzo dei Conseratori and Palazzo Nuovo) are in two buildings (one L10,000 ticket is good for both museums, free entrance on the last Sun of the month, closed in 1999 but they plan to open for 2000, Tue–Sun 9:00–19:00 or later, closed Mon, tel. 06-6710-2071).

The **Palazzo dei Conservatori** (the building nearest the river, on Marcus Aurelius' left side) is one of the world's oldest museums, at 500 years old. Outside the entrance, notice the marriage announcements and, very likely, wedding-party photo ops. Inside the free courtyard, have a look at giant chunks of a statue of Emperor Constantine. (A rare public toilet hides near the museum ticket-taker.) The museum is worthwhile, with lavish rooms housing several great statues. Tops is the original (500 B.C.) Etruscan *Capitoline Wolf* (the little statues of Romulus and Remus were added in the Baroque age). Don't miss the *Boy Extracting a Thorn* or the enchanting *Commodus as Hercules*. The second-floor painting gallery—except for one Carravagio—is forgettable.

Across the square, the **Palazzo Nuovo** houses mostly portrait busts of forgotten emperors. But it has two must-sees: the *Dying Gaul* (first floor up) and the restored gilded bronze equestrian statue of Marcus Aurelius (behind glass in museum courtyard). This greatest surviving equestrian statue of antiquity was the original centerpiece of the square. While most such pagan statues were destroyed by Dark Age Christians, Marcus was mistaken as Constantine (the first Christian emperor) and therefore spared.

Descend the stairs leading to Piazza Venezia. At the bottom of the stairs, look up the long stairway to your right (which pilgrims climb on their knees) for a good example of the earliest style of Christian church. While pilgrims find it worth the climb, sightseers can skip it.

Also from the bottom of the stairs, look left several blocks down the street to see a condominium actually built around surviving ancient pillars and arches of Teatro Marcello—perhaps the oldest inhabited building in Europe. Farther ahead (toward Piazza Venezia), look down into the ditch on your right and see how everywhere modern Rome is built on the forgotten frescoes and mangled mosaics of ancient Rome.

Piazza Venezia—This vast square is the focal point of modern Rome. The Via del Corso, starting here, is the city's axis,

The Dolce Vita Stroll down Via del Corso

This is the city's chic and hip "cruise" from Piazza del Popolo (Metro: Flaminio) down a wonderfully traffic-free section of Via del Corso and up Via Condotti to the Spanish Steps each evening around 18:00 (Sat and Sun are best). Strollers, shoppers, and flirts on the prowl fill this neighborhood of Rome's most fashionable stores (open after siesta 16:30–19:30).

Throughout Italy, early evening is time to stroll. While elsewhere in Italy this is called the *passeggiata*, in Rome it's a cruder big-city version called the *struscio* (*struscio* means "rubing"). Unemployment among Italy's youth is very high; many stay with their parents even into their thirties. They spend a lot of time being trendy and hanging out. Hard-core cruisers who live in the suburbs, which lack pleasant public spaces, congregate on Via del Corso to make the scene. The hot vroom vroom motorscooter is their symbol; haircuts and fashion are follow-the-leader. They are the *coatto*. In a more genteel small town, the *passeggiata* comes with sweet whispers of *"bella"* and *"bello"* ("pretty" and "handsome"). In Rome, the admiration is stronger, oriented toward consumption—*"buona"* and *"buono"*—meaning "good" (used to describe food).

Historians note that Piazza del Popolo was just inside medieval Rome's main entry. The delightfully car-free square is marked by an obelisk brought to Rome by Augustus after conquering Egypt (it once stood in the Circus Maximus). The Baroque Church of Santa Maria del Popolo (with Raphael's Chigi Chapel and two Caravaggio paintings) is next to the gate in the old wall, on the far side of Piazza del Popolo. Nonshoppers hike a mile down Via del Corso—straight since Roman times—to the Victor Emmanuel Monument. Climb Michelangelo's stairway to his glorious (especially when floodlit) square atop Capitol Hill and catch the lovely views of the Forum (from either side of the mayor's palace) as the horizon reddens and cats prowl the unclaimed rubble of ancient Rome.

---

surrounded by Rome's classiest shopping district. From the Palazzo Venezia's balcony above the square (to your left with back to Victor Emmanuel Monument), Mussolini whipped up the nationalistic fervor of Italy. Fascist masses filled the square screaming, "Four more years!" or something like that. (Fifteen years later, they hung him from a meat hook in Milan.)

Victor Emmanuel Monument—This oversized monument to an Italian king was part of Italy's rush to overcome the new country's strong regionalism and to create a national identity after unification in 1870. Romans think of it not as an altar of the fatherland but as "the wedding cake," "the typewriter," or "the dentures." It wouldn't be so bad if it weren't sitting on a priceless acre of ancient Rome and if they chose better marble (this is too in-your-face white and picks up the pollution horribly). Soldiers guard Italy's Tomb of the Unknown Soldier as the eternal flame flickers. Stand directly in front of it and see how Via del Corso bisects Rome.

▲Trajan's Column and Forum—This is the grandest column and best example of "continuous narration" from antiquity. Over 2,500 figures scroll around the 40-meter-high column telling of Trajan's victorious Dacian campaign (circa A.D. 103, in present-day Romania), from the assembling of the army at the bottom to the victory sacrifice at the top. The ashes of Trajan and his wife were held in the mausoleum at the base while the sun once glinted off a polished bronze statue of Trajan at the top. Today St. Peter is on top. Study the propaganda that winds up the column like a scroll, trumpeting Trajan's wonderful military exploits. You can view this close-up for free across Mussolini's busy Via dei Fori Imperiali from the Victor Emmanuel Monument. Viewing balconies once stood on either side, but it seems likely Trajan fans only came away with a feeling that the greatness of their emperor and empire was beyond comprehension (for a rolled-out version of the Column's story, visit the Museum of Roman Civilization at E.U.R., below). This column marked Trajan's Forum, built to handle the shopping needs of a wealthy city of over a million. Commercial, political, religious, and social activities all mixed in the Forum. Rome is in the slow process of excavating Trajan's Forum, closing down Via dei Fori Imperiali (controversial for the traffic problems this would create), and turning the entire area into a vast archaeological park.

Sights—Heart of Rome

▲▲▲Pantheon—For the greatest look at the splendor of Rome, antiquity's best-preserved interior is a must (free, Mon–Sat 9:00–18:30, Sun 9:00–13:00, tel. 06-6830-0230). Because it became a church dedicated to the martyrs just after the fall of Rome, the barbarians left it alone, and the locals didn't use it as a quarry. The portico is called Rome's umbrella—a fun local gathering in a rainstorm. Walk past its one-piece granite columns (biggest in Italy, shipped from Egypt) and through the original bronze doors. Sit inside under the glorious skylight and enjoy classical architecture at its best.

The dome, 142 feet high and wide, was Europe's biggest until the Renaissance. Michelangelo's dome at St. Peter's, while much higher, is one meter smaller. The brilliance of its construction astounded architects through the ages. During the Renaissance, Brunelleschi was given permission to cut into the dome (see the

Heart of Rome

Map legend:
1. Hotel Campo dei Fiori
2. Albergo del Sole
3. Hotel Navona
4. Casa di Santa Brigida
5. Il Delfino Rest.
6. Giolitti
7. Hotel Nazionale
8. Rist. Pallaro, Filettaro S. Barb. & Grotte Teatro Pomp.

little square hole above and to the right of the entrance) to analyze the material. The concrete dome gets thinner and lighter with height—the highest part is volcanic pumice.

This wonderfully harmonious architecture greatly inspired the artists of the Renaissance, particularly Raphael. Raphael, along with Italy's first two kings, chose to be buried here.

As you walk around the outside of the Pantheon, notice the "rise of Rome"—about 15 feet since it was built.

▲▲**Curiosities near the Pantheon**—The only Gothic church you'll see in Rome is **Santa Maria sopra Minerva**. On a little square behind the Pantheon to the east, past the Bernini statue of an elephant carrying an Egyptian obelisk, this Dominican church was built *sopra* (over) a pre-Christian temple of Minerva. Before stepping in, notice the high-water marks on the wall (right of door). Inside you'll see that the lower parts of the frescoes were lost to floods.

(After the last great flood, in 1870, Rome built the present embankments, finally breaking the spirit of the Tiber River.)

Rome was at its low ebb, almost a ghost town, through much of the Gothic period. Little was built during this time (and much of what was built was redone Baroque). This church is a refreshing exception.

St. Catherine's body lies under the altar (her head is in Siena). In the 1300s, she convinced the pope to return from France to Rome, thus saving Italy from untold chaos.

Left of the altar stands a little-known Michelangelo statue, *Christ Bearing the Cross*. Michelangelo gave Jesus an athlete's or warrior's body (a striking contrast to the more docile Christ of medieval art) but left the face to one of his pupils. Fra Angelico's simple tomb is farther to the left, on the way to the back door. Before leaving, head over to the right (south transept), pop in a L500 coin for light, and enjoy a fine Filippo Lippi fresco showing scenes from the life of St. Thomas Aquinas.

Exit the church via its rear door (behind the Michelangelo statue), walk down Fra Angelico lane (spy any artisans at work), turn left, and walk to the next square. On your right you'll find the **Chiesa di St. Ignazio** church, a riot of Baroque illusions. Study the fresco over the door and the ceiling in the back of the nave. Then stand on the yellow disk on the floor between the two stars. Look at the central (black) dome. Keeping your eyes on the dome, walk under and past it. Church building project runs out of money? Hire a painter to paint a fake, flat dome. (Both churches open early, take a siesta—Santa Maria sopra Minerva closes at 12:00, St. Ignazio at 12:30—reopen around 15:30, and close at 19:00. Modest dress recommended.)

A few blocks away, back across Corso Vittorio Emanuele, is the rich and Baroque **Gesu Church**, headquarters of the Jesuits in Rome. The Jesuits powered the Church's Counter-Reformation. While Protestants were teaching that all roads to heaven didn't pass through Rome, the Baroque churches of the late 1500s were painted with spiritual road maps that said they did.

Walk out the Gesu Church and two blocks down **Corso V. Emanuele** to the **Sacred Area** (Largo Argentina), an excavated square facing the boulevard, about four blocks south of the Pantheon. Walk around this square, looking into the pit at some of Rome's oldest ruins. Caesar was assassinated here. Today this is a refuge for some 250 cats, cared for by volunteers. You'll see them (and their refuge) at the far (west) side of the square.

Sights—Near the Train Station

These sights are within a three- to ten-minute walk northwest of the train station. By Metro, use the Piazza Repubblica stop for all of these sights except the National Museum (Metro: Termini).

▲▲▲**National Museum of Rome in Palazzo Massimo**—
Rome's National Museum houses the greatest collection of ancient Roman art I've seen anywhere. The ground floor is a historic yearbook of marble statues from the second century B.C. to the second century A.D., with rare Greek originals.

The first floor is peopled by statuary from the first through fourth centuries A.D. The second floor (which requires an appointment) offers an intimate peek into Roman domestic life 2,000 years ago through exquisite mosaics and delightful garden paintings from high-society houses. The decor, designed to create a public image, is more than simply decoration. Finally, descend into the basement (where you can use a free audio guide) to see the mummy of an eight-year-old girl, fine gold jewelry, dice, an abacus, and vault doors leading into the best coin collection in Europe, with fancy magnifying glasses maneuvering you through cases of coins from ancient Rome to modern times (L12,000, daily 9:00–19:45, tel. 06-481-5576, 2nd floor can be visited only with escort, get time for 45-minute tour upon arrival, not possible to reserve in advance, Metro: Termini).

Baths of Diocletian—Around A.D. 300 Emperor Diocletian built the largest baths in Rome. This sprawling meeting place, with baths and schmoozing spaces to accommodate 3,000 bathers at a time, was a big deal in ancient Rome. While most of it is still closed, two sections—both facing Piazza della Repubblica—are open and worth a visit: the Octagonal Hall and the Church of St. Mary of the Angels and Martyrs.

▲▲**Octagonal Hall**—The Aula Ottagona or Rotunda of Diocletian was a private gymnasium in the Baths of Diocletian. Built around A.D. 300, these functioned until 537, when the barbarians cut Rome's aqueducts. The floor would have been 20 feet lower (look down the window in the center of the room). The graceful iron grid supported the canopy of a 1928 planetarium. Today, the hall's a gallery, showing off fine bronze and marble statues—the kind that would have decorated the baths of imperial Rome. Most are Roman copies of Greek originals... gods, atheletes, portrait busts. Two merit a close look: the *Defeated Boxer* (first century B.C., Greek and textbook Hellenistic) and the *Roman Aristocrat*. The aristocrat's face is older than the body. This cat-bronze statue is typical of the day: Take a body modeled on Alexander the Great and pop on a portrait bust. (Free, Tue–Sat 9:00–14:00, Sun 9:00–13:00, closed Mon.)

▲**Church of St. Mary of the Angels and Martyrs (Santa Maria degli Angeli e dei Martiri)**—From Piazza della Repubblica step through the Roman wall into what was the great central hall of the baths and is now a church (since the 16th century), designed by Michelangelo. When the church entrance was moved to Piazza Repubblica, the church was reoriented 90 degrees, turning the nave into long transepts and the transepts into a short nave. The

12 red granite columns still stand in their ancient positions. The classical floor was 15 feet lower. Project the walls down and imagine the soaring shape of the Roman vaults.

▲**Santa Maria Della Vittoria**—This church houses Bernini's statue of a swooning *St. Theresa in Ecstasy* (free, daily 6:30–11:30, 16:30–19:00, Largo Susanna, about 5 blocks northwest of the train station, Metro: Repubblica).

Sights—North Rome

▲**Villa Borghese**—Rome's unkempt "Central Park" is great for people watching (plenty of modern-day Romeos and Juliets). Take a row on the lake or visit its fine museums.

▲▲▲**Borghese Gallery**—This private museum, filling a cardinal's mansion in the park, is newly restored and offers one of Europe's most sumptuous art experiences. Because of the gallery's slick mandatory reservation system, you'll enjoy its collection of world-class Baroque sculpture, including Bernini's *David* and his exciting statue of Apollo chasing Daphne, as well as paintings by Caravaggio, Raphael, Titian, and Rubens, without any crowds.

The essence of the collection is the connection of the Renaissance with the classical world. Notice the second-century Roman reliefs with Michelangelo-designed panels above either end of the portico as you enter. The villa was built in the early 17th century by the great art collector Cardinal Borghese, who wanted to prove that the glories of ancient Rome were matched by the Renaissance.

In the main entry hall, opposite the door, notice the thrilling relief of the horse falling (first century A.D., Greek). Pietro Bernini, father of the famous Bernini, completed the scene by adding the rider.

Each room seems to feature a Baroque masterpiece. The best of all is in Room 3: Bernini's Apollo chasing Daphne. It's the perfect Baroque subject—capturing a thrilling, action-filled moment. In the mythological story Apollo races after Daphne. Just as he's about to reach her, she turns into a tree. As her toes turn to roots and branches spring from her fingers, Apollo is in for one rude surprise. Walk slowly around. It's more air than stone.

Cost, Hours, and Reservations: L12,000, Tue–Fri 9:00–21:00, Sat 9:00–23:30, Sun 9:00–20:00, closed Mon. Admission is limited to 360 people every two hours (entry times: 9:00, 11:00, 13:00, 15:00, 17:00, 19:00, Jun–Sept the museum may stay open until 23:30). You can reserve guided English tours (L8,000, at 11:10 and 15:10), with your entry reservation. Reservations are easy to get in English over the Internet (www.ticketeria.it) or by phone (dial 06-32810; if you get a recording, English follows the Italian, Mon–Fri 9:00–19:00, Sat 9:00–13:00). Appointments at 11:00 and on weekends book up first. You'll be given a time and a claim number. While you'll be advised to come 30 to 60 minutes early, you can arrive a few minutes beforehand. Just don't be late, as no-show tickets are given to standbys. The CD-wand audio tour is excellent (L8,000). No photos are allowed. For general info, call 06-854-8577.

Visits are strictly limited to the two-hour window on your ticket. Do the first floor first but leave yourself 30 minutes—maximum time allowed—for the paintings of the pinacoteca on the top floor (to get to the pinacoteca, exit the first floor, go outside and down to the basement—the entry is opposite café and shop). Visit the fine bookshop and cafeteria outside your two-hour entry window.

If you don't have a reservation, show up and get on the waiting list. No-shows are released a few minutes after the top of the hour. Generally out of 360 reservations, a few fail to show (but more than a few may be waiting to grab them).

▲**Cappuccin Crypt**—If you want bones, this is it. It's below the church Santa Maria della Immaculata Concezione on Via Veneto, just off Piazza Barberini. The bones of over 4,000 monks who died between 1528 and 1870 are in the basement, all artistically arranged for the delight—or disgust—of the always-wide-eyed visitor. The soil in the crypt was brought from Jerusalem 400 years ago, and the monastic message on the wall explains that this is more than just a macabre exercise. Pick up a few of Rome's most interesting postcards (donation, Fri–Wed 9:00–12:00, 15:00–18:00, closed Thu, Metro: Barberini). A painting of St. Francis by Caravaggio is upstairs. Just up the street you'll find the American embassy, Federal Express, and fancy Via Veneto cafés filled with the poor and envious looking for the rich and famous.

Sights—Near the Vatican

Castel Sant' Angelo—Built as a tomb for Emperor Hadrian; used through the Middle Ages as a castle, prison, and place of last refuge for popes under attack; and a museum today, this giant pile of ancient bricks is packed with history (L10,000, Tue–Fri 9:00–21:00, Sat 9:00–24:00, Sun 9:00–20:00, closed Mon, Metro: Lepanto, or bus #64, #80, #87, #280 or #492, near Vatican City, tel. 06-681-9111).

Sights—Vatican City

This tiny independent country of just over 100 acres, contained entirely within Rome, has its own postal system, armed guards, helipad, mini–train station, and radio station (KPOP). Politically powerful, the Vatican is the religious capital of 800 million Roman Catholics. If you're not one already, become a Catholic for your visit. A helpful tourist office is just to the left of St. Peter's Basilica (Mon–Sat 8:30–19:00, closed Sun, tel. 06-6988-4466, Vatican switchboard tel. 06-6982, www.vatican.va). Telephone the Vatican TI if you're interested in their sporadic but good tours of the Vatican grounds or the church interior or the pope's schedule

Italy

> ## Holy Year at the Vatican
>
> At midnight on Christmas Eve, 1999, the pope hit the Holy Door with a silver hammer, symbolically opening it and kicking off the Holy Year. The door stays open throughout the year 2000, which starts and ends with all the world's Catholic churches ringing their bells. The pope will be in Rome all year, except for a short trip to the Holy Land. Each evening (God willing) he'll lead a prayer and bless the pilgrims on St. Peter's Square. Among the many Church festivities planned, the biggies are June 29 (St. Peter's Feast Day, when 250,000 will pack Piazza San Pietro) and August 19 (the start of a weeklong Youth Jubilee, when 2 million young pilgrims gather to pray).
>
> The Vatican is ready for the crowds. A new Metro stop drops visitors closer to the Vatican Museum; the scaffolding recently came off of St. Peter's, revealing a pristine and powerful facade; the Vatican Museum has a new entrance to accommodate larger crowds; and the Vatican's Web site (www.vatican.va) explains more details.

(see below). If you don't care to see the pope, minimize crowd problems by avoiding these times.

The shuttle bus between St. Peter's and the Vatican Museum may begin running again (the stop is outside St. Peter's TI, to the left as you face the church). These little buses save you a 15-minute walk around the wall, give you a pleasant peek at the garden-filled Vatican grounds, and allow you to bypass the line outside the Vatican Museum. When running, the service costs L2,000 (2/hrly, 8:45–13:45, or 12:45 when museum closes early). The neighborhood's new Metro stop, Cipro–Musei Vaticani, is closer to the Vatican Museum, while the Ottaviano stop is closer to St. Peter's.

▲▲▲**St. Peter's Basilica**—There is no doubt: This is the richest and most impressive church on earth. To call it vast is like calling God smart. Marks on the floor show where the next-largest churches would fit if they were put inside. The ornamental cherubs would dwarf a large man. Birds roost inside, and thousands of people wander about, heads craned heavenward, hardly noticing each other. Don't miss Michelangelo's *Pietà* (behind bullet-proof glass) to the right of the entrance. Bernini's altar work and seven-story-tall bronze canopy (*baldacchino*) are brilliant.

For a quick self-guided walk through the basilica, follow these points (see map on page 429):

1. The atrium is larger than most churches. Notice the

St. Peter's Basilica

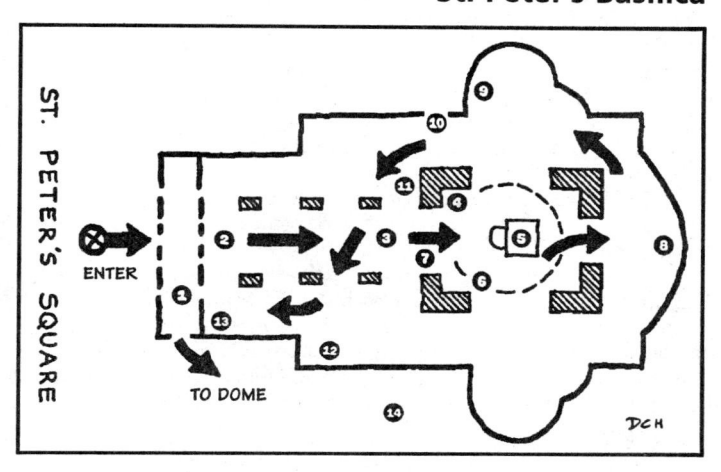

historic doors (the Holy Door, on the right, is open throughout the special year 2000—see point 13 below). Guided tours depart from the desk nearby.

2. The purple circular porphyry stone marks the site of Charlemagne's coronation in A.D. 800 (in the first St. Peter's church that stood on this site). From here get a sense of the immensity of the church, which can accommodate 95,000 worshipers standing on its six acres.

3. Michelangelo planned a Greek-cross floor plan rather than the Latin cross standard in medieval churches. A Greek cross, symbolizing the perfection of God, and by association the goodness of man, was important to the humanist Michelangelo. But accommodating large crowds was important to the Church in the fancy Baroque age, which followed Michelangelo, so the original nave length was doubled. Stand halfway up the nave and imagine the stubbier design Michelangelo had in mind.

4. View the magnificent dome from the statue of St. Andrew. See the vision of heaven above the windows: Jesus, Mary, a ring of saints, rings of angels, and, on the very top, God the Father.

5. The main altar sits directly over St. Peter's tomb and under Bernini's 70-foot-tall bronze canopy.

6. The stairs lead down to the crypt foundation, chapels, and tombs of popes. (Do this last—it leads you out of the church.)

7. The statue of St. Peter, with an irresistibly kissable toe, is one of the few pieces of art that predate this church. It adorned the first St. Peter's church.

8. St. Peter's throne and Bernini's star-burst dove window is the site of a daily Mass (Mon–Sat at 17:00, Sun at 17:45).

9. St. Peter was crucified here when this location was simply "the Vatican Hill." The obelisk now standing in the center of St. Peter's square marked the center of a Roman racecourse long before a church stood here.

10. For most, the treasury (in the sacristy) is not worth the admission.

11. The church is filled with mosaics, not paintings. Notice the mosaic version of Raphael's *Transfiguration*.

12. Blessed Sacrament Chapel.

13. Michelangelo sculpted his *Pietà* when he was 24 years old. A pietà is a work showing Mary with the dead body of Christ taken down from the cross. Michelangelo's mastery of the body is obvious in this powerfully beautiful masterpiece. Jesus is believably dead, and Mary, the eternally youthful "handmaiden" of the Lord, still accepts God's will... even if it means giving up her son.

The Holy Door (just to the right of the *Pietà*), usually bricked shut, is open for the year 2000, symbolizing the "Jubilee Year." Every 25 years the Church celebrates this especially festive year derived from the Old Testament idea of the Jubilee Year (originally every 50 years), which encourages new beginnings and the forgiveness of sins and debts. In this particularly monumental Jubilee Year, the pope is tirelessly calling for the World Bank and the world's rich countries to usher in the new millennium by forgiving or relieving the crippling debt burden that keeps much of the Third World in squalor (see end of this book for details).

14. An elevator leads to the roof and the stairway up the dome. The dome, Michelangelo's last work, is (you guessed it) the biggest anywhere. Taller than a football field is long, it's well worth the sweaty climb for a great view of Rome, the Vatican grounds, and the inside of the basilica—particularly heavenly while there is singing. Look around—Rome has no modern skyline. No building is allowed to exceed the height of St. Peter's. The elevator takes you to the rooftop of the nave. From there a few steps bring you to a balcony at the base of the dome looking down into the church interior. After that the one-way 300-step climb (for some people claustrophobic) to the cupola begins. The rooftop level (below the dome) has a gift shop, WC, drinking fountain, and a commanding view (L8,000 elevator, allow an hour to go up and down, May–Sept daily 8:30–19:00, Oct–Apr daily 8:30–18:00, ticket booth closes a half hour earlier).

The church strictly enforces its dress code. Dress modestly—a dress or long pants, shoulders covered (men and women). You are usually required to check any bags at a free cloakroom near the entry.

Hours: St. Peter's is open daily May through September from

7:00 to 19:00, until 18:00 October through April (ticket booth to treasury closes 1 hour earlier). All are welcome to join in the hour-long Mass at the front altar (Mon-Sat at 17:00, Sun at 17:45).

The church is particularly moving at 7:00, while tourism is still sleeping. Volunteers who want you to understand and appreciate St. Peter's give free 90-minute "Pilgrim Service" tours in English, usually at 10:00 and 12:30; these are generally excellent but non-Christians can find them preachy. Check for the day's schedule at the desk just after the dress-code check as you're entering. Seeing the *Pietà* is neat; understanding it is divine.

▲▲▲Vatican Museum—Too often the immense Vatican Museum is treated as an obstacle course, with four nagging miles of displays separating the tourist from the Sistine Chapel. Even without the Sistine, this is one of Europe's top three or four houses of art. It can be exhausting, so plan your visit carefully, focusing on a few themes. Allow two hours for a quick visit, three or four for time to enjoy it. The museum has a nearly-impossible-not-to-follow one-way system (although for the rushed visitor, the museum does clearly mark out 4 color-coded visits of different lengths—A is shortest, D longest).

You'll start, as civilization did, in Egypt and Mesopotamia. Next, the Pio Clementino collection features Greek and Roman statues. Decorating its courtyard are some of the best Greek and Roman statues in captivity, including the *Laocoön* group (1st century B.C., Hellenistic) and the *Apollo Belvedere* (a 2nd-century Roman copy of a Greek original). The centerpiece of the next hall is the *Belvedere Torso* (just a 2,000-year-old torso, but one that had a great impact on the art of Michelangelo). Finishing off the classical statuary are two fine fourth-century porphyry sarcophagi; these royal purple tombs hold the remains of Constantine's mother and daughter. Crafted in Egypt at a time when a declining Rome was unable to do such fine work, the details are fun to study.

After long halls of tapestries, old maps, broken penises, and fig leaves, you'll come to what most people are looking for: the Raphael *stanza*, or rooms, and Michelangelo's Sistine Chapel.

These outstanding works are frescoes. A fresco (meaning "fresh" in Italian) is technically not a painting. The color is mixed into wet plaster, and, when the plaster dries, the painting is actually part of the wall. This is a durable but difficult medium, requiring speed and accuracy as the work is built slowly, one patch at a time.

After fancy rooms illustrating the "Immaculate Conception of Mary" (a hard-to-sell, 19th-century Vatican doctrine) and the triumph of Constantine (with divine guidance, which led to his conversion to Christianity), you enter the first room completely done by Raphael and find the newly restored *School of Athens*. This is remarkable for its blatant pre-Christian classical orientation wallpapering the apartments of Pope Julius II. Raphael honors the

Vatican City, St. Peter's, and the Museum

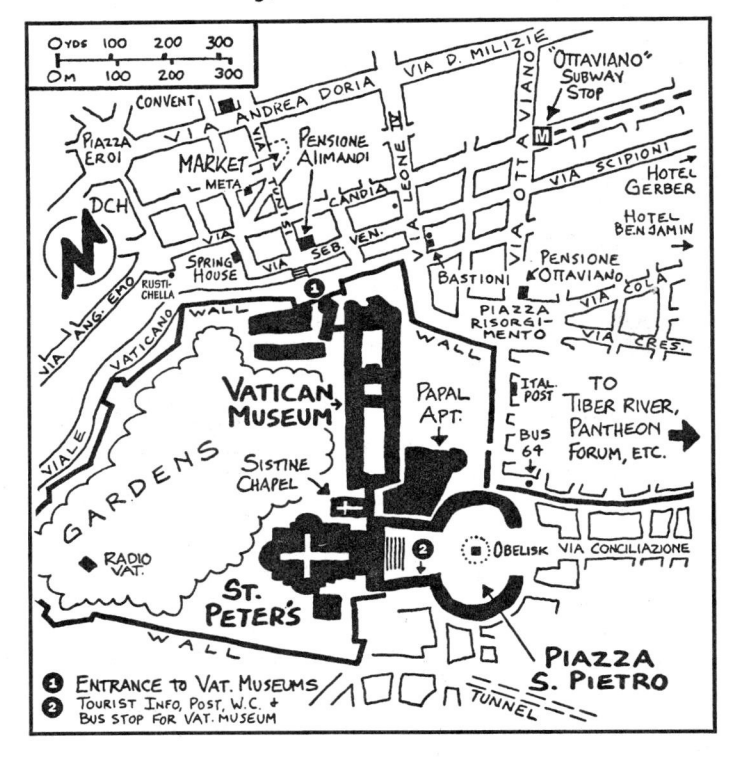

great pre-Christian thinkers—Aristotle, Plato, and company—who are portrayed as the leading artists of Raphael's day. The bearded figure of Plato is Leonardo da Vinci. Diogenes, history's first hippie, sprawls alone in bright blue on the stairs, while Michelangelo broods in the foreground—supposedly added late. Apparently Raphael snuck a peek at the Sistine Chapel and decided that his arch competitor was so good he had to put their personal differences aside and include him in this tribute to the artists of his generation. Today's St. Peter's was under construction as Raphael was working. In the *School of Athens*, he gives us a sneak preview of the unfinished church.

Next (unless you detour through the refreshingly modern Catholic art section) is the brilliantly restored Sistine Chapel. The Sistine Chapel, the pope's personal chapel, is where, upon the death of the ruling pope, a new pope is elected. The College of

Cardinals meets here and votes four times a day until a two-thirds-plus-one majority is reached and a new pope is elected.

The Sistine is famous for Michelangelo's pictorial culmination of the Renaissance, showing the story of Creation, with a powerful God weaving in and out of each scene through that busy first week. This is an optimistic and positive expression of the High Renaissance and a stirring example of the artistic and theological maturity of the 33-year-old Michelangelo, who spent four years on this work.

Later, after the Reformation wars had begun and after the Catholic army of Spain had sacked the Vatican, the reeling Church began to fight back. As part of its Counter-Reformation, a much older Michelangelo was commissioned to paint the *Last Judgment* (behind the altar). Brilliantly restored, the message is as clear as the day Michelangelo finished it: Christ is returning, some will go to hell and some to heaven, and some will be saved by the power of the rosary.

In the recent and controversial restoration project, no paint was added. Centuries of dust, soot (from candles used for lighting and Mass), and glue (added to make the art shine) were removed, revealing the bright original colors of Michelangelo. Photos are allowed elsewhere in the museum (without a flash or tripod), but as part of the deal with the company who did the restoration, no photos are allowed in the Sistine Chapel.

From the Sistine, a long walk routes you back to the entrance. Here, you'll find the Vatican's small but fine collection of paintings—the Pinacoteca (with Raphael's *Transfiguration*, Leonardo's unfinished *St. Jerome*, and Caravaggio's *Deposition*)—a cafeteria, and the underrated early-Christian-art section before you exit via the souvenir shop.

Vatican Museum nitty-gritty: A new entryway has been designed to handle 2000 crowds. Museum admission costs L18,000 (Apr–mid-Jun and Sept–Oct: Mon–Fri 8:45–16:30, Sat 8:45–13:45, closed Sun, except last Sun of the month, when museum is free; the rest of the year it's open Mon–Sat 8:45–13:45. Last entry 45 minutes before closing. The Sistine Chapel closes 30 minutes before the rest of the museum. Closed May 1, Jun 29, Aug 15, Nov 1, Dec 8, and on church holidays. Tel. 06-6988-3333, www.vatican.va.)

The rentable CD-ROM tour (L8,000) is a great new system, letting you dial whichever piece of art you'd like commentary on as you come across numbered pieces in the museum. It offers a fine coverage of the Raphael rooms and Michelangelo's Sistine masterpiece.

A small door at the rear of the Sistine Chapel allows tour groups and speedy individuals (without CD-ROM tour) to escape directly to St. Peter's Basilica (ignore sign saying "Tour Groups

Only"). If you squirt out here, you're done with the museum. The Pinacoteca is the only important part left. Consider doing it at the start. Otherwise it's a 10-minute heel-to-toe slalom through tourists from the Sistine Chapel to the entry/exit.

The Vatican post, with an office in the museum and one on Piazza San Pietro (comfortable writing rooms, Mon–Fri 8:30–19:00, Sat 8:30–18:00), is more reliable than the Italian mail service. The stamps are a collectible bonus (Vatican stamps are good throughout Rome; Italian stamps are not good at the Vatican). The Vatican bank has sinful rates. The modern cafeteria is handy but comes with long lines and mediocre food.

To see the pope: During Holy Year, the pope will bless the crowds on Piazza San Pietro almost daily. In normal summers, the pope (when in town) reads a prayer and blesses the gathered masses from his library window overlooking Piazza San Pietro Sundays at noon and Wednesday mornings. In the winter this is done in the 7,000-seat Aula Paola VI Auditorium (free, Wed at 11:00, call 06-698-83273 for details and reservations). Smaller ceremonies celebrated by the pope require reservations. The weekly entertainment guide *Romanc'e* always has a "Seeing the Pope" section.

Self-Guided Walk of Rome

▲▲▲**Floodlit Rome Hike: Trastevere to the Spanish Steps**—
Rome can be grueling. But a fine way to enjoy this historian's rite of passage is an evening walk lacing together Rome's floodlit night spots. Fine urban spaces, real-life theater vignettes, sitting so close to a Bernini fountain that traffic noises evaporate, water flickering its mirror on the marble, jostling with local teenagers to see all the gelato flavors, enjoying lovers straddling more than the bench, jaywalking past flak-proof vested *polizia*, marveling at the ramshackle elegance that softens this brutal city for those who were born here and can imagine living nowhere else—these are the flavors of Rome best tasted after dark. This walk is about two miles long; for a shortcut, start at Campo de' Fiori.

Taxi or ride the bus (from Vatican area, #23; from Via Nazionale hotels, take #64, #70, #115, or #640 to Largo Argentina and then transfer to #8) to Trastevere, the colorful neighborhood across (*tras*) the Tiber (*tevere*) river. Trastevere offers the best look at medieval-village Rome. The action all marches to the chime of the church bells. Go there and wander. Wonder. Be a poet. This is Rome's Left Bank.

The proud neighborhood of **Trastevere** was long an independent working-class area. Now becoming trendy, high rents are driving out the source of so much color. Still, it's a great people scene, especially at night. Start your exploratory stroll at Piazza di Santa Maria in Trastevere. While today's fountain is 17th century, there's been a fountain here since Roman times.

Santa Maria in Trastevere, one of Rome's oldest churches, was made a basilica in the fourth century, when Christianity was legalized (free, daily 7:30–13:00, 15:00–19:00). It was the first church dedicated to the Virgin Mary. The portico (covered area just outside the door) is decorated with fascinating ancient fragments filled with early Christian symbolism. Most of what you see today dates from around the 12th century, but the granite columns come from an ancient Roman temple, and the ancient basilica floor plan (and ambience) survives. The 12th-century mosaics behind the altar are striking and notable for their portrayal of Mary—the first showing her at the throne with Jesus in Heaven. Look below the scenes from the life of Mary to see ahead-of-their-time paintings (by Cavallini, from 1300) that predate the Renaissance by 100 years.

Before leaving Trastevere, wander the back streets (if you're hungry, see "Eating," below). Then, from the church square (Piazza di Santa Maria), take Via del Moro to the river and cross on Ponte Sisto, a pedestrian bridge with a good view of St. Peter's dome. Continue straight ahead for one block. Take the first left, which leads down Via di Capo di Ferro through the scary and narrow darkness to Piazza Farnese, with its imposing Palazzo Farnese. Michelangelo contributed to the facade of this palace, now the French embassy. The fountains on the square feature huge one-piece granite hot tubs from the ancient Roman Baths of Caracalla.

One block from there (opposite the palace) is **Campo de' Fiori** (Field of Flowers), which is my favorite outdoor dining room after dark (see "Eating," below). The statue of Giordano Bruno, a heretic who was burned in 1600 for believing the world was round and not the center of the universe, marks the center of this great and colorful square. Bruno overlooks a busy produce market in the morning and strollers after dark. This neighborhood is still known for its free spirit. When the statue of Bruno was erected in 1889, local riots overcame Vatican protests against honoring a heretic. Bruno faces his executioner, the Vatican Chancellory (the big white building in the corner a bit to his right), while his pedestal reads: "And the flames rose up." The square is lined and surrounded by fun eateries. Bruno also faces La Carbonara, which gave birth to pasta carbonara. The Forno, next door, is a popular place for hot and tasty take-out *pizza bianco* (plain but spicy pizza bread).

If Bruno did a hop, step, and jump forward and turned right and marched 200 yards, he'd cross the busy Corso Vittorio Emanuele and find **Piazza Navona**. Rome's most interesting night scene features street music, artists, fire eaters, local Casanovas, ice cream, outdoor cafés (splurge-worthy if you've got time to sit and enjoy the human river of Italy), and fountains by Bernini, the father of Baroque art. The Tartufo "death by chocolate" ice cream (L5,500 to go, L12,000 at a table) made the Tre Scalini café (left of obelisk) world famous among connoisseurs of ice cream and chocolate alike. This oblong square is molded around the long-gone stadium of Domitian, an ancient chariot racetrack.

Leave Piazza Navona directly across from Tre Scalini café, go (east) past rose peddlers and palm readers, jog left around the guarded building, and follow the brown sign to the **Pantheon** straight down Via del Salvatore (cheap pizza place on left just before the Pantheon, easy WC at McDonald's). Sit for a while under the Pantheon's flood- and moonlit portico.

With your back to the Pantheon, head right, passing Bar Pantheon on your right. The Tazza d'Oro Casa del Caffè, one of Rome's top coffee shops, dates back to the days when this area was licensed to roast coffee beans. Look back at the fine view of the Pantheon from here.

With the coffee shop on your right, walk down Via degli Orfani to Piazza Capranica, with the big plain Florentine Renaissance-style Palazzo Capranica. Big shots, like the Capranica family, built stubby towers on their palaces—not for any military use...just to show off. Leave the piazza to the right of the palace, between the palace and the church. Via in Aquiro leads to a sixth-century B.C. Egyptian **obelisk** (taken as a trophy by Augustus after his victory in Egypt over Mark Antony and Cleopatra). Walk into the guarded square past the obelisk and face the huge parliament building. A short detour to the left (past Albergo National) brings you to some of Rome's best gelato. Gelateria Caffè Pasticceria Giolitti is cheap to go or elegant and splurge-worthy for a sit among classy locals (open daily until very late, your choice: cone or *bicchierini*—cup, Via Uffici del Vicario 40). Or head directly from the parliament into the next, even grander square.

Piazza Colonna features a huge second-century column honoring Marcus Aurelius. The big, important-looking palace is the prime minister's residence. Cross Via del Corso, Rome's noisy main drag, and jog right (around the Y-shaped shopping gallery from 1928) and head down Via dei Sabini to the roar of the water, light, and people of the Trevi fountain.

The **Trevi fountain** is an example of how Rome took full advantage of the abundance of water brought into the city by its great aqueducts. This watery Baroque avalanche was built in 1762 by a pope celebrating his reopening of the ancient aqueduct that powers it. Romantics toss two coins over their shoulder thinking it will give them a wish and assure their return to Rome. That may sound silly, but every year I go through this touristic ritual...and it actually seems to work.

Take some time to people watch (whisper a few breathy *bello*s or *bella*s) before leaving. Facing the fountain, go past it on the right down Via delle Stamperia to Via del Triton. Cross the busy street and continue to the Spanish Steps (ask, *"Dov'è Piazza di*

Spagna?"; doh-vay pee-aht-zah dee spahn-yah) a few blocks and thousands of dollars of shopping opportunities away.

The **Piazza di Spagna** (rhymes with "lasagna"), with the very popular Spanish Steps, got its name 300 years ago, when this was the site of the Spanish Embassy. It's been the hangout of many Romantics over the years (Keats, Wagner, Openshaw, Goethe, and others). The Boat Fountain at the foot of the steps, which was done by Bernini's father, Pietro Bernini, is powered by an aqueduct. (All of Rome's fountains are aqueduct powered; their spurt is determined by the water pressure provided by the various aqueducts. This one, for instance, is much weaker than Trevi's gush.) This is a thriving night scene. Facing the steps, walk to your right about a block to tour one of the world's biggest and most lavish McDonald's. About a block on the other side of the steps is the Metro, which (usually until 23:30) will zip you home.

Sights—Away from the Center

▲▲**Ostia Antica**—Rome's ancient seaport, less than an hour from downtown, is the next best thing to Pompeii. Ostia had 80,000 people at the time of Christ, later became a ghost town, and is now excavated. Start at the 2,000-year-old theater, buy a map, explore the town, and finish with its fine little museum (note that museum closes at 14:00). To get there take the subway's B Line to the Piramide stop and then catch the Lido train to Ostia Antica (2/hrly), walk over the overpass, go straight to the end of that road, and follow the signs to (or ask for) "*scavi* Ostia Antica" (L8,000, Tue–Sun 9:00 until an hour before sunset, closed Mon, museum closes at 14:00, tel. 06-5635-8099). Just beyond is Rome's filthy beach (*lido*).

E.U.R.—In the late 1930s, Italy's dictator, Mussolini, planned an international exhibition to show off the wonders of his fascist society. But the "wonders of fascism" brought us World War II first, and Il Duce's celebration never happened. Italy made the best of the unfinished mega-project, finishing it in the 1950s to house government offices and big obscure museums. If Hitler and Mussolini had won the war, our world might look like E.U.R. (pronounced "ai-oor"). From the Magliana subway stop, stairs lead uphill to E.U.R.'s skyscraper, the blocky **Palace of the Civilization of Labor** (Palazzo del Civilta del Lavoro). With its giant, no-questions-asked, patriotic statues and its black-and-white simplicity, this is the essence of fascist architecture. It's understandably nicknamed the "Square Colosseum."

The **Museum of Roman Civilization** (Museo della Civilta Romana) fills 59 rooms with casts and models illustrating the greatness of classical Rome. It has a scrolled-out version of Trajan's Column, but the highlight is the 1/250 scale model of Constantine's Rom (L5,000, Tue–Sat 9:00–19:00, Sun 9:00–13:30, closed Mon, Piazza G. Agnelli, Metro: E.U.R. Fermi, tel. 06-592-6041).

Italy

Sleeping in Rome
(L1,900 = about $1)
Sleep Code: **S** = Single, **D** = Double/Twin, **T** = Triple, **Q** = Quad, **b** = bathroom, **t** = toilet only, **s** = shower only, **CC** = Credit Card (Visa, MasterCard, Amex), **SE** = Speaks English, **NSE** = No English. Breakfast is normally included in the expensive places.

The absolute cheapest doubles in Rome are L70,000, without shower or breakfast. You'll pay L30,000 in a backpacker-filled dorm or hostel. A nicer hotel (L240,000 with a bathroom and air-conditioning) provides an oasis and refuge, making it easier to enjoy this intense and grinding city. If you're going door to door, prices are soft—so bargain. Built into a hotel's official price list is a kickback for a room-finding service or agency; if you're coming direct, they pay no kickback and may lower the price for you. Many hotels have high-season (mid-Mar–Jun, Sept–Oct) and low-season prices. Easter and September are most crowded and expensive. Room rates are lowest in sweltering August. Most of my recommended hotels are small, with huge, murky entrances that make you feel like a Q-Tip in a gas station. English works in all but the cheapest places. Traffic in Rome roars. My challenge has been to find friendly places on quiet streets. With the recent arrival of double-paned windows and air-conditioning, night noise is not the problem it was. Even so, light sleepers should always ask for a *tranquillo* room. Many prices here are promised only to people who show this book, pay in lire (no credit cards), and come direct without using a room-finding service. On Easter, April 25, and May 1 the entire city gets booked up.

If you need help, Scala Reale, the company that runs tours (see "Tours of Rome," above), can help you find short-term accommodations in private apartments (toll-free number in U.S.: 888/467-1986, Italy tel. 06-445-1477, fax 06-4470-0898, www.scalareale.org).

Sleeping on Via Firenze

I generally stay on Via Firenze because it's tranquil, safe, handy, and central. It's a short walk from the central train station and airport shuttle and two blocks beyond the Piazza della Repubblica and TI. The defense ministry is nearby, and you've got heavily armed guards all night. Virtually all the orange buses that rumble down Via Nazionale (#64, #70, #115, #640) take you to Piazza Venezia (Forum) and Largo Argentina (Pantheon). From Largo Argentina, #8 goes to Trastevere (first stop after crossing the river), and #64 (jammed with people and thieves) continues to the Vatican.

Hotel Oceania is a peaceful slice of air-conditioned heaven. This nine-room manor house–type hotel is spacious and quiet, with newly renovated and spotless rooms, run by a pleasant father-and-son team (Sb-L190,000, Db-L240,000, Tb-L300,000, Qb-L355,000, these prices through 2000 with this book only, additional 20 percent off in Aug and winter, breakfast included, phones, English newspaper, CC:VMA, Via Firenze 38, 00184 Roma, tel. 06-482-4696, fax 06-488-5586, www.hoteloceania.it, e-mail: hoceania@tin.it, son Stefano SE, dad Armando serves world-famous coffee).

Hotel Aberdeen is classier and more professional for about the same price. It has minibars, phones, and showers in its 36 modern, air-conditioned, and smoke-free rooms; includes a fine breakfast buffet; and is warmly run by Annamaria, with support from her cousins Sabrina and Cinzia, and trusty Reda riding shotgun after dark (Sb-L180,000, Db-L240,000, Tb-L280,000, prices through 2000 with this book only, L50,000 less per room in Aug and winter, CC:VMA, garage-L40,000, Via Firenze 48, 00184 Roma, tel. 06-482-3920, fax 06-482-1092, e-mail: hotel.aberdeen@travel.it, SE).

Residence Adler, with its wide halls, garden patio, and eight quiet, elegant, and air-conditioned rooms in a great locale, is another good deal. It's run the old-fashioned way by a charming family (Db-L200,000, Tb-L280,000, Qb-L340,000, includes breakfast, prices through 2000 with this book only, CC:VMA, additional 5 percent off if you pay cash, elevator, Via Modena 5, 00184 Roma, tel. 06-484-466, fax 06-488-0940, NSE).

Here are three basic and sleepable hotels each wonderfully located on Via Firenze: **Hotel Nardizzi Americana** has a backpacker-friendly roof terrace and decent rooms. But it won't win any cleanliness awards, and traffic noise can be a problem in the front rooms (Sb-L150,000, Db-L200,000, Tb-L240,000, Qb-L260,000, prices through 2000 with this book only, includes breakfast, discounts for off-season and long stays, CC:VMA, additional 10 percent off with cash, air-con, elevator, drinks available evenings, Via Firenze 38, 00184 Roma, tel. 06-488-0368, fax 06-488-0035, SE). **Hotel Seiler** is a quiet, serviceable place with 30 basic rooms (Sb-L190,000, Db-L250,000, Tb-L300,000, CC:VMA, fans, elevator, Via Firenze 48, tel. 06-485550, fax 06-4880688, e-mail: acropoli@rdn.it, Silvio SE). **Hotel Texas Seven Hills**, a stark institutional throwback to the 1960s, rents 18 quiet but depressing rooms (D-L160,000, Db-L200,000, CC:VMA, often soft prices, Via Firenze 47, elevator, tel. 06-481-4082, fax 06-481-4079, e-mail: what's that?, NSE).

Sleeping between Via Nazionale and Basilica Santa Maria Maggiore

Hotel Rex is a business-class Art Deco fortress—a quiet, plain, and stately four-star place with all the comforts but too many sconces (48 rooms, Sb-L300,000, Db-L400,000, Tb-L500,000, prices through 2000 with this book only, CC:VMA, elevator, air-con, some smoke-free rooms, just off Via Nazionale at Via Torino 149, tel. 06-482-4828, fax 06-488-2743, e-mail: hotel.rex@alfanet.it, SE).

Hotel Britannia stands like a marble fruitcake, offering all the comforts in tight quarters on a quiet and safe-feeling street. Lushly renovated with over-the-top classical motifs, its 32 air-conditioned rooms are small but comfortable, with bright, modern bathrooms (Db-L410,000 in May–Jun and Sept–Oct, Db-L360,000 the rest of the year, even less in Aug, CC:VMA, extra bed-L90,000, children up to 10 stow away for free, baby-sitting service, free parking, Via Napoli 64, tel. 06-488-3153, fax 06-488-2343, e-mail: britannia @venere.it).

Hotel Sonya is a small, family-run, but impersonal place with a dozen comfortable, well-equipped rooms, a great location, and low prices; reserve well in advance (Db-L200,000, Tb-L240,000, Qb-L290,000, CC:VMA, air-con, elevator, facing the Opera at Via Viminale 58, tel. 06-481-9911, fax 06-488-5678, Francesca SE).

Hotel Pensione Italia, in a busy, interesting, handy locale and placed safely on a quiet street next to the Ministry of the Interior, is comfortable, airy, bright, clean, and thoughtfully run by English-speaking Andrea and Abdul (31 rooms, Sb-L130,000, Db-L180,000, Tb-L240,000, Qb-L280,000, includes breakfast, prices through 2000 with this book and cash only, all rooms 20 percent off in Aug and winter, elevator, air-con for L15,000 extra, Via Venezia 18, just off Via Nazionale, tel. 06-482-8355, fax 06-474-5550, e-mail: hitalia@pronet.it). Their singles are all on the quiet courtyard, and the nine annex rooms across the street are a cut above the rest.

Hotel Cortina rents 14 simple, comfortable, air-conditioned rooms for a decent price (Db-L240,000, includes breakfast, CC:VMA, 10 percent discount with this book and cash, Via Nazionale 18, 00184 Roma, tel. 06-481-9794, fax 06-481-9220, e-mail: hotelcortina@pronet.it, John Carlo and Angelo SE).

YWCA Casa Per Studentesse accepts men and women. It's an institutional place filled with white-uniformed maids, more-colorful Third World travelers, and 75 single beds. It's closed from midnight to 7:00 in the morning; the locked doors with no way out trouble some travelers (L40,000 per person in 3- and 4-bed rooms, S-L60,000, Sb-L80,000, D-L100,000, Db-L120,000, includes breakfast except on Sun, Via C. Balbo 4, 00184 Roma, tel. 06-488-0460, fax 06-487-1028). The YWCA faces a great little street market.

Suore di Santa Elisabetta is a heavenly Polish-run convent booked long in advance, but it's a great value (Sb-L63,000, Db-L115,000, Tb-L148,000, Qb-L180,000, includes breakfast, CC:VM, elevator, fine roof terrace, a block south of Santa Maria Maggiore at Via dell' Omata 9, tel. 06-488-8271, fax 06-488-4066).

Hotel Montreal is a bright, solid, business-class place on a big street a block in front of Santa Maria Maggiore (Db-L220,000, CC:VMA, 18 of its 22 rooms have air-con, a block from Metro: Vittorio at Via Carlo Alberto 4, 00185 Roma, tel. 06-445-7797, fax 06-446-5522, www.venere.it, e-mail: info@hotelmontrealroma.com).

Rome

Sleeping Cheap, Northeast of the Station
The cheapest hotels in town are northeast of the train station. Some travelers feel this area is weird and spooky after dark. With your back to the train tracks, turn right and walk two blocks out of the station.

Hotel Fenicia rents 11 comfortable, well-equipped rooms at a fine price. Some are on fourth floor—quiet, but there's no elevator (Sb-L80,000, Db-L130,000, Tb-L180,000, prices through 2000 with this book only, air-con-L20,000/day, breakfast-L10,000, CC:VMA, 2 blocks from station at Via Milazzo 20, tel. & fax 06-490-342, Anna and Georgio).

Hotel Magic, a tiny place run by a mother-daughter team, is clean and high enough off the road to escape the traffic noise (10 rooms, Sb-L90,000, Db-L130,000, Tb-L170,000, prices through 2000 with this book only, less in Aug, CC:VM, no breakfast, thin walls, midnight curfew, Via Milazzo 20, 3rd floor, 00185 Roma, tel. & fax 06-495-9880, little English spoken, reportedly unreliable for reservations).

Albergo Sileo is a shiny-chandeliered, 10-room place with an elegant touch that has a contract to house train conductors who work the night shift. With maids doing double time, they offer rooms from 19:00 to 9:00 only. If you can handle this, it's a great value. During the day they store your luggage, and though you won't have access to a room, you're welcome to hang out in their lobby or bar (D-L75,000, Db-L90,000, Tb-L115,000, breakfast extra, elevator, Via Magenta 39, tel. & fax 06-445-0246, Alessandro and Maria Savioli NSE).

Fawlty Towers is a backpacker-type place well run by the Aussies from Enjoy Rome. It's young, hip, and English-speaking, with a rooftop terrace, lots of information, and no curfew (shared co-ed 4-bed dorms for L30,000 per bed, S-L60,000, Sb-L75,000, D-L90,000, Ds-L100,000, Db-L120,000, Ts-L130,000, Tb-L145,000, reservations by credit card but pay in cash, dorm beds reserved only to those calling at 21:00 the night before, elevator, Internet access, Via Magenta 39, tel. & fax 06-445-0374, e-mail: info@enjoyrome.com).

Sleeping near the Colosseum
(zip code: 00184)
One stop on the subway from the train station (to Metro: Cavour), these places are buried in a very Roman world of exhaust-stained medieval ambience. The handy *electrico* bus line #117 connects you with the sights.

Hotel Duca d'Alba is a tight and modern pastel-marble-hardwood place just half a block from the Metro station (Sb-L260,000, Db-L350,000, extra bed-L40,000, breakfast buffet, CC:VMA, air-con, Via Leonina 14, tel. 06-484-471, fax 06-488-4840, e-mail: duca.dalba@venere.it, SE).

Rome's Train Station Neighborhood

1. HOTEL OCEANIA & NARDIZZI
2. HOTEL ABERDEEN
3. RESIDENCE ADLER
4. HOTEL REX
5. HOTEL BRITTANIA
6. HOTEL SONYA
7. HOTEL PENSIONE ITALIA
8. HOTEL CORTINA
9. YMCA CASA STUDENTESSE
10. SUORE SANTA ELISABETTA
11. HOTEL MONTREAL
12. HOTEL FENICIA & MAGIC
13. ALBERGO SILEO & FAWLTY TOWERS
14. HOTEL DUCA D'ALBA
15. HOTEL GRIFO
16. SUORE DI SANT ANNA
17. SNACK BAR GASTRONOMIA
18. PASTICCERIA DAGNINO
19. HOSTARIA ROMANA
20. RISTORANTE GIOVANNI
21. GRILL TARGET PIZZA
22. EST EST EST PIZZERIA
23. RIST. CINESE INT'L.

Hotel Grifo has a homey but tangled floor plan, 20 simple, modern rooms, and a roof terrace. The double-paned windows don't quite keep out the Vespa noise (Db-L230,000, L210,000 in Jul–Aug, CC:VMA, elevator, air-con planned for 2000, 2 blocks off Via Cavour at Via del Boschetto 144, tel. 06-487 1395, fax 06-474 2323, e-mail: zuccale@freemail.it, son Alessandro SE).

Suore di Sant Anna was built for Ukrainian pilgrims. The sisters are sweet. It's clumsy and difficult (23:00 curfew), but once you're in, you've got a comfortable home in a classic Roman-village locale (Sb-L60,000, Db-L120,000, Tb-L180,000, includes breakfast, consider a monkish dinner for L26,000, off the corner of Via dei Serpenti and Via Baccina at Piazza Madonna dei Monti 3, Metro: Cavour, tel. 06-485-778, fax 06-487-1064).

Sleeping near Campo de' Fiori and Piazza Navona (zip code: 00186)

For hotel locations, see map on page 442.

Hotel Campo de' Fiori is ideal for wealthy bohemians who value centrality over peace and comfort. It's just off Campo de' Fiori and has an unreal rooftop terrace and rickety windows and furniture (D-L160,000, Db-L220,000, includes breakfast, CC:VM, lots of stairs and no elevator, Via del Biscione 6, tel. 06-6874886, fax 06-687-6003, SE). They also have apartments nearby that can house five or six people (L250,000 for 2 people, extra person-L50,000).

Albergo del Sole is impersonal and filled with German groups but well located (D-L150,000, small Db-L180,000, Db-L220,000, no breakfast, Via del Biscione 76, tel. 06-6880-6873, fax 06-689-3787, e-mail: sole@italyhotel.com).

Casa di Santa Brigida, also near the characteristic Campo de' Fiori, overlooks the elegant Piazza Farnese. With soft-spoken sisters gliding down polished hallways and pearly gates instead of doors, this lavish convent makes the exhaust-stained Roman tourist feel like he's died and gone to heaven. If you're unsure of your destiny (and don't need a double bed), this is worth the splurge (Sb-L125,000, Db-L250,000, 4 percent extra with CC, great-value dinners, roof garden, plush library, air-con, walk-in address: Monserrato 54, mailing address: Piazza Farnese 96, reserve long in advance, tel. 06-6889-2596, fax 06-6889-1573, www.brigidine.org, e-mail: brigida@mclink.it, many of the sisters are from India and speak English).

Piazza Navona: The **Hotel Navona**, a ramshackle 25-room hotel occupying an ancient building in a perfect locale a block off Piazza Navona, is a fine value (S-L90,000, D-L130,000, Db-L160,000, Db with air-con-L200,000, breakfast, family rooms, lots of student groups, Via dei Sediari 8, tel. 06-686-4203, fax 06-6880-3802, run by an Australian named Corry).

Hotel Nazionale, a four-star landmark, is a 16th-century palace sharing a well-policed square with the national parliament. Its 87 rooms are served by lush public spaces, fancy bars, and a uniformed staff. I think it's the only place with a revolving front door I've ever recommended, but if you want security, comfort and the heart of old Rome at your doorstep (the Pantheon is 3 blocks away, Rome's top gelateria is just around the corner), this is a worthy splurge. Its room furnishings are a bit tired, keeping the price out of orbit (Sb-L340,000, Db-L400,000–500,000, extra person-L100,000, fancier rooms and suites available for much more, CC:VMA, air-con, elevator, Piazza Montecitorio 131, tel. 06-695-001, fax 06-678-6677, www.nazionaleamontecitorio.it, e-mail: nazionale@micanet.it).

Sleeping "Three Stars" near the Vatican Museum
(zip code: 00192)

Hotel Alimandi is a good value, run by the friendly and entrepreneurial Alimandi brothers: Paolo, Enrico, Luigi, and Germano (35 rooms, Sb-L160,000, Db-L220,000, Tb-L260,000, 5 percent discount with this book and cash, CC:VMA, grand breakfast-L15,000 elevator, great roof garden, self-service washing machines, Internet access, pool table, parking-L30,000/day, down the stairs directly in front of Vatican Museum, Via Tunisi 8, near Metro: Cipro–Musei Vaticani, reserve by phone, no reply to fax means they are full, tel. 06-3972-6300, toll free in Italy tel. 800-12212, fax 06-3972-3943, www.lcnet.it/initaly/alimandi/hoteling.htm, e-mail: alimandi@tin.it, SE). They offer their guests free airport pickup and drop-off (saving you L80,000 if you were planning on taking a taxi), though you must reserve when you book your room and conform to their schedule (which can mean waiting). Maria Alimandi rents out three rooms in her apartment a 20-minute bus ride from the Vatican (Db-L140,000, see Web site above).

Hotel Spring House, offering fine rooms with balconies and refrigerators, has an impersonal staff. Confirm prices and mention this book ("superior" Db-L250,000, includes breakfast, 5 percent discount for cash payment, 15 percent discount Jul-Aug, simple doubles a bit cheaper, CC:VMA, air-con, elevator, parking-L25,000/day, Metro: Cipro–Musei Vaticani, Via Mocenigo 7, a block from Alimandi, tel. 06-3972-0948, fax 06-3972-1047, www.hotelspringhouse.com).

Hotel Gerber is sleek, modern, air-conditioned, businesslike, and set in a quiet residential area (27 rooms, S-L120,000, Sb-L180,000, Db-L235,000, Tb-L285,000, Qb-L330,000, 10 percent discount with this book, includes breakfast buffet, CC:VMA, 1 block from Lepanto subway stop, Via degli Scipioni 241, tel. 06-321-6485, fax 06-321-7048, Peter SE).

Eating in Rome

Romans spend their evenings eating rather than drinking, and the preferred activity is to simply enjoy a fine slow meal buried deep in the old city. Rome's a fun and cheap place to eat, with countless little eateries serving fine $20 meals. Tourists wander the streets just before midnight wondering, "Why did I eat so much?"

Eating in Trastevere

My best dinner tip is to go for Rome's Vespa street ambience and find your own place in Trastevere or on Campo de' Fiori (below). Guidebooks list Trastevere's famous places, but I'd wander the fascinating maze of streets near Piazza Santa Maria in Trastevere and find a mom-and-pop place with barely a menu. Check out the tiny streets north of the church. You might consider these places before making a choice:

For outdoor seating on romantic Piazza della Scala, check out **Taverna della Scala**, the local choice for pizza (closed Tue, tel. 06-581-4100), and **La Scala Restaurant**, chic and popular with Generation X Romans. Don't miss the fine little *gelateria* with oh-wow pistachio (north end of Piazza della Scala).

At **Taverna del Moro**, Tony scrambles—with a great antipasto table—to keep his happy eaters well fed and returning (but too much mayo on bruschetta, off Via del Moro at Vicolo del Cinque 36, tel. 06-580-9165). For a basic meal with lots of tourists, you can eat cheap at **Mario's** (Mon–Sat 19:00–24:00, closed Sun, 3 courses with wine and service for L18,000, Via del Moro 53, tel. 06-580-3809).

Ristorante Alle Fratte di Trastevere is lively and inexpensive (closed Tue, Via dell Fratte di Trastevere, tel. 06-583-5775). **La Cisterna**—bragging it's the oldest restaurant in Rome and has served the rich and famous—is more expensive but serves tasty food in a lively, pleasant setting (Via Della Cisterna 13, tel. 06-581-2543).

Eating near Campo de' Fiori

For the ultimate romantic square setting, eat at whichever place looks best on Campo de' Fiori. Circle the square, considering each place. **La Carbonara** claims to be the birthplace of pasta carbonara (closed Tue). Meals on small nearby streets are a better value but lack that Campo de' Fiori magic. Bars and pizzerias seem to be overwhelming the popular square. The **Taverna** or **Vineria** at numbers 16 and 15 offer good perches from which to people watch and nurse a glass of wine.

Nearby, on the more elegant and peaceful Piazza Farnese, **Ostaria Da Giovanni Ar Galletto** has a dressier local crowd, great outdoor seating, moderate prices, and fine food (closed Sun, tucked in corner of Piazza Farnese at #102, tel. 06-686-1714).

Dar Filettaro a Santa Barbara is a tradition for many Romans. This is basically a fish bar with paper tablecloths and cheap prices, and its grease-stained hurried waiters serve old-time favorites—fried cod fillets, a strange bitter *puntarelle* salad, and delightful anchovies with butter—to nostalgic locals (Mon–Sat 17:30–23:10, closed Sun, a block east of Campo de' Fiori, tumbling onto a tiny and atmospheric square, Largo dei Librari 88, tel. 06-686-4018).

Ristorante del Pallaro has no menu but plenty of return eaters. Paola Fazi, with a towel wrapped around her head turban-style, and her family serve up a five-course festival of typically Roman food for L33,000, including wine, coffee, and a wonderful mandarin liquor. Their slogan: "Here, you'll eat what we want to feed you." Look like Oliver asking for more soup and get seconds on the mandarin liqueur (Tue–Sun 12:00–15:30, 19:30–24:00, closed Mon, indoor/outdoor seating on quiet square, a block south of Corso Vittorio Emanuele down Largo del Chiavari to Largo del Pallaro 15, tel. 06-6880-1488).

Ristorante Grotte del Teatro di Pompeo, sitting atop an ancient theater, serves good food at fair prices with a smile (closed Mon, Via del Biscione 73, tel. 06-6880-3686).

For interesting bar munchies, try **Cul de Sac** on Piazza Pasquino (a block southwest of Piazza Navona). **L'Insalata Ricca**, a popular chain that specializes in hearty and healthy salads, is next door (Piazza Navona 72, tel. 06-6830-7881). Another branch is nearby and has more spacious outdoor seating (just off Corso Vittorio Emanuele on Largo del Chiavari).

Near the Pantheon, facing Largo Argentina, **Il Delfino** is a handy self-service cafeteria (daily 7:00–21:00, not cheap but fast). Across the side street, **Frullati Bar** sells refreshing fruity frappés. The *alimentari* (grocery store) on the Pantheon square will make you a sandwich for a temple-porch picnic.

Eating near Via Firenze and Via Nazionale Hotels

Snack Bar Gastronomia is a great local hole-in-the-wall for lunch or dinner (open until 20:00, closed Sun, really cheap hot meals dished up from under the glass counter, tap water with a smile, Via Firenze 34). There's an *alimentari* (grocery store) across the street.

Pasticceria Dagnino, popular for its top-quality Sicilian specialties—especially pastries and ice cream—is where those who work at my recommended hotels eat (daily 7:00–22:00, in Galleria Esedra off Via Torino, a block from hotels, tel. 06-481-8660). Their *arancino*—a rice, cheese, and ham ball—is a greasy Sicilian favorite. Direct the construction of your meal at the bar, pay for your trayful at the cashier, and climb upstairs, where you'll find the dancing Sicilian girls (free).

Hostaria Romana is a great place for traditional Roman cuisine. For an air-conditioned classy local favorite run by a jolly group of men who enjoy their work, eat here (closed Sun, midway between Trevi fountain and Piazza Barberini, Via del Boccaccio 1, at intersection with Via Rasella, no reservations needed before 20:00, tel. 06-474-5284). Go ahead and visit the antipasto bar in person to assemble your plate. They're happy to serve an *antipasti misto della casa* and pasta dinner. Take a hard look at their *Specialita Romane* list.

Ristorante da Giovanni is a serviceable, hardworking place feeding locals and travelers now for 50 years (L23,000 menu, Mon–Sat 12:00–15:00, 19:00–22:30, closed Sun, just off Via XX Septembre at Via Antonio Salandra 1, tel. 06-485-950).

Restaurant Grill Target Pizza is a modern, efficient place with a good antipasti buffet (L7,000 per plate) and a mix-and-match pasta and sauce menu and offers a fast alternative to the burger joints (daily 12:00–15:00, 18:00–23:00, air-con, Via Torino 33, tel. 06-474-0066).

Est Est Est Antica Pizzeria, with a traditional old-Roman ambience and quiet street-side tables outside, serves good pizza and crostini as well as heavier meals (Tue–Sun 19:00–24:00, closed Mon, 32 Via Genova, a block off Via Nazionale, tel. 06-4881107).

Ristorante Cinese Internazionale is your best neighborhood bet for Chinese (daily 18:00–23:00, inexpensive, no pasta, just off Via Nazionale behind Hotel Luxor at Via Agostino de Pretis 98, tel. 06-474-4064).

The **McDonald's** restaurants on Piazza della Repubblica (free piazza seating outside), Piazza Barberini, and Via Firenze offer air-conditioned interiors and salad bars.

Flann O'Brien Irish Pub is a great place for a quick light meal (pasta or something OTHER than pasta), fine Irish beer, and the most Italian crowd of all (daily 7:00–24:00, Via Nazionale 18, at intersection with Via Napoli, tel. 06-488-0418).

Eating near the Vatican Museum

Antonio's Hostaria dei Bastioni is tasty and friendly. It's conveniently located midway between your walk from St. Peter's to the Vatican Museum, with noisy street-side seating and a quiet interior (hot when hot—no air-con, Mon–Sat 12:00–15:00, 19:00–23:30, closed Sun, L10,000–12,000 pastas, L15,000 *secondi*, no cover charge, at corner of Vatican wall, Via Leone IV 29, tel. 06-3972-3034).

La Rustichella has a great and fresh antipasti buffet (L15,000, enough for a meal) and fine pasta dishes. Arrive when they open at 19:30 to avoid a line and have the pristine buffet to yourself (Tue–Sun 12:30–15:00, 19:30–23:00, closed Mon, near new Metro: Cipro–Musei Vaticani stop, opposite church at end of Via Candia,

Via Angelo Emo 1, tel. 06-3972-0649). Consider the fun and fruity **Gelateria Millennium** next door.

Avoid the restaurant pushers handing out flyers near the Vatican: bad food, expensive menu tricks. Viale Giulio Cesare is lined with cheap **Pizza Rustica** shops and other fun eateries, such as **Cipriani Self-Service Rosticcería** (closed Mon, pleasant outdoor seating, near Ottaviano subway stop, Viale Guilio Cesare 195).

Turn your nose loose in the wonderful **Via Andrea Doria** open-air market two blocks north of the Vatican Museum (Mon–Sat roughly 7:00–13:30, later on Tue and Fri, between Via Tunisi and Via Andrea Doria). If the market is closed, try the nearby **Meta supermarket** (Mon–Wed and Fri–Sat 8:30–13:15, 16:15–19:30, Thu 8:30–13:15, closed Sun, a half block straight out from Via Tunisi entrance of open-air market, Via Francesco 18).

Transportation Connections—Rome

By train to: Venice (6/day, 5–8 hrs, overnight possible), **Florence** (12/day, 2 hrs), **Pisa** (8/day, 3–4 hrs), **Genova** (7/day, 6 hrs, overnight possible), **Milan** (12/day, 5 hrs, overnight possible), **Naples** (6/day, 2 hrs, L33,000 2nd class), **Brindisi** (2/day, 9 hrs), **Amsterdam** (2/day, 20 hrs), **Bern** (5/day, 10 hrs), **Frankfurt** (4/day, 14 hrs), **Munich** (5/day, 12 hrs), **Nice** (2/day, 10 hrs), **Paris** (5/day, 16 hrs), **Vienna** (3/day, 13–15 hrs). **Civita:** Take the Rome–Orvieto train (every 2 hrs, 75 min), catch the bus from Orvieto to Bagnoregio (8/day, 50 min, no service on Sun), and walk to Civita. Train information: tel. 1478-88088.

Rome's Airport

A slick direct train link connects Rome's Fiumicino (a.k.a. Leonardo da Vinci) airport and the central Termini train station's track 22 (L16,000 or free with first-class railpass, departures last year from train station 20 min after every hr, 7:20–21:20, 30-min ride, buy ticket from machine of Alitalia desk at track 22). Your hotel can arrange a taxi to the airport at any hour for about L80,000. To get from the airport into town cheaply by taxi, try teaming up with any tourist also just arriving (most are heading for hotels near yours in the center). Splitting a taxi and hopping out once downtown at a taxi stand to take another to your hotel will save you L30,000. You could also save money taking the train to the station and then catching a taxi to your hotel, but you probably won't save time: The airport train runs only once hourly.

Airport information (tel. 06-65951) can connect you directly to your airline. (British Air tel. 06-6595-4195, Alitalia tel. 06-65643, Delta tel. 06-6595-4104, KLM tel. 06-652-9286, SAS tel. 06-6501-0771, TWA tel. 06-6595-4901, United tel. 0266-7481, Lufthansa tel. 06-6595-4156, Swiss Air tel. 06-6595-4099.)

FLORENCE (FIRENZE)

Florence, the home of the Renaissance and birthplace of our modern world, is a "supermarket sweep," and the groceries are the best Renaissance art in Europe.

Get your bearings with a Renaissance walk. Florentine art goes beyond paintings and statues—there's food, fashion, and handicrafts. You can lick Italy's best gelato while enjoying some of Europe's best people watching.

Planning Your Time

If you're in Europe for three weeks, Florence deserves a well-organized day. (Siena, an easy hour away by bus, has no awesome sights but is a more enjoyable home base.) For a day in Florence, see Michelangelo's *David*, tour the Uffizi Gallery (best Italian paintings anywhere), tour the underrated Bargello (best statues), and do the Renaissance ramble (explained below). Art lovers will want to chisel another day out of their itinerary for the many other Florentine cultural treasures. Shoppers and ice-cream lovers may need to do the same. Plan your sightseeing carefully. Mondays and afternoons can be sparse. While many spend several hours a day in lines, thoughtful travelers do not. Consider eating long and slow at lunch (it's hot out and prices are better). See any sights in the evening that you can.

Orientation

The Florence we're interested in lies mostly on the north bank of the Arno River. Everything is within a 20-minute walk of the train station, cathedral, or Ponte Vecchio (Old Bridge). The less impressive but more characteristic Oltrarno (south bank) area is just over the bridge. The huge red-tiled dome of the cathedral (the Duomo) and its tall bell tower (Giotto's Tower) mark the center of historic Florence.

Tourist Information

There are three TIs in Florence. The one at the train station is usually plagued by long lines (Mon–Sat 8:15–19:15; it'll likely move across the square in 2000). The Hotel Reservations "TI" near the McDonald's is not a real TI but a hotel reservation business. Avoid it. The TI near Santa Croce Church is pleasant, helpful, and uncrowded (Mon–Sat 8:30–19:15, and maybe Sun 8:30–13:45, Borgo Santa Croce 29 red, tel. 055-234-0444). Another winner is the TI three blocks north of the Duomo (Mon–Sat in summer 8:15–19:15, Sun 8:15–13:45, Via Cavour 1 red, tel. 055-290-832 or 055-290-833). There's a fine international bookstore (with American guidebooks) across the street at Via Cavour 20 red.

At the TI pick up a map, a current museum-hours listing (extremely important since hours are constantly in flux), and the periodical entertainment guide or tourist magazine. The free monthly *Florence Concierge Information* magazine lists museums plus lots that I don't: concerts and events, markets, sporting events, church services, shopping ideas including conversions, bus and train connections, and an entire similar section on Siena. Get yours at the TI or from any expensive hotel (pick one up, as if you're staying there).

Arrival in Florence

By Train: The station soaks up time with its dazed and sweaty crowds. Try to get your tourist information and train tickets elsewhere. (You can get onward tickets at American Express—see below.) With your back to the tracks, buses, most recommended hotels, and the escape tunnel (marked Galleria S.M. Novella) are on your left.

By Car: From the *autostrada* (north or south) take the Certosa exit (follow signs to Centro, at Porta Romana go to the left of the arch and down Via Francesco Petrarca). After driving and trying to park in Florence, you'll understand why Leonardo never invented the car. Cars flatten the charm of Florence. Don't drive in Florence. The city has plenty of lots. For a short stay, consider the underground lot at the train station (L3,000/hr). The Fortezza da Basso is clearly marked in the center (L36,000/24 hrs). The least expensive lot is Parcheggio Parterre (Firenze Parcheggi, L15,000/24 hrs with hotel reservation). For parking information, call 055-234-0444.

Helpful Hints

Museums and Churches: See everyone's essential sight, *David*, right off. In Italy a masterpiece seen and enjoyed is worth two tomorrow; you never know when a place will unexpectedly close for a holiday, strike, or restoration. The Uffizi has one- to two-hour lines on busy days; by 17:00 lines are normally gone (go late or make reservations, see Uffizi, under "Sights," below). Some museums close at 14:00 and stop selling tickets 30 minutes before that. The biggies (Uffizi and Accademia) close on Monday. The *Concierge Information* magazine thoughtfully lists which sights are open afternoons, Sundays, and Mondays (best attractions open Mon: Michelangelo's Casa Buonarroti, Dante's House, Giotto's Tower, Museo dell' Opera del Duomo, and Palazzo Vecchio). Churches usually close from 12:30 to 15:00 or 16:00. Local guidebooks are cheap and give you a map and a decent commentary on the sights.

Theft Alert: Florence has particularly hardworking thief gangs. They specialize in tourists and hang out where you do: near the train station, the station's underpass (especially where the tunnel surfaces), and major sights. American tourists—especially older ones—are considered the easiest targets.

Medical Help: For a doctor who speaks English, call 055-475-411 (reasonable hotel calls, cheaper if you go to the clinic at Via L. Magnifico 59, 24-hour pharmacy at the train station). The TI has a list of English-speaking doctors.

Addresses: Street addresses list businesses in red and residences in black or blue (color coded on the actual street number and indicated by a letter following the number in printed addresses: n = black, r = red). *Pensioni* are usually black but can be either.

American Express: Amex offers all the normal services but is most helpful as an easy place to get your train tickets, reservations, or supplements (same price as at station). It's near the Palazzo Vecchio on Via Dante Alighieri 22 red (Mon–Fri 9:00–17:30, Sat 9:00–12:30, CC:A!, tel. 055-50981).

Long-Distance Telephoning: Little shops all over town sell PIN phone cards for cheap (3 min/$1) phone calls to the U.S.A.

Books: Paperback Exchange is at the corner of Via Fiesolana and Via dei Pilastri (6 blocks east of the Duomo).

Getting around Florence

I organize my sightseeing geographically and do it all on foot. A L1,500 ticket gives you one hour on the buses, L2,500 gives you three hours, and L6,000 gets you 24 hours (tickets not sold on bus, buy in tobacco shops or newsstands, validate on bus). Minimum taxi ride: L7,000, or after 22:00, L9,500 (rides in the center of town should be charged as tarif #1). A taxi ride from the train station to Ponte Vecchio costs about L15,000.

A Florentine Renaissance Walk

Even during the Dark Ages people knew they were in a "middle time." It was especially obvious to the people of Italy—sitting on the rubble of Rome—that there was a brighter age before them. The long-awaited rebirth, or Renaissance, began in Florence for good reason. Wealthy because of its cloth industry, trade, and banking; powered by a fierce city-state pride (locals would pee into the Arno with gusto, knowing rival city-state Pisa was downstream); and fertile with more than its share of artistic genius (imagine guys like Michelangelo and Leonardo attending the same high school)—Florence was a natural home for this cultural explosion.

Take a walk through the core of Renaissance Florence by starting at the Accademia (home of Michelangelo's *David*) and cutting through the heart of the city to Ponte Vecchio on the Arno River. (A 10-page, self-guided tour of this walk is outlined in my museum guidebook, *Rick Steves' Mona Winks*; otherwise, you'll find brief descriptions below.)

At the Accademia you'll look into the eyes of Renaissance man—humanism at its confident peak. Then walk to the cathedral (Duomo) to see the dome that kicked off the architectural Renaissance. Step inside the baptistery to view a ceiling covered with preachy, flat, 2-D, medieval mosaic art. Then, to learn what happened when art met math, check out the realistic 3-D reliefs on the doors. The painter, Giotto, designed the bell tower—an early example of how a Renaissance genius excelled in many areas. Continue toward the river on Florence's great pedestrian mall, Via de' Calzaioli (or "Via Calz"), which was part of the original grid plan given the city by the ancient Romans. Down a few blocks, compare medieval and Renaissance statues on the exterior of the Orsanmichele Church. Via Calz connects the cathedral with the central square (Piazza della Signoria), the city palace (Palazzo Vecchio), and the Uffizi Gallery, which contains the greatest collection of Italian Renaissance paintings in captivity. Finally, walk through the Uffizi courtyard—a statuary think tank of Renaissance greats—to the Arno River and Ponte Vecchio.

Sights—On Florence's Renaissance Walk

▲▲▲**Accademia (Galleria dell' Accademia)**—This museum houses Michelangelo's *David* and powerful (unfinished) *Prisoners*. Eavesdrop as tour guides explain these masterpieces. More than any other work of art, when you look into the eyes of *David*, you're looking into the eyes of Renaissance man. This was a radical break with the past. Man was now a confident individual, no longer a plaything of the supernatural. And life was now more than just a preparation for what happened after you died.

The Renaissance was the merging of art and science. In a humanist vein, *David* is looking at the crude giant of medieval darkness and thinking, "I can take this guy." Back on a religious track (and speaking of veins), notice *David*'s large and overdeveloped right hand. This is symbolic of the hand of God that

Florence

powered David to slay the giant... and enabled Florence to rise above its crude neighboring city-states.

Beyond the magic marble are two floors of interesting pre-Renaissance and Renaissance paintings, including a couple of dreamy Botticellis (L12,000, Tue–Fri 8:30–21:00, Sat 8:30–24:00, Sun 8:30–20:00, closed Mon, off-season: Tue–Sat 8:30–19:00, Sun 8:30–14:00, closed Mon, Via Ricasoli 60, tel. 055-238-8609).

Behind the Accademia, the Piazza Santissima Annunziata features lovely Renaissance harmony. Brunelleschi's Hospital of the Innocents (Spedale degli Innocenti, not worth going inside), with terra-cotta medallions by Luca della Robbia, was built in the 1420s and is considered the first Renaissance building.

▲▲**Museum of San Marco**—One block north of the Accademia on Piazza San Marco, this museum houses the greatest collection anywhere of medieval frescoes and paintings by the early Renaissance master Fra Angelico. You'll see why he thought of painting as a form of prayer and couldn't paint a crucifix without shedding tears. Each of the monks' cells has a Fra Angelico fresco. Don't miss the cell of Savonarola, the charismatic monk who rode in from the Christian right, threw out the Medici, turned Florence into a theocracy, sponsored "bonfires of the vanities" (burning books, paintings, and so on), and was finally burned himself when Florence decided to change channels (L8,000, daily 8:30–13:50 but closed the 1st, 3rd, and 5th Sun and the 2nd and 4th Mon of each month).

▲▲**Duomo**—Florence's mediocre Gothic cathedral has the third-longest nave in Christendom (free, Mon–Sat 10:00–17:00, Sun 13:00–17:00, 1st Sat of month 10:00–15:00). The church's noisy neo-Gothic facade from the 1870s is covered with pink, green, and white Tuscan marble. Since nearly all of its great art is stored in the Museo dell' Opera del Duomo, behind the church, the best thing about the interior is the shade. The inside of the dome is decorated by what must be the largest painting of the Renaissance, a huge (and newly restored) *Last Judgment* by Vasari and Zuccari. The cathedral's claim to artistic fame is Brunelleschi's magnificent dome—the first Renaissance dome and the model for domes to follow. Ascend 463 steps and enjoy an inside look at the construction (L10,000, Mon–Fri 8:30–19:00, Sat 9:30–17:00, first Sat of month 9:30–15:20). When planning St. Peter's in Rome, Michelangelo said, "I can build a dome bigger, but not more beautiful, than the dome of Florence."

Giotto's Tower—Climbing Giotto's 82-meter-tall tower (or Campanile) beats climbing the neighboring Duomo's dome because it's 50 fewer steps, faster, not so crowded, and offers the same view plus the dome (L10,000, daily 8:30–18:50).

▲▲**Museo dell' Opera del Duomo**—The underrated cathedral museum, behind the church at #9, is great if you like sculpture. It has masterpieces by Donatello (a gruesome wood carving of Mary Magdalene clothed in her matted hair, and the *cantoria*, a delightful choir loft bursting with happy children) and della Robbia (another choir loft, lined with the dreamy faces of musicians praising the Lord). Look for a late Michelangelo *Pietà* (Nicodemus, on top, is a self-portrait), Brunelleschi's models for his dome, and the original restored panels of Ghiberti's doors to the baptistery. This is one of the few museums in Florence open on Monday (L10,000, Mon–Sat 9:00–18:50, Sun 9:00–13:20, tel. 055-230-2885).

▲**Baptistery**—Michelangelo said its bronze doors were fit to be the gates of Paradise. Check out the gleaming copies of Ghiberti's bronze doors facing the Duomo and the famous competition

Florence

doors around to the right (north). Making a breakthrough in perspective, Ghiberti used mathematical laws to create the illusion of receding distance on a basically flat surface. Go inside Florence's oldest building and sit and savor the medieval mosaic ceiling. Compare that to the "new, improved" art of the Renaissance (L5,000 interior open 12:00–18:30, bronze doors are on the outside so always "open"; original panels are in the Museo dell' Opera del Duomo).

▲**Orsanmichele**—Mirroring Florentine values, this was a combination church-granary. The glorious tabernacle by Orcagna takes you back (1359). Notice the grain spouts on the pillars inside. Also study the sculpture on its outside walls. You can see man stepping out of the literal and figurative shadow of the church in the great Renaissance sculptor Donatello's *St. George* (free, daily 9:00–12:00, 16:00–18:00, closed 1st and 4th Mon, on Via Calzaioli; often closed due to staffing problems, try going through the back door).

▲**Museo Orsanmichele**—For some peaceful time alone with the original statues that filled the niches of Orsanmichele, climb to the top of the church (entry behind the church, across the lane). Be there during the few minutes at 9:00, 10:00, and 11:00 when the door is open and art lovers in the know scamper up to this little known museum (free, closed 1st and 4th Mon).

▲**Palazzo Vecchio**—This fortified palace, once the home of the Medici family, is a Florentine landmark. But if you're visiting only one palace interior in town, the Pitti Palace is better. The Palazzo Vecchio interior is wallpapered with mediocre magnificence, worthwhile only if you're a real Florentine art and history fan (L10,000, Mon–Wed and Fri–Sat 9:00–19:00, Sun and Thu 9:00–14:00, summer weeknights maybe until 23:00, WC inside on ground floor). Do step into the free courtyard (behind the fake *David*) just to feel the Medici. Until 1873 Michelangelo's *David* stood at the entrance, where the copy is today. While the huge statues in the square are important only as the whipping boys of art critics and rest stops for pigeons, the nearby Loggia dei Lanzi has several important statues. Look for Cellini's bronze statue of Perseus (with the head of Medusa). The plaque on the pavement in front of the fountain marks the spot where Savonarola was burned in MCCCCXCVIII.

▲▲▲**Bargello (Museo Nazionale)**—This underrated sculpture museum is behind Palazzo Vecchio in a former prison that looks like a mini–Palazzo Vecchio. It has Donatello's painfully beautiful *David* (the very influential first male nude to be sculpted in a thousand years), works by Michelangelo, and rooms of Medici treasures cruelly explained in Italian only—request English descriptions (L8,000, daily 8:30–13:40 but closed 1st, 3rd, and 5th Sun and 2nd and 4th Mon of each month, Via del Proconsolo 4).

▲▲▲**Uffizi Gallery**—The greatest collection of Italian paintings anywhere is a must, with plenty of works by Giotto, Leonardo, Raphael, Caravaggio, Rubens, Titian, and Michelangelo and a roomful of Botticellis, including his *Birth of Venus*. There are no official tours, so buy a book on the street before entering (or follow *Mona Winks*). Because only 600 visitors are allowed inside the building at any one time, during the day there's generally a very long wait. The good news: no Louvre-style mob scenes. The museum is nowhere near as big as it is great: Few tourists spend more than two hours inside. The paintings are displayed on one comfortable floor in chronological order from the 13th through 17th centuries.

Essential stops are (in this order) the Gothic altarpieces (narrative, prerealism, no real concern for believable depth); Giotto's altarpiece in the same room, which progressed beyond "totempole angels"; Uccello's *Battle of San Romano*, an early study in perspective (with a few obvious flubs); Fra Filippo Lippi's cuddly Madonnas; the Botticelli room, filled with masterpieces, including a pantheon of classical fleshiness and the small *La Calumnia*, showing the glasnost of Renaissance freethinking being clubbed back into the darker age of Savonarola; two minor works by Leonardo; the octagonal classical sculpture room with an early painting of Bob Hope and a copy of Praxiteles' *Venus de Medici*—considered the epitome of beauty in Elizabethan Europe; Michelangelo's only surviving easel painting, the round *Holy Family*; Raphael's noble *Madonna of the Goldfinch*; Titian's voluptuous *Venus of Urbino*; and views from the café terrace at the end (L12,000, Tue–Fri 8:30–21:00, Sat 8:30–23:45, Sun 8:30–20:00, closed Mon; Nov–Apr 8:30–19:00, until 18:00 on Sun and closed Mon, last ticket sold 45 minutes before closing, go late to avoid crowds and heat, take elevator or climb 4 long flights of stairs).

Avoid the two-hour peak-season midday wait by making a reservation. It's easy, slick, and costs only L2,000. Simply telephone during their office hours, choose a time, leave your name, and they'll give you a 15-minute entry time window and a five-digit confirmation number (call 055-294-883, Mon–Fri 8:30–18:30, Sat 9:00–12:00). At the Uffizi, walk briskly past the 200-meter-long line to the special entrance for those with reservations, give your name and number, pay (cash only), and scoot right in. You can reserve from 24 hours to months in advance. This can also be done for other museums (including the Bargello, Accademia, and Medici Chapel). Note: They don't take reservations for evening visits because there is never a line after 18:00. The Uffizi is all yours at night. Visit then.

Enjoy the Uffizi square, full of artists and souvenir stalls. The surrounding statues honor the earthshaking: artists, philosophers (Machiavelli), scientists (Galileo), writers (Dante), explorers

Florence

(Amerigo Vespucci), and the great patron of so much Renaissance thinking, Lorenzo (the Magnificent) de Medici.

▲**Ponte Vecchio**—Florence's most famous bridge is lined with shops that have traditionally sold gold and silver. A statue of Cellini, the master goldsmith of the Renaissance, stands in the center, ignored by the flood of tacky tourism. Notice the "prince's passageway" above. In less secure times, the city leaders had a fortified passageway connecting the Palace Vecchio and Uffizi with the mighty Pitti Palace, to which they could flee in times of attack. This passageway is not open to the public.

More Sights—Central Florence

▲▲**Santa Croce Church**—This 14th-century Franciscan church, decorated by centuries of precious art, holds the tombs of great Florentines (free, Mon–Sat 9:30–17:30, Sun 15:00–17:30, modest dress code enforced). The loud 19th-century Victorian Gothic facade faces a huge square ringed with tempting touristy shops and littered with tired tourists. Escape into the church.

Working counterclockwise from the entrance you'll find the tomb of Michelangelo (with the allegorical figures of painting, architecture, and sculpture), a memorial to Dante (no body... he was banished by his hometown), the tomb of Machiavelli (the originator of hardball politics), a relief by Donatello of the Annunciation, and the tomb of the composer Rossini. To the right of the altar, step into the sacristy, where you'll find the bit of St. Francis' cowl (he is supposed to have founded the church around 1290) and old sheets of music with the medieval and mobile C clef (two little blocks on either side of the line determined to be middle C). In the bookshop notice the photos high on the wall of the devastating flood of 1966. Beyond that is a touristy—but mildly interesting— "leather school." The chapels lining the front of the church are richly frescoed. The Bardi Chapel (far left of altar) is a masterpiece by Giotto featuring scenes from the life of St. Francis. On your way out you'll pass the tomb of Galileo (allowed in by the church long after his death). The neighboring Pazzi Chapel (by Brunelleschi) is considered one of the finest pieces of Florentine Renaissance architecture.

▲**Medici Chapel (Cappelle dei Medici)**—This chapel, containing two Medici tombs, is drenched in incredibly lavish High Renaissance architecture and sculpture by Michelangelo (L10,000, daily 8:30–16:50 but closed the 2nd and 4th Sun on the 1st, 3rd, and 5th Mon of each month). Behind San Lorenzo on Piazza Madonna is a lively market scene that I find just as interesting. Don't miss a wander through the huge double-decker central market one block north.

Science Museum (Museo di Storia della Scienza)—This is a fascinating collection of Renaissance and later clocks, telescopes, maps, and ingenious gadgets. One of the most talked-about bottles in Florence is the one here containing Galileo's finger. English guidebooklets are available. It's friendly, comfortably cool, never crowded, and just downstream from the Uffizi (L10,000, Mon, Wed, and Fri 9:30–13:00, 14:00–17:00, Tue and Thu 9:30–13:00, closed Sun, Piazza dei Giudici 1).

▲**Michelangelo's Home, Casa Buonarroti**—Fans enjoy Michelangelo's house, which has some of his early, much-less-monumental statues and sketches (L12,000, Wed–Mon 9:30–13:30, closed Tue, English descriptions, Via Ghibellina 70).

Casa di Dante—Dante's house is five rooms in an old building with little of substance to show but lots of photos relating to the life and work of Dante. Although it's well described in English, it's interesting only to his fans (L5,000, Mon and Wed–Sat 10:00–18:00, Sun 10:00–14:00, closed Tue, across the street and around the corner from Bargello, at Via S. Margherita 1).

Church of Santa Maria Novella—This 13th-century Dominican church is rich in art. Along with crucifixes by Giotto and Brunelleschi, there's the textbook example of early Renaissance mastery of perspective: *The Holy Trinity* by Masaccio (free, daily 9:00–14:00).

A palatial perfumery is around the corner at 16 Via della Scala. Thick with the lingering aroma of centuries of spritzes, it started as the herb garden of the Santa Maria Novella monks. Well-known even today for its top-quality products, it is extremely Florentine. Pick up the history sheet at the desk and wander deep into the shop. From the back room you can see the S. M. Novella cloister, with its dreamy frescoes, and imagine a time before Vespas and tourists.

Museum of Precious Stones (Museo delle Pietre Dure)—This unusual gem of a museum features mosaics of inlaid marble and semiprecious stones, along with oil-painting copies (L4,000, Tue–Sat 9:00–14:00, closed Sun–Mon, Via degli Alfani 78, around the corner from the Accademia).

Sights—Florence, South of the Arno River

▲▲**Pitti Palace**—From the Uffizi follow the elevated passageway (closed to non-Medicis) across the Ponte Vecchio bridge to the gargantuan Pitti Palace, which has five separate museums.

The **Palatine Gallery/Royal Apartments** features palatial room after chandeliered room, its walls sagging with paintings by the great masters. Its Raphael collection is the biggest anywhere (1st floor, L12,000, Tue–Sat 8:30–24:00, Sun 8:30–20:00, closed Mon, shorter hours off-season).

The **Modern Art Gallery** features Romanticism, neoclassicism, and Impressionism by 19th- and 20th-century Tuscan painters (2nd floor, L8,000, daily 8:30–13:50 but closed 2nd and 4th Sun and 1st, 3rd, and 5th Mon).

The **Grand Ducal Treasures,** or Il Museo degli Argenti, is the Medici treasure chest entertaining fans of applied arts with jeweled crucifixes, exotic porcelain, gilded ostrich eggs, and so on (ground floor, L4,000, same hours as Modern Art Gallery).

Behind the palace, the huge landscaped **Boboli Gardens** offer a cool refuge from the city heat (L4,000, Tue–Sun 9:00–17:30, closed 1st and 4th Mon).

▲**Brancacci Chapel**—For the best look at the early Renaissance master Masaccio, see his restored frescoes here (L5,000, Mon and Wed–Fri 10:00–17:00, Sun 13:00–17:00, closed Tue, cross Ponte Vecchio and turn right a few blocks to Piazza del Carmine). Since only a few tourists are let in at a time, seeing the chapel often involves a wait. The neighborhoods around here are considered the last surviving bits of old Florence.

▲**Piazzale Michelangelo**—Across the river overlooking the city (look for the huge statue of *David*), this square is worth the 30-minute hike, drive, or bus ride (either #12 or #13 from the train station) for the view. After dark it's packed with local schoolkids feeding their dates slices of watermelon. Just beyond it is the stark and beautiful, crowd-free Romanesque San Miniato Church.

Experiences—Florence

▲▲**Gelato**—Gelato is an edible art form. Italy's best ice cream is in Florence—one souvenir that can't break and won't clutter your luggage. But beware of scams turning a simple request of a cone into a L15,000 "tourist special." Gelateria Carrozze is very good (30 yards from Ponte Vecchio toward the Uffizi, Via del Pesce 3). Gelateria dei Neri—considered by many to be the best in central Florence—is worth finding (open daily in summer, behind Palazzo Vecchio at Via Dei Neri 20r). Vivoli's is a longtime favorite (Tue–Sun 8:00–01:00, closed Mon, the last 3 weeks in August, and winter; opposite the Church of Santa Croce, go down Via Torta a block, turn right on Via Stinche; before ordering, try a free sample of their *riso*—rice). The Cinema Astro, across the street from Vivoli's, plays English/American movies in their original language (closed Mon).

Shopping—Florence is a great shopping town. Busy street scenes and markets abound, especially near San Lorenzo, on Ponte Vecchio, and near Santa Croce. Leather (often better quality for half the U.S. price), gold, silver, art prints, and tacky plaster "mini-*Davids*" are most popular. Many spend entire days shopping. Shops usually have promotional stalls in the market squares. Prices are soft in the markets. For ritzy Italian fashions, browse along Via de Tornabuoni, Via de la Vigna Nouva, and Via Strozzi. For many shopping ideas and aids, see the *Florence Concierge Information* magazine described under "Tourist Information," above (free from TI and many hotels).

Side Trips to Fiesole and Siena

For a candid peek at Fiesole—a Florentine suburb—ride bus #7 (3/hrly, from Piazza Adua, northeast side of the station and from Piazza San Marco) for about 25 minutes through neighborhood gardens, vineyards, orchards, and large villas to the last stop—Fiesole. Fiesole is a popular excursion from Florence for its small eateries and good views of Florence. Catch the sunset from the terrace just below the La Reggia restaurant; from the Fiesole bus stop, face the bell tower and take the very steep Via San Francisco on your left. The view terrace is near the top of the hill.

Connoisseurs of peace and small towns who aren't into art or shopping (and who won't be seeing Siena otherwise) should consider riding the bus to Siena (75 minutes if you take the *"corse rapide"* via the autostrada). This can be a day trip or an evening trip. Siena is magic after dark. Confirm when the last bus returns.

Sleeping in Florence
(L1,900 = about $1)
Sleep Code: **S** = Single, **D** = Double/Twin, **T** = Triple, **Q** = Quad, **b** = bathroom, **s** = shower only, **CC** = Credit Card (Visa, MasterCard, Amex), **SE** = Speaks English, **NSE** = No English. Unless otherwise noted, breakfast is included (but usually optional). English is generally spoken.

The hotel scene varies wildly with the season. Spring and fall are very tight and expensive, while mid-July through August are wide open and discounted. November through February is also generally empty. With good information and a phone call ahead, you can find a stark, clean, and comfortable double with breakfast for L90,000, with a private shower for L120,000. You get roof-garden elegance for L150,000. Many places listed are old and rickety. I can't imagine Florence any other way. Rooms with air-conditioning cost around L200,000—worth the extra lire in the summer. Virtually all of the places are central, within minutes of the great sights.

Call direct to the hotel. Do not use the tourist office, which costs your host and jacks up the price. In slow times, budget travelers call around and find soft prices. If you're staying for three or more nights, ask for a discount. The optional and over-priced breakfast can be a bargaining chip, as can paying in cash. Call ahead. I repeat, call ahead. Places will hold a room until early afternoon. If they say they're full, mention you're using this book.

The Wash & Dry Lavarapido chain offers long hours and efficient self-service Laundromats at several locations (daily 8:00–22:00, tel. 055-580-480). Close to recommended hotels: Via Dei Servi 105r (near *David*), Via del Sole 29r and Via Della Scala 52r (between station and river), and Via Dei Serragli 87r (across the river). East of the station another handy modern launderette is just

Florence

off Via Cavour at Via Guelfa 22 red (daily 8:00–22:00, 12 wash and dry for L12,000).

Sleeping near the San Lorenzo Market
(zip code: 50123)

Hotel Accademia is an elegant two-star hotel with marble stairs, parquet floors, attractive public areas, pleasant rooms, and a floor plan that defies logic (S-L140,000, Sb-L160,000, Db-L220,000, Tb-L270,000, CC:VMA, air-con, Via Faenza 7, tel. 055-293-451, fax 055-219-771, e-mail: hotaccad@tin.it).

Hotel Nuova Italia Firenze is a slumber mill in all the guidebooks, with 20 quiet, well-maintained rooms (Sb-L140,000, Db-L190,000, Tb-L250,000, 8 percent discount for cash, cheaper off-season, CC:VMA, air-con, triple-paned windows, Via Faenza 26, tel. 055-268-430, fax 055-210-941, e-mail: hotel.nuovo:italia @data.it).

Sleeping near the Central Market
(zip code: 50129)

Casa Rabatti is the ultimate if you always wanted to be a part of a Florentine family. It's simple, clean, friendly, and run with motherly warmth by Marcella and her husband, Celestino, who speak minimal English (4 rooms, D-L85,000, Db-L100,000, L35,000 per bed in shared quad or quint, prices good with this book, no breakfast, closed Nov–Mar, 5 blocks from station, Via San Zanobi 48 black, tel. 055-212-393). Her daughter runs a similar place with much street noise.

Soggiorno Pezzati Daniela is another quiet little place with six homey rooms (Sb-L70,000, Db-L98,000, Tb-L135,000, Qb-L160,000, no breakfast, marked only by small sign near door, Via San Zanobi 22, tel. 055-291-660, fax 055-287-145, Daniela SE). If you get an Italian recording when you call, hang on—your call is being transferred to a cell phone.

Soggiorno delle Rondini rents five quiet, comfy rooms up four flights of stairs (S-L60,000, Ds-L80,000, Ts-L100,000, Qs-L120,000, near Via XXVII Aprile at Via San Zanobi 43, tel. 055-4620226). Carlotta Messini speaks a little English and promises these special prices through 2000 to those with this book.

Hotel Enza rents 16 quirky, unpredictable rooms. While Eugenia's chihuahua, Tricky, is tiny, her rooms are particularly spacious—though sometimes dirty (S-L75,000, Sb-L80,000, D-L95,000, Db-L130,000, T-L130,000, Tb-L170,000, family loft, no breakfast, Via San Zanobi 45 black, tel. 055-490-990, fax 055-473-672).

Central and humble **Soggiorno Magliani** feels and smells like a great-grandmother's place (7 rooms, S-L56,000, D-L77,000, double-paned windows don't keep out street noise, at corner of Via

Italy

Florence Hotels and Restaurants

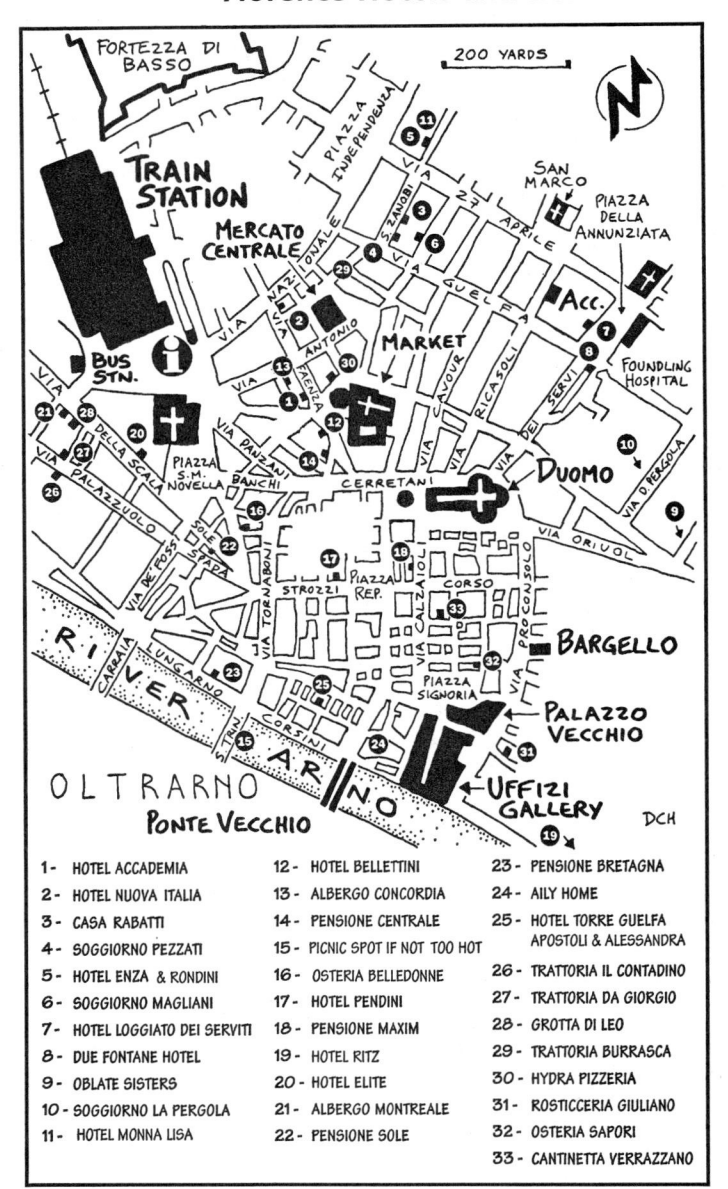

1. HOTEL ACCADEMIA
2. HOTEL NUOVA ITALIA
3. CASA RABATTI
4. SOGGIORNO PEZZATI
5. HOTEL ENZA & RONDINI
6. SOGGIORNO MAGLIANI
7. HOTEL LOGGIATO DEI SERVITI
8. DUE FONTANE HOTEL
9. OBLATE SISTERS
10. SOGGIORNO LA PERGOLA
11. HOTEL MONNA LISA
12. HOTEL BELLETTINI
13. ALBERGO CONCORDIA
14. PENSIONE CENTRALE
15. PICNIC SPOT IF NOT TOO HOT
16. OSTERIA BELLEDONNE
17. HOTEL PENDINI
18. PENSIONE MAXIM
19. HOTEL RITZ
20. HOTEL ELITE
21. ALBERGO MONTREALE
22. PENSIONE SOLE
23. PENSIONE BRETAGNA
24. AILY HOME
25. HOTEL TORRE GUELFA APOSTOLI & ALESSANDRA
26. TRATTORIA IL CONTADINO
27. TRATTORIA DA GIORGIO
28. GROTTA DI LEO
29. TRATTORIA BURRASCA
30. HYDRA PIZZERIA
31. ROSTICCERIA GIULIANO
32. OSTERIA SAPORI
33. CANTINETTA VERRAZZANO

Florence

Guelfa and Via Reparata, Via Reparata 1, tel. 055-28
Vincenza and her English-speaking daughter, Cristir

Sleeping East of the Duomo

The first two listings are near the Accademia, on Piazza Annunziata (zip code: 50122).

Hotel Loggiato dei Serviti, at the most prestigious address in Florence on the most Renaissance square in town, gives you Renaissance romance with a place to plug in your hair dryer (29 rooms, Sb-L240,000, Db-L350,000, family suites from L500,000, book a month ahead, big discounts in Aug, CC:VMA, elevator, square noisy at night, Piazza S.S. Annunziata 3, tel. 055-289-592, fax 055-289-595, e-mail: loggiato_serviti@italyhotel.com, SE). Stone stairways lead you under open-beam ceilings through this 16th-century monastery's elegant public rooms. The cells, with air conditioning, TVs, minibars, and telephones, wouldn't be recognized by their original inhabitants.

Le Due Fontane Hotel faces the same great square but fills its old building with a smoky, 1970s, business-class ambience. Its 57 air-conditioned rooms are big and comfortable (Sb-L180,000, Db-L250,000, Tb-L360,000, buffet breakfast, CC:VMA, elevator, phones, TVs, Piazza S.S. Annunziata 14, tel. 055-210-185, fax 055-294-461, SE).

Hotel Monna Lisa, my only four-star listing in this neighborhood, is an art-filled convent-turned-palace with an elegant garden, palatial public spaces, and professional service. It's steeped in history. Judging from the guest book, its visitors are happy to have paid the ransom (30 rooms, Db-L350,000 most of the year but L480,000 mid-Mar–mid-Jul and Sept–Oct, CC:VMA, air-con, parking, 3 blocks east of Duomo at Borgo Pinti 27, tel. 055-2479751, fax 055-2479755, www.monnalisa.it).

The **Oblate Sisters of the Assumption** run a 50-bed hotel in a Renaissance building with a dreamy garden and a quiet, institutional feel (S-L55,000, D-L110,000, Db-L130,000, big L20,000 dinners, elevator, Borgo Pinti 15, 50121 Firenze, tel. 055-248-0582, fax 055-234-6291).

Soggiorno La Pergola di Letitia Barlozzi is an extremely homey place with kitchenettes in the rooms and the cheapest air-conditioned rooms in town (Db-L120,000, Via della Pergola 23, tel. & fax 055-213-886).

Sleeping between the Station and Duomo
(zip code: 50123)

Hotel Bellettini has 28 bright, cool, well-cared-for rooms with tile floors, inviting lounges, and a touch of class (Sb-L150,000, Db-L200,000, Tb-L270,000, Qb-L340,000, CC:VMA, 5 percent discount with this book, buffet breakfast, air-con, free Internet access, Via de' Conti 7, tel. 055-213-561, fax 055-283-551, e-mail: hotel.bellettini@dada.it).

Albergo Concordia is modern, well run, and conveniently located, though noisy, next to a night club. Confirm prices (16 rooms, 1 fine Sb-L95,000, Db-L150,000, Tb-L205,000, CC:VMA, no elevator, popular with school groups Feb–Apr, Via dell' Amorino 14, tel. & fax 055-213-233, e-mail: concordia@fol.it, Fabrizio SE).

Pensione Centrale, a happy and traditional-feeling place, is indeed central. Run by aristocratic Marie Therese Blot, spunky Margherita, and Franco, you'll feel right at home (D-L150,000, Db-L180,000 with an "American" breakfast, some air-con rooms, often filled with American students, CC:VMA, elevator, Via de' Conti 3, tel. 055-215-761, fax 055-215-216).

Sleeping on or near Piazza Repubblica
(zip code: 50123)

These are the most central of my accommodations recommendations, though given Florence's walkable core, nearly every hotel can be considered central.

Hotel Pendini, a three-star hotel with 42 elegant rooms (8 with views of the square), is popular and central, overlooking Piazza Repubblica (Sb-L140,000–180,000, Db-L190,000–260,000, depending on season, CC:VMA, elevator, fine lounge and breakfast room, air-con, Via Strozzi 2, reserve at least a month in advance, tel. 055-211-170, fax 055-281-807, www.tiac.net/users/pendini).

Pensione Maxim is a big, institutional-feeling place as close to the sights as possible. You'll feel like a mouse in a maze navigating its narrow halls (23 rooms, Sb-L140,000, Db-L150,000, Tb-L190,000, Qb-L240,000, with breakfast, add L10,000 per person per day for air-con Jun–Sept, CC:VMA but pay 1st night in cash, e-mail service, laundry service, elevator, Via dei Calzaiuoli 11, tel. 055-217-474, fax 055-283-729, e-mail: hotmaxim@tin.it, Paolo and Nicola Maioli).

Sleeping South of the Train Station near Piazza Santa Maria Novella
(zip code: 50123)

From the station, follow the Galleria S.M. Novella tunnel (with back to tracks, outside on the left) to Piazza Santa Maria Novella, a pleasant square by day that becomes a little sleazy after dark. *Note: Theft alert in the tunnel, where the tunnel surfaces, and at night.* The square is handy—only three blocks from the cathedral and near a good launderette (La Serena, Mon–Sat 8:30–20:00, closed Sun, L20,000 for 11 pounds, Via della Scala 30 red, tel. 055-218-183) and cheap restaurants (on Via Palazzuolo, see below).

Hotel Pensione Elite, with eight comfortable rooms and a charm rare in this price range, is a fine basic value run warmly by Maurizio and Nadia (Ss-L80,000, Sb-L100,000, Ds-L110,000, Db-L130,000, breakfast-L10,000, at south end of square with back to church, go right to Via della Scala 12, 2nd floor, tel. & fax 055-215-395, SE).

The nearby **Albergo Montreal** is OK for backpackers, with clean, airy, characterless, although renovated, rooms (18 rooms, S-L60,000, D-L80,000, Db-L98,000, Tb-L135,000, with this book through 2000, Via della Scala 43, tel. 055-238-2331, fax 055-287-491, e-mail: info@hotelmontreal.com, SE).

Pensione Sole, a clean, cozy, family-run place with seven bright rooms, is just off Santa Maria Novella toward the river (Db-L120,000–130,000, no breakfast, elevator, Via del Sole 8, 3rd floor, lots of stairs, tel. & fax 055-239-6094, Anna NSE).

Sleeping on/near the Arno River and Ponte Vecchio (zip code: 50123)

Pensione Bretagna is an Old World–elegant place with thoughtfully appointed rooms. The hotel is run by the helpful, English-speaking Antonio, Maura, and Sara. Imagine eating breakfast under a painted, chandeliered ceiling overlooking the Arno River (S-L80,000, Ss-L85,000, Sb-L95,000, D-L120,000, Ds-L140,000, Db-L165,000, Tb-L210,000, Qb-L240,000, including optional L10,000 breakfast, family deals, prices special with this book through 2000, CC:VMA, elevator, just past Ponte San Trinita, Lungarno Corsini 6, tel. 055-289-618, fax 055-289-619, e-mail: hotelpens.bretagna@agora.stm.it). They also run a cheaper place, Althea, near Piazza San Spirito in the Oltrarno neighborhood (Db-L110,000, no breakfast, call Bretagna to book).

Aily Home is a humble, homey, grandmotherly five-room place tucked away on a peaceful square a block from Ponte Vecchio (3-night minimum, D-L60,000, showers-L3,000, scary elevator, Piazza San Stefano 1, tel. 055-239-6505, Rosaria Franchis NSE).

Hotel Torre Guelfa is topped with a fun medieval tower with a panoramic rooftop terrace and a huge living room. Its 12 rooms vary wildly in size (small Db-L200,000, Db-L250,000). Number 15, with a private terrace—L270,000—is worth reserving several months in advance (elevator, air-con, a couple blocks northwest of Ponte Vecchio, Borgo S.S. Apostoli 8, tel. 055-239-6338, fax 055-239-8577, e-mail: zucconi@fol.it, Giancarlo, Carlo, and Luigi all SE).

Residenza Apostoli, a new B&B in the same building, is bright, spacious, and modern, with parquet floors and 12 air-conditioned rooms in a very old building on a quiet street one block off the river (Db-L180,000–200,000, light breakfast in room, CC:VM, 10 percent discount with this book, TV lounge, elevator, Borgo Santi Apostoli 8, tel. 055-284-837, fax 055-268-790).

Hotel Pensione Alessandra is an old, peaceful place with

Oltrarno Neighborhood

1 - HOTEL LA SCALETTA
2 - HOTEL SILLA
3 - PENSIONE SORELLE BANDINI
4 - SOGGIORNO PEZZATI #2
5 - INSTITUTE GOULD
6 - OSTELLO SANTA MONICA
7 - TRATTORIA CASALINGA
8 - TRATTORIA SABATINO
9 - OSTERIA CINGHIALE BIANCO
10 - TRATTORIA BORDINO
11 - RISTORANTE BIBO

25 big rooms (S-L100,000, Sb-L150,000, D-L150,000, Db-L200,000, Tb-L270,000, Qb-L330,000, includes breakfast, CC:VMA, most rooms have air-con, Borgo S.S. Apostoli 17, tel. 055-283-438, fax 055-210-619, www.hotelalessandra.com).

Hotel Ritz, a grand, riverside, four-star place with all the comforts, often advertises special deals on the Web (Db-L180,000–280,000 Lungarno della Zecca 24, 50122 Firenze, tel. 055-234-0650, fax 055-24-0863, www.tiac.net/users/pendini/ritz).

Sleeping in Oltrarno, South of the River
(zip code: 50125)

Across the river in the Oltrarno area, between the Pitti Palace and Ponte Vecchio, you'll still find small traditional crafts shops, neighborly piazzas, and family eateries. The following places are a few minutes' walk from Ponte Vecchio.

Hotel La Scaletta is elegant, friendly, and clean, with a dark, cool, labyrinthine floor plan, lots of Old World lounges, and a romantic and panoramic roof terrace. Owner Barbara, her son Manfredo, and daughters Bianca and Diana run this well-worn but loved place. If Manfredo is cooking dinner, eat here (Ss-L80,000, Sb-L140,000, D-L140,000, Db-L180,000–200,000, Tb-L210,000–240,000, Qb-L250,000–270,000, L20,000 extra for rooms on garden side, CC:VM, from L10,000–20,000 discount if you pay cash, elevator, Via Guicciardini 13 black, 150 yards up the street from Ponte Vecchio, tel. 055-283-028, fax 055-289-562, www.italyhotel.com/firenze/lascaletta). Reserve by phone, confirm by fax, then send a personal or traveler's check.

Hotel Silla, a classic three-star hotel with cheery, spacious, pastel, and modern rooms, is a fine value. It faces the river and overlooks a park opposite the Santa Croce Church (36 rooms, Db-L250,000 with breakfast, CC:VMA, elevator, nearly all rooms have air-con, Via dei Renai 5, 50125 Florence, tel. 055-234-2888, fax 055-234-1437, e-mail: hotelsilla@tin.it, manager Gabriele SE).

Pensione Sorelle Bandini is a ramshackle, 500-year-old palace on a perfectly Florentine square, with cavernous rooms, museum-warehouse interiors, a musty youthfulness, cats, a balcony lounge-loggia with a view, and an ambience that, for romantic bohemians, can be a highlight of Florence. Mimmo or Sr. Romeo will hold a room until 16:00 with a phone call (D-L160,000, Db-L200,000, T-L220,000, Tb-L270,000, includes breakfast, elevator, Piazza Santo Spirito 9, tel. 055-215-308, fax 055-282-761).

Soggiorno Pezzati Alessandra (a.k.a. Soggiorno Pezzati #2) is a warm and friendly place renting five great rooms in the Oltrarno neighborhood (Sb-L70,000, Db-L98,000, Tb-L135,000, Qb-L160,000, Via Borgo San Frediano 6, tel. 055-290-424, fax 055-783-0607, Alessandra). If you get an Italian recording when you call, hang on—your call is being transferred to a cell phone.

Institute Gould is a Protestant Church–run place with 89 beds in 27 rooms and clean, modern facilities (S-L50,000, Sb-L57,000, D-L75,000, Db-L80,000, Tb-L110,000, L34,000 in quads, L29,000 in quints, Via dei Serragli 49, tel. 055-212-576). You must arrive when the office is open (Mon–Fri 9:00–13:00, 15:00–19:00, Sat 9:00–13:00, no check-in Sun).

Pension Ungherese, warmly run by Sergio and Rosemary, is good for drivers. It's outside the city center (near Stadio, on route to Fiesole), with easy, free street parking and quick bus access (#11 and #17) into central Florence (Sb-L110,000, Db-L200,000 with this book, 20 percent less off-season, pay cash with this book for a 7 percent discount, includes breakfast, CC:VM, Via G. B. Amici 8, tel. & fax 055-573-474, e-mail: hotel.ungherese@dada.it, NSE). It has great singles and a backyard garden terrace (ask for a room on the garden).

Last alternatives: **Ostello Santa Monaca** (L25,000 beds, 10-bed rooms, no breakfast, midnight curfew, a few blocks past Ponte Alla Carraia, Via Santa Monaca 6, tel. 055-268-338, fax 055-280-185) and the classy **Villa Camerata** IYHF hostel (L25,000 per bed with breakfast, 4- to 8-bed rooms; ride bus #17A or B to Salviatino stop, Via Righi 1, tel. 055-601-451) are on the outskirts of Florence.

Eating in Florence

To save money and time for sights, you can keep meals fast and simple, eating in one of the countless self-service places and pizzerias or just picnicking (try juice, yogurt, cheese, and a roll for L8,000). Or consider the following.

Eating in Oltrarno, South of the River

For a change of scene, I'd eat across the river in Oltrarno. Here are a few good places just over Ponte Vecchio and on or near Piazza Santo Spirito.

A block past Ponte Vecchio is the unpretentious and happy Piazza San Felicita, with two great restaurants to consider. **Ristorante Bibo** serves *"cucina tipica Fiorentina"* with smart and friendly service, an air-conditioned interior, and leafy candlelit outdoor seating (good L25,000 3-course meal, CC:VMA, reserve for outdoor seating, daily 12:00–14:30, 19:00–22:30, Piazza San Felicita 6r, tel. 055-239-8554). The cosier **Trattoria Bordino**, just up the street, is similar, serving fine Florentine cuisine (L40,000 dinners, closed Sun, Via Stracciatella 9 red).

Piazza Santo Spirito is a classic Florentine square (and therefore touristy) with two classy and popular little restaurants offering good local cuisine every night of the week, indoor and on-the-square seating (reserve for on-the-square), moderate prices, and impersonal service: **Borgo Antico** (Piazza Santo Spirito 6 red, tel. 055-210-437) and **Osteria Santo Spirito** (Piazza Santo Spirito 16r, tel. 055-2382383).

The **Ricchi bar**, next to Borgo Antico on the same square, has fine homemade gelati and shady outdoor tables. Notice how plain the facade of the Brunelleschi church facing the square is. Then step inside, grab a coffee, and ponder the many proposals on how it might be finished.

Trattoria Casalinga is an inexpensive and popular standby. Famous for its home cooking, it's now filled with tourists rather than locals. But it sends them away full, happy, and with lire left for gelato (closed Sun, plus Sat in Jul–Aug, just off Piazza Santo Spirito, near the church at Via dei Michelozzi 9 red, tel. 055-218-624).

Other places to consider: **Osteria del Cinghiale Bianco**

(Borgo S. Jacopo 43, closed Tue–Wed, tel. 055-215706), **Trattoria Sabatino** (Borgo S Frediano 17), **Trattoria Angiolino** (closed Mon, Via S. Spirito 36r, tel. 055-239-8976), or several other inviting places along Via Santo Spirito.

Eating North of the River
Eating near Santa Maria Novella and the Train Station
Osteria Belledonne is a crowded and cheery hole-in-the-wall serving great food at good prices. I loved the meal but had to correct the bill—read it carefully (Mon–Fri 12:00–14:30, 19:00–22:30, closed Sat–Sun, Via delle Belledonne 16r, tel. 055-238-2609). **Ristorante La Spada,** nearby, is also a local favorite serving typical Tuscan cuisine with less atmosphere and more menu (L20,000 lunch special, air-con, near Via della Spada at Via del Moro 66r, tel. 055-218-757).

Twin chow houses for local workers offer a L17,000, hearty, family-style, fixed-price menu with a bustling working-class/budget-Yankee-traveler atmosphere (Mon–Sat 12:00–14:30, 18:15–21:30 or 22:00, closed Sun, 2 blocks south of the train station): **Trattoria il Contadino** (Via Palazzuolo 69 red, tel. 055-238-2673) and **Trattoria da Giorgio** (across the street at Via Palazzuolo 100 red). Arrive early or wait.

The touristy **La Grotta di Leo** (a block away) has a cheap, straightforward menu and edible food and pizza (daily 11:00–23:00, Via della Scala 41 red, tel. 055-219-265).

Eating near the Central and San Lorenzo Markets
For mountains of picnic produce or just a cheap sandwich and piles of people watching, visit the huge, multistoried Central Market—**Mercato Centrale** (Mon–Sat 7:00–14:00, closed Sun), a block north of the San Lorenzo street market.

Trattoria la Burrasca is a small, inexpensive place serving local-style dishes in a characteristic setting (Fri–Wed 12:00–15:00, 19:00–22:00, closed Thu, Via Panicale 6 red, Panicale borders Central Market on the north, tel. 055-215-827).

Hydra Pizzeria Spaghetteria, two blocks south, is brighter and more modern (closed Tue, across from Medici Chapel, entrance amid San Lorenzo street market, Canto de' Nelli 38r, tel. 055-218-922).

Eating near Palazzo Vecchio
The cozy **Rosticceria Guilano Centro,** a few blocks east of the Palazzo Vecchio, serves fine food to go or enjoy there (Tue–Sat 8:00–15:30, 17:00–21:30, closed Sun–Mon, Via Dei Neri 74 red).

Osteria Vini e Vecchi Sapori is a colorful hole-in-the-wall serving traditional food, including plates of mixed sandwiches (L1,500 each), half a block north of the Palazzo Vecchio (Tue–Sun 9:30–22:30, closed Mon, Via dei Magazzini 3 red, facing the equestrian statue in Piazza della Signoria, go behind its tail to your left).

Cantinetta dei Verrazzano is a long-established bakery/café/wine bar serving elegant sandwich plates and hot focaccia sandwiches in an elegant old-time setting (until 21:00, closed Sun, just off Via Calzaiuoli directly across from Orsanmichele at Via dei Tavolini 18, tel. 055-268-590).

For a reasonably priced pizza with a Medici-style view, consider one of the pizzerias on Piazza della Signoria.

Transportation Connections—Florence

By train to: Assisi (10/day, 2.5–3 hrs), **Orvieto** (6/day, 2 hrs), **Pisa** (2/hrly, 1 hr), **La Spezia** (for the Cinque Terre, 2/day direct, 2 hrs, or change in Pisa), **Venice** (7/day, 3 hrs), **Milan** (12/day, 3–5 hrs), **Rome** (hrly, 2.5 hrs), **Naples** (2/day, 4 hrs), **Brindisi** (3/day, 11 hrs with change in Bologna), **Frankfurt** (3/day, 12 hrs), **Paris** (1/day, 12 hrs overnight), **Vienna** (4/day, 9–10 hrs). Train info: tel. 147-888-088.

Buses: The SITA bus station, a block from the Florence train station, is very user-friendly (but remember, bus service drops dramatically on Sunday). Schedules are posted everywhere with TV monitors indicating imminent departures. You'll find buses to: **San Gimignano** (hrly at :40 past the hour, 1.75 hrs), **Siena** (hrly at :10 past the hour, 75-min *corse rapide* fast buses, avoid the 2-hr *diretta* slow buses, faster than the train, L11,000), and the **airport** (hrly, 15 min). Bus info: tel. 055-214-721 from 9:30–12:30; some schedules are in *Florence Concierge Information* magazine.

VENICE (VENEZIA)

Soak all day in this puddle of elegant decay. Venice is Europe's best-preserved big city. This car-free urban wonderland of 100 islands—laced together by 400 bridges and 2,000 alleys—survives on the artificial respirator of tourism.

Born in a lagoon 1,500 years ago as a refuge from barbarians, Venice is overloaded with tourists and slowly sinking (unrelated facts). In the Middle Ages, the Venetians, becoming Europe's clever middlemen for east-west trade, created a great trading empire. By smuggling in the bones of St. Mark (San Marco, in about A.D. 830), Venice gained religious importance as well. With the discovery of America and new trading routes to the Orient, Venetian power ebbed. But as Venice fell, her appetite for decadence grew. Through the 17th and 18th centuries Venice partied on the wealth accumulated through earlier centuries as a trading power.

Today Venice is home to about 70,000 people in its old city, down from a peak population of around 200,000. While there are about 500,000 in greater Venice (counting the mainland, not counting tourists), the old town has a small-town feel. Locals seem to know everyone. To see small-town Venice through the touristic flak, get away from the Rialto–San Marco tourist zone and savor the town early and late without the hordes of vacationers day-tripping in from nearby beach resorts. A 10-minute walk from the madness puts you in an idyllic Venice few tourists see.

Planning Your Time

Venice is worth at least a day on even the speediest tour. Hyperefficient train travelers take the night train in and/or out. Sleep in the old center to experience Venice at its best: early and late. For

Venice

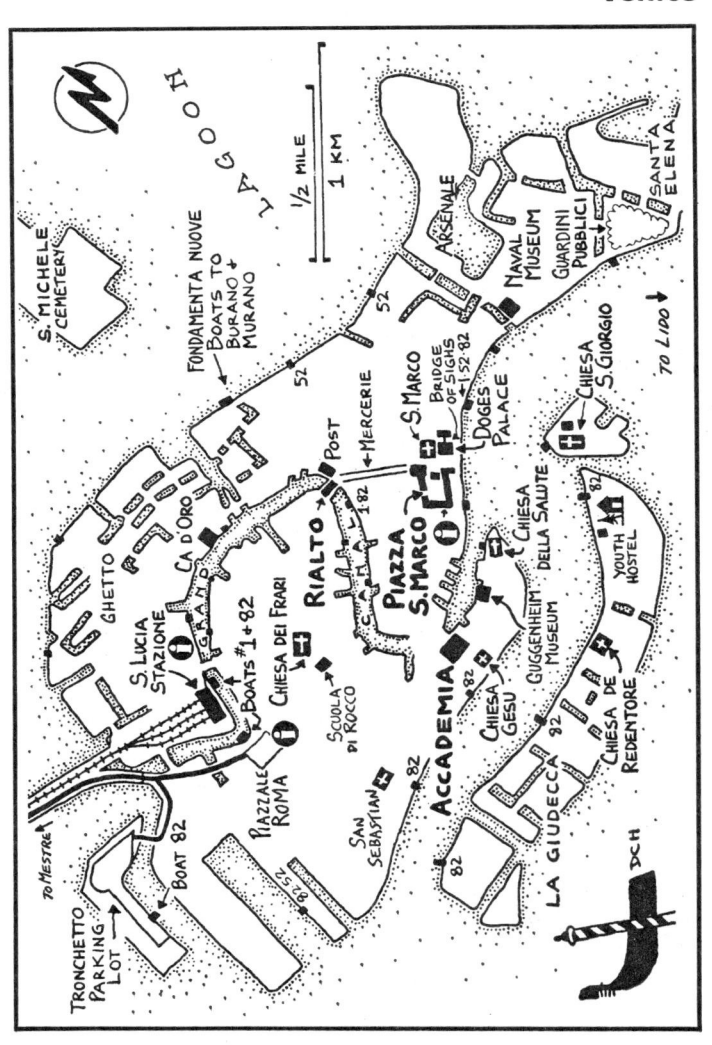

a one-day visit, cruise the Grand Canal, do the major sights on St. Mark's Square (the square itself, Doge's Palace, St. Mark's Basilica), see the Church of the Frari (Chiesa dei Frari) for art, and wander the back streets on a pub crawl (see "Eating," below).

Venice

Venice's greatest sight is the city itself. Make time to simply wander. While doable in a day, Venice is worth two. It's a medieval cookie jar, and nobody's looking.

Orientation

The island city of Venice is shaped like a fish. Its major thoroughfares are canals. The Grand Canal winds through the middle of the fish, starting at the mouth where all the people and food enter, passing under the Rialto Bridge, and ending at St. Mark's Square (San Marco). Park your 20th-century perspective at the mouth and let Venice swallow you whole.

Venice is a carless kaleidoscope of people, bridges, and odorless canals. The city has no real streets, and addresses are hopelessly confusing. There are six districts: San Marco (most touristy), Castello (behind San Marco), Cannaregio (from the station to the Rialto), San Polo (other side of the Rialto), Santa Croce, and Dorsoduro. Each district has about 6,000 address numbers. Luckily it's easy to find your way, since many street corners have a sign pointing you to the nearest major landmark, such as San Marco, Accademia, Rialto, and Ferrovia (the train station). To find your way, navigate by landmarks, not streets. Obedient visitors stick to the main thoroughfares as directed by these signs and miss the charm of backstreet Venice.

Tourist Information

There are TIs at the train station (daily 8:10–18:50, crowded and surly) and at the far end of St. Mark's Square (daily 9:00–17:00, friendly). For a quick question save time by phoning (tel. 041-529-8711 or 041-526-5721). At either TI, pick up a free city map, the week's events, and the latest museum hours and confirm your sightseeing plans. Ask for the fine brochure outlining three offbeat Venice walks. The free periodical entertainment guide *Un Ospite de Venezia* (a monthly listing of events, nightlife, museum hours, train and *vaporetto*—motorized bus-boat—schedules, emergency telephone numbers, and so on) is available at the TI or fancy hotel reception desks. The cheap Venice map on sale at postcard racks has much more detail than the TI map. Also consider the little guidebook (sold alongside the postcards), which comes with a city map and explanations of the major sights.

Walking Tours: Enjoy Venice offers walking tours giving a rundown on the Doges, Marco Polo, Casanova, casinos, canals, and building gondolas (10:00 any day except Sun, meet in front of Thomas Cook, a few steps from Rialto Bridge *vaporetto* stop, L30,000, L25,000 if under 26, 3 hrs, toll-free tel. 167-274-819). Local guide Alessandro Schezzini is good at getting beyond the clichés and into offbeat Venice (L150,000, 2.5 hrs, tel. & fax 041-923-626, cellular 033-5530-9024).

Arrival in Venice

A two-mile-long causeway (with highway and train lines) connects Venice to the mainland. Mestre, Venice's sprawling mainland industrial base, has fewer crowds, cheaper hotels, plenty of parking lots, but no charm. Don't stop here (unless you're parking your car in a lot). Trains regularly connect Mestre with Venice's Santa Lucia station (6/hrly, 5 min).

By Train: Venice's Santa Lucia train station plops you right into the old town on the Grand Canal, an easy *vaporetto* ride or fascinating 40-minute walk from St. Mark's Square. Upon arrival, skip the station's crowded TI (St. Mark's Square's is better), confirm your departure plan (good train info desk), consider stowing unnecessary heavy bags at the *deposito* (baggage check), and then walk straight out of the station to the canal. The dock for *vaporetti* #1 and #82 is on your left. Buy a L6,000 ticket at the window and hop on a boat for downtown (direction: Rialto or San Marco).

By Car: At Venice, the freeway ends like Medusa's head. Follow the green lights directing you to a parking lot with space. The standard place is Tronchetto (across the causeway and on the right), which has a huge, new, multistoried garage (L30,000 per day, half-price with a discount coupon from your hotel). From there you'll find travel agencies masquerading as tourist information offices and *vaporetto* docks for the boat connection (#82) to the town center. Don't let taxi boatmen con you out of the cheap (L6,000) *vaporetto* ride. Parking in Mestre is easy and much cheaper (open-air lots L8,000 per day, L10,000-a-day garage across from the Mestre train station).

By Plane: A handy shuttle bus (L5,000, 20 min, blue ATVO bus) or the cheaper bus #5 (L1,500, 40 min, orange ICTV bus) connects the airport with the Tronchetto *vaporetto* stop. Romantics jetting in can get directly to St. Mark's Square by Alilaguna speedboat (L17,000, hrly, 70 min, running 6:15–24:00 from the airport, 4:50–22:50 from San Marco). Airport general information tel. 041-2606111 or flight information 041-2609260.

Helpful Hints

The Venice fly trap lures us in and takes our money any way it can. Count your change carefully—I catch someone shortchanging me about once a day. Accept the fact that Venice was a tourist town 400 years ago. It was, is, and always will be crowded. While 80 percent of Venice is actually an untouristy place, 80 percent of the tourists never notice. Hit the back streets.

Get Lost: Venice is the ideal town to explore on foot. Walk and walk to the far reaches of the town. Don't worry about getting lost. Get as lost as possible. Keep reminding yourself, "I'm on an island and I can't get off." When it comes time to find your way, just follow the directional arrows on building corners or simply ask a local, *"Dov'è San Marco?"* ("Where is St. Mark's?"). People in the tourist business (that's most Venetians) speak some English. If they don't, listen politely, watching where their hands point, say *"Grazie,"* and head off in that direction. If you're lost, pop into a hotel and ask for their business card—it comes with a map and a prominent "you are here."

Rip-Offs, Theft, and Help: While pickpockets work the crowded main streets, docks, and *vaporetti*, the dark, late-night streets of Venice are safe. A service called Venezia No Problem aids tourists who've been mistreated by any Venetian business (toll-free tel. 800-355-920).

Water: Venetians pride themselves on having pure, safe, and tasty tap water piped in from the foothills of the Alps (which you can actually see from Venice bell towers on crisp, clear winter days).

Money: Bank rates vary. I like the Banca di Sicilia, a block toward St. Mark's Square from Campo San Bartolomeo. The American Express change desk is just off St. Mark's Square (Mon–Sat 8:30–20:00). Thomas Cook's two offices waive their commission on Thomas Cook checks but charge 4.5 percent for others (Mon–Sat 9:00–20:00, Sun 9:30–17:00, at St. Mark's Square, nearly under the tower with digital clock; or Mon–Sat 9:00–19:45, Sun 9:30–17:00, at Rialto *vaporetto* dock). Nonbank exchange bureaus like Exacto will cost you $10 more than a bank for a $200 exchange. A 24-hour cash machine near the Rialto *vaporetto* stop exchanges U.S. dollars and other currencies for lire at fair rates. ATMs are plentiful.

Travel Agencies: If you need to get train tickets, pay supplements, or make reservations, try Kele & Teo Viaggi e Turismo (cash only, Mon–Fri 8:30–12:30, 15:00–18:00, Sat 9:00–12:00, at Ponte dei Bareteri on the Mercerie midway between Rialto and St. Mark's Square, tel. 041-520-8722) or American Express (Mon–Fri 9:00–17:30, Sat 9:00–12:30, just off St. Mark's Square at 1471, en route to the Accademia, tel. 041-520-0844). Either agency saves travelers with railpasses time-consuming trips to the train station for supplements and reservations (sold at the same price as at the station).

Post Office: A large post office is off the far end of St. Mark's Square (on the side of square opposite the church), and a branch is near the Rialto (on St. Mark's side, Mon–Fri 8:10–13:30, Sat 8:10–12:30).

English-Language Church Service: The San Zulian Church offers a mass in English at 9:30 on Sunday (May–Sept, 2 blocks toward Rialto off St. Mark's Square).

Internet Access: Internet@cafe is a block off Piazza Santa Maria di Formosa on Calle Lunga (daily 9:30–13:00, 15:30–19:30, tel. 041-520-4711).

The "Rolling Venice" Youth Discount Pass: This worthwhile L5,000 pass gives those under 30 discounts on sights and transportation plus information on cheap eating and sleeping (Mon–Fri 9:30–13:00, across the street from Alloggi Masetto—see "Sleeping"—at Corte Contarina 1529, 3rd floor, tel. 041-274-7651). They also have an office at the train station (Mon–Fri, 8:30–12:30, 15:00–19:00).

Pigeon Poop: If bombed by a pigeon, resist the initial response to wipe it off immediately—it'll just smear into your hair. Wait until it dries and flake it off cleanly.

Laundry: Near St. Mark's Square and many of my hotel listings is the full-service Lavanderia Gabriella (Mon–Fri 8:00–19:00, 985 Rio Terra Colonne, off the Mercerie near San Zulian Church, over Ponta dei Ferali, 1st right down Calle dei Armeni, tel. 041-522-1758). Near the Rialto is Lavanderia S.S. Apostoli (Mon–Sat 8:30–12:00, 15:00–19:00, closed Sun, on Campo S.S. Apostoli, tel. 041-522-6650). At either place you can get nine pounds of laundry washed and dried for L30,000—confirm price carefully. Drop it by in the morning; pick it up that afternoon. (Call to be sure they're open.) Don't expect to get your clothes back ironed, folded, or even entirely dry. The modern and much cheaper Bea Vita self-serve *lavanderia* is across the canal from the station (daily 8:00–22:00).

Shopping: If you're buying a substantial amount from a glass/art shop, bargain. It's accepted and almost expected.

Etiquette: Walk on the right. Don't loiter on bridges. Picnics are technically forbidden (keep a low profile). Dress modestly. Men should keep their shirts on. When visiting any major church, men and women should cover their knees and shoulders.

Haircuts: I've been getting my hair cut at Coiffeur Benito for 15 years. Everyone knows Benito, who's been keeping locals trim for 25 years. He's an artist—actually a "hair sculptor"—and a cut (L30,000) is a fun diversion from the tourist grind (behind the San Zulian Church near St. Mark's Square, tel. 041-5286221).

Getting around Venice

The public transit system is a fleet of motorized bus-boats called *vaporetti*. They work like city buses except that they never get a flat, the stops are docks, and if you get off between stops, you may drown. For most, only two lines matter: #1 is the slow boat, taking 45 minutes to make every stop along the entire length of the Grand Canal; and #82 is the fast boat that zips down the Grand Canal in 25 minutes, stopping mainly at Tronchetto (car park), Piazzale Roma (bus station), Ferrovia (train station), Rialto Bridge, and San Marco. Buy a L6,000 ticket before boarding or (for an extra fee) from a conductor on board. There are 24-hour (L18,000) and 72-hour (L35,000) passes. Families get a group ticket for L5,000 per person. Technically, luggage costs the same as dogs—L6,000—but I've never been charged. Riding free? There's a one-in-six chance a conductor will fine you L32,000.

Venice 477

Downtown Venice

LODGING:

1. GUERATTO
2. STURION
3. CANADA
4. ASTORIA
5. CANEVA
6. RIVA
7. PIAVE
8. FONTANA
9. DONI
10. CORONA
11. MASETTO
12. MARIN
13. LEVI
14. GAMBERO
15. CAMPIELLO
16. PAGANELLI
17. ACCADEMIA
18. GALLERIA
19. ALBORETTI
20. ALLA SCALA
21. GIORGIONE
22. AMERICAN
23. BELLE ARTI
24. LA CALCINA
25. CHIESA VALDESE

● 1·82 VAPORETTI STOPS W/LINE #'S
●·····● TRAGHETTO ROUTES

Only three bridges cross the Grand Canal, but *traghetti* (little L700 ferry gondolas, marked on better maps) shuttle locals and in-the-know tourists across the Grand Canal at several handy locations (see Downtown Venice map). Take advantage of these time savers. They can also save money. For instance, while most tourists take the L6,000 *vaporetto* to connect St. Mark's with Salute Church, a L700 *traghetto* also does the job.

Grand Canal Tour of Venice

For a ▲▲▲ joyride, introduce yourself to Venice by boat. You can ride boat #82 (too fast, 25 minutes, be certain you're on a "San Marco via Rialto" boat) or #1 (slow, 45 minutes). Either way, cruise the entire Canale Grande from Tronchetto (car park) or Ferrovia (train station) to San Marco. If you can't snag a front seat, lurk nearby and take one when it becomes available or find an outside seat in the stern. This ride has the best light and least crowds early in the morning. Twilight is also good. While Venice is a barrage on the senses that hardly needs a narration, these notes give the cruise a little meaning and help orient you to this great city. Some city maps (on sale at postcard racks) have a handy Grand Canal map on the back.

Venice, built in a lagoon, sits on pilings—pine trees driven 15 feet into the clay. About 25 miles of canals drain the city, dumping like streams into the Grand Canal. Technically, there are three canals (Grand, Giudecca, and Cannaregio), and the other 45 "canals" are rivers.

Venice is a city of palaces. The most lavish were built fronting this canal. This cruise is the only way to really appreciate the front doors of this unique and historic chorus line of mansions from the days when Venice was the world's richest city. Strict laws prohibit any changes in these buildings, so while landowners gnash their teeth, we can enjoy Europe's best-preserved medieval city—slowly rotting. Many of the grand buildings are now vacant. Others harbor chandeliered elegance above mossy, empty ground floors.

Start at Tronchetto (the bus and car park) or the train station. The station, one of the few modern buildings in town, was built in 1954. It's been the gateway into Venice since 1860, when the first station was built. *F.S.* stands for "Ferrovie dello Stato," the Italian state railway system. The bridge at the station is the first of only three that cross the Canale Grande.

The ghetto is shortly after the station, on the left. Look down Cannareggio Canal (opposite the Riva di Biasio stop). The twin pink six-story buildings (known as the "skyscrapers") are a reminder of how densely populated the world's original ghetto was. Set aside as the local Jewish quarter in 1516, the area became extremely crowded. This urban island (behind the San Marcuola stop) developed into one of the most closely knit business and cultural quarters of all Jewish communities in Italy.

As you cruise, notice the traffic signs. Venice's main thoroughfare is busy with traffic. You'll see all kinds of boats: taxis, police boats, garbage boats, and even brown-and-white UPS boats. Venice's sleek, black, graceful gondolas are a symbol of the city. While used gondolas cost around $10,000, new ones run up to $30,000 apiece. They're built with a slight curve so that one oar propels them in a straight line. Today, with over 500 gondoliers joyriding around the churning *vaporetti*, there's a lot of congestion on the Grand Canal. Watch your *vaporetto* driver curse the gondoliers.

Opposite the San Stae stop look for the faded frescoes. Imagine the facades of the Grand Canal in its day: frescoed by masters like Tintoretto and glittering with mosaics.

At the Ca d'Oro stop notice the lacy Gothic palace. Named the **"House of Gold"**—the frilly edge of the roof was once gilded—it's considered the most elegant Venetian Gothic palace on the canal. Unfortunately there's little to see inside.

On the right, the outdoor **fish and produce market** bustles with people in the morning but is quiet the rest of the day. (This is a great scene to wander through—even though new European hygiene standards require a less-colorful remodeling job in 2000.) Can you see the *traghetto* gondola ferrying shoppers—standing like Washingtons crossing the Delaware—back and forth? Ahead, above the post office, the golden angel of the Campanile faces the wind and marks St. Mark's Square (where this tour ends). The huge **post office**, with *servizio postale* boats moored at its blue posts, is on the left just before the Rialto Bridge.

A major landmark of Venice, the **Rialto Bridge** is lined with shops and tourists. The third bridge on this spot, it was built in 1592. Earlier Rialto Bridges could open to let in big ships. After 1592, the Grand Canal was closed to shipping and became a canal of palaces. With a span of 42 meters and foundations stretching 200 meters on either side, the Rialto was an impressive engineering feat in its day. Locals call the summit of this bridge the "icebox of Venice" for its cool breeze. Tourists call it a great place to kiss. *Rialto* means "high river." The restaurants beyond the bridge feature high prices and low quality.

The Rialto, a separate town in the early days of Venice, has always been the commercial district, while San Marco was the religious and governmental center. Today a street called the Mercerie connects the two, providing travelers with human traffic jams and a gauntlet of shopping temptations.

Beyond the Rialto on the left notice the long stretch of merchants' palaces, each with proud and different facades. Many feature the Roman palace design of twin towers flanking a huge set of central windows. These were light-filled showrooms.

Take a deep whiff of Venice. What's all this nonsense about stinky canals? All I smell is my shirt. By the way, how's your captain? Smooth dockings? To get to know him, stand up in the bow and block his view.

The rising water level takes its toll. Many canal-level floors are abandoned. Notice how many buildings have a foundation of waterproof white stone (*pietra d'Istria*) upon which the bricks sit high and dry. The posts—historically painted gaily with the equivalent of family coats of arms—don't rot under water. But the wood at the water line does rot. Notice how the rich marble facades are just a veneer covering no-nonsense brick buildings. And notice the characteristic chimneys.

After the San Silvestro stop you'll see (on the right) a 13th-century admiral's palace. Venetian admirals marked their palaces with twin obelisks.

After the San Tomá stop look down the side canal (on the right) before the bridge to see the traffic light, the fire station, and the fireboats ready to go.

These days, when buildings are being renovated, huge murals with images of the building mask the ugly scaffolding. Corporations hide the scaffolding out of goodwill (and get their name—e.g., Frette—on the mural).

The wooden Accademia Bridge crosses the Grand Canal and leads to the **Accademia Gallery** (neoclassical facade just after the British consulate on the right), filled with the best Venetian paintings. The bridge was put up in 1932 as a temporary fix for the original iron one. Locals liked it, so it stayed.

Cruising under the bridge, you'll get a classic view of the **Salute Church** (ahead), built as a thanks to God when the devastating plague of 1630 passed. It's claimed that more than a million trees were piled together to build a foundation upon the solid clay 35 meters below sea level. Much of the surrounding countryside was deforested by Venice. Trees were needed both to fuel the furnaces of its booming glass industry and to prop up this city in the mud.

The low white building on the right (between the bridge and the church) is the **Peggy Guggenheim Gallery**. She willed the city a fine collection of modern art. The Salviati building (with the fine mosaic) is a glass factory.

Just before the Salute stop (on the right), the house with the big view windows and the red and wild Andy Warhol painting on the living-room wall (often behind white drapes) was lived in by Mick Jagger. In the 1970s this was famous as Venice's rock-and-roll-star party house.

The building on the right with the golden ball is the Dogana da Mar, a 16th-century customs house. Its two bronze Atlases hold a statue of Fortune riding the ball. While there are no hotels on this side, all the buildings on the left are fancy Grand Canal hotels.

As you prepare to deboat at San Marco, look from left to right out over the lagoon. A wide harbor-front walk leads past the town's most elegant hotels to the green area in the distance. This is the public garden, the only sizable park in town. Farther out is

Venice

the lido, Venice's beach. It's tempting, with its sand and casinos, but its car traffic breaks into the medieval charm of Venice.

The dreamy church that seems to float is the architect Palladio's **San Giorgio**. It's just a scenic *vaporetto* ride away. Find the Tintoretto paintings in the church (such as the *Last Supper*) and take the elevator up the bell tower for a terrific, crowd-free view (L3,000, daily 9:30–13:00, 14:30–18:30, tel. 041-522-7827). Beyond San Giorgio (to your right) is a residential chunk of Venice called the Guidecca.

Get out at the San Marco stop. Directly ahead is Harry's Bar. Hemingway drank here when it was a characteristic no-name *osteria* and the gondoliers' hangout. Today, of course, it's the overpriced hangout of well-dressed Americans who don't mind paying triple for their Bellini (peach juice with Prosecco wine) drinks to make the scene. St. Mark's Square is just around the corner.

For more *vaporetto* fun, ride a boat around the city and out into the lagoon and back (ask for the *circulare*; pron. cheer-koo-LAH-ray). Plenty of boats leave from San Marco for the beach (lido), and speedboats offer tours of nearby islands: Burano is a quiet, picturesque fishing and lace town, Murano specializes in glassblowing, and Torcello has the oldest churches and mosaics but is otherwise dull and desolate. Boat #12 takes you to these remote points slower and cheaper.

Sights—Venice, on St. Mark's Square

▲▲▲**St. Mark's Square (Piazza San Marco)**—Surrounded by splashy and historic buildings, Piazza San Marco is filled with music, lovers, pigeons, and tourists by day and is your private rendezvous with the Middle Ages late at night. Europe's greatest dance floor is the romantic place to be. This is the first place to flood, has Venice's best TI (with your back to the church, go to the far corner on your left), and offers fine public rest rooms (Albergo Diorno—"day hotel," L500 WC, between St. Mark's Square and American Express office, en route to Accademia).

With your back to the church, survey one of Europe's great urban spaces and the only square in Venice to merit the title "Piazza." Nearly two football fields long, it's surrounded by the offices of the republic. On the right are the "old offices" (16th-century Renaissance). On the left are the "new offices" (17th-century Baroque). Napoleon, after enclosing the square with the more simple and austere neoclassical wing across the far end, called this "the most beautiful drawing room in Europe."

The clock tower, a Renaissance tower built in 1496, marks the entry to the Mercerie, the main shopping drag, which connects St. Mark's Square with the Rialto. From the piazza you can see the bronze men (Moors) swing their huge clappers at the top of each hour. In the 17th century one of them knocked an unsuspecting worker off the top and to his death—probably the first-ever killing by a robot. Notice the world's first "digital" clock on the tower facing the square (with dramatic flips every five minutes).

For a slow and pricey evening thrill, invest L12,000 (plus L7,000 if the orchestra plays) in a beer or coffee in one of the elegant cafés with the dueling orchestras. If you're going to sit awhile and savor the scene, it's worth the splurge. For the most thrills L2,000 can get you in Venice, buy a bag of pigeon seed and become popular in a flurry. To get everything airborne, toss your sweater in the air.

▲▲St. Mark's Basilica—Since about A.D. 830 this basilica has housed the saint's bones. The mosaic above the door at the far left of the church shows two guys carrying Mark's coffin into the church. Mark looks pretty grumpy after the long voyage from Egypt. The church has 4,000 square meters of Byzantine mosaics, the best and oldest of which are in the atrium (turn right as you enter and stop under the last dome). Face the piazza, gape up (it's OK, no pigeons), and study the story of Noah, the ark, and the flood (two by two, the wicked being drowned, Noah sending out the dove, a happy rainbow, and a sacrifice of thanks). Now face the church and read clockwise the story of Adam and Eve that rings the bottom of the dome. Step inside the church (stairs on right lead to bronze horses) and notice the rolling mosaic marble floor. As you shuffle under the central dome, look up for the Ascension. (Modest dress, no shorts or bare shoulders, free, Mon–Sat 9:45–17:30, Sun 14:00–16:00, tel. 041-522-5205.) See the schedule board in the atrium listing two free English guided tours of the church each week. The church is particularly beautiful when lit at the 18:45 Mass on Saturday, from 14:00 to 17:00 on Sunday, and some middays.

In the museum upstairs (L3,000, daily 10:00–17:00), you can see an up-close mosaic exhibition, a fine view of the church interior, a view of the square from the horse balcony, and (inside, in their own room) the newly restored original bronze horses. These well-traveled horses, made during the days of Alexander the Great (fourth century B.C.), were taken to Rome by Nero, to Constantinople/Istanbul by Constantine, to Venice by crusaders, to Paris by Napoleon, back "home" to Venice when Napoleon fell, and finally indoors and out of the acidic air.

The treasury and altarpiece of the church (L4,000 each, daily 10:00–17:00) give you the best chance outside of Istanbul or Ravenna to see the glories of Byzantium. Venetian crusaders looted the Christian city of Constantinople and brought home piles of lavish loot (until the advent of TV evangelism, perhaps the lowest point in Christian history). Much of this plunder is stored in the treasury (*tesoro*) of San Marco. As you view these treasures, remember most were made in A.D. 500, while Western Europe was still rutting in the mud. Beneath the high altar lies the body of St. Mark ("Marxus") and the Pala d'Oro, a golden altarpiece made with 80 Byzantine enamels (A.D. 1000–1300). Each shows a religious scene set in gold and precious stones. Both of these sights are interesting and historic, but neither is as much fun as two bags of pigeon seed.

▲▲▲**Doge's Palace (Palazzo Ducale)**—The seat of the Venetian government and home of its ruling duke, or doge, this was the most powerful half acre in Europe for 400 years (daily 9:00–19:00, last entry at 17:30, shorter hours off-season). The L18,000 combo ticket includes admission to a number of lesser museums: Museo Correr (see below), Palazzo Mocenigo (costumes), Museo Vetrario di Murano (glass museum on Murano), and Museo del Merletto di Burano (lace museum on Burano).

While each room in the Doge's Palace has a short English description, the fast-moving, 90-minute, tape-recorded guided tour wand is wonderfully done and worth the L7,000 if you don't have *Rick Steves' Mona Winks* and you're planning to really understand the Palace. (Vagabond lovers, sightseeing cheek to cheek, can crank up the volume and split one wand.)

The palace was built to show off the power and wealth of the republic and remind all visitors that Venice was number one. In typical Venetian Gothic style, the bottom has pointy arches, and the top has an Eastern or Islamic flavor. Its columns sat on pedestals, but in the thousand years since they were erected, the palace has settled into the mud, and the bases have vanished.

Enjoy the newly restored facades from the courtyard. Notice a grand staircase (with nearly naked Moses and Paul Newman at the top). Even the most powerful visitors climbed this to meet the doge. This was the beginning of an architectural power trip. The doge, the elected-for-life king of this "dictatorial republic," lived with his family on the first floor near the halls of power. From his lavish quarters you'll follow the one-way tour through the public rooms of the top floor, finishing with the Bridge of Sighs and the prison. The place is wallpapered with masterpieces by Veronese and Tintoretto. Don't worry much about the great art. Enjoy the building.

In room 12, the Senate Room, the 200 senators met, debated, and passed laws. From the center of the ceiling, Tintoretto's *Triumph of Venice* shows the city in all her glory. Lady Venice, in heaven with the Greek gods, stands high above the lesser nations who swirl respectfully at her feet with gifts.

The Armory shows remnants of the military might the empire employed to keep the east-west trade lines open (and the local economy booming). Squint out the window at the far end for a fine view of Palladio's San Georgio Church and the lido (cars, casinos, crowded beaches) in the distance.

After the huge brown globes, you'll enter the giant Hall of

the Grand Council (180 feet long, capacity 2,000), where the entire nobility met to elect the senate and doge. Ringing the room are portraits of 76 doges (in chronological order). One, a doge who opposed the will of the Grand Council, is blacked out. Behind the doge's throne, you can't miss Tintoretto's monsterpiece, *Paradise*. At 1,700 square feet, this is the world's largest oil painting. Christ and Mary are surrounded by a heavenly host of 500 saints.

Walking over the Bridge of Sighs, you'll enter the prisons. Doges could sentence, torture, and jail opponents secretly and in the privacy of their own homes. As you walk back over the bridge, squeeze your arm outside and wave to the gawking tourists.

▲▲**Museo Civico Correr**—The city history museum is now included (whether you like it or not) with the Doge's Palace admission. In the Napoleon Wing you'll see fine neoclassical works by Canova. Then peruse armor, banners, and paintings recreating festive days of the Venetian Republic. The top floor lays out a fine overview of Venetian art. And just before the cafeteria a room is filled with traditional games. There are fine English descriptions and great Piazza San Marco views throughout (L18,000 combo ticket with Doge's Palace, enter in arcade directly opposite church, daily 9:00–19:00, Nov–Mar daily 9:00–17:00, tel. 041-5224951).

▲**Campanile di San Marco**—Ride the elevator 300 feet to the top of the bell tower for the best view in Venice. This tower crumbled into a pile of bricks in 1902, a thousand years after it was built. For an ear-shattering experience, be on top when the bells ring (L8,000, daily 9:00–21:00 in summer, until 19:00 otherwise). The golden angel at its top always faces into the wind. Beat the crowds and enjoy crisp air at 9:00.

More Sights—Venice

▲▲**Galleria dell' Accademia**—Venice's top art museum, packed with highlights of the Venetian Renaissance, features paintings by Bellini, Veronese, Tiepolo, Giorgione, Testosterone, and Canaletto. It's just over the wooden Accademia Bridge (L15,000, Mon 9:00–14:00, Tue–Fri 9:00–21:00, Sat 9:00–23:00, Sun 9:00–20:00; shorter hours off-season; expect late morning delays, as they allow only 300 visitors at a time; visit late to miss crowds, tel. 041-522-2247). Hour-long guided tours run Monday through Friday at 10:00, 11:00, and 12:00 for L8,000 (you can skip to the front of the line if buying a tour). There's a decent pizzeria at the bridge (Pizzeria Accademia Foscarini; see "Eating," below), a public WC under it, and a classic shell game going on on top of it (study the system as partners in the crowd win big money).

▲**Peggy Guggenheim Collection**—This popular collection of far-out art, including works by Picasso, Chagall, and Dalí, offers one of Europe's best reviews of the art styles of the 20th century (L12,000, Wed–Mon 11:00–18:00, closed Tue, near the Accademia).

Venice

▲▲**Chiesa dei Frari**—This great Gothic Franciscan church, an artistic highlight of Venice featuring three great masters, offers more art per lira than any other Venetian sight. Freeload on English-language tours to get the most out of the Titian *Assumption* above the high altar. Then move one chapel to the right to see Donatello's wood carving of St. John the Baptist almost live. And for the climax, continue right through an arch into the sacristy to sit before Bellini's *Madonna and the Saints*. The genius of Bellini, perhaps the greatest Venetian painter, is obvious in the pristine clarity, believable depth, and reassuring calm of this three-paneled altarpiece. Notice the rich colors of Mary's clothing and how good it is to see a painting in its intended setting. For many, these three pieces of art make a visit to the Accademia Gallery unnecessary (or they may whet your appetite for more). Before leaving, check out the neoclassical, pyramid-shaped tomb of Canova and (opposite that) the grandiose tomb of Titian the Venetian. Compare the carved marble Assumption behind his tombstone portrait with the painted original above the high altar (L3,000, Mon–Sat 9:00–18:00, Sun 13:00–18:00).

▲**Scuola di San Rocco**—Next to the Frari Church, another lavish building bursts with art, including some 50 Tintorettos. The best paintings are upstairs, especially the *Crucifixion* in the smaller room. View the neck-breaking splendor with one of the mirrors (*specchio*) available at the entrance (L9,000, daily 9:00–17:30). For *molto* Tiepolo (14 stations of the cross), drop by the nearby Church of San Polo.

Ca' Rezzonico—This 18th-century Grand Canal *palazzo* is the Museo del '700 Veneziano, offering a good look at the life of Venice's rich and famous in the 1700s (at a *vaporetto* stop of the same name, tel. 041-522-4543). It will probably be closed for restoration in 2000.

▲**Gondola Rides**—This is a rip-off for some but a traditional must for romantics. Gondoliers charge about L120,000 for a 40-minute ride (L150,000 to 200,000 at night, from 20:00 on). You can divide the cost—and the romance—among up to six people (some take seven if you're cute, blonde, and female). Glide through nighttime Venice with your head on someone else's shoulder. Follow the moon as it sails past otherwise unseen buildings. Silhouettes gaze down from bridges while window glitter spills onto the black water. You're anonymous in the city of masks as the rhythmic thrust of your striped-shirted gondolier turns old crows into songbirds. This is extremely relaxing (and I think worth the extra to experience at night). Since you'll be enjoying a narration and some chat with your gondolier, talk with a few and choose one you like who speaks English well.

For a glimpse at a gondola workshop in the Accademia neighborhood, walk down the Accademia side of the canal Fondamente

Nani. As you approach Giudecca Canal you'll see the beached gondolas on your right across the Nani Canal.

For cheap gondola thrills, stick to the L700 one-minute ferry ride on a Grand Canal *traghetto* or hang out on a bridge along the gondola route and wave at (or drop leftover pigeon seed on) romantics.

▲Glassblowing—Don't go all the way to Murano Island to see glassblowing demonstrations. A demo's a demo. For the handiest show, wait by one of several glassworks near St. Mark's Square and follow any tour group into the furnace room for a fun and free 10-minute show. (Two big companies that welcome individuals are 200 yards behind St. Mark's Basilica; facing the church, go left alongside it and continue straight.) You'll usually see a vase and a "leetle 'orse" made from molten glass. The commercial that always follows in the showroom is actually entertaining. Prices around St. Mark's have a sizable tour-guide commission built in. Serious glass shoppers buy at small shops on Murano Island.

Santa Elena—For a pleasant peek into a completely untouristy residential side of Venice, catch the boat from St. Mark's Square to the neighborhood of Santa Elena (at the fish's tail). This 100-year-old suburb lives as if there were no tourism. You'll find a kid-friendly park, a few lazy restaurants, and beautiful sunsets over San Marco.

Sights—Venice Lagoon

Several interesting islands hide out in the Venice Lagoon. **Burano,** famous for its lace making, is a sleepy island with a sleepy community—village Venice without the glitz. Lace fans enjoy Burano's Scuola di Merletti (L8,000, Wed–Mon 10:00–17:00, closed Tue, tel. 041-730-034).

Torcello, another lagoon island, is dead except for its church, which claims to be the oldest in Venice (L5,000, daily 10:30–17:30, tel. 041-730-084). It's impressive for its mosaics but not worth a look on a short visit unless you really have your heart set on Ravenna but can't make it there.

The island of **Murano,** famous for its glass factories, has the Museo Vetrario, which displays the very best of 700 years of Venetian glassmaking (L8,000, Thu–Tue 10:00–17:00, closed Wed, tel. 041-739-586). The islands are reached easily but slowly by *vaporetto* (from the Fondamente Nuove or San Zaccaria docks). Four-hour speedboat tours of these three lagoon destinations leave twice a day from the dock near the Doge's Palace.

Nightlife in Venice

Venice is quiet at night, as tour groups are back in the cheaper hotels of Mestre, the masses of day-trippers return to their beach resorts, and the East Europeans are busing home overnight. Gondolas cost nearly double but are doubly romantic and relaxing

Venice Lagoon

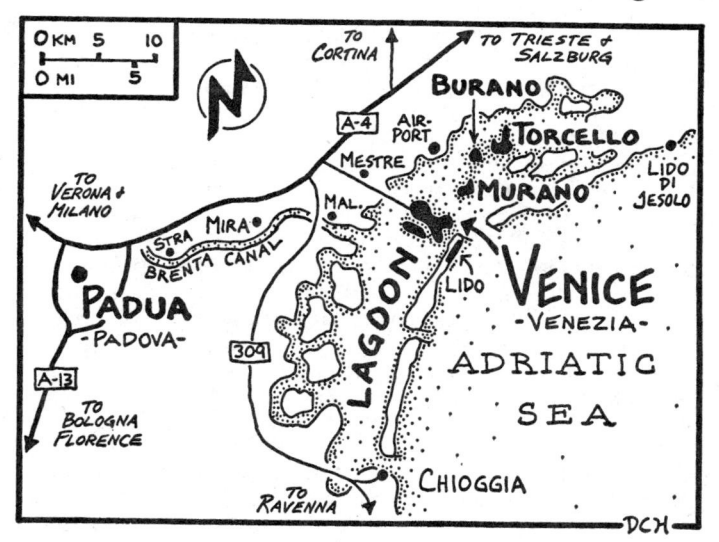

under the moon. *Vaporettos* are nearly empty, and it's a great time to cruise the Grand Canal on the slow boat #1.

Take your pick of traditional Vivaldi concerts in churches throughout town. Vivaldi is as trendy here as Strauss in Vienna and Mozart in Salzburg. In fact you'll find frilly young Vivaldis all over town hawking concert tickets. The TI has a list of this week's concerts (tickets from L30,000). If you see a concert at Scuola di San Rocco, you can enjoy the art (which you're likely to pay L9,000 for during the day) for free during the intermission.

On St. Mark's Square the dueling café orchestras entertain. Hang out for free behind the tables or spring for a seat and enjoy a fun and gorgeously set concert. If you sit awhile it can be L20,000 well spent (drink L12,000 plus a onetime L7,000 fee for entertainment).

You're not a tourist, you're a living part of a soft Venetian night... an alley cat with money. Streetlamp halos, live music, floodlit history, and a ceiling of stars make St. Mark's magic at midnight. Shine with the old lanterns on the gondola piers where the sloppy Grand Canal splashes at the Doge's Palace... reminiscing. Comfort the four frightened tetrarchs (ancient Byzantine emperors) under the moon where the Doge's Palace hits the basilica. Cuddle history.

Sleeping in Venice
(L1,900 = about $1)
Sleep Code: **S** = Single, **D** = Double/Twin, **T** = Triple, **Q** = Quad, **b** = bathroom, **t** = toilet only, **s** = shower only, **CC** = Credit Card (Visa, MasterCard, Amex), **SE** = Speaks English, **NSE** = No English. Breakfast is included unless otherwise noted. Air conditioning, when available, is usually only turned on in summer. See map on page 477 for hotel locations.

Reserve a room as soon as you know when you'll be in town. Call first to see what's available. Follow up with a fax unless you're already on the road. Most places will take a credit card for a deposit. If everything's full, don't despair. Call a day or two in advance and fill in a cancellation. If you arrive on an overnight train, your room may not be ready. Drop your bag at the hotel and dive right into Venice.

I've listed prices for peak season: April, May, June, September, and October. July and August are low season, and rooms are discounted about 25 percent. Book direct—not through any tourist agency. Prices may be cheaper (or soft) off-season. If on a budget, ask for a cheaper room or a discount. Many places give up to a 10 percent discount for cash ("tax-free" income). Always ask. I've listed rooms in two basic neighborhoods: in the Rialto–San Marco action and in a quiet Dorsoduro area behind the Accademia Gallery.

Sleeping near St. Mark's Square
(zip code: 30122)

Hotel Riva, with gleaming marble hallways and bright modern rooms, is romantically situated on a canal along the gondola serenade route. You could actually dunk your breakfast rolls in the canal (but don't). Sandro may hold a corner (*angolo*) room if you ask. Confirm prices and reconfirm reservations, as readers have had trouble with both (2 4th-floor view D with adjacent showers-L140,000, Db-L170,000, Tb-L250,000, Ponte dell' Angelo, #5310 Castello, 30122 Venezia, tel. 041-522-7034, fax 041-528-5551, unenthusiastic receptionists don't speak English). Face St. Mark's cathedral, walk behind it on the left along Calle de la Canonica, take the first left (at blue "Pauly & C" mosaic in street), continue straight, go over the bridge, and angle right to the hotel.

Locanda Piave, with 15 fine rooms above a bright and classy lobby, feels fresh, modern, and comfortable (Db-L240,000, family suites-L350,000–420,000 for 3–5 people, prices with this book, CC:VMA but 10 percent discount with cash, air-con; *vaporetto* #82 to San Zaccaria, find Campo Santa Maria Formosa; then—with Hotel Scandinavia on your left and the church on your right—cross the bridge and follow Ruga Giuffa 50 yards to #4838/40, Castello, 30122 Venezia, tel. 041-528-5174, fax 041-523-8512, e-mail: hotel.alpiave@iol.it, Mirella, Paolo, and Ilaria SE, faithful

Molly NSE). They have a couple of apartments for L350,000–420,000 (cash only, includes kitchenette).

Locanda Gambero, with 27 rooms, is the biggest one-star hotel in the San Marco area (S-L85,000, old D-L140,000, new Db-L210,000, T-L190,000, Tb-L283,000, CC:VM, rooms with bath also have TV and air-con; from Rialto *vaporetto* #1 dock go straight inland on Calle le Bembo, which becomes Calle dei Fabbri; or from St. Mark's Square go through Sotoportego dei Dai then down Calle dei Fabbri to #4687, at intersection with Calle del Gambero, tel. 041-522-4384, fax 041-520-0431, e-mail: hotgamb@tin.it). Gambero runs the pleasant Art Deco "La Bistrot" on the corner, which serves old-time Venetian cuisine.

Alloggi Alla Scala, a comfy and tidy five-room place run by Senora Andreina della Fiorentina, is homey, central, and tucked away on a quiet square that features a famous spiral stairway called Scala Contarini del Bovolo (small Db-L120,000, big Db-L140,000, extra bed-L40,000, breakfast-L10,000, CC:VM, Campo Manin #4306, San Marco, tel. 041-521-0629, fax 041-522-6451, daughter SE). From Campo Manin follow signs to (on statue's left) "Scala Contarini del Bovolo."

Hotel Astoria is a clean, simple place with 28 comfortable rooms tucked away a few blocks off St. Mark's Square (D-L160,000, Db-L210,000, Jul–Aug Db-L150,000, closed mid-Nov–mid-Mar, CC:VMA, 2 blocks from San Zulian Church at Calle Fiubera #951, tel. 041-522-5381, fax 041-520-0771).

Hotel Fontana is a cozy, two-star, family-run place with lots of stairs on a touristy square two bridges behind St. Mark's Square (Db-L210,000–260,000, family rooms, CC:VMA, 10 percent discount with cash, fans, 2 bridges behind St. Mark's Square on Campo San Provolo, Castello 4701, tel. 041-522-0579, fax 041-523-1040, www.hotelfontana.it).

Hotel Caneva is an institutional, vinyl feeling, canal-side place with plain, big, bright rooms and a tired management (S-L70,000, Sb-L110,000, Db-L155,000, Tb-L205,000, prices good with this book and cash, CC:VMA but prices increase with a credit card; midway between Rialto and St. Mark's Square near Chiesa la Fava, Ramo Dietro La Fava #5515, 30122 Venezia, tel. 041-522-8118, fax 041-520-8676).

Albergo Corona is a clean, confusing Old World place with eight basic rooms (D-L115,000, lots of stairs, tel. 041-522-9174, SE). Coming from St. Mark's Square, find Campo SS Filippo e Giacomo, go down Calle Sacristia, take the first right, and then go left on Calle Corona to #4464.

Alloggi Masetto is well located and has four dirt-cheap rooms. It's an eccentric grandmotherly place filled with birds, goldfish, and stacks of magazines. Irvana Artico, the erratic landlady, surprises you with pretty good English. Your mission: charm Irvana (D-L55,000, Db-L75,000, T-L75,000, Tb-90,000, confirm prices carefully, breakfast?... You wouldn't want it, shower *rapido* or suffer Irvana's wrath; from American Express head toward St. Mark's Square, first left, first left again through "Contarina" tunnel, follow white sign to Commune di Venezia and see her sign, Sotoportego Ramo Contarina #1520a, Frezzeria, tel. 041-523-0505). One-night stays make Irvana angry.

Sleeping near the Waterfront and Doge's Palace

These places, about one canal down from the Bridge of Sighs on or just off the Riva degli Schiavoni waterfront promenade, rub drainpipes with Venice's most palatial five-star hotels. Each—while pricey for the location and not particularly friendly—is professional and comfortable. Ride *vaporetto* #82 to San Zaccaria.

Hotel Campiello is a lacy and bright little 16-room place, ideally located 50 yards off the waterfront (Sb-L190,000, Db-L230,000–280,000, CC:VMA, 5 percent discount with cash, air-con; behind Hotel Savoia, up Calle del Vin off Riva Schiavoni, San Zaccaria #4647, tel. 041-520-5764, fax 041-520-5798, e-mail: campiello@hcampiello.it, run by sisters Monica and Nicoletta).

Albergo Paganelli is right on the Riva degli Schiavoni and has a few incredible view rooms (S-L150,000, Sb-L190,000, D-L190,000, Db-L240,000–280,000, Db with view-L300,000, T-L205,000, Tb-L390,000, request *"con vista"* for view, CC:VMA, air-con, prices often soft, at San Zaccaria *vaporetto* stop, Riva degli Schiavoni #4182, Castello, 30122 Venezia, tel. 041-522-4324, fax 041-523-9267, e-mail: hotelpag@tin.it). With spacious rooms, carved and gilded headboards, chandeliers, and hair dryers, this hotelesque place is a good value. Seven of their 22 rooms are in a less interesting but equally comfortable *dependencia* a block off the canal.

Albergo Doni is a dark, hardwood, clean, and quiet place with 12 dim-but-classy rooms run by a likable smart aleck named Gina (D-L130,000, Db-L170,000, T-L170,000, Tb-L220,000, ceiling fans, air-con for L10,000 extra, use credit card to secure telephone reservations but must pay in cash, Riva Schiavoni, San Zaccaria N. #4656 Calle del Vin, tel. & fax 041-522-4267, Nick and Gina SE). Leave Riva Degli Schiavoni on Calle del Vin and go 100 yards with a left jog.

Sleeping near the Rialto Bridge
(zip code: 30125)

Locanda Sturion, with air-conditioning and all the modern comforts, is pricey because it overlooks the Grand Canal (Db-L310,000, L250,000 in low season, Tb-405,000, Qb-L520,000, canal-view rooms cost about L60,000 extra, CC:VMA, miles of

Venice

stairs, 100 yards from the Rialto Bridge opposite *vaporet* San Polo, Rialto, Calle Sturion #679, 30125 Venezia, tel 6243, fax 041-522-8378, e-mail: sturion@tin.it, SE). They require a personal check or traveler's check for a deposit. The similar **Hotel Locanda Ovidius** is one floor below (9 rooms, Db-L180,000–350,000, CC:VMA, air-con, Calle del Sturion #677a, tel. 041-523-7970, fax 041-5204101, www.hotelovidius.com).

Hotel Canada has 25 small, pleasant rooms (Sb-L190,000, 2 D with adjacent bath-L220,000, Db-L250,000, CC:VM, air-con L15,000 extra, rooms on canal come with view, noise, and aroma, rooms facing church are quiet and fresh, Castello San Lio #5659, 30122 Venezia, tel. 041-522-9912, fax 041-523-5852, SE). Canada is ideally located on a small, lively square, just off Campo San Lio between the Rialto and St. Mark's Square.

Albergo Guerrato, overlooking a handy and colorful produce market, one minute from the Rialto action, is run by friendly, creative, and hardworking Roberto and Piero. Georgio takes the night shift. Their 800-year-old building is Old World simple, airy, and wonderfully characteristic (D-L130,000, Db-L175,000, T-L170,000, Tb-L230,000, Q-L190,000, Qb-L270,000, including a L4,000 city map, prices promised through 2000 with this book, cash only, no double beds; walk over the Rialto away from St. Mark's Square, go straight about 3 blocks, turn right on Calle drio la Scimia—not Scimia, the block before—and you'll see the hotel sign, Calle drio la Scimia #240a, 30125 San Polo, tel. & fax 041-522-7131 or 528-5927, e-mail: hguerrat@tin.it, SE). My tour groups book this place for 50 nights each year. Sorry. If you fax without calling first, no reply within three days means they are booked up. (It's best to call first.)

Hotel Giorgione, a four-star hotel in a 15th-century palace on a quiet lane, is superprofessional, with plush public spaces, pool tables, Internet access, a garden terrace, and 70 spacious over-the-top rooms with all the comforts (Sb-L230,000–270,000, Db-L350,00–400,000, pricier suites, extra bed-L100,000, 20 percent off in July and August, check the Web for discounts, CC:VMA, elevator, air-con, Piazza SS Apostoli #4587, tel. 041-522-5810, fax 041-523-9092, www.hotelgiorgione.com).

Sleeping near the Accademia

When you step over the Accademia Bridge, the commotion of touristy Venice is replaced by a sleepy village laced with canals. This quiet area, next to the best painting gallery in town, is a 10-minute walk from St. Mark's Square and the Rialto. All are within 12 minutes from the station or car park and 3 minutes from St. Mark's Square on the fast boat #82.

Pension Accademia fills the 17th-century Villa Maravege. While its 27 comfortable and air-conditioned rooms are nothing extraordinary, you'll feel aristocratic gliding through its grand public spaces and lounging in its breezy garden (Sb-L185,000, standard Db-L255,000–300,000, superior Db-L300,000–350,000, family deals, CC:VMA; on the corner of Rio della Toletta and Rio di San Trovaso 200 yards from gallery, Dorsoduro #1058, 30123 Venezia, tel. 041-523-7846, fax 041-523-9152, e-mail: pensione .accademia@flashnet.it).

Hotel Galleria is a compact and velvety little 10-room place (S-L100,000, D-L140,000–150,000, Db-L170,000–200,000, depending upon size of room, CC:VMA, breakfast in room, some views overlooking canal next to Accademia Gallery, fans, Dorsoduro #878a, 30123 Venezia, tel. 041-523-2489, tel. & fax 041-520-4172, e-mail: galleria@tin.it, SE).

Hotel Agli Alboretti is a cozy, family-run, 25-room place in a quiet neighborhood a block behind the Accademia Museum (Sb-L168,000, 2 small Db-L210,000, Db-L260,000, Tb-L315,000, CC:VMA, air-con; 100 yards from the Accademia *vaporetto* stop on Rio Terra a Foscarini at #884 Accademia, tel. 041-523-0058, fax 041-521-0158, e-mail: alborett@gpnet.it, SE).

Hotel American is a small, cushy, three-star place on a lazy canal next to the delightful Campo San Vio (a tiny overlooked square facing the Grand Canal). It's an Old World hotel with 18 rooms and better rates on weekdays (Sb-L130,000–250,000, Db-L250,000–400,000—rates vary with canal view and season, extra bed-L50,000–85,000, buffet breakfast, CC:VMA, air-con, 30 meters off Campo San Vio and 200 meters from Accademia Gallery, 628 Accademia, 30123 Venezia, tel. 041-520-4733, fax 041-520-4048, www.hotelamerican.com for deals).

Hotel Belle Arti is the place if you want to be in the old center without the commotion and intensity of Venice. With all the American hotel comforts, it's a big, modern, three-star place sitting on a former schoolyard (Db-L340,000, Jul–Aug Db-L280,000, Tb-L330,000–420,000, CC:VMA, buffet breakfast, plush public areas, air-con, elevator, 100 meters immediately behind the Accademia Gallery, at Via Dorsoduro 912, tel. 041-522-6230, fax 041-528-0043).

Pensione La Calcina, the home of English writer Ruskin in 1876, comes with all the three-star comforts in a professional yet intimate package. It's squeaky clean, with hardwood floors and a peaceful canalside setting facing the Giudecca at the south end of Rio di San Vio (Sb-L140,000–160,000, Db-L180,000–280,000 depending upon the size, season, and view, CC:VMA, air-con, canalside buffet breakfast terrace, Dorsoduro #780, tel. 041-520-6466, fax 041-522-7045). From the car park or station catch *vaporetto* #51 to Zattere.

Fondazione Levi, a guest house run by a foundation that promotes research on Venetian music, offers 18 quiet, comfortable

Venice **493**

rooms (Sb-L110,000, Db-L180,000, Tb-L210,000, Qb-L240,000, only twin beds, elevator, 80 meters from San Marco side of Accademia Bridge, cross Ponte Giustinian and go down Calle Giustinian directly to the Fondazione, buzz the "Foresteria" door to the right, San Vidal #2893, 30124 Venezia, tel. 041-786-711, fax 041-786-766, SE).

Sleeping near the Train Station

Hotel Marin is three minutes from the train station but completely out of the touristic bustle of the Lista di Spagna. Just renovated, cozy, and cheery, it seems like a 19-bedroom home the moment you cross the threshold and is one of the best values in town (S-L90,000, D-L115,000, Db-L145,000, T-L160,000, Tb-L190,000, Q-L195,000, Qb-L215,000, prices good with this book and if you pay cash, CC:VMA, San Croce #670b, tel. 041-718-022, fax 041-721-485, www.hotelmarin.it). It's family run by helpful, friendly English-speaking Bruno, Nadia, and son Samuel (they have city maps). It's immediately across the canal from the train station, behind the green dome (over bridge, right, first left, first right, first right). There's an Internet café and handy Laundromat nearby.

Dormitory Accommodations

Foresteria della Chiesa Valdese, warmly run by a Protestant church, offers dorm beds at youth hostel prices in a handy location (halfway between St. Mark's Square and Rialto). This run-down but charming old palace has elegant paintings on the ceilings (L30,000 dorm beds or L85,000 doubles with sheets and breakfast, more expensive for 1-night stays, some larger "apartments" for families or small groups, office open Mon–Sat 9:00–13:00, 18:00–20:00, Sun 9:00–13:00, from Campo Santa Maria di Formosa, walk past Bar all' Orologio to the end of Calle Lunga and cross the bridge, Castello #5170, tel. & fax 041-528-6797).

Foresteria Domus Cavanis, near the Accademia, is a simple church-run dorm offering cheap beds June 15 through September 15 only (S-L50,000, D-L75,000, breakfast-L5,000, next to Hotel Agli Alboretti, listed above, at #896 on Rio Antonio Foscarini, tel. & fax 041-522-2826).

The **Venice youth hostel,** on Giudecca Island, is crowded, cheap, and newly remodeled (L25,000 beds with sheets and breakfast in 10- to 16-bed rooms, membership required, office open 7:00–9:30, 13:30–23:00, catch *vaporetto* #82 from station or San Marco to Zittele, tel. 041-523-8211). Their budget cafeteria welcomes nonhostelers (nightly 18:00–23:00).

Eating in Venice

While touristy restaurants are the scourge of Venice, there are plenty of good alternatives. The first trick: Walk away from triple-language menus. For budget eating, I like small *cicchetti* bars (see "Pub Crawl," below) or simple pizzalike dinners at scenic locations. For speed, value, and ambience, you can get a filling plate of local-style tapas at nearly any of the bars described below.

A key to cheap eating in Venice is bar snacks, especially stand-up minimeals in out-of-the-way bars. Order by pointing. *Panini* (sandwiches) are sold fast and cheap at bars everywhere. Pizzerias are cheap and easy.

The **produce market** that sprawls for a few blocks just past the Rialto Bridge (best 8:00–13:00, closed Sun) is a great place to assemble a picnic. The nearby street, Ruga Vecchia, has good bakeries and cheese shops. Side lanes in this area are speckled with fine little hole-in-the-wall munchie bars.

The **Mensa DLF,** the public transportation workers' cafeteria, is cheap and open to the public (daily 11:00–14:30, 18:00–22:00). Leaving the train station, turn right on the Grand Canal, walk about 150 yards along the canal, up eight steps, and through the unmarked door.

The Stand-Up Progressive Venetian Pub-Crawl Dinner

A tradition unique to Venice in Italy is a *giro di ombre* (pub crawl)—ideal in a city with no cars. My favorite Venetian dinner is a pub crawl. I've listed plenty of pubs in walking order for a quick or extended crawl below. If you've crawled enough, most of these bars make a fine one-stop, sit-down dinner. *Ombre* means shade, from the old days when a wine bar scooted with the shadow of the Campanile across St. Mark's Square.

Venice's residential back streets hide plenty of characteristic bars with countless trays of interesting toothpick-munchie food (*cicchetti*). This is a great way to mingle and have fun with the Venetians. Real *cicchetti* pubs are getting rare in these fast-food days, but locals appreciate the ones that survive.

Try fried mozzarella, gorgonzola, calamari, artichoke hearts, and anything ugly on a toothpick. Ask for a *piatto misto* (mixed plate). Or try *"Un classico piatto di cicchetti misti da dieci mila lire"* (a plate of assorted appetizers for L10,000, depending upon how much food you want). Drink house wines. A small glass of house red or white wine (*ombre rosso* or *ombre bianco*) or a small beer (*birrino*) costs about L2,000. *Vin bon,* Venetian for "fine wine," may cost L3,000 to L5,000 per little glass. Meat and fish (*pesce:* PAY-shay) munchies are expensive; veggies (*verdura*) are cheap, around L6,000 for a meal-sized plate. Bread sticks (*grissini*) are free. A good last drink is *fragolino,* the local sweet wine—*bianco* or *rosso.* A liter of house wine costs around L7,000. Bars don't stay open late, and the *cicchetti* selection is best early, so start your evening by 18:00. Most bars are closed on Sunday. You can stand around the bar or grab a table in the back—usually for the same price.

Venice 495

Venice Pub Crawl

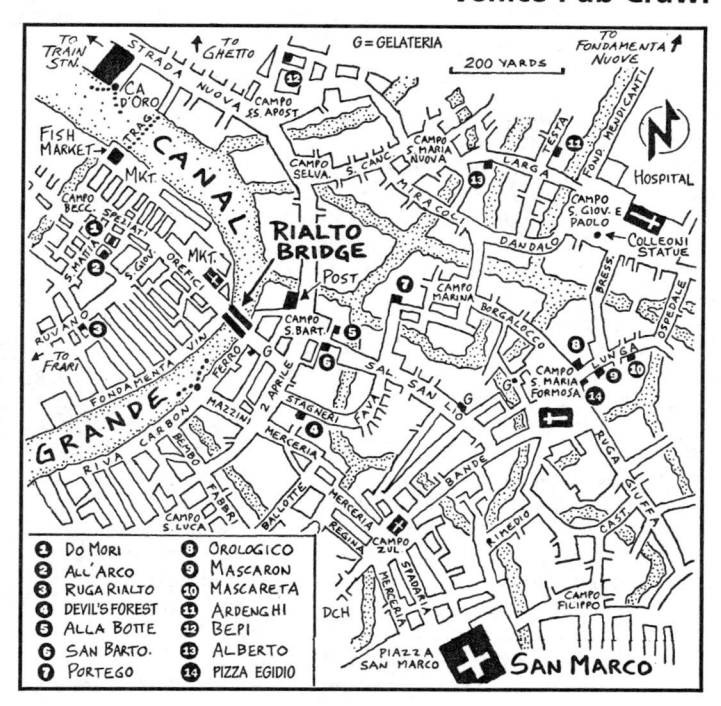

Cicchetteria *West of the Rialto Bridge*

Cantina Do Mori is famous with locals (since 1462) and savvy travelers (since 1962) as a classy place for fine wine and *francobollo* (a spicy selection of 20 tiny sandwiches called "stamps"). Choose from the featured wines in the barrel on the bar. Order carefully, or they'll rip you off. From Rialto Bridge walk 200 yards down Ruga degli Orefici away from St. Mark's Square—then ask (Mon–Sat 17:00–20:30, closed Sun, stand-up only, arrive early before *cicchetti* are gone, San Polo 429, tel. 041-522-5401). The rough-and-tumble **Cantina All' Arco** across the lane is worth a quick *ombra*.

Antica Ostaria Ruga Rialto is less expensive than Do Mori and offers tables, a busier/younger crowd, and a better selection of munchies (closed Mon, past the blue Chinese restaurant sign, on corner of Ruga Vecchia S. Giovanni and Ramo del Sturion, San Polo 692, tel. 041-521-1243).

There are several other *cicchetti* bars within a block or two.

You could track down **Ostaria Sora al Ponte** (closed Mon, San Polo 1588, tel. 041-718-208), **Cantina Do Spade, Vini da Pinto,** and **Osteria Enoteca Vivaldi** (on Campo A. Aponal).

Eating near Campo San Bartolomeo, East of the Rialto Bridge

Osteria "Alla Botte" Cicchetteria is an atmospheric place packed with a young, local, bohemian jazz clientele. It's good for a light meal or a *cicchetti* snack with wine (2 short blocks off Campo San Bartolomeo in the corner behind the statue—down Calle de la Bissa, tel. 041-520-9775, notice the "day after" photo showing a debris-covered Venice after the notorious 1989 Pink Floyd open-air concert).

If the statue on the Campo San Bartolomeo walked backward 20 yards, turned left, and went under a passageway, he'd hit **Rosticceria San Bartolomeo.** This cheap—if confusing—self-service restaurant on the ground floor has a likably surly staff (good L8,000 pasta, great fried mozzarella *al* prosciutto for L2,300, delightful fruit salad, and L2,000 glasses of wine from a cute wine list, prices listed at the door, no cover or service charge, daily 9:30–21:30, tel. 041-522-3569). Good but pricier meals are served at the full-service restaurant upstairs. Take out or grab a table.

From Rosticceria San Bartolomeo, continue over a bridge to Campo San Lio (a good landmark), go left at Hotel Canada, and walk straight over another bridge into **Osteria Al Portego** (at #6015). This fine, friendly, and local-style bar has plenty of *cicchetti* (Mon–Fri 9:00–22:00, closed Sat–Sun, tel. 041-522-9038). The *cicchetti* here can make a great meal. If pub crawling from here, ask *"Dov'è Santa Maria di Formosa?"*

The **Devil's Forest Pub,** an air-conditioned bit of England tucked away a block from the crowds, is—strangely—more Venetian these days than the *tipico* places. Locals come here for good English and Irish beer on tap, big salads (L12,000, lunch only), hot bar snacks, and an easygoing ambience (no cover or service charge, fine prices, backgammon and chess boards available-L3000, meals daily 12:00–15:30, bar snacks all the time, a block off Campo San Bartolomeo on Calle dei Stagneri, tel. 041-5200623). Across the street, the **Bora Bora Pizzeria** serves pizza and salads from an entertaining menu (daily 12:00–15:00, 19:00–22:30, tel. 041-523-6583).

Eating near Campo Santa Maria di Formosa

Campo Santa Maria di Formosa is just plain atmospheric (as most squares with a Socialist Party office seem to be). For a balmy outdoor sit, you could split a pizza with wine on the square. **Bar all' Orologio** has a good setting and friendly service but mediocre "freezer" pizza (happy to split a pizza for pub crawlers, Mon–Sat 6:00–23:00, closed Sun). **Pizzeria da Egidio** has the best pizza on the square (closed Wed, tel. 041-528-9169). For a pizza snack on the square, cross the bridge behind the canalside *gelateria* and grab a slice to go from **Cip Ciap Pizza** (open until 21:00, closed Tue, Calle del Mondo Novo). Pub crawlers get a salad course at the fruit-and-vegetable stand next to the water fountain (open until about 19:30).

From Campo S.M. di Formosa, follow the yellow sign to "SS Giov e Paolo" down Calle Longa Santa Maria di Formosa and head down the street to **Osteria Mascaron** (Gigi's bar, best selection by 19:30, closes at 24:00 and on Sun). Gigi also runs **Enoteca Mascareta**, with less food and more wine, 30 yards farther down the street (#5183, closed Sun, tel. 041-523-0744). The piano sounds like they dropped it in the canal, but the wine was saved.

Eating between Campo Santi Apostoli and Campo SS Giovanni e Paolo

Trattoria da Bepi caters to a local crowd and specializes in fresh seafood and Venetian cuisine. Bepi's son, Loris, who speaks English, makes a smooth *panna cotta* and a mean licorice grappa (Fri–Wed 19:00–22:00, closed Thu, CC:VM, allow L65,000 per person, on Calle Pistar next to Santi Apostoli Church, tel. 041-528-5031).

Antiche Cantine Ardenghi de Lucia e Michael is an excellent splurge. Michael, an effervescent former Murano glass salesman, and his wife, Lucia, cook for a handful of people each night by reservation only. You must call first. You pay L70,000 per person and trust them to wine, dine, and serenade you with Venetian class. The evening can be quiet or raucous. When you call, ask for a festival of fruit and vegetables or you'll get nothing but crustaceans. There's no sign, and the door's locked. Find #6369 and knock. The password: La Republica Serenissima. From Campo SS Giovanni e Paolo, pass the churchlike hospital (notice the illusions painted on its facade), go over the bridge to the left, and take the first right to #6369 (Tue–Sat 20:00–02:00, closed Sun–Mon, tel. 041-523-7691).

Two colorful *osterias* are good for *cicchetti*, wine tasting, or a simple, rustic, sit-down meal surrounded by a boisterous local ambience: **Osteria da Alberto** (Mon–Sat 18:00–21:30, closed Sun, midway between Campo Santi Apostoli and Campo SS Giovanni e Paolo, next to Ponte de la Panada on Calle Larga Giacinto Gallina) and **Osteria Candela** on Calle de l'Oca. You'll find local pubs in the side streets opposite Campo St. Sofia across Strada Nueva.

For great local cuisine in a rustic Venetian setting, hike to **Osteria Al Bacco** in Cannaregio (closed Mon, Fondamenta Capuzine, Cannaregio #3054, reservations wise, tel. 041-717-493).

Eating near the Accademia

Restaurant/Pizzeria Accademia Foscarini, next to the Accademia Bridge and Galleria, offers decent L10,000 pizzas in a great canalside setting (Wed–Mon 7:00–23:00, closed Tue, tel. 041-522-7281).

Trattoria Al Cugnai is an unpretentious place run by three sisters serving good food at a good price with friendly service (Tue–Sun 12:00–15:00, 19:00–22:00, closed Mon, midway between the Accademia Gallery and the forgotten and peaceful Campo San Vio, tel. 041-528-9238). They are happy to let you sip your sweet *fragolino bianco* (L2,000) on Campo San Vio (benches with Grand Canal view) and return the glass.

Taverna San Trovaso is a restaurant/pizzeria with nice gnocchi and a good L27,000 menu (12:00–14:00, 19:00–22:00, 100 meters from the Accademia Gallery on San Trovaso canal across from Pensione Accademia).

Just west of St. Mark's Square, consider **Pietro Panizzolo**, a fun and very local hole-in-the-wall where the food is good, the price is right, and Carla mothers you (closed Sun, straight through Sotoportego e Corte Contarina off Calle la Frezzeria, for directions, see recommended Alloggi Masetto in "Sleeping," above).

Gelato

There's a decent *gelateria* canalside on Santa Maria Campo di Formosa, or even better, try **La Botique del Gelato,** one of the best in Venice (2 blocks off Campo di Formosa on the corner of Saliza da San Lido and Calle Paradiso, next to Hotel Bruno, #5727).

For late-night gelato in the center go to **Michaelangelo** (next to McDonald's on the San Marco side of the Rialto Bridge) or head toward San Marco, where the *gelaterias* stay open later (opposite Doge's Palace).

Transportation Connections—Venice

By train to: Verona (hrly, 90 min), **Florence** (6/day, 3 hrs), **Dolomites** (8/day to Bolzano, 4 hrs with 1 transfer; catch bus from Bolzano into mountains), **Milan** (hrly, 3–4 hrs), **Rome** (6/day, 5 hrs, slower overnight), **Naples** (change in Rome, plus 2–3 hrs), **Brindisi** (3/day, 11 hrs), **Cinque Terre** (2 La Spezia trains go directly to Monterosso al Mare daily, 6 hrs, at 9:58 and 14:58), **Bern** (4/day, change in Milan, 8 hrs), **Munich** (5/day, 8 hrs), **Paris** (3/day, 11 hrs), **Vienna** (4/day, 9 hrs). Train and *couchette* reservations (L30,500) are easily made at the American Express office near St. Mark's Square. Venice train information: tel. 147-888-088 or 041-785-570.

HILL TOWNS OF CENTRAL ITALY

Break out of the Venice-Florence-Rome syndrome. There's more to Italy! Experience the slumber of Umbria, the texture of Tuscany, and the lazy towns of Lazio. For starters, here are a few of my favorites.

Siena seems to be every Italy connoisseur's pet town. In my office, whenever Siena is mentioned, someone moans, "Siena? I luuuv Siena!" San Gimignano is the quintessential hill town, with Italy's best surviving medieval skyline. Assisi—visited for its hometown boy, St. Francis, who made very good—is best after dark. Orvieto, one of the most famous hill towns, is an ideal springboard for a trip to tiny Civita. Stranded alone on its pinnacle in a vast canyon, Civita's the most lovable.

Planning Your Time

Siena, the must-see town, has the easiest train and bus connections. On a quick trip, consider spending three nights in Siena (with a whole-day side trip into Florence and a day to relax and enjoy Siena). Whatever you do, enjoy a sleepy medieval evening in Siena. After an evening in Siena, its major sights can be seen in half a day. San Gimignano is an overrun, pint-sized Siena. Don't rush Siena for San Gimignano (with less than 24 hours for Siena, skip San Gimignano).

Assisi has half a day of sightseeing and another half a day of wonder. While a zoo by day, it's a delight at night.

Orvieto, an easy train stop, is worth a short visit and provides the carless traveler with the best launchpad for a trip to Civita.

Civita di Bagnoregio is the great pinnacle town. A night in Bagnoregio (via Orvieto bus) with time to hike to the town and spend three hours makes the visit worthwhile.

Hill Towns of Central Italy

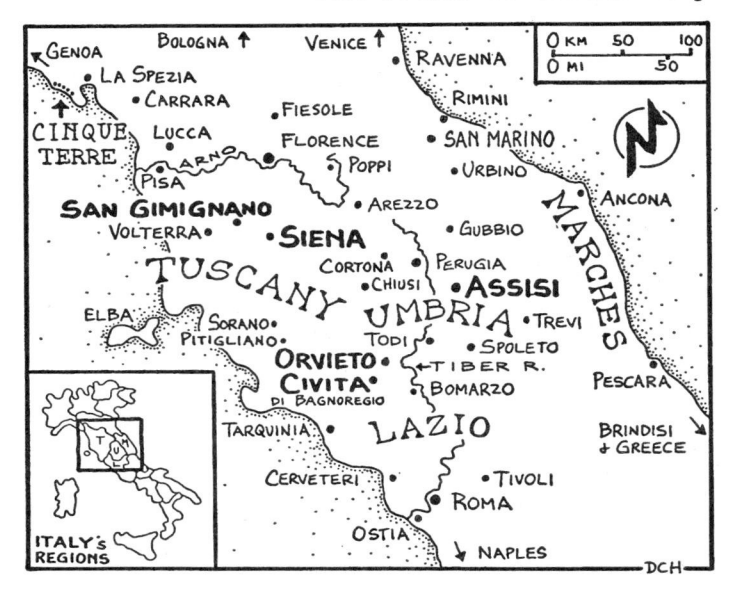

SIENA

Seven hundred years ago, Siena was a major military power in a class with Florence, Venice, and Genoa. With a population of 60,000, it was even bigger than Paris. In 1348 a disastrous plague weakened Siena. Then, in the 1550s, her bitter rival, Florence, really salted her, making Siena forever a nonthreatening backwater. Siena's loss became our sightseeing gain, as its political and economic irrelevance pickled it purely Gothic. Today Siena's population is still 60,000, compared to Florence's 420,000.

Siena's thriving historic center, with red-brick lanes cascading every which way, offers Italy's best Gothic city experience. Most people do Siena, just 30 miles south of Florence, as a day trip, but it's best experienced after dark. While Florence has the blockbuster museums, Siena has an easy-to-enjoy soul: Courtyards sport flower-decked wells, alleys dead-end at rooftop views, and the sky is a rich blue dome. Right off the bat, Siena becomes an old friend.

For those who dream of a Fiat-free Italy, pedestrians rule in the old center of Siena. Sit at a café on the red-bricked main square. Take time to savor the first European city to eliminate automobile traffic from its main square (1966) and then, just to be silly, wonder what would happen if they did it in your city.

Orientation

Siena lounges atop a hill, stretching its three legs out from Il Campo. This main square, the historic meeting point of Siena's neighborhoods, is pedestrians-only. And most of those pedestrians are students from the local university. Everything I mention is within a 15-minute walk of the square. Navigate by landmarks, following the excellent system of street-corner signs. The typical visitor sticks to the San Domenico–Il Campo axis.

Siena is one big sight. Its essential individual sights come in two little clusters: the square (city hall, museum, tower) and the cathedral (baptistery, cathedral museum with its surprise viewpoint). Check these sights off and you're free to wander. Hours may be expanded for 2000 (ask at TI upon arrival).

Tourist Information: Pick up the excellent and free topographical town map from the main TI on Il Campo (#56, look for the yellow "Change" sign—bad rates, good information, Mon–Sat 8:30–19:30 plus sometimes Sun 8:30–14:00 in spring and fall; mid-Nov–mid-Mar Mon–Sat 8:30–14:00, 15:00–19:00, tel. 057-728-0551). The little TI at San Domenico is for hotel promotion only and sells a Siena map for L1,000.

Local Guide: Roberto Bechi, a hardworking Sienese tour guide, offers off-the-beaten-path tours of Siena and the region. After marrying an American and running a restaurant in the U.S., Roberto communicates well with Americans. His passions are Sienese culture and local cuisine. Depending on the size of the group and type of tour, prices range from $50 to $90 per person for a full day and from $20 to $50 per person for a half day. For more info or to book a tour, contact him at Tours by Roberto, tel. & fax 057-770-4789, www.zaslon.si/roberto, or e-mail: tourrob@tin.it.

Arrival in Siena

By Train: From Siena's train station, buy a L1,400 bus ticket from the blue machine near the exit (exact change needed), cross the square, and board any orange city bus heading for Piazza del Sale. The cost of a taxi from the station to your hotel is about L15,000. Siena taxi numbers: at the station (tel. 057-744-504), Piazza Matteotti (tel. 057-728-9350), and elsewhere (tel. 057-749-222).

Day-trippers can check baggage at the Deposito Bagagli at the train station or, for those using the buses, under Piazza Gramsci in Sotopassage la Lizza (L5,000, 7:00–19:45, no overnight).

By Car: Drivers coming from the autostrada take the Porta San Marco exit and follow the "Centro" then "Stadio" signs (stadium, soccer ball). The soccer-ball signs take you to the stadium lot (Parcheggio Stadio, L2,500/hour, L24,000/day) at the huge, bare-brick San Domenico Church. The Fortezza lot nearby charges the same (you pay 8:00–20:00, nights are free). You can drive into the pedestrian zone (a pretty ballsy thing to do) only to drop bags at your hotel. You can park free in the lot below the Albergo Lea, in white-striped spots behind Hotel Villa Liberty, and behind the fortezza. (Note the L200,000 tow-fee incentive to learn the days of the week in Italian).

Sights—Siena's Main Square

▲▲▲Il Campo—Siena's great central piazza is urban harmony at its best. Like a people-friendly stage set, its gently tilted floor fans out from the tower and city hall backdrop. It's the perfect invitation to loiter. Think of it as a trip to the beach without sand or water. Il Campo was located at the historic junction of Siena's various competing districts, or *contrada*, on the old marketplace. The brick surface is divided into nine sections, representing the council of nine merchants and city bigwigs who ruled medieval Siena. Don't miss the Fountain of Joy at the square's high point, with its pigeons politely waiting their turn to gingerly tightrope down slippery snouts to slurp a drink and with the two naked guys about to be tossed in. At the base of the tower, the Piazza's chapel was built in 1348 as a thanks to God for ending the Black Plague (after it killed more than a third of the population). The market area behind the city hall, a wide-open expanse since the Middle Ages, originated as a farming area within the city walls to feed the city in times of siege.

To say Siena and Florence have always been competitive is an understatement. In medieval times a statue of Venus stood on Il Campo (where the Fountain of Joy is today). After the plague hit Siena, the monks blamed this pagan statue. The people cut it to pieces and buried it along the walls of Florence.

▲Museo Civico—The Palazzo Pubblico (City Hall), at the base of the tower, has a fine and manageable museum housing a good sample of Sienese art. In the following order you'll see the Sala Risorgimento, with dramatic scenes of Victor Emmanuel's unification of Italy (surrounded by statues that don't seem to care); the chapel, with impressive inlaid wood chairs in the choir; and the Sala del Mappamondo, with Simone Martini's *Maesta* (Enthroned Virgin) facing the faded *Guidoriccio da Fogliano* (a mercenary providing a more concrete form of protection). Next is the Sala della Pace—where the city's fat cats met. Looking down on the oligarchy during their meetings were two interesting frescoes showing *The Effects of Good and Bad Government*. Notice the whistle-while-you-work happiness of the utopian community ruled by the utopian government (in the best-preserved fresco) and the fate of a community ruled by politicians with more typical values (in a terrible state of repair). The message: Without justice there can be no prosperity. The rural view out the window is essentially the view from the top of the big stairs—enjoy it from here (L10,000, Mon–Sat 10:00–18:00, likely 10:00–23:00

Hill Towns of Central Italy 503

Siena

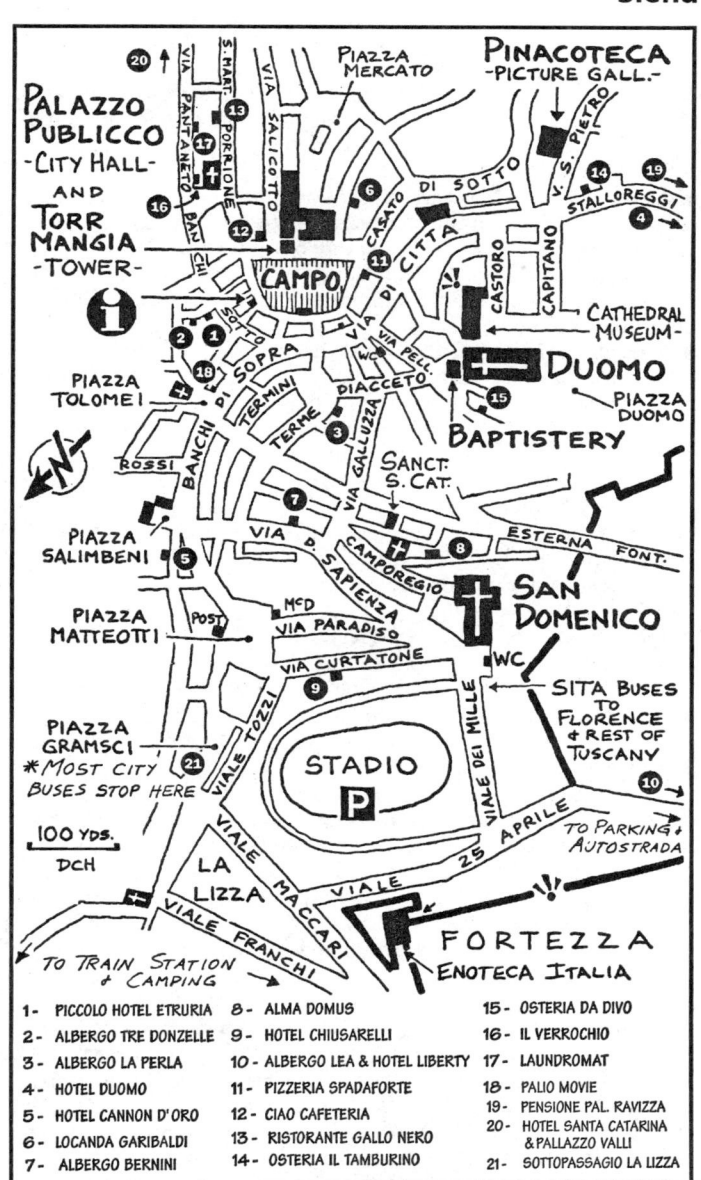

#	Name	#	Name	#	Name
1 -	PICCOLO HOTEL ETRURIA	8 -	ALMA DOMUS	15 -	OSTERIA DA DIVO
2 -	ALBERGO TRE DONZELLE	9 -	HOTEL CHIUSARELLI	16 -	IL VERROCHIO
3 -	ALBERGO LA PERLA	10 -	ALBERGO LEA & HOTEL LIBERTY	17 -	LAUNDROMAT
4 -	HOTEL DUOMO	11 -	PIZZERIA SPADAFORTE	18 -	PALIO MOVIE
5 -	HOTEL CANNON D'ORO	12 -	CIAO CAFETERIA	19 -	PENSIONE PAL. RAVIZZA
6 -	LOCANDA GARIBALDI	13 -	RISTORANTE GALLO NERO	20 -	HOTEL SANTA CATARINA & PALLAZZO VALLI
7 -	ALBERGO BERNINI	14 -	OSTERIA IL TAMBURINO	21 -	SOTTOPASSAGIO LA LIZZA

mid-Jul–mid-Sept, Sun 9:30–13:30, off-season Mon–Sat 10:00–16:00, tel. 057-729-2111). Leave Mauro Civai (the director of this museum) a polite note requesting that a little English information be shared with his paying guests.

▲**City Tower (Torre del Mangia)**—Siena gathers around its city hall, not its church. It was a proud republic, and its "declaration of independence" is the tallest secular medieval tower in Italy, the 100-yard-tall Torre del Mangia (named after a hedonistic watchman who consumed his earnings like a glutton consumes food; his chewed-up statue is in the courtyard, to the left as you enter). Its 300 steps get pretty skinny at the top, but the reward is one of Italy's best views (L8,000, daily 10:00–19:30, off-season Mon–Sat 10:00–17:00, closed in rain, long lines, limit of 30 towerists at a time, avoid the midday crowd).

▲**Pinacoteca (National Picture Gallery)**—Siena was a power in Gothic art. But the average tourist, wrapped up in a love affair with the Renaissance, hardly notices. This museum takes you on a walk through Siena's art, chronologically from the 12th through the 15th centuries. For the casual sightseer, the Sienese art in the city hall and cathedral museums is adequate. But art fans enjoy this opportunity to trace the evolution of Siena's delicate and elegant art (L8,000, Mon 8:30–13:30, Tue–Sat 9:00–19:00, Sun 8:30–13:00, less in winter, tel. 0577-281-161). From the Campo, walk out Via di Citta to Piazza di Postierla and go left on San Pietro.

Sights—Siena's Cathedral Area

▲▲▲**Duomo**—Siena's cathedral is as Baroque as Gothic gets. The striped facade is piled with statues and ornamentation; the interior is decorated from top to bottom. The heads of 172 popes peer down from the ceiling over the fine inlaid art on the floor. This is one busy interior.

To orient yourself in this *panforte* of Italian churches, stand under the dome and think of the church floor as a big clock. You're the middle, and the altar is high noon: you'll find the *Slaughter of the Innocents* roped off on the floor at 10:00, Pisano's pulpit between two pillars at 11:00, Bernini's chapel at 3:00, two Michelangelo statues (next to snacks, shop, and WC) at 7:00, the library at 8:00, and a Donatello statue at 9:00. Take some time with the floor mosaics in the front. Nicola Pisano's wonderful pulpit is crowded with delicate Gothic storytelling from 1268. To understand why Bernini is considered the greatest Baroque sculptor, step into his sumptuous *Cappella della Madonna del Voto*. This last work in the cathedral, from 1659, is enough to make a Lutheran light a candle. Move up to the altar and look back at the two Bernini statues: St. Jerome playing the crucifix like a violinist lost in beautiful music, and Mary Magdalene in a similar state of spiritual ecstasy. The Piccolomini altar is most interesting for its two Michelangelo statues (the lower big ones).

Paul, on the left, may be a self-portrait. Peter, on the right, resembles Michelangelo's more famous statue of Moses. Originally contracted to do 15 statues, Michelangelo left the project early (1504) to do his great *David* in Florence. The Piccolomini Library (worth the L2,000 entry), brilliantly frescoed with scenes glorifying the works of a pope from 500 years ago, contains intricately decorated, or illuminated, music scores and a Roman copy of three Greek graces. Donatello's bronze statue of St. John the Baptist, in his famous rags, is in a chapel to the right (church open daily 9:00–19:30, Nov–mid-Mar 10:00–13:00, 14:30–17:00, modest dress required).

▲▲**Santa Maria della Scala**—This renovated old hospital (opposite the Duomo entrance) displays a rich treasury and a lavishly frescoed hall. The frescoes in the Pellegrinaio Hall show medieval Siena's innovative health care and social welfare system in action (c. 1442, wonderfully described in English). Downstairs are statues from the *Fountain of Gaia* by Jacopo della Quercia (L8,000, daily 10:00–18:00, maybe until 23:00 in summer, off-season 11:00–17:00).

▲**Baptistery**—Siena is so hilly that there wasn't enough flat ground on which to build a big church. What to do? Build a big church and prop up the overhanging edge with the baptistery. This dark and quietly tucked-away cave of art is worth a look (and L3,000) for its cool tranquility and the bronze carvings by Ghiberti and Donatello (the six women, or angels) on the baptismal font (daily 9:00–19:30, Oct 9:00–18:00, Nov–mid-Mar 10:00–13:00, 14:30–17:00).

▲▲**Cathedral Museum (Museo dell'Opera)**—Siena's most enjoyable museum, on the Campo side of the church (look for the yellow signs), was built to house the cathedral's art. The ground floor is filled with the cathedral's original Gothic sculpture by Giovanni Pisano (who spent 10 years here carving and orchestrating the decoration of the cathedral in the late 1200s) and a fine Donatello *Madonna and Child*. Upstairs to the left awaits a private audience with Duccio's *Maesta* (Enthroned Virgin). Pull up a chair and study one of the great pieces of medieval art. The flip side of the *Maesta* (displayed on the opposite wall), with 26 panels—the medieval equivalent of pages—shows scenes from the Passion of Christ. Climb onto the "Panorama dal Faccitone." From the first landing, take the skinnier second spiral for Siena's surprise view. Look back over the Duomo and consider this: When rival republic Florence began its grand cathedral, proud Siena decided to build the biggest church in all Christendom. The existing cathedral would be used as a transept. You're atop what would have been the entry. The wall below you, connecting the Duomo with the museum of the cathedral, was as far as Siena got before a plague killed the city's ability to finish the project. Were it completed, you'd be looking straight down the nave—white stones mark where columns would have stood (L6,000, worthwhile L5,000 audio guide, daily 9:00–19:30, Oct 9:00–18:00, Nov–mid-Mar 9:00–13:30, tel. 057-728-3048).

Sights—Siena's San Domenico Area

Church of San Domenico—This huge brick church is worth a quick look. The simple, bland interior fits the austere philosophy of the Dominicans. Walk up the steps in the rear of the church for a look at various paintings from the life of Saint Catherine, patron saint of Siena. Halfway up the church on the right you'll see a wooden bust of Saint Catherine and her finger in a case. And in the adjacent chapel, you'll see her actual head (free, daily 7:00–13:00, 15:00–18:30, less in winter).

Sanctuary of Saint Catherine—A few downhill blocks toward the center from San Domenico (follow signs to the Santuario di Santa Caterina), step into Catherine's cool and peaceful home. Siena remembers its favorite hometown girl, a simple, unschooled, but almost mystically devout girl who, in the mid-1300s, helped get the pope to return from France to Rome. Pilgrims have come here since 1464. Wander around to enjoy art depicting scenes from her life. Her room is downstairs (free, daily 9:00–12:30, 14:30–18:00, winter 9:00–12:00, 15:30–18:00, Via Tiratoio).

Siena's Palio

In the Palio, the feisty spirit of Siena's 17 *contrada* (neighborhoods) lives on. These neighborhoods celebrate, worship, and compete together. Each even has its own historical museum. *Contrada* pride is evident any time of year in the colorful neighborhood banners and parades. But *contrada* pride is most visible twice a year—on July 2 and August 16 (with a rare third Jubilee Palio in May—or maybe September—of 2000), when they have their world-famous Palio di Siena. Ten of the 17 neighborhoods compete (chosen by lot), hurling themselves with medieval abandon into several days of trial races and traditional revelry. On the big day, Il Campo is stuffed to the brim with locals and tourists, as the horses charge wildly around the square in this literally no-holds-barred race. Of course, the winning neighborhood is the scene of grand celebrations afterward. The grand prize: simply proving your *contrada* is numero uno. All over town, sketches and posters depict the Palio. This is not some folkloristic event. It's a real medieval moment. If you're packed onto the square with 15,000 people who each really want to win, you won't see much, but you'll feel it. While the actual Palio packs the city, you could side trip in from Florence to see horse-race trials each of the three days before the big day (usually at 9:00 and 19:45).

▲**Palio al Cinema**—This 20-minute film helps recreate the craziness of the Palio. See it at the Cinema Moderno (L10,000, L8,000 or 2 for L15,000 with this book, Mon–Fri 9:30–17:30, Sat 9:30–15:00, closed Sun, English showings generally hourly at :30 past the hour, 2 blocks from the Campo, on Piazza Tolomei, tel. 057-728-9201). Call or drop by to confirm when the next English showing is scheduled—there are usually nine each day.

Nightlife in Siena

Don't miss the evening *passeggiata* (peak strolling time is 19:00) along Via Banchi di Sopra with gelato in hand. **Nannini's** at Piazza Salimbeni has fine gelato (daily 11:00–24:00).

The **Enoteca Italiana** is a good wine bar in a cellar in the Fortezza (Mon 12:00–20:00, Tue–Sat 12:00–01:00, closed Sun, glasses cost L3,000–8,000, bottles and snacks available).

Sleeping in Siena
(L1,900 = about $1, zip code: 53100)
Sleep Code: **S** = Single, **D** = Double/Twin, **T** = Triple, **Q** = Quad, **b** = bathroom, **t** = toilet only, **s** = shower only, **CC** = Credit Card (Visa, MasterCard, Amex), **SE** = Speaks English, **NSE** = No English. Breakfast is generally not included. Have breakfast on Il Campo or in a nearby bar.

Finding a room is tough during Easter or for the Palio in early July and mid-August (and May or September in 2000). Call ahead any time of year, as Siena's few budget places are listed in all the budget guidebooks. While day-tripping tour groups turn the town into a Gothic amusement park in midsummer, Siena is basically yours in the evenings and off-season. Nearly all listed hotels lie between Il Campo and the Church of San Domenico.

Siena has two modern, self-service Laundromats with daily long hours: Lavarapido Wash and Dry (Via di Pantaneto 38) and Onda Blue (Casato di Soto 17).

Sleeping near Il Campo
Each of these first listings is forgettable but inexpensive and just a horse wreck away from one of Italy's most wonderful civic spaces.

Piccolo Hotel Etruria, a good bet for a hotel with decent rooms but not much soul, is just off the square (S-L60,000, Sb-L70,000, Db-L110,000, Tb-L145,000, Qb-L180,000, breakfast-L7,000, CC:VMA, with your back to the tower, leave Il Campo to the right at 2:00, Via Donzelle 1–3, tel. 057-728-8088, fax 057-728-8461).

Albergo Tre Donzelle is a plain, institutional, but decent place next door to Piccolo Hotel Etruria that makes sense only if you think of Il Campo as your terrace (S-L47,000, D-L75,000, Db-L95,000, extra bed-L30,000, CC:VMA, Via Donzelle 5, tel. 057-728-0358, fax 057-722-3933, Senora Iannini SE).

Albergo La Perla is a funky, jumbled, 13-room place. Its narrow maze of hallways, stark rooms, cramped bathrooms, and laissez-faire environment works for backpackers (Sb-L75,000, Db-L105,000, Tb-L145,000, a block off the square on Piazza Independenza at Via della Terme 25, tel. 057-747-144). Attilio and his American wife, Deborah, take reservations only a day or two ahead. Ideally, call the morning you'll arrive.

Hotel Duomo is the best in-the-old-town splurge, a classy place with 23 spacious, elegant rooms (Sb-L145,000, Db-L220,000, Tb-L290,000, Qb-L330,000, includes breakfast, CC:VMA, air-con, picnic-friendly roof terrace, follow Via di Citta, which becomes Via Stalloreggi, to Via Stalloreggi 38, tel. 057-728-9088, fax 057-743-043, e-mail: hduomo@comune.siena.it, Stefania SE). If you arrive by train, take a taxi (L15,000; if you drive, go to Porta San Marco and follow the signs to hotel, drop off bags, and then park in nearby "Il Campo" lot).

Pensione Palazzo Ravizza has an aristocratic feel and a peaceful garden. It's classy yet friendly and decent for drivers who want to be a short walk from the Campo (Db-L240,000 with breakfast and parking, CC:VMA, elevator, great garden, back rooms face open country, restaurant offers a good 3-course L45,000 dinner, Via Pian dei Mantellini 34, tel. 057-728-0462, fax 057-722-1597).

Hotel Cannon d'Oro, a few blocks up Via Banchi di Sopra, is spacious and group-friendly (30 rooms, Sb-L105,000, Db-L128,000, Tb-L170,000, prices promised through 2000 with this book, family deals, breakfast-L10,000, CC:VMA, Via Montanini 28, tel. 057-744-321, fax 057-728-0868, e-mail: cannonsi@tin.it, Maurizio and Debora SE).

Locanda Garibaldi is a modest, very Sienese restaurant/ *albergo*. Gentle Marcello wears two hats, as he runs a fine, busy restaurant downstairs and seven newly renovated rooms up a funky metal staircase (D-L120,000, T-L165,000, family deals, no CC, takes reservations only a few days in advance, half a block downhill off the square at Via Giovanni Dupre 18, tel. 057-728-4204, NSE).

Sleeping Closer to San Domenico Church

These hotels are listed in order of closeness to Il Campo—max 10-minute walk. The first two enjoy views of the old town and cathedral (which sits floodlit before me as I type) and are the best values in town.

Albergo Bernini makes you part of a Sienese family in a modest, clean home with nine fine rooms. Friendly Nadia and Mauro welcome you to picnic on their spectacular view terrace for breakfast or dinner. The mynah bird (Romeo) actually says *"ciao"* as you come and go from the terrace (Sb-L95,000, D-L110,000, Db-L130,000, family deals, less in winter, midnight curfew, on the main San Domenico–Il Campo drag at Via Sapienza 15, tel. & fax 057-728-9047, e-mail: hbernin.tin.it, their son, Alessandro, SE).

Alma Domus is ideal—unless nuns make you nervous, you need a double bed, or you plan on staying out past the 23:30 curfew. This quasi-hotel (not a convent) is run with firm but angelic smiles by sisters who offer clean and quiet rooms for a steal and save the best views for foreigners. Bright lamps, quaint balconies, fine views, grand public rooms, top security, and a friendly atmosphere make this a great value. The check-out time is strictly 10:00, but they have a *deposito* for luggage (Db-L100,000, Tb-L125,000, Qb-L150,000, breakfast-L11,000, from San Domenico walk downhill with the church on your right toward the view, turn left down Via Camporegio, make a U-turn at the little chapel down the brick steps to Via Camporegio 37, tel. 057-744-177 and 057-744-487, fax 057-747-601, NSE).

Hotel Chiusarelli is a proper hotel in a beautiful building with a handy location, but it comes with lots of night noise, flimsy beds, and an indifferent management (50 rooms, Sb-L115,000, Db-L185,000, Tb-L250,000, includes breakfast, CC:VMA, air-con, pleasant garden terrace, across from San Domenico at Viale Curtone 15, tel. 057-728-0562, fax 057-727-1177, SE).

Albergo Lea is a run-down but sleepable place in a residential neighborhood a few blocks away from the center (past San Domenico) with easy parking (S-L75,000, Db-L120,000, Tb-L150,000 Qb-L180,000, includes breakfast, CC:VMA, Viale XXIV Maggio 10, tel. & fax 057-728-3207, SE). **Hotel Villa Liberty** has big, bright, and comfortable rooms (Db-L200,000, includes breakfast, CC:VMA, elevator, air-con, TVs, minibars, etc., facing the fortress at Viale V. Veneto 11, tel. 057-744-966, fax 057-744-770, SE).

Sleeping Farther from the Center

Hotel Santa Caterina is a three-star place best for drivers who need air-conditioning. It's peaceful and professionally run, with real attention to quality and a delightful garden (Sb-L170,000, small Db-L185,000, Db-L230,000, Tb-L290,000, includes breakfast, CC:VMA, request garden side for no traffic noise, fridge in room, 100 meters outside Porta Romana at Via E.S. Piccolomini 7, tel. 057-722-1105, fax 057-727-1087, e-mail: hsc@sienanet.it, Stefania SE). Easy parking and shuttle bus (4/hrly) to town center.

Palazzo di Valli is a newly opened hotel a mile or two beyond Porta Romana. It feels like it's in the country (and has simple parking) but is a straight shot into town on the shuttle bus (4/hrly). The Camarda family has a great vision for this place, with 11 big, peaceful rooms, a fine TV lounge, and garden (Db-L220,000 with breakfast for travelers with this book in 2000, CC:VMA, Via E.S. Piccolomini, tel. 057-722-6102, fax 057-722-2255). From the autostrada exit at Siena Sud in the direction of Porta Romana.

Siena's **Guidoriccio Youth Hostel** has 120 cheap beds, but, given the hassle of the bus ride and the charm of downtown Siena at night, I'd skip it (office open 7:00–9:00, 15:00–23:30, L21,000 beds in doubles, triples, and dorms with sheets and breakfast, bus #10 from Piazza Gramsci or the train station to Via Fiorentina 89 in the Stellino neighborhood, tel. 057-752-212, SE).

The TI lists private homes that rent rooms for around L30,000 per person. Many require a stay of several days, but some are central and a fine value (tel. 057-728-0551).

Eating in Siena

Restaurants are reasonable by Florentine and Venetian standards. Budget eaters look for *pizza al taglio* shops, scattered throughout Siena, selling pizza by the slice.

Even with higher prices, lousy service, and lower-quality food, consider eating on Il Campo—a classic European experience. **Pizzeria Spadaforte** has a fine setting, mediocre pizza, and tables steeper than its prices (daily 12:00–16:00, 19:30–22:30, tel. 057-728-1123). At the bottom of the Campo, a **Ciao** cafeteria offers cheap meals, no ambience, and no views; the neighboring **Spizzicato** serves huge, inexpensive quarter pizzas (daily 12:00–15:00, 19:00–21:00, to the left of the city tower as you face it).

For authentic Sienese dining at a fair price, eat at **Locanda Garibaldi**, down Via Giovanni Dupre a few steps from the square (L27,000 menu, open at 12:00 for lunch and 19:00 for dinner, arrive early to get a table, closed Sat). Marcello does a nice little L5,000 *piatto misto dolce*, featuring several local sweets with sweet wine.

Ristorante Gallo Nero, a friendly "grotto" for authentic Tuscan cuisine, is a good student-type place. This "black rooster" serves a mean *ribollita* (hearty Tuscan bean soup), offers a "medieval menu," and has cheap Chianti (daily 19:00–24:00, CC:VMA, 3 blocks down Via del Porrione from the Campo at #65, tel. 057-728-4356). Just around the corner, **Il Verrochio** serves a decent L24,000 menu (Logge del Papa 1).

Osteria il Tamburino is friendly, small, and intimate and serves up tasty meals (Mon–Sat 12:00–14:30, 19:00–20:30, closed Sun, follow Via Citta off Campo, becomes Stalloreggi, Via Stalloreggi 11, tel. 057-728-0306).

Antica Osteria Da Divo is the place for a fine L80,000 meal. The kitchen is creative, the food is fresh and top notch, and the ambience is candlelit. You'll get a basket of exotic fresh breads. The "black pearls"—with a truffle sauce—are sumptuous. The lamb goes baaa in your mouth. And the chef is understandably proud of his desserts (daily 12:00–14:30, 19:00–22:00, CC:VMA, facing baptistery door, take the far right, Via Franciosa 29, tel. 057-728-4381).

Osteria la Chiacchera, while touristy, is an atmospheric, tasty, and affordable hole-in-the-brick-wall (daily 12:00–15:00, 19:00–24:00, below Pension Bernini at Costa di San Antonio 4, reservations wise, tel. 057-728-0631).

Le Campane, two blocks off the Campo, is also good (indoor/outdoor seating, Via delle Campane 6, tel. 057-728-4035).

Snack with a view from a balcony overlooking the Campo. Survey these three places from the Campo to see which has a free table: **Gelateria Artigiana La Costarella** (perhaps Siena's best ice cream), **Bar Paninoteca** (sandwiches), or **Bar Barbero d'Oro** (*panforte*—L3,500/100 grams—and cappuccino, best balcony open in summer), all of which are on Via di Citta.

Siena's claim to caloric fame is its *panforte*, a rich, chewy concoction of nuts, honey, and candied fruits that impresses even fruitcake haters (although locals prefer a white macaroon-and-almond cookie called *ricciarelli*). All over town Prodotti Tipici shops sell Sienese specialties.

Transportation Connections—Siena

To: Rome (by SENA bus, 6/day, 3 hrs, L22,000, tel. 057-724-7934; by train, 8/day, 3 hrs), **Viterbo** (for Civita, 1 bus/day), **Assisi** (4 direct SENA buses/day, 2 hrs, L16,000), **San Gimignano** (hrly Trans-Sita buses, 1.25 hrs, change in Poggibonsi, tel. 057-720-4111). Both SENA and Trans-Sita bus companies have offices under Piazza Gramsci in Sottopassaggio La Lizza.

To Florence: Take the *rapide* SITA bus from Siena's Piazza San Domenico to downtown Florence's bus station (12/day, 75 min, L10,000, buy ticket before boarding at nearby *biglietteria* or office on ground floor of church, 057-720-4111 or 057-720-4245). Don't confuse the blue (intercity) and orange (city) buses. If you're going to Florence, you want blue. Don't panic if there are too many people. They generally add buses when necessary. The fastest buses are marked *"corse rapide,"* the *diretto* makes two stops en route, and the misnamed *accellerata* stops everywhere. These milk-run buses are much slower but more scenic, offering an interesting glimpse of small-town and rural Tuscany.

Trains, which take longer than SITA buses, sometimes require a change in Empoli. City buses connect Siena's train station with its old town center (look for buses marked "Piazza del Sale" or "Piazza Gramsci").

SAN GIMIGNANO

The epitome of a Tuscan hill town, with 14 medieval towers still standing (out of an original 72!), San Gimignano is a perfectly preserved tourist trap so easy to visit and visually pleasing that it's a good stop. In the 13th century, back in the days of Romeo and Juliet, towns were run by feuding noble families. They'd periodically battle things out from the protective bases of their respective family towers. Pointy skylines were the norm in medieval Tuscany. But in San Gimignano, fabric was big business, and many of its towers were built simply to hang dyed fabric out to dry.

While the basic three-star sight here is the town of San Gimignano itself, there are a few worthwhile stops. From the town gate, shop straight up the traffic-free town's cobbled main drag to Piazza del Cisterna (with its 13th-century well). The town sights cluster around the adjoining Piazza del Duomo.

The TI is in the old center on Piazza Duomo (daily 9:00–13:00, 15:00–19:00, Nov–Feb 9:00–13:00, 14:00–18:00, changes money, tel. 057-794-0008, www.sangimignano.com, e-mail: prolocsg@tin.it).

Sights—San Gimignano

The **Collegiata,** with the round windows and wide steps, is a Romanesque church filled with fine Renaissance frescoes (free, daily 9:30–12:30, 15:00–17:30, closed during Mass). In **Palazzo del Popolo** (facing the same piazza) you'll find the city museum and San Gimignano's tallest tower, Torre Grossa. You can climb this 180-foot-tall tower for L8,000, but the free *rocca* (castle), a short climb behind the church, offers a better view and a great picnic perch, especially at sunset.

The **Museo Civico** has a classy little painting collection with a 1422 altarpiece by Taddeo di Bartolo honoring Saint Gimignano. You can see him with the town in his hands surrounded by events from his life (L12,000-combined entry for Torre Grossa and Museo Civico, L8,000-tower only, L5,000-museum only, daily 9:30–19:20, Nov–Feb Tue–Sun 9:30–12:50, 14:30–16:50, closed Mon). Thursday is market day (8:00–13:00), but for local merchants, every day is a sales frenzy.

Sleeping and Eating in San Gimignano
(L1,900 = about $1, zip code: 53037)
Senora Carla Rossi offers rooms—some with views—throughout the town (Db-from L90,000, Via di Cellole 81, tel. 057-795-5041, cellular 036-8352-3206, fax 057-794-1268). For a listing of private rooms, stop by or call **Associazione Strutture Extralberghiere** (L50,000 per person, Piazza della Cisterna, tel. 057-794-3190). **Osteria del Carcere** has good food and prices (Via del Castello 13, just off Piazza della Cisterna, tel. 057-794-1905). Shops guarded by wild boar statues sell it by the gram; carnivores buy some boar (*cinghiale*—cheen-GAH-lay), cheese, bread, and wine and enjoy a picnic in the garden by the castle.

Transportation Connections—San Gimignano
To: Florence (hrly buses, 75 min, change in Poggibonsi; or catch the frequent 20-min shuttle bus to Poggibonsi and train to Florence), **Siena** (hrly buses, 90 min, change in Poggibonsi to bus or train), **Volterra** (6 buses/day, 2 hrs, change in Poggibonsi and Colle di Val d'Elsa). Bus tickets are sold at the bar just inside the town gate. San Gimignano has no baggage-check service.

Drivers: You can't drive within the walled town of San Gimignano, but a car park awaits just a few steps outside.

ASSISI

Around the year 1200, a simple friar from Assisi challenged the decadence of church government and society in general with a powerful message of nonmaterialism, simplicity, and a "slow down and smell God's roses" lifestyle. Like Jesus, Francis taught by example. A huge monastic order grew out of his teachings, which were gradually embraced (some would say co-opted) by the church. Clare, St. Francis' partner in poverty, founded the Order of the Poor Clares. Catholicism's purest example of simplicity is now glorified in beautiful churches. In 1939 Italy made Francis and Clare its patron saints.

Francis' message of love and sensitivity to the environment has a broad and timeless appeal. But any pilgrimage site will be commercialized, and the legacy of St. Francis is Assisi's basic industry. In summer the town bursts with flash-in-the-pan Francis fans and Franciscan knickknacks. Those able to see past the tacky friar mementos can actually have a "travel on purpose" experience. Most visitors are day-trippers. Assisi after dark is closer to a place Francis could call home.

Orientation

Assisi, crowned by a ruined castle, is beautifully preserved and rich in history. The 1997 earthquake did more damage to the tourist industry than to the local buildings. But it's back to business as usual for 2000, and that quake should be of no concern to anyone planning a visit.

Tourist Information: The TI is in the center of town on Piazza del Comune (Mon–Sat 8:00–14:00, 15:30–18:30, Sun 9:00–13:00, tel. 075-812-534), along with the Roman temple of Minerva, a Romanesque tower, banks, a finely frescoed pharmacy, the Pinacoteca (with obscure Umbrian art, not worth the admission for most), and a Roman Forum (see "Sights," below). Market day is Saturday on Piazza Mateotti.

Arrival in Assisi: Buses, which connect Assisi's train station (near Santa Maria degli Angeli) with the old town center (L1,200, 2/hrly, 5 km), stop at Piazza Unita d'Italia (Basilica di San Francisco), Largo Properzio (Santa Chiara), and Piazza Matteotti (top of old town). Buses usually leave from both the station and Piazza Matteotti at :10 and :40 past the hour. Taxis into town run about L16,000 (beware: many taxis rip off tourists with tarif #2; the meter should be set on tarif #1, L5,000 drop). You can check bags at the train station but not in town. Drivers just coming in for the day should follow the signs to Piazza Matteotti's wonderful underground parking garage at the top of the town (which comes with bits of ancient Rome in the walls, L1,500/hr, open 7:00–21:00, until 23:00 in summer).

Travel Agency: You can get bus and train tickets within a

Assisi

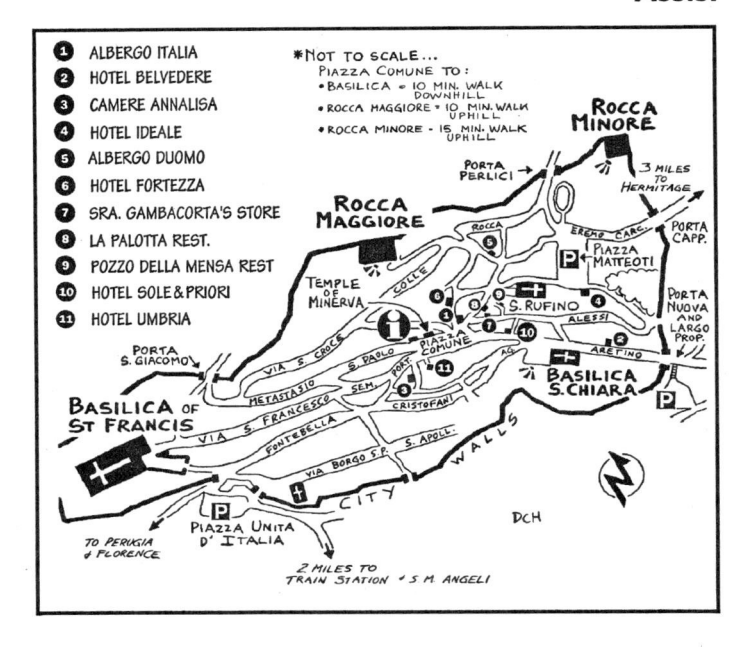

- ① ALBERGO ITALIA
- ② HOTEL BELVEDERE
- ③ CAMERE ANNALISA
- ④ HOTEL IDEALE
- ⑤ ALBERGO DUOMO
- ⑥ HOTEL FORTEZZA
- ⑦ SRA. GAMBACORTA'S STORE
- ⑧ LA PALOTTA REST.
- ⑨ POZZO DELLA MENSA REST
- ⑩ HOTEL SOLE & PRIORI
- ⑪ HOTEL UMBRIA

*NOT TO SCALE...
PIAZZA COMUNE TO:
- BASILICA = 10 MIN. WALK DOWNHILL
- ROCCA MAGGIORE = 10 MIN. WALK UPHILL
- ROCCA MINORE - 15 MIN. WALK UPHILL

block of the Basilica St. Clare at Agenzia Viaggi Stoppini (Corso Mazzini 31, tel. 075-812-597).

Local Guide: Anne Robichaud, an American Elderhostel lecturer who has lived in Italy for 25 years, offers personalized tours of Assisi and the Umbrian countryside with a focus on history, art, crafts, folklore, and food—your choice (half-day tours are $260 and full-day tours are $380 with this book, tel. & fax 075-802-334—best from 6:30–7:30 and 20:00–23:00, www.bloto.com/anne/).

Assisi Welcome Walk

There's much more to Assisi than St. Francis and what all the blitz tour groups see. This self-guided short walk, rated ▲▲, covers the town from Piazza Matteotti at the top to the Basilica of St. Francis at the bottom. Ride the bus from the train station to Piazza Matteotti, the last stop, or drive your car there (underground parking with Roman ruins).

1. The Roman Arena: Start 50 meters beyond Piazza Matteotti (under the castle). A lane leads to a cozy circular neighborhood built around a Roman arena. Assisi was an important

Roman town. Circle the arena counterclockwise. Imagine how colorful the town laundry must have been in the last generation when the women of Assisi gathered here to do their wash. Adjacent is the old fountain under the coats of arms of the town's leading families. Twenty meters later, hike up the steps to the top of the hill for an aerial view of the oval arena. The Roman stones have long been absorbed into the medieval architecture. It was Roman tradition to locate the arena outside of town...which this was. Continue on. The lane leads down to a city gate.

2. Umbrian view: Leave Assisi at the Porta Perlici for a commanding Umbrian view. This state is called the "green heart of Italy": the geographical center of the country and only state completely landlocked by other Italian states. Enjoy the greens: silver green on the valley floor (olives), emerald green 10 meters below you (grape vines), and deep green on the hillsides (evergreen oak trees). Also notice the Rocca Maggiore (big castle), a fortress providing townsfolk a refuge in times of attack and, behind you, the Rocca Minore (little castle). Now walk back to Piazza Matteotti. You'll see the square bell tower (a little to the right in the distance) of your next stop. It's easiest to get there by walking past the square and turning right on Via del Torrione.

3. Church of San Rufino: While Francis is Italy's patron saint, Assisi's is Rufino, the town's first bishop (in the third century, he was martyred and buried here). The church is 12th-century Romanesque with a neoclassical interior. As you enter, look left (under the bell tower) at the Roman cistern—the town's water source when under attack. Both Francis and Clare were baptized at the simple font (front right corner). Traditionally, the children of Assisi are still baptized right here.

4. Medieval Architecture: Follow the sign down Via Dono Doni toward St. Clare. After 20 meters, hike down the steps on the right. At the bottom notice the pink limestone pavement. The medieval town survives. The pointed arches are from the 12th through the 14th century. The vaults that turn lanes into tunnels are reminders of medieval urban expansion (mostly 15th century). While the population grew, people wanted to live protected within the walls, so Assisi became more dense. Medieval Assisi had five times the population density of today's Assisi. Notice the floating gardens. Assisi has a flowering balcony competition each June. From here, hike down to the Church of St. Clare.

5. Basilica di Santa Chiara (Saint Clare): Dedicated to the founder of the order of the Poor Clares, this Umbrian Gothic church is simple, in keeping with the Poor Clares' dedication to a life of contemplation. (For description, see "Sights," below.)

6. Another Umbrian View: Belly up to the viewpoint in front of the church. On the left is the monastery of St. Clare; below you, the olive grove of the Poor Clares since the 13th century; and in the distance, a grand Umbrian view. Assisi overlooks the richest and biggest valley in otherwise hilly and mountainous Umbria. The municipality of Assisi has 29,000, but only 1,000 live in the old town. The lower town grew up with the coming of the railway in the 19th century. In the haze, the blue-domed church is St. Mary of the Angels (Santa Maria degli Angeli), the cradle of the Franciscan order, marking the place St. Francis lived and worked. (For description, see below.) This church, a popular pilgrimage sight today, is the first Los Angeles. Think about California. The Franciscans named L.A. (after this church), San Francisco, and even Santa Clara.

7. Artisans: From Via Santa Chiara you can see three arches. The arch next to the church dates from 1265. Beyond that, the Parta Nuova, from 1316, marks the final expansion of Assisi. Toward the center (on Via Santa Chiara, the high road) an arch indicates the site of the Roman wall. Forty meters before this arch, pop into the souvenir shop at #1b. The plaque over the door explains that the old printing press (a national monument now, just inside the door) was used to make fake documents for Jews escaping the Nazis in 1943 and 1944. The shop is run by a couple of artisans: the man makes frames out of medieval Assisi timbers; the woman makes the traditional Assisi or Franciscan cross-stitch. Just past the gate, the Lisa Assisi shop (at Corso Mazzini 25b) has a delightful bargain basement with surviving bits of a 2000-year-old mortarless Roman wall. Cooks love the La Pasteria natural products shop at Corso Mazzini 18b. Here you can peruse Umbrian wines, herbs, pâtés, and truffles and sample an aromatic "fruit infusion." Ahead at Corso Mazzini 14d, the small shop (Poiesis) sells olive-wood carvings. Drop in. It's said that St. Francis made the first nativity scene to help teach the Christmas message. That's why you'll see so many of these in Assisi. Even today, nearby villages are enthusiastic about their "living" manger scenes. Ahead of you, the columns of the Temple of Minerva mark the Piazza del Comune (described below). Walk there. Sit at the fountain for a few minutes of people watching—don't you love Italy? Within 200 meters of this square, on either side, were the medieval walls. Imagine a commotion of 5,000 people confined within these walls. No wonder St. Francis needed an escape for some peace and quiet. I'll meet you over at the temple.

8. Roman Temple/Christian Church: Assisi has always been a spiritual center. The Romans went to great lengths to make this Temple of Minerva a centerpiece of their city. Notice the columns cutting into the stairway. It was a tight fit here on the hilltop. The stairs went down probably triple the distance you see today. The store facing the temple has a basement with the original pavement stones of the Roman square. There was a church of Santa Maria *sopra* (over) Minerva here in the ninth century. The bell tower is 13th century. Pop inside. Today's church interior is 17th-century Baroque. Flanking the altar are the original Roman temple floor stones. You can even see the drains for the bloody sacrifices that took place here. Behind the statues of Peter and Paul, the original Roman embankment peeks through.

The Keramos store (filled with typical ceramics and textiles) welcomes "shoppers" into its classy basement, where the actual Roman pavement is artfully incorporated into the shop. A few doors back toward the fountain, step into the 16th-century vaults from the old fish market. Notice the Italian flair for design. Even a smelly fish market was finely decorated. The art style is "grotesque"—literally a painting in a grotto. This was painted in the early 1500s, a few years after Columbus brought turkeys back from the New World. The turkeys painted here may just be that bird's European debut.

9. Church of San Stefano: From the main square, hike past the temple up the high road, Via San Paolo. After 200 meters a sign directs you down a lane to San Stefano, which used to be outside the town walls in the days of St. Francis. Legend is that its bells miraculously rang on October 3, 1226, the day St. Francis died. Surrounded by cypress, fig, and walnut trees, it's a delightful bit of offbeat Assisi. Step inside. This is the typical rural Italian Romanesque church—no architect, just built by simple stone masons who put together the most basic design. The lane zigzags down to Via San Francesco. Turn right and walk under the arch toward the Basilica of St. Francis.

10. Via San Francesco: This was the main drag leading from the town to the basilica holding the body of St. Francis. Francis was a big deal even in his own day. He died in 1226 and was made a saint in 1228—the same year the basilica's foundations were laid—and his body was moved in by 1230. Assisi was a big-time pilgrimage center, and this street was a booming place. Notice the fine medieval balcony just below the arch. A few yards farther down (on the left), cool yourself at the fountain. The hospice next door was built in 1237 to house pilgrims. Notice the three faces of its fresco to survive: Jesus, Francis, and Clare.

Sights—Assisi
▲▲▲**Basilica of St. Francis**—In 1226 St. Francis was buried (with the outcasts he had stood by) outside of his town on the "hill of the damned." Now called the "Hill of Paradise," this is one of the artistic highlights of medieval Europe. It's frescoed from top to bottom by the leading artists of the day: Cimabue, Giotto, Simone Martini, and Pietro Lorenzetti. A 13th-century historian wrote "No more exquisite monument to the Lord has been built."

From a distance you see the huge arcades "supporting" the basilica. These were 15th-century quarters for the monks. The arcades lining the square leading to the church housed medieval pilgrims. For 2000, the Franciscans have opened a new subterranean welcome center below this square.

There are three parts to the church: the upper basilica, the lower basilica, and the saint's tomb (below the lower basilica). In the 1997 earthquake, the lower basilica (with nine-foot-thick walls) was undamaged. The upper basilica (with three-foot-thick walls and bigger windows) was damaged. Restoration was completed in November 1999, and the entire church is ready for visitors again (free, daily 7:00–19:00, sometimes closed for Mass, modest dress required, tel. 075-819-001).

The Basilica of St. Francis—a theological work of genius—is difficult for the 20th-century tourist/pilgrim to appreciate. Since the basilica is the reason most visit Assisi and the message of St. Francis has even the least devout blessing the town Vespas, I've designed a *Mona Winks*-type tour with the stress on the place's theology rather than art history. It's adapted from the excellent little *The Basilica of Saint Francis—A Spiritual Pilgrimage*, by Goulet, McInally, and Wood (L5,000 in the bookshop).

Enter the church from the parking lot at the lower level. At the doorway look up and see St. Francis, who greets you with a Latin inscription. Sounding a bit like John Wayne, he says the equivalent of "Slow down and be joyful, pilgrim. You've reached the Hill of Paradise, and this church will knock your spiritual socks off." Start with the tomb (turn left into the nave and go down the *"Tomba"* stairs). Grab a pew right in front of his tomb.

The message: Francis' message caused a stir. He traded a life of power and riches for one of obedience, poverty, and chastity. The Franciscan existence (Brother Sun, Sister Moon, and so on) is a space where God, man, and the natural world frolic harmoniously. Franciscan friars, known as the "Jugglers of God," were a joyful part of the community. In an Italy torn by fighting between towns and families, Francis promoted peace and the restoration of order. (He set an example by reconstructing a crumbled chapel.) While the Church was waging bloody Crusades, Francis pushed ecumenism and understanding. Even today the leaders of the world's great religions meet here for summits.

This rich building seems to contradict the teachings of the poor monk it honors, but it was built as an act of religious and civic pride to remember the hometown saint. It was also designed, and still functions, as a pilgrimage center and a splendid classroom.

The tomb: Holy relics were the "ruby slippers" of medieval Europe. They gave you power—got your prayers answered and helped you win wars—and ultimately helped you get back to your eternal Kansas. For obvious reasons of security, you didn't flaunt your relics. In fact, Francis' tomb was hidden until 1818, when this crypt was opened to the public. The saint's remains are above the altar in the stone box with the iron ties. His four closest friends are buried in the corners of the room. Opposite the altar, up four steps in between the entrance and exit, notice the remains of Francis' rich Roman patron, Jacopa dei Settesoli, in an urn behind the black metal grill. Climb back to the lower nave.

The lower basilica is appropriately Franciscan, subdued and Romanesque. The nave was frescoed with parallel scenes from the lives of Christ and Francis—connected by a ceiling of stars. Unfortunately, after the church was built and decorated, the popularity of the Franciscans meant side chapels needed to be built. Huge arches were cut out of some scenes, but others survive. The first panels show Jesus being stripped of his clothing—across the nave from the famous scene of Francis stripping off his clothes in front of his father. In the second arch fresco on the right wall, Christ is being taken down from the cross (just half his body can be seen), and it looks like the story is over. Defeat. But in the opposite fresco we see Francis preaching to the birds, reminding the faithful that through baptism, the message of the Gospel survives.

These stories directed the medieval pilgrim's attention to the altar, where, through the sacraments, he met God. The Church was a community of believers sailing toward God. The prayers coming out of the nave (*navis*, or ship) fill the triangular sections of the ceiling (*vele*, or sails) with spiritual wind. With a priest for a navigator and the altar for a helm, faith propels the ship.

Stand behind the altar (toes to the bottom step) and look up. The three scenes in front of you are, to the right, "Obedience" (Francis wearing a yoke); to the left, "Chastity" (in a tower of purity held up by two angels); and straight ahead, "Poverty." Here Jesus blesses the marriage as Francis slips a ring on Lady Poverty. In the foreground two "self-sufficient" merchants (the new rich of a thriving North Italy) are throwing sticks and stones at the bride. But Poverty, in her patched wedding dress, is fertile and strong, and even those brambles blossom into a rosebush crown.

Putting your heels to the altar and bending back like a drum major, look up at Francis, who traded a life of earthly simplicity for glory in heaven. Now, turn to the right and march....

In the corner, steps lead into the relic chapel. Circle the room clockwise. You'll see the silver chalice and plate Francis used for the bread and wine of the Eucharist. Francis explained that while his possessions should be very simple, these were to be made of the finest materials. In the corner is a rag of "hair cloth" worn by Francis as penitence. In the next corner is the tunic and slippers Francis wore during his last days. Next find a prayer St. Francis wrote for Brother Leo, signed with his tau cross. Next is a papal document (1223) legitimizing the Franciscan order and assuring his followers that they were not risking a (deadly) heresy charge. Finally, see the tunic lovingly patched and stitched by followers of the five-foot, four-inch-tall St. Francis.

Back upstairs, look around at the painted scenes in this transept. In 1300 this was radical art—believable homespun scenes, landscapes, trees, real people. Check out the crucifix (by Giotto) with the eight sparrowlike angels. For the first time, holy people are expressing emotion: One angel turns her head sadly at the sight of Jesus, and another scratches her hands down her cheeks, drawing blood. Mary, who'd been in control until now, has fainted in despair. The Franciscans, with their goal of bringing God to the people, found a natural partner in Europe's first modern painter, Giotto.

To see the Renaissance leap, look at the painting to the right. This is by Cimabue—it's Gothic, without the 3-D architecture, natural backdrop, and slice-of-life reality of the Giotto work. Cimabue's St. Francis is considered by some to be the earliest existing portrait of the saint.

This church brought together the greatest Sienese (Martini and Lorenzetti) and Florentine (Cimabue and Giotto) artists of the day. Enjoy the Martini saints and their exquisite halos at eye level on the left.

Francis' friend, "Sister Death," was really not that terrible. In fact, he'd like to introduce you to her now (above, to the right of the door to the relic chapel). Go ahead, block the light and meet her. I'll wait upstairs in the courtyard. By the way, robed monks are not my idea of easy-to-approach people, but the Franciscans are God's jugglers (and most of them speak English).

From the courtyard, climb the stairs to the upper basilica. The upper basilica, built later than the lower, is brighter, Gothic (the first Gothic church in Italy, 1228), and nearly wallpapered by Giotto. This gallery of frescoes by Giotto and his assistants shows 28 scenes from the life of St. Francis.

Look for these scenes:

• **A common man spreads his cape before Francis** (immediately to right of altar) out of honor and recognition to a man who will do great things. Symbolized by the rose window, God looks over the 20-year-old Francis, a dandy imprisoned in his selfishness. A medieval pilgrim fluent in symbolism would understand this because the Temple of Minerva (which you saw today on Assisi's Piazza del Comune) was a prison at that time. The rose window, which never existed, is symbolic of God's eye.

• **Francis offers his cape to a needy stranger** (next panel). Prior to this act of kindness, Francis had been captured in battle, held as a prisoner of war, and then released.

• **Francis is visited by the Lord in a dream** (next panel) and told to leave the army and go home.

• **Francis relinquishes his possessions** (two panels down), giving his dad his clothes, his credit cards, and even his time-share condo on Capri. Naked Francis is covered by the bishop, symbolizing his transition from a man of the world to a man of the church.

- **The pope has a vision** of a simple man propping up his teetering church. This led to the papal acceptance of the Franciscan reforms.
- **Christ appears to Francis** being carried by a seraph—a six-winged angel (other side of church, fourth panel from the door). For the strength of his faith, Francis is given the marks of his master, the "battle scars of love"... the stigmata. Throughout his life Francis was interested in chivalry; now he's joined the spiritual knighthood. The weeds in the foreground were an herb that, in olden days, "drove away sadness and made men merry and joyful." Pilgrims smiled.
- **Francis preaches to the birds** (to the right of the exit). Francis was more than a nature lover. The birds, of different species, represent the diverse flock of humanity and nature, all created and loved by God and worthy of each other's love.

Near the outside of the upper basilica is the Latin pax (peace) and the Franciscan tau cross in the grass. Tau, the last letter in the Hebrew alphabet, is symbolic of faithfulness to the end. Francis signed his name with this simple character. Tau and pax. (For more pax, take the high lane back to town, up to the castle, or into the countryside.)

▲**Basilica di Santa Chiara (Saint Clare)**—Dedicated to the founder of the order of the Poor Clares, this Umbrian Gothic church is simple, in keeping with the Poor Clares' dedication to a life of contemplation. The church was built in 1265, and the huge buttresses were added in the next century. The interior's fine frescoes were whitewashed in Baroque times. The Chapel of St. George, on the right (actually an earlier church incorporated into this one), has the crucifix that supposedly spoke to St. Francis, leading to his conversion in 1206. In the back of that chapel are some important Franciscan relics, including Clare's robe. Stairs lead from the nave down to the tomb of Saint Clare. The attached cloistered community of the Poor Clares has flourished for 700 years (church open 7:00–12:00, 14:00–19:00, Sun till 18:00).

For a change of pace, from Porta Nuova (behind the church) climb Via Sermei to #6 and dip into the wondrous mechanical, water-powered manger scene of Silvano Gionbolina. (He may relocate nearer the church in 2000. It's worth asking about.)

Roman Forum (Foro Romano)—For a look at Assisi's Roman roots, tour the Roman Forum, which is actually under the Piazza del Comune. The floor plan is sparse, the odd bits and pieces obscure, but it's well explained in English, and you can actually walk an ancient Roman road (L4,000, daily 10:00–13:00, 15:00–19:00).

▲**Rocca Maggiore**—The "big castle" offers a good look at a 14th-century fortification and a fine view of Assisi and the Umbrian countryside (L5,000, daily 10:00–19:00, closes earlier off-season). If you're counting lire, the view is just as good from outside the castle, and the interior is pretty bare. For a picnic with the same birdsong and views that inspired St. Francis, leave all the tourists and hike to the Rocca Minore (small castle) above Piazza Matteotti.

▲▲**Santa Maria degli Angeli**—This huge church, towering above the buildings below Assisi, was built around the tiny but historic Porziuncola Chapel. When the pope gave Francis his blessing, he was given this *porziuncola*, or "small portion"—a little land with a fixer-upper chapel—from which Francis and his followers established their order. As you enter St. Mary of the Angels, notice the sketch on the door showing the original little chapel with the monks' huts around it and Assisi before it had its huge basilica. Francis lived here after he founded the Franciscan Order in 1208, and this was where he consecrated St. Clare as the Bride of Christ. The other "sights" in the church (a chapel on the spot where Francis died, the rose garden, a museum that has a few monastic cells upstairs) are most interesting to pilgrims (daily 7:00–18:30, Nov–Apr 7:00–12:00, 14:00–sunset).

Sleeping in Assisi
(L1,900 = about $1, zip code: 06081)
Sleep Code: **S** = Single, **D** = Double/Twin, **T** = Triple, **Q** = Quad, **b** = bathroom, **s** = shower only, **CC** = Credit Card (Visa, MasterCard, Amex), **SE** = Speaks English, **NSE** = No English.

The town accommodates large numbers of pilgrims on religious holidays. Finding a room any other time should be easy. See map on page 514 for hotel locations.

Albergo Italia is clean and simple, with great beds and delightful owners. Some of its 13 rooms overlook the town square (Ss-L37,000, D-L50,000, Db-L70,000, T-L63,000, Tb-L90,000, Qb-L100,000, CC:VM, no breakfast, just off Piazza del Comune's fountain at Vicolo della Fortezza 2, tel. 075-812-625, fax 075-804-3749, SE).

Hotel Belvedere offers 16 comfortable rooms and good views and is run by friendly Enrico and his American wife, Mary (Db-L110,000, breakfast-L10,000, 2 blocks past St. Clare's church at Via Borgo Aretino 13, tel. 075-812-460, fax 075-816-812, SE). Their attached restaurant is also good.

Camere Annalisa Martini is a cheery home swimming in vines, roses, and bricks in the town's medieval core. Annalisa speaks English and enthusiastically accommodates her guests with a picnic garden, a washing machine, a refrigerator, and six homey, lived-in-feeling rooms (S-L38,000, Sb-L40,000, D-L58,000, Db-L65,000, Tb-L90,000, Qb-L100,000, 5 rooms share 3 bathrooms, no breakfast, one block below Piazza del Comune, then left on Via S. Gregorio to #6, tel. 075-813-536).

Hotel Ideale is on the top edge of town, overlooking the valley, and has 12 bright, modern rooms, view balconies, a peaceful garden, free parking, and an English-speaking welcome (Sb-L80,000, Db-L140,000, includes breakfast, CC:VMA, Piazza Matteotti 1, tel. 075-813-570, fax 075-813-020, Lara SE).

Albergo Il Duomo is tidy and quiet on a stair-step lane one block up from San Rufino (9 rooms, S-L49,000, Sb-L50,000, D-L61,000, Db-L73,000, breakfast-L8,000, saggy beds, CC:VM, Vicolo S. Lorenzo 2, tel. 075-812-742, fax 075-812-762, e-mail: ilduomo@krenit.it, Carlo SE).

Hotel La Fortezza is a simple, modern, and quiet place with seven rooms (Db-L95,000, Tb-L130,000, Qb-L150,000 CC:VMA, a short climb above Piazza del Comune at Vicolo della Fortezza 19b, tel. 075-812-993, fax 075-819-8035, e-mail: fortezza@krenet.it, SE).

La Pallotta has clean, bright rooms above its busy restaurant (see "Eating," below). Rooms #12 and #18 have views (Db-L90,000, CC:VMA, Via San Ruffino 4, tel. & fax 075-812-307).

Senora Gambacorta rents several decent rooms and has a roof terrace on a quiet lane (Via Sermei 9) just above St. Chiara. There is no sign and no reception desk, so you'll need to check in at her shop one-half block off Piazza Comune at San Gabriele 17—look for the sign "Bottega di Gambacorta" (Db-L60,000, tel. 075-812-454, fax 075-813-186, e-mail: geo@krenet.it, NSE). She also has an apartment for longer stays.

Hotel Sole is also well located, with 35 spacious and comfortable rooms (Sb-L70,000, Db-L100,000, Tb-L130,000, breakfast-L10,000, CC:VMA, half its rooms are in a quieter annex across the street, 100 meters before St. Clare church, Corso Mazzini 35, tel. 075-812373, fax 075-813706, e-mail: sole@tecnonet.it).

Hotel Umbra, the best splurge in the center, feels like a quiet villa in the middle of town (25 rooms, Sb-L130,000, Db-L170,000–200,000, depending upon size of room, Tb-L210,000, includes breakfast, CC:VMA, air-con, peaceful garden and view terrace, good restaurant, very quiet, 100 meters below Piazza di Comune at Via degli Archi 6, tel. 075-812-240, fax 075-813-653, e-mail: humbra@mail.caribusiness.it, family Laudenzi).

Hotel Dei Priori is another family-run, three-star, palace-type place in the old center with big, quiet rooms that have all the comforts (Db-L170,000–190,000, deluxe Db-L230,000–L250,000, includes breakfast, CC:VMA, elevator, air-con, Corso Mazzini 15, tel. 075-812-237, fax 075-816-804, e-mail: hpriori@edisons.it).

Francis probably would have bunked with the peasants in Assisi's **Ostello della Pace** (L22,000 beds in 4- to 8-bed rooms, 2 D-L54,000, a family room with bathroom-L27,000, includes breakfast, dinner-L14,000, a 15-minute walk below town at Via di Valethye 177, at the San Pietro stop on the station-town bus, tel. & fax 075-816-767, SE).

Eating in Assisi

For a fine Assisian perch and good regional cooking, relax on a terrace overlooking Piazza del Comune at **Taverna dei Consoli** (L25,000 menu, closed Wed, across from Albergo Italia, tel. 075-812-516, laid-back owner Moreno SE).

La Pallotta is a local favorite run by a friendly, hardworking family. It offers excellent regional specialties, such as *piccione* (pigeon), *coniglio* (rabbit), and more (L27,000 menu, closed Tue, a block above Piazza del Comune, Via San Rufino 4, tel. 075-812-649).

Osteria Piazzetta Dell Erba is a fun little family-run place a block above Piazza del Comune serving good, basic Umbrian specialties next to the farmer's market (daily L10,000 pasta specials, *bruschetta* and focaccia sandwiches, closed Mon, Via San Gabriele dell' Addolorata, tel. 075-815-352). **Pizzeria/Tavola Calda Dal Carro** is similar and also friendly (good pizzas and L22,000 menu, closed Wed, Vicolo di Nepis 2, tel. 075-815249).

Ristorante San Francesco is the place to splurge for dinner (facing the basilica at Via San Francesco 52, tel. 075-812-329).

Pozzo della Mensa has a good L20,000 menu and simple, hearty cooking (hidden down a quiet alley 1 block from San Rufino Church at Via della Menza 11, tel. 075-816-247).

Transportation Connections—Assisi

To: Rome (2 direst trains/day, 2.5 hrs, consider taxi to nearby Foligno for more-frequent trains), **Florence** (10 trains/day, 2.5 hrs, sometimes changing at Terontola-Cortona), **Siena** (4 buses/day, 2 hrs, L16,000, departing 8:45, 10:20, 15:40, 20:45, departing from Assisi train station), **Orvieto** (4 trains/day, 2–3 hrs). Train info: tel. 147-888-088. There are one or two buses a day to Rome and Florence.

ORVIETO

Umbria's grand hill town, while no secret, is still worth a quick look. Just off the freeway, with three popular claims to fame (its cathedral, Classico wine, and ceramics), it's loaded with tourists by day and quiet by night. Drinking a shot of wine in a ceramic cup as you gaze up at the cathedral lets you experience Orvieto all at once.

Ride the back streets of Orvieto into the Middle Ages. The town sits majestically on a big chunk of tufa. Streets lined with buildings made from the exhaust-stained volcanic stuff seem to grumble Dark Ages.

Piazza Cahen is a key transportation hub at the entry to the hilltop town. It has a ruined fortress with a garden, a commanding view, and the Pozzo San Patrizio, an impressive, although overpriced, double helix well carved into tufa rock.

Tourist Information: The TI is at Piazza Duomo 24 on the cathedral square (Mon–Fri 8:15–13:50, 16:00–19:00, Sat

10:00–13:00, 16:00–19:00, Sun 10:00–12:00, 16:00–18:00, tel. 076-334-1772).

Arrival in Orvieto: A handy funicular/bus shuttle takes visitors quickly from the train station and car park to the top of the town (4/hrly, L1,500 ticket includes Piazza Cahen–Piazza Duomo minibus transfer, where you'll find everything that matters; or L1,200 for funicular only—best choice if you're staying at Hotel Corso; funicular runs Mon–Sat 7:15–20:30, Sun 8:00–20:30).

Buy your ticket at the entrance to the funicular (look for *"biglietteria"* sign) or at the train station *tabacchi* shop across the street. At the top of the funicular, get on the waiting orange bus. The shuttle bus drops you at the TI (last stop, in front of Duomo). Drivers park at the base of the hill at the huge, free lot behind the Orvieto train station (follow the "P" and *"funicolare"* signs) or at the pay lot to the right of Orvieto's cathedral (L1,500 for the 1st hr, L1,000/hrly thereafter).

Sights—Orvieto

▲▲**Duomo**—Orvieto's cathedral has Italy's most striking facade (from 1330). Grab a gelato (to the left of the church) and study this fascinating mass of mosaics and sculpture (daily 7:30–12:45, 14:30–19:15, closes at 18:15 Mar and Oct, closes at 17:15 Nov–Feb). Inside the cathedral notice how the downward-sloping floor diminishes the perspective, giving it the illusion of being shorter than it is. Notice also the alabaster windows.

To the right of the altar, the Chapel of St. Brizio features Luca Signorelli's brilliantly lit and recently restored frescoes of the Apocalypse. Step into the chapel and you're surrounded by vivid scenes showing the Preaching of the Antichrist, the End of the World, the Resurrection of the Bodies, the Last Judgment, and a gripping pietà. For a bonus, check out Fra Angelico's painting of Jesus, the angels, and the prophets on the ceiling. This room is Orvieto's artistic must-see (get L3,000 ticket at the TI or the shop across the square, see TI hours above; chapel sometimes free 7:30–10:00—drop by to check). A good book about the chapel is Dugald McLellan's *Signorelli's Orvieto Frescoes*.

Public toilets are just off the square, down the stairs from the left transept. To find the viewpoint park, face the cathedral and go right (past parking lot) for a one-minute walk.

Archaeological Museum (Museo Civico)—Across from the entrance of the cathedral is a fine Etruscan art museum combined with a city history museum (L7,000, Tue–Sun 10:00–13:00, 14:00–18:00, closed Mon; Oct–Mar Tue–Sun 10:00–13:00, 14:30–17:00).

Underground Orvieto Tours (Parco delle Grotte)—Guides weave archaeological history into a look at about 100 meters of Etruscan and medieval caves (L10,000, daily at 11:00, 12:15, 16:00,

Orvieto

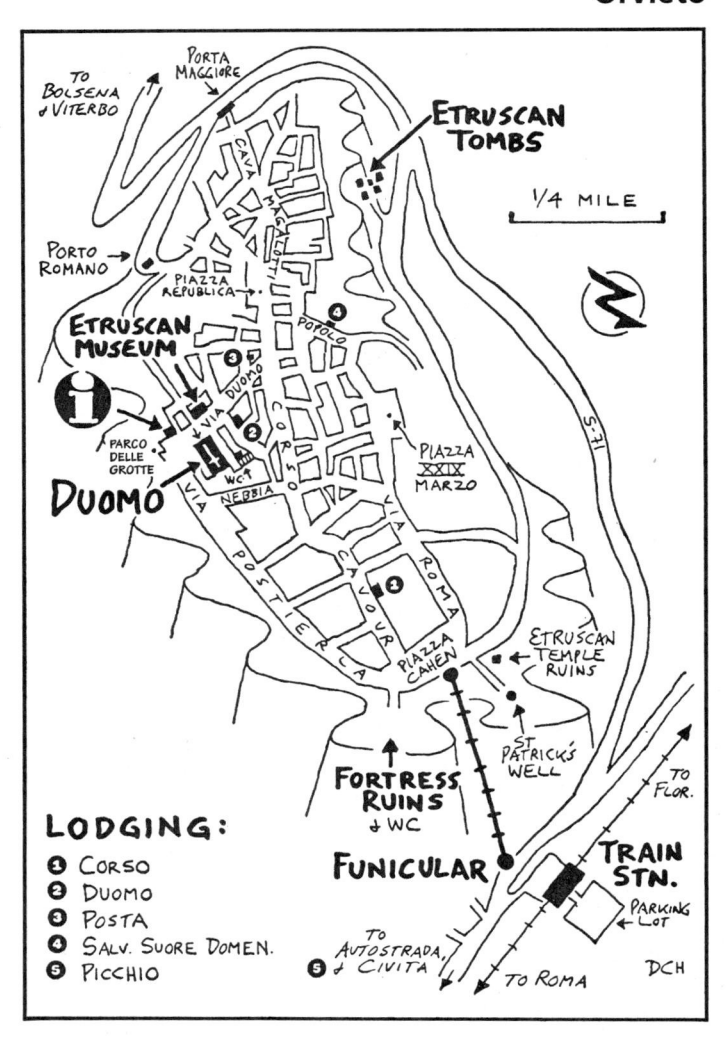

LODGING:
1. Corso
2. Duomo
3. Posta
4. Salv. Suore Domen.
5. Picchio

and 17:15 from TI, tel. 076-337-5084 or the TI). Orvieto is honeycombed with caves. You'll see only the remains of an old olive press, two 40-meter-deep Etruscan well shafts, and the remains of a primitive cement quarry, but if you want underground Orvieto, you'll get it.

Wine Tasting—Orvieto Classico wine is justly famous. For a short tour of a local winery, visit Tenuta Le Velette, where English-speaking Corrado and Cecilia Bottai will welcome you—if you call ahead to set up an appointment (L15,000 for tour and tasting, Mon–Fri 8:30–12:00, 14:00–17:00, Sat 8:30–12:00, closed Sun, tel. 076-329-090, fax 076-329-114). From their sign (5 minutes past Orvieto at top of switchbacks just before Canale, on Bagnoregio Road) cruise down a long, tree-lined drive and then park at the striped gate (must call ahead; no drop-ins).

Sleeping in Orvieto
(L1,900 = about $1, zip code: 05018)

Here are five places in the old town and one in a more modern neighborhood near the station.

Hotel Virgilio is a decent hotel with bright and modern—if overpriced—rooms shoehorned into an old building ideally located on the main square facing the cathedral (Sb-L120,000, Db-L175,000, includes breakfast, send personal or traveler's check for 1st night's deposit, CC:VM, elevator, Piazza Duomo 5, tel. 076-334-1882, fax 076-334-3797, SE). They also have a cheaper *"dependencia"*—a double and quad in a one-star hotel a few doors away (Db-L110,000, Qb-L200,000).

Hotel Corso is small, clean, and friendly, with comfy modern rooms, some with balconies and views (Sb-L100,000, Db-L140,000, 10 percent discount if you show this book, CC:VM, elevator, garage on the main street up from the funicular toward the Duomo at Via Cavour 339, tel. & fax 076-334-2020).

Hotel Duomo is a funky, brightly colored, Old World place with not-quite-clean rooms and a great location (17 rooms, S-L40,000, D-L60,000, Db-L85,000, a block from the Duomo, behind *gelateria* at Via di Maurizio 7, tel. 076-334-1887, fax 076-334-1105).

Hotel Posta is a five-minute walk from the cathedral into the medieval core. It's a big, old, formerly elegant but well-cared-for-in-its-decline building with a breezy garden, a grand old lobby, and spacious, clean, plain rooms with vintage rickety furniture and springy beds (20 rooms, D-L75,000, Db-L95,000, Via Luca Signorelli 18, tel. & fax 076-334-1909).

The sisters of the **Instituto Salvatore Suore Domenicane** rent 15 spotless twin rooms in their heavenly convent (Sb-L50,000, Db-L80,000, 2-night minimum, breakfast-L5,000, just off Piazza del Populo at Via del Populo 1, tel. & fax 076-334-2910).

Hotel Picchio is a concrete-and-marble place, more comfortable but with less character than others in the area. It's in the lower, plain part of town, 300 yards from the train station (D-L50,000, Db-L80,000, Tb-L90,000, Via G. Salvatori 17, 05019 Orvieto Scalo, tel. 076-330-1144 or 076-390-246, family-run by Marco and Picchio). A trail leads from here up to the old town. Ask for the Rick Steves discount.

For a long list of rural B&Bs, farms, and apartments in Canale, Bagnoregio, and Lubriano, contact Cecilia Bottai at the winery (Db-L80,000, tel. 076-329-090, fax 076-329-114, SE).

Transportation Connections—Orvieto

By train to: Rome (14/day, 75 min, consider leaving your car at the large car park behind the Orvieto station), **Florence** (14/day, 90 min), **Siena** (10/day, 2–3 hrs, change in Chiusi).

By bus to Bagnoregio: It's a 50-minute, L3,000 bus ride (1999 departures from Orvieto's Piazza Cahen on blue Cotral bus: 9:10, 12:40, 13:55, 15:45, 17:40, and 18:35, each bus stops at Orvieto's train station five minutes later, runs daily except Sun, buy tickets on bus or from "café snack bar" at station, confirm return times with the conductor, tel. 076-379-2237). If the bus is empty, develop a relationship with your driver. He may let you jump out in Lubriano for a great photo of distant Civita.

CIVITA DI BAGNOREGIO

Perched on a pinnacle in a grand canyon, the traffic-free village of Civita is Italy's ultimate hill town. Curl your toes around its Etruscan roots.

Civita is terminally ill. Only 15 residents remain, as, bit by bit, it's being purchased by rich big-city Italians who escape here. Apart from its permanent (and aging) residents and those who have weekend homes here, there is a group of Americans—introduced to the town through a small University of Washington architecture program—who have bought into the rare magic of Civita. When the program is in session, 15 students live with residents and study Italian culture and architecture.

Civita is connected to the world and the town of Bagnoregio by a long pedestrian bridge. While Bagnoregio lacks the pinnacle-town romance of Civita, it is a pure and lively bit of small-town Italy. It's actually a healthy, vibrant community (unlike Civita, the suburb it calls "the dead city"). Get a haircut, sip a coffee on the square, walk down to the old laundry (ask, *"Dov'è la lavanderia vecchia?"*). A lively market fills the parking lot each Monday.

From Bagnoregio, yellow signs direct you along its long, skinny spine to its older neighbor, Civita. Enjoy the view as you walk up the bridge to Civita. Be prepared for the little old ladies of Civita, who have become aggressive at getting lire out of visitors—tourists are their only source of support. Off-season Civita, Bagnoregio, and Al Boschetto (see "Sleeping," below) are all deadly quiet—and cold. I'd side trip in quickly from Orvieto or skip the area altogether.

Civita Orientation Walk

Civita was once connected to Bagnoregio. The saddle between the separate towns has eroded away, but photographs around town show the old donkey path, the original bridge. It was bombed in World War II and was replaced in 1965 with the new bridge, which you'll climb today. The hearty old folks of the town hang onto the bridge's hand railing when fierce winter weather rolls through.

Entering the town you'll pass through a cut in the rock (made by Etruscans 2,500 years ago) and under a 12th-century Romanesque arch. This was the main Etruscan road leading to the Tiber Valley and Rome.

Inside the town gate on the left notice the old laundry (in front of the WC). On the right a fancy door and windows lead to thin air. This was the facade of a Renaissance palace—one of five that once graced Civita. It fell into the valley riding a chunk of the ever-eroding rock pinnacle. Today the door leads to a remaining chunk of the palace—complete with Civita's first hot tub—owned by the "Marchesa," a countess who married into Italy's biggest industrialist family.

Poke through the museum next door and check out the viewpoint around the corner near the long-gone home of Civita's one famous son, Saint Bonaventure, known as the "second founder of the Fransciscans."

Now wander to the town square in front of the church, where you'll find Civita's only public phone, bar, and restaurant—and a wild donkey race on the first Sunday of June and the second Sunday of September. The church marks the spot where an Etruscan temple, and then a Roman temple, once stood. The pillars that stand like giants' bar stools are ancient—Roman or Etruscan.

Go into the church and find Anna. She'll give you a tour, proudly pointing out frescoes and statues from "the school of Giotto" and "the school of Donatello," a portrait of the patron saint of your teeth (notice the scary-looking pincers), and an altar dedicated to Marlon Brando (or St. Ildebrando). Tip her and buy your postcards from her.

The basic grid street plan of the ancient town survives. Just around the corner from the church, on the main street, is Rossana and Antonio's cool and friendly wine cellar. Pull up a stump and let them or their children, Arianna and Antonella, serve you *panini* (sandwiches), *bruschetta* (garlic toast with optional tomato topping), wine, and a local cake called *ciambella*. Climb down into the cellar and note the traditional wine-making gear and the provisions for rolling huge kegs up the stairs. Tap on the kegs in the cool bottom level to see which are full.

The rock below Civita is honeycombed with ancient cellars (for keeping wine at the same temperature all year) and cisterns (for collecting rainwater, since there was no well in town). Many of these date from Etruscan times.

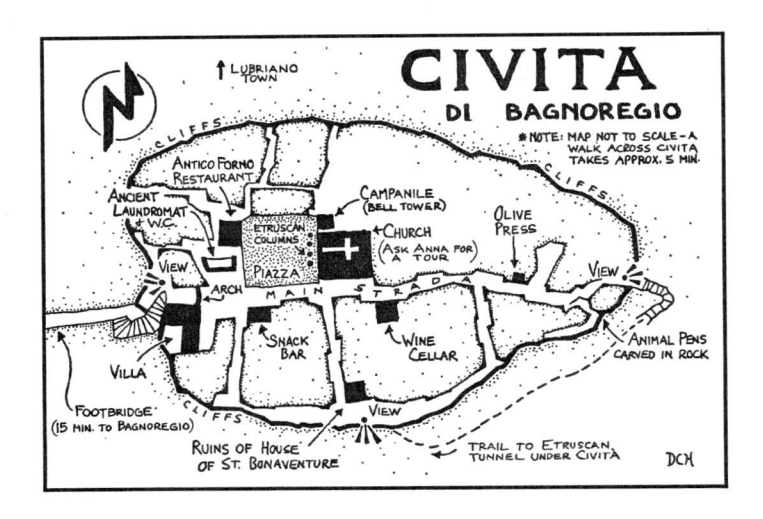

Explore farther down the street but remember, nothing is abandoned. Everything is still privately owned. After passing an ancient Roman tombstone on your left, you'll come to Vittoria's Antico Mulino, an atmospheric collection of old olive presses (donation requested, give about L1,500). Her sons Sandro and Felice, running the local equivalent of a lemonade stand, toast delicious *bruschetta* on weekends and holidays. Choose your topping (chopped tomato is super) and get a glass of wine for a fun, affordable snack.

Farther down the way, Maria (for a donation of about L1,500) will show you through her garden with a grand view (Maria's Giardino) and share historical misinformation (she says Civita and Lubriano were once connected).

At the end of town the main drag peters out, and a trail leads you down and around to the right to a tunnel that has cut through the hill under the town since Etruscan times. It was widened in the 1930s so farmers could get between their scattered fields easier.

Evenings on the town square are a bite of Italy. The same people sit on the same church steps under the same moon, night after night, year after year. I love my cool late evenings in Civita. If you visit in the cool of the morning, have cappuccino and rolls at the small café on the town square.

Whenever you visit, stop halfway up the donkey path and listen to the sounds of rural Italy. Reach out and touch one of the monopoly houses. If you know how to turn the volume up on the crickets, do so.

Sleeping in Civita, Bagnoregio and Beyond
(L1,900 = about $1, zip code: 01022)

When you leave the tourist crush, life as a traveler in Italy becomes easy, and prices tumble. Finding a room is easy in small-town Italy.

Franco, who runs Civita's only restaurant, **Antico Forno,** rents three newly remodeled rooms on Civita's main square. Call a minimum of two days in advance. Franco will meet you at the base of the bridge to beam up your luggage (Db-L120,000, D-L100,000, the more expensive rooms overlook the square, L20,000 more for optional half-pension, CC:VM, Piazza Del Duomo Vecchio, 01022 Civita di Bagnoregio, tel. 076-176-0016, cell phone: 034-7611-5426, e-mail: fsala@pelagus.it, Franco Sala SE).

For information about a fully furnished and equipped two-bedroom **Civita apartment** with a terrace and cliffside garden that's rentable May through October ($700/week, $2,200/month, one-week minimum), call Carol Watts in Kansas (tel. 785/539-0815, evenings).

Hotel Fidanza, in Bagnoregio near the bus stop, is tired but decent and the only hotel in town. Of its 25 rooms, #206 and #207 have views of Civita (Sb-L70,000, Db-L100,000, breakfast-L20,000, attached restaurant, Via Fidanza 25, Bagnoregio/Viterbo, tel. & fax 076-179-3444).

Just outside Bagnoregio is **Al Boschetto.** The Catarcia family speaks no English. Have an English-speaking Italian call for you (D-L85,000, Db-L95,000, breakfast-L6,000, CC:V, Strada Monterado, Bagnoregio/Viterbo, tel. 076-179-2369, walking and driving instructions below). Most rooms, while very basic, have private showers (no curtains, slippery floors—be careful not to flood the place; sing in search of your shower's resonant frequency). The Catarcia family (Angelino, his wife Perina, sons Gianfranco and Domenico, daughter-in-law Giuseppina, and the grandchildren) offer a candid look at rural Italian life. Meals are sometimes hearty, and the men are often tipsy. If the men invite you down deep into the gooey, fragrant bowels of the cantina, be warned: The theme song is *"Trinka Trinka Trinka,"* and there are no rules unless the female participants set them. The Orvieto bus drops you at the town gate. (Remember, no bus service at all on Sunday.) Al Boschetto is a 15-minute walk out of town past the old arch (follow *"Viterbo"* signs); turn left at the pyramid monument and right at the first fork (follow *"Montefiascone"* sign). Civita is a pleasant 45-minute walk (back through Bagnoregio) from Al Boschetto.

Casa San Martino, in the village of Lisciano Niccone (near Cortona and Perugia), is a 250-year-old farmhouse run as a B&B by American Italophile Lois Martin. Using this comfortable hilltop countryside as a home base, those with a car can tour

Assisi, Orvieto, and Civita. While Lois reserves the summer for one-week stays, she'll take guests staying a minimum of two nights for the rest of the year (Db-$100, includes breakfast, views, pool, washer/dryer, house rental available, Casa San Martino 19, Lisciano Niccone, tel. 075-844-288, fax 075-844-422). When she's booked, she refers people to her neighbors Ernestina and Gisbert **Schwanke**, who rent a two-bedroom apartment cheaper than Lois' (minimum 4-night stay, San Martino 36, tel. & fax 075-844-309, SE).

Eating in and near Civita

In Civita, try **Trattoria Antico Forno,** which serves up pasta at affordable prices (daily for lunch at 12:30 and dinner at 19:30, on the main square, tel. 076-176-0016).

Hostaria del Ponte offers light, creative cuisine at the car park at the base of the bridge to Civita (Tue–Sat 12:30–16:00, 19:30–24:00, Sun 12:30–16:00, closed Mon, great view terrace, tel. 076-179-3565).

In Bagnoregio, check out **Ristorante Nello il Fumatore** (closed Fri, on Piazza Fidanza). You'll get hearty country cooking—such as bunny—served at **Al Boschetto,** just outside Bagnoregio (see "Sleeping," above).

Transportation Connections—Bagnoregio

To Civita: It's a 30-minute walk. Taking the shuttle bus from Bagnoregio (10-min ride, first bus at 7:45, last at 17:50, 2/hrly except during 13:00–15:00 siesta) still involves a 15-minute walk up the pedestrian bridge from the bus stop.

To Orvieto: Public buses (8/day, 50 min) connect Bagnoregio to the rest of the world via Orvieto (1999 departures from Bagnoregio: 5:30, 6:35, 6:55, 9:30, 10:15, 13:00, 13:35, 14:25, 16:40, 17:20, runs daily except Sun). While there's no official baggage-check service in Bagnoregio, I've arranged with Laurenti Mauro, who runs the Bar Enoteca just outside the Bagnoregio old-town gate, to let you leave your bags there (open 6:00–24:00 with a short lunch break, closed Thu, from the Orvieto bus stop walk downhill and turn right on 1st street). Pay him L2,000 per bag or buy breakfast there.

THE CINQUE TERRE

The Cinque Terre (CHINK-wuh TAY-ruh), a remote chunk of the Italian Riviera, is the traffic-free, lowbrow, underappreciated alternative to the French Riviera. There's not a museum in sight. Just sun, sea, sand (well, pebbles), wine, and pure unadulterated Italy. Enjoy the villages, swimming, hiking, and evening romance of one of God's great gifts to tourism. For a home base, choose among five villages, each of which fills a ravine with a lazy hive of human activity—calloused locals, sunburned travelers, and no Vespas. While the place is now well discovered, I've never seen happier, more relaxed tourists. Vernazza is my favorite home base.

The area was first described in medieval times as "the five castles." Tiny communities grew up in the protective shadows of the castles ready to run inside at the first hint of a Turkish "Saracen" pirate raid. Many locals were kidnapped and ransomed or sold into slavery somewhere far to the east. As the threat of pirates faded, the villages grew, with economies based on fish and grapes. Until the advent of tourism in this generation, the towns were very remote. Even today, traditions survive, and each of the five villages comes with a distinct dialect and proud heritage. The region has just become a national park, and its natural and cultural wonders will be carefully preserved.

Sadly, a few ugly, noisy Americans are giving tourism a bad name here. Even hip young locals are put off by loud, drunk tourists. They say (and I agree), the Cinque Terre is a special place. It deserves a special dignity. Party in Viareggio but be mellow in the Cinque Terre. Talk softly. Help keep it clean. In spite of the tourist crowds, it's still a real community, and we are guests.

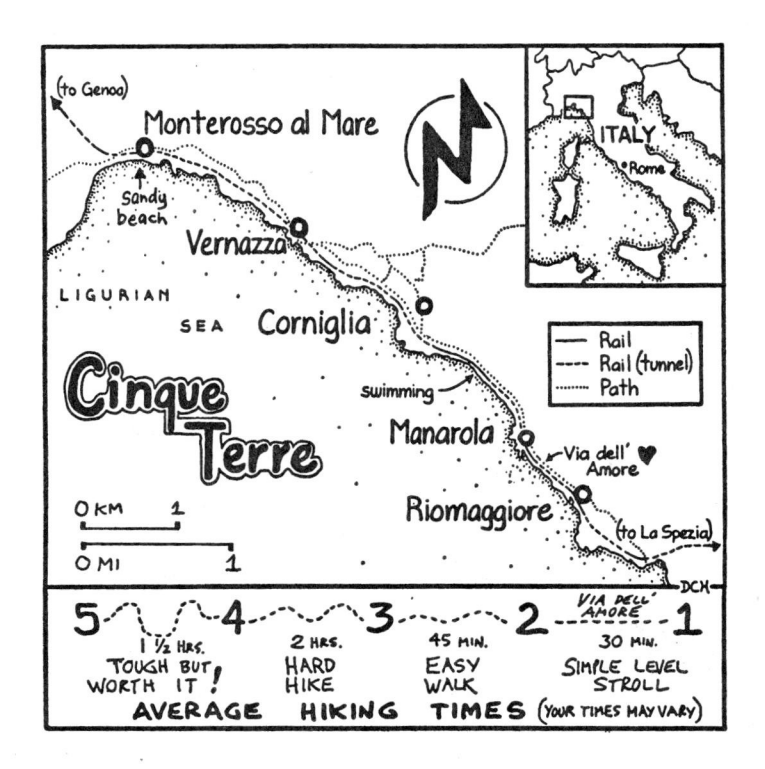

Planning Your Time

The ideal minimum stay is two nights and a completely uninterrupted day. The Cinque Terre is served by the milk-run train from Genoa and La Spezia. Speed demons arrive in the morning, check their bag in La Spezia, take the five-hour hike through all five towns, laze away the afternoon on the beach or rock of their choice, and zoom away on the overnight train to somewhere back in the real world. But be warned: The Cinque Terre has a strange way of messing up your momentum.

The towns are each just a few minutes apart by hourly train or boat. There's no checklist of sights or experiences; just a hike, the towns, and your fondest vacation desires. Study this chapter in advance and piece together your best day, mixing hiking, swimming, trains, and a boat ride. For the best light and comfort, start your hike early.

Market days perk up the towns (Tue in Vernazza, Thu in Monterosso, and on Fri a big market sprawls near the station at La Spezia, 8:00–13:00).

Getting around the Cinque Terre

The city of La Spezia is the gateway to the Cinque Terre. In La Spezia's train station, the milk-run Cinque Terre train schedule is posted at the information window. Take the L2,000, half-hour train ride into the Cinque Terre town of your choice. Once in the villages you'll get around cheapest by train but more conveniently and scenically by boat.

Cinque Terre Train Schedule: Since the train is the Cinque Terre lifeline, many shops and restaurants post the current schedule (train info tel. 018-781-7458). Pick up a photocopied schedule—it'll come in handy.

Trains leave La Spezia for the Cinque Terre villages (last year's schedule) at 6:15, 7:17, 8:10, 9:53, 11:23, 12:31, 13:20, 15:00, 16:30, 17:18, 18:16, 19:16, 20:14, 21:10, and 23:02.

Trains leave Monterosso al Mare for La Spezia (departing Vernazza about 10 minutes later, last year's schedule) at 6:30, 7:03, 8:13, 9:14, 10:16, 11:00, 12:16, 13:07, 14:08, 15:12, 16:15, 17:33, 18:25, 19:14, 20:12, 21:18, 22:13, and 23:31.

Do not rely on these train times. Check the current posted schedule and then count on half the trains being 15 minutes or so late (unless you're late, in which case they are right on time).

To orient yourself, remember that directions are *"per* [to] Genoa" or *"per* La Spezia," and any train that stops at any of the villages other than Monterosso will stop at all five. (Note that many trains leaving La Spezia skip them all or stop only in Monterosso.) The five towns are just minutes apart by train. Know your stop. After leaving the town before your destination, go to the door to slip out before mobs pack in. Since the stations are small and the trains are long, you might need to get off the train deep in a tunnel, and you might need to open the door yourself.

If the train station is not staffed (which is often the case in Vernazza, Corniglia, and Manarola), buy your ticket from the nearest newsstand or tobacco shop (in Vernazza, near the harbor) or on board from the conductor. If you buy from the conductor, explain, *"La stazione era chiusa"* (the station was closed); otherwise you'll pay a bit more.

Since a one-town hop costs the same as a five-town hop (L1,800) and every ticket is good for six hours with stopovers, save money and explore the region in one direction on one ticket. Stamp the ticket at the station machine before you board. Stations sell a L5,500, all-day Cinque Terre pass. Don't spend one of your railpass flexi-days on the Cinque Terre.

Boats: From Easter to late October a regular boat service connects the five towns and Portovenere. This provides a scenic way to get from town to town and survey what you just hiked. It's also the only efficient way to visit the nearby resort of Portovenere (alternative: a tedious train/bus connection via La Spezia). In good weather, the boats are more reliable than the trains. Boats go about hourly, from 10:00 until 18:30 (about L5,000 per single hop or L20,000 for an all-day pass to the 5 towns, buy tickets at little harborside card tables, tel. 018-781-7456). A more frequent boat service connects Monterosso and Vernazza (tel. 018-781-7452). Schedules are posted at docks, harbor bars, and hotels. If you're in a jam, Gianni in Monterosso runs a taxi boat service (cell phone 033-9761-0022).

VERNAZZA

With the closest thing to a natural harbor—overseen by a ruined castle and an old church—and only the occasional noisy slurping up of the train by the mountain to remind you of the modern world, Vernazza is my Cinque Terre home.

The action is at the harbor, where you'll find a kids' beach, plenty of sunning rocks, outdoor restaurants, a bar hanging on the edge of the castle (great for evening drinks), and a tailgate-party street market each Tuesday morning. In the summer, the beach becomes a soccer field where teams fielded by local bars and restaurants provide late night entertainment.

The town's 500 residents, proud of their Vernazzan heritage, brag that "Vernazza is locally owned. Portofino has sold out." Fearing the change it would bring, keep-Vernazza-small proponents stopped the construction of a major road into the town and region. Families are tight and go back centuries; several generations stay together. Leisure time is devoted to the *passegiata*: strolling lazily together up and down the main street. Sit on a bench and study the passersby. Then explore the characteristic alleys called *carugi*. In October the cantinas are draped with drying grapes. In the winter the population shrinks, as many people move to more comfortable big-city apartments.

A steep five-minute hike in either direction from Vernazza gives you a classic village photo op (for the best light, head toward Corniglia in the morning, toward Monterosso in the evening). Franco's Bar, with a panoramic terrace, is at the tower on the trail toward Corniglia.

Vernazza has ATMs and two banks (center and top of town). The Blue Marlin bar (run by Franco and Massimo) offers Internet access and a self-service laundry (L9,000 to wash 5 kilos, L9,000 to dry 10 kilos, supereasy machines with automatic detergent and clear English instructions, buy tokens at the adjacent bar, Via Roma 49, 30 meters below the train station, Fri–Wed 7:00–22:00, closed Thu). Accommodations are listed at the end of this chapter.

Sights—Vernazza

▲▲**Vernazza Town Top-Down Orientation Walk**—Walk uphill until you hit the parking lot—with a bank, a post office, and a barrier that keeps all but service vehicles out. The tidy new

The Cinque Terre

Vernazza

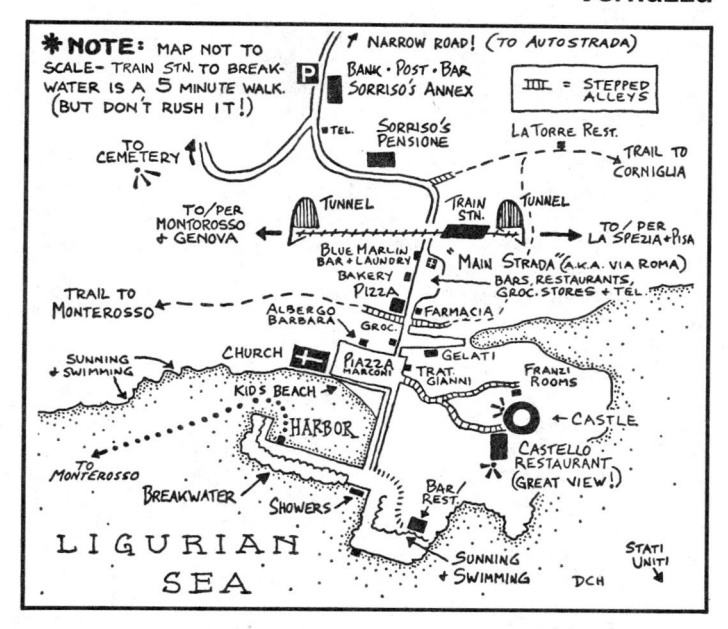

square is called Fontana Vecchia, after a long-gone fountain. Older locals remember the river filled with townswomen doing their washing. Begin your saunter downhill to the harbor.

Just before the "Pension Sorriso" sign you'll see the ambulance barn on the right. A group of volunteers is always on call for a dash to the hospital, 30 minutes away in La Spezia. Opposite that is a big empty lot behind Pension Sorriso. Like many landowners, Sr. Sorriso had plans to expand, but the government said no. The old character of these towns is carefully protected.

Across from Pension Sorriso is the honorary clubhouse for the ANPI (members of the local WWII resistance). Only five ANPI old-timers survive. Cynics consider them less than heroes. After 1943 Hitler called up Italian boys over 15. Rather than die on the front for Hitler, they escaped to the hills. Only to remain free did they become "resistance fighters."

A few steps farther you'll see a monument to those killed in World War II. Not a family was spared. Study this: Soldiers *"morti in combat timento"* fought for Mussolini, some were deported to Germania, and "partisans" were killed later fighting against Mussolini.

The tiny monorail *trenino* is parked quietly here except in September and October, when it's busy helping locals bring down the grapes. From here the path leads to Corniglia. The school bus picks up children from the many tiny neighboring villages. Today only about 25 children attend the Vernazza elementary school. The tiny square playground is decorated with three millstones, which no longer grind local olives into oil. From here, Vernazza's tiny river goes underground.

In the tunnel under the railway tracks you'll find the Croce Verde, the list of volunteers ready for ambulance duty each day of the month. The second track was recently renovated to lessen the disruptive noise.

Until the 1950s Vernazza's river ran open through the center of town from here to the *gelateria*. You can see where it once flowed.

Wandering through the main business center you'll pass many locals doing their *vasca* (laps) past the tiny Chapel of Santa Marta, where Mass is celebrated only on special Sundays; the entrepreneurial Blue Marlin bar (about the only nightspot in town); and the bakery, grocery, and pharmacy.

On the left an arch leads to what was a beach and where the river used to flow out of town. Continue on down to the harbor square and breakwater. Vernazza, with the only natural harbor of the Cinque Terre, was established as the only place boats could pick up the fine local wine. It's named for a kind of wine. Peek into the tiny street behind the Vulneta restaurant with the commotion of arches. The most characteristic of Vernazza's side streets, called *carugi*, lead up from here. The trail (above the church toward Monterosso) leads to the classic view of Vernazza (best photos just before sunset).

▲▲▲**The Burned-Out Sightseer's Visual Tour of Vernazza—**
Sit on the harbor breakwater (perhaps with a glass of local white wine or something more interesting from Bar Capitano—borrow the glass, they don't mind), face the town, and see…

The harbor: In a moderate storm you'd be soaked, as waves routinely crash over the *molo* (breakwater, built in 1972). The train line, constructed 130 years ago to tie a newly united Italy together, linked Turin and Genoa with Rome. A second line (hidden in a tunnel at this point) was built in the 1960s. The yellow building was Vernazza's first train station. You can see the four bricked-up waiting alcoves. Vernazza's fishing fleet is down to three small fishing boats (with the net spools); the town's restaurants buy up everything they catch. Vernazzans are more likely to own a boat than a car. In the '70s tiny Vernazza had one of the top water polo teams in Italy, and the harbor was their "pool." Later, when a real pool was required, Vernazza dropped out of the league.

The castle: On the far right, the castle, which is now a grassy park with great views, still guards the town (L2,000, daily 9:00 or 10:00–19:00, see the photo and painting gallery rooms). It's called *Belforte*, or "loud screams," for the warnings it made back in pirating days. The lowest deck is great for a glass of wine (follow the rope to the Belforte Bar, open until 24:00, closed Tue; inside the submarine-strength door, a photo of a major storm shows the entire tower under a wave). The highest umbrellas mark the recommended Castello restaurant (see "Eating," below).

The town: Vernazza has two halves—*"sciuiu,"* on the left (literally "flowery"), is the sunny side, and *"luvegu,"* on the right (literally "dank"), is the shady right side. From the lower castle the houses were interconnected with an interior arcade—ideal for fleeing attacks. The pastel colors are regulated by a commissioner of good taste in the community government. The square before you is locally famous for some of the region's finest restaurants. The big red central house, the 12th-century site where Genoan warships were built, used to be a kind of guardhouse.

Above the town: The ivy-covered tower, another part of the city fortifications, reminds us of Vernazza's importance in the Middle Ages, when it was an important ally of Genoa (whose arch enemies were the other maritime republics of Pisa, Amalfi, and Venice). Franco's Bar, just behind the tower, welcomes hikers finishing, starting, or simply contemplating the Corniglia–Vernazza hike with great town views. Vineyards fill the mountainside beyond the town. Notice the many terraces. Someone calculated that the vineyard terraces of the Cinque Terre have the same amount of stonework as the Great Wall of China. Wine production is down nowadays, as the younger residents choose less physical work. But locals still work their plots and proudly serve their family wine. A single steel train line winds up the gully behind the tower. This is for the vintner's *trenino*, the tiny service train.

The church and city hall: Vernazza's Ligurian Gothic church, built with black stones quarried from Puenta Mesco (the distant point behind you), dates from 1318. The grey-and-red house above and to the left of the spire is the local grade school. High school is in the "big city," La Spezia. The red building to the right is the former monastery and present city hall. Vernazza and Corniglia function as one community. Through most of the 1990s the local government was Communist. In 1999 they elected a coalition of many parties working to rise above ideologies and simply make Vernazza a better place. Finally, on the top of the hill, with the best view of all, is the town cemetery, where most locals plan to end up.

Cinque Terre Hiking and Swimming

▲▲▲**Hiking**—All five towns are connected by good trails. Experience the area's best by hiking from one end to the other. The entire 11-kilometer hike can be done in about four hours, but allow five for dawdling. While you can detour to dramatic hilltop sanctuaries (one trail leads from Vernazza's cemetery uphill), I'd keep it simple by following the easy red-and-white-marked low trails between the villages. A good L7,000 hiking map (sold everywhere, not necessary for this described walk) covers the expanded version of this hike, from Porto Venere through all five Cinque Terre towns to Levanto, and more serious hikes in the high country.

Since I still get the names of the Cinque Terre towns mixed up, I think of the towns by number: Riomaggiore (town #1), Manarola (#2), Corniglia (#3), Vernazza (#4), and resorty Monterosso (#5).

Riomaggiore–Manarola (20 min): Facing the front of the train station in Riomaggiore (town #1), go up the stairs to the right, following signs for the Via dell' Amore. The film-gobbling promenade—wide enough for baby strollers—leads down the coast to Manarola. While there's no beach here, stairs lead down to sunbathing rocks.

Manarola–Corniglia (45 min): The walk from the Manarola (#2) to Corniglia (#3) is a little longer and a little more rugged than that from #1 to #2. The high alternative via the hamlet of Volastra takes two hours and offers sweeping views and a closer look at the vineyards. Ask locally about the more difficult six-mile inland hike to Volastra. This tiny village, perched between Manarola and Corniglia, offers great views and the Five-Terre wine co-op; stop by the Cantina Sociale.

Corniglia–Vernazza (90 min): The hike from Corniglia (#3) to Vernazza (#4)—the wildest and greenest of the coast—is most rewarding. From the Corniglia station and beach, zigzag up to the town. Ten minutes past Corniglia toward Vernazza you'll see the well-hung Guvano beach far below (see below). The trail leads past a bar and picnic tables, through lots of fragrant and flowery vegetation, and scenically into Vernazza.

Vernazza–Monterosso (90 min): The trail from Vernazza (#4) to Monterosso (#5) is a scenic up-and-down-a-lot trek. Trails are rough (and some readers report "very dangerous") but easy to follow. Camping at the picnic tables midway is frowned upon. The views just out of Vernazza are spectacular.

▲**Swimming**—Wear your walking shoes and pack your swim gear. Each beach has showers that may work better than your hotel's. Underwater sightseeing is full of fish (goggles sold in local shops). Here's a beach review:

Monterosso's beaches, immediately in front of the train station, are easily the best (and most crowded). It's a sandy resort with everything rentable... lounge chairs, umbrellas, paddleboats, and usually even beach access (L2,000). Beach access is free only where you see no umbrellas.

Vernazza has a sandy children's cove, sunning rocks, and

showers by the breakwater. There's a ladder on the breakwater for deepwater access. The tiny *acque pendente* (waterfall) cove which locals call their *laguna blu*, between Vernazza and Monterosso, is accessible only by small hired boat.

Corniglia has a rocky man-made beach below its station. It's clean and less crowded than the Monterosso beach, and the beach bar has showers, drinks, and snacks.

The nude Guvano (GOO-vah-noh) beach (between Corniglia and Vernazza) made headlines in Italy in the 1970s as clothed locals in a makeshift armada of dinghies and fishing boats retook their town beach. But big-city nudists still work on all-around tans in this remote setting. From the Corniglia train station (follow the road north, zigzag below the tracks, follow signs to the tunnel), travelers buzz the intercom, and the hydraulic *Get Smart*–type door is opened from the other end. After a 15-minute hike through a cool, moist, and dimly lit unused old train tunnel, you'll emerge at the Guvano beach—and be charged L5,000 (L4,000 with this guidebook, water, no WC). A steep (free) trail also leads from the beach up to the Corniglia–Vernazza trail. The crowd is Italian counterculture: pierced nipples, tattooed punks, hippie drummers in dreads, and nude exhibitionist men. The ratio of men to women is about three to two. About half the people on the pebbly beach keep their swimsuits on.

Manarola has no sand but the best deepwater swimming of all. The first beach with a shower, ladder, and wonderful rocks (with daredevil high divers) is my favorite. The second (follow paved path around the point) has tougher access and no shower but feels more remote and pristine.

Riomaggiore's beach is rocky but clean and peaceful and has a shower (follow the roped path from the harbor 100 meters to the left).

Cinque Terre Cuisine 101

A few menu tips: *Accuighe* (ah-CHOO-gay) are anchovies, a local specialty—always served the day they're caught. If you've always hated anchovies (the harsh, cured-in-salt American kind), try them fresh here. *Tegame alla Vernazza* is the most typical main course: anchovies, potatoes, tomatoes, white wine, oil, and herbs. *Pansotti* is ravioli with ricotta and spinach, often served with a hazelnut sauce...delightful. While antipasto is cheese and salami in Tuscany, here you'll get *antipasti di mare*, a big plate of mixed fruits of the sea and a fine way to start a meal. For many, splitting this and a pasta dish is plenty. A fun local dessert: "grandmother's cake" with a glass of *sciacchetrà* for dunking (see "Wine," below).

▲▲**Pesto**—This is the birthplace of pesto. Basil, which loves the temperate Ligurian climate, is mixed with cheese (half *Parmigiano* cow cheese and half pecorino sheep cheese), garlic, olive oil, and

Riomaggiore and Manarola

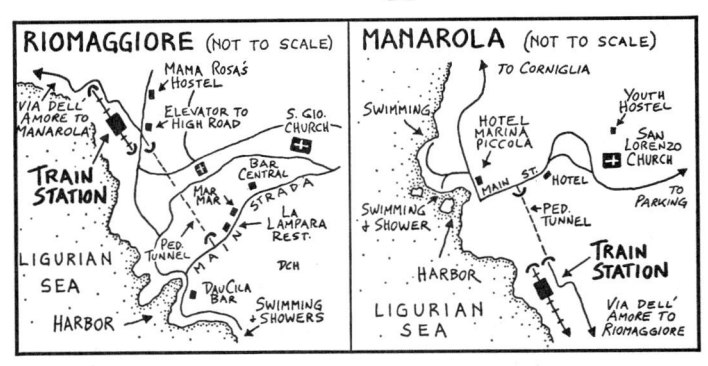

pine nuts and then poured over pasta. Try it on spaghetti, *trenette*, or *trofie* (made of flour with a bit of potato, designed specifically for pesto). Many also like pesto lasagna. If you become addicted, small jars of pesto are sold in the local grocery stores.

▲▲**Wine**—The *vino delle Cinque Terre*, famous throughout Italy, flows cheap and easy throughout the region. It is white—great with the local seafood. D.O.C. is the mark of top quality. For a sweet, sherrylike wine, the local *sciacchetrà* wine is worth the splurge (L5,000 per glass, often served with a cookie). While 10 kilos of grapes yield seven liters of local wine, *sciacchetrà* is made from near-raisins, and 10 kilos of grapes make only 1.5 liters of *sciacchetrà*. The word means "push and pull"... push in lots of grapes, pull out the best wine. If your room is up a lot of steps, be warned: *sciacchetrà* is 18 percent alcohol, while regular wine is only 11 percent. In the cool, calm evening, sit on the Vernazza breakwater with a glass of wine and watch the phosphorescence in the waves. While red wine is sold as Cinque Terre wine, it's a fantasy designed to please the tourists.

Cinque Terre Towns

(Note: Readers of this book fill Vernazza. For this reason you might prefer to stay in one of these towns with fewer Americans. See "Sleeping," below.)

▲▲**Riomaggiore (town #1)**—The most substantial nonresort town of the group, Riomaggiore is a disappointment from the train station. But walk through the tunnel next to the train tracks (or ride the elevator through the hillside to the church square at the top of town) and you land in a fascinating tangle of pastel homes leaning on each other as if someone stole their crutches. There's homemade gelato at the Bar Central on main street, and

Corniglia and Monterosso

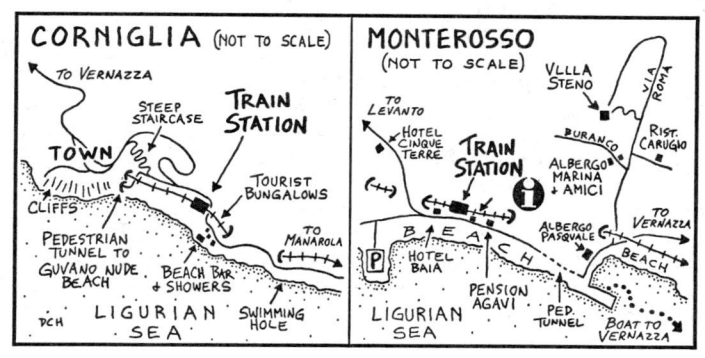

[Map of Corniglia showing: To Vernazza, Steep Staircase, Train Station, Town, Cliffs, Tourist Bungalows, Pedestrian Tunnel to Guvano Nude Beach, Beach Bar & Showers, To Manarola, Swimming Hole, Ligurian Sea]

[Map of Monterosso showing: To Levanto, Villa Steno, Via Roma, Hotel Cinque Terre, Buranco, Rist. Carugio, Train Station, Albergo Marina, Amici, Beach, Hotel Baia, Albergo Pasquale, To Vernazza, Pension Agavi, Ped. Tunnel, Boat to Vernazza, Ligurian Sea]

if Ivo is there you'll feel right at home. When Ivo closes, the gang goes down to the harborside with a guitar. A cliff-hanging trail leads from the beach to a hilltop botanical garden and old WWII bunkers. Another climbs scenically to the Madonna di Montenero sanctuary high above the town. A free electric bus shuttles locals and tourists from the top to the bottom of town. Riomaggiore's TI is harborside below the station (tel. 018-792-0633).

▲**Manarola (town #2)**—Like town #1, #2 is attached to its station by a 200-yard-long tunnel. Manarola is tiny and rugged, a tumble of buildings bunny-hopping down its ravine to the fun-loving harbor. Notice how the I-beam crane launches local boats. Punta Bonfiglio is an entertaining park/game area/bar.

▲▲**Corniglia (town #3)**—From the station a footpath zigzags up 370 stairs to the only town of the five not on the water. Originally settled by a Roman farmer who named it for his mother, Cornelia (which is how Corniglia is pronounced), its ancient residents produced a wine so famous that vases found at Pompeii touted its virtues. Today its wine is still its lifeblood. Follow the pungent smell of ripe grapes into an alley cellar and get a local to let you dip a straw into her keg. Remote and less visited, Corniglia has cooler temperatures, a windy belvedere, a few restaurants, and more than enough private rooms for rent. Past the train station is the Corniglia beach and Albergo Europa, a bungalow village filled with Italians doing the Cinque Terre in 14 days.

▲▲**Monterosso al Mare (town #5)**—This is a resort with cars, hotels, rentable beach umbrellas, and crowds. The new town is near the station. Walk east through the tunnel for the Old World charm (and the nearly hourly boats to Vernazza). The TI is near the station (Mon–Sat 10:00–12:00, 15:30–17:30, Sun 10:00–12:00, exit station and go left, tel. 018-781-7506).

Sleeping and Eating on the Cinque Terre
(L1,900 = about $1)
Sleep Code: **S** = Single, **D** = Double/Twin, **T** = Triple, **Q** = Quad, **b** = bathroom, **t** = toilet only, **s** = shower only, **CC** = Credit Card (Visa, MasterCard, Amex), **SE** = Speaks English, **NSE** = No English. Breakfast is included only in real hotels.

If you're trying to avoid my readers, stay away from Vernazza. Rich, sun-worshiping softies like Monterosso. Winos and mountain goats prefer Corniglia. Students sleep cheap in Riomaggiore. Sophisticated Italians and Germans take over Manarola.

While the Cinque Terre is too rugged for the mobs that ravage the Spanish and French coasts, it's popular with Italians, Germans, and Americans in the know. Hotels charge the most and are packed on Easter, in August, and on summer Fridays and Saturdays. August weekends are worst. But L40,000 beds in private rooms abound throughout the year. Outside of August weekends, I think you can land a comfortable L80,000 double in a private home any day by just arriving and asking around. This seems scary, but it's correct.

If you want the security of a reservation, do it long in advance for a hotel. If faxing, assume no reply means they are full. Small places generally don't bother with reservations long in advance. Without reservations, arrive in the morning and ask at bars or restaurants or simply people on the street. For the best value, visit three private rooms and snare the best. Going direct cuts out a middleman and softens prices. Plan on paying cash. Private rooms are generally bigger and more comfortable than those offered by the pensions.

Sleeping in Vernazza
(zip code: 19018)
Vernazza, the essence of the Cinque Terre, is my favorite. There are three pensions and piles of private rooms for rent. Anywhere you stay here will require some climbing. Night noises can be a problem if you're near the station or the church bell tower. Address letters to 19018 Vernazza, Cinque Terre, La Spezia. If you get no reply to your fax, assume they are full.

Albergo Barbara, on the harbor square, is run by kindly Giuseppe and his Swiss wife, Patricia. The nine rooms share three public showers and WCs (S-L60,000, tiny loft D-L70,000, D-L80,000, bigger D-L90,000, bunky family Q-L120,000, loads of stairs, fans, closed Dec–Jan, Piazza Marconi 21, tel. & fax 018-781-2398, cellular 032-8221-9688, SE). The big doubles come with grand harbor views and are the best value. The office is on the top floor of the big, red, vacant-looking building facing the harbor.

Trattoria Gianni rents 23 small rooms just under the castle. The funky ones are artfully decorated à la shipwreck and are up lots of tight, winding, spiral stairs, and most have tiny balconies and grand views. The new, comfy rooms lack views but have modern bathrooms and a superscenic, cliff-hanger private garden. Marisa (who doles out smiles like a rich gambler on a losing streak) requires a two-night minimum and check-in before 16:00 (S-L65,000, D-L90,000, Db-L115,000, Tb-L150,000, CC:VMA but 10 percent discount for cash, Piazza Marconi 5, closed Jan–Feb, tel. & fax 018-781-2228, tel. 018-782-1003). Pick up your keys at Trattoria Gianni's restaurant/reception on the harbor square and hike up the stairs to #41 (funky) or #47 (new) at the top. As a matter of principle, no English is spoken here. (Note: My tour company books this place 50 nights of the season.) Telephone three days in advance and leave your first name and time of arrival.

Pension Sorriso knows it's the only real pension in town. Don't expect an exuberant welcome. Prices include breakfast and an obligatory dinner (D-L150,000, Db-L180,000, cash only, 50 yards up from station, closed Nov–Feb, tel. 018-781-2224, fax 018-782-1198, some English spoken). While train sounds rumble through the front rooms of the main building, the annex up the street is quieter.

Affitta Camere are the best values in Vernazza. The town is honeycombed year-round with pleasant, rentable private rooms and apartments (cheap for families, with kitchens). They are reluctant to reserve rooms far in advance. It's easiest to call a day or two in advance or simply show up by morning and look around. All are comfortable and inexpensive (L30,000–50,000 per person, depending on the view and plumbing). Some are lavish, have killer views, and cost the same as a small dark place on a back lane over the train tracks. Little or no English is spoken at these places. Any main-street business has a line on rooms for rent.

Affitta Camere da Filippo is a good network of 15 rooms and apartments run by Antonio and his mother, Rita (D-L70,000, Db-L80,000, apartments-L100,000, Via A. Del Santo 62—take the stairs across from the phone booths by the railroad tracks or ask at the Blue Marlin bar, tel. 018-781-2244). For rooms with some of the best harbor views in town, stop by the harbor-front **Gambero Rosso** restaurant (closed Mon, tel. 018-781-2265, ask for Valerio). You can also try **Affitta Camere da Anna-Maria** (D-L80,000, Db-L100,000 with view or terrace; turn left at pharmacy, climb Via Carattino to #64, tel. 018-782-1082). The lady at the grocery store has a line on rooms; **Giuseppina's Villa** is a modern, deluxe apartment without a view (Db-L80,000, Qb-L140,000, Via S. Giovanni Battista 7, tel. 018-781-2026). **Mike Castiglione**, who speaks New Yorkish, rents a room (Via Carratino 16, tel. 018-781-2374). **Martina Callo** rents three expensive rooms overlooking the square up miles of steps next to the church bell tower—dong, dong, dong, all through the night (Db-L110,000, room #1-Db with harbor view, room #2-Qb is huge family room, room #3-Db with fine view terrace, Piazza Marconi 26, tel. & fax 018-781-2365). **Franca Maria Dimartino** rents three comfortable rooms on or near the harbor (Db-L110,000, Piazza Marconi 30, tel. 018-781-1002). **Pizzeria Vulnetina** on the harbor rents two rooms, one with a view (call for details, tel. 018-782-1193).

Eating in Vernazza

If you're into Italian cuisine, Vernazza's restaurants are worth the splurge. All take pride in their cooking and have similar prices. At about 20:00 wander around and compare the ambience.

The **Castello**, run by gracious and English-speaking Monica, her new husband Massimo, gracious Mario, and the rest of her family, serves great food with great views just under the castle (Thu–Tue 12:00–22:00, closed Wed and Nov–Apr, tel. 018-781-2296).

Three fine places fill the harbor front with happy eaters: **Gambero Rosso**, considered Vernazza's best restaurant, feels classy and costs only a few thousand lire more than the others (Valerio will take very good care of you). **Trattoria del Capitano** might serve the best food for the lire (Paolo speaks English). **Trattoria Franzi** is also good. **Pizzeria Vulnetia** serves the best harborside pizza (closed Mon).

Trattoria da Sandro mixes Genovese and Ligurian cuisine with friendly service but no view (closed Tue, Via Roma 60, tel. 018-781-2223). The more offbeat and intimate **Trattoria da Piva** may come with late-night guitar strumming (closed Mon).

For great food, a grand view, and perfect peace, hike to Franco's **Ristorante "La Torre"** for a dinner at sunset (Wed–Mon 20:00–21:30, closed Tue, tel. 018-782-1082).

The main street is creatively finding tourist needs and filling them. The **Blue Marlin** bar offers a good selection of sandwiches, salads, and *bruschetta*. Try the bakery and bars for good focaccia and pizza by the slice. Grocery stores make inexpensive sandwiches to order (Mon–Sat 7:30–13:00, 17:00–19:30, Sun 7:30–13:00). The town's two *gelaterias* are good. Most harborside bars will let you take your glass on a breakwater stroll.

Breakfast: Locals take breakfast about as seriously as flossing. A cappuccino and a pastry or a piece of focaccia does it. The two harbor-front bars offer the most ambience. The bakery is open early and makes ham and cheese on toast. Most tourists start their day at the Blue Marlin. Consider their L12,000 breakfast special: grilled ham and cheese focaccia; tiny slices of three local pastries—apple tart, chocolate coffee cake, and fruit cake; juice; and cappuccino (Fri–Wed 6:30–01:00, closed Thu, just below the station, tel. 018-782-1149).

Sleeping and Eating in Riomaggiore
(zip code: 19017)

Riomaggiore has organized its private room scene better than its neighbors. Several agencies within a few yards of each other on the main drag (with regular office hours, English-speaking staff, and e-mail addresses) manage a corral of local rooms for rent.

Edi's Rooms is open daily from 8:00 to 20:00 and has a line on 10 fine rooms (Db-L80,000, pricier apartments, Via Colombo 111, tel. & fax 018-792-0325, cellular 033-8619-0434, e-mail: edi-vesigna@iol.it).

Mar Mar Rooms is run by Mario Franceschetti (Db-L80,000, bunky family deals, you can request kitchen, balcony, minihostel dorms with L30,000 beds in shared apartments, 30 meters above the train tracks on the main drag next to Lampara restaurant, Via Malborghetto 8, tel. & fax 018-792-0932). Mar Mar also rents kayaks (double kayaks L15,000/hr, cheaper by the half day).

Michielini Anna rents three rooms (Db-L80,000) and two apartments with kitchens (L40,000–45,000 per person, up to 5; across from Bar Central at Colombo 143, tel. 018-792-0950, tel. & fax 018-792-0411, e-mail: cammichie@tin.it, Daniela SE).

Luciano and Roberto Fazioli have five apartments, nine rooms, and a basic seven-bed minihostel (L30,000 for dorm bed, D-L70,000, Db-L80,000; prices can increase with view and demand, Via Colombo 94, tel. 018-792-0587 or 018-792-0904).

At **Bar Central,** friendly Ivo and Alberto can help you find a room (Via Colombo 144, tel. 018-792-0208, e-mail: barcentr @tin.it). Ivo lived in San Francisco, fills his bar with only the best San Francisco rock, and speaks great English. His Bar Central, a good stop for breakfast, cheeseburgers, and Internet access (L350/ minute, L10,000/30 min), is a shady place to relax with other travelers. It's the only lively late-night place in town. And there's prizewinning gelato next door.

Youth Hostel Mama Rosa is a hard-to-forget slum that gives vagabonds a reason to bond. It's run by Rosa Ricci (an aggressively friendly character who snares backpackers at the train station), her husband, Carmine (a.k.a. "Papa Rosa"), and their English-speaking son, Silvio. It's a jumble of bunk beds with the ambience of a YMCA locker room (L30,000 beds in 9 co-ed, poorly ventilated dorms; meager washroom; 20 yards directly in front of the station; no curfew; just show up without a reservation—the earlier, the better; no telephone). This is one of those rare places where perfect strangers become good friends with the slurp of spaghetti, and wine supersedes the concept of ownership—organize and cook a co-op dinner.

Eating: Eat well at **Ristorante La Lampara.** Check out the *frutti di mare* pizza, the *trenete al pesto*, and my favorite 5-Terre pasta experience: the aromatic *spaghetti al cartoccio*—spaghetti with mixed seafood cooked in foil (L25,000 tourist menu, closed Tue, on Via Colombo just above the tracks, tel. 018-792-0120). The **pizzeria** at Via Colombo 26 serves thick and delicious pizza by the slice. While the late-night action is at Ivo's **Bar Central**, for jazz, nets, and mellow *limoncello*, walk down to the harborside **Dau Cila** bar.

Sleeping in Manarola
(zip code: 19010)

Manarola has plenty of private rooms. Ask in bars and restaurants. Otherwise you'll find a modern three-star place halfway up the main drag, a cluster of great values around the church at the peaceful top of town a five-minute hike above the train tracks, and a salty old place on the harbor.

Up the hill, the utterly normal **Albergo ca' d'Andrean** is quiet, comfortable, modern, and very hotelesque, with 10 big, sunny rooms and a cool garden oasis complete with lemon trees (Sb-L90,000, Db-L115,000, breakfast-L9,000, closed Nov, Via A. Discovolo 101, tel. 018-792-0040, fax 018-792-0452, Simone SE).

Affitta Camere de Baranin rents seven comfortable rooms (Db-L80,000, climb the steps beyond the church, Via Rollandi 35a, tel. & fax 018-792-0595, www.5terre-vacanze.com/baranin.html, Sara and Silvia).

La Torretta has two compact apartments with kitchens (L95,000), two doubles (L70,000), and a single (L40,000), all designed by the young English-speaking architect/manager Gabriele Baldini (views, big garden, breakfast-L8,000, with your back to church, look left across the square, Piazza della Chiesa, Vico Volto 14, tel. & fax 018-792-0327, e-mail: torretta@cdn.it).

Casa Capellini rents four rooms (D-L80,000, L70,000 for 2 or more nights, Db-L90,000, L80,000 for 2 or more nights; the *alta camera* on the top, with a kitchen, private terrace, and knockout view-L100,000; 2 doors down the hill from the church, on your right, Via Ettore Cozzani 12, tel. 018-792-0823 or 018-773-6765, NSE).

Ostello 5-Terre, Manarola's modern and well-run hostel, stands like a Monopoly hotel behind the church square. Reserve well in advance by fax or e-mail (beds-L25,000, CC:VMA, 48 beds in 4- to 6-bed rooms, office closed 13:00–17:00, rooms closed 10:00–17:00, open to anyone of any age, laundry, Internet access, elevator, breakfast and dinner, great roof terrace with showers and sunsets, Via B. Riccobaldi 21, tel. 018-792-0215, fax 018-792-0218, www.cinqueterre.net/ostello/, e-mail: ostello@cdh.it).

Marina Piccola has 10 bright, modern rooms on the water, so they figure a warm welcome is unnecessary (Db-L130,000, extra for required dinner Jul–Sept and whenever else they think they can get it, CC:VMA, tel. 018-792-0103, fax 018-792-0966).

Sleeping in Corniglia
(zip code: 19010)
Parked high above the sea on a hilltop, this town has plenty of private rooms (generally D-L80,000, Db-L90,000). **Maria Guelfi** (Via Fieschi 222, tel. 018-781-2178) and **Senora Silvana** (tel. 018-751-3830) offer rooms on Via Fieschi near the town-end promontory. The **Lanterna** rents a dozen rooms (bar on the main square, tel. 018-781-2291). **Affittasi Vista Mare** has rooms scattered all over town (Via Villa 3, tel. 018-781-2293). Try **Domenico Spora** (Via Villa 19, tel. 018-781-2293), **Pellegrini** (3 rooms, Via Solferino 34, tel. 018-781-2184), or **Villa Sandra** (Via Fieschi 212, tel. 018-781-2384). **Villa Cecio** is more of a hotel (on the main road 200 yards toward Vernazza, views, tel. 018-781-2043). There is a slim chance someone will be waiting for stray travelers at the station with a car to run you up to their place in the town—otherwise, prepare for a 15-minute uphill hike.

Louisa Christiana rents a great apartment with three doubles and a big comfy living room/kitchen with view terrace on the tiny soccer court at the top of the town. Two can rent the whole thing for L150,000 or rent a room and share the rest for L90,000 (Via Fieschi 215, tel. 018-781-2345 or English-speaking daughter Christiana at the bar, tel. 018-781-2236).

Sleeping in Monterosso
(zip code: 19016)
Monterosso al Mare, the most beach-resorty of the five Cinque Terre towns, offers maximum comfort and ease. There are plenty of hotels and rentable beach umbrellas, shops, and cars. The TI (Pro Loco) can find you a L40,000-per-person room in a private home (below the station, Mon–Sat 10:00–12:00, 15:30–17:30, Sun 10:00–12:00, tel. 018-781-7506). Monterosso is 30 minutes off the freeway (exit: Carrodano). Parking is easy in the huge beachfront guarded lot (L12,000/day). Via Roma at the top of the old town has banks, a post office, and a self-serve laundry.

The following hotel listings are in the order you'll see them as you leave the station heading right (two hotels) or left (the rest of the hotels).

Turn right leaving the station to the grumpy, money-grubbing **Hotel Baia** (beachfront balconies, Db-L200,000, CC:VMA, Via Fegina 88, tel. 018-781-7512, fax 018-781-8322). Farther on, **Hotel Cinque Terre**, a slick new building with 54 similar rooms, is often the last to fill (Db-L200,000–240,000, includes breakfast, dinner deals for guests, closed Nov–Mar, CC:VM, reconfirm reservations, easy parking, 300 meters off the beach, Via IV Novembre 21, tel. 018-781-7543, fax 018-781-8380).

Turn left out of the station to the bright, airy **Pension Agavi** (8 rooms, Db-L140,000, refrigerators, tel. 018-781-7171, fax 018-

781-8264, spunky Hillary SE). The tunnel then leads to the old town and two unexceptional places that require dinner in August: **Albergo Marina** (Db-L130,000–160,000, includes breakfast, CC:VM, Via Buranco 40, tel. & fax 018-781-7242 or 018-781-7613) and the fancier **Albergo degli Amici** (Db-L160,000 with breakfast, CC:VMA, no views, next door at Via Buranco 36, tel. 018-781-7544, fax 018-781-7424). **Ristorante al Carugio** rents 10 blocky, no-view rooms in an apartment flat at the no-character top end of town (Db-L110,000, office at Via S. Pietro 15, rooms at Via Roma 100, tel. & fax 018-781-7453). **Hotel La Colonnina,** a comfy, modern place, mainly takes only long-term reservations but rents fine rooms to those who call a day in advance (Db-L145,000, no breakfast, elevator, Via Zuecca 6, tel. 018-781-7439).

Farther on is the best place in town: the lovingly managed **Hotel Villa Steno**, featuring great view balconies, private gardens off some rooms, TVs, telephones, air-conditioning, and the friendly help of English-speaking Matteo. Of his 16 rooms, 12 have view balconies (Sb-L130,000, Db-L200,000, Tb-L230,000, Qb-L260,000, with hearty buffet breakfast, CC:VMA, L20,000 discount per room, per night if you pay with cash and show this book; Internet access; 10-minute hike from the station at the top of the old town at Via Roma 109, tel. 018-781-7028 or 018-781-8336, fax 018-781-7354, www.pasini.com, e-mail: steno@pasini.com). Readers get a free glass of the local sweet wine, *sciacchetrà*, when they check in—ask. The Steno has a tiny parking lot (free, but call to reserve a spot).

The Pasini family also runs the **Albergo Pasquale,** a decent place with less character but that's plenty comfortable and closer to the beach (1st place after tunnel, air-con, Via Fegina 4, tel. 018-781-7550 or 018-781-7477, fax 018-781-7056, Felicita and Matteo SE).

Transportation Connections—Cinque Terre

The five towns of the Cinque Terre are on a milk-run train line described earlier in this chapter. Hourly trains connect each town with the others, La Spezia, and Genoa. While a few of the milk-run trains go to more distant points (Milan or Pisa), it's faster to change in La Spezia or Monterosso to a bigger train.

From La Spezia by train to: Rome (10/day, 4 hrs), **Pisa** (hrly, 1 hr), **Florence** (hrly, 2.5 hrs, change at Pisa), **Milan** (hrly, 3 hrs, change in Genoa), **Venice** (2 direct 6-hr trains/day—also from Monterosso). Many major trains now run from Monterosso (e.g., direct express to Milan and Venice, train info tel. 018-781-7458).

AMSTERDAM

Amsterdam is a progressive way of life housed in Europe's most 17th-century city. Physically, it's a city built upon millions of pilings. But, more than that, it's a city built on good living, cozy cafés, great art, street-corner jazz, stately history, and a spirit of live and let live. It has 800,000 people and as many bikes it; has more canals than Venice—and as many tourists. While Amsterdam may box your Puritan ears, this great, historic city is an experiment in freedom.

Planning Your Time

While I'd sleep in nearby Haarlem (see next chapter), Amsterdam is worth a full day of sightseeing on even the busiest itinerary. While the city has a couple of must-see museums, its best sight is its own breezy ambience. The city's a joy on foot. It's a breezier and faster joy by bike. And the sights are conveniently laced together by the circular tram #20. Here are the essential stops for a day in Amsterdam:

Start the day with a circular orientation tour on tram #20 (described below). Break this morning overview with a stop at the city's two great art museums: Van Gogh and the Rijksmuseum (cafeteria for lunch). Pick up tram #20 where you got off and complete the circle back to the station (or walk to Spui from the museums via Leidsestraat).

Spend midafternoon taking a relaxing hour-long canal cruise (from the dock at Spui). Near Spui consider seeing the peaceful Begijnhof, the Amsterdam Historical Museum, and the flower market.

Visiting the Anne Frank House after 18:00 (it's open until 21:00) will save you an hour in line. On a balmy evening,

Amsterdam Overview

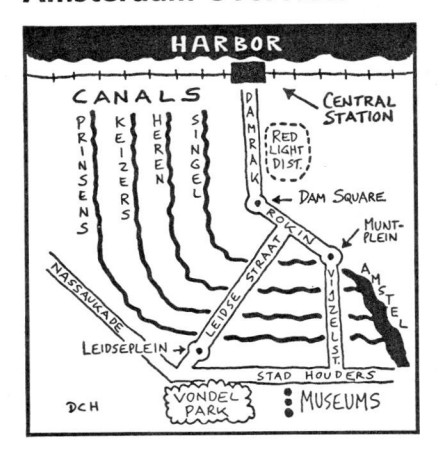

Amsterdam has a Greek island ambience. Wander the Jordaan for the idyllic side of town and wander down Leidsestraat to Leidseplein for the roaring café and people scene. Wander the Red Light District while you're at it.

With extra time: With two days in Holland, I'd side-trip by bike, bus, or train to an open-air folk museum and visit Haarlem. With a third day I'd do the other great Amsterdam museums. With four days I'd visit The Hague.

Orientation (tel. code: 020)

Amsterdam's central train station is your starting point (TI, bike rental, and tram #20 and others fanning out to all points). Damrak is the main street axis, connecting the station with Dam Square and its Royal Palace. From this spine the city spreads out like a fan, with 90 islands, hundreds of bridges, and a series of concentric canals (named "Prince's," "Gentleman's," and "Emperor's") laid out in the 17th century, Holland's Golden Age. Amsterdam's major sights are within walking distance of Dam Square.

Tourist Information

Avoid inefficient VVV offices if you can. (VVV is Dutch for tourist information office; TI in train station open Mon–Sat 8:00–20:00, Sun 9:00–17:00). Most people wait 30 minutes just to pick up brochures and get a room. At the VVV in front of the station, avoid this line by studying the wall display of publications for sale and going straight to the sales desk (where everyone ends up anyway, since any information of substance will cost you). Consider buying a city map (f4), *What's On* (f4, monthly entertainment calendar), and any of the f4 walking-tour brochures ("Discovery Tour through the Center," "The Former Jewish Quarter," "Walks through Jordaan"). The Amsterdam Culture & Leisure Pass, offering free or discounted admissions to some sights and boat rides, isn't worth the clutter or cost (f40, doesn't include Anne Frank House). Nor does it make sense to stand in line at the VVV to buy prepaid same-cost admissions to various Amsterdam sights.

The TI on Leidsestraat is less crowded (Mon–Fri 9:00–19:00, closes at 17:00 Sat–Sun). But for f1 a minute, you can save yourself a trip by calling the tourist information toll line at 0900-400-4040 (Mon–Fri 9:00–17:00). If you're staying in nearby Haarlem, use the helpful Haarlem TI (see the Haarlem chapter) to answer most of your Amsterdam questions and provide you with the brochures.

At Amsterdam's Central Station, GWK Change has two hotel reservations windows that sell phone cards and cheaper city maps (f3) and answer basic tourist questions. The lines are shorter. They also change money, including coins, for a hefty f5 fee (near the lockers, at the right end of the station as you leave the platform).

Don't use the TI (or GWK) to book a room (you'll pay f5 and your host loses the 13 percent deposit). The phone system is easy, everyone speaks English, and the listings in this book are a better value than the potluck booking you'd be charged for at the TI.

Helpful Hints

Many shops close all day Sunday and Monday morning. A *plein* is a square, *gracht* means canal, and most canals are lined by streets with the same name. Handy telephone cards (f10, f25, or f50) are sold at the TI, the GVB public-transit office, tobacco shops, post offices, and train stations (calling the United States from a phone booth is now very cheap—you'll get about 5 minutes for a dollar). Internet access is easy at cafés all over town (Internet Café, a couple blocks from the station, is at Martelaarsgracht 11, f2.50 per 20 min, daily, long hours, waits 16:00–21:00, tel. 020/627-1052). Coffee-shops are also into surfing the Web. Tourists are considered green and rich, and the city has more than its share of hungry thieves—especially on the trams.

Arrival in Amsterdam

By Train: Amsterdam swings, and the hinge that connects it to the world is its perfectly central Central Station. Walk out the door and you're in the heart of the city. You'll nearly trip over trams ready to take you anywhere your feet won't. Straight ahead is Damrak Street, leading to Dam Square. With your back to the entrance of the station, the TI and GVB public-transit offices and circular tram #20A are just ahead and to your left.

By Plane: From Schiphol Airport, take the train to Amsterdam (6/hrly, 20 min, f6.25). If you're staying in Haarlem, take a direct express bus to Haarlem (#236 or #362, 2/hrly, 30 min, f7).

Getting around Amsterdam

The helpful GVB transit-information office is next to the TI (the glass building with the revolving sign in front of the train station). Its free multilingual *Tourist Guide to Public Transport* includes a transit map, explains ticket options and tram connections to all the sights, and describes the circle tram #20 route, listing all the stops (and nearby sights, #20A goes clockwise, #20B goes counter-clockwise).

By Bus, Tram, and Metro: Individual tickets cost f3 and give you an hour on the buses, trams, and metro system (on trams and buses pay as you board; buy metro tickets from machines). **Strip cards** are cheaper than individual tickets. Any downtown ride costs two strips (good for an hour of transfers). A card with 15 strips costs f12 at the GVB public-transit office, train stations, post offices, airport, or tobacco shops throughout the country; shorter strip tickets (two, three, and eight strips) are also sold on some buses and trams. Strip cards are good on buses all over Holland (e.g., six strips for Haarlem to the airport), and you can share them with your partner. An f10 **Day Card** gives you unlimited transportation on the buses and metro for a day in Amsterdam; you'll almost break even if you take three trips (valid until 6:00 the following morning; buy as you board or at the GVB public-transit office, which also sells a 2-day version for f15). If you get lost in Amsterdam, 10 of the city's 17 trams take you back to the central train station.

By Foot: The longest walk a tourist would take is 45 minutes from the station to the Rijksmuseum. Watch out for silent but potentially painful bikes, trams, and crotch-high curb posts.

By Bike: One-speed bikes, with "brrringing" bells and two locks (use them both; bike thieves are bold and brazen here), rent for f9.50 per day at the central train station (daily 8:00–22:00; deposit of f200 or your credit-card imprint and passport required; entrance to the left down the ramp as you leave the station, tel. 020/624-8391). In the summer, arrive early or make a telephone reservation (they hold bikes until 10:30).

By Boat: While the city is great on foot or bike, there is a "Museum Boat" and a similar "Canal Bus" with an all-day ticket that shuttles tourists from sight to sight. Tickets cost f25 (with discounts to sights worth about f5). The sales booths in front of the central train station (and the boats) offer handy free brochures with museum times and admission prices. The narrated ride takes 90 minutes if you don't get off (every 30 min in summer, every 45 min off-season, 7 stops, live quadrilingual guide, departures 10:00–17:00, discounted after 13:00 to f20, tel. 020/622-2181). If you're looking for a floating (nonstop) tour, the real canal tour boats (without the stops) give more information, cover more ground, and cost less (see below).

By Taxi: Amsterdam's taxis are expensive (f6 drop and f3 for each km). Given the fine tram system, taxis are only a good value for airport connections (Schiphol Airport to Amsterdam costs f55).

By Car: Forget it—frustrating one-ways, terrible parking.

Circle Tram #20 Orientation Tour

For a ▲▲ self-guided tour, orient yourself for f3 in less than an hour by riding this designed-for-tourists circle route from the station. Catch #20A (not #20B) from tram lane (or *spoor*) #2 on the left as you leave the station. The free tourist guidebooklet—there's a stack on the desk in the transit office 50 meters away—comes with a route map and lists each stop. You could buy the f6 one-day tram #20 pass. Tram #20 runs every 10 minutes from 9:00 to 18:00 only.

0. Train Station: Leaving the station you pass both the canal bus and museum boat docks (left). *Rondvaart* sign (right) means round-trip. Boats like these all over town offer similar one-hour city tours. Gliding up the tacky commercial cancan called the Damrak you're following the same route taken by boats loaded with spices and goodies from the East Indies in the city's early trading days. The buildings across the water are Amsterdam's oldest. Behind them is the Red Light District and old sailor's quarter. The huge redbrick Beurs building (left) is the Dutch stock exchange.

1. The Dam Square: This is the city center, where the original dam was built across the Amstel River, giving the town its name. To your right is the Royal Palace (1655); next to it is the New Church, the coronation church of Dutch royalty. To your left is the World War I Memorial (1956), now becoming a generic peace memorial; behind that is a strip of head shops. Straight ahead is one of many "diamond polishing centers." Beyond the Dam Square you continue down Rokin. Parallel and a block to the right is the thriving Kalverstraat pedestrian shopping mall.

2. Spui Square: This marked the end of the city in the 14th century. It's near the Begijnhof and the University of Amsterdam's archaeology museum, which has a fine Egyptian collection.

3. Muntplein: This lively area is marked by the Mint Tower from 1620 (on the right). Behind that a charming flower market lines the Singel Canal (see the row of greenhouses, thriving Mon–Sat 9:00–17:00). Turning left you enter a noisy neon nightlife center.

4. Rembrandtplein: Look for Rembrandt's statue in the leafy park (right). This is the center of gay Amsterdam. You'll pass lots of discos and a Planet Hollywood, and a bridge will take you over the Amstel River. The modern brown and white building (left) is the city hall. Adjacent is the round Opera House. Notice the charming counterbalance bridges (right).

5. Waterlooplein: This is famous for its flea market (daily except Sun, on left). The Jewish Quarter (right) features the impressive new Jewish History Museum (renovated brick synagogues with blue and white banner). Crossing the bridge (funny paintings revealed when opened) you enter green Amsterdam (gardens and hothouses of University of Amsterdam all around, zoo nearby).

6. Plantage Kerklaan: Immediately to the right of this tram stop, the white facade of the old Dutch Theater (Hollandsche

Amsterdam

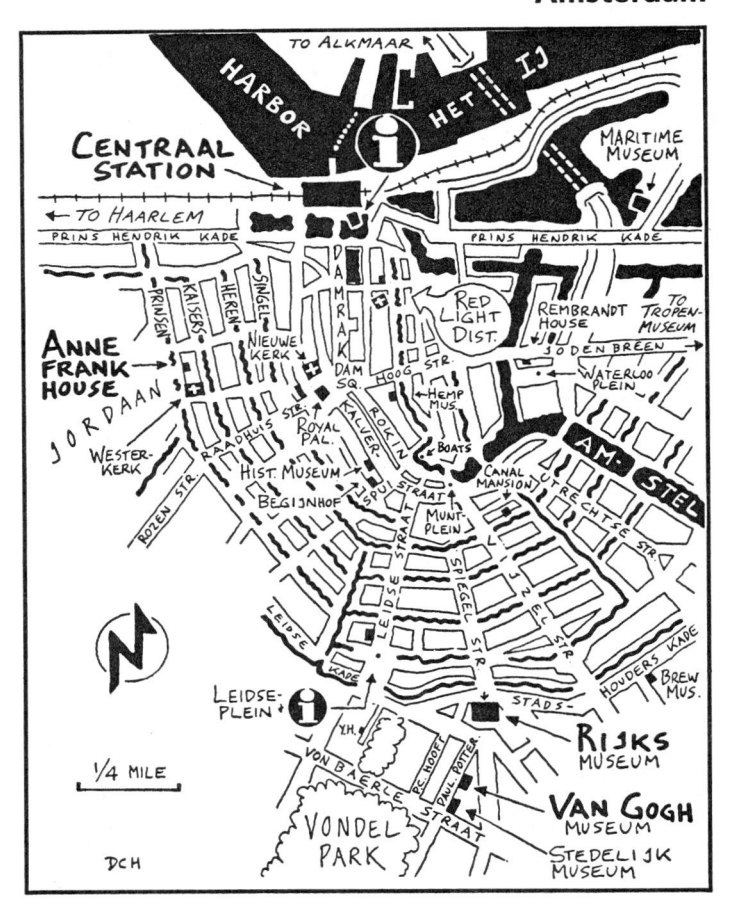

Schouwburg) survives. Used by Nazis as a holding zone for Jews being deported, today it's a memorial. The Dutch Resistance Museum and the zoo are half a block to the left. Passing through many University of Amsterdam buildings, notice the "XXX" symbol of the city (the three Xs stand for the adversities the Amsterdammers have overcome throughout their history: fire, plague, and floods). Crossing the Amstel River again, see the city hall and the opera house again in the distance (right), the palatial Amstel Hotel (behind on the left) and, in the distance, Holland's tallest skyscraper—the Phillips corporate headquarters.

7. Frederiksplein: Notice the houseboats; they're a common sight in Amsterdam. Also at Frederiksplein, you'll see the huge Albert Cuyp Market, perhaps the town's most interesting market, showing off the town's ethnic mix daily except Sunday. Now, passing through a nondescript area, notice how the city works: shops at street level—with homes above—keep neighborhoods vital, people-friendly, and safe. Bike lanes even have their own little traffic lights. New buildings still lean out and come with planks and pulleys for hoisting furniture past too-narrow stairways. Many of these are brick and built in the Art Deco "Amsterdam School" from the 1920s—a time when architects considered entire blocks as integrated works of art. Notice street signs with the district listed. You're in the *oud-zuid* (old south) quarter. Mail slots have green and orange decals saying yes or no to junk mail. And now public phone booths stand next to curbside computers for Internet access (locals use "chip cards"—the first step toward the cash-free society of the future—to access things like these).

8. Museumplein: A huge park (right) leads to the grand redbrick Rijksmuseum (built in 1885 by the same guy who designed Central Station). The new addition to the Van Gogh Museum (opened 1999) juts into the park in the foreground. The Concertgebouw (on the left) is Amsterdam's main concert hall. A huge underground parking lot keeps things uncluttered.

9. Van Baerlestraat: Rounding the corner, you stop at the Stedelijk Modern Art Museum (right) and the Van Gogh Museum (see crowd on right). An ice rink (right) faces the Coster Diamond House (left).

10. Hobbenmastraat: This is the stop for the Rijksmuseum (right). A fancy gate marks the entrance to the sprawling, in-love-with-life Vondelpark (left). Pass a casino (right) as you cross a canal and enter the noisy, people-filled Leidseplein area.

11. Leidseplein: Your tram just skirts Amsterdam's liveliest café, people-watching, and entertainment district. Be sure to loiter in Leidseplein later on. The huge modern parking lot (Texaco station, left) marks the line between the protected old town (right) and the anything-goes new one (left). Turning right you cut through the proud, fashionable, and trendy Jordaan district. Ahead stands the much-loved tallest church spire in town, marking the Westerkerk (West Church). Anne Frank hid out just down the street. As you continue ahead, the canal system is evident as you cross the Prince's, Keizers (kings), Herren (medieval business fat cats), and Singel canals and head toward the back side of the Royal Palace we saw at the Dam Square. Hop out here or glide back to your starting point at the Central Station.

Sights—Amsterdam's Museum Neighborhood

▲▲▲**Rijksmuseum**—Built to house the nation's greatest art, the Rijksmuseum packs several thousand paintings into 200 rooms.

To survive, focus on the Dutch masters: Rembrandt, Hals, Vermeer, and Steen. For a list of the top 20 paintings, pick up the cheap f1 leaflet "A Tour of the Golden Age" and plan your attack (or follow the self-guided tour, one of 20, in my *Mona Winks* guidebook). CD tours are available, allowing you to dial up descriptions of over 200 paintings (f7.50).

Follow the museum's chronological layout to see painting evolve from narrative religious art to religious art starring the Dutch love of good living and eating to the Golden Age, when secular art dominated. With no local church or royalty to commission big canvases in the post-1648 Protestant Dutch republic, artists had to find different patrons. They specialized in portraits of the wealthy city class (Hals), pretty still lifes (Claesz), and non-preachy slice-of-life art (Steen). The museum has four quietly wonderful Vermeers. And, of course, a thoughtful brown soup of Rembrandt, including *Night Watch*. Works by Rembrandt show his excellence as a portraitist for hire (*De Staalmeesters*) and offer some powerful psychological studies, such as *St. Peter's Denial*—with a betrayed Jesus in the murky background (f15, daily 10:00–17:00, great bookshop, decent cafeteria; tram #2, #5, or #20 from the station; Stadhouderskade 42).

The Rijksmuseum celebrates 2000 with a year of special exhibits. Through most of the tourist season (Apr 15–Sept 17) the *Glory of the Golden Age* exhibit will amass an extravaganza of 17th-century Dutch art: the permanent collection—already the world's best—plus much much more. The result: too much art, long lines, and higher prices. Admission will jump to f25, and they threaten to dole out entry times only by advance reservation (for details: info@rijksmuseum.nl or call upon arrival, tel. 020/674-7000).

▲▲▲**Van Gogh Museum**—Next to the Rijksmuseum, this outstanding and user-friendly museum was opened in 1973 to house the 200 paintings owned by Vincent's younger brother, Theo. Newly renovated in 1999, it's a stroll through a beautifully displayed garden of van Gogh's work and life (f12.50, daily 10:00–18:00, Paulus Potterstraat 7, tel. 020/570-5200). The museum also focuses on the late 19th-century art that influenced van Gogh (it happened to be in his brother Theo's collection). The new exhibition hall (included with admission) features art from 1840 to 1920. The f8.50 audio guide includes insightful commentaries about van Gogh's paintings along with related quotations from Vincent himself.

Stedelijk Modern Art Museum—Next to the Van Gogh Museum, this place is fun, far-out, and refreshing. It has mostly post-1945 art but also a sometimes-outstanding collection of Monet, van Gogh, Cézanne, Picasso, and Chagall and a lot of special exhibitions (f9, daily 11:00–19:00, closes at 17:00 Nov–Mar, tel. 020/573-2737).

Sights—Near Dam Square

▲▲Anne Frank House—A virtual pilgrimage for many, this house offers a fascinating look at the hideaway of young Anne when the Nazis occupied the Netherlands. Pick up the English pamphlet at the door. Recently expanded, the exhibit now offers more thorough coverage of the Frank family, the diary, the stories of others who hid out, and the Holocaust. Why do thousands endure hour-long daytime lines when they can walk right in by arriving after 18:00? Last entrance is 20:30. Visit after dinner (f10, Apr–Aug daily 9:00–21:00, closes daily at 19:00 Sept–Mar, 263 Prinsengracht, tel. 020/556-7100). For an interesting glimpse of Holland under the Nazis, rent the powerful movie *Soldier of Orange* before you leave home.

Westerkerk—Near the Anne Frank House, this landmark church has a barren interior, Rembrandt somewhere under the pews, and Amsterdam's tallest steeple. It's worth climbing for the view (f3, ascend only with a guide, departures on the hour, Apr–Sept Mon–Sat 10:00–17:00, closed Sun, tel. 020/612-6856).

Royal Palace (Koninklijk Paleis)—The palace, right on Dam Square, was built as a lavish city hall for Amsterdam, part of the proud new Dutch Republic. Amsterdam was awash in profit from trade, and, when it was built (around 1660), this building was one of Europe's finest. Today it's the official (but not actual) residence of the queen. Its sumptuous interior is worth a look (f5, Jun–Aug daily 12:30–17:00, less off-season).

▲Begijnhof—Step into this tiny, idyllic courtyard in the city center to escape into the charm of old Amsterdam. Notice house #34, a 500-year-old wooden structure (rare since repeated fires taught city fathers a trick called brick). Peek into the hidden Catholic church, opposite the English Reformed church, where the pilgrims worshiped while waiting for their voyage to the New World (marked by a plaque near the door). Be considerate of the people who live here (free, on Begijnensteeg Lane, just off Kalverstraat between #130 and #132, pick up flyer at office near entrance).

Amsterdam Historical Museum—Offering the town's best look into the age of the Dutch masters, this creative and hardworking museum features Rembrandt's paintings, fine English descriptions, and a carillon loft. The loft comes with push-button recordings of the town bell tower's greatest hits and a self-serve carillon "keyboard" to ring a few bells yourself (f11, Mon–Fri 10:00–17:00, Sat–Sun 11:00–17:00, good-value restaurant, next to Begijnhof, Kalverstraat 92, tel. 020/523-1822). Its free pedestrian corridor is a powerful teaser.

Sights—East Amsterdam

To reach these sights from the train station, ride tram #9, #14, or #20. The first six sights listed make an interesting walk.

Central Amsterdam

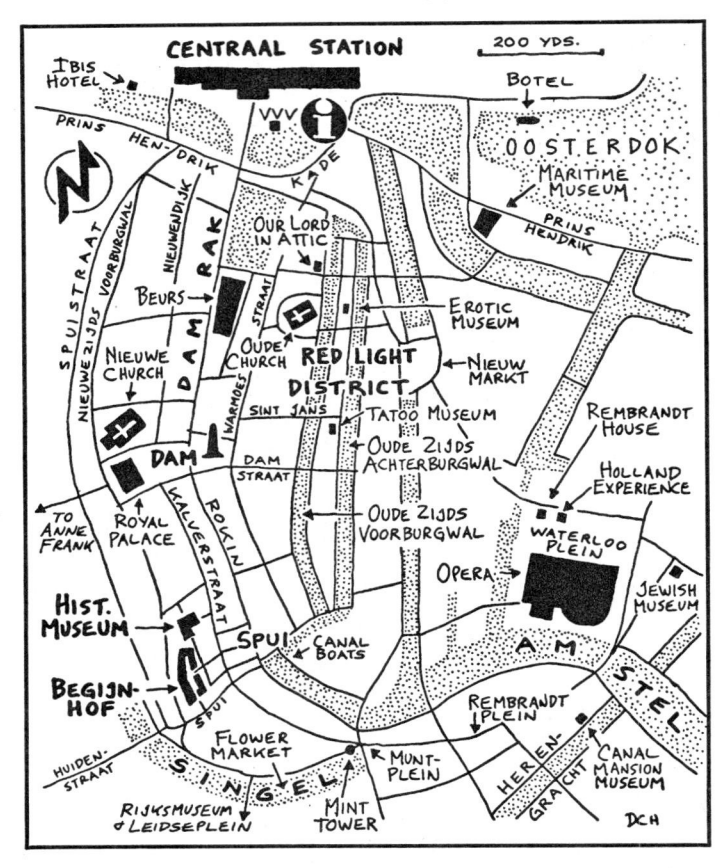

Rembrandt's House—Rembrandt's reconstructed house is filled with exactly what his bankruptcy inventory of 1656 said he owned. You'll find no paintings but 65 of his etchings (f12.50, Mon–Sat 10:00–17:00, Sun 13:00–17:00, 10-min English video upon request, Jodenbreestraat 4, tel. 020/638-4668).

Holland Experience—Bragging "Experience Holland in 30 minutes," this show takes you traveling with three clowns through an idealized montage of Dutch clichés. No words but lots of images and special effects as you rock with the boat and get spritzed with perfume while viewing the tulips (f17.50, 2 enter for the price of 1 with this book, or show this book and get f2.50 off the f25 combo Rembrandt's House/Experience ticket, daily 10:00–18:30, Jodenbreestraat 8, near Rembrandt's House and Waterlooplein street market, metro: Waterlooplein, tel. 020/422-2233). The men's urinal is a trip to the beach. Plan for it.

Waterlooplein Flea Market—For over a hundred years, the flea market of the Jewish Quarter has raged daily except Sunday behind the Rembrandt House.

Jewish History Museum—Four historic synagogues have been joined by steel and glass to make one modern complex telling the story of the Jews in Amsterdam through the centuries (f8, daily 11:00–17:00, good kosher café, Jonas Daniel Meijerplein 2, tel. 020/626-9945).

Dutch Theatre (Hollandsche Schouwburg)—This is a moving memorial. Once a great theater in the Jewish neighborhood, this was used as an assembly hall for local Jews destined for Nazi concentration camps. On the wall, 6,700 family names pay tribute to the 104,000 Jews deported and killed by the Nazis. There's little to actually see but plenty to think about (free, daily 11:00–16:00, Plantage Middenlaan 24, tel. 020/626-9945).

▲▲**Dutch Resistance Museum (Verzetsmeuseum)**—This is a new and impressive look at how the Dutch resisted their Nazi occupiers from 1940 to 1945. You'll see propaganda movie clips, study forged ID cards under a magnifying glass, and read of ingenious, clever, and courageous efforts to hide local Jews from the Germans (f8, Tue–Sun 12:00–17:00, closed Mon, well described in English, tram #9 or #20A from station, Plantage Kerklaan 61, tel. 020/620-2535). Amsterdam's famous zoo is just across the street.

▲**Tropenmuseum (Tropical Museum)**—As close to the Third World as you'll get without lots of vaccinations, this imaginative museum offers wonderful re-creations of tropical-life scenes and explanations of Third World problems (f12.50, Mon–Fri 10:00–17:00, Sat–Sun 12:00–17:00, tram #9 to Linnaeusstraat 2, tel. 020/568-8215).

Netherlands Maritime (Scheepvaart) Museum—This huge collection of model ships, maps, and sea-battle paintings fills the 300-year-old Dutch Navy Arsenal. Given the Dutch seafaring heritage, I expected a killer museum but found it lifeless and boring. Sailors may disagree, but—even with its re-creation of an 18th-century Dutch East India Company ship manned with characters in old costumes—the museum disappoints (f12.50, daily 10:00–17:00, closed Mon off-season, English explanations, don't waste your time with the 30-min movie, bus #22 or #32 to Kattenburgerplein 1, tel. 020/523-2222).

Sights—Red Light District

Our Lord in the Attic (Amstelkring)—Near the station, in the Red Light District, you'll find a fascinating hidden church

filling the attic of a hollowed-out row of 17th-century merchant's houses. This dates from 1661, when post-Reformation Dutch Catholics couldn't worship in public (f7.50, Mon–Sat 10:00–17:00, Sun 13:00–17:00, Oude Zijds Voorburgwal 40, tel. 020/624-6604).
▲**Red Light District**—Europe's most touristed ladies of the night shiver and shimmy in display-case windows between the Oudezijds Achterburgwal and Oudezijds Voorburgwal, surrounding the Oude Kerk (Old Church). Druggies make the streets uncomfortable late at night, but it's a fascinating walk at any other time after noon (S&F, f50).

Amsterdam has two sex museums, one in the Red Light District and one a block in front of the train station on Damrak. While visiting one can be called sightseeing, visiting both is hard to explain. Here's a comparison:

The Red Light District sex museum is less offensive, with five sparsely decorated rooms relying heavily on badly dressed dummies acting out the roles that women of the neighborhood play. It also has videos, phone-sex phones, and a lot of uninspired paintings, old photos, and sculpture (f5, daily 11:00–24:00, along the canal at Oude Zijds Achterburgwal 54).

The Damrak sex museum goes deeper and has more rooms. It tells the story of pornography from Roman times through 1960. Every sexual deviation is uncovered in its various displays, and the nude and pornographic art is a cut above the other sex museum's. Also interesting are the early French pornographic photos and memorabilia from Europe, India, and Asia. You'll find a Marilyn Monroe tribute and some S&M displays, too (f5, daily 10:00–23:30, Damrak 18, a block in front of the station).

More Sights—Amsterdam

▲**Herengracht Canal Mansion (Willet Holthuysen Museum)**—This 1687 patrician house offers a fine look at the old rich of Amsterdam, with a good 20-minute English introductory film and a 17th-century garden in back (f7.50, Mon–Fri 10:00–17:00, Sat–Sun 11:00–17:00, tram #1, #2, #4, #5, or #9 to Herengracht 605, tel. 020/523-1870).

Vondelpark—This huge and lively city park is popular with the Dutch—families with little kids, romantic couples, hippies sharing blankets and beers, and oldsters strolling. It's the scene of free concerts in the summer (tel. 020/523-7790).

Leidseplein—Brimming with cafés, this people- and pigeon-watching square is an impromptu stage for street artists, accordionists, jugglers, and unicyclists. Sunny afternoons are the liveliest. Stroll nearby Lange Leidsedwarsstraat (1 block north) for a taste-bud tour of ethnic eateries from Greece to Indonesia.

Shopping—Amsterdam brings out the browser even in those who were not born to shop. Ten general markets, open six days a week, keep folks who brake for garage sales pulling U-ies. Shopping highlights include Waterlooplein (the flea market); the huge Albert Cuyp street market; various flower markets (daily except Sun, along Singel Canal near the mint tower, or Munttoren); diamond dealers (free cutting and polishing demos at shops behind the Rijksmuseum and on Dam Square); and Kalverstraat, Amsterdam's teeming walking/shopping street (parallel to Damrak).

Tours of Amsterdam

▲▲Canal-Boat Tour—These long, low, tourist-laden boats leave continually from several docks around the town for a good, if uninspiring, one-hour quadrilingual introduction to the city (f13, 2/hrly, more frequent in summer). One very central company is at the corner of Spui and Rokin, about five minutes from Dam Square (daily 10:00–22:00, tel. 020/623-3810). No fishing allowed—but bring your camera for this relaxing orientation. Some prefer to cruise at night, when the bridges are illuminated.

Biking and Walking Tours—The Yellow Bike Tour company offers bike tours (f33 for 3-hour city tour; f42.50 for 6.5-hour, 35-kilometer countryside tour; daily Apr–Nov) and city walking tours for groups by arrangement (f200, 2 hrs, Nieuwezijds Kolk 29, 3 blocks from train station, tel. 020/620-6940).

Brewery Tour—The infamous Heineken brewery tours are in full slosh Monday through Friday at 9:30 and 11:00 (f2; tours also afternoons and Sat in summer; must be 18 years old, tram #16, #24, or #25, Stadhouderskade 78, near Rijksmuseum, tel. 020/523-9666). Try to arrive a little early.

Wetlands Safari, Nature Canoe Tours Near Amsterdam—If you'd like to "turn your back on Amsterdam" and get a dose of the *polder* country and village life along with some exercise, consider this tour. Majel Tromp, a village girl who speaks great English, takes groups of no more than 15. The program: Meet at the VVV tourist office outside the station, catch a bus, stop for coffee, take a canoe trip with several stops, munch a village picnic lunch (included), canoe, and bus back into the big city by 14:30 (f58, May–mid-Sept Mon–Fri, call to reserve, tel. 020/686-3445 or 06/53-552-669, http://members.xoom.com/wet_lands).

Sleeping in Amsterdam
(f1 = about 50 cents, tel. code: 020)

Sleep Code: **S** = Single, **D** = Double/Twin, **T** = Triple, **Q** = Quad, **b** = bathroom, **t** = toilet only, **s** = shower only, **CC** = Credit Card (Visa, MasterCard, Amex). Nearly everyone speaks English in the Netherlands, and prices include breakfast unless noted.

While I prefer sleeping in cozy Haarlem (see next chapter),

Amsterdam Hotels

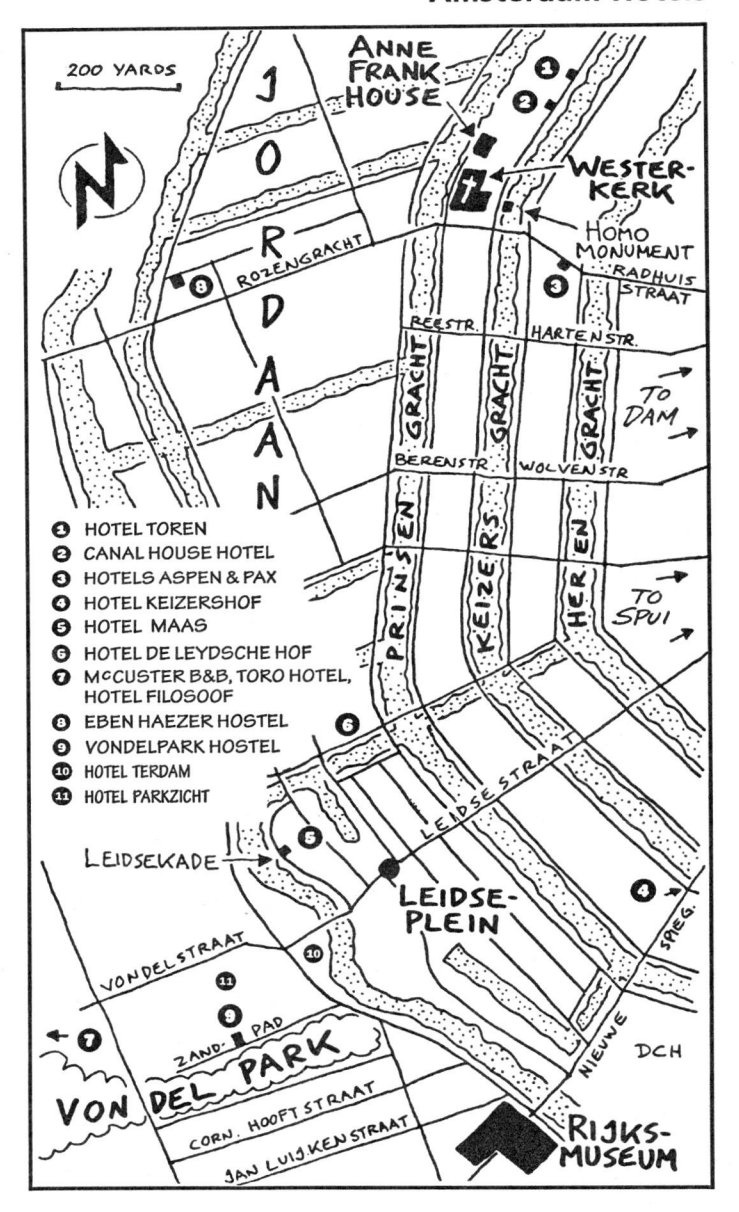

- ❶ HOTEL TOREN
- ❷ CANAL HOUSE HOTEL
- ❸ HOTELS ASPEN & PAX
- ❹ HOTEL KEIZERSHOF
- ❺ HOTEL MAAS
- ❻ HOTEL DE LEYDSCHE HOF
- ❼ McCUSTER B&B, TORO HOTEL, HOTEL FILOSOOF
- ❽ EBEN HAEZER HOSTEL
- ❾ VONDELPARK HOSTEL
- ❿ HOTEL TERDAM
- ⓫ HOTEL PARKZICHT

Amsterdam 565

those into more urban charms will find that Amsterdam has plenty of beds. Summer weekends are booked well in advance.

Sleeping near the Station

Amstel Botel, the city's only remaining "boat hotel," is a shipshape, bright, and clean floating hotel with 175 rooms (Sb-f130, Db-f147, Tb-f180, worth the extra f10 for canal-side view, breakfast-f12, f33/day parking pass, CC:VMA, elevator, 400 yards from the station, exit left as you leave station, you'll see the sign, Oosterdokskade 2-4, 1011 AE Amsterdam, tel. 020/626-4247, fax 020/639-1952).

Ibis Amsterdam Hotel is a modern and efficient 180-room place towering over the station. It's perfectly central but out of the bustle and quiet—all comfort and value without a hint of charm (Db-f274, family-f358, skip breakfast and save f22 per person, CC:VMA, book long in advance, air-con, smoke-free floors, Stationsplein 49, tel. 020/638-3080, fax 020/620-0156, www.ibishotel.com).

Sleeping between Dam Square and the Anne Frank House

Hotel Toren is a chandeliered historic mansion in a pleasant canalside setting in downtown Amsterdam. This splurge is classy yet friendly, quiet, two blocks northeast of the Anne Frank House, and still run by the Toren family: Elsje, Lisa, and Eric (Sb-f200, Db-f225–350, Tb-f270; bridal suites for f310–410 make you want to get married; prices vary with view and Jacuzzi; 10 percent discount for 3 nights and cash with this book, CC:VMA, air-con, Keizersgracht 164, 1015 CZ Amsterdam, tel. 020/622-6352, fax 020/626-9705, e-mail: hotel.toren@tip.nl).

Well-heeled readers enjoy the similar 17th-century **Canal House Hotel**, a few doors down, with its beautiful antique interiors, candlelit evenings, and soft music (Db-f265–345, CC:VMA, elevator, Keizersgracht 148, 1015 CX Amsterdam, tel. 020/622-5182, fax 020/624-1317, e-mail: canalhousehotel @compuserve.com).

Cheap hotels line the convenient but noisy main drag between the town hall and the Anne Frank House. Expect a long, steep, and depressing stairway, with quieter rooms in the back. **Hotel Aspen**, a good value for a budget hotel, is tidy, stark, and well maintained (S-f55, D-f80, Db-f125, Tb-f130–150, Qb-f180, no breakfast, CC:MA, Raadhuisstraat 31, 1016 DC Amsterdam, tel. 020/626-6714, fax 020/620-0866, run by Esam). A few doors away, **Hotel Pax** has large, plain, but airy backpacker-type rooms (S-f55–75, D-f80–110, T-f110–130, Q-f120–150, no breakfast, prices vary with size and season, CC:VMA, 2 showers for 8 rooms, Raadhuisstraat 37, tel. 020/624-9735, run by 2 brothers: Philip and Peter).

Calendula Goldbloom's B&B, run by an American couple,

offers two comfortable rooms in a classy old home in a quiet Jordaan neighborhood a five-minute walk northwest of the Anne Frank House (D-f180, extra bed f50, 2-night minimum, good breakfasts, Goudsbloemstraat 132, tel. 020/428-3055, fax 020/776-0075, www.calendulas.com, Lynn and Dennis).

Sleeping in the Leidseplein Area

The area around Amsterdam's museum square (Museumplein) and the rip-roaring nightlife center (Leidseplein) is colorful, comfortable, convenient, and affordable. These three canalside places are 5 or 10 minutes from Leidseplein.

Hotel Keizershof is a wonderfully Dutch place, with six bright, airy rooms in a 17th-century canal house. A steep spiral staircase leads to rooms named after old-time Hollywood stars. The enthusiastic hospitality of the De Vries family has made this place a treat for 38 years (S-f75, D-f125, Ds-f135, Db-f150, T-f175, Tb-f200, CC:VM, nonsmoking, classy breakfast, nice garden; tram #16, #24, or #25 from station; where Keizers canal crosses Spiegelstraat at Keizersgracht 618, 1017 ER Amsterdam, tel. 020/622-2855, fax 020/624-8412, e-mail: keizershof@vdwp.nl).

Hotel Maas is a big, well-run, elegant, quiet, and stiffly hotelesque place (S-f110, 1 D-f135, Db-f250–275, suite-f375, prices vary with view and room size, extra person-f50, CC:VMA, hearty breakfast, air-con, elevator, tram #1, #2, #5, or #20 from station, Leidsekade 91, 1017 PN Amsterdam, tel. 020/623-3868, fax 020/622-2613, www.hotelmaas.nl).

Hotel De Leydsche Hof is canalside with simple, quiet rooms. Its peaceful demeanor almost helps you overlook the flimsy cots and old carpets (Ds-f110, Tb-f150, Qb-f200, no breakfast, near where Keizersgracht hits Leidsegracht, Leidsegracht 14, 10-minute walk from Leidseplein, 1016 CK Amsterdam, tel. 020/623-2148, run by friendly Mr. Piller).

Sleeping near Vondelpark

These options connect you with the sights via an easy tram ride, a pleasant 15-minute walk, or a short bike ride through Vondelpark.

Karen McCuster, a friendly Englishwoman, rents cozy rooms in her shoes-off home. Rooms are clean, white, and bright, with red carpeting and green plants; one room has a private rooftop patio (D-f90–120, depending on room size, little or no breakfast, tram #2 from station to Amstelveenseweg, Zeilstraat 22, third floor, 1075 SH Amsterdam, tel. 020/679-2753, fax 020/670-4578).

Toro Hotel, in a peaceful residential area at the edge of Vondelpark, is your personal turn-of-the-century hotel/mansion, with a plush lounge, elegant dining hall, and 22 rooms with TVs, safes, and phones. Rooms in the back overlook the park, canal, and garden, which is yours for relaxing. Mr. Plooy fusses over his guests

(Ss-f165, Sb-f200, Db-f250, Tb-f300, CC:VMA, elevator, metered parking at the door, tram #2 from station to Koningslaan, then walk to intersection of Emmalaan and Koningslaan, Koningslaan 64, 1075 AG Amsterdam, tel. 020/673-7223, fax 020/675-0031).

Hotel Filosoof greets you with Aristotle and Plato in the foyer and classical music in its lobby. Its 25 rooms are decorated with themes; the Egyptian room has a frieze of hieroglyphics. Philosophers' sayings hang on walls as thoughtful travelers wander down the halls or sit in the garden, rooted deep in discussion. The rooms are small (and split between two buildings), but the hotel is endearing (Sb-f155, Db-f185, Tb-f235, Qb-f275, CC:VMA, cheaper off-season, all rooms have TV and phone, Anna Vondelstraat 6, 5-minute walk from tram #1 line, get off at Constantyn Huygenstraat, tel. 020/683-3013, fax 020/685-3750, e-mail: filosoof@sx4all.nl).

Best Western Hotel Terdam is a 90-room American-style hotel well situated on a quiet street just across the bridge from bustling Leidseplein (Db-f260–305, depending on season and air-con, CC:VMA, elevator, Tesselschadestraat 23, tel. 020/612-6876, fax 020/683-8313, www.hospitality.nl/ams).

Hotel Parkzicht is an old-time place with lots of extremely steep stairs and 14 big plain rooms on a quiet street bordering Vondelpark (S-f65, Sb-f95, Db-f140–170, as low as f100 in winter, Tb-f220, Qb-f250, CC:VMA, tram #1, #2 or #5 from station, Roemer Visscherstraat 33, tel. 020/618-1954, fax 020/618-0897).

Hostels

The Shelter Jordan (also known as Hostel Eben Haezer) is scruffy, with 20-bed dorms. Friendly, well run, and in a great neighborhood, offering Amsterdam's best rock-bottom budget beds (f28 per bed with sheets and breakfast, maximum age 35, nonsmoking, near the Anne Frank House, Bloemstraat 179, tel. 020/624-4717, www.shelter.nl, e-mail: jordan@shelter.nl). It serves cheap, hot meals, runs a snack bar, offers lockers to all, leads nightly Bible studies, and closes the dorms from 10:00 to 12:30. Its sister Christian hostel, **The Shelter City**, in the Red Light District, is similar but definitely not preaching to the choir (open to any traveler, f28 per bed, tel. 020/625-3230, e-mail: city@shelter.nl).

The city's two IYHF hostels are **Vondelpark**, Amsterdam's top hostel (f38 with breakfast, S-f85, D-f125, nonmembers pay f5 extra, lots of school groups, 6 or 8 beds per dorm, right on the park at Zandpad 5, tel. 020/589-8996, fax 020/589-8955), and **Stadsdoelen YH** (f29 with breakfast, f5 extra without YH card, f6.25 for sheets, just past Dam Square, closed Jan, Kloveniersburgwal 97, tel. 020/624-6832, fax 020/639-1035). Each accepts travelers only under 35. While generally booked long in advance, a few beds open up each day at 11:00.

Eating in Amsterdam

Dutch food is basic and hearty. *Eetcafés* are local cafés serving budget sandwiches, soup, eggs, and so on. Cafeterias, *broodje* (sandwich shops), and automatic food shops are also good bets for budget eaters. Picnics are cheap and easy. A central supermarket is **Albert Heijn**, at the corner of Koningsplein and Singel canal near the flower market (Mon–Sat 10:00–20:00, Sun 12:00–18:00).

Of Amsterdam's thousand-plus restaurants, no one knows which are best—especially me. I pick an area and wander. The major action is around Leideseplein. Wander along restaurant row: Leidsedwarsstraat. For fewer crowds and more charm, find something in the Jordaan. The best advice: your hotel's. Most keep a reliable eating list for their neighborhood. Consider these:

Eating near Spui in the Center

The city university's **Atrium** is a great budget cafeteria (f9 meals, Mon–Fri 12:00–14:00, 17:00–19:30; from Spui, walk west down Landebrug Steeg past the canalside Café 't Gasthuys 3 blocks to Oudezijds Achterburgwal 237, go through arched doorway on the right, tel. 020/525-3999). **Café 't Gasthuys**, one of Amsterdam's many "brown" cafés (named for their smoke-stained walls), makes good sandwiches and offers indoor or canalside seating (daily 12:00–01:00, walk west down Landebrug Steeg to Grimburgwal 7).

La Place, a cafeteria on the ground floor of the Vroom Dreesmann department store, has islands of entrées, veggies, fruits, desserts, and beverages (Mon–Sat 10:00–21:00, Thu until 22:00, Sun 11:00–21:00, near Mint Tower, corner of Rokin and Muntplein).

Eating in the Train Station

The train station has a surprisingly classy budget self-service **Stationsrestauratie** on platform 1 (Mon–Sat 7:00–22:00, Sun from 8:00).

Eating near the Anne Frank House

For pancakes in a family atmosphere, try the **Pancake Bakery** (f18 pancakes, splitting is OK, offers an Indonesian pancake for those who want 2 experiences in 1, daily 12:00–21:30, Prinsengracht 191, 1 block north of A.F. House, tel. 020/625-1333). Across the canal, **De Bolhoed** serves serious vegetarian food (daily 12:00–22:00, Prinsengracht 60, tel. 020/626-1803). **Dimitri's** is the place for a hearty salad (f18 main course salads, daily 8:00–22:00, reservations smart, Prinsenstraat 3, tel. 020/627-9393).

Eating near the Rijksmuseum, on Leideseplein

The Art Deco **American Hotel** dining room serves an all-you-can-eat f16 salad bar (available 12:00–14:30, 18:00–22:00, where Leideseplein hits Singel Canal). On the café-packed street called

Lange Leidsedwarsstraat, **Bojo** is a reasonably-priced Indonesian restaurant at #51 (daily from 16:00, 020/622-7434). If hunger hits in the **Rijksmuseum**, head for the cafeteria in the west wing's ground floor.

Bars
Try a *jenever* (Dutch gin), the closest thing to an atomic bomb in a shot glass. While cheese gets harder and sharper with age, *jenever* grows smooth and soft. Old *jenever* is best.

Drugs
Amsterdam, Europe's counterculture mecca, thinks the concept of a "victimless crime" is a contradiction. While hard drugs are definitely out, marijuana causes about as much excitement as a bottle of beer. Throughout the Netherlands "coffee shops" are pubs selling marijuana. Menus dangling from strings look like the inventory of a drug bust. Display cases show various joints or baggies for sale. The Dutch roll a little tobacco into their joints. To avoid that you need to get a baggie and papers. Baggies usually cost f25—smaller contents... better quality. Walk east from Dam Square on Damstraat for a few blocks and then down to Nieuwmarkt. While several touristy Bulldog Cafés are hits with tourists, less-glitzy neighborhood places (farther from the tourists) offer a better value and a more comfortable atmosphere.

Pot should never be bought on the street in Amsterdam. Well-established coffee shops are considered much safer. Up to five grams of marijuana per person per day can be sold in coffee shops. Minimum age for purchase: 18 years.

The tiny **Grey Area** coffee shop is a cool, welcoming, and smoky hole-in-the-wall appreciated among local aficionados as a seven-time winner of Amsterdam's Cannabis Cup award. Judging by the proud autographed photos on the wall, many of America's most famous heads have dropped in. You're welcome to just nurse a bottomless cup of coffee (open high noon to 21:00, closed Mon, between Dam Square and the Anne Frank House at Oude Leliestraat 2, tel. 020/420-4301, www. greyarea.nl, Steven and John).

Near the corner of Leidsestraat and Prinsengracht, **Tops** coffee shop has Internet access. **Homegrown Fantasy's** coffee shop and gallery, about two blocks northwest of Dam Square, has a gentle Dutch atmosphere and cosmic restroom (daily 9:00–24:00, Nieuwe Zijds Voorburgwal 87a, tel. 020/627-5683). They also have a grow shop next door.

▲**Marijuana and Hemp Museum**—This is a collection of dope facts, history, science, and memorabilia (f8, daily 11:00–22:00, Oudezijds Achterburgwal 148, tel. 020/623-5961). While small, it has a shocker finale: the high-tech grow room in which dozens of varieties of marijuana are cultivated in optimal hydroponic (among other) environments. Some plants stand five feet tall and shine under the intense grow lamps. The view is actually through glass walls into the neighboring "Sensi Seed Bank" Grow Shop (which sells carefully cultivated seeds and all the gear needed to grow them). It's an interesting neighborhood. The Cannabis College Foundation "dedicated to ending the global war against the cannabis plant through public education" is next door at #102 (www.cannabiscollege.org). As you wander, ponder the 400,000 Americans in jail because of U.S. marijuana laws.

Transportation Connections—Amsterdam

Amsterdam's train-information center requires a long wait. Save lots of time by getting train tickets and information in a small-town station or travel agency. For phone information, 0900-9292 for local trains or 0900-9296 for international trains (75 cents/min, daily 7:00–24:00, wait through recording and hold... hold... hold...).

By train to: Schiphol Airport (6/hrly, 20 min, f6.25), **Haarlem** (6/hrly, 15 min, f10.50 round trip), **The Hague** (4/hrly, 45 min), **Rotterdam** (4/hrly, 1 hr), **Brussels** (hrly, 3 hrs), **Oostende** (hrly, 4 hrs, change in Roosendaal), **Paris** (5/day, 5 hrs, required fast train from Brussels with f21 supplement; the only cheap no-supplement option is the overnight train), **London** (4/day, 10–12 hrs), **Copenhagen** (5/day, 11 hrs), **Frankfurt** (10/day, 5 hrs), **Munich** (8/day, 8 hrs, change in Mannheim), **Bonn** (10/day, 3 hrs), **Bern** (8/day, 9 hrs, change in Basel).

Amsterdam's Schiphol Airport: The airport, like most of Holland, is English speaking, user-friendly, and below sea level. Its banks offer fair rates (24 hours daily, in the arrival area). Schiphol Airport has easy bus and train connections (7 miles) into Amsterdam or Haarlem. The airport also has a train station of its own. (You can validate your Eurailpass and hit the rails immediately or, to stretch your train pass, buy the short ticket today and start the pass later.) Schiphol flight information (tel. 0900-0141) can give you flight times and your airline's Amsterdam number for reconfirmation before going home (f1 per minute to climb through its phone tree). KLM tel. 020/649-9123, Martainair tel. 020/601-1222.

HAARLEM

Cute, cozy, yet real and handy to the airport, Haarlem is a fine home base, giving you small-town, overnight warmth with easy access (15 minutes by train) to wild and crazy Amsterdam.

Haarlem is a busy Dutch market town buzzing with shoppers biking home with fresh bouquets. Enjoy Saturday (general) and Monday (clothing) market days, when the square bustles like a Brueghel painting with cheese, fish, flowers, and families. Make yourself at home here. Buy some flowers to brighten your hotel room.

Orientation (tel. code: 023)

Tourist Information: Haarlem's VVV, at the train station, is friendlier, more helpful, and less crowded than Amsterdam's. Ask your Amsterdam questions here (Mon–Fri 9:30–17:30, Sat 10:00–14:00, closed Sun, tel. 0900-616-1600, f1 a minute, their f4 *Haarlem* magazine is not necessary).

Arrival in Haarlem: As you walk out of the train station, the TI is on your right and the bus station is across the street. Two parallel streets flank the train station (Kruisweg and Jansweg). Head up either one and you'll reach the town square and church within 10 minutes. If you're uncertain of the way, ask a local person, "*Grote Markt?*" ("Main Square?"), and they'll point you in the right direction.

Helpful Hints: The handy GWK change office at the station offers fair exchange rates (Mon–Sat 8:00–20:00, Thu–Fri until 21:00, Sun 9:00–17:00). The train station rents bikes (f9.50/day, f100 deposit, Mon–Sat 6:00–24:00, Sun 7:30–24:00). For Internet access (f7.50/30 min), nonguests are welcome to use Hotel Amadeus' computer (facing market square), and nonsmokers are welcome at High Times (Lange Veerstraat 47). My Beautiful Launderette is handy, self-service, and cheap (f11 wash and dry, daily 8:30–20:30, bring coins, including 6 Dutch quarters for dryer, near Vroom Dreesman department store at Boter Markt 20). The VVV and local hotels have a helpful parking brochure.

Sights—Haarlem

▲▲Market Square (Grote Markt)—Haarlem's market square is the town's delightful centerpiece. To enjoy a coffee or beer here simmering in Dutch good living is a quintessential European experience. In a recent study, the Dutch were found to be the most content people in Europe. And later, the people of Haarlem were found to be the most content in the Netherlands. Observe. Just a few years ago trolleys ran through the square and cars were parked everywhere. But today it's a people zone, with market stalls filling the square on some days and café tables on others. The local drunk used to hang out on the bench in front of the town hall, where he'd expose himself to newlyweds. The Dutch, rather than arrest the man, moved the bench. The big statue in the square is of Coster, the man only Haarlemers think invented printing. The little shops around the cathedral have long been church owned and rented to bring in a little cash. The fine building nearest the cathedral is the old meat hall—decorated with carved bits of early advertising.

▲Church (Grote Kerk)—This 15th-century Gothic church (now Protestant) is worth a look, if only for its Oz-like organ (from 1738, 30 meters high, its 5,000 pipes impressed both Handel and Mozart). Note how the organ, which fills the west end, seems to steal the show from the altar. Pick up the English flyer, which lists spots of interest, including Frans Hals tomb (under the black lantern in the choir). To enter, find the small "*Entrée*" sign behind the church (f2.50, Mon–Sat 10:00–16:00). Consider attending (even part of) a concert to hear Holland's greatest pipe organ (regular free concerts Tue mid-May–mid-Oct at 20:15; additional concerts Jul–Aug on Thu at 15:00; confirm schedule at TI).

▲▲Frans Hals Museum—Haarlem is the hometown of Frans Hals, and this refreshingly easy museum—an almshouse for old men back in 1610—displays many of his greatest paintings (f10, Mon–Sat 11:00–17:00, Sun 12:00–17:00, tel. 023/511-5775). Enjoy lots of Frans Hals group portraits (rooms 21, 26, 28) and take-me-back paintings of old-time Haarlem (room 22). Peter Brueghel the Younger's painting *Proverbs* (outside room 24) illustrates 72 old Dutch proverbs. To peek into old Dutch ways, identify some with the help of the English-language key.

History Museum—Across the street from the Frans Hals Museum, this small, free museum gives a peek into old Haarlem. Request the English version of the 10-minute video. Study the large-scale model of Haarlem in 1822 before the town's fortifications were demolished

Haarlem 573

Haarlem

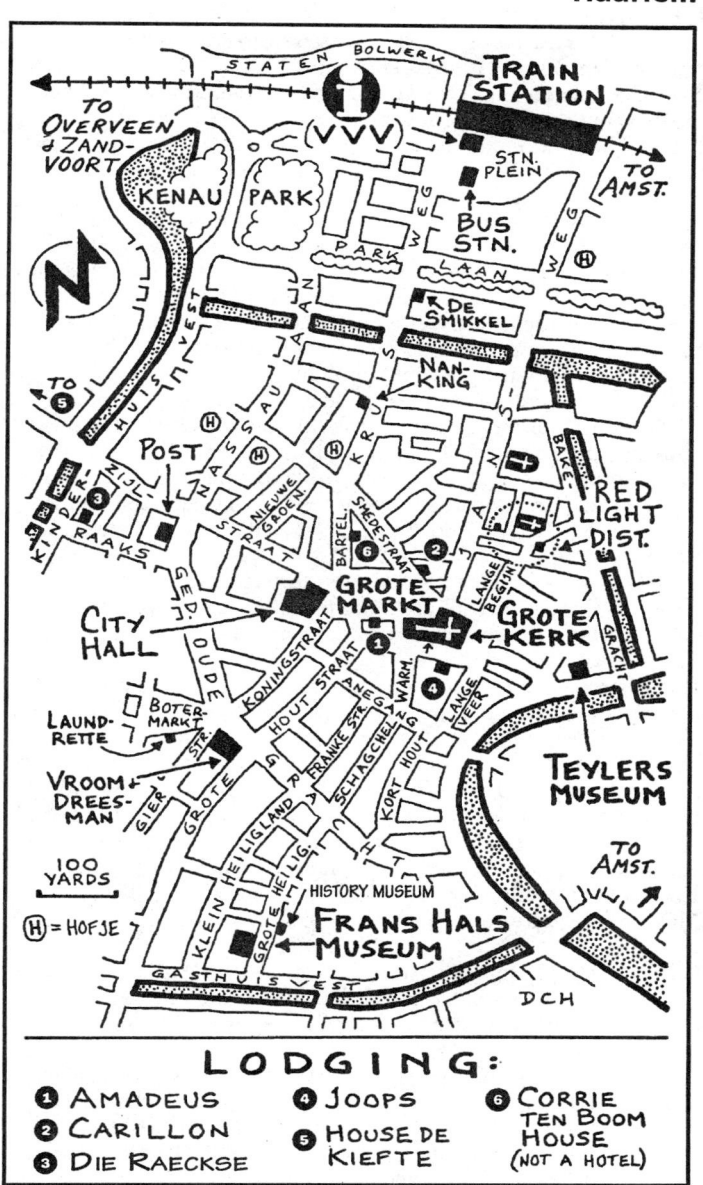

LODGING:
- ❶ AMADEUS
- ❷ CARILLON
- ❸ DIE RAECKSE
- ❹ JOOPS
- ❺ HOUSE DE KIEFTE
- ❻ CORRIE TEN BOOM HOUSE (NOT A HOTEL)

(Tue–Sat 12:00–17:00, Sun 13:00–17:00, closed Mon, Groot Heiligland 47, tel. 020/542-2427). The adjacent architecture museum (also free) is of conceivable interest to architects.

Corrie Ten Boom House—Haarlem is also home to Corrie Ten Boom, popularized by *The Hiding Place*, an inspirational book and movie about the Ten Boom family's experience hiding Jews from Nazis. The Ten Boom House is open for hourlong English tours (donation accepted, Tue–Sat 10:00–16:00, Nov–Mar Tue–Sat 11:00–15:00, 50 meters off market square at Barteljorisstraat 19; the clock shop people get all wound up if you go inside—wait at the door, where tour times are posted, tel. 023/531-0823). The Ten Boom family had for generations hosted a prayer meeting for peace here for Jews and Christians. On the 100th anniversary of the prayer meetings, the Gestapo came, looking for the hiding place. It's a great and inspirational story (although non-Christians may be put off by the preaching mixed in).

▲**Teylers Museum**—Famous as the oldest museum in Holland, it's interesting mainly as a look at a 200-year-old museum—fossils, minerals, and primitive electronic gadgetry. New exhibition halls (with rotating exhibits) have freshened up the place. Stop by if you enjoy mixing, say, Renaissance sketches with pickled coelacanths (f10, Tue–Sat 10:00–17:00, Sun 12:00–17:00, Spaarne 16, tel. 023/531-9010).

Canal Cruise—Making a scenic loop through and around Haarlem, these little trips are more relaxing than informative (f12.50, 70 min, 5/day, across from Teylers Museum at Spaarne 11a, tel. 023/535-7723).

Red Lights—For a little red-light district precious as a Barbie doll, wander around the church in Haarlem's cutest Begijnhof (two blocks northeast of big church, off Lange Begijnestraat, no senior or student discounts). Don't miss the mall marked by the red neon sign reading "*t'Steegje*." The nearby t'Poortje (office park) costs f7.50.

Global Hemp Museum—More a hemp-products store and hub of Haarlem's coffee-shop action, this friendly place runs a humble hemp museum out back (shop free, museum f5, Mon–Sat 11:00–18:00, summer Sun 12:00–18:00, down the canal from Teylers Museum at Spaarne 94, tel. 023/534-9939).

Nightlife in Haarlem

Haarlem's evening scene is great. The bars around the Grote Kerk and Lange Veerstraat are colorful and lively. You'll find plenty of music.

The best show in town: the café scene on the market square. In good weather, café tables tumble happily out of the bars.

For trendy local crowds, consider a drink at the **Studio** (on the square, next to Hotel Carillon) or **Café 1900** (across from the Corrie Ten Boom House (live music Sun night).

Haarlem

Coffee Shops: Haarlem has 16 "coffee shops," where marijuana is casually sold and smoked by easygoing noncriminal types. The **Frans Hals Coffee Shop** is one of the best established (in front of station at 46 Kruisweg). The display case–type "menu" explains what's on sale (f5 joints, f25 baggies, space cakes—but no alcohol, only soft drinks). At **High Times**, smokers can choose from 16 varieties of joints in racks behind the bar (neatly prepacked in trademarked "Joint Packs," f4-7.50, daily 12:00–23:00, Internet access, 47 Lange Veerstraat). If you don't like the smell of pot, avoid places sporting Rastafarian yellow, red, and green colors; wildly painted walls; or plants in the windows.

Crack is the wild and leathery place to go for loud music, pool, darts, and smoking (Lange Veerstraat 32). **Imperial Café and Bar** has live music every Monday, Wednesday, Thursday, and Friday (a few doors down from Crack, at Korte Veerstraat 3).

Sleeping in Haarlem
(f1 = about 50 cents, tel. code: 023)
Sleep Code: **S** = Single, **D** = Double/Twin, **T** = Triple, **Q** = Quad, **b** = bathroom, **t** = toilet only, **s** = shower only, **CC** = Credit Card (Visa, MasterCard, Amex).

The helpful Haarlem tourist office ("VVV" at the train station, Mon–Fri 9:30–17:30, Sat 10:00–14:00, tel. 0900-616-1600, f1/minute) can nearly always find you a f35 bed in a nearby private home (for a f10-per-person fee plus a cut of your host's money). Avoid this if you can; it's cheaper to call direct.

Haarlem is most crowded in April, on Easter weekend, in May, and in August. Nearly every Dutch person you'll encounter speaks English. The listed prices include breakfast (unless otherwise noted) and usually include the f3.50-per-person-per-day tourist tax. To avoid this town's louder-than-normal street noises, forgo views for a room in the back.

Hotel Amadeus, on the market square, has 15 small, bright, and basic rooms. Some have views of the square. This characteristic hotel, ideally located above a turn-of-the-century dinner café, is relatively quiet. Its lush old lounge/breakfast room, on the second floor, overlooks the square (Sb-f97.50, Db-f140, Tb-f180, Qb-f200, includes tax, 2-night stay and cash get you a 5 percent discount, a 12-min walk from train station, CC:VMA, steep climb to lounge, then an elevator, Grote Markt 10, 2011 RD Haarlem, tel. 023/532-4530, fax 023/532-2328, www.amadeus-hotel.com, Mike takes good care of his guests).

Hotel Carillon also overlooks the town square but comes with a little more traffic and bell-tower noise. Many of the well-worn rooms are small, and the stairs are ste-e-e-p. The front rooms come with great town-square views and street noise (22 rooms, tiny loft singles-f57.50, Db-f137, Tb-f180.50, Qb-f194, includes tax, no elevator, 12-min walk from train station, CC:VMA, Grote Markt 27, 2011 RC Haarlem, tel. 023/531-0591, fax 023/531-4909, e-mail: fra.baars@wxs.nl). The Carillon also runs the nearby **Die Raeckse Hotel**, which has fewer stairs, less character, more traffic noise, and decent rooms (Sb-f92.50–110, Db-f135–160, baths cost more than showers, CC:VMA, Raaks 1, 2011 VA Haarlem, tel. 023/532-6629, fax 023/531-7937).

Hotel Joops is an innovative concept. From a reception desk in his furniture store, just behind the cathedral, Mr. Joops administers a corral of 80 rooms, all within a block of the church. He has cheap, well-worn, spacious rooms (S-f75, D-f105, T-f140) and new suites with kitchenettes (Db-f122–152, depending upon size, Tb-f165–195, breakfast—with the furniture—is f17.50 extra, save about 5 percent with cash, CC:VM, Oude Groenmarkt 20, 2011 HL Haarlem, tel. 023/532-2008, fax 023/532-9549, e-mail: joops@hotelinformation.com).

Bed and Breakfast House de Kiefte, your get-into-a-local-home budget option, epitomizes the goodness of B&Bs. Marjet (mar-yet) and Hans, a fun-to-know Dutch couple who speak English fluently, rent four bright, cheery, nonsmoking rooms (with good breakfast and travel advice) in their quiet, 100-year-old home (Ds-f90, T-f130, Qs-f165, Quint/s-f190, cash only, minimum 2 nights, family loft sleeps up to 5, very steep stairs, kid-friendly, Coornhertstraat 3, 2013 EV Haarlem, tel. 023/532-2980, cellular 06-5474-5272). It's a 15-minute walk or f12 taxi ride from the train station and a five-minute walk from the center. From Grote Markt (market square), walk straight out Zijlstraat and over the bridge and take a left on the fourth street.

Hotel Lion D'Or is a classy business hotel with all the professional comforts and a handy location. Don't expect a warm welcome (34 rooms, Sb-f210, Db-f275, extra beds-f50, often 10 percent off on weekends and slow times, CC:VMA, elevator, some nonsmoking rooms, across the street from the station at Kruisweg 34, 2011 LC Haarlem, tel. 023/532-1750, fax 023/532-9543).

The 300-room, very American **Hotel Haarlem Zuid** is sterile but a good value for those interested only in sleeping and eating. It sits in an industrial zone, a 20-minute walk from the center on the road to the airport (Db-f153–173, depending upon size of room, add f10 each for a 3rd or 4th person, breakfast included or skip and save f15 each, CC:VMA, elevator, easy parking, inexpensive hotel restaurant, Toekenweg 2, 2035 LC Haarlem, tel. 023/536-7500, fax 023/536-7980). Buses #70, #72, and #75 connect the hotel to the station and market square every 10 minutes.

Sleeping near Haarlem

Pension Koning, a 15-minute walk north of the station or a quick hop on bus #71, has five simple rooms in a row house in a residential

Haarlem 577

area (S-f45, D-f90, T-f120, 2-night minimum, includes breakfast, Kleverlaan 179, 2023 JC Haarlem, tel. 023/526-1456).

Hostel Jan Gijzen, completely renovated and with all the youth-hostel comforts, charges f34 for beds (breakfast) in six-bed dorms (f5 extra for nonmembers) and f6.50 for sheets (a few D-f82, daily 7:00–24:00, closed Nov–Feb, Jan Gijzenpad 3, 2 miles from Haarlem station—take bus #2, or a 5-minute walk from Santpoort Zuid train station, tel. 023/537-3793, fax 023/537-1176).

Eating in Haarlem

Eating between Market Square (Grote Markt) and Train Station

Enjoy an Indonesian rijsttafel feast at the **Nanking Chinese-Indonesian Restaurant** (daily 16:00–22:00, Kruisstraat 16, a few blocks off Grote Markt, tel. 023/532-0706). Couples eat plenty, heartily, and cheaply by splitting a f24.50 Indonesian "rice table" for one; each eater should order a drink. Say hi to gracious Ai Ping and her daughter, Fan. Don't let them railroad you into a Chinese (their heritage) dinner. They also do cheap and tasty takeout.

Pancakes for dinner? **Pannekoekhuis "De Smikkel"** serves a selection of over 50 dinner (meat, cheese, etc.) and dessert pancakes. The pancakes (f16 each) are filling. With the f2.50-per-person cover charge, splitting is OK (daily 16:00–22:00, closed Mon in winter, 2 blocks in front of station, Kruisweg 57, tel. 023/532-0631).

Eat well and surrounded by trains and 1908 architecture in the classy **Brasserie Haarlem** Station Restaurant (f30 for 3 courses, daily 12:00–23:00, between tracks #3 and #6).

Eating on or near Zijlstraat

Eko Eet Café is great for a cheery, tasty vegetarian meal (f19 *menu*, daily 17:30–21:30, Zijlstraat 39). Because they serve only fresh food, the menu gets sparse by 21:00.

Vincent's Eethuis serves the best cheap, basic Dutch food in town. This former St. Vincent's soup kitchen now feeds more gainfully employed locals than poor (f9, free seconds on veggies, friendly staff, Mon–Fri 12:00–14:00, 17:00–19:30, Nieuwe Groenmarkt 22).

The friendly **De Buren** offers handlebar-mustache fun and traditional Dutch food (such as *draadjesvlees*—beef stew with applesauce—and *oma's kippetje*—grandmother's chicken) to happy locals (f25 dinners, Wed–Sun 17:00–22:00, closed Mon–Tue, outside the tourist area at Brouwersvaart 146, near the intersection with Zijlsingel, across the canal from Die Raeckse Hotel and close to House de Kiefte B&B, tel. 023/534-3364). Gerard and Marjo love their work. Enjoy their creative menu, made especially for you.

Eating between the Market Square and Frans Hals Museum

Jacobus Pieck Eetlokaal is popular with locals for its fine-value "global cuisine" (f18 plate of the day, Mon–Sat 10:00–22:00, Sun 12:00–22:00, Warmoesstraat 18, tel. 023/532-6144).

For a (f2) cone of old-fashioned French fries, drop by **Friethuis de Vlaminck** on Warmoesstraat 3 (Tue–Sat until 18:00). Notice the old-time shop sign cobbled into Warmoesstraat's brick sidewalk.

La Plume steak house is noisy with a happy, local, and very carnivorous crowd (f28 meals, daily from 17:30, CC:VMA, Lange Veerstraat 1).

Bastiaan serves good "Mediterranean" cuisine in a classy atmosphere (f30 dinners, Tue–Sun from 18:00, closed Mon, CC:VMA, Lange Veerstraat 8).

De Lachende Javaan ("The Laughing Javanese") serves the best real Indonesian food in town. Their f35 rijsttafel is great (light eaters can split this extravaganza—f5 for the extra plate, Tue–Sun from 17:00, closed Mon, CC:VMA, Frankestraat 25, tel. 023/532-8792).

For a candlelit dinner of cheese and wine, consider **In't Goede Uur** (Tue–Sun from 17:30, closed Mon, Korte Houtstraat 1).

For a healthy budget lunch with Haarlem's best view, eat at **La Place**, on the top floor or roof garden of the Vroom Dreesman department store (Mon–Sat 9:30–18:00, Thu until 21:00, closed Sun, on the corner of Grote Houtstraat and Gedempte Oude Gracht).

Picnic shoppers head to the **DekaMarkt** supermarket (Mon–Sat 8:30–20:00, closed Sun, Gedemple Oude Gracht 54, between Vroom Dreesman department store and post office).

Transportation Connections—Haarlem

By train to: Amsterdam (6/hrly, 15 min, f6 one way, f10.50 same-day return, ticket not valid on "Lovers Train," a misnamed private train that runs hrly), **Delft** (2/hrly, 38 min), **Hoorn** (4/hrly, 1 hr), **The Hague** (4/hrly, 35 min), **Alkmaar** (2/hrly, 30 min), **Schiphol Airport** (2/hrly, 40 min, f10, transfer at Amsterdam-Sloterdijk); the direct buses #236 (use a strip card) and #362 (local cash) to the airport are faster (2/hrly, 30 min, f6.25); by taxi it's f70.

Sights—Near Haarlem and Amsterdam

▲**Zaanse Schans**—This 17th-century Dutch village turned open-air folk museum puts Dutch culture—from cheese making to wooden-shoe carving—on a lazy Susan. Take an inspiring climb to the top of a whirring windmill (gather a group and ask for a tour). Located in the town of Zaandijk, this is your easiest one-stop look at traditional Dutch culture and the Netherlands' best collection

Day Trips from Haarlem and Amsterdam

of windmills (free, daily 8:30–18:00, until 17:00 in winter, parking f7.50/1 hr, f15/day, tel. 075/616-8218). Fifteen minutes by train north of Amsterdam: Take the Alkmaar-bound train to Station Koog-Zaandijk and then walk, following the signs—past a fragrant chocolate factory—for 10 minutes.

▲▲Aalsmeer Flower Auction—Get a bird's-eye view of the huge Dutch flower industry. Wander on elevated walkways (through what's claimed to be the biggest building on earth) over literally trainloads of freshly cut flowers. About half of all the flowers exported from Holland are auctioned off here in six huge auditoriums (f7.50, Mon–Fri 7:30–11:00; the auction wilts after 9:30, but the warehouse swarms; gift shop, cafeteria; bus #172 from Amsterdam's station, 2/hrly, 1 hr; from Haarlem take bus #140, 2/hrly, 1 hr, tel. 0297/393-939). Aalsmeer is close to the airport and a handy last fling before catching a morning weekday flight.

▲▲▲Keukenhof—This is the greatest bulb-flower garden on earth. Each spring 6 million flowers, enjoying sandy soil behind the Dutch dunes, conspire to make even a total garden hater enjoy them. This 100-acre park is packed with tour groups daily from about March 23 to May 21 for the spring show (f18, 8:00–19:30, last tickets sold at 18:00) and from August 18 to September 18 for the

summer exhibition (f12.50, 9:00–18:00; bus #50 or #51 from Haarlem then transfer at Lisse; tel. 0252/465-555, www.keukenhof.nl).
▲**Alkmaar**—Holland's cheese capital is especially fun (and touristy) during its weekly cheese market (Friday 10:00–12:00).
▲▲**The Hague (Den Haag)**—Locals say the money is made in Rotterdam, divided in The Hague, and spent in Amsterdam. The Hague is the Netherlands' seat of government and the home of several engaging museums. The Mauritshuis' delightful, easy-to-tour art collection stars Vermeer and Rembrandt (f12.50, Tue-Sat 10:00–17:00, Sun 11:00–17:00, Korte Vijverberg 8, tel. 070/302-3456). Across the pond, the Torture Museum (Gevangenpoort) shows the medieval mind at its worst (f6, Tue–Fri 10:00–16:00, Sat–Sun 12:00–16:00, closed Mon, required tours on the hour, last one at 16:00; confirm with the ticket taker if the film and talk will be in English before you commit, tel. 070/346-0861). For a look at the 19th century's attempt at virtual reality, tour Panorama Mesdag, a 360-degree painting of the nearby town of Scheveningen in the 1880s with a 3-D sandy-beach foreground (f7.50, Mon–Sat 10:00–17:00, Sun 12:00–17:00, Zeestraat 65, tel. 070/310-6665). Scheveningen, the Dutch Coney Island, is liveliest on sunny summer afternoons (take tram #7); and Madurodam, a mini-Holland amusement park, is a kid pleaser (f21, kids 4–11 f14, daily 9:00–18:00, until 20:00 in Jun, until 23:00 Jul–Aug, tram #1 or #9, tel. 070/355-3900). The Hague's TI is at the train station (Mon–Sat 9:00–17:30, later in summer, Sun 10:00–17:00, tel. 06/3403-5051, f1 a minute).
▲▲**Arnhem's Open-Air Dutch Folk Museum**—An hour east of Amsterdam, Arnhem has Holland's first and biggest folk museum. You'll enjoy a huge park of windmills, old farms, traditional crafts in action, and a pleasant education-by-immersion in Dutch culture. The English guidebook (f7.50) explains each historic building (f18, Apr–Oct daily 10:00–17:00, tel. 026/357-6111). Its rustic Pancake House serves hearty (splittable) Dutch flapjacks.

Trains make the 70-minute trip from Amsterdam to Arnhem twice an hour (likely transfer in Utrecht). At Arnhem station, take bus #13 (4/hrly, 15 min) to the Openlucht Museum.
▲▲**Kröller-Müller Museum and Hoge Veluwe National Park**—Near Arnhem, the Hoge Veluwe National Park is Holland's largest (13,000 acres) and is famous for its Kröller-Müller Museum. This huge, impressive modern-art collection, including 55 paintings by van Gogh, is set deep in the forest. The park has hundreds of white bikes you're free to use to make your explorations more fun. After you pay f8.50 at the park entrance, the museum is "free" (Tue–Sun 10:00–17:00, easy parking, tel. 055/378-1441). Pick up information at the Amsterdam or Arnhem TI (tel. 026/442-6767). Bus #12 connects the Arnhem train station with the Kröller-Müller Museum (Mar–Oct). A visit to the park and the open-air museum makes a great day trip from Amsterdam.

LISBON

Lisbon is a ramshackle but charming mix of now and then. Old wooden trolleys shiver up and down its hills, bird-stained statues mark grand squares, taxis rattle and screech through cobbled lanes, and well-worn people sip coffee in Art Nouveau cafés.

Lisbon, like Portugal in general, is underrated. The country seems somewhere just beyond Europe. The pace of life is noticeably slower than in Spain. Roads are rutted. Prices are cheaper. While the unification of Europe is bringing sweeping changes, the traditional economy is based on fishing, cork, wine, and textiles. Be sure to balance your look at Iberia with enough Portugal.

While Lisbon's history goes back to the Romans and Moors, its glory days were the 15th and 16th centuries, when explorers such as Vasco da Gama opened new trade routes around Africa to India, making Lisbon one of Europe's richest cities. (These days, in the wake of the 500th anniversary of his 1498 voyage, da Gama has a higher profile.) Portugal's "Age of Discovery" fueled an economic boom, which fueled the flamboyant art boom called the Manueline period—named after King Manuel I (ruled 1495–1521). In the early 18th century, the gold and diamonds of Brazil, one of Portugal's colonies, made Lisbon even wealthier.

Then, on All Saints' Day in 1755, while most of the population was in church, the city was hit by a tremendous earthquake. Candles quivered as far away as Ireland. Lisbon was dead center. Two-thirds of the city was leveled. Fires started by the many church candles raged through the city, and a huge tidal wave blasted the waterfront. Of Lisbon's 270,000 people, 30,000 were killed.

Under the energetic and eventually dictatorial leadership of Prime Minister Marques de Pombal—who had the new city

Lisbon

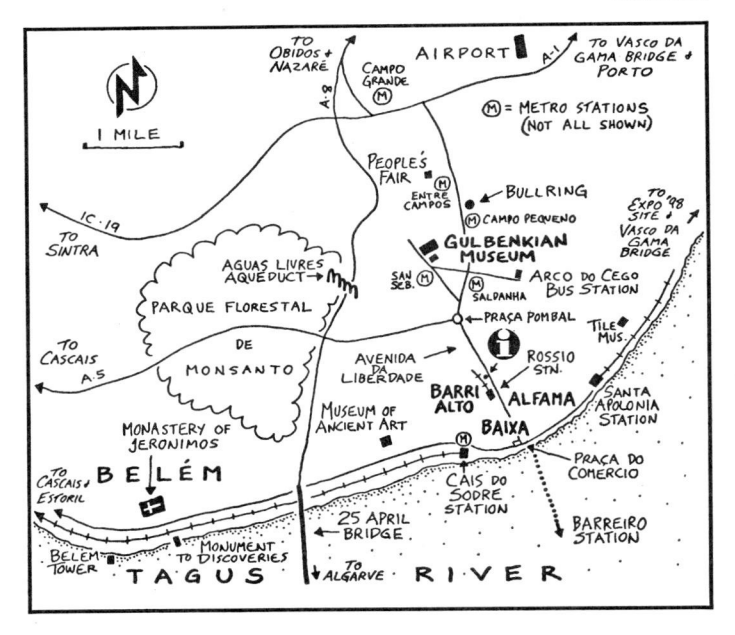

planned within a month of the quake—Lisbon was rebuilt in a progressive grid plan, with broad boulevards and square squares. Remnants of pre-earthquake Lisbon charm survive in Belém, the Alfama, and the Baírro Alto district.

The heritage of Portugal's Age of Discovery was a vast colonial empire. Except for Macao and the few islands off the Atlantic coast, the last bits of the empire disappeared with the 1974 revolution, which delivered Portugal from the right-wing Salazar dictatorship. Emigrants from former colonies such as Mozambique and Angola have added diversity and flavor to the city, making it more likely that you'll hear African music than Portuguese fados these days.

But Lisbon's heritage survives. The city seems better organized, cleaner, and more prosperous and people-friendly than ever. With its elegant outdoor cafés, exciting art, entertaining museums, a hill-capping castle, the saltiest sailors' quarter in Europe, and the boost given the city after hosting the 1998 World's Fair, Lisbon is a world-class city. And with some of Europe's lowest prices, enjoying Lisbon is easy on the budget.

Lisbon

Planning Your Time

With three weeks in Iberia, Lisbon is worth two days.
Day 1: Start by touring Castle São Jorge, at the top of the Alfama, and surveying the city from its viewpoint. Hike down to another fine viewpoint, Miradouro de Santa Luzia, and descend into the Alfama. Explore. Back in the Baixa (bai-shah; "lower city"), have lunch on or near Rua Augusta and walk to the funicular near Praça dos Restauradores. Start the described walk through the Baírro Alto with a ride up the funicular. Take a joyride on trolley #28. If it's not later than 14:00, art lovers can Metro or taxi to the Gulbenkian Museum. Consider dinner at a fado show in the Baírro Alto. If one of your nights is a summer Thursday, consider a bullfight.
Day 2: Trolley to Belém and tour the Tower, Monastery, and Coach Museum (note: Most of Belém's sights are closed Monday). Have lunch in Belém. You could catch the train or drive to Sintra to tour the Pena Palace and explore the ruined Moorish castle. If you're itchy for the beach, drive four hours from Sintra to the Algarve.

A third day could easily be spent at the Museum of Ancient Art and browsing through the Rossio, Baírro Alto, and Alfama neighborhoods.

Orientation

Greater Lisbon has around 3 million people and some frightening sprawl, but for the visitor, Lisbon can be a delightful small-town series of parks, boulevards, and squares bunny-hopping between two hills down to the waterfront. The main boulevard, Avenida da Liberdade, goes from the high-rent district downhill, ending at the grand square called Praça dos Restauradores. From here the Baixa—the post-earthquake, grid-planned lower town, with three fine squares—leads to the riverfront. Rua Augusta is the grand pedestrian promenade running through the Baixa to the river.

Most travelers focus on the three characteristic neighborhoods that line the downtown harborfront: Baixa (flat, in the middle), the Baírro Alto (literally "high town," Lisbon's "Latin Quarter" on a hill to the west), and the tangled, medieval Alfama (topped by the castle on the hill to the east).

From ye olde Lisbon, Avenida da Liberdade storms into the no-nonsense real world, where you find the airport, bullring, popular fairgrounds, Edward VII Park, and breezy botanical gardens.

Tourist Information

Lisbon's city TI is in the peach-colored Palacio Foz at the bottom of Praça dos Restauradores (daily 9:00–18:00, 21-346-3314). The national TI for Portugal is in the same office (daily 9:00–20:00, tel. 21-346-3658). The free city map lists all museums and has a helpful inset of the town center. The free biweekly *Follow Me Lisboa* is better than the TI's *Cultural Agenda*. The Falk Map, sold for 1,200$ at bookstores (*livrerias*), is excellent. Each summer cheery little "Ask Me about Lisbon" info booths, staffed by tourism students, pop up all over town (less busy and jaded, actually eager to help you enjoy their town). The city has no regular walking tours, but for a private guide you can call the Guides' Union (13,000$/4 hrs, 24,000$/full day, tel. 21-346-7170). Angela da Silva is a good local guide (tel. 21-479-3597, cellular tel. 96-605-9518).

Arrival in Lisbon

By Train: Lisbon has four train stations—Santa Apolonia (to Spain and most points north), Rossio (for Sintra, Obidos, and Nazaré), Barreiro (for Algarve), and Cais do Sodre (Cascais and Estoril). If leaving Lisbon by train, see if your train requires a reservation (boxed "R" in timetable).

Santa Apolonia Station covers international trains and nearly all of Portugal (except the south). It's just past the Alfama and includes foreign-currency change machines and good bus connections to the town center (buses #9, #39, #46, and #90 go from station through center, up Avenida da Liberdade). A taxi from Santa Apolonia to any hotel I recommend should cost around 700$. If there's a long taxi-stand lineup, walk a block away and hail one off the street.

Rossio Station is in the town center (within walking distance of most of my hotel listings) and handles trains from Sintra (and Óbidos and Nazaré, with transfers at Cacém). It has a handy all-Portugal train information office on the ground floor (Mon–Fri 9:15–13:00, 14:00–18:30).

Barreiro Station, a 30-minute ferry ride across the Tagus River (Rio Tejo) from Praça do Comércio, is for trains to the Algarve and points south (the 170$ ferry ticket is generally sold to you with a train ticket).

Caís do Sodre Station handles the 40-minute rides to Cascais and Estoril.

By Bus: Lisbon's bus station is at Arco do Cego (200 meters from Metro: Saldanha, tel. 21-354-5439).

By Plane: Lisbon's easy-to-manage airport is eight kilometers northeast of downtown, with a 24-hour bank, ATMs, a tourist office, reasonable taxi service (1,800$ to center), good city bus connections into town (#44 and #45, 160$), and an airport bus.

The Aero-Bus #91 runs from the airport to Restauradores, Rossio, and Praça do Comércio (450$, 3/hrly, 30 min, 7:00–21:00, buy ticket on bus). Your ticket is actually a one-day Lisbon transit pass that covers bus, tram, and elevator rides. If you fly in on TAP airline, show your ticket at the TAP welcome desk on the arrivals level to get a free one-way voucher for the Aero-Bus (TAP tel. 21-841-6990). A Lisbon transit pass (sold in one-day and three-day versions) covers the Aero-Bus trip to the airport if you're

Central Lisbon

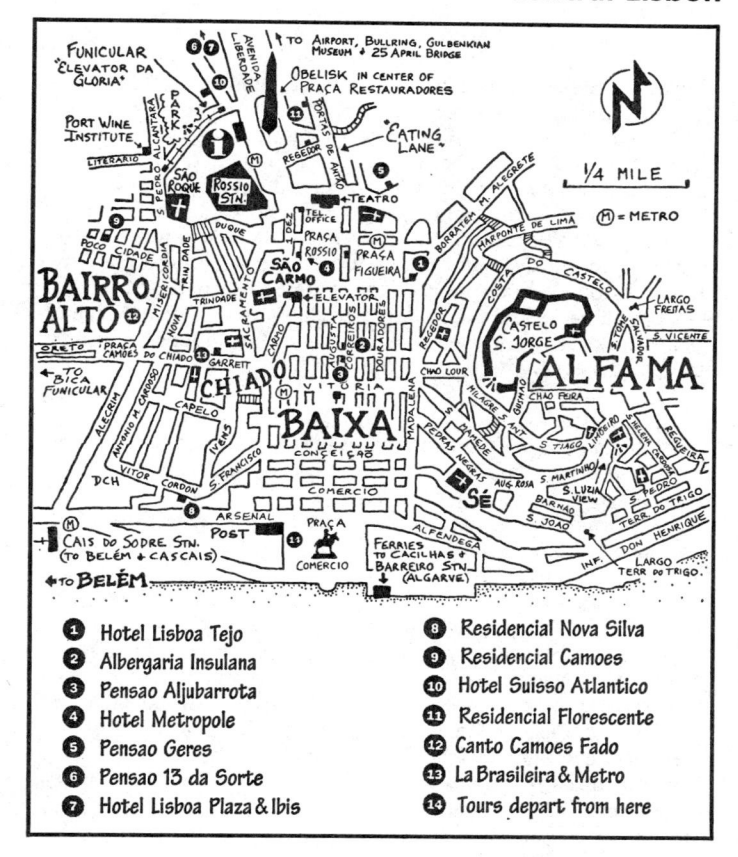

1. Hotel Lisboa Tejo
2. Albergaria Insulana
3. Pensao Aljubarrota
4. Hotel Metropole
5. Pensao Geres
6. Pensao 13 da Sorte
7. Hotel Lisboa Plaza & Ibis
8. Residencial Nova Silva
9. Residencial Camoes
10. Hotel Suisso Atlantico
11. Residencial Florescente
12. Canto Camoes Fado
13. La Brasileira & Metro
14. Tours depart from here

flying out of Lisbon. (Airport information: tel. 21-841-3500; flight info: tel. 21-841-3700.)

Getting around Lisbon

By Metro: Lisbon's simple, fast subway is handy for trips to the Gulbenkian Museum, the fairgrounds, bullfights, the Colombo mall, the Expo '98 site, and the long-distance bus station. Bring change for the machines, as many stations are not staffed (100$ per ride or 250$ all day). Remember to stamp your ticket in the machine. Metro stops are marked with a red "M." *Saida* means exit.

By Trolley, Funicular, and Elevator: For fun and practical public transport, use the trolley, the funicular, and the Eiffelesque elevator (might be closed in 2000; otherwise, tickets at the door, going every few minutes) that connect the lower and upper towns. One ride costs 160$ (no transfers). The 450$ day pass and the 1,060$ three-day transit pass cover all public transportation (including the extensive city bus system) except for the Metro.

The 160$ Bilhete Unico de Coroa gives you two trips on the trolley, bus, or elevator for the cost of one. Buy these tickets at green-and-yellow Carris booths (on Praça Figueira or at the base of the Santa Justa elevator—up a few stairs and behind the elevator).

By Taxi: Lisbon cabbies are good-humored and abundant, and they use their meters. Rides start at 280$, and you can go anywhere in the center for under 500$. Especially if there are two of you, Lisbon cabs are a great, cheap time saver. For an average trip, couples save less than a dollar by taking public transport and spend an extra 20 minutes to get there—bad economics. If time is limited, taxi everywhere.

Helpful Hints

Bullfights take place most summer Thursdays in Lisbon and most Sundays nearby. Tuesdays and Saturdays are flea-market days in the Alfama.

Museums: Most museums are free on Sunday until 14:00 and closed all day Monday (a good day to explore Lisbon's neighborhoods or Sintra's Moorish ruins).

LisboaCard: This card covers all public transportation (including the Metro), allowing free entrance to most museums and discounts on others, plus discounts on city tours. If you plan to museum-hop, the card is a good value, particularly for a day in Belém (covers your transportation and every worthwhile sight in Belém). Don't use one on a Monday, when virtually all sights are closed, or on a Sunday, when many sights are free until 14:00 (24-hour card/1,900$; 48-hour card/3,100$; 72-hour card/4,000$; includes excellent explanatory guidebook). Buy it at the city TI (in Palacio Foz at Praça do Restauradores). You can choose what date and time you want it to "start."

Pedestrian Warning: Sidewalks are narrow, and drivers are daring; cross streets with care. Avoid nighttime strolls through the seedy area near Rossio station and San Vincente Church.

Language: Remember to try to start conversations in Portuguese. Fortunately, many people in the tourist trade speak some English. Otherwise, try Portuguese, French, or Spanish, in that order. Lisbon comes with some tricky pronunciations. Locals call their city Lisboa (LEEZH-bo-ah) and their river the Tejo (TAY-zhoo). Squares are major navigation points and are called *praça* (PRA-sah).

Time Zone Change: Portuguese time is usually one hour earlier than Spanish time.

Lisbon

Banking: ATMs are the way to go, giving more escudos per dollar all over Lisbon. Banks offer fine rates but high fees to change checks or cash. Shop around and minimize trips to the bank by changing large amounts (bank hours are generally Mon–Fri 8:30–15:00). American Express cashes any kind of traveler's check at a decent rate without a commission, but the office is not central (Mon–Fri 9:30–13:00, 14:30–18:30, in Top Tours office at Avenida Duque de Loule 108, Metro: Rotunda, tel. 21-315-5885). Automatic bill-changing machines are available and seductive, offering fair rates but high fees.

Post Office and Telephones: The post office, at Praça dos Restauradores 58, has easy-to-use metered phones (Mon–Fri 8:00–22:00, Sat–Sun 9:00–18:00). The telephone center, on the northwest corner of Rossio Square, sells phone cards and also has metered phone booths (daily 8:00–23:00, accepts credit cards).

Internet Access: Ciber Ciado is at Largo de Picadero in the Baírro Alto (600$/hr).

Do-It-Yourself Walking Tours

▲▲**The Baírro Alto and Chiado Stroll**—This colorful upper-city walk starts at the funicular and ends with the elevator (might be closed in 2000), each a funky 160$ experience in itself. Leave the lower town on the funicular, called Elevator da Gloria, near the obelisk at Praça dos Restauradores. (Notice the plaque inside near the ceiling from the car's 100th birthday in 1985.) Leaving the funicular on top, turn right to enjoy the city view from Miradouro de São Pedro Alcantara (San Pedro Park belvedere). Wander over to the tile map, which helps guide you through the view, stretching from the castle birthplace of Lisbon on the right to the towers of the new city in the distance on the left. The centerpiece of the park is a statue honoring a 19th-century local writer. This district is famous for its writers, poets, and bohemians.

If you're into port (the fortified wine that takes its name from the city of Oporto), you'll find the world's greatest selection directly across the street from the lift at **Solar do Vinho do Porto** (run by the Port Wine Institute, Mon–Fri 10:00–23:30, less on Sat, closed Sun, Rua São Pedro de Alcantara 45). In a plush, air-conditioned living room you can, for 200$ to 3,000$ per glass (poured by an English-speaking bartender), taste any of 300 different ports—though you may want to try only 150 or so and save the rest for the next night. Fans of port describe it as "a liquid symphony playing on the palate."

Follow the main street (Rua São Pedro de Alcantara) downhill a couple of blocks; it turns into the Rua Misericordia. The grid plan of streets to your right is 16th-century Renaissance town planning—predating the earthquake and grid plan of the lower town by two centuries.

São Roque Church is on your left at Largo Trindade Coelho (8:00–17:00). It looks like just another church, but wander slowly under its flat, painted ceiling and notice the rich side chapels. The highlight is the Chapel of St. John the Baptist (left of altar, gold and blue), which looks like it came right out of the Vatican. It did. Made in Rome out of the most precious materials, it was the site of one papal Mass; then it was shipped to Lisbon—probably the most costly chapel per square inch ever constructed. Notice the beautiful mosaic floor and the three paintings that are actually intricate mosaics—a Vatican specialty (designed to avoid damage from candle smoke that would darken paintings). The São Roque Museum, with some impressive old paintings and church riches (150$, Tue–Sun 10:00–17:00, closed Mon) is not as interesting as the church itself.

After a visit with the poor pigeon-drenched man in the church square (TI and WC), continue downhill along Rua Misericordia into the more elegant shopping district called the **Chiado** (SHEE-ah-doo).

When you reach Praça Luis de Camões (named after Portugal's best-loved poet), turn left to a small square (Largo Chiado) past **A Brasileira café** and the classy Rua Garrett. The statue is of a famous local poet (Fernando Pessoa) who was a regular at Brasileira. Coffee-house aficionados enjoy this grand old café, which reeks with smoke and the 1930s (open daily). Drop in for a *bica* (Lisbon slang for an espresso) and a *pastel de Belém* (140$ cream cake—a local specialty).

Browse downhill for two blocks on Rua Garrett, peeking into the classy shops. Notice the lamps with the symbol of Lisbon: a ship, or caravel—carrying the remains of St. Anthony—guarded by two ravens. This street was one of Lisbon's best shopping streets before the fire of 1988.

At Calle Sacramento, go left uphill to another pleasant square, Largo dos Carmo, with the ruins of the **Convento do Carmo** (if it's open, pop in to see the elegant, earthquake-ruined Gothic arches for free or pay 300$ to get all the way in and see the museum, Mon–Sat 10:00–17:30, closed Sun).

Trolley tracks lead from the square past the church to the Santa Justa elevator. At the elevator, climb the spiral stairs one floor to the small observatory deck or to the top of this Eiffelian pimple for a great view café (daily, English spoken, reasonable coffee, expensive eats). The elevator (built by a pupil of Eiffel) takes you down into the Baixa.

▲▲▲**Alfama Stroll**—Europe's most colorful sailors' quarter goes back to Visigothic days. It was a rich district during the Arabic period and finally the home of Lisbon's fisherfolk (and of the poet Luis de Camões, who wrote, "our lips meet easily high across the narrow street"). The tangled street plan is one of the few aspects of Lisbon to survive the 1755 earthquake, helping make the Alfama a cobbled playground of Old World color. A visit is best during the busy midmorning market time or in the late afternoon/early evening, when the streets teem with locals.

Consider riding a taxi or bus #37 from Praça Figueira to the castle—the highest point in town—and walking from there down to the Alfama viewpoint and into the Alfama.

Start at **Castle São Jorge**. Lisbon's castle is boring as far as castles go. But it's the birthplace of the city, it offers a fine view, and it's free (open daily until sunset). Straddle a cannon, enjoy the view and park, and wander the sterile ramparts if you like. Within the castle, **Olisiponia** (the Roman name for Lisbon) is a high-tech syrupy multimedia presentation offering a sweeping video overview of the city's history in English (600$, daily 10:00–17:30).

It's a five-minute walk downhill to another great Alfama viewpoint, at **Largo Santa Luzia**. (This square is a stop for trolleys #12 and #28; some prefer to start their Alfama exploration here and take the steep but worthwhile 10-minute uphill hike to the castle.) Admire the panoramic view from the square's small terrace, Miradouro de Santa Luzia, where old-timers play cards in the shade of the bougainvillea amid lots of tiles. Probably the most scenic cup of coffee in town is enjoyed from the nearby Cerca Moura bar/café terrace (after 11:30, Largo das Portas do Sol 4).

The **Museum of Decorative Arts**, next to the Cerca Moura bar, offers a unique (but nearly meaningless with its lack of decent English descriptions) stroll through aristocratic households richly decorated in 16th- to 19th-century styles (800$, Tue–Sun 10:00–17:00, closed Mon, Largo das Portas do Sol 2, tel. 21-886-2183).

From the Largo das Portas do Sol (Cerca Moura bar), stairs lead deep into the Alfama. To descend from the viewpoint: Behind the Santa Luzia church, take Rua Norberto de Araujo down a few stairs and go left under the arch and you'll hook up with Beco Santa Helena, an alley of steps leading downhill.

The Alfama's urban jungle roads are squeezed into tangled, confusing alleys; bent houses comfort each other in their romantic shabbiness; and the air drips with laundry and the smell of clams and raw fish. Get lost. Poke aimlessly, sample ample grapes, peek through windows, buy a fish. Don't miss Rua de São Pedro, the liveliest street around. On Tuesday and Saturday mornings the fun Feira da Ladra flea market rages on Campo de Santa Clara (a 20-minute walk; worth it only if it's flea-market day).

Tours—Lisbon
▲▲**Ride a Trolley**—Lisbon's vintage trolleys, most from the 1920s, shake and shiver all over town, somehow safely weaving within inches of parked cars, climbing steep hills, and offering sightseers breezy views of the city. Line #28 is a Rice-A-Roni Lisbon joyride. Tram #28 stops from west to east include Estrela (the 18th-century late-Baroque Estrela Basilica and Estrela Park—

cozy neighborhood scene with pond-side café and a "garden library kiosk"), the top of the Bica funicular (drops steeply through a rough-and-tumble neighborhood to the riverfront), Chiado square (Lisbon's café and "Latin Quarter"), Baixa (on Rua da Conceicão between Augusta and Prata), the cathedral (*sè*), the Alfama viewpoint (Santa Luzia belvedere), Portas do Sol, Santa Clara Church (flea market), and the pleasant and untouristy Graca district. Just pay the conductor as you board, sit down, and catch the pensioners as they lurch at each stop. For a quicker circular Alfama trolley ride, catch #12 on Praça da Figueira (departs every few minutes, 20-minute circle, driver can tell you when to get out for the viewpoint near the castle—about three-quarters through the ride).

City Bus Tours—Two tours give tired tourists a lazy overview of the city. Neither is great, but both are handy, daily, and inexpensive. **Tagus Tour** lets you hop on and off their topless double-decker buses (2,000$, hrly beginning at 11:00 May–Sept, 90-minute tour covers the town and Belém, taped, English, Portuguese, and French). On the **Hills Tour** you follow the rails on restored turn-of-the-century trams through the Alfama and Baírro Alto (2,800$; live, trilingual guide; 4 or 5 departures daily in summer, less off-season). While the ride is scenic, the information is sparse. Both leave from the Praça do Comércio (tel. 21-363-2021).

Sights—Lisbon

▲▲▲**Gulbenkian Museum**—This is the best of Lisbon's 40 museums. Gulbenkian, an Armenian oil tycoon, gave his art collection (or "harem," as he called it) to Portugal in gratitude for the hospitable asylum granted him during World War II. This great collection, spanning 2,000 years and housed in a classy modern building, offers the most purely enjoyable museum experience in Iberia. It's cool, uncrowded, gorgeously lit, and easy to grasp, displaying only a few select and exquisite works from each epoch.

Savor details as you stroll chronologically through the ages past the delicate Egyptian, vivid Greek (fascinating coins), and exotic Oriental sections and the well-furnished Louis land. There are masterpieces by Rembrandt, Rubens, Renoir, Rodin, and artists whose names start with other letters. The nubile finale is a dark room filled with Art Nouveau jewelry by the French designer Rene Lalique (500$, free Sun, Tue 14:00–18:00, Wed–Sun 10:00–18:00, closed Mon, pleasant gardens, good air-con cafeteria, take Metro from Rossio to São Sebastião and walk 200 meters, or 500$ taxi from downtown, Berna 45, tel. 21-793-5131).

▲▲**Museum of Ancient Art (Museu Nacional de Arte Antiga)**—This is the country's best for Portuguese paintings from her glory days, the 15th and 16th centuries. (Most of these works were gathered in Lisbon after the dissolution of the abbeys and convents in 1834.) You'll also find the great European masters—

Lisbon

such as Bosch, Jan van Eyck, and Raphael—and rich furniture, all in a grand palace. Highlights include the *Temptations of St. Anthony* (a three-paneled altarpiece fantasy by Bosch, c. 1500); *St. Jerome* (by Dürer); the *Adoration of St. Vincent* (a many-paneled altarpiece by the late-15th-century Portuguese master Nuno Goncalves, showing everyone from royalty to sailors and beggars surrounding Portugal's patron saint); and the curious Namban screens (16th-century Japanese depictions of Portuguese traders in Japan). The museum has a good cafeteria, with seating in a shaded garden overlooking the river (500$, Tue 14:00–18:00, Wed–Sun 10:00–18:00, closed Mon, tram #15, bus #40, or #60 from Praça Figueira, Rua das Janeles Verdes 9, tel. 21-397-6002).

▲**National Tile Museum (Museu Nacional do Azulejo)**—This museum, filling the Convento da Madre de Deus, features piles of tiles, which, as you've probably noticed, are an art form in Portugal. The presentation is very low tech, but the church is sumptuous, and the tile panorama of pre-earthquake Lisbon (upstairs) is fascinating (350$, Tue 14:00–18:00, Wed–Sun 10:00–18:00, closed Mon, 10 minutes on bus #105 from Praça Figueira, Rua da Madre de Deus 4, tel. 21-814-7747).

Cathedral (Sè)—Just a few blocks east of Praça do Comércio, it's not much on the inside, but its fortresslike exterior is a textbook example of a stark and powerful Romanesque fortress of God. Started in 1150, after the Christians reconquered Lisbon from the Islamic Moors, its crenellated towers made a powerful statement: The Reconquista was here to stay. St. Anthony—the patron saint of Portugal but known to most of us as the saint in charge of helping you find lost things—is buried in the church. In the 12th century his remains were brought to Lisbon on a ship, as the legend goes, guarded by two sacred black ravens...the symbol of the city. The **cloisters** are peaceful and an archaeological work in progress—uncovering Roman ruins (100$). The humble **treasury** shows off relics of St. Anthony but is worthwhile only if you want to support the church and climb some stairs (400$).

Expo '98 Grounds and Aquarium—Lisbon celebrated the 500th anniversary of Vasco da Gama's voyage to India by hosting Expo '98. The theme was "The Ocean and the Seas," with an emphasis on the importance of healthy, clean waters in our environment. The riverside fairgrounds are east of the Santa Apolonia train station in an area suddenly revitalized with luxury condos and crowd-pleasing terraces and restaurants. Ride the Metro to the last stop (Oriente—meaning east end of town) to join the riverside promenade and visit Europe's biggest aquarium.

Vasco da Gama Bridge—The second-longest bridge in Europe (14 km) was opened in 1998 to connect the Expo grounds with the south side of the Tagus and to alleviate the traffic jams on Lisbon's only other bridge over the river. As the 25th of April Bridge (see below) was modeled after the Golden Gate bridge in San Francisco (same company built it and was paid off by years of tolls), this new Vasco da Gama Bridge was designed with engineering help from the people building the new San Francisco Bay Bridge.

▲25th of April Bridge—At a mile long, this is one of the longest suspension bridges in the world. Built in 1966, it was originally named for the dictator Salazar but was renamed for the date of Portugal's 1974 revolution and freedom. For over 30 years locals could show their political colors by choosing what name to use. While conservatives called it the Salazar Bridge, liberals called it the 25th of April Bridge. Those who preferred to keep their politics private simply called it "the bridge over the river." Now, with the opening of the second bridge over the Tagus in 1998, everyone has to choose a name...and show their politics.

Cristo Rei—A huge statue of Christ (à la Rio de Janeiro)—with outstretched arms, symbolically blessing the city—overlooks Lisbon from across the Tagus River. It was built as a thanks to God, funded by Lisboetas grateful that Portugal stayed out of World War II. While it's designed to be seen from a distance, a lift takes visitors to the top for a great view (250$, daily 9:00–18:00). Catch the ferry from downtown Lisbon (6/hrly, from Praça do Comércio) to Cacilhas then take a bus marked "Cristo Rei" (4/hrly, from ferry dock). Because of bridge tolls, taxis to or from the site are expensive. For drivers, the most efficient visit is a quick stop on your way south to the Algarve.

Sights—Lisbon's Belém District

Three miles from downtown Lisbon, the Belém District is a sprawling pincushion of important sights from Portugal's Golden Age, when Vasco da Gama and company made it Europe's richest power. Belém was the send-off point for voyages from the Age of Discovery. Sailors would stay and pray here before embarking. The tower would welcome them home. For some reason, the grand buildings of Belém survived the great 1755 earthquake. Consequently, this is the only place to experience the grandeur of pre-earthquake Lisbon. Safety-conscious royalty lived here after the earthquake, and the modern-day president of Portugal has his house here today. To celebrate the 300th anniversary of independence from Spain, a grand exhibition was held here in 1940, resulting in the fine parks, fountains, and monument.

While the monastery is great, Belém's several museums are somewhere between good and mediocre, depending upon your interests. Belém's sights are closed on Monday, except for the Coach Museum, which closes on Tuesday instead.

Get to Belém by taxi (800$ from downtown), bus (#27, #28,

Belém

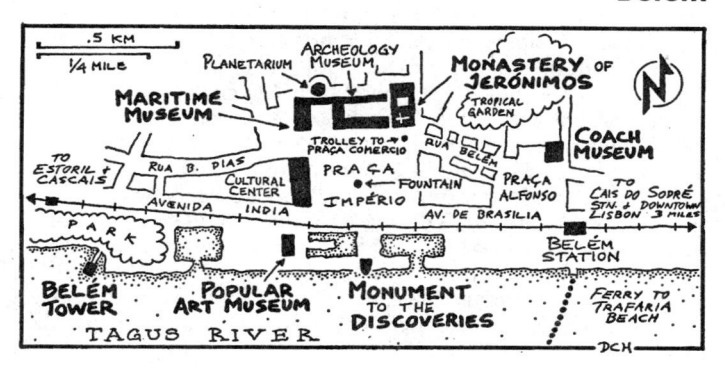

#29, #43, #49, and #51), or the sleek new tram #15 from Praça da Figueira (buy 160$ tickets from machine onboard, no change). The first stop is the Coach Museum; the second is the monastery. Consider doing Belém in this order: the Coach Museum, pastry and coffee break, Monastery of Jerónimos, (Maritime Museum if interested), Monument to the Discoveries, Belém Tower.

▲▲**Coach Museum (Museu dos Coches)**—In 1905 the Queen of Portugal decided to use the palace's riding-school building to preserve this fine collection of royal coaches. Claiming to be the most visited sight in Portugal, it is impressive, with more than 70 dazzling carriages (well described in English). The oldest is the crude and simple coach used by King (of Spain and Portugal) Philip II to shuttle between Madrid and Lisbon around 1600. Imagine how slow and rough the ride would be with bad roads and no suspension. Study the evolution of suspension and the highly symbolic ornamentation of the coaches. The newly restored "Ocean Coach" has figures symbolizing the Atlantic and Indian Oceans holding hands, in recognition of Portugal's mastery of the sea (450$, free Sun until 14:00, Wed–Mon 10:00–17:30, closed Tue, tel. 21-361-0850).

Rua de Belém leads from the coach museum and the monastery past the guarded entry to Portugal's presidential palace, some fine pre-earthquake buildings, and a famous pastry shop. This shop, **Casa Pasties de Belém** (Rua de Belém 88), is the birthplace of the wonderful cream tart called *pastel del Nata* throughout Portugal. In Lisbon they're called *pastel del Belém*. Since 1837 locals have come here to get them warm out of the oven. Sit down and order one with a *café com leite*. Sprinkle on the cinnamon and powdered sugar.

▲▲▲**Monastery of Jerónimos**—This is Portugal's most exciting building. King Manuel (who ruled from 1495) had this giant church and its cloisters built (starting in 1501) with "pepper money"—a 5 percent tax on spices brought back from India—as a thanks for the discoveries. Sailors would spend their last night here in prayer before embarking on their frightening voyages.

1. South portal: The ornate south portal, facing the street, is a great example of the Manueline style. Manueline—like Spain's Plateresque but with motifs from the sea—bridged Gothic and Renaissance. Henry the Navigator stands in the middle of the door with his patron saint, St. Jerome (with the lion), up in the tympanum. This door is used only used when Mass lets out.

2. Church interior: The interior is best viewed from the high altar in the middle. Look back down the nave to see how Manueline is a transition between Gothic and Renaissance. While in Gothic architecture huge columns break the interior into a nave with low-ceilinged ambulatories on either side, here the slender palm-tree-like columns don't break the interior space, and the ceiling is all one height. Find some of the Manueline motifs from the sea: the shells providing ceilings for the niches, the ropelike arches, the ships, coral, and seaweed. It is, after all, the sea that brought Portugal its 16th-century wealth and power and made this art possible.

3. Front of church: Now turn 180 degrees toward the front and see how the rest of the church is Renaissance. Everything but a cupola and the stained glass (replacement glass is from 1940) survived the earthquake. In the apse lions support two kings and two queens (King Manuel I is front left).

4. Tombs: The rear of the nave (near the entry) sports two memorial tombs. Closest to the street is the one for Portugal's much-loved poet, Camões (he's buried elsewhere). Vasco da Gama might be buried in the other. Check out its richly symbolic carving: The proud sailboat is a Portuguese caravel (a technological marvel in its day, with a sail that could pivot to catch the wind efficiently). The sphere is a common Manueline symbol. Some say the diagonal slash is symbolic of the unwritten pact and ambition of Spain and Portugal to split the world evenly. Even the ceiling—a Boy Scout handbook of rope and knots—comes with a whiff of the sea.

5. Cloisters: Leave the church (turn right, buy a ticket) and enter the cloisters. These cloisters, my favorite in all of Europe, are the architectural highlight of Belém. The lacy lower arcade is textbook Manueline; the simpler top floor is Renaissance. Study the carvings. The 12 doors lead to confessionals in the church. Traditionally girls put their right hand on the left paw of St. Jerome's lion (in the corner of the courtyard) and were married within six months. Upstairs you'll find better views and the bookshop (church free, 400$ for cloisters, Tue–Sun 10:00–17:00, closed Mon; women's WC upstairs, men's downstairs).

Maritime Museum (Museu de Marinha)—If you're interested in the ships and navigational tools of Portugal's Age of Discovery, this museum, which fills the east wing of the monastery, is worth a

Lisbon

look. Sailors love it (500$, Tue–Sun 10:00–18:00, closed Mon, Praça do Império).

▲**Monument to the Discoveries**—This giant riverside monument was built in 1960 to honor Prince Henry the Navigator on the 500th anniversary of his death. Huge statues of Henry, Magellan, Vasco da Gama, and other heroes of Portugal's Age of Discovery line the giant concrete prow of a caravel. Note the marble map chronicling Portugal's empire building (on the ground in front). Follow the years as Portuguese explorers gradually worked their way around Africa. In 1999 Portugal granted Macau its independence, leaving only the Azores and Madeira (whose original inhabitants were Portuguese) as Portuguese possessions. Inside the monument, a TV plays footage of the 1940 Expo, and you can ride a lift to a fine view (330$, Tue–Sun 9:30–18:30, closed Mon, tel. 21-362-0034).

▲**Belém Tower**—The only purely Manueline building in Portugal (built 1515–1520), this tower protected Lisbon's harbor and symbolizes the voyages that made Lisbon powerful. This was the last sight sailors saw as they left and the first when they returned with gold, spices, and social diseases. When the tower was built, the river went nearly to the walls of the monastery and the tower was midriver. Its interior is pretty bare, but the view from its top is fine (400$, Tue–Sun 10:00–17:00, closed Mon, tel. 21-362-0034). The floatplane on a pedestal is a monument to the first flight across the South Atlantic (Portugal to Brazil), in 1922. The original is across the street in the Maritime Museum.

Popular Art Museum (Museu de Arte Popular)—This museum takes you through Portugal's folk art one province at a time, providing a sneak preview of what you'll see throughout the country (300$, Tue–Sun 10:00–12:30, 14:00–17:00, closed Mon, between the monument and the tower on Avenida Brasilia).

Shopping

Flea Market—On Tuesday and Saturday, the Feira da Ladra flea market hops in the Alfama on Campo de Santa Clara.

Colombo Shopping Mall—While Lisbon offers decaying but still elegant department stores, a teeming flea market, and classy specialty shops, nothing is as impressive as the enormous Centro Colombo, the largest shopping center in Spain and Portugal. More than 400 shops, 10 cinemas, 60 restaurants, and a health club sit atop Europe's biggest underground car park and under a vast and entertaining play center (daily until midnight, pick up a map at the info desk, Metro: Colegio Militar takes you right there, tel. 21-711-3636).

Nightlife

Nightlife in the Baixa seems to be little more than loitering prostitutes and litter stirred by the wind. But head up into the Baírro Alto

and you'll find plenty of action. The Jardím do São Pedro is normally festive and the Rua Diario de Noticias is lined with busy bars.
▲**Fado**—Fado is the folk music of Lisbon's back streets. Since the mid-1800s it's been the Lisbon blues—mournfully beautiful, haunting ballads about lost sailors, broken hearts, and sad romance. To the lilting accompaniment of the Portuguese *guitarra* (like a 12-string mandolin), the singer longs for what's been lost.

These days, the fado songs come with a new casualty—a tourist's budget. Fado has become one of Lisbon's favorite late-night tourist traps, but it can still be a great experience. The Alfama has a few famous touristy fado bars, but the Baírro Alto is better (and safer late at night). Wander around Rua Diario de Noticias and neighboring streets either for a late dinner (after 22:00) or later for just drinks and music. Homemade "fado tonight" signs in Portuguese are good news, but even a restaurant filled with tourists can come with good food and fine fado. Prices for a fado performance vary greatly. Many have a steep cover charge, while others have a minimum purchase. Any place a hotel sends you to has a bloated price for the kickback.

Canto do Camões is my favorite, run by friendly Gabriel (2,000$ minimum, 3,900$ menu, Travessa da Espera 38, call ahead to reserve—ask for Mr. Rick's table, tel. 21-346-5464, e-mail: cantodocamoes@ip.pt). The meal is punctuated with sets of three fado songs with different singers. For a snack, a good vintage Porto goes nicely with a plate of *queso de cera* (sheep cheese) and pancetta (salt-cured ham). Relax, spend some time, make eye contact with the singer. Let the music and wine work together.

▲▲▲**Portuguese Bullfight**—If you always felt sorry for the bull, this is Toro's Revenge—in a Portuguese bullfight, the matador is brutalized along with the bull. After an exciting equestrian prelude in which the horseman (*cavaleiro*) skillfully plants barbs in the bull's back while trying to avoid the padded horns, a colorfully clad eight-man team (suicide squad called a *forcado*) enters the ring and lines up single file facing the bull. The leader prompts the bull to charge and then braces himself for a collision that can be heard all the way up in the cheap seats. As he hangs onto the bull's head, his buddies then pile on, trying to wrestle the bull to a standstill. Finally, one guy hangs on to el toro's tail and "water-skis" behind him. Unlike at the Spanish *corrida*, the bull is not killed in front of the crowd at the Portuguese *tourada* (but it is killed later).

You'll most likely see a bullfight in Lisbon or Estoril or on the Algarve (Easter–Oct, flyers at TI). In Lisbon's Campo Pequeno, fights are on Thursday at 22:00 mid-June through September. Tickets cost 1,000$ to 10,000$. The ring is small. There are no bad seats. To sit nearly at ringside, try the cheapest *bancada* seats, on the generally half-empty and unmonitored main floor.

Note: Half the fights are simply Spanish-type *corridas* without

Lisbon

the killing. For the real slam-bam Portuguese-style fight, confirm that there will be *grupo de forcados*. Tickets are nearly always available at the door (no surcharge, tel. 21-793-2143 to confirm). For an 11 percent surcharge you can buy them at the green ABEP kiosk above Lisbon's central TI (bottom of Praça dos Restauradores).

▲**People's Fair (Feira Popular)**—Consider spending a lowbrow evening at Lisbon's Feira Popular, which bustles on weekends with Portuguese families at play. Pay the entry fee then enjoy rides, munchies, people watching, and music—basic Portuguese fun. Have dinner among the chattering families, with endless food and wine paraded frantically in every direction. Fried ducks drip, barbecues spit, and dogs squirt the legs of chairs while, somehow, local lovers ignore everything but each other's eyes. (300$, nightly 19:00–24:00 May–Sept, on Avenida da República at Metro: Entre-Campos.)

Movies—Lisbon reels with theaters, and, unlike in Spain, most films are in the original language with subtitles. Many of Lisbon's theaters are classy, complete with assigned seats and ushers, and the normally cheap tickets go for half price on Monday. Check the cinema listings in the monthly magazine *Lisboaem* (free at TI).

Sleeping in Lisbon
(190$ = about $1)
Sleep Code: **S** = Single, **D** = Double/Twin, **T** = Triple, **Q** = Quad, **b** = bathroom, **t** = toilet only, **s** = shower only, **CC** = Credit Card (Visa, MasterCard, Amex), **SE** = Speaks English, **NSE** = No English. Breakfast is usually included.

With the exception of a few splurges, rooms downtown feel like Lisbon does downtown: tired and well worn. To sleep in a well-located place with local character, you'll be climbing dark stairways into a world of cracked plaster, taped handwritten signs, dingy carpets, cramped and confusing floor plans, and ramshackle plumbing. If you're on a tight budget, arrive without a reservation and bargain. While old Lisbon seems a little sleazy at night, with normal discretion my listings are safe.

Singles cost nearly the same as doubles. As in France, bathtubs and twin beds can cost more than showers and double beds. Addresses like 26-3 stand for street #26, third floor (which is fourth floor in American terms). Never judge a place by its entryway.

Sleeping Downtown in Baixa
(zip code: 1100)
Central as can be, this area bustles with lots of shops, traffic, people, buskers, pedestrian areas, and urban intensity.

Near Praça da Figueira: The **Lisboa Tejo**, tastefully refurbished, has 58 comfortable rooms and an attentive and welcoming staff (Sb-14,000–16,000$, Db-16,000–18,000$, prices vary according to room size, includes huge buffet breakfast, 8 percent discount with this book, air-con, CC:VMA, Poço do Borratém 4, from southeast corner of Praça da Figueira, walk 1 block down Rua Dos Condes de Monsanto and turn left, tel. 21-886-6182, fax 21-886-5163, SE). Manolo Carrera is justifiably proud of his historic fountain and wine shop.

On Rua da Assunção: The **Albergaria Residencial Insulana**, on a pedestrian street, is very professional, with 32 quiet and comfortable—if a bit smoky—rooms (Sb-9,000$, Db-10,000$, Tb-14,000$, includes continental breakfast, CC:VMA, elevator, air-con, Rua da Assunção 52, tel. & fax 21-342-3131, SE).

Pensão Aljubarrota is a fine value if you can handle the long climb up four floors, claustrophobic hallways, and the black-vinyl flooring. Once you're on top it's a happy world of small rustically furnished rooms with cute take-my-photo balconies from which to survey the Rua Augusta scene (S-3,500–4,500$, D-5,800–7,000$, Ds-7,000–8,500$, T-8,100–10,800$, 10 percent discount with cash and this book, includes breakfast, all but singles have balconies, CC:VM, priority given for stays of 2 or more nights, Rua da Assunção 53-4, tel. & fax 21-346-0112, Italian Pino and lovely Rita SE).

On or near Rossio Square: The **Hotel Metropole**, right on Rossio Square, offers 1920s-style elegance and 36 big, beautiful rooms, some of which overlook the square (Sb-16,900–21,100$, Db-18,800–23,200$, extra bed-5,000$, includes breakfast, CC:VMA, air-con, elevator, double-paned windows, spacious bathrooms, Rossio 30, tel. 21-346-9164, fax 21-346-9166, SE).

Pensão Residencial Gerês, a good budget bet downtown, has bright, basic, cozy rooms with older plumbing. Recently remodeled, it lacks the dingy smokiness that pervades Lisbon's cheaper hotels (S-6,500$, Sb-8,000$, D-8,000$, Db-10,000$, T-9,500$, Tb-12,000$, Qb-14,000$, 10 percent discount for cash with this book, CC:VMA, Calçada do Garcia 6, uphill a block off the northeast corner of Rossio, tel. 21-881-0497, fax 21-888-2006, Nogueira family speaks some English).

Near Praça dos Restauradores: The **Hotel Suisso Atlantico** is formal, hotelish, and stuffy, but it's a functional hotel with a practical location (Sb-7,900$, Db-10,000$, Tb-11,800$, includes breakfast, CC:VMA, no fans or air-con, Rua da Gloria 3-19, 1250 Lisbon, behind funicular station, on a quiet street near a peep show 1 block off Praça dos Restauradores, tel. 21-346-1713, fax 21-346-9013, SE).

Residencial Florescente rents 72 rooms on a thriving pedestrian street a block off Praça dos Restauradores. It's a slumber mill, but rooms are clean, and some are nearly charming (S-4,000$, Ss-5,000$, Sb-7,000$, D-5,000$, Ds-6,000$, Db-8,000$, no breakfast, most Db with air-con, CC:VMA, Rua Portas S. Antão 99, 1150 Lisbon, tel. 21-346-3517, fax 21-342-7733, SE).

Sleeping Uptown along Avenida da Liberdade

These listings are a 10-minute walk or short Metro ride from the center.

Pensão Residencial 13 da Sorte, a simple but cheery place, has full bathrooms in each of its 22 rooms and bright tiles throughout (Sb-6,500$, Db-8,000$, Tb-9,500$, no breakfast, CC:VM, elevator, just off Avenida da Liberdade near the Spanish Embassy at Rua do Salitre 13, 1250 Lisbon, 50 meters from Metro: Avenida, tel. 21-353-9746, fax 21-353-1851, Alexandra SE).

Hotel Lisboa Plaza, a four-star gem, is by far my classiest Lisbon recommendation. It's a spacious and plush mix of traditional style with bright-pastel modern elegance, and offers a warm welcome without the stuffiness you'd expect in this price range (Db-30,000–34,000$, CC:VMA, air-con, well located on a quiet street off busy Avenida da Liberdade, a block from Metro: Avenida at Travessa do Salitre 7, 1250 Lisbon, tel. 21-346-3922, fax 21-347-1630, e-mail: plaza.hotels@mail.telepac.pt).

Sleeping in Baírro Alto
(zip code: 1200)

Just west of downtown, this area is a bit seedy but full of ambience, good bars, local fado clubs, music, and markets. The area may not feel comfortable for women alone at night, but the hotels themselves are safe.

Residencial Nova Silva, a quiet, ramshackle place on the crest of the Baírro Alto, overlooks the river. The borderline dumpy rooms with grand little balconies give you bird noises rather than traffic noises (priority for longer stays). It's three blocks from the heart of Chiado on the #28 tram line and has the easiest street parking (12 hrs/1,200$) of my listings (S-4,500$, Ss-5,000$, Sb-6,000$, D-5,000$, Ds-5,500$, Db-6,000–6,500$, T-7,500$, Ts-7,000$, Tb-8,500$, breakfast-400$, no elevator, lots of stairs, Rua Victor Cordón 11, tel. & fax 21-342-4371, Fatima SE).

Residencial Camões lies right in the seedy thick of the Baírro Alto but offers sleepable rooms. Street-side rooms have balconies and noise (S-3,500$, D-7,000$, Db-8,500$, includes breakfast, Travessa Poco da Cidade 38, 1 block south of São Roque Church and to the west, tel. 21-346-7510, fax 21-346-4048, some English spoken).

Sleeping away from the Center

Hotel Ibis Lisboa-Centro is big, concrete, modern, and practical in a soulless area far from the center but near a Metro station. It offers plain, modern comforts and no stress for a good price (Db-9,100$, without breakfast, CC:VMA, air-con, next to Novotel and Metro: Palhava, Avenida Jose Malhoa, tel. 21-727-3181, fax 21-727-3287, SE). Forgive me.

Eating in Lisbon

Eating in the Alfama

This gritty chunk of pre-earthquake Lisbon is full of interesting eateries, especially along Rua San Pedro and on Largo de São Miguel. Eat fast, cheap, and healthy at **Comidas de Santiago**, a little salad bar with great gazpacho (choose 2 salads on a small plate for 530$ or 4 on a big plate for 860$, open from 11:00, 1 block uphill from Santa Luzia viewpoint terrace, Largo do Contador Mor 21, tel. 21-887-5805).

For a seafood feast, consider dining high in the Alfama at the **Farol de Santa Luzia** restaurant (2,600$ fixed-price *menu turistico*, closed Sun, Largo Santa Luzia 5, across from Santa Luzia viewpoint terrace, no sign but many window decals, tel. 21-886-3884).

For cheap and colorful dinners, walk past Portas do Sol and follow the trolley tracks along Rua da São Tome to a square called Largo Rodrigues Freitas, where **Nossa Churrasqueira** is busy feeding chicken to finger-lickin' locals on rickety tables and meager budgets (closed Mon).

Arco Do Castello, an Indo-Portuguese restaurant, dishes up delicious fish and shrimp curries from Goa, a former Portuguese colony in India. A complete meal for two costs around 5,000$. Top it off with a shot of the Goan firewater, *feni*, made from cashews (located just across from ramp leading into the castle, tel. 21-887-6598).

While in the Alfama, brighten a few dark bars. Have an aperitif, taste the *branco seco* (local dry white wine). Make a friend, pet a chicken, read the graffiti, and pick at the humanity ground between the cobbles.

Eating in Baírro Alto

Lisbon's "high town" is full of small, fun, and cheap places. Fishermen's bars abound. Just off São Roque's Square you'll find two fine eateries: the very simple and cheap **Casa Trans-Montana** (closed Sun, down the steps of Calcada do Duque at #43) and the bright and touristy **Cervejaría da Trindade**, a Portuguese-style beer hall covered with historic tiles and full of seafood (3,000$ meals, good *bacalhau*—cod, daily 12:00–24:00, CC:VMA, 1 block down from São Roque at Rua Nova da Trindade 20C, tel. 21-342-3506). You'll find many less-touched restaurants deeper into the Baírro Alto on the other (west) side of Rua Misericordia.

Eating in Rossio and Beyond

In Rossio: For cod and vegetables prepared faster than a Big Mac and served with more energy than a soccer team, stand or sit at **Restaurant Beira-Gare** (a greasy spoon in front of Rossio train station at the end of Rua 1 de Dezembro, Mon–Sat 6:00–24:00, closed Sun). To get a house-special pork sandwich, ask for a *bifane no pão*. Farther down the same street is **Celeiro**, a handy and bigger-than-it-looks supermarket (Mon–Fri 8:30–20:00, Sat 9:00–18:00, closed Sun, Rua 1 de Dezembro 67-83). Across the street at #65 (same hours), Celeiro runs a **health-food store** with a bleak but healthy cafeteria in its basement. The Rossio's Rua dos Correeiros is lined with competitive local cafés.

The "eating lane" is a galaxy of eateries with small zoos hanging from their windows for you to choose from (opposite Rossio station, just off Praça dos Restauradores down Rua do Jardím do Regedor and Rua das Portas de St. Antão). The seafood is among Lisbon's best. **Restaurant da Casa do Alentejo**, part of a cultural and social center for people from the traditional southern province of Portugal living in Lisbon, fills an old ballroom and specializes in dry and salty meat and potatoes—Alentejo cuisine (3-course 2,500$ menu, open from 19:30, Rua das Portas de St. Antao 58).

On Praça da Figueria: Casas Suissa is a bright, modern, air-conditioned place popular with locals because it's classy but affordable (cheap at the bar, reasonable at tables, good salads and fruit cups, 7:00–22:00, entries on both Praça da Figueria and Rossio squares). For a gritty snack, stand with the locals at **Pastelaria Tentacão** and munch a *prato do dia* (daily specials, all under 1,000$, daily 7:00–22:00, east side of Praça Figueria). The house specialty to try—or avoid—is *leitão*, a suckling pig sandwich. Pick up the tally sheet as you enter, eat what you like, and turn it in to pay up as you leave. A few doors down, **Mercado da Figueira** is a great grocery.

Drinks

Ginjinha (zheen-ZHEEN-yah) is the diminutive name for a favorite Lisbon drink. *Ginjinha* is a sweet liquor made from the sour cherry-like *ginja* berry, sugar, and schnapps. It's sold for 150$ a shot in funky old hole-in-the-wall shops throughout town. The only choices are with or without berries (*com* or *sem fruta*) and *gelada* (if you want it from a chilled bottle out of the fridge—very nice). In Portugal, when someone is impressed by the taste of something, they say, "*Sabe melhor que nem ginjas*" ("It tastes even better than *ginja*").

Transportation Connections—Lisbon

Remember to reserve ahead if your train requires a reservation.

By train to: Madrid (1/day, overnight 21:56–8:35), **Paris** (1/day, 17:56–15:00, 21 hrs), **Lagos** (5/day, 3.5 hrs, overnight possible, likely transfer in Tunes). Train info tel. 21-888-4025.

COPENHAGEN

Copenhagen (København) is Scandinavia's largest city. With over a million people, it's home to more than a quarter of all Danes. A busy day cruising the canals, wandering through the palace, taking a historic walking tour, and strolling the Strøget (Europe's greatest pedestrian shopping mall) will get you oriented, and you'll feel right at home. Copenhagen is Scandinavia's cheapest and most fun-loving capital, so live it up.

Planning Your Time
A first visit deserves two days.
Day 1: If staying in Christianshavn, start the day browsing through the neighborhood, called Copenhagen's "Little Amsterdam." Catch the 10:30 city walking tour. After a Riz-Raz lunch, visit the Use It information center and catch the relaxing canal boat tour out to *The Little Mermaid*. Spend the rest of the afternoon tracing Denmark's cultural roots in the National Museum and/or touring the Ny Carlsberg Glyptotek art gallery; spend the evening strolling or biking Strøget (follow "Heart and Soul" walk described below) or Christianshavn.
Day 2: At 10:00 explore the subterranean Christiansborg Castle ruins under today's palace. At 11:00 take the 50-minute guided tour of Denmark's royal Christiansborg Palace. The afternoon is free, with many options, including a *smørrebrød* lunch, tour of the Rosenborg Castle/crown jewels, brewery tour, or Nazi Resistance museum (free tour often at 14:00). Evening at Tivoli Gardens before catching a night train out.

With a third day, side trip out to Roskilde and Frederiksborg. Remember the efficiency of sleeping in and out by train. Most flights from the States arrive in the morning. After you arrive, head for Stockholm and Oslo (both are connected to Copenhagen by overnight trains). Kamikaze sightseers see Copenhagen as a Scandinavian bottleneck. They sleep in and out heading north and in and out heading south, with two days and no nights in Copenhagen. Considering the joy of Oslo and Stockholm, this isn't that crazy if you have limited time. You can check your bag at the station and take a 10-kr shower in the Interail Center.

You can set yourself up in my best rooms for your entire Scandinavian tour with a quick trip to a pay phone. This is probably a wise thing to do.

Orientation

Nearly all of your sightseeing is in Copenhagen's compact old town. By doing things by bike or on foot you'll stumble into some surprisingly cozy corners, charming bits of Copenhagen that many miss. Study the map. The medieval walls are now roads that define the center: Vestervoldgade (literally, "western wall street"), Nørrevoldgade, and Østervoldgade. The fourth side is the harbor and the island of Slotsholmen where København ("merchants' harbor") was born in 1167. The next of the city's islands is Amager, where you'll find the local "Little Amsterdam" district of Christianshavn. What was Copenhagen's moat is now a string of pleasant lakes and parks, including Tivoli Gardens. To the north is the old "new town," where the Amalienborg Palace is surrounded by streets on a grid plan, and *The Little Mermaid* poses relentlessly, waiting for her sailor to return and the tourists to leave.

The core of the town, as far as most visitors are concerned, is the axis formed by the train station, Tivoli Gardens, the Rådhus (city hall) square, and the Strøget pedestrian street. It's a great walking town, bubbling with street life and colorful pedestrian zones. But be sure to get off the Strøget.

The character in Copenhagen's history who matters most is Christian IV, who ruled from 1588 to 1648. He was Denmark's Renaissance king, the royal Danish party animal whose personal energy kindled a golden age when Copenhagen prospered and many of the city's grandest buildings were built. Locals love to tell great stories of everyone's favorite king.

Tourist Information

The tourist office is now run by a for-profit consortium called "Wonderful Copenhagen." This colors the advice and information it provides. Still, it's worth a quick stop for the top-notch freebies it provides, such as a city map and *Copenhagen This Week* (a free, handy, and misnamed monthly guide to the city, worth reading for its good maps, museum hours with telephone numbers, sightseeing tour ideas, shopping suggestions, and calendar of events, including free English tours and concerts). The TI is across from the train station, near the corner of Vesterbrogade and Bernstorffsgade, next to the Tivoli entrance (daily May–Aug 9:00–20:00, Sept–Apr Mon–Fri 9:00–16:30, Sat 9:00–13:30, closed Sun, tel. 33 11 13 25, www.ctw.dk, www.dt.dk). Corporate dictates prohibit the TI from freely offering other brochures (such as walking-tour schedules and brochures on any sights of special interest), but ask and you shall receive. The TI's room-finding service charges you and the hotel a fee and cannot give hard opinions. Do not use it. Get on the phone and call direct—everyone speaks English.

Use It is a better information service, though it's a 10-minute walk from the train station. This "branch" of Huset, a hip, city government–sponsored, student-run cluster of cafés, theaters, and galleries, caters to Copenhagen's young but welcomes travelers of any age. It's a friendly, driven-to-help, energetic, no-nonsense source of budget travel information, offering a free budget room-finding service, free Internet access (slow with long lines), a back-packer's breakfast for 25 kr, a jazz bar, a ride-finding board, a pen-pals-wanted scrapbook, free condoms, and free luggage lockers. Their free *Playtime* publication is full of Back Door–style travel articles on Copenhagen and the Danish culture, special budget tips, and events. They have brochures on just about everything, including self-guided tours for bikers, walkers, and those riding scenic bus #6. They have a list of private rooms (225–300-kr doubles without breakfast). To get to Use It from the station, head down Strøget then turn right on Rådhustræde for three blocks to #13 (daily mid-Jun–mid-Sept 9:00–19:00; otherwise Mon–Wed 10:00–15:00, Thu 10:00–18:00, Fri 10:00–14:00, closed Sat–Sun; tel. 33 15 65 18, fax 33 15 75 18). After hours, their computer touch screen lists the cheapest rooms available in town.

The **Copenhagen Card** covers the public transportation system and admissions to nearly all the sights in greater Copenhagen, (Helsingør to Roskilde). It includes virtually all the city sights, Tivoli, and the bus from the airport. It's available at any TI (including the airport's) and the train stations: 24 hours, 155 kr; 48 hours, 255 kr; 72 hours, 320 kr (www.woco.dk). It's hard to break even, unless you're planning to side trip on the included (and otherwise expensive) rail service. It comes with a book explaining the 60 included sights, such as Christiansborg Palace (normally 40 kr), Christiansborg Castle ruins (20 kr), National Museum (40 kr, free Wed), Ny Carlsberg Glyptotek (30 kr, free Wed and Sat), Rosenborg Castle (45 kr), Tivoli (45 kr), Frederiksborg Castle (45 kr), and Roskilde Viking Ships (50 kr). It also includes round-trip train rides to Roskilde (70 kr) and Frederiksborg Castle (70 kr).

Arrival in Copenhagen

By Train: The main train station is called Hovedbanegården (HOETH-ban-gorn; learn that word—you'll need to recognize it).

It's a temple of travel and a hive of travel-related activity, offering lockers (25–35 kr/day), a garderobe (40 kr/day per rucksack), a post office, a grocery store (daily 8:00–24:00), 24-hour thievery, and bike rentals. The Interail Center, a service the station provides for mostly young travelers (but anyone with a Eurailpass, Scanrail, student BIGE or Transalpino ticket, or Interail pass is welcome), is a pleasant lounge with 10-kr showers, free (if risky) luggage storage, city maps, snacks, information, and other young travelers (Jun–mid-Sept 6:30–22:00). If you just need the map and *Playtime*, a visit here is quicker than going to the TI.

Most travelers arrive in Copenhagen after an overnight train ride. Look for an ATM when you get off the train. If you need to change traveler's checks, the station has two exchange desks. Den Danske Bank is fair, charging the standard 40-kr-minimum or 20-kr-per-check fee for traveler's checks (daily 8:00–20:00). FOREX, which has a worse rate but charges only 10 kr per traveler's check with no minimum, is better for small exchanges (daily 8:00–21:00). On a $100 exchange, I saved 23 kr at FOREX. (The American Express office—a 20-minute walk away, off Strøget—may be even better; see "Helpful Hints," below.) While you're in the station, reserve your overnight train seat or *couchette* out (at Rejse-bureau). International rides and all IC trains require reservations (usually 20 kr). Bus #8 (in front of the station on the station side of Bernstorffsgade) goes to Christianshavn B&Bs. Note the time the bus departs, then stop by the TI (across the street on the left) and pick up a free city map that shows bus routes.

By Plane: Copenhagen's International Airport is a traveler's dream, with a tourist office, bank (standard rates), post office, telephone center, shopping mall, grocery store, and bakery. You can use U.S. dollars at the airport and get change back in kroner. (Phone service for all airline offices is split between two switchboards: SAS services, tel. 32 32 31 25; and Copenhagen Air Service, tel. 32 47 47 47. SAS ticket hotline, tel. 32 32 68 00.) Need to kill a night at the airport? Try the fetal rest cabins, called *hvilekabiner* (Sb-325 kr, Db-480 kr for 8 hours, prices vary for 4- to 16-hour periods, reception open 6:00–22:00, easy telephone reservations, CC:VMA, sauna and showers also available, tel. 32 31 32 31, fax 32 31 31 09).

Getting Downtown from the Airport: Taxis are fast and easy, accept credit cards, and, at about 150 kr to the town center, are a good deal for foursomes. Both the new Air Rail train (17 kr, 3/hrly, 10 min) and new metro services (17 kr, 3/hrly, 12 min) link the airport with the train station. City bus #250s gets you downtown (City Hall Square, TI) in 30 minutes for 17 kr (12/hrly, across the street and to the right as you exit the airport). If you're going from the airport to Christianshavn, ride #9 just past Christianshavn Torv to the last stop before Knippels Bridge.

Helpful Hints

Ferries: Book any ferries you plan to use in Scandinavia now. Any travel agent can book the boat rides you plan to take later on your trip, such as the Denmark–Norway ferry (ask for special discounts on this crossing) or the Stockholm–Helsinki–Stockholm cruise; Silja Line's office is at Nyhavn 43a (Mon–Thu 9:00–16:30, Fri 9:00–16:00, tel. 33 14 40 80). Drivers heading to Sweden by ferry before July 2000 should call for a reservation (two competing lines: 33 15 15 15 and 49 26 01 55); reservations are free and easy and assure that you won't be stuck in a long line. As of July 2000, the new Øresund bridge opens, linking Denmark and Sweden (toll-210 kr), making the ferry obsolete.

Jazz Festival: The Copenhagen Jazz Festival—10 days starting the first Friday in July (Jul 7–16 in 2000)—puts the town in a rollicking slide-trombone mood. The Danes are Europe's jazz enthusiasts and, more than most music festivals, this one fills the town with happiness. The TI prints up an extensive listing of each year's festival events (as well as a listing of other festivals).

Telephones: Use the telephone liberally. Everyone speaks English, and *This Week* and this book list phone numbers for everything you'll be doing. All telephone numbers in Denmark are eight digits, and there are no area codes. Calls anywhere in Denmark are cheap; calls to Norway and Sweden cost 6 kr per minute from a booth (half that from a private home). Coin-op booths are often broken. Get a phone card (from newsstands, starting at 20 kr).

American Express: Amex recently moved to Nyman & Schultz (Mon–Fri 9:00–17:00, Sat 9:00–12:00, May–Aug till 14:00 on Sat, Nørregade 7a, 3rd floor, tel. 33 12 23 01).

Pharmacy: Steno Apotek is across from the train station (open 24 hours daily, on Vesterbrogade).

Getting around Copenhagen

By Bus and Subway: Take advantage of the fine bus (tel. 36 45 45 45) and subway system called S-tog (Eurail valid on S-tog, tel. 33 14 17 01). A joint fare system covers greater Copenhagen. You pay 11 kr as you board for an hour's travel within two zones, or buy a blue two-zone *klippekort* from the driver (75 kr for 10 one-hour "rides"). A 24-hour pass costs 70 kr. Don't worry much about "zones." Assume you'll be within the middle two zones. Board at the front, tell the driver where you're going, and he'll sell you the appropriate ticket. Drivers are patient, have change, and speak English. City maps list bus and subway routes. Locals are friendly and helpful. Copenhagen is a bit torn up as it puts together a slick new subway system to celebrate the year 2000.

By Bus Tour: "The Official Copenhagen Sightseeing Tour" runs continuously in a one-hour hop-on hop-off loop each day from 9:00 to 18:00. The trip connects all the major sights: Tivoli,

Royal Palace, National Museum, *The Little Mermaid*, Rosenborg Castle, Nyhavn, and more. Catch the bus on the left side of city hall behind the *Lur Blowers* statue, or at many other stops throughout the city (100 kr for 1-day pass, free for kids under 12, tel. 38 28 01 88).

Budget do-it-yourselfers simply ride city bus #6: from the Carlsberg Brewery, it stops at Tivoli, city hall, National Museum, Royal Palace, Nyhavn, Amalienborg Castle, Kastellet, and *The Little Mermaid* (11 kr for 1 stop-and-go hour). The entire tour is described in a free Use It brochure.

By Taxi: Taxis are plentiful and easy to call or flag down (22-kr drop charge, then 9 kr per km). For a short ride, four people can travel cheaper by taxi than by bus (e.g., 50 kr from train station to Christianshavn B&Bs). Taxis accept all major credit cards. Calling 35 35 35 35 will get you a taxi within minutes.

Free Bikes! Copenhagen's radical "city bike" program is great for sightseers (though bikes can be hard to find at times). Two thousand clunky but practical little bikes are scattered around the old-town center (basically the terrain covered in the Copenhagen map in this chapter). Simply locate one of the 150 racks, unlock a bike by popping a 20-kr coin into the handlebar, and pedal away. When you're done, park the bike at any other rack, pop in the lock, and you get your deposit coin back (if you can't find a rack, leave the bike on the street anywhere and a bum will take it back and pocket your coin). These simple bikes come with "theft-proof" parts (unusable on regular bikes) and—they claim—computer tracer chips embedded in them so bike patrols can retrieve strays. These are constructed with prison labor and funded by advertisements painted on the wheels and by a progressive electorate. Try this once and you'll find Copenhagen suddenly a lot smaller and easier.

For a serious bike tour, rent a more comfortable bike at Central Station's Cykelcenter (50 kr/day, Mon–Fri 8:00–18:00, Sat 9:00–13:00, summer Sun 10:00–13:00, closed Sun off-season, tel. 33 33 86 13). In the summer, City Safari offers guided bike tours (prices and routes vary, depart from train station Mon–Fri at 16:00, tel. 33 23 94 90, www.citysafari.dk, or ask at Use It).

Do-It-Yourself Orientation Walk: "Strøget and Copenhagen's Heart and Soul"

Start from **Rådhuspladsen** (City Hall Square), the bustling heart of Copenhagen, dominated by the city hall spire. This used to be the fortified west end of town. The king cleverly quelled a French Revolution–type thirst for democracy by giving his people Europe's first great public amusement park. **Tivoli** was built just outside the city walls in 1843. When the train lines came, the station was placed just beyond Tivoli. The **golden girls** high up on the building on the square opposite the Strøget's entrance tell the weather: on a bike

Copenhagen

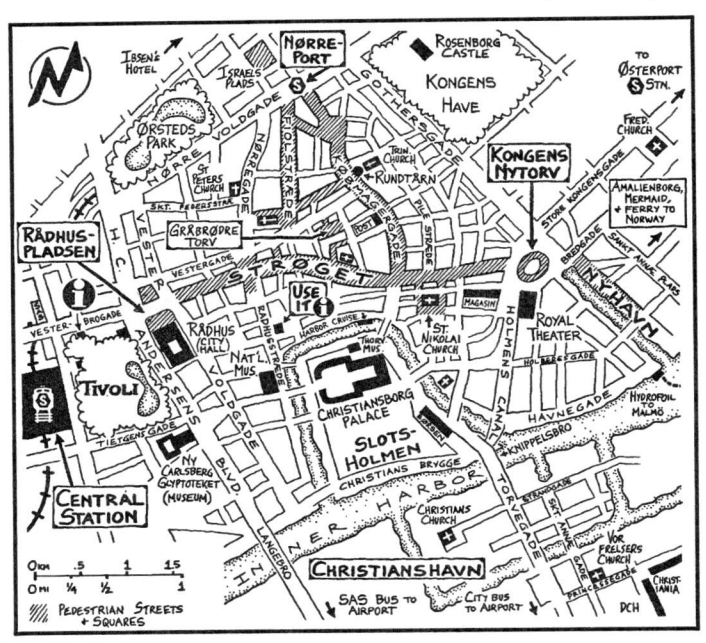

(fair) or with an umbrella. These two have been called the only women in Copenhagen you can trust. Here in the traffic hub of this huge city you'll notice...not many cars. Denmark's 200 percent tax on car purchases makes the bus or bike a sweeter option.

Old Hans Christian Andersen sits to the right of the city hall, almost begging to be in another photo (as he did in real life). On a pedestal left of the city hall, note the *Lur Blowers* sculpture. The *lur* is a horn that was used 3,500 years ago. The ancient originals (which still play) are displayed in the National Museum.

The American trio of Burger King, 7-Eleven, and McDonald's marks the start of the otherwise charming **Strøget**. Copenhagen's 25-year-old experimental, tremendously successful, and most-copied pedestrian shopping mall is a string of lively (and individually named) streets and lovely squares that bunny-hop through the old town from the city hall to Nyhavn, which is a 15-minute stroll (or "*strøget*") away.

As you wander down this street, remember that the commercial focus of a historic street like Strøget drives up the land value, which generally tears down the old buildings. While Strøget has become quite hamburgerized, charm lurks in adjacent areas and many historic bits and pieces of old Copenhagen are just off this commercial cancan.

After one block you can side trip two blocks left up Larsbjørnsstræde into Copenhagen's colorful **university district**. Formerly the old brothel area, today this is Soho chic.

Back on Strøget, the first segment, Frederiksberggade, ends at **Gammel Torv and Nytorv** (Old Square and New Square). This was the old town center. The Oriental-looking kiosk was one of the city's first community telephone centers before phones were privately owned. The squirting woman and boy on the very old fountain was so offensive to people from the Victorian age that the pedestal was added, raising it—they hoped—out of view. The brick church at the start of Amager Torv is the oldest building you'll see here.

Side trip two blocks north of Amager Torv to the leafy and caffeine-stained **Gråbrødretorv** (Grey Brothers' Square). At the next big intersection, Købmagergade—an equally lively but less-touristy pedestrian street—is worth exploring.

The final stretch of Strøget leads past **Pistolstræde** (a cute street of shops in restored 18th-century buildings leading off Strøget to the right from Østergade), McDonald's (good view from top floor), and major department stores (Illum and Magasin—see "Shopping," below) to a big square called Kongens Nytorv, where you'll find the Royal Theater.

Nyhavn, a recently gentrified sailors' quarter, is just opposite Kongens Nytorv. This formerly sleazy harbor is an interesting mix of tattoo parlors, taverns, and trendy (mostly expensive) cafés lining a canal filled with glamorous old sailboats of all sizes. Any historic sloop is welcome to moor here in Copenhagen's ever-changing boat museum. Hans Christian Andersen lived and wrote his first stories here.

Continuing north along the harborside (from end of Nyhavn canal, turn left), you'll pass a huge ship that sails to Oslo every evening (for information, see "Transportation Connections," near end of chapter). Follow the water to the modern fountain of Amaliehave Park.

The **Amalienborg Palace and Square** (a block inland, behind the fountain) is a good example of orderly Baroque planning. Queen Margrethe II and her family live in the palace to your immediate left as you enter the square from the harbor side. Her son and heir to the throne, Frederik, recently moved into the palace directly opposite his mother's. While the guards change with royal fanfare at noon only when the queen is in residence, they shower every morning.

Leave the square on Amaliegade, heading north to Kastellet (Citadel) Park and a small museum about Denmark's World War II resistance efforts. A short stroll past the Gefion fountain (showing the mythological story of the goddess who was given one night to carve a chunk out of Sweden to make into Denmark's main island, Zealand—which you're on) and a church built of flint brings you to the overrated, overfondled, and overphotographed symbol of Copenhagen, *Den Lille Havfrue*—**The Little Mermaid**.

You can get back downtown on foot, by taxi, or on bus #1, #6, or #9 from Store Kongensgade on the other side of Kastellet Park (a special bus may run from the mermaid in summer).

Tours of Copenhagen

▲**Walking Tours**—Once upon a time, American Richard Karpen visited Copenhagen and fell in love with the city (and one of its women). He gives daily two-hour walking tours of his adopted hometown covering its people, history, and contemporary scene. He offers four entertaining tours: three city walks—each about 1.5 miles with breaks, covering different parts of the city center—and a Rosenborg Castle tour (city tours leave TI daily at 10:30 Mon–Sat May–Sept, 50 kr, kids under 12 free; Rosenborg Castle tour leaves TI at 13:30 Mon and Thu, 100 kr, 50 kr with Copenhagen Card, prices include castle admission; pick up schedule at TI or call Richard at tel. 32 97 14 40). All of Richard's tours, while different, complement each other and are of equal "introduction" value.

▲▲**Harbor Cruise and Canal Tours**—Two companies offer basically the same live, three-language, 50-minute tours through the city canals (daily 10:00–17:00, later in Jul, 2/hrly, Apr–late Oct; dress warmly—boats are open-top). Both boats leave from near Christiansborg Palace, cruise around the palace and Christianshavn area, and then proceed into the wide-open harbor. It's a pleasant way to see the mermaid and take a load off those weary feet. The low-overhead 20-kr Netto-Bådene Tour boats (tel. 38 87 21 33) leave from Nyhavn. The competition, Canal Tours Copenhagen, does a 42-kr harbor tour with a hop-on-and-hop-off version. It leaves from Gammel Strand near Christiansborg Palace and Nyhavn (tel. 33 13 31 05). Don't be confused. If you don't plan to get off the boat, go with Netto. There's no reason to pay double. Tour boats also start at Nyhavn.

Sights—Copenhagen

▲**Copenhagen's City Hall (Rådhus)**—This city landmark, between the station/Tivoli/TI and Strøget pedestrian mall, offers private tours and trips up its 350-foot-high tower. It's draped, inside and out, in Danish symbolism. Bishop Absalon (the city's founder) stands over the door. The polar bears climbing on the rooftop symbolize the giant Danish protectorate of Greenland. The city hall is free and open to the public (Mon–Fri 10:00–15:00). Tours are given in English and get you into otherwise-closed rooms (30 kr, 45 min, Mon–Fri at 15:00, Sat at 10:00). Tourists romp up the tower's 300 steps for the best aerial view of Copenhagen (20 kr, Mon–Fri 10:00, 12:00, and 14:00, Sat 12:00; off-season Mon–Sat 12:00, tel. 33 66 25 82).

▲**Christiansborg Palace**—This modern *slot*, or palace, built on the ruins of the original 12th-century castle, houses the parliament, supreme court, prime minister's headquarters, and royal reception rooms. Guided 40-minute English tours of the queen's reception rooms let you slip-slide on protect-the-floor slippers through 22 rooms and gain a good feel for Danish history, royalty, and politics in this 100-year-old, still-functioning palace (40 kr, Jun–Aug daily 11:00, 13:00, and 15:00; May and Sept daily 11:00 and 15:00; off-season Tue, Thu, Sat, and Sun 11:00 and 15:00, tel. 33 92 64 92). For a rundown on contemporary government, you can also tour the parliament building. From the equestrian statue in front, go through the wooden door, past the entrance to the Christiansborg Castle ruins, into the courtyard, and up the stairs on the right.

▲**Christiansborg Castle ruins**—An exhibit in the scant remains of the first castle built by Bishop Absalon—the 12th-century founder of Copenhagen—lies under the palace (20 kr, daily 9:30–15:30, closed off-season Mon, Wed, and Sat, good 1-kr guide). Early birds note that this sight opens 30 minutes before other nearby sights.

▲▲▲**National Museum**—Focus on the excellent and curiously enjoyable Danish collection, which traces this civilization from its ancient beginnings. Exhibits are laid out chronologically and are described in English. Pick up the museum map and consider the 10-kr miniguide that highlights the top stops. Find room 1 opposite the new entrance and begin your walk by following the numbers through the "prehistory" section on the ground floor—oak coffins with still-clothed and armed skeletons from 1300 B.C., ancient and still-playable *lur* horns, the 200-year old Gunderstrup Cauldron of art-textbook fame, lots of Viking stuff, and a bitchin' collection of well-translated rune stones. Then go upstairs, find room 101, and carry on—fascinating dirt on the Reformation, everyday town life in the 16th and 17th centuries, and, in room 126, a unique "cylinder perspective" of the royal family (from 1656) and two peep shows. The next floor takes you into modern times (40 kr, Tue–Sun 10:00–17:00, free Wed, closed Mon; mandatory bag check, 10-kr locker deposit, refunded with returned key; enter at Ny Vestergade 10, tel. 33 13 44 11). Occasional free English tours are offered in the summer—call ahead.

▲**Ny Carlsberg Glyptotek**—Scandinavia's top art gallery, with especially intoxicating Egyptian, Greek, and Etruscan collections; the best of Danish Golden Age (early 19th century) painting; and a heady, if small, exhibit of 19th-century French paintings (in the new "French Wing," including Géricault, Delacroix, Manet,

Impressionists, Gauguin before and after Tahiti) is an impressive example of what beer money can do. Linger with marble gods under the palm leaves and glass dome of the very soothing winter garden. Designers, figuring Danes would be more interested in a lush garden than classical art, used this wonderful space as leafy bait to cleverly introduce locals to a few Greek and Roman statues. (It works for tourists, too.) One of the original Rodin *Thinker*s (wondering how to scale the Tivoli fence?) can be seen for free in the museum's backyard. This collection is artfully displayed and thoughtfully described—good even after a visit to Rome (30 kr, Mon–Sat 10:00–16:00, free Wed and Sun; mandatory bag check, 10-kr locker deposit, refunded with returned key; 2-kr English brochure/guide, classy cafeteria under palms, behind Tivoli, Dantes Plads 7, tel. 33 41 81 41).

▲▲Rosenborg Castle—This finely furnished Renaissance-style castle houses the Danish crown jewels and 500 years of royal knickknacks. It's musty with history (including some great Christian IV lore...like the shrapnel he pulled from his eye after a naval battle and made into earrings for his girlfriend) and would be fascinating if anything was explained in English. Consider purchasing the guide. The castle is surrounded by the royal gardens, a rare plant collection, and, on sunny days, a minefield of sunbathing Danish beauties and picnickers (45 kr, daily May–Sept 10:00–16:00, Oct 11:00–15:00, Nov–Apr 11:00–14:00; there's no electricity inside, so visit at a bright time; Richard Karpen—see "Walking Tours," above—does 2 Rosenborg tours a week; S-train: Nørreport, tel. 33 15 32 86). When the royal family is in residence, there is a daily changing-of-the-guard miniparade from Rosenborg Castle (at 11:30) to Amalienborg Castle (at 12:00). The King's Rosegarden (across the canal from the palace) is a royal place for a picnic (for cheap open-face sandwiches to go, walk a couple of blocks to Lorraine's at the corner of Borgergade and Dronningenstværgade). The fine statue of Hans Christian Andersen in the park, actually erected in his lifetime (and approved by H.C.A.), is meant to symbolize how his stories had a message even for adults.

▲Denmark's Resistance Museum (Frihedsmuseet)—The fascinating story of a heroic Nazi resistance struggle (1940–1945) is well explained in English (free, May–mid-Sept Tue–Sun 10:00–16:00, closed Mon; off-season Tue–Sun 11:00–15:00; between the Queen's Palace and *The Little Mermaid*, bus #1, #6, or #9, tel. 33 13 77 14). If prioritizing, the Resistance Museum in Oslo is more interesting.

▲Our Savior's (Vor Frelsers) Church—The church's bright Baroque interior is worth a look (free, daily Mar–Nov 9:00–16:30, Dec–Feb 10:00–14:00, closed during church functions, bus #8, tel. 31 57 27 98). The unique spiral spire that you'll admire from afar can be climbed for a great city view and a good aerial view of the Christiania commune below. It's 311 feet high, claims to have 400 steps, and costs 20 kr.

Lille Mølle—This tiny intimate museum shows off a 1916 house in Christianshavn (open Tue–Sun afternoons, closed Mon; mandatory guided tours at 13:00, 14:00, 15:00, 16:00; just off south end of Torvgade, tel. 33 47 38 38). A fine café serves light lunches and dinners in its terrace garden. On Saturday and Sunday, enjoy their huge brunch (95 kr, 10:00–14:00).

Carlsberg Brewery Tour—Denmark's beloved source of legal intoxicants, Carlsberg provides free one-hour brewery tours followed by 30-minute "tasting sessions" (Mon–Fri 11:00 and 14:00, bus #6 to Ny Carlsberg Vej 140, tel. 33 27 12 74).

Museum of Erotica—This museum's focus: the love life of *Homo sapiens*. Better than the Amsterdam equivalents, it offers a chance to visit a porno shop and call it a museum. It took some digging, but they've documented a history of sex from Pompeii to present day. Visitors get a peep into the world of 19th-century Copenhagen prostitutes and a chance to read up on the sex lives of Martin Luther, Queen Elizabeth, Charlie Chaplin, and Casanova. After reviewing a lifetime of *Playboy* centerfolds, visitors sit down for the arguably artistic experience of watching the "electric *tabernakel*," a dozen silently slamming screens of porn seething to the gentle accompaniment of music (worth the 59-kr entry fee only if fascinated by sex, daily May–Sept 10:00–23:00, Oct–Apr 11:00–20:00, a block north of Strøget at Købmagergade 24, tel. 33 12 03 11). For the real thing—unsanitized but free—wander Copenhagen's dreary little red-light district along Istedgade behind the train station.

Hovedbanegården—The great Copenhagen train station is a fascinating mesh of Scandinanity and transportation efficiency. Even if you're not a train traveler, check it out (fuller description under "Orientation," above).

Nightlife—For the latest on Copenhagen's hopping jazz scene, ask at the TI or get *Playtime* magazine at Use It.

Tivoli

The world's grand old amusement park—which just turned 156 years old—is 20 acres, 110,000 lanterns, and countless ice-cream cones of fun. You pay one admission price and find yourself lost in a Hans Christian Andersen wonderland of rides, restaurants, games, marching bands, roulette wheels, and funny mirrors. Tivoli is wonderfully Danish. It doesn't try to be Disney (45 kr, Apr–mid-Sept Sun–Thu 10:00–24:00, Fri–Sat 10:00–01:00; also open for Christmas market mid-Nov–Dec daily 11:00–21:00, with ice skating on Tivoli Lake; tel. 33 15 10 01, www.tivoli.dk). Rides range in price from 10 to 50 kr (205 kr for all-day pass). All children's amusements are in full swing by 11:30; the rest of the amusements open by 13:30.

Entertainment in Tivoli: Upon arrival, go directly to the Tivoli Service Center (through main entry, on left) to pick up a map and events schedule. Take a moment to sit down and plan your entertainment for the evening (events on the half hour 18:30–23:00; 19:30 concert in concert hall can be free or cost up to 500 kr, depending on performer). Free concerts, mime, ballet, acrobats, puppets, and other shows pop up all over the park, and a well-organized visitor can enjoy an exciting evening of entertainment without spending a single krone (though occasionally the schedule is a bit sparse). The children's theater, Valmuen, plays excellent traditional fairy tales (daily except Mon, 12:00, 13:00, and 14:00). If the Tivoli Symphony is playing, it's worth paying for. Friday evenings feature a 22:00 rock or pop show. On Wednesday and Saturday at 23:45, fireworks light up the sky. If you're taking an overnight train out of Copenhagen, Tivoli (across from the station) is the place to spend your last Copenhagen hours.

Eating at Tivoli: Generally, you'll pay amusement-park prices for amusement park–quality food inside. **Søcafeen**, by the lake, allows picnics if you buy a drink. The *pølse* (sausage) stands are cheap. **Færgekroen** is a good lakeside place for a beer or some typical Danish food. The Croatian restaurant, **Hercegovina**, is a decent value (119-kr lunch buffet includes glass of beer or wine; 199-kr dinner buffet includes half a bottle of wine). For a cake and coffee, consider the **Viften** café. **Georg**, to the left of the Concert Hall, has tasty 40-kr sandwiches and 100-kr dinners (dinner includes glass of wine).

Christiania

In 1971 the original 700 Christianians established squatters' rights in an abandoned military barracks just a 10-minute walk from the Danish parliament building. A generation later this "free city"—an ultra-human mishmash of 1,000 idealists, anarchists, hippies, dope fiends, nonmaterialists, and people who dream only of being a Danish bicycle seat—not only survives, it thrives. This is a communal cornucopia of dogs, dirt, soft drugs, and dazed people—or haven of peace, freedom, and no taboos, depending on your perspective. Locals will remind judgmental Americans that a society must make the choice: allow for alternative lifestyles... or build more prisons.

For 25 years Christiania was a political hot potato... no one in the Danish establishment wanted it—or had the nerve to mash it. Now that Christiania is no longer a teenager, it's making an effort to connect better with the rest of society. The community is paying its utilities and even offering daily walking tours (see below).

Passing under the city gate you'll find yourself on "Pusher Street"... the main drag. This is a line of stalls selling hash, pot, pipes, and souvenirs leading to the market square and a food circus beyond. Make a point of getting past this "touristy" side of Chris-

Copenhagen

tiania. You'll find a fascinating ramshackle world of moats and earthen ramparts, alternative housing, unappetizing falafel stands, carpenter shops, hippie villas, children's playgrounds, and peaceful lanes. Be careful to distinguish between real Christianians and Christiania's uninvited guests—motley lowlife vagabonds from other countries who hang out here in the summer, skid row–type Greenlanders, and gawking tourists.

Soft Drugs: While hard drugs are out, hash and pot are sold openly (huge joints for 20 kr, senior discounts) and smoked happily. While locals will assure you you're safe within Christiania, they'll remind you that it's risky to take pot out—Denmark is required by Uncle Sam to make a token effort to snare tourists leaving the "free city" with pot. Beefy marijuana plants stand on proud pedestals at the market square. Beyond that an open-air food circus (or the canal-view perch above it, on the earthen ramparts) creates just the right ambience to lose track of time. Graffiti on the wall declares "a mind is a wonderful thing to waste."

Nitty-Gritty: Christiania is open all the time and visitors are welcome (follow the beer bottles and guitars down Prinsessegade behind Vor Frelsers' spiral church spire in Christianshavn). Photography is absolutely forbidden on Pusher Street (if you value your camera, don't even sneak a photo). Otherwise, you are welcome to snap photos, but ask residents before you photograph them. Guided tours leave from the front entrance of Christiania at 15:00 (daily Jun–Aug, 25 kr, in English and Danish, tel. 32 95 65 07 to confirm). Morgenstedet is a cheap and good vegetarian place (left after Pusher Street). Spiseloppen is the classy good-enough-for-Republicans restaurant (see "Eating," below).

More Sights—Copenhagen

Thorvaldsen's Museum features the early 18th–century work of Denmark's greatest sculptor (20 kr, Tue–Sun 10:00–17:00, closed Mon, next to Christiansborg Palace). The noontime **changing of the guard** at the Amalienborg Palace is boring—all they change is places. **Nyhavn**, with its fine old ships, tattoo shops (pop into Tattoo Ole at #17—fun photos, very traditional), and jazz clubs, is a wonderful place to hang out. The **Round Tower**, built in 1642 by Christian IV, connects a church, library, and observatory (the oldest functioning observatory in Europe) with a ramp that spirals up to a fine view of Copenhagen (15 kr; Jun–Aug Mon–Sat 10:00–20:00, Sun 12:00–20:00; Sept–May Mon–Sat 10:00–17:00, Sun 12:00–17:00; nothing to see but the ramp and the view, just off Strøget on Købmagergade).

Copenhagen's **Open Air Folk Museum (Frilandsmuseet)** is a park filled with traditional Danish architecture and folk culture (40 kr, Mar–Sept Tue–Sun 10:00–17:00, closed Mon, shorter hours off-season, outside of town in the suburb of Lyngby, tel. 33 13 44 11). From Copenhagen, hop on the S-train to Sorgenfri; then either take a 20-minute walk to the museum (as you exit the station, turn right and walk about a kilometer to next traffic light, turn left and go 2 blocks to museum) or catch bus #184 from the north end of Nørreport station (this bus takes a circuitous route through several towns before stopping at museum).

Danes gather at Copenhagen's other great amusement park, **Bakken** (free, daily late Mar–Aug 12:00–24:00, 30 minutes by S-train to Klampenborg, then walk through the woods, tel. 39 63 35 44).

For a look at small-town Denmark, consider a trip to the tiny fishing village of **Dragør** (30 minutes on bus #30 or #33 from Copenhagen's City Hall Square).

Shopping

Copenhagen's colorful flea market is small but feisty and surprisingly cheap (summer Sat 8:00–14:00 at Israels Plads). An antique market enlivens Nybrogade (near the palace) every Friday and Saturday. For other street markets, ask at the TI.

Shops are open Monday through Friday from 10:00 to 19:00 and Saturday from 9:00 to 16:00. For a street's worth of shops selling "Scantiques," wander down Ravnsborggade from Nørrebrogade. At UFF on Kultorvet you can buy nearly new clothes for peanuts and support charity at the same time.

The city's top department stores (Illum at Østergade 52, tel. 33 14 40 02, and Magasin at Kongens Nytorv 13, tel. 33 11 44 33) offer a good, if expensive, look at today's Denmark. Both are on Strøget and have fine cafeterias on their top floors. The department stores and the Politiken Bookstore on the Rådhus Square have a good selection of maps and English travel guides.

If you buy more than 300 kr ($50) worth of stuff from a shop displaying the Danish Tax-Free Shopping emblem, you can get back 80 percent of the 25 percent VAT (MOMS in Danish). If you have your purchase mailed, the tax can be deducted from your bill. Call 32 52 55 66 (Mon–Fri 7:00–22:00), see the shopping-oriented *Copenhagen This Week*, or ask a merchant for specifics.

Sleeping in Copenhagen
(7 kr = about $1)
Sleep Code: **S** = Single, **D** = Double/Twin, **T** = Triple, **Q** = Quad, **b** = bathroom, **CC** = Credit Card (Visa, MasterCard, Amex). Breakfast is often included at hotels and rarely included with private rooms and hostels.

I've listed the best budget hotels in the center, cheaper rooms in private homes an easy bus ride or 15-minute walk from the station, and even cheaper dormitory options.

Ibsen's Hotel is a cheery and central budget hotel, run by three women who treat you like you're paying top dollar

Copenhagen 617

Copenhagen Hotels

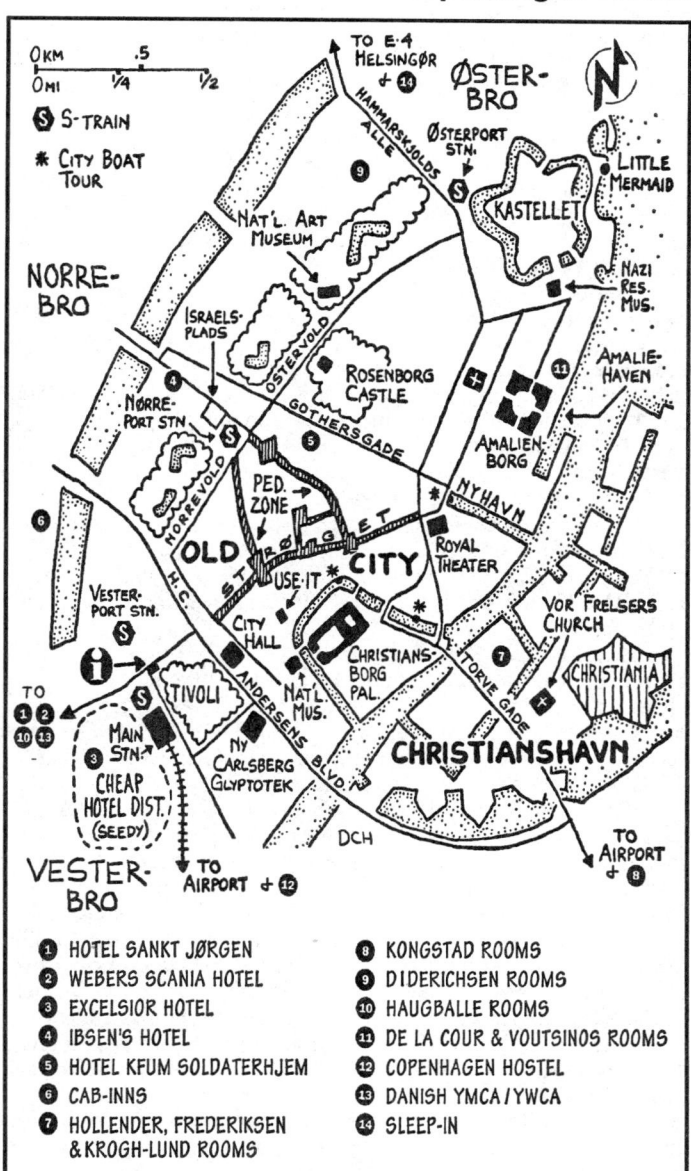

[Map of Copenhagen showing hotel locations with landmarks including Østerbro, Kastellet, Little Mermaid, Nazi Res. Mus., Amalie-Haven, Nørrebro, Nat'l. Art Museum, Israels Plads, Rosenborg Castle, Nørreport Stn., Amalienborg, Nyhavn, Old City, Ped. Zone, Use-it, Royal Theater, Vesterport Stn., City Hall, Christiansborg Pal., Nat. Mus., Vor Frelsers Church, Christiania, Tivoli, Main Stn., Ny Carlsberg Glyptotek, Christianshavn, Cheap Hotel Dist. (seedy), Vesterbro]

- ① HOTEL SANKT JØRGEN
- ② WEBERS SCANIA HOTEL
- ③ EXCELSIOR HOTEL
- ④ IBSEN'S HOTEL
- ⑤ HOTEL KFUM SOLDATERHJEM
- ⑥ CAB-INNS
- ⑦ HOLLENDER, FREDERIKSEN & KROGH-LUND ROOMS
- ⑧ KONGSTAD ROOMS
- ⑨ DIDERICHSEN ROOMS
- ⑩ HAUGBALLE ROOMS
- ⑪ DE LA COUR & VOUTSINOS ROOMS
- ⑫ COPENHAGEN HOSTEL
- ⑬ DANISH YMCA/YWCA
- ⑭ SLEEP-IN

(Sb-845–945 kr, Db-1,050–1,250 kr, 3rd person-200 kr, CC:VMA, Vendersgade 23, DK-1363 Copenhagen, bus #5, #7E, #16, or #40 from the station, or S-train: Nørreport, tel. 33 13 19 13, fax 33 13 19 16, e-mail: hotel@ibsenshotel.dk).

Hotel Sankt Jørgen has big, friendly-feeling rooms with plain old wooden furnishings. Brigitte and Susan offer a warm welcome and a great value, though the rooms are musty from smokers (S-450 kr, D-550 kr, 3rd person-150 kr, 5-bed family rooms, 10 percent less in winter, breakfast served in your room, elevator, a 12-minute walk from station or catch bus #13 to first stop after lake, Julius Thomsensgade 22, DK-1632 Copenhagen V, tel. 35 37 15 11, fax 35 37 11 97).

Webers Scania Hotel is my best fine hotel by the train station. Just a five-minute walk down Vesterbrogade from the station, it offers breakfast in a peaceful garden courtyard (if sunny); a classy, modern but inviting interior; and generous weekend/summer rates (late Jun–Jul and Fri–Sun all year: Sb-875 kr, Db-1,150 kr, 1,250 kr, and 1,350 kr depending on size/grade of room; high season: Sb-from 1,195 kr, Db-from 1,395 kr; CC:VMA, sauna/exercise room, Vesterbrogade 11B, DK-1620 Copenhagen, tel. 31 31 14 32, fax 31 31 14 41, e-mail: webers@webers-hotel.dk).

Excelsior Hotel is a big, mod, normal, tour-group hotel a block behind the station, in a sleazy but safe area just half a block off the decent, bustling Vesterbrogade (Sb-995 kr, Db-1,195 kr, CC:VMA, Colbjørnsensgade 4, DK-1652 Copenhagen, tel. 33 24 50 85, fax 33 24 50 87).

Hotel KFUM Soldaterhjem, originally for soldiers, rents eight singles and three doubles on the 5th floor, with no elevators (S-315 kr, S plus hideabed-425 kr, D-480 kr, no breakfast, Gothersgade 115, Copenhagen K, tel. 33 15 40 44). The reception is on the first floor up (Mon–Fri 8:30–23:00, Sat–Sun 15:00–23:00) and is next to a budget cafeteria.

Cab-Inn is a radical innovation: 86 identical, mostly collapsible, tiny but comfy, cruise ship–type staterooms, all bright, molded, and shiny with TV, coffeepot, shower, and toilet. Each room has a single bed that expands into a twin with one or two fold-down bunks on the walls. The staff will hardly give you the time of day, but it's tough to argue with this efficiency (S-470 kr, D-640 kr, T-810 kr, Q-980 kr, includes breakfast, easy parking-30 kr, CC:VMA). There are two virtually identical Cab-Inns in the same neighborhood: **Cab-Inn Copenhagen** has a nicer locale (Danasvej 32-34, 1910 Frederiksberg C, 5 minutes on bus #29 to center, tel. 33 21 04 00, fax 33 21 74 09). **Cab-Inn Scandinavia** has a bigger building with a bigger cafeteria. Some rooms come with a real double bed for 100 kr extra (Vodroffsvej 55, tel. 35 36 11 11, fax 35 36 11 14). E-mail either at cabinn @inet.uni-c.dk.

Sleeping in Rooms in Private Homes
Following are a few leads for Copenhagen's best accommodations values. Most are in the lively Christianshavn neighborhood. While each TI has its own list of B&Bs, by booking direct you'll save yourself and your host the tourist-office fee. Always call ahead—they book in advance. Most are run by single professional women supplementing their income. All speak English and afford a fine peek into Danish domestic life. Rooms generally have no sink. Don't count on breakfast.

Private Homes in Christianshavn
This area—my Copenhagen home—is a never-a-dull-moment hodgepodge of the chic, artistic, hippie, and hobo, with beer-drinking Greenlanders littering streets in the shadow of fancy government ministries. Colorful with lots of shops, cafés, and canals, it's an easy 10-minute walk to the center and has good bus connections to the airport and downtown.

Annette and Rudy Hollender enjoy sharing their 300-year-old home with my readers. Even with a long and skinny staircase, sinkless rooms, and three rooms sharing one toilet/shower, it's a comfortable and cheery place to call home (S-250 kr, D-350 kr, T-400 kr, Wildersgade 19, 1408 Copenhagen K, closed Nov–Apr, tel. 32 95 96 22, fax 32 57 24 86). Take bus #9 from the airport, bus #8 from the station, or bus #2 from the city hall. From downtown, push the button immediately after crossing Knippels Bridge, and turn right off Torvegade down Wildersgade.

Morten Frederiksen, a laid-back, ponytailed sort of guy, rents five spacious rooms and two four-bed suites in a mod-funky-pleasant old house. The furniture is old-time rustic but elegant. The posters are Mapplethorpe. It's a clean, comfy, good look at today's hip Danish lifestyle in a great location right on Christianshavn's main drag (S-200 kr, D-300 kr, T-400 kr, Q-500 kr, no breakfast, 2 minutes from Annette's, Torvegade 36, tel. 32 95 32 73, cellular 20 41 92 73).

Britta Krogh-Lund rents two spacious doubles in an old Christianshavn house (S-250 kr, D-350 kr, T-400 kr, kitchen for self-serve breakfast only, Amagergade 1, C-1423 Copenhagen K, tel. 32 95 55 85).

South of Christianshavn, **Gitte Kongstad** rents two apartments, each taking up an entire spacious floor in her flat. You'll have a kitchenette, little garden, and your own bike (D-350 kr, family deals, no breakfast, bus #9 or #19 from airport, bus #12 or #13 from station, a 10-minute ride past Christianshavn to Badensgade 2, 2300 Copenhagen, tel. & fax 32 97 71 97, e-mail: g.kongstad@post.tele.dk). While it's not central, you'll feel at home here and the bike ride into town is a snap.

More Private Rooms

Puk (pook) **De La Cour** rents two rooms in her mod, bright, and easygoing house near Amalienborg Palace. It's in a stately embassy neighborhood—no stress but a bit bland and up lots of stairs. You can look out your window to see the queen's palace (and the guards changing). It's a 10-minute walk north of Nyhavn and Strøget (D-350 kr with no breakfast but tea, coffee, and a kitchen/family room available, Amaliegade 34, 4th floor, tel. 33 12 04 68). Puk's friend **Line** (lee-nuh) **Voutsinos** offers a similar deal May through September only (D-400 kr, extra bed-100 kr, enough room for four people, good for family with two kids; each room comes with a double bed, tea and coffee in the morning, long-term parking—5 kr/hr or 50 kr/day on street, Amaliegade 34, third floor, tel. & fax 33 14 71 42).

Annette Haugballe rents three modern, pleasant rooms in the quiet, green, residential Frederiksberg area (summer only, D-325 kr, no breakfast, easy parking, Hoffmeyersvej 33, 2000 Frederiksberg, on bus line #1 from station or City Hall Square, and near Peter Bangsvej S subway station, tel. 38 74 87 87).

Gørli and Viggo Hannibel, Annette's parents, have two rooms in the same neighborhood (D/Db-325 kr, from train station take bus #1 to P. G. Rammsalle plus 3-minute walk, or S-tog to Peder Bangsvej station plus 7-minute walk, Folketsalle 17, 2000 F Copenhagen, tel. 31 86 13 10).

Solveig Diderichsen rents three rooms in her comfortable, high-ceilinged, ground-floor apartment home. It's located in a quiet embassy neighborhood next to a colorful residential area with fun shops and eateries behind Østre Anlæg park. Unfortunately, Solveig can be rude, distracted, and unreliable (S-300 kr, D-350 kr, extra bed-125 kr, no breakfast, direct train from the airport or 3 stops on the subway from train station to Østerport station, then a 3-minute walk to Upsalagade 26, 2100 Copenhagen Ø, tel. 35 43 39 58, fax 35 43 22 70, cellular 40 11 39 58). If her place is full she can find you a room in a B&B nearby. An avid sledder, Solveig shares her home with her sled dog, Maya.

Sleeping in Hostels

Copenhagen energetically accommodates the young vagabond on a shoestring. The Use It office is your best source of information. Each of these places charges about 100 kr per person for a bed and breakfast. Some don't allow sleeping bags, and if you don't have your own hostel bedsheet you'll normally have to rent one for around 30 kr. IYHF hostels normally sell noncardholders a "guest pass" for 25 kr.

The modern **Copenhagen Hostel** (IYHF) is huge, with 60 220-kr doubles and five-bed dorms at 85 kr per bed (sheets extra, no curfew, excellent facilities, cheap meals, self-serve laundry). Unfortunately, it's on the edge of town (bus #10 from the station to Mozartplads, then #37; or, daytime only, ride bus #46 direct from the station; no breakfast; Vejlands Alle 200, 2300 Copenhagen S, tel. 32 52 29 08, fax 32 52 27 08).

The **Danish YMCA/YWCA**, open only in July and August, is a 10-minute walk from the train station or a short ride on bus #3, #6, or #16 (dorm bed-75 kr, 4- to 10-bed rooms, breakfast-25 kr, Valdemarsgade 15, tel. 33 31 15 74).

The **Sleep-In** is popular with the desperate or adventurous (80 kr with sheets, Jul–Aug, 4-bed cubicles in a huge 452-bed coed room, no curfew or breakfast, pretty wild, lockers, always has room and free condoms, Blegdamsvej 132, bus #1 or #6 to "Triangle" stop and look for sign, tel. 35 26 50 59).

Eating in Copenhagen

Copenhagen's many good restaurants are well listed by category in *Copenhagen This Week*. Since restaurant prices include a 25 percent tax, your budget may require alternatives. These survival ideas for the hungry budget traveler in Copenhagen will save lots of money.

Picnics

Irma (in arcade on Vesterbrogade next to Tivoli) and **Brugsen** are the two largest supermarket chains. **Netto** is a cut-rate outfit with the cheapest prices. The little grocery store in the central station is expensive but handy (daily 8:00–24:00).

Viktualiehandler (small delis) and bakeries, found on nearly every corner, sell fresh bread, tasty pastries (a *wienerbrød* is what we call a "Danish"), juice, milk, cheese, and yogurt (drinkable, in tall liter boxes). Liver paste (*leverpostej*) is cheap and a little better than it sounds.

Smørrebrød

While virgins no longer roll around carts filled with delicate sandwiches, Denmark's 300-year-old tradition of open-face sandwiches survives. Open-face sandwiches cost a fortune in restaurants, but the many *smørrebrød* take-out shops sell them for 8 kr to 30 kr. Drop into one of these no-name, family-run budget savers, and get several elegant OFSs to go. The tradition calls for three sandwich courses: herring first, then meat, then cheese. It makes for a classy—and cheap—picnic. Downtown you'll find these handy local alternatives to Yankee fast-food chains: **Centrum** (open long hours, Vesterbrogade 6C, across from station), **Tria Cafe** (Mon–Fri 8:00–14:00, closed Sat–Sun, Gothersgade 12, near Kongens Nytorv), **Domhusets Smørrebrød** (Mon–Fri 7:00–14:30, Kattesundet 18), and one in Nyhavn, on the corner of Holbergsgade and Peder Skrams Gade.

The Pølse

The famous Danish hot dog, sold in *pølsevogn* (sausage wagons) throughout the city, is one of the few typically Danish institutions to resist the onslaught of our global fast-food culture. "Hot dog" is a Danish word for wienie—study the photo menu for variations. These are fast, cheap, tasty, easy to order, and almost worthless nutritionally. Even so, the local "dead man's finger" is the dog kids love to bite.

By hanging around a *pølsevogn* you can study this institution. Denmark's "cold feet café" is a form of social care: only people who have difficulty finding jobs, such as the handicapped, are licensed to run these wiener-mobiles. As they gain seniority they are promoted to work at more central locations. Danes like to gather here for munchies and *pølsesnak* ("sausage talk"), the local slang for empty chatter.

Inexpensive Restaurants

Riz-Raz, around the corner from Use It at Kompagnistræde 20, serves a healthy all-you-can-eat 49-kr Mediterranean/vegetarian buffet lunch (daily 11:30–17:00) and an even bigger 59-kr dinner buffet (until 24:00, tel. 33 15 05 75). The dinner has to be the best deal in town. And they're happy to serve free water with your meal. Department stores serving cheery, reasonable meals in their cafeterias include **Illum**, an elegant top-floor circus of reasonable food under a glass dome (Østergade 52), **Magasin** (Kongens Nytorv 13), and **Dælls Varehus** (Nørregade 12).

Det Lille Apotek, the "little pharmacy," is a reasonable, candlelit place that has been popular with locals for 200 years (sandwich lunches, bigger dinners, just off Strøget, between Frue Church and Round Tower at St. Kannikestræde 15, tel. 33 12 56 06). Their specialty is "Stone Beef," a big slab of tender, raw steak plopped down in front of you on a scalding-hot lava stone. Flip it over a few times and it's cooked within minutes.

At **El Porron**, you'll find good Spanish tapas (Vendersgade 10, 1 block from Ibsen's Hotel). **Nemsis**, across the street from Ibsen's Hotel, has cheap, tasty sandwiches and a friendly staff.

Bryggeriet, a lively brew pub, serves meals light (50–100 kr) or hearty (115–160 kr), has an impressive salad bar, and brews a tasty beer of the month on site (kitchen open Mon–Sat 11:30–14:00, 17:30–22:00, Sun 17:30–22:00, located around the corner from the train station and the TI at Vesterbrogade 3, tel. 33 12 33 13).

To explore your way through a world of traditional Danish food, try a Danish *koldt bord* (an all-you-can-eat buffet). The central station's **Bistro Restaurant** is handy but touristy (145-kr dinner, served daily 11:30–22:00, tel. 33 14 12 32).

Eating in Christianshavn
This neighborhood is so cool, it's worth combining an evening wander with dinner even if you don't live here. **Café Wilder** serves creative and hearty dinner salads by candlelight to a trendy local clientele (corner of Wildersgade and Skt. Annæ Gade, a block off Torvegade). To avoid having to choose just one of their interesting salads, try their three-salad plate (61 kr with bread). They also feature a budget dinner plate for around 85 kr and are happy to serve free water. Across the street, **Luna Café** is also good and serves a slower-paced meal. Choose one of three good dinner salads and bread for 45 kr.

Ravelin Restaurant, on a tiny island on the big road just south of Christianshavn, serves good and traditional Danish-style food at reasonable prices to happy local crowds. Either dine indoors or on the lovely lakeside terrace (*smørrebrød* lunches 40–100 kr, dinners 100–170 kr, Torvegade 79, tel. 32 96 20 45). A block away, at the little windmill (Lille Mølle), **Bastionen & Løven** serves Scandinavian nouveau cuisine on a Renoir terrace or in its Rembrandt interior (55-kr lunch specials, 130–160-kr dinners, 265 kr for 3-course menu, menu is small but fresh, Voldgade 50, walk to the end of Torvegade and follow the ramparts up to the restaurant, at south end of Christianshavn, tel. 32 95 09 40).

Lagkagehuset, with a big selection of pastries and excellent fresh-baked bread and focaccia, is a great place for breakfast (coffee and pastries for 15 kr, Torvegade 45).

In Christiania, the wonderfully classy **Spiseloppen** (meaning "the flea eats") serves great 100-kr vegetarian meals and 140-kr meaty ones by candlelight. Christiania is the free city/squatter town, located three blocks behind the spiral spire of Vor Frelser's church (restaurant open Tue–Sun 17:00–22:00, closed Mon, on the top floor of an old brick warehouse, turn right just inside Christiania's gate, reservations often necessary on weekends, tel. 31 57 95 58).

Base Camp offers an unusual eating/drinking/partying experience in an old military barracks that has been converted into three sprawling restaurants with enough seating for you and 800 travel companions. Dance under an enormous disco ball inside, or head outside to where the food is served raw. Grill it at your table and play beach volleyball in the sand. Were it not for the off-the-beaten-path location, Base Camp would be filled with the American-Aussie-Brit frat party crowd. But it's tucked away, 10 minutes on foot from Christiania, making it a great place to mingle with young, festive Danes. From Christianshavn, follow Prinsessegade past Christiania. You'll cross a canal at Trangravsvej. Continue till you see the big "BASE CAMP" sign in camouflage stencil on the right-hand side of the road (disco usually Fri-Sat, occasionally closes for private parties, call ahead for evening's events, tel. 70 23 23 28).

Morten, who runs a local B&B, recommends: **Long Feng** (good, cheap Chinese, south end of Torvegade) and **Skipperkroen** (cheap traditional Danish, east end of Strandgade). Right on the community square you'll find a huge grocery store, fruit stands under the Greenlanders monument, and a delightful bakery (facing the square at Torvegade 45).

Transportation Connections—Copenhagen
By train to: Hillerød/Frederiksborg (6/hrly, 30 min), **Louisiana Museum** (Helsingør train to Humlebæk, 3/hrly, 30 min), **Roskilde** (1–3/hrly, 30 min), **Odense** (2/hrly, 2 hrs), **Helsingør** (ferry to Sweden, 40/day, 50 min), **Stockholm** (5/day, 8 hrs), **Oslo** (4/day, 9 hrs), **Växjö** (via Alvesta, 10/day, 5 hrs), **Kalmar** (10/day, via Alvesta and Växjö, 7 hrs), **Berlin** (via Hamburg, 4/day, 9 hrs), **Amsterdam** (2/day, 11 hrs), **Frankfurt/Rhine** (4/day, 8 hrs). Through June 2000 all Norway- and Sweden-bound trains go right onto the Helsingør–Helsingborg ferry. (You get 20 minutes to romp on the deck, eat the wind, grab a bite, and change money.) The crossing is included in any train ticket. As of July 2000, trains will take the slick new Øresund bridge linking Denmark with Sweden. Convenient overnight trains from Copenhagen run directly to Stockholm, Oslo, Amsterdam, and Frankfurt. National train info tel. 70 13 14 15. International train info tel. 70 13 14 16. Cheaper bus trips are listed at Use It.

A quickie cruise from Copenhagen to Oslo: A luxurious cruise ship leaves daily from Copenhagen (departs 17:00, returns 2 days later by 9:15; 16 hours sailing each way and 7 hours in Norway's capital). Special packages give you a bed in a double cabin, a fine dinner, and two *smørgåsbord* breakfasts for around $175 in summer ($210 for single, Fri–Sat cost more). Call DFDS Scandinavian Seaways (tel. 33 42 30 00). It's easy to make a reservation in the United States (tel. 800/5DF-DS55).

STOCKHOLM

If I had to call one European city home, it would be Stockholm. Surrounded by water and woods, bubbling with energy and history, Sweden's stunning capital is green, clean, and underrated.

Crawl through Europe's best-preserved old warship and relax on a canal-boat tour. Browse the cobbles and antique shops of the lantern-lit Old Town and take a spin through Skansen, Europe's first and best open-air folk museum. Marvel at Stockholm's glittering city hall, modern department stores, and art museums.

While progressive and sleek, Stockholm respects its heritage. In summer, mounted bands parade daily through the heart of town to the royal palace, announcing the changing of the guard and turning the most dignified tourist into a scampering kid. The Gamla Stan (Old Town) celebrates the midsummer festivities (late June) with the vigor of a rural village, forgetting that it's part of a gleaming 20th-century metropolis.

Planning Your Time

On a two- to three-week trip through Scandinavia, Stockholm is worth two days. Efficient train travelers sleep in and out for two days in the city with only one night in a hotel. (The Copenhagen train arrives at about 8:00 and departs at about 22:00 or 23:00.) To be even more economical and efficient, you could use the luxury Stockholm–Helsinki boat as your hotel for two nights (spending a day in Helsinki) and have two days in Stockholm without a hotel (e.g., Copenhagen; night train to Stockholm, day in Stockholm; night boat to Helsinki, day in Helsinki; night boat to Stockholm, day in Stockholm; night train to Copenhagen). That schedule may sound crazy, but it gives you three interesting and inexpensive days of travel fun.

Spend two days in Stockholm this way:
Day 1: Arrive by train (or the night before by car), do station chores (reserve next ride, change money, pick up map, *Stockholm This Week*, and a Stockholm Card at the Hotellcentralen TI), check into hotel, 10:30–Catch 50-minute bus tour from Opera, 11:30–Tour Vasa warship and have a picnic, 13:30–Tour Nordic Museum, 15:00–Skansen Open-Air Museum (ask for tour), 19:00–Folk dancing, possible *smørgåsbord*, and popular dancing, or wander Gamla Stan.
Day 2: 10:00–City hall tour, climb city hall tower for a fine view, 12:00–Catch the changing of the guard at the palace, tour royal palace and armory, explore Gamla Stan, or picnic on one-hour city boat tour, 16:00–Browse the modern city center around Kungsträdgården, Sergels Torg, Hötorget market and indoor food hall, and Drottninggatan area.

Orientation (tel. code: 08)

Greater Stockholm's 1.8 million residents live on 14 islands that are woven together by 54 bridges. Visitors need only concern themselves with five islands: **Norrmalm** is downtown, with most of the hotels, shopping areas, and the train station. **Gamla Stan** is the old city of winding lantern-lit streets, antique shops, and classy, glassy cafés clustered around the royal palace. **Södermalm**, aptly called Stockholm's Brooklyn, is residential and not touristy. **Skeppsholmen** is the small, central, traffic-free park island with the Museum of Modern Art and two fine youth hostels. **Djurgården** ("deer garden"), now officially a national city park, is Stockholm's wonderful green playground with many of the city's top sights (bike rentals just over bridge as you enter island).

Tourist Information

Hotellcentralen is primarily a room-finding service (in the central train station), but its friendly staff adequately handles all your sightseeing and transportation questions. This is the place for anyone arriving by train to arrange accommodations, buy the Tourist Card or Stockholm Card (see below), and pick up a city map, *Stockholm This Week* (which lists open hours and directions to all the sights, special events, and much more), and brochures on whatever else you need (city walks, parking, jazz boats, excursions, bus routes, shopping, and so on). While *This Week* has a decent map of the sightseeing zone, the 15-kr map covers more area and bus routes. It's worth the extra money if you'll be using the buses (daily Jun–Sept 7:00–21:00, May 8:00–19:00, off-season 9:00–18:00, tel. 08/789-2425 or 08/789-2456, fax 08/791-8666, www.stoinfo.se).

Sverige Huset (Sweden House), Stockholm's official TI (a short walk from the station on Kungsträdgården), is good but usually more crowded than Hotellcentralen. They've got pamphlets

Stockholm's Islands

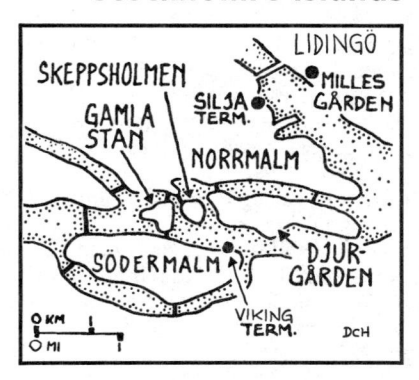

on everything; an "excursion shop" for transportation, day-trip, and bus-tour information and tickets; and an English library and reading room upstairs with racks of information on various aspects of Swedish culture and one state's attempt at cradle-to-grave happiness (Jul–Aug Mon–Fri 8:00–19:00, Sat–Sun 9:00–17:00, less off-season, Hamngatan 27, T-bana: Kungsträdgården, tel. 08/789-2490 for info, 08/789-2415 for tickets).

The **City Hall TI** is smaller but with all the information and a bit less chaos (May–Oct daily 9:00–17:00, off-season Fri–Sun 9:00–15:00, closed Jan, at the Stadshuset or City Hall, tel. 08/5082-9000).

Arrival in Stockholm

By Train: Stockholm's central train station is a wonderland of services, shops, and people going places. The Hotellcentralen TI is as good as the city TI nearby. If you're sailing to Finland, check out the Viking Line office. The FOREX long-hours exchange counter changes traveler's checks for a 15-kr fee (2 offices, upstairs and downstairs, in the station).

By Plane: Stockholm's Arlanda Airport is 45 kilometers north of town. Shuttle buses run between the airport and City Terminal, which is next to the station (6/hrly, tel. 08/600-1000). Airport info tel. 08/797-6000 (SAS tel. 020/727-727, British Air tel. 020/770-098).

Helpful Hints

There are three kinds of public phones: coin-op, credit card, and phone card. For operator assistance, call 0018. Numbers starting with 020 are toll free. For around-the-clock medical help, call 08/463-9100. There's a 24-hour pharmacy near the central station at Klarabergsgatan 64 (tel. 08/454-8130). To get a taxi within three minutes, call Taxi Stockholm (tel. 08/150-000) or Taxi Kurir (tel. 08/300-000). Rent bikes, inline skates, and boats at Skepp & Hoj on Djurgådsbron Bridge next to Vasa Museum (summer 9:00–21:00, tel. 08/660-5757). For Internet access, try Fröken Matildas (open until 23:00, Stora Nygatem 6 in Gamla Stan, tel. 08/206-020).

Getting around Stockholm

By Bus and Subway: Stockholm complements her many sightseeing charms with great information services, a fine bus and subway system, and special passes that take the bite out of the city's cost (or at least limit it to one vicious budgetary gash).

Buses and the subway work on the same tickets. Ignore the zones since everything I mention (except Drottningholm and Carl Millesgården) is in Zone One. Each 14-kr ticket is valid for one hour (10-packs cost 95 kr). The subway, called T-bana or Tunnelbana, gets you where you want to go quickly. Ride it just for the futuristic drama of being a human mole and to check out the modern public art (for instance, in Kungsträdgården station, transit info tel. 08/600-1000). The **Tourist Card**, which gives you free use of all public transport and the harbor ferry (24 hrs/60 kr, 72 hrs/120 kr, sold at TIs and newsstands), is not necessary if you're getting the Stockholm Card (see below). The 72-hour pass includes admission to Skansen, Gröna Lund, and the Kaknäs Tower.

It seems too good to be true, but each year I pinch myself and the **Stockholm Card** is still there. This 24-hour, 199-kr pass (sold at TIs and ship terminals) gives you free run of all public transit, free entry to virtually every sight (70 places), free parking, a handy sightseeing handbook, and the substantial pleasure of doing everything without considering the cost (many of Stockholm's sights are worth the time but not the steep individual ticket costs). This pays for itself if you do Skansen, the Vasa, and the Royal Palace and Treasury. If you enter Skansen on your 24th hour (and head right for the 55-kr aquarium), you get a few extra hours. (Parents get an added bonus: Two children under 18 go along for 35 kr with each adult pass.) The same pass comes in 48-hour (398 kr) and 72-hour (498 kr) versions.

By Harbor Shuttle Ferry: Throughout the summer, ferries connect Stockholm's two most interesting sightseeing districts. They sail from Nybroplan and Slussen to Djurgården, landing next to Vasa and Skansen (20 kr, not covered by Stockholm Card, 3/hrly).

Sights—Downtown Stockholm

▲**Kungsträdgården**—The King's Garden Square is the downtown people-watching center. Watch the life-size game of chess and enjoy the free concerts at the bandstand. Surrounded by the Sweden House, the NK department store, the harborfront, and tour boats, it's the place to feel Stockholm's pulse (with discretion).

▲▲**Sergels Torg**—The heart of modern Stockholm, between Kungsträdgården and the station, is worth a wander. Enjoy the colorful, bustling underground mall and dip into the Gallerien mall. Visit the Kulturhuset, a center for reading, relaxing, and socializing designed for normal people (but welcoming tourists), with music, exhibits, hands-on fun, and an insight into contempo-

Stockholm

rary Sweden (free, Wed and Fri–Sat 11:00–17:00, Tue and Thu 11:00–19:00, Sun 12:00–17:00, often open later, closed Mon, tel. 08/700-0100). From Sergels Torg, walk up the Drottninggatan pedestrian mall to Hötorget (see "Eating," below).

▲▲**City Hall**—The Stadshuset is an impressive mix of 8 million bricks, 19 million chips of gilt mosaic, and lots of Stockholm pride. One of Europe's finest public buildings (built in 1923) and site of the annual Nobel Prize banquet, it's particularly enjoyable and worthwhile for its entertaining tours (40 kr, daily Jun–Aug at 10:00, 11:00, 12:00, and 14:00; Sept at 10:00, 12:00, and 14:00; off-season at 10:00 and 12:00; just behind the station, bus #48 or #62, tel. 08/5082-9059). Climb the 350-foot tower (an elevator takes you halfway) for the best possible city view (15 kr, daily 10:00–16:30 May–Sept only). The city hall also has a TI and a good cafeteria with complete lunches for 60 kr (Mon–Fri 11:00–14:30).

▲**Orientation Views**—Try to get a bird's-eye perspective on this wonderful urban mix of water, parks, concrete, and people from the city hall tower (see above), the Kaknäs Tower (at 500 feet, the tallest building in Scandinavia, 25 kr, daily May–Aug 9:00–22:00, daily Sept–Apr 10:00–21:00, bus #69 from Nybroplan or Sergels Torg, tel. 08/789-2435), the observatory in Skansen, or the Katarina elevator (5 kr, Mon–Sat 7:30–21:00, Sun 10:00–21:00, circa 1930s, ride 40 meters to the top; near Slussen subway stop—walk behind Katarinavagen for grand views, a classy residential neighborhood, and a lively Mosebacke evening of strolling, dancing, and beer gardens).

▲**Quickie Orientation Bus Tour**—Several different city-bus tours leave from the Royal Opera House. Your choices: 50 minutes for 90 kr with a Swedish/English guide (mid-Jun–mid-Aug 10:30–18:30 at half past the hour), 90 minutes for 130 kr (mid-Apr–Oct at 10:00, 12:00, 14:00; in summer also at 11:00, 13:00, 15:00, 17:00; tel. 08/411-7023), or a 75-minute Old Town walk (75 kr, daily in summer at 11:30 and 14:30). For a free self-guided tour, follow the Gamla Stan walk laid out below.

▲**City Boat Tour**—For a good floating look at Stockholm, and a pleasant break, consider a sightseeing cruise. Tour boats leave regularly from in front of the Grand Hotel (tel. 08/240-470). The "Historical Canals of Stockholm" tour offers the best informative introduction (90 kr, 1 hour, departing on the half hour 10:30–16:30 mid-Jun–mid-Aug). The "Under the Bridges" tour goes through two locks and under 15 bridges (live guide, 140 kr, 2 hours, hrly departures mid-Apr–mid-Oct). The "Royal Canal" tour is a scenic joyride through lots of greenery (90 kr, 1-hour tape-recorded spiel, departing on the half hour 10:30–18:30 mid-May–Aug).

▲**National Museum**—Though mediocre by European standards, this museum is small, central, uncrowded, and user-friendly. The highlights of the collection are several Rembrandts, Rubens, a fine

Stockholm

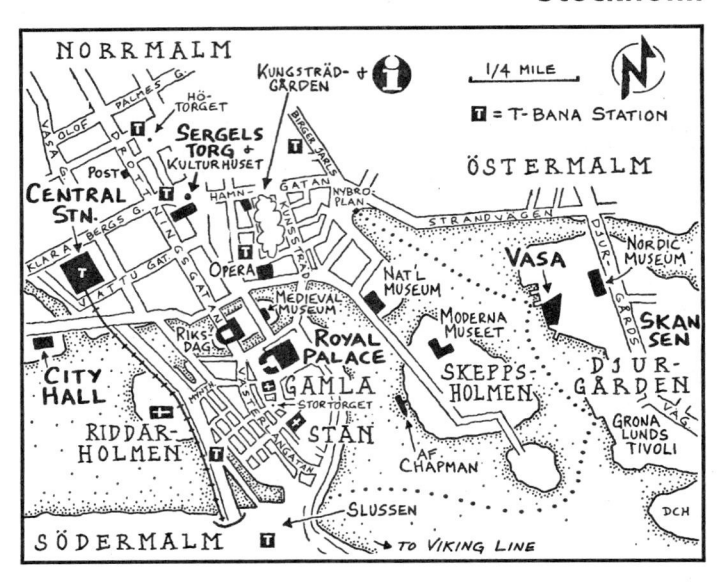

group of Impressionists, and works by the popular and good-to-get-to-know local artists Carl Larsson and Anders Zorn (60 kr, Tue–Sun 11:00–17:00, Tue and Thu until 20:00, closed Mon, tel. 08/5195-4300). A free and worthwhile CD guides you through a 50-minute tour of the collection's highlights. In summer, free guided tours in English begin at 13:00.

Museum of Modern Art—Newly reopened after a major renovation, this bright and cheery gallery is as far out as can be, with Picasso, Braque, and lots of goofy Dada art (such as the *Urinal* and the *Goat with Tire*). It's in a pleasant park on Skeppsholmen (60 kr, Tue–Thu 11:00–22:00, Fri–Sun 11:00–18:00, closed Mon, tel. 08/5195-5200).

Sights—Stockholm's Gamla Stan

▲▲**Gamla Stan self-guided walk**—Stockholm's old island core is charming, fit for a roll of film, and full of antique shops, street lanterns, painted ceilings, and surprises. While you could just happily wander, try this guided walk first:

Slottsbacken: Start at the base of the palace (bottom of Slottsbacken) where a statue of King Gustav III gazes at the palace, formerly the site of Stockholm's first castle. Walk up the broad cobbled boulevard. Behind the obelisk stands the Storkyrkan, Stockholm's cathedral (and most interesting church, which we'll visit later in the walk). Opposite the palace (orange building on left) is the Finnish church (Finska Kyrkan), which originated as the royal tennis hall. Walk behind the church into the shady churchyard where you'll find the three-inch-tall "iron boy," the tiniest statue in Stockholm (often with a little gift). Continue through the yard onto Trädgårdsgatan, which leads (turn right) to the old stock exchange.

Stortorget: Left of the stock exchange is the oldest square in town, Stortorget. The town well is now dry but this is still a popular meeting point. Scan the fine old facades. This square has a notorious history. It was the site of Stockholm's bloodbath of 1520—during a royal power grab, most of the town's aristocracy was beheaded. Rivers of blood were said to have run through the streets. Later, this was the location of the town's pillory. At the far end of the square (under the finest gables) turn right and follow Trangsund toward the cathedral.

Cathedral: Just before the church you'll see my favorite phone booth (Rikstelefon) and the gate to the churchyard being guarded by statues of Caution and Hope. Enter the cathedral (10 kr, daily 9:00–18:00, until 16:00 off-season, pick up free English flyer describing interior). The fascinating interior is paved with centuries-old tombstones; more than 2,000 people are buried under the church. In front on the left is an impressive sculpture of *Saint George and the Dragon* made of oak, gilded metal, and elk horn (1489). Near the exit is a painting with the oldest existing depiction of Stockholm (from 1535, showing a walled city filling only today's Gamla Stan).

Prastgatan: Exiting through the churchyard, continue down Trangsund. At the next corner go downhill on Storkyrkobrinken and take the first left—where the priests used to—on Prastgatan. Enjoy a quiet wander down this peaceful lane. After two blocks (at Kakbrinken) you'll see a cannon on the corner guarding a prehistoric rune stone. (In case you can't read ancient Nordic script, it says: "Torsten and Trogun erected this stone in memory of their son.") Continue farther down Prastgatan until you see the German-strength brick steeple of the Tyska Kyrkan (German church). This is a reminder of the days when German merchants worked here. Wander through its churchyard and out the back onto Svartmangatan. Follow it downhill to its end at a couple of benches and an iron railing overlooking Österlånggatan.

Österlånggatan: From this perch, survey the street to the left and right. Notice how it curves. This marks the old shoreline. In medieval times piers stretched out like many fingers into the harbor. Gradually, as land was reclaimed and developed, these piers were extended and what were originally piers became lanes leading to piers farther away. Walk left along Österlånggatan. At the cobbled Y in the road head uphill (up Kopmanbrinken) past a copy of *George and the Dragon*. (Or, for a quick finish, Österlånggatan takes you back to your starting point at the palace.)

Shopping, Jazz, and Food: From Kopmantorget (the statue), Kopmangatan leads past fine antique shops (some with their medieval painted ceilings still visible) back to Stortorget. Crossing the square, follow the crowds downhill two blocks to Stora Nygatan. This is Gamla Stan's main commercial drag, a festival of distractions that keeps most visitors from seeing the historic charms of the Old Town—which you just did. Now you can shop and eat.

▲▲**Military Parade and Changing of the Guard**—Starting at the Army Museum (daily at 12:00), the parade marches over either Norrbro Bridge or Strombron Bridge and up to the palace courtyard where the band plays and the guard changes (every other day the band is mounted . . . on horses). These days, the royal family lives out of town at Drottningholm, but the guards are for real. If the guard by the cannon in the semicircular courtyard looks a little lax, try wandering discreetly behind him.

▲▲**Royal Palace**—The palace is a complex of sights. Drop by the info booth in the semicircular courtyard (at the top where the guard changes) for an explanatory brochure with a map marking the different entrances. In a nutshell: The Apartments of State are lavish, as worthwhile as any; the Royal Treasury is the best in northern Europe; the chapel is no big deal; skip Gustav III's Museum of Antiquities; and plan to spend some time in the awesome Royal Armoury. An 80-kr combo ticket covers the apartments, treasury, and antiquities (more info below). To add the Royal Armory, get the 100-kr combo ticket (tel. 08/5877-1000, www.royalcourt.se).

▲▲**Apartments of State**—The stately palace exterior encloses 608 rooms (one more than Britain's Buckingham Palace) of glittering Baroque and rococo decor. Clearly the palace of Scandinavia's superpower, it's richly decorated (18th century) and steeped in royal history. The guided tour is heavy and tedious; the place is more interesting on your own—pick up English descriptions where available and don't miss the Bernadotte rooms (50 kr, daily Jun–Aug 10:00–16:00; off-season Tue–Sun 12:00–15:00, closed Mon; free English-language tours at 12:00 and 13:15).

▲▲**Royal Treasury**—You'll find great crowns, scepters, jeweled robes, and plenty of glitter that's gold. Nothing is explained, so get the 2-kr description at the entry (50 kr, May–Aug 10:00–16:00, off-season 12:00–15:00, no samples, often tours at 11:00 and 14:15, tel. 08/402-6000).

Gustav III's Museum of Antiquities—In the 1700s, Gustav III traveled through Italy and brought home impressive classical Roman statues. This was a huge deal if you'd never been out of Sweden. It's worth a look only if you've never been to the rest of Europe. Nothing is explained in English (50 kr, same hours as Apartments).

▲▲▲**Royal Armoury (Livrust Kammaren)**—This, the oldest museum in Sweden, has the most interesting and best-displayed collection of medieval royal armor I've seen anywhere in Europe. The incredible, original 17th-century gear includes royal baby wear, outfits kings wore when they were killed in battle or assassinated, and five centuries of royal Swedish armor—all wonderfully described in English. An added bonus is a basement lined with royal coaches, including coronation coaches, all beautifully preserved and richly decorated (60 kr, daily 10:00–16:00; winter Mon–Sat 11:00–16:00, closed Mon; tours daily in summer at 11:00, entry at bottom of Slottsbacken at base of palace, tel. 08/5195-5544).

Riksdaghuset—You can tour Sweden's parliament buildings if you'd like a firsthand look at its government (free hrly tours in English Jun–Aug, usually Mon–Fri at 12:30 and 14:00, some Sat–Sun at 13:30, enter at Riksgatan 3a, but call 08/786-4000 to confirm times).

Museum of Medieval Stockholm (Medeltidsmuseet)—This may be grade-schoolish, but it gives you a good look at medieval Stockholm (40 kr, daily Jul–Aug 11:00–16:00, Tue–Thu until 18:00; Sept–Jun Mon–Sat 11:00–16:00, Wed until 18:00, closed Mon; free 30-min English tours at 14:00 daily in summer enlivens the exhibits; enter from park in front of Parliament, tel. 08/5083-1790). The Stromparterren park, with its Carl Milles statue of the *Sun Singer* greeting the day, is a pleasant place for a sightseeing break (but an expensive place for a potty break—use the free WC in the museum).

Riddarholm Church—This final resting place for about 600 years of Sweden's royalty is pretty lifeless (20 kr, daily May–Aug 10:00–16:00, Sept Sat–Sun 12:00–15:00, closed in winter, tel. 08/402-6130). In a futile attempt to make this more interesting, they'll loan you the church guidebooklet. The cathedral next to the palace (see "Gamla Stan self-guided walk," above) is far more interesting.

Sights—Stockholm's Djurgården

▲▲▲**Skansen**—Europe's original and best open-air folk museum, Skansen is a huge park gathering more than 150 historic buildings (homes, churches, shops, and schoolhouses) transplanted from all corners of Sweden. Tourists can explore this Swedish-culture-on-a-lazy-Susan, seeing folk crafts in action and wonderfully furnished old interiors (lively only in the summer). In the town quarter (top of the escalator), craftspeople such as potters are busy doing their traditional thing in a re-created Old World Stockholm. Seek out the glassblowers if you'll be missing Sweden's glass country to the south.

Spreading out from there, the sprawling park is designed to show northern Swedish culture and architecture in the northern part of the park (top of park map) and southern Sweden in the south (bottom of map). Free one-hour guided walks (from Bollnästorget info stand at top of escalator) paint a fine picture of old Swedish lifestyles (usually daily at 14:00 and 16:00 Jun–Aug). There's fiddling nightly (except Sun) at 18:15; folk dancing demonstrations daily in summer at 19:00, Sunday at 14:30 and 16:00; and public dancing to live bands three nights a week (20:30–23:30, call for evening theme—jazz, folk, rock, or disco). Admission to the aquarium is the only thing not covered on your entry ticket (55 kr, opens daily at 10:00, closes between 16:00 and 20:00 depending on season and day of the week, call for times, tel. 08/660-1082).

Kids love Skansen, especially its zoo (ride a life-size wooden Dala-horse and stare down a hedgehog) and Lill' Skansen (Punch 'n' Judy, Mon–Fri at 12:00 and 14:00, minitrain, and pony ride fun daily from 11:00 till at least 16:00). There are lots of special events and several restaurants. The main restaurant serves a grand *smørgåsbord* (200 kr) and the Ekorren café offers the least expensive self-service lunches with a view. Tre Byttor (next to Ekorren) serves 18th century–style food in a candlelit setting. Another cozy inn, the old-time Stora Gungan Krog, at the top of the escalator, has better food (60- to 90-kr indoor or outdoor lunches with a salad and cracker bar).

Skansen is great for people watching and picnicking, with open and covered benches all over (especially at Torslunden and Bollnästorget, where peacenik local toddlers don't bump on the bumper cars). Get the map or the 30-kr museum guidebook that has the same map, and check the live crafts schedule at the information stand at Bollnästorget to confirm your Skansen plans.

Use the west entrance (Hazeliusporten) if you're heading to or from the Nordic Museum. (60 kr; winter weekdays-30 kr, weekends-40 kr; daily May–Aug 10:00–22:00, buildings 11:00–17:00; winter 10:00–16:00, some buildings 11:00–15:00; take bus #47 or #44 from the station; call 08/5789-0005 for recording of the day's tour, music, and dance schedule, or tel. 08/442-8000.) You can miss Gröna Lund, the second-rate amusement park across the street.

▲▲▲*Vasa*—Stockholm turned a titanic flop into one of Europe's great sightseeing attractions. This glamorous but unseaworthy warship—top-heavy with a tacked-on extra cannon deck—sank 20 minutes into her 1628 maiden voyage when a breeze caught the sails and blew her over in the Stockholm harbor. After 333 years she rose again from the deep (with the help of marine archaeologists) and today is the best-preserved ship anywhere, housed in a state-of-the-art museum. The masts on the roof are placed to show their actual height.

Catch the 25-minute English-subtitled movie (in English at 11:30 and 13:30, other languages with English subtitles every half hour) and, for more information, take the free 25-minute English tours (at the bottom of each hour from 10:30, fewer tours

Stockholm 635

off-season, call for times) to best enjoy and understand the ship. Learn about ship's rules (bread can't be older than eight years), why it sank (heavy bread?), how it's preserved, and so on. Private tours are easy to freeload on, but the displays are so well described that a tour is hardly necessary. (60 kr, daily mid-Jun–mid-Aug 9:30–19:00; off-season 10:00–17:00, winter Wed until 20:00, tel. 08/666-4800.) Take bus #47 to the big brick Nordic Museum or catch the boat from Nybroplan or Slussen, or walk from Skansen.

▲▲**Nordic Museum**—This museum, built to look like a Danish palace, offers a look at how Sweden lived over the last 500 years. Ask for a free audio guide when you enter. Highlights include the Food and Drink section, with its stunning china and crystal table settings; the Nordic folk art (2nd and 3rd floors); the huge statue of Gustav Vasa, father of modern Sweden, by Carl Milles (top of 2nd flight of stairs); and the Sami (Lapp) exhibit in the basement (Tue–Sun 10:00–21:00, summer Tue and Thu until 21:00, closed Mon, free guided tour in English Tue–Thu at 15:00 and 17:00, or ask for a free audio guide when you enter, tel. 08/51 95 6000). It's worth your time if you have the Stockholm Card, but it's overpriced at 60 kr per admission.

▲**Thielska Galleriet**—If you liked the Larsson and Zorn art in the National Gallery and/or if you're a Munch fan, this charming mansion on the water at the far end of the Djurgården park is worth the trip (40 kr, Mon–Sat 12:00–16:00, Sun 13:00–16:00, bus #69 from the central station, tel. 08/662-5884).

Sights—Outer Stockholm

▲▲**Carl Millesgården**—The home and garden housing a museum and the major work of Sweden's greatest sculptor is dramatically situated on a cliff overlooking Stockholm. Milles' entertaining, unique, and provocative art was influenced by Rodin. There's a classy café and a great picnic spot (60 kr, daily May–Sept 10:00–17:00; off-season Tue–Sun 12:00–16:00, closed Mon, tel. 08/446-7590.) Catch the T-bana to Ropsten, then take any bus (except #203 and #213) to the first stop (Torsvik). It's a five-minute walk from there (follow the signs).

▲▲**Drottningholm**—The queen's 17th-century summer castle and present royal residence has been called, not surprisingly, Sweden's Versailles. The adjacent, uncannily well-preserved Baroque theater is the real highlight, especially with its 50-kr guided tours (Jun–Aug English theater tours normally depart half past each hour 11:30–16:30, fewer tours off-season). Get there by a relaxing but overpriced boat ride (85 kr round-trip, two hrs) or take the subway to Brommaplan and bus #301 to #323 to Drottningholm. (50-kr entry, palace open daily May–Aug 12:00–16:30, Sept 12:00–15:30, tel. 08/402-6280 for palace tours in English, Jun–Aug often at 11:00, Sept at 12:00.)

The 18th-century Drottningholm court theater performs perfectly authentic operas (about 30 performances each summer). Tickets for this popular, time-tunnel musical and theatrical experience cost 100 kr to 470 kr, and go on sale each March. For information, contact Drottningholm's Theater Museum (Box 27050, 10251 Stockholm, tel. 08/660-8225, fax 08/665-1473).

▲▲Archipelago—The world's most scenic islands (24,000 of them!) surround Stockholm. Europeans who spend entire vacations in and around Stockholm rave about them. If you cruise to Finland, you'll get a good dose of this island beauty. Otherwise, consider the pleasant hour-long cruise (80 kr each way, buy tickets on boat) from Nybroplan downtown to the quiet town of Vaxholm. The TI has a free archipelago guidebooklet.

Sauna

Sometime while you're in Sweden or Finland, you'll have to treat yourself to Scandinavia's answer to support hose and a face-lift. (A sauna is actually more Finnish than Swedish.) Simmer down with the local students, retired folks, and busy executives. Try to cook as calmly as the Swedes. Just before bursting, go into the shower room. There's no lukecold, and the trickle-down theory doesn't apply—only one button, bringing a Niagara of liquid ice. Suddenly your shower stall becomes a Cape Canaveral launch pad, as your body scatters to every corner of the universe. A moment later you're back together. Rejoin the Swedes in the cooker, this time with their relaxed confidence; you now know that exhilaration is just around the corner. Only very rarely will you feel so good.

Any TI can point you toward the nearest birch twigs. Good opportunities include a Stockholm–Helsinki cruise, any major hotel you stay in, some hostels, or (cheapest) a public swimming pool. In Stockholm, consider Eriksdalsbadet (Hammarby Slussväg 8, near Skanstull T-bana, tel. 08/5084 0275). Use of its 50-meter indoor/outdoor pool and first-rate sauna costs 55 kr.

For a classier experience, the newly refurbished Centralbadet lets you enjoy an extensive gym, "bubblepool," sauna, steam room, and an elegant Art Nouveau pool from 1904 (Mon–Fri-79 kr, Sat-99 kr, long hours, last entry 20:30, closed Sun, Drottningsgatan 88, 5 minutes up from Sergels Torg, tel. 08/242-403). The steam room is mixed; the sauna is not. Bring your towel into the sauna—not for modesty but to separate your body from the bench. Massage and solarium cost extra, and the pool is more for floating than for jumping and splashing. The leafy courtyard is an appropriately relaxing place to enjoy their restaurant (reasonable and healthy light meals).

Shopping

Modern design, glass, clogs, and wooden goods are popular targets for shoppers. Browsing is a free, delightful way to enjoy Sweden's brisk pulse. Cop a feel at the Nordiska Kompaniet (NK, also meaning "no kroner left") just across from the Sweden House or close by in the Gallerian mall. The nearby Åhlens is less expensive. Swedish stores are open weekdays from 10:00 to 18:00 and Saturdays until 15:00, but are closed on Sundays. Some of the bigger stores (like Åhlens and NK) are open later on Saturdays and on Sunday afternoons. Take a short walk to Norrmalms Torg to the new bank branch of Scandia Insurance for its ATMs, Internet access, and free coffee, tea, or chocolate.

For a *smørgåsbord* of Scanjunk, visit the Loppmarknaden (northern Europe's biggest flea market) at the planned suburb of Skärholmen (free on weekdays, 10 kr on weekends, Mon–Fri 11:00–18:00, Sat 9:00–15:00, Sun 10:00–15:00, busiest on weekends, T-bana: Skärholmen, tel. 08/710-0060).

Sleeping in Stockholm
(7 kr = about $1, tel. code: 08)
Sleep Code: **S** = Single, **D** = Double/Twin, **T** = Triple, **Q** = Quad, **b** = bathroom, **CC** = Credit Card (Visa, MasterCard, Amex). "Summer rates" mean mid-June to mid-August, and Friday and Saturday (sometimes Sunday) the rest of the year. Prices include breakfast unless otherwise noted.

Stockholm has plenty of money-saving deals for the savvy visitor. Its hostels are among Europe's best ($15 a bed), and plenty of people offer private accommodations ($50 doubles). Peak season for Stockholm's expensive hotels is business time—workdays outside of summer. Rates drop by 30 to 50 percent in the summer or on weekends. If business is slow, ask for a discount. To sort through all of this, the city has helpful, English-speaking room-finding services with handy locations and long hours (see Hotellcentralen and Sweden House, above).

The **Stockholm Package** (limited to Jun–Aug and Fri and Sat throughout the year) offers business-class doubles with buffet breakfasts from 870 kr, includes two free Stockholm Cards, and lets two children up to 18 years old sleep for free. Assuming you'll be getting two Stockholm Cards anyway (398 kr), this gives you a $200 hotel room for about $50. This is for real (summertime is that dead for business hotels). The procedure (through either TI) is easy: a 100-kr advance-booking fee (you can arrange by fax, pay when you arrive) or a 40-kr in-person booking fee if you just drop in. Arriving without reservations in July is never a problem. It gets tight during the Water Festival (10 days in early Aug) and during a convention stretch for a few days in late June.

My listings are a good value only outside of Stockholm Package time, or if the 790 kr for a double and two cards is out of your range and you're hosteling. Every place listed here has staff who speak English and will explain their special deals to you on the

Stockholm Hotels

Map Legend:
- ❶ QUEEN'S HOTEL
- ❷ BENTLEY'S HOTEL
- ❸ STUREPARKENS GÄSTVÅNING
- ❹ HOTEL GUSTAV VASA
- ❺ DROTTNING VICTORIAS ORLOGSHEM
- ❻ PRIZE HOTEL
- ❼ RICA CITY HOTEL
- ❽ HOTELLJÄNST ROOM FINDING
- ❾ SUNDIN ROOMS
- ❿ LICHTSTEINER ROOMS
- ⓫ AF CHAPMAN HOSTEL
- ⓬ SKEPPSHOLMEN HOSTEL
- ⓭ ZINKENSDAMM HOSTEL
- ⓮ BRYGGHUSET HOSTEL
- ⓯ KRISTINA RESTAURANG
- ⓰ HERMITAGE REST.

phone. If money is limited, ask if they have cheaper rooms. It's not often that a hotel will push their odd misfit room that's 100 kr below all the others. And at any time of year, prices can be soft.

About the only Laundromat in central Stockholm is Tvättomaten, at Västmannagatan 61 on Odenplan (60 kr, full serve-80 kr, Mon–Fri 8:30–18:30, Sat 9:30–15:00, closed Sun, across from Gustav Vasa church, bus #53 from Upplandsgaten to Central Station, T-bana: Odenplan, helpful manager, tel. 08/346-480).

Sleeping in Hotels

Queen's Hotel is cheery, clean, and just a 10-minute walk from the station, located in a great pedestrian area across the street from the Centralbadet (city baths, listed on all maps). With a fine TV and piano lounge, coffee in the evenings, and a staff that enjoys helping its guests, this is probably the best cheap hotel in town (summer and Fri–Sat rates: S-525 kr, Ss-550 kr, Sb-675 kr, D-575–680 kr,

Ds-625 kr, Db-775 kr, winter rates: D-575–680 kr, Ds-625 kr, Db-1,100–1,250 kr, CC:VMA, Drottninggatan 71A, tel. 08/249-460, fax 08/217-620, e-mail: queenshotel@queenshotel.se). Their simple rooms have no sinks. If you're arriving early from the train or boat, you're welcome to leave your bags and grab a 45-kr breakfast.

Bentley's Hotel is an interesting option with old-English flair and renovated rooms (summer rates include winter Sundays: very small Db-750 kr, Db-775 kr, Db suite-915 kr, winter Db-1,175 kr, CC:VMA, 2 blocks up the street from Queen's at Drottninggatan 77, 11160 Stockholm, tel. 08/141-395, fax 08/212-492). Klas and Agi Källström attempt to mix elegance, comfort, and simplicity into an affordable package. Each room is tastefully decorated with antique furniture but has a modern full bathroom.

The proud little **Stureparkens Gästvåning** is a carefully run, traditional-feeling place with lots of class and 10 thoughtfully appointed rooms. (S-460 kr, D-695–750 kr, Db-950 kr, 2-night minimum, elevator, CC:VM, near T-bana: Stadion, across from Stureparken at Sturegatan 58, tel. 08/662-7230, fax 08/661-5713). They rent an apartment for 1,500 kr per night (7-night minimum).

Hotel Gustav Vasa has classy Old World rooms in a listed building with a family-run feel on a convenient square just 15 minutes on foot from the center (Ss-575 kr, Sb-650 kr, D-680 kr, Db-900 kr, includes breakfast, rates up to 150-kr higher outside of summer and weekends, they have some cheaper tiny doubles, family deals, CC:VMA, elevator, subway to Odenplan, exit Västmannagatan, to Västmannagatan 61, tel. 08/343-801, fax 08/307-372, e-mail: gustov.vasa@wineasy.se).

Drottning Victorias Orlogshem, formerly a hotel for navy personnel, now accepts the public. It offers functional, quiet rooms with hardwood floors and naval decor in a great neighborhood behind the National Museum, just a block off the central harbor (35 rooms, Sb-500 kr, Db-700 kr, Tb-900 kr, extra bed-150 kr, family deals, same prices all year, breakfast-40 kr, no double beds—only twins, Teatergatan 3, 11148 Stockholm, tel. 08/611-0113, fax 08/611-3150).

Prize Hotel is unique—a super-modern, happy place with tight 'n' tidy rooms two blocks from the station in Stockholm's World Trade Center. Designed for business travelers, it has mostly singles (with wall-beds that fold down to make doubles) and major summer and weekend discounts (not worth the high-season price; low prices Fri, Sat, and Jun 8–Aug 8: Sb-680 kr, Db-835 kr; high-season price: Sb-1,195 kr, Db-1,350 kr; they have a few real doubles for the same price as their wall-bed doubles; low rates offered during slow winter times; breakfast-55 kr, CC:VMA, Kungsbron 1, tel. 08/566-22200, fax 08/5662-2444, e-mail: prize.sth@prize.se, www.prize.se).

Rica City Hotel is also unique. Filling the top floors of a downsized department store and a leader in environmental friendliness, this modern place offers hardwood floors and all the comforts in a "one-star delux" package (200 rooms, discount rates weekends and Jun 20–Aug 9: Sb-700 kr, Db-880 kr, Qb-970–1,280 kr, some rooms lack windows but have good ventilation: Sb-550 kr, Db-700 kr, all D are twins shoved together, high-season Db-1,360 kr, breakfast-50 kr, CC:VMA, free loaner bikes, overlooking Hötorget market at Kungsgatan 47, tel. 08/723-7220, fax 08/723-7299).

Sleeping in Rooms in Private Homes

Stockholm's centrally located private rooms are nearly as expensive as discounted hotels—a deal only in the high season. More reasonable rooms are a few T-bana stops just minutes from the center. Stockholm's TIs refer those in search of a room in a private house to **Hotelljånst** (near station, Vasagatan 15, tel. 08/104-467, fax 08/213-716). They can set you up for about 450 kr per double without breakfast for a minimum two-night stay. Go direct—you'll save your host the listing service's fee. Be sure to get the front door security code when you call, as there's no intercom connection with front doors.

Else Mari Sundin, an effervescent retired actress, rents her homey apartment just two blocks from the bridge to Djurgården (Db-700 kr for up to 4 people, bus #47 or #69 to Torstenssonsgatan 7, go through courtyard to "garden house" and up to 2nd floor, tel. 08/665-3348, 0884 door code). Since she lives out of town, this can be complicated. But once you're set up, it's great.

Mrs. Lichtsteiner offers rooms with kitchenettes and has a family room with a loft (S-from 300 kr, D-from 400 kr without breakfast, a block from T-bana: Rådhuset, exit T-bana direction: Polishuset, at Bergsgatan 45, once inside go through door on left and up elevator to 2nd floor, tel. 08/746-9166, call ahead to get the security code, e-mail: rooms@user.bip.net).

Sleeping in Hostels

Stockholm has Europe's best selection of big-city hostels offering good beds in simple but interesting places for 100 kr. If your budget is tight, these are right. Each has a helpful English-speaking staff, pleasant family rooms, good facilities, and good leads on budget survival in Stockholm. All will hold rooms with a phone call. Hosteling is cheap only if you're a member (guest membership: 40 kr per night; necessary only in IYHF places); bring your own sheet (paper sheets rent for 30 kr, cotton sheets-50 kr) and plan on a picnic for breakfast (or pay 45 kr). Several of the hostels are often booked up well in advance but hold a few beds for those who are left in the lurch.

Af Chapman (IYHF), Europe's most famous youth hostel, is a permanently moored cutter ship. Just a five-minute walk from

Stockholm 641

downtown, this floating hostel has 140 beds—two to eight per stateroom. A popular but compassionate place, it's often booked far in advance, but saves some beds each morning for unreserved arrivals (given out at 7:00) and gives away unclaimed rooms each evening after 18:00. If you call at breakfast time and show up before 12:00, you may land a bed, even in summer (130 kr per bed, D-300 kr, bike rental-90 kr/day or 50kr/half day, open Apr–mid-Dec, sleeping bags allowed, has a lounge and cafeteria that welcomes nonhostelers, reception open 24 hours, rooms locked 11:00–15:00, STF Vandrarhem Af Chapman, Skeppsholmen, 11149 Stockholm, tel. 08/08/679-5015 for advance booking).

Skeppsholmen Hostel (IYHF), just ashore from the Af Chapman, is open all year. It has better facilities and smaller rooms (150 kr per bed in doubles, 130 kr in triples or quads, only 100 kr in dorms, nonmembers-40 kr extra, tel. 08/463-2266), but it isn't as romantic as its seagoing sister.

Bed and Breakfast is Stockholm's newest cozy hostel, with only 20 beds (145 kr per bed in 8- to 12-bed rooms, breakfast-20 kr, sheets-40 kr, near Rådmansgatan T-bana stop, just off Sveavägen at Rehnsgatan 21, tel. & fax 08/152-838). Friendly Bjørn and Daniela also offer eight single (295 kr) and double (395 kr) rooms with breakfast.

Zinkensdamm Hostel (IYHF) is a big, basic hostel in a busy suburb, with 135-kr dorm beds (40 kr extra for sheets and nonmembers), plenty of 360-kr doubles without sheets, a Laundromat, and the best hostel kitchen facilities in town (STF Vandrarhem Zinken, open 24 hours all year, restaurant, Zinkens Väg 20, T-bana: Zinkensdamm, tel. 08/616-8100, fax 08/616-8120, e-mail: info:zinkensdamm@Sweden.hotels.se). This is a great no-nonsense, user-friendly value.

Vandrarhemmet Bryggghuset, in a former brewery near Odenplan, is small (57 beds in 12 spacious rooms), bright, clean, and quiet, with a Laundromat and a kitchen. Since this is a private hostel, its two- to six-bed rooms are open to all for 130 kr per bed (no sleeping bags allowed, sheets rent for 45 kr). Sheetless doubles are 320 kr. (Open Jun–mid-Sept 7:00–12:00, 15:00–23:00, 02:00 curfew, Norrtullsgatan 12 N, tel. 08/312-424.)

Stockholm has 12 campgrounds (located south of town) that are a wonderful solution to your parking and budget problems. The TI's "Camping Stockholm" brochure has specifics.

Eating in Stockholm

Stockholm's elegant department stores (notably NK and Åhlens, near Sergels Torg) have cafeterias for the kroner-pinching local shopper. Look for the 50-kr "rodent of the day" (*dagens rätt*) specials. Most museums have handy cafés. The café at the **Af Chapman** hostel serves a good salad/roll/coffee lunch in an unbeatable deck-of-a-ship atmosphere—if the weather's good (open to the public Jun 28–Aug 2 11:30–18:00, off-season closed at 16:00). **Restaurang Al Forno** on Drottningsgatan, across from Queen's Hotel, has tasty 50-kr pizzas and pasta.

In Gamla Stan: The Old Town (Gamla Stan) has lots of restaurants. Try the wonderfully atmospheric **Kristina Restaurang** (Västerlånggatan 68, tel. 08/208-086). In this 1625 building, under a leather ceiling steeped in a turn-of-the-century interior, you'll find good dinners from 145 kr, including a salad and cracker bar and a cheaper "summer" menu. They serve a great 55-kr lunch (Mon–Fri 11:00–15:00) that includes an entrée, salad bar, bread, a drink, and live jazz. You can enjoy the music over just a beer or coffee, too. **Hermitage** has good vegetarian food and daily specials (Stora Nygatan 11). **Paganini** has a good mix of Swedish and Italian food, and great people watching if you snare a window seat (80-kr lunch specials, Västerlånggatan 75, tel. 08/406-0607).

Picnics

With higher taxes almost every year, Sweden's restaurant industry is suffering. You'll notice many fine places almost empty. Swedes joke that the "local" cuisine is now Chinese, Italian, and hamburgers. Here more than anywhere, budget travelers should picnic.

Stockholm's major department stores and the many small corner groceries are fine places to assemble a picnic. **Åhlens** department store has a great food section (open until 21:00, near Sergels Torg). The late-hours supermarket downstairs in the central train station is picnic friendly, with fresh, ready-made sandwiches (Mon–Fri 7:00–23:00, Sat–Sun 9:00–23:00).

The market at **Hötorget** is a fun place to picnic shop, especially in the indoor, exotic, and ethnic **Hötorgshallen** (fun café and restaurant in fish section). The outdoor market closes at 18:00, and many merchants put their unsold produce on the push list (earlier closing and more desperate merchants on Sat).

For a classy vegetarian buffet, often with a piano serenade, try **Ørtagården**—literally "the herb garden"—above the colorful old Østermalms food market at Østermalmstorg (70-kr lunch Mon–Fri until 17:00, 85-kr dinner evenings and weekends, Nybrogatan 31, tel. 08/662-1728).

Transportation Connections—Stockholm

By train to: Copenhagen (6/day, 8 hrs, night service 22:30–7:05), **Oslo** (2/day, 7 hrs, plus a 15-hour night train via Göteborg: 20:15–10:52). Train info tel. 020/757-575 (toll free in Sweden) or 08/227-940 (outside Sweden).

By boat to: Helsinki (daily/nightly boats, 16 hrs; see www.vikingline.fi and www.silja.com/english), **Turku** (daily/nightly boats, 11 hrs).

# OSLO

Oslo is the smallest and least earthshaking of the Nordic capitals, but this brisk little city offers more sightseeing thrills than you might expect. Sights of the Viking spirit—past and present—tell an exciting story. Prowl through the remains of ancient Viking ships and marvel at more peaceful but equally gutsy modern boats like the *Kon-Tiki*, *Ra*, and *Fram*. Dive into the country's folk culture at the open-air folk museum and get stirred up by Norway's heroic spirit at the Norwegian Resistance Museum.

For a look at modern Oslo, browse through the new yuppie-style harbor shopping complex, tour the striking city hall, take a peek at sculptor Vigeland's people pillars, and climb the towering Holmenkollen ski jump.

Situated at the head of a 60-mile-long fjord, surrounded by forests, and populated by more than 500,000 people, Oslo is Norway's cultural hub and an all-you-can-see *smørgåsbord* of historic sights, trees, art, and Nordic fun.

Planning Your Time

Oslo offers an exciting two-day slate of sightseeing thrills. Ideally, spend two days and leave on the night train to Copenhagen or take a third day to do "Norway in a Nutshell" for the fjord scenery (see end of Chapter). Spend two days in Oslo like this:
Day 1: Set up. Visit the TI. Tour the Akershus Castle and Norwegian Resistance Museum. Take a picnic on the ferry to Bygdøy and enjoy a view of the city harbor. Tour the *Fram*, *Kon-Tiki*, and Viking ships. Finish the afternoon at the Norwegian Open Air Folk Museum. Boat home. For evening culture, consider the folk music and dance show (20:30 Mon and Thu).
Day 2: At 10:00 catch the city hall tour, then browse through the

National Gallery. Spend the afternoon at Vigeland Park and at the Holmenkollen ski jump and museum. Browse Karl Johans Gate (all the way to the station) and Aker Brygge harbor in the early evening for the Norwegian paseo. Consider munching a fast-food dinner on the harbor minicruise.

Orientation

Oslo is easy to manage, with nearly all its sights clustered around the central "barbell" street (Karl Johans Gate, with the Royal Palace on one end and the train station on the other) or in the Bygdøy district, a 10-minute ferry ride across the harbor.

Tourist Information

The **Norwegian Information Center** displays Norway as if it were a giant booth at a trade show (daily 9:00–19:00, shorter hours off-season, on the waterfront between city hall and Aker Brygge, tel. 22 83 00 50). Stock up on brochures for Oslo and all of your Norwegian destinations. Pick up the free Oslo map, Sporveiskart transit map, *What's on in Oslo* monthly (for the most accurate listing of museum hours and special events), *Streetwise* magazine (hip, fun to read, and full of offbeat ideas), and the free annual *Oslo Guide* (with plenty of details on sightseeing, shopping, and eating). Consider buying the Oslo Card (unless your hotel provides it for free). The info center has a handy public toilet and rooms showcasing various crafts and ways you can spend your money. The TI window in the central station is much simpler and deals only with Oslo but can handle your needs just as well (daily in summer 8:00–23:00, less off-season).

Use It is a hardworking youth information center, providing solid, money-saving, experience-enhancing information to young, student, and vagabond travelers (mid-Jun–mid-Aug Mon–Fri 7:30–17:00, closed Sat–Sun; otherwise Mon–Fri 11:00–17:00, Møllergata 3, tel. 22 41 51 32, fax 22 42 63 71, www.unginfo.oslo.no). They have telephones and e-mail, and can find you the cheapest beds in town (no booking fee). Read their free *Streetwise* magazine for ideas on eating and sleeping cheap, good nightspots, the best beaches, and so on.

The **Oslo Card** gives you free use of all city public transit and boats, free entry to all sights, a free harbor minicruise tour, free parking, and many more discounts—and is also a handy handbook (24 hours-150 kr, 48 hours-220 kr, 72 hours-250 kr). Almost any two-day visit to Oslo will be cheaper with the Oslo Card (which costs less than 3 Bygdøy museum admissions, the ski jump, and 1 city bus ride). Students with an ISIC card may be better off without the Oslo Card. The TI's special Oslo Package hotel deal (described under Sleeping, below) includes this card with your discounted hotel room.

Oslo

Arrival in Oslo

By Train: Oslo S, the modern central train station, is slick and helpful, with a late-hours TI (daily in summer 8:00–23:00, less off-season), room-finding service, and a late-hours bank (fair rates, normal fee). Pick up leaflets on the Flåm and Bergen Railway. For a handy supermarket, head down the escalator across from tracks 13 through 19 to Østbanehallen (Mon–Fri 9:00–21:00, Sat 9:00–20:00, Sun 12:00–20:00).

By Plane: The super speedy "Flytog" train zips travelers from Oslo's Gardermoen Airport to the central train station in 22 minutes (120 kr, 6/hrly, not covered by railpass). InterCity trains cost about half as much and take about twice the time (1/hrly, covered by railpass). "Flybuss" airport buses make several downtown stops including the train station (65 kr, 6/hrly). For a taxi from the airport to downtown, allow 600 kr.

Getting around Oslo

By Public Transit: Oslo's transit system is made up of buses, trams, ferries, and a subway. Tickets cost 20 kr and are good for one hour of use on any combination of the above. Flexicards give eight rides for 105 kr. Buy tickets as you board (bus info tel. 22 17 70 30, daily 8:00–23:00). **Trafikanten**, the public transit information center, is under the ugly tower immediately in front of the station. Their free "Sporveiskart for Oslo" transit map is the best city map around and makes the transit system easy. The similar but smaller "Visitor's Map Oslo" (available at TI) is easier to use and also free. The **Dagskort Tourist Ticket** is a 40-kr, 24-hour transit pass that pays for itself in the second hour. The Oslo Card (see "Tourist Information," above) gives you free run of the entire transit system. Note how gracefully the subway lines fan out after huddling at Stortinget. Take advantage of the way they run like clockwork, with schedules clearly posted and followed.

By Bike: Oslo is a good biking town, especially if you'd like to get out into the woods or ride a tram uphill out of town and coast for miles back. Glåmdal Cycle rents bikes (3 hrs/90–130 kr, 6 hrs/140–180 kr, 24 hrs/180–230 kr depending on bike, 20 percent discount for readers of this book; May–Sept Mon–Fri 8:00–21:00, Sat–Sun 10:00–18:00, closes earlier off-season; between Norway Info Center and Akerbrygge Shopping Center, through the iron gates, tel. 23 11 51 08).

Helpful Hints

To get a taxi, call 22 38 80 90, then dial 1. Jernbanetorgets Apotek is a 24-hour pharmacy directly across from the train station (on Jernbanetorget, tel. 22 41 24 82). Kilroy Travel is everyone's favorite for student and discounted air tickets (Nedre Slottsgate 23, tel. 23 10 23 10).

Oslo

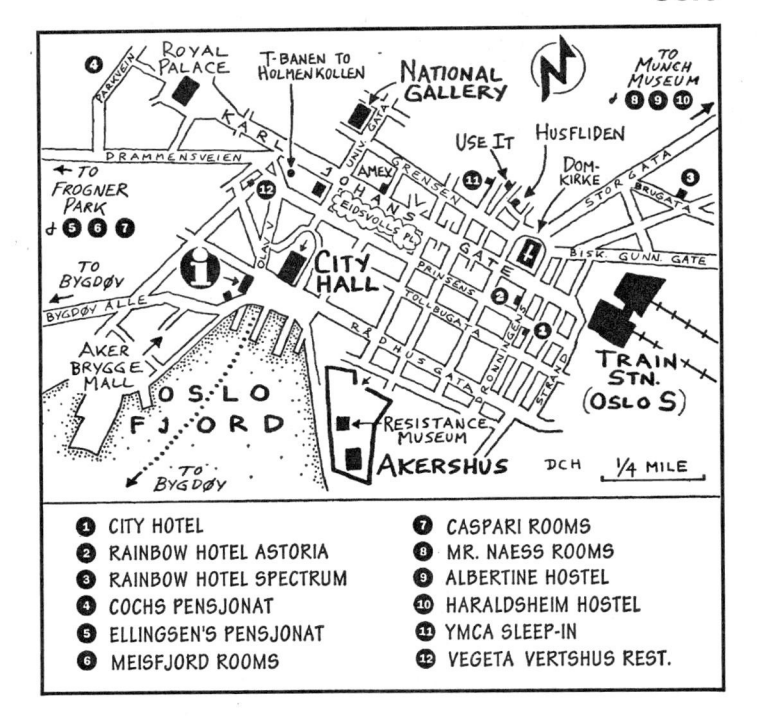

- **1** CITY HOTEL
- **2** RAINBOW HOTEL ASTORIA
- **3** RAINBOW HOTEL SPECTRUM
- **4** COCHS PENSJONAT
- **5** ELLINGSEN'S PENSJONAT
- **6** MEISFJORD ROOMS
- **7** CASPARI ROOMS
- **8** MR. NAESS ROOMS
- **9** ALBERTINE HOSTEL
- **10** HARALDSHEIM HOSTEL
- **11** YMCA SLEEP-IN
- **12** VEGETA VERTSHUS REST.

Sights—Downtown Oslo

Note: Because of Norway's passion for minor differences in opening times from month to month, I've generally listed only the peak-season hours. Assume opening hours shorten as the days do. The high season in Oslo is mid-June to mid-August. (I'll call that "summer" in this chapter.)

▲▲**City Hall**—Construction on Oslo's richly decorated Rådhuset began in 1931 and was finished in 1950 in time to celebrate the city's 900th birthday. Norway's leading artists (including Edvard Munch) all contributed to what was an avant-garde thrill in its day. The interior's 2,000 square yards of bold and colorful "socialist modernism" murals (which take you on a voyage through the collective psyche of Norway, from its simple rural beginnings through the scar tissue of the Nazi occupation and beyond) are meaningful only with the excellent, free guided tours (offered Mon–Fri at 10:00, 12:00, and 14:00; open Mon–Sat 9:00–17:00, Sun 12:00–17:00, until 16:00 in off-season, entry on Karl Johans side, tel. 22 86 16 00). Ever notice how city halls rather than churches are the dominant buildings in the your-government-loves-you northern corner of Europe? The main hall of Oslo's city hall actually feels like a temple to good government (the altarlike mural celebrates "work, play, and civic administration"). The Nobel Peace Prize is awarded each December in this room.

▲**Akershus Fortress Complex**—This parklike complex of sites scattered over Oslo's fortified center is still a military base. But dodging patrolling guards and vans filled with soldiers you'll see war memorials, the castle, a prison, the Nazi resistance museum, an armed forces museum, and cannon-strewn ramparts affording fine harbor views and picnic perches. Immediately inside the gate is an information center with an interesting exhibit on medieval Oslo's fortifications. In summer, free 45-minute tours of the grounds leave from the center (10:00, 12:00, 14:00, 16:00, daily but not Sun morning, tel. 23 09 39 17). There's a small changing of the guard daily at 13:30.

Akershus Fortress—One of the oldest buildings in town, this castle overlooking Oslo's harbor is mediocre by European standards. The big, empty rooms remind us of Norway's medieval poverty. Behind the chapel altar, steps lead down to the tombs of some Norwegian kings. The castle is interesting only with the tour (20 kr for castle entry, May–mid-Sept Mon–Sat 10:00–16:00, Sun 12:30–16:00; open in Jul until 18:00 Mon–Thu; open Sun only in spring and fall; closed in winter; free 50-min English tours offered in summer Mon–Sat at 11:00, 13:00, and 15:00, Sun at 13:00 and 15:00, tel. 22 41 25 21).

▲▲**Norwegian Resistance Museum (Norges Hjemmefrontmuseum)**—A stirring story about the Nazi invasion and occupation is told with wonderful English descriptions. This is the best look in Europe at how national spirit endured total German occupation (20 kr, Mon–Sat 10:00–17:00, Sun 11:00–17:00, closes 1 hour earlier off-season, next to castle in building overlooking harbor, tel. 23 09 31 38).

Armed Forces Museum—Across the fortress parade ground, a large museum traces Norwegian military from Viking days to post-WWII. The early stuff is very sketchy but the WWII story is fascinating (free, Mon–Fri 10:00–18:00, Sat–Sun 11:00–16:00, shorter hours Sept–May, tel. 23 09 35 82).

▲**National Gallery**—Located downtown, this easy-to-handle museum gives you an effortless tour back in time and through Norway's most beautiful valleys, mountains, and villages, with the help of its romantic painters (especially Dahl). The gallery also has several Picassos, a noteworthy Impressionist collection, some Vigeland statues, and a representative roomful of Munch paintings, including one of his famous *Scream* paintings. His artwork here makes a trip to the Munch museum unnecessary for most.

Greater Oslo

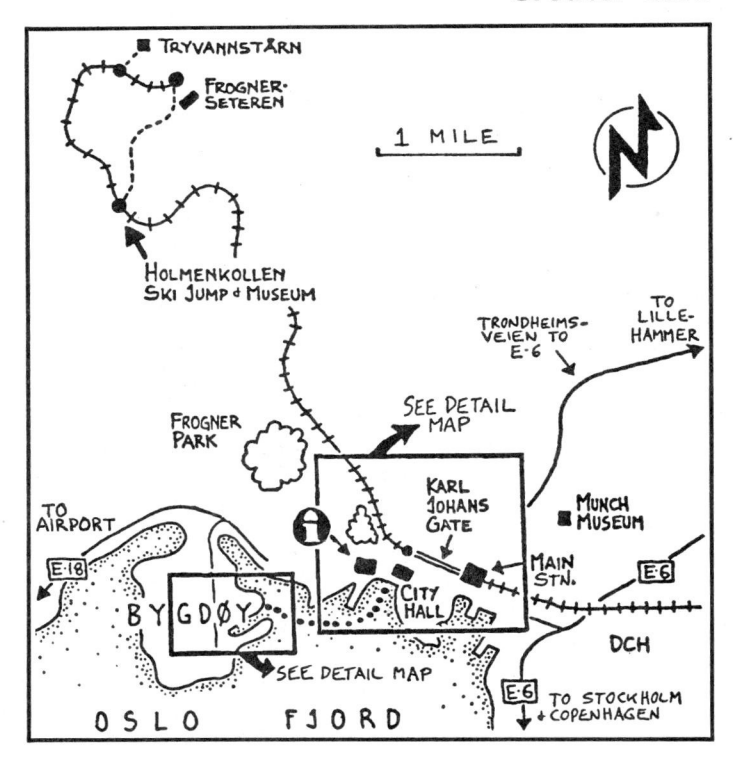

For an entertaining survey of 2,500 years of sculpture, go through the museum gift shop and down the stairs to the right for a room filled with plaster copies of famous works (free, Mon, Wed, Fri 10:00–18:00, Thu 10:00–20:00, Sat 10:00–16:00, Sun 11:00–16:00, closed Tue, Universitets Gata 13, tel. 22 20 04 04).

▲▲**Browsing**—Oslo's pulse is best felt along and near the central Karl Johans Gate (from station to palace), between the city hall and the harbor, and in the trendy harborside Aker Brygge Festival Market Mall—a glass-and-chrome collection of sharp cafés and polished produce stalls just west of the city hall (trams #10 and #15 to/from train station). The buskers are among the best in Europe. Aker Brygge is very lively late evenings.

▲▲▲**Vigeland Sculptures and the Vigeland Museum in Frogner Park**—The 75-acre park contains a lifetime of work by Norway's greatest sculptor, Gustav Vigeland. From 1924 to 1942

he sculpted 175 bronze and granite statues—each nude and unique. Walking over the statue-lined bridge you'll come to the main fountain. Trace the story of our lives in the series of humans intertwined with trees around the fountain. The maze in the pavement around the fountain starts opposite the monolith and comes out, three kilometers later, closest to the monolith. Try following it...you can't go wrong. Vigeland's 60-foot-high tangled tower of 121 bodies called *The Monolith of Life* is the centerpiece of the park. While it seems the lower figures are laden with earthly concerns and the higher ones are freed to pursue loftier, more spiritual adventures, Vigeland gives us permission to interpret it any way we like. Pick up the free map from the box on the kiosk wall as you enter. The park is more than great art. It's a city at play. Enjoy its urban Norwegian ambience. Then visit the Vigeland Museum to see the models for the statues and more in the artist's studio. Photos on the wall show the construction of the monolith (30 kr for museum, Tue–Sat 10:00–18:00, Sun 12:00–19:00, closed Mon; off-season Tue–Sun 12:00–16:00 and free, tel. 22 44 11 36). The park is always open and free. Take bus #20 or #45 or tram #12 or #15—get off at Frogner Plass for the museum or Vigeland Park for outdoor statues—or take the T-bane to "Majorstuen."
Oslo City Museum—Located in the Frogner Manor farm in Frogner Park, this museum tells the story of Oslo. A helpful free English brochure guides you through the exhibits (30 kr, Tue–Fri 10:00–18:00, Sat–Sun 11:00–17:00, closed Mon, shorter hours off-season, tel. 22 43 06 45).
▲▲**Edvard Munch Museum**—The only Norwegian painter to have had a serious impact on European art, Munch (monk) is a surprise to many who visit this fine museum. The emotional, disturbing, and powerfully expressionist work of this strange and perplexing man is arranged chronologically. You'll see paintings, drawings, lithographs, and photographs. Don't miss *The Scream*, which captures the fright many feel as the human "race" does just that (50 kr, daily 10:00–18:00; off-season closes at 16:00 and all day Mon; take T-bane from station to "Tøyen," tel. 22 67 37 74). If the price or location is a problem, you can see a roomful of Munch paintings in the free National Gallery downtown.

Sights—Oslo's Bygdøy Neighborhood
▲▲▲**Bygdøy**—This exciting cluster of sights is on a parklike peninsula just across the harbor from downtown. To get to Bygdøy, either take bus #30 from the station and National Theater or, more fun, catch the ferry from City Hall (20 kr, free with transit pass or Oslo Card, 3/hrly, 8:30–21:00). The Folk Museum and Viking ships are a 10-minute walk from the ferry's first stop, Dronningen. The other museums are at the second stop, Bygdøynes. All Bygdøy sights are within a 15-minute walk of each other. While an overpriced

tourist train shuttles visitors around Bygdøy (3/hrly, 50 kr for all-day pass), the *Fram*-Viking ships walk gives you a fine feel for rural Norway.

▲▲Norwegian Folk Museum

Brought from all corners of Norway, 150 buildings have been reassembled on these 35 acres. While Stockholm's Skansen was the first to open to the public, this museum is a bit older, started in 1885 as the king's private collection. You'll find craftspeople doing their traditional things; security guards disguised in cute, colorful, and traditional local costumes; endless creative ways to make do in a primitive log-cabin-and-goats-on-the-roof age; a 12th-century stave church; and a museum filled with toys and fine folk costumes. The place hops in the summer but is dead off-season. Catch the free one-hour guided walks (call for times). Otherwise, glean information from the 10-kr guidebook and the informative attendants who look like Rebecca Boone's Norwegian pen pals (50 kr, daily Jun–Aug 9:00–18:00; off-season 10:00–17:00 or less). For folk dance performances, tour, and crafts demonstration schedules, call 22 12 37 00.

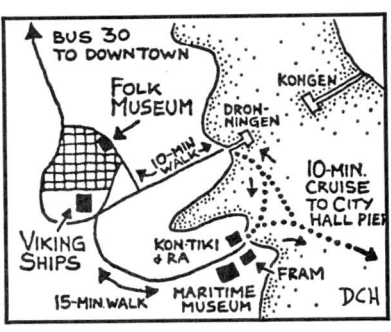

▲▲Viking Ships

Three great ninth-century Viking ships are surrounded by artifacts from the days of rape, pillage, and—ya sure, you betcha—plunder. There are no museum tours, but everything is well described in English, and it's hard not to hear the English-speaking bus tour guides. There was a time when much of a frightened Europe closed every prayer with "And deliver us from the Vikings, Amen." Gazing up at the prow of one of these sleek, time-stained vessels, you can almost hear the screams and smell the armpits of those redheads on the rampage (30 kr, daily summer 9:00–18:00, spring and fall 11:00–17:00, closes in winter at 15:00, tel. 22 43 83 79). To miss the tour-group crowds, come early, late, or at lunchtime.

▲▲The *Fram*

This great ship took modern-day Vikings Amundsen and Nansen deep into the Arctic and Antarctic, farther north and south than any ship before. For three years the *Fram* was part of an Arctic ice drift. The exhibit is fascinating. Read the ground-floor displays, then explore the boat (25 kr, daily summer 9:00–18:45, shorter hours off-season). You can step into the lobby and see the ship's hull for free. The **polar sloop *Gjøa*** is dry-docked next to the ferry dock. This is the boat Amundsen and a crew of six used from 1903 to 1906 to "discover" the Northwest Passage (*Fram* ticket gets you aboard).

▲▲***Kon-Tiki* Museum**—Next to the *Fram* are the *Kon-Tiki* and the *Ra II*, the boats Thor Heyerdahl built and sailed 4,000 and 3,000 miles, respectively, to prove that early South Americans could have sailed to Polynesia and Africans could have populated Barbados. Both are well displayed and described in English. A short "adventures of Thor Heyerdahl" movie plays constantly (30 kr, daily 9:30–17:00, off-season 10:30–16:00).

▲**Norwegian Maritime Museum**—If you like the sea, this museum is a salt lick, providing a fine look at Norway's maritime heritage (30 kr, 60 kr for a family, daily 10:00–19:00, off-season 10:30–16:00 and sometimes later). Consider viewing the wide-screen nature film on Norway's coast called *The Ocean, A Way of Life* (free, 20 min, on the half hour).

Other Oslo Sights and Activities

▲**Henie-Onstad Art Center**—Norway's best private modern art collection, donated by the famous Norwegian Olympic skater/movie star Sonja Henie (and her husband), combines modern art, a stunning building, a beautiful fjord-side setting, and the great café/restaurant Pirouetten. Don't miss Henie's glittering trophy room near the entrance of the center (about 50 kr, depending on exhibit, Tue–Thu 10:00–21:00, Fri–Mon 11:00–18:00, tel. 67 54 30 50). It's in Høvikodden, eight miles southwest of Oslo (catch bus #151, #161, #251, #252, or #261 from the Oslo train station or from Universitets Plass by the National Theater).

▲▲**Holmenkollen Ski Jump and Ski Museum**—Overlooking Oslo is a tremendous ski jump with a unique museum of skiing. The T-bane #1 gets you out of the city, into the hills and forests that surround Oslo, and to the jump. After touring the history of skiing in the museum, ride the elevator and climb the 100-step stairway to the top of the jump for the best possible view of Oslo—and a chance to look down the long and frightening ramp that has sent so many tumbling into the agony of defeat. The **ski museum**—a must for skiers—traces the evolution of the sport from 4,000-year-old rock paintings to crude 1,500-year-old skis to the slick and quickly evolving skis of our century (60 kr, museum is at ski jump, both open daily Jun–Aug 9:00–20:00 and close earlier off-season).

For a thrill, step into the **Simulator** and fly down the French Alps in a Disneyland-style downhill ski race. My legs were exhausted after the four-minute terror. This stimulator, parked in front of the ski museum, costs 40 kr. (Japanese tourists, who wig out over this one, are usually given a free ride after paying for four.)

To get to the ski jump, ride the T-bane line #1 to the Holmenkollen stop and hike up the road 10 minutes. For a longer walk, ride to the end of the line (Frognerseteren) and walk 10 minutes down to the **Frognerseteren Hovedrestaurant**. This classy, traditional old place, with a terrace that offers a commanding view of the city, is a popular stop for apple cake and coffee or a splurge dinner (café open 10:30–22:30, restaurant open 12:00–15:00 and 16:30–22:00, tel. 22 14 05 50). From the restaurant it's a 30-minute walk downhill through the woods on a gravel path that runs generally parallel to Holmenkollenveien.

The nearby **Tryvannstårnet observatory tower** offers a lofty 360-degree view of Oslo in the distance, the fjord, and endless forests, lakes, and soft hills. It's impressive but not necessary if you climbed the ski jump, which gives you a much better view of the city (Mon–Fri 10:00–20:00, Sat–Sun 10:00–18:00, 10-min walk from Voksenkollen T-bane stop; tel. 22 14 67 11).

Forests, Lakes, and Beaches—Oslo is surrounded by a vast forest dotted with idyllic little lakes, huts, joggers, bikers, and sun worshipers. Mountain bike–riding possibilities are endless (as you'll discover if you go exploring without a guide or good map). For a quick ride, you can take the T-bane (with your bike; it needs a ticket too) to the end of line #1 (Frognerseteren, 30 min from the National Theater, gaining you the most altitude possible) and follow the gravelly roads (mostly downhill but with some climbing) past several dreamy lakes to Sognsvann at the end of T-bane line #3. Farther east, from Maridalsvannet, a bike path follows the Aker River all the way back into town. For plenty of trees and none of the exercise, ride the T-bane #3 to Sognsvann (with a beach towel rather than a bike) and join in the lakeside scene. Other popular beaches (such as Bygdøy Huk—direct boat from city hall pier, and others on islands in the harbor) are described in Use It's *Streetwise* magazine.

Harbor and Fjord Tours—Several tour boats leave regularly from Pier 3 in front of the city hall. A relaxing and scenic 50-minute minicruise with a boring three-language commentary departs hourly and costs only 75 kr (free with Oslo Card, daily 11:00–20:00, tel. 22 20 07 15). They won't scream if you bring something to Munch. The cheapest way to enjoy the scenic Oslofjord is to simply ride the ferries that regularly connect the nearby islands with downtown (free with Oslo Card or transit pass).

▲▲▲**Folk Entertainment**—A group of amateur musicians and dancers (called "Leikarringen Bondeungdomslaget"—Oslo's country youth society) gives a sweet, caring, and vibrant 90-minute show at the Oslo Concert Hall. Several traditional instruments are explained and demonstrated. While folk dancing seems hokey to many, if you think of it as medieval flirting set to music and ponder the complexities of village social life back then, the experience takes you away (140–180 kr, Mon and Thu Jul–early Sept at 20:30, tel. 23 11 31 11). Look for the big, brown, glassy overpass on Munkedamsveien; the recommended Vegeta Vertshus restaurant is just up the street. For their off-season concert schedule (different locales), call 22 41 40 70.

Tusenfryd/Vikinglandet—A giant amusement complex just out of town offers a world of family fun—sort of a combo Norwegian Disneyland/Viking Knott's Berry Farm. It's one big company. While the Tusenfryd entry includes the Vikings, you can do just the Viking park if you like. Tusenfryd offers more than 50 rides, plenty of entertainment, family fun, and restaurants. Vikinglandet is a Viking theme park. A coach shuttles fun seekers to the park from behind the train station (25 kr, 2/hrly, 20-min ride). The entry, 195 kr, is not covered by the Oslo Card (daily 10:30–19:00 in summer, closed in winter). Tickets for Viking Land cost only 100 kr (tel. 64 97 64 97).

Wet Fun—Oslo offers lots of water fun for 40 kr (kids half price). In Frogner Park, the Frognerbadet has a sauna, outdoor pools, high dives, a cafeteria, and lots of young families (free with Oslo Card, daily late May–mid-Aug Mon–Fri 7:00–19:00, Sat–Sun 11:00–17:00, last entry 1 hour before closing, Middelthunsgate 28, tel. 22 44 74 29). Tøyenbadet is a modern indoor pool complex with minigolf and a 100-yard-long water slide (40 kr, free with Oslo Card, open at odd hours throughout the year, Helgengate 90, a 10-minute walk from Munch Museum, tel. 22 68 24 23). Oslo's free botanical gardens are nearby. (For more ideas on swimming, pick up *Streetwise* magazine.)

Nightlife—They used to tell people who asked about nightlife in Oslo that Copenhagen was only an hour away by plane. Now Oslo has sprouted a nightlife of its own. The scene is always changing. The TI has information on Oslo's many cafés, discos, and jazz clubs. It's the best source of information for local hot spots.

Shopping—For a great selection (but high prices) of sweaters and other Norwegian crafts, shop at Husfliden, the retail center for the Norwegian Association of Home Arts and Crafts (Mon–Wed and Fri 10:00–17:00, Thu 10:00–18:00, Sat 10:00–15:00, Den Norske Husflidsforening, Møllergata 4, behind the cathedral, tel. 22 42 10 75). Shops are generally open 10:00–17:00. Many stay open until 20:00 on Thursday and close early on Saturday and all day Sunday. Shopping centers are open Monday through Friday from 10:00 to 20:00, Saturday from 10:00 to 18:00. The first Saturday of the month is Super Saturday, when shops are open later and have sales.

Sleeping in Oslo
(7 kr = about $1)
Sleep Code: **S** = Single, **D** = Double/Twin, **T** = Triple, **Q** = Quad, **b** = bathroom, **CC** = Credit Card (Visa, MasterCard, Amex).

Yes, Oslo is expensive. In Oslo, the season dictates the best deals. In low season (Jul–mid-Aug, and Fri–Sun the rest of the year), fancy hotels are the best value for softies, when rooms go for 600 kr for a double with breakfast. In high season (business days outside of summer), your affordable choices are dumpy-for-Scandinavia (but still nice by European standards) doubles for around 500 kr in hotels and 350 kr in private homes. For experience and economy (but not convenience), go for a private home. Oslo's Albertine Hostel (see below) is well located, cheap, and normally has beds available.

Like those in its sister Scandinavian capitals, Oslo's hotels are designed for business travelers. They're expensive during our off-season (fall through spring), full in May and June for conventions (get reservations), and empty otherwise. Only the TI can sort through all the confusing hotel "specials" and get you the best deal possible on a fancy hotel—push-list rooms at about half price. Half price is still 600 kr to 700 kr, but that includes a huge breakfast and a lot of extra comfort for a few extra kroner over the cost of a cheap hotel. Cheap hotels, whose rates are the same throughout the year, are a bad value in summer but offer real savings in low season.

The TI's **Oslo Package** advertises 700-kr discounted doubles in business-class rooms (normally priced at 1,200 kr) and includes a free Oslo Card (worth 150 kr/day). The Oslo Package is a good deal for couples and an incredible deal for families with children under 16 who are traveling between early June and late August or on weekends. Two kids under 16 sleep free, breakfast included, and up to four family members get Oslo Cards, covering admission to sights and all public transportation. The clincher is that the cards are valid for four days, even if you stay at the hotel for one night (technically, you should stay two nights, but this is not enforced). Buy this through your travel agent at home, ScanAm World Tour in the United States at 800/545-2204, or, easier, upon arrival in Oslo (at the TI). If it's late in the day, ask about any half-price last-minute deals.

Use the TI only for these push-list deals, not for cheap hotels or private homes. Some of the cheaper hotels (my listings) tell the TI (which gets a 10 percent fee) they're full when they're not. Go direct. A hotel getting 100 percent of your payment is more likely to have a room. July and early August are easy, but June can be crammed by conventions and September can be tight.

A Laundromat is on Ullevalsvein 15, one kilometer north of the train station (8:00–21:00, tel. 94 22 29 74).

Sleeping in Hotels near the Train Station

Each of these places is within a five-minute walk of the station, in a neighborhood your mom probably wouldn't want you hanging around in at night. The hotels themselves, however, are secure and comfortable. Leave nothing in your car. The Paleet parking garage is handy but not cheap—120 kr per 24 hours.

City Hotel, clean, basic, very homey, and with a wonderful lounge, originated 100 years ago as a cheap place for Norwegians to sleep while they waited to sail to their new homes in America. It now serves the opposite purpose with good if well-worn rooms and a great location (S-395 kr, Sb-510 kr, D-560 kr, Db-695 kr, includes breakfast, CC:VMA, Skippergata 19, enter from Prinsens Gate, tel. 22 41 36 10, fax 22 42 24 29, e-mail: chotea@online.no).

Rainbow Hotel Astoria is a comfortable, modern place, and part of the quickly growing Rainbow Hotel chain that understands which comforts are worth paying for. There are umbrellas, televisions, telephones, and full modern bathrooms in each room. Ice machines! Designed for businessmen, the place has mostly singles. Most "twins" are actually "combi" rooms with a regular bed and a fold-out sofa bed (Sb-470–680 kr, Db/twin-590–780 kr, Db-690–880 kr, rates vary with season, includes buffet breakfast, CC:VMA, 3 blocks in front of the station, 50 yards off Karl Johans Gate, Dronningensgate 21, 0154 Oslo, tel. 22 42 00 10, fax 22 42 57 65).

Rainbow Hotel Spectrum is also conveniently located and a good value (discounted prices Fri–Sun and throughout Jul: "combi" Twin/b-590–780 kr, full doubles-100 kr more, CC:VMA, four blocks to the right as you leave the station on Lilletorget, Brugata 7, 0186 Oslo, tel. 22 17 60 30, fax 22 17 60 80). **Rainbow Hotel Terminus** is similar and closer to the station, but has a less-exciting low-season deal (Fri, Sat, or Sun anytime or reservations within 48 hours any day during the May–Aug period: Sb-470 kr, small bed Db-590 kr, Db-690 kr, regular Db rate-880 kr, includes breakfast, Stenersgate 10, tel. 22 05 60 00, fax 22 17 08 98).

Sleeping in the West End

Cochs Pensjonat has 68 plain rooms (plus 9 remodeled doubles) with fresh paint and stale carpets. It's right behind the palace (S-340 kr, Sb-430–480 kr, D-480 kr, Db-580–640 kr, all Dbs have kitchenettes, no breakfast, CC:VM, tram #11, #13, #17, or #18 to Parkveien 25, tel. 22 33 24 00, fax 22 33 24 10, www.hurra.no \html\cochs_pensjonat.html).

Ellingsen's Pensjonat has no lounge, no breakfasts, and dreary halls. But its rooms are great, with fluffy down comforters. It's located in a residential neighborhood four blocks behind the Royal Palace (a lot of S-280 kr, D-420 kr, Db-460–530 kr, extra bed-110 kr, call well in advance for doubles, Holtegata 25, 0355 Oslo 3, tel. 22 60 03 59, fax 22 60 99 21). Located near the Uranienborg church, it's #25 on the east side of the street (T-bane #19 from the station).

Sleeping in Rooms in Private Homes

The TI at the train station can find you a 300-kr double for a 20-kr fee (minimum two-night stay). My listings are pretty funky, but full of memories.

Marius Meisfjord, a retired teacher deeply interested in imparting Norse culture, rents rooms behind the palace. Beds, which cost 200 kr per person, are in a house stuffed with ancient furniture and pictures of European royalty. This eccentric place feels more like a museum than a B&B, and friendly Mr. Meisfjord looks more like Ibsen than a B&B host (breakfast extra, take tram #12 or #15 to Elisenbergveien, walk 2 blocks to Thomas Heftes Gate 46, tel. 22 55 38 46).

The **Caspari family** rents four comfortable rooms in their home (D-320 kr, no breakfast). Loosely run, it's set in a lush green yard in a peaceful suburb behind Frogner Park, a quick T-bane ride away (get off at Borgen and walk 100 yards more on the right-hand side of the tracks, Heggelbakken 1, tel. 22 14 57 70).

Sleeping in Hostels

Albertine Hostel, a huge student dorm open to travelers of any age, offers the best cheap doubles in town. It feels like a bomb shelter, but each room is spacious, simple, and clean. There are kitchens, free parking, and elevators (Sb-265 kr, Db-340 kr, beds in quads-140 kr, beds in 6-bed rooms-115 kr, sheets-40 kr, towel-10 kr, breakfast-50 kr; catch tram #11, #12, #15, or #17, or bus #27 or #30 from the station; Storgata 55, N-0182 Oslo, tel. 22 99 72 00, fax 22 99 72 20, www.anker.oslo.no). In winter they use the adjacent Anker Hotel reception desk.

Haraldsheim Youth Hostel (IYHF), a huge, modern hostel open all year, is situated far from the center on a hill. It comes with a grand view, laundry, and self-service kitchen. Its 270 beds (four per room) are often completely booked. Beds in the new fancy quads with private showers and toilets are 180 kr per person, including buffet breakfast. (Beds in simple quads-160 kr, includes breakfast, sheets-45 kr, guest membership-25 kr; tram #10 or #11 from station to Sinsen, 4 km out of town, 5-min uphill hike, Haraldsheimveien 4, tel. 22 15 50 43, fax 22 22 10 25.) Eurailers can train (2/hrly, to Grefsen) to the hostel with their railpass.

YMCA Sleep-In Oslo, located near the train station, offers the cheapest mattresses in town in three large rooms with 15 to 30 mattresses each, plus a left-luggage room, kitchen, and piano lounge (earplugs for sale). It's as pleasant as a sleep-in can be (100 kr, Jul–mid-Aug only, reception open daily 8:00–11:00 and 17:00–24:00, no bedding provided, you must bring a sleeping bag, Møllergata 1, entry from Grubbegata, 1 block beyond the cathedral behind Use It, tel. 22 20 83 97). They don't take reservations, but you should call to see if there's room.

Sleeping on the Train

Norway's trains offer 110-kr beds in triple compartments and 210-kr beds in doubles. Eurailers who sleep well to the rhythm of the rails have several scenic overnight trips to choose from

Oslo

(it's light until midnight for much of the early summer at Oslo's latitude). If you have a train pass, use the station's service center (across from the ticket windows) and avoid the long lines.

Eating in Oslo

My strategy is to splurge for a hotel that includes breakfast. A 50-kr Norwegian breakfast is fit for a Viking. Have a picnic for lunch or dinner, using one of the many grocery stores. Basements of big department stores have huge first-class supermarkets with lots of picnic dinner–quality alternatives to sandwiches. The little yogurt tubs with cereal come with collapsible spoons. The train station has a late-hours grocery.

Oslo is awash with clever little budget eateries (modern, ethnic, fast food, pizza, department-store cafeterias). Here are several places for those who want to eat like my Norwegian grandparents:

Kaffistova is an alcohol-free cafeteria serving simple, hearty, and typically Norwegian (read "bland") meals for the best price around. You'll get your choice of an entrée (meatballs) and all the salad, cooked vegetables, and "flat bread" you want (or, at least, need) for around 80 kr (Mon–Fri 12:00–20:30, until 17:00 Sat and 18:00 Sun in summer, closes earlier off-season, Rosenkrantzgate 8).

Norrøna Cafeteria is another traditional budget saver (75-kr *dagens rett*, before 14:00 you'll get the same thing for 65 kr with a cup of coffee tossed in; Mon–Fri until 18:00, later off-season; central at Grensen 19).

Stortorvets Gjæstgiveri offers good Norwegian food. Entrées in the café start at 60 to 90 kr (Grensen 1). For a classier traditional meal with a grand view, consider the **Frognerseteren** restaurant (described above with the ski jump).

Vegeta Vertshus, which has been keeping Oslo vegetarians fat, happy, and low on the food chain for 60 years, serves a huge selection of hearty vegetarian food that would satisfy even a hungry Viking. Fill your plate once (small plate-80 kr, large plate-90 kr) or eternally for 125 kr. How's your balance? One plate did me fine (daily 11:00–23:00, no smoking, no meat, Munkedamsveien 3B, near top of Stortingsgata between palace and city hall, tel. 22 83 42 32).

Lofotstua has a drab interior, but cooks up tasty, traditional fish dishes (entrées 150–190 kr, Mon–Fri 13:00–22:00, located on Kirkeveien between Majorstuen T-bane stop and Frogner Park; exiting subway station, turn right and walk 2 blocks on Kirkeveien).

The **Aker Brygge** (harborfront mall) development isn't cheap, but it has some cheery cafés, classy delis, open-till-22:00 restaurants, and markets.

For a grand and traditional breakfast, consider the elegant spread at the **Bristol Hotel** (105 kr, dinner specials 14:00–19:00 for 125 kr, a block off Karl Johans Gate behind the Grand Hotel).

Transportation Connections—Oslo

For train info, call 81 50 08 88 (7:00–23:00, phone tree, press 1 and wait) or use their Web site: www.nsb.no.

By train to Bergen: Oslo and Bergen are linked by a spectacularly scenic seven-hour train ride. Reservations (20 kr) are required on all long and IC (express) trains. Departures are roughly at 7:30, 10:45, 14:55, 16:10, and 23:00 daily in both directions (530 kr; 335 kr if you buy 5 days in advance and don't travel at peak times like Fri or Sun).

By boat to Copenhagen: Consider the cheap quickie cruise that leaves daily from Copenhagen (departs 17:00, returns 9:15 two days later; 16 hrs sailing each way and 7 hrs in Norway's capital). For specifics, see "Transportation Connections" in the Copenhagen chapter.

NORWAY IN A NUTSHELL

If you go to Oslo and don't get out to the fjords, you should have your passport revoked. For the best one-day look at Norway's greatest claim to scenic fame, do Norway in a Nutshell. This series of well-organized train, ferry, and bus connections lays this most beautiful fjord country spread-eagle on a scenic platter.

Every morning at 7:30, northern Europe's most spectacular train ride leaves Oslo for Bergen. Cameras smoke as this train roars over Norway's mountainous spine. The barren, windswept heaths, glaciers, deep forests, countless lakes, and a few rugged ski resorts create a harsh beauty. The railroad is an amazing engineering feat. Completed in 1909, it's 300 miles long and peaks at 4,266 feet—which, at this Alaskan latitude, is far above the tree line. You'll go under 18 miles of snow sheds, over 300 bridges, and through 200 tunnels in just under seven hours (530kr, free with railpass).

At Myrdal, "Nutshellers" take a 12-mile spur line (50 kr supplement for Eurailpass holders), dropping 2,800 breathtaking feet in 50 minutes to the village of Flåm on Sognefjord. This is a party train. The engineer even stops the train for photographs at a particularly picturesque waterfall.

From Flåm, Nutshellers catch the most scenic of fjord cruises. Sightseeing boats leave throughout the day (135 kr one way, half off with a student card or full-fare spouse). For 90 minutes, camera-clicking tourists scurry on the drool-stained deck like nervous roosters, scratching fitfully for a photo to catch the magic. Waterfalls turn the black-rock cliffs into a bridal fair. You can nearly reach out and touch the sheer towering walls. The ride is one of those fine times, like being high on the tip of an Alp, when a warm camaraderie spontaneously combusts between the strangers who came together for the experience. The boat takes you up one narrow arm (Aurlandsfjord) and down the next (Nærøyfjord) to the town of Gudvangen, where waiting buses (60 kr) shuttle you back to the

Norway in a Nutshell

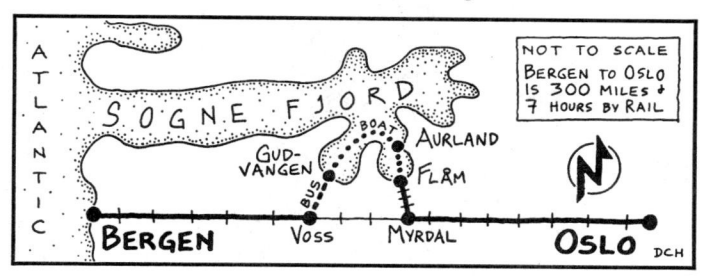

main train line at Voss. From Voss, return to Oslo (arriving about 22:00) or carry on into Bergen for the evening before catching the overnight train back to Oslo.

Tourist offices in Oslo and Bergen have souvenir-worthy brochures with photos, descriptions, and exact times. Trains depart from both Oslo and Bergen several times daily; if you want to do the Nutshell as a day trip from either Oslo or Bergen, start with the earliest train (about 7:30). Nutshell connections are made even if trains/boat/buses are running late.

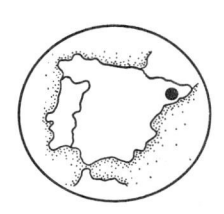

BARCELONA

Barcelona is Spain's second city and the capital of the proud and distinct region of Catalunya. With Franco's fascism now history, Catalunyan flags wave once again. Language and culture are on a roll in Spain's most cosmopolitan and European corner.

Barcelona bubbles with life in its narrow Gothic Quarter alleys, along the grand boulevards, and throughout the chic, grid-planned new town. While Barcelona had an illustrious past as a Roman colony, Visigothic capital, 14th-century maritime power, and, in more modern times, a top Mediterranean trading and manufacturing center, it's most enjoyable to throw out the history books and just drift through the city. If you're in the mood to surrender to a city's charms, let it be in Barcelona.

Planning Your Time

Sandwich Barcelona between flights or overnight train rides. There's little of earth-shaking importance within eight hours by train. It's as easy to fly into Barcelona as into Madrid, Lisbon, or Paris for most travelers from the United States. Those renting a car can cleverly start here, sleep on the train or fly to Madrid, see Madrid, and pick up the car there.

On the shortest visit Barcelona is worth one night, one day, and an overnight train out. The Ramblas is two different streets by day and by night. Stroll it from top to bottom at night and again the next morning, grabbing breakfast on a stool in a café in the market. Wander the Gothic Quarter, see the cathedral, and have lunch in Eixample (ay-SHAM-pla). The top two sights in town, Gaudí's Sacred Family Church and the Picasso Museum, are usually open until 20:00. The illuminated fountains (on Montjuïc, near Plaça Espanya) are a good finale for your day.

Barcelona 661

Barcelona

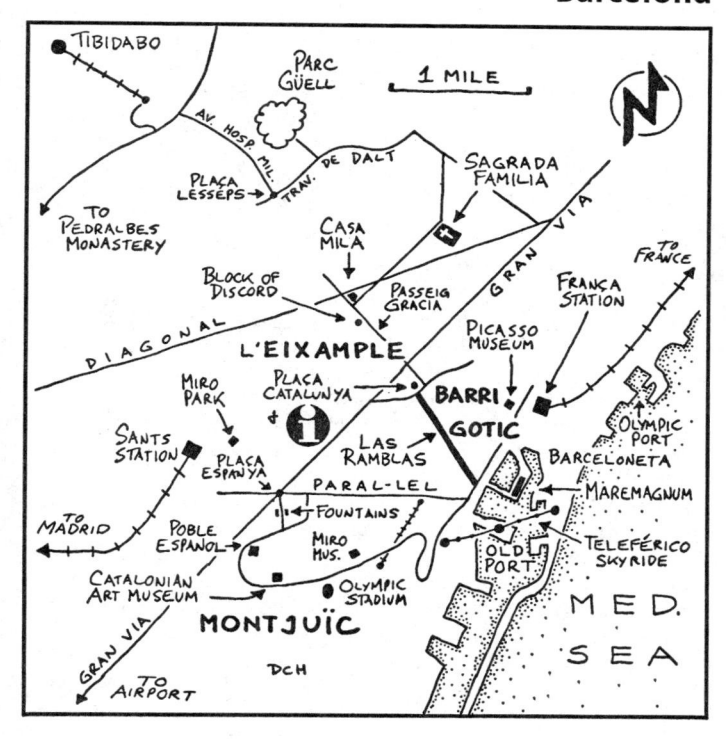

[Map of Barcelona showing Tibidabo, Parc Güell, Av. Hosp. Mil., Plaça Lesseps, Trav. de Dalt, Sagrada Familia, To Pedralbes Monastery, Casa Mila, Block of Discord, Passeig Gracia, Gran Via, To France, França Station, Diagonal, L'Eixample, Picasso Museum, Miro Park, Plaça Catalunya, Barri Gotic, Sants Station, Plaça Espanya, Las Ramblas, Olympic Port, Barceloneta, Maremagnum, To Madrid, Paral-lel, Fountains, Poble Espanyol, Miro Mus., Old Port, Teleférico Skyride, Catalonian Art Museum, Olympic Stadium, Montjuïc, Gran Via, To Airport, Med. Sea]

Of course, Barcelona in a day is a dash. To better appreciate the city's ample charm, spread your visit over two days.

Orientation
Orient yourself mentally by locating these essentials on the map: Barri Gòtic/Ramblas (Old Town), Eixample (fashionable modern town), Montjuïc (hill covered with sights and parks), and Sants Station (train to Madrid). The soul of Barcelona is in its compact core—the Barri Gòtic (Gothic Quarter) and the Ramblas (main boulevard). This is your strolling, shopping, and people-watching nucleus. The city's sights are widely scattered, but with a map and a willingness to figure out the sleek subway system, all is manageable.

Tourist Information
There are three useful TIs in Barcelona: at the airport, at the Sants train station (daily 8:00–20:00, off-season 8:00–14:00, at the access

to platform 6), and on—actually under—Plaça de Catalunya, across from the El Corte Inglés store (daily 9:00–21:00, city walking tours in English Sat–Sun at 10:00, 950 ptas, 2 hrs, call to reserve, tel. 90-630-1282; fair rates at TI exchange desk, room-finding service worthwhile if you're desperate). Pick up the large city map and brochures on public transport, Gaudí, Miró, Dalí, Picasso, and the Barri Gòtic. Ask for the free quarterly Barcelona guide with practical information (museum hours, restaurants, transportation) and cultural information (history, festivals, and points of interest grouped by neighborhood).

Arrival in Barcelona

By Train: Although many international trains use the França Station, all domestic (and some international) trains use Sants Station. Both França and Sants have subway stations: França's is "Barceloneta" (two blocks away), and Sants' is "Sants Estacio" (under the station). Both stations have baggage lockers. Sants Station has a good TI, a world of handy shops and eateries, and a classy "Sala Euromed" lounge for travelers with first-class reservations (quiet, plush, TV, free drinks, study tables, coffee bar). There is nothing of interest within easy walking distance of either train station. Subway or taxi to your hotel.

By Plane: Barcelona's El Prat de Llobregat Airport is 12 kilometers southwest of town and connected cheaply and quickly by Aerobus (immediately in front of arrivals lobby, 4/hrly, 20 min to Plaça de Catalunya, buy 485-ptas ticket from driver, tel. 93-412-0000) or by RENFE train (walk the tunnel overpass from airport to station, 2/hrly, 20 min to Sants Station and Plaça de Catalunya, 310 ptas). A taxi to or from the airport costs about 3,000 ptas.

Getting around Barcelona

Barcelona's subway (the Metro), among Europe's best, can be faster than a taxi and connects just about every place you'll visit. It has five color-coded lines (L1 is red, L2 is lilac, L3 is green, L4 is yellow, L5 is blue). Rides cost 145 ptas each. A T-1 Card gives you 10 tickets good for the bus or Metro for 795 ptas. Pick up the TI's guide to public transport.

The handy Tourist Bus (Bus Turistic) shuttles tourists on a 24-stop circuit covering the must-sees, with stops at the funicular and *teleférico* to Montjuïc (Apr–Dec 9:00–21:30, buy tickets on bus). The one-day (1,800 ptas) and two-day (2,300 ptas) tickets include some serious discounts on the city's major sights. Buses run every 10 to 20 minutes and take three hours to do the entire circuit.

Taxis are plentiful and honest (300 ptas drop charge, 100 ptas/km). You can go from the Ramblas to Sants Station for 600 ptas (100 ptas extra for each piece of luggage).

Helpful Hints

Theft Alert: Barcelona, after recently illuminating many of its seedier streets, is not the pickpocket paradise it was a few years back, but it's good to be alert—especially on the Ramblas.

American Express: Amex offices are at Paseo de Gràcia 101 (Mon–Fri 9:30–18:00, Sat 10:00–12:00, tel. 93-415-2371, Metro: Diagonal) and on the Ramblas opposite the Liceu Metro station (daily 9:00–24:00, with a small TI, tel. 98-301-1166).

U.S. Consulate: Designed to be low profile, it's hard to find at Passeig Reina Elisenda 23 (tel. 93-280-2227).

Pharmacy: At the corner of Ramblas and Carrer de la Portaferrissa (daily 9:00–22:00).

Language: Although Spanish is understood here (and the basic survival words are the same), Barcelona speaks a different language—Catalan. (Most place-names in this chapter are listed in Catalan.) Here are the essential Catalunyan phrases:

Hello	*Hola*	(OH-lah)
Please	*Si us plau*	(see oos plow)
Thank you	*Gracies*	(GRAH-see-es)
Goodbye	*Adeu*	(ah-DAY-oo)
Exit	*Sordida*	(sor-DEE-dah)
Long live Catalunya!	*Visca Catalunya!*	(BEE-skah...)

Sights—The Ramblas

More than a Champs-Élysées, this grand boulevard takes you from rich at the top to rough at the port in a 20-minute walk. You'll find the grand opera house, ornate churches, plain prostitutes, pickpockets, con men, artists, street mimes, an outdoor bird market, elegant cafés, great shopping, and people willing to charge more for a shoeshine than you paid for the shoes. Take 15 minutes to sit on a white metal chair for 50 ptas and observe. When Hans Christian Andersen saw this street more than 100 years ago, he wrote that there could be no doubt that Barcelona was a great city.

Rambla means "stream" in Arabic. The Ramblas was a drainage ditch along the medieval wall that used to define what is now called the Gothic Quarter. It has five separately named segments, but addresses treat it as a mile-long boulevard.

Walking from Plaça de Catalunya downhill to the harbor, you'll see the following Ramblas highlights.

▲**Plaça de Catalunya**—This vast central square is the divider between old and new and the hub for the Metro, bus, and airport shuttle. The grass around its fountain is considered the best public place in town for serious necking. Overlooking the square, the huge El Corte Inglés department store offers everything from bonsai trees to a travel agency, plus one-hour photo developing, haircuts, and cheap souvenirs (Mon–Sat 10:00–21:30, closed Sun, supermarket in basement, 9th-floor terrace cafeteria with great city view—take elevator from west entrance, tel. 90-112-2122). Four great boulevards start here: the Ramblas, the fashionable Passeig de Gràcia, the cozier but still fashionable Rambla Catalunya, and the stubby, shop-filled, pedestrian-only Portal de L'Angel.

▲▲**La Boqueria**—This lively produce market (a.k.a. Mercat de Sant Josep) is an explosion of chicken legs, bags of live snails, stiff fish, delicious oranges, and sleeping dogs (Mon–Sat 8:00–20:00, best in the morning after 9:00, closed Sun). The Conserves shop sells 25 kinds of olives (go straight in; it's near the back on the right; 100-gram minimum, 40–70 ptas). Full legs of ham (*jamón serrano*) abound; *Paleta Iberica de Bellota* are best—strictly acorn-fed, about 15,000 ptas ($100) each. Beware: *Huevos de toro* are bull testicles—surprisingly inexpensive... but oh so good. Drop by Mario and Alex's Café Central for breakfast or an *espresso con leche* (far end of main aisle on left).

Café de L'Ópera—One of Barcelona's mainstays, this serves a good *café con leche* (daily 9:00–02:30, La Rambla 74, tel. 93-317-7585).

Gran Teatre del Liceu—Spain's only real opera house is luscious but closed for a few years for renovation because of a 1994 fire (tourable when it reopens).

Plaça Reial—This elegant neoclassical square comes complete with old-fashioned taverns, modern bars with patio seating, a Sunday coin and stamp market (10:00–14:00), and characters who don't need the palm trees to be shady. Escudellers, a street one block toward the water from the square, is lined with bars whose counters are strewn with vampy ladies. The area is well policed, but if you tried, you could get into trouble.

▲▲**Palau Güell**—The only look at a Gaudí Art Nouveau interior, and for me, it's the most enjoyable look at Barcelona's organic architect (300 ptas, combo ticket for 600 ptas covers a guided visit—beginning at Casa Lleo Morera, Paseo de Gràcia #35—to 3 Moderniste sights, 50 percent discount at 3 others, worthwhile for fans; usually open Mon–Fri 10:00–14:00, 16:00–20:00, Carrer Nou de la Rambla 3–5, tel. 93-317-3974). If you're tired and will see/have seen Casa Milà, skip the climb to the rooftop.

Chinatown (Barri Xines)—Farther downhill, on the right-hand side, is the world's only Chinatown with nothing even remotely Chinese in or near it. Named this for the prejudiced notion that Chinese immigrants go hand in hand with poverty, prostitution, and drug dealing, the actual inhabitants are poor Spanish, Arab, and Gypsy people down on their luck. At night the area is full of prostitutes, many of them transvestites, who cater to sailors wandering up from the port. Don't venture in at night.

Columbus Monument (Monument a Colóm)—Marking the point where the Ramblas hits the harbor, this 50-meter-tall monument built for an 1888 exposition offers an elevator-assisted view from its top (250 ptas, daily 9:00–20:30; off-season 10:00–14:30, 15:30–19:30; skip the ascent if you plan on riding the harbor gondola to Montjuïc, which offers a far better view). It's interesting that Barcelona would so honor the man whose discoveries ultimately led to its downfall as a great trading power. It was here in Barcelona that Ferdinand and Isabel welcomed Columbus home after his first trip to America.

Maritime Museum (Museo Maritim)—This museum covers the salty history of ships and navigation from the 13th to 20th centuries. Its 45-minute infrared headphone multimedia tour in English shows off the Catalan role in the development of maritime technology (e.g., the first submarine was Catalan). With fleets of seemingly unimportant replicas of old boats explained in Catalan and Spanish, landlubbers may find it dull (800 ptas, daily 10:00–19:00, closed Mon in off-season).

Golondrinas—Little tourist boats at the foot of the Columbus Monument make half-hour tours of the harbor every 20 to 30 minutes from 11:00 to 20:00 (285 ptas one way to other side of harbor or 485 ptas round-trip). Consider this ride or the harbor steps here for a picnic. They offer a glass-bottom, four-language, 90-minute port tour for 1,275 ptas.

Maremagnum—This modern Spanish monstrosity of a mall (with a cinema, aquarium, and restaurants) offers fine city views. It's connected to the waterfront by a slick wooden pedestrian drawbridge next to the *golondrina* boats.

Sights—Gothic Quarter (Barri Gòtic)

The Barri Gòtic is a bustling world of shops, bars, and nightlife packed between hard-to-be-thrilled-about 14th- and 15th-century buildings. Except for the part closest to the port, the area now feels safe, thanks to police and countless streetlights. There is a tangled grab bag of undiscovered courtyards, grand squares, schoolyards, Art Nouveau storefronts, baby flea markets, musty junk shops, classy antique shops, and balconies with domestic jungles behind wrought-iron bars. Go on a cultural scavenger hunt. Write a poem.

▲**Cathedral**—The colossal cathedral, a fine example of Catalan Gothic, was started in about 1300 and took 600 years to complete. Rather than stretching toward heaven, it makes a point to be simply massive (similar to the Gothic churches of Italy). Under towering arches, 28 richly ornamented chapels ring the finely carved 15th-century choir (*coro*). While you can see the *coro* from the back for free, paying the 125-ptas entry fee turns on the lights and lets you get close up to the ornately carved stalls and the emblems representing the various Knights of the Golden Fleece who once sat here. Don't miss the cloister, with its wispy garden, protective geese, and WC, or the dark, barrel-vaulted Romanesque Chapel of Santa

Barcelona's Gothic Quarter

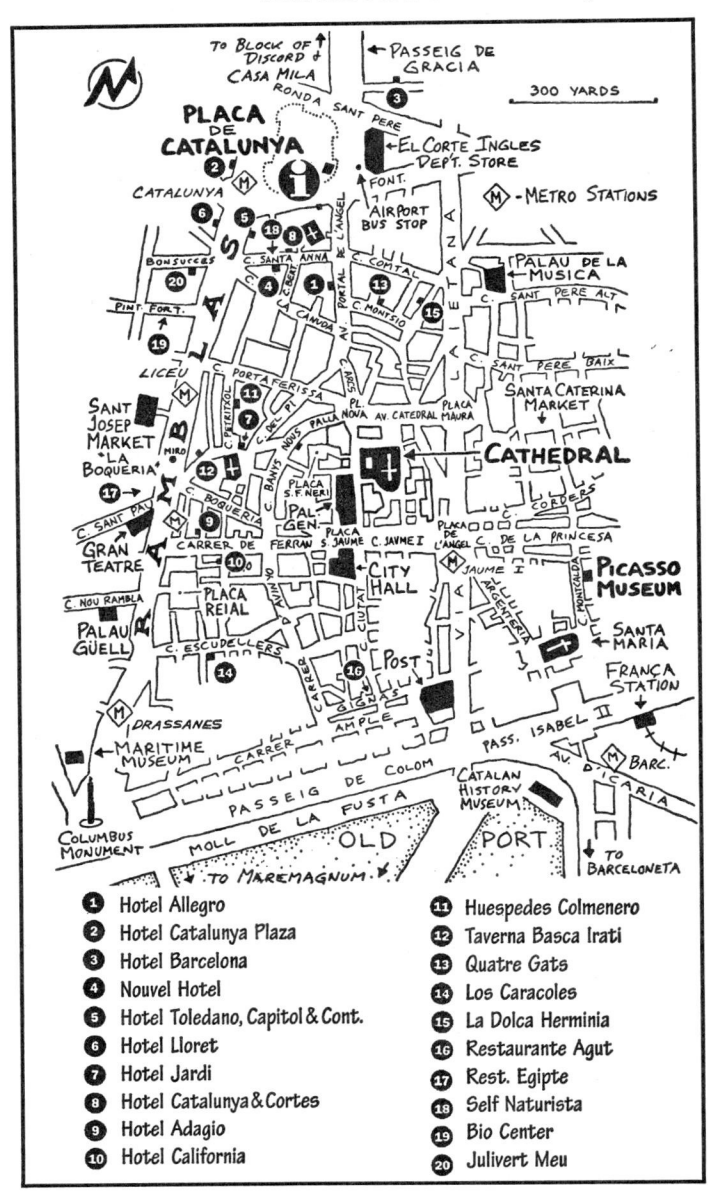

1. Hotel Allegro
2. Hotel Catalunya Plaza
3. Hotel Barcelona
4. Nouvel Hotel
5. Hotel Toledano, Capitol & Cont.
6. Hotel Lloret
7. Hotel Jardi
8. Hotel Catalunya & Cortes
9. Hotel Adagio
10. Hotel California
11. Huespedes Colmenero
12. Taverna Basca Irati
13. Quatre Gats
14. Los Caracoles
15. La Dolca Herminia
16. Restaurante Agut
17. Rest. Egipte
18. Self Naturista
19. Bio Center
20. Julivert Meu

Lucia, with its great old tombstone floor. The tiny 100-ptas museum is one plush room with a dozen old religious paintings (cathedral 8:00–13:30, 16:00–19:30; cloisters 9:00–13:00, 16:00–19:00; museum 10:00–13:00, 16:00–19:00; tel. 93-315-1554).

▲**Sardana Dances**—The stirring and patriotic Sardana dances are held at the cathedral (18:30 Sat, 12:00 Sun) and at Plaça de Sant Jaume (18:30 Sun). Locals of all ages seem to spontaneously appear. They gather in circles after putting their things in the center—symbolic of community and sharing. Then they raise and hold hands as they hop and sway gracefully to the band. The band (*cobla*) consists of a long flute, tenor and soprano oboes, strange-looking brass instruments, and a tiny bongolike drum (*tambari*). The rest of Spain mocks this lazy circle dance, but it is a stirring display of local pride and patriotism.

Shoe Museum (Museu del Calcat)—Shoe lovers enjoy this two-room shoe museum (with a we-try-harder attendant) on the delightful Plaça Sant Felip Neri (200 ptas, Tue–Sun 11:00–14:00, closed Mon, 1 block beyond the outside door of the cathedral cloister, behind Plaça de G. Bachs).

Royal Palace (Palau Reial)—Several museums are in the old Royal Palace complex next to the cathedral. The city history museum shows off Barcelona's Roman and medieval history along with piles of medieval documents in the Arxiu de la Corona d'Aragon (Archives of the Kingdom of Aragon). The Frederic Mares Museum combines a classy collection of medieval religious art with a quirky bundle of more modern artifacts—old pipes, pin-ups, toys, and so on (both museums open Tue–Sun 10:00–15:00, some nights until 18:00, closed Mon).

Plaça de Sant Juame—On this stately central square of the Gothic Quarter, two of the top governmental buildings in Catalan face each other: the Barcelona city hall (Ayuntamento) and the seat of the autonomous government of Catalan (Palau de la Generalitat). Sardana dances take place here Sunday at 18:30 (see "Sardana Dances," above).

▲▲**Picasso Museum**—Far and away the best collection of Picasso's (1881–1973) work in Spain, and the best collection of his early works anywhere, is scattered through two Gothic palaces a short walk from the cathedral. This is a great chance to see his earliest sketches and paintings and better understand his genius. You'll find no English information inside but if you follow the rooms in numerical order you can trace the evolution of his work. Picasso lived in Barcelona from 1895 to 1904. The first rooms show the 14-year-old hard at work. Room 13 holds a museum highlight: *Science and Charity*. Pablo painted this in 1897 at age 16. Note the tiny studies inside the doorway. The man in the painting is Pablo's first teacher—his dad. The baby was rented. From this point on, young Pablo Ruiz called himself Picasso, moved to Paris in 1900, and sharpened the cutting edge.

The next rooms show Picasso romping through various styles and into his popular Blue Period (named for the tone and tint of his 1901–1904 works). After the Rose Period (1904–1905) we see Picasso the cubist (1917, room 21). In 1957 Picasso began a series of variations on Velázquez's famous *Las Meninas*. Study the copy of the realistic Velázquez original and the Velázquez/Picasso comparison chart. Then see if you can follow Picasso as he plays paddleball with perspective in the next few rooms. Before leaving, drop by the video room—opposite the café—to see Picasso at work. (700 ptas, Tue–Sat 10:00–20:00, Sun 10:00–15:00, closed Mon, Montcada 15–19, Metro: Jaume, tel. 93-319-6310.)

Textile and Garment Museum (Museu Textil i de la Indumentaria)—If fabrics from the 4th to 16th centuries leave you cold, have a *café con leche* on the museum's beautiful patio (museum, 400 ptas, Tue–Sat 10:00–20:00, Sun 10:00–15:00, closed Mon; patio is outside the museum but within the walls, 30 meters from Picasso Museum at Montcada 12–14).

▲**Catalana Concert Hall (Palau de la Música Catalana)**—This colorful hall is an extravagant burst of Modernisme, with a floral ceramic ceiling, colored-glass columns, and detailed mosaics. Admission is by tour only (1 hr, in English, 700 ptas, daily 10:00–15:30 through peak season, shorter hours off-season, call to reserve, tel. 93-268-1000). Ask about concerts.

Sights—Eixample

Uptown Barcelona is a unique variation on the common grid-plan city. Barcelona snipped off the building corners to create light and spacious eight-sided squares at every intersection. Wide sidewalks, hardy shade trees, chic shops, and plenty of Art Nouveau fun make the Eixample a refreshing break from the Old Town. For the best Eixample example, ramble Rambla Catalunya (unrelated to the more famous Ramblas) and pass through Passeig de Gràcia (described below, Metro: Passeig de Gràcia).

The 19th century was a boom time for Barcelona. By 1850 it was busting out of its medieval walls. A new town was planned to follow a gridlike layout. The intersection of three major thoroughfares—Gran Vía, Diagonal, and the Meridiana—would shift the city's focus uptown.

The Eixample, or "Enlargement," was a progressive plan in which everything was accessible to everyone. Each 20-block-square district would have its own hospital and large park, each 10-block-square area would have its own market and general services, and each five-block-square grid would house its own schools and daycare centers. The hollow space found inside each "block" of apartments would form a neighborhood park.

While much of that vision never quite panned out, the Eixample was an urban success. Rich and artsy big shots bought

Barcelona

plots along the grid. The richest landowners built as close to the center as possible. For this reason, the best buildings are near the Passeig de Gràcia. Adhering to the height, width, and depth limitations, they built as they pleased—often in the trendy new Moderniste style.

Sights—Gaudí's Art and Architecture

Barcelona is an architectural scrapbook of the galloping gables and organic curves of hometown boy Antonio Gaudí. A devoted Catalan and Catholic, he immersed himself in each project, often living on-site. He called Parc Güell, La Pedrera, and the Sagrada Familia all home.

▲▲Sagrada Familia (Sacred Family) Church—Gaudí's most famous and persistent work is this unfinished landmark. He worked on the church from 1891 to 1925; your 800 ptas admission helps pay for the ongoing construction (daily 9:00–20:00, off-season 9:00–18:00, Metro: Sagrada Familia, tel. 93-207-3031).

When finished, 12 100-meter spires (representing the Apostles) will stand in groups of four marking the three ends of the building. The center tower (honoring Jesus), reaching 170 meters up, will be flanked by 125-meter-tall towers of Mary and the four Evangelists. A unique exterior ambulatory will circle the building like a cloister turned inside out.

The nativity facade really shows the vision of Gaudí. It was finished in 1904, before Gaudí's death, and shows scenes from the birth and childhood of Jesus along with angels playing musical instruments. (Because of ongoing construction, you may need to access this area—opposite the entrance, viewed from outside—by walking through the museum. Don't miss it.)

The little on-site museum displays physical models used for the church's construction. Gaudí lived on the site for more than a decade and is buried in the crypt. When he died in 1926, only one spire stood. Judge for yourself how the controversial current work fits in with Gaudí's original formulation.

With the cranking cranes, rusty forests of rebar, and scaffolding requiring a powerful faith, the Sagrada Familia Church offers a fun look at a living, growing, bigger-than-life building. Take the lift (200 ptas) or the stairs (free but can be miserably congested) up to the dizzy lookout bridging two spires. You'll get a great view of the city and a gargoyle's-eye perspective of the loopy church. If there's any building on earth I'd like to see, it's the Sagrada Familia—finished.

▲Palau Güell—This is the best chance to enjoy a Gaudí interior (see above under "Sights—The Ramblas"). Curvy.

▲Casa Milà (La Pedrera)—This house and nearby Casa Battlo have Gaudí exteriors that laugh down on the crowds filling Passeig de Gràcia. Casa Milà, also called La Pedrera (The Quarry), has a much-photographed roller coaster of melting-ice-cream eaves. This is Barcelona's quintessential Moderniste building. An elevator will whisk you to the top, where you can wander under brick arches, frolic on the fanciful rooftop, and enjoy the fascinating *Espai Gaudí*, a multimedia exhibit—in English—of models, photos, and videos of Gaudí's works. An apartment fully furnished from the Gaudí era was recently added. It contains a well-presented display on life in Barcelona in the early 1900s (600 ptas for museum and roof, 1,000 ptas includes the apartment, daily 10:00–20:00; the 1,500-ptas fee for 21:30–24:00 viewing includes a glass of wine; Passeig de Gràcia 92, Metro: Diagonal, tel. 93-484-5995). At the ground level of Casa Milà is the original entrance courtyard for the Fundacio Caixa de Caluyna, dreamily painted in pastels (free).

The Street of Discord—Four blocks from Casa Milà you can survey a noisy block of competing turn-of-the-century facades. Several of Barcelona's top Moderniste mansions line Passeig de Gràcia (Metro: Passeig de Gràcia). Because the structures look as though they are trying to outdo each other in creative twists, locals nicknamed the block between Consell de Cent and Arago "The Street of Discord." First (at #43) and most famous is Gaudí's Casa Battlo, with skull-like balconies and a tile roof of cresting waves... or is it a dragon's back? (If you're tempted to frame your photos from the middle of the street, be careful—Gaudí died under a streetcar.) Next door, at Casa Amatller (#41), check out architect Puig i Cadafalch's creative mix of Moorish and Gothic and iron grillwork. On the corner (at #35), Casa Lleo Morera (by Lluís Domènechi Muntaner) offers more of a sense of a Moderniste interior; you can nose into the lobby and often climb to the first floor (combo ticket for 600 ptas covers a guided visit—beginning at Casa Lleo Morera, Passeig de Gràcia #35—to 3 Moderniste sights and a 50 percent discount at 3 others). The perfume shop halfway down the street has a free and interesting little perfume museum in the back.

Parc Güell—Gaudí fans find the artist's magic in this colorful park (free, daily 9:00–20:00) and small Gaudí Museum (200 ptas, daily 10:00–20:00, closes off-season at 18:00, Metro: Vallarca but easier by bus #24 from Plaça de Catalunya; 1,000 ptas by taxi). Gaudí intended this to be a planned garden city rather than a park. As a high-income housing project, it flopped. As a park... even after I reminded myself that Gaudí's work is a careful rhythm of color, shapes, and space, it was disappointing.

Modern Art Museum (Museu d'Art Modern)—East of the França train station in Parc de la Ciutadella, this manageable museum exhibits Catalan sculpture, painting, glass, and furniture by Gaudí, Casas, Llimona, and others (500 ptas, Tue-Sat 10:00–19:00, Sun 10:00–14:30, closed Mon).

Barcelona

Sights—Barcelona's Montjuïc

The Montjuïc (Mount of the Jews), overlooking Barcelona's hazy port, has always been a show-off. Ages ago it had the impressive fortress. In 1929 it hosted an international fair, from which most of today's sights originated. And in 1992 the Summer Olympics directed the world's attention to this pincushion of attractions.

There are many ways to reach Montjuïc: on the Bus Turistic (see "Getting around Barcelona," above); bus #50 from the corner of Gran Vía and Passeig de Gràcia (145 ptas, every 10 minutes); subway to Metro: Parallel and catch the funicular (250 ptas one way, 375 ptas round-trip, daily 11:00–22:00, shorter hours in winter); or taxi. The first three options leave you at the *teleférico*, which you can take to the Castle of Montjuïc (425 ptas one way, 625 ptas round-trip). Alternatively, from the same spot, you can walk uphill 20 minutes through the pleasant park. Only a taxi gets you doorstep delivery. From the port, the fastest and most scenic way to Montjuïc is via the 1929 Trasbordador Aereo (at the tower in the port, ride an elevator up to catch the dangling gondola, 1,200 ptas round-trip, 4/hrly, daily 10:30–20:00).

Castle of Montjuïc—This offers great city views and a military museum (200 ptas, Tue–Sun 9:30–19:30, closed Mon). The seemingly endless museum houses a dull collection of guns, swords, and toy soldiers. An interesting section on the Spanish-American War covers Spain's valiant fight against American aggression (from its perspective). Unfortunately, there are no English descriptions. Those interested in Jewish history will find a fascinating collection of ninth-century Jewish tombstones.

▲**Fountains (Fonts Lluminoses)**—Music, colored lights, and huge amounts of water make an artistic and coordinated splash on summer nights (Thu–Sun, 30-minute shows start on the half-hour, 21:30–24:00, from Metro: Plaça Espanya, walk toward the towering National Palace).

Spanish Village (Poble Espanyol)—This tacky five-acre model village uses fake traditional architecture from all over Spain as a shell to contain gift shops. Craftspeople do their clichéd thing only in the morning (9:00–19:30, not worth the time or the 950 ptas). After hours it becomes a popular local nightspot.

▲▲**Catalonian Art Museum (Museo Nacional d'Art de Catalunya)**—Often called "the Prado of Romanesque art," this is a rare, world-class collection of Romanesque art collected mostly from remote Catalan village churches in the Pyrenees (saved from unscrupulous art dealers).

The Romanesque wing features frescoes, painted wooden altar fronts, and ornate statuary. This classic Romanesque art—with flat 2-D scenes, each saint holding his symbol, and Jesus (easy to identify by the cross in his halo)—is now impressively displayed on replicas of the original church ceilings.

In the Gothic wing, fresco murals give way to vivid 14th-century paintings of Bible stories on wood. A roomful of paintings by the Catalan master Jaume Huguet (1412–1492) deserves a close look.

Before you leave, ice skate under the huge dome over to the air-conditioned cafeteria. This was the prime ceremony room and dance hall for the 1929 International Exposition (800 ptas, Tue–Sat 10:00–19:00, Thu until 21:00, Sun 10:00–14:30, closed Mon, tel. 93-423-7199). The museum is in the massive National Palace building above the fountains, near Plaça Espanya (Metro: Plaça Espanya, then hike up or ride the bus; the Bus Turistic and bus #50 stop close by).

▲Fundació Joan Miró—For something more up-to-date, this museum showcases the modern art talents of yet another Catalunyan artist and is considered the best collection of Joan Miró art anywhere. You'll also see works by other modern Spanish artists; don't miss the Mercury Fountain by Alexander Calder. This museum leaves those who don't like abstract art scratching their heads (800 ptas, Tue–Sat 10:00–20:00, Thu until 21:30, Sun 10:00–14:30, closed Mon, closes at 19:00 off-season).

Sleeping in Barcelona
(160 ptas = about $1)
Sleep Code: **S** = Single, **D** = Double/Twin, **T** = Triple, **Q** = Quad, **b** = bathroom, **t** = toilet only, **s** = shower only, **CC** = Credit Card (Visa, MasterCard, Amex), **SE** = Speaks English, **NSE** = No English. Book ahead in July and August or run the risk of paying dearly for a room nicer than you need. If you strike out, try the room-finding service at the TI at Plaça de Catalunya.

Barcelona is Spain's most expensive city. Still, it has reasonable rooms. A few places raise their rates in August and deal off-season. Assume prices listed do not include the 7 percent tax or breakfast. While many recommended places are on pedestrian streets, night noise is a problem almost everywhere. Most places charge more for a balcony overlooking a people-filled street. To save money and gain sleep ask for *"tranquilo"* rather than *"con vista."*

Sleeping near the Ramblas and in the Gothic Quarter
(zip code: 08002)
These accommodations are listed in roughly geographical order downhill from Plaça de Catalunya. See map on page 666.

Hotel Allegro fills a renovated old palace with wide halls, marble and hardwood floors, and elegant, modern rooms with all the comforts. It overlooks a busy pedestrian boulevard (Db-25,000 ptas plus tax, extra bed-3,000 ptas, CC:VMA, family rooms, satellite TV, air-con, elevator, a block down from Plaça de Catalunya at Portal de l'Angel 17, tel. 93-318-4141, fax 93-301-2631, SE).

Catalunya Plaza, a business hotel, has all the air-conditioning and minibar comforts (Sb-19,000 ptas, Db-22,000 ptas, includes breakfast, CC:VMA, elevator, free nuts at the desk, on the square at Plaça de Catalunya 7, tel. 93-317-7171, fax 93-317-7855, SE).

Hotel Barcelona is another big, American-style hotel (Sb-17,000 ptas, Db-25,000 ptas, 32,000 ptas with a terrace, CC:VMA, air-con, 1 block away at Caspe 1–13, tel. 93-302-5858, fax 93-301-8674).

Nouvel Hotel, an elegant Victorian-style building on a fine pedestrian street, has royal lounges and comfy rooms (Sb-12,125 ptas, Db without balcony-15,350 ptas, Db with balcony-18,000 ptas, includes breakfast, manager Gabriel promises 10 percent discount with this book; no balcony = quieter and cheaper; air-con, hair dryers, CC:VMA, Carrer de Santa Ana 18, tel. 93-301-8274, fax 93-301-8370, SE).

Hotel Toledano's elevator takes you high above the noise. View balcony rooms overlook the Ramblas. Suitable for backpackers, this small and folksy, and at times dumpy, hotel is run by the helpful English-speaking owner Juan Sanz, his son Albert, and Jordi (Sb-3,900 ptas, Db-6,900 ptas, Tb-8,600 ptas, Qb-9,600 ptas, cheaper off-season, CC:VMA, Rambla de Canaletas 138, tel. 93-301-0872, fax 93-412-3142, e-mail: Toledano@idgrup.ibernet.com). They run **Hostal Residencia Capitol** one floor above—quiet, plain, cheaper, and also appropriate for backpackers (S-2,900 ptas, D-4,600 ptas, Ds-5,200 ptas, cheap 5-bed room).

Hotel Continental has comfortable rooms, double-thick mattresses, wildly clashing carpets and wallpaper, an all-day complimentary coffee bar, and a good location at the top of the Ramblas (Db-10,000–13,000 ptas with breakfast, CC:VMA, fans in rooms, elevator, Las Ramblas 138, tel. 93-301-2570, fax 93-302-7360, www.hotelcontinental.com).

Hotel Lloret is a big, dark, Old World place on the Ramblas with plain, air-conditioned rooms—confirm prices first (Sb-6,000 ptas, Db-9,000 ptas, extra beds-1,000 ptas each up to quints, buffet breakfast-400 ptas, choose between a noisy Ramblas balcony or *tranquilo* in the back, CC:VMA, elevator dominates the stairwell, Rambla de Canaletas 125, tel. 93-317-3366, fax 93-301-9283, SE).

Hotel Jardi is a hardworking, clean, plain place on the happiest little square in the Gothic Quarter. Room prices vary with newness, views, and balconies (Sb-3,500–4,000 ptas, Db-7,000–8,000 ptas, Tb-7,800–9,500 ptas, breakfast-700 ptas, CC:VM if bill totals at least 15,000 ptas, no elevator, halfway between the Ramblas and cathedral on Plaça Sant Josep Oriol #1, tel. 93-301-5900, fax 93-318-3664, NSE). Rooms with balconies enjoy a classic plaza setting and minimal noise.

These sister hotels straddle a pedestrian street in buildings that reek of concrete. Run by the same company, they have good but plain rooms with mod bathrooms (Sb-7,000 ptas, Db-11,500 ptas includes tax and breakfast, CC:VMA, elevator): **Hotel Catalunya** (Carrer de Santa Ana 24, tel. 93-301-9120, fax 93-302-7870) and **Hotel Cortes** (Carrer de Santa Ana 25, tel. 93-317-9112, fax 93-302-7870).

Deeper in the Gothic Quarter, these two new, modern neighbors suffer from street noise but keep businesspeople happy with TV, telephone, and air-conditioning: **Hotel Adagio** (Sb-9,000 ptas, Db-11,000 ptas, Tb-13,000 ptas, saggy beds, includes breakfast, CC:VMA, elevator, Ferran 21, tel. 93-318-9061, fax 93-318-3724) and, across the street, the **Hotel California** (Sb-6,500 ptas, Db-10,000 ptas, Tb-13,500 ptas, includes breakfast, CC:VMA, Raurich 14, tel. 93-317-7766, fax 93-317-5474, email: hotel _california@seker.es, SE). The California lacks an elevator but has bigger and brighter halls and bathrooms. Hike halfway down the Ramblas (just past Metro: Liceu), then turn left at McDonald's.

Humble Places Buried in Gothic Quarter with Youth Hostel Prices

Pensio Vitoria has loose tile floors and 12 humble rooms, each with a tiny balcony. It's a fine line between homey and dumpy, but consider the price (D-3,000 ptas, Db-3,500 ptas, CC:VM, a block off the day-dreamy Plaça dei Pi at Carrer la Palla 8, tel. & fax 93-302-0834).

Hostal Campi, big, quiet, and ramshackle, is a few doors off the Ramblas (D-4,500 ptas, Db-5,500 ptas, no elevator, Canuda 4, tel. & fax 93-301-3545, NSE). **Huéspedes Santa Ana** is plain and claustrophobic, with head-to-toe twins (S-2,800 ptas, D-5,000 ptas, Db-6,000 ptas, T-7,000 ptas, Carrer de Santa Ana 23, tel. 93-301-2246). **Hostal Residencia Lausanne**, filled with backpackers, has only its location and price going for it (S-2,500 ptas, D-3,500 ptas, Ds-5,000 ptas, Db-6,500 ptas, TV room, Avenida Portal de l'Angel 24, tel. 93-302-1139, SE). **Hostal Residencia Rembrandt** keeps countless backpackers happy with simple rooms and a good location (S-2,800 ptas, Sb-3,800 ptas, D-4,500 ptas, Db-6,300 ptas, Tb-7,500 ptas, breakfast-400 ptas, Portaferrisa 23, tel. & fax 93-318-1011, SE). **Huéspedes Colmenero**, on a noisy pedestrian street, is a homey little place with five rooms, each with a tiny balcony (S-3,000–4,000 ptas, D-5,000–6,000 ptas, Db-6,000–7,000 ptas, less off-season, 2 streets toward the cathedral from the Ramblas at Petritxol 12, tel. 93-302-6634, fax: What's that?, Rosa NSE).

Sleeping in Eixample

For a more elegant and boulevardian neighborhood, sleep on or near Gran Vía de les Corts Catalanes in Eixample, a 10-minute walk from the Ramblas action.

Hotel Gran Vía, filling a palatial mansion built in the 1870s, offers Botticelli and chandeliers in the public rooms; a sprawling, peaceful sun garden; and spacious, comfy, air-conditioned rooms. It's an excellent value (Sb-10,000 ptas, Db-13,500 ptas, tax and breakfast extra, CC:VMA, book long in advance, elevator, Gran Vía de les Corts Catalanes 642, 08007 Barcelona, tel. 93-318-1900, fax 93-318-9997, SE).

Hotel Residencia Neutral, with a classic Eixample location, 35 cheery rooms, plush public rooms, and a passion for cleanliness, is the poor man's Hotel Gran Vía (tiny Sb-3,400 ptas, big Sb-6,000 ptas, Ds-5,000 ptas, Db-6,000 ptas, Ts-6,100 ptas, Tb-7,275 ptas, tax included, breakfast extra, CC:VM, elevator, elegantly located 2 blocks north of Gran Vía at Rambla Catalunya 42, 08007 Barcelona, tel. 93-487-6390, SE).

Eating in Barcelona

Barcelona, the capital of Catalunyan cuisine, offers a tremendous variety of colorful places to eat. The harbor area, especially Barceloneta, is famous for fish. Good tapas bars are all over the Gothic Quarter. Many restaurants are closed in August (or sometimes July), when the owners, like you, are on vacation.

Eating in the Gothic Quarter

Taverna Basca Irati serves 25 kinds of hot and cold Basque *pintxos* for 130 ptas each. These are open-face sandwiches—like Basque sushi but on bread. Muscle in through the hungry local crowd. Get an empty plate from the waiter, then help yourself. It's a Basque honors system: You'll be charged by the number of toothpicks left on your plate when you're done. Wash it down with a delicate glass of *sidra* (apple wine, 125 ptas) poured from on high to bring out the flavor (Tue–Sat 12:00–15:00, 19:00–23:00, Sun 12:00–15:00, closed Mon, a block off the Ramblas, behind the noisy amusement arcade at Calle Cardenal Casanyes 17, near Metro: Liceu, tel. 93-302-3084). **Juicy Jones**, next door, is a tutti-fruity vegetarian place with a hip menu (#7, great fresh juices).

Two popular but touristy places are side by side, just down from the Plaça Reial: **Los Caracoles** is a pricey Spanish wine cellar dripping in atmosphere (daily 13:00–24:00, Escudellers 14, a block toward the harbor from Plaça Reial in red-light bar country, Metro: Drassanes, tel. 93-302-3185). The neighboring **La Fonda** is brighter and more modern, with high-quality traditional cuisine at better prices and even more tourists. Arrive early or make a reservation to avoid the very long waits (Escudellers 10, daily 13:00–15:30, 20:30–23:30, tel. 93-301-7515).

The owner of the wildly successful La Fonda has opened **La Dolca Herminia** and **Les Quinze Nitz**—both serving good local food at good prices in a classy modern bistro setting. La Dolca Herminia, already popular but not yet touristy, is two blocks toward the Ramblas from the Palau de la Música at Magdalenes 27 (tel. 93-317-0676). Les Quinze Nitz is on the trendy La Plaça Reial at #6—you'll see the line (tel. 93-317-3075); after a late dinner here, head across the square (after midnight) to the speakeasy at the **Barcelona Pipa Club** at #3. Ring the bell to be let in and head upstairs to a world of velvet and jazz unknown to tourists and most locals. Dress appropriately and pay a 600-ptas-per-person cover charge with your drinks.

At **El Portalon**, a tapas bar at Banys Nous 20, locals clatter away evenings with dominoes, oblivious to the tourist mecca outside.

Restaurant Agut is a fine place for huge servings of local-style food in a local-style setting (inexpensive, closed in July or August, Calle Gignas 16, tel. 93-315-1709).

Egipte, with its late-19th-century ambience, attracts the opera crowd. Local stars' portraits are on the walls. Try the *pebrots amb bacalao*—red bell peppers stuffed with cod and served over rice (daily 13:00–16:00, 20:00–24:00, Rambla 79, downhill from the Boqueria, Metro: Liceu, tel. 93-317-7480).

Els Quatre Gats, Picasso's hangout, is famous but has become uppity and expensive. Before it was founded in 1897, the idea of a café for artists was mocked as a place where only *quatre gats* ("four cats," meaning nobody) would go (3,000 ptas meals, Mon–Sat 8:30–02:00, Sun 17:00–01:30, live piano nightly from 21:00, CC:VMA, Montsio 3, tel. 93-302-4140).

Eating near Plaça de Catalunya

Self Naturista is a bright and cheery buffet that will make vegetarians and health-food lovers feel right at home. Others may find a few unidentifiable plates and drinks. The food's already out—pick what you like and microwave it (Mon–Sat 11:30–22:00, closed Sun, near several recommended hotels, just off the top of Ramblas at Carrer de Santa Ana 11–17). Another vegetarian choice is **Bio Center** (Mon–Sat 9:00–17:00, closed Sun, Pintor Fortuny 25, Metro: Catalunya, tel. 93-301-4583).

Julivert Meu teams up regional specialties like *pan con tomate* (bread with tomato and olive oil), *jamón serrano* (cured ham), and *escalivadas* (grilled vegetables) in a rustic interior (Mon–Sat 13:00–01:00, Sun 13:00–17:00, 20:00–01:00, off the Ramblas at Bonsuccés 7, Metro: Catalunya, tel. 93-318-0343).

Eating Elsewhere in Barcelona

In the Eixample at **La Bodegueta**, have a *carajillos* (coffee with rum) and a *flauta* (sandwich on flute-thin baguette) in this authentic below-street-level bodega (Mon–Sat 8:00–2:00, Sun 19:00–1:00, Rambla Catalunya 100, at intersection with Provenza, Metro: Diagonal, tel. 93-215-4894). Or slip into the classy **Quasi Queviures** for upscale tapas, sandwiches, or the whole nine yards—

classic food with modern decor (Passeig de Gràcia 24).

El Café de Internet provides an easy way to munch a sandwich while sending e-mail messages to Mom (600 ptas for a half-hour, Mon–Sat 9:00–24:00, closed Sun, Gran Vía 656, Metro: Passeig de Gràcia, tel. 93-412-1915, www.cafeinternet.es).

For a quick meal, pick up a healthy sandwich at **Pans & Company**. Its sister establishment, **Pastafiore**, dishes up salads and pasta at a fair price (500–800 ptas). Both are lifesavers on Sunday, when many restaurants are closed (daily 8:00–24:00, opens at 9:00 Sun, located on Plaça Urquinaona, Provenza, La Rambla, Portal de l'Angel, and just about everywhere else).

Eating in Barceloneta

This charming beach suburb of the big city has long been famous for its fresh-fish restaurants. Lately, the big money has shifted to new, more trendy locales, and Barceloneta has gone back to being a big, easygoing neighborhood. A grid plan of long, narrow, laundry-strewn streets surrounds the central Plaça Poeta Boscan. For an entertaining evening, start here (15-minute walk or Metro: Barceloneta). During the day a lively produce market fills one end of the square. At night kids play soccer and Ping-Pong.

Cova Fumada is the neighborhood eatery. Josep Maria and his family serve famously fresh fish (Mon–Fri 17:30–20:30, closed Jul, Carrer del Baluarte 56, on the corner at Carrer Sant Carles, tel. 93-221-4061). Their *sardinas a la plancha* (grilled sardines, 350 ptas) are fresh and tasty. *Bombas* (potato croquets with pork, 150 ptas) are the house specialty. It's macho to have it *picante* (spicy with chili sauce); gentler taste buds prefer it with garlic cream (all-i-oli). If you're not sure how you like it, get it *marica*. Catalunyan bruschetta is *pan tostado* (toast with oil and garlic, 140 ptas). Wash it down with *vino tinto* (house red wine, 80 ptas).

At **Bar Electricidad**, Arturo Jordana Barba is the neighborhood source for cheap wine. Drop in. It's 180 ptas per liter; the empty plastic water bottles are for take-away. Try a 75-ptas glass of Torroja Tinto, the best local red, or Priorato Dulce, a wonderfully sweet red (Mon–Sat 8:00–13:00, 15:00–19:00, across the square from Cova Fumada, Plaça del Poeta Bosca, #61, NSE).

Tapas in the Gothic Quarter

Tapas aren't as popular in Catalunya as they are in the rest of Spain, but Barcelona boasts great *tascas*—colorful local tapas bars. Get small plates (for maximum sampling) by asking for "*tapas*," not "*raciones*." For the most fun and flavorful route through the Gothic Quarter, go to Plaça de la Merce (Metro: Drassanes) then follow the small street that runs along the right side of the church (Carrer Merce), stopping at whichever *tascas* look fun.

La Jarra is known for its tender *jamón canario con patatas* (baked ham with salty potatoes). Across the street, **La Pulperia** serves up fried fish. A block down the street, **Tasca El Corral** makes one of the neighborhood's best chorizo *al diablo* (hell sausage), which you sauté yourself. It's great with the regional specialty *pan con tomate*. Across the street, **La Plata** keeps things wonderfully simple, serving extremely cheap plates of sardines and small glasses of keg wine. **La Socarrena** serves northern Spain mountain favorites (like *queso de cabrales*—very moldy cheese) with *sidra* (apple wine). You can smell **Las Campanas'** fragrant sausage a block away. Have a chat with the parrot at **Bar la Choza del Sopas**. At the end of Carrer Merce, **Bar Vendimia** serves up tasty clams and mussels. Carrer Ample, the street paralleling Carrer Merce, has more-refined bar-hopping possibilities.

La Cava del Palau, also in the Gothic Quarter, is a great wine bar, bubbling with Spain's sparkling wine (Verdaguer i Callis 10, near Palau de la Música Catalana).

Transportation Connections—Barcelona

By train to: Lisbon (1/day, 15 hrs with change in Madrid), **Madrid** (6/day, 7–9 hrs, $50 with *couchette*), **Paris** (3/day, 11–15 hrs, $70, night train, reservation required), **Sevilla** (4/day, 11 hrs), **Málaga** (3/day, 14 hrs), **Nice** (1/day, 12 hrs, change in Cerbere). Train info: tel. 93-490-0202; international train info: tel. 93-490-1122.

By bus to: Madrid (6/day, 8 hrs, half the price of a train ticket).

By plane: To avoid 10-hour train trips, check the reasonable flights from Barcelona to Sevilla or Madrid. Iberia Air (tel. 93-412-5667) and Air Europe (tel. 90-224-0042) offer $80 flights to Madrid. Airport info: tel. 93-298-3838.

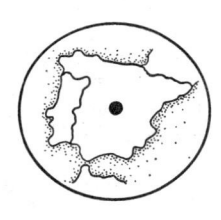

MADRID

Today's Madrid is upbeat and vibrant, still enjoying a post-Franco renaissance. You'll feel it. Even the statue-maker beggars have a twinkle in their eyes.

Madrid is the hub of Spain. This modern capital—Europe's highest, at more than 2,000 feet—has a population of more than 4 million and is young by European standards. Only 400 years ago, King Philip II decided to move the capital of his empire from Toledo to Madrid. One hundred years ago Madrid had only 400,000 people, so nine-tenths of the city is modern sprawl surrounding an intact, easy-to-navigate historic core.

Dive headlong into the grandeur and intimate charm of Madrid. The lavish Royal Palace, with its gilded rooms and frescoed ceilings, rivals Versailles. The Prado has Europe's top collection of paintings. The city's huge Retiro Park invites you for a shady siesta and a hopscotch through a mosaic of lovers, families, skateboarders, pets walking their masters, and expert bench sitters. Make time for Madrid's elegant shops and people-friendly pedestrian zones. Enjoy the shade in an arcade. On Sundays, cheer for the bull at a bullfight or bargain like mad at a mega-flea market. Lively Madrid has enough street singing, barhopping, and people-watching vitality to give any visitor a boost of youth.

Planning Your Time

Madrid's top two sights, the Prado and the palace, are worth a day. If you hit the city on a Sunday, allot extra time for a bullfight. Ideally, give Madrid two days and spend them this way:
Day 1: Breakfast of *churros* (see "Eating," below) before a brisk, good-morning-Madrid walk for 20 minutes from Puerta del Sol to the Prado; 9:00–12:00 at the Prado; afternoon siesta in Retiro

Park or modern art at the Centro Reina Sofia (*Guernica*) and/or the Thyssen-Bornemisza Museum; Tapas for dinner around Plaza Santa Ana.

Day 2: Follow this book's "Puerta del Sol to Royal Palace Walk" (see below); tour the Royal Palace, lunch near Plaza Mayor; afternoon free for other sights or shopping.

Note that the Prado and Thyssen-Bornemisza Museum are closed on Monday.

Orientation

The historic center can easily be covered on foot. No major sight is more than a 20-minute walk from the Puerta del Sol, Madrid's central square. Your time will be divided between the city's two major sights—the Royal Palace and the Prado—and its barhopping, car-honking, contemporary scene.

The Puerta del Sol is at the dead center of Madrid and of Spain itself; notice the "kilometer zero" marker, from which all of Spain is surveyed (southwest corner). The Royal Palace to the west and the Prado Museum and Retiro Park to the east frame Madrid's historic center.

Southwest of Puerta del Sol is a 17th-century district with the slow-down-and-smell-the-cobbles Plaza Mayor and plenty of relics from pre-industrial Spain.

North of Puerta del Sol runs the Gran Vía, and between the two are lively pedestrian shopping streets. The Gran Vía, bubbling with expensive shops and cinemas, leads to the modern Plaza de España. North of Gran Vía is the gritty Malasana quarter, with its colorful small houses, shoemakers' shops, sleazy-looking hombres, milk vendors, bars, and hip night scene.

Tourist Information

Madrid has four Turismos (all closed on Sunday): one on the Plaza Mayor at #3 (Mon–Fri 10:00–20:00, Sat 10:00–14:00, tel. 91-588-1636); another near the Prado Museum, behind the giant Palace Hotel (Mon–Fri 9:00–19:00, Sat 9:00–13:00, Duque de Medinaceli 2, tel. 91-429-4951); and smaller offices at the Chamartin train station (Mon–Fri 8:00–20:00, Sat 9:00–13:00, tel. 91-315-9976) and at the airport (same hours, tel. 91-305-8343). During the summer you'll also find small temporary stands with yellow umbrellas and yellow-shirted student guides happy to help out lost tourists (there's a handy booth on Puerta del Sol). Confirm your sightseeing plans and pick up a map and *Enjoy Madrid*, the free monthly city guide. (The TI's free guide to city events, *En Madrid*, is not as good as the easy-to-decipher Spanish weekly entertainment guide, *Guía del Ocio*, on sale at street-side newsstands for 125 ptas.) If interested, ask at the TI about bullfights and Zarzuela (the local light opera). The free

Madrid

Madrid

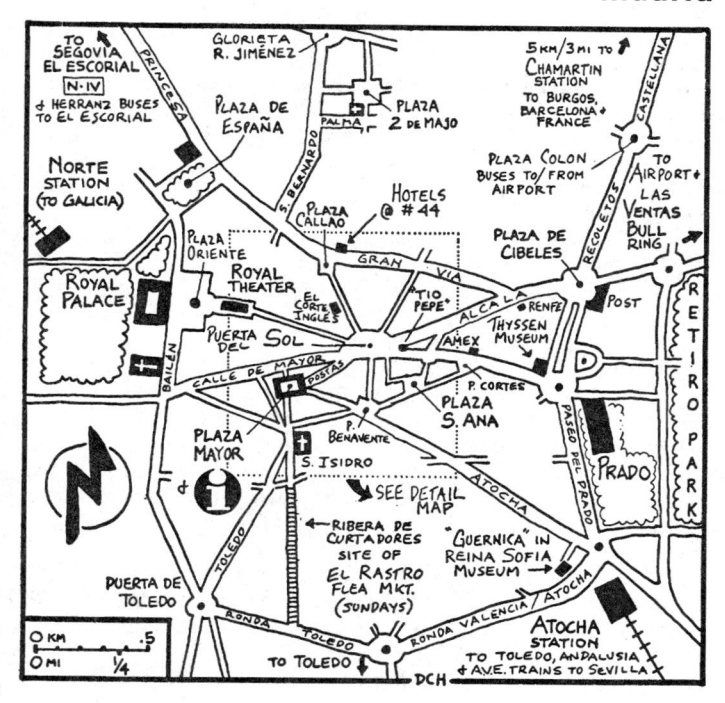

and amazingly informative *Mapa de Comunicaciones España* lists all the Turismos and highway SOS numbers with a road map of Spain. (If they're out, ask for the Paradores Hotel chain-sponsored route map.) If you're heading to other destinations in Spain, see if the Madrid TI has free maps and brochures. Since many small-town TIs keep erratic hours and run out of these pamphlets, get what you can here. Get bus schedules, too, to avoid unnecessary trips to the various bus stations.

Arrival in Madrid

By Train: The two main rail stations, Atocha and Chamartin, are both on subway lines with easy access to downtown Madrid. Each station has all the services, though there is no TI at Atocha. In Spain, train rides longer than about three hours require reservations, even if you have a Eurailpass. To avoid needless running around, arrange your departure upon arrival.

Chamartin handles most international trains, and Atocha runs

AVE trains to Sevilla. Both stations offer long-distance trains (*largo recorrido*) as well as local trains to nearby destinations (*cercanías*). Atocha is more clearly split into two halves (local and long-distance trains) with separate schedules; this can be confusing if you're in the wrong side of the building. Atocha also has two helpful (necessary) customer-service offices called Atención al Cliente (daily 7:00–23:00)—one office for each half of the building. The Chamartin station is less confusing. Its customer-service office is beside the ticket windows, in the middle of the building, and the helpful TI is opposite track #20.

Club AVE in Atocha (upstairs) is a lounge reserved solely for AVE business or first-class ticketholders or Eurailers with a reservation (free drinks, newspapers, showers, info service, and so on). Club Intercity in Chamartin is less exclusive—you can get in if you have a first-class railpass and first-class seat or sleeper reservations.

Both train stations have Metro stops: Chamartin and Atocha RENFE. (Note that there are two Atocha Metro stops in Madrid; the train station's Metro station is "Atocha RENFE"). If you're traveling between Chamartin and Atocha, use the Cercanias trains (6/hrly, 12 min, free with railpass—show it at ticket window in the middle of all the turnstiles); they're far quicker than the subway. Trains depart from Atocha's track #2. At Chamartin, check the Salidas Immediatas board for the next departure.

At the downtown RENFE office you can get train information, reservations, and tickets (Mon–Fri 9:30–19:00, credit cards accepted, best to go in person, 2 blocks north of the Prado Museum at Calle Alcala 44, tel. 91-328-9020).

By Bus: Madrid's three key bus stations, all connected by Metro, are: Larrea (handles Segovia; Metro: Príncipe Pío), the brand-new Estación Sur Autobuses (covers Toledo, Avila, and Granada; Metro: Méndez Alvaro), and Estación Herranz (serves El Escorial; in the Metro: Moncloa).

By Plane: Madrid's Barajas Airport, 10 miles east of downtown, comes well equipped to help new arrivals. It has a 24-hour bank with fair rates, an ATM, a TI, a telephone office where you can buy a phone card, a RENFE desk for rail information, a pharmacy, on-the-spot car-rental agencies, and easy public transportation into town. Airport info: tel. 91-393-6000. By public transport, take the yellow bus from the airport to Madrid (to Plaza Colón, 4/hrly, 20 min, 385 ptas); then, from Plaza Colón, take a taxi or subway to your hotel (to get to the subway, walk up the stairs and face the blue "URBIS" sign high on a building—the subway stop, M. Serrano, is 50 yards to your right).

The airport' new Metro stop, Aeropuerto, provides a cheap (135 ptas) but time-consuming (45 min) way into town (access Metro at check-in level, transfer at Mar de Cristal to brown line #4—direction Arguelles, transfer at Goya to red line #3 to Sol).

Heart of Madrid

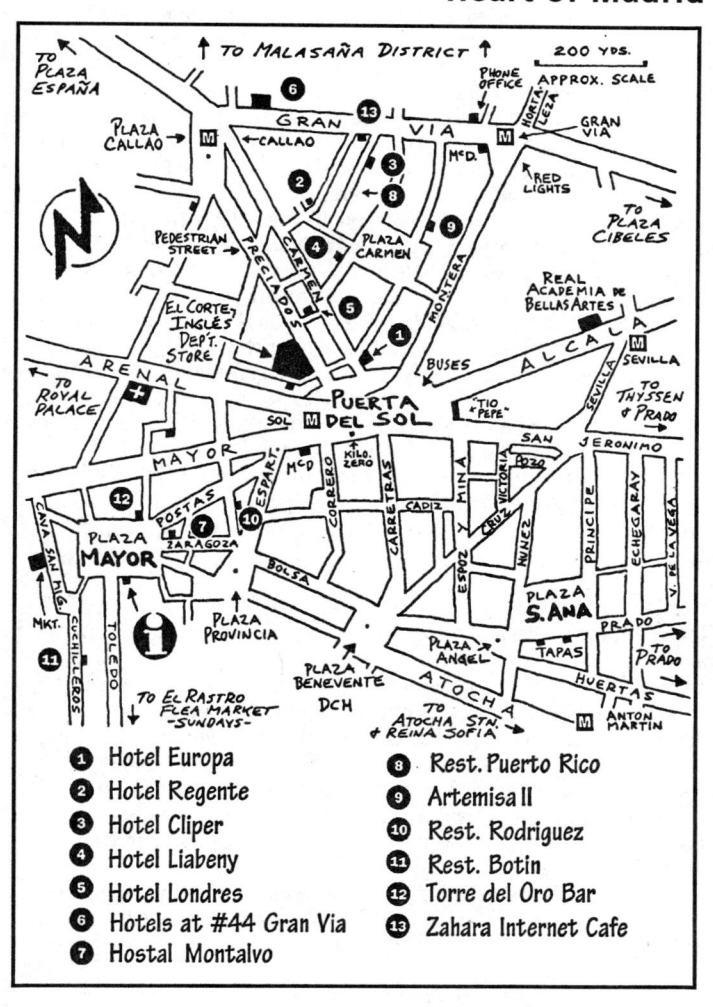

1. Hotel Europa
2. Hotel Regente
3. Hotel Cliper
4. Hotel Liabeny
5. Hotel Londres
6. Hotels at #44 Gran Via
7. Hostal Montalvo
8. Rest. Puerto Rico
9. Artemisa II
10. Rest. Rodriguez
11. Rest. Botin
12. Torre del Oro Bar
13. Zahara Internet Cafe

If you take a taxi (easily available from the airport bus station at Plaza Colón), insist on the meter; a ride through town should be less than 1,000 ptas. For a taxi to or from the airport, allow at least 3,000 ptas (5,000 ptas is a rip-off). At the airport, get a rough idea of the price before you hop in. Ask "*¿Cuanto cuesta a Madrid, más o menos?*" ("How much is it to Madrid, more or less?")

Getting around Madrid

By Subway: Madrid's subway is simple, speedy (outside of rush hour), and cheap (135 ptas/ride). For 680 ptas, buy the 10-ride Metrobus ticket, which can be shared by several travelers and works on both the Metro and buses (available at kiosks or tobacco shops or in Metro). The city's broad streets can be hot and exhausting. A subway trip of even a stop or two can save time and energy. Pick up a free map (*Plano del Metro*) at most stations. Navigate by subway stops (shown on city maps). To transfer, follow signs to the next subway line (numbered and color-coded). End stops are used to indicate directions. Insert your ticket in the turnstile, then retrieve it as you pass through. Green *Salida* signs point to the exit. Use the neighborhood maps and street signs to exit smartly.

By Bus: City buses, while not as easy as the Metro, can be useful. If you're interested, get a bus map at the TI or the info booth on Puerta del Sol. Tickets are 135 ptas (buy on bus) or 680 ptas for a 10-ride Metrobus (buy at kiosks, in tobacco shops, or in the Metro). The Madrid Vision bus provides transportation and a tour (see "Tours of Madrid," below).

By Taxi: While taxis are easy to hail and reasonable (175 ptas drop, 85 ptas per km, late night 115 ptas per km; supplements for airport, train station, and bags), you'll go just as fast and a lot cheaper by subway.

Helpful Hints

Theft Alert: Be wary of pickpockets, anywhere, anytime, but particularly on Puerta del Sol (main square), the subway, and crowded streets. Wear your money belt. In crowds, keep your day bag in front of you. Some thieves "accidentally" spill something on your clothes, then pick your pocket as they help you clean up. The small streets north of Gran Vía are particularly dangerous even before nightfall. Fortunately, violent crime against tourists is very rare.

Museum Pass: If you plan to visit the Prado, Reina Sofia (*Guernica*), and Thyssen-Bornemisza museums, save 33 percent by buying the Paseo del Arte pass (1,200 ptas, available at all three).

Monday Plans: If you're in Madrid on a Monday (when the Prado is closed), you can visit the Royal Palace and Reina Sofia, rent a boat at Retiro Park, tour the nearby botanical gardens, shop, or café-hop.

Travel Agency and Free Maps: The grand department store, El Corte Inglés, has a travel agency (Mon–Sat 10:00–21:30, just off Puerta del Sol) and gives free Madrid maps (at the information desk, just inside the door at the northwest corner of the intersection of Preciados and Tetuan).

Telephones: The telephone office, centrally located at Gran Vía 30, has metered phones and accepts credit cards for charges over 500 ptas (daily 10:00–23:00).

Madrid 685

Plaza Mayor to Royal Palace

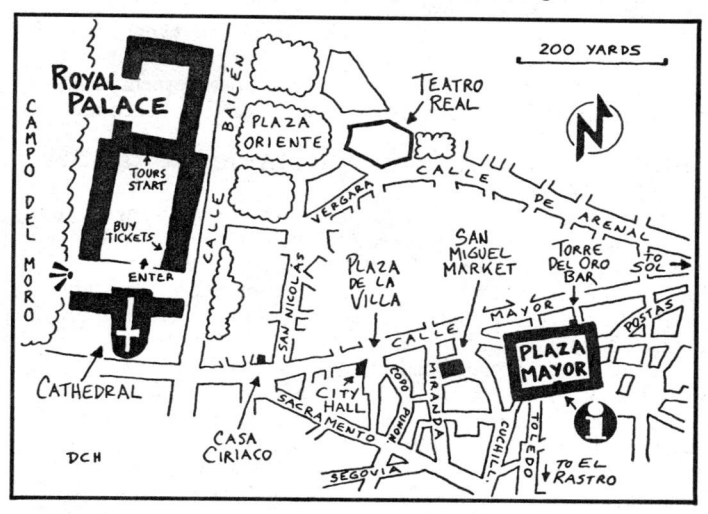

American Express: The Amex office is at Plaza Cortes 2 (opposite Palace Hotel, 6 blocks from Metro: Sevilla, Mon–Fri 9:00–17:30, Sat 9:00–12:00, tel. 91-322-5455).

Embassies: The U.S. Embassy is at Serrano 75 (tel. 91-587-2200); the Canadian Embassy is at Nuñez de Balboa 35 (tel. 91-431-2350).

Laundromat: The self-service Lavamatique is funky but central (Mon–Fri 9:00–20:00, Sat 9:00–17:00, Cervantes 1).

Internet Access: Zahara is at the corner of Gran Vía and Mesoneros (Mon–Fri 9:00–0:30, Sat–Sun 9:00–01:30).

Tours of Madrid

Bus Tour—The Madrid Vision Bus takes tourists on a big hop-on hop-off sightseeing loop with a multilingual tape-recorded narration (2,200 ptas for all-day pass, departures from Gran Vía 32 every 45 minutes, 9:15–17:15, tel. 91-767-1743).

Walking Tour—British expatriate Stephen Drake-Jones gives entertaining, informative walks of historic old Madrid almost nightly (along with several other more specialized tours). A historian with a passion for the memory of Wellington (the man who stopped Napoleon), Stephen is the founder of the Wellington Society. For 2,500 ptas you become a member of the society for one year and get a free two-hour tour that includes stops at two bars for local drinks and tapas. Stephen, in his nearly eccentric style, takes you back in time to sort out the Habsburg and Bourbon history of this underappreciated city. Stephen likes his drink—if you feel he's had too much, skip the tour. Tours start at the statue on Puerta del Sol (tel. 60-914-3203—a cell phone number that will cost you 200 ptas—to confirm tour and reserve a spot; Stephen also does inexpensive private tours for small groups; e-mail: sdrake_jones@hotmail.com).

Sights—From Madrid's Puerta del Sol to the Royal Palace

Connect the sights with the following walking tour. Allow an hour for this half-mile walk, not including your visit to the palace.

▲▲**Puerta del Sol**—Even without its "kilometer zero" plaque, Puerta del Sol is ground zero for Madrid. Standing by the statue of Charles III, survey the square. Because of his enlightened urban policies, King Charles III (who ruled until 1788) is affectionately called the "best mayor of Madrid." He decorated the city squares with fine fountains, got the meddlesome Jesuits out of city government, established a public education system, made the Retiro a public park rather than a royal retreat, and generally cleaned up Madrid. The huge palace he faces was the first post office (which he established in the 1760s). Today the building is remembered for being a police headquarters during the reign of Franco. An amazing number of those detained and interrogated by the Franco police "tried to escape" by flying out the windows to their deaths. You'll see civil guardsmen at the entry. (It's said their hats have square backsides so they can lean against the wall while enjoying a cigarette.)

On New Year's Eve, crowds gather on this square, and, as the big clock atop the post office chimes 12 times, Madrillinos eat one grape for each ring to bring good luck through the coming year.

A plaque on the post office wall marks the spot where the war against Napoleon started. Napoleon wanted his brother to be king of Spain. Trying to finagle this, Napoleon brought nearly the entire Spanish royal family (the Bourbons) to Paris for negotiations. An anxious crowd gathered outside the post office awaiting word of the fate of their royal family. This was just after the French Revolution, and there was a general nervousness between France and Spain. The French guard appeared and the 2nd of May, 1808, massacre took place. Goya, who lived just up the street, observed the massacre and captured the tragedy in his paintings *2nd of May, 1808*, and *3rd of May, 1808*, which you'll see in the Prado.

Puerta del Sol is a hub for the Metro, buses, and pickpockets. Look up at the surveillance camera. In summer you'll see a yellow-umbrella TI booth with student tour guides helping visitors. The statue of the bear pawing the strawberry bush is the symbol of Madrid.

Walking from Puerta del Sol to Plaza Mayor: On the

Madrid

corner of Calle Mayor and Puerta del Sol, step into the busy Confiteria. It's famous for its savory, meat-filled *agujas* pastries (175 ptas); notice the racks with goodies hot out of the oven. Look back toward the entrance and notice the tile above the door with the 18th-century view of the Puerta del Sol. Compare this with the view out the door. This was before the square was widened, when a church stood where the Tío Pepe sign stands today. The French used this church to hold local patriots awaiting execution.

Continue down Calle Mayor. At McDonald's veer left up the pedestrian alley called Calle de Postas. The street sign shows the post coach heading for that famous first post office. Take a left up Calle San Cristobal. At the square notice the big brick 17th-century Ministry of Foreign Affairs building—originally a prison for rich prisoners who could afford the best cells. Look right and walk under the arch into...

Plaza Mayor—This square, built in 1619, is a vast, cobbled, traffic-free chunk of 17th-century Spain. Each side of the square is uniform, as if a grand palace were turned inside out. The statue is of Philip III, who ordered the square's construction. Upon this stage, much Spanish history was played out: bullfights, fires, royal pageantry, and events of the gruesome Inquisition. Carved reliefs under the lampposts tell the story. During the Inquisition, many were tried here. The guilty would parade around the square (bleachers were built for bigger audiences) with billboards listing their many sins. They were then burned. Some were slowly strangled with a garrotte; they'd hold a crucifix and hear the reassuring words of a priest as this life was squeezed out of them. The square is painted a lovely shade of burgundy—the result of a city-wide vote. Since Franco's 1975 death, there has been a passion for voting here. Three different colors were painted as samples on the walls of this square, and the city voted for its favorite. Visit the subterranean museum of city exhibitions (free, hours depend on exhibition) under the fanciest facade (the Casa de la Panaderia—Royal Bakery).

Throughout Spain, lesser *plazas mayores* provide peaceful pools for the river of Spanish life. A stamp-and-coin market bustles here on Sundays from 10:00 to 14:00, and on any day it's a colorful and affordable place to enjoy a cup of coffee. The TI is at #3.

Finish your Plaza Mayor visit with a drink at the Torre del Oro Bar Andalu. This is Madrid's temple to bullfighting. You'll get a free tapa if Mariano is serving you between the hours of 11:00 and 13:00. Warning: They tend to order for tourists, serving them expensive dishes they didn't order; I ended up with a $10 plate I didn't want. To ask if the food is free, ask, *"¿Libero?"* The bar's ambience is *"Andalu"*...Andalusian. Look under the stuffed head of "Barbero" the bull. At eye level you'll see a *puntilla*, the knife used to put a bull out of its misery at the arena. This was the knife used to kill Barbero.

Notice the incredible action caught in the bar's many photographs. Near Barbero, follow the photo series of a wanna-be bullfighter who jumped into the ring and was killed by the bull. Below that is a series of photos showing the scandalous fight in which a banderillero (the guy who puts the arrows into the bull's back) was in trouble and his partners just stood by watching in horror as the man was killed. At the end of the bar in a glass case is the "suit of lights" El Cordobes wore in his ill-fated 1967 fight. With Franco in attendance, El Cordobes went on and on, long after he could have ended the fight, until finally the bull gored him. El Cordobes survived, the bull didn't. Find Franco with El Cordobes at the far end.

Walking from Plaza Mayor to the Royal Palace: Leave the Plaza Mayor on Calle Cuidad Rodrigo (left of Royal Bakery), passing a series of fine turn-of-the-century storefronts. From the archway you'll see Mercado de San Miguel, covered since 1900 (on left). Wander through this produce market, leaving on the downhill side and following the street left. At the corner, turn right, continuing downhill. A right on Calle de Punonrostro gives a feeling of medieval Madrid and eventually becomes Calle del Codo (where those in need of bits of armor shopped), before hitting Plaça de la Villa, the city hall square. Notice the Moorish arch where Calle del Codo hits the square. Ahead the flags of city, state, and nation grace the city hall. In the lovely garden there's a statue of Don Bazan—mastermind of the Christian victory over the Muslims at the naval battle of Lepanto in 1571. This pivotal battle ended the Muslim threat to Christian Europe.

From here Calle Mayor leads downhill a couple more blocks to the Royal Palace. Halfway down there's a tiny square opposite the recommended Casa Ciriaco restaurant (#84). The statue memorializes the 1906 anarchist bombing that killed about 50 people as the royal couple paraded by on their wedding day. While the crowd was throwing flowers, an anarchist threw a bomb from the top floor of #84 (which was a pension at the time). Amazing photos of the event are on the wall in the dining room of the restaurant.

▲▲▲**Royal Palace (Palacio Real)**—Europe's third-greatest palace (after Versailles and Vienna's Schonbrunn) is packed with tourists and royal antiques. After a fortress burned down on this site, King Phillip V commissioned this huge 18th-century palace as a replacement. How huge is it? Two thousand rooms with miles of lavish tapestries, a king's ransom of chandeliers, priceless porcelain, and paintings. Nowadays it's used only for formal state receptions and tourist's daydreams.

You can wander on your own or join an English tour (get time of next tour and decide as you buy your ticket; tours depart about every 20 minutes). The museum guidebook and the tour guides are equally dry, each showing a passion for meaningless data (850 ptas without a tour, 950 ptas with a tour, Mon–Sat

Madrid

9:00–18:00, Sun 9:00–15:00; Oct–Mar Mon–Sat 9:30–17:00, Sun 9:00–14:00; Metro: Opera, tel. 91-542-0059). Your ticket includes the armory (most likely closed for restoration) and the pharmacy, both on the courtyard.

Sights—Madrid's Museum Neighborhood

These three worthwhile museums are in east Madrid. From Prado to the Thyssen-Bornemisza Museum is a five-minute walk; Prado to Reina Sofia is a 10-minute walk.

▲▲▲**Prado Museum**—The Prado is my favorite collection of paintings anywhere. With more than 3,000 canvases, including entire rooms of masterpieces by Velázquez, Goya, El Greco, and Bosch, it's overwhelming. Take a tour or buy a guidebook (or bring me along by ripping out and packing the Prado chapter from *Rick Steves' Mona Winks*). Focus on the Flemish and northern (Bosch, Dürer, Rubens), the Italian (Fra Angelico, Raphael, Botticelli, Titian), and the Spanish art (El Greco, Velázquez, Goya).

Follow Goya through his stages, from cheery (*The Parasol*), to political (*2nd of May, 1808* and *3rd of May, 1808*), to dark ("Negras de Goya": e.g., *Saturn Devouring His Children*). In each stage, Goya asserted his independence from artistic conventions. Even the standard court portraits from his "first" stage reflect his politically liberal viewpoint, subtly showing the vanity and stupidity of his royal subjects by the looks in their goony eyes. His political stage, with paintings like the *3rd of May, 1808*, depicting a massacre of Spaniards by Napoleon's troops, makes him one of the first artists with a social conscience. Finally, in his gloomy "dark stage," Goya probed the inner world of fears and nightmares, anticipating the 20th-century preoccupation with dreams. Also, seek out Bosch's *The Garden of Earthly Delights*. The art is constantly rearranged by the Prado's fidgety management, so even the Prado's own maps and guidebooks are out of date. Regardless of the latest location, most art is grouped by painter, and any guard can point you in the right direction if you say "*¿Dónde está...?*" and the painter's name as Españoled as you can (e.g., Titian is "Ticiano" and Bosch is "El Bosco"). Show up 30 minutes after it opens to avoid the initial flood (the Murillo entrance—at the end closest to Retiro Park—always has shorter line) or go at lunchtime, from 14:00 to 16:00, when the Prado is quietest (500 ptas, Tue–Sat 9:00–19:00, Sun 9:00–14:00, closed Mon; Paseo de Prado, Metro: Banco de España or Atocha—each a 15-minute walk from the museum, tel. 91-330-2800 or 91-420-2836).

▲▲**Thyssen-Bornemisza Museum**—This stunning museum displays the impressive collection that Baron Thyssen (a wealthy German married to a former Miss Spain) sold to Spain for $350 million. It's basically minor works by major artists and major works by minor artists (the real big guns are over at the Prado).

But art lovers appreciate how the good baron's art complements the Prado's collection by filling in where the Prado is weak (Impressionism). For a fine walk through art history, ride the elevator to the top floor and do the rooms in numerical order. It's located across from the Prado at Paseo del Prado 8 in the Palacio de Villahermosa (700 ptas, Tue–Sun 10:00–19:00, closed Mon, Metro: Banco de España or Atocha, tel. 91-369-0151). Tired ones can hail a cab at the gate and zip straight to Centro Reina Sofia.

▲▲**Centro Reina Sofia**—This exceptional modern-art museum covers the art of our century. Ride the elevator to the second floor and follow the room numbers for art from 1900 to 1950. The fourth floor continues the collection from 1950 to 1980. The museum is most famous for Picasso's *Guernica*, a massive painting showing the horror of modern war. Guernica, a village in northern Spain, was the target of the world's first saturation-bombing raid, approved by Franco and carried out by Hitler. Notice the two rooms of studies for *Guernica* filled with iron-nail tears and screaming mouths. *Guernica* was exiled in America until Franco's death, and now it reigns as Spain's national piece of art. The museum also houses an easy-to-enjoy collection of other modern artists, including more of Picasso (three rooms divided among his pre-civil-war work, *Guernica*, and his post-civil-war art) and a mind-bending room full of Dalís. Enjoy a break in the shady courtyard before leaving (500 ptas, Mon and Wed–Sat 10:00–21:00, Sun 10:00–14:30, closed Tue, Santa Isabel 52, Metro: Atocha, across from Atocha train station, look for exterior glass elevators, tel. 91-467-5062).

More Sights—Madrid

▲▲**Retiro Park**—Siesta in this 350-acre green and breezy escape from the city. At midday on Saturday and Sunday the area around the lake becomes a street carnival, with jugglers, puppeteers, and lots of local color. These peaceful gardens offer great picnicking and people watching. From the Retiro Metro stop, walk to the big lake (El Estanque), where you can rent a rowboat (450 ptas for 45 min). Past the lake, a grand boulevard of statues leads to the Prado. Charles III's Botanical Garden (Real Jardín Botánico) is a pleasant extension of Retiro Park (entry just opposite the Atocha end of the Prado). For 200 ptas you can escape all the commotion of Madrid and wander through a lush forest with trees from around the world (daily 10:00–19:00, Plaza de Murillo 2, Metro: Atocha or Retiro).

Parque de Atracciones—This colorful amusement park comes complete with Venetian canals, dancing, eating, games, free shows, and top-notch people watching (600 ptas admission, Super Napy all-inclusive ticket for rides-2,675 ptas, 1,500 ptas for kids, Jul–Aug daily 12:00–01:00, except Sat until 02:00, shorter hours off-season, Metro: Batan, tel. 91-463-2900 for exact times). This fair

Madrid

and Spain's best zoo (1,615 ptas entrance, daily 10:30–21:00, dolphin shows in good, new aquarium, tel. 91-512-3770) are in the vast Casa de Campo Park just west of the Royal Palace.

Shopping

Shoppers focus on the pedestrian area between Gran Vía and Puerta del Sol. The giant department store, El Corte Inglés, is a block off Puerta del Sol (Mon–Sat 10:00–21:30, closed Sun, supermarket in basement).

▲**El Rastro**—Europe's biggest flea market, held on Sundays and holidays, is a field day for shoppers, people watchers, and thieves (9:00–15:00, best before 12:00). Thousands of stalls titillate more than a million browsers with mostly new junk. Start at the Plaza Mayor and head south or take the subway to Tirso de Molina. Hang on to your wallet. Europe's biggest stamp market thrives simultaneously on Plaza Mayor.

Nightlife

▲▲▲**Bullfight**—Madrid's Plaza de Toros hosts Spain's top bullfights on most Sundays and holidays from Easter through October and nearly every day mid-May through early June. Top fights sell out in advance. Fights usually start punctually at 19:00. Tickets range from 500 to 10,000 ptas. There are no bad seats at Plaza de Toros; paying more gets you in the shade and/or closer to the gore (*filas* 8, 9, and 10 tend to be closest to the action). Booking offices add 20 percent and don't sell the cheap seats (Plaça del Carmen 1, tel. 91-531-2732). If you want to save money, buy your ticket at the bullring. Tickets go on sale the day of the fight at 10:00; 10 percent of the seats are kept available to be sold two hours before the fight (Calle Alcala 237, Metro: Ventas, tel. 91-356-2200). The bullfighting museum (Museo Taurino) is next to the bullring (free, Sun and Tue–Fri 9:30–14:30, closed Sat and Mon, Calle Alcala 237, tel. 91-725-1857).

▲▲**Zarzuela**—For a delightful look at Spanish light opera that even English speakers can enjoy, try an evening of Zarzuela. Guitar-strumming Napoleons in red capes, buxom women with masks and fans, castanets and stomping feet, Spanish-speaking pharaohs, melodramatic spotlights, aficionados singing along from the cheap seats, where the acoustics are best—this is the people's opera. That's Zarzuela. Madrid's Theater Zarzuela is at Jovellanos 4 (Metro: Banco de Espana, tel. 91-524-5400). The TI's monthly guide has a special Zarzuela listing.

Flamenco—Taberna Casa Patas is small, intimate, smoky, and powerful, with one drink included and no hassling after that (tickets around 3,000 ptas, shows at 22:00, Canizares 10, near Plaza Santa Ana, reservations tel. 91-369-0496). The Flamenco House is more touristy (Calle Torija 7, just off Plaza Mayor).

Sleeping in Madrid
(160 ptas = about $1)
Sleep Code: **S** = Single, **D** = Double/Twin, **T** = Triple, **Q** = Quad, **b** = bathroom, **t** = toilet only, **s** = shower only, **CC** = Credit Card (Visa, MasterCard, Amex), **SE** = Speaks English, **NSE** = No English. Breakfast is not included unless noted. In Madrid, the 7 percent IVA tax is generally, but not always, included in the price.

Madrid has plenty of centrally located budget hotels and *pensiónes*. You'll have no trouble finding a sleepable double for $30, a good double for $60, and a modern air-conditioned double with all the comforts for $100. Prices are the same throughout the year, and it's almost always easy to find a place. The accommodations I've listed are all within a few minutes' walk of Puerta del Sol. Competition is stiff. Those on a budget can bargain. Nighttime Madrid's economy is brisk. Even decent areas are littered with shady-looking people after dark. Just don't invite them in.

Sleeping in the Pedestrian Zone between Puerta del Sol and Gran Vía
(zip code: 28013)

Predictable and away from the seediness, these are good values for those wanting to spend a little more. Especially for these hotels, call first to see if the price is firm. Their formal prices may be inflated, and some offer weekend deals. Use Metro: Sol for these five hotels. See map on page 683 for location.

Hotel Europa has red-carpet charm: a quiet courtyard, royal salon, plush halls with happy Muzak, polished wood floors, attentive staff, and 80 squeaky-clean rooms with balconies overlooking the pedestrian zone or an inner courtyard. All rooms have TVs (CNN) and big, modern bathrooms. Many rooms face an inner courtyard that amplifies voices and TV noise. Caution: Your words will travel. For a better night's sleep, feel free to remove their rubber-coated undersheets—then toss them into the hallway to make a statement (Sb-6,400 ptas, Db-8,500 ptas, Tb-12,000 ptas, Qb-14,000 ptas, breakfast-600 ptas, fine lounge on 2nd floor, elevator, fans in rooms, easy phone reservations with credit card, CC:VMA, Calle del Carmen 4, tel. 91-521-2900, fax 91-521-4696, e-mail: hoteleuropa@genio.infor.es, Sr. Garaban and his very helpful staff SE). The convenient Europa cafeteria/restaurant next door is a good value.

Hotel Regente is a big, traditional, and impersonal place with 145 plain but comfortable air-conditioned rooms and a great location (Sb-6,200 ptas, Db-9,500 ptas plus tax, CC:VMA, midway between Puerta del Sol and Plaza del Callao at Mesonero Romanos 9, tel. 91-521-2941, fax 91-532-3014).

Nearby, the **Hotel Cliper** is faded-elegant and bordering on run-down but has character and comfortable rooms on a fairly quiet street (Sb-5,800 ptas, Db-7,800 ptas, most rooms have air-con, elevator, CC:VMA, Chincilla 6, near Plaza Carmen, tel. 91-531-1700, fax 91-531-1707, SE).

The huge **Hotel Liabeny** feels classy and new, with 222 plush, spacious rooms and all the comforts. It's a business-class hotel that decided to lower its prices to get the tourist trade (Sb-11,900 ptas, Db-16,200 ptas, CC:VMA, air-con, if one room is smoky they can usually switch you to another, off Plaza Carmen at Salud 3, tel. 91-531-9000, fax 91-532-7421, www.apunte.es/liabeny, fax is better than Web access, SE).

Hotel Londres is a sad business-class hotel: dark, stark, and a little smoky and unfriendly (Db-10,100 ptas, renovated Db-11,700 ptas, ask for 15–20 percent off Jan–Mar and Jul–Aug, CC:VMA, elevator, air-con, don't trust their safes, Galdo 2, tel. 91-531-4105, fax 91-531-4101; e-mail: hotellondres@cempresarial.com).

Sleeping at Gran Vía #44
(zip code: 28013)

The pulse (and noise) of today's Madrid is best felt along the Gran Vía. This main drag in the heart of the city stays awake all night. Despite the dreary pile of prostitutes just a block north, there's a certain urban decency about it. My choices (all at Gran Vía #44) are across from Plaza del Callão, which is four colorful blocks (of pedestrian malls) from Puerta del Sol. Although many rooms are high above the traffic noise, cooler and quieter rooms are on the back side. The Café & Te next door provides a classy way to breakfast. The Callão Metro stop is at your doorstep, and the handy Gran Vía stop (direct to Atocha) is two blocks away.

Hostal Residencia Miami is clean and quiet, with lovely, well-lit rooms, padded doors, and plastic-flower decor throughout. It's like staying at your eccentric aunt's in Miami Beach. The bubbly landlady, Sra. Sanz, and her too-careful husband, who dresses up each day for work here, speak no English (S-2,500–3,000 ptas, D-3,500 ptas, Db-4,500 ptas; closed mid-Jul–Aug—if they take reservations then, they're booking you elsewhere; 8th floor, tel. 91-521-1464).

Across the hall, **Hostal Alibel**, like Miami with less sugar, rents seven big, airy, quiet rooms (D-4,000 ptas, Ds-4,500 ptas, Db-5,000 ptas, tel. 91-521-0051, grandmotherly Terese NSE).

Hostal Residencia Valencia is run like a hotel with 32 big stark rooms. The friendly manager, Antonio Ramirez, speaks English (Sb-4,400 ptas, Ds-5,800 ptas, Db-6,200 ptas, Tb-8,200 ptas, Qb-9,200 ptas, CC:VMA, 5th floor, tel. 91-522-1115, fax 91-522-1113). Also a good value but a bit smoky and with less character is **Hostal Residencia Continental** (Sb-4,000 ptas, Db-5,200 ptas, CC:VMA, 3rd floor, tel. 91-521-4640, fax 91-521-4649, e-mail: continental@mundivia.es, SE).

Sleeping on or near Plaza Santa Ana
(zip code: 28012)

The Plaza Santa Ana area has plenty of cheap places and a couple of splurges. While noisy at night, it has a rough but charming ambience, with colorful bars and a central location (3 minutes from Puerta del Sol's "Tío Pepe" sign; walk down Calle San Jeronimo and turn right on Príncipe; Metro: Sol). At most of these hotels, fluent Spanish is spoken, bathrooms are usually down the hall, and there's no heat during winter. To locate hotels, see map on page 698.

Hopeless romantics might enjoy playing corkscrew around the rickety cut-glass elevator to the very simple yet homey **Pensión La Valenciana**'s old and funky rooms with springy beds. All rooms have balconies; three of them overlook the square (S-1,600 ptas, D-3,500 ptas, Príncipe 27, 4th floor, right on Plaza Santa Ana next to the theater with flags, tel. 91-429-6317, Esperanza NSE).

In the beautifully tiled building at **Plaza Santa Ana 15**, up a dark wooden staircase, are two good places. Unfortunately, a disco thumps Thursday through Saturday nights. **Hostal Filo** is squeaky clean and has a nervous but helpful management and 20 rooms hiding in a confusing floor plan (S-2,100 ptas, D-3,600 ptas, Ds-4,600 ptas, T-5,400 ptas, Ts-5,400 ptas, closed Aug, 2nd floor, tel. 91-522-4056). **Hostal Delvi** is simple, clean, and homey (S-1,800–2,000 ptas, D-3,200 ptas, Ds-3,700 ptas, Ts-4,700 ptas, 3rd floor, tel. 91-522-5998, Maria NSE). Maria offers these already-discounted prices to readers with this book.

The cheapest beds are across the street at **Hostal Lucense** (S-1,500 ptas, D-2,300 ptas, Ds-3,000 ptas, T-3,500 ptas, 200 ptas per shower, cheaper for 2 nights, Nuñez de Arce 15, tel. 91-522-4888, run by Sr. and Sra. Muñoz, both interesting characters, Sr. SE) and **Casa Huéspedes Poza** (same prices and owners, Nuñez de Arce 9, tel. 91-522-4871). Because of these two places, I list no Madrid youth hostels.

Hostal R. Veracruz II, between Plaza Santa Ana and Puerta del Sol, rents decent, quiet rooms (Sb-3,700 ptas, Db-5,200 ptas, Tb-6,900 ptas, CC:VM, elevator, air-con, Victoria 1, 3rd floor, 28012 Madrid, tel. 91-522-7635, fax 91-522-6749, NSE).

Splurges: To be on the same square and spend in a day what others spend in a week, luxuriate in **Hotel Reina Victoria** (Sb-21,000 ptas, Db-26,250 ptas, prices generally discounted to Db-18,000 in Jul–Aug, when this becomes a fine value, ask about "corporate rates," CC:VMA, Plaza Santa Ana 14, tel. 91-531-4500, fax 91-522-0307, SE). For a royal, air-conditioned breather and some cheap entertainment, spit out your gum, step into its lobby, grab a sofa, and watch the bellboys push the beggars back out of the revolving doors.

Suite Prado, two blocks toward the Prado from Plaza Santa Ana, is a better value, offering 18 sprawling, air-conditioned suites

Madrid   695

with a homier feel (Db suite-20,400 ptas, suites are modern and comfortable with fridges and sitting rooms, 2 extra kids sleep for free or 1 extra adult for 3,000 ptas, elevator, CC:VMA, Manuel Fernandez y Gonzalez 10, at the intersection with Venture de la Vega, 28014 Madrid, tel. 91-420-2318, fax 91-420-0559, Sylvia SE).

Sleeping Elsewhere in Central Madrid

Halfway between the Prado Museum and Plaza Santa Ana are two good places in the same building. At #34 Cervantes (28014 Madrid, Metro: Anton Martin) you'll find the spotless, friendly, and comfortable **Hotel Cervantes** (Sb-5,000 ptas, Db-6,000 ptas, CC:VMA, 2nd floor, tel. & fax 91-429-2745, NSE); and the equally polished and friendly **Hotel Gonzalo** (Sb-4,500 ptas, Db-5,700 ptas, CC:VMA, 3rd floor, tel. 91-429-2714, fax 91-420-2007, NSE).

Just off Plaza Mayor, **Hostal Montalvo** is sprawling; run by the Caraballo family; comfortable, with tons of extras; and just half a block east of the elegant Plaza Mayor on a quiet, traffic-free street (S-3,340 ptas, Sb-4,490 ptas, D-5,080 ptas, Db-5,750 ptas, Tb-8,490 ptas, elevator, CC:VM, Zaragoza 6, 28012 Madrid, 3rd floor, Metro: Sol, tel. 91-365-5910, fax 91-364-5260, SE).

Eating in Madrid

In Spain only Barcelona rivals Madrid for taste-bud thrills. You have three dining choices: an atmospheric sit-down meal in a well-chosen restaurant, an unmemorable basic sit-down meal, or a stand-up meal of tapas in a bar or (more likely) in several bars. Many restaurants are closed in August.

Eating near Puerta del Sol

Restaurante Puerto Rico has fine food, great prices, and few tourists (Mon–Sat 13:00–16:30, 20:30–24:00, closed Sun, Chinchilla 2, off Gran Vía, on same street as Hotel Cliper, tel. 91-532-2040).

Artemisia II is a hit with vegetarians who like good, healthy food in a smoke-free room (closed Aug, CC:VMA, Tres Cruces 4, just off Plaza Carmen, tel. 91-521-8721). **Artemisia I** is its sister (daily 13:30–16:00, 21:00–24:00, nonveggie options available, CC:VMA, Ventura de la Vega 4 off San Jeronimo, tel. 91-429-5092).

Eating near Plaza Mayor

At **Restaurante Rodriguez**, the food's not fancy but is hearty (closed Jul, San Cristobal 15, 1 block toward Puerta del Sol from Plaza Mayor, tel. 91-231-1136). Many Americans are drawn to Hemingway's favorite, **Sobrino del Botín** (daily 13:00–16:00, 20:00–24:00, Cuchilleros 17, a block downhill from Plaza Mayor, tel. 91-366-4217). It's touristy, pricey, and the last place he'd go now, but still, people love it, and the food is excellent. If phoning to make a reservation, ask for downstairs (for dark, medieval-cellar ambience) or upstairs (for a still-traditional but airier and lighter elegance). Those in need of a dirt-cheap but tasty *bocadillo* (sandwich) or *calamares* (squid) line up at the **Casa Rua** on Plaza Mayor's southwest corner (behind and to the right of the horse statue). Picnic shoppers forage at the **San Miguel market** (see "Picnics," below). For a great scene and reasonable prices, consider eating right on the Plaza Mayor.

For a fine meal with no tourists and locals who appreciate good local-style cooking, try **Casa Ciriaco** (2,000-ptas meals, Thu–Tue 13:30–16:00, 20:30–24:00, closed Wed, halfway between Puerta del Sol and the Royal Palace at Calle Mayor 84, tel. 91-548-0620). It was from this building in 1906 that an anarchist threw a bomb at the royal couple on their wedding day. Photos of the carnage are on the wall in the dining room.

Eating near the Prado

Each of the big three art museums has a decent cafeteria. After a long visit to the Prado, consider a meal on the tiny Plaza de Platarias de Matinez (directly across the busy highway from the Atocha end of the Prado), where two little eateries share the square and shade. **La Plateria** is a hardworking little café/wine bar with a good menu for light meals or a hearty salad. The chalkboard shows a list of items in three different sizes (daily 13:00–15:00, 17:00–24:00). The **Bar Museu**, a simpler place, serves tapas and sandwiches.

Tapas: The Madrid Pub Crawl Dinner

For maximum fun, people, and atmosphere, go mobile and do the "tapa tango," a local tradition of going from one bar to the next, munching, drinking, and socializing. Tapas are the toothpick appetizers, salads, and deep-fried foods served in most bars. Madrid is Spain's tapa capital—tapas just don't get any better. Grab a toothpick and stab something strange—but establish the prices first. Some items are very pricey, and most bars offer larger *raciónes* rather than smaller tapas. *Un pincho* is a bite-sized serving (not always available), *una tapa* is a snack, and *una ración* is half a meal. Say *"un bocadillo,"* and it comes on bread as a sandwich. A *caña* is a small glass of draft beer.

Prowl the area between Puerta del Sol and Plaza Santa Ana. There's no ideal route, but the little streets (see map on page 683) between Puerta del Sol, San Jeronimo, and Plaza Santa Ana hold tasty surprises. Below is an eight-stop tapa crawl. These places are good, but don't be blind to making discoveries on your own.

1. From Puerta del Sol, head east down Carrera de San Jeronimo to the corner of Victoria Street. Across from Museo del Jamón you'll find **La Tourina Cervecería**, a bullfighter's Planet Hollywood. Wander among trophies and historic photographs. Each stuffed bull's head is named, along with its farm, awards, and who killed him. Among the photos you can see Che Guevara, Orson Welles, and Salvador Dalí all enjoying a good fight. Find the Babe Ruth of bullfighters, El Cordobes, wounded in bed. The photo below shows him in action. Kick off your pub crawl with *rabo del toro* (bull-tail stew, 1,100 ptas) and a glass of red wine. Across the street at San Jeronimo 5 is...

2. Museo del Jamón (Museum of Ham), which is tastefully decorated, unless you're a pig. This frenetic, cheap, stand-up bar is an assembly line of fast and deliciously simple *bocadillos* and *raciónes*. Options are shown in photographs with prices. For a small sandwich, ask for a *chiquito* (95 ptas). Just point and eat (daily 9:00–24:00, sit-down restaurant upstairs). Next, head halfway up Calle Victoria to the tiny...

3. La Casa del Abuelo, for shrimp lovers who savor sizzling plates of tasty little *gambas*. Try *gambas a la plancha* (grilled shrimp, 560 ptas) and *gambas al ajillo* (shrimp version of escargot, cooked in oil and garlic and ideal for bread dipping—700 ptas) and a 150-ptas glass of red wine (daily 11:30–15:30, 18:30–23:30, Calle Victoria 12). Continue uphill and around the corner to...

4. Casa Toni for refreshing bowls of gazpacho (200 ptas, closed mid-Jun–mid-Jul, Calle Cruz 14). This cold tomato-and-garlic soup is slurped by locals throughout the summer. Backtrack halfway down Calle Victoria and turn left, walking through an alley littered with dining tables to...

5. La Ria, a tapas bar that sells plates of 10 mussels—toss the shells on the floor as you smack your lips (19:00–23:00, Pasaje Matheu 5). *Mejillones picantes* is spicy (460 ptas). Wash each down with the crude, dry, white Ribeiro wine from Galicia. It's served in a ceramic bowl to disguise its lack of clarity. The place is draped in mussels. Notice the photo showing the floor filled with litter—a reminder that mussel bars have seen better days. In the 1970s they sold 14 tons a month. Now—with other, more trendy evening activities entertaining the cruising youth—it takes a year to sell 14 tons.

6. Jump to stop #7 or, for a classy side trip, follow Nuñez de Arce up to Plaza Santa Ana. Cross the square (past lots of trendy pubs) and continue one block down Calle Príncipe to the venerable **Casa Alberto**. It's been serving tasty tapas since 1827 (11:00–01:00, closed Sun evening, all day Mon, and most of Aug, Huertas 18, tel. 91-429-9356). It's hard to stop at just one *canape de salmon ahumado* (smoked salmon appetizer, 275 ptas). The popular dining room in the back has a different, pricier menu.

7. Head to Plaza Mayor for **La Torre del Oro Bar Andalu** (26 Plaza Mayor, tel. 91-366-5016). Bullfight aficionados hate the gimmicky Bull Bar across from Museo del Jamón (stop #1). This one has more soul. The walls are lined with grisly bullfight photos from annual photo competitions. Read the complete description above in

Plaza Santa Ana Area

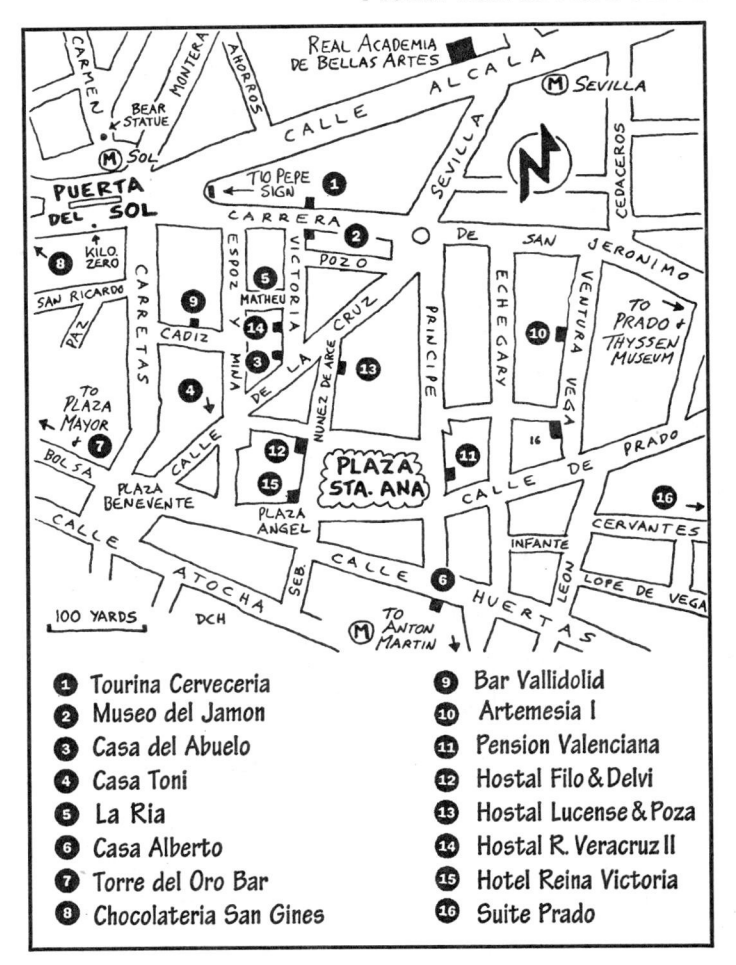

1. Tourina Cerveceria
2. Museo del Jamon
3. Casa del Abuelo
4. Casa Toni
5. La Ria
6. Casa Alberto
7. Torre del Oro Bar
8. Chocolateria San Gines
9. Bar Vallidolid
10. Artemesia I
11. Pension Valenciana
12. Hostal Filo & Delvi
13. Hostal Lucense & Poza
14. Hostal R. Veracruz II
15. Hotel Reina Victoria
16. Suite Prado

the Plaza Mayor section. Be careful not to let the aggressive staff bully you into food you don't want.

8. The classy **Chocolatería San Ginés** is much loved locally for its *churros* (greasy cigar-shaped fritters) and chocolate. Open nightly from 22:00 to 7:00, it caters to the late-night crowd (mostly disco— the popular Joy disco is next door). Finish off your crawl with this sweet treat, dunking your *churros* into the pudding-like hot

Madrid

chocolate, as locals have done here for over 100 years (from Plaza Mayor, cross Calle Mayor and go down Calle P. de San Ginés to #5, off Calle Arenal, tel. 93-365-6546).

Fast Food, Picnics, and Breakfast

Fast Food: For an easy, light, cheap meal, try **Rodilla**—a popular sandwich bar on the northeast corner of Puerta del Sol at #13 (daily 8:30–20:30). **Pans & Company**, with shops throughout Spain, offers healthy, tasty sandwiches and great chef's salads (daily 9:00–24:00, on Puerta del Sol, Plaza Callão, Gran Vía 30, and many more).

Picnics: The department store **El Corte Inglés** has a well-stocked **deli**, but its produce is sold only in large quantities (Mon–Sat 10:00–21:00, closed Sun). A perfect place to assemble a cheap picnic is downtown Madrid's neighborhood market, **Mercado de San Miguel**. How about breakfast surrounded by early morning shoppers in the market's café? (Mon–Fri 9:00–14:00, 16:00–19:00, Sat 9:00–14:00, closed Sun; from Plaza Mayor, face the colorful building and exit from the upper left-hand corner.)

Churros con chocolate **for breakfast:** If you like hash browns and eggs in American greasy-spoon joints, you must try the Spanish equivalent: greasy *churros* dipped in thick, hot chocolate at **Bar Valladolid** (open from 7:00, closed Sun, 2 blocks off the Tío Pepe end of Puerta del Sol, south on Espoz y Mina, turn right on Calle de Cadiz). If you arrive early, it's *churros* and hookers. You'll see the changing of the guard, as workers of the night finish their day by downing a cognac and workers of the day start theirs by dipping *churros* or *porras* (simply fatter *churros*) into chocolate. (One serving is often plenty for two.) With luck, the *churros* machine in the back will be cooking. Throw your napkin on the floor like you own the place. For something with less grease and more substance, ask for a *tortilla española* (potato omelet), *zumo de naranja* (orange juice), and *café con leche* (coffe with milk). Notice the expressive WC signs.

Transportation Connections—Madrid

By train to: Toledo (6/day, 1 hr, from Madrid's Atocha station), **Segovia** (8/day, 2 hrs, both Chamartin and Atocha stations), **Ávila** (6/day, 90 min, from Chamartin and Atocha), **Salamanca** (3/day, 2.5 hrs, from Chamartin), **Barcelona** (7/day, 8 hrs, mostly from Chamartin), **Granada** (6–9 hrs, a daily day train from Chamartin and a nightly train from Atocha), **Sevilla** (15/day, 2.5 hrs by AVE, 3.5 hrs by Talgo, from Atocha), **Córdoba** (16 AVE trains/day, 2 hrs, from Chamartin and Atocha), **Lisbon** (1/day, 10 hrs, overnight from Chamartin), **Paris** (4/day, 12–16 hrs, 1 direct overnight, from Chamartin). Train information: tel. 91-328-9020.

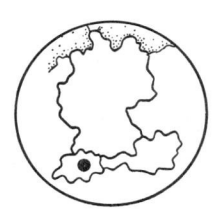

GIMMELWALD AND THE BERNER OBERLAND

Frolic and hike high above the stress and clouds of the real world. Take a vacation from your busy vacation. Recharge your touristic batteries up here in the Alps, where distant avalanches, cowbells, the fluff of a down comforter, and the crunchy footsteps of happy hikers are the dominant sounds. If the weather's good (and your budget's healthy), ride a gondola from the traffic-free village of Gimmelwald to a hearty breakfast at Schilthorn's 10,000-foot revolving Piz Gloria restaurant. Linger among Alpine whitecaps before riding, hiking, or hang gliding down (5,000 feet) to Mürren and home to Gimmelwald.

Your gateway to the rugged Berner Oberland is the grand old resort town of Interlaken. Near Interlaken is Switzerland's open-air folk museum, Ballenberg, where you can climb through traditional houses from every corner of this diverse country.

Ah, but the weather's fine and the Alps beckon. Head deep into the heart of the Alps and ride the gondola to the stop just this side of heaven—Gimmelwald.

Planning Your Time

Rather than tackling a checklist of famous Swiss mountains and resorts, choose one region to savor—the Berner Oberland. Interlaken is the administrative headquarters (fine transportation hub, banking, post office, laundry, shopping). Use it for business and as a springboard for Alpine thrills. With decent weather, explore the two areas (south of Interlaken) that tower above either side of the Lauterbrunnen Valley: Kleine Scheidegg/Jungfrau and Schilthorn/Mürren. Ideally, home-base three nights in the village of Gimmelwald and spend a day in each area. On a speedy train trip you can overnight into and out of Interlaken. For the fastest look, consider a night in Gimmelwald, breakfast at the Schilthorn, an afternoon doing the Männlichen-to-Wengen hike, and an evening or night train out. What? A nature lover not spending the night high in the Alps? Alpus-interruptus.

Getting around the Berner Oberland

For more than 100 years, this has been the target of nature-worshiping pilgrims. And the Swiss have made the most exciting Alpine perches accessible by lift or train. Part of the fun (and most of the expense) here is riding the many lifts. Generally, scenic trains and lifts are not covered on train passes, but a Eurail or Europass gets you a 25 percent discount on even the highest lifts. Ask about discounts for early (and late) birds, youths, seniors, families, groups, and those staying awhile. The Family Card pays for itself on the first hour of trains and lifts: Children under 16 travel free with parents, children ages 16 to 23 pay half price (20 SF at Swiss train stations but not available at gondola stations). Get a list of discounts and the free fare and time schedule at any train station. Study the Alpine Lifts in the Berner Oberland chart in this chapter. Lifts generally go at least twice hourly, from about 7:00 until about 20:00 (sneak preview: www.jungfrau.ch). Drivers can park at the gondola station in Stechelberg for the lift to Gimmelwald, Mürren, and the Shilthorn (5 SF/day), or at the train station in Lauterbrunnen for trains to Wengen and Kleine Scheidegg.

INTERLAKEN

When the 19th-century Romantics redefined mountains as something more than cold and troublesome obstacles, Interlaken became the original Alpine resort. Ever since then, tourists have flocked to the Alps because they're there. Interlaken's glory days are long gone, its elegant old hotels eclipsed by the new, more jet-setty Alpine resorts. Today its shops are filled with chocolate bars, Swiss Army knives, and sunburned backpackers.

Orientation (tel. code: 033)

Efficient Interlaken is a good administrative and shopping center. Take care of business, give the town a quick look, and view the live TV coverage of the Jungfrau and Schilthorn weather in the window of the Schilthornbahn office on the main street (at Höheweg 2, also on TV in most hotel lobbies). Then head for the hills. Stay in Interlaken only if you suffer from alptitude sickness (see "Sleeping," at the end of this chapter).

Tourist Information: The TI has good information for the region, advice on Alpine lift discounts, and a room-finding service (Jul–Sept Mon–Fri 8:00–12:15, 13:30–18:30, Sat 8:00–17:00, Sun 17:00–19:00; off-season Mon–Fri 8:00–12:00, 14:00–18:00, Sat 8:00–12:00, closed Sun, tel. 033/822-2121, on main street,

Interlaken

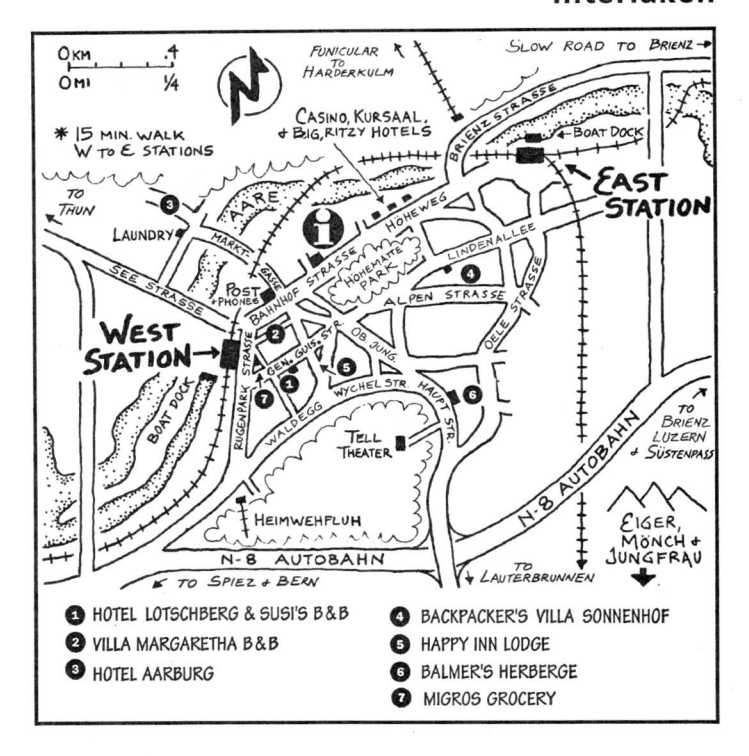

- **1** HOTEL LOTSCHBERG & SUSI'S B&B
- **2** VILLA MARGARETHA B&B
- **3** HOTEL AARBURG
- **4** BACKPACKER'S VILLA SONNENHOF
- **5** HAPPY INN LODGE
- **6** BALMER'S HERBERGE
- **7** MIGROS GROCERY

five-minute walk from West station). While the Jungfrau region map costs 2 SF, a good miniversion is included in the free Jungfrau region train timetable. Pick up a Bern map if that's your next destination. The TI organizes daily town walks in English (10 SF, 18:00, 60 min, depart from TI).

Arrival in Interlaken: Interlaken has two train stations: East and West. Most major trains stop at the Interlaken-West station. This station's train information desk answers tourists' questions (Mon–Sat 8:00–19:00, Sun 8:00–12:00, 14:00–18:00), and there's a fair exchange booth next to the ticket windows. Ask at the station about discount passes, special fares, Eurail discounts, and schedules for the scenic mountain trains (tel. 033/826-4750). A Migros supermarket is across the street with a self-service cafeteria upstairs (Mon–Thu 8:00–18:30, Fri 8:00–21:00, Sat 7:30–16:00, closed Sun).

It's a pleasant 15-minute walk between the West and East

stations, or an easy, frequent train connection. From the Interlaken-East station, private trains take you deep into the mountainous Jungfrau region (see "Transportation Connections," at the end of this chapter).

Helpful Hints

Telephone: Phone booths cluster outside the post office near the West station. Inside the office you'll find metered phone booths (talk first, pay later; Mon–Fri 7:45–18:15, Sat 8:30–11:00, closed Sun). For efficiency, buy a phone card from a newsstand. (There's a card phone that doesn't take coins in Gimmelwald.)

Laundry: Helen Schmocker's *Wäscherei* (laundry) has a change machine, soap, English instructions, and a pleasant riverside locale (daily 7:00–22:00 for self-service, or Mon–Sat 8:00–12:00, 13:30–18:00 for full service: Drop off 10 pounds in the morning and pick up clean clothes that afternoon; from post office, follow Marktgasse over two bridges to Beatenbergstrasse; tel. 033/822-1566).

Sights—Interlaken

Boat Trips—*Interlaken* means "between the lakes." Lazy boat trips explore these lakes (8/day, fewer off-season, free with Eurail, schedules at TI). The Lake Thun boat stops at Beatushöhlen (interesting caves, 30 min from Interlaken) and two visit-worthy towns: Spiez (one hr from Interlaken) and Thun (1.75 hrs away). The Lake Brienz boat stops at the super-cute and quiet village of Iseltwald (45 min away) and Brienz (1.25 hrs away, near Ballenberg Open-Air Folk Museum).

Adventure Trips—For the adventurer with money and little concern for personal safety, several places offer high-adrenaline trips such as rafting, canyoneering (rappelling down watery gorges), bungee jumping, and paragliding. Most adventure trips cost from 88 to 150 SF. Alpin Raft offers trips (Postfach 78, tel. 033/823-4100, www.alpinraft.ch).

GIMMELWALD

Saved from developers by its "avalanche zone" classification, Gimmelwald is one of the poorest places in Switzerland. Its economy is stuck in the hay, and its farmers, unable to make it in their disadvantaged trade, are subsidized by the Swiss government (and work the ski lifts in the winter). For some travelers there's little to see in the village. Others enjoy a fascinating day sitting on a bench and learning why they say, "If heaven isn't what it's cracked up to be, send me back to Gimmelwald." Gimmelwald is my home base in the Berner Oberland (see "Sleeping," at the end of this chapter).

Take a walk through the town. This place is for real. Most of the 130 residents have the same last name—von Allmen. They are

Gimmelwald

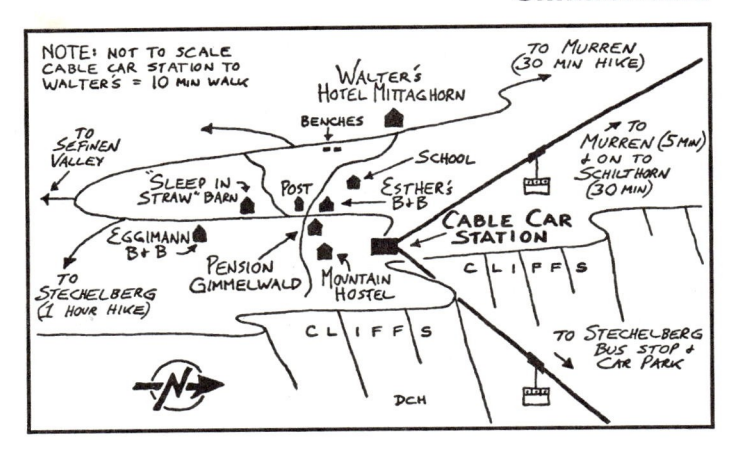

tough and proud. Raising hay in this rugged terrain is labor intensive. One family harvests enough to feed only 15 or 20 cows. But they'd have it no other way and, unlike absentee landlord Mürren, Gimmelwald is locally owned. (When word got out that urban planners wished to develop Gimmelwald into a town of 1,000, locals pulled some strings to secure the town's bogus avalanche-zone building code.)

Notice the traditional log-cabin architecture and blond-braided children. The numbers on the buildings are not addresses, but fire-insurance numbers. The cute little hut near the station is for storing and aging cheese, not hostelers. In Catholic-Swiss towns, the biggest building is the church. In Protestant towns, it's the school. Gimmelwald's biggest building is the school (1 teacher, 17 students, and a room that doubles as a chapel when the pastor makes his monthly visit). Do not confuse obscure Gimmelwald with touristy and commercialized Grindelwald just over the Kleine Scheidegg ridge.

Evening fun in Gimmelwald is found at the youth hostel (lots of young Alp-aholics and a good chance to share information on the surrounding mountains) or at Pension Gimmelwald's terrace restaurant next door. Walter's bar is a local farmers' hangout. When they've made their hay, they come here to play. They look like what we'd call hicks (former city slicker Walter still isn't fully accepted by the gang), but they speak some English and can be fun to get to know. Sit outside (benches just below the rails, 100 yards down the lane from Walter's), and watch the sun tuck the mountaintops into bed as the moon rises over the Jungfrau.

Lauterbrunnen Valley: West Side Story

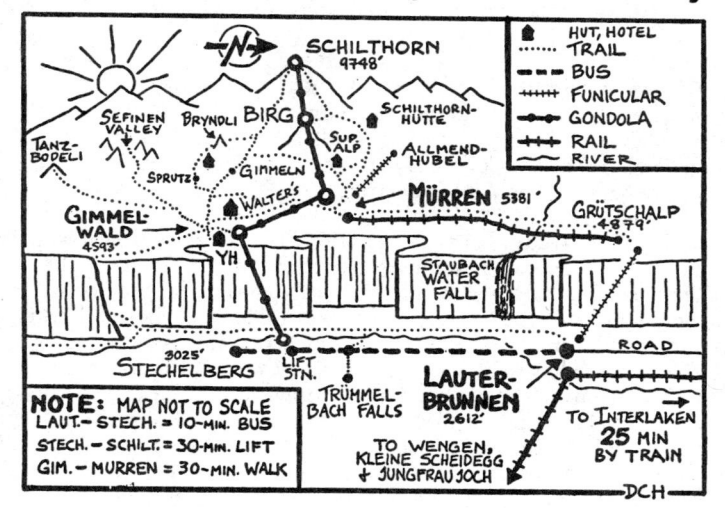

Alpine Hikes

There are days of possible hikes from Gimmelwald. Many are a fun combination of trails, mountain trains, and gondola rides. Don't mind the fences (but wires can be electrified); a hiker has the right-of-way in Switzerland. But as late as early June, snow can curtail your hiking plans (the Männlichen lift doesn't even open until June 6). Before setting out on any hike, get advice from a knowledgeable local to confirm that it is safe and accessible. Clouds can roll in anytime, but skies are usually clearest in the morning.

▲▲▲**Hike 1: The Schilthorn: Hikes, Lifts, and a 10,000-Foot Breakfast**—If the weather's good, have breakfast atop the Schilthorn in the slowly revolving, mountaintop restaurant (of James Bond movie fame). The early-bird and afternoon-special gondola tickets (about 55 SF, before 9:00 or after 15:30) take you from Gimmelwald to the Schilthorn and back at a discount (normal rate is 69 SF, and 87 SF from Stechelberg where you can park, 5 SF/day). Nag the Schilthorn station in Mürren for a gondola souvenir decal (Schilthorn info: tel. 033/823-1444).

Breakfast costs from 13.50 to 22 SF; a cup of coffee is 3.40 SF. Expect slow service, and ask for more hot drinks if necessary. If you're not revolving, ask them to turn it on. Linger on top. Piz Gloria has a souvenir shop, the rocks of the region on the restaurant wall, telescopes, and a "touristorama" film room showing a multiscreen slideshow and explosive highlights from the James

Bond thriller that featured the Schilthorn (free and self-serve; push the button for slides or, after a long pause for the projector to rewind, push for 007).

Watch hang gliders set up, psych up, and take off, flying 30 minutes with the birds to distant Interlaken. Walk along the ridge out back. This is a great place for a photo of the "mountain-climber you." For another cheap thrill, ask the gondola attendant to crank down the window. Then stick your head out and pretend you're hang gliding, ideally over the bump going down from Gimmelwald.

Lifts go twice hourly, and the ride (including two transfers) to the Schilthorn takes 30 minutes. Watch the altitude meter in the gondola. (The Gimmelwald–Schilthorn hike is free if you don't mind a 5,000-foot altitude gain.) You can ride up to the Schilthorn and hike down, but I wouldn't (weather can change; have good shoes). For a less scary hike, go halfway down by cable car and walk down from the Birg station. Buy the round-trip excursion early-bird fare (cheaper than the Gimmelwald-Schilthorn-Birg ticket) and decide at Birg if you want to hike or ride down.

Hiking down from Birg is very steep and gravelly. Just below Birg is Schilthorn-Hutte. Drop in for soup, cocoa, or a coffee schnapps. You can spend the night in the hut's crude loft (bed-20 SF, plus 45 SF if you want breakfast and dinner, open Jul–Sept, tel. 033/855-1167). Youth hostelers scream down the ice fields on plastic-bag sleds from the Schilthorn. (English-speaking doctor in Mürren.)

The most interesting trail from Birg to Gimmelwald is the high one via Grauseewli Lake and Wasenegg Ridge to Brünli and down to Spielbodenalp and the Sprutz waterfall. From the Birg lift, hike toward the Schilthorn, taking your first left down to the little, newly made Grauseewli Lake. From the lake a gravelly trail leads down the rough switchbacks until it levels out. When you see a rock painted with arrows pointing to "Mürren" and "Rotstockhütte," follow the path to Rotstockhütte, traversing the cow-grazed mountainside. Follow Wasenegg Ridge left/down and along the barbed-wire fence to Brünli. (For maximum thrills, stay on the ridge and climb all the way to the knobby little summit where you'll enjoy an incredible 360-degree view and a chance to sign your name on the register stored in the little wooden box.) A steep trail winds directly down from Brünli toward Gimmelwald and soon hits a bigger, easy trail. The trail bends right (just before the popular restaurant/mountain hut at Spielbodenalp), leading to Sprutz. Walk under the Sprutz waterfall then follow a steep, wooded trail that will deposit you in a meadow of flowers at the top side of Gimmelwald.

For an expensive thrill, you can bungee-jump from the Stechelberg-Mürren service gondola (100 SF for a 330-foot drop,

Gimmelwald and the Berner Oberland

220 SF for 590 feet, drop head first or feet first, have photos taken, daily 8:00–18:00, tel. 033/826-7711).

▲▲▲Hike 2: The Männlichen–Kleine Scheidegg Hike—This is my favorite easy Alpine hike. It's entertaining all the way with glorious Jungfrau, Eiger, and Mönch views. (That's the Young Maiden being protected from the Ogre by the Monk.)

If the weather's good, descend from Gimmelwald bright and early. Catch the post bus to the Lauterbrunnen train station, or park there (synchronized to depart with the arrival of each lift—3.60 SF; or drive, parking at the large multistoried pay lot behind the Lauterbrunnen station). Buy a ticket to Männlichen and catch the train. Ride past great valley views to Wengen, where you'll walk across town (buy a picnic, but don't waste time here if it's sunny), and catch the Männlichen lift (departing every 15 minutes, after June 6) to the top of the ridge high above you.

From the tip of the Männlichen lift hike 20 minutes north to the little peak for that king- or queen-of-the-mountain feeling. It's an easy hour's walk from there to Kleine Scheidegg for a picnic, restaurant lunch, or the night. If you've got an extra 100 SF and the weather's perfect, ride the train from Kleine Scheidegg through the Eiger to the towering Jungfraujoch and back. Check for discount trips up to Jungfraujoch (3 trips a day early or late, tel. 033/826-4750, trilingual weather info: tel. 033/855-1022). Jungfraujoch crowds can be frightening. The price has been jacked up to reduce the mobs, but sunny days are still a mess.

From Kleine Scheidegg, ride the train or hike downhill (30 gorgeous minutes to Wengeralp; 90 more steep minutes from there into the town of Wengen) while enjoying the ever-changing Alpine panorama of the north faces of the Eiger, Jungfrau, and Mönch. The views will probably be accompanied by the valley-filling mellow sound of Alp horns and distant avalanches. If the weather turns bad or you run out of steam, catch the train early at the little Wengeralp station along the way. After Wengeralp, the trail to Wengen is steep and, while not dangerous, requires a good set of knees. Wengen is a good shopping town. The boring final descent from Wengen to Lauterbrunnen is knee-killer steep—catch the train. Trails may be snowbound into early June. Ask about conditions at the lift stations or local TI. If the Männlichen lift is closed, take the train straight from Lauterbrunnen to Kleine Scheidegg. Many risk slipping and enjoy the Kleine Scheidegg-to-Wengeralp hike even with a little snow.

▲▲Hike 3: Schynige Platte to First—The best day I've had hiking in the Berner Oberland was when I made the demanding six-hour ridge walk high above Lake Brienz on one side and all that Jungfrau beauty on the other. Start at Wilderswil train station (just above Interlaken) and catch the little train up to Schynige Platte (2,000 meters). Walk through the Alpine flower display

Berner Oberland

garden and into the wild Alpine yonder. The high point is Faulhorn (2,680 meters, with its famous mountaintop hotel). Hike to a small gondola called "First" (2,168 meters), then descend to Grindelwald and catch a train back to your starting point, Wilderswil. Or, if you have a regional train pass or no car but endless money, return to Gimmelwald via Lauterbrunnen from Grindelwald over Kleine Scheidegg. For an abbreviated ridge walk, consider the Panoramaweg, a short loop from Schynige Platte to Daub Peak.

▲▲Hike 4: Cloudy Day Lauterbrunnen Valley Walk—For a smell-the-cows-and-flowers lowland walk, ideal for a cloudy day, weary body, or tight budget, follow the riverside trail five kilometers from Lauterbrunnen's Staubach Falls (just after the town church) to the Schilthornbahn station at Stechelberg. Detour to Trümmelbach Falls en route (see below).

If you're staying in Gimmelwald: To get to Lauterbrunnen, walk up to Mürren (30 min), walk or ride the train to Grütschalp

Alpine Lifts in the Berner Oberland

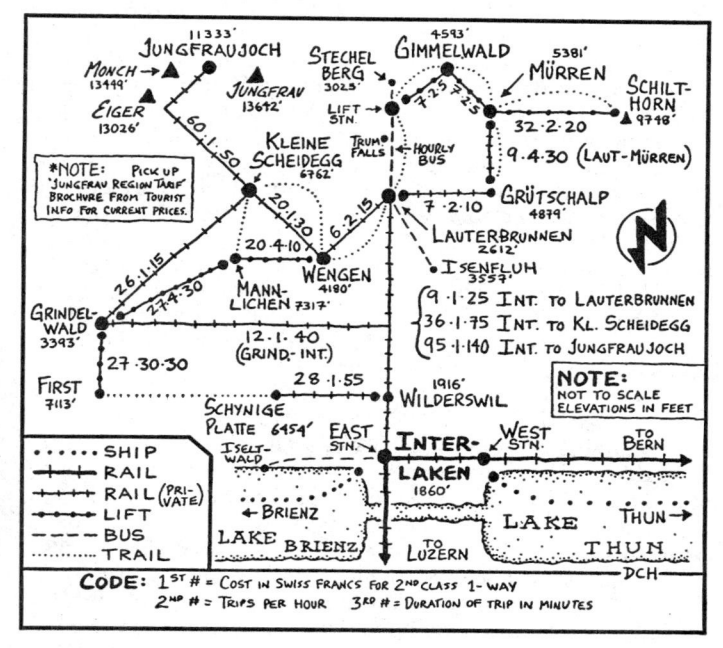

(Map showing Alpine lifts, rail, ship, bus, and trail connections in the Berner Oberland region, including Jungfraujoch (11333'), Mönch (13449'), Eiger (13026'), Jungfrau (13642'), Stechelberg (3025'), Gimmelwald (4593'), Mürren (5381'), Schilthorn (9748'), Kleine Scheidegg (6762'), Grütschalp (4879'), Lauterbrunnen (2612'), Isenfluh (3557'), Wengen (4190'), Männlichen (7317'), Grindelwald (3393'), First (7113'), Schynige Platte (6454'), Wilderswil (1916'), Interlaken (1860'), with connections to Bern, Thun, Luzern, and Brienz.)

*NOTE: Pick up 'Jungfrau Region Tarif' Brochure from Tourist Info for Current Prices.

9 ·1·25 Int. to Lauterbrunnen
36 ·1·75 Int. to Kl. Scheidegg
95 ·1·140 Int. to Jungfraujoch

NOTE: NOT TO SCALE ELEVATIONS IN FEET

- ····· SHIP
- —+— RAIL
- —+— RAIL (PRIVATE)
- —•— LIFT
- — — — BUS
- ········ TRAIL

CODE: 1ST # = Cost in Swiss Francs for 2ND Class 1-way
2ND # = Trips per Hour   3RD # = Duration of Trip in Minutes

—DCH—

(60-min hike), ride the funicular down to Lauterbrunnen (10 min), walk through town, and take the riverside trail ending up at Stechelberg (75 min) where you can ride the lift back up to Gimmelwald (10 min).

Biking the Valley: You can rent bikes at the Interlaken station, and for 5 SF extra you can take your bike on the train to Lauterbrunnen and enjoy a scenic ride downhill back into Interlaken via a peaceful bike path over the river from the road. I prefer biking the valley between Stechelberg and Lauterbrunnen (rentals at Imboden Bike on Lauterbrunnen's main street, 25–35 SF/day, daily 9:00–21:00, tel. 033/855-2114). Mountain bikes are available in Mürren (Salomon Sports, at gondola station, 35 SF/half day, 45 SF/full day, 8:30–17:00, tel. 033/855-2330).

▲**More Hikes near Gimmelwald**—For a not-too-tough three-hour walk (but there's a scary 20-minute stretch) with great Jungfrau views and some mountain farm action, ride the funicular from Mürren to Allmendhübel (1,934 meters), and walk to Marchegg, Saustal, and Grütschalp (a drop of about 500 meters), where you can catch the panorama train back to Mürren. An easier version is the lower Bergweg from Allmenhübel to Grütschalp via Winteregg. For an easy family stroll with grand views, walk from Mürren just above the train tracks to either Winteregg (40 min, restaurant, playground, train station) or Grütschalp (60 min, train station), and catch the panorama train back to Mürren. An easy, go-as-far-as-you-like trail from Gimmelwald is up the Sefinen Valley. Or you can wind from Gimmelwald down to Stechelberg (60 min).

You can get specifics at the Mürren TI. For a description of six diverse hikes on the west side of Lauterbrunnen, pick up the fine and free *Mürren-Schilthorn Hikes* brochure (at stations, hotels, and TIs). The 3-D map of the Mürren mountainside, which includes hiking trails, makes a useful and attractive souvenir (2 SF at TI and lift station). For an extensive rundown on the region, get Don Chmura's fine 5-SF Gimmelwald guidebook (includes info on hikes, flora, fauna, culture, and travel tips; available at Hotel Mittaghorn in Gimmelwald).

Rainy-Day Options

If clouds roll in, don't despair. They can roll out just as quickly, and there are some good bad-weather options. There are easy trails and pleasant walks along the floor of the Lauterbrunnen Valley (see above). If all the waterfalls have you intrigued, sneak a behind-the-scenes look at the valley's most powerful one, **Trümmelbach Falls** (10 SF, Apr–Jun and Sept–Nov daily 9:00–17:00, Jul–Aug daily 8:00–18:00, on Lauterbrunnen-Stechelberg road, tel. 033/855-3232). You'll ride an elevator up through the mountain and climb through several caves to see the melt from the Eiger, Mönch, and Jungfrau grinding like God's band saw through the mountain at the rate of up to 20,000 liters a second (nearly double the beer consumption at Oktoberfest). The upper area is the best, so if your legs ache you can skip the lower ones and ride the lift down.

Lauterbrunnen's **Heimatmuseum** shows off the local folk culture (3 SF, mid-Jun–Sept Tue, Thu, Sat–Sun 14:00–17:30, just over bridge). Mürren offers a variety of rainy-day activities, from its shops to its slick **Sportzentrum** (sports center) with pools, steam baths, squash, and a fitness center (for details, see "Sleeping in Mürren," below). Or consider taking a boat trip from Interlaken (see "Interlaken," above).

▲▲**Swiss Open-Air Folk Museum at Ballenberg**—Near Interlaken, the Swiss Open-Air Museum of Vernacular Architecture, Country Life, and Crafts in the Bernese Oberland is a rich collection of traditional and historic farmhouses from every region of the country. Each house is carefully furnished, and many feature traditional craftspeople at work. The sprawling 50-acre park, laid out roughly as a huge Swiss map, is a natural preserve providing a wonderful setting for this culture-on-a-lazy-Susan look at Switzerland.

The Thurgau house (#621) has an interesting wattle-and-daub (half-timbered construction) display and house #331 has a fun bread museum. Use the 2-SF map/guide. The more expensive picture book is a better souvenir than guide. (14-SF entry, half price after 16:00, mid-Apr–Oct daily 10:00–17:00, houses close at 17:00, park stays open later, craft demonstration schedules are listed just inside the entry, tel. 033/951-1123.) A reasonable outdoor cafeteria is inside the west entrance, and fresh bread, sausage, mountain cheese, and other goodies are on sale in several houses. Picnic tables and grills with free firewood are scattered throughout the park. The little wooden village of Brienzwiler (near the east entrance) is a museum in itself with a lovely little church. Trains run frequently from Interlaken to Brienzwiler, an easy walk from the museum.

Sleeping and Eating in the Berner Oberland
(1.40 SF = about $1, tel. code: 033)
Sleep Code: **S** = Single, **D** = Double/Twin, **T** = Triple, **Q** = Quad, **b** = bathroom, **t** = toilet only, **s** = shower only, **CC** = Credit Card (Visa, MasterCard, Amex), **SE** = Speaks English, **NSE** = No English. Unless otherwise noted, breakfast is included.

Sleeping and Eating in Gimmelwald
(4,500 feet, tel code: 033, zip code: 3826)
To inhale the Alps and really hold it in, sleep high in Gimmelwald. Poor but pleasantly stuck in the past, the village has a creaky hotel, happy hostel, decent pension, and a couple of B&Bs. The bad news is that the lift costs 7.40 SF each way to get there.

Hotel Mittaghorn, the treasure of Gimmelwald, is run by Walter Mittler, a perfect Swiss gentleman. Walter's hotel is a classic, creaky, Alpine-style place with memorable beds, ancient down comforters (short and fat; wear socks and drape the blanket over your feet), and a million-dollar view of the Jungfrau Alps. The Yodelin' Seniors' loft has a dozen real beds on either side of a divider, with several sinks, down comforters, and a fire ladder out the back window. The hotel has one shower for 10 rooms (1 SF for 5 minutes). Walter is careful not to let his place get too hectic or big and enjoys sensitive Back Door travelers. He runs the hotel with a little help from Rosemary from the village, and keeps it simple but classy. This is a good place to receive mail from home (check the mail barrel in entry hall).

To some, Hotel Mittaghorn is a fire waiting to happen with a kitchen that would never pass code, lumpy beds, teeny towels, and nowhere near enough plumbing, run by an eccentric old grouch. These people enjoy Interlaken, Wengen, or Mürren, and that's where they should sleep. Be warned, you'll see more of my readers than locals here, but it's a fun crowd—an extended family (D-60–70 SF, T-85 SF, Q-105 SF, Yodelin' Seniors' loft beds-25 SF, all with breakfast, 3-SF surcharge for one-night stays, closed Nov–Apr, CH-3826 Gimmelwald/Bern, tel. 033/855-1658, SE). Reserve by telephone only, then reconfirm by telephone the day before your arrival. Walter usually offers his guests a simple 15-SF dinner. Off-season only, lofters pay just 20 SF for a bed with breakfast. Hotel Mittaghorn is at the top of Gimmelwald, a five-minute climb up the steps from the village intersection.

Mountain Hostel is a beehive of activity, simple and as clean as its guests, cheap, and very friendly. Phone ahead (two days maximum) to secure one of its 60 dorm beds (call after 9:30 and just leave your name). The hostel has low ceilings, a self-service kitchen, a minigrocery, and healthy plumbing. A new Internet station is planned for 2000. Petra Brunner has filled the place with flowers. This relaxed hostel survives with the help of its guests. Read the signs (please clean the kitchen), respect Petra's rules, and leave it cleaner than you found it. Guests do a small duty. The place is one of those rare spots where a family atmosphere spontaneously combusts, and spaghetti becomes communal as it softens (16 SF per bed in 6- to 15-bed rooms, showers-1 SF, no breakfast and no sheets—bring your own, hostel membership not required, 20 yards from lift station, tel. & fax 033/855-1704, e-mail: mountainhostel@tcnet.ch).

Pension Restaurant Gimmelwald, next door, offers 12 basic rooms under low, creaky ceilings (D-90 SF, Db-110 SF). It also has sheetless backpacker beds (25 SF in D, T, and Q rooms). Prices include breakfast. The pension has Gimmelwald's scenic terrace overlooking the Jungfrau and the hostel, and is the village's only restaurant (fine meals—their specialty is sweet *Waffeln*): great for camaraderie but not for peace (closed Nov and first half of May, CC:VM, nonsmoking, 50 meters from gondola station; reserve by phone, plus obligatory reconfirmation by phone 2 or 3 days in advance of arrival, tel. & fax 033/855-1730, run by Liesi and Männi).

Maria and Olle Eggimann rent two rooms—Gimmelwald's most comfortable—in their Alpine-sleek chalet. Twelve-year town residents Maria and Olle, who job-share the village's only teaching position and raise three kids of their own, offer visitors a rare inside peek at this community (D-100 SF, Db with kitchenette-180 SF for 2 or 3 people, optional breakfast-18 SF, no CC, last check-in 18:30, 3-night minimum for advance reservations; from gondola continue straight 100 meters past town's only intersection, B&B on left, CH-3826 Gimmelwald, tel. 033/855-3575, e-mail: oeggimann@bluewin.ch, SE fluently).

Esther's B&B, overlooking the main intersection of the village, is like an upscale, minihostel with five clean, basic, but comfortable rooms sharing two bathrooms and a great kitchen (S-30 SF, D-70–80 SF, T-90 SF, Q-140 SF, 2-night minimum stay, make your own breakfast, tel. 033/855-5488, fax 033/855-5492, e-mail: evallmen@bluewin.ch, some English spoken).

Gimmelwald and the Berner Oberland

Schalf im Stroh ("Sleep in Straw") offers exactly that in an actual barn. After the cows head for higher ground in the summer, the friendly von Allmen family hoses out their barn and fills it with straw and budget travelers. Blankets are free, but bring your own sheet, sleep sack, or sleeping bag. No beds, no bunks, no mattresses, no kidding (19 SF, 13 SF for kids under 12, includes breakfast, showers-2 SF, open mid-Jun–mid-Oct, depending on grass and snow levels; from lift, continue straight through intersection, barn marked "1995" on right, tel. 033/855-5488, fax 033/855-5492).

Eating in Gimmelwald: Pension Gimmelwald, the only restaurant in town, serves a hearty breakfast buffet for 11 SF, fine lunches, and good 15-SF dinners featuring a fine *Rösti* and a sampling of organic produce from the local farmers. The hostel has a decent members' kitchen and a small grocery but serves no food. Consider packing in food from the larger towns. Hotel Mittaghorn serves dinner only to its guests (15 SF). Follow dinner with a Heidi Cocoa (cocoa *mit* peppermint schnapps) or a Virgin Heidi. The farmers sell their produce. Esther (at the main intersection of the village) sells cheese, sausage, and Gimmelwald's best yogurt—but only until the cows go up in June.

Sleeping and Eating in Mürren
(5,500 feet, tel. code: 033, zip code: 3825)

Mürren—pleasant as an Alpine resort can be—is traffic free, filled with bakeries, cafés, souvenirs, old-timers with walking sticks, GE employees enjoying incentive trips, and Japanese making movies of each other with a Fujichrome backdrop. Its chalets are prefab-rustic. Sitting on a ledge 2,000 feet above the Lauterbrunnen Valley, surrounded by a fortissimo chorus of mountains, it has all the comforts of home (for a price) without the pretentiousness of more famous resorts. With a gondola, train, and funicular, hiking options are endless from Mürren. Mürren has an ATM (by the Co-op grocery), and there are lockers at both the train and gondola stations (located a 10-minute walk apart, on opposite ends of town).

Mürren's **TI** can find you a room, give hiking advice, and change money (mid-Jul–mid-Sept Mon–Wed 9:00–12:00, 13:00–18:30, Thu until 20:00, Sat 13:00–18:00, Sun 13:00–17:30, less off-season, above the village, follow signs to Sportzentrum, tel. 033/856-8686, www.muerren.ch). The slick **Sportzentrum** (sports center) that houses the TI offers a world of indoor activities (12 SF to use pool and whirlpool, 7 SF for Mürren hotel guests, mid-Jun–Oct Mon–Sat afternoon).

Salomon Sports, right at the gondola station, rents mountain bikes (35 SF/half day, 45 SF/full day), hiking boots (12 SF/day), and is the village Internet station (12 SF/hr, 8:30–17:00, tel. 033/855-2330). **Top Apartments** will do your laundry (14:00–

Mürren

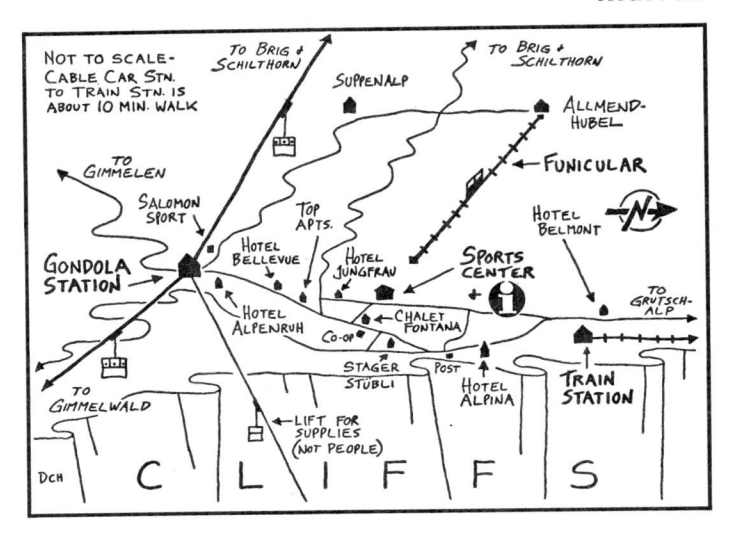

17:30, across from Hotel Bellevue's backside, look for blue triangle, tel. 033/855-3706). They also have a few cheap rooms (25–35 SF per person).

All prices are higher during the ski season and from July 15 to August 15.

Guesthouse Belmont offers good budget rooms. This is a friendly, creaky, very wooden home away from home (S-45 SF, D-90 SF, Db-130 SF, 39-SF beds in 2-, 4- and 6-bunk rooms, with sheets and breakfast, closed Nov, CC:VMA, across from train station, tel. 033/855-3535, fax 033/855-3531, well-run by Verena). The Belmont serves good, reasonably priced dinners and its pool room is a popular local hangout.

Hotel Alpina is a simple, modern place with comfortable rooms and a concrete feeling—a good thing, given its cliff-edge position (Sb-75-85 SF, Db-130–170 SF, Tb-160 SF, Qb-180 SF with awesome Jungfrau views and balconies, CC:VMA, exit left from station, walk 2 minutes gradually downhill, tel. 033/855-1361, fax 033/855-1049, Frau and Herr Taugwalder).

Chalet Fontana, run by a charming Englishwoman, Denise Fussell, is a rare budget option in Mürren with simple, crispy-clean, and comfortable rooms (35–45 SF per person in small doubles or triples with breakfast, 5 SF cheaper without breakfast, 1 3-bed room with kitchenette-45 SF per person, closed Nov–mid-May, across street from Stägerstübli restaurant in town center, tel. 033/855-2686, e-mail: 106501.2731@compuserve.com). If no one's home, check at the Ed Abegglen shop next door (tel. 033/855-1245, off-season only).

Hotel Jungfrau offers a variety of options: a hotel with pricey, modern, and comfortable rooms (Db-162 SF with view, 142 SF without, elevator); a lodge in a basic, blocky 20-room annex with well-worn but fine rooms and better Jungfrau views (Db-116 SF, family apartments-213 SF); and the **Staff House**. Outside of ski season, half the industrial-strength employees' quarters are empty and rented to budget travelers stark and basic with only sinks in the rooms (S-50 SF, D-80 SF). All rooms include the same fancy buffet breakfast and free entrance to the Sports Center pools. Without breakfast, deduct 10 SF per person (CC:VMA, near TI and Sportzentrum, tel. 033/855-4545, fax 033/855-4549, www.muerren.ch/jungfrau).

Hotel Alpenruh—expensive and yuppie-rustic—is about the only hotel in Mürren open year-round. The comfortable rooms come with views and some balconies (Sb-80–100 SF, Db-140–200 SF depending on season, CC:VMA, elevator, attached restaurant, sauna, free tickets for breakfast atop Schilthorn, 10 meters from gondola station, tel. 033/856-8800, fax 033/856-8888, e-mail: alpruh@tcnet.ch).

Hotel Bellevue-Crystal has a homey lounge, great view terrace, and good rooms at fair rates, most with balconies and views. The more expensive rooms are newly renovated and larger (Db-110–120 SF, a few family apartments 225–345 SF, tel. 033/855-1401, fax 033/855-1490, e-mail: bellevue-crystal@bluewin.ch).

Eating in Mürren: For a rare bit of ruggedness, eat at the **Stägerstübli** (10–30 SF lunches and dinners, closed Tue off-season). The **Kandhar Snack Bar** at the Sports Center has fun, creative, and inexpensive light meals, a good selection of teas and pastries, and impressive views. The **Edelweiss** self-serve restaurant is reasonable and wins the best view award (next to Hotel Alpina). Mürren's bakery is excellent. For picnic fixings, shop at the Co-op (normally Mon and Wed–Fri 8:00–12:00, 14:00–18:30, Tue and Sat 8:00–12:00 only, closed Sun).

Sleeping in Interlaken
(tel. code: 033, zip code: 3800)

I'd head for Gimmelwald or at least Lauterbrunnen (20 min by train or car). Interlaken is not the Alps. But if you must stay....

Hotel Lotschberg, with a sun terrace and wonderful rooms, is run by English-speaking Susi and Fritz and is the best real hotel value in town. Information abounds, and Fritz organizes wonderful adventures (Sb-100 SF, Db-145–180 SF, extra bed-20–25 SF, family deals, cheaper Nov–May, CC:VMA, elevator, bar, non-smoking, laundry service-8 SF, bike rental, cheap e-mail access, free pickup at station or a 4-minute walk, exit right from West Station, on General Guisanstrasse 31, tel. 033/822-2545, fax 033/822-2579, www.beo-swiss.ch/lotschberg, e-mail: lotschberg @interlakentourism.ch). **Guest House Susi's B&B** is Hotel Lotschberg's no-frills annex, run by the same people (same address and phone number). It has simple, cozy, cheaper rooms (Db-110 SF, apartments with kitchenettes for 2 people-100 SF; for 4 or 5 people-175 SF, cheaper off-season).

Villa Margaretha B&B, warmly mothered by English-speaking Frau Kunz-Joerin, offers the best cheap beds in town. It's a big Victorian house with a garden on a quiet residential street three blocks directly in front of the West Station (D-80 SF, T-120 SF, 4 rooms share a big bathroom, minimum 2-night stay, kitchenette, Aarmühlestrasse 13, tel. 033/822-1813).

Hotel Aarburg offers 13 plain, peaceful rooms in a beautifully located but run-down old building five minutes' walk from the West Station (D-80 SF, Db-100 SF, next to Laundromat at Beatenbergstrasse 1, tel. 033/822-2615, fax 033/822-6397).

Backpackers' Villa Sonnenhof is a creative guesthouse run by a Methodist Church group. It's fun and youthful but without the frat-party ambience of Balmer's (below). Rooms are comfortable, and half come with Jungfrau-view balconies (D-86 SF, dorm beds in 4- to 6-bed rooms with lockers and sheets-27 SF each, cheaper if you BYO sheets, includes breakfast, kitchen, garden, Internet access, game room, no curfew, check-in from 16:00–21:00, open all day, 10-minute walk from either station across grassy field from TI, Alpenstrasse 16, tel. 033/826-7171, fax 033/826-7172, www.villa.ch).

Happy Inn Lodge has cheap rooms a five-minute walk from the West Station (D-60–70 SF, dorm beds-18–27 SF, breakfast-7 SF, Rosenstrasse 17, tel. 033/822-3225, fax 033/822-3268).

For many, **Balmer's Herberge** is backpacker heaven. This Interlaken institution comes with movies, Ping-Pong, a Laundromat, bar, restaurant, swapping library, Internet stations, tiny grocery, bike rental, currency exchange, rafting excursions, a shuttle-bus service (which meets every arriving train), and a friendly, hardworking staff. This little Nebraska is home for those who miss their fraternity. Particularly on summer weekends, it's a mob scene (dorm beds-22–25 SF, S-40 SF, D, T, or Q-26–32 SF per person, includes sheets and breakfast, CC:VMA, nonsmoking, no reservations, open year-round, Hauptstrasse 23, in Matten, 15-minute walk from either Interlaken station, tel. 033/822-1961, fax 033/823-3261, e-mail: balmers@tcnet.ch).

Transportation Connections—Interlaken
By train to: Spiez (2/hrly, 15 min), **Brienz** (hrly, 20 min), **Bern** (hrly, 1 hr). While there are a few long trains from Interlaken, you'll generally connect from Bern.

By train from Bern to: Lausanne (hrly, 70 min), **Zurich** (hrly, 75 min), **Salzburg** (4/day, 8 hrs, transfers include Zurich), **Munich** (4/day, 5.5 hrs), **Frankfurt** (hrly, 4.5 hrs, transfers in Basel and Mannheim), **Paris** (4/day, 4.5 hrs).

Interlaken to Gimmelwald: Take the train from the Interlaken East (Ost) Station to Lauterbrunnen, then cross the street to catch the funicular to Mürren. Ride up to Grütschalp, where a special scenic train (Panorama Fahrt) will roll you along the cliff into Mürren. From there, either walk an easy, paved 30 minutes downhill to Gimmelwald, or walk 10 minutes across Mürren to catch the gondola (7.40 SF and a 5-minute steep uphill backtrack). A good bad-weather option (or vice versa) is to ride the post bus from Lauterbrunnen (hrly departure coordinated with arrival of train) to Stechelberg and the base of the Schilthornbahn (a big, grey gondola station, tel. 033/823-1444 or 033/555-2141), which will whisk you in five thrilling minutes up to Gimmelwald.

By car it's a 30-minute drive from Interlaken to Stechelberg. The pay parking lot (5 SF/day) at the gondola station is safe. Gimmelwald is the first stop above Stechelberg on the Schilthorn gondola (7.40 SF, 2 trips/hrly at :25 and :55, get off at 1st stop). Note that for a week in early May and from mid-November through early December, the Schilthornbahn is closed for servicing.

APPENDIX

European National Tourist Offices in the United States

Austrian National Tourist Office: Box 1142, New York, NY 10108-1142, tel. 212/944-6880, fax 212/730-4568, www.anto.com. Ask for their "Vacation Kit" map. Fine hikes and Vienna material.
Belgian National Tourist Office: 780 Third Ave. #1501, New York, NY 10017, tel. 212/758-8130, fax 212/355-7675, www.visitbelgium.com.
British Tourist Authority: 551 Fifth Ave., Seventh floor, New York, NY 10176, tel. 800/462-2748, fax 212/986-1188, www.visitbritain.com. Free maps of London and Britain. Meaty material. Responsive to individual needs.
Czech Tourist Authority: 1109 Madison Ave., New York, NY 10028, tel. 212/288-0830, fax 212/288-0971, www.czechcenter.com. To get a weighty information package (1–2 lbs, no advertising), send a check for $3.20 to cover postage and specify places of interest.
Denmark: (see Scandinavia)
French Tourist Office: For general information, call 410/286-8310 or write to the nearest office: 444 Madison Ave., 16th floor, New York, NY 10022; 676 N. Michigan Ave., #600, Chicago, IL 60611; 9454 Wilshire Blvd., #715, Beverly Hills, CA 90212. Web site: www.francetourism.com.
German National Tourist Office: 122 E. 42nd St., 52nd floor, New York, NY 10168, tel. 212/661-7200, fax 212/661-7174, www.germany-tourism.de. Maps, Rhine schedules, events; very helpful.
Irish Tourist Board: 345 Park Ave., 17th floor, New York, NY 10154, tel. 800/223-6470 or 212/418-0800, fax 212/371-9059, www.ireland.travel.ie.
Italian Government Travel Office: Contact nearest office: 630 Fifth Ave., #1565, New York, NY 10111, brochure hotline tel. 212/245-4822, tel. 212/245-5618, fax 212/586-9249; 500 N. Michigan Ave., #2240, Chicago, IL 60611, brochure hotline tel. 312/666-0990, tel. 312/644-0996, fax 312/644-3019; 12400 Wilshire Blvd., #550, Los Angeles, CA 90025, brochure hotline tel. 310/820-0098, tel. 310/820-1898, fax 310/820-6357. Web site: www.italiantourism.com.
Netherlands National Tourist Office: 225 N. Michigan Ave., #1854, Chicago, IL 60601, tel. 888/GO-HOLLAND (automated) or 312/819-1500 (live), fax 312/819-1740, www.goholland.com Send a $3 check to receive info within one week (call first to request). Great country map.

Appendix

Norway: (see Scandinavia)
Portuguese National Tourist Office: 590 Fifth Ave., Fourth floor, New York, NY 10036, tel. 800/PORTUGAL, 212/354-4403, fax 212/764-6137, www.portugal.org.
Scandinavian Tourism: P.O. Box 4649, Grand Central Station, New York, NY 10163, tel. 212/885-9700, fax 212/885-9710, www.goscandinavia.com. Good booklets on all the Scandinavian countries, be sure to ask for specific country info and city maps.
Spanish National Tourist Office: For general info, call 888/OKSPAIN; 666 Fifth Ave., 35th floor, New York, NY 10022, tel. 212/265-8822, fax 212/265-8864; 845 N. Michigan Ave., Chicago, IL 60611, tel. 312/642-1992, fax 312/642-9817; 1221 Breckell Ave., #1850, Miami, FL 33131, tel. 305/358-1992, fax 305/358-8223; San Vicente Plaza Bldg., 8383 Wilshire Blvd., #960, Beverly Hills, CA 90211, tel. 323/658-7188, fax 323/658-1061, www.okspain.org.
Sweden: (see Scandinavia)
Swiss National Tourist Office: Call the nearest office: New York, tel. 212/757-5944, fax 212/262-6116; Chicago, tel. 312/332-9900; San Francisco, tel. 415/362-2260; Los Angeles, tel. 310/640-8900. Or write to 608 Fifth Ave., New York, NY 10020 or visit www.switzerlandtourism.com. Great maps and hiking material.

Let's Talk Telephones

In Europe, you can make your calls from public phone booths using a phone card or coins. At post offices in major cities, you'll sometimes find easy-to-use "talk now, pay later" metered phones.

Avoid using hotel room phones, which are rip-offs for anything other than local calls, PIN card calls, or calling-card calls.

International Access Codes

When dialing direct, first dial the international access code of the country you're calling from. For the U.S.A. and Canada, it's 011. Virtually all European countries use "00" as their international access code; the only exceptions are Finland (990), Estonia (800), and Lithuania (810).

Country Codes

After you've dialed the international access code, dial the code of the country you're calling.

Austria—43	Finland—358	Norway—47
Belgium—32	France—33	Portugal—351
Britain—44	Germany—49	Spain—34
Canada—1	Greece—30	Sweden—46
Czech Repub.—420	Ireland—353	Switzerland—41
Denmark—45	Italy—39	U.S.A.—1
Estonia—372	Netherlands—31	

Calling Card Operators

	AT&T	MCI	SPRINT
Austria	022-903-011	022-903-012	022-903-014
Belgium	0800-100-10	0800-100-12	0800-100-14
Britain	0800-89-0011	0800-89-0222	0800-89-0877
Czech Rep.	00420-00101	00420-00112	00420-87187
Denmark	8001-0010	8001-0022	8001-0877
Estonia	800-800-1001	800-800-1122	—
France	0800-990-011	0800-990-019	0800-990-087
Germany	0800-225-5288	0800-888-8000	0800-888-0013
Ireland	1800-550-000	1800-551-001	1800-552-001
Italy	172-1011	172-1022	172-1877
Netherlands	0800-022-9111	0800-022-9122	0800-022-9119
Norway	800-19-011	800-19-912	800-19-877
Portugal	0800-800-128	050-171-234	0800-800-187
Spain	900-990-011	900-99-0014	900-99-0013
Sweden	020-795-611	020-795-922	020-799-011
Switzerland	0800-89-0011	0800-89-0222	0800-89-9777

Numbers and Stumblers

- Europeans write a few of their numbers differently than we do: 1 = 1 , 4 = 4, 7= 7. Learn the difference or miss your train.
- In Europe, dates appear as day/month/year, so Christmas is 25/12/00.
- Commas are decimal points and decimals commas. A dollar and a half is 1,50. There are 5.280 feet in a mile.
- When pointing, use your whole hand, palm downward.
- When counting with fingers, start with your thumb. If you hold up your first finger to request one item, you'll probably get two.
- What we Americans call the second floor of a building is the first floor in Europe.
- Europeans keep the left "lane" open for passing on escalators and moving sidewalks. Keep to the right.

Metric Conversion (approximate)

1 inch = 25 millimeters
1 foot = 0.3 meter
1 yard = 0.9 meter
1 mile = 1.6 kilometers
1 centimeter = 0.4 inch
1 meter = 39.4 inches
1 kilometer = .62 mile

32 degrees F = 0 degrees C
82 degrees F = about 28 degrees C
1 ounce = 28 grams
1 kilogram = 2.2 pounds
1 quart = 0.95 liter
1 square yard = 0.8 square meter
1 acre = 0.4 hectare

Climate

Here is a list of average temperatures and days of no rain. This can be helpful in planning your itinerary, but I have never found European weather to be particularly predictable, and these charts ignore humidity.

(1st line, average daily low; 2nd line, average daily high; 3rd line, days of no rain)

	J	F	M	A	M	J	J	A	S	O	N	D
France	32°	34°	36°	41°	47°	52°	55°	55°	50°	44°	38°	33°
Paris	42°	45°	52°	60°	67°	73°	76°	75°	69°	59°	49°	43°
	16	15	16	16	18	19	19	19	19	17	15	14
Germany	29°	31°	35°	41°	48°	53°	56°	55°	51°	43°	36°	31°
Frankfurt	37°	42°	49°	58°	67°	72°	75°	74°	67°	56°	45°	39°
	22	19	22	21	22	21	21	21	21	22	21	20°
Great Britain	35°	35°	37°	40°	45°	51°	55°	54°	51°	44°	39°	36°
London	44°	45°	51°	56°	63°	69°	73°	72°	67°	58°	49°	45°
	14	15	20	16	18	19	18	18	17	17	14	15
Italy	39°	39°	42°	46°	55°	60°	64°	64°	61°	53°	46°	41°
Rome	54°	56°	62°	68°	74°	82°	88°	88°	83°	73°	63°	56°
	23	17	26	24	25	28	29	28	24	22	22	22
Netherlands	34°	34°	37°	43°	50°	55°	59°	59°	56°	48°	41°	35°
Amsterdam	40°	41°	46°	52°	60°	65°	69°	68°	64°	56°	47°	41°
	12	13	18	16	19	18	17	17	15	13	11	12
Switzerland	29°	30°	35°	41°	48°	55°	58°	57°	52°	44°	37°	31°
Geneva	39°	43°	51°	58°	66°	73°	77°	76°	69°	58°	47°	40°
	20	19	21	19	19	19	22	21	20	20	19	21

Faxing Your Hotel Reservation

Faxing is more accurate and cheaper than telephoning. Use this handy form for your fax (or find it on-line at www.ricksteves.com/reservation). Photocopy and fax away.

One-Page Fax

To: _____ @ _____
        hotel   *fax*

From: _____ @ _____
         name   *fax*

Today's date: ____ / _____ / ____
              day *month* *year*

Dear Hotel _____,

Please make this reservation for me:

Name: _____

Total # of people: _____   # of rooms: _____   # of nights: _____

Arriving: ____ / _____ / ____   My time of arrival (24-hr clock): _____
          day *month* *year*   (I will telephone if I will be late)

Departing: ____ / _____ / ____
           day *month* *year*

Room(s): Single___ Double___ Twin___ Triple___ Quad___

With: Toilet___ Shower___ Bath___ Sink only___

Special needs: View___ Quiet___ Cheapest Room___

Credit card: Visa___ MasterCard___ American Express___

Card #: _____

Expiration date: _____

Name on card: _____

You may charge me for the first night as a deposit. Please fax or mail me confirmation of my reservation, along with the type of room reserved, the price, and whether the price includes breakfast. Thank you.

_____
Signature

_____
Name

_____
Address

_____
City   **State**   **Zip Code**   **Country**

_____
E-mail Address

Road Scholar Feedback for BEST OF EUROPE 2000

We're all in the same travelers' school of hard knocks. Your feedback helps us improve this guidebook for future travelers. Please fill this out (or use the on-line version at www.ricksteves.com/feedback), include more info or any tips/favorite discoveries if you like, and send it to us. As thanks for your help, we'll send you our quarterly travel newsletter free for one year. Thanks! **Rick**

Of the recommended accommodations/restaurants used, which was:

Best _____

    Why? _____

Worst _____

    Why? _____

Of the sights/experiences/destinations recommended by this book, which was:

Most overrated _____

    Why? _____

Most underrated _____

    Why? _____

Best ways to improve this book:

_____

I'd like a free newsletter subscription:

____ Yes   ____ No   ____ Already on list

_____
Name

_____
Address

_____
City, State, Zip

_____
E-mail Address

Please send to: ETBD, Box 2009, Edmonds, WA 98020

Jubilee 2000—Let's Celebrate the Millennium by Forgiving Third World Debt

Let's ring in the millennium by convincing our government to forgive the debt owed to us by the world's poorest countries. Imagine spending over half your income on interest payments alone. You and I are creditors, and poor countries owe us more than they can pay.

Jubilee 2000 is a worldwide movement of concerned people and groups—religious and secular—working to cancel the international debts of the poorest countries by the year 2000.

Debt ruins people: In the poorest countries, money needed for health care, education, and other vital services is diverted to interest payments.

Mozambique, with a per-capita income of $90 and life expectancy of 40, spends over half its national income on interest. This poverty brings social unrest, civil war, and often costly humanitarian intervention by the United States. To chase export dollars, desperate countries ruin their environment. As deserts grow and rain forests shrink, the world suffers. Of course, the real suffering is among local people born long after some dictator borrowed (and squandered) that money. As interest is paid, entire populations go hungry.

Who owes what and why? Mozambique is one of 41 countries defined by the World Bank as "Heavily Indebted Poor Countries." In total, they owe $200 billion. Because these debts are unlikely to be paid, their market value is only a tenth of the face value (about $20 billion). The United States' share is under $2 billion.

How can debt be canceled? This debt is owed mostly to the United States, Japan, Germany, Britain, and France, either directly or through the World Bank. We can forgive the debt owed directly to us and pay the market value (usually 10 percent) of the debts owed to the World Bank. We have the resources. (Norway, another wealthy creditor nation, just unilaterally forgave its Third World debt.) All the United States needs is the political will...people power.

While many of these poor nations are now democratic, corruption is still a concern. A key to Jubilee 2000 is making certain that debt relief reduces poverty in a way that benefits ordinary people—women, farmers, children, and so on.

Let's celebrate the new millennium by giving poor countries a break. For the sake of peace, fragile young democracies, the environment, and countless real people, forgiving this debt is the right thing for us in the rich world to do.

Tell Washington, D.C.: If our government knows this is what we want, it can happen. Learn more, write letters, lobby legislators, or even start a local Jubilee 2000 campaign. For details, contact Jubilee 2000 (tel. 202/783-3566, www.j2000usa.org). For information on lobbying Congress on J2000, contact Bread for the World (tel. 800/82-BREAD, www.bread.org).

INDEX

Aalsmeer, 579
Alkmaar, 580
Amsterdam, 551–570
Appendix, 718–724: climate chart, 721; hotel reservation fax form, 722; Jubilee 2000, 724; metric conversions, 720; national tourist offices, 718–719; Road Scholar Feedback Form, 723; telephone information, 719–720
Arnhem, 580
Austria, 24–74: Hallstatt, 70–74; Reutte, 263–269; Salzburg, 56–70; Salzkammergut Lake District, 70–74; Vienna, 24–55

Bacharach, 196–199, 204–206
Banking, 5–7
Barcelona, 660–678
Bath, 327–339
Bavaria, 252–269
Bed-and-Breakfasts, 19–20
Beilstein, 211
Belgium, Bruges, 75–89
Bruges, 75–89
Burano, 486

Camping, 20
Channel, English, 89, 320–321
Chartres, 143
Cinque Terre, 533–550
Cochem, 209–210, 211–212
Copenhagen, 602–624: eating, 621–624; sightseeing, 607–616; sleeping, 616–621; transportation, 604–605, 606–607, 624
Corniglia, 543, 549
Costs, trip, 2–3
Czech Republic, Prague, 90–112

Denmark, Copenhagen, 602–624
Dingle, Peninsula, 389–404; Town, 389–399
Driving, 15
Dublin, 371–388
Dun Laoghaire, 383

Eating European, 20–22: picnics, 21–22; restaurants, 21
Edinburgh, 352–370, Festival, 363–364
English Channel Tunnel, 89, 320–321
Europe Through the Back Door, 9
Europe's Best Three-Week Trip, 6, 7
Eurostar, 89, 320–321
Exchange rates, 3

Florence, 449–470
France, 113–186: airports, 169–170; Arles, 173–181; Avignon, 181–184; Chartres, 143; Disneyland Paris, 145–147; Giverny, 143–145; Glanum, 185; Les Baux, 184–185; orange, 186; Paris, 113–170, Pont du Gard, 185–186; Provence, 171–186; St. Rémy, 185; Uzès, 186; Versailles, 139–143
Frankfurt, 227–231
Füssen, 254–263

Germany, 187–263: Bacharach, 196–199, 204–206; Bavaria, 252–269; Beilstein, 211; Burg Eltz, 210–211; Cochem, 209–210, 211–212; Dachau, 243–244; Frankfurt, 227–231; Füssen, 254–263; Hohenschwangau, 259, 262–263; Linderhof, 259; Loreley, 193–195; Mosel Valley, 208–213; Munich, 232–251; Neuschwanstein, 242–243, 255–257; Oberammergau, 258–259; Oktoberfest, 241–242; Rhine Valley, 187–208; Romantic Road, 214–231; Rothenburg, 214–226; St. Goar, 119–203, 206–208; Tirol, 252–269; Wieskirche, 258; Zell, 211, 212–213; Zugspitze, 260
Giverny, 143–145
Great Britain, 270–370: Bath, 327–339; Edinburgh, 352–370, Edinburgh Festival, 363–364;

English Channel Tunnel, 320–321; Gatwick Airport, 319, Greenwich, 321–326; Heathrow Airport, 317–319; London, 270–321; York, 340–351
Greenwich, 321–326
Guidebooks, 8–10

Haarlem, 571–578
The Hague (Den Haag), 580
Hallstatt, 70–74
Hill Towns of Italy, 499–532: Assisi, 513–524; Civita di Bagnoregio, 528–532; Orvieto, 524–528; San Gimignano, 511–512; Siena, 500–511;
Hostels, 20
Hotels, 18–19; fax form, 722; reservations, 19

Ireland, 371–404: Dingle, Peninsula, 389–404, Dingle Town, 389–399; Dublin, 371–388, Dun Laoghaire, 383; ferry connections, 388
Italy, 405–550: Assisi, 513–524; Burano, 486; Cinque Terre, 533–550; Civita di Bagnoregio, 528–532; Corniglia, 543, 549; Florence, 449–470; Hill Towns, 499–532; Italian Riviera, 533–550; Jubilee 2000, 410; Manarola, 543, 548; Monterosso al Mare, 543, 549–550; Murano, 486; Orvieto, 524–528; Ostia Antica, 437; Riomaggiore, 542–543, 547–548; Rome, 405–448; San Gimignano, 511–512; Siena, 500–511; Torcello, 486; Vatican City, 427–434; Venice, 471–498; Vernazza, 536–539, 544–546

Jubilee 2000, 414, 724

Linderhof, 242–243, 259
Lisbon, 581–601
London, 270–321: eating, 311–317, "Hello London" Walk, 280–283, sightseeing, 280–296; sleeping, 301–311; transportation, 274–279, 280, 317–321

Madrid, 679–699
Mail, 17
Manarola, 543, 548
Monterosso al Mare, 543, 549–550
Mosel Valley, 208–213
Munich, 232–251
Murano, 486

Netherlands, 551–581: Aalsmeer, 579; Alkmaar, 580; Amsterdam, 551–570; Arnhem, 580; Haarlem, 571–578; The Hague (Den Haag), 580; Marijuana, 569–570; Schiphol Airport, 570; Zaanse Schans, 578–579
Neuschwanstein, 242–243, 255–257
Norway, 643–659: Norway in a Nutshell, 658–659; Oslo, 643–658

Oktoberfest, 241–242
Ostia Antica, 437

Paris, 113–170: day trips, 139–146; eating, 158–165; "Historic Core of Paris" Walk, 122–129; sightseeing, 122–139; sleeping, 146–158; transportation, 116–117, 118–121, 168–170
Philosophy, Back Door, 23
Picnics, 21–22
Portugal: Alfama, 588–589; Belém District, 592–595; Bullfight, Portuguese, 596–597, Lisbon, 581–601

Restaurants, 21
Reutte, 263–269
Rhine Valley, 187–208
Riomaggiore, 543–543, 547–548
Romantic Road, 214, 226–231
Rome, 405–448: eating, 445–448; sightseeing, 415–437; sleeping, 438–444; transportation, 412–414, 448

Index

Rothenburg, 214–226
Salzburg, 56–70; Festival, 63
Salzkammergut Lake District, 70–74
Scotland, Edinburgh, 352–370
Sightseeing priorities, 5
Sleep Code, 18
Sound of Music, country, 70–74; tour, 62
Spain, 660–699: AVE bullet train, 681–682; Barcelona, 660–678; Madrid, 679–699
St. Goar, 199–203; 206–208
Stockholm, 625–642
Sweden, Stockholm, 625–642
Switzerland, 700–717: Ballenberg, 710–711; Berner Oberland, 700–717; Gimmelwald, 703–713; Interlaken, 701–703, 715–717; Lauterbrunnen, 707, 708–709, 710; Mürren, 709–710; 713–715

Telephones, 15–17
Tirol, 252–269

Torcello, 486
Tourist information offices, 8,
Transportation, 10; car rental, 10–11, 14–15; Eurailpass, 11, 12–14; train, 11–14

Vatican City, 427–434
Venice, 471–498: eating, 493–498; sightseeing, 478–486; sleeping, 488–493; transportation, 474, 476, 498
Vernazza, 536–539, 544–546
Versailles, 139–143
Vienna, 24–55: eating, 45–46, 53–55; sights, 33–45; sleeping, 47–53; transportation, 28–29, 55

When to go, 4–5
Wieskirche, 258

York, 340–351

Zaanse Schans, 578–579
Zell, 211, 212–213

Rick Steves' Postcards from Europe
25 Years of Travel Tales from America's Favorite Guidebook Writer

1978   1998

TRAVEL GURU RICK STEVES has been exploring Europe through the Back Door for 25 years, sharing his tricks and discoveries in guidebooks and on TV. Now, in *Rick Steves' Postcards from Europe*, Rick shares stories—ranging from goofy to inspirational—of his favorite moments and his off-beat European friends.

Postcards takes you on the fantasy trip of a lifetime, and it gives you a close-up look at contemporary Europeans.

You'll meet Marie-Alice, the Parisian restaurateur who sniffs a whiff of moldy cheese and says, "It smells like zee feet of angels." In an Alpine village, meet Olle, the schoolteacher who lets Rick pet his edelweiss, and Walter, who schemes with Rick to create a fake Swiss tradition. In Italy, cruise with Piero through his "alternative Venice" and learn why all Venetian men are mama's boys.

Postcards also tracks Rick's passion for wandering—from his first "Europe-through-the-gutter" trips, through his rocky early tours, to his career as a travel writer and host of a public-television series.

These 240 pages of travel tales are told in that funny, down-to-earth style that makes Rick his Mom's favorite guidebook writer.

Rick Steves' Postcards from Europe is available at your local bookstore. To get Rick's free travel newsletter, call (425) 771-8303 or visit www.ricksteves.com. For a free catalog or to order any John Muir Publications book, call (800) 888-7504.

Rick Steves' Phrase Books

Unlike other phrase books and dictionaries on the market, my well-tested phrases and key words cover every situation a traveler is likely to encounter. With these books you'll laugh with your cabby, disarm street thieves with insults, and charm new European friends.

Each book in the series is 4" x 6", with maps.

RICK STEVES' GERMAN PHRASE BOOK & DICTIONARY
U.S. $6.95/Canada $10.95

RICK STEVES' FRENCH PHRASE BOOK & DICTIONARY
U.S. $6.95/Canada $10.95

RICK STEVES' ITALIAN PHRASE BOOK & DICTIONARY
U.S. $6.95/Canada $10.95

RICK STEVES' SPANISH & PORTUGUESE PHRASE BOOK & DICTIONARY
U.S. $8.95/Canada $13.95

RICK STEVES' FRENCH, ITALIAN & GERMAN PHRASE BOOK & DICTIONARY
U.S. $8.95/Canada $13.95

You'll Feel Like a Local
When You Travel with Guides from John Muir Publications

TRAVEL✦SMART®
Trip planners with select recommendations to:
Alaska, American Southwest, Arizona, Carolinas, Colorado, Deep South, Eastern Canada, Florida Gulf Coast, Hawaii, Illinois/Indiana, Iowa/Nebraska, Kentucky/Tennessee, Maryland/Delaware, Michigan, Minnesota/Wisconsin, Montana/Wyoming/Idaho, New England, New Mexico, New York State, Northern California, Ohio, Pacific Northwest, Pennsylvania/New Jersey, South Florida and the Keys, Southern California, Texas, Utah, Virginias, Western Canada

CiTY·SMaRT™ GUIDEBOOKS
Pick one for your favorite city:
Albuquerque, Anchorage, Austin, Baltimore, Boston, Calgary, Charlotte, Chicago, Cincinnati, Cleveland, Denver, Indianapolis, Kansas City, Memphis, Milwaukee, Minneapolis/St. Paul, Nashville, Pittsburgh, Portland, Richmond, Salt Lake City, San Antonio, San Francisco, St. Louis, Tampa/St. Petersburg, Toronto, Tucson, Vancouver

Rick Steves' GUIDES
See **Europe Through the Back Door** *and take along guides to:*
France, Belgium & the Netherlands; Germany, Austria & Switzerland; Great Britain & Ireland; Italy; Scandinavia; Spain & Portugal; London; Paris; Rome; or The Best of Europe

Live Well
Learn how to relocate, retire, and increase your standard of living in:
Honduras, Mexico, Ireland
Also available:
The World's Top Retirement Havens

ADVENTURES IN NATURE
Plan your next adventure in:
Alaska, Belize, British Columbia, the Caribbean, Costa Rica, Ecuador, Guatemala, Hawaii, Honduras, Mexico, New Zealand

---

JMP travel guides are available at your favorite bookstores. For a FREE catalog or to place a mail order, call: **800-888-7504**.

John Muir Publications • P.O. Box 613 • Santa Fe, NM 87504